图书在版编目(CIP)数据

罗马帝国编年史/〔古罗马〕塔西佗著;贺严,高书
文译.—北京:中国社会科学出版社,2007.8
(西方学术经典译丛)
ISBN 978-7-5004-6300-9

Ⅰ.罗… Ⅱ.①塔…②贺…③高… Ⅲ.罗马帝国—编年
史 Ⅳ.K126

中国版本图书馆 CIP 数据核字(2007)第 097621 号

出版策划 曹宏举
责任编辑 丁玉灵
责任校对 尹 力
技术编辑 李 建

出版发行 中国社会科学出版社
社　　址 北京鼓楼西大街甲 158 号　　邮　编 100720
电　　话 010—84029450(邮购)
网　　址 http://www.csspw.cn
经　　销 新华书店
印　　刷 北京京晟纪元印刷有限公司
版　　次 2007 年 8 月第 1 版
印　　次 2007 年 8 月第 1 次印刷
开　　本 630×970 1/16
印　　张 73
字　　数 786 千字
定　　价 138.00 元

【英汉对照全译本】

THE ANNALS OF IMPERIAL ROME

罗马帝国编年史

[古罗马] 塔西佗 著

贺 严 高书文 译

（一）

中国社会科学出版社

出版说明

　　为了进一步促进中西文化交流，构建全新的西学思想平台，我们出版了这套《西方学术经典译丛》（英汉对照全译本）。本译丛精选西方学术思想流变中最有代表性的部分传世名作，由多位专家学者选目，内容涵盖了哲学、宗教学、政治学、经济学、心理学、法学、历史学等人文社会科学领域，收录了不同国家、不同时代、不同体裁的诸多名著。

　　本译丛系根据英文原著或其他文种的较佳英文译本译出，在国内第一次以英汉对照的形式出版。与以往译本不同的是，本译丛全部用现代汉语译出，尽量避免以往译本时而出现的文白相间、拗口难懂的现象；另外出于尊重原作和正本清源的目的，本译本对原作品内容一律不做删节处理，全部照译。以往译本由于时代和社会局限，往往对原作品有所删节，因此，本译本也是对过去译本的补充和完善。

　　为加以区别，原文中的英文注释，注释号用①、②……形式表示；中文译者注释则以〔1〕、〔2〕……形式表示。至于英译本中出现的原文页码和特殊索引等问题，中文译者在"译者后记"中将予以解释、说明。另外，在英文原著或原英译本中，有一些表示着重意义的斜体或大写等字体，考虑到读者可以在英汉对照阅读中注意到，在本译文中没有照样标出，还望读者理解。

中国社会科学出版社

The Annals Of Imperial Rome
By *Tacitus*
English Translation
By Michael Grant

本书根据 Penguin Books Ltd. 1988 年版本译出

CONTENTS

目　录

（一）

PART One　　Tiberius

第一部分　　提贝里乌斯

PART One   Tiberius

CHAPTER 1

From Augustus To Tiberius

When Rome was first a city, its rulers were kings. Then Lucius Junius Brutus created the consulate and free Republican institutions in general. Dictatorships were assumed in emergencies. A Council of Ten did not last more than two years; and then there was a short-lived arrangement by which senior army officers—the commanders of contingents provided by the tribes—possessed consular authority.

第一部分　提贝里乌斯[1]

第一章　从奥古斯都到提贝里乌斯[2]

罗马建城之初,是由国王进行统治的。然后,路奇乌斯·尤尼乌斯·布鲁图斯建立了执政官制度和自由政体,独裁只是在紧急情况下所采取的措施。十人团的任期不能超过两年,部落议事会所授予的军团将领的权力也是临时性的安排。

---

〔1〕　这一部分记述的是提贝里乌斯(前42~37年)在位期间的事。提贝里乌斯于公元14年登上帝位,一直到公元37年去世。有历史学家称其为"虐政时期"的开始。

〔2〕　塔西佗在本章所提到的事件列简表如下:

公元前753年,传说罗马建城。

公元前510年,路奇乌斯·布鲁图斯担任执政官。

公元前451~前449年的一部分,十人团执政。

公元前444~前367年(中间有间断),设置拥有执政官权力的军团将领的职位。

公元前87~前84年,路奇乌斯·秦纳四次连任执政官。

公元前82~前79年,苏拉的独裁时期。

公元前60/59~前53年,庞培·玛尔库斯·利奇尼乌斯·克拉苏斯和尤利乌斯·恺撒的第一次三人执政时期。

公元前49~前44年,尤利乌斯·恺撒的独裁时期。

公元前43年,安东尼·屋大维(即后来的奥古斯都)和马尔库斯·艾米利乌斯·列庇都斯的第二次三人执政时期。

公元前43年,布鲁图斯和卡西乌斯横死。

公元前36年,庞培被击败,列庇都斯被排除。

公元前30年,安托尼乌斯自杀。

Subsequently Cinna and Sulla set up autocracies, but they too were brief. Soon Pompey and Crassus acquired predominant positions, but rapidly lost them to Caesar. Next, the military strength which Lepidus and Antony had built up was absorbed by Augustus. He found the whole state exhausted by internal dissensions, and established over it a personal regime known as the Principate.

Famous writers have recorded Rome's early glories and disasters. The Augustan Age, too, had its distinguished historians. But then the rising tide of flattery exercised a deterrent effect. The reigns of Tiberius, Gaius, Claudius, and Nero were described during their lifetimes infictitious terms, for fear of the consequences; whereas the accounts written after their deaths were influenced by still raging animosities. So I have decided to say a little about Augustus, with special attention to his last period, and then go on to the reign of Tiberius and what followed. I shall write without indignation or partisanship: in my case the customary incentives to these are lacking.

The violent deaths of Brutus and Cassius left no Republican forces in the field. Defeat came to Sextus Pompeius in Sicily, Lepidus was dropped, Antony killed. So even the Caesarian party had no leader left except the 'Caesar' himself, Octavian. He gave up the title of Triumvir, emphasizing instead his position as consul; and the powers of a tribune, he proclaimed, were good enough for him—powers for the protection of ordinary people.

He seduced the army with bonuses, and his cheap food policy was successful bait for civilians. Indeed, he attracted everybody's goodwill by the enjoyable gift of peace. Then he gradually pushed ahead and absorbed the functions of the senate, the officials, and even the law. Opposition did not exist. War or judicial murder had disposed

后来,秦纳和苏拉建立了专制统治,但是也都很短暂,不久就被庞培和克拉苏斯夺得,而且庞培和克拉苏斯的大权也很快又落入了恺撒之手。接着,列庇都斯和安托尼乌斯建立起来的军事大权被奥古斯都获取。奥古斯都又重整由于内争而纷乱不堪的城邦,并以普林凯普斯[1]的名义建立了一个王国。

著名的历史学家已经记录下了早期罗马的光荣和不幸,奥古斯都时代,也已经有了优秀的历史学家。但阿谀奉承之风一旦兴起,其后果就是记录真实历史的传统消失了。在提贝里乌斯、盖乌斯、克劳狄乌斯和尼禄活着的时候,人们怀着恐惧的心情编写他们统治的历史,而在他们死后,人们撰述的作品又受到余怒未消的愤恨情绪的影响,两者都有失历史的客观性。因此,我想说一说奥古斯都,特别是他当政的后期。接下来再谈一谈提贝里乌斯和他的继承者们的统治。在我撰写这些历史时,既没有什么愤慨,也没有任何派性偏见,因为在我身上缺乏通常足以引起愤慨和偏见的那一种动机。

布鲁图斯和卡西乌斯的横死使共和国丧失了武装作战的力量,塞克斯图斯·庞培在西西里战败,[2]列庇都斯被清除,安东尼被杀死。这样,恺撒党除了"恺撒"本人,即屋大维以外已没有其他领导者了。屋大维放弃了三头之一头衔,他声称自己只是一个普通的执政官,而且一个执政官所拥有的权力只要足以用来保护普通民众就可以了。

他用奖励来笼络军队,用廉价的粮食来平息市民们的情绪。而实际上,他用和平博得了人们对他的好感。然后,他逐渐地提

---

〔1〕 普林凯普斯这个称号只代表一种头衔,并不能拥有任何行政和军事权力,拥有这个头衔的人被列为首席元老。

〔2〕 公元前36年,塞克斯图斯·庞培在佩洛鲁姆海角附近海面上被阿格里帕打败。

of all men of spirit. Upper-class survivors found that slavish obedience was the way to succeed, both politically and financially. They
had profited from the revolution, and so now they liked the security of
the existing arrangement better than the dangerous uncertainties of the
old regime. Besides, the new order was popular in the provinces.
There, government by Senate and People was looked upon sceptically
as a matter of sparring dignitaries and extortionate officials. The legal
system had provided no remedy against these, since it was wholly incapacitated by violence, favouritism, and—most of all—bribery.

To safeguard his domination Augustus made his sister's son Marcellus a priest and a curule aedile—in spite of his extreme youth—and
singled out Marcus Agrippa, a commoner but a first-rate soldier who had
helped to win his victories, by the award of two consecutive consulships;
after the death of Marcellus, Agrippa was chosen by Augustus as his son-
in-law. Next the emperor had his stepsons Tiberius and Nero Drusus
hailed publicly as victorious generals. When he did this, however, there
was no lack of heirs of his own blood: there were Agrippa's sons Gaius
Caesar and Lucius Caesar. Augustus had adopted them into the imperial
family. He had also, despite pretended reluctance, been passionately eager that, even as minors, they should be entitled Princes of Youth and
have consulships reserved for them. After Agrippa had died, first Lucius Caesar and then Gaius Caesar met with premature natural deaths—

高自己的地位和声望,把元老院、高级长官甚至司法权都集中在自己手里。反对者消失了,他用战争或者法律制裁的手段将具有独立自主精神的人全部消除掉,剩下的贵族们认为奴隶般的服从是升官发财的最好途径。他们既然从革命中获得了好处,因此也就乐于在现行制度中苟且偷安,甚于喜欢那种旧体制能带来的危险。而且新统治在各行省都很受欢迎,元老院和人民的管理,反而由于权贵之间的互相倾轧和官吏们的敲诈盘剥而得不到信任。法制对此也提供不了什么有效的制止措施,因为暴力、偏私,特别是各式各样的贿赂,已经使它无能为力了。

为了加强自己的统治,奥古斯都让他姐姐的儿子玛尔凯路斯,[1]一个十分年轻的小伙子担任祭司和高级行政官;[2]又提拔虽是平民出身但粗通军事,曾经帮助他获得胜利的玛尔库斯·阿格里帕,给予他两次连任领事的殊荣。玛尔凯路斯死后,奥古斯都又选择了阿格里帕作为自己的女婿。接下来,皇帝又公然授予他的继子提贝里乌斯和尼禄·杜路苏斯两人以凯旋将军的头衔。然而,他这样做并没有削弱他自己的家族:阿格里帕的两个儿子盖乌斯·恺撒和路奇乌斯·恺撒被奥古斯都纳入他的帝王之家中。[3]尽管假装不情愿,他却是十分渴望在他们尚未成年时就授予他们青年元首的称号,并为他们保留执政官的位置。阿格里帕死后,先是路奇乌斯·恺撒,接着是盖乌斯·恺撒也相继死

---

〔1〕 克劳狄乌斯·玛尔凯路斯是维吉尔的叙事诗《埃涅伊特》中的重要人物,他娶了奥古斯都的女儿优利娅,20 岁的时候就死了。

〔2〕 古罗马掌管公共建筑物、道路、供水、社会秩序和文娱活动等的民选行政官。

〔3〕 盖乌斯和路奇乌斯是阿格里帕和优利娅的两个儿子,是奥古斯都的外孙。

unless their stepmother Livia had a secret hand in them. Lucius died on his way to the armies in Spain, Gaius while returning from Armenia incapacitated by a wound.

Nero Drusus was long dead. Tiberius was the only surviving stepson; and everything pointed in his direction. He was adopted as the emperor's son and as partner in his powers (with civil and military authority and the powers of a tribune) and displayed to all the armies. No longer was this due to his mother's secret machinations, as previously. This time she requested it openly. Livia had the aged Augustus firmly under control—so much so that he exiled his only surviving grandson to the island of Planasia. That was the young, physically tough, indeed brutish, Agrippa Postumus. Though devoid of every good quality, he had been involved in no scandal. Nevertheless, it was not he but Germanicus, the son of Nero Drusus, whom the emperor placed in command of the eight divisions on the Rhine—and, although Tiberius had a grown son of his own, he ordered him to adopt Germanicus. For Augustus wanted to have another iron in the fire.

At this time there was no longer any fighting—except a war against the Germans; and that was designed less to extend the empire's frontiers, or achieve any lucrative purpose, than to avenge the disgrace of the army lost with Publius Quinctilius Varus. In the capital the situation was calm. The titles of officials remained the same. Actium had been won before the younger men were born. Even most of the older generation had come into a world of civil wars. Practically no one had

去——或许是因为他们的继母利维拉的毒害,也或许是因为两人是先天的短命。路奇乌斯死于去西班牙军队的途中,盖乌斯在从亚美尼亚回来的途中受伤致死。

尼禄·杜鲁苏斯早就死了,提贝里乌斯是唯一幸存的继子,事情的发展完全在他的预料之中。他被皇帝认作继子,在权力方面成了皇帝的伙伴(他拥有管理行政和军事的权力,还拥有护民官的权力)而且可以在全军面前展现自己的才能。以前,这些都是由他母亲秘密谋划,但是,现在已成为公开要求的理所当然的事情。利维拉把年老的奥古斯都调理得言听计从,以至于把他仅存的一个外孙都流放到了皮亚诺扎岛。尽管这个外孙阿格里帕·波斯图姆斯幼稚、粗暴、蛮横,没有多少优点,也并没有什么丑闻恶行。但是这位帝王却不让他的继子,而是让尼禄·杜鲁苏斯的儿子日耳曼尼库斯成为莱茵河一带八个军团的统帅,虽然提贝里乌斯有一个已经成年的儿子,奥古斯都却仍然让提贝里乌斯将日耳曼尼库斯收为继子。奥古斯都如此安排,是想在继承方面获得多一层的保障。

这时除了对日耳曼人的战争外,已基本没有任何战争了。这场战争与其说是为了扩充帝国的疆土或者获取任何实利,倒不如说是要为普布里乌斯·克温克提里乌斯·伐鲁斯军队的失败[1]洗雪耻辱。在都城,形势是平静的。官员们的职务依然如旧,没有什么变动。年轻人都出生在阿克提乌姆一战的胜利之后,甚至多数老一代

---

[1] 普布里乌斯·克温克提里乌斯·伐鲁斯是奥古斯都的侄孙女婿,公元9年,他和他的三个军团在威斯特伐利亚的森林中与阿尔米尼乌斯作战,结果被阿尔米尼乌斯全部歼灭。

ever seen truly Republican government. The country had been transformed, and there was nothing left of the fine old Roman character. Political equality was a thing of the past; all eyes watched for imperial commands.

Nobody had any immediate worries as long as Augustus retained his physical powers, and kept himself going, and his House, and the peace of the empire. But when old age incapacitated him, his approaching end brought hopes of change. A few people started idly talking of the blessings of freedom. Some, more numerous, feared civil war; others wanted it. The great majority, however, exchanged critical gossip about candidates for the succession. First, Agrippa Postumus—a savage without either the years or the training needed for imperial responsibilities. Tiberius, on the other hand, had the seniority and the military reputation. But he also possessed the ancient, ingrained arrogance of the Claudian family; and signs of a cruel disposition kept breaking out, repress them as he might. Besides, it was argued, he had been brought up from earliest youth in an imperial household, had accumulated early consulships and Triumphs, and even during the years at Rhodes—which looked like banishment but were called retirement—his thoughts had been solely occupied with resentment, deception, and secret sensuality. And then there was that feminine bully, his mother. ' So we have got to be slaves to a woman', people were saying, ' and to the two half-grown boys Germanicus and Drusus. First they will be a burden to the State—then they will tear it in two !'

Amid this sort of conversation the health of Augustus deteriorated. Some suspected his wife of foul play. For rumour had it that a few months earlier, with the knowledge of his immediate circle but accom-

人也是在内战时期出生的。实际上,他们中没有人能真正了解什么是共和政府。国家改变了,古罗马的风格已荡然无存。政治上的平等已成为过去,所有的眼睛都在观望着帝王的命令。

只要奥古斯都还年富力强,还能保持着他自己的、他的家庭的以及帝国的和平现状,就不会存在什么忧虑。但是,当他年老体弱、能力衰退,当他的末日迫近之时,人们就产生变革的希望。一些人开始谈论自由的福祉,更多的人则在担心会发生内战,还有一些人在期盼战争。尽管如此,绝大多数人还是在交换着关于候选继任者的闲言碎语。首先,阿格里帕·波斯图姆斯粗暴残忍,既太过年幼又没有受过应有的帝王之责所需的训练。而提贝里乌斯正当壮年,又有着良好的军事声誉,但他又有着克劳狄乌斯家族那种古老的、天生的傲慢,尽管他想极力压制,也仍然会时时表现出一些残忍的迹象。另外,人们认为,从一出生就是在帝王的家庭中受到抚育培养。早年,提贝里乌斯头脑中想的就全是执政官的职位和胜利凯旋等事,甚至在他住在罗德岛的那几年的时间里——[1]这种生活表面上看起来是隐退,实际上却是被放逐,他心中也充满了愤恨、诡诈,而且还暗中纵欲放荡。人们还谈到他的母亲,指责她的盛气凌人。"如果让他继任,我们以后就要受这个女人的奴役了。"人们窃窃私语,"而且还要成为日耳曼尼库斯和杜鲁苏斯这两个毛头小子的奴隶! 他们不只是给国家增加负担,还将会制造国家的分裂!"

正当人们纷纷谈论着这一类话题的时候,奥古斯都的健康状况却越来越糟糕了。一些人怀疑是他的妻子在暗中捣鬼。因为有谣传说,就在几个月之前,在只有身边的几个亲信了解的情况下,仅

---

〔1〕 提贝里乌斯从公元前 6 年到公元 2 年住在罗德岛。

panied only by Paullus Fabius Maximus, he had gone to Planasia to visit Agrippa Postumus; and that there had been such a tearful display of affection on both sides that the young man seemed very likely to be received back into the home of his grandfather. Maximus, it was further said, had told his wife, Marcia, of this, and she had warned Livia—but the emperor had discovered the leakage, and when Maximus died shortly afterwards (perhaps by his own hand) his widow had been heard at the funeral moaning and blaming herself for her husband's death. Whatever the true facts about this, Tiberius was recalled from his post in Illyricum (immediately after his arrival there) by an urgent letter from his mother. When he arrived at Nola, it is unknown whether he found Augustus alive or dead. For the house and neighbouring streets were carefully sealed by Livia's guards. At intervals, hopeful reports were published—until the steps demanded by the situation had been taken. Then two pieces of news became known simultaneously: Augustus was dead, and Tiberius was in control.

The new reign's first crime was the assassination of Agrippa Postumus. He was killed by a staff-officer—who found it a hard task, though he was a persevering murderer and the victim taken by surprise unarmed. Tiberius said nothing about the matter in the senate. He pretended that the orders came from Augustus, who was alleged to have instructed the colonel in charge to kill Agrippa Postumus as soon as Augustus himself was dead. It is true that Augustus' scathing criticisms of the young man's behaviour were undoubtedly what had prompted

由帕乌鲁斯·法比乌斯·玛克西姆斯陪同,皇帝到了普拉纳西亚岛去会见阿格里帕·波斯图姆斯。据说两个人见面时都很激动,两人都痛哭了一场,因此这个年轻人很有可能会被接回他的外祖父家中。更有甚者,有人说,玛克西姆斯把这件事告诉了他的妻子玛尔奇娅,玛尔奇娅又告诉了利维拉。恺撒发现有人泄了密,不久之后,玛克西姆斯就死了(可能是自杀)。据说他的寡妇玛尔奇娅在丈夫的葬仪上放声痛哭,并为丈夫的死自责不已。不管这件事的真相如何,提贝里乌斯被母亲的一封急信从他在伊里利库姆的营地召了回来(在他刚刚到达那儿之后)。已经无法确定,在他到达诺拉看到奥古斯都时,奥古斯都是否还活着。因为利维拉的卫队已经将皇帝的行宫和附近的街道都严密封锁了起来。使人乐观的消息也时常发布出来,危急的局势要求必须采取最后的措施。于是两个消息同时发布出来:奥古斯都逝世,提贝里乌斯登基。[1]

　　新皇帝继位后所犯下的第一桩罪行就是暗杀了阿格里帕·波斯图姆斯。阿格里帕·波斯图姆斯在毫无防备的情况下,受到了一名百人团长的进攻,尽管他发现这是一项艰难的任务,但是,他是一个顽强的杀手,不达目的绝不罢休。而阿格里帕·波斯图姆斯手里当时并没有武器,尽管奋力抵抗,最后还是断送了自己的性命。提贝里乌斯在元老院里根本没有提起这件事情,他谎称这是他父亲奥古斯都发出的命令,他说他父亲曾命令负责监视阿格里帕的一位军团将领,要这位将领在他一去世的时候,就把阿格里帕·波斯图姆斯杀死。毫无疑问,奥古斯都对这个年轻人的品行所进行的严厉责

---

〔1〕　此事发生于公元 14 年 8 月 19 日。

the senate to decree his banishment. But the emperor had never been callous enough to kill any of his relations, and that he should murder his own grandchild to remove the worries of a stepson seemed incredible. It would be nearer the truth to suppose that Tiberius because he was afraid, and Livia through stepmotherly malevolence, loathed and distrusted the young Agrippa Postumus and got rid of him at the first opportunity. But when the staff-officer reported in military fashion that he had carried out his orders, Tiberius answered that he had given no orders and that what had been done would have to be accounted for in the senate.

This came to the notice of Tiberius' confidant, Gaius Sallustius Crispus. It was he who had sent instructions to the colonel, and he was afraid that the responsibility might be shifted to himself—in which case either telling the truth or lying would be equally risky. So he warned Livia that palace secrets, and the advice of friends, and services performed by the army, were best undivulged; and Tiberius must not weaken the throne by referring everything to the senate. The whole point of autocracy, Crispus observed, is that the accounts will not come right unless the ruler is their only auditor.

Meanwhile at Rome consuls, senate, knights, precipitately became servile. The more distinguished men were, the greater their gency and insincerity. They must show neither satisfaction at the death of one emperor, nor gloom at the accession of another: so their features were carefully arranged in a blend of tears and smiles, mourning and flattery. The first to swear allegiance to Tiberius Caesar were the consuls Sextus Pompeius (II) and Sextus Appulcius; then in their

难,曾促使元老院作出了放逐他的决定。但是,这位皇帝却从来也没有冷酷无情到杀死他的任何一个亲人的程度。而且,为了减轻继子的担忧而把自己的外孙杀死,这也确实令人难以置信。比较可能的情况是,提贝里乌斯是由于恐惧,而利维拉是出于继母的恶毒,厌恶、不信任阿格里帕·波斯图姆斯,因此急忙将这个年轻人除掉。但是当这位百人团长在例行的军事报告中,说已经完成了他的命令的时候,提贝里乌斯却说他从来没有发过这样的命令,并且表示这件事必须向元老院作出充分的解释。

皇帝的心腹盖乌斯·撒路斯提乌斯·克利司普斯[1]听到了皇帝讲的这些话,正是他把这个命令传达给那个军团将领的,因此他害怕自己会受到这件事的连累,因为无论他讲真话还是说谎话,对他来说都同样非常危险。因而他就劝利维拉最好不要把这桩宫廷秘事、朋友们的劝告以及军队干的事情声张出去。而且,不要把任何事情都交给元老院,这样会削弱提贝里乌斯的权力。克利司普斯指出,专制统治的总的宗旨就是,统治者必须是唯一的仲裁者,这样一切事情才能够顺利进行。

这时,在罗马,执政官、元老和骑士都在争先恐后地去奴颜婢膝。而且地位越高的人,越是急不可待,越是虚伪。他们需要十分恰当地控制自己的表情:既不能对皇帝的去世表示不合时宜的欣慰,也不能为另一位继位者的登基表示不当的忧郁。因此他们要将眼泪和微笑、哀悼和谄媚这些表情恰如其分地糅合在一起。首先向提贝里乌斯·恺撒宣誓效忠的是执政官塞克斯图斯·彭佩乌斯(二世)和塞克斯图斯·阿普列乌斯二人;然后在这两位执政官的面前,近

---

[1] 他是著名历史学家撒路斯提乌斯的侄子和继子。

presence the commander of the Guard, Lucius Seius Strabo, and the controller of the corn-supply, Gaius Turranius; next the senate, army, and public. For Tiberius made a habit of always allowing the consuls the initiative, as though the Republic still existed and he himself were uncertain whether to take charge or not. Even the edict with which he summoned the senate to its House was merely issued by virtue of the tribune's power which he had received under Augustus. His edict was brief, and very unpretentious. In it he proposed to arrange his father's last honours, and stay by the side of his body. This, He said, was the only State business which he was assuming.

Nevertheless, when Augustus died Tiberius had given the watchword to the Guard as its commander. He already had the trappings of a court, too, such as personal bodyguards and men-at-arms. When he went to the Forum, or into the senate, he had soldiers to escort him. He sent letters to the armies as though he were already emperor. He only showed signs of hesitation when he addressed the senate. This was chiefly because of Germanicus, who was extremely popular and disposed of a large Roman force and hordes of auxiliary troops. Tiberius was afraid Germanicus might prefer the throne to the prospect of it. Besides, in deference to public opinion, Tiberius wanted to seem the person chosen and called by the State—instead of one who had wormed his way in by an old man's adoption, and intrigues of the old man's wife. Afterwards it was understood that Tiberius had pretended to be hesitant for another reason too, in order to detect what leading men were thinking. Every word, every look he twisted into some criminal significance—and stored them up in his memory.

卫军长官路奇乌斯·塞乌斯·斯特拉波和粮务长官盖乌斯·图尔拉尼乌斯宣誓效忠；接下来是元老、军队和普通民众。因为提贝里乌斯有个习惯，就是不管做什么事情，总是先让执政官主动提出来，仿佛共和体制依然存在，而他本人还不能确定是否由他掌握统治大权似的。甚至在发布敕令、召集元老到元老院开会时，他所使用的也只不过是奥古斯都赋予他的保民官的权力。他的布告十分简洁，而且非常谦逊。在布告中他说，他打算料理父亲的后事，而且要守在他父亲的遗体旁，这是他敢擅自处理的唯一一件国家大事。

但事实却并非如此，在奥古斯都逝世的时候，提贝里乌斯就已经以统帅的身份向近卫军发布了口令。并且还已经掌握了宫廷的一切，拥有诸如哨兵、卫士等等宫廷的全套装备。他到广场或者是元老院去的时候，都有士兵护卫；他给军队写信时，已经完全是一副皇帝的口吻。只有在元老院里讲话时，他才表现出一些犹豫不决的神态。他这样做的原因主要是因为日耳曼尼库斯，因为日耳曼尼库斯这时在国内拥有极高的声誉，他还拥有许多罗马军团和行省的大批辅助军队。提贝里乌斯担心日耳曼尼库斯会立刻夺取帝位，而不愿在那里静静地等待自己将来再将帝位传给他。除此以外，提贝里乌斯为了博取舆论对他的支持，还极力想让人们把自己看成是被公众推选出来的，是国家的召唤。他的继位既不是由于奥古斯都在晚年收养了他的缘故，也不是老奥古斯都的妻子阴谋暗算的结果。后来我们才看到，提贝里乌斯之所以假装出那种犹豫不决的神态还有一个原因，那就是他想弄清楚贵族们的想法，他把他们的每一句话、每一个表情都曲解成犯罪的迹象，并且深深地牢记在脑海里。

At the senate's first meeting he allowed no business to be discussed except the funeral of Augustus. But first the emperor's will was brought in by the priestesses of Vesta. Tiberius and Livia were his heirs, and Livia was adopted into the Julian family with the name of 'Augusta'. Grandchildren and great-grandchildren had been named as heirs in the second degree. In the third degree came the most prominent men in the State; Augustus had detested a good many of them, but their inclusion bragged to posterity that he had been their friend. His legacies were in keeping with the standards of ordinary citizens, except that he left 43,500,000 sesterces to the nation and people of Rome, a thousand to every Guardsman, five hundred each to the troops of the capital, three hundred to every citizen soldier, whether he belonged to a regular brigade or to an auxiliary battalion.

A discussion of the funeral followed. The proposals regarded as most noteworthy were those of Gaius Asinius Gallus and Lucius Arruntius. What Gallus wanted was that the procession should pass through a triumphal arch. Arruntius proposed that the body should be preceded by placards showing the titles of every law Augustus had passed and the names of every people he had conquered. Marcus Valerius Messalla Messallinus (I) also suggested that the oath of allegiance to Tiberius should be repeated every year. When Tiberius . asked him to confirm that he, Tiberius, had not prompted this proposal, Messalla answered that it was his own idea—and that in matters of public importance he intended to use his own judgement and no

在元老院的第一次会议上,他不谈论别的事情,只允许人们讨论有关奥古斯都的葬礼的问题。首先,维司塔贞女把皇帝的遗嘱拿了出来。[1] 遗嘱中指定提贝里乌斯和利维拉为继承人,利维拉被接纳为尤利乌斯家族的一员,并被加上奥古斯塔的称号。遗嘱还确立了他的孙子和重孙作为第二亲等的继承人。奥古斯都还指定了国内一些显要贵族为第三亲等的继承人,虽然其中大多数人其实是他所讨厌的。他把他们纳入他的后裔之列,目的是想表明他一直是他们的朋友。如果不把他赠赐的钱计算在内的话,他的遗产的数目和罗马普通公民的财产水平相一致。赠赐的钱的分配情况是:给罗马国家和人民 4350 万谢司特尔提乌斯,近卫军士兵每人 1000 谢司特尔提乌斯,驻在罗马城的士兵每人 500 谢司特尔提乌斯,还有罗马的军团士兵或辅助步兵中队的士兵,[2] 每人 300 谢司特尔提乌斯。

接下来,人们开始讨论有关葬仪的问题。其中,人们认为盖乌斯·阿西尼乌斯·伽路斯和路奇乌斯·阿尔伦提乌斯两人的提议最有价值。伽路斯建议葬仪的仪仗队应当穿过一座凯旋门,阿尔伦提乌斯建议,在遗体前面应当用一些布告牌子列出奥古斯都在生前所制定的一切法律,以及他所征服的所有民族的名称。玛尔库斯·瓦列里乌斯·美撒拉·美撒里努斯(一世)则建议每年人们都应该向提贝里乌斯反复宣誓效忠。当提贝里乌斯问他提出这样的建议,是否是出于提贝里乌斯的授意的时候,美撒拉说,这完全是他自己的想法,并且坚决表示,只要是涉及公众利益的时候,他发表的永

---

〔1〕 按照古罗马的惯例,遗嘱和条约都存放在神庙里,特别是维司塔神庙里,维司塔贞女则是维司塔神庙的住持。

〔2〕 辅助步兵中队不属于军团的编制,在帝国时期有 30 多个这样的步兵中队,其地位和待遇与军团相同。

one else's, even at the risk of causing offence. This show of independence was the only sort of flattery left.

Members clamoured that the body of Augustus should be carried
to the pyre on the shoulders of senators. Tiberius, with condescending
leniency, excused them. He also published an edict requesting the
populace not to repeat the disturbances—due to over-enthusiasm—at
the funeral of Julius Caesar, by pressing for Augustus to be cremated
in the Forum instead of the Field of Mars, his appointed place of rest.
On the day of the funeral the troops were out, apparently for protec-
tive purposes. This caused much jeering from people who had witnessed, or heard from their parents, about that day (when the nation's enslavement was still rudimentary) of the ill-starred attempt to
recover Republican freedom by murdering the dictator Caesar—a fearful crime? or a conspicuously glorious achievement? Now, they said,
this aged autocrat Augustus seems to need a military guard to ensure
his undisturbed burial, in spite of his lengthy domination and the
foresight with which his heirs, too, have been allocated resources for
the suppression of the old order.

Then there was much discussion of Augustus himself. Most people
were struck by meaningless points such as the coincidence between the
dates of his first public office and his death, and the fact that he died

远是自己的独立见解,而不会为任何人代言,即使这样做是冒着得罪人的危险他也义无反顾。其实他这番关于所谓独立见解的表白,正是人们早已司空见惯的一种谄媚方式。

元老们吵吵嚷嚷地说,奥古斯都的遗体应该由元老们抬到火葬用的柴堆上去。提贝里乌斯以屈尊纡贵的温和态度免除了他们这项义务,并且发布敕令说,为了避免如先前为圣尤利乌斯(即尤利乌斯·恺撒)举行葬仪时,人们由于过分热心反而掀起了骚乱那样的情况再度发生,他要求人民不要强迫在罗马广场上火葬奥古斯都,而是在奥古斯都,生前指定的葬地玛尔斯广场举行。[1]在举行葬礼的那一天,军队全部出动,处于武装戒备状态。这种情况引起了那些亲眼看到过,或是听老一辈的人们谈起过恺撒被刺杀[2]那一天的情况的人们的嘲笑(在人们刚开始受奴役)想恢复自由但又运气不佳的日子里,刺杀独裁者恺撒这件事在一些人眼里就成了极为可怕的罪行,而在另一些人眼里却又成了极其光荣的功勋。现在他们说:"尽管统治了很久,甚至能事先富有预见性地进行妥善安排,使他的继承者能拥有足够的力量来制服国家,这个年老的专制君主奥古斯都却仍然还需要卫队的护卫,来保证葬仪的平安无事。"

然后,更多的谈论集中在奥古斯都本人身上。大多数人注意的只是那些毫无意义的事情,比如说,他取得皇帝大权的日子和他去世的日子是相同的;他和他的父亲盖乌斯·屋大维一样,死在诺

---

〔1〕 奥古斯都的陵地是他在第六次担任执政官的时候(公元前28年),在玛尔斯广场北部修建起来的。

〔2〕 恺撒是在公元前44年被刺杀,死时56岁。

in the same house and room at Nola as his father, Gaius Octavius. There was also talk about his numerous consulships—which equalled the combined totals of Marcus Valerius Corvus and Gaius Marius—of his tribune's power continuous for thirty-seven years, of the twenty-one times he was hailed as victor, and of his other honours, traditional or novel, single or repeated. Intelligent people praised or criticized him in varying terms. One opinion was as follows, Filial duty and a national emergency, in which there was no place for law-abiding conduct, had driven him to civil war—and this can be neither initiated nor maintained by decent methods. He had made many concessions to Antony and to Lepidus for the sake of vengeance on his father's murderers. When Lepidus grew old and lazy, and Antony's selfindulgence got the better of him, the only possible cure for the distracted country had been government by one man. However, Augustus had put the State in order not by making himself king or dictator but by creating the Principate. The empire's frontiers were on the ocean, or distant rivers. Armies, provinces, fleets, the whole system was interrelated. Roman citizens were protected by the law. Provincials were decently treated. Rome itself had been lavishly beantified. Force had been sparingly used—merely to preserve peace for the majority.

The opposite view went like this. Filial duty and national crisis had been merely pretexts. In actual fact, the motive of Octavian, the future Augustus, was lust for power. Inspired by that, he had mobilized ex-army settlers by gifts of money, raised an army—while he was

拉的同一所房子、同一间屋子里等等。人们还谈论他担任执政官的众多的次数——这等于瓦列里乌斯·考尔武斯和盖乌斯·马利乌斯二人担任次数的总和,[1]谈论他保持保民官的权力达连续37年之久,还有关于他取得的21次的胜利;关于其他的旧的、新的,唯一的或多次取得的荣誉,人们也谈论得非常多。具有聪明才智的人们各自用不同的术语去颂扬或批评他。一种意见是:"对继父的孝心和当时法纪废弛的国家紧急情况,驱使他发动了内战——而不论发动内战还是进行内战,都是无法采用正当的手段的。为了追究谋杀他继父的凶手,他向安托尼乌斯、列庇都斯都作出了很大的让步。当列庇都斯越来越老,越来越懒散起来而安托尼乌斯的自我放纵也更加剧的时候,唯一可以补救这个陷于混乱的国家的办法就是由一个人来全权统治。但是奥古斯都在治理国家时并不是使自己成为君主或是独裁者,而是创立了普林凯普斯的名义。帝国的边陲是海洋或遥远的河流。军团、行省、舰队、全部行政机构的统治权都被集中起来。罗马公民受到法律的保护,行省的人民受到尊重,罗马城也被装点得极为富丽堂皇。那时很少使用武力去解决问题,只有在需要保证全国人民的和平时才会使用武力。"

但是另一方面,一些反对者认为:"对继父的孝心和国家的危急情况,只不过是一种借口。事实上,屋大维,这位未来的奥古斯都,他这样做的动机正是为了取得统治大权。出于此,他才用金钱的赏赐刺激老兵,在他尚未成年而且还没有担任过任何公职的

---

〔1〕 考尔乌斯六次担任执政官,马利乌斯七次,两人的总和是13次。

only a half-grown boy without any official status—won over a consul's brigades by bribery, pretended to support Sextus Pompeius (I) , and by senatorial decree usurped the status and rank of a practor. Soon both consuls, Gains Vibius Pansa and Aulus Hirtius, had met their deaths—by enemy action; or perhaps in the one case by the deliberate poisoning of his wound, and in the other at the hand of his own troops, instigated by Octavian. In any case it was he who took over both their armies. Then he had forced the reluctant senate to make him consul. But the forces given him to deal with Antony he used against the State. His judicial murders and land distributions were distasteful even to those who carried them out. True, Cassius and Brutus died because he had inherited a feud against them; nevertheless, personal enmities ought to be sacrificed to the public interest. Next he had cheated Sextus Pompeius by a spurious peace treaty, Lepidus by spurious friendship. Then Antony, enticed by the treaties of Tarentum and Brundusium and his marriage with Octavian's sister, had paid the penalty of that delusive relationship with his life. After that, there had certainly been peace, but it was a bloodstained peace. For there followed the disasters of Marcus Lollius (I) and Publius

时候便征募了一支军队,靠贿赂收买了一位执政官〔1〕的军团,并装出一副支持塞克斯图斯·庞培(一世)的样子。在他通过元老院的命令夺取到行政长官的身份和权力之后不久,两位执政官盖乌斯·维比乌斯·庞撒和奥路斯·希尔提乌斯就死了。〔2〕这两个人或许是被敌人杀死的,或许是被谋害致死的:庞撒的伤口被故意撒上了毒药,希尔提乌斯则是被自己手下那些受到屋大维教唆的士兵杀死的。无论如何,最后是他接管了两位执政官的军队。接着,他又强迫那些内心不情愿的元老院任命他担任执政官,而那些交给他用来制服安托尼乌斯的军队,却被他用来反对共和国了。对于他所宣判的谋杀者和土地的分配,人们并不满意,甚至连执行这些任务的人也不赞同。事实上,卡西乌斯和布鲁图斯的丧命是因为他们与他长期仇恨的结果,尽管私人之间的仇恨应当服从于公众的利益。接下来,他又以一项虚伪的和平条约〔3〕欺骗了塞克斯图斯·庞培,列庇都斯则受到了一种虚假的友谊的欺骗。继而安托尼乌斯又受到双重诱惑:塔伦特和布伦地西乌姆条约的签订,〔4〕以及屋大维把自己的妹妹嫁给他,结果这一骗人的裙带关系却断送了他的性命。在这之后,国家确实是获得了和平,但这是一种充满血腥的和平,因为接踵而至的是马尔库斯·洛里乌斯(一世)和普

---

〔1〕 指安托尼乌斯,事情发生在公元前44年。

〔2〕 事情发生在公元前44年的木提那战役之后,传说两人都是死在他的奸细之手。当时安托尼乌斯逃亡在外,共和国又没有执政官,因此,作为唯一的胜利者,屋大维便夺取了三军的统率权。

〔3〕 这是指公元前39年屋大维、安托尼乌斯和庞培三人缔结的米塞努姆条约,条约尚未履行,第二年就发生了战争。

〔4〕 公元前37年,缔结塔伦特条约;公元前40年,缔结布伦地西乌姆条约,屋大维和安托尼乌斯瓜分了罗马世界。

Quinctilius Varus; and there were the assassinations, for example, of Aulus Terentius Varro Murena, Marcus Egnatius Rufus and Iullus Antonius.

And gossip did not spare his personal affairs—how he had abducted the wife of Tiberius Claudius Nero, and asked the priests the farcical question whether it was in order for her to marry while pregnant. Then there was the debauchery of his friend Publius Vedius Pollio. But Livia was a real catastrophe, to the nation, as a mother and to the house of the Caesars as a stepmother.

Besides, critics continued, Augustus seemed to have superseded the worship of the gods when he wanted to have himself venerated in temples, with god-like images, by priests and ministers. His appointment of Tiberius as his successor was due neither to personal affection nor to regard for the national interests. Thoroughly aware of Tiberius' cruelty and arrogance, he intended to heighten his own glory by the contrast with one so inferior. For a few years earlier, when Augustus had been asking the senate to re-award tribune's powers to Tiberius, the emperor had actually let drop in a complimentary oration certain remarks about Tiberius' deportment, style of dressing, and habits. Ostensibly these were excuses; in fact they were criticisms.

布里乌斯·克温克提利乌斯·伐鲁斯的灾难,[1]还有谋杀,比如奥路斯·特伦提乌斯·瓦罗·穆列纳、玛尔库斯·埃格纳提乌斯·路福斯和优鲁斯·安托尼乌斯在罗马被处死。"[2]

人们的闲言碎语还涉及他个人家庭的私事:他是怎样诱拐了提贝里乌斯·克劳狄乌斯·尼禄的妻子,并且他还向祭司们提出过引人发笑的滑稽问题,那就是她在怀有身孕的时候,结婚是否合法。还有他的朋友普布里乌斯·维狄乌斯·波里欧[3]的胡作非为。但是利维拉是一个真正的祸害:作为一个母亲,利维拉是国家的祸害,而作为一个继母,她又是恺撒一家的祸害。

除此以外,人们还议论说,奥古斯都想建立个人崇拜以取代人们对诸神的崇拜,他要求在神庙中给他设立神像,受祭司和僧侣的膜拜。他过继提贝里乌斯为自己的继承人,他这样做既不是因为他个人喜欢提贝里乌斯,也不是从国家的利益考虑,而是因为他已经透彻地了解,提贝里乌斯内心是多么残忍和傲慢,因此他就想选他作为继承人,以便在对比之下,可以提高他本人的声誉。早在几年前,当奥古斯都请求元老们重新授予提贝里乌斯保民官的权力的时候,这位帝王就在作为祝词的一次发言中提到了提贝里乌斯的品行、衣着和习惯,这些话表面上看起来是在为提贝里乌斯的缺点作辩解,但实则是一种责难。

---

〔1〕 公元前 16 年,马尔库斯·洛里乌斯溃败于日耳曼。普布里乌斯·克温克提利乌斯·伐鲁斯则是在公元 9 年在威斯特伐利亚的森林中被阿尔米尼乌斯歼灭。

〔2〕 公元前 23 年穆列纳被处死,公元前 19 年路福斯被处死,公元前 2 年安托尼乌斯因与优利娅通奸自杀。

〔3〕 普布里乌斯·维狄乌斯·波里欧是奥古斯都的朋友,他出身卑微,但拥有巨额财富。

After an appropriate funeral, Augustus was declared a god and decreed a temple. But the target of every prayer was Tiberius. Addressing the senate, he offered a variety of comments on the greatness of the empire and his own unpretentiousness. Only the divine Augustus, he suggested, had possessed a personality equal to such responsibilities—he himself, when invited by Augustus to share his labours, had found by experience what hard hazardous work it was to rule the empire. Besides, he said, a State which could rely on so many distinguished personages ought not to concentrate the supreme power in the hands of one man—the task of government would be more easily carried out by the combined efforts of a greater number.

But grand sentiments of this kind sounded unconvincing. Besides, what Tiberius said, even when he did not aim at concealment, was—by habit or nature—always hesitant, always cryptic. And now that he was determined to show no sign of his real feelings, his words became more and more equivocal and obscure. But the chief fear of the senators was that they should be seen to understand him only too well. So they poured forth a flood of tearful lamentations and prayers, gesticulating to heaven and to the statue of Augustus, and making reverent gestures before Tiberius himself.

At this juncture he gave instructions for a document to be produced and read. It was a list of the national resources. It gave the numbers of regular and auxiliary troops serving in the army; the strength of the navy; statistics concerning the provinces and dependent kingdoms;

葬礼顺利结束后,元老院宣布将奥古斯都作为神供奉,并且还决定建一座神庙来奉祀他。但是提贝里乌斯却成了人们祈祷的对象。他在元老院发言时,极力赞美了帝国的伟大,而且对自己的能力作出了十分谦逊的说明。他说,只有圣奥古斯都这样伟大的人才能承担起这样一个伟大国家的责任。当他本人奉奥古斯都之召前来同他分担责任的时候,他根据自己的经验了解到,治理国家是一件多么艰难、多么需要冒风险的事情。除此以外,他认为,一个要依靠许多杰出人物来维持的国家,是不应该把全部责任都集中到一个人身上去的。如果大家能齐心协力、共同分担国家的责任的话,那么国家的治理就会容易多了。

但是这种冠冕堂皇的话,实际上并没有说服力。而且提贝里乌斯的讲话方式,或许是出于习惯,或许是天性使然,即便在他不是故意隐瞒自己的真实意图时,也总是含糊其辞。既然现在他是在一意隐藏自己的真实感情,他的话也就变得更加暧昧模糊、不可捉摸了。元老们也非常害怕皇帝会认为他们似乎已猜透了他的心思,因此他们涕泪纵横地悲叹、痛哭并祈求。他们向上苍和奥古斯都的神像伸手祷告,又匍匐在提贝里乌斯本人面前虔诚乞怜。

而就在这个关键时刻,他下令取出并宣读一个文件。[1] 这是一个记录着国家力量的清单,里面列举了正规军队和辅助军队的人数;海军军力;行省和罗马保护下的王国的数目;直接的和间接

---

〔1〕 奥古斯都死后留下了三个遗嘱,一个是关于他的葬仪问题的,一个记述了他本人的业绩,另一个就是这份清单。

direct and indirect taxation; recurrent expenditure and gifts. Augustus had written all this out in his own hand. Furthermore, he had added a clause advising that the empire should not be extended beyond its present frontiers. Either he feared dangers ahead, or he was jealous.

The senate now wallowed in the most abject appeals. Tiberius remarked incidentally that, although he did not feel himself capable of the whole burden of government, he was nevertheless prepared to take on any branch of it that might be entrusted to him. 'Then I must ask, Caesar,' called out Gaius Asinius Gallus, 'which branch you desire to have handed over to you.' This unexpected question threw Tiberius off his stride. For some moments he said nothing. Then, recovering his balance, he replied that, since he would prefer to be excused from the responsibility altogether, he felt much too diffident to choose or reject this or that part of it. Gallus, however, who had guessed from Tiberius' looks that he had taken offence, protested that the purpose of his question had not been to parcel out functions which were inseparable; it had been to obtain from the lips of Tiberius himself the admission that the State was a single organic whole needing the control of a single mind. Gallus went on to praise Augustus and remind Tiberius of his own victories, and his long and splendid achievements as a civilian. All the same he failed to appease the indignation he had caused. Tiberius had hated him for years, feeling that Gallus' marriage to his own former wife, Marcus Agrippa's daughter Vipsania, was a

的税收;每年必要的开支和例行的奖赏等。所有这些数目都是奥
古斯都亲自誊定的,最后他还附加了一个条款,条款规定帝国今
后不许再扩充现有的疆土。这或许是因为他害怕会有危险,或许
是由于他的嫉妒。

到了这时,元老院更加堕落了,以至于提出了最卑鄙的请求。
提贝里乌斯偶然说了这样一句话,他说尽管他觉得自己没有能力
承担起整个国家的重任,但他仍然做好了充分的准备去承担起可
能分配给他的任何一个部门的工作。于是盖乌斯·阿西尼乌
斯·伽路斯[1]就问道:"那就要请问恺撒,你希望把哪个部门的
工作分配给你呢?"这种突如其来的提问使他一时间茫然无措,不
知该怎样回答。他好长一段时间没说一句话,过了一会儿,他才
定了定神,回答道,他宁愿把全副重担都卸下来,对于这副重担中
的任何一个部分的工作,选择接受还是推辞,他都深感困难。伽
路斯从提贝里乌斯的脸色猜出他冒犯了他,于是就辩解说,他向
提贝里乌斯提出这个问题,目的并不是要他把那不可分割的职权
分割开来,而是想得到提贝里乌斯的亲口承认,国家是一个需要
由一个人来统治的完整的有机体。接着伽路斯就颂扬了奥古斯
都,并且请求提贝里乌斯不要忘记他自己过去的胜利,以及他作
为一个执政官长久以来所取得的辉煌成就。他所有的这些努力
并未能平息他所激起的皇帝的恼怒,提贝里乌斯多年以来就已经对
伽路斯非常恼恨了,伽路斯娶了他的前妻,即玛尔库斯·阿格里帕
的女儿维普撒尼娅,[2]这种做法使提贝里乌斯觉得,他和他的

---

〔1〕 盖乌斯·阿西尼乌斯·伽路斯是奥古斯都的好朋友盖乌斯·阿
西尼乌斯·波里欧的儿子,是当时著名的演说家。

〔2〕 维普撒尼娅·阿格里披娜是玛尔库斯·维普撒尼乌斯·阿格里
帕的女儿,起初嫁给了提贝里乌斯,奥古斯都为了让提贝里乌斯和他的女儿
优利娅结婚而进行干预,提贝里乌斯于是和维普撒尼娅离婚。

sign that Gallus had the arrogance of his father Gaius Asinius Pollio (I)—and was over-ambitious.

Next Lucius Arruntius spoke in rather the same vein as Gallus. He too gave offence. Tiberius, in his case, had no longstanding hostility. But he was suspicious of Arruntius, whose wealth, activity, and talents were celebrated. Augustus, in one of his last conversations, had gone over the names of men who would be fit and willing to become emperor, or unfit and unwilling, or fit but unwilling. He had described Marcus Aemilius Lepidus (IV) as suitable but disdainful, Gaius Asinius Gallus as eager but unsuitable, and Lucius Arruntius as both fit and capable of making the venture, if the chance arose. (There is agreement about the first two names; but in some versions Arruntius is replaced by Cnaeus Calpuius Piso.) All those mentioned, apart from Lepidus, were soon struck down on one charge or another, at the instigation of Tiberius. Others who chafed his suspicious temperament were Quintus Haterius and Mamercus Aemilius Scaurus. What Haterius did was to ask: ' How long, Caesar, will you allow the State to have no head?' The fault of Scaurus was to say that, since Tiberius had not vetoed the consuls' motion by his tribune's power, there was hope that the senate's prayers would not be unrewarded. Tiberius lost no time in abusing Haterius. But the intervention of Scaurus, against whom his anger was more implacable, he passed over in silence.

父亲盖乌斯·阿西尼乌斯·波里欧(一世)同样心怀傲慢,并且野心勃勃。

路奇乌斯·阿尔伦提乌斯接着发言,他发言的内容与伽路斯的发言基本相同,因此他也触怒了提贝里乌斯。尽管提贝里乌斯对他并没有怀着积久的怨愤,但是阿尔伦提乌斯却引起了他的怀疑,因为阿尔伦提乌斯是一个财富丰饶、深具魄力、才华出众的人物。原来奥古斯都在他逝世前的一次谈话中,曾经历数了一些人的名字。这些人中谁是适合、也愿意当皇帝的,哪些人不适合、也不想当皇帝,还有哪些人适于担任、而又不愿意担任皇帝的,奥古斯都都一一进行了评说。他评述道,马尔库斯·艾米利乌斯·列庇都斯(四世)有这样的能力,但是他不想担任;盖乌斯·阿西尼乌斯·伽路斯非常渴望这个帝位,可是他不适合;路奇乌斯·阿尔伦提乌斯不但适合并具有这样的能力,而且只要有机会,他也会冒险一试(关于前面两个人大家没有异议;但是在另一些版本中记载的,奥古斯都说的是格涅乌斯·卡尔普伊乌斯·披索,而不是阿尔伦提乌斯)。上面提到的那些人,除了列庇都斯以外,不久都在提贝里乌斯的主使之下借着这样或那样的罪名除掉了。其他引起提贝里乌斯猜忌的人还有克温图斯·哈提里乌斯和玛美尔库斯·艾米利乌斯·司考路斯。原来哈提里乌斯曾经提出过这样的问题:"恺撒啊,你要让国家这样没有首脑的时间延续多长呢?"司考路斯的错误就在于也说过同样的话,他曾说,既然提贝里乌斯从来没有利用自己保民官的权力否决过执政官的提议,因此人们就有希望看到元老院的请求都会得到答复。提贝里乌斯立刻就把哈提里乌斯辱骂了一顿。由于司考路斯的多嘴,提贝里乌斯的怒火就更加难以平息了,但是他当时一句话也没说就把司考路斯放在一边了。

Finally, exhausted by the general outcry and individual entreaties, he gradually gave way—not to the extent of admitting that he had accepted the throne, but at least to the point of ceasing to be urged and refuse. There is a well-known story about Haterius. He went into the palace to apologize, and, as Tiberius walked by, grovelled at his feet. Thereupon Tiberius crashed to the ground, either by accident or because he was brought down by the grip of Haterius—who was then all but killed by the guards. However, the emperor's feelings were not softened by the dangerous predicament of the senator, until Haterius appealed to the Augusta—as Livia was now called—and, at her urgent entreaty, was saved.

She, too, was flattered a great deal by the senate. It was variously proposed that she should be called 'parent' and 'mother' of her country; and a large body of opinion held that the words 'son of Julia' ought to form part of the emperor's name. He, however, repeatedly asserted that only reasonable honours must be paid to women—and that, in regard to compliments paid to himself, he would observe a comparable moderation. In reality, however, he was jealous and nervous, and regarded this elevation of a woman as derogatory to his own person. He would not even allow her to be allotted an official attendant, and forbade an Altar of Adoption and other honours of the kind. For Germanicus, however, he requested a special command. A

到了最后，提贝里乌斯终于对这些平庸的大声疾呼和个人的乞求感到厌倦了，他开始一点一点地逐渐让步——不是让步到接受帝位的程度，而是让步到大家不再恳求、自己不再拒绝的程度。哈提里乌斯的故事是众所周知的，他到宫殿里去向皇帝请罪的时候，看到提贝里乌斯正走过来，他便匍匐跪倒在提贝里乌斯脚下。于是提贝里乌斯也趴倒在地上，这或许是出于偶然，或许是因为哈提里乌斯紧紧抓着提贝里乌斯而将他带倒了，因此他差点儿被卫兵们杀死。尽管这位元老陷入如此危险的困境，皇帝的心也并没有为之所动。万般无奈，最后哈提里乌斯又去恳求奥古斯塔——这是利维拉现在的称呼——在她的迫切恳求下，哈提里乌斯才终于保住了性命。

奥古斯塔也是元老院极力谄媚的一个对象。人们纷纷提出各种不同的建议，有些人建议称她为"太后"；有些人建议给她加上"国母"的尊号；大多数的人则提议说"优利娅之子"这个词应该成为帝王名字的一个组成部分。不过提贝里乌斯反复强调说，公众给予妇人的荣誉必须是合理的，而对于人们加到他本人身上的荣誉，他也将会保持着一种比较谦逊的态度。然而，实际上，他是心怀妒忌而多疑的，他认为如此提高一个妇人的地位会贬低他自己的威信。他甚至不允许分配给她一名侍从，禁止修建一座纪念过继的祭坛，[1]也不允许给她以诸如此类的其他荣誉。但是对日耳曼尼库斯·恺撒，他却为他提出一些特殊的请求，他请求授予他

---

〔1〕 修建这种祭坛是用来纪念利维拉过继到尤利乌斯家族的。

mission was sent to confer it and at the same time to console Germanicus' sorrow at the death of Augustus. The same request was not made for Drusus because he was consul elect and in Rome.

The elections were now transferred from the Assembly to the senate. With regard to the number of praetors Tiberius adhered to the precedent established by Augustus and nominated twelve candidates. The senate asked him to increase the number, but he declared on oath that he would never do so.

Up to this time, although the most important elections were settled by the emperor, some had been left to the inclinations of the national Assembly drawn up by 'tribes'. The public, except in trivial talk, made no objection to their deprival of this right. The senate acquiesced gladly, since it relieved them from the necessity of undignified canvassing and outlay. Tiberius guaranteed that he himself would not recommend more than four candidates, who would have to be appointed without competition or rejection.

At the same time the tribunes petitioned to offer, at their own expense, an annual display which would take its name from the late emperor and be added to the calendar as the Games of Augustus. But it was decided to pay for them from public funds, and to allow the tribunes to wear triumphal robes in the Circus Maximus (they were

总督的权力,[1]并且派出一个使团去授予他这些权力,同时他还安慰日耳曼尼库斯,要他为奥古斯都的去世而节哀顺变。提贝里乌斯并没有为杜路苏斯[2]提出同样的请求,因为这时杜路苏斯正是下一任执政官的候选人,而且本人正在罗马。

现在,选举权由民团会议转到了元老院。关于候选人的数目,提贝里乌斯坚持奥古斯都生前规定的人数,他指定了 12 个人为候选行政长官。元老院请求他增加候选人的数目,但是提贝里乌斯声明说,他发誓决不增加人数。

在此以前,虽然最重要的选举都是由皇帝亲自裁决的,但还有一些是由各特里布斯[3]族团会议斟酌决定的。人民对于自己被剥夺了这种权利,只是絮絮叨叨地嘟哝几句,除此之外,他们并没有任何抗议的表示。而元老院因此可以从那种有损尊严的拉选票和收买的活动中解放出来,所以他们也很高兴地默许了这种变革。提贝里乌斯则保证说推荐候选人不超过 4 名,[4]并且候选人被指定后,就不允许再竞争,也不能拒绝。

与此同时,几位保民官请愿,要求允许他们每年自费举办一次赛会,赛会是以故去的皇帝的名字来命名的,并且还把这一赛会列入了岁时表,称为奥古斯都赛会。但是经过讨论后人们决定,赛会的费用仍由国库担负。在赛会举行时,并且还允许保民

---

[1] 远方军队的将领常常被授予总督的权力,这里所要求的是恢复日耳曼尼库斯在高卢和日耳曼已经享有了三年的特殊的总督权力。

[2] 杜路苏斯是提贝里乌斯的儿子。

[3] 全体罗马人民分为 35 个特里布斯,农村 31 个,城市 4 个。城市特里布斯包括无产者,还有全体罗马细民(是指那些地位较低的人,包括被释奴隶)。

[4] 这里的 4 名候选人是从 12 名行政长官候选人中间选出的。

not, however, to be permitted the use of chariots). It was not long before the organization of this show was transferred to the praetor who is concerned with lawsuits between citizens and non-citizens.

官在大赛马场中穿凯旋袍(但是不允许他们乘坐马车)。可是不久之后,每年举办这种赛会的权力便转到行政长官手里去了,这些行政长官本来是负责审判罗马公民与异邦人之间的争讼的。

CHAPTER 2

Mutiny On The Frontiers

While these events were taking place at Rome, mutiny broke out in the regular army in Pannonia. There were no fresh motives for this, except that the change of emperors offered hopes of rioting with impunity and collecting the profits afforded by civil wars. Three brigades were stationed together in a summer camp with Quintus Junius Blaesus in command. When he heard of the death of Augustus and accession of Tiberius, he suspended normal duty for public mourning (or rejoicing). This was when insubordination and altercation began.

Before long, easy living and idleness were all the troops wanted; the idea of work and discipline became distasteful. There was a man called Percennius in the camp. Having become a private soldier after being a professional applause-leader in the theatre, he was insolent of tongue, and experienced in exciting crowds to cheer actors. The soldiers, simple men, were worried—now that Augustus was dead—about their future terms of service. Percennius gradually worked on them. After dark or in the evening twilight, when the better elements had dispersed to their tents and the riff-raff collected, they talked with him.

第二章　发生在边防军中的兵变

　　以上所述事件都是发生在罗马城内的情况,接下来要说的是在潘诺尼亚的正规军团里爆发的一次兵变。兵变并没有什么新的动机,只是新皇帝的继位使他们产生了一种新的想法,那就是他们可以为非作歹而不受惩罚,并且还可以在内战中大肆聚敛财富。在克温图斯·尤尼乌斯·布莱苏斯统率下的三个军团全部驻扎在夏营里。当布莱苏斯听到奥古斯都逝世和提贝里乌斯继位的消息后,便下令停止日常例行的一切事务,以表示大家的哀悼(或者说是庆祝)。从此他们就开始了不顺从,队伍不听命令并且吵吵闹闹。

　　不久,整个军队里便充满了贪图安逸享乐的不良风气,他们厌恶工作的劳苦,不愿意受纪律的约束。军营里有一个叫佩尔肯尼乌斯的人,来军营之前专门在剧场里干领头喝彩的行当,以后来到了军营中当兵。他最喜欢搬弄是非,为舞台上演员捧场的丰富经验使他具有一套鼓动群众的非凡本领。士兵们,那些单纯的普通的士兵们都在担心,奥古斯都的死会给他们在部队中服役的未来生活带来什么影响。佩尔肯尼乌斯看到有机可乘,就不断地鼓动他们。他利用黄昏后的时间或者是在夜间又或者是在黎明时分,这时那些比较正派的人都已经各自回到了自己的营帐,而那些军队里的乌合之众都纠集在他的周围,他们就与他鬼鬼祟祟地交谈。

Finally Percennius had acquired a team of helpers ready for mutiny. Then he made something like a public speech. 'Why', he asked, 'obey, like slaves, a few commanders of companies, fewer still of battalions? You will never be brave enough to demand better conditions if you are not prepared to petition—or threaten—an emperor who is new and still faltering. Inactivity has done quite enough harm in all these years. Old men, mutilated by wounds, are serving their thirtieth or fortieth year. And even after your official discharge your service is not finished; for you stay on with the colours as a reserve, still under canvas—the same drudgery under another name! And if you manage to survive all these hazards, even then you are dragged off to a remote country and "settled" in some waterlogged swamp or untilled mountainside. Truly the army is a harsh, unrewarding profession! Body and soul are reckoned at two and a half sesterces a day—and with this you have to find clothes, weapons, tents, and bribes for brutal companycommanders if you want to avoid chores.

'Heaven knows, lashes and wounds are always with us! So are hard winters and hardworking summers, grim war and unprofitable peace. There will never be improvement until service is based on a contract—pay,

最后,佩尔肯尼乌斯拉起了一支准备发动兵变的队伍,于是他就发表了一篇公开演说。"为什么?"他问道,"为什么我们要像奴隶一样地服从一些百人团长和几个军团将领的命令? 如果你们现在还没有足够的勇气,向一个地位尚未稳固的新皇帝提出请求或者进行武力威胁,那么什么时候才敢要求改善现状呢? 这些年的消极无为,已经给你们自己造成了够多的伤害。身体已经是多处重伤的老兵们,在军队里已经服役了三四十年。但是甚至在你们的长官宣布你们正式退役之后,你们的作战任务也仍然还没有结束;因为你们还要作为后备军带着满身伤痕继续留在营地的军旗之下,以另一个名义做着和先前一样的苦差事。[1] 即使你们幻想在经历了这么多的危险之后能够侥幸活下来,你们也仍然还要被强送到边远的地方去,你们'定居'在一块积水的沼泽地或者是一个寸草不生的荒山边。说实在话,在军队服役可真是一个既艰苦又毫无益处的工作啊。肉体加上灵魂,一天才值 10 个谢司特尔提乌斯;[2] 而且你们还必须用这点钱来购置衣服、武器、帐篷,去贿赂那些残暴的百人团长,以免他们会分配给你们一些苦差事!

但是天知道,鞭子和伤痕总是与我们形影不离,严寒的冬天和难熬的夏天,残酷的战争和无利可图的和平,这些东西也都是我们永远摆脱不掉的。改进的办法只有一个,那就是实施应征入

---

〔1〕 奥古斯都创建了常备军后,在公元前 16 年规定,军团士兵的服役期为连续 16 年,近卫军士兵为 12 年。20 年后,服役期限又分别延长到 20 年和 16 年,但在期满时士兵可以领到一笔退役金,以代替过去半个世纪中间施行的授予土地的办法。退役时愿意留下来的老兵可以留下,不过他们没有军旗,而只有自己的队旗。从理论上来说,他们可以不再做军团士兵所做的日常工作,可以另行组成一支精锐的老兵战斗队伍。

〔2〕 古代罗马的货币单位。

four sesterces a day; duration of service, sixteen years with no subsequent recall; a gratuity to be paid in cash before leaving the camp. Guardsmen receive eight sesterces a day, and after sixteen years they go home. Yet obviously their service is no more dangerous than yours. I am not saying a word against sentry-duty in the capital. Still, here are we among tribes of savages, with the enemy actually visible from our quarters!'

Percennius had an enthusiastic reception. As one point or another struck home, his hearers indignantly showed their lash-marks, their white hair, their clothes so tattered that their bodies showed through. Finally, in frenzied excitement, they clamoured that the three brigades should be merged into one. But jealousy wrecked this suggestion, because everyone wanted it to take his own brigade's name. So the proposal was altered, and instead the three Eagles, and the standards of the battalions, were put side by side. Turf was piled up, and a platform erected so as to make the place as conspicuous as possible. As they were hurrying ahead with this, Blaesus came up and began to revile them. Seizing hold of one man after another, he cried: 'Dye your hands in my blood instead! It would be less criminal to kill your general than to rebel against the emperor. As long as I live I shall keep my troops loyal—if I die, my death will help to bring them to their senses.'

伍时由契约明确规定的,饷银是每天 4 个谢司特尔提乌斯;服役期限是 16 年,期满之后不得再留为后备军;而且在离开军队前还应当以现金形式支付一笔养老金。近卫军士兵的军饷是每天 8 个谢司特尔提乌斯,并且是在 16 年服役期满后就回家。但是很明显你们所冒的危险要比近卫军多得多,我说这些话并非是针对在都城的警卫工作。可是在这里我们是置身在野蛮的部族中间的,而且敌人近在眼前,从我们自己的营帐中就可以清楚地望见!"

佩尔肯尼乌斯激起了士兵们的义愤,他的演说收到了预期的效果。因为他的话中有这一点或那一点正说到他们的心坎里去了。这时他的听众们有的愤怒地把鞭痕袒露出来,另一些人展示出他们的白头发,有的人给人们看他们那多处漏洞不能遮体的褴褛的衣衫。最后,他们群情激昂,纷纷要求把三个军团合并为一。但是强烈的嫉妒心使这个建议未能通过。因为每个人都想以自己的军团命名,而把其余的军团合并到自己的军团里面来。于是他们便采取了一个变通的建议,这就是把军团的三面军旗[1]和步兵中队的队旗[2]都并排地悬挂在一起。他们把草根土堆积起来,搭成了一个土台,以便尽可能地使这个集合的地方能够引人注目。正当他们热火朝天地忙活的时候,布莱苏斯来了。他严厉地斥责他们,还一个一个地用力把人们拉开。他咆哮着喊道:"把你们的手浸泡在我的血里吧,杀死你们的将领的罪行总比反叛皇帝的罪行轻一些!只要我还活着,我就要坚决保持我的军队的绝对忠诚,如果我死了,我的死亡将会唤起他们理性的觉醒。"

---

〔1〕 军团的军旗有一个鹰形的标记。
〔2〕 这里指每个步兵中队里三个步兵小队的旗帜,每一个军团有 30 面这样的队旗。

Nevertheless, the mound of turf kept rising. But when it was already breast-high, the stubborn perseverance of Blaesus won the day and they gave up the project. Then he made a tactful appeal to them. Rioting and mutiny were not, he said, the best ways of bringing grievances to the emperor's notice. The army had never in former days put such unheard-of-proposals to its commanders. Nor had they themselves ever put them to the divine Augustus. Besides, at this early stage of the reign it was untimely to add to the emperor's burdens. If, however (Blaesus continued) it was their firm intention to claim, in peacetime, what even the winners of civil wars had never claimed, then they must not plan violent, undisciplined, insubordinate measures—they must appoint delegates and brief them, in his presence. There was a clamorous reply that Blaesus' own son (a colonel) should be the delegate and should request the sixteen-year term of service, his further instructions to follow when the first had produced results. The colonel left for Rome. Then things became fairly peaceful. But the men were pleased with themselves, since the fact that the general's son had gone to speak in the common cause showed clearly that force had secured more than correct behaviour could ever have.

Before the disturbances began, detachments had been sent to Nauportus for various tasks such as road-making and bridge-building. When these men heard of the troubles in camp, they tore down their

尽管如此,但土台却仍在不断加高。但是当土台已经堆到齐胸高的时候,布莱苏斯坚定不移地坚持终于赢得了胜利,他们放弃了原来的计划。布莱苏斯随即向他们发表了一个十分机智的讲话。他说,暴动和兵变并不是让皇帝注意到自己的委屈的最好办法。在以前,罗马士兵从来没有向自己的指挥官提出过这样骇人听闻的要求,他们自己本身对已故的奥古斯都也从来没有做过这样的事,而在皇帝新即位不久就给他增加麻烦,这种做法更是不合时宜的。但是(布莱苏斯继续说)如果在和平时期他们一定要坚决地提出一些甚至内战的胜利者都从来没有提出的要求的话,那么他们一定不能采取暴力手段,采取那些破坏纪律原则和不服从的措施。他们可以委派一些使者,当面简短地转达他们的意愿。于是士兵们便纷纷叫嚷着回答说,应该派布莱苏斯(那位担任军团将领)的儿子去执行这个任务,先要请求服军役满16年就可以退役。如果这一请求得到批准,接下来他再提出进一步的要求。这个年轻人动身去了罗马以后,军队中就比较平静了。但企图骚乱的人是洋洋自得的,因为他们的统帅的儿子已经为了他们的共同利益去和皇帝谈话,而这一点清楚地表明,武力是比以前那种循规蹈矩的行为更见成效的。

在军队发生骚乱之前,几股特遣小分队曾被派到纳乌波尔图斯[1]去执行各种任务,诸如修建公路、建筑桥梁之类。当这些人一听到在军营中发生了骚乱的消息后,他们就立刻扯下了军队的旗

---

[1] 凯拉利乌斯认为该地就是现在的欧柏莱巴赫,大约在莱巴赫也就是现在的卢布尔雅那西南30英里。

colours and looted the villages nearby and even Nauportus itself, a community large enough to rank as a town. Company-commanders who tried to restrain them were jeered at arid abused, and finally beaten. The principal object of their anger was the corps chief-of-staff, Aufidienus Rufus. They pulled him out of his carriage, piled baggage on his back and drove him along at the head of the column, with frequent mocking inquiries whether he enjoyed these heavy burdens and protracted marches. For Rufus, promoted to company-commander and then to his present post after long service in the ranks, was all for reviving strict old-fashioned service conditions. He had won free from drudgery himself—but what he had endured made him all the more ruthless.

The arrival of the men from Nauportus revived the mutiny. Now marauders began to roam about ransacking the whole district. A few who had looted more than the rest were ordered by Blaesus to be flogged and confined to cells, in order to frighten the others; for he was still obeyed by the company-commanders and the steadier ordinary soldiers. As they were dragged away they offered resistance and grabbed at the legs of bystanders. Shouting out the names of their friends, and of their companies, battalions, and brigades, they cried that the same fate was in store for everybody—all this with repeated insults against the general and invocations of the gods. In fact, they did everything possible to arouse sympathy, indignation, ill-feeling, and panic. Everyone surged to their rescue. The cells were forced open, and deserters and condemned murderers were released and joined them.

帜,抢劫了附近的村庄,甚至连纳乌波尔图斯本地也遭到了他们的劫掠。这地方很大,差不多可以称得上是一个城镇了。那些百人团长出来制止他们,结果却遭到了嘲笑、侮辱、谩骂,最后甚至遭受到了攻击。使他们恼火的主要对象是营帅[1]奥菲迪耶努斯·路福斯,他们把他从马车上拖了下来,把行李一股脑儿堆在他的背上,驱赶着他走在队伍的最前面,并且不断地用嘲笑的口吻问他,他是否喜欢这些重负和令人厌倦的行军。路福斯是在经历了多年的普通士兵生涯以后才升任百人团长,后来又提拔到现在的营帅的位置上的。因此,他也一直想恢复过去那种极其严格的陈旧的军纪,他本人是从军队的苦役中熬出来的,而正是由于他自己受过苦,因此他对别人也就更加残酷无情。

这群人从纳乌尔波尔图斯回来后,又重新挑起了叛乱。掠夺者开始到处游荡,他们抢劫了附近的所有地区。当时百人团长和那些比较规矩的士兵还是服从布莱苏斯的,因此为了震慑一下其他作乱者,布莱苏斯便下令鞭打那几个劫掠了更多赃物的士兵,并把这些人关进了牢房。当这些人被卫兵拉走时,他们拼命挣扎,而且抓住旁观者的腿。他们呼喊着他们的朋友的名字,呼叫着他们所属的百人团、步兵中队和军团的名称,他们哭喊着说所有的人在不久的将来都会遭到同样的命运。他们一边还在不断地辱骂着他们的统帅,恳求着上帝。实际上,他们是在尽可能地利用一切办法来引起人们的同情、义愤、憎恶和恐慌。人们奔涌而来解救他们,他们冲破了牢房。这样,开小差的士兵和因重罪而被判刑的囚犯就被救了出来,并且他们会合在了一起。

---

〔1〕 这是为常备军的军营而设置的一种官职,负责设营、运输、战械、伤病等事宜。这种官职在公元前两个世纪才开始设置,一般都是从有长期作战经验的百人团长中选任。

Now the mutiny gained momentum. More and more leaders came forward. A private soldier called Vibulenus was hoisted on the shoulders of the men standing round the general's dais. The excited crowd, watching to see what he would do, heard him speak:

'I know you have brought these poor innocent men back to life and daylight. But you can't give my brother back to me, or me to him! The army in Germany sent him to talk to you about our common interests—and the general had him murdered last night by the gladiators whom he keeps armed to butcher us soldiers. Answer, Blaesus— where have you put his corpse? Even enemies don't refuse a grave. Later, when I have embraced his corpse and mourned my fill, you can tell them to murder me as well. But they mustn't grudge us burial. We are not dying because of any crime. We are dying because we worked for the army's good !'

To add to the inflammatory effect, Vibulenus wept and struck his face and beat his chest. Then he pushed aside those who were holding him on their shoulders, and hurled himself flat in front of one man after another, appealing to them. They went frantic with impassioned hostility. One group arrested the gladiators who were slaves in the service of Blaesus while others captured the rest of Blaesus' household, and a further band rushed off in search of the body. Indeed if it had not rapidly come to light that there was no body to be found, that the slaves denied the murder even under torture, and that Vibulenus had never had a brother, they were not far from killing the general himself.

现在兵变获得了动力,越来越多的军官们挺身而出。一个叫做维布列努斯的普通士兵被一些围在统帅的座坛前面旁观的人抬在肩膀上。人们群情激奋,纷纷好奇地望着他,看他要做什么,只听他向人群演讲道:

"我知道是你们使得这些可怜的、无辜的人们重新得到了阳光和生命。但是你们无法使我的兄弟起死回生,回到我的身边,也无法让我回到我兄弟的身边去。日耳曼的军队派他到你们这里来讨论我们的共同利益,但是在昨天夜里,统帅却命令剑奴〔1〕把我的兄弟杀死了,这些剑奴是他武装起来用以屠杀士兵的。回答我吧,布莱苏斯,你把他的尸体抛到什么地方去了?即使是敌人,也不能不给他一个葬身的坟墓啊!等一下吧,当我拥抱了他的尸体,尽情地痛哭一场之后,你就叫他们把我也杀掉吧。但是请他们将我们埋葬,不要让我们抛尸荒野。我们不是由于犯罪而死,我们是为了军团的利益而战,因而送掉了性命的。"

为了增加自己的话的煽动性效果,维布列努斯大声哭泣,他泪流满面、捶胸顿足。然后他猛烈地推开那些用肩膀抬着他的人们,一直横冲到前面去,他跪在人们面前一个一个地恳求。人们对他寄予了极大的同情,被维布列努斯激起的愤怒冲昏了他们的头脑,于是一群人把为布莱苏斯服务的剑奴抓了起来,他们本来都是些奴隶。还有一群人去抓捕布莱苏斯家中的其他人。更多的人则四散出去寻找尸体。老实说,如果不是很快就真相大白,那么他们差一点就要把统帅本人也杀死了。人们清楚地知道了,根本就没有什么尸体会被发现,奴隶们即使受到了酷刑拷问也仍然否认杀过人,而且维布列努斯也根本就没有这样一个兄弟。

---

〔1〕 古罗马公开表演的格斗者,他们通常都是奴隶和俘虏。

As it was, they turned out the other senior officers, including the chief-of-staff—looting their luggage as they fled. The company-commander Lucilius lost his life. In joking army talk his nickname was 'Another-please', because every time he broke a stick over a soldier's back he used to shout loudly for another and then another. His fellowofficers found safe hiding-places, except only Julius Clemens, who was kept because his intelligence was thought to qualify him for presenting the mutineers' demands. The eighth and fifteenth brigades nearly came to blows when one shouted for the death of a company-commander, Sirpicus by name, and the other protected him. Finally, the men of the ninth brigade intervened with appeals—and with threats of violence against those who ignored them.

The natural inscrutability of Tiberius was always particularly impenetrable in a crisis. However, this news impelled him to send to the scene his son Drusus with a distinguished staff and two battalions of the Guard. Drusus was given no definite instructions—he was to act as the circumstances required. The Guard battalions were strengthened beyond their usual numbers by picked drafts, and were further augmented by a substantial part of the horse Guards and also by the best

尽管如此,他们还是赶跑了其余的军团将领包括营帅,劫掠了逃跑者的行李。百人团长路奇里乌斯也在这场暴乱中丢了性命。对于路奇里乌斯,军队中有人给他起了个戏谑的绰号"下一个",因为在每次抽打士兵后背[1]的时候,他总是习惯地大声呼喊"下一个",然后又是"下一个"。他的同僚们都为了获得安全而躲藏起来。在这场动乱中,只有尤利乌斯·克利门斯是个例外,叛乱者饶了他的性命,因为叛乱的士兵们认为,他的机智会对他们提出自己的要求发挥一些恰当的用处。因为第八军团要求处死一个名叫西尔披库斯的百人团长时,第十五军团却出面保护他,因此第八军团和第十五军团之间也差一点火并起来。最后幸亏是第九军团出面干预,连请求加威胁地说谁要再惹怒他们,他们就会用武力来对付他,这样才把双方的争吵平息下来。

本性就让人难以捉摸的提贝里乌斯,在遇到危机的时候就更加隐秘,高深莫测。尽管如此,从潘诺尼亚传来的叛乱消息还是迫使他不得不把他的儿子杜路苏斯派到出事的地方。和杜路苏斯同行的,是一批杰出的贵族,还有近卫军的两个步兵中队。杜路苏斯没有得到什么明确的指示,他到那里将见机行事。这两个近卫军的步兵中队是由选拔出来的精锐士兵组成的,军力得到了极大的加强,要远胜于平常的近卫军步兵中队。此外还增添了一大部分近卫军骑兵和最优良精锐的日耳曼军队,这些日耳曼军队

---

[1] 葡萄蔓的棍子是百人团长的常用标志,他们经常用这种藤棍抽打士兵。

of the Germans who at that time guarded the emperor's person. With them went a man whose influence over Tiberius was very great, Lucius Aelius Sejanus, joint commander of the Guard with his father, Lucius Seius Strabo. He was to be the prince's adviser, and not to let the rest of the party forget what they stood to gain—or lose.

As Drusus approached, the soldiers met him. Ostensibly this was a mark of respect. But there were none of the customary demonstrations of pleasure and glittering full-dress decorations. The men were disgustingly dirty, and their expressions, intended merely to display dejection, looked virtually treasonable. As soon as Drusus had passed inside the outworks, they picketed the gates, and set armed detachments at key points of the camp. Everyone else crowded round the dais in a gigantic mob. Drusus mounted it with a gesture calling for silence. The mutineers, looking round at the great crowd, set up a truculent roar. But the next instant, as they caught sight of the Caesar, their nerve faltered. Violent yells alternated with confused mutterings, and then silence. They were terrifying and terrified in turn, as their feelings shifted. When Drusus finally got the better of the noise, he read out a letter from his father. It stated that the heroic Roman

在当时是直接护卫皇帝的。和他们同行的还有一个人,此人对提贝里乌斯的影响力是很大的,他就是路奇乌斯·埃利乌斯·谢雅努斯,他和他的父亲路奇乌斯·塞乌斯·斯特拉波一道担任近卫军长官。他这次随同前去的任务是担任皇子的顾问,并且使同行的其他人不要忘记,他们怎样做才能得到奖赏,怎样又会受到惩罚。[1]

当杜路苏斯快要到达营地的时候,军团的士兵们出去迎接他。表面上看来这种做法是尊重的表示,但是他们这时并没有丝毫平时的那种欢乐的神情,也没有佩戴光彩夺目的装饰品、衣冠整洁地出来迎接。他们的肮脏不堪令人恶心,他们的表情只是要故意表明他们内心的忧郁沮丧,但实际上,他们看起来却更像是图谋不轨的样子。杜路苏斯刚一进入外围的堡垒,他们就在各个门口设下了哨兵警戒,并且在营地的各个要口部署了全副武装的部队,作好了战斗的准备。其他的人则全部簇拥在他的座坛周围集结成一个巨大的骚动的人群。杜路苏斯登上座坛用手势要求大家安静下来,叛乱的士兵们四处张望,看到四周有这么多人,就发出一阵粗暴的喊声。接下来的刹那,当他们看到了恺撒,神经马上却又紧张起来。猛烈粗暴的叫喊与嘈杂混乱的私语交替出现,随即一切吵嚷戛然而止,周围一片寂静。正如他们内心不断交织的复杂矛盾一样,他们一会儿非常惊恐,一会儿又会成为别人恐怖的对象。杜路苏斯等喧嚣声终于稍微平静下来的时候,便宣读了他父亲写的一封信。信中写道,英雄的罗马军团的士兵们,在多次战

---

〔1〕 因为路奇乌斯·埃利乌斯·谢雅努斯对提贝里乌斯具有非同一般的影响力,因此他的随行就带有着提贝里乌斯本人的权威。

soldiers, his comrades in so many campaigns, were particularly near his heart, and that as soon as the shock of his bereavement was over, he would refer their claims to the senate. Meanwhile he had sent his son to grant without delay any concessions that could be awarded immediately. The remaining points must be saved up for the senate, which was as capable, they must understand, of generosity as of severity.

The answer came from the crowd that the company-commander Julius Clemens was briefed to put forward their demands. He started by proposing a sixteen-year term of service, with gratuities at its completion, pay of four sesterces a day, and no recalls after release. Drusus urged that the senate and emperor must have their say. This caused uproar. 'Why have you come', they shouted, 'if you are not going to raise salaries, improve terms of service, or help us at all? Anyone, on the other hand, is allowed to murder and flog! It used to be Tiberius who blocked the regular army's grievances by citing Augustus. Now Drusus has revived the same old trick. It looks as though our visitors will always be young men with fathers How cutious it is that the only army matters which the emperor refers to the senate are reforms in service conditions! If he does this, he ought also to consult them when death penalties or battles are in store. Clearly when rewards are concerned, he is not his own master—whereas no one controls punishments. '

役中和他并肩作战的伙伴们，[1]是特别和他心心相连，等他的悲痛情绪镇定下来以后，他将会立即把他们的要求提交元老院。现在，他先把他的儿子派到这里来，以便保证那些可以当场做出答复的要求不会再有任何拖延。剩下的其他各项要求，则必须提交有能力裁决的元老院定夺，他们必须弄清楚，哪些是应予宽容应允的，哪些又必须是应该严肃拒绝的。

士兵们回答说，百人团长尤利乌斯·克利门斯已经被推选代他们简明地提出他们的要求。于是他由服役期限为 16 年和退役时发给养老金的要求开始谈起，接着又说到要求规定兵饷每天为 4 谢司特尔提乌斯，以及退役后不再被留下来服兵役的问题。杜路苏斯解释说元老院和皇帝一定会作出妥善的处理。但是这种说法被士兵们的怒吼打断了。"那么你为什么要到这里来?"他们说，"如果你不能提高我们的军饷，不能改善我们的服役期限，换句话说，也就是你对我们不能有丝毫帮助，那么你又何必到这里来呢? 从另一方面来说，你来就是为允许任何人随便杀人、鞭打人! 把士兵们的请愿推诿到奥古斯都身上是提贝里乌斯先前惯用的伎俩，现在杜路苏斯又来故伎重演了。看起来好像总是那些谨遵父命的年轻人来作我们的说客，难道就派不出别的人到这里来了吗? 只要是有关改善士兵服役条件的事情，皇帝就一定要把它交给元老院去处理，这是多么奇怪的事情! 如果这件事他也这样交给元老院处理的话，那么在判处死刑和进行战争的问题上，他也应当征求元老院的意见才是。很显然，当涉及奖赏的时候，他便不能自己做主;而在谈到惩罚的时候，又没有任何人能够插手。"

---

〔1〕 这是指公元前 12 ~ 前 9 年，当时提贝里乌斯将国境推到上多瑙河，以及公元 6 ~ 9 年，当时潘诺尼亚和达尔马提亚发动了起义，形势极为严峻。

At last they left the dais. But if they came upon any Guardsmen on Drusus' staff, they made menacing gestures, to create ill-feeling and give a pretext for open hostilities. They were particularly bitter against Gnaeus Cornelius Lentulus (II), whose seniority and military distinction made them think that, being more disgusted than anyone with the scandalous conduct of the army, he was stiffening Drusus' attitude. Shortly afterwards they caught him leaving, escorted to the gate by Drusus. Lentulus had seen danger ahead and was withdrawing to the winter camp. The men gathered round him and asked him where he was going. Was he on his way to the emperor, or to the senate—to oppose army reforms there too? Then they closed in on him and began throwing large stones. One hit him and drew blood. He was convinced that his end had come. But the hasty arrival of Drusus' main force saved him.

The night looked like ending in a disastrous criminal outbreak. But this was averted by a stroke of luck. Suddenly, in a clear sky, the light of the moon was seen to decline. The soldiers did not know why this was, and detected an omen of their own situation. The waning moon seemed to provide an analogy to their own efforts: success would only crown the measures they were adopting if the moon-goddess shone brightly again. To produce this result they made a clattering of brass instruments and blew blasts on every sort of trumpet. The light seemed stronger, and they were happy. Then it looked dimmer, and

最后他们离开了座坛。但如果在路上碰到任何一个杜路苏斯的随从人员时，他们就会挥动拳头威胁，制造事端、寻衅闹事。他们最痛恨的是格涅乌斯·考尔尼利乌斯·楞图路斯(二世)，这个人年龄比较大，军事上也享有很高的声誉,[1]他们认为，因为此人对于士兵们的叛乱行为比其他人更为厌恶，所以他是会进一步增强杜路苏斯的顽固态度的。不久之后，他们就发现他已离开，由杜路苏斯陪同着一起向大门走去。原来楞图路斯已经预感到了自己所面临的危险处境，正想向冬营撤退。叛乱的士兵们围住了他，问他要到哪里去，是到皇帝那里去，还是到元老院去，再到那里去干反对军队的正当要求的勾当？他们把他团团围在中心，开始扔大石头砸他。一块石头向他砸去，他顿时流出了血。他想这次他是死定了。就在这时，杜路苏斯的主力卫士们迅速赶到，将他解救了出来。

这一夜形势极为险恶，看起来一场会带来灭顶之灾的暴乱将要无可避免地发生。但是一次突如其来的幸运却使形势发生了逆转。原来在晴朗皎洁的夜空中，人们发现月亮的光亮突然变暗了。士兵们不知道这是什么原因，便认为这是他们当前情况的一个不好的兆头，这个光辉暗淡下来的月亮，正是向他们暗示着他们自身努力的结果:如果月亮女神能重新现出皎洁的光辉，那么他们将能够获得他们所期望的胜利。因此为了使月亮能够重新放出光辉，他们便敲起了铜器，并且把各种号角全都吹了起来。月光亮一些，他们就欢欣鼓舞;月光暗淡一些，他们就悲伤沮丧。

---

〔1〕 格涅乌斯·考尔尼利乌斯·楞图路斯这时已经60多岁,他曾在多瑙河罗马军队对南方的达奇人的作战中取得了荣誉。

they were mournful. Finally clouds hid it from view altogether. Men's minds, once unbalanced, are ready to believe anything; and now they howled that heaven was sickened by their crimes, and endless hardships were in store for them.

Drusus felt that advantage must be taken of this turn of events; a lucky chance could be exploited in the interests of good sense. Summoning Julius Clemens and any other officers whose kind natures had made them popular, he ordered them to go round the tents. Insinuating themselves among the watches and pickets and sentries they worked on the men's hopes and fears. Was it desirable, they questioned, to go on besieging the emperor's son? Where would these disputes end? Were they going to swear loyalty to Percennius and Vibulenus? Percennius and Vibulenus were not going to replace Neros and Drususes as lords of the Roman world. They were not going to pay the army and give ex-soldiers land. 'We were the last to give offence,' the officers suggested, 'so let us be the first to be sorry. Reform by collective agitation is slow in coming: individuals can earn goodwill and win its rewards straightaway.' This made a profound impression. Mutual suspicions began to udermine the solidarity between one brigade and another, between young and old. A sense of obedience gradually came back. The gates were left unguarded, and the Eagles and standards set up side by side at the beginning of the mutiny were returned to where they belonged.

At daybreak Drusus called a meeting. Though not a practised orator, he spoke with natural dignity. He censured their former behaviour, and expressed approval of their new attitude. Intimidation and

最后云层完全遮住了月亮,月亮一点也看不见了。人们的心理一旦失去平衡,是会很容易陷入迷信中的。现在,他们开始哭泣起来,认为他们所犯的罪过触怒了上天,等待着他们的将会是无穷无尽的苦难。

杜路苏斯感觉必须及时利用天象变化这一好时机;聪明人是不会放过任何一个幸运的机会的。他下令对军营进行一次巡视。他把尤利乌斯·克利门斯和其他一些由于良好的品质而在士兵中享有普遍的威信的百人团长招来,让他们去巡视周围各个营帐。他们在卫兵、巡逻兵、守门的哨兵们中间作出种种暗示,以燃起他们的希望,又用叛乱会受到的惩罚以引起他们的恐惧。"继续包围皇子会有什么希望呢?"他们问,"我们的这场纠纷要到什么时候才能结束呢?我们是不是要向佩尔肯尼乌斯和维布列努斯宣誓效忠?佩尔肯尼乌斯和维布列努斯能代替尼禄和杜路苏斯成为罗马的帝王吗?他们是不会给士兵发军饷,不会给退伍士兵分配土地的。我们是最后一批参加叛乱的人,就让我们作第一批悔改的人吧。集体要求的改革实现起来是很缓慢的,但是个人要赢得好感却很容易并且是很快就能得到报偿的。"他们散布的这些言论在士兵中间产生了很大的影响。军团和军团、新兵和老兵相互之间产生了猜疑,这种猜疑破坏了他们之间的团结,瓦解了他们的凝聚力。他们心中服从的本能又渐渐地恢复了。他们不再去警戒堡垒的门,而在兵变开始时被集中起来、并列竖立的大小旗帜也都被送回了各自原来的地方。

天亮时分,杜路苏斯召集了一次会议。尽管他并不是一个熟练的演说家,但说起话来却带有一种天生的尊严。他责备了兵士们过去的行为,但对他们当前的态度表示了他的赞许。他说,恫

menaces, he said, made no impression on him. If, however, he found that discipline had prevailed and they were pleading for pardon, he would write to his father recommending a merciful hearing for their pleas. They begged him to do this. So the younger Blaesus was again sent to Tiberius, accompanied by a Roman knight on Drusus' staff, Lucius Aponius, and a senior company-commander, Catonius Justus. There was now a division of opinion. One proposal was that the return of this delegation should be awaited, and that meanwhile the soldiers should be treated gently and humoured. Others favoured a more forceful solution, arguing that the masses only dealt in extremes and would terrorize unless they were terrorized—once intimidated, they could be disregarded with impunity: now, when superstition had a hold of them, was the time for the general to intensify their panic by striking down the leaders of the mutiny. Drusus had a natural preference for severe measures. Summoning Vibulenus and Percennius, he ordered them to be executed. Report has it that they were buried inside the general's tent. According to another account, however, the bodies were thrown outside the lines to be exhibited. Then all the chief instigators of the mutiny were hunted up. Some were killed by company-commanders or Guardsmen as they wandered blindly about outside the camp. Others were given up by their own units as a proof of loyalty.

The hardships of the soldiers were made worse by an early winter with unceasing rain. It rained so hard that they could hardly leave their tents to confer. They could only barely save the standards from being carried away by hurricane and flood. Besides, they were still afraid of divine wrath—extinguished planets and torrential downpours seemed directly connected with their criminal actions. The only cure for their misfortunes appeared to be the evacuation of this

吓和威胁对他是不能产生任何影响的,但是如果他能看到他们大家都遵守军纪,并且对自己过去的行为有悔改的表现,那他就会写信给他的父亲,建议皇帝以怜悯的态度考虑军团的要求。士兵们恳求他这样做,于是小布莱苏斯便再一次被派到提贝里乌斯那里去,陪同他一起前往的还有杜路苏斯随从中的一个罗马骑士路奇乌斯·阿波尼乌斯和一个地位较高的百人团长卡托尼乌斯·优斯图斯。这时在如何对待兵士们的意见上又产生了分歧。一种意见主张应该等使节们回来后再作定夺,在这期间对士兵们要温和幽默。另一种意见则主张采取比较严厉的措施,他们认为群众总是走极端的,如果不给他们点颜色看看,他们就会制造恐怖。他们一旦被镇服下来,就会接受应有的处罚的。现在,他们由于迷信而情绪沮丧,这对于统帅来说,正是一个好时机,应该趁此时机杀掉兵变的罪魁祸首,杀一儆百,以加强士兵们的恐惧情绪。杜路苏斯的内心更倾向于采取严厉的措施。他将维布列努斯和佩尔肯尼乌斯招来,下令将他们立即处决。报告说他们被埋葬在统帅的营帐里,另外一种说法却说他们的尸体被抛到了营地外面示众。接着就是搜捕所有的主要罪犯。有些人向营地外盲目地四处逃窜,被百人团长或近卫军士兵发现后杀死了。另一些人却是他们所在的部队为了证明自己的忠诚而主动交了出来。

　　这年冬天来得特别早,而且又不停地下雨,士兵们的处境也就更加糟糕了。大雨下个不停,以致他们都无法离开帐篷集合到一块儿商量事情。狂风大作、洪水泛滥,他们几乎都无法保住队旗。此外,他们还依然非常害怕上天的震怒——他们认为,月亮星斗被遮住和这次奔流而下的倾盆大雨都是与他们的犯罪行为有直接关系的。祛除不幸的唯一办法,看来就是离开这个不吉利

sinister, defiled camp and their return, purged of guilt, to their various winter quarters. First the eighth brigade left, then the fifteenth. The men of the ninth had loudly favoured waiting fore reply from Tiberius. But the withdrawal of the rest left them stranded, and they did voluntarily what they would soon have been forced to do anyway.

Drusus felt that the situation had become reasonably calm. So, without awaiting the delegation's return, he left for Rome.

At just about this time, and for the same reasons, the regular brigades in Germany mutinied too. They were more numerous, and the outbreak was proportionately graver. Moreover they were in high hopes that Germanicus, unable to tolerate another man as emperor, would put himself at the disposal of the forces, which would then sweep all before them. There were two armies on the Rhine bank. The army of Upper Germany was under the command of Gaius Silius (I), the army of Lower Germany under Aulus Caecina Severus. Their supreme commander was Germanicus, but he was occupied at this time in assessing the property-tax in the Gallic provinces.

The forces of Silius did not regard the mutiny as their own concern and watched it with mixed feelings. But the army of Lower Germany lost its senses. The two brigades which took the initiative, the twentyfirst and fifth, brought in the first and twentieth, which shared their summer camp upon the borders of the Ubii and were occupied on light duty, or none at all. When the death of Augustus became known,

的、被罪行玷污了的营地,回心转意,肃清自己的罪恶,返回各自的冬营。第八军团首先回去了,接着第十五军团也这样做了。起初第九军团的士兵还高声叫喊着要坚持等候提贝里乌斯的回音。可是其他的人都退出了,因此他们便陷入了困境。与其不久他们会被迫去做,不如索性现在就主动地去做。

杜路苏斯看到局势已经安定下来,于是便不等使节返回就赶回罗马去了。

几乎就在同时,而且由于同样的原因,日耳曼的正规军团也发动了叛乱。他们的人数更多,[1]所以叛乱也就更加严重。此外,他们抱着很大的期望,因为他们知道日耳曼尼库斯不会容忍另一个人成为帝王的,如此一来他就会任凭自己的部队以横扫天下之势扫除他们面前的一切障碍。在莱茵河岸一带驻扎有两支军队,上日耳曼军是在盖乌斯·西里乌斯(一世)统率之下,下日耳曼军则由奥路斯·凯奇纳·塞维路斯统率。他们的最高统帅是日耳曼尼库斯,但是他当时正在高卢行省征收财产税。[2]

西里乌斯麾下的士兵并没有加入叛乱的队伍之中,对于别人发动的这次兵变只是怀着复杂的心情冷眼旁观。但是下日耳曼军丧失了理智,两支部队主动发起了兵变。最先发动兵变的是第二十一军团和第五军团;接着第一军团和第二十军团也揭竿而起,这两个军团那时都在乌比伊人居住区边界的一个夏营里,他们的工作任务很轻或干脆没有什么职责。因此听到奥古斯都

---

〔1〕 上军有四个军团,下军也有四个军团,而潘诺尼亚只有三个军团。在莱茵河左岸的两个军区当中,上日耳曼从康斯坦茨湖到布罗尔;下日耳曼从布罗尔直到大海。

〔2〕 财产税是根据财产的多少而规定的定期税金。

the simple minds of the majority came under the influence of the masses of town-slaves who had recently been conscripted in the capital. Naturally insolent and lazy, they now argued that the moment had come for old soldiers to demand long-overdue demobilization, and for the younger men to demand an increase in pay. Everyone should insist on relief from their hardships, and retaliate against the savagery of their company-commanders. Here it was not just a matter of one Percennius, as in the army of Pannonia, or of soldiers nervously thinking of other and more powerful armies. This was a massive outbreak. There was a universal cry that they had won Rome's victories, her fate rested with them, and army commanders used a surname (Germanicus) derived from them.

The general, Caecina, took no counter-measures. The scale of the disturbances broke his nerve. Suddenly, in a passionate frenzy, swords drawn, the men attacked their company-commanders—the customary targets of the army's ill-will, and the first victims of any outbreak. They were hurled to the ground and given the lash, sixty strokes each, one for each of them in the brigade. Then, broken and mutilated, they were cast outside the lines or thrown into the Rhine, more dead than

逝世的消息,大多数头脑简单的人就受到了那些新兵的影响,这些新兵是在城市里长大,不久前刚从首都征募来的,[1]他们一贯傲慢无礼、好逸恶劳。他们大肆宣扬,现在是到了提出自己的要求的时候了,老兵应当要求早已延期的退伍,而新兵应当要求提高自己的待遇。他们每个人都应当要求减轻他们的苦难,对百人团长对他们所施加的野蛮行为也应该进行报复了。这次并不像那起只有佩尔肯尼乌斯单枪匹马在潘诺尼的军团士兵中所进行的煽动,而士兵们也不像潘诺尼军队中的士兵那样惴惴不安,顾虑重重,惧怕另一支势力更强大的军队。这是一起更为大规模的兵变,在这次叛乱中全体人员都叫嚣着:罗马的胜利是通过他们而取得的;罗马的命运就掌握在他们手里;统帅们所使用的(日耳曼尼库斯)这一称号也是从他们那儿僭取来的。[2]

副帅凯奇纳没有及时采取任何应对的措施。叛乱的庞大规模和气势把他吓坏了。突然地,怒不可遏的士兵们抽出剑来向着百人团长们冲了过去,这些百人团长过去一直都是士兵们最憎恨的对象,也成为叛乱中人们宣泄愤怒的第一批牺牲者。这些百人团长被打倒在地遭受鞭打,他们每人被鞭打60下,因为每个军团里有60个百人团,每人所遭受的鞭打数目就代表一个军团对他们的集体惩罚。之后,那些给打得皮开肉绽的百人团长就被抛到堡垒外面,或者被投进了莱茵河中,大多数都死去了。一个叫

---

〔1〕 伐鲁斯损失了第十七、十八、十九军团之后,奥古斯都又征募了第二十一和二十二军团:第二十一军团由凯奇纳率领,第二十二军团驻在埃及。

〔2〕 这些军团是 Germanicae,元老院曾把 Germanicus 的头衔授予提贝里乌斯的兄弟杜路苏斯和他的后人。因此他们现在的统帅和他的兄弟克劳狄乌斯都有这个头衔,提贝里乌斯本人有时也使用这个头衔。

alive. One, Septimius, took refuge on the general's dais and fell at Caecina's feet. But he was shouted for so violently that he had to be given up to his fate. Gaius Cassius Chaerea, who later went down to history as the murderer of the emperor Gaius and was at this time young and fiery, fought his way through the armed mob which held him up. Colonels, corps chiefs-of-staff had no control any longer. Patrols and sentries, and whatever else circumstances demanded, were organized by the men themselves. Students of army psychology could see the momentous and implacable character of the revolt from the fact that its instigators were not few and far between, but there was universal, silent fury, as resolute and unanimous as if they were acting on orders.

At this time Germanicus, as I have said, was engaged upon assessments in Gaul. There he learnt that Augustus was dead. Germanicus was married to his granddaughter Agrippina (I) and had several children by her; and since he was the son of Tiberius' brother Nero Drusus, one of his grandparents was the Augusta. Yet Germanicus suffered from the fact that his grandmother and uncle hated him, for reasons which were unfair but all the more potent. For Nero Drusus still lived on in Roman memories. It was believed that if he had obtained control of the empire he would have brought back the free Republic. The

谢普提米乌斯的百人团长逃到统帅的座坛那里去,跌倒在凯奇纳的脚下,但是人们猛烈地叫喊着要求把他交出来,因此凯奇纳只好将他交出去任凭听天由命。盖乌斯·卡西乌斯·凯列亚,这个不久之后因为杀死盖乌斯而名传史册的人,在当时还是一个年轻暴躁的小伙子,[1]他手持利剑从围攻他的武装暴徒中杀出了一条血路。军团将领和营帅现在已经完全无法控制局面了。巡逻、岗哨以及当时情况所需要的任何重要部门和事务都已由叛乱的士兵们自己组织起来。研究军队心理学的专家会发现,每次特别重大的、不能平息的叛乱都具有相似的特征,那就是:叛乱的发动者不是少数几个人,也并非各不相干,而是到处都爆发同样的强烈愤怒情绪,并且都表现出沉默的狂怒,他们的表现是那样地坚决、一致,他们的行动就好像是在执行着统一的命令。

我已经说过,日耳曼尼库斯这时正忙于在高卢整顿税收。在那里他得悉了奥古斯都去世的消息。他的妻子是这位故去的皇帝的外孙女阿格里披娜(一世),并且她还给他生了几个孩子,而他本人又是提贝里乌斯的兄弟尼禄·杜路苏斯的儿子,他的祖母是皇太后奥古斯塔。虽然关系是这样,但是日耳曼尼库斯内心却承受着这样的痛苦,那就是他的叔父和祖母都憎恨他,他们憎恨他的理由非常不公平,但惟其如此对他伤害的效力才更大。要知道,尼禄·杜路苏斯仍然活在人们心中,而且大家相信,如果是他获得了罗马帝国的统治权,他一定已恢复了自由共和制度。因此人们也把这种希望和爱戴的心情,从他身上

---

〔1〕 塔西佗记载他杀死卡里古拉的部分已佚,因此只能参看其他史书有关的记载,如《卡里古拉传》《犹太古代史》等。

hopes and goodwill thus engendered passed to his son, Germanicus. For this young man's unassuming personality and popular manner were very different from the haughty, ambiguous looks and words of Tiberius. Ill-feeling among the women made things worse. The Augusta had a stepmother's aversion to Agrippina. Agrippina herself was determined, and rather excitable. But she turned this to good account by her devoted faithfulness to her husband.

At all events Germanicus' proximity to the summit of ambition only made him work more enthusiastically on behalf of Tiberius. After taking the oath of loyalty himself, he administered it to his immediate subordinates and to the Belgic communities. Then came the news that the army was rioting. He set out for it hurriedly.

The men met him outside the camp. They kept their eyes fixed on the ground, ostensibly remorseful. As soon as he entered their lines, however, they assailed him with all manner of complaints. Some grasped his hand as though to kiss it, but instead thrust his fingers into their mouths to make him touch their toothless gums. Others showed how old age had deformed them. They crowded round him to listen in no sort of order. Germanicus told them to divide into their units. But they shouted back that they would hear better where they were. He said that they must at least bring their standards to the front so that it could be seen which battalion was which. Slowly they obeyed. Then Germanicus, after paying a reverent tribute to Augustus' memory, praised the victories and triumphs of Tiberius and, by way of

转移到他的儿子日耳曼尼库斯身上来。因为这个年轻人的谦逊的性格和极为平易近人的作风,同提贝里乌斯那种傲慢的、暧昧的表情和语言恰恰形成了极为鲜明的对比。女性之间的互相仇视使形势更加紧张,奥古斯塔像个继母似的对阿格里披娜十分厌恶。阿格里披娜本人也非常固执,而且容易冲动。但是她对丈夫的忠诚,使她能将自己这些不利的情绪转化到好的方面来。

不过无论如何,日耳曼尼库斯越是在雄心即将实现的时候,就越是更加热心地为提贝里乌斯的事业效劳。他自己在向皇帝宣誓效忠之后,又劝告紧随他的属下和比尔伽伊人的城市都向皇帝宣誓效忠。他一听到军团发生叛乱的消息,就急忙火速起身赶回叛乱的军营。

士兵们都跑到营地的外边来迎接他,眼睛死盯着地面,表面看来好像是很后悔的样子。但是当他刚一走到队伍中间,士兵们就纷纷以抱怨的语气向他诉起苦来。一些人抓住了他的手好像要亲吻的样子,但实际上是要他把手指伸到他们嘴里,要让他触摸他们掉了牙的牙龈。另一些人则要他看年老已使他们的身体变形得多么严重。最后他们终于杂乱地围在他的四周听他的命令。日耳曼尼库斯让他们分成队伍排列,但是士兵们叫喊着回答,他们这样站着能听得更清楚些。日耳曼尼库斯坚持说,无论如何他们至少也得把他们的队旗立到前面来,以便使他能够识别他们是属于哪些步兵中队的。慢慢地他们听从了日耳曼尼库斯的要求各自站好。日耳曼尼库斯首先是对奥古斯都表示了衷心的怀念,接着赞扬了提贝里乌斯的胜利和凯旋,顺便特别赞

climax, his glorious achievements in German lands with those very brigades. He spoke appreciatively of Italy's unanimous support for the government, and of the loyalty of the Gauls—of the perfect harmony and order prevailing everywhere.

This was received in silence or with indistinct muttering. But then Germanicus passed on to the mutiny. What on earth had happened, he asked, to their famous, traditional military discipline, and where had they driven their colonels and company-commanders? The soldiers' reply was to tear off their clothes one after another, and point abusively to the scars left by their wounds and floggings. There was a confused roar about their wretched pay, the high cost of exemptions from duty, and the hardness of the work. Specific references were made to earthworks, excavations, foraging, collecting timber and firewood, and every other camp task that is either necessary or invented to occupy spare time. The most violent outcry came from the old soldiers, who pointed to their thirty years' service and more, and appealed for relief from their exhaustion before death overtook them in the same old drudgery. 'End this crushing service!' they begged. 'Give us rest—before we are utterly destitute!'

Some asked Germanicus for the legacies which the divine Augustus had left them—adding expressions of personal support for Germanicus. If he wanted the throne, they showed they were for him. At this

扬了他率领的这些军团在日耳曼取得的辉煌胜利。[1] 在之后,他又以赞赏的语气说起了意大利对政府同心协力的支持,说到高卢行省的忠诚不渝,那些地方都非常安宁和谐,命令都得到了很好的贯彻和执行。

士兵们听着他这些话,默不作声或喃喃私语。但是当日耳曼尼库斯谈到了叛变,问到底是怎么回事,并且问他们那种过去闻名天下的严整的纪律都跑到哪里去了的时候,当他问他们把军团将领、百人团长都赶到什么地方去了的时候,士兵们的回答是一个一个地把外衣脱掉、把自己满身的伤疤和鞭痕显露出来,嘴里谩骂着指给他看。于是就掀起了一片混乱的叫嚷声,他们乱糟糟地喊成一片,向他抱怨着饷银的微薄、豁免任务时的高额费用以及工作的艰苦等。他们还特别提出,有些任务诸如修筑工事、挖掘战壕、准备粮草,搜集建筑用的木料和薪柴,还有营地里的许多其他苦役,这些苦役有些是必需的,有些却只不过是用来占据空余时间,不让人休息而已。最强烈的呼声来自老兵,他们在指出他们已服了 30 年、甚至更多年的兵役的时候,请求他把他们从精疲力竭的状态中解救出来,不要让他们再像过去那样在悲惨环境里因过度劳苦而死。“结束我们这种无休止的服役吧!”他们请求他:“让我们极度困乏的生活稍微得到一丝喘息吧。”

有一些人竟然向日耳曼尼库斯要求圣奥古斯都遗赠给他们的钱,并且向他表示了自己对他的支持。如果他想取得皇位的话,他们表示他们是准备站到他这一边的。听到这种话之后,他

---

〔1〕 提贝里乌斯曾在公元前 9～前 8 年、公元 4～5 年和公元 9～11 年几次对日耳曼人作战。

point he leapt off the dais as if their criminal intentions were polluting him, and moved away. But they blocked his path and menaced him until he went back. Then, however, shouting that death was better than disloyalty, he pulled the sword from his belt and lifted it as though to plunge it into his chest. The men round him clutched his arm and stopped him by force. But the close-packed masses at the back of the crowd, and even, remarkably enough, certain individuals who had pushed themselves into prominent positions, encouraged him to strike. A soldier called Calusidius even drew his own sword and offered it, remarking that it was sharper. But even in their demented frame of mind the men found this a brutal and repellent gesture. There was a pause; and Germanicus' friends had time to hurry him into his tent.

There they considered what was to be done. The soldiers were reported to be organizing a deputation to bring over the army of Upper Germany. They were also, it was said, planning to destroy the capital of the Ubii, and after that taste of looting to burst into the Gallic provinces and plunder them too. The situation was all the more alarming because the Germans knew of the mutiny in the Roman army: the abandonment of the Rhine bank would mean invasion. Yet to arm auxiliaries and loyal tribesmen against the rebellious regulars would be civil war. Severity appeared dangerous. But large concessions would be criminal. It would be just as desperately risky for Rome to give way about everything or about nothing. When all the arguments had been weighed and compared, it was decided to make a statement in the

立刻从座坛上跳了下来,就好像他已经被这种罪恶的想法玷污了似的,立即准备离开。他们挡住了他的去路,并威胁说如果他不回到座坛上,他们就要动武了。但是他高声说道,他宁肯死也绝不叛国,并且从腰间抽出了佩剑,高高举起好像要将它插入自己的胸口的样子,围在他旁边的人们抓住他的胳膊,用力将他制止。但是人群后面的一些人密密麻麻地围上来,尤为引人注目的是,他们当中有些人还挤到了非常显著的位置上,这些人竟然极力地鼓励他自杀。一个名叫卡路西狄乌斯的士兵甚至还把自己的剑拔出来交给他,说他这把剑更加锋利。但是即使是在这些头脑已经疯狂的人看来,这也是一种残忍的,不怀好意的举动。人群暂时出现了一个间歇,日耳曼尼库斯的朋友们迅速地冲过去将他拉回了营帐。

他们在那里商讨应该采取怎样的措施。根据报告,叛乱的士兵正在组织一个代表团,准备去拉拢上日耳曼军队;据说他们还打算捣毁乌比伊人的首都,[1]而在尝到了抢掠的甜头后,他们还计划闯入高卢行省,到那些地方进行抢劫。此外还有更加使人感到不安的情况,因为日耳曼人也知道了罗马军中发生兵变的事情:如果放弃了莱茵河岸一带的防线,敌人是肯定要入侵的。可是要把辅助部队和联盟者的军队武装起来,以对付叛乱的士兵,就势必会引起一场内战了。对于这场叛乱如果采取严厉的手段看来是很危险的,但大的让步也会是一种犯罪行为。答应叛乱士兵的所有要求或全部拒绝他们的要求,都同样会使罗马面临极大的危险。在反复衡量和比较了各种意见的利弊得失之后,最后

---

〔1〕 乌比伊人的首都是科隆,即科洛尼亚·阿格里披嫩西斯。

emperor's name. In this, demobilization was promised after twenty years' service. Men who had served sixteen years were to be released but kept with the cdours with no duties except to help beat off enemy attacks. Moreover, the legacies which they had requested were to be paid—twice over.

The soldiers saw that these were hastily improvised and demanded their immediate implementation. The discharges were speedily arranged by the senior officers. The cash payments, however, were held up until the troops reached winter camps. Two brigades, the fifth and the twenty-first, refused to move from their summer quarters until, there and then, the whole sum was paid. It had to be scraped together from the travelling funds of Germanicus himself and his staff. The general Caecina took the remaining two brigades, the first and the twentieth, back to the Ubian capital. It was a scandalous march—Eagle, standards, and the cash stolen from the commander, all were carried along together.

Then Germanicus moved on to the army of Upper Germany. He had no difficulty in inducing the second, thirteenth and sixteenth brigades to take the oath; the fourteenth only took it after hesitation. Though there were no demands for discharges and money payments, both were conceded. In the territory of the Chauci, however, a fresh outbreak occurred, among a garrison consisting of detachments from the insubordinate brigades. The trouble was soon stamped out by two prompt executions. This illegal but salutary measure was carried out on the orders of the corps chief-of-staff Manius Ennius. Then, as the

决定以皇帝的名义发出一道敕令,敕令申明凡是服役满 20 年的,可以一律退役,服兵役满 16 年的则可以免除日常的服役,但是要留在军中。他们虽然免除了日常服役,但是仍然需要协助击退敌人的进攻。此外,他们所要求的遗赠不但照付,而且还会得到加倍的支付。

士兵们看出这一切让步不过是应付当前局势的权宜之计,因而要求立刻予以兑现。军团将领们即刻迅速地安排好了退役事宜。然而,关于钱的问题,则要等士兵们各自返回他们的冬营之后才予发放。但是有两个军团,第五军团和第二十一军团拒绝离开夏营,无论如何要等到全数发给他们饷银后,才肯回到冬营。因此不得不从日耳曼尼库斯本人和他的随从人员的私人行囊中拿出钱筹集饷银,并全部付给他们。副帅凯奇纳则率领保存下来的两个军团,第一军团和第二十军团回到乌比伊人的首府。这是一次具有讽刺意义的行军——鹰形标志、大小军旗,还有从统帅手里偷来的钱,都夹杂在一起。

接着,日耳曼尼库斯动身到上日耳曼军去,他很容易地就劝服了第二军团、第十三军团和第十六军团三个军团宣誓效忠;第十四军团只是犹豫了一会儿后,就同意了。虽然他们并没有提出退役和饷银的要求,日耳曼尼库斯也主动地让老士兵们退役,并发给他们金钱。可是在卡乌奇人[1]的地区,在一支由从叛乱的军团那里派出来的士兵组成的卫成部队中,一场新的叛乱又爆发了。但是这一叛乱很快就由于果断地处决了两个士兵而被镇压下去了。处决的命令是营帅玛尼乌斯·恩尼乌斯发出的,这在法律上是不合法

---

〔1〕 指住在艾姆斯河与威悉河之间的小卡乌奇人。

mutiny began to swell, he got away. But he was discovered. Relying on a bold course for the safety which his hiding-place had failed to provide, he cried out that their offence was not just against an officer, it was against Germanicus their commander—against Tiberius their emperor! At the same time, intimidating all opposition, he seized the standard and pointed it towards the Rhine. Then, shouting that everyone who fell out would be treated as a deserter, he conducted his men back to their winter camp—still rebellious, but frustrated.

Meanwhile the senate's mission to Germanicus found him back at the Ubian altar and capital. The first and the twentieth brigades were in winter quarters there, and also the soldiers who had recently been released but not yet demobilized. Mad with anxiety and bad conscience, these men were also terrified that the concessions which they had won by mutinous methods would be concelled by the senatorial dsselegation. Crowds habitually find scapegoats, however unjustifiably, and now they attacked the chief envoy, the former consul Lucius Munatius Plancus, charging him with instigating sanctions against them in the senate. Early in the night they began to clamour for their standard, which was hept in Germanicus' residence. They rushed the door and forced him to get up and—under threat of death—to hand it over. Then,

的,但是在当时情况下采取这样的措施却是有益的。后来随着兵变的规模越来越大,他就跑开了,但是被士兵们发现了。他想躲起来以得到安全,但是失败了。于是他就索性大着胆子叫喊着说,他们的行动不仅仅是侮辱了他一个营帅,而是侮辱了他们的统帅日耳曼尼库斯和他们的皇帝提贝里乌斯。就在这时,趁反抗者刚刚被镇服,他一下子抓住军旗,将它直指向莱茵河,然后他大声地说所有擅自离开队伍的人都将被视为逃兵,他就这样把队伍带回了冬营——这时士兵们尽管心中仍有不服,但是已被挫败,不敢再轻举妄动了。

就在这个时候,已经来到日耳曼尼库斯这里的元老院派来的使团,发现日耳曼尼库斯这时已经返回了乌比伊人的祭坛[1]和首府。第一军团和第二十军团正在自己的冬营里,而最近刚刚被免除军役的老兵也还留在营地里。士兵们已经意识到了自己的罪行,心里惴惴不安,充满了焦虑,而且还有使他们感到害怕的事情,那就是元老院派来的使团会全部取消他们在叛乱时争得的让步。群众总是习惯找一个替死鬼,不管对这个替死鬼来说是多么不公平。现在他们就攻击这一使团的团长、前任执政官路奇乌斯·穆纳提乌斯·普朗库斯,指责他说正是在他的鼓动之下,元老院才发布了反对他们的命令的。刚刚入夜,他们就开始高喊要求拿回存放在日耳曼尼库斯住所的队旗[2]。他们冲进了日耳曼尼库斯住所的大门,把普朗库斯从床上拖起来,并且以死亡威胁他把军

---

〔1〕 在乌比伊人的首府,也就是后来的科隆设置的奥古斯都的祭坛,是罗马在日耳曼行省的祭祀中心。

〔2〕 他们要求队旗是为了保证他们的地位,以防备使团对他们做出不利的举动。

roaming the streets, they encountered the members of the delegation, who had heard the uproar and were on their way to Germanicus. The soldiers heaped abuse on them. Indeed they had it in mind to kill them, and especially Plancus. His high rank made it impossible for him to run away; and in his extreme danger the only available refuge was the camp of the first brigade. There he found sanctuary, grasping the Eagle and standards. But if a colour-sergeant named Calpurnius had not protected him from his fate, then, without precedent even between enemies, the altars of the gods would have been stained with the blood of an emissary of the Roman people, in a Roman camp.

At last morning arrived; and commanders and private soldiers, and the night's doings, were seen for what they were. Germanicus came into the camp and ordered Plancus to be brought to him. Escorting him on to the dais, he assailed this disastrous, maniacal revival of violence. 'It shows how angry the gods are', he said, 'rather than the soldiers!' Then he explained why the delegation had come, and spoke with gloomy eloquence about the rights of envoys, and the deplorable and unfair treatment of Plancus himself—a disgrace to the brigade. The gathering was hardly pacified, but it was cowed; and Germanicus sent the delegates away under the protection of auxiliary cavalry.

In this alarming situation Germanicus was generally criticized for not proceeding to the upper army, which obeyed orders and would help against the rebels. Enough and more than enough mistakes had been made, it was felt, by releases and payments and mild measures.

旗交给他们。稍后,他们在街道上游荡时,遇到了使团的成员,这些成员是在听到骚乱的消息之后,正向日耳曼尼库斯这里赶过来的。士兵们对这些人大加侮辱谩骂。实际上他们很想把使团成员杀死,特别是普朗库斯。普朗库斯所具有的高级地位使他不能逃走,在这种极其危险的时刻,最可靠的安全去处就是第一军团的驻地。他到了那里,发现了避难所,他抓住了保存在营地圣所里的军旗和队旗。[1] 如果不是一个名叫卡尔普尼乌斯的旗手保护了他,使他免于不幸的命运的话,在罗马军队的营地里,诸神的祭坛上就将会洒下罗马人民的使者的鲜血,[2] 这甚至是在敌人之间也是从来没有发生过的先例。

后来,天亮了,军官、士兵和夜间所发生的一切也都终于弄清楚了。日耳曼尼库斯来到营地,命令把普朗库斯请到他这里来,并且陪同普朗库斯登上座坛。他质问这种灾难性的、疯狂的暴行何以会重新爆发。"这表明诸神是如何的愤怒",他说,"而不是士兵的愤怒。"接下来他又向士兵们解释了使团此行的目的,并以忧郁的口吻陈述了使节们应有的权利和普朗库斯本人所遭受到的非常严重的、不公平的侮辱,而这对于军团来说也是一件极不光彩的事情。聚集的士兵们很难安静下来,但最后总算是被镇服了;日耳曼尼库斯就派遣辅助的骑兵部队护送着使节离开了。

在这样危急的时刻,所有的人都一致责怪日耳曼尼库斯,批评他没有能够听从命令并且可以协助他镇压叛军到上军那里去。人们认为遣散、赠赐和善意的措施已经造成了很多甚至太多的错误。

---

[1] 军旗和队旗被认为是神圣不可侵犯的。
[2] 这个祭坛和军旗等都在营地的司令部。

And even if he did not value his own life, people asked why, among these madmen who had broken every law, he kept with him his baby son and his pregnant wife. Surely he owed it to the nation and their imperial grandfather to send them back! Germanicus was long hesitant. His wife scorned the proposal, reminding him that she was of the blood of the divine Augustus and would live up to it, whatever the danger. Then he burst into tears—and clasping to him the expectant mother and their child, persuaded her to go. It was a pitiable feminine company that set out. The supreme commander's own wife, a refugee, clutched his infant son to her breast. Her escorts, his friends' wives—forced to leave with her—were in tears. Those who remained were equally mournful. The scene suggested a captured city rather than a highly successful Caesar in his own camp.

The women's sobbing and lamentation attracted the attention of the soldiers, who came out of their tents and asked why they were crying and what was wrong. Here were these distinguished ladies with no staff-officers or soldiers to look after them, none of the usual escort or other honours due to the supreme commander's wife. And they were off to the Treviri, to be looked after by foreigners! The men felt sorry for them, and ashamed, when they thought of her ancestry—her father was Agrippa, her grandfather Augustus, her father-in-law Nero Drusus—and of her impressive record as wife and mother. Besides, there was her baby son, Gaius, born in the camp and brought up with the regular troops as his comrades. In their army fashion they had

他可以不爱惜自己的生命,但是人们责问他,他为什么竟然将他那年幼的儿子[1]和怀孕的妻子也置身于这些不把任何法律放在眼中的疯狂的人中间呢?无论如何他也应当把他们送回帝国、送回到他们的祖父那里去。日耳曼尼库斯犹疑了很久。他的妻子阿格里披娜则嘲笑这样的建议,提醒他说她是圣奥古斯都的后裔,不论有多大危险她都会坚持气节的。于是,日耳曼尼库斯放声大哭,他拥抱着他怀孕的妻子和他们的孩子,劝她离开这里。于是一群可怜的妇女出发了。统帅夫人,一个逃难者,将自己的孩子紧紧地搂在自己的怀抱里。在她身边的则是统帅朋友们的妻子,她们是被迫和她一道离开自己的丈夫的,一个个满脸泪水。留下来的人们也是同样地悲痛。这情景使人仿佛置身于一座被攻克的城市,而不像是有着赫赫战功的恺撒置身于自己的营地里。

妇女们的抽泣声和悲叹声引起了士兵们的注意,他们都从营帐里跑出来问她们为什么哭泣,发生了什么事情。她们都是地位显赫的夫人,身边却没有一个百人团长或一个士兵来保护照顾她们,统帅夫人身边也没有日常护从的卫队或其他任何证明她的这一身份的标志物。她们正被送到特列维利人[2]那里去,去让外国人保护!对于这种情况,人们感受到又羞耻又同情,当他们想到她的家族血统——他的父亲是阿格里帕,她的祖父是奥古斯都,她的公公是尼禄·杜路苏斯,还有她本人作为妻子和母亲所给人的深刻印象。此外还有她的小儿子盖乌斯,出生在营地里,并且在军团的环境中是被当作他们的伙伴抚养起来的。按照士兵们的习

---

[1] 即未来的皇帝卡里古拉。
[2] 高卢的一个部族,他的首都是今天的特里夫斯。

nicknamed him 'little Boots' (Caligula), because as a popular gesture he was often dressed in miniature army boots. But their jealousy of the Treviri was what affected them most.

So now they wanted to prevent Agrippina's departure, and appealed that she should stop and come back. Some ran to intercept her, the majority returned to Germanicus. He stood among them, still smarting with grief and anger. 'My wife and son', he told them, 'are not more dear to me than my father and my country. But my father has his august dignity to protect him, and the Roman empire has its other armies. I would willingly see my wife and children die for your greater glory. Now, however, I am taking them out of your demented reach. Whatever atrocities are impending, my life alone must atone for them. Do not make your guilt worse by murdering the great-grandson of Augustus, the daughter-in-law of Tiberius!

'In these last days you have committed every possible crime and horror. I do not know what to call this gathering! You men who have used your fortifications and weapons to blockade your emperor's son can hardly be called soldiers. And "citizens" is not the name for people who cast aside the authority of the senate. The international code too, rights due even to enemies, the sanctity of ambassadors—you have outraged them. The divine Julius Gaesar suppressed a mutiny by one word: when his men would not take the oath he called them "civilians". The divine Augustus put fear into his troops at Actium by a

惯还给他起了一个绰号"小靴子"(卡里古拉),〔1〕因为当作一种普遍的装束,他通常穿的就是和士兵们一模一样的靴子。但是给他们所带来的最大的触动还是他们对特列维利人的妒忌。〔2〕

因此,现在他们企图阻止阿格里披娜的离开,请求她无论如何也要回来,留在这里。一些人跑过去阻拦她,但大多数人则是跑回到日耳曼尼库斯那里去。他站在士兵中间,依然沉浸在悲伤而又生气的情绪中,他对他们说:"我爱自己的妻子和儿子,但并非甚于爱自己的父亲和国家。但是,我父亲有帝王的尊严保护他,我的国家还有其他的军队保护它。我是很高兴看到我的妻子和孩子为你们的光荣事业献出生命的。但是现在我要让她们到远离你们的疯狂所能及的地方。不管你们的暴行要发展到何种程度,只能由我一个人的生命来抵偿,不要让你们的罪行深重到杀死奥古斯都的重孙,提贝里乌斯的儿媳!

最近几天里,你们尽其所能地制造了每一个罪恶和恐怖。我不知道,对于你们这样一群人,应当称作什么才合适呢!你们这些用堡垒和武器把你们皇帝的儿子包围起来的人,简直不配称作士兵。'公民'也不是那些废除了元老院权力的人所应享有的称号。全世界都共同遵守的法则、敌人也能享受到的权利、使节的神圣,所有这些都被你们用暴乱的行动统统破坏掉了。神圣的尤利乌斯·恺撒用一个词就平定了兵变:当士兵们拒绝向他宣誓效忠时,他就称他们为'公民'。〔3〕神圣的奥古斯都只是目光

---

〔1〕 "卡里古拉"意思是小靴子,这种靴子一般只有普通士兵才穿。

〔2〕 特列维利人比他们受到更大的信任。

〔3〕 公民是同士兵相对的,士兵大多非常珍惜自己军人的称号。文中所说是公元前47年第十军团的一次兵变。

look. I cannot yet compete with them. But I am their descendant; and if the soldiers even in Spain or Syria—where I am not known—were disrespectful to me, it would be surprising and scandalous enough. And here we have you, the first brigade, which received its colours from Tiberius, and you, the twentieth, his comrades in many battles. He rewarded you amply. How splendidly you are repaying your old commander! This, it seems, is the report I must make to my father—amid the good news that he has from every other province—that his own old soldiers, his own recruits, they and they alone, not content with releases and gratuities, are slaughtering their company-commanders, ejecting their colonels, arresting their generals, until the camp and the river are soaked in blood, and I myself, surrounded by hatred, live only on sufferance!

'When, at that first day's meeting, you pulled away the sword I was preparing to plunge into my body, your friendly solicitude was inconsiderate. A better, truer friend was the man who offered me his own sword. At any rate I should have died with my conscience spared all my army's crimes! The leader whom you would then have chosen need not have avenged my death. Instead he could have avenged Publius Quinctilius Varus and his three brigades. For heaven forbid that the distinction and glory of having helped Rome, and suppressed the peoples of Germany, should go to the Belgae—Gauls and foreigners—for all their offers. Divine Augustus, I call upon your spirit now in

一扫,就使阿克提乌姆的士兵感到了恐惧。[1] 我还无法和他们相比,但我是他们的子孙。即使是在不了解我身份的西班牙或叙利亚的士兵不尊重我,也已经够令人吃惊和气愤的了。然而在这儿,我的部下,从提贝里乌斯手里领到了军旗的第一军团,还有你们第二十军团,[2] 随他战斗过多次的同伴们,他曾经给予过你们丰厚的赠赐。可是对于你们过去的统帅,你们的报答是多么慷慨啊!我的父亲从各个行省都得到很好的消息,可是在这儿,我却必须向我的父亲报告说,他的老兵们、他自己亲手招募来的士兵们,他们每个人在豁免了劳役、得到了金钱之后还是不满足,他们还要屠杀百人团长,驱逐军团将领,拘捕他们的副帅,让营地和河流浸透在血泊之中,而我本人也被仇恨包围着,艰难地生活在忍辱负重之中。

在第一天见面的时候,你们从我手中把我准备刺入胸膛的宝剑夺走了,你们的友好和热心是草率的、不明智的。那位把自己的剑拿出来交给我的人才是更好的、真正的朋友!那时我自杀身死,至少我可以看不到在这之后我的军队所犯下的种种的罪行!到时候你们给自己再选出来的统帅,也大可不必选择为我的死亡报仇,相反,他却应该给普布里乌斯·克温克提里乌斯·伐鲁斯和他的三个军团报仇。尽管比尔伽伊人—高卢人和外国人表示愿意效劳,但上天是不允许那维护罗马的尊严和征服日耳曼诸民族的荣誉和光荣落到这些外族人身上的。神圣的奥古斯

---

〔1〕 这是公元前 30 年冬天在布林迪西发生的事情。

〔2〕 提贝里乌斯为了应付公元 6 年潘诺尼亚的起义而征募了第二十军团。

heaven! Nero Drusus my father, I invoke your image that is in our memories! Come to these soldiers of yours (into whose hearts shame and pride are making their way); wash clean this stain! Direct these revolutionary passions against enemy lives instead. And you men: I see your looks and hearts have changed. Will you give the senate back its delegates, be obedient to the empetor again—and return me my wife and son? Then shake off the contagion. Single out the culprits! That will show you are sorry, and prove you are loyal. '

At this they petitioned for mercy. Admitting the justice of his rebuke, they begged him to punish the guilty, and forgive those who had slipped. He must lead them against the enemy, they urged. And first his wife must be summoned back—the boy they bred must also return, and not be given to Gauls as a hostage. Germanicus agreed that his son should return, but excused his wife since her confinement was at hand, and so was winter. The rest, he said, was up to them. Changed men, they hastened round arresting the leading rebels and dragging them before the commander of the first brigade, Gaius Caetronius. Each ringleader in turn was tried and punished by him in the following fashion. The men, with drawn swords, stood in a mass. One after another the prisoners were paraded on the platform by a colonel. If they shouted 'Guilty', he was thrown down and butchered. The soldiers revelled in the massacre as though it purged them of their

都,我请求您的在天之灵！尼禄·杜路苏斯,我的父亲,我向您那我们作为纪念的雕像[1]恳求！让您的精神进入这些您的士兵中(他们的心已经懂得耻辱,并且让您的骄傲为他们指明正确的道路);洗刷尽他们的这种污点吧！指点他们把这种发动内乱的情绪变成击溃外敌的精神吧！而你们各位,我看得出你们的表情和内心已经发生了转变。你们愿意把使节送回给元老院,重新听从皇帝的命令,你们愿意将我的妻儿交还给我吗？那么就摆脱那些坏影响,把坏人孤立起来！那样才是真正的悔过,才能真正证明你们的忠诚。"

听了这番话之后,士兵们就开始请求他的宽恕。他们承认他对他们的指责是正当的,他们请求惩办罪犯,请求他原谅他们所犯的错误。他们还恳求他带领他们去杀敌。而且他们还要求他首先把妻子召回来,把他那在军团士兵中抚养起来的儿子也召回来,无论如何也不能把他妻子和儿子送到高卢人那里去作人质！日耳曼尼库斯同意让他的儿子回来,但他还是希望他的妻子能够离开,因为她产期将近,[2]而这儿却是冬天。至于其他的事情该怎样做,那就由他们自己来决定。这些士兵现在回心转意了,他们立刻奔向各处,将兵变的罪魁祸首逮住,并且把他们拖到第一军团的副帅盖乌斯·凯特洛尼乌斯面前。凯特洛尼乌斯则采用以下的办法对这些罪魁祸首依次加以审讯和惩罚。军团士兵们手持长剑,集合在一起,军团将领把这些罪犯一个一个地拉到座坛上面来展示。如果士兵们高呼"有罪",那么这个人就被打倒在地,并立即杀死。士兵们迷醉在这种屠杀中,好像如此就是对

---

〔1〕 雕像就放在军旗和队旗之中。
〔2〕 蒙森认为这可能是一次死产。

offences. And Germanicus, though the orders had not been his, did not intervene. For the disgust caused by this savagery would be directed against its perpetrators, and not against him.

The discharged men acted similarly. Soon afterwards, they were sent to Raetia. The pretext was defence against a threat from the Suebi; but the real intention was to remove them from a camp with hateful memories of crimes and of their equally appalling retribution. Then Germanicus revised the roll of company-commanders. Each in turn came before him and reported his name, company, birth-place, length of service, and any battle distinctions and decorations. If the colonels and men spoke favourably of his work and character, then the company-commander kept his job. If, however, he was unanimously described as grasping and brutal, he was dismissed from the service.

This relieved the immediate crisis. But there was still equally serious trouble from the truculent attitude of the fifth and twenty-first brigades wintering sixty miles away at Vetera. It was they who had started the mutiny and committed the worst atrocities. Now they were as angry as ever, undeterred by the punishment and contrition of their fellow-soldiers. So Germanicus, ready to use force if his authority were set aside, prepared to transport auxiliary troops and arms down the Rhine.

自己罪行的一种洗刷。而日耳曼尼库斯虽然没有发布这样的命令,却也对他们的做法不加干涉。因为对这种残暴罪行的痛恨不是针对他,而是针对那些罪犯的。

那些允许退役的老兵们也这样做了,而在不久之后,他们就给派到莱提亚[1]去了。这种安排表面上是为了防御苏埃比人[2]的入侵,但实际上却是为了使他们离开这样一个营地:在这个营地有对所犯下的种种罪行的深刻的记忆,还有对进行清洗时的恐怖行为的同样深刻的印象。在这之后,日耳曼尼库斯又重新修订了一下百人团长的名单。每个人都被统帅挨个召到面前,向他报告自己的姓名,队伍的番号、籍贯、服役年限以及他建立下的所有战功和得过的勋章。如果军团将领和他所在的军团的士兵对他的工作和品性都能加以肯定的话,那么他的地位就得以保留。然而,如果大家都一致认为他贪得无厌或者残暴成性的话,那么他就被解除职务。

这种做法立刻平息了当时的危机。但是还有一个同样严重的情况,仍然没有得到解决。这就是第五军团和第二十一军团的桀骜不驯的态度,他们这时正驻扎在离这里大约60英里的维特拉的一个名叫"老营"[3]的冬营里。他们最早开始发动兵变,也最残暴无情。现在他们仍然像以前一样满腔怒火,他们尚未受到惩罚,对于其他士兵的悔过表现也无动于衷。因此日耳曼尼库斯便着手沿莱茵河一带运送军队、辅助部队和武器装备,时刻准备着,如果这些士兵不听从他的命令,他就会诉诸武力。

---

〔1〕 这一行省包括多瑙河和伊恩河上游地带的格利松斯、蒂罗尔和巴伐利亚的一部分。

〔2〕 苏埃比人是居住在易北河以东,多瑙河以北的部族。

〔3〕 在克桑顿附近。

When Rome heard of the rebellion in Germany—before the final developments in Illyricum were known—the whole population rounded panic-striken on Tiberius. Here was he with his insincere hesitation, making fools of the helpless, unarmed senate and Assembly; while the soldiers mutinied! Two half-grown boys, they felt, could not control these rebellions. Tiberius ought to have gone himself, and confronted them with his imperial dignity: they would have given way when they saw their experienced emperor, with sovereign powers of retribution and reward. It was recalled that Augustus had made several visits to the Germanies in later life—yet here was Tiberius, in his prime, sitting in the senate quibbling at members' speeches! The enslavement of Rome, men said, was well in hand. Now something must be done to calm the troops and make peace.

Such talk made no impression on Tiberius. He was determined not to jeopardize the nation and himself by leaving the capital. His worries were various. Germany had the stronger army, Pannonia the nearer. The former had Gaul's resources behind it, the latter threatened Italy. So which should he visit first? And what if the one placed second should take serious offence? Whereas, through his sons, he could deal with both simultaneously and keep intact his imperial dignity—which

罗马方面在还不知道伊里利库姆[1]骚乱事件的结果如何的时候，却又得到了日耳曼兵变的消息。惊慌失措的所有罗马居民于是把话题转到提贝里乌斯的身上来了。你看，他利用虚假的犹豫不决来愚弄软弱无助而又手无寸铁的元老院和民团大会；但是士兵们却发动了叛乱！他们认为，两个没有成年的男孩子，是没有能力平定这些叛乱的。提贝里乌斯应当亲自去一趟，用他的帝王的尊严去征服他们。当他们看到他们经验丰富又有着至高无上的赏罚大权的皇帝的时候，他们就会屈服的。人们回忆说奥古斯都在晚年还多次访问日耳曼，可是现在提贝里乌斯在他的盛年时期[2]反而总坐在元老院里挑剔元老们的发言。人们还说，他对罗马的奴役已经足够了，现在应该出去做点事情，去平息部队的情绪，为国家创造和平的生活。

这些不满的言论并没有对提贝里乌斯产生任何影响。他已经下定了决心，无论如何也不离开首都，以免使他的国家和他本人受到危害。他的担心很多，涉及方方面面的事情。日耳曼拥有比较强大的军队，潘诺尼亚则离罗马比较近。日耳曼在它背后拥有高卢诸行省的丰富资源，潘诺尼亚则对意大利构成一个严重的威胁。所以他应当先到哪个地方去呢？如果他先到一个地方去，但另一个地方的士兵又发动起事端来了，他又该怎么办呢？可是，如果通过自己的儿子去处理这些事情，那他就可以同时处理两个地方的问题，同时又不致使自己的皇帝尊严发生危险，因

---

[1] 伊里利库姆在这里是泛指潘诺尼亚、达尔马提亚和美西亚等地。

[2] 奥古斯都最后到日耳曼是公元前 8 年，当时他是 54 岁，但提贝里乌斯此时已经 56 岁了。

was, indeed, more awe-inspiring at a distance. Besides, it was excusable for the young Germanicus and Drusus to refer some points to their father, and resistance offered to them could be conciliated or broken by himself. If, on the other hand, the emperor were treated contemptuously, no expedient was left.

All the same, as though he were going to start at any moment, he chose his staff, collected equipment, and prepared ships. Then, however, he offered various excuses about the weather, and pressure of business. The deception worked—on intelligent people for a little, on most people for some time, and on those in the provinces for longest of all.

Germanicus had brought his troops together and was ready for counter-measures against the mutineers. But he decided to give them more time in case they might profit by the example of the other brigades. So he sent word to Caecina saying that he was coming with a strong force and that, unless they first punished the agitators, he would execute them indiscriminately. Caecina read the letter privately to the colour-sergeants and sergeant-majors and other reliable elements in the camp, and appealed to them to save the army's honour, and their own lives. 'In peace-time', he said, 'backgrounds and justifications are considered; but when war comes, the innocent fall with the guilty.' Sounding the men whom they thought reliable, they found that the greater part of the two brigades was loyal. So in consultation with the general, they fixed a time at which the grossest offenders were

为说实话,身在一个距离遥远的地方更使人畏惧。而且,如果年轻的皇子日耳曼尼库斯和杜路苏斯将一些问题推到他们父亲身上去,那是更容易交代过去的,而且对皇子们的反抗还可以由他出面安抚或打破。另一方面,如果士兵们对皇帝本人也投以蔑视,完全不放在眼里,那么他就无计可施了。

但是同时,他又作出了一种在任何时候都可能会出发的姿态,他选拔护卫人员,装备所有用品装置,并准备船只。可是接着又找出了各种各样的借口,诸如天气的原因,事务太繁忙等等来进行欺骗,这种欺骗对机警的人来说,持续不了多长时间。而对大多数人而言,则会持续较长一段时间。对各行省的人,欺骗的时间最长。

日耳曼尼库斯这时已经把他的军队集结在了一起,准备用武力来解决这些叛乱者了。但是他决定还是给他们一些时间来考虑,这样,他们也许会从其他军团的榜样中得到鼓励,主动屈服。因此,他给凯奇纳写了一封信,信中说他即将率领一支强有力的军队前来,到时候如果不是他们事先处决了惹是生非的罪魁祸首,他就要不加区别地把他们一律处死。凯奇纳偷偷地把这封信念给军旗的旗手、中队的旗手和营地里他最信任的人们听,并且请求他们维护全军的荣誉、珍惜他们自己的生命。"如果和平解决,"他说,"处理时会考虑到各人过去功劳的大小,会公平对待的;可是如果动起武来,则无辜的人也会被当作罪犯处理,大家就会一同遭殃了。"听了他们所信任的人的一番话,他们便分头对他们认为合适的人进行了试探。他们发现两个军团中的多数人仍然是忠诚的。于是在得到了副帅的同意之后,他们便约定了一个时间,决定在那个时间里向那些最顽固的

to be struck down. At a given signal, they burst into the tents, and surprised and killed their victims. Only those in the secret knew how the massacre had begun—or where it would end.

This was unlike any other civil war. It was not a battle between opposing forces. Men in the same quarters, who had eaten together by day and rested together by night, took sides and fought each other. The shrieks, wounds, and blood were unmistakable. But motives were mysterious, fates unpredictable. There were casualties among the loyalists, too; for the culprits also had seized weapons when they realized who were being attacked. Generals, colonels, offered no restraining hand. Mass vengeance was indulged and glutted.

Soon afterwards Germanicus arrived in the camp. Bursting into tears, he cried: 'This is no cure; it is a catastrophe!' Then he ordered the bodies to be cremated.

和最活跃的叛兵发动突然袭击。在约定的信号传出去之后，他们便冲进了营帐，出其不意地消灭了那些牺牲品。只有那些参与了此次机密的人才知道，这次屠杀是怎样开始，又是做到什么程度才结束的。

这次内战与其他任何内战都不一样。它不是发生在两个敌对阵营之间的战斗，大家都是同营的士兵，白天同吃，夜晚同住。但是现在他们各自站到对立面相互攻击，到处是惨叫声，到处是创伤，血流遍地，触目惊心！偶然性主宰着一切，即使是忠于皇帝的士兵也有不少命丧黄泉的，因为当叛兵看清楚什么人正在遭受着攻击的时候，他们也拿起了武器。副帅、军团将领冷眼旁观，毫不制止这种杀戮。他们对人们的大肆报复采取纵容的态度，任由士兵们胡作非为。

不久之后，日耳曼尼库斯到达了营地，看到这种情景他不禁泪流满面。他哭喊着说："这不是平息叛乱，这简直是一场灾难！"于是下令将这些尸体焚烧掉。

CHAPTER 3
War With The Germans

THERE was still a savage feeling among the troops—and a desire to make up for their lunacy by attacking the enemy. Honourable wounds, they felt, on their guilty breasts, were the only means of appeasing the ghosts of their fellow-soldiers. Germanicus encouraged these ambitions, and built a bridge across the Rhine.

Across it he transported twelve thousand regular troops, twenty-six auxiliary battalions, and eight cavalry regiments, of which the loyalty had not been affected during the rising. While we were immobilized, first by the mourning for Augustus and then by the mutinies, the Germans were in high spirits—and not far off. But a rapid march through the Caesian forest brought the Roman army across the line begun by Tiberius. Germanicus pitched camp on the line with earthworks to his front and rear, and palisades on his flanks. Ahead were dark forests

第三章　与日耳曼人的战争

弥漫在部队里的野蛮之性还没有平息,人们渴望上战场杀敌来弥补他们的疯狂行为所犯下的过失。他们认为,只有让自己罪恶的胸膛光荣地负伤,才是安慰他们同伴们灵魂的好办法。日耳曼尼库斯鼓励士兵们这种雄心,就在莱茵河上架起了一座桥。

1.2 万名正规军团士兵,辅助军队的 26 个步兵中队和 8 个骑兵中队跨过了这座桥。这次兵变中,士兵们的忠诚并没有受到影响。先是由于对奥古斯都逝世的哀悼,后来又由于兵变,我们这方面一直没有采取什么军事行动。在这期间,日耳曼人却得意洋洋,他们就在我们边界不远处大肆活动。但是罗马军队进行了一次穿过凯西亚森林的急行军,然后就通过了从提贝里乌斯就开始构筑的边界。[1] 日耳曼尼库斯就在这道边界上安营扎寨,营地的前后都修筑了土垒防卫,两侧则竖起了栅栏。再往前走则是阴暗的森林和两条小路:

---

〔1〕 凯西亚森林和这道边界到底是在什么地方,目前还没能确定。福尔诺认为:"超过下述的情况几乎是不可能的,即罗马人也许从维提拉沿着利珀河左岸行进,然后穿过一个比较生僻的地区向南,朝着上鲁尔行进,而在利珀河以北的部族却企图截断他们的退路。"

and two paths—one the short, usual route, and the other so hard and unfamiliar that the enemy left it unwatched. After a conference the Romans chose the longer way. Their advance was rapid, since according to intelligence reports there was a German festival that night with ceremonial banquets and performances. Caecina was instructed to go on ahead with light-armed auxiliary battalions to clear a passage through the forests, the regular brigades to follow not far behind. A starry night helped. Each village they came to in the country of the Marsi found itself surrounded by a ring of Roman pickets. The Germans were lying in bed or beside their tables, unafraid, with no sentries posted. There was careless disorganization everywhere. Of war there was not a thought. Their condition was one of peace—in this case, an uncontrolled, drunken prostration.

To increase the scope of the raid, Germanicus divided his enthusiastic troops into four columns. These ravaged and burnt the country for fifty miles around. No pity was shown to age or sex. Religious as well as secular centres were utterly destroyed—among them the temple of Tanfana, the most revered holy place of those tribes. There were no Roman casualties, since their victims were scattered, unarmed and half-asleep. But neighbouring tribes, the Bructeri, Tubantes, and Usipetes, disturbed by the massacre, occupied the woods on their way back. Germanicus discovered this and took the road in readiness

一条较短,是人们通常走的道路;另一条路偏僻难行,是没有人走过,敌人也没有防守的路。罗马士兵在研究之后,选择了较长的那条道路。但是他们行军的速度非常迅速,因为根据侦察兵的报告,那一晚正是日耳曼人的一个节日,节日中有盛大的宴会,还有各种表演。凯奇纳奉命率领一些轻装的辅助步兵中队打前锋,在森林里清除障碍,开辟出一条通道,正规军团士兵就跟在他们后面不远处。晴朗多星的夜晚对行军非常有利。他们每到达一处玛尔喜人的村庄,就派出前哨将村庄团团包围。这时日耳曼人有的正躺在床上,有的正在桌旁,他们没有丝毫恐惧,也没有设置岗哨。到处都是毫无戒备的松散混乱状态。他们根本没有想到会发生战争,他们的情况呈现出一片和平的景象。在这种情况下,他们无所节制,甚至烂醉如泥,卧倒在地。

为了扩大进攻的规模,日耳曼尼库斯将他的士气高涨的军团士兵分成了四个部分,这些士兵在周围 50 英里的地方大肆烧杀抢掠。没有因年龄和性别而对烧杀对象产生丝毫的怜悯。不论是宗教的还是世俗的居住区都遭到了彻底的摧毁。在这些被摧毁的建筑物中间,有这些部族最著名的宗教中心坦法那神庙。[1] 罗马的军队没有受到任何损伤,因为他们所屠杀的敌人都是分散的,他们手无寸铁,正处在半睡半醒之中。但是,邻近的部族,布路克提里人、图邦提斯人和乌西皮提斯人都被这一屠杀所惊扰,他们也投入到战场上来了。他们占领了森林中罗马军队回去时必经的道路。日耳曼尼库斯发现了这种情况,便整装待

---

〔1〕 关于坦法那这个名称,仅见于日耳曼 9 世纪或 10 世纪文献中的一个诗句:"赞(坦)法那在早上送去了一只小肥羊。"

either to march or fight. A cavalry force and auxiliary battalions went ahead, followed by the first brigade in the centre, the twenty-first and the fifth on the left and right flanks respectively, and the twentieth in the rear. Behind came the remaining auxiliaries.

The enemy did not budge until the whole column was strung out in the wood. Then, feinting against the vanguard and flanks, they directed their full force against the rear. The massed German attacks disorganized the light-armed auxiliary battalions. Germanicus rode up to the twenty-first brigade and shouted that now was the time to wipe out the mutiny—by one rapid stroke, their disgrace could be turned into glory. Then the brigade by a single, passionate attack broke through the German army and drove it with heavy losses into open country. Simultaneously the vanguard emerged from the woods and established a fortified camp. From then on, the journey was without incident. The troops settled into winter quarters, their morale improved and the past forgotten.

Tiberius' reaction to German developments included worry as well as relief. He was glad the mutiny had been put down. But he was not pleased that Germanicus had courted the army's goodwill by money payments and accelerated discharges—not to speak of his military success. Tiberius reported the achievements of Germanicus to the senate. But what he said, though complimentary, was so ostentatiously elaborate that it did not ring true. The few words with which he praised Drusus for ending the mutiny in Illyricum sounded more heartfelt and sincere; and he extended to the regular troops in Pannonia the concessions which Germanicus had granted to those on the Rhine.

发,摆出了一副准备进军或作战的阵势。一队骑兵和辅助部队的步兵中队在前头开路。后面跟着的第一军团走在中间,第二十一军团和第五军团分别在左右两侧。第二十军团断后,其余的辅助部队则都跟在后面。

敌人一直安静地埋伏着,直到罗马全军都单列行进到森林里去的时候,他们才对前锋和两翼作了小规模的进攻,并且全力进攻后卫部队。日耳曼大军的集中进攻,使轻武装的罗马辅助步兵中队的队伍陷入了混乱。这时日耳曼尼库斯骑着马来到了第二十一军团,他高声呐喊着对他们说,现在到了他们以迅速的攻击洗刷他们叛乱污点的时候了,他们的耻辱将会因此而变成光荣。军队的战斗热情被鼓舞了起来,他们一下子就冲进了日耳曼的队伍,并给他们以沉重的打击,将其赶到了空旷的地方。与此同时,先锋部队已经走出了森林,而且还建起了一座构筑了防卫工事的营地。从那时起,行军就没有再遇见什么麻烦事了。士兵们住进了冬营,他们的士气提高了,过去的事也都抛到了脑后。

在日耳曼取得胜利的消息使提贝里乌斯既感到欣慰,同时又有些不安。他很高兴叛乱被镇压下去了。但另一方面,日耳曼尼库斯发放金钱、加速遣散工作——更不用说他在军事上取得的胜利,从而取得了士兵们的好感,这些又使他感到不快!提贝里乌斯向元老院报告了日耳曼尼库斯的战绩。他在报告中虽然对日耳曼尼库斯大加称赞,但是他言过其实的夸张之辞,使人怀疑他说的不是真心话。他称赞杜路苏斯在伊利库姆平息叛乱的话比较简短,但听起来却真挚诚恳得多了。此外,他又把日耳曼尼库斯在莱茵河对士兵所作的一切让步,也给予了潘诺尼亚的士兵。

This was the year when Julia (Ⅲ) died. Her father Augustus had imprisoned her—for immorality—first on the island of Pandateria and then in the town of Rhegium on the straits opposite Sicily. While Gaius Caesar and Lucius Caesar were still alive, she had been married to Tiberius, but had looked down on him as an inferior. That had been the fundamental reason for his retirement to Rhodes. When he became emperor, he eliminated her last hope by the removal of Agrippa Postumus. Then he let her waste away to death, exiled and disgraced, by slow starvation. He calculated that she had been banished for so long that her death would pass unnoticed.

There were similar motives behind his harsh treatment of Sempronius Gracchus. This shrewd, misguidedly eloquent aristocrat had seduced Julia while she was Marcus Agrippa's wife. Nor was that the end of the affair, for when she was transferred to Tiberius this persistent adulterer made her defiant and unfriendly to her new husband. A letter abusing Tiberius, which Julia wrote to her father Augustus, was believed to have been Gracchus' work. So he had been dismissed to the African island of Cercina, where he endured fourteen

这一年,优利娅(三世)死了。[1] 由于她的行为放荡,她的父亲奥古斯都先是把她囚禁在庞达提里亚这个小岛上,[2]继而又把她囚禁在与西西里海峡相对的城市列吉乌姆。[3] 在盖乌斯·恺撒和路奇乌斯·恺撒还活着的时候,她就嫁给了提贝里乌斯,但是她却瞧不起他,认为他的身份低人一等。而这一点实际上也正是他隐退到罗德岛去的根本原因。但当提贝里乌斯成为皇帝的时候,他铲除了阿格里帕·波司图姆斯,将她最后的一点希望也破灭了。后来他使得她在贫困与饥饿中慢慢死去。他认为如此长时期的放逐会使人们对她的死亡也不再注意。

他残酷地虐待显普洛尼乌斯·格拉古也是出于同样的动机。这个精明的、富有善于误导人的好口才的显贵人物在优利娅还是玛尔库斯·阿格里帕的妻子时,便曾经引诱过她。不过奸情还没有到此结束,当优利娅再嫁给提贝里乌斯的时候,她的这个旧情未了的情夫唆使她对自己新嫁的丈夫居高临下,百般瞧不起和憎恶。优利娅写给她父亲奥古斯都的一封信中,对提贝里乌斯大肆污蔑,据说就是出自格拉古的手笔。因此最后显普洛尼乌斯·格拉古被放逐到了阿非利加海上的凯尔奇那岛,[4]在那里他承受了

---

〔1〕 优利娅是奥古斯都和司克里波尼娅所生的女儿,也是他唯一的孩子(前39~14年)。公元前25年她和堂兄玛尔库斯·玛尔凯路斯结婚(无子嗣),后者死后两年她又嫁给了玛尔库斯·维普撒尼乌斯·阿格里帕,他们生了三个儿子:盖乌斯·恺撒、路奇乌斯·恺撒、阿格里帕·波斯图姆斯,两个女儿:优利娅和日耳曼尼库斯的妻子阿格里披娜。阿格里帕死后,她又被迫嫁给提贝里乌斯(公元前11年),提贝里乌斯为此竟不得不和自己的妻子维普撒尼娅离婚。公元前2年被贬黜放逐。

〔2〕 那不勒斯湾西北部的一个荒岛,现称万多提那或温托提尼。

〔3〕 即现在意大利的勒佐。

〔4〕 加贝斯湾的两个小岛凯尔凯纳。

years of exile. Now soldiers were sent to kill him. They found him standing on a promontory, fearing the worst. When they landed, he asked for a few moments so that he could write his wife Alliaria certain last requests. Then he offered his neck to the assassins. His life had fallen short of the prestige of the Sempronii. His brave death, however, was worthy of them. According to another account the soldiers did not come from Rome, but were sent by the governor of Africa, Lucius Nonius Asprenas. This version, however, originated from Tiberius—who hoped (unsuccessfully) to blame the murder on the governor.

In the same year, there was a religious innovation: a new Brotherhood of Augustus was created, on the analogy of the ancient Titian Brotherhood founded by King Titus Tatius for the maintenance of Sabine ritual. Twenty-one members were appointed by lot from the leading men of the State; and Tiberius, Drusus, Claudius, and Germanicus were added. The annual Games established in honour of Augustus were also begun. But their inauguration was troubled by disorders due to rivalry between ballet-dancers. Augustus had tolerated such performances out of indulgence to Maecenas, who was passionately fond of a contemporary star, Bathyllus. Besides, Augustus himself liked this sort of entertainment, and thought it looked democratic to join in the people's amusements. Tiberius' character took a different course. But he did not yet venture to introduce the longpampered Romans to austerity.

14年的流放生活的痛苦。现在,一些士兵被派到那里去结束他的性命,他们发现他正站在一个海岬上,等待着最坏情况的来临。士兵们登陆之后,他请求他们给他一些时间,让他给他的妻子阿利亚里亚写一封信作最后的交代。信写好后,他便把脖子伸过去,让那些刽子手动手。他堕落的生活行径玷污了显普洛尼乌斯一家的名声,但他面对死亡的勇敢镇定却是配得上这种声名的。还有另一种说法,说这些士兵不是来自罗马,而是阿非利加的总督路奇乌斯·诺尼乌斯·阿司普列那斯派来的。不过这种说法是提贝里乌斯所授意的,他是想(没有成功)把谋杀的罪名转嫁到总督身上。

也就在这一年,在宗教仪式方面也有了一些改革:设置了奉祀奥古斯都的一个新的祭司团,这与先前金·提图斯·塔提乌斯为了保护萨比尼人的祭仪而设置的古老的提齐乌斯祭司团一样。从罗马的显要家族中用抽签的方式选出了21人,此外,又加上了提贝里乌斯、杜路苏斯、克劳狄乌斯和日耳曼尼库斯。并第一次举行了为纪念奥古斯都而设立的每年一度的赛会。但是这初次举行的赛会却半途而废了,因为优伶之间的竞争引起了极大的混乱。以前奥古斯都对这些戏剧表演采取宽容的态度,乃是出于对迈凯纳斯的放任:迈凯纳斯迷上了当时的明星巴图路斯。[1] 而且,奥古斯都本人也喜欢这一类的娱乐,他认为参加民众的娱乐活动看起来会有些民主气氛。提贝里乌斯的性格则使他采取了不同的态度,但是他还不敢冒险去迫使那些多年来过惯了养尊处优生活的罗马人再去过节俭朴素的生活。

---

〔1〕 巴图路斯是一个被释的奴隶,奥古斯都的朋友皮拉迪斯的劲敌,哑剧的创始人。

In the next year, when the consuls were Drusus and Gaius Norbanus, a Triumph was decreed to Germanicus. The war, however, was not over. Its next stage was a sudden raid on the Chatti in early spring. But he was planning a large-scale summer campaign against the major enemy, the Cherusci. It was hoped that their allegiance was split between Arminius and Segestes. These two leaders stood respectively for treachery and goodwill to Rome. Arminius was Germany's troublemaker. Segestes had often warned Publius Quinctilius Varus that rebellion was planned. At the feast which immediately preceded the rising Segestes had advised Varus to arrest Arminius and the other chiefs, and also himself, on the grounds that their removal would immobilize their accomplices and Varus could then take his time in sorting out the guilty from the innocent. However, Varus was destined to fall to Arminius.

Segestes had been forced into the war by the unanimous feeling of the Cherusci. But relations between the two Germans were still bad. Domestic ill-feeling contributed because Segestes' daughter, engaged to another man; was stolen by Arminius. The girl's father and husband detested each other. The marriage relationship, which brings friends closer, increased the bitterness of these two enemies.

For the operation against the Chatti, Germanicus transferred to Aulus Caecina Severus four brigades with 5000 auxiliaries, also some

第二年,当杜路苏斯·恺撒和盖乌斯·诺尔巴努斯做执政官的时候,[1]他们把凯旋的荣誉授予了日耳曼尼库斯,但是战争还没有结束。他原计划对主要敌人凯路斯奇人[2]在夏天发起一次大规模的战争,但却在初春便出其不意地向卡提伊人[3]发动了进攻。他期望着阿尔米尼乌斯和塞盖司特斯之间的联合会发生分裂。这两个部族领袖都十分出名,不过一个是由于对罗马背信弃义,而另一个则是由于忠诚不渝。阿尔米尼乌斯是日耳曼叛乱的制造者。塞盖司特斯则屡次提醒波布里乌斯·克温克提里乌斯·伐鲁斯注意正在策划中的叛乱。在就要进行武力镇压的那次盛大宴会上,塞盖司特斯请求伐鲁斯把他本人、阿尔米尼乌斯和其他主要人物都逮捕起来,理由是在领袖们被逮捕之后,参加的群众便会老实了,而之后伐鲁斯也就可以有充裕的时间从无辜者之中辨认出罪犯了。然而伐鲁斯命中注定要死在阿尔米尼乌斯的手里。

在凯路斯奇人民团结一致的意志的压力下,塞盖司特斯不得不参加了战争。但是这两个日耳曼人之间的关系依然很糟糕。他们之间的矛盾主要是因为,塞盖司特斯的女儿已经许配给了别人,可是阿尔米尼乌斯却将她拐跑了,这样便使岳父和女婿成了冤家。婚姻关系本来会使双方的友情更加密切,但现在却更增加了这两个仇人之间的敌对情绪了。

为了对付卡提伊人,日耳曼尼库斯于是给了阿乌路斯·凯奇纳·塞维路斯四个军团外加 5000 名辅助士兵以及在莱茵河西岸

---

〔1〕 罗马建城 768 年,即公元 15 年。
〔2〕 住在卡提伊人东北,在威悉河与易北河之面。
〔3〕 住在莱茵河右岸黑森—拿骚地区。敌视罗马的这个部族,对阿尔米尼乌斯和凯路斯奇人是同样敌视的。

German emergency levies from this side of the Rhine. He himself retained the same number of brigades with twice as many auxiliary troops. He built a fort on Mount Taunus—on the remains of a construction of his father's—and proceeded with rapid, lightly equipped forces against the Chatti. He left a force under Lucius Apronius to put roads and bridges in order, since rain and floods were feared on the return journey; but now a drought, rare in those parts, had emptied the rivers, and gave him an uninterrupted advance.

Germanicus completely surprised the Chatti. Helpless women, children, and old people were at once slaughtered or captured. The younger men swam across the river Eder and tried to prevent the Romans from building a bridge. But they were driven back by missiles and arrows. An unsuccessful attempt was made by the tribesmen to come to terms. Then there were some desertions to the Roman side. But the majority evacuated their towns and villages, dispersed and took to the woods. Germanicus burnt their capital, Mattium, and, ravaging the open country, started back for the Rhine. The enemy did not dare to harass the rearguard, as they are fond of doing when they have retreated for strategic purposes rather than in a panic.

The Cherusci had been inclined to help the Chatti; but a series of swift manoeuvres by Caecina deterred them. He also defeated the Marsi who had ventured to engage him. Soon afterwards a deputation arrived appealing for the rescue of Segestes, besieged by his hostile compatriots. Arminius was in power. He was leader of the war-party—in disturbed times uncivilized communities trust and prefer leaders

紧急征募的一些日耳曼人。他自己则率领着同样多的军团士兵和两倍的辅助部队。他在陶努斯山[1]上他父亲修筑的要塞的废址上建立了一座要塞,随即便向卡提伊人轻装进行全速进军。他命令路奇乌斯·阿普洛尼乌斯带领一支部队留在后面修路架桥,因为人们担心暴雨和洪水会阻碍归路。但是现在由于那些地区发生了一次罕见的旱灾,河道干涸,因此日耳曼尼库斯进军时毫无阻碍。

卡提伊人看到日耳曼尼库斯的到来完全惊呆了,无助的妇女、儿童和老人立刻被抓获或残杀了。青壮年男子游过了埃德尔河,[2]力图阻止罗马人架桥,但是被投射的器械和射出的箭击退了。他们想求和,但是日耳曼尼库斯的军队没有答应。有人投到罗马军队这边来,其他多数人则逃出自己的小镇和村庄,四处逃散跑到森林里去了。日耳曼尼库斯先烧掉了他们的首府玛提乌姆,[3]随后又洗劫了广大的乡村,接着就返回了莱茵河。敌人不敢骚扰撤退部队的后卫,虽然他们出于战略上的考虑在敌方撤退时总喜欢如此,但他们现在是处于恐惧之中。

凯路斯奇人打算前来援助卡提伊人,但是凯奇纳发动的一连串迅速的军事行动阻止了他们的增援。他还击败了胆敢向他发动攻击的玛尔喜人。不久之后,一个代表团前来请求对塞盖司特斯进行援助,因为对他怀有敌意的同族人将他包围了。这时阿尔米尼乌斯已经当权,他是主战派的领袖。在发生骚乱的时候,外族人信任、喜欢那些不怕危险的人,于是拥戴他作领袖。塞盖司特

---

〔1〕 在莱茵河和尼达河之间。
〔2〕 这条河流入威悉河支流富尔达河。
〔3〕 在埃德河以北。

who take risks. Segestes had included his own son Segimundus in the deputation. The latter, reflecting on his record, had hesitated. For in the year of the German rebellion he had taken off the insignia of his Roman priesthood at the Ubian altar, and had run away to the rebels. However, he was persuaded to hope for Roman indulgence, and served as his father's envoy. He was well received, and escorted across to the left bank of the river.

Germanicus thought it worth his while to wheel round, engage the besieging force, and rescue Segestes and many of his relations and dependants. These included women of high rank, among whom was Segestes' daughter, the wife of Arminius. She was temperamentally closer to her husband than to her father. From her came no appeals, no submissive tears; she stood still, her hands clasped inside her robe, staring down at her pregnant body. The party brought with them trophies from Varus' disaster, many of them distributed on that occasion as loot to those who were now surrendering.

And then there was Segestes himself, a huge figure, fearlessly aware he had been a good ally. 'This is not the first day I have been a true friend to Rome,' he cried. 'Ever since the divine Augustus made me a Roman citizen, my choice of friends and enemies has been guided by your advantage. My motive has not been hatred of my people—for traitors are distasteful even to the side they join—but the belief that Roman and German interests are the same, and that peace is better than war. That is why I denounced to your former commander Varus the man who broke the treaty with you—Arminius, the robber of

斯让自己的儿子西吉孟都斯也参加了这个使团,但是西吉孟都斯因为对自己过去的行为有顾虑而犹豫不决。原来在日耳曼人发动叛乱的那一年里,他被罗马人任命为乌比伊人的祭坛的祭司,但他却在乌比伊祭坛把作为祭司圣职标志的饰带扯下来,逃到叛变者那边去了。然而,在别人的劝说下他相信罗马人会宽恕他,于是就接受了作为父亲的外交特使的任务。他受到了友好的接待,并且被护送到了莱茵河左岸去。[1]

日耳曼尼库斯认为回师解围是值得的,于是便进攻包围塞盖司特斯的外族,并救出了塞盖司特斯以及他的许多亲族和侍从。这些人当中包括一些门第很高的妇女,其中有塞盖司特斯的女儿、也就是阿尔米尼乌斯的妻子。她的脾气不太像她的父亲,倒是比较像她的丈夫。她不作任何恳求,不掉一滴眼泪;她静静地站在那里,双手在外袍的衣褶里紧握着,她的两只眼睛则向下凝望着自己怀孕的腹部。这些人带来了因伐鲁斯战败而获得的战利品,这些战利品有许多在当时曾拿来分配给现在前来投降的人们。

还有塞盖司特斯本人,他身材高大魁梧,毫无畏惧之色,因为他知道,他始终是罗马忠诚的联盟者。他叫喊着说:"我并不是从今天才开始成为罗马人民的忠诚朋友的,自从神圣的奥古斯都使我成为罗马的公民,我就以你们的利益为标准来选择朋友和敌人了。我这样做,并不是由于我憎恨我的人民——卖国贼甚至在他加入的那一边的人们看来也是可憎的,而是因为我相信罗马和日耳曼的利益是一致的,而且我认为和平总是比战争要好一些。这也就是我在你们先前的统帅伐鲁斯面前指责阿尔米尼乌斯的原

---

〔1〕 高卢人所在的那一边。

my daughter!

'But Varus indolently put me off. I lost faith in due processes of law, and begged him to arrest Arminius, and his partisans—and myself. May that night confirm my story—I wish I had not survived it! What followed is matter for mourning rather than excuses. But I did imprison Arminius; and his supporters have imprisoned me. And now, at my first meeting with you, I tell you I favour the old not the new—peace, not trouble. I am not after rewards; I want to clear myself of double-dealing. And if the Germans prefer remorse to suicide, I am a fitting agent. For my son's youthful misdeeds I ask pardon. My daughter, I admit, was brought here by force. It is for you to say which shall count the more, the son she is bearing to Arminius, or the fact that I am her father.'

Germanicus answered kindly, promising safety to Segestes' children and relations, and a home in Gaul for himself. Then Germanicus withdrew his forces, allowing himself to be hailed as victor on Tiberius' initiative. A son was born to Arminius' wife; he was brought up at Ravenna. I shall write elsewhere of the ironical fate in store for him.

因,他破坏了同你们缔结的条约,霸占了我的女儿!

可是伐鲁斯不慌不忙的推脱,使我的指责没有得到什么结果。我并不相信法律能给予什么真正的保护,于是我请求他把阿尔米尼乌斯、他的同谋者和我都逮捕起来。那一夜可以为我的话作证,我真希望那一夜里我并没有活下来!接下来所发生的事情只能使人哀伤,而无法寻找任何借口。但我还是把阿尔米尼乌斯逮捕起来,可是我自己也被他的同党逮捕了。而现在,在我同你们第一次会面的时候,我告诉你们我仍然希望恢复过去的和平,而不是当前的这种骚乱。我不是来要求报酬的,我只是想来澄清自己,我并不是一个口是心非的两面派。同时如果日耳曼人愿意悔改而不去自寻死路的话,那么我就是一个合适的代理人。我为我的儿子因年轻而犯下的过错请求你们的宽恕。我的女儿,我承认,是被我强迫带到这里来的。但是她的哪一种身份更重要一些,就请你们判断吧:她将要生养的是阿尔米尼乌斯的儿子,可事实我又是她的父亲。"

日耳曼尼库斯的回答宽宏大量,他答应会保证塞盖司特斯的孩子和亲属们的安全,并答应他定居高卢境内。[1] 随后他就将军队撤回,并接受了在提贝里乌斯的建议之下所授予的凯旋的称号。阿尔米尼乌斯的妻子后来生了一个儿子,这个孩子在拉温那被抚养长大。我在以后的其他地方还要谈到这个孩子所遭受到的具有讽刺意味的不幸命运。[2]

―――――――――

〔1〕 左岸高卢境内属于日耳曼行省。伐鲁斯战败后,日耳曼的领土在实际上已经不再是一个行省,但在理论上仍被视为一个行省。

〔2〕 塔西佗关于这部分的作品已佚,从16卷可以看出,这个孩子已经死了。

The news of Segestes' submission and good reception pleased those who did not want fighting, distressed those who did. Arminius' violent nature was maddened by his wife's abduction and the prospect of servitude for their unborn child. He made a rapid tour of the Cherusci, demanding war against Segestes and Germanicus. These were some of his savage taunts: 'What a fine father! What a glorious commander of a valiant army, whose united strength has kidnapped one helpless woman! I, on the other hand, have annihilated three divisions and their commanders. My fighting has been open, not treacherous—and it has been against armed men and not pregnant women. The groves of Germany still display the Roman Eagles and standards which I hung there in honour of the gods of our fathers.

'Let Segestes live on the conquered bank, and make his son a Roman priest again. With this warning before them Germany will never tolerate Roman rods, axes, and robes between Rhine and Elbe. Other countries, unacquainted with Roman rule, have not known its impositions or its punishments. We have known them—and got rid of them! Augustus, now deified, and his "chosen" Tiberius have gone away frustrated. There is nothing to fear in an inexperienced youth and a mutinous army. If you prefer your country, your parents, and the old ways to settlement under tyrants abroad, then do not follow Segestes to shameful slavery—follow Arminius to glory and freedom!'

Besides the Cherusci, the tribes around responded to his call. It also won over Arminius' uncle, Inguiomerus, long respected by the

塞盖司特斯投诚的消息以及他所受到的友好对待,使那些不想看到战争的人充满了欢欣,而那些主张战争的人却感到忧伤。妻子被俘和尚未出生的儿子将要因此遭受到奴役的命运的现实,将脾气暴躁的阿尔米尼乌斯气得发疯了。他迅速前往凯路斯奇人那里联络,要求对塞盖司特斯和日耳曼尼库斯作战。以下是他的一些野蛮的谩骂之词:"一个多么好的父亲!一支多么勇敢的军队的一个多么了不起的统帅!他们竟然联合起来绑架一个软弱无助的女人!另一方面,我虽然曾经消灭了他们三个军团和他们的统帅,但是我的战斗是光明正大地进行的,我与之作战的是全副武装的战士,而不是怀孕的妇女。我所悬挂起来的、以纪念我们祖先灵魂的各种罗马的旗帜,还在日耳曼的森林里陈列着。"

"让塞盖司特斯定居在被征服的河岸地区,让他的儿子继续重新做罗马祭司吧。但是我还要提醒他们,日耳曼人是永远不会容忍罗马人的棍棒、斧头和出现在莱茵河和易北河之间的地区的长袍的。其他没有经受过罗马统治的民族地区的人们,他们不熟悉罗马的统治,不了解他们会对人们施以怎样的压迫和惩罚。可是我们深深地了解,并且我们已经摆脱了他们的压迫和惩罚。奥古斯都以及他现在选定的接班人提贝里乌斯,已经战败而还。对这样一个没有经验的年轻人和这样一支充满叛乱的军队,我们没有什么好怕的。如果你们还爱你们的国家,还爱你们的父母,还向往你们原先古朴的生活而不愿受外族暴君的统治的话,就不要追随塞盖司特斯去做令人羞耻的奴隶,跟着我阿尔米尼乌斯去争取我们的光荣和自由吧!"

不仅仅是凯路斯奇人,周围的各个部族也都对他的呼吁做出了积极的回应。不仅如此,阿尔米尼乌斯的叔父,音吉奥美路斯,

Romans. This increased Germanicus' alarm. To create a diversion, and break the force of the expected blow, he sent Caecina with forty regular battalions through the territory of the Bructeri to the river Ems, while cavalry under Pedo Albinovanus crossed the Frisian borderland. Germanicus himself sailed with four brigades across the lakes. Then infantry, horse, and fleet effected a junction on the Ems, and a contingent offered by the Chauci was incorporated. A flying column under Lucius Stertinius, sent by Germanicus against the Bructeri when they started burning their possessions, went killing and looting, and found the Eagle of the nineteenth brigade, lost with Varus. Then the army ravaged all the country between the Ems and the Lippe, marching to the extremity of Bructeran territory.

Now they were near the Teutoburgian Wood, in which the remains of Varus and his three divisions were said to be lying unburied. Germanicus conceived a desire to pay his last respects to these men and their general. Every soldier with him was overcome with pity when he thought of his relations and friends and reflected on the hazards

这位在罗马人中长久以来一直享有很高威信的人也被他争取了过去。这一点使得日耳曼尼库斯大为吃惊。为了对敌人进行牵制，破坏他们未来的袭击可能要会合成一支巨大的力量，他命令凯奇纳率领40个正规步兵中队〔1〕通过布路克提里人的地区到埃姆斯河去。指挥官佩多·阿尔比诺瓦努斯〔2〕则率领着骑兵穿过弗里喜人地区〔3〕的边境前进。日耳曼尼库斯本人则带领四个军团乘船穿过湖区。〔4〕步兵、骑兵和舰队都在上述埃姆斯河会合。在罗马的军队里，还有卡乌奇人所组成的一个士兵分遣队。路奇乌斯·司特尔提尼乌斯曾奉日耳曼尼库斯之命率领一支轻武装队伍攻打布路克提里人。当布路克提里人焚烧他们的财物时，路奇乌斯·司特尔提尼乌斯率部赶到，将他们赶跑了。当这支队伍正在烧杀掳掠的时候，他们发现了第十九军团的军旗，这是伐鲁斯丢下的。于是全军又洗劫了埃姆斯河和里普河之间的整个地区，从这里一直行进到布路克提里人地区的最边远的地带。

现在他们离提乌托布尔格森林〔5〕已经很近了，据说伐鲁斯和他的军团士兵的尸体还留在那里没有得到掩埋。日耳曼库尼斯很想对这些阵亡的士兵和他们的统帅表示最后的敬意。他所率领的全部士兵们则想到了他们的亲属和朋友，想到了战争的灾难和人类生活所遭受的不幸，于是也不由自主地为感伤怜悯之情所征

---

〔1〕 指下军的四个军团。

〔2〕 佩多·阿尔比诺瓦努斯是奥维狄乌斯的朋友，他写过一篇有关日耳曼尼库斯的战役的叙事诗。

〔3〕 弗里喜人居住的地区是在沮伊德湖和埃姆斯河之间的沿岸地区。

〔4〕 这四个军团是指上军的四个军团，湖区大约是今天的沮伊德湖。

〔5〕 关于乌托布尔格森林的确切地点争议颇多，迄今为止还没有最后的定论，一般认为是在威斯特伐利亚的荷恩附近。

of war and of human life. Caecina was sent ahead to reconnoitre the dark woods and build bridges and causeways on the treacherous surface of the sodden marshland. Then the army made its way over the tragic sites. The scene lived up to its horrible associations. Varus' extensive first camp, with its broad extent and headquarters marked out, testified to the whole army's labours. Then a half-ruined breastwork and shallow ditch showed where the last pathetic remnant had gathered. On the open ground were whitening bones, scattered where men had fled, heaped up where they had stood and fought back. Fragments of spears and of horses' limbs lay there—also human heads, fastened to tree-trunks. In groves nearby were the outlandish altars at which the Germans had massacred the Roman colonels and senior company-commanders.

Survivors of the catastrophe, who had escaped from the battle or from captivity, pointed out where the generals had fallen, and where the Eagles were captured. They showed where Varus received his first wound, and where he died by his own unhappy hand. And they told of the platform from which Arminius had spoken, and of his arrogant insults to the Eagles and standards—and of all the gibbets and pits for the prisoners.

So, six years after the slaughter, a living Roman army had come to bury the dead men's bones of three whole divisions. No one knew if the remains he was burying belonged to a stranger or a comrade. But in their bitter distress, and rising fury against the enemy, they looked on them all as friends and blood-brothers. Germanicus shared in the

服。凯奇纳被派为先锋去阴暗的森林中探察,并在这块叛乱发生地,在那到处是水的沼泽地和不坚实的地面上铺路架桥。之后,军队就开进了这一悲惨的地方。这场景使人很自然地与恐怖联系在一起。他们看到伐鲁斯的第一个营地,这个营地占地广阔,军营的宽阔的边界和安放军旗的地方都规划分明,这一情况表明这乃是整个军队的劳动成果。此外那些已经半颓败的土墙上和浅水沟里,留下了那些残兵败将们在被击溃之前用作掩护的可怜的残余物。在这广阔的平原上到处是白骨,那些四散逃跑的人的尸骨分散在他们所逃往的各处,那些站在那儿回身反击的人的白骨则堆在他们反击之处。时时可见长矛断折的碎片和战马残损的肢体,还有吊在树干上的髑髅,十分显眼。在附近的森林里还有一些蛮族的祭坛,就是在这里,日耳曼人大肆屠杀了罗马军队的军团将领和主力的百人团长。

那些从战斗中逃脱出来或者是挣脱了他们的囚禁的幸免于难的人,则向人们指点着,副帅们是在什么地方被杀死的,军旗又是在什么地方被夺走的。他们向人们讲述着伐鲁斯第一次负伤是在什么地方,又是在什么地方用自己那不幸的手结束了自己的生命。他们还指出阿尔米尼乌斯是在哪个座坛上发表演说的,还说起他是如何以傲慢的态度侮辱军旗和队旗的,还向人们介绍那些为囚犯准备的所有绞架和地牢。

就这样,在那场屠杀发生的六年之后,生还的罗马军队来到这个灾难场所掩埋了这三个军团的士兵的遗骨。谁也不知道自己掩埋的是一个陌生人还是一个同伴的遗骨,但是,他们在内心中怀着深深的悲哀,同时也满怀着对敌人的愤怒,他们以尊敬的心情把这些尸骨全部作为朋友和血肉相连的同胞兄弟埋葬起

general grief, and laid the first turf of the funeral-mound as a heartfelt tribute to the dead. Thereby he earned Tiberius' disapproval. Perhaps this was because the emperor interpreted every action of Germanicus unfavourably. Or he may have felt that the sight of the unburied dead would make the army too respectful of its enemies, and reluctant to fight—nor should a commander belonging to the antique priesthood of the Augurs have handled objects belonging to the dead.

Arminius retreated into pathless country. Germanicus followed. When opportunity arose, he instructed the cavalry to move forward and rush the flat ground where the enemy were stationed. Arminius first ordered his men to fall back on the woods in close order. Then he suddenly wheeled them round, and a force he had secretly posted in the forest was given the signal to charge. The Roman cavalry were disorganized by this new front. Reserve battalions were sent up. But, battered by the retreating mass, they only added to the panic, and were almost forced on to marshy ground, well known to their victorious opponents but perilous for strangers. Then, however, Germanicus brought up his regular brigades in battle formation. This intimidated the enemy, and gave the Romans heart. The battle was broken off without a decision.

Germanicus now withdrew his forces to the Ems. The regular troops which had come by ship returned by the same means. Part of the cavalry were instructed to return to the Rhine along the sea-coast. Caecina took back his own force. His route was familiar, but he was told to proceed as quickly as possible across the Long Bridges. This was the name of a narrow causeway built some years back through a

来。日耳曼尼库斯也和大家一样悲伤,在修建坟山的时候,他捧上了第一把泥土,用以表示对死者的衷心尊敬。但是他的这些做法却没有赢得提贝里乌斯的称许,这或许是因为皇帝从恶意方面来解释日耳曼尼库斯的一切行为,也或许是因为他感觉,看到未被掩埋的死者的场景,会使军队更加重视敌人、厌恶战争。或许他还认为,一位担任着古老的祭坛祭司之职、主持严肃的宗教仪式的统帅是不应当处理任何与死人有关的事务的。

阿尔米尼乌斯退到了没有路的荒野,日耳曼尼库斯在后面紧追不舍。机会一到,他便下令骑兵出击,冲进平原上的敌人阵地里。但是,阿尔米尼乌斯先是命令自己的队伍尽量靠拢在一起,退入森林,之后却突然间又包抄到了日耳曼尼库斯的背后,并且向秘密埋伏在森林里面的士兵发出信号,命令他们向罗马军队发动袭击。罗马的骑兵队伍被面前的这个新情况一下子扰乱了。后备的步兵中队也被派遣了上去,但是这支军队被败退的士兵冲乱了阵脚,他们只是增加了队伍的惊恐情绪,他们一直被压迫着,几乎退到了沼泽地带上去,这种地带是胜利的敌人所熟悉的,然而对于外人来说却非常危险。然而,就在这时,日耳曼尼库斯率领着正规军团赶到了,他把他的士兵排成了正规的战斗行列。这种阵势吓住了敌人,振作起了罗马军队的士气,最后双方不分胜负,各自收兵结束了战斗。

不久以后,日耳曼尼库斯率领他的军队返回了埃姆斯河。就和来的时候乘船而来一样,他的军团在撤退时也是乘船而退的。他命令一部分骑兵沿着海岸线向莱茵河后撤。凯奇纳则率领着自己的军队返回,他们走的是一条熟悉的道路,但他却依然被提醒,要尽快地穿过长桥。所谓长桥,就是一条狭窄的堤道的

vast swamp by Lucius Domitius Ahenobarbus (I). All round was slimy, treacherous bog, clinging mud intersected by streams. Beyond lay gently sloping woods. These were now occupied by Arminius, who by forced marches, using short-cuts, had outstripped the baggageladen, heavily armed Roman column. Caecina was not sure how he could repair the old, broken causeway and at the same time keep the enemy off. So that repairs and fighting could proceed simultaneously, he decided to pitch his camp on the spot.

The Germans, by fierce pressure on front and flanks, tried to break through the outposts and attack the working party. Workers and combatants combined made a terrible din. Everything was against the Romans. The waterlogged ground was too soft for a firm stand and too slippery for movement. Besides, they wore heavy armour and could not throw their javelins standing in the water. The Cherusci, on the other hand, were used to fighting in marshes. They were big men, too, whose thrusts with their great lances had a formidable range. The Roman brigades were wavering when night rescued them from defeat.

Made tireless by success, the Germans did not rest even now. They started to divert towards the low ground streams rising in the surrounding hills. Floods overwhelmed what work the Romans had

名称，是几年之前路奇乌斯·多米提乌斯·埃诺巴尔布斯（一世）[1]在一片辽阔的沼泽地带上铺设起来的。除了堤道以外，所有的地方都是泥泞难行的沼泽地，到处都是纵横交错的小河。远处则是从平原地带缓缓出现在眼帘的森林，它们现在已被阿尔米尼乌斯占领，原来他的军队是以急行军的方式抄近路走过去的，这样他们便超过了辎重装备都很重的罗马军队。如何修补这条旧的已经塌陷的堤道，同时又要与敌人保持一段距离，不直接发生冲突，在这一点上凯奇纳是没有把握的。因此他决定就地停驻下来构筑一个营地，这样一部分人进行修补堤道的工作，同时另一部分人随时准备迎击敌人。

日耳曼人以小规模的战斗，采取正面进攻或者是两翼包抄的办法对罗马军队发动了猛烈的攻势，他们企图突破罗马军队的外围据点，并强攻正在修路的部队。修路的士兵和作战的士兵的叫喊声嘈杂地响成一片。一切都对罗马人不利。满处都是水洼和很深的淤泥地面，松软而又黏滑，士兵们站立不住，要前进而又总是滑倒无法移动。而且他们穿戴的盔甲太重，更无法站在水里把投枪用力投出去。但另一方面，凯路斯奇人却习惯于沼泽地的战斗。他们也是一些身材高大的人，可以将很大的投枪投到很远的地方去刺伤敌人。罗马军团的战斗力越来越弱，已经快要支持不住了，这时夜幕的降临结束了这场战斗，将他们解救了出来。

胜利使得日耳曼人不知疲倦，甚至到了此刻他们也不休息。他们开始着手把发源于周边小山中的小河的水都引到下面这个平原上来。大水淹没了罗马人修补的堤道，而士兵的工作也

---

〔1〕 路奇乌斯·多米提乌斯·埃诺巴尔布斯是皇帝尼禄的祖父。

done, and the soldiers' task was doubled. However, Caecina remained unperturbed. In his forty years of service as soldier and commander, he had known crisis as well as success. Looking ahead he could see nothing for it but to keep the enemy in the woods until his wounded and the heavier part of his force had passed on. Between the hills and the swamp there was enough flat ground for a slender line of battle. The fifth brigade was chosen for the right flank and the twenty-first for the left; the first was to be vanguard, and the twentieth to hold off pursuers.

The night brought no rest. And there was a contrast between the echoes resounding in the low-lying valleys and the forests, as the natives feasted with their savage shouting and triumphant songs, and the occasional murmuring of the Romans round their smouldering fires, as they lay here and there by the breastwork or wandered around the tents, dazed but sleepless. The general had a horrible dream—Varus, covered with blood, seemed to rise out of the morass, and call him: but he would not obey; and when Varus held out his hand he pushed it back. When dawn came, the Roman brigades on the flanks, frightened or disobedient, withdrew from their positions, hastily occupying a level space beyond the swampy ground. This gave Arminius a clear approach. At first he did not attack, until he saw the Romans' heavy equipment stuck in the mud and the ditches. The men round it became disorganized. Units overlapped, and as usual in such

就倍加艰难了。好在凯奇纳并没有惊慌失措,他在军队里服役已经有40年了,不管是作为被领导的士兵或作为统帅,他亲身经历过许多危险和胜利,因此他能够保持足够的镇定。在对目前的情况作出全面的分析和斟酌之后,他知道唯一的办法就是把敌人遏阻在森林里,直到他的军队中负伤的和辎重较多的一部分人渡过河去。在小山和沼泽地之间有一块足够平坦的地面,可以在那里布置一道微弱的战线。第五军团奉命担任右翼,第二十一军团担任左翼,第一军团当先锋,第二十军团断后,以阻止必然会发生的追击。

这一夜,双方都没有休息,但是双方的情况却大相径庭。低谷和森林里到处都回荡着强烈的呼喊声和胜利的歌声,这是这些外族在大张宴席庆贺。而在罗马人这边,兵士们围着有气无力的篝火,发出的是断断续续的抱怨声,一些人这儿一个那儿一个地躺在栅栏旁边,还有一些人在营帐的四周踱来踱去,他们虽然迷迷糊糊,却难以入睡。统帅在这一夜里做了一个阴森可怕的梦——他梦见了伐鲁斯,他浑身是血,看起来似乎是刚从沼泽地里站起身来,他叫着他,但他没有听从伐鲁斯的呼唤,当伐鲁斯向他伸出手来的时候,他把伐鲁斯推了回去。天将破晓的时候,被派到两翼去的罗马军团,或是由于害怕或是由于纪律混乱,从他们原来的阵地上撤了下来,却匆匆忙忙地去占领沼泽地外面的一块平地,这就成为了阿尔米尼乌斯明确的进攻目标。但是阿尔米尼乌斯并没有立刻发动进攻。直到当他看到罗马军队的辎重陷在淤泥里和水沟里的时候,他们才发动进攻。于是周围的士兵立刻陷入了混乱,各个军团搅在了一起。队旗的次序被打乱了,叠放在一

circumstances everyone was hurrying about his own interests, deaf to orders.

Then Arminius ordered the Germans to attack. At the head of a picked force, crying that here was another Varus and his army caught in the same trap again, he broke through the Roman column. His chief targets were the horses, which slipped in their own blood and the slimy bog and threw their riders, scattering everyone in their way and trampling on those who had fallen. The Eagles caused particular difficulty, as the rain of missiles held the colour-sergeants back, and they could not plant them in the mud. While Caecina was struggling to maintain the line, his horse was killed under him. As he fell he was nearly surrounded; but the first brigade rescued him. Fortunately, the greedy Germans stopped killing and went after loot. So towards evening the Romans forced their way out on to firm, open ground. But their hardships were not yet ended. Earthworks had to be constructed, and their material collected; and most of the equipment for moving soil and cutting turf had been lost.

Units had no tents, the wounded no dressings. As the muddy, bloodstained rations were handed round, men spoke miserably of the deathly darkness, and the end which tomorrow would bring to thousands. A horse broke loose and cantered around, frightened of the shouting. It struggled when men tried to stop it, and caused a panic-stricken belief that the Germans had broken in. There was a stampede for the gates, especially the main gate—farthest from the enemy and

块儿,正像平时发生混乱的情形一样,每个人都在急急忙忙地为自己寻求安全的地方,对于长官的命令则置若罔闻。

于是,阿尔米尼乌斯向日耳曼人下达了发动进攻的命令。他率领着一支精锐部队冲在前面,一面叫道:"另一个伐鲁斯和他的军团又陷入了和先前一样的困境啦!"一面杀向罗马的队伍。他首要的目标是马。一匹匹战马滑倒在它们自己的血泊和泥泞的沼泽里,这样骑在它们身上的骑兵也被掀翻在地,马的狂奔冲散了它们路上遇到的所有人,并把倒在地上的人践踏在蹄下。军旗引起的麻烦最大,因为密集的投枪的冲击,一次次将旗手打了回来,并且他们也没有办法把军旗插在淤泥中。当凯奇纳极力想保持队形完整的时候,他的坐骑被杀死了。他从马上摔下来之后,差一点就被敌人包围了起来;但是幸亏第一军团将他解救了出来。不过幸运的是,贪婪的日耳曼人放弃了屠杀而去掳掠战利品。因此到了晚上,罗马的军团才终于杀出了一条路,来到了一块坚实、敞亮的土地上。但是罗马士兵的艰难困苦还没有结束。必须修筑工事堡垒,并且需要搜集修筑工事的材料,而运土或割草的工具却已经丢失了大半。

队伍没有营帐,伤兵得不到必要的包扎。当那满是泥土又沾染着鲜血的口粮被分配到士兵们手中的时候,他们悲惨地谈论起这死亡一般的黑夜,谈论着明天将要带给成千上万人的死亡。一匹挣脱了缰绳的马又在四处乱跑,它被人们的叫喊声吓坏了。有一些人跑来想拉住它,但是它极力挣扎,这给队伍造成了很大的混乱,引起了人们的惊恐。人们以为是日耳曼人又冲进来了。于是大家一齐向几个营门口蜂拥而去,想夺路而逃。特别是全营的那个主要的大门,这个门离敌人最远,因而

so best for escape. Caecina discovered that there was no cause for fear. But his authority and appeals, and even force, did not suffice to hold the men back. Then he blocked the gate by throwing himself down across it. The men were not hard-hearted enough to go over the general's body. Then colonels and company-commanders explained that it was a false alarm.

Caecina collected the men at his headquarters, and called for silence. He described the critical situation. The only way out was to fight, he said. But the fighting must be planned. They must stay inside the defences until the enemy approached to storm them. Then the entire force must break out—and so to the Rhine! Running away would only mean more forests, worse swamps, savage attacks; but success would be glorious. Caecina spoke of their dear ones at home, of their victorious battles. Of setbacks nothing was said. Then, without respect of persons, he distributed the horses of the generals and colonels-starting with his own—to the best fighters in the army. They were to charge first, the infantry to follow.

On the German side, too, there were commotions—because of clashes of opinion among the greedy, optimistic chiefs. Arminius' plan was to let the Romans come out, and then trap them again on difficult swampy ground. Inguiomerus was for the more sensational measures which natives enjoy—surround the camp, he said, and you can easily storm it; that is the way to win more prisoners, and collect loot undamaged. Following his advice, at daybreak they filled in the

是最适于逃跑的。凯奇纳发现这种恐惧是毫无必要的，但是他的命令、他的请求，甚至他动用武力，都不能挡住士兵们的逃跑。于是他自己就横躺在大门间。士兵们没有足够的狠心从自己副帅的身体上踏过去。这时军团将领和百人团长们也都解释说，这次的惊惶是一个误会。

凯奇纳把士兵集合在他的营帐前面，他要求他们安静下来听他讲话。他阐明了当前所面临的局面的危险性。他说，要想冲出一条活路，唯一的办法就是勇敢地作战。但是作战必须先要有一个计划。如果敌人没有对他们发动猛攻而逼近的话，他们一定要留在营地内部。接下来，他们就要积蓄力量，全力冲出去，这样一直冲到莱茵河那里。如果他们逃跑的话，那就只会意味着遇到更多的森林、更糟糕的泥沼和敌人凶猛的攻击。只要他们获得了成功，就会得到荣勋。凯奇纳向他们提起了他们所爱的家人，提到他们一次次取得的胜利。但是关于过去的挫折，他却只字未提。在这之后，他便大公无私地把统帅和军团将领们的马——先从他自己的马开始，分配给军中作战最勇敢的人。得到马的人将冲在最前面，步兵随后。

在日耳曼人的阵营中，情况也是同样的混乱——因为贪婪和盲目乐观在领袖人物之间造成了意见冲突。阿尔米尼乌斯的意见是先让罗马人出来，然后把他们再次围困在一个泥泞难行的沼泽地里。因吉奥美路斯则主张采取本民族所乐于使用的那些更加激烈的办法。他说，如果把营地包围起来，就可以轻而易举地对他们发起猛攻。这是一种不但可以得到更多的俘虏，而且还可以把战利品毫无损伤地收集过来的好方法。最后大家听从了他的主张，

ditches, constructed bridges, and poured across them.

When they grasped the top of the parapet they saw only a few Roman soldiers, apparently paralysed with fright. But as they went clambering over, the battalions received their signals, and the horns and bugles sounded. Shouting, the Romans fell upon the German rear. 'Here there are no woods or swamps,' they jeered. 'It's a fair field, and a fair chance !' The enemy had been imagining the easy slaughter of a few badly armed men. The blare of trumpets, the glitter of weapons, was all the more effective because it was totally unexpected. The Germans went down—as defenceless in defeat as success had made them impetuous. Arminius got away unhurt, Inguiomerus badly wounded. The massacre of rank and file went on as long as fury and daylight lasted. Finally, at night-fall, the Romans re-entered their camp. They were as hungry as ever, and their wounds were worse. But they had their cure, nourishment, restorative, everything in one—victory.

Meanwhile behind the Rhine a rumour had spread that the army was cut off and a German force was on the way to invade Gaul. Some, in panic, envisaged the disgraceful idea of demolishing the bridge. But Agrippina put a stop to it. In those days this great-hearted woman

天一亮,他们就开始填壕沟、建桥梁,并且把树枝荆条编的篱笆填充进去以利于攀登。

当他们抓住栏杆的顶端攀登了上去的时候,他们看到堡垒上只有寥寥几个罗马士兵,很显然他们毫无战斗的意志。不过当他们爬上了堡垒的时候,各步兵中队都收到了信号,号角声和喇叭声立刻都响了起来,罗马的军队呼啦一下子就冲向了日耳曼人的后方。"这里既没有森林,也没有沼泽地",他们用嘲笑的口吻说,"地形对双方都是平等的,机会也是公正的。"敌人原以为对付这样少数几个装备极差的部队很容易。喇叭声大声吹响,武器熠熠闪光,这突如其来的一切产生了很大的效果。日耳曼人被打败了,他们在胜利时得意忘形,失败时则又手足无措。阿尔米尼乌斯逃出去了,他没有受伤,因吉奥美路斯则伤得很严重。日耳曼人遭到了残酷的屠杀,直到罗马人的怒气随着白日渐渐消失的时候,屠杀才告结束。最后,夜幕降临了,罗马军团又返回了他们的营地。他们还是和以前一样口粮缺乏,他们的伤员也更多了。但是这一次胜利治愈了他们受伤的心灵,他们从中又焕发了新的力量、得到了新的精神给养,找到了一切。

同时在莱茵河对岸,却流传着这样一个谣言:罗马军队遭到了敌人的伏击,日耳曼军队正在向高卢挺进,要进犯高卢了。一些人听到这个消息万分恐慌,竟然恬不知耻地想把莱茵河上的桥[1]拆毁。但是阿格里披娜出面坚决地制止,桥才没有被拆毁。

---

[1] 在维提拉。

acted as commander. She herself dispensed clothes to needy soldiers, and dressed the wounded. Pliny the elder, the historian of the German campaigns, writes that she stood at the bridge-head to thank and congratulate the returning column. This made a profound impression on Tiberius. There was something behind these careful attentions to the army, he felt; they were not simply because of the foreign enemy. 'The commanding officer's job', he reflected, 'is a sinecure when a woman inspects units and exhibits herself before the standards with plans for money-distributions. ' As though it were not pretentious enough to parade the commander's son around in private soldier's uniform and propose to have him called 'little Boots' Caesar! Agrippina's position in the army already seemed to outshine generals and commanding officers; and she, a woman, had suppressed a mutiny which the emperor's own signature had failed to check. Lucius Aelius Sejanus aggravated and intensified his suspicions. He knew how Tiberius' mind worked. Inside it, for the eventual future, he sowed hatreds. They would lie low, but one day bear fruit abundantly.

Meanwhile Germanicus handed over the second and fourteenth brigades, which he had brought by ship, to Publius Vitellius, who was to take them back by land. This was designed to lighten the fleet, in case of shallow water and grounding at low tide. At first Vitellius had

在那些日子里,这位心地高贵的妇人一直像一个统帅一样处理着一切事情。她亲自把衣服送给无衣的士兵,给伤兵们包扎伤口。写日耳曼战争史的历史学家老普列尼[1]记述说,她亲自站在桥头上,向回师的军队表示感谢并给予热情的赞美。她的这种做法在提贝里乌斯心里留下了深深的印象。"在她对士兵的这种悉心关怀的背后肯定还另有企图",提贝里乌斯揣想,"她对军队这样讨好绝不仅仅是为了对付外敌那么简单"。他想:"如果由一个妇人去做巡视的工作,并且亲自出现在队旗近前,给士兵颁赐奖赏的话,那么统帅的职位岂不就形同虚设了吗?"就好像统帅的儿子穿着普通士兵的衣服,站在队列中,并且还要人们称他为"小靴子"恺撒,这样的做法还不够哗众取宠吗? 阿格里披娜在军队士兵眼中的地位看来已经超过了任何将领或最高统帅;而且她,一位小妇人,竟然平定了连皇帝亲自签署的命令都不能平定的兵变。路奇乌斯·埃利乌斯·谢雅努斯极力地煽动并加深着提贝里乌斯的怀疑情绪。他非常清楚提贝里乌斯内心是怎样想的。为了未来可能的事件,他要在提贝里乌斯心里播下仇恨的种子。这种仇恨现在是藏在皇帝的内心深处,但有朝一日它是会大量地开花结果的。

这时,日耳曼尼库斯把他装载在船上的两个军团,即第二和第十四军团,交给了普布里乌斯·维提里乌斯,让他把他们从陆路带回去。这是由于他考虑到舰船必须要减轻负担,才能避免在浅水中航行时或在退潮时搁浅。开始,维提里乌斯行进得还

---

〔1〕 这里是指老普列尼(23~79年),他的《自然历史》保存到了现在,他还写了记述战争的作品《日耳曼战争》,现已佚。

an easy journey. The ground was dry or only slightly waterlogged. But then at the autumnal equinox, when the North Sea is always at its roughest, his column was harassed and confused by a northerly gale. The country was deluged. Sea, land, and shore all looked the same. There was no way to distinguish solid from treacherous ground, shallow water from deep. Men were knocked down by waves and dragged under. Pack-animals, baggage, dead bodies floated about and struck against each other. Units lost their identity. Men stood up to the chest or even the neck in water. Then they lost their footing, and were carried away or went under. Their shouts to encourage one another were unavailing against the floods. Brave men or cowards, good sense or bad, planning or the lack of it, were all one, in the grip of the raging elements.

Finally Publius Vitellius and his column struggled out on to higher ground. They spent the night without fire or other necessities. Many men were naked or hurt—as badly off as a besieged army, indeed worse, since for such an army death is at least glorious, not squalid as it was here. With daybreak land reappeared, and they got through to a river, where they found Germanicus' fleet and embarked. Reports that they had been drowned persisted until Germanicus and his army were back and on view.

By now Segestes' brother Segimerus, whose submission Lucius Stertinius had been sent ahead to accept, had been escorted back to the Ubian capital with his son. Both were amnestied. Segimerus' case was

很顺利,因为他经过的地方都是干地,或者只有很浅的水洼地。但是不久,秋分来临,这时的北海是最粗暴的,狂骤的北风劲吹,掀起了猛烈的海浪,扰乱了他的队伍。整个土地上都弥漫着大水,海洋、陆地和海岸的景色看起来都是一样的。人们根本无法辨别哪里是陆地、哪里是能使人陷下去的泥淖,哪里是浅水、哪里是深水。人们被浪头冲倒或被卷到水中。驮着重物的牲畜、行李和死尸在水面上到处飘荡,互相撞击着。队伍无法一致行动。人们站在齐胸深的水中,甚至还站在没到脖颈深的水中。因此他们就无法站稳,或者是被水冲走,或者就没入水下了。相互激励的叫喊声也不能帮助他们对付洪水的冲击。勇敢的人和怯懦的人,聪明的人和愚蠢的人,谨慎的人和缺乏计谋的人,这时都一样,都陷入了一种狂乱的情绪之中。

最后,普布里乌斯·维提里乌斯和他的士兵们终于挣扎到了一块较高的地面上去,队伍在那里集合起来。他们在那里过了一夜,没有火,也没有其他的生活必需品。许多人赤身裸体或是受了重伤——这种狼狈情况与被敌人包围的其他军队一样糟糕,事实上还更糟,因为对那些军队中的士兵来说,死亡至少还是一种荣誉,不像这里士兵这样在洪水中窝囊地丧失了性命。天亮时水退了,陆地重新出现了,他们来到河边,在那里他们看到了日耳曼尼库斯的舰队,军队登上了船。但外面的消息却都传说,这些军队都被淹死了,直到看到日耳曼尼库斯率领军队回来,出现在他们的眼前,人们才打消了疑虑。

就在这个时候,那位被指派去接受塞盖司特斯的兄弟塞吉美路斯的投降的路奇乌斯·司特尔提尼乌斯,已把塞吉美路斯和他的儿子护送到乌比伊人的首都来了。这两个人都得到了赦

simple, but his son caused more hesitation since he was alleged to have treated Varus' corpse insultingly.

The Gallic and Spanish provinces and Italy competed to make good the army's losses, offering weapons, horses, or gold, as their resources permitted. Germanicus commended their public spirit, but only accepted arms and horses for the war. He assisted his men from his private means, and tried to distract them from thoughts of their past hardships by personal kindness—inspecting the wounded and their injuries, praising individual feats, playing on their pride or ambition. By these attentions and conversations all round, he intensified their fighting spirit and their loyalty to himself.

In this year honorary Triumphs were awarded to Aulus Caecina Severus, Lucius Apronius, and Gaius Silius (I) for their service with Germanicus.

In spite of repeated popular pressure, Tiberius refused the title 'Father of his Country'. He also declined the senate's proposal that obedience should be sworn to his enactments. All human affairs were uncertain, he protested, and the higher his position the more slipper

免。对于塞吉美路斯的处罚问题，大家的意见都是比较一致的，但是对于他的儿子，人们意见则有一些分歧，因为据说他曾经侮辱过伐鲁斯的遗体。

至于其他地方，如高卢、西班牙诸行省和意大利，则都争相努力弥补军队的损失，他们尽其所有地为罗马军队提供武器、马匹或是黄金。日耳曼尼库斯高度赞扬了他们大公无私的精神，但他只接受了武器和马匹这些作战的用品。他用自己私人的力量帮助士兵，并且用他个人的友好关心将他的士兵们从对不久之前所遭受的灾难的痛苦回忆中拉出来——他巡视伤员，检查他们的伤口，称赞他们个人立下的功绩，并鼓励起他们对未来的希望和荣誉感。日耳曼尼库斯到处都给予亲切的关切和慰问，这极大地增强了他们作战的信心，也使士兵们的心对他更加忠诚。

在这一年里，奥路斯·凯奇纳·谢维路斯、路奇乌斯·阿普洛尼乌斯和盖乌斯·西里乌斯（一世）由于他们随同日耳曼尼库斯作战的功勋而被授予了光荣的凯旋式。[1]

尽管人民一再要强加给他，提贝里乌斯还是拒绝了"国父"[2]的称号。他还拒绝了元老院提出的人们要宣誓服从他的法令的建议。[3] 他解释说，人间的万事万物都变幻无常，他的地位越高，

〔1〕 取得这种荣誉的统帅在典礼上和一些特殊的日子里有权穿凯旋袍，人们还给他们竖立穿着这种袍和头戴桂冠的像，但是不为他们举行凯旋仪式。因为在帝国时期，只有掌握统治大权的皇帝和他的共治者才有特权举行正式的凯旋仪式。

〔2〕 公元前2年，元老院曾授予奥古斯都这样的称号。提贝里乌斯则始终未答应接受这样的称号，在他的钱币上也没有出现过这样的头衔。

〔3〕 每年元旦，高级长官和元老院都要宣誓承认皇帝和包括独裁官尤利乌斯·恺撒在内的前任皇帝的一切裁断有效。

it was.

Nevertheless, he did not convince people of his Republicanism. For he revived the treason law. The ancients had employed the same name, but had applied it to other offences—to official misconduct damaging the Roman State, such as betrayal of an army or incitement to sedition. Action had been taken against deeds, words went unpunished. The first who employed this law to investigate written libel was Augustus, provoked by Cassius Severus, an immoderate slanderer of eminent men and women. Then Tiberius, asked by a praetor, Quintus Pompeius Macer, whether cases under the treason law were to receive attention, replied: *the laws must take their course.* Like Augustus he had been annoyed by anonymous verses. These had criticized his cruelty, arrogance, and bad relations with his mother.

The tentative charges against Falanius and Rubrius, members of the order of knights, are worth recording. For they illustrate the beginnings of this disastrous institution—which Tiberius so cunningly insinuated, first under control, then bursting into an all-engulfing

就越会容易跌倒。

虽然如此,他依然未能使人民相信他是共和制度的拥护者。因为他恢复了大逆法。[1]古人的法律中也有过这个名称,不过它所针对的罪行与古代的有所不同——它原来所针对的都是玷污了"罗马人民的尊严"的官吏渎职的罪行,诸如军队的背叛,煽动人民发动叛乱等等。这种法的施行是针对具体的行动,但言论自由是无须要受到惩罚的。第一个利用这一法律追究在文字上进行诽谤罪行的是奥古斯都。惩罚的是一个名叫卡西乌斯·谢维路斯[2]的人,一个曾经肆无忌惮地诽谤过显要男女人士的人,因此他激怒了奥古斯都。后来一位行政长官克温图斯·彭佩乌斯·玛凯尔曾经请示提贝里乌斯,还应当不应当受理涉及大逆法的案件,提贝里乌斯回答说:"这一法律是必须要得到坚决的执行的。"和奥古斯都一样,他也曾经对一些匿名的诗深感震怒。这些诗批评了他的残酷、骄傲和他与自己的母亲的恶劣关系。

值得记录的是大逆法最初在法拉尼乌斯和卢布里乌斯两人身上的施行,他们是两个普通的罗马骑士。这件事可以表明这种灾难性的实施是怎样开始的——提贝里乌斯是怎样巧妙地逐步地予以实行的,这个措施在开头还是不声不响地有节制地执

---

〔1〕 提贝里乌斯想使人们相信他愿意作为一个普通的公民,但"大逆法"与此相矛盾,因为从"大逆法"的观点来看,皇帝本人已不是公民,而是国家了。

〔2〕 著名演说家,公元8年(一说12年)被奥古斯都放逐到克里特,提贝里乌斯将他移至塞里波司,并在公元24年没收了他的财产。他在放逐后的第二十五年死去。

blaze. Falanius was charged, first, with admitting among the worship-
pers of Augustus, in the cult maintained by households on the analogy
of priestly orders, an actor in musical comedies named Cassius who
was a male prostitute, and, secondly, with disposing of a statue of
Augustus when selling some garden property. Rubrius was charged
with perjury by the divinity of Augustus.

When Tiberius heard of these accusations, he wrote to the consuls saying that Augustus had not been voted divine honours in order
to ruin Roman citizens. The actor, he observed, together with others,
had regularly taken part in the Games which his mother the Augusta
had instituted in Augustus' honour—and to include the latter's statues (like those of other gods) in sales of houses or gardens was not
sacrilegious. As regards the perjury, it was parallel to a false oath in
Jupiter's name: the gods must see to their own wrongs.

Shortly afterwards Marcus Granius Marcellus, governor of Bithynia, was accused of treason by his own assistant, Aulus Caepio
Crispinus. But it was the latter's partner Romanius Hispo who created a career which was to be made notorious by the villainous products
of subsequent gloomy years. Needy, obscure, and restless, he wormed
his way by secret reports into the grim emperor's confidence. Then
everyone of any eminence was in danger from him. Over one man he

行,接着就爆发为全面燃烧的熊熊大火。法拉尼乌斯被告发的罪名是:首先,在一个奥古斯都奉祀团中,这种奉祀团是所有的显贵人家按照教团一样的方式参加的,而他曾经允许一个演滑稽戏的同时又是娈童的名叫卡西乌斯的人也参加了;其次,他在出售他的花园私有财产时,把奥古斯都的一座雕像也卖掉了。卢布里乌斯则是由于伪誓而亵渎了奥古斯都的圣名,因此遭到了惩罚。

当提贝里乌斯听到了这些控诉后,就写信给执政官说,对奥古斯都给予神圣的崇敬,并不是为了使他的国人遭殃。他还分析说,那个优伶和与他同一行业的其他人经常参加他的母亲奥古斯塔为纪念奥古斯都而举行的赛会——关于在出卖房屋或花园时,把奥古斯都的像(如同其他诸神的神像那样)与财产一齐卖掉,这并不能算是冒渎天神的行为。至于伪誓,这就如以朱庇特神的名义发伪誓一样,诸神会对他们的错误进行报复的。

不久之后,玛尔库斯·格拉尼乌斯·玛尔凯路斯,比提尼亚的行政长官,被他自己手下的官员奥路斯·凯皮欧·克利司披努斯指控以大逆罪。但是,后来他的同伙洛玛努斯·希斯波也参加了对他的控告。他发明了这样一种行业,在以后阴暗的年代里,厚颜无耻的人们很快地就使这种臭名昭著的行业成了时髦的勾当[1]这个贫穷、阴暗、不安分守己的人物蠕蠕爬行着,他因为告密而取得了那位严酷皇帝的信任。后来连那些最显要的人物也都人人自危,害怕陷入他的魔掌。这样,他通过一个人而取得了一个优宠

---

〔1〕 罗马当时没有检察官,所以法律的应用必须通过私人之手,于是便出现了职业的告密人,告密人在得逞之后按规定是有奖赏的。

enjoyed an ascendancy; all others loathed him. His was the precedent which enabled imitators to exchange beggary for wealth, to inspire dread instead of contempt, to destroy their fellow-citizens—and finally themselves.

He alleged that Marcus Granius Marcellus had told scandalous stories about Tiberius. The charge was damning. The descriptions the accuser imputed to him recounted the most repulsive features in the emperor's character. Since these were not fictitious it seemed plausible that Marcellus should have described them. Hispo added that Marcellus had placed his own effigy above those of the Caesars, and that on one statue he had cut off the head of Augustus and replaced it by Tiberius.

The emperor lost his temper and, voluble for once, exclaimed that he personally would vote, openly and on oath. This would have compelled other senators to do the same. But, since there still remained some traces of declining freedom, Cnaeus Calpurnius Piso asked a question; 'Caesar, will you vote first or last? If first, I shall have your lead to follow; if last, I am afraid of inadvertently voting against you. ' This struck home, and Tiberius, regretting his impetuous outburst, meekly voted for acquittal on the treason counts. Charges of embezzlement were referred to the proper court.

However, investigations in the senate were not enough for Tiberius. He also began to sit in the law courts—at the side of the platform, so

的地位,但是却遭到所有其他人的憎恨。他是这一行当的先驱,自从他开了这种风气之后,仿效他的人们就从叫花子变成富翁,从被人轻蔑的人变成了被人仰慕的人。他们在毁灭了别人之后,最后也把自己毁掉了。

他宣称玛尔库斯·格拉尼乌斯·玛尔凯路斯讲了许多诽谤提贝里乌斯的话。这种指控是具有毁灭性的。他把皇帝的品行中那些最令人厌恶的特征搜集起来,然后绘声绘色地归罪于被控诉的人,说是他们讲出来的。因为,所说的这些事情并非是虚构的,所以看起来说玛尔凯路斯曾经讲过这些话,那也就完全可信的了!希斯波还添油加醋地说玛尔凯路斯把自己的像放在恺撒的像的上面,而且还把一座奥古斯都雕像的头去掉,换上了提贝里乌斯的头像。

提贝里乌斯听了这话之后勃然大怒。他一下子变得健谈起来,声称在这样的情况下,他要公开地发誓表示自己的意见。他这样说的目的就是要迫使其他元老也都这样做。但是正在走向衰弱的自由这时还保留着一些痕迹,因此格涅乌斯·卡尔普尔尼乌斯·披索就提出了一个问题:"恺撒啊,你是第一个还是最后一个提出自己的意见呢?如果你第一个发表意见,我就按照你的意见发表我个人的意见;如果你最后发表意见,我害怕会不小心而发表了和你相反的意见。"这番话正中要害,提贝里乌斯后悔他刚才不该那样冲动地表现出暴怒,于是他便温和地表示同意赦免被告者的大逆罪。而侵吞公款的案子则交给有关的法庭去处理。

然而,提贝里乌斯并不满足于仅仅在元老院里审理案件,他还开始到一般的法庭去出席案件的审理。为了不至于把行政长官从

as not to oust the praetor from his official chair. His presence success-fully induced many verdicts disregarding influential pressure and in-trigue. Nevertheless, it also infringed on the independence of judges.

At about this time also, a junior senator named Aurelius Pius protested that his house had been undermined by the government's construction of a road and aqueduct. He appealed to the senate. The praetors in charge of the Treasury resisted the claim, but Tiberius came to his help and paid him the value of his house. For the emperor was prepared to spend in a good cause, and kept this good quality long after his others were gone. When an ex-praetor, Propertius Cel-er, asked to resign from the senate on grounds of poverty, Tiberius, finding that his lack of means was inherited, presented him with one million sesterces. Others then applied. But he requested them to prove their case to the senate. Even when he acted fairly his austerity made a harsh impression; and the applicants preferred silent impover-ishment to publicized subsidy.

In the same year the Tiber, swollen by persistent rain, flooded lowlying parts of the city. When it receded, much loss of life and build-ings was apparent. Gaius Asinius Gallus proposed consultation of the Sibylline Books. Tiberius, with his preference for secrecy—in heavenly

其席位上驱逐下去,他坐在行政长官的审判台的边上。他的出席,成功地使行政长官可以不顾别人的压力和事先的勾结而作出许多公正的判决。尽管如此,它也侵犯了法官的独立。

大概也就是在这个时候,有一个名叫奥列里乌斯·披乌斯的元老抱怨说,由于一条公用的道路和水道的修筑,他的房屋竟然遭到了破坏。他向元老院要求给予赔偿。管理国库的官吏[1]坚持反对他的请求,但是提贝里乌斯却帮了他的忙,付给了与他的房屋相当的价钱。因为只要是有充足的理由,这位皇帝是愿意支付金钱的,而且他的这种美德在他的其他优点丧失以后还保持了很久。当一位卸任的行政长官普洛佩尔提乌斯·凯列尔由于贫穷的缘故而请求解除他的元老职务的时候,提贝里乌斯知道他的贫困确实是因为他并没有继承到任何财产,于是就赐给了他100万谢司特尔提乌斯[2] 随后,其他人也做了同样的申请,但是他却要求他们向元老院去证实他们自己的情况。由于他的性格严峻,因此甚至当他公正地行事的时候,他也仍旧给人以苛刻的印象。而且这样一来,那些申请者就宁肯在默默中忍受贫困,也不想去用公开坦白本身情况的办法以取得补助了。

就在这一年,连绵的阴雨造成了台伯河河水的泛滥,淹没了罗马城地势低洼的地方。水退去以后,有大量房屋和生命遭受了明显的损失。因此盖乌斯·阿西尼乌斯·伽路斯就建议去看一下西比拉预言书。提贝里乌斯不同意,因为他无论在世俗生活中

---

〔1〕 罗马建城726年,奥古斯都任命两位行政长官负责国库的管理。

〔2〕 这是奥古斯都规定的元老应有的最低的财产数目,约合1万英镑。

as in earthly matters—demurred. Instead, Gaius Ateius Capito and Lucius Arruntius were instructed to control the water-level. Achaea and Macedonia begged for relief from their tax burdens, and it was decided, for the present, to transfer them from senatorial to imperial government.

A gladiator-show was given in the names of Germanicus and Drusus. The latter was abnormally fond of bloodshed. Admittedly it was worthless blood, but the public were shocked and his father was reported to have reprimanded him. Tiberius himself kept away. Various reasons were given—his dislike of crowds, or his natural glumness, or unwillingness to be compared with Augustus, who had cheerfully attended. It was also suggested, though I would scarcely believe it, that he deliberately gave his son a chance to show his forbidding character—and win unpopularity.

Disorders connected with the stage had started in the previous year, and now their violence increased. There were civilian casualties. Soldiers, too, and a company-commander were killed, and a colonel of the Guard injured, in keeping order and protecting officials from disrespect. The senate discussed the disturbance, and it was moved that

还是宗教事务上都是宁愿保守秘密，而不愿公开的。[1] 然而盖乌斯·阿泰乌斯·卡皮托和路奇乌斯·阿尔伦提乌斯却被指派去抗洪。由于阿凯亚和马其顿请求减轻沉重的租税负担，因此决定暂时将对这两个地方的统治治理权，由总督直接转交给皇帝。[2]

一场剑斗士的比赛以日耳曼尼库斯和杜路苏斯的名义举行。杜路苏斯特别喜欢这种流血的表演，当然，无可否认，这种流血毫无价值。但是，这种表演使公众感到胆战心惊，据说他的父亲曾为此斥责过他。提贝里乌斯本人没有来参观，人们猜测着各种各样的理由。一些人认为他不喜欢到人多的地方去；一些人认为是他阴郁性格的表现；还有人认为他不愿意人们将他和奥古斯都相比。奥古斯都兴致勃勃地出席了这种赛事。还有一种说法，我个人是不太认同的，是说他故意给他儿子一个表现他残忍性格的机会，以便引起人民对他的反感。

舞台上的混乱从上一年起就开始出现了，而现在变得更加严重了。市民中间发生了伤亡事故，几名士兵和一名百人团长也被杀，近卫军的一个军官受了伤，因为他们想维持秩序、保护高级官吏，使他们不会受到侮辱。元老院对这次暴乱进行了讨论，

〔1〕 提贝里乌斯对西比拉预言书总是抱着怀疑态度。过去搜集的各种西比拉预言书在公元 12 年由奥古斯都从卡披托里乌姆神庙移至帕拉努斯山的阿波罗神庙。而这些预言书只有十五人团经元老院批准才能查阅。

〔2〕 公元前 27 年，奥古斯都把行省分成国家的和皇帝的行省两类。前者仍然用抽签的办法由担任过执政官或行政长官的人治理，这些官吏受元老院的监督。后者则由直接向皇帝负责的副帅治理。阿凯亚当时已与马其顿分开并且被变成了元老院行省。在公元 15 年，它成了皇帝的行省并在这种情况下继续了 29 年。由于这一改变而引起的财政情况的好转，部分是由于维持这个机构的费用省下了，因为这一行省由美西亚的长官代管，但主要的，也还是由于行政上的更有效的改革。

the praetors should be empowered to have ballet-dancers flogged. When the tribune Decimus Haterius Agrippa vetoed the proposal, he was attacked by Gaius Asinius Gallus. Tiberius, who allowed the senate such pretences of freedom, did not speak. But the veto stood, for the divine Augustus had once ruled that these people were exempt from corporal punishment—and to Tiberius his decisions were sacred. However, numerous measures were passed to limit the salaries of this profession and check the violence of their partisans. In particular, senators were debarred from entering the houses of ballet-dancers, and knights from escorting them when they appeared in public. Moreover, performances outside the theatre were forbidden. The praetors were also empowered to exile spectators who misbehaved.

A Spanish application to build a Temple of Augustus at the settlement of Tarraco was granted, thus providing a precedent for every province. There was public discontent with the I per cent auction tax instituted after the Civil Wars. But Tiberius pointed out that the Military Treasury needed these funds, and added that the national resources were still insufficient unless the troops served for a full twenty years. So the misguided concession of a sixteen-year term, extorted in the recent mutinies, was cancelled. The next question discussed was whether the Tiber floods should be checked by diverting the streams

有人建议说,应当授权行政长官鞭打那些优伶。当护民官德奇穆斯·哈提里乌斯·阿格里帕否决了这个提议后,他受到了盖乌斯·阿西尼乌斯·伽路斯的攻击。提贝里乌斯则一言不发,他这样做,目的在于在元老院里造成一种自由的假象。不过反对的意见还是通过了,因为神圣的奥古斯都曾经规定,要免除对人民的肉体所进行的体罚。而对于提贝里乌斯来说,奥古斯都的一切决定都是神圣的。尽管如此,还是制定了很多措施来限制娱乐业方面的开支和限制捧角人的猛烈行为。特别值得注意的是,规定任何元老都不能到优伶的家里去。而且如果优伶在公众场合出现,不允许骑士作他们的护卫队。除此以外还进一步规定,只能在剧院之内,而不能到剧院外的任何地方去进行表演。观众如果行为不端,行政长官也有权将其放逐。

西班牙人在塔尔拉科移民地[1]为奥古斯都修建一座神庙的要求,获得了批准,这就给所有的行省开了一个先例。人民群众普遍反对在内战之后制定的、对拍卖的商品征收百一税的政策。但是提贝里乌斯却指出,军用库[2]是需要这笔款项的。他还补充说,除非老兵在服役期满 20 年之后才退伍,否则国库是没有足够的力量担负起这样的重担的。这样一来,由于最近的兵变而作出的军团士兵服役期最多不超过 16 年的错误的指示,在今后就被取消了。接下来开始讨论的问题是,台伯河的水患是否可以通过改变涨水的上游河流和湖泊的水路的办法加以控制,这

---

〔1〕 西班牙东北部的首府,今天的塔拉戈纳。

〔2〕 公元 6 年,由奥古斯都捐资设立,目的是用来支付退役士兵的养老金和赏金。

and lakes which nourished it. The discussion was led by Lucius Arruntius and Gaius Ateius Capito. Deputations from the country towns
were heard. The Florentines begged that the river Chiana should not
be moved from its natural bed into the Arno, with disastrous effect on
themselves. Interamna's case was similar: acceptance of the plan to
spread the waters of the Nera far and wide in small channels would ruin the best land in Italy. The people of Reate protested equally vigorously against the damming of the Veline Lake (at its outlet into the
Nera), since it would burst its banks into the surrounding country.
Nature, they said, had done best for humanity by allotting to each
river its appropriate mouth, course, and limits too; and respect must
be paid to the religious susceptibilities of the inhabitants, who had
honoured the rivers by their homes with rites, and groves, and altars—and indeed Tiber himself would scarcely be glad to flow less
majestically, deprived of his associate tributaries. Because of the
pleas from towns, or superstitious scruples, or engineering difficulties, the senate carried a proposal by Cnaeus Calpurnius Piso that
nothing should be changed.

个问题是由路奇乌斯·阿尔伦提乌斯和盖乌斯·阿泰乌斯·凯皮托提出的。又听取了自治市和移民地的代表们发表的意见。佛罗伦萨人请求不要改变克拉尼斯河[1]的自然河床而将其导入阿尔诺河，因为这样做会使他们遭受到巨大的灾害。印提拉姆那提斯人[2]的意见也与此相似：如果接受这个计划把纳尔河[3]远远地分散疏导到各条小河里去，就将会毁掉意大利最肥沃的土地。列阿提尼斯人也同样强烈地反对筑坝截堵维里涅湖的入河口[4]（它通过入河口流入纳尔河）的计划，因为筑坝截堵，它的支流水流就会泛滥到周围的地方去。他们认为，为了最好地实现人类的利益，大自然给每一条河流安排了它们适当的河口、适当的河道、适当的起讫界限。而且对于居民们的宗教信仰也应当给予尊重，因为他们曾把宗教仪式、森林和祭坛献给了流过他们家乡的河流。而且，切断了台伯河本身与其他支流的联系，这条河就缺乏那种令人愉悦的一泻千里的庄严宏伟的气势了。最后，由于各种各样的理由：由于自治市的请求，由于迷信方面的考虑，或者是由于工程方面的困难，元老院通过了格涅乌斯·卡尔普尔尼乌斯·披索提出的这样一个"一切原封不动"的建议。

----

〔1〕 现在的奇亚纳河。

〔2〕 他们是翁布利亚的印提拉姆那·纳哈尔提乌姆（今天的特尔尼）地方的居民。由于这里是塔西佗的故乡，故而在这里也给历史学家塔西佗修建了一座坟墓，但这座坟墓后来因教皇庇护五世的命令而被毁，因为他是基督教的敌人。

〔3〕 今天的内拉河。

〔4〕 位于列阿特和印提拉姆那之间。

In his imperial governorship of Moesia, with which Achaia and Macedonia were merged, Gaius Poppaeus Sabinus was kept on. It was one of Tiberius' customs to prolong the tenures of these posts; both military and other governors were often left unchanged until their dying day. Different explanations of this practice have been offered. According to one account Tiberius found recurrent problems tedious, and preferred making a single permanent decision. Others attribute his policy to a jealous desire that not too many people should benefit. An alternative suggestion is that his natural subtlety placed him in a dilemma: he disliked bad characters, but did not search out exceptional ability. Misconduct he deplored, as likely to cause public scandal—but outstanding merits would be a threat to himself. In the end his indecisiveness became so pronounced that he gave governorships to men whom he was never going to allow outside Rome.

About the elections to consulships, from this first year of Tiberius until his death, I hardly venture to make any definite statement. The evidence in historical accounts, and indeed in his own speeches, is conflicting. Sometimes he suppressed candidates' names, but described their social positions, antecedents, and service records-in terms revealing their identity. On other occasions he suppressed even these clues, but merely warned candidates not to invalidate the elections by bribery—promising his own assistance to the same end. He usually stated that those whose names he had passed to the consuls were the only applicants for nomination. But others, he would say, were still entitled to apply, if their popularity or record encouraged them to do so. Such pronouncements sounded plausible. Yet in relation to the facts they were meaningless, if not disingenuous. The impressiveness of the Republican facade only meant that the slave

　　盖乌斯·波培乌斯·撒比努斯继续治理美西亚行省,[1]阿凯亚和马其顿也划归入这个行省的统辖。提贝里乌斯有一个习惯,就是喜欢延长他分派的职位的期限,军事和政府的长官往往一成不变直到他们去世的日子。对他的这种行为,人们作出了各种各样的解释。一种意见认为提贝里乌斯觉得要不断地重复作出决定是单调乏味的,因此他宁愿一次性作出一个永远生效的决定。还有些人将此归因于他的嫉妒心,提贝里乌斯不愿意看到有过多的人得到提拔。对这两者进行折中的意见认为,他那机敏的才智反而使他处于进退两难的境地:一方面,他不喜欢恶劣的品行,另一方面却又不愿简拔突出的才智。对不正当的行为他感到悲哀,因为任用这样的人会引起公众的非议;但是具有优秀品质的人物对他本人又是一种威胁。最后,他的优柔寡断竟使他把行省的统治权断然交给了他从来不允许离开罗马的人物。

　　至于执政官的选举,则从这第一年直到提贝里乌斯去世为止,我并不能做出什么确定的陈述,因为历史学家所提供的材料,和皇帝自身的发言都非常混乱。有时他不说出竞选人的名字,但是描述他们每个人的社会地位、生平和战事上的经历,很清楚地揭示出此人的身份。另一些时候他连这些线索也不提,但却警告竞选人不要用行贿的手段来糟蹋选举,而且他自己也承诺协助做到这一点。他总是说,他已经把向他申请的人的名字全部提交给执政官了。他还会说,但是如果别的人对自己的声望或资历很有信心的话,也是完全可以提出参加竞选的。这种声明听起来是可信的。然而事实上即使不是虚伪的,也是毫无意义的。这种共和的表象表面上一本

---

〔1〕　属于皇帝的行省,大约相当于今天的保加利亚和今天的塞尔维亚。

state, which was to grow out of them, would be all the more loathsome.

Next year the consuls were Sisenna Statilius Taurus and Lucius Scribonius Libo. Trouble broke out among the dependent kingdoms and provinces of the East. The Parthians were the originators. They had requested and received a king from Rome; and though he was a member of their Arsacid royal house, they despised him as a foreigner. This was Vonones I. He had been given to Augustus as a hostage by King Phraates IV, who, for all his expulsions of Roman armies and generals, had shown the emperor conspicuous respect. As a bond of friendship he had sent Augustus several of his children—not so much from fear of Rome as from doubts of his own people's loyalty.

When domestic disputes removed Phraates and his successors, a deputation from the Parthian leaders had visited Rome to invite Vonones, his eldest child, to the throne. Augustus regarded this as a compliment and presented Vonones with valuable gifts on his departure. The Parthians gave him the good reception that they habitually give new kings. But this was soon replaced by an ashamed feeling of national humiliation at having accepted, from another world, a king

正经,但只是意味着从中产生的奴役,将会更加令人厌恶。

第二年,西森纳·司塔提里乌斯·塔乌路斯和路奇乌斯·里波担任执政官。[1] 这时在东方的独立王国和罗马行省里发生了骚乱。帕尔提亚人是始作俑者。他们向罗马要求并且从罗马得到了一位国王,尽管这个人是他们的阿尔撒奇达伊王族中的一员,[2] 但是他们却把他当作一个外族人而瞧不起他。这个人是沃诺尼斯一世,先前他是被普拉提斯四世[3] 作为人质送到奥古斯都那里去的。普拉提斯这位曾经把罗马的军队和统帅们打退的人,[4] 对于皇帝,仍然是倍加尊敬的。为了进一步巩固友谊,他把自己的几个孩子送到奥古斯都这里来,这并不是因为他害怕罗马人,而是因为他不信任自己臣民的忠诚。

在国内的争执中,普拉提斯和他的继承者们都被除掉了,帕尔提亚的首领们便派遣了一个使团来到罗马,请普拉提斯的长子沃诺尼斯回去继承王位。奥古斯都认为这对他本人是一种荣誉,于是就在这位年轻人离开时给了他十分贵重的赠赐。帕尔提亚人也十分高兴地接待了他,在每一位新国王即位时他们总是这样热情接待的。但是帕尔提亚人的兴奋情绪很快就被国家蒙受的耻辱感所代替,那就是他们竟然接受一个来自另一个世界的沾染了

---

〔1〕 公元16年,罗马建城769年。
〔2〕 帕尔提亚的阿尔撒奇达伊王族,统治时期约当公元前250年到公元230年,亡于萨萨尼朝的新波斯帝国。他们的祖先是王国的建立者阿尔撒凯斯。
〔3〕 普拉提斯四世,公元前37年~公元2年在位。
〔4〕 指公元前36年安托尼乌斯对帕尔提亚失败的出征。

tainted with enemy customs. A monarch was being imposed on the Parthian throne, they told themselves. It was being allocated like a Roman province. If their ruler was to be a man who for years had been Augustus' slave, then the glory of Crassus' slayers and Antony's conquerors was dead.

Their scorn was intensified because their national habits were alien to Vonones. He rarely hunted and had little interest in horses. When passing through a city he rode in a litter. The traditional banquets disgusted him. Moreover, he was laughed at because his entourage was Greek, and because he kept even ordinary household objects locked up. The Parthians, unfamiliar with his good qualities—accessibility and affable manners—took them for unusual vices. His good and bad points alike were alien and hateful.

So another royalty, Artabanus III, was produced. He had been brought up among the Dahae. Now, after an initial defeat he rallied and seized the throne. The defeated Vonones took refuge in Armenia. This buffer-state between the Roman and Parthian empires was at the time without a ruler. Armenia was no friend of ours because Antony,

敌人习气的人来当国王。他们告诉自己,竟然将一个君主加在帕尔提亚人的王权之上,他们就像罗马的一个行省一样给人任意摆布!如果他们的统领是一个多年来一直在奥古斯都的手下当奴隶的人,那么曾经杀死过克拉苏斯[1]并且打败过安东尼的人们的光荣也就不复存在了。

他们对沃诺尼斯这个人的轻蔑越来越强烈,因为沃诺尼斯对于他本国世代相传的风俗习惯非常陌生。他很少出去狩猎,而且对马也不感兴趣。当他走过一个城市时总要乘坐肩舆,本国传统的宴会也令他反感。[2]更有甚者,他的随从都是希腊人,他还把他日常使用的普通的家用器具都封存起来,这也引起了帕尔提亚人对他的嘲笑。另一方面,对他的一些良好的品质,帕尔提亚人也感到非常陌生。他十分平易近人,待人非常温和有礼,这在对之不习惯的帕尔提亚人看来也是与众不同的恶习。帕尔提亚人对他身上的好的和坏的品质都同样感觉陌生和厌恶。

结果,另一个属于阿尔撒奇达伊王族的人阿尔塔巴努斯三世[3]就出来和沃诺尼斯争雄了。阿尔塔巴努斯是在达阿伊人[4]中间抚养长大的。他起初虽然战败了,但现在又重新集合了自己的力量,夺取了王位。被打败的沃诺尼斯跑到了亚美尼亚去避难。亚美尼亚位于帕尔提亚帝国和罗马帝国之间,因为没有一个统治者,当时帝位便空虚了。由于安东尼的罪恶,亚美尼亚不做

---

〔1〕 帕尔提亚人在公元前53年,在美索不达米亚的卡尔莱战胜并杀死了玛尔库斯·里奇尼乌斯·克拉苏斯。

〔2〕 指国王和他的贵族的宴会。

〔3〕 阿尔塔巴努斯三世,公元11~40年在位。

〔4〕 居住在里海东南面的一个西徐亚人的部落。

pretending friendship, had treacherously trapped its king Artavasdes I, only to arrest and kill him. The latter's son Artaxias II, remembering his father, hated us, and called in the Parthian monarchy to protect himself and his throne. When Artaxias II fell by the treachery of his own relations, Augustus made Tigranes II king of Armenia and Tiberius settled him on the throne. But his reign was brief and so was that of his two children, though according to foreign custom they were husband and wife as well as joint rulers. Next Artavasdes II had been made king, by imperial order. His deposition, which followed, was a setback to us; and Gaius Caesar was appointed by Augustus to

我们的朋友了。原来安东尼曾经假装是朋友,使用奸诈的计谋设圈套竟然将前国王阿尔塔瓦斯一世抓起来,并且把他杀了。[1] 他的儿子阿尔塔克西亚斯二世,牢记着他的杀父之仇,对我们充满了仇恨,于是他邀请帕尔提亚君主政体保卫他自己和他的王位。在阿尔塔克西亚斯二世由于他的亲族的阴谋而被暗杀之后,奥古斯都便让提格拉尼斯二世做了亚美尼亚的国王,而提贝里乌斯[2]又安排他做了他本国的国王。但是提格拉尼斯做国王的时间非常短,而且他的两个孩子尽管根据东方的惯例结为夫妻并做了共同的统治者,[3]但他们的统治时期也很快便结束了。接下来,由于罗马皇帝的命令,阿尔塔瓦斯德斯二世成为了国王。但是随之他也被废除了,这对我们来说是一次挫折。继而

---

〔1〕 公元前36年,阿尔塔瓦斯德斯一世在与安东尼在帕尔提亚作战时欺骗过安东尼,但两年之后被安东尼设计抓住,并交给了克利欧帕特拉,克利欧帕特拉在公元前30年将其处死。

以下是有关亚美尼亚统治者的一览表:

公元前56年或55年至公元前34年:阿尔塔瓦斯德斯一世。

公元前33年至公元前20年:阿尔塔克西亚斯二世。

约公元前20年至公元前6年:提格拉尼斯二世;提格拉尼斯三世和埃拉托王后。

约公元前6年至公元前1年:阿尔塔瓦斯德斯二世;提格拉尼斯三世和埃拉托王后复位。

约公元前1年至公元11年:阿里奥巴尔扎尼斯;阿尔塔瓦斯德斯三世;提格拉尼斯四世;埃拉托王后复位。

公元11年或12年:沃诺尼斯。

〔2〕 即后来的皇帝提贝里乌斯。

〔3〕 阿尔撒奇达伊族中有兄弟姐妹通婚的习惯,提格拉尼斯三世和埃拉托王后就是遵照这种习俗,兄妹通婚,两人共同执政。

solve the Armenian problem. Gaius' nominee Ariobarzanes, a Mede by origin, had a fine character and splendid appearance which endeared him to the Armenians. But when he died a natural death they would not have his child. Instead they tried feminine government, under Erato. However, she was soon deposed. Drifting into chaos, anarchic rather than free, its people accepted the fugitive Vonones as king. But they could do little against Artabanus' threats, and if Rome gave them armed support it would mean war with Parthia. So the imperial governor of Syria, Quintus Caecilius Metellus Creticus Silanus, extricated him, allowing him royal state and rank, but keeping him under guard. Vonones' effort to escape from this undignified situation will be described at the appropriate place.

Tiberius was not sorry that the Eastern situation was disturbed. For this provided a pretext for separating Germanicus from his familiar army and subjecting him to the intrigues and hazards of a new provincial command. Germanicus, however, as his troops (in contrast to the emperor) became increasingly enthusiastic about him, grew all the more ambitious for a quick victory in Germany. Reflecting on invasion routes in the light of his successes and failures during the past

盖乌斯·恺撒[1]受奥古斯都之命前去处理亚美尼亚的问题。他把王位授予了阿里奥巴尔扎尼斯，一个出生于米地亚[2]的人。这个人品质很好，又有一副极好的外表，这使他很受亚美尼亚人的喜爱。但是当阿里奥巴尔扎尼斯自然死亡之后，他们却不同意他的孩子继续接任做国王。相反，他们在埃拉托王后的统治之下，试行女性当政。但是她也不久就被驱逐了。这些在混乱中彷徨不定、无人统治但也并不自由的人民，又把逃亡在外的沃诺尼斯迎接回来做国王。但是他们对阿尔塔巴努斯的威胁毫无办法，而如果罗马给予他们武力支持，那就会意味着对帕尔提亚发动战争。于是叙利亚行省的统治者克温图斯·凯奇里乌斯·米特尔路斯·克列提库斯·西拉努斯便把他接了出来，承认他的帝王之位和头衔，但是将他置于自己的监护之下。沃诺尼斯努力想摆脱掉这种没有尊严的傀儡朝廷的生活。这在后面适当的地方我还要谈到的。

东方的局势搞得一片混乱，对此提贝里乌斯并不感觉愧疚。这正好给了他一个很好的借口，可以使日耳曼尼库斯离开他所熟悉的那些军团，把他派到一个新的他生疏的充满各种阴谋和危险的行省去。但是日耳曼尼库斯的士兵（与皇帝相反）对他更加忠诚不二，因此他本人也就越增加了想在日耳曼迅速取得胜利的野心。于是他便根据过去的两次战争中所取得的成功的和失败

[1] 盖乌斯·恺撒在公元前1年被授予总督的权力并以副王的身份被派往东方行省。公元3年，他在亚美尼亚负伤，公元4年2月12日，还没到意大利就死了。

[2] 米地亚·阿特洛帕提尼，即今阿塞拜疆，位于亚美尼亚和米地亚本土之间，是阿尔撒奇达伊族的属地。

two campaigns, he saw that, though in open battle and fair country the Germans were beaten, their forests, swamps, short summers, and early winters favoured them. His own men had suffered less from wounds than from protracted marches and shortages of arms. The supply of horses from Gaul was exhausted. Besides, long baggagetrains were vulnerable to surprise, with the odds against their defenders.

The sea, he felt, provided a better route. It was easily controlled—and inaccessible to enemy intelligence. Besides, arrival by sea would mean an earlier start to the campaign and simultaneous transportation of Roman infantry and supplies; while cavalry, horses, and men alike could be taken up-river from the coast and landed intact in midGermany. So Germanicus decided accordingly. Two generals, Publius Vitellius and Gaius Antius, were sent to assess Gaul for taxation; Gaius Silius (I) , Anteius, and Aulus Caecina Severus were entrusted with the building of a fleet. A thousand ships were calculated to be enough. They were constructed quickly. Some were short and broad—with little prow or stern—to stand a rough sea. Some were flat-bottomed, so as to run aground undamaged. Others, more numerous, had rudders at each end, so that the oarsmen could suddenly reverse direction and land them on either side of a river. Many had decks for catapults and also served to carry horses and supplies. The fleet was well adapted for rapid sailing or rowing. It was formidable and impressive, the more so because of the soldiers' high morale. The rendezvous decided upon was the Batavian island. Its good landing places made it well-suited

的经验,仔细考虑今后的作战方法;他看到,在公开的战斗中以及在对双方来说都算公平的平地上作战时,日耳曼人总是要打败仗的,然而森林、沼泽地、短促的夏天和提早到来的冬天却对他们有利。他自己的士兵们承受着负伤所受的痛苦,但是令人厌倦的长途行军和武器的丢失给他们带来的痛苦比负伤更大。高卢诸行省已不能再供应马匹了。另外,长长的辎重队很容易受到出其不意的伏击,与敌人对抗处于不利的形势。

他认为,走海路是一种比较好的选择。如果他们走海路的话,就比较容易发动进攻,还不容易被敌人侦察到。而且走海路早些到达可以提前开始战斗,罗马的步兵军团和军需也可以同时运送;骑兵的人员马匹可以从入海口逆流而上,完整无缺地在日耳曼腹地登陆。于是日耳曼尼库斯决定就这样做。普布里乌斯·维提里乌斯和盖乌斯·安提乌斯这两位副帅被派到高卢去征收赋税;盖乌斯·西里乌斯、安提乌斯和奥路斯·凯奇纳·塞维路斯则被委派负责建造一支舰队。估计 1000 只船就足够用了,船很快就造好了。有一些船短而宽,船头或者船尾很小,这是为了使它们能经得住海上的风浪。有一些船是平底的,以便保证它们在被冲到陆上时不致受到损坏。还有更多的舰船在两端都安装上了舵,这样划手就可以突然改变划行的方向,也可以在河的任何一边着陆。许多舰船上有安置放射机械的甲板,这种甲板还可以用来运送马匹和军需。整个舰队装备得既可以迅速航行,也可以用桨划行,它宏伟壮观、令人敬畏,给人的印象十分深刻,这种气势也更是士兵们极其旺盛的士气所致。集合地点定在巴塔维亚岛,[1]那里

---

〔1〕 即莱茵河口的三角洲。

for receiving troops and carrying the war into Germany. The Rhine, which has until this point flowed in a single channel—broken only by unimportant islands—divides into two main streams at the Batavian frontier. The branch bordering Germany keeps its name: it goes on flowing swiftly down to the sea. The broader, slower stream on the Gallic side is called the Waal in this region, and then, lower down, the Meuse; it discharges into the same sea, in the great estuary of the latter river.

While the fleet was assembling, Gaius Silius was instructed to take a light force and raid the Chatti, but owing to sudden rains a-chieved nothing except a little loot and the capture of the wife and daughter of Arpus their chief. Germanicus himself heard that a fort upon the river Lippe was besieged, and proceeded towards it with six divisions. But the besieging force gave him no opportunity at all for a battle since it melted away at news of his approach. First, however, it destroyed the funeral mound recently raised to commemorate Varus' army, and an earlier altar in honour of Nero Drusus. Germanicus re-constructed the altar and himself headed a procession of his force in honour of his father. It was decided not to erect the mound again. The whole region between Fort Aliso and the Rhine was heavily forti-fied by new highways and embankments.

The fleet had now collected. Supplies were sent ahead, and the regu-

是一个极好的登陆之处,在那个地方最便于集合军队,而且适于作为渡河与日耳曼人作战的基地。原来莱茵河在这个地方以上是一个单纯的河道,河里只有一些不重要的小岛,但是到巴塔维亚边界处,它就分成了两条主要的河流。作为日耳曼边界的那一条支流,它的名字没有改变,它一直汹涌地往下流入北海。在高卢的这一面,河道比较宽,水流也比较缓慢,当地人称它为瓦尔河,再往下游,又称为默兹河了,默兹河也是通过它的巨大的河口流入同一个大海的。

当舰队刚刚开始集合的时候,副帅盖乌斯·西里乌斯就接到了命令让他率领一支轻装部队去进攻卡提伊人的地区。但是由于突然下起雨来,西里乌斯并没有获得成功,只是获得了一点极少的战利品,并俘虏了卡提伊人的首领阿尔普斯的妻子和女儿。而日耳曼尼库斯本人在听到里普河上的要塞[1]被包围的消息后,就率领着六个军团前去救援。但是包围要塞的敌军并未给予日耳曼尼库斯以任何交战的机会,因为他们一听见日耳曼尼库斯到来,就偷偷溜掉了。不过他们却首先毁坏了不久之前修筑起来的坟山,这是最近为了纪念伐鲁斯的军团士兵而刚刚修建的,还毁坏了较早修建的一座纪念尼禄·杜路苏斯的祭坛。日耳曼尼库斯修复了祭坛,并且亲自领导着军团士兵列队举行了纪念他父亲的仪式。不过那座大坟山却决定不再修复了。此外,在阿里索要塞和莱茵河之间的整个地区,也都用一条新修的大路和工事牢固地防御了起来。

舰队现在已经集合了起来,军需粮草被先送了出去,军团士

---

〔1〕 即阿里索要塞。

lar brigades and auxiliaries allotted their ships. Germanicus himself, entering the channel called Drusiana after his father, called on the memory and example of his words and deeds to give generous and auspicious aid to this enterprise modelled on his achievements. Then, setting sail through lakes and sea, he reached the Ems without incident. The troops disembarked in the more easterly arm of the Ems. But a mistake was made in not transporting the troops upstream or landing them farther south, nearer to their destination. As it was, days were wasted in bridge-building. The cavalry and regular infantry made a well-disciplined crossing of the first tidal marshes, before the tide rose. But then the auxiliaries in the rear, including Batavians, jumped into the water—to show off their swimming—and there was confusion and loss of life. While Germanicus was laying out his camp, it was reported that a tribe, the Angrivarii, had revolted in his rear, and auxiliary cavalry and light infantry were at once sent under Lucius Stertinius to burn and kill in revenge for this treachery.

Now the Weser separated the Romans from the Cherusci. On its bank stood Arminius and the other chieftains. He inquired whether Germanicus had come, and, hearing that he had, asked to be allowed to speak to his brother Flavus in the Roman army. Flavus was very loyal; he had lost an eye some years earlier, fighting under Tiberius.

兵和辅助军队也都分配了船只。日耳曼尼库斯本人然后就进入了以他父亲的名字命名的被称做杜路苏斯的运河[1]。他向士兵们唤起了对他父亲以及他的智慧和英勇事迹的遗范的怀念,并向他父亲祈祷,恳求他施予恩惠赐予他幸运,来帮助他的这个继承了他的事业的儿子像他一样取得成功[2]。随后他便航行穿过湖[3]和海洋继续他的行程,并安然无事地到达了艾姆斯河。舰队停泊在了艾姆斯河东边的海湾。但是他没有使军队进一步逆流上行,或者在靠近他们的目的地的更远的南方登陆,这是一个错误。结果是有好几天都耗费在了修桥上面。骑兵和军团士兵穿过了第一次浪潮,在涨潮之前十分勇敢地渡过了附近的河口。但是最后面的辅助部队,包括一些巴塔维亚人,跳到水里去表现他们的游泳技能,结果军队陷入了混乱,他们当中有一些人溺水死了。当日耳曼尼库斯正在安排营地的时候,有消息说安格里瓦利人在他部队的后方发动了叛乱,于是他立刻派路奇乌斯·司特尔提尼乌斯率领一支骑兵和一支轻武装的步兵,去焚烧和杀戮,以对这一叛乱进行报复。

现在,威悉河将罗马军队和凯路斯奇人隔开了。阿尔米尼乌斯和其他的同僚将领们一道站到河岸上。他问日耳曼尼库斯是否已经来了,当听到日耳曼尼库斯就在这里的回答后,他便请求和他的兄弟说说话,他的兄弟名叫弗拉乌斯,当时正在罗马军队中服役。弗拉乌斯对罗马人非常忠诚,几年前在提贝里乌斯统

----

〔1〕 尼禄·杜路苏斯建造了一条运河,它将阿恩海姆附近的莱茵河北部支流和依赛尔河连接了起来,日耳曼尼库斯继续沿此行进。

〔2〕 杜路苏斯在担任财务官和行政长官的时候,曾经领导过莱提亚的战争和后来日耳曼的战争。在罗马统帅中,他是第一个在北海上航行的人。

〔3〕 指沮伊德湖。

Permission was granted, and Flavus came forward to the river-bank. Arminius greeted him and, dismissing his own attendants, asked that the bowmen stationed along our bank should likewise withdraw.

When they had gone he asked his brother to explain his face-wound. The place and the battle were told him. Then he asked what reward Flavus had got. Flavus mentioned his higher pay, chain, and wreath of honour and other military decorations. 'The wages of slavery are low,' sneered Arminius.

Then they argued their opposing cases. Flavus spoke of Rome's greatness, the emperor's wealth, the terrible punishment attending defeat, the mercy earned by submission—even Arminius' own wife and son were not treated like enemies. His brother dwelt on patriotism, long-established freedom, the national gods of Germany—and their mother, who joined him in imploring that Flavus should not choose to be the deserter and betrayer, rather than the liberator, of his relatives and his country. The discussion soon became abusive: blows would have followed—in spite of the river barrier—if Lucius Stertinius had not hastened up and restrained Flavus, who was angrily calling for his horse and weapons. Across the river Arminius was to be seen, shouting threats and challenges to fight—a good many of them in Latin, since he had formerly commanded a Cheruscan force in the Roman army.

On the next day, the German army drew up beyond the Weser. Germanicus believed it would be bad strategy to risk the regular in

帅下的一次战斗中受伤失掉了一只眼睛。阿尔米尼乌斯的请求得到了允许,弗拉乌斯就向河岸那边走过去。阿尔米尼乌斯向他打招呼,他命令自己的卫队撤下去,又要求我们这边配置在河岸上的弓箭手也都撤走。

当这些弓箭手都退下去的时候,他就问他的兄弟脸上的伤是怎么回事儿。弗拉乌斯就把在何处的哪次战斗中受的伤都告诉了他。然后他又问弗拉乌斯得到了什么样的赏赐。弗拉乌斯向他提起了得到的更高的饷银,以及项链、象征荣誉的花冠和其他军事勋章。"为人奴役所取得的报酬是很低的。"阿尔米尼乌斯嘲笑他说。

于是他们站在相反的立场上展开了争论。弗拉乌斯强调罗马的伟大,帝王的威力,对于战败者的严厉惩罚以及对于归顺者的仁慈。甚至阿尔米尼乌斯的妻子和孩子也没有被当作敌人看待。他的兄弟则详细叙述了对于他们的祖国应有的爱国精神,他们长时期以来一直坚持的自由,保卫日耳曼民族的神灵——而他们的母亲,则和他本人一起祈求弗拉乌斯不要甘心充当叛徒和卖国贼,背叛他的亲戚和他的民族,请求他去做一个民族的解放者。争论不久就变成了辱骂:尽管在他们二人中间隔着一条河流,如果不是路奇乌斯·司特尔提尼乌斯迅速跑上前来并制止了弗拉乌斯的话,紧接着他们就会格斗起来的,因为弗拉乌斯已怒气冲冲地要人把他的武器和马匹送过来。在河对岸,人们看到阿尔米尼乌斯也在高声叫喊着发出威胁,向他的兄弟提出挑战——在他的话里夹杂着许多拉丁语,先前他曾经在罗马的军队中服过役,指挥过凯路斯奇人的军队。

第二天,日耳曼人就在威悉河的那一面摆开了阵势。日耳曼尼库斯认为,如果不适当地修造一些具有足够保卫力量的桥梁,

fantry without properly guarded bridges. So he first sent over the cavalry under Lucius Stertinius with a senior staff officer, Aemilius. They crossed by fords at different points so as to divide the enemy. The Batavians under their leader Chariovalda plunged through where the current was strongest. The Cherusci pretended to give way and drew them on to a level space with wooded hills around. There they made an enveloping attack, and drove in the Batavians' front. The latter, falling back hard-pressed, formed a circle, but suffered severe casualties both at close quarters and from missiles. Chariovalda resisted this savage assault steadfastly. Finally, commanding his men to force a way through the attackers in mass formation, he plunged into the thick of the battle and fell beneath a rain of javelins, with his horse killed under him. Many of his chieftains fell with him. The rest of the force was preserved partly by its own exertions and partly by the arrival of the cavalry to relieve them.

When Germanicus crossed the Weser, a deserter gave him information. Arminius had chosen his battle-ground. Other tribes too had collected, in a wood sacred to Hercules. And a night attack on the camp was planned. The informant was believed. Indeed, German fires were visible and a reconnaissance party which went near reported the neighing of horses and the noise of a vast, undisciplined advance. So now the critical moment was at hand.

Germanicus decided he must test his troops' morale. He considered

就使正规的军团士兵冒险前去作战,这是一个很糟糕的策略。于是他先派出了一支骑兵,率领这支骑兵的是路奇乌斯·司特尔提尼乌斯和一个年长的主力百人团长埃米里乌斯。他们穿过了浅滩,从四面八方的不同地点展开了对敌人的进攻,以分散敌人的注意力。巴塔维亚人在他们的首领卡利奥瓦尔达的率领下,直接从水流最湍急的地方穿插过去。凯路斯奇人假装撤退,把他们引到了一块周围都是林木茂密的小山的平地上。在那里他们对巴塔维亚人展开了围攻,在巴塔维亚人的前方步步紧逼。巴塔维亚人在强大的压力下节节败退,他们集合成一个圆形的队伍,但是,在对方四面八方的攻击下,在密集的枪、箭的投射中,他们遭受了重大的伤亡。卡利奥瓦尔达对于敌人的猛烈进攻坚持抗击,最后他激励他的士兵全体集合到一处,从进攻的敌人中间杀出一条血路,随后他便投身到战斗最激烈的地方去,死在了密集的投枪的攻击之下,他的坐骑也被杀死了。他身边的许多贵族也都和他一同牺牲了。军队中其余的人之所以能够脱险,部分是由于他们自己的力量,部分是由于司特尔提尼乌斯和埃米里乌斯麾下的骑兵的到来,将他们解救了出来。

日耳曼尼库斯渡过威悉河之后,一个逃跑过来的人告诉了他一个消息。说阿尔米尼乌斯已经选好了作战的场所,其他的民族也都在赫尔克里士的圣林里集合起来了。他们计划要对营地发动一次夜袭。这个人的报告是可以相信的,人们确实看见了日耳曼人的篝火,而那些曾经逼近敌人营地的侦察兵也报告说,他们听到了马嘶声和一大群杂乱无章的军队行进中的嘈杂的声音。因此,现在危急的时刻临近了。

日耳曼尼库斯认为他必须要试探一下他的军队的士气。他

how this could be done authentically—reflecting that the reports of colonels and company-commanders are cheerful rather than reliable, ex-slaves remain slaves at heart, friends are flatterers. If he called a meeting, initiative would be shown by a handful, the majority would applaud them. Mess-time, he decided, was the time to discover what they really thought, as the men talked intimately, unsupervised, of their hopes and fears. So after dark, dressed in an animal-skin, he left the general's tent by an exit unknown to the sentries, with one attendant. As he walked the camp lines and stood near the tents, he basked in his own popularity, as he heard admiring remarks about his great origins and splendid looks. There was general praise of his endurance, his friendliness, his equability in serious and relaxed moments alike. All agreed that they must show their gratitude by fighting well: the treacherous treaty-breakers must be offered up to vengeance and glory.

An enemy who knew Latin now rode up to the stockade. In Arminius' name he called out, promising every deserter a wife, some land, and a hundred sesterces a day for the rest of the war. This insulting suggestion infuriated the Roman soldiers. 'Wait until tomorrow and the battle,' they shouted. 'We will help ourselves to German lands and wives. This is a good omen ! Their women and their wealth are going to come to us as loot.'

在考虑怎样才能真正做到这一点——军团将领和百人团长的报告中所反映的情况是令人高兴的,然而却不可靠;那些已被释放的奴隶在内心里还是保留着奴隶的卑躬;朋友则是一些阿谀奉承者。如果他召集一次会议,即使是少数人提出建议,其余的人也一定会拍手附和。只有在一片混乱的时间里,他认为,才是能发现士兵们心里在想些什么的最好时候,因为那时他们觉得没有人监视他们,因此会互相亲密的交谈,毫无顾忌地说出他们的希望和恐惧。因此,到了晚上,他就披上了一张野兽皮,[1]从哨兵们所不知道的一个秘密小门偷偷地溜出营帐,身边只带着一名侍从。当他在营地的各条通路上巡视,站在营帐的附近的时候,他在自己的士兵中间感到非常温暖舒适,因为他听到了士兵们对他的高贵的身世和美好的外表的赞美的言词。大多数的人则在称赞他的耐性、他的友爱、无论在严肃的场合还是在休闲的时间里他都一以贯之的平等态度。他们都说他们一定要以英勇的战斗来报答他:他们一定要让那些背信毁约的叛变者成为光荣和复仇之下的牺牲品。

就在这时,一个懂得拉丁语的敌人骑马来到了壁垒面前,他代表阿尔米尼乌斯高声宣布说,凡是投顺过去的人都可以得到一个妻子和一些土地,参加战斗的每天还可以得到100谢司特尔提乌斯的饷银。这种侮辱性的话激起了军团士兵极大的激怒。"等到天亮之后吧,战斗打响的时候,"他们说,"我们自己会取得日耳曼的土地,带回日耳曼人的妻子的。这是一个好兆头啊! 他们的女人和他们的财物注定将成为我们的战利品啦!"

---

〔1〕 他可能想把自己打扮成一个当地的辅助军队的士兵的样子。

At about midnight an attempt was made on the Roman camp. But not a spear was thrown. The attackers found vigilance everywhere, the fortifications lined with men. During the same night, Germanicus had a pleasant dream. He dreamt that he was sacrificing, and, as his robe was spattered with the victim's blood, his grandmother the Augusta handed him another, finer robe. The omen encouraged him. The auspices, too, proved favourable. So, parading his army, he announced the steps his experience had dictated together with such remarks as seemed called for on the eve of battle.

'Open ground is not the only battle-field favourable to a Roman,' he said. 'Woods, wooded hills, are good too, if he acts sensibly. The natives' great shields and huge spears are not so manageable among tree-trunks and scrub as Roman swords and javelins and tight-fitting armour. You must strike repeatedly, and aim your points at their faces. The Germans wear no breastplates or helmets. Even their shields are not reinforced with iron or leather, but are merely plaited wickerwork or flimsy painted boards. Spears, of a sort, are limited to their front rank. The rest only have clubs burnt at the end, or with short metal points. Physically, they look formidable and are good for a short rush. But they cannot stand being hurt. They quit and run unashamedly, regardless of their commanders. In victory they respect no law, human or divine; in defeat they panic. If you are tired of marching and sailing,' went on Germanicus, 'this is the battle to relieve you of them ! Already we are nearer the Elbe than the Rhine. Once you

在半夜时分,敌人对罗马的营地发起了一次试探性的攻击行动。但是他们并没有投掷一支投枪。进攻的敌人发现这里处处都有非常高的警惕性,防御工事上也都有步兵中队严密把守着。就在这一夜里,日耳曼尼库斯做了一个令人高兴的梦。他梦见自己正在献上祭品,而且当他的外袍上溅上了牺牲的血的时候,他的祖母奥古斯塔又赐给了他一件更漂亮的外袍。这一征兆激励他精神振奋。同时,各种占卜也都证明他处于非常有利的运势当中。于是他便把他的全部军队召集起来,向他们宣布了根据自己的经验所制定的作战措施并为即将到来的战争发表了讲话。

"平原并不是有利于罗马士兵的唯一的战场",他说,"如果罗马士兵在行动中能随时保持机敏的话,森林和林木覆盖的山地也同样是有利的战场。在树木和丛生的灌木林中,蛮族的巨大的盾和长枪是不可能像我们罗马人的剑、标枪和贴身的盔甲那样灵活方便的。你们必须反复攻击并把你们的矛头指向敌人的正面。日耳曼人既没有胸甲也没有头盔,甚至他们的盾牌下面都没有金属或牛皮垫着,而只是柳条编成的盾牌或是薄薄的涂了色的板子。一种短的投枪,也只是最前面的一排士兵使用。其余的人只有长棍,而且这种长棍不是在端头用火煅烧尖了的就是装上了一截非常短的铁尖。他们的体格虽然看起来很可怕,而且很有爆发力,可是他们不能忍受伤痛。一旦受伤,他们就会撤退,转身逃跑,一点也不以为耻,根本不把他们的首领放在心里。胜利时他们蔑视一切法律,不论是人间世俗的还是宗教神圣的;而在失败的时候,他们又会惊慌失措,垂头丧气。如果你们已经厌倦了陆地上和海上的行军生活的话,那么这次战争就会使你们从中摆脱出来了。现在我们离易北河已经比莱茵河更近了,一旦你们踏着

give me victory where my father and uncle have trodden before me,
the fighting will be over!' The speech was enthusiastically received,
and the signal for battle rang out.

Arminius and the other German chiefs also each addressed their
men, reminding them that these Romans were Varus' runaways—men
who had mutinied to escape battle. Some had backs covered with
wounds, others were crippled by storm and sea; and now, hopeless,
deserted by the gods, they were again pitted against a relentless enemy. They had taken to ships and remotest waters to evade attack—
and escape pursuit after disaster. 'But once battle comes', cried
Arminius, 'winds and oars cannot prevent their defeat !' He urged
his troops to remember how greedy, arrogant, and brutal Rome was.
The only alternatives, he insisted, were continued freedom or—in
preference to slavery —death.

Excited by this appeal, the Germans clamoured to fight. They
were marched to a level area called Idistaviso, which curves irregu-
larly between the Weser and the hills; at one point an outward bend
of the river gives it breadth, at another it is narrowed by projecting
high ground. Behind rose the forest, with lofty branches but clear
ground between the tree-trunks. The Germans occupied the plain
and the outskirts of the forest. The Cherusci alone occupied the
heights, waiting to charge down when the battle started. The Roman
army moved forward in the following order: first, Gallic and German
auxiliaries followed by unmounted bowmen; next, four Roman brigades, and Germanicus with two battalions of the Guard and picked
cavalry; then four more brigades, each brought by light infantry and

我的父亲和叔父曾经走过的足迹,在他们作战的地区为我取得了胜利,那么战争就会结束了!"他的话得到了士兵们热烈的响应,士兵们群情激奋;于是战斗的信号就发出了。

阿尔米尼乌斯和日耳曼的其他首领也都给他们的士兵粉饰着美好的前景,提醒他们说,这些罗马士兵只不过是伐鲁斯麾下善于逃跑的军队而已——他们靠发动叛乱来逃避战斗。他们中,一些人有着伤痕累累的后背,还有一些人被海上的暴风雨伤残了肢体;现在,他们已是毫无成功的希望了,他们的行为遭到了上天的厌弃!他们已经陷入了他们的敌人的无情的包围中了。他们借助于船只和最辽远的水域来逃避攻击——并且逃避灾难的追逐。"但是一旦战斗打响了",阿尔米尼乌斯喊道,"风和桨也阻止不了他们的失败!"他要求他的部队记住罗马人是如何的贪婪、自傲、残忍。他坚决地宣称,目前唯一的选择就是,或者是继续坚持为自由而战,或者是放弃,被奴役而死。

为这番讲演所激励,日耳曼人喧嚷着要进行战斗。他们行进到一个叫做伊狄希亚维索的平原上。这个平原不规则地蜿蜒在威悉河和众山之间;在一个地方河流的弯曲,使它变得非常宽阔,而在另一个地方平原又被凸出的高地挤得非常狭窄。在它的后面挺立着一片森林,树枝高耸入云,但树干和树干之间却都是干净的空地。日耳曼人占据了平原和森林的边缘地带。凯路斯奇人独自占据着高地,准备在战斗开始后从上面向下冲击。罗马的军队是按照如下序列向前推进的:最前面是高卢人和日耳曼人的辅助部队,他们后面跟着徒步的弓箭手;接下来,是四个罗马军团,日耳曼尼库斯带领着两个近卫军步兵中队以及精锐的骑兵部队;再次又是四个更大的军团、每个军团后面跟着一个轻武

mounted bowmen to divisional strength; and the remaining auxiliary battalions. The troops were alert and ready to deploy from column of march into battle order.

Units of the Cherusci charged impetuously. Seeing this, Germanicus ordered his best cavalry to attack their flank, while the rest of the cavalry, under Lucius Stertinius, was to ride round and attack them in the rear: and he himself would be there at the right moment. He saw a splendid omen—eight eagles flying towards and into the forest. 'Forward,' he cried, 'follow the birds of Rome, the Roman army's protecting spirits !' The infantry attacked, and the cavalry, which had been sent ahead, charged the enemy's flanks and rear. It was a strange sight. Two enemy forces were fleeing in opposite directions, those from the woods into the open, those from the open into the woods.

The Cherusci between began to be dislodged from the slopes: among them Arminius, striking, shouting, wounded, trying to keep the battle going. His full force was thrown against the bowmen, and it would have broken through if the standards of the Raetian, Vindelician, and Gallic auxiliary battalions had not barred the way. Even so, by sheer physical strength aided by the impetus of his horse, he got through. To avoid recognition he had smeared his face with his own blood. One story is that Chauci among the Roman auxiliaries recognized him and let him go. Inguiomerus was likewise saved, by his own bravery or by treachery. The rest were massacred. Many tried to swim the Weser. They were battered by javelins, or carried away by the current, or finally overwhelmed by the mass of fugitives and collapse of the river banks. Some ignominiously tried to escape by

装的军队、骑马的弓箭手;还有其余的联盟军步兵中队。士兵们都处于高度的戒备状态之中,他们可以随时从行军状态中变化成战斗的序列。

凯路斯奇人的队伍不顾一切地向前冲来。日耳曼尼库斯看到了这种情况,便下令他的骑兵精锐部队进攻他们的侧面;其余的骑兵队伍则由路奇乌斯·司特尔提尼乌斯率领迂回到敌人的后面去发动进攻,而他本人将瞅准适当的时机下手。他看到了一个极其鼓舞人心的征兆——有八只鹰向森林飞去并飞进了森林中。"前进,"他喊道:"跟着这些罗马的鸟,它们是罗马军团的保护神呀!"就在这时,步兵的队伍开始进攻,而被派到前方去的骑兵也都向敌人的后方和两翼展开了进攻。这是一种十分奇怪的场景。两支敌人的军队向两个相反的方向逃跑,森林里的军队冲向平原,而平原上的军队却冲向森林。

夹在这两支军队中间的凯路斯奇人则被从山坡上赶了下来:在他们当中就有阿尔米尼乌斯,他攻击着、叫喊着,他已经受了伤,但还仍在努力想坚持这场战斗。他奋力向弓箭手那里冲去,如果不是莱提亚人、文戴里奇人和高卢人的步兵中队用队旗挡住了他的去路的话,弓箭手的阵地就会被突破了。即使如此,由于他具有惊人的力气,又有精良的坐骑的冲力的辅助,他终于突围而出。为了避免给别人认出他来,他满脸都涂抹上了自己的血。根据一些人的说法,在罗马辅助军队中服役的卡乌奇人虽然认出了他是谁,但还是把他放走了。音吉奥美路斯也由于同样的勇气或同样的诡计而得以逃命。其他的人则被大批地杀死。许多人企图游过威悉河,他们中一些人遭到了投枪的猛击,一些人则被急流冲走,最后,许多人被大量跳到河里去逃生的人和塌

climbing trees. As they cowered among the branches, bowmen a-
mused themselves by shooting them down. Others were brought to the
ground by felling the trees.

It was a great victory, and it cost us little. The slaughter of the
enemy continued from midday until dusk. Their bodies and weapons
were scattered for ten miles round. Among the spoils were found
chains which they had brought for the Romans in confident expectation of the result. The troops hailed Tiberius as victor on the battle-
field, and erected a mound on which, like a trophy, they set arms
with the names of the defeated tribes. The sight of this upset and enraged the Germans more than all their wounds and losses and destruction. Men who had just been planning emigration across the Elbe now
wanted to fight instead, and rushed to arms.

Germans of every rank and age launched sudden and damaging
attacks against the Romans on the march. Finally they selected a narrow swampy open space enclosed between a river and the forest—
which in its turn was surrounded by a deep morass (except on one
side where a wide earthwork had been constructed by the Angrivarii to
mark the Cheruscan frontier). Here the Germans stationed their infantry. The cavalry took cover in the woods nearby, so as to take the
Romans in the rear when they came into the forest. Germanicus was
aware of all this. He knew their plans, positions, their secret as well
as their visible arrangements; and he planned to use their strategy for

陷的河岸压死了。一些人不光彩地爬到树上去逃命,当他们想躲到树枝中间去的时候,弓箭手向他们射箭把他们射下来嘲弄他们,另一些人则是由于砍倒树木而被摔了下来。

这是一次辉煌的胜利,而且付出的代价也并非是惨重的。对敌人的屠杀从中午一直持续到夜幕的降临。敌人的尸体和武器在周围 10 英里的地段上到处分散着。在战利品当中发现了一些为罗马人准备的锁链,这些锁链是他们用来增强对于战争的胜利的信心的。军队在战场上把提贝里乌斯欢呼为统帅,[1] 又在上面筑起了一座土丘,把刻有打败的部族的名字的武器作为战利品竖在上面作为装饰。这种情景比负伤、损失和毁灭更使日耳曼人感到沮丧和愤怒。刚才正准备移居到易北河对岸去的人,现在却渴望作战并冲进去拿起武器了。

日耳曼人,无论是何种身份、何种年龄,都突然地向着正在行进的罗马军队发动了进攻,并且使罗马的队伍受到了损伤。最后,他们选择了一个狭窄的、夹在河流和森林中间的布满沼泽的平原地带作为阵地,而且森林也被深深的沼泽地包围着。(只有一面是例外,在那里安格里瓦利人早就修筑了一道很宽的土堤,作为他们与凯路斯奇人的边界。)在这里,日耳曼人驻守着他们的步兵。他们的骑兵则隐蔽在附近的丛林里,以便在罗马军团进入森林时,可以紧紧将他们的后面部分咬住。日耳曼尼库斯对他们的这一切布置了如指掌。他了解他们的计划、他们的地势、他们秘密的和可见的一切部署。于是他将计就计,打算用敌人自己的计划

---

〔1〕　在此,士兵们之所以这样欢呼,是因为日耳曼尼库斯是以提贝里乌库斯的名义,在他的授权之下指挥作战的。

their own ruin. His cavalry, under the command of Lucius Seius Tubero, was allotted the open ground. The infantry were divided. Part were to proceed along the level ground to the wood, the rest were to scale the earthwork. He undertook this more difficult project himself, leaving the remaining tasks to his generals.

Those allocated the level ground broke into the wood easily. But the men scaling the earthwork were virtually climbing a wall, and received severe damage from above. Seeing that fighting conditions were unfavourable at close quarters, Germanicus withdrew his brigades a short way, and ordered his slingers into action to drive off the enemy. Simultaneously, spears were launched from machines. Exposure cost the defenders heavy casualties; they were beaten back, the earthwork was captured, and Germanicus personally led the Guard battalions in a charge into the woods. There, hand-to-hand fighting began. The enemy were hemmed in by the marsh behind them, the Romans by the river or hills. Both sides had to fight it out on the spot. Bravery was their only hope, victory their only way out.

The Germans were as brave as our men, but their tactics and weapons proved their downfall. With their vast numbers crammed into a narrow space they could neither thrust nor pull back their great pikes. They were compelled to fight as they stood, unable to exploit their natural speed by charging. The Romans on the other hand, with shields close to their chests and sword-hilts firmly grasped, rained blows on the enemy's huge forms and exposed faces, and forced a murderous passage.

Either Arminius had been through too many crises, or his recent

把他们自己消灭掉。他的骑兵,在他的副帅路奇乌斯·塞乌斯·图倍罗带领下,分配在平原地带。步兵分成两部分,一部分继续沿着平地向森林方向行进,另一部分则要攀越土堤这一障碍。他亲自承担这一更加艰难的任务,而把其余的任务留给了他的将领们。

被分配在平地上的那部分军队没有费太大的力气便攻入了森林。攻打土堤的罗马士兵,实际上是攀登一道城墙,因此他们受到了来自土堤上面的有力反击,因而受到了严重的损失。看到这种近距离的交锋对自己相当不利,日耳曼尼库斯于是就让他军团的士兵稍稍后撤,然后下令投射手进入行动将敌人驱散。与此同时,器械也开动起来把投枪射了出去,此时,防御者自身暴露得越明显,他们的死伤也就越严重。敌人被打退了,土堤也被攻占下来,日耳曼尼库斯亲自率领着近卫军士兵攻进到森林里面去。在那里,他们与敌人面对面展开了一场白刃战。敌人的后方被一片沼泽地包围着,罗马人的后方则是河流和小山。双方都只能在这样的情势下战斗,寻找自己的出路。只有勇敢杀敌才会有希望,取得战斗的胜利是他们可以得救的唯一办法。

日耳曼人也和我们一样勇敢,但是他们的战术和他们的武器却使他们遭受到了失败。他们那么多的人拥挤在一块狭小的地方,无法刺出或是拉回他们那巨大的投枪。他们被迫站在一点固定的地方作战,在那里他们也不能发挥他们迅速敏捷的能力。但另一方面,罗马的士兵把盾牌紧紧贴在他们的胸前,手里紧握着刀柄,暴风雨般地砍杀着敌人高大的躯体和暴露着的脸,杀出了一条血路。

阿尔米尼乌斯或许是因为接连不断地经历了太多的危险,或

wound was troubling him: he did not show his usual vigour. Inguiomer-us, however, was in every part of the battle at once. His courage did not fail him—but he had bad luck. Germanicus, who had torn off his helmet so as to be recognized, ordered his men to kill and kill. No prisoners were wanted. Only the total destruction of the tribe would end the war. Finally, late in the day, he withdrew one brigade from the battle to make a camp. Apart from the cavalry, whose battle was inde-cisive, the rest sated themselves with enemy blood until nightfall.

Germanicus congratulated the victorious troops and piled up a heap of arms with this proud inscription: DEDICATED TO MARS AND THE DIVINE AUGUSTUS BY THE ARMY OF TIBERIUS CAESAR AFTER ITS CONQUEST OF THE NATIONS BETWEEN THE RHINE AND THE ELBE. Of himself he said nothing. He may have feared jealousy; or perhaps he felt that the knowledge of what he had done was enough. Shortly afterwards he sent Lucius Stertinius to fight the Angrivarii unless they rapidly surrendered. They begged for mercy unconditionally and received an unqualified pardon. Next, summer being already at its height, part of the army were sent back to winter quarters overland, while the majority embarked on the Ems and sailed with Germanicus down to the sea.

At first only the sound of a thousand ships' sails, and the motion of their oars, disturbed the calm. But then, from dense black clouds, descended a hailstorm. Squalls blew up from every side, and the ris-ing waves destroyed visibility and upset steering. The troops, terri-fied and unfamiliar with the perils of the sea, impeded the professional

许是因为不久前负的伤妨碍了他：这时他已没有了往常所有的那种旺盛的活力。音吉奥美路斯在战场上杀来杀去，尽管他作战十分勇敢，但是却总是运气不佳。把头盔摘了下来，以便使自己容易被士兵辨认出来的日耳曼尼库斯，命令他麾下的士兵尽自己的力量杀杀杀，一个战俘也不要。他认为只有把这个部族全部杀光，才能够结束这场战争。最后到傍晚的时候，他把一个军团从战场上撤了下来以便设营。直到夜间，除了骑兵团的战斗还没有分出胜负外，而其余的士兵则都已经痛痛快快地将敌人杀了个够。

日耳曼尼库斯先是向胜利的军队表示了祝贺，然后就把武器堆了起来，并且刻了这样自豪的碑铭："提贝里乌斯·恺撒的军队在征服了莱茵河和易北河之间的各族之后，献给玛尔斯和圣奥古斯都。"但是在铭文上，他却一句话也没有提及他本人。这或许是因为害怕别人的妒忌，或许是因为他觉得人们已经知道了他自己所做的一切，这就足够了。不久之后，他又派路奇乌斯·司特尔提尼乌斯出去对安格里瓦利人作战，除非他们能赶快投降。对方无条件地投降，请求他们的仁慈，结果他们也就在一切方面都得到了宽恕。随之，时间已行进到了盛夏，一部分军团经由陆路调回了冬营，而大部分的军队却在埃姆斯河上乘船，随同日耳曼尼库斯一道下行到了北海。

最初，浩瀚的海洋上一片寂静，只有上千只船航行的声音和船桨摇动的声音偶尔会打破这种宁静。不一会儿，从一片厚厚的乌云中落下了冰雹。从四面八方刮起的狂风和卷起的巨浪使得人们无法看清楚任何东西，并且也无法驾驶船只。惊恐万状并且没有经历过海上的风险的士兵们碍手碍脚或是帮忙帮不到点子

sailors by getting in the way and offering unwanted help. Soon sea and sky were swept by a southerly gale—nourished by waterlogged Germany and its deep rivers and mighty clouds, and aggravated by the savage North Sea just beyond. The gale caught the ships and scattered them over the open sea or on to islands with sharp cliffs and treacherous sunken shoals. Scarcely had these hazards been avoided when the tide turned and ran in the same direction as the gale.

Now the anchors held no longer, and no bailing could keep the torrential waters out. Horses, baggage, animals, even arms were jettisoned to lighten the ships as they leaked at the joints and were deluged by waves. The North Sea is the roughest in the world, and the German climate the worst. The disaster was proportionately terrible—indeed it was unprecedented. On one side were enemy coasts, on the other a sea so huge and deep that it is held to be the uttermost, with no land beyond. Some ships went down. Others, more numerous, were cast on to remote islands, where the men were obliged to eat the horses washed up with them or starve to death. Germanicus' warship landed alone in the realm of the Chauci. He spent days and nights on the rocky headlands—cursing himself for the catastrophe. His friends could scarcely prevent him from drowning himself in the same sea.

At last, when the tide turned and a favourable wind blew, the crippled ships came back with most of their oars lost, or with clothes

上，从而妨碍了专业水手及时地处理面临的变故。接着，天空和海洋都被南风裹挟着——这种风从日耳曼的沼泽，从它深深的河流，从强有力的云中取得了力量，而不远处的严酷的北海更加重了它的威力。南风袭击了船舶，将它们冲散在辽阔的海洋上，或是把它们冲到岩石嶙峋、又布满了危险的暗滩的岛屿上。[1] 当潮水开始改变而与风暴的方向相一致的时候，这些危险总算是躲过去了。

现在，船锚没有了，人们极力往外舀也无法将涌入船中的洪水弄出去。战马、行李、驮马甚至武器都被投到了海里，以便减轻船的重量，因为它们的接缝处都漏水，并且都已经被浪头淹没了。北海是世界上最狂暴的海，而日耳曼的气候又是一切气候当中最恶劣的。所以这一灾难是多么巨大也就可想而知，而事实上这一灾难也确实是空前未有的。一面是充满敌意的海岸，一面是一片又深又阔的海洋，以致人们认为这是天涯海角，在它以外再也没有什么陆地了。一些船沉没了，更多的船被狂风吹到了遥远的岛屿上去，在那里，他们不得不以和他们一起被冲上来的马为食，或者就饿死在那里。只有日耳曼尼库斯的那只舰船在卡乌奇人居住的地区靠了岸。在布满山岩的向水中凸出的一块陆地上所度过的那些日日夜夜当中，日耳曼尼库斯一直在责怪自己是这次大灾难的罪魁祸首。他的朋友们好不容易才阻止了他在此投海自尽。

最后当潮水改变了流向并且又刮起了和顺的风的时候，残破的船才开始转了回来，其中，一些船只剩下了几把桨，另一些船

---

〔1〕 这些岛屿在威悉河和荷兰之间。

for sails, or towed by less damaged craft. Rapidly repaired, they were sent by Germanicus to search the islands, and in this way many men were recovered. Many more were ransomed from remoter tribes. The Angrivarii, who had recently submitted, acted as intermediaries. Others had been carried to Britain, and were sent back by its chieftains. Men coming from these remote regions told strange stories—of hurricanes, unknown birds, sea-monsters, and shapes half-human and half-animal, which they had seen or in their terror had imagined.

Rumours that the fleet was lost raised the Germans' military hopes and led Germanicus to take repressive measures. Gaius Silius (I) was ordered to attack the Chatti with a force of 30,000 infantry and 3,000 horse. Germanicus himself, with the larger of the two forces, proceeded against the Marsi, whose chief, Mallovendus, had recently submitted and now reported that the Eagle of one of Varus' brigades lay buried in a neighbouring grove, protected by only a small guard. A detachment was at once sent to provide a frontal diversion, while another went round behind and dug. Both achieved success. This encouraged Germanicus to penetrate further into the interior, plundering and exterminating an enemy who either did not dare to encounter him or was routed wherever he attempted a stand. Prisoners reported unprecedented demoralization. The Romans were said to be invincible and proof against every misfortune—their fleet and their arms were lost, the shores heaped with bodies of men and horses, and yet they had returned to the attack with undiminished courage and ferocity, apparently more numerous than ever.

则是用衣服作船帆,还有一些船被损伤较少的船拖着。迅速作了修补以后,这些船又被日耳曼尼库斯派到了各个岛上去搜寻。由于采取了这一措施,许多人得救了。还有更多的人则是从较远的部落赎回来的,刚刚降服的安格里瓦利人从中作媒介。还有一些船一直被吹到了不列颠,被那里的酋长们送了回来。从远处回来的人,讲述着各种各样奇异的故事——飓风、从未听说过的鸟儿、海怪和半人半兽的怪物,这是他们亲眼看到的,或者是他们在恐惧中自己想象出来的。

罗马舰队遇难的谣传使日耳曼人蠢蠢欲动,想再打一仗,另一方面这也促使日耳曼尼库斯采取了制服他们的措施。他命令盖乌斯·西里乌斯(一世)率领 3 万步兵和 3000 骑兵去攻打卡提伊人,日耳曼尼库斯本人则率领两支更庞大的军队去进攻玛尔喜人,玛尔喜人的将领玛洛文都斯不久之前刚向罗马人投降,现在他报告说,伐鲁斯的一个军团的军旗被埋葬在附近的一个丛林里面,而且只有一小队人在那里看守。日耳曼尼库斯立刻派了一队人马到敌人的前方活动,以便把敌人牵制住,同时他又派出一队人绕到敌人后面去挖掘军旗。这两队人都取得了成功。这极大地激励了日耳曼尼库斯,他更加精神振奋地率军向内地挺进,抢劫敌人的财物,并歼灭了敌人。这些人或是不敢与他作战,或是在陷入绝境时被击溃。据被俘的人员说,日耳曼人的士气从来还没有这样沮丧过。罗马人被他们说成是不可战胜的,是能够经受得住任何的灾难的。他们的舰队和武器都失去了,海岸上到处都堆积着他们的人和马的尸体。但是他们还是返回来以毫无削减的勇敢和凶猛向敌军发起了进攻,而且人数显然比从前还要多。

Then the army returned to its winter-camps, gratified to have compensated the disasters at sea by this successful expedition. Germanicus treated them generously, satisfying every claim for losses. It was felt certain that the enemy were collapsing and about to sue for peace-one more summer's campaign would end the war. But repeated letters from Tiberius instructed Germanicus to return for the Triumph that had been voted to him. 'There have been enough successes,' wrote the emperor, 'and enough misfortunes. You have won great victories. But you must also remember the terrible, crippling losses inflicted by wind and wave—through no fault of the commander. I was sent into Germany nine times by the divine Augustus, and I achieved less by force than by diplomacy; thereby the Sugambri were forced to submit, and the Suebi and their King Maroboduus compelled to keep the peace. Similarly the Cherusci and other rebellious tribes, now that we have duly punished them, can be left to their own internal disturbances.'

When Germanicus asked for another year to complete the job, Tiberius subjected his unpretentious adoptive son to even stronger pressure by offering him the prize of a second consulship—to be occupied personally at Rome. The emperor added that, if the war must continue, Germanicus should leave his brother, Drusus, some chance of distinction; for, in the absence of enemies elsewhere, Germany was the only place in which Drusus could earn a salutation as victor and the triumphal laurels. Germanicus knew that this was hypocritical, and that jealousy was the reason why Tiberius denied him a victory that was already won. But he acquiesced without further delay.

随后军队就返回了冬营。令他们感到高兴的是,他们这次出征的成功,使在海上受到的灾难得到了补偿。日耳曼尼库斯对他们非常慷慨,每个人只要申明自己受到了什么损失,他都会给予充分的补偿。人们普遍深信不疑地感觉到,敌人已经崩溃了,而且正在讨论向他们求和——只要来年夏天再努力打一仗,就可以结束战争了。但是从提贝里乌斯那里却不断有信给日耳曼尼库斯,命令他回去接受已经授予他的凯旋的荣誉。"你取得的成功已经够多了,"提贝里乌斯在信中说道,"而你遭受的灾难也够多的了。你取得了伟大的胜利。但是你也不要忘了由于海上的风浪所遭受的可怕而严重的损失。当然这自始至终都不是统帅的过错。我曾经九次被圣奥古斯都派到日耳曼,我在外交方面的成就多于武力方面的成功。通过这种努力,苏甘布利人被迫投降,苏埃比人和他们的国王玛洛波都斯也被促使保持和平。同样的,对于凯路斯奇人和其他背叛的部族,既然已经受到了我们的适当的惩罚,就让他们自己去内乱吧。"

当日耳曼尼库斯请求再给他一年的时间来完成这里的工作时,提贝里乌斯就对他这个谦逊的养子施加了更大的压力。他建议,让日耳曼尼库斯第二次担任执政官,以此将他拴在罗马城。同时这位皇帝还进一步说道,如果战争非得继续下去不可的话,他也应该留给他的兄弟杜路苏斯一点崭露头角的机会。因为目前其他地方已经没有敌人了,只有在日耳曼,杜路苏斯才能赢得统帅的称号和凯旋的荣誉。日耳曼尼库斯虽然知道他的这些客套话都是伪善的,而且正是由于嫉妒使提贝里乌斯否认了他那已经到手的成功,但他还是不再犹豫,同意了提贝里乌斯的决定。

CHAPTER 4

The First Treason Trials

It was about now that Marcus Scribonius Libo Drusus was accused of subversive plotting. Since this case initiated an evil which for many years corroded public life, I will give details of its beginnings, progress, and conclusion. Libo was a fatuous young man with a taste for absurdities. One of his closest friends, a junior senator named Firmius Catus, interested him in astrologers' predictions, magicians' rites, and readers of dreams. Catus reminded Libo that the Caesars were his cousins—besides being a great-grandson of Pompey, he was grandnephew of Scribonia, at one time the wife of Augustus—and that his own house, too, was full of ancestral statues.

By encouraging Libo's extravagances and debts and sharing his dissipations and embarrassments, Catus accumulated damning evidence. When he had collected enough witnesses—including slaves to corroborate the account—he requested an interview with the emperor. Tiberius already knew who was accused, and why, through a knight, Vescularius Flaccus, who was more intimate with the emperor than Catus was. Tiberius did not refuse the information of Catus but declined personal contact, indicating that they could continue to com-

第四章　第一次叛国罪的审判

　　几乎就在同时,玛尔库斯·司克里波尼乌斯·里波·杜路苏斯被控犯有密谋颠覆国家的叛国罪行。因为从这件案子开始,公民的生活就受到了长达多年的侵蚀,所以我下面就将要对这件事的起因、经过和结果,做出比较详细的叙述。里波是一个喜欢做荒唐事的糊涂的年轻人,他的最亲密的朋友之一,一个名字叫费尔米乌斯·卡图斯的元老激起了他对占星术士的预言、魔法师的礼节以及圆梦人的兴趣。卡图斯提醒里波说,除了庞培是他的曾祖父外,恺撒们也都是他的堂兄弟,他是司克里波尼娅的侄孙子——司克里波尼娅一度曾是奥古斯都的妻子。在他家里也摆满了许许多多祖先的雕像。

　　卡图斯不但教唆里波奢侈浪费、欠债,而且还拉他一块儿过放荡生活,一块儿陷入窘境。卡图斯积累着他的毁灭性的证据。当他召集了足够多的证人——包括一些可以确证这些证据的奴隶的时候,他就请求觐见皇帝。原来皇帝早已经知道了谁将受到控告以及为什么受到控告了,他是通过一个骑士得到这些情报的。这位骑士名叫维司库拉里乌斯·佛拉库斯,比卡图斯和皇帝更亲近。提贝里乌斯并不拒绝卡图斯所提供的情报,但是拒绝与卡图斯进行个人接触,他表示他们之间可以通过佛拉库斯做中间

municate through the knight as intermediary. Meanwhile he made Libo praetor and invited him to dinner. No unfriendliness was apparent in Tiberius' expression or talk. His malevolence was completely concealed. He could have stopped all Libo's actions and words. Instead, he preferred to note them.

Finally, however, a certain Junius whom Libo had approached to practise necromancy reported him to Lucius Fulcinius Trio, a man known for his talents as a prosecutor—and eager for notoriety. Trio immediately pounced on Libo, applied to the consuls, and demanded an inquiry by the senate: which was summoned, to discuss a grave and terrible matter. Meanwhile Libo put on mourning and, with an escort of aristocratic ladies, went from house to house appealing to his wife's relatives and seeking for an advocate in his perilous position. Everyone refused. Their excuses were different, but they were all afraid. On the day of the meeting he was prostrate with fear and ill-health (possibly, as some said, assumed), and had to be carried in a litter to the senate-house door. Leaning on his brother's arm he stretched out his hand to Tiberius and cried for mercy. The emperor, without altering his expression, read out the accusation and its signatures in a toneless voice calculated neither to aggravate nor to extenuate the charges.

Trio and Catus had now been joined by further accusers, Fonteius Agrippa and Gaius Vibius Serenus (I). They all competed for the principal speech. Finally, as none of them would give way and Libo was undefended, Vibius announced that he would take the charges

人,继续保持联系。同时,他提拔了里波担任行政长官,并且几次召他来和自己共同进餐。在提贝里乌斯的表情和言谈间都没有任何对他疏远的表现,他将恶意完全掩藏了起来。他可以制止里波所有的言行,但是他没有这样做,他更喜欢将这些记录下来。

然而,后来,有一个曾被里波请去为他念咒招魂的名叫尤尼乌斯的人把他的事情报告给了路奇乌斯·富尔奇尼乌斯·特里奥,特里奥是一个以告密才能而著名的人,而且臭名昭著。特里奥立刻就猛扑向了里波,他到执政官那里去控告并且要求元老院进行调查。元老们被召集起来,讨论一个十分严重的、骇人听闻的案件。与此同时,里波穿上丧服,[1]在一些贵族妇女的陪伴下,挨家挨户地恳求他的妻子的亲戚,请他们出来为他的危险处境讲讲情。没有一个人肯帮忙,他们的借口各不相同,但他们有着相同的一点就是害怕。元老院开会那天,他因恐惧和身体不舒服而极为衰弱(也许像有些人所说的那样,他是装病),以至于不得不坐着肩舆被人抬到了元老院的门口。斜倚在他的兄弟的胳膊上,他伸出手向提贝里乌斯请求宽恕。但是皇帝脸上的表情没有丝毫改变,仍用单调的声音宣读起诉书的控告和证人的名字,人们无法估计他是想减轻还是想加重他所控诉的罪行。

除了特里奥和卡图斯之外,丰提乌斯·阿格里帕和盖乌斯·维比乌斯·塞伦努斯(一世)也参加了这次控诉。他们争相做主控,最后,由于他们争执不下、各不相让,而里波又没有正式的辩护人,于是维比乌斯就宣布说,他要把控诉的条款一项一项地提出来。

---

〔1〕 这是为了引起人们对他的同情。

one by one; and he produced the documents. They were preposterous. In one, Libo asked a fortune-teller if he would become rich enough to pave the Via Appia with money as far as Brundisium. Other stupidities were equally pointless—indeed, if indulgently regarded, pitiable. But in one paper, mysterious or sinister marks against the names of imperial personages and senators were alleged by the prosecutor to be in Libo's handwriting. Libo denied this. But slaves identified his hand; and it was decided to interrogate them under torture. Since, however, there was an ancient senatorial decree forbidding such investigations of slaves in capital charges against their masters, Tiberius—by an astute legal innovation—ordered the slaves to be sold individually to the Treasury Agent. And all this in order to use slaves' evidence against a man of Libo's position, without infringing a senatorial decree !

The defendant thereupon requested an adjournment until the following day, and left for his home. He entrusted his relative Publius Sulpicius Quirinius with a final appeal to Tiberius. The emperor's answer was that Libo should apply to the senate. Meanwhile his house was surrounded by Guardsmen. The sound and sight of them, clanking about in front of the door, plagued the dinner-party which Libo had arranged as his last pleasure on earth. Gripping his slaves' hands and thrusting his sword into their grasp, he cried out for someone to kill him. The slaves shrank away in terror, and knocked over the table-lamp. For Libo it was the darkness of death. He stabbed himself twice in the stomach, and fell moaning. Ex-slaves ran up. The soldiers saw he was dead, and left.

In the senate, however, the prosecution continued with undi-

于是他便把里波的那些公文拿了出来。这些公文非常荒谬,在一份文书里,里波竟然问占卜者他会不会富到能用钱把直到布伦地西乌姆的阿披亚大道给遮盖起来。其他的东西也都同样的愚蠢、无聊。事实上,如果宽容一些来看,这其实是很可怜的东西。但是在一份文书里,在皇族的成员和一些元老的名字上作了一些神秘的,或用心险恶的记号,检控官宣称这是出自里波的笔迹。里波否认了这种说法,但是奴隶们确认这就是里波的笔迹,这是他们在拷打的审讯之下进行的辨认。然而,既然有一条古老的法令禁止在涉及奴隶的主人的重大案件中对奴隶们进行调查审问,于是提贝里乌斯便十分巧妙地作出了一种法律上的创新——他下令把奴隶们个别地转售给掌理国库的官员。他这样做的目的只不过是要让奴隶有资格证明里波的罪行,同时却又不致破坏元老院的法令!

被告于是请求延期一天审理,他离开元老院回家去了。他托付他的一个亲戚普布里乌斯·苏尔皮奇乌斯·克维里尼乌斯留在那里向提贝里乌斯作最后的恳求。皇帝的回答是,里波应该提交给元老院处理。同时,里波的家也被卫兵包围起来了。这些士兵在门口走来走去的身影和声音,全家人都看得见、听得见,这使里波安排的他在世上的最后一次享乐的宴会充满了灾难的气息。里波抓住了他的奴隶们的手,将他的剑塞入他们手中,他叫嚷着,要他们中的一个来杀死他。他的奴隶们在慌乱中后退,碰翻了桌子上的烛台。这对里波来说,是一种死亡的黑暗。就在这时,他用刀子向自己的腹部刺了两下,便呻吟着倒了下去。被释放的奴隶们跑了过来。士兵们看到他已经死了,就离开了。

但是,在元老院里,控诉依然以丝毫没有减弱的真诚在继续

minished earnestness. Tiberius pronounced on oath that, whatever Libo's guilt, he himself would have interceded for his life if he had not so hastily killed himself. Libo's property was divided among the accusers, and those of them who were senators received supernumerary praetorships. Then Marcus Aurelius Cotta Maximus Messallinus proposed that Libo's statue should be excluded from his descendants' funeral-parades, and Cnaeus Cornelius Lentulus (II) that no Scribonius should ever again bear the name of Drusus. On the motion of Lucius Pomponius Flaccus, days were appointed for public thanksgiving. Lucius Munatius Plancus, Gaius Asinius Gallus, Marcus Papius Mutilus, and Lucius Apronius voted thank-offerings to Jupiter, Mars, and Concord, and a resolution that 13 September—the day of Libo's suicide—should become a public holiday. I have listed these distinguished proposers and their servilities to show how long ago this national disgrace started. The senate also ordered the expulsion of astrologers and magicians from Italy. One, Lucius Pituanius, was thrown from the Tarpeian Rock, another, Publius Marcius, executed by the consuls in traditional fashion to the sound of the bugle, outside the Esquiline Gate.

At the senate's next meeting Quintus Haterius and Octavius Fronto, a former consul and praetor respectively, denounced current extravagance. The use of gold plate for private entertainments was prohibited, and so were the silk clothes into which male costume had degenerated. Fronto went further and demanded restrictions on silver plate, furniture, and slaves. (It was still a usual practice for senators, when their

着。提贝里乌斯发誓宣称，不论里波犯了什么罪，他本人都会出面干预来挽救他的，如果他不是这样快就自杀了的话。里波的财产分配给了那些控诉者，临时增加的那些行政长官的职位则由他们当中一些元老担任。接着，玛尔库斯·奥列利乌斯·马克西姆斯·科塔·美撒里努斯提出建议，在里波的后人为里波举行的葬仪行列中，不得把里波的像抬出来，格涅乌斯·科尔涅里乌斯·楞图路斯(二世)建议司克里波尼乌斯家族的任何成员今后不应再使用杜路苏斯的姓氏。根据路奇乌斯·彭波尼乌斯·佛拉库斯的建议，设立了全民感恩的节日。路奇乌斯·穆纳提乌斯·普朗库斯、盖乌斯·阿西尼乌斯·伽路斯、玛尔库斯·帕披乌斯·木提路斯和路奇乌斯·阿普洛尼乌斯等人则倡议，9月13日，即里波自杀的日子，这一向朱庇特、玛尔斯和协和神感恩、上供还愿的日子应定为全民的节日。我把这些显赫的提议者的名字和奴颜婢膝的行为一一列出，就是为了显示出，这种耻辱的行径在我们的国家，是多久以前就已经开始的啊。元老院还形成了另外的决议，那就是，下令把占星术士和魔法师逐出意大利。其中一个叫做路奇乌斯·皮杜亚尼乌斯的人被从塔尔培亚岩上抛了下去，另一个叫做普布里乌斯·玛尔奇乌斯的人则按照古老的习俗在喇叭声中被执政官在埃斯克维里努斯门外执行了处决。

元老院召集下一次会议时，克温图斯·哈提里乌斯和奥克塔维乌斯·佛隆托，他们分别是前任执政官和前任行政长官，发表了演说，反对当前国内的奢华风习。决定在私人的招待宴会上不许使用黄金制造的食具，男子的服装也不应该再用丝织品，因为这会使他们堕落下去。佛隆托更进一步提出建议，要求用法律明文限定银器、家具和奴仆方面的规制。(在轮到自己发言时，

turn came to speak, to put forward any matter that they believed to be in the public interest.) Gaius Asinius Gallus spoke in opposition. 'The extension of the empire', he argued, 'has meant the growth of private fortunes. This is nothing new; indeed it is in keeping with the most ancient history. Wealth meant one thing to the Fabricii, another to the Scipios. It must be judged in relation to the country. When the nation was poor, people's houses were small. In its present grandeur individuals, too, expand.

'In slaves, plate, or any other article for use, the only criterion of moderation or excess is the owner's means. Senators and knights have special property qualifications, not because they are intrinsically different, but because their precedence in station, rank, and honours warrants special provision for their mental and physical well-being. Otherwise leading men would have all the worries and dangers, and none of their compensations.' This euphemistic admission of debauchery readily won his audience, since extravagance was widespread. Moreover, Tiberius had observed that this was not the time for a censorship: but if morality deteriorated, he said, his services as reformer would be available.

At this meeting Lucius Calpurnius Piso (Ⅱ) denounced official sharp practices—corruption in the courts, and bullying by advocates, with their continual threats of prosecution. He himself was going to leave Rome, he said, and retire to some remote, inaccessible country place. Then he proceeded to walk out of the senate-house.

元老们可以提出任何他认为对公众有利的事情,这在当时仍然是元老院的一种惯例。)盖乌斯·阿西尼乌斯·伽路斯反对他的看法。"帝国的扩大,"他说,"也意味着私人财富的增长。这绝不是什么新鲜事;事实上,这与大多数古老的历史是相一致的。财产对法布里奇乌斯家族意味着一件事情,对斯奇比奥家族又有另一种意义。这一切都应当与国家的情况联系起来判断。当国家贫穷的时候,人们的房屋矮小简陋,可是国家一旦达到目前这样强大的地步,每个个人当然也就发达富有起来了。

在奴隶、食具或任何其他用品方面,是浪费还是适度的评断必须由主人的财产情况如何而定。元老和骑士都有他们自己特殊的财产资格,[1]这并不是因为他们和他们的同国人在本质上有什么不同之处,而是因为他们在地位、官阶和高贵的身份方面的优先地位提供给了他们在精神和物质上幸福安乐的保证。否则那些肩负领导责任的人们,承担着所有的忧虑和风险,但是却没有得到任何补偿。"伽路斯对恶习所做的这种委婉的赞许,很容易赢得听众的同情,因为奢侈之风在当时是普遍流行的。再者,提贝里乌斯经过一番慎重考虑后也说,现在还不是动用审查制度的时候:如果公民有道德败坏的地方,他说,他还会采取改正的措施的。

在会上的辩论中,路奇乌斯·卡尔普尔尼乌斯·披索(二世)痛斥官员的不端行为——法官的贪污,控诉者的欺凌弱小,还有告密者不断带来的威胁。他本人则要离开罗马,他说,他要退休,去住到一个偏僻、难以到达的乡村过清净的生活。接着,他就要走出元

---

〔1〕 元老的财产资格是100万谢司特尔提乌斯,骑士的是40万谢司特尔提乌斯。

Tiberius was upset and made every effort to mollify Piso, besides requesting his relations to use their influence and entreat him to stay.

Soon afterwards Lucius Piso gave another, equally remarkable display of outspoken indignation. For he summoned to court Urgulania, whose friendship with the Augusta had placed her above the law. Urgulania defied Lucius Piso, refused to obey, and drove to the palace. Thereupon the Augusta complained that it was an insult to her dignity. However, Lucius Piso persisted. Tiberius decided that, without acting autocratically, he could back his mother up to the point of promising to appear before the praetor and support Urgulania. Ordering his military escort to follow at a distance, he left the palace, and was seen by the crowd walking composedly and discussing various matters to pass the time. But Lucius Piso's relatives could not induce him to desist—and the Augusta gave instructions that the sum demanded should be paid. Thus ended an incident which did Lucius Piso credit and increased the emperor's popularity. However, Urgulania's influence remained so excessive that on one occasion, when she was summoned to the senate as witness in a case, she refused to attend. A praetor was dispatched to interrogate her at her home—though even priestesses of Vesta traditionally attend legal proceedings in the Forum to give evidence.

The senate's adjournment this year is only noteworthy because of

老院。提贝里乌斯为此深感不安,他尽一切努力来对披索进行抚慰,还要他的亲属也利用他们对他的影响力或通过努力的恳求使他留下来。

不久之后,路奇乌斯·披索再一次同样明显地表现了他的那种坦率直言的义愤。他向法院控告了乌尔古拉尼娅,她仗着同奥古斯塔的友谊关系而将自己凌驾于法律之上,胡作非为。乌尔古拉尼娅不把披索放在眼里,她拒绝服从法院的传唤,却径直乘坐肩舆到皇宫去了。在此她对奥古斯塔抱怨说,披索的这种做法冒犯和侮辱了她本人的尊严。但是路奇乌斯·卡尔普尔尼乌斯·披索在这方面仍然毫不让步,坚持自己的立场。提贝里乌斯认为,对于自己的母亲他能够支持到这样一种程度,那就是他答应公开出现在行政长官的面前去为乌尔古拉尼娅辩护,这不能算是独裁行为。于是他命令他的侍卫远远地跟着他,他便离开了皇宫。聚拢来观看的人群看到他带着十分镇静的神色一面走着,一面谈论着各种各样的事情以打发时间。路奇乌斯·披索的亲属劝告他放弃诉讼,却没有成功。奥古斯塔下令归还应付的款项,这才结束了这一事件。披索所争取到的这一结果增强了人们对皇帝的信任,也提高了皇帝的声望。不过乌尔古拉尼娅在国内的势力仍然是如此之大,以致后来偶尔地在一次审判中又需要她到元老院去作证的时候,她竟然拒绝出席。于是不得不派一位行政长官亲自到她家里去询问——尽管按照正式的规定,甚至维司塔贞女在被审问时都应当亲自到罗马广场和法庭上去作证。

这一年元老院的休会特别值得注意,因为在格涅乌斯·卡尔普尔

the dispute regarding it between Gaius Asinius Gallus and Cnaeus
Calpurnius Piso. Tiberius had said he would be away. But Cnaeus Piso considered this an additional reason for business to continue, it being in the public interest that senate and knights should be able to undertake their proper duties in the emperor's absence. Gallus, forestalled by Piso in the display of independence, protested that to conduct
business without the emperor's presence and supervision was incompatible with the national dignity; so the numerous Italian and provincial visitors ought to await his presence. Tiberius listened in silence
as the argument raged. Finally, the adjournment was carried.

A dispute next arose between Gallus and the emperor. Gallus
moved that officials should be elected five years in advance, and
praetorships should immediately be earmarked for major-generals who
had not yet held them, the emperor nominating twelve candidates a
year. This proposal obviously had profound implications attacking the
whole unspoken premises of autocracy. But Tiberius replied as if the
suggestion actually envisaged an enlargement of his powers. He could not
presume, he said, to make so many selections and postponements—e-
ven the annual system easily caused offence, but its rebuffs were mitigated by hopes of an early reversal. Rejection for five years would indeed cause ill-feeling. 'So far ahead', protested Tiberius, 'a man'
s attitude, family connections, and resources are unpredictable. Even

尼乌斯·披索和盖乌斯·阿西尼乌斯·伽路斯之间在这个问题上发生了争执。提贝里乌斯曾经表示他要离开一段时间,但格涅乌斯·披索却认为这更加有理由让国事继续下去,元老和骑士在皇帝离开罗马时,为了国家的利益,应该承担起他们本身的职责。在表现独立不倚的精神方面后于披索一步的伽路斯却反对说,没有皇帝的出席和亲自监督就处理国事,这种做法是同罗马人民的尊严不相容的。因此,从意大利及各个行省前来的大群的访问者必须等待皇帝的到来。在辩论激烈进行的时候,提贝里乌斯在那里默默地听着,最后就决定休会了。

接下来,在伽路斯和皇帝之间又发生了一次争论。伽路斯建议选举应当把今后五年的高级官吏预先确定下来,[1] 而军团的将领如果还不是行政长官,那么就应当立刻把当选的行政长官这个职位授给他们,而皇帝每年都要任命十二名候补者。这一建议很显然是有着更深远的含义的,它实际上触犯了未被明言的皇帝的独裁大权的基础。不过提贝里乌斯在答复他的建议时,却把这种建议解释成是将自己的权力进行了扩张。他说,他无法假设由他一个人作出这么多的选举和延期的决定——甚至在每年一次的选举制度中,也是很容易对人产生冒犯的,虽然这种挫折会因很快又能当选的希望而减轻。第一次没有当选,就要再多等五年,这会让人产生怨恨。"而在面前这么长的一段时间里",提贝里乌斯反对说,"一个人的态度、他的家庭关系、他的财产等各方面会有

---

〔1〕 这种选举还是需要每年都举行,首先是确定今后五年的全部高级官吏职位,而在第二年的选举中,则要确定从当时起第五年的高级官吏,如此一直顺延下去。

when nomination is one year before office, men become haughty in the interval—what if they had five years of putting on airs? The proposal invalidates the laws establishing time-tables for canvassing, and seeking or holding office. It also virtually multiplies officials five-fold. "This speech had a popular ring. But its effect was to safeguard Tiber-rius' dominant position.

He also gave certain senators financial assistance. So it was curious that he dealt high-handedly with the appeal of Marcus Hortensius Hortalus, a young nobleman who was obviously poor. Hortalus was a grandson of the orator Quintus Hortensius, and had been persuaded by a grant of a million sesterces from Augustus to marry and have children, thus preventing the extinction of his famous family. When Hortalus' affairs were debated in the senate and his turn came to speak, his four sons were posted at the door of the hall. Hortalus turned towards the statue of Augustus, and also to that of Hortensius among the orators (for they were meeting on the Palatine). ' Senators,' he cried, ' these boys—you see how numerous they are—have been brought up at the emperor's wish, not mine. And he was right; for my ancestors deserved to have descendants! In these changed days, I myself have not been able to inherit or acquire money, or popularity, or even our family characteristic—eloquence. If my small resources neither disgraced me nor encumbered others, I was content. Then I married, because the emperor told me to. Behold the descendants of all those consuls and dictators! I say this in no competitive spirit but

什么变化都是难以预料的。甚至当任官只有一年时,人们在这短暂的期间就已经很骄傲了——如果连续五年任官,他们又会呈现出一种如何夸耀的神气呢?这一建议实际上破坏了为选举拉选票、为候选人的竞选活动以及为争取和保持高级官吏职位建立了适当的时间议程表的法律的效力。它在实质上也使高级官吏的人数增加到了五倍之多。"这番言论高唱着一种受欢迎的声调,但实际上提贝里乌斯的目的还是在于捍卫他的独裁大权。

此外,他又给了几名元老一些金钱方面的帮助。因此,下面的做法便更加使人感到惊讶了:原来他非常横暴地拒绝了一个显然是十分贫穷的年轻贵族玛尔库斯·霍尔田西乌斯·霍尔塔路斯的请求。霍尔塔路斯是演说家克温图斯·霍尔田西乌斯的孙子,已故的奥古斯都曾赐给他100万谢司特尔提乌斯,劝他结婚生子,由此防止了这一著名的家族遭受到灭亡的命运。当元老院辩论他的问题而且就要轮到他本人发言的时候,他的四个儿子正在会场的门口站着。霍尔塔路斯转向奥古斯都的像,又望着演说家的像中间那幅霍尔田西乌斯的像(因为元老院的会议是在皇宫举行的),然后才发言。"元老们",他高声说道,"这些孩子——请你们自己看看,是多么多啊——生养他们并不是我的本愿,而是因为皇帝希望我这样做。而且皇帝是对的,因为我的祖先也享有繁衍后世子孙的权力啊!在这个已经变化了的世界里,我不能继承也不能取得金钱、声望,甚至连我们家族生来就有的优点——口才,我也没有。只要我的微薄的资产能使我摆脱耻辱,能使我对他人不再是一种负担,那我便感到满足了。于是皇帝让我结婚,我就遵命而行了。现在就请你们看一看这些执政官和独裁者的子孙吧!我说这些话的目的并不是要和谁一争高低,而是要

to arouse your compassion. Under your glorious rule, Caesar, they will win whatever honours you choose to give. Meanwhile I beg you to save from destitution the great-grandsons of Quintus Hortensius, the prot g s of the deified Augustus. '

The senate received this so favourably that the emperor lost no time in objecting. ' If every poor man is to come here ', he said in effect, ' and start requesting money for his children, the applicants will never be satisfied and the nation's finances will collapse. When our ancestors authorized senators to digress sometimes from their subject-matter and raise matters of public importance when it was their turn to speak, this was not to enable us to promote our private interests and personal finances. Such attempts are invidious for senate and emperors alike, whether they grant the subsidies or refuse.

' Besides, this is not an appeal but an ultimatum—and an unforeseen and untimely one. A member interrupts a session—convened for other purposes—by rising and embarrassing the senate with a list of his children and their ages ! I am involved, and a determined attempt is made on the Treasury. But if we empty it by favouritism, we shall need criminal methods to fill it. Hortalus: the divine Augustus gave you money, but he did so spontaneously—and with no guarantee of a permanent supply. For permanent concessions would mean an end of all effort and all enterprise, because their incentives, fear and ambition, would be gone. Everyone would look irresponsibly elsewhere

唤起你们的同情。在你光辉的统治之下,恺撒啊,这些孩子将来会赢得你愿意授予他们的任何荣誉的。因此现在就请你救一救克温图斯·霍尔田西乌斯的曾孙和神圣的奥古斯都抚育起来的人们,使他们免受贫困之苦吧。"

元老院对他产生了如此同情的态度以致使提贝里乌斯不容迟延地就提出了反对的意见。"如果世界上所有的穷人都到这里来",他不容分辩地说,"并且为他们的孩子乞求金钱,我们是永远也满足不了这些乞求者的,而我们国家的财富也将会被耗尽。当我们的祖先规定,元老在发言的时候,有时可以离开他们的主要议题,而提出有利于公众的重要问题来的时候,这并不是为了让我们能在这里提出我们的私人利益和我们个人财富的问题。面对这样的企求,元老院和皇帝的确都同样感到左右为难,不知道是应该给还是不应该给这笔救济金。

"而且这根本不是什么恳求,而是一种最后通牒——一种出人意料的和不合时宜的要求。试想当大家正在开会讨论其他提议的时候,一个元老站起来打断了会议,列举自己孩子的数目和年龄,以此向元老院施加压力,这是多么荒谬!而且我本人也被卷了进去,他这种强硬的要求是指向国库的。但是,如果我们因为照顾别人而使国库空虚了,我们就不得不用罪恶的手段来把它重新填满了。霍尔塔路斯:圣奥古斯都给了你钱,但他这样做是出于自愿的,同时他也没有声明说,这种钱应当永远给下去。因为这种永远的许诺,将使人们不再注意勤勉,懒惰也就滋长起来,因为他们勤勉的动机、对未来生活的担忧和雄心壮志都失去了。如此,则在全国各地,每个人都会因为有别人能免除他们的困苦而毫无责任心,对于自己的事情即使是举手之劳也不肯为之——如

for relief, without lifting a finger for himself—a dead weight on the community. '

This sort of argument was applauded by those who habitually applaud emperors, right or wrong. But the majority received it in silence or with suppressed mutters. Tiberius perceived this. After a pause, he announced that, though he had given the applicant his answer, he would, if the senate approved, bestow two hundred thousand sesterces on each of Hortalus' male children. There were grateful acknowledgements. But Hortalus said nothing. Perhaps he was frightened. Or perhaps, even in his reduced circumstances, he preserved some inherited dignity. The house of the Hortensii continued to sink into abject destitution. But Tiberius showed it no further pity.

In the same year, the country was nearly plunged into the horrors of civil war by the daring of a single slave—only prompt measures prevented disaster. He was called Clemens. He had belonged to Agrippa Postumus, and when he heard of Augustus' death he had formed the very un-slave-like scheme of proceeding to the island of Planasia, rescuing Agrippa Postumus by force or a trick, and conducting him to the armies in Germany. The slowness of a cargo-boat upset his plans: when he arrived his master had already been assassinated. Then Clemens fell back on a more ambitious and desperate project. He stole Agrippa's ashes, and proceeded to Cosa on a promontory of Etruria, where he hid himself until his hair and beard had grown. For in age and appearance he resembled his master.

此,对于我们整个社会来说,就造成了一个极大的负担。"

诸如此类的话得到了一部分人的赞同,因为这些人对于皇帝的行为,已经习惯于趋奉,不管是对的还是错的。但大多数的人对他的话却保持沉默,只是暗地里小声嘀咕一些不同意的话。提贝里乌斯感觉到了这种冷淡的反应。因此在停了一会儿之后,他就宣称说虽然他已经对霍尔塔路斯作出了这样的答复,但如果元老院赞成的话,他是愿意给霍尔塔路斯的儿子每人以 20 万谢司特尔提乌斯的赠赐。其他元老对这一点表示了带着谢意的认可,但是霍尔塔路斯本人却一句话也没有说。这或许是因为他害怕了,或许是因为他即使在时运不济时,也仍旧坚持他从家族继承来的尊严。后来,霍尔田西乌斯一家越来越深地陷入到很不体面的贫困境地中,但是提贝里乌斯没有再进一步地表示对他们的同情。

就在这同一年里,由于一个奴隶的胆大妄为,国家差点儿就卷入了一场可怕的内战中,幸亏迅速采取了紧急的措施才使国家幸免于难。这个奴隶名叫克利门斯,他是阿格里帕·波斯图姆斯的奴隶,当他听到奥古斯都去世的消息时,在他脑子里就形成了一个完全不像是一个奴隶所能想到的计划,那就是立刻就去普拉纳西亚岛,用武力或是用计谋救出阿格里帕·波斯图姆斯,然后把他送到日耳曼的军队里去。运货船的迟到,打乱了他的计划:当他到达时他的主人已经被杀死了。于是克利门斯便想出了一个野心更大和更加冒险的计划。他偷走了阿格里帕的骨灰,并且航行到埃特路里亚沿岸海角上的一个叫科撒的城市躲了起来,在那里他一直待到他的胡须和头发都长长了的时候。这样就年纪和相貌而论,他就都很像他的主人了。

Then selected companions from his hiding-place spread the rumour that Agrippa Postumus was alive. It was first whispered secretly, as forbidden stories are. Then the news spread to every fool with cocked ears, every subversive malcontent. Clemens himself would appear in a town after dark. He never showed himself openly or stayed in one place; no sooner was he heard of than he was gone, to spread the rumour in a new place. Publicity and immobility bring out the truth too clearly—impostures need mystery and movement.

So the story that, by heaven's intervention, Agrippa Postumus was safe, spread throughout Italy. It had believers at Rome. Great crowds welcomed Clemens at Ostia—and met him secretly in the capital. Tiberius was in two minds whether to use the army to suppress his own slave or to let time eliminate the naive public credulity. At one moment he was alarmed, and felt that no measure should be omitted. At another, he would reflect ashamedly that all things were not terrifying.

Finally he entrusted the matter to Gaius Sallustius Crispus. The latter selected two of his own dependants—soldiers according to some accounts—and instructed them to approach Clemens and, pretending complicity, to offer him money and support, come what might. They carried out their instructions. Then, awaiting a night when Clemens was unguarded, they took an adequate detachment, bound and gagged him, and brought him to the palace. When Tiberius asked how he had made himself into Agrippa Postumus, Clemens is reported to have answered: 'As you made yourself into a Caesar.' He could not be

于是他从藏身的地方,挑选了一些和他共同进行这一阴谋的同伙,去四处散布谣言,说阿格里帕·波斯图姆斯还活着。起初,像那些禁止传播的消息那样,人们只是秘密地窃窃私语。不久之后,消息就传到了什么都相信的愚人和总想造反的不逞之徒那里。克利门斯本人则一到天黑下来的时候就在行省的各个城市中出现。他从来不公开地暴露自己,也绝不会在一个地方长久地待下去。在新的地方,不断地有人说,一会儿看到他出现了,一会儿又不见了,谣言在不断地传播着。公开露面和静止不动,会使真相大白,他的乔装是需要扑朔迷离的神秘和行踪不定地到处游动来掩盖的。

这样一来,阿格里帕·波斯图姆斯由于上天特殊的保佑而得救的消息就传遍了整个意大利。在罗马有很多相信这个消息的人。大批群众正在奥斯蒂亚等着欢迎克利门斯,首都的人们也在暗中准备迎接他。这时在提贝里乌斯心中两种思想在不断交锋,他不知道是该用军事力量镇压他自己的一个奴隶,还是应该让时间自然而然地消除国内人们的轻信。他时而感到惊恐,认为此事绝不可等闲视之;时而又感到羞愧,觉得这一切并不足畏惧。

最后,他把这件事交给了盖乌斯·撒路斯提乌斯·克利司普斯,克利司普斯又选出了自己的两名食客——也有人说是士兵,指令他们装作同谋者接近克利门斯,给他金钱,并且尽可能地给他以他所需要的支持。他们执行了这些命令。于是等到了一天夜里,当克利门斯身边没有人员警卫的时候,他们就带着一支足够的士兵分队跳过去将他绑住并堵塞住了他的嘴,然后押送到皇宫。提贝里乌斯问他,他是如何将自己变成阿格里帕·波斯图姆斯的,据说他是这样回答的:"这和你使你自己变成为恺撒的做法

compelled to reveal his associates. Tiberius dared not execute him publicly, but ordered him to be killed in a secluded part of the palace, and his body to be removed secretly. Many members of the emperor's household, and also senators and knights, were alleged to have advised and subsidized Clemens. But no inquiries followed.

At the end of this year an arch was dedicated near the temple of Saturn celebrating the recapture, under the leadership of Germanicus and the auspices of Tiberius, of the Eagles lost with Varus. Other dedications included a temple of Fors Fortuna near the Tiber—in the gardens which the dictator Caesar had left to the nation—and a shrine to the Julian house and statue of the divine Augustus at Bovillae.

In the following year the consuls were Gaius Caelius Rufus and Lucius Pomponius Flaccus. On 26 May Germanicus celebrated a triumph over the Cherusci, Chatti, Angrivarii, and all other German tribes this side of the Elbe. The procession included spoils, prisoners, and pictures of mountains, rivers, and battles. The war, which he had not been allowed to complete, was regarded as terminated. Attention was riveted on the splendid figure of the commander, accompanied by five children in his chariot. And yet there were unspoken misgivings. Men recalled that popularity had not helped his father Nero Drusus. And that great favourite his uncle, Marcellus, had been carried off at

一样。"无论怎样逼迫他也不肯把他的同谋者招供出来。提贝里乌斯不敢公开处决他,而是下令在宫中一个僻静的地方将他处死。他的尸体被秘密地运走了。虽然据说皇室中的许多人,以及骑士和元老都曾资助过克利门斯,给他出过主意,但是接下来并没有继续追究下去。

这一年年底,在撒图尔努斯神庙附近修建了一座凯旋门,用以纪念失去了的伐鲁斯军旗的重新夺回,因为这件事是在日耳曼尼库斯的领导之下并在提贝里乌斯的吉兆赞助之下实现的。其他的奉献物还包括在台伯河河畔为幸运之神修建的神庙——神庙是在独裁官恺撒留给罗马人民的花园里面,还有奉献给尤利乌斯家族的一座圣堂和在波维莱〔1〕这个地方的圣奥古斯都的一座雕像。

第二年,〔2〕担任执政官的是盖乌斯·凯里乌斯·路福斯和路奇乌斯·彭波尼乌斯·佛拉库斯。那一年的 5 月 26 日,日耳曼尼库斯庆祝他对凯路斯奇人、卡提伊人、安格里瓦人和易北河以西其他所有日耳曼部族的胜利。在游行的行列里有战利品,有俘虏,有山脉、河流和战役的图画。这场战争,既然不允许他完成,因此就当作已经结束了。统帅本人的高贵形象和跟他一起在马车里的五个孩子是人们注意的中心。但是在人们心中却隐藏着一种说不出的担忧。人们回想起,在民众中的崇高声望并没能帮得了他的父亲尼禄·杜路苏斯,而他那为众人所爱戴的舅父玛尔

---

〔1〕 传说波维莱这个地方是作为阿尔巴·隆伽的移民地而建立起来的,而当地人自己则声称阿尔巴·隆伽是优路斯家族的创始人建立起来的。

〔2〕 即公元 17 年,罗马建城 770 年。

an early age. The loves of the Romans seemed brief and ill-omened.

In the name of Germanicus, the emperor distributed three hundred sesterces a head to the population, and proposed to serve personally as his fellow-consul. But people did not believe his affection was sincere. Next he decided to find honourable excuses for the young man's elimination. Some pretexts were invented, others happened to be available. Archelaus had been king of Cappadocia for fifty years. He was hated by Tiberius, to whom, during the latter's residence at Rhodes, he had shown no attention. This omission had not been intended insultingly, but was prompted by associates of Augustus, because while Gaius Caesar was in the ascendant and on a mission to the East it had been considered inadvisable to be Tiberius' friend.

However, the house of the Caesars became extinct, and Tiberius reigned. He now made his mother write luring Archelaus to Rome. She did not conceal her son's resentment but held out hopes of indulgence if he came to beg for it. He came without delay, being either unsuspicious of treachery or afraid of suffering violence if he showed he anticipated it. The emperor's reception of Archelaus was unrelenting, and before long he was prosecuted before the senate. He was worn out, not by the charges—which were fictitious—but by distress and old

凯路斯也是很早便去世了。[1] 罗马人民所爱戴的人物似乎都是那么短命、不幸。

此外,皇帝又以日耳曼尼库斯的名义,发给每个罗马人300谢司特尔提乌斯,同时又提议让日耳曼尼库斯和他自己一同担任执政官。但是,罗马人民并不相信他的这种友爱会是真心实意的。接下来,他决定找一些冠冕堂皇的借口来除掉这个年轻人。他自己制造了一些借口,而其他的又恰是他可以利用的事件。阿尔凯拉乌斯做卡帕多奇亚的国王已有50年之久。由于提贝里乌斯居住在罗德岛时,阿尔凯拉乌斯根本不把他放在眼里,因此提贝里乌斯对他怀恨在心。对提贝里乌斯的这种忽视并不是由于对方故意无礼的对待,而是奥古斯都的亲信们促使其如此。因为当时盖乌斯·恺撒占据着优势,而且他正被派到东方来做大使,因此这时同提贝里乌斯表示友好绝对是一种很失策的行为。

但是,恺撒家族灭绝了,提贝里乌斯继承了王位。现在,他让他的母亲写信给阿尔凯拉乌斯,把他从卡帕多奇亚引诱到罗马来。她并不隐瞒她的儿子对阿尔凯拉乌斯的仇视,但她说如果他到这里来恳请的话,是有希望得到她的儿子的宽恕的。他毫不迟延,立刻就赶了来。这也许是由于他并不怀疑会有什么阴谋诡计,或者是由于害怕遭受武力攻击,如果他在事先已感到有武力行动的话。皇帝以冷酷无情的态度接待了阿尔凯拉乌斯,不久之后,阿尔凯拉乌斯又被人向元老院提出了起诉。使他垮掉的并不是那些控告——因为它们是毫无根据的,而是不幸的遭遇和衰老的年

---

〔1〕 玛尔凯路斯在公元前21年去世,当时才20岁。杜路苏斯在公元前9年去世,时年30岁。

age. Kings are not used even to equality, much less to subordination. So Archelaus died, by his own hand or the course of nature. His kingdom was turned into a province; and the emperor announced that its revenue enabled him to reduce the I per cent auction tax, which was fixed at 1/2 per cent for the future.

At about the same time Commagene and Amanus were unsettled by the deaths of their dependent kings, Antiochus Epiphanes III and Philopator II respectively. Royal rule still had some supporters, but most of the inhabitants wanted annexation by Rome. Other problems had arisen in Syria and Judaea, where the provincials were finding their financial burdens oppressive and petitioning for a reduction of direct taxation.

These developments, and the Armenian situation mentioned above, were brought before the senate by Tiberius. The eastern troubles, he said, could only be put right by the wisdom of Germanicus. For he himself, he said, was of advancing years, whereas Drusus was not yet sufficiently mature. So the senate entrusted the overseas provinces to Germanicus, with powers superior (wherever he might go) to those of all governors of imperial and senatorial provinces alike. But Tiberius had removed Syria's imperial governor Quintus Caccilius Metellus Creticus Silanus (who had betrothed his daughter to Germanicus' eldest son, Nero Caesar), replacing him by Cnaeus Calpurnius Piso. This ferocious, insubordinate man inherited his violent character from his father (of the same name), who during the civil war had vigorously helped the revived Republican party in Africa against Julius Caesar, and then supported Brutus and Cassius. Nevertheless

龄。国王是不能容忍别人和自己处于平等地位的,当然更不用说屈辱了。因此,阿尔凯拉乌斯就死了,他可能是自杀的,也可能是自然老死的。他死之后,他的王国就被变成了一个行省,皇帝宣称从这里所取得的收入可以使他减轻 1% 的贩卖税,将来要把它规定为 0.5% 。

　　大约就在这个时候,孔玛盖尼和阿马努斯由于两国国王,即安提奥库斯·埃皮普哈尼斯三世和庇洛帕托尔二世的死,发生了混乱。大多数的人都想合并入罗马,只有少数的人还希望保持王国的体制。叙利亚和犹太两行省也发生了其他问题,那里的人们感到他们的赋税负担太重了,他们请求减轻赋税。

　　这些事情的发展以及如上所述的亚美尼亚发生的事件,提贝里乌斯都向元老院做了汇报。关于东方的骚乱,他还说,只有日耳曼尼库斯的智慧才能解决。他说因为他本人年纪已经老了,而杜路苏斯又还不够成熟。[1] 于是元老院便发布命令,把海外诸行省委托给日耳曼尼库斯,并给予他超越于所有官员的权力,(他不管到什么地方去)都有权节制元老院所委派或皇帝所任命的地方长官。不过提贝里乌斯却把克温图斯·凯奇利乌斯·米提尔乌斯·克列提库斯·西拉努斯调离了叙利亚,因为他将自己的女儿西拉努斯许配给了日耳曼尼库斯的长子尼禄·恺撒。接替他这一职位的是格涅乌斯·卡尔普尔尼乌斯·披索。这个凶猛的、一点都不驯顺的人物从他父亲(他们的名字相同)那里继承了一种暴烈的性格。这个老披索在内战时期曾极其有力地帮助过在阿非利加复活起来的共和派以反对尤利乌斯·恺撒,后来又支持布鲁

---

〔1〕　这时提贝里乌斯是 59 岁,日耳曼尼库斯 31 岁,杜路苏斯 29 岁。

he had been allowed to return to Rome; at first he had not sought office, but finally, when Augustus personally solicited him to take the consulship, he accepted it. In addition to his father's spirit, Piso had his wife Plancina's lineage and wealth to spur him on. He grudgingly allowed Tiberius first place, but looked down on Tiberius' children as far beneath him.

Piso was certain that the purpose of his Syrian appointment was the repression of Germanicus' ambitions. According to one view, he received secret instructions from Tiberius to that effect. Plancina certainly received advice from the Augusta, whose feminine jealousy was set on persecuting Agrippina. For the court was disunited, split by unspoken partisanships for Drusus or Germanicus. Tiberius supported Drusus, as the son of his own blood. But the popularity of Germanicus had increased, partly owing to his uncle's hostility, and partly because his mother's family gave him precedence. He could point to Augustus as great-uncle and Antony as grandfather, whereas Drusus was great-grandson of a knight, Titus Pomponius Atticus, who hardly added lustre to the Claudian genealogy. Besides, Ger-

图斯和卡西乌斯,但是以后他得到允许返回了罗马。一开始他不去请求任何官职,但是最后奥古斯都诚恳地邀请他出来做执政官,他才接受了这一职位。然而,除了从父亲那里继承来的性格之外,披索的妻子普朗奇娜也拥有高贵的身世和大量的财富,这也助长了他的脾气。他很勉强地允许提贝里乌斯占了先,但是他认为提贝里乌斯的孩子们比自己的身份是远远为低的。

披索当然知道,他这次被任命主管叙利亚的目的,是为了抑制日耳曼尼库斯的野心。有一种看法认为,他在这方面是从提贝里乌斯那里得到过秘密指令的。普朗奇娜也毫无疑问曾从奥古斯塔那里接受过指示,奥古斯塔是由于妇女的妒忌而一心想迫害阿格里披娜的。因为在宫廷里面的人们,虽然不公开说,但实际上是分成拥护日耳曼尼库斯和拥护杜路苏斯两派的。提贝里乌斯支持杜路苏斯,因为这是他的亲生儿子。而日耳曼尼库斯却有着很高的声望,这一部分原因是由于他的叔父对他的敌意,反而提高了他在人们中的声望,一部分原因是由于他的母亲一家的显赫地位给了他很大的优势。从母系来说,奥古斯都是他的外舅祖父,安东尼是他的外祖父。然而另一方面,杜路苏斯的外曾祖父辈却只是一个普通骑士,他的名字叫提督斯·彭波尼乌斯·阿提库斯,[1]这个人几乎是不能给克劳狄乌斯家族的谱系增加任何光彩的。另外,日耳曼尼库斯的妻子阿格里披娜

---

〔1〕 他是西塞罗的朋友和信使。阿提库斯的女儿彭波尼娅或者叫凯奇利娅·阿提卡,是阿格里帕的第一个妻子,她是杜路苏斯的母亲维普撒尼娅的母亲。阿格里帕的第二任妻子是玛尔塞拉一世,第三任妻子是优利娅三世。

manicus' wife Agrippina was more distinguished than Drusus' wife Livilla—and had more children. However, the brothers were good friends, unperturbed by the rivalries around them.

Drusus was now sent to Illyricum, to be introduced to army life-and win favour among the troops. Tiberius also considered that the camp would be better for him than his present frivolous life of juvenile extravagance in Rome. Besides, he himself would feel safer with both his sons commanding armies.

But the pretext for Drusus' departure was an appeal by the Suebi for help against the Cherusci. For now that the Romans had gone and there was no external threat, national custom and rivalry had turned the Germans against one another. The two nations were well matched in strength, and their leaders equally capable. But the Suebi did not like the royal title of their leader Maroboduus, whereas Arminius was popular as champion of freedom. So in addition to his old soldiers—the Cherusci and their allies—two Suebian tribes, the Semnones and Langobardi, from the kingdom of Maroboduus also entered the war on Arminius' side. These additions looked like turning the scale. However, Inguiomerus and a group of his followers deserted to the Suebi, merely because the old man was too proud to serve

在声誉方面也超过了杜路苏斯的妻子利维拉[1]，而且阿格里披娜还生了更多的孩子。尽管如此，他们兄弟二人却是十分要好的朋友，他们的情谊也并没有受到周围亲属的各种敌对态度的影响。

现在，杜路苏斯也被派到了伊里利库姆去，去熟悉军队的生活——目的是让他取得军队的好感。同时提贝里乌斯认为，年轻人在罗马的豪华奢侈养成了他轻浮的生活习惯，到军队里去会更有利于他的成长。除此之外，让他的两个儿子都去指挥军队，他本人也会觉得更加安全些。

不过，他这样做的借口却是苏埃比人要求他给予帮助，以对付凯路斯奇人。原来现在既然罗马人已经撤走，就已经没有了外来的威胁，这样一来，各自遵守本国的风俗习惯并且为了争夺领导地位而反目的部族，就互相动起武来了。这两个部族的实力可算是旗鼓相当，而它们的领袖的才能也可说是棋逢对手。不过苏埃比人并不喜欢他们的领袖的玛洛波都斯国王的称号，而阿尔米尼乌斯作为一个拥护自由的人却在国内享有很高的声望。结果不仅是阿尔米尼乌斯的老兵，即凯路斯奇人和他们的联盟者参加了战斗，就是两个苏埃比人的部族谢姆诺尼斯和朗哥巴狄人也叛离了他们的玛洛波都斯王国，也加入到了阿尔米尼乌斯这一边的战斗中。这一投奔过来的行动看起来好像是改变了双方的军事规模，使阿尔米尼乌斯这一方面确保了优势地位。可是音吉奥美路斯和他手下的一队人却又投到苏埃比人那边去了，他的这一行动的唯一理由仅仅是作为一位老年人，他太骄傲自大了，以致不愿

---

[1] 日耳曼尼库斯和克劳狄乌斯的姐妹，杜路苏斯的妻子，后来把杜路苏斯毒死了。

under his young nephew.

Each army had high hopes as it drew up for battle. The old German unsystematic battle-order and chaotic charges were things of the past. Their long wars against Rome had taught them to follow the standards, keep troops in reserve, and obey commands. Arminius rode round inspecting his whole army. He reminded each unit, as he came to it, that freedom was back again, that they had annihilated Roman armies—that many of his men were actually carrying Roman spoils and spears. He denounced Maroboduus as a runaway who, lurking in the Hercynian forest without a single fight, had begged Rome for peace with presents and deputations. ' He is a traitor, an imperial agent!' cried Arminius. ' Eject him as fiercely as you killed Varus. Remember all those battles and their result—the expulsion of the Romans. That shows who won ! '

Maroboduus too spoke, praising himself and reviling the enemy. Grasping Inguiomerus by the hand, he credited him with all the glory of the Cherusci—the brain behind their successes. Arminius, he said, was a senseless inexperienced man who took the credit due to others because he had treacherously trapped three straggling divisions and an unsuspecting commander, an action disastrous to Germany and dishonourable to Arminius himself, since his wife and son were still

意服从他的年轻侄子的统治。

当两军都整队摆开战斗阵势准备战斗时,双方的军队都情绪高昂。过去日耳曼人作战时的那种不成体统的战斗秩序和混乱的战斗都已经成为过去了。对罗马进行的长期的战争,已经教会了他们听从军旗的指挥作战,教会了他们配备后备部队来接应主力部队,并遵守将领们发出的号令。阿尔米尼乌斯骑马在周围走动以巡视全军,当他在走近每一队的士兵时,他都提醒他们说,他们已经恢复了自由了,他们曾歼灭过罗马的军团,而且实际上他的许多军人们的手中还拿着从罗马战死者手中取得的战利品和投枪呢。他还公然抨击说,玛洛波都斯是一个逃兵,他一次仗都不打,却躲在赫尔库尼亚森林里,[1]还派使节带着厚礼到罗马那里去乞求和平。"他是一个祖国的叛徒,是罗马皇帝的走狗!"阿尔米尼乌斯叫喊道,"就像你们当年勇猛地杀死伐鲁斯那样,现在就毫不留情地把他驱逐出去吧。请记住过去所有的那些战争以及这些战争的结果吧——罗马人最后还是被驱逐出去了。这些结果都已经明显地表明了,谁将在战场上取得胜利!"

玛洛波都斯也发表了演说。他称赞自己,咒骂敌人。他拉着音吉奥美路斯的手,说他相信他才是真正代表了凯路斯奇人的全部荣誉,正是由于他的聪明才智,凯路斯奇人才取得了他们过去的一切成功。他说,阿尔米尼乌斯是个没有头脑没有经验的人,他背信弃义地给三个迷乱的军团和对他毫无疑心的统帅设下了圈套,这才窃取到了别人的名誉。他的这一行动给日耳曼人带来的是灾难,而对阿尔米尼乌斯本人来说也是可耻的,因为他的妻子和

---

〔1〕 即波希米亚。

in slavery. 'But I myself', he continued, 'when attacked by twelve divisions under Tiberius, maintained German honour unblemished. We parted on equal terms ! As regards Rome we have the choice, I am proud to say, between war with our resources intact, and peace without oppression. '

Besides these speeches, the armies had motives of their own to excite them. The Cherusci had the glorious past to fight for, and their new allies, the Langobardi, their freshly acquired freedom from the Suebi. Their enemy's aim was expansion. Never had a result been so unpredictable. Both right wings were routed. However, instead of renewing the battle, as was expected, Maroboduus transferred his camp to the hills. This showed he was beaten. Then, weakened by a series of desertions, he retreated to the territory of the Marcomanni and sent a delegation to Tiberius requesting help. The answer was that, since he had not helped Rome against the Cherusci, he was not justified in claiming Roman support against them. However Drusus, as I have said, was sent to establish peaceful conditions.

In the same year twelve famous cities in the province of Asia were

儿子到现在还在受着奴役呢。"但是我本人",他继续说道,"当我受到提贝里乌斯所率领的 12 个军团的进攻时,我坚持日耳曼的尊严并没有玷污我们的荣誉。不久我们双方便在打成平手的情况下各自收兵了。[1] 在对待罗马的问题上,我们可以自由地选择,我也可以自豪地宣布,我们既可以用自己充足的军事力量与其作战,还可以轻松地同它缔结和约。"

　　除了受到演说的鼓动之外,军队的士兵们也都各有自己的作战动机激励着自己。凯路斯奇人是为他们过去的光荣和现在的联合而战斗,朗哥巴狄人则是为他们不久之前刚刚从苏埃比那里争取到的自由而战斗的。而他们的敌人作战的目的就是为了扩张国土。从来都没有一场战争的结果是这样不可预料的。双方的右翼全都被击溃了。人们认为战斗会重新开始,但是这时玛洛波都斯却把营地移转到小山上。这表明他已经被击败了。士兵的临阵脱逃逐渐削弱了他的实力,于是他便退到玛尔科曼尼人[2]的地区中去,并且派出一个使团到提贝里乌斯那里去请求援助。但是他所得到的回答却是,因为他不曾帮助过罗马人对付凯路斯奇人,因此现在在他也不应该来请求罗马人帮助他对凯路斯奇人作战。虽然如此,就如上面我已经说过的那样,杜路苏斯还是被派了出去,安排双方缔和事宜。

　　就在这一年,亚细亚行省的 12 座著名的城市被一次地震给摧毁

---

　　〔1〕 这里指公元 6 年的事件,玛洛波斯在罗马的占绝对优势的兵力的进攻下幸存了下来,因为提贝里乌斯必须撤回去平定潘诺尼亚和达尔马提亚的更大的动乱,当时意大利本土已受到了威胁。
　　〔2〕 他们是一个强大的部落,但是在作战中被日耳曼尼库斯的父亲从美因河畔赶到波希米亚。他们则把凯尔特人从波希米亚赶走。

overwhelmed by an earthquake. Its occurrence at night increased the surprise and destruction. Open ground—the usual refuge on such occasions—afforded no escape, because the earth parted and swallowed the fugitives. There are stories of big mountains subsiding, of flat ground rising high in the air, of conflagrations bursting out among the debris. Sardis suffered worst and attracted most sympathy. Tiberius promised it ten million sesterces and remitted all taxation by the Treasury or its imperially controlled branches for five years. Magnesia-by-Sipylus came next, in damage and compensation. Exemptions from direct taxation were also authorized for Temnus, Philadelphia, Aegeae, Apollonis, Mostene (the Macedonian Hyrcanians), Hierocaesarea, Myrina, Cyme, and Tmolus. It was decided to send a senatorial inspector to rehabilitate the sufferers. The choice fell on an ex-praetor, Marcus Aletius. The governor of Asia was a former consul, so the embarrassments of rivalry between equals were avoided.

Tiberius supplemented this impressive official generosity by an e-qually welcome private benefaction. The wealthy Aemilia Musa died intestate, and her property was claimed for the emperor. But he transferred it to Marcus Aemilius Lepidus (IV), with whose house she was apparently connected. Again, when a rich member of the order of knights named Pantuleius died, Tiberius was named as one of the

了。地震是在夜里发生的,所以也就更增加了灾害来临的突然性,而且造成的损害也更加惨重。通常在遇到地震时,人们可以赶忙逃到平地上去,但这次他们却无处可逃。因为大地裂开了,吞没了那些逃跑的人。据记载,大山沉陷,平原高高隆起在空中,大火喷射,周围是一片残片、废墟。撒尔迪斯人受害最重,因而也就得到最大的同情。提贝里乌斯答应赐给他们 1000 万谢司特尔提乌斯,并且在五年间免除了他们向国家以及向皇室缴纳的租税。西皮路斯河畔的玛格涅喜人在损失方面以及所得的补偿都占第二位。同样地得到了赋税的豁免的,还有铁姆尼人、披拉德尔佩涅斯人、埃吉亚提斯人、阿波洛尼迪人和(莫司提尼和叙尔卡尼亚的)马其顿人,以及希耶洛恺撒利亚、米利纳、库美和特莫路斯诸城市[1]并且决定由元老院派一名要员去视察当地的情况,救济他们所遭受的苦难。这一次选择的结果是落到了一位前任的行政长官玛尔库斯·阿泰乌斯身上。因为亚细亚的总督是一位前任的执政官,所以这样做是为了避免在两位身份相等的官吏之间会因相互竞争而产生麻烦。

提贝里乌斯除了代表国家所作出的给人以深刻印象的慷慨作风之外,他在私人方面也同样表现出了受人欢迎的善行。一位很有钱的妇人埃米里娅·姆撒死的时候没有立下遗嘱,按照规定她的财产便归皇帝所有。但是他却把这笔钱转赠给了玛尔库斯·埃米里乌斯·列庇都斯(四世),因为这个妇人很显然属于列庇都斯家族。又一次,一位富有的名字叫庞图列乌斯的罗马骑士,他死时

---

〔1〕 在这 12 个城市当中,铁姆诺斯、埃吉阿伊、米利纳和库美是在埃奥利斯,其他城市是在吕地亚内地。

legatees; but he handed over the whole property on finding that an earlier and evidently authentic will had named Marcus Servilius Nonianus (I) sole heir. Moreover, he refused to accept any bequests which he had not earned by friendship. He had no truck with strangers, or with people who named the emperor their heir because they had quarrelled with others.

While relieving honourable and unoffending poverty, he removed from the senate (or allowed to resign) persons whose means had vanished through extravagance or misbehaviour, namely Vibidius Virro, Marius Nepos, Appius Appianus, Cornelius Sulla, and Quintus Vitellius.

In this period, too, he dedicated certain temples which Augustus had begun to restore when they had decayed or been burnt down. These were the temples of Liber, Libera, and Ceres near the Circus Maximus (vowed by Aulus Postumius Tubertus and Marcus Poblicius Malleolus when they were aediles); and of Janus (built in the vegetable market by Gaius Duilius, who gained the first Roman naval victory—

在遗嘱中指定把他的遗产的一部分给予皇帝,但是皇帝却把他的全部财产都给了玛尔库斯·塞尔维里乌斯·诺尼亚努斯(一世),因为他发现,在更早的和显然是真实确凿的一份遗嘱上提出了他的名字。更何况除非他和死者有交情,他是不肯接受任何遗赠的。对于那些陌生的人,以及那些因为和别人不合才指定他为遗产继承人的那些人,他是不准备和他们打交道的。

他一方面使一些清白的元老免除了光荣的贫困,另一方面却又免掉了一些元老的职务(或是同意了他们的辞职),因为这些人生活奢侈腐化,行为不检。他们是维比狄乌斯·维尔罗、马利乌斯·涅波斯、阿庇乌斯·阿庇亚努斯、科尔涅里乌斯·苏拉和克温图斯·维提里乌斯。

就在这一时期,他又奉献了一些神庙,这些神庙原来由于年深日久或因火灾而毁坏,[1]当时奥古斯都就已经开始修复。其中有在马克西姆斯大跑马场附近献给里倍尔、里倍拉和凯列司的一座神庙[2](它是由奥路斯·波司图米乌斯·吐波尔图斯和玛尔库斯·普布利奇乌斯·玛列奥路斯在做行政长官时发愿修建的);[3]雅努斯神庙(它是由盖乌斯·杜伊里乌斯在菜市场修建的,[4]杜伊里乌斯使罗马第一次在海上战胜了迦太基人并且为此得到

---

〔1〕 这里所说的火灾可能是指公元前 31 年的一次,起因据说是由于征收财产税而引起的被释奴隶的一次暴动。

〔2〕 即狄奥尼西乌斯、佩尔赛波妮和戴美特尔。据说这是在列吉路斯湖一役(公元前 496 年)前由波司图米乌斯发愿修建的,三年之后才建成。

〔3〕 公元前 240 年左右。

〔4〕 在卡庇托里努斯山和台伯河之间,杜伊里乌斯统率下的罗马舰队的第一次胜利是在西西里的米莱附近海面上取得的(公元前 260 年),船头柱就是纪念这次胜利的。

over the Carthaginians—and won a Triumph for it). The temple of Hope, which Aulus Atilius Calatinus had vowed in the same war, was consecrated by Germanicus.

Meanwhile, the treason law was maturing. Appuleia Varilla was charged under it for speaking insultingly about the divine Augustus (whose sister was her aunt), as well as about Tiberius and his mother, and for committing adultery. The latter offence was ruled to be a matter for the Julian adultery law. As regards the treason, Tiberius insisted on a distinction between disrespectful remarks about Augustus — for which she should be condemned—and about himself, on which he desired no inquiry to be held. Asked by the consul what his ruling was about Appuleia's alleged slanders against his mother, he did not reply. But at the next meeting of the senate he requested in his mother's name also that no words uttered against her should in any circumstances be made the subject of a charge. He released Appuleia from liability under the treason law. For her adultery he deprecated the severer penalty, but recommended that according to traditional practice her relatives should remove her two hundred miles from Rome. Her lover, Manlius by name, was banned from Italy and Africa.

了海战凯旋的荣誉);希望神庙,它是奥路斯·阿提里乌斯·卡拉提努斯[1]在同一战争期间许愿修建的,它是日耳曼尼库斯奉献给神明的。

这时,大逆法开始发挥了作用;(奥古斯都的姊妹的外甥女)阿普列娅·瓦莉拉[2]被人根据大逆法告发,因为她对圣奥古斯都,还有提贝里乌斯和他的母亲都讲了侮辱性的话,此外她还被指控与人通奸。根据规定,通奸罪是要按照尤利乌斯法[3]来处理的。至于大逆罪,皇帝则坚持说应当区别对待,如果她对奥古斯都发表了一些不敬的言论,那就应当治罪;如果是针对他本人说了些什么话,那他是不希望再作什么调查的。执政官问他,据说阿普列娅也诽谤过他的母亲,对于这件事他如何答复,他没有回答。但是在元老院下一次集会的时候,他代表他的母亲提出要求,对她进行过诽谤的人,在任何情况下都无须受到法律的追究。这样他就免除了阿普列娅免可能受到的大逆罪的惩罚。在通奸方面,他也不主张对她进行严厉的惩罚,[4]不过他建议根据传统的惯例,她的亲属们应该将她迁移到离罗马200英里之外的一个地方去。她的情夫曼里乌斯则被禁止居住在意大利或阿非利加[5]。

---

〔1〕 是公元前258年、254年的执政官,公元前249年的独裁官。

〔2〕 塞克斯图斯·阿普列伊乌斯和玛尔塞拉的女儿,玛尔塞拉的母亲是奥古斯都的姐姐奥克塔维娅。

〔3〕 这种优利斯法是奥古斯都在公元前18年制定的惩治通奸的一项措施。

〔4〕 即没收她的一半嫁妆和她的1/3的财产,并把她放逐到一个岛上去。

〔5〕 应剥夺他的一半财产,并且放逐到同阿普列娅不同的另一个岛上去。

When the praetor Vipstanus Gallus died, the appointment of his substitute was disputed. Germanicus and Drusus, who were still both at Rome, supported Decimus Haterius Agrippa, who was related to Germanicus. However, it was strongly urged—and was legally correct—that the number of the candidates' children should be the decisive factor. Tiberius enjoyed seeing the senate divided between his sons and the law. Naturally the law lost, but it took time and the majority was small; and after all, that is how laws had been overruled even when they still meant something.

In the same year war broke out in the province of Africa, under a Numidian leader called Tacfarinas. He had deserted from service as a Roman auxiliary. His first followers were vagabonds and marauders who came for loot. Then he organized them into army units and formations, and was finally recognized as the chief, no longer of an undisciplined gang, but of the Musulamian people—a powerful nomad tribe on the edge of the African desert. Taking up arms, they brought in the neighbouring Mauretanians, under their leader Mazippa. Their army was in two parts. Tacfarinas retained in camp an lite force equipped in Roman fashion, which he instructed in discipline and obedience; while Mazippa's light-armed troops burnt, killed, and intimidated. The substantial tribe of the Cinithii came over to the rebels.

At this stage Marcus Furius Camillus, governor of Africa, confronted Tacfarinas with his Roman brigade and its auxiliaries. Though

一位名叫维普斯塔努斯·伽路斯的行政长官去世以后,在继任人选方面发生了意见分歧。当时还在罗马的日耳曼尼库斯和杜路苏斯两个人都支持德奇穆斯·哈提里乌斯·阿格里帕,这个人是日耳曼尼库斯的一个亲戚。另一方面,又有许多人坚决主张,而且还有法律上的充足的依据,认为候补者的孩子的数目应是起决定作用的因素。提贝里乌斯很高兴看到元老院分成拥护他的儿子和拥护法律的两派的局面。拥护法律的一派自然是遭到了失败。不过另一派也是花了很长时间才取得了胜利,而且表决时在票数方面也只占很小的优势。这件事清楚地表明了法律甚至在其已经生效以后,是以什么样的方式被毁弃的!

就在同一年,阿非利加行省在努米地亚人的领袖,一个名叫塔克法里那斯的人的带领下爆发了一场战争。他曾在罗马的辅助军队中服过役,后来逃跑了。他的第一批追随者是一群流浪汉和劫匪。后来,他把这些人像军队那样组成了一支支的队伍。最后,他就被承认是穆苏拉米人的领袖,而不是一个无组织无纪律的团伙的头目了——穆苏拉米是一个居住在阿非利加沙漠边缘地带的强大的游牧部族。他们拿起武器,并使邻近的玛乌列塔尼亚人也参加了他们的战斗。玛乌列塔尼亚人的领袖的名字是玛吉帕。联盟的军队分成两部分,塔克法里那斯把一支按照罗马方式装备起来的精锐部队留在营地,在那里训练他们的纪律性和服从性;另一方面,玛吉帕则率领一队轻武装的士兵到处进行烧杀和恐吓等活动。一个相当大的奇尼提人的部族也参加到叛乱中来。

这时,阿非利加行省的总督玛尔库斯·福利乌斯·卡米路斯把他的罗马军团士兵和全部辅助军队都集合了起来,对抗塔克法

this was a small army compared to the masses of Numidians and Mauretanians, his chief concern was to prevent the enemy from cautiously evading battle. Actually, the Africans were optimistic-and this lured them into an unsuccessful engagement. The Roman brigade was posted in the centre, the auxiliary infantry battalions and two cavalry regiments on the wings. Tacfarinas accepted the challenge, and the Numidians were routed. After centuries the Furian family had won military glory again. For ever since the great Marcus' to whom Rome had owed its revival, and his son Lucius, success in the field had passed to other families; and the present commander was believed to be no general. So Tiberius was all the readier to praise his victory in the senate. Camillus was voted an honorary Triumph—and lived so unassumingly that he survived it.

里那斯。尽管与努米地亚人和玛乌列塔尼亚人的大批人马相比，这支军队是一支非常小的部队，但是总督主要担心的情况却是，敌人会因害怕而回避同他进行正式的武装较量。事实上，阿非利加人是乐观的，但这却诱使他们投入了一场没有获得成功希望的交战。罗马的军队部署在中央，辅助的步兵中队和两个骑兵中队则部署在两翼。塔克法里那斯接受了挑战，而且努米地亚人被赶走了。几个世纪以后，福利乌斯家族又再一次获得了军事的荣誉。因为自从罗马的伟大复兴者玛尔库斯[1]和他的儿子路奇乌斯那时以来，在指挥战争中取得军事胜利的荣誉便转到其他家族的身上去了。人们认为现在的指挥者卡米路斯并不是一位军人。因此提贝里乌斯就更加愿意在元老院称颂他的胜利了。卡米路斯被授予了凯旋的标记，卡米路斯不会装腔作势，因此坦然接受下来。

---

〔1〕 在公元前 387 年，他打败了高卢人，被人习惯地称为"解放者"，后来又被称作罗马的重建者。他的儿子和孙子都叫路奇乌斯。

CHAPTER 5

The Death of Germanicus

In the following year Tiberius was consul for the third time, Germanicus for the second. The latter assumed office at Nicopolis in the province of Achaia, which he had reached along the Adriatic coast after visiting his brother Drusus, then stationed in Dalmatia. Since both the Adriatic and the Ionian seas had been stormy, he spent a few days at Nicopolis overhauling the fleet. He employed this opportunity to visit the gulf famous for the victory of Actium, and its spoils dedicated by Augustus, and Antony's camp. The place brought memories of his ancestors, for (as I have pointed out) he was the grand-nephew of Augustus, and the grandson of Antony. Here his imagination could re-enact mighty triumphs and mighty tragedies.

第五章　日耳曼尼库斯之死

在接下来的一年里,[1]提贝里乌斯第三次担任执政官,日耳曼尼库斯第二次担任执政官。不过日耳曼尼库斯是在阿凯亚行省的一个城市尼科波利斯[2]就职的,他是在看望了当时在达尔马提亚的他的兄弟杜路苏斯之后,才沿着伊里利亚的海岸到达了尼科波利斯的。由于在亚得里亚海以及后来在爱奥尼亚海一路上都有风暴,所以他就在尼科波利斯停留了几天,整顿自己的舰队。利用这个机会,他参拜了以阿克提乌姆一役的胜利而名垂千古的海湾,以及奥古斯都献给神的战利品和安托尼乌斯的营地,[3]以缅怀先人的业绩。这个地方唤起了他对祖先的回忆,(正如我曾经指出的)奥古斯都是他的外舅祖父,安东尼则是他的外祖父。在这里,过去所发生的灾难和胜利的伟大场面又一幕幕在他脑海中重新上演。

---

〔1〕　指公元18年,当时是罗马建城771年。以下部分叙述的中心事件是日耳曼尼库斯之死。

〔2〕　奥古斯都为纪念阿克提乌姆之役而在他的营地的原址上建立起来的移民地,在今阿尔塔湾入口处的北岸。人们在普列维扎—维奇亚附近曾发现这一城市的废墟。

〔3〕　在海湾南岸的阿克提乌姆。

Then he visited Athens, contenting himself with one official attendant, out of regard for our treaty of alliance with that ancient city. The Greeks received him with highly elaborate compliments, and flattery all the more impressive for their emphasis on the bygone deeds and words of their own compatriots. Next, after crossing by way of Euboca to Lesbos (where Agrippina gave birth to her last child Julia Livilla), he skirted the coast of the Asian province, and after calling at the Thracian ports of Perinthus and Byzantium passed into the Bosphorus and the Black Sea. He visited famous historical sites enthusiastically. He also worked to rehabilitate these provinces, exhausted as they were from internal disputes and misgovernment. On the way back, he tried to visit the religious centre of Samothrace, but northerly winds drove him off. However, he inspected Troy's venerable reminders of fortune's vicissitudes and Rome's origins. Then, coasting again along the Asian province, he put in at Colophon, to consult the oracle of Apollo at Clarus. Here there is no priestess, as at Delphi, but a male priest, chosen from certain families (usually from Miletus). He is told the number and names (only) of his consultants, and then descends into a cave, drinks water from a sacred spring, and —though generally illiterate and ignorant of metre—produces a set of verses on whatever subject the visitor has in mind. Rumour had it

随后他又访问了雅典。出于对我们和这一古老名城所缔结的盟约的敬意,他身旁只带了一名侍从。[1] 希腊人以崇高的庆典礼仪接待了他,为使他们的奉承给他留下更深的印象,他们特别强调了他们自己的同胞的事业和言论。接下来,他离开雅典,经过优卑亚,然后渡海到了列斯波司(在那里,阿格里披娜最后一次分娩时生了优利娅·利维拉)。[2] 他巡视了亚细亚行省的沿海地带,访问了佩林图斯和拜占庭城市的港口色雷斯,随后便穿过博斯普鲁斯海峡进入了黑海。他充满热情地参观了那些著名的历史古迹,同时又努力设法对这些因内战或暴政而残破不堪的行省给予救助。在回来的路上,他想去参观撒莫色雷斯的宗教中心,[3] 但是他遇到的北风使他无法靠岸。于是他就到特洛伊去游历,在那里参观了那些足以证明变幻无常的命运和罗马的源流的远古遗迹。然后再度巡视了亚细亚行省的沿岸并在科罗彭登陆,以便在克拉路斯向阿波罗请示神谕。这里不同于戴尔波伊,没有女祭司,传达神谕的是一个男祭司,他是从一些家族中(通常都是米利都的家族中)选拔出来的。这个祭司只问一下前来请示神谕的人的人数和名字,然后就钻到一个地穴里去,喝圣泉的水,虽然这个人一般来说既不识字也不识数,但是却能针对每个请示神谕的人心里想的问题用一组诗作出答复。谣传说克拉路斯的神谕曾经预言了日

---

〔1〕 按照惯例,罗马高级官吏在进入雅典这样的自由城市时,是不应当有持束棒的侍从的。

〔2〕 公元33年,优利娅·利维拉和玛尔库斯·维尼奇乌斯结婚,4年后被她的兄弟卡里古拉放逐,虽然被她的叔父克劳狄乌斯召回,但后来却又因美撒里娜的教唆以所谓同塞内加私通的罪名被处死。

〔3〕 指卡比里人的祭仪。

that the oracle of Clarus (in the cryptic fashion of oracles) foretold Germanicus' early death.

Cnaeus Calpurnius Piso was in a hurry to execute his designs. His impact on the Athenians was alarmingly violent. In a speech savagely attacking them, he criticized Germanicus (without naming him) for excessive compliments, incompatible with Roman dignity, to a people whom he called Athenians no longer (since successive catastrophes had exterminated them), but the dregs of the earth: allies of Mithridates VI of Pontus against Sulla, of Antony against the divine Augustus. And he even brought up ancient accusations—their failures against Macedonia and oppression of their own countrymen. He had personal reasons also for his hostility. For they had refused to release a certain Theophilus whom the Athenian High Court had condemned for forgery.

Then a quick sea-journey by a short cut through the Cyclades brought him to Germanicus at the island of Rhodes. Though aware of Piso's attacks on him, Germanicus behaved so forgivingly that when a storm was driving Piso on to the rocks—so that his death could have been put down to accident—Germanicus sent warships to rescue his enemy. However, Piso was not mollified. Grudging even a single day's delay, he left Germanicus and went on.

On reaching the army in Syria he was lavish with gifts, bribes, and

耳曼尼库斯的早丧(虽然所用的是神谕的那种含义模糊的神秘语言)。

格涅乌斯·卡尔普尔尼乌斯·披索正要赶快执行他的计划,他强烈地使雅典人受到了震惊。他在一次对他们进行恶毒攻击的演说当中,(没有指名道姓地批评了日耳曼尼库斯)说他的过分客气是与罗马的尊严不相称的,他所客气的对象他称之为雅典人的人已经不存在了(雅典人由于一再遭难已经灭绝了),当前存在的全是地球上的一些渣滓:这些人曾经与米特利达特斯六世结成联盟,和庞都斯一起反对苏拉,[1]又曾经和安东尼一起反对圣奥古斯都。[2]他甚至对他们远古的历史也进行责难——他们反对马其顿人的失败和他们对本国人民的压迫。他个人也有理由仇视雅典,因为他们的当局曾经拒绝释放一个名叫提欧披路斯的人,雅典最高法庭因伪造文件的罪名而将他判了罪。

在这之后,披索利用海上的一条捷径,迅速地穿过基克拉季斯岛来到了罗德岛的日耳曼尼库斯这里。尽管日耳曼尼库斯已经知道披索对他进行的恶毒的攻击,然而他仍然如此宽容,以致当一次暴风把披索吹到一些嶙峋的岩石上面去的时候——而他本来可以把他的对头死亡的原因归之于意外事故,日耳曼尼库斯还是派了战船过去,解救出了他的敌人。尽管如此,披索的态度也仍然没有缓和。甚至只在那里勉强待了一天,就离开日耳曼尼库斯走了。

他一到达叙利亚的军团,就到处慷慨地送礼、行贿,甚至对最

---

〔1〕 公元前 87 ~ 前 86 年。
〔2〕 在阿克提乌姆。

favours even to the humblest soldiers. He replaced company-commanders of long service, and the stricter among the colonels, by his own dependants and bad characters. He allowed the camp to become slack, the towns disorderly, and the men to wander in undisciplined fashion round the countryside. The demoralization was so bad that he was popularly called 'father of the army'. And Plancina went beyond feminine respectability by attending cavalry exercises—and insulting Agrippina and Germanicus. Yet some even of the better soldiers were misguided enough to support her, because of secret rumours that the emperor's approval was not lacking.

Germanicus knew what was happening. But his more urgent concern was to reach Armenia first. The national character and geographical position of that country have long been equally equivocal. It shares an extensive frontier with Roman provinces. It also stretches as far as Media Atropatene. So it is between the two great empires of Rome and Parthia—and often opposed to them, since the Armenians hate Rome and are jealous of Parthia. At this moment they were kingless, Vonones having been turned out. Popular feeling—among high and low alike—favoured Zeno, the son of King Polemo I of Pontus, because he had copied Armenian customs and clothes since earliest childhood: he loved hunting and feasting and other barbarian pastimes. So at a great gathering in the city of Artaxata, with the agreement of the aristocracy, Germanicus crowned him king. The Armenians paid him homage and acclaimed him as King Artaxias III, after

下级的士兵也表示关切。用他自己的人或品行恶劣的人,替换掉久经战场的百人团长和要求比较严格的将领。他纵容营地的人们懒散下去,城市陷于混乱放纵,士兵在附近地方到处毫无纪律的游荡。在这里纪律松弛到如此坏的程度,以致许多人竟然称他为"军团之父"。普朗奇娜的行为也远离了一个庄重的妇人应有的作风,她参加骑兵演习,她侮辱阿格里披娜和日耳曼尼库斯。甚至一些比较正派的士兵都被深深地误导而支持她了,因为人们都在暗中传说,这些做法都少不了是得到皇帝认可的。

日耳曼尼库斯知道这里发生的一切,但是他当前更迫切的事情是先要到亚美尼亚去。亚美尼亚这个地方的民族性格和地理形势,很久以来就都是难以捉摸的。因为它同罗马各行省接壤的边界很长,它还向内地一直伸展到米地亚阿特罗帕提尼的地方。这样一来,亚美尼亚人就被夹在罗马和帕尔提亚两大帝国之间——而且经常反对这两个帝国,因为亚美尼亚既厌恶罗马,又妒忌帕尔提亚。这时由于沃诺尼斯被赶下王位,他们正没有国王。全国上上下下都喜欢庞都斯国王波列莫一世[1]的儿子吉诺,因为吉诺从很小的时候,在习惯和衣着方面就喜欢模仿亚美尼亚人:他喜欢狩猎、饮宴和蛮族喜爱的其他各种娱乐活动。因此,在征得了贵族的同意之后,日耳曼尼库斯就在阿尔塔克撒塔城[2]向集会的庞大人群,宣布吉诺为国王。亚美尼亚人都向他致敬,并且给他加上国王阿尔塔克西亚斯三世的称号,这一称号是根据这个城市的名

---

〔1〕 死去已久,当时是他的未亡人在统治着。

〔2〕 在阿拉克西斯河上,阿勒拉特山下,它的遗址目前仍然叫阿尔达斯卡尔。

the city. Cappadocia, on the other hand, was converted into an imperial province with Quintus Veranius (I) as governor. To make Roman
rule seem the preferable alternative, certain of its royal taxes were diminished. Commagene was annexed to the province of Syria, and put
under Quintus Servaeus. So Germanicus had solved every eastern
question.

Yet his satisfaction was ruined by Piso's arrogance. Germanicus
had ordered him to conduct part of the Roman army to Armenia, or
send it with his son. Piso had done neither. Finally, at the winter
quarters of the tenth brigade at Cyrrhus, they met. Their features
were carefully composed, Piso's to show no fear, Germanicus' not to
seem menacing. He was, as I have said, a kind-hearted man. But
his friends knew how to work up ill-feeling, and piled up a variety of
exaggerated facts and hostile fictions against Piso, Plancina, and their
sons. A few friends were present at their meeting. Germanicus spoke
first, with ill-concealed indignation. Piso apologized—insolently.
They parted in undeclared enmity. Subsequently, Piso rarely sat on
Germanicus' dais, and, when he did, he looked sullen and critical. At a

字而取得的。但是,另一方面,卡帕多奇亚却被变成了帝国的一个行省,由克温图斯·维拉尼乌斯一世担任长官。[1] 为了使罗马人的统治给人以比过去还要温和些的印象,日耳曼尼库斯减少了一些王室先前所征收的赋税。孔玛盖尼第一次被并入叙利亚行省,交给行政长官克温图斯·谢尔瓦埃乌斯统治。这样,日耳曼尼库斯就圆满地解决了所有的东方问题。

不过,披索的傲慢无礼破坏了日耳曼尼库斯因此事而带来的好心情。日耳曼尼库斯曾命令披索本人或他的儿子率领一部分罗马军队到亚美尼亚去,披索没有服从命令,他自己没有去,也不派他的儿子去执行这一命令。然而最后在库尔路斯[2]第十军团的冬营里,他们两人终于相遇了。他们应当有怎样的表情都是经过了一番考虑的,披索故意表现得无所畏惧,而日耳曼尼库斯看起来则没有一点威胁的神气。因为我在前面已经讲过,他实际上是一个心地善良的人。但是他的朋友们很清楚地了解应该怎样去激起他的憎恨情绪。这些人堆积了许多夸大其词的事例,制造了种种假象,千方百计地中伤披索、普朗奇娜和他们的儿子。只有几个友人参加他们的会议上,日耳曼尼库斯首先说话,他强压着自己心中的愤怒情绪。但是披索傲慢地进行辩解。他们于是就在各自暗含的敌意中分手了。从这时起,披索就很少坐到日耳曼尼库斯的坐席这边来。即使有时坐到日耳曼尼库斯的坐席这边来,他的表情也是很阴郁的,充满了敌对情绪。在一次纳

---

〔1〕 不久他和谢尔瓦埃乌斯便又回到日耳曼尼库斯的麾下去了。

〔2〕 在叙利亚北部,现在的科洛司。

banquet given by the dependent king of the Nabataci, when heavy gold crowns were presented to Germanicus and Agrippina and lighter ones to Piso and the others, Piso was heard to say that the guest of honour was son of a Roman emperor, not of a Parthian king. He pushed his own crown aside, with a prolonged denunciation of extravagance. This was irritating for Germanicus. But he endured it.

A deputation now came to him from the Parthian king Artabanus III. Its mission was to recall the friendship and alliance between the two empires, and to request a renewal of pledges. The king would pay Germanicus the compliment of coming to the bank of the Euphrates. But meanwhile he asked that Vonones should not be kept in Syria, from which, at short range, his agents were inciting tribal chieftains to disloyalty. Germanicus answered with courtesy about the alliance between Rome and Parthia, and with becoming modesty as regards the king's visit and politeness to himself. Vonones was moved to the Cilician coastal town of Pompeiopolis. This was not just because of Artabanus' request. It was also a rebuff to Piso, whose friend Vonones had made himself by numerous attentions and gifts to Plancina.

While Germanicus was spending the summer in various provinces, Drusus distinguished himself by inducing the Germans to fight among

巴泰伊人[1]国王举行的宴会上,当主人把沉重的金冠送给日耳曼尼库斯和阿格里披娜,把较轻的金冠送给披索和其他人的时候,有人听到披索说,这是为罗马皇帝的儿子,而不是为帕尔提亚的国王的儿子举行的宴会。他还把他的金冠推到一边去,同时以冗长的言词对奢侈之风进行了猛烈的抨击。这些话使日耳曼尼库斯非常恼火,但他还是忍耐了下来。

这时从帕尔提亚的国王阿尔塔巴努斯三世那里来了一些使节。代表团此行的目的,是要这里记起两国之间的友谊和缔结的盟约,并且要求双方重新交换信誓。帕尔提亚的国王向日耳曼尼库斯致敬,表示欢迎日耳曼尼库斯来幼发拉底河岸对他们进行访问。但同时他又要求把沃诺尼斯从叙利亚驱逐出去,因为在近旁的各地,沃诺尼斯正在煽动一些部族的酋长们背信弃义。关于罗马和帕尔提亚之间的联盟的问题、关于国王的来访和国王对他的致敬,他都作了十分得体的、谦逊有礼的回应。沃诺尼斯被迁移到奇里奇亚沿海的一个叫做庞培欧波里斯[2]的城市去。这一举措不仅仅是由于阿尔塔巴努斯的要求,同时也是使披索感到难堪的一种举动。沃诺尼斯是披索的朋友,他曾经向普朗奇娜大献殷勤并赠送了大量礼物,从而取得了披索的好感。

正当日耳曼尼库斯在各个行省过夏时,杜路苏斯由于诱使日耳曼人自相残杀而取得了很高的声望;他又利用玛洛波都斯的力

---

[1] 纳巴泰伊人这时在阿拉伯西北部成立了一个附属王国,公元105年改为阿拉伯·佩特莱亚行省。

[2] 以前的索里,现在的美泽特路。

themselves; and he thereby put an end to the already broken Maroboduus. Among the Gotones there was a young German nobleman called Catualda who had been expelled by Maroboduus, and now, seeing him in difficulties, was eager for revenge. Invading Marcomannic territory with a strong force, Catualda bribed the leading men to co-operate, and broke into the palace and adjoining fort. There he found old Suebian loot. There, too, were business-men and campfollowers from the Roman provinces. They had been induced first by a trade agreement, then by hopes of making more money, to migrate from their various homes to enemy territory. Finally they had forgotten their own country.

Maroboduus, completely deserted, was obliged to appeal to the emperor's mercy. Crossing the Danube—at the point where it borders on the province of Noricum—he wrote to Tiberius. His tone was not that of a refugee or petitioner, but reminiscent of his former greatness. When he had been a powerful monarch, he said, and many nations had made approaches to him, he had preferred the friendship of Rome. The emperor answered that he should have a secure and honourable home in Italy as long as he stayed there, and if it became advantageous for him to leave Italy he could go as freely as he had come. In the senate, however, he asserted that Maroboduus had been more dangerous

量业已摇摇欲坠的情况,使他彻底垮台。在哥特尼斯人[1]中间有一个名叫卡图阿尔达的年轻的日耳曼贵族,这个人先前被玛洛波都斯驱逐了出去,现在看到玛洛波都斯已经处于极端困难的境地,于是他就渴望着复仇。他带领一支强有力的士兵队伍进入了玛尔科曼尼人的领土,卡图阿尔达贿赂那里的部落首领和他合作,然后就一起攻进王宫和附近的要塞。他们在那里发现了古老的苏埃比人的战利品,还有从罗马各个行省来的许多商贩和随军的人。他们先是被商业上的许诺引诱过来,继而又为能挣到更多金钱的希望所诱惑,他们从各自的故乡移居到了这一敌人的地区。最后,他们就把自己的祖国忘掉了。

玛洛波都斯现在遭到了彻底的抛弃,没有别的办法,他被迫向皇帝请求宽恕。在渡过了作为诺里库姆行省[2]的边境的多瑙河之后,他便上书给提贝里乌斯。他的口气一点都不像是一个避难的人或是一个乞求者,他还仍然在回忆他过去的辉煌伟大。当他是一个强大的国王的时候,他说,许多国家都愿意拉拢他,但是他却宁愿得到罗马的友谊。皇帝回答说,只要他愿意来罗马,他将会在这儿得到一个安全和体面的住处。如果他认为离开意大利对他更加有利,那么他也可以像来时一样自由地离开。不过,在元老院里他却明确地表示,玛洛波都斯比菲利浦斯[3]对于雅典,或

_____

〔1〕 居住在维斯杜拉河下游东岸。在公元 2 世纪后期的移居之后,他们来到黑海地带,并有了一个更著名的名称"哥特人"。

〔2〕 在莱提亚和潘诺尼亚之间,它的北界是从帕绍几乎到维也纳的这一段多瑙河。

〔3〕 指马其顿的菲利浦斯·亚历山大大帝的父亲。

than Philip had been to Athens, or Pyrrhus and Antiochus III to Rome. The speech has survived. It emphasizes the king's power, the ferocity of his subject peoples, Italy's peril from so near an enemy— and the emperor's skill in eliminating him.

Maroboduus was kept at Ravenna, and whenever the Suebi became disorderly they were threatened with his restoration. But for eighteen years he never left Italy, growing old, his reputation dimmed by excessive fondness for life. Catualda's fate and refuge were similar. Overthrown shortly afterwards by the Hermunduri under Vibilius, he was admitted inside the empire and lodged at Forum Julii, a Roman settlement in Narbonese Gaul. The native followers of the two princes were not allowed to inhabit and disturb peaceful provinces: they were settled beyond the Danube between the rivers Morava and Vá-h and a king, Vannius from the Quadi, was provided for them.

News now arrived of Germanicus' coronation of Artaxias III. The senate voted that Germanicus and Drusus should receive ovations on entering the city. Moreover, arches bearing their statues were erected on either side of the temple of Mars the Avenger.

庇鲁斯[1]与安提奥库斯三世之对于罗马人民,还要危险。这一讲话已留传下来,其中着重强调了这位国王的伟大,他所统治的人民的凶猛残忍,这样近的敌人对意大利所构成的危险——还有皇帝除掉他的技巧。

玛洛波都斯还被拘留在拉文纳,每当苏埃比人表现得不驯服的时候,玛洛波都斯的复位就会对他们起到一些震慑的作用。但是在18年中间他从没有离开过意大利,人已经越来越衰老了,由于过分贪生怕死,他的声望也降低了。卡图阿尔达也和玛洛波都斯相似,遇到了同样的不幸命运和灾难。不久之后,他就被在维比里乌斯领导之下的赫尔孟都利人[2]打败,而逃到了罗马去避难。结果他就被安置在纳尔波高卢的一个移民地佛路姆·优里乌姆。[3]这两个国王的本国的追随者却没有被允许住在罗马行省,这会使和平的生活受到侵害,因此他们便被移居到多瑙河对岸摩拉瓦河和瓦格河之间的地方,并且给他们立了一个克瓦地人[4]出身的国王万尼乌斯。

这时,传来了日耳曼尼库斯让阿尔塔克西亚斯三世做了亚美尼亚国王的消息。元老院决定,日耳曼尼库斯和杜路苏斯二人在进入罗马的时候要受到小凯旋式的欢迎。而且还决定,在复仇者玛尔斯神[5]的神庙的两边,竖立起雕刻着他们二人的像的拱门。

---

〔1〕 埃庇路斯的国王,公元前278年曾进攻过意大利。

〔2〕 苏埃比人的一支,住在莱提亚以北的地方。

〔3〕 位于通向阿尔和奥列里娅大道的边上,现在是瓦特县的弗雷儒斯。

〔4〕 住在莫拉维亚和上匈牙利,和玛尔科曼尼人相邻。他们曾领导蛮族的大联合同玛尔库斯·奥列里乌斯治下的罗马对抗。

〔5〕 奥古斯都为纪念他对谋杀独裁官恺撒的人们的复仇而在广场上修建的。

Tiberius was happier to have secured peace by prudent negotiation than if he had fought a victorious war. So now he used the same diplomatic methods with Rhescuporis, king of Thrace. On the death of the previous king, Rhoemetalces I, who had controlled the whole country, Augustus had divided it between his brother Rhescuporis and his son Cotys IV. The partition gave Cotys the cultivated parts, the towns, and the vicinity of the Greek cities, while Rhescuporis got a wild, savage land with hostile neighbours. The kings' characters were similarly contrasted, the former being attractive and civilized, and the latter grim, ambitious, and an unwilling partner. At first, however, there was ostensible harmony. But soon Rhescuporis began to encroach and annex territory allotted to Cotys, meeting resistance with force. He proceeded tentatively during the lifetime of Augustus, who had created the two kingdoms and might (Rhescuporis feared) punish disrespect. But when he heard of the change of ruler he provoked war, by infiltrating bandit groups and demolishing forts.

Tiberius, whose greatest horror was an upset arrangement, sent a staff-officer to tell the kings to keep the peace. Cotys at once dismissed the force which he had mobilized. Rhescuporis, pretending to be reasonable, requested a conference at which disputed matters could

提贝里乌斯不喜欢通过在战场上取得的胜利而结束战争,而比较喜欢通过谨慎的外交手段保持和平。因此,现在他就利用自己的这一巧妙手法来对付色雷斯[1]的国王列司库波里斯。以前,前国王莱美塔尔凯斯一世统治着整个地区,但是在他死后,奥古斯都将这块地方一分为二,一半送给了他的兄弟列司库波里斯,另一半则送给了他的儿子科提斯四世。给予科提斯的这一部分是耕种过的土地、城市和邻接希腊诸城市的各个地区,而列司库波里斯得到的却是贫瘠荒凉的土地,民风粗野而且邻邦满怀敌意。两个国王的性格也形成了同样鲜明的对照,科提斯平易近人、彬彬有礼,列司库波里斯则阴郁、贪婪而又不能容忍别人。虽然,开始的时候,他们在表面上还是和谐的。但是过了不久,列司库波里斯便开始越过自己的国界,暗中侵占、吞并分给科提斯的地区,因而遭到了对方的武力反抗。在奥古斯都活着的时候,他还是试试探探地去这样做,因为奥古斯都缔造了这两个王国,对于那些对他不尊重的人,(列司库波里斯害怕)他会施以惩罚的。但是当他一听到奥古斯都去世,已经改换了皇帝的时候,就立刻把打劫的队伍渗透到国境之外,摧毁要塞,公然挑起了战争。

提贝里乌斯最担心的是,局面安定下来以后又会发生变故。他选派一名百人团长通知两个国王,要保持和平。科提斯得到了这项通知后,立刻把他已经征募起来的部队解散了,但是列司库波里斯却装出一副很通情达理的样子,要求会晤协商解决他们之

---

〔1〕 在提贝里乌斯时期,除了连接爱琴海的南岸(属马其顿行省)和色雷斯的凯尔索尼斯(这是皇帝的私产)之外,它是被一些半独立的土著王公统治着。直到克劳狄乌斯当政时期(公元46年)它才成为一个行省。

be settled verbally. Place and time were soon fixed, and agreement was reached. Concessions were readily made, for Cotys was goodnatured—and Rhescuporis treacherous. He gave a banquet, ostensibly to ratify the treaty; and when the festivities and drinking had continued far into the night, Cotys, off his guard, was imprisoned.

As soon as Cotys realized the trick, he appealed to the sacred right of kings, to the gods their family shared, to the laws of hospitality. But Rhescuporis now possessed all Thrace. He wrote to Tiberius alleging that there had been a plot against himself, but that he had forestalled its instigator. Meanwhile, on the excuse of a tribal campaign against the Bastarnae and Scythians, he reinforced his infantry and cavalry. Tiberius replied gently that, if he had acted in good faith, he need not worry since he was not culpable; but neither he himself nor the senate would judge the rights and wrongs of the case until they heard it. So Rhescuporis must give up Cotys, come to Rome, and relinquish to others the unpopular task of criminal investigation.

The emperor's letter was sent to Thrace by Latinius Pandusa, imperial governor of Moesia, together with a force to take over Cotys. Rage and fear battled in Rhescuporis' mind. Finally he thought it better to be charged with a crime committed than a crime attempted, and ordered Cotys to be killed, alleging suicide. Tiberius' policy however, once fixed, remained unmodified. Pandusa (whom Rhescuporis had

间的问题,说他们之间的争端是可以在会晤中通过口头解决的。会晤的时间和地点很快就定了下来,和解的一致意见也很快就形成了。会晤中很容易地实现了让步,因为科提斯的脾气非常好,能作出一切让步;而列司库波里斯阴险奸诈,能接受一切让步。列司库波里斯举行了一次宴会,表面上是为了批准这一条约。正当宴会进行到深夜的时候,他却把没有任何防备的科提斯逮捕了起来。

当科提斯意识到自己竟然被骗的时候,他就诉诸国王的神圣权利、他们共同的家神和被款待的客人的豁免权为自己申诉,但是现在列司库波里斯占有了整个色雷斯。之后,他就写信给提贝里乌斯,声称这里组织了反对他的一次阴谋,但是阴谋的煽动者已经在事先被他逮捕起来了。与此同时,他又借口对巴斯塔尔奈人和西徐亚人作战,重新征募步兵和骑兵,从而加强了自己的军事力量。提贝里乌斯很温和地给他回了一封信,信中说,如果他对自己是满怀信心的,那么他就不必担心,因为他是不会受到指责的。但是不论是皇帝本人还是元老院,除非亲自审问清这一案件,他们是无法对谁对谁错做出裁决的。因此要他一定把科提斯释放出来,亲自到罗马来,把调查犯罪事实这一不受欢迎的任务交由其他人去处理。

皇帝的这封信是由拉提尼乌斯·潘杜撒送到色雷斯来的;潘杜撒是美西亚的长官,他带着一队士兵,来接管科提斯。列司库波里斯这时心里是既害怕,又恼怒。最后他决定,与其被指控为有犯罪的企图,倒不如索性被指控为犯了罪更好些,因此他决定在宣称科提斯自杀的托词之下把科提斯处死。不过提贝里乌斯的策略是,一旦作出了什么安排,就无论如何也绝不会改变的。

accused of hostile bias) died, and his successor in Moesia was Lucius Pomponius Flaccus, an old soldier whose close friendship with the king made it easy to trap him. Flaccus crossed into Thrace, and by large promises induced Rhescuporis (who had hesitated, when he considered his offences) to enter the Roman lines.

A strong guard was attached to him, ostensibly as a courtesy. Its colonels and company-commanders advised and coaxed him. As Thrace receded, their surveillance became increasingly apparent, until at last he saw, as they conducted him into Rome, that there was no choice. He was accused in the senate by the widow of Cotys, and exiled from his kingdom. Thrace was divided between his son Rhoemetalces II, who was known to have opposed his father's policy, and the children of Cotys. Since, however, these last were not of age, a former praetor, Titus Trebellenus Rufus, was to act as their regent. (In the same way, at an earlier epoch, Marcus Aemilius Lepidus (I) had been sent to Egypt to look after the children of Ptolemy IV Philopator.) Rhescuporis was deported to Alexandria, where he was killed while attempting (so it was said) to escape.

In the following year (the consuls were Marcus Junius Silanus Tor

（但这时被列司库波里斯说成是敌视自己的）潘杜撒死了，于是提贝里乌斯就派路奇乌斯·彭波尼乌斯·佛拉库斯来接替他担任美西亚的长官。佛拉库斯是一位久经沙场的老军人，他和列司库波里斯有着深厚的交情，这样他也就更容易成功地将对方诱捕了。佛拉库斯渡海进入了色雷斯，他用许多慷慨的许诺引诱列司库波里斯（想到自己的冒犯行为，他也有些犹豫）进入到罗马的防线上来。

一队强壮的卫士被派到他的身边来，这从表面上看来，是对于他的国王身份的尊敬。军团将领和百人团长们不断地对他进行耐心的忠告和劝说。看到他有些退却了，他们对他的监视就变得越来越明显了。最后，列司库波里斯终于认识到他必须面临的事情。当他们把他押解到罗马去的时候，他也就无可选择了。科提斯的寡妇向元老院控告了他的罪行，他被判处流放到他的王国之外的一个地方。色雷斯则分给了他的儿子莱美塔尔凯斯，据说他曾反对过他的父亲的做法。关于科提斯的孩子们，由于还没有成年，一位卸了任的行政长官提图斯·特列贝列努斯·路福斯便负责照管这些孩子，治理王国（在前代也有过类似的事件，那就是把玛尔库斯·埃米利乌斯·列庇都斯派到埃及去监护托勒米的孩子庇洛美特尔。）[1]列司库波里斯被押送到亚历山大去，并且在一次据说是逃跑的企图中被杀死了。

在接下来的一年里，[2]（玛尔库斯·尤尼乌斯·西拉努斯·托

---

〔1〕 这里指托勒米·埃披帕尼斯（死于公元前 18 年）的儿子庇洛美特尔和庇司孔。

〔2〕 公元 19 年，即罗马建城 772 年。

quatus and Lucius Norbanus Balbus) Germanicus went to Egypt to look at the antiquities. His ostensible object, however, was the country's welfare; by opening the public granaries he lowered the price of corn. His behaviour was generally popular. He walked about without guards, in sandalled feet and Greek clothes, imitating Scipio Africanus, who is said to have done likewise in Sicily though the Second Punic War was still raging.

Tiberius criticized Germanicus mildly for his clothes and deportment, but reprimanded him severely for infringing a ruling of Augustus by entering Alexandria without the emperor's permission. For one of the unspoken principles of Augustus' domination had been the exclusion of senators and knights from Egypt without his leave. He had thereby isolated Egypt, to minimize the threat from any hostile power which, however weak itself and however powerful its opponents, might by holding that country—with its key-positions by land and sea—starve Italy.

Germanicus, still unaware that his expedition was frowned upon, visited the nearest of the Nile mouths, which is sacred to Hercules; the inhabitants say that others of comparable prowess later took his name, but that its original bearer came from their country. Germanicus then proceeded upstream, starting from Canopus, founded by the Spartans

尔克瓦图斯和路奇乌斯·诺尔巴努斯·巴尔布斯担任执政官）日耳曼尼库斯到埃及去参观古迹。不过在表面上，他此行的目的是为了关心行省的福利安全。他用开放国家粮仓的办法压低了粮价，他的行为受到了人民的普遍欢迎。他到各处去的时候不带侍卫，脚上穿着便鞋，身上穿着希腊人的服装。这种做法是模仿普布里乌斯·斯奇比奥·阿佛里卡努斯。据说，第二次布匿战争还在激烈进行的时候，斯奇比奥在西西里就是这样打扮的。

提贝里乌斯温和地批评了他的这种衣着和作风，但是对于他未经皇帝的许可便进入了亚历山大一事，却作出了极为严厉的谴责，因为这违背了奥古斯都制定的规则。作为从未明言的保持专制统治的手法之一，奥古斯都曾禁止任何元老和高级骑士进入埃及，除非是得到了他的许可。他通过这种做法封锁了埃及，[1]以便尽量减少外来的敌人的威胁，不管它本身的力量是如何弱小，而它要抗击的兵力又有多么强大，他也不让任何一个人有可能通过控制这一行省以及海上和陆上的枢纽地点而陷意大利于饥饿之地。[2]

此时，日耳曼尼库斯还没有意识到他的这次远访皇帝是不赞同的，因此他访问了尼罗河口最近处一个奉献给赫尔克里士的神庙。当地的居民们说，赫尔克里士是埃及人，这个名字最早起源于他们的国家，后来与他同样勇敢的那些人也采用了他的名字。接着，日耳曼尼库斯又逆着尼罗河上行，他首先开始访问的是一个叫做卡诺普斯的城市，这个城市是斯巴达人为了纪念埋藏在那

〔1〕 埃及从来不是一个真正的行省，而是皇帝的私人领地。
〔2〕 海上要地是帕鲁斯，陆上要地是佩路西乌姆。

to commemorate the burial there of the steersman Canopus when Me-
nelaus, returning to Greece, had been driven off his course on to the
Libyan coast. Next Germanicus inspected the imposing remains of
ancient Thebes. On its massive masonry, in Egyptian writing, are
testimonies to ancient splendour. One of the older priests, requested
to interpret the native tongue, told how the country had once possessed 700,000 men of military age, with whom King Rameses II had
made his conquests. The tribute-list of the subject lands (they were
Libya, Ethiopia, Media, Persia, Bactria, and Scythia; his empire
had also included Syria, Armenia, and its neighbour Cappadocia,
and had extended to the Bithynian and Lycian coasts) could be
read—the weight of gold and silver was recorded, and the numbers of
weapons and horses, the temple-offerings of ivory and spices, the
quantities of corn and other materials contributed by every country:
revenues as impressive as those exacted nowadays by Parthian compulsion or Roman imperial organization.

Germanicus was interested in other remarkable sights, too, particularly the stone statue of Memnon which gives out the sound of a
voice when the sun's rays strike it; the pyramids, mountainous monuments of royal competition and wealth, erected on drifting and almost

里的一个名叫卡诺普斯的舵手而建立起来的,这一段时期,正是
美涅劳斯在返回希腊的途中,被狂风吹离了他的航程,从而来到
了利比亚海岸的时候。在这之后,日耳曼尼库斯又视察了古老的
底比斯的那些巨大的遗迹。[1] 在那些巨大的石造建筑物上,还有
埃及的字母刻在上面,记述了古埃及昔日的壮丽辉煌。而奉命把
埃及语传译过来的一位老高级祭司对他述说了这个一度曾拥有
70万服兵役的人的国家,在那个时代是怎样的一种盛况;而国王
拉姆吉斯二世就是依靠着这一支军队完成了他的多次征服伟业。
他还能读出被征服的部族的名单(他们是:利比亚人、埃塞俄比亚
人、米地亚人、波斯人、巴克妥利亚人和西徐亚人,他还征服了叙
利亚人、亚美尼亚人以及相邻的卡帕多奇亚人所居住的国土,这
样他的统治范围就延伸到了从比提尼亚海到吕奇亚海的全部土
地);还有他治下各民族的贡物表所记录的各个部族贡献的黄金
和白银的分量、武器和马匹的数目、在神庙中作供物用的象牙和
香料的数目,还有粮食和其他日用品的数量。这种税收规模之
大,与今天强大的帕尔提亚王国或是罗马帝国征收的赋税恰恰
相当。

　　日耳曼尼库斯对其他一些著名的景点也非常感兴趣,特别是
美姆农的巨大石像,[2]这座石像每当太阳光照射到它上面的时
候,它便会发出一声巨大的响声;象征着国王们的竞争和财富的
像山那样高的金字塔,是那些争强好胜的国王们花钱像旋风吹过一

---

〔1〕 今天卡尔纳克、路克索尔和美迪尼特—哈布的废墟。

〔2〕 阿门—赫提普三世(约公元前1450年)在美迪尼特—哈布的两座
大石像的靠北的一座。

pathless sands; artificial lakes to receive the Nile's overflow ; and elsewhere gorges and depths unplumbed. He came to Elephantine and Syene, once the frontier-posts of the Roman Empire, which now, however, extends to the Red Sea.

At about this time Vonones, whose deportation to Cilicia has been mentioned, bribed his guards with a view to escaping, via Armenia, to the lands of the Albani and Heniochi and to a Scythian tribal chieftain who was related to him. Under the pretence that he was going hunting, he moved inland, aiming for the trackless woods. With a fast horse he made quick time to the river Ceyhan. But on the news of his escape the local inhabitants had destroyed its bridges, and the river was unfordable. So he was arrested on the bank, by a cavalry colonel, Vibius Fronto. Soon afterwards a reservist called Remmius stabbed him to death—ostensibly in a fit of anger, but the man's former position as the king's chief guard increased suspicions that he had connived at the escape and had murdered Vonones to avoid detection.

On leaving Egypt Germanicus learnt that all his orders to divisional commanders and cities had been cancelled or reversed. Between him

样,在几乎无路可走的沙漠上修建起来的;将尼罗河泛滥的河水引了进来的人工湖[1];还有别的地方的那些人们无法测量的狭窄的峡谷和深渊。他又来到了埃列芳提尼和昔耶涅,[2]这里曾一度是罗马帝国的边界,不过现在这个边界已经扩展到红海[3]了。

大概就在这个时候,沃诺尼斯,他被放逐到奇里奇亚的事情我在上面已经提到过,企图通过贿买看守人的办法逃走,经由亚美尼亚,去到阿尔巴尼亚、赫尼欧奇人的领土,再到一个和他有亲属关系的西徐亚的国王那里去。在出去打猎的借口之下,他进入到了内地,直奔无路可通的森林地带。然后他骑上一匹快马,急速向吉罕河赶去。但是当地的居民在接到他逃跑的消息之后,就拆毁了那里的桥,而河流本身则是无法涉水而过的。因此他就在河岸的地方,被一个名叫维比乌斯·佛隆托的骑兵长官捉住了。不久之后,一个叫做列米乌斯的退伍老兵,便用刀把他戳死了——他这样做从表面看起来像是出于一时的盛怒,但这个人此前的职务就是看守沃诺尼斯的那些士兵的头目,他的这种行动更加深了人们对他的怀疑,那就是他曾受沃诺尼斯的贿买,这次是害怕沃诺尼斯会把这件事揭发出来,被人们察觉,才故意杀人灭口的。

在离开埃及的时候,日耳曼尼库斯才得悉,他给军团和各城市所发出的所有的命令,不是被取消,就是被换掉了。于是在他

---

〔1〕 即希罗多德所说的莫伊利斯湖,位于孟斐斯之南。现在法尤姆的比尔凯特·阿尔—卡伦。

〔2〕 阿苏安,埃列芳提尼是同它相对的一个岛。

〔3〕 塔西佗在这里所说的"红海",人们有各种各样的解释,有的说就是现在的红海,还有人说是指波斯湾。

and Piso there were violent reciprocal denunciations. Then Piso decided to leave Syria. But Germanicus fell ill, and so Piso stayed on. When news came that the prince was better and vows offered for his recovery were being paid, Piso sent his attendants to disperse the rejoicing crowds of Antioch, with their sacrificial victims and apparatus. Then he left for Seleucia Pieria, to await the outcome of Germanicus' illness. He had a relapse—aggravated by his belief that Piso had poisoned him. Examination of the floor and walls of his bedroom revealed the remains of human bodies, spells, curses, lead tablets inscribed with the patient's name, charred and bloody ashes, and other malignant objects which are supposed to consign souls to the powers of the tomb. At the same time agents of Piso were accused of spying on the sickbed.

Germanicus, alarmed and angry, reflected that if his own house was besieged and his enemies were actually watching as he died, the prospects of his unhappy wife and babies were gloomy. Apparently poisoning was too slow; Piso was evidently impatient to monopolize the province and its garrison. But Germanicus felt he was not so feeble as all that-the murderer should not have his reward. He wrote to Piso

和披索之间,就发生了相互间的猛烈抨击,双方各不相让。这样一来,披索便决定离开叙利亚了。但是日耳曼尼库斯病倒了,于是披索又留了下来。但是后来,当他听到日耳曼尼库斯的病情有了好转,并且人们为了他的好转而正在通过祭献以还愿的时候,披索便派遣自己的侍从驱散了安提奥克地方为日耳曼尼库斯病情的好转而欢欣鼓舞的人群,并且把他们献上的牺牲以及奉献牺牲的明器都夺走了。后来他便离开那里到塞琉西亚·披耶里亚[1]去了,在那里等候日耳曼尼库斯病情的结果。由于日耳曼尼库斯过分相信披索给他吃了毒药,因此病情就更加严重了。而人们在检查日耳曼尼库斯的卧室的地面和墙壁的时候,也确实发现了人的尸骸、符咒、咒语、上面刻有病人名字的铅饼[2]、烧焦的和带血的骨灰[3]以及其他施行恶意的巫术的用具,人们相信这些东西会使活人的灵魂被坟墓中的幽灵攫去。就在这个时候,有人控诉说,披索还派来了密使追根问底地打探日耳曼尼库斯的病情。

日耳曼尼库斯既吃惊又气愤,他想到如果他自己的住宅被人包围着,他的敌人就一直在窥视着他,亲眼看着他死去,那么他那不幸的妻子和那些年幼的孩子们将来的命运就会非常惨淡了。[4]很显然,毒药的效力看来是太慢了。披索显然是迫不及待地想独揽统治行省和卫戍部队的大权。但是日耳曼尼库斯认为他自己还没有虚弱无力到对谋杀者一点都不能加以报

---

〔1〕 安提奥克的港口。

〔2〕 主要是在施行降神术时使用的,术者把钉子或针钉在被诅咒的人的像或名字上面,以致对方于死命。

〔3〕 这是从火葬堆上取来的。

〔4〕 这时在日耳曼尼库斯身边,除了年幼的优利娅以外,还有卡里古拉。

renouncing his friendship, and it is usually believed that he ordered him out of the province. Piso now delayed no longer, and sailed. But he went slowly, so as to reduce the return journey in case Germanicus died and Syria became accessible again.

For a time Germanicus' condition was encouraging. But then he lost strength, and death became imminent. As his friends stood round him, he spoke to them. 'Even if I were dying a natural death', he said, 'I should have a legitimate grudge against the gods for prematurely parting me, at this young age, from my parents, children, and country. But it is the wickedness of Piso and Plancina that have cut me off. I ask you to take my last requests to your heart. Tell my father and brother of the harrowing afflictions and ruinous conspiracies which have brought my wretched life to this miserable close. My relatives, those who shared my prospects, even those who envied me in my life, will lament that the once flourishing survivor of many campaigns has fallen to a woman's treachery!

'You will have the opportunity to protest to the senate and to invoke the law. The chief duty of a friend is not to walk behind the corpse pointlessly grieving, but to remember his desires and carry out his instructions. Even strangers will mourn Germanicus. But if it was I that you loved, and not my rank, you must avenge me! Show Rome my wife—the divine Augustus' granddaughter. Call the roll of our six children. Sympathy will go to the accusers. Any tale of criminal instructions given to Piso will seem unbelievable or, if believed, unforgivable.'

复的程度。他给披索写了一封信,宣布和他绝交,通常的说法是,他命令披索离开行省。现在,披索毫不耽搁地拔锚起程了。但是他却故意走得很慢,这样当他听到日耳曼尼库斯死讯的时候,就可以减少旅程,较快地回到叙利亚来了。

在一段时期里,日耳曼尼库斯的病情有了起色。但是随后他的体力便支持不住了,死亡即将来临。当他的朋友们站在了他的病榻旁边的时候,他对他们说了这样的话:"即使我是自然死亡,我仍然有正当的理由抱怨上天,因为它正当我盛年之时就过早地把我从我的父母、子女和祖国的手中夺走了。然而现在,是因为披索和普朗奇娜的罪恶将我杀死的。我希望你们能牢牢地记住我最后的恳求:请你们把我身受的痛苦以及我所受的阴谋陷害告诉我的父亲和我的弟弟,是他们给我这不幸的一生带来了这样悲惨的结局。我的那些亲属们,那些共同分享过我的美好希望的人,甚至那些在我的一生中羡慕、嫉妒过我的人,当他们在听到一个曾在这样多次的战争的厮杀中仍能幸运地活下来的人却死于一个妇人的阴谋之手,是会悲伤流泪的。

你们必将会有机会向元老院控诉并且运用法律的力量来解决问题的。一个朋友的主要责任并非是跟在死者的尸体后消极地哀悼,而是要记住他的愿望并执行他的命令。甚至不相识的人也会对日耳曼尼库斯的死亡表示悲痛的。但是如果你们爱的是我,而不是爱我的地位的话,那么你们就一定要给我报仇啊!把我的妻子——也就是圣奥古斯都的外孙女,指给罗马人民看吧。把我们的六个子女都一一指出来吧。人们会将同情给予控告者的,谋杀者如果捏造出什么谎言为披索辩护的话,也没有人会相信他们,而且就是相信他们,也不会原谅他们的。"

His friends touched the dying man's right hand, and swore to perish rather than leave him unavenged. Turning to his wife, Germanicus begged her—by her memories of himself and by their children—to forget her pride, submit to cruel fortune, and, back in Rome, to avoid provoking those stronger than herself by competing for their power. That was his public utterance. Privately he said more—warning her of danger (so it was said) from Tiberius. Soon afterwards he died.

The province and surrounding peoples grieved greatly. Foreign countries and kings mourned his friendliness to allies and forgiveness to enemies. Both his looks and his words had inspired respect. Yet this dignity and grandeur, befitting his lofty rank, had been unaccompanied by any arrogance or jealousy. At his funeral there was no procession of statues. But there were abundant eulogies and reminiscences of his fine character. Some felt that his appearance, short life, and manner of death (like its locality) recalled Alexander the Great. Both were handsome, both died soon after thirty, both succumbed to the treachery of compatriots in a foreign land. But Germanicus, it was added, was kind to his friends, modest in his pleasures, a man with one wife and legitimate children. Though not so rash as Alexander, he was no less of a warrior. Only, after defeating the Germans many times, he had not been allowed to complete their subjection. If he had been in sole control, with royal power and title, he would have equalled Alexander in military renown as easily as he outdid him in

他的朋友们摸着垂死的病人的右手发誓说,他们即使是拼出性命也要给他报仇的。然后,日耳曼尼库斯又转向他的妻子,请求她说,为了纪念他,为了他们两人的孩子,忘掉自己的骄傲,向残酷的命运屈服。返回罗马以后,无论如何也不要去争夺权力以致激怒那些比她更有势力的人们。以上这些话是他当着大家的面讲的。在私下里他还讲了更多——(据说)他曾警告她提防来自提贝里乌斯方面的危险。不久之后他就去世了。

他的死亡引起了行省和周围各族人民的极大悲痛。国外各民族和他们的国王哀悼他对联盟国家的友善和对于敌人的宽厚仁慈。他的相貌和言谈都令人肃然起敬。他有着与他的高贵的身份相称的威严和伟大,但是并不骄傲,也从不妒忌。在他的葬仪上没有祖宗的雕像,但是却有大量人们对他的美德的称颂和怀念。有些人感到,他的风采、他的早丧和他去世时的种种情况(甚至他去世的地点),都让人联想起亚历山大大帝。都长得十分漂亮,都在 30 岁刚出头就死去,[1] 又都是在外国的土地上由于本国人的谋害而死。不过日耳曼尼库斯还有其他优点,他对他的朋友很友好,在享乐方面很有节制,作为一个男人他只娶了一个妻子,而且孩子都是合法婚姻的结晶。然而他也是一个相当出色的战士,尽管他不像亚历山大那样勇猛。当他多次打败了日耳曼人的时候,他却没有得到允许把对方彻底加以制服。但是如果他拥有皇帝的权力和头衔,能够独立自主地处理问题,那么他在军事上的声望也可以很容易地超过亚历山大,就如同他可以轻而易举地在仁慈、自制

---

〔1〕 亚历山大比日耳曼尼库斯少活了一年。

clemency, self-control, and every other good quality.

Before cremation the body of Germanicus was exposed in the main square of Antioch, which was to be its resting-place. It is uncertain if the body showed signs of poisoning. People came to opposite conclusions according to their preconceived suspicions, inspired by sympathy for Germanicus or support for Piso.

The other senior officials, generals and senators present now discussed who should govern Syria. The only two who pressed their claims were Gaius Vibius Marsus and Cnaeus Sentius Saturninus. Between them, competition was prolonged. Finally, as Sentius was the older and more insistent, Vibius withdrew. Publius Vitellius, Quintus Veranius (I) and others began preparing charges and indictments against Piso and Plancina as though the trial was already on. At their demand, Sentius dispatched to Rome a woman called Martina who was notorious in the province as a poisoner: Plancina was very fond of her.

Agrippina, exhausted by grief and unwell, but impatient of anything that postponed revenge, took ship with Germanicus' ashes and her children. Everyone was sorry for this very great lady, splendidly

和所有其他优秀品质方面超过他一样。

在火葬之前,日耳曼尼库斯的遗体被安放在安提奥克的广场上,这里也就是将要举行葬仪的地方。尸体是否显示出中毒而死的迹象,还不能确定。对这件事,因为同情心和先入为主的怀疑,大家还有不同的意见:同情心使得一些人站在日耳曼尼库斯的一面,而对披索的支持又使一些人站在披索的一面。

其他的高级官员、副帅和在场的元老随后便就叙利亚的新的统治人选问题进行了商谈。只有两个人提出了自己的主张,他们各持己见,这两个人就是盖乌斯·维比乌斯·玛尔苏斯[1]和格涅乌斯·森提乌斯·撒吐尔尼努斯。[2]人们在他们二人提出的意见之间争论了很久,仍不能确定下来。最后由于森提乌斯年纪较长,而且又更坚持,维比乌斯就让步了。普布里乌斯·维提里乌斯、克温图斯·维拉尼乌斯(一世)和其他一些人于是开始准备对披索和普朗奇娜的指控和上诉,就仿佛审讯已经开始了似的。在他们的请求之下,森提乌斯把一个叫做玛尔提娜的女人派到罗马去,这个女人在行省这里因制造毒药而声名狼藉,但普朗奇娜对这个女人却十分赏识。

悲痛和疾病虽然使阿格里披娜精疲力竭,但她还是没有耐心处理任何足以拖延她的复仇行动的事情,她带着日耳曼尼库斯的骨灰和她的孩子们登上了船。每个人都十分同情这位了不起的妇人,她出身帝王家族,迄今为止一直有着一个显赫的婚姻,过去

―――――――――――――

〔1〕 公元 17 年的补缺执政官,27～30 年(?)是阿非利加总督;克劳狄乌斯时期是叙利亚的长官。

〔2〕 公元 4 年的补缺执政官。一个铭文证明他的任命被提贝里乌斯承认为有效。

married hitherto, accustomed to attracting the gaze of respectful and admiring crowds. Now, she clasped to her bosom the remains of the dead. The prospects of vengeance were dubious, her own future perilous, her fertility accursed—for it only multiplied hostages to fortune.

Meanwhile Piso heard at Cos that Germanicus was dead. Temples were visited, victims sacrificed, in an orgy of celebration. His own extravagant pleasure was eclipsed by that of Plancina, who chose this moment to exchange her mourning (for the death of a sister) for festive clothes. Company-commanders flocked in from Syria, urging that the Roman garrison was for Piso and that he should reoccupy the province, improperly taken from him and now masterless. He took counsel what to do. His son Marcus recommended a speedy return to Rome, since so far he had done nothing irremediable—unconfirmed suspicions or empty rumours were nothing to be frightened of. 'Your quarrel with Germanicus', said Marcus, 'may earn you unpopularity, but not punishment. Besides, your enemies have satisfied themselves, by annexing your province. Return to Syria, on the other hand, means civil war, if Sentius resists. And you can expect no lasting support from company-commanders and soldiers. They still vividly remember their commanding officer, and their dominant emotion is a profound attachment to the Caesars. '

But one of Piso's closest friends, Domitius Celer, opposed this advice. ' Use your opportunity', he said. 'You, not Sentius, were made imperial governor of Syria, with its insignia, its jurisdiction, and its

所到之处总会吸引许多尊敬的目光的注视和羡慕她的群众对她的注意。现在，她把亡人的遗骨抱在胸前，她对于复仇的前景感觉很迷茫，她自己的前途也充满了危机，她的多子成了一件可憎的事情——因为这些孩子只是加倍增加了命运的抵押品。

而与此同时，披索在科斯岛上得到了日耳曼尼库斯去世的消息。他参拜了神庙，奉献了牺牲，纵酒狂饮以表庆祝，简直表达不尽他欣喜若狂的心情。但是他过度的狂喜在普朗奇娜的面前却显得黯然失色了。因为刚刚还正在（给自己的一位姊妹）戴孝的普朗奇娜，在这时竟然脱掉了孝服，换上了节日的服装。百人团长们于是纷纷从叙利亚聚集到他这里来献策。他们说罗马的军团士兵们都支持披索，因此他应当回到被非法从他手中夺走并且现在没有领导者的行省去，重新占领它。他向他们询问这时应当如何行动，他的儿子玛尔库斯建议他应当快速返回罗马去，因为到现在为止，他根本并没有做什么不可挽回的事情——那些没有根据的怀疑或没有实际内容的谣言是没有什么好怕的。"您和日耳曼尼库斯之间的争吵"，玛尔库斯说，"也许会使您不太受欢迎，但是不会受到惩罚。而且您的敌人已经对获得了您的行省感到满足了。另一方面，回到叙利亚去，如果遭到森提乌斯的抗拒的话，这将会意味着引起内战。您也不要指望百人团长和普通士兵会坚定不移地站在您的这一边。因为这些人还清晰地记着他们的统帅，而且他们对恺撒的感情是特别深厚的，这种爱戴在他们身上比其他任何情绪都占着更加重要的地位。"

但是披索最亲密的友人之一，多米提乌斯·凯列尔却反对这个建议。"你要充分利用这个机会"，他说，"被任命为叙利亚长官的是你，而不是森提乌斯。长官的标记、行政长官的职权以及军

garrison. In event of opposition, the man with the post of governor (not to speak of private instructions) is pre-eminently entitled to take up arms. Besides, it is advisable to give rumours time to fade; when indignation is fresh it often overwhelms even the innocent. But if you keep and strengthen the army, chance might take an unforeseen favourable turn. Why hasten to reach Rome at the same instant as Germanicus' ashes? If you do, the weeping Agrippina and the witless crowd will bring you down at once on hearsay, your defence unheard. You have the Augusta's complicity, the emperor's sympathy—secretly. No one is so delighted by Germanicus' death as its most ostentatious mourners. "

Piso, naturally impetuous, was easily converted to this course. He wrote to Tiberius accusing Germanicus of extravagance and haughtiness, and asserting that he himself had been expelled to leave the way clear for a rebellion, and that he had now resumed his command as loyally as he had held it before. He put Domitius Celer on board a warship with instructions to proceed to Syria across the open sea, avoiding the coasts and islands. Deserters, streaming in, were organized in units; and weapons were distributed to camp-followers.

Piso crossed to the mainland and intercepted a force of recruits on its way to Syria. He also wrote requesting the Cilician princelings to send him reinforcements. His son Marcus, though he had advised

团都是交给你的。如果有人用武力抗拒你，那么一个接受了副帅的权力（不是指私人指授）的人物岂不是比任何人都有权力首先发动战争吗？而且，经过一段时间之后，谣言自然就会消失的；当人们的义愤刚刚起来的时候，是远远盖过了无辜者的清白的。但是，如果他能保持并加强军队的实力，那么命运就可能会带来许多难以预见到的有利的转机的。为什么要急急忙忙地赶回罗马去，弄得和日耳曼尼库斯的骨灰同时到达呢？如果你这样做了，那么哭哭啼啼的阿格里披娜和愚昧的人群立刻就会用谣言搞得你身败名裂，而且根本没有人会听你的辩解。你是有奥古斯塔的同谋，皇帝也支持你，但这只是私下里的情况。越是在表面上为日耳曼尼库斯的命运而悲痛的人，越是对他的死亡感到高兴。"

本性好冲动的披索是很容易接受这样的意见的。他写信给提贝里乌斯，控诉日耳曼尼库斯的奢侈和傲慢无礼，声称说他本人遭到驱逐，以致那里发生了叛乱，但是现在他已经重新取得兵权，他和从前领导军队时一样，对皇帝忠诚不贰。在这同时，他要多米提乌斯·凯列尔乘上一艘战船，命令他从海上穿过诸岛一直到叙利亚去，一路要避开海岸和岛屿。那些逃亡者、流窜人员都集中到了他这里来，他把他们组成了小队，又把武器分配给随军的非战斗人员。

随后披索便率领着海军横渡大海到大陆上去，在路上他还截留了开到叙利亚去的一支新兵。他又写信给奇里奇亚的小国王们，[1]要他们派出援军来支援他。他的儿子玛尔库斯虽然不主张

---

〔1〕 在庞洛帕托尔死后，这样的小王国还有两个：庞培欧波里斯以北的欧尔巴和奇里奇亚西部的特拉凯亚。

against war, helped actively in its preparations. As they coasted along Lycia and Pamphylia they met the ships taking Agrippina to Italy. The meeting was hostile, and both squadrons prepared to fight. But mutual fears limited them to recriminations. A message from Gaius Vibius Marsus urged Piso to return home to plead his cause. Piso sarcastically replied that he would attend when the praetor in charge of poisoning cases notified accused and accusers of a date.

Meanwhile Domitius had landed at the Syrian city of Laodicea. He made for the winter camp of the sixth brigade which seemed to him the likeliest for his rebellious designs. But he was forestalled by its commander Pacuvius. Sentius wrote informing Piso of this and warning him to keep subversive agents away from the army, and war away from the province. Then, collecting together all whom he knew to cherish Germanicus' memory or dislike his enemies, and emphasizing that this was a forcible attack on the emperor's majesty, he took personal command of a strong force, ready for battle.

Piso's project had started badly. However, he took the safest course in the circumstances by seizing a fortified Cilician town, Celenderis. The Cilician chiefs had sent troops. By adding deserters, the recently intercepted recruits, and his and Plancina's slaves, Piso had brought

作战,但是却也积极地帮助他做好作战前的准备工作。他们沿着吕奇亚和潘披里亚的海岸航行时,遇到了送阿格里披娜到意大利去的船队。他们一见面就充满了敌意,双方都准备动手。但是由于双方都还有所顾忌,所以他们也只是相互责骂,没有动起手来。在责骂的时候,盖乌斯·维比乌斯·玛尔苏斯透露出一个信息,就是要披索回到罗马去准备应付控诉。披索则讽刺地回答说,等到审理放毒案的行政长官确定地通知了原告和被告到庭的日期时,他会到那里去的。[1]

在这期间,多米提乌斯在叙利亚的一个叫做拉欧狄凯亚的城市登陆了。他到第六军团的冬营那里去,因为他认为这个军团看起来是最便于实现他的兵变计划的。但是他的这个计划在事先被军团的一个将领帕库维乌斯识破了。于是森提乌斯便写信把这一事件通知披索,并警告他让他那些来搞破坏的代理人离他的军队远一点,不要企图在行省挑起战争。随后,他便把他所知道的所有怀念日耳曼尼库斯的那些人,或至少是反对他的敌人的那些人都召集到一起来,他强调说披索的这种行为正是对皇帝的最高权威的一次武装侵犯,他亲自率领着这支强大的军队,随时准备投入战斗。

披索的计划进行得并不顺利。但是在这种情况下,他采取了一种最稳妥的办法,就是夺取奇里奇亚的名叫凯伦德利斯的一座极为坚固的要塞。奇里奇亚的小国王们已经派来了援助部队。他又将逃亡者、不久之前截获的新兵、他本人和普朗奇娜的奴隶

---

[1] 玛尔苏斯所提出的传讯并没有法律的效力,而只有在法庭庭长正式受理这一诉讼,并定出了双方出庭的日期(受理后第十天)时,传讯才有效力。

them to the strength of a division. He insisted to them that he, the emperor's governor, was kept out of the province the emperor had given him—not by the army (he was returning at its invitation), but by Sentius, whose slanders were a cloak for personal ill-will. 'Stand in line', he said, 'and the soldiers will not fight, when they see Piso whom they themselves formerly called "Father"! If right is what matters, my cause will prevail—and if it comes to force, too, it is not a weak one!'

Then Piso drew up his troops in front of the city's fortifications, at the top of a precipitous hill bounded on the other sides by the sea. Against him were old soldiers in regular units, backed by reserves. Piso's position was favourable; but his men, unlike the good troops on the other side, were dispirited and unhopeful, with rustic or makeshift weapons. When the battle started, suspense only lasted while the Roman battalions were clambering up to level ground. Then the Cilicians fled and shut themselves into the fortress. Meanwhile Piso tried to attack the fleet which was lying close by—but without success. Returning, he stood on the walls and beat his breast, calling on individuals by name with offers of reward. These incitements to mutiny had the effect of bringing over the colour-sergeant of the sixth brigade with his Eagle.

But then Sentius ordered the trumpets and bugles to sound. At his command a mound was thrown up, ladders planted and mounted by chosen men supported by a rain of spears, stones, and firebrands from

都加入到这支援助部队中,这样就将这支军队的力量加强到了一个军团的规模。他要他们来作证,他这个受皇帝委派来的统治者,现在却被排除在恺撒交给他的行省之外,不过他不是被军团(因为他是应军团之请而来的),而是被一个叫做森提乌斯的人排除在行省之外的,这个人对他进行的那些诽谤底下掩盖着他私人的仇恨。"你们要坚守自己的战线",他说,"如果对方士兵看到他们以前曾一度称为'父亲'的披索在这里,他们是绝对不会对我们作战的!"他还说,如果公理得以伸张的话,那毫无疑问他是会占上风的。如果对方悍然动用武力的话,那么他也绝对不会示弱的。

接着,披索就在城市工事前面一座陡峭的小山上面部署了自己的小队,山的其他各个侧面因为临海所以是安全的。和他相对的是他的正规部队的老兵和他们的后备部队。披索的地理位置是极为有利的,但是他的士兵却不像敌人方面那支精良的部队那样,他们无精打采,没有希望,甚至可以说没有武器,只是一些农家用具或者勉强凑合的兵器。战斗开始时,只有在罗马的步兵中队爬到平地上来以前的一段时间里,双方的战斗还算是有点悬念。接着奇里奇亚人就逃进要塞,把自己关在要塞的门内不再出来了。与此同时,披索企图向附近的一支舰队发动进攻,但是没有成功。他回来之后,便站在要塞的壁垒上,捶打着自己的胸脯,向对面召唤着个别士兵的名字,答应给他们以奖励,想用这种办法勾引对方发动叛变。他的这些煽动也产生了一定的效果,第六军团的一名旗手带着军旗投到了他这面来。

但是这时森提乌斯却下令吹起了号角和喇叭,在他的指挥下,人们就在城下堆起了一座土山,在山上架起了梯子,精选出来的士兵一直爬上了梯子,其他的士兵则用战斗器械把投枪、石

the engines. Finally Piso's stubbornness gave way. He pleaded to be allowed to stay in the fortress if he gave up his arms, while the verdict on the Syrian governorship was referred to the emperor. These terms were refused. All that was granted to him was a naval escort and safe conduct home.

At Rome, when the news of Germanicus' illness spread, with all the sinister exaggerations customary for distant events, there was grief and indignation. So this then, it was angrily said, was why he had been dismissed to a remote country, and Piso given the governorship. This had been the purpose of the Augusta's private talks with Plancina. So it was true what older men said about Nero Drusus, that rulers do not like affability in their sons! Germanicus and Nero Drusus had been struck down precisely because they had planned to give Romans back their freedom, with equal rights for everyone.

This sort of talk was greatly aggravated by the news of Germanicus' death. Without awaiting an official edict or senatorial decree, all business was suspended, the courts emptied, houses shut. There was universal silence and sorrow—no organized display or outward tokens of mourning, but profound, heartfelt grief. Some business-men who had left Syria while Germanicus was still alive happened to come with a more hopeful report of his progress. It was immediately believed and repeated at every chance encounter, and the uncritical hearers

块和引火物不断地向对方的城上投射过去,掩护他们登城。披索最后终于坚持不下去了,于是他作出了让步。他请求对方如果他把武器交出去,请允许他自己留在要塞内,以便等候皇帝对治理叙利亚的人选的确定。这些条件并未为对方所接受,所给予他的全部保证就是答应给他一些船只,把他安全地送回老家。

在罗马,当日耳曼尼库斯得病的消息传开以后,正像从远道传来的所有消息那样,每种情况都被夸大到很严重的程度,人们都感到非常悲痛和愤慨。于是在这时人们就都愤怒地说,难怪他被派到边远的地方去,而且还把一个行省的统治权交给披索,原来是为了这件事啊。奥古斯都和普朗奇娜在一起私下密谋,原来也是为了这个目的啊!因此老一辈的人所谈论的关于尼禄·杜路苏斯的话也是真的了,他们都说当政的统治者是不喜欢具有民主作风的儿子的。[1] 日耳曼尼库斯和杜路苏斯之所以被斥,原因就是他们两个人都正是想把自由还给罗马,使罗马人民人人都能享有同等的权力。

日耳曼尼库斯去世的消息使人们的这类谈论更加激烈了。人们还没有等到高级长官发布任何命令,没有等到元老院的决定公布出来,所有的事务就都停了下来,法庭里面没有人了,家家户户也都关上了大门。全城一片沉默,大家都沉浸在悲伤之中。但是他们并没有组织起来表达他们的哀悼或者打出一些哀悼的标志,但是他们的内心却怀着更深的哀悼之情。在日耳曼尼库斯还在世的时候离开叙利亚的一些商人们,偶然又带来了一些说他病情有了好转的比较令人高兴的消息。这个消息立刻就会为人们所相信,并且每当人们相遇时,总喜欢谈起这样的好消息,不加辨

---

〔1〕 杜路苏斯是奥古斯都的继子,日耳曼尼库斯是提贝里乌斯的继子。

spread it again, with joyful embellishments. Crowds ran through the city and broke open temple doors. Night encouraged credulity, and assertions waxed readier in the dark. Tiberius left the false rumours uncontradicted, for time to dispose of. Then, disillusioned, the people were all the more sorrowful—as though they had lost Germanicus a second time.

He was decreed every honour which love or ingenuity could devise. His name was introduced into the Salian hymn: curule chairs, crowned by oak-wreaths, were to be placed in his honour among the seats of the Brotherhood of Augustus; his statue in ivory was to head the processions at the Circus Games; his posts of priest of Augustus and augur were to be filled by members of the Julian family only. The knights of Rome gave the name 'Germanicus' to the block of seats, in the theatre, which had been called the 'junior block'; and they laid down that on 15th July every year his likeness should head their parade. There were to be arches at Rome, on the Rhine bank, and on Mount Amanus in Syria, with inscriptions recording his deeds and his death for his country. Antioch, where he had been cremated, was to have a sepulchre: Epidaphne, where he died, a funeral monument. His statues and cult-centres were almost innumerable. It was also proposed to place a huge golden medallion-portrait among the busts of the great orators. But Tiberius announced that he himself would

别的听者一遍又一遍兴高采烈地传播给别人,于是越传越广,而且不断地加以润饰。人们在街上跑来跑去,强行冲开了神庙的大门。夜晚激励了人们对这件事的信心,而人们在黑暗中也容易作出最大胆的肯定。提贝里乌斯并没有制止这些谣言,因为这些谣传会随着时间的流逝而自然消失的。因此,当人们醒悟过来,知道日耳曼尼库斯确实已经死了的时候,就觉得好像又一次失去了日耳曼尼库斯一样,陷入了更深的痛苦之中。

或是出于爱戴,或是由于机敏,日耳曼尼库斯被冠以了各种哀荣。他的名字将放进撒利人的赞美诗,让大家歌唱;在奉祀奥古斯都的祭司们有权坐的地方,也都要为日耳曼尼库斯设置显贵的专席,上面还要安放上桂冠;在举行赛马时的仪仗中,他的象牙雕像要摆在最前面。继承他生前担任的祭司或占卜师之职的人,必须是尤利乌斯家族出身的人。罗马的骑士阶级把剧场中他们坐的那一部分座位,即先前所谓的“低级座位”,都以“日耳曼尼库斯”为名字来命名;他们还规定每年的 7 月 15 日,他的像要举在骑兵队伍的前面。[1] 在罗马,在莱茵河畔,在叙利亚的阿玛努斯山上都修造了拱门,上面铭记着他的功勋和他殉国的事迹。在安提奥克,他被火葬的地方,修造了一座坟墓;在埃披达普尼,他去世的地方,人们为他竖立了一座墓碑。人们给他造的像和奉祀他的地方几乎可以说是不计其数。还有人建议为他铸造一个巨大的金质圆形浮雕像,放置在那些伟大的演说家的半身像中间。但是提贝里乌斯这时却说他本人只想奉献一个像其他人的一样的普

---

〔1〕 这是一个已经废除了的传统的骑士的庆典,奥古斯都又重新将它恢复。

dedicate one of the usual sort—like the rest—since opulence was no criterion of eloquence and it was compliment enough to be ranked with the classic writers. A good many of these honours are still paid, but some were discontinued, at once or in course of time.

While the mourning was still fresh, Germanicus' sister Livilla— the wife of Drusus—gave birth to twin sons. This happy event, rare even in ordinary homes, gratified the emperor so much that he could not resist boasting to the senate that twins had never been born to so distinguished a Roman father before. He extracted material for self-congratulation from everything—even accidents! But among the people even this, at such a time, was unwelcome. The increase in Drusus' family seemed a further blow to that of Germanicus.

In the same year the senate passed stringent decrees against female immorality. The granddaughters, daughters, and wives of Roman gentlemen were debarred from prostitution. A woman called Vistilia, belonging to a family that had held the praetorship, had advertised her availability to the aediles, in accordance with the custom of our ancestors who believed that an immoral woman would be sufficiently punished by this shameful declaration. Her husband Titidius Labeo was also requested to state why, when his wife was obviously guilty, he had refrained from enforcing the statutory penalty. He alleged, however, that the sixty days allowed him for consultation had not expired. It was therefore decided to take action regarding the

通的雕像,因为外表的豪华并不能作为口才的标准,而且把他和古代的大师并列,这种光荣也已经足够了。许多这样的荣誉一直保留了下来,但是也有一些没有保留下来,有的是立刻被废掉了,有的是过了一段时间后渐渐湮没了。

正当公众还沉浸在对日耳曼尼库斯的死亡的深深的哀悼中的时候,日耳曼尼库斯的姊妹、杜路苏斯的妻子利维拉却生了一对双胞胎的儿子。这样令人高兴的喜事,甚至在普通人家也都极为罕见,皇帝是如此心满意足,以致禁不住向元老们夸耀说,双胞胎得以生在这样一个显贵的罗马父亲家里的事,以前还从来没有过。他利用任何事情,来进行自我吹捧,即便是偶然发生的事情,也为他所利用。但是,在人民中间,在这样的时刻,即使这件事也是不受欢迎的。因为杜路苏斯家中人口的增加,只会进一步加重对日耳曼尼库斯一家的打击。

同年,元老院发布严厉的法令,限制女人们的不道德行为。法令规定,凡是罗马贵族的孙女、女儿和妻子,一律禁止卖淫。原来有一个行政长官家庭出身的妇女维司提里娅曾到营造官那里去公开登记申请卖淫,这是符合我们的祖先的传统规定的,因为我们的祖先认为,这样耻辱的申请本身,已经是对一个放荡的女人足够严厉的惩罚了。她的丈夫提提狄乌斯·拉贝欧也受到质询,为什么他的妻子已经是明显地犯了罪,而他却还阻止法律强制执行的惩罚呢? 然而,他的理由却是,法律所允许他的 60 天的考虑期限还没有届满[1] 于是元老院便决定对维司提里娅采取行动,将

---

[1]　罗马的法律规定,妻子犯罪后,丈夫可以在 60 天中间准备起诉事宜。

woman only, and she was deported to the island of Seriphos.

Another discussion concerned the expulsion of Egyptian and Jewish rites. The senate decreed that four thousand adult ex-slaves tainted with those superstitions should be transported to Sardinia to suppress banditry there. If the unhealthy climate killed them, the loss would be small. The rest, unless they repudiated their unholy practices by a given date, must leave Italy.

The emperor reported that a priestess of Vesta had to be chosen in place of Occia, whose saintly priesthood had lasted fifty-seven years. He thanked Fonteius Agrippa and Comicius Pollio for the patriotic rivalry with which they had offered their daughters. The choice fell on Pollio's child, the reputation of Agrippa's family having suffered from his divorce. However, Tiberius consoled the rejected girl by a dowry of a million sesterces.

There was popular agitation against the terrible expense of corn. Tiberius fixed the sale price and promised a subsidy of two sesterces a bushel for dealers. But he still rejected the title 'Father of his Country', which was not offered him again because of this. He also severely reproved people who spoke of his occupations as 'divine' and himself as 'master'. So the paths of speech were narrow and slippery. For though the emperor dreaded freedom, he detested flattery.

I find from the writings of contemporary senators that a letter was read in the senate from a chieftain of the Chatti named Adgandestrius, offering to kill Arminius if poison were sent him for the job. The reported answer was that Romans take vengeance on their enemies,

她流放到塞里波司岛去了。

讨论的另一件事情是关于禁止埃及的和犹太的礼节。元老院还规定把4000名沾染上这种宗教信仰的被释放的成年奴隶用船送到撒丁去,在那里执行镇压盗匪的任务。如果他们死于当地的不利于健康的气候,那么这一损失也是很小的。其他信奉异教的人们,除非到规定的日期声明放弃他们那不敬的礼节,他们就必须要离开意大利。

皇帝建议挑选一位维司塔贞女来接替欧克奇娅,她对维司塔祭仪的圣洁无瑕地主持已经延续了57年。他感谢丰提乌斯·阿格里帕和考米奇乌斯·波里欧两人,因为他们出于爱国的热忱争着要把自己的女儿献出来。结果选定了波里欧的女儿,因为阿格里帕的离婚使他家的声誉受到了影响。而为了安慰失败的女孩子,提贝里乌斯赠给了她100万谢司特尔提乌斯,作为嫁妆。

对于粮价的昂贵,人们都激烈地表示反对。于是他便做了一些平议粮价的工作,他本人答应粮商每一蒲式耳的粮食由他给予两谢司特尔提乌斯的补贴。但他还是拒绝接受先前建议过的要授给他"国父"的尊号,因此,授予"国父"尊号的事也就再一次作罢。他还严厉斥责那些把他的事业说成是"神圣的",又称他本人为"主人"的行为。因为这位皇帝害怕自由,却又讨厌谄媚的言语,人们的言路也就十分狭窄而又容易摔跤了。

从同时代担任过元老的作家的作品中,我发现,在元老院里曾宣读过从卡提伊人的名字叫阿德刚德司特利乌斯的酋长那里来的一封信。信里提出说,如果给他送去毒药,他可以把阿尔米尼乌斯害死。但是给他的回答却是,罗马人民对他们的敌人进行

not by underhand tricks, but by open force of arms. By this elevated sentiment Tiberius invited comparison with generals of old who had forbidden, and disclosed, the plan to poison King Pyrrhus. However, the Roman evacuation of Germany and the fall of Maroboduus had induced Arminius to aim at kingship. But his freedom-loving compatriots forcibly resisted. The fortunes of the fight fluctuated, but finally Arminius succumbed to treachery from his relations.

He was unmistakably the liberator of Germany. Challenger of Rome —not in its infancy, like kings and commanders before him, but at the height of its power—he had fought undecided battles, and never lost a war. He had ruled for twelve of his thirty-seven years. To this day the tribes sing of him. Yet Greek historians ignore him, reserving their admiration for Greece. We Romans, too, underestimate him, since in our devotion to antiquity we neglect modern history.

Agrippina pressed on with her journey over the wintry sea. When she reached the island of Corcyra, opposite the Calabrian coast, she paused for a few days to calm herself. Her misery was unendurable. Meanwhile, at the news of her approach, people flocked to Brundusium, the nearest and safest port of disembarkation. Close friends came, and many officers who had served under Germanicus; also

报复时从来不使用阴谋诡计,而是进行公开的作战。通过这种崇高的情操,提贝里乌斯把自己置身于那些古代统帅的行列以邀誉,这些人曾经阻止并且揭发了毒死国王庇鲁斯的建议。然而,罗马人从日耳曼的撤军,以及玛洛波都斯的被放逐,使阿尔米尼乌斯又开始有了做国王的野心。但是他的那些热爱自由的人民用武力反抗他,战争的命运摇摆不定,但最后阿尔米尼乌斯还是死在他的亲戚的阴谋之中。

他毫无疑问是日耳曼的解放者,他和他先前的那些首领和国王不同,他面对的挑战者不是童年时期的罗马,而是一个势力正如日中天的罗马,他与罗马进行了无数次未决出胜负的战斗,而且整个战争没有失败过。在他 37 年的生命里程中,他统治了这一民族 12 年,[1]直到今天他本族的歌谣还在传颂他的事迹。但是那些将赞美给予了希腊历史事件的希腊历史学家们却忽略了他,而我们这些罗马人,也没有对他给予足够的重视,因为我们只醉心颂扬往古而漠视我们当前时代的历史。

阿格里披娜日夜兼程地在冬天的海上赶路[2],到达与卡拉布里亚的海岸相对峙的科尔启拉岛时,阿格里披娜停了下来,在那里休息了几天,以便使自己的心情平静下来,她所遭遇的不幸和悲惨是难以承受的。这时,人们听说她的到来,立刻都拥到布伦地西乌姆来,因为这里是航行者最近的、最安全的登陆地点。亲近的朋友们都来了,还有许多曾在日耳曼尼库斯的领导下服过军

---

〔1〕 他在位的时间应当从他击败伐鲁斯的时候算起,这样他的卒年应当是公元 21 年。

〔2〕 公元 20 年,罗马建城 773 年。

many strangers from towns nearby, some to pay duty to the emperor, others (more numerous) imitating them. As soon as her squadron was seen out to sea, huge sorrowing crowds filled the harbours and shallows, walls, house-tops—every vantage point.

They wondered whether they ought to receive her landing in silence or with some utterance. As they still hesitated about the appropriate course, the fleet gradually came nearer. There was none of the usual brisk rowing, but every deliberate sign of grief. Agrippina, with her two children, stepped off the ship, her eyes lowered, the urn of death in her hands. Her companions were worn out by prolonged grieving; so the sorrow of the fresh mourners who now met her was more demonstrative. Otherwise everyone's feelings were indistinguishable; the cries of men and women, relatives and strangers, blended in a single universal groan.

Tiberius had sent two battalions of the Guard, and had ordered the officials of Calabria, Apulia and Campania to pay their last respects to his adoptive son. So, as his ashes were borne on the shoulders of colonels and company-commanders, preceded by unadorned standards and reversed axes, at each successive settlement—in proportion to its wealth—the populace clothed in black and the knights in purplestriped tunics burnt garments, spices, and other funeral offerings. Even people from towns far away came to meet the procession, offering sacrifices and erecting altars to the dead man's soul, and showing their grief by tears and lamentations.

Drusus came out to Tarracina with Germanicus' brother Claudius and those of his children who had been at Rome. The consuls Marcus

役的官员,甚至还有从附近各个市镇赶来的陌生人。有些人这样做是为了向皇帝致敬,而其他(大多数的)人则是模仿他们的榜样。当阿格里披娜的船队出现在海上的时候,巨大的悲哀的人群就充满了海港、海湾、城墙、屋顶和所有能据以瞭望的地方。

他们拿不定主意。当阿格里披娜登岸时,他们是沉默好呢,还是用声音来表示悲痛情绪好呢。当他们还在犹豫,在这种情况下怎样才算得体时,舰队已经逐渐靠近了海岸。这次没有了常见的那种欢快活泼的热烈的摇桨场面,而是所有的人都一致表现出早有准备的悲伤的表情。阿格里披娜带着两个孩子走下船,她两只眼睑低垂着,手里捧着骨灰瓶。和阿格里披娜同行的人们由于长时间沉浸在悲痛中,已经筋疲力尽了,因此前来迎接她的新的悼念者们的悲痛情绪反而表现得更加显著了。这时人们齐声发出了悲痛的呼号,分不清哪是男人的哭声,哪是女人的,也分不清谁是亲属,谁是陌生人,各种哭声叹息声都混合在了一起。

提贝里乌斯派来了近卫军的两个步兵中队,并且命令卡拉布里亚、阿普里亚和康帕尼亚等地的高级官吏们为他的继子举行追悼仪式。因此日耳曼尼库斯的骨灰便由军团将领和百人团长们抬在肩头上,行进在他们前面的则是举着不加装饰的军旗和倒持着斧头的仪仗队,每当他们经过一个居民区的时候,穿着黑色衣服的平民和紫条的外袍的骑士,便根据自己的经济状况焚烧衣服、香料和其他用来送葬的供物。甚至远处各个市镇的居民也赶来迎接送葬的队伍,为死者的亡灵奉献牺牲,修造祭坛,并且用泪水和恸哭表示自己的悲痛心情。

杜路苏斯偕同日耳曼尼库斯的亲兄弟克劳狄乌斯和他的留在罗马的孩子们来到了特拉契纳。执政官玛尔库斯·瓦列里乌

Valerius Messalla Messallinus (II) and Marcus Aurelius Cotta Maximus Messallinus had now begun their term of office, and they, the senate, and a great part of the population thronged the roadside in scattered groups, weeping as their hearts moved them. There was no flattery of the emperor in this. Indeed everyone knew that Tiberius could scarcely conceal his delight at the death of Germanicus.

He and the Augusta made no public appearance. Either they considered open mourning beneath their dignity, or they feared that the public gaze would detect insincerity on their faces. I cannot discover in histories or official journals that Germanicus' mother Antonia (II) played a prominent part in these happenings, although the names not only of Agrippina, Drusus and Claudius, but of all his other bloodrelations as well are recorded. Ill-health may have prevented her. Or perhaps she was too overcome by grief to endure visible evidence of her bereavement. But it seems to me more plausible that Tiberius and the Augusta, who remained at home, kept her there too, so that the dead man's grandmother and uncle might seem, by staying indoors, only to be following the mother's example, and grieving no less than she.

On the day when the remains were conducted to the Mausoleum of Augustus there was a desolate silence—rent only by wailing. The streets were full, the Field of Mars ablaze with torches. Everyone—

斯·羌撒拉·美撒利努斯（二世）和玛尔库斯·奥列里乌斯·科特·玛克西姆斯·美撒利努斯现在已经就任，他们、元老们和很大一部分人民都三五一组地群集在路旁，他们尽情地哭泣着，宣泄着自己内心的悲哀。他们这种表现根本没有讨好皇帝的意思，因为这里的每个人都知道，提贝里乌斯在接到日耳曼尼库斯的死讯时，差一点就掩饰不住自己的喜悦心情了。

他和奥古斯塔没有在公开的场合出现。这或者是因为他们认为公开表示哀悼有失他们的尊严，或者是害怕公众的凝视会探察到他们的不真诚。无论在历史学家的著作，还是在官方的官报中，[1]我都未能发现日耳曼尼库斯的母亲安托尼娅（二世）[2]曾在整个这些事件中起过任何显著的作用，虽然，在阿格里披娜和杜路苏斯和克劳狄乌斯之外，还记录了他的别的有血缘关系的亲属的名字。她也许由于身体不好而无法参加仪式，也许是因为太悲伤过度了，以致不能承受眼前各种亲子丧亡的真实证物。但是我觉得更有可能的理由则是，留在家里的提贝乌斯和奥古斯塔让她待在那里的，他们这样做以便给人以这样的印象：祖母和叔父留在家里而不出去参加葬礼的做法，只不过是老老实实地模仿了母亲的榜样而已，因为他们的哀恸一点也不比他的母亲少。

骨灰被送到奥古斯都灵庙去的那一天，所到之处是一片凄凉的宁静，只有一阵阵的哀号声不时地打破这种宁静。所经过的街

---

〔1〕　这些官报是从尤利乌斯·恺撒的第一次共同执政时期，即公元前59年就已经开始了的。

〔2〕　安托尼娅大约生在公元前36年，她是安东尼和奥古斯都的姊妹屋大维娅二人所生的两个女儿中间的幼女，嫁给了提贝里乌斯的兄弟杜路苏斯，她一直活到卡里古拉当政的时候。

armed soldiers, officials without their insignia, the people organized in their tribes—reiterated that Rome was done for, all hope gone. In the readiness and openness of their talk, they seemed to forget their rulers. But what upset Tiberius most was the popular enthusiasm for Agrippina. The glory of her country, they called her—the only true descendant of Augustus, the unmatched model of traditional behaviour. Gazing to heaven, they prayed that her children might live to survive their enemies.

Some people missed the pageantry of a state funeral. How different, they said, had been the magnificent rites devoted by Augustus to Germanicus' father, Nero Drusus! In deepest winter the emperor had gone to Ticinum, and had not left the body until it entered Rome. Statues of Claudii and Livii had surrounded the bier. Nero Drusus had been mourned in the Roman Forum, praised from its dais—every honour ever thought of, ancient or modern, had been his. Yet Germanicus had not even received the honours due to any nobleman. Certainly, he had died so far from Rome that his body had to be cremated unceremoniously in a foreign land. ' But if due marks of respect were thus at first fortuitously denied him, they should be all the more numerous later. His brother went only one day's journey to

道上挤满了人,玛尔斯广场上火把的光芒在不时地闪耀着。所有的人——武装的士兵、不佩戴勋章的官吏、按照族群组织起来的公民,人人都在那里反复地大声叫道,罗马垮了,一点希望也没有了。他们在大庭广众之下,公开地大声叫喊,看起来似乎是完全忘记了统治者的存在。但是最使提贝里乌斯心烦意乱的是人们对阿格里披娜所表现出的普遍的爱戴。人们称她为祖国的光荣,奥古斯都仅存的后裔、无与伦比的传统美德的典范。人们凝视上苍,向上天和诸神祷告,希望她的后人能活得比他们的敌人更为长久。

有些人觉得这次葬礼没有一个国葬应有的壮观气派。他们说,这次葬礼和奥古斯都为日耳曼尼库斯的父亲尼禄·杜路苏斯所举行的宏伟壮观的仪式相比,差别简直是太大了。在最寒冷的严冬季节里,皇帝亲自到提奇努姆去,[1]而且一路陪着遗骨,送到罗马之前,一步也没有离开过。棺架的四周摆满了克劳狄乌斯家族和里维乌斯家族的胸像。尼禄·杜路苏斯的追悼会是在罗马广场举行的,人们在讲坛上对他作了各种各样的赞颂,凡是所能想到的,古代或者是现代的所有的一切的荣誉都被加到了他的身上。但是日耳曼尼库斯却连任何一个普通贵族所应得到的荣誉都没有得到! 当然,他死在远离罗马的异地,因而没有任何仪式就在外地把遗体火化了,这也勉强还算是在情理之中。"但是如果说偶然的情况使得当初未能授予他这些哀荣,但是在事后也应当大量地追授他所有的哀荣啊。他的兄弟只不过仅仅是走了一

---

[1] 今天的帕维亚。公元前 9 年,杜路苏斯死于日耳曼,提贝里乌斯到 200 里外去奔丧。

meet him. Even the gate was too far for his uncle! What had happened to the traditional customs? The image at the head of the bier,
the formal poems of eulogy, the panegyrics—the tears, which at least
simulated sorrow?'

Tiberius heaid of all this. Then, to silence the widespread talk,
he issued the following statement. 'Many famous Romans have died
for their country. But none has ever been so ardently lamented before. That seems admirable to all, myself included—provided that
moderation is observed. For the conduct of ordinary households or
communities is not appropriate for rulers or an imperial people. Tearful mourning was a proper consolation in the first throes of grief. But
now be calm again. Remember how Julius Caesar, when he lost his
only daughter, and Augustus, when he lost his grandsons, hid their
sorrow—not to mention Rome's courageous endurance (on earlier occasions) of the loss of armies, the deaths of generals, the total destruction of great families. Rulers die; the country lives for ever. So
return to your ordinary occupations—and since the Megalesian Games
are nearly due, to your pleasures. '

So business started again. People went back to work; and Drusus

天的路程,去迎他的遗骨。他的叔父甚至连大门都没有迈出！那些传统习俗到底出了什么问题了呢？在灵床的头部放置的胸像,歌颂死者的德行的那些例行的诗篇、颂词,甚至至少能假情假意也流出一些悲伤的泪水,又都到哪里去了呢?"

所有这些话,提贝里乌斯全都听到了。于是,为了平息这些到处传播的言论,他发表了这样的一个声明:"许多显赫的罗马人为国捐躯,但是以前从来没有任何一个人像日耳曼尼库斯今天这样受到如此深切的哀悼。这种尊敬的表示使所有的人,也包括我,都感到十分欣慰,但是这件事情要做得适当。因为普通家庭或社群的行为并不适合于一个国家领袖或是皇室的成员。人们在刚刚遇到极大痛苦的时候,痛哭流涕的哀悼是一种适当的安慰。但是现在到了必须克制自己的时候了。请大家不要忘记,当尤利乌斯恺撒在失去他唯一的女儿时,[1]以及奥古斯都在失去他的外孙时,[2]是怎样抑制自己的悲痛的。更不用说罗马人民(在过去的历史上)在军队被歼、将领阵亡和名门世家灭门绝族时表现得是何等的英勇坚强。首领们是会死去的,但国家却会永世长存。因此大家还是各自回到自己的本业上去吧,因为美伽利修斯节就要来临了,[3]你们也可以恢复娱乐活动了。"

因此生活又开始恢复了正常,人们又各自回去做自己的事情

---

〔1〕 恺撒和科尔涅里娅的女儿,生于公元前83(或82)年,公元前59年嫁给庞培,5年后去世。

〔2〕 盖乌斯与路奇乌斯·恺撒。

〔3〕 是纪念诸神之母,伟大的母神库倍列的节日,每年4月4～10日举行,节日活动以演剧为主。

left for the armies of Illyricum. Everyone looked forward to retribution for Piso. It was widely complained that he was insolently and treasonably loitering in pleasure trips round Asia and Achaia, and meanwhile suppressing the proofs of his crimes. For it had become known that the notorious poisoner Martina (sent to Rome, as I have mentioned, by Cnaeus Sentius Saturninus) had suddenly died at Brundusium; and that, although her body bore no signs of suicide, poison had been found hidden in a knot of her hair.

Meanwhile Piso sent his son Marcus ahead to Rome with soothing messages for the emperor. He himself visited Drusus, from whom he hoped to find gratitude for the removal of a rival rather than estrangement because of a brother's death. Tiberius, to show his open mind, received Piso's son courteously, with the presents customarily given to young noblemen. Drusus said to Piso that, if the rumours were accurate, his own fury would be greater than anybody's—but that he prayed they were false and baseless, and that Germanicus' death would ruin no one. This was said openly; Drusus avoided a private interview. It was generally believed that his answer, which displayed an old man's diplomacy foreign to his youthful affability and directness, was prompted by Tiberius.

Piso crossed the Adriatic, left his ships at Ancona, and caught up a brigade marching from Pannonia to Rome on its way to join the

了。杜路苏斯动身回伊里利库姆的军队。大家都很希望看到披索能够得到应有的制裁。人们都普遍地指责说，披索在这段时期里却侮慢无礼、背信弃义地在亚细亚和阿凯亚地区到处游山玩水，同时利用这个漫游的机会掩人耳目地把罪证消灭掉。因为人们已经知道，那个臭名昭著的投毒犯玛尔提娜（我在前面说过，她是被格涅乌斯·森提乌斯·撒图尔尼乌斯送到罗马来的），突然在布伦地西乌姆死了。虽然在她的尸体上看不出任何自杀的痕迹，[1]但是在她的一个发结里却发现了隐藏着的毒药。

这时，披索派他的儿子玛尔库斯先到罗马来，打探皇帝的真实意图。而披索自己又去拜会了杜路苏斯，他希望发现杜路苏斯不会由于兄弟的死亡而疏远他，反而会由于除掉一个敌手而对他表示满意。提贝里乌斯为了表示公正不倚，很有礼貌地接见了这个年轻的贵族，并且赐给他不少的东西，他通常对于名门子弟都是这样对待的。杜路苏斯对于披索的回答却是，如果外面的传说确有其事，那么他的愤怒将会比任何人都要强烈，但是他但愿那些说法是虚假的毫无根据的谣传，并且希望日耳曼尼库斯的去世不会殃及任何人。这些话是他当着众人的面讲的，杜路苏斯避免一切私下的会晤。大家都认为，杜路苏斯所讲的这些话显示出一个温和而又直截了当的青年人所不可能有的老练的外交手腕，其背后肯定是提贝里乌斯在指使。

披索在渡过了亚得里亚海之后，就在安科纳登陆了，他赶上了从潘诺尼亚到罗马去的一个军团，这个军团是准备以后到阿非利加

―――――――――

〔1〕 有人说，她是在披索的逼迫下服毒自杀的。

army in Africa. Gossip stressed that he persistently brought himself to the troops' attention during the march from Narnia. But then, to avoid suspicion—or perhaps because frightened men change their plans—he embarked on the Nera, and subsequently the Tiber, and increased his unpopularity by landing beside the imperial Mausoleum. It was a busy time of day and the river-bank was crowded. But Piso with a large escort of dependants, and Plancina surrounded by women, went on their way with cheerful expressions. Moreover, his house, which overlooked the Forum, was festively decorated; and a dinnerparty followed. In that crowded area nothing was private—and indignation mounted.

On the next day Lucius Fulcinius Trio applied to the consuls for leave to accuse Piso. Germanicus' staff, led by Publius Vitellius and Quintus Veranius (I), objected that Trio had nothing to do with the matter, but that they themselves were available—not as accusers, but as witnesses to the facts, and bearers of Germanicus' instructions. Trio waived his proposal to prosecute on this charge, but obtained authority to attack Piso's previous career. The emperor was then asked to take over the inquiry. The accused was not sorry. He anticipated malevolence among senators and others, but believed that Tiberius

去参加那里的防务的。[1] 从纳尔尼亚一直到这儿的一路行军中，披索一直在显示自己以引起士兵们的注意，因此人们在闲谈中对他的议论特别多。继而，或许是为了逃避嫌疑，或许是由于心怀恐惧的人容易改变主意，他在纳尔尼坐上了船，沿纳尔河、继而是台伯河下行，不过更加使大家感到不满的是，他在恺撒们的灵庙所在地的附近下船登上了岸。当时正是一天当中最忙碌的时候，河岸上挤满了人。可是带着一大群侍从的披索和有许多妇女簇拥着的普朗奇娜却一副兴高采烈的样子。还有他那俯瞰着广场的住宅被披上了节日的盛装，紧接着在那里举行了招待客人的宴会。在那样人多眼杂的地方，任何事情都是逃不过大家的眼睛的，人们对他们这种得意的行为非常愤怒。

第二天，路奇乌斯·富尔奇尼乌斯·特里奥就向执政官请求控告披索。[2] 不过，日耳曼尼库斯的下属，以普布里乌斯·维提里乌斯和克温图斯·维拉尼乌斯（一世）为首的一些人却提出反对意见，认为特里奥与此事无关。而他们自己也不打算担任控诉人，他们只是做一个目睹这一事实的证人，一个日耳曼尼库斯临终指令的执行者。特里奥在控诉披索这件事情上的建议也并不坚定，但是他却取得了对披索早先的行为作风加以抨击的权力。于是，皇帝被请求来主持这次调查。被告对此并不感到遗憾，他早已经预见到在元老院和其他人中间，对他是存在

---

〔1〕 为了戒备塔克法里那斯。以后这个军团过早地被提贝里乌斯撒走了。

〔2〕 路奇乌斯·富尔奇尼乌斯·特里奥请求元老院听取此案情况，此前，首先由皇帝听取原被告双方的简单陈述。在重大案件中这两种新程序都被法院的常规处理所取代。

had the strength to ignore gossip and was also immobilized by his mother's complicity. Besides, he argued, it was easier for a single judge to distinguish truth from defamation: numbers encourage prejudice and hostile emotion.

Tiberius was fully aware of the problems of the investigation and of the malignant rumours about himself. So, after listening-with the help of a few close friends—to the accusations and pleas of defence, he referred the whole case to the senate. (At this stage Drusus returned from Illyricum and entered the city, postponing the ovation decreed him by the senate for the suppression of Maroboduus and his other achievements in the summer before last.) Men asked by Piso to defend him—Lucius Arruntius, Publius Vinicius, Gaius Asinius Gallus, Marcus Claudius Marcellus Aeserninus, and Sextus Pompeius (II)- declined on various pretexts. But he received support from Marcus Aemilius Lepidus (IV), Lucius Calpurnius Piso (I), and Livincius Regulus (I). The whole of Rome was excitedly asking: would Germanicus' friends keep their word? What was Piso's defence? Would Tiberius succeed in repressing his feelings? Never had there been so much intense public interest, and so much private criticism and unspoken suspicion of the emperor.

On the day of the senate's meeting the emperor spoke with studied moderation. 'Cnaeus Piso', he said, 'was my father's friend and

着很深的厌恶情绪的,但是他相信,提贝里乌斯有力量驳回这种闲言碎语似的诉讼,而且皇帝也会由于他自己的母亲共同参加了这个阴谋而将这件事压下来的。此外他还认为,皇帝做出一个把真相和外面相信的诽谤区分开来的简单的判决是非常容易的。而如果参加断案的人很多,憎恶和敌视的情绪也就多了。

提贝里乌斯完全清楚所调查的各种问题,对于外面流传的关于他本人的各种十分不利的谣言,他也心知肚明。因此他就在他的几位密友的帮助下,先听取了原告的控告和被告的请求,随后便把这个案件全部交给元老院去处理了。(就在这时,杜路苏斯从伊里库姆回来并进入了罗马。由于他平定了玛洛波都斯以及他在前一年的夏天所取得的成功,元老院决定为他举行小凯旋式;但是他却将这一小凯旋式推迟而回到了罗马。)披索请求路奇乌斯·阿尔伦提乌斯、普布里乌斯·维尼奇乌斯、盖乌斯·阿西尼乌斯·伽路斯、玛尔库斯·克劳狄乌斯·玛尔凯路斯·埃塞尔尼努斯和塞克斯图斯·彭佩乌斯(二世)五个人做他的辩护人,但是这五人却用各种不同的借口回绝了他。不过玛尔库斯·埃米利乌斯·列庇都斯(四世)、路奇乌斯·卡尔普尔尼乌斯·披索(一世)和李维涅乌斯·列古路斯(一世)却愿意为他效劳。整个罗马上上下下都在关切地问:日耳曼尼库斯的朋友们是否信守他们对日耳曼尼库斯的诺言? 披索是如何为自己进行申辩的? 提贝里乌斯是不是还能压制自己心里的感情? 人民群众对国家的事情的兴趣从来没有这样强烈过,对于皇帝本人所做出的个人的批评意见也从来没有这样多,暗地里对他的怀疑也从来没有这深过。

元老院集会的那天,皇帝以仔细琢磨过的分寸发表了讲话。他说:"格涅乌斯·披索过去是我的父亲的朋友和副帅,而我本人又是

governor, and I myself, with the senate's approval, made him Germanicus' helper in his eastern duties. It must be decided objectively whether, having upset the prince by disobedience and quarrelsomeness, he rejoiced at his death, or whether he murdered him. For if he has exceeded his position, failed in respect to his senior, and exulted in his death—and my sorrow—then I will renounce his friendship and close my doors against him, but not use a ruler's power to avenge personal wrongs. If, however, there is proof of murder, a crime which would require vengeance whatever the victim's rank, it will be your duty to give proper satisfaction to the children of Germanicus and to us his parents.

'You must also consider these questions. Did Piso incite his troops to mutiny and rebellion? Did he bribe them to support him? Did he make war to recover the province? Or are these lies spread and elaborated by the accusers? Their excessive vigour has given me cause for irritation. For to strip the body and expose it to the stares of the public, thus encouraging—among foreigners—the report that he was poisoned, served no good purpose since this question is still undecided, and the subject of inquiry.

'I grieve for my son, and always shall. But I offer the accused every opportunity of producing evidence which may establish his innocence or Germanicus' unfairness, if there was any. And I implore you not to regard charges as proofs because my personal grief is involved. Those whose blood-relationship or loyalty to Piso have made them his defenders should help him in his peril with all the eloquence and indus-

在征得元老院的同意之后,任命披索为日耳曼尼库斯的助手以处理东方的事务的。担任这一职务的披索是由于固执己见和喜好争论而惹怒了王子,从而欣喜于他的去世,还是他谋害了他的性命,这个问题一定要得到一个客观公正地判别。如果实际的情况是他曾经僭越行事,藐视上级并且对日耳曼尼库斯的去世欢欣雀跃——而我正沉浸于悲痛之中,那么我就要同他断绝友情,将他拒之门外。但是我不会利用帝王的权力去报复个人的仇怨。如果有证据证明日耳曼尼库斯确实是他害死的,则不管被害者是什么样的身份,罪犯也是应当受到报复的,那么就请你们酌情处理吧,应当如何恰当地给予日耳曼尼库斯的孩子们以及我们,也就是他的双亲以抚慰,就是你们的职责所在了。

"同时你们应当仔细考量这些问题:披索是否煽动过军队发动骚乱或是叛变?他是否曾贿买过军团的士兵来支持他?他是否曾挑起了战争以重新恢复他行省的统治权?还是这些说法都是控诉者散布的谎言,而且是精心编织的谎言?对于他们的这种过分粗莽的做法,我本人是有理由感到生气的。因为剥去尸体的衣服,把他暴露在公众的目光之下,这样便激起了议论——甚至是在异邦人中间,说他是被毒死的,在争论还没有最后确定而还需要调查的时候,这样的做法是不怀好意的。

"我为我儿子的死亡感到悲痛,并且会永远这样。但是我会给被告一个机会,来提出足以证明他的无辜和日耳曼尼库斯的不公正的证据,如果确实有的话。我请求你们不要因为这一件事牵涉到我个人的悲痛,就把别人的指控径直地当成是他犯罪的证据。如果同披索有亲属关系或是忠诚于他的那些人,站出来为他辩护,在他身处危险的时候施展自己的全部口才并用出全部的精

try they possess; and I urge the accusers to be no less industrious and determined. I propose that Germanicus should be placed outside the law in one respect only: the investigation of his death is being conducted by the senate in its House and not by judges in a law court. Let similar restraint mark the rest of the case, regardless of the tears of Drusus or my own sorrow—or slanders invented against us. '

It was decided to allow the prosecution two days and then-after an interval of six days—the defence three. Lucius Fulcinius Trio opened with an ancient, pointless story of corruption and extortion during Piso's Spanish governorship. Proofs of this would not damage the accused if he refuted the recent charges, and likewise its disproof would not exonerate him if he were convicted of the graver offences. Then Quintus Servaeus, Quintus Veranius, and Publius Vitellius spoke, all earnestly and Vitellius brilliantly. They alleged that Piso, hating Germanicus and hankering after rebellion, had allowed the troops to become undisciplined and overbearing to the provincials, corrupting them into calling him, as the riff-raff did, 'father of the army'. Against every good man, on the other hand, he had borne malice—and particularly against the staff and friends of Germanicus. Finally, they continued, he had killed Germanicus by spells and poison. Then, after his and Plancina's evil rites and sacrifices, he had made war on the State, and had to be defeated before he could be prosecuted.

Under every head except one the defence faltered. Bribery of the

诚来帮助他,那么我希望,原告这方面的人也能表现出同样地勤勉和坚定。我建议,关于日耳曼尼库斯的案件,我们不按一般的法律程序,只作出一种处理,这就是:对他的死亡案件的调查审理只在元老院内部由元老们进行,而不是交给法官们在法庭上审理。有关这一案件的其他方面也应当有同样的限制,而不要考虑杜路苏斯的眼泪和我自己的悲伤,也不要受到人们对我们的恶意诽谤的影响。"

于是决定给原告两天的时间提出控诉,休会 6 天后,再给被告 3 天的时间进行辩护。路奇乌斯·富尔奇尼乌斯·特里奥首先讲了一大篇陈腐的、不得要领的话,历数披索在统治西班牙时的腐败作风和强取豪夺的行径。如果被告驳倒了这些对最近的事情的指控,那么这些证据就不会对他造成任何损害;同样的,如果他被确认为犯了更严重的罪行,那么这些反证也仍然不能给他开脱罪名。接下来是克温图斯·塞尔瓦埃乌斯、克温图斯·维拉尼乌斯和普布里乌斯·维提里乌斯所作的发言,他们的情绪都显得十分激动,其中维提里乌斯表现得最有才华。他们指控披索说:"他由于憎恨日耳曼尼库斯和企图制造叛乱,而使军队纪律松弛,他纵容士兵凌辱行省居民,造成普通士兵们思想涣散堕落,致使一些乌合之众竟称他为'军团之父'。而另一方面,对于每一个品行良好的人,特别是日耳曼尼库斯的同僚和朋友,他却残忍得很。最后,部队依然一片混乱,而他竟然借助于毒药和巫术害死了日耳曼尼库斯。这之后他本人和普朗奇娜就举行了用心邪恶的仪式和祭献,随后他又发动了对国家的叛乱,不过为了使他受到应得的起诉,人们在战场上将他打败了。"

对于上述的各项指控,除去一项之外,其他辩护都是站不住

troops, abandonment of the province to every rascal, and insults a-gainst the commander, was undeniable. The poisoning charge alone was refuted. No conviction was carried by the story of the accusers that, at a party of Germanicus, Piso, his neighbour at dinner, had himself put poison into his food. It seemed fantastic that he should have attempted this, with many people looking on—including another man's slaves—and under Germanicus' own eyes. Piso offered his own slaves for torture and demanded that the waiters should be tortured too.

But for various reasons the judges were implacable—Tiberius because he had made war on the province, the senate because it remained unconvinced that Germanicus had died naturally. Both the emperor and Piso refused to produce private correspondence. Outside the senate-house the crowd were shouting that, if the senate spared him, they would lynch him. They dragged statues of him to the Gemonian Steps and began to destroy them; but on the emperor's orders they were saved and put back. Piso was set in a litter and escorted home by a colonel of the Guard, whose role was variously interpreted as protector of his life or supervisor of his execution.

脚的。他曾经贿买过士兵,他曾经放任那些流氓无赖在行省胡作非为,他甚至还曾经侮辱过统帅,这些事实都是无可否认的。他唯一可以驳回的一条指控就是关于放毒的问题。控诉者说在日耳曼尼库斯举行的一次宴会上,和他相邻而坐的披索把毒药放入了他吃的东西里面,这种说法是难以令人信服的。他竟敢在众目睽睽之下,包括在另一个人的奴隶之中,在日耳曼尼库斯本人的眼皮子底下,试图投毒,那简直是不可思议的事情。为了证实自己的说法,披索要求对他自己的奴隶进行拷问,同时还要求拷问当时那些参加宴会的侍者。

不过,由于各种不同的原因,判决难以做出。提贝里乌斯之所以这样,是因为披索对行省发动了战争;而元老院委决不下,则是因为他们对日耳曼尼库斯是自然死亡之说,始终是不能确信的。皇帝和披索都否认他们在私下通过信。[1] 这时就听见拥挤在元老院门外的人民群众高声呼叫道,如果元老院免除了对他的惩罚,他们就将会自行把他处死。实际上他们已经把他的像拖到了盖莫尼埃台阶,[2]开始将它们毁坏。但是皇帝下了命令,这些胸像于是被保全下来,并且被放了回去。披索则被放到肩舆上,在近卫军中队的一名军官的护送之下回了家,对于这名军官的角色,人们有着各种不同的解释,有人说他是披索的生命的保护者,也有人说他是执行披索的死刑的监督者。

〔1〕 这个地方原文脱落了一段,而且显然是很长的一段。这段话的内容可能涉及停审以后与第二次审讯之间的事情。控诉者要求交出普朗奇娜写给提贝里乌斯和奥古斯塔的信件,但被告和皇帝都拒绝这样做。
〔2〕 从卡披托里乌姆神庙通向广场的一列台阶。监狱中被绞死的罪犯的尸体在投入台伯河之前都要先在这里示众。

Plancina was equally loathed, but she had more influence. So it was doubted how far Tiberius could act against her. As long as Piso's fate was uncertain, she swore she would share whatever happened to him, and if necessary die with him. But the Augusta's private appeals secured her pardon. Thereafter she gradually dissociated herself from her husband, and treated her defence separately.

Piso saw that this was a fatal sign, and hesitated whether to continue the struggle. Finally, pressed by his sons, he steeled himself to enter the senate again. Renewed charges, hostile cries from senators, relentless enmity everywhere, he endured. But what horrified him most was the sight of Tiberius, pitiless, passionless, adamantly closed to any human feeling. Piso was carried home. He wrote a brief note—ostensibly preparation for the next day's defence—and handed it, sealed, to an ex-slave. Then he performed his usual toilet. Late at night, when his wife had left the bedroom, he ordered the door to be shut. At dawn he was found with his throat cut. A sword lay on the floor.

I remember hearing older men speak of a document often seen in Piso's hands. He never made it known. But his friends insisted that it contained a letter from Tiberius with instructions relating to Germanicus. If, they alleged, Piso had not been deceived by insincere promises from Sejanus, he had intended to disclose this to the senate—thereby convicting the emperor. Moreover, his death, according to this story, was not by his own hand, but by an assassin's. I cannot vouch for either version. But I have felt bound to repeat this account

普朗奇娜同样遭人憎恨,但是她却拥有更大的势力。因此人们就不知道皇帝对她到底要追究到什么程度。她发誓说,只要披索的命运还没有最后确定,那么不管披索的遭遇如何,她都要与他共同承担,必要时可以与他共同赴死。但是奥古斯塔在私下里的请求,使她获得了皇帝的宽恕和保护。因此她就逐步地把自己从和丈夫的联系中分离出来,并把自己的辩护作为一个单独的案件进行。

披索看出这是一个不祥的征兆,于是他犹豫是否还有必要再继续进行争辩。最后,在他的儿子们的催促之下,他才下了狠心,再次走进了元老院。在重新审理中,他忍受了元老们不断的攻击、敌意的叫声,还有到处充斥的对他的无情的憎恨。但是最使他感到恐惧的却是提贝里乌斯的目光,这种目光中没有怜悯,也没有热情,丝毫没有一点人类的情感。披索被送回了家。他写了一个便条——这显然是为了第二天的辩护作准备的,并且把写的东西封了起来,交给了一个被释的奴隶。随后他自己就像通常那样梳洗打扮了一番。后来到了深夜,当他的妻子已经离开了寝室以后,他就叫人把门关上。第二天黎明时分,人们发现他已割断了自己的喉咙,一把刀放在地上。

我记得听老一辈人讲过,人们常常看到披索手里拿着一份文件。他自己从来不让人们知道里面的内容。但是他的朋友们却坚持说,这些文件中有一封信,那是提贝里乌斯写给他的,其内容是对有关日耳曼尼库斯的问题所做出的指示。他们说,如果披索不是受了谢雅努斯的空洞诺言的欺骗,他是已经打算将这封信公开,交给元老院的——这样做就将会证明皇帝本人也有罪了。而且人们还认为,他这次的死亡并不是自杀,而是死于一个刺客之手。我不能确定哪一种说法正确。但是我认为我有义务把我在年轻时听

given by people who were still alive when I was young.

In the senate Tiberius wore a sad expression. The manner of Piso's death, he complained, was calculated to discredit him. He repeatedly interrogated Marcus Piso concerning his father's behaviour during that last day and night. Apart from a few indiscretions, the young man answered prudently. Tiberius then read aloud a memorandum written by Piso, of which this was the gist:

'Conspiracy among my enemies, and the odium caused by a lying charge, have ruined me. There is no place for my guiltless honesty. But I call heaven to witness, Caesar, that I have always been loyal to you, and dutiful to your mother. I beg you both to protect my children. Cnaeus has not shared my doings, good or bad, since he has been in Rome all this time. Marcus urged me not to return to Syria. How I wish I had given way to my young son, rather than he to his old father! I pray, therefore, all the more earnestly that he, who is innocent, should not be punished for my mistakes. By my forty-five years of loyalty, by our joint consulship, I, whom your parent the divine Augustus favoured, whom you yourself befriended, beg you to spare my unlucky son. It is the last thing I shall ask.' Of Plancina nothing was said.

Tiberius exonerated Marcus from the charge of civil war, pointing

到的,当时还在世的老一辈的人们的那些叙述忠实地再重复一遍。

在元老院,提贝里乌斯表现出一份十分悲伤的表情。他指责说披索的这种死法,目的就是要引起人们对皇帝的不信任。他反复地向玛尔库斯·披索询问他父亲在死前的一天一夜里的种种行为。尽管有一些回答显得有些轻率,这个年轻人的应对大体上来说还是十分谨慎的。然后,提贝里乌斯就大声念了披索写给他的一个便条,内容大致是这样的:

"我的敌人们的合谋和他们的谎话连篇的控诉所激起的对我的憎恨毁了我。我的无辜的真诚在这个世界上也已无容身之地了。但是我敢请上天作证,恺撒啊,我对你始终是忠心耿耿的,对于你的母亲也一直是恪尽职守的。我恳求你们两位保护我的孩子们。我所做的事情无论是好的还是坏的,都与格涅乌斯没有任何关系,因为在这一段时期里他一直在罗马。玛尔库斯则劝说过我不要回到叙利亚去。我是多么希望当时是我对我年轻的儿子作出了让步,而不是让他听从了他的年老的父亲啊!因此,我更加恳切地请求您,他这样一个无辜的孩子是不应该因为我自己的罪过而受到惩罚的。凭着我过去 45 年来的忠诚,凭着我曾和你一道担任执政官,[1]我,一个曾得到过你的父亲圣奥古斯都欣赏的人,一个你自己也当作朋友的人,现在向你恳求,请饶恕我的不幸的儿子。这是我向您所做出的最后一个要求。"对于普朗奇娜信中却只字未提。

提贝里乌斯赦免了对玛尔库斯内战罪责的指控。他指出,儿

---

〔1〕 公元前 7 年,他和提贝里乌斯曾经同任执政官。

out that the son could not have disobeyed his father's orders. He also expressed pity for this great family and for the terrible end, merited or otherwise, of Piso himself. On behalf of Plancina he made a deplorable and embarrassed appeal, pleading his mother's entreaties. All decent people were, in private, increasingly violent critics of the Augusta—a grandmother who was apparently entitled to see and talk to her grandson's murderess, and rescue her from the senate. The feeling was that Germanicus alone had been refused the rights which every citizen possesses by law. 'His mourners were Publius Vitellius and Quintus Veranius', people said, 'and meanwhile the Augusta and the emperor were protecting Plancina. Now, no doubt, it is Agrippina's turn, and her children's, to suffer from Plancina's wiles and poisons, so satisfactorily tested! And so this fine grandmother and uncle will have their fill of the unhappy family's blood. '

Two days were spent on the sham investigation of Plancina. Tiberius encouraged Piso's sons to defend their mother. But accusers and witnesses competed in their attacks, and no one answered. People felt sorry for her rather than hostile. The consul Marcus Aurelius Cotta Maximus Messallinus was asked to speak first (for when the emperor presided, it was his custom to include officials among those called upon for their views). The consul's proposal was that Piso's name could be deleted from the calendar; that half his property should be confiscated

子是不能不服从父亲的命令的。同时,他还对于这样一个显贵的家族和它最后的悲惨命运,不论是披索本人应得的下场还是其他情况,表示了同情。他还以他的母亲的恳求作为理由,为普朗奇娜作了可叹的、极为尴尬的辩解。这样一来,所有正派的人士都在私下里对奥古斯塔进行了更加强烈的指责,一个表面上有着祖母称号的奥古斯塔,竟然眼看着他人谋害自己的孙子,并且还为凶手讲话,还去元老院解救她! 人们感觉,在法律上每个公民都能拥有的权利,却唯独日耳曼尼库斯不能拥有。"日耳曼尼库斯的哀悼者是普布里乌斯·维提里乌斯和克温图斯·维拉尼乌斯",人们都在说,"同时,皇帝和奥古斯塔则是普朗奇娜的保护者。现在,毫无疑问,普朗奇娜的阴谋诡计和投毒既然如此称心如意,那么下一个遭受这种毒害之苦的就要轮到阿格里披娜和她的孩子们了! 而且这悲惨的一家的鲜血将会充分满足这个出色的祖母和叔父的心愿。"

对普朗奇娜的这次装腔作势的审讯一共进行了两天。提贝里乌斯怂恿披索的儿子们为他们的母亲进行辩护。但是原告和证人争先恐后地进行控诉,没有一个人能站出来回答。人们为她感到遗憾,而不是憎恨。被请求最先发言的是执政官玛尔库斯·奥列里乌斯·科塔·马科西姆乌斯·米撒利努斯(因为如果会议是由皇帝主持的话,按照规定,甚至高级长官也必须发表自己的意见)。[1] 科塔建议应当把披索的名字从编年表中删除;[2]他的财产

---

〔1〕 如果不是皇帝主持,则应由执政官主持。这时首先发言的是次年度当选的执政官而不是现任的高级官吏。

〔2〕 罗马的编年表是用执政官的名字标示的,披索担任过执政官,因此那里有他的名字。

and the other half allowed to his son Cnaeus, who should change his first name; that Marcus Piso should be deprived of his rank and sent away for ten years, with a subsidy of five million sesterces; and that owing to the Augusta's pleas Plancina should be pardoned.

The emperor reduced the proposed penalties in various respects. He would not have Piso's name removed from the calendar, when it still contained the names of Antony, who had made war on his country, and his son Iullus Antonius, who had outraged Augustus' family. Tiberius excused Marcus from degradation and allowed him his father's property. For, as I have often mentioned, he was no miser, and now his shame at Plancina's acquittal increased his leniency. Similarly, he rejected proposals by Marcus Valerius Messalla Messallinus (I) and Aulus Caecina Severus for a golden statue in the temple of Mars the Avenger, and an Altar of Vengeance, on the grounds that such monuments were appropriate for foreign victories but that domestic disasters were occasions for silent mourning.

The former of these proposals had added that Tiberius, the Augusta, Antonia (II), Agrippina, and Drusus should be thanked for avenging Germanicus. Claudius was left out; and it was only when Lucius Nonius Asprenas publicly asked whether the omission was deliberate that his name was included. The more I think about history, ancient or modern, the more ironical all human affairs seem. In public opinion,

应当一半充公,一半给他的儿子格涅乌斯,不过格涅乌斯的第一个名字应该予以更改;玛尔库斯·披索应当被剥夺所拥有的头衔,并且把他黜免10年,[1]同时要给他500万谢司特尔提乌斯的补助金;由于奥古斯塔的请求,普朗奇娜则应当得到赦免。

皇帝减轻了执政官在各个方面提出的那些惩罚提议。他说,既然曾经对祖国宣战的安东尼和曾经侮辱过奥古斯都家族的他的儿子优路斯·安托尼乌斯的名字,还保留在编年表上,那么他就不能将披索的名字从年表上面删掉了。提贝里乌斯免除了对玛尔库斯·披索的降职惩罚,并允许他继承他父亲的遗产。因为正像我常常提到的,他并不是一个吝啬的人,而且现在对普朗奇娜无罪的宣判使他感到的羞愧,也更增加了他的宽厚仁慈的行为。同样,当玛尔库斯·瓦列里乌斯·美撒拉·美撒里努斯(一世)建议在复仇者玛尔斯的神庙立一座金像,而奥路斯·凯奇纳·谢维路斯建议修筑一座复仇祭坛时,他都予以否决了。他的理由是,这些纪念物是为在国外取得的胜利而建的,而对于国内发生的灾难,大家只应默默致哀。

美撒里努斯还建议说,提贝里乌斯、奥古斯塔、安托尼娅(二世)、阿格里披娜和杜路苏斯都应当因为替日耳曼尼库斯复仇有功,而受到国人的感谢。不过在这里他没有提到克劳狄乌斯,而只有在路奇乌斯·诺尼乌斯·阿司普列那斯在元老院公开询问他是不是故意把克劳狄乌斯的名字漏掉的时候,这个名字才又被包括了进去。至于我本人,我越是深入思考古往今来的所有历史,越是感到人间的所有事物看起来都是一种莫大的讽刺。从外界的舆论

---

[1] 被黜免的人可以保留公民权和自己的财产。

expectation, and esteem no one appeared a less likely candidate for the throne than the man for whom destiny was secretly reserving it.

Some days later, Tiberius recommended the senate to admit Publius Vitellius, Quintus Veranius, and Quintus Servaeus to the Pontifical Order. He also promised to back Lucius Fulcinius Trio for office, but warned him not to ruin his eloquence by excessive forcefulness. So the avenging of Germanicus ended. Contradictory rumours have raged around it among contemporaries and later generations alike. Important events are obscure. Some believe all manner of hearsay evidence; others twist truth into fiction; and both sorts of error are magnified by time.

和人们的期望来看,从一个人所受的尊重程度来看,任何人都比克劳狄乌斯更有资格来充当皇帝的候选人,但冥冥中命运却正是安排了这位默默无闻的克劳狄乌斯成为了罗马未来的统治者。

几天之后,提贝里乌斯建议元老院授予普布里乌斯·维提里乌斯、克温图斯·维拉尼乌斯和克温图斯·谢尔瓦埃乌斯大祭司的圣职。他还答应支持路奇乌斯·富尔奇尼乌斯·特里奥取得官职,但是又警告富尔奇尼乌斯,不要因为过分的激烈而毁坏了自己的口才。这样,为日耳曼尼库斯的复仇就至此结束了。不论是在当代人中间,还是在后代人那里,围绕着这件事所散布的那些传言都表现出针锋相对的两种观点。其中重要的事实都是模糊不清的。一些人相信所有的传闻都是真实的;另一些人则又把真相歪曲成虚构的东西,而且这两种错误到后来都会随着时间的推移而更加夸大。

CHAPTER 6

Tiberius And The Senate

Drusus left the city to resume his command, and returned soon afterwards to receive a formal ovation. A few days later his mother Vipsania died. Of Agrippa's children, she alone died peacefully. The rest were either killed in battle or allegedly poisoned or starved to death.

In the same year Tacfarinas, whose defeat in the previous summer by Marcus Furius Camillus I have recorded, resumed hostilities. After nomad raids—too swift for reprisals—he began destroying villages and looting extensively. Finally, he encircled a Roman regular battalion near the river Pagyda. The energetic and experienced commander of the fort, Decrius, considered the siege a disgrace, and ordered his men to fight in the open, forming line in front of the camp. The battalion succumbed to the first attack, but Decrius hurled himself into the rain of missiles to bar its flight, cursing the sergeant-majors for letting Roman soldiers run away from irregulars and deserters. He turned towards the enemy, wounded in body and face (one eye was pierced), and went on fighting until he fell. His men abandoned him.

第六章 提贝里乌斯和元老院

　　杜路苏斯离开罗马去重新接管他的统帅大权,不久之后他又回到了罗马接受一个正式的小凯旋式。几天之后,他的母亲维普撒尼娅去世。在阿格里帕所有的孩子当中,她是唯一一个平静地死去的人。其余的孩子,或者在战争中被杀死,或者被毒死或饿死。

　　就在同一年,塔克法里那斯,我在前面曾经记录过,他在去年夏天曾经被玛尔库斯·富里乌斯·卡米路斯(一世)打败——又挑起了战争。他先是进行了出其不意的袭击,他的袭击是如此迅速,以至于根本来不及反击。接着就毁坏村落并且进行大规模的劫掠。最后,他竟然在帕吉打河附近的地方包围了一支正规的罗马步兵中队。这个驻防地点的将领是戴克里乌斯,这个人行动敏捷而又富有作战经验,他把这次被包围看成是一次耻辱,于是,他就在自己的营地前面拉开战线,命令自己的士兵在空地上公开和敌人作战。中队的士兵在敌人第一次进攻的时候就溃退了,但是戴克里乌斯本人却不顾一切地冲到密雨般的投枪中间去,企图阻止住逃跑的士兵。他咒骂旗手,因为他们竟然使罗马士兵从一群乌合之众和逃亡者那里逃跑了。他又转身冲向敌人,带着身体和面部的伤(他的一只眼睛已被刺穿),继续奋勇战斗,一直到最后阵亡的时候。他的士兵则抛开他逃走了。

When Lucius Apronius, the successor of Camillus, heard of this, he was less worried by the enemy's success than by the Roman disgrace. Adopting an ancient procedure, now rare, he drew lots in the discredited battalion and had every tenth man flogged to death. The severity was effective. When the same force of Tacfarinas attacked the fort of Mala, a detachment of only five hundred old soldiers routed it. In the battle a private soldier, Helvius Rufus, won the honour of saving a citizen's life. Apronius decorated him with the honorific chain and spear, and the Citizen's Oak-wreath was added by Tiberius. The emperor pretended to deplore that Apronius, as governor and commander-in-chief, had not made this award, like the others, on his own initiative.

Since the Numidians were demoralized and impatient of siege warfare, Tacfarinas conducted a guerrilla campaign, giving way under pressure and then attacking from the rear. The tired Romans, frustrated and ridiculed by these tactics, could not retaliate. But finally Tacfarinas turned aside to the coast and, immobilized by all the plunder he had collected, kept close to a stationary base: and then the Roman

当卡米路斯的继任者路奇乌斯·阿普洛尼乌斯听到了这次
失败的消息时,让他深感忧虑的与其说是敌人的胜利,毋宁说是
他自己的罗马军队的不光彩的表现。于是他采用了古时用过、但
当时已很少使用的一项措施,就是在不光彩的中队里,采用抽签
的办法,将抽中的 1/10 的士兵鞭笞至死。[1] 这种严厉的措施产
生了很好的效果,以致当塔克法里那斯以同样的兵力进攻称为塔
拉的要塞时,他只用了一支不到 500 人的老兵组成的小分队就把他们
打败了。在战斗中,一个名叫赫尔维乌斯·路福斯的普通士兵由于救
了一个罗马公民的性命而赢得了荣誉,阿普洛尼乌斯赏给了他象征荣
誉的项圈和投枪,提贝里乌斯又给他加上了市民的荣冠。提贝里乌斯
假装对这件事情表示悲痛,因为身为行省长官兼统帅的阿普洛尼乌斯
没有像其他人一样,行使自己的权力把这种荣誉也授予这个士兵。[2]

由于努米地亚人的士气低落了下去并且失去了耐心,不愿意
再进行围攻的时候,塔克法里那斯便重新使用游击战术指挥战斗。
敌人进攻,他就退却,然后再进攻敌人的后方。疲于奔命的罗马人
被这种战术挫败、受着他的愚弄,但却无能为力,没有办法报复他。
可是最后,当塔克法里那斯转移到海岸边的时候,由于携带着大量
的掳获物而行动不便,因此便靠近一个固定阵地停了下来。这

---

〔1〕 最先实施这个十中杀一的办法的是阿庇乌斯·克劳狄乌斯,后来
也偶然实行过。

〔2〕 项圈和投枪是一般的军事赏赐,但用橡皮树叶编成的"市民的荣
冠"却是人们最向往的很高的赏赐。取得这种赏赐的必要条件是受赏者必
须是罗马公民,必须在战场上救过罗马公民的性命,必须在救命时杀死过一
个敌人,而且在立功的地点,必须是坚持到底不曾后退的。由于阿非利加在
元老院的行省中是唯一长官麾下有一个军团的行省,因此阿普洛尼乌斯就
有权将荣冠授予市民,否则就只有皇帝才有这样的权力。

governor's son, Lucius Apronius Caesianus, sent against him with cavalry, auxiliary infantry, and the most mobile Roman regulars, won a victory and drove the Numidians into the desert.

Aemilia Lepida (II) was now indicted. In addition to her glorious Aemilian lineage, she was great-granddaughter of both Sulla and Pompey. She was accused of falsely claiming to bear a son to the rich and childless Publius Sulpicius Quirinius. There were additional charges of adultery, poisoning, and consultation of astrologers regarding the imperial house. She was defended by her brother Manius Aemilius Lepidus. Though disreputable and guilty, she attracted compassion since Quirinius, even after their divorce, had treated her vindictively.

The emperor's attitude during the trial is not easy to reconstruct. Alternately, or simultaneously, both anger and indulgence were perceptible. First he asked the senate not to consider the charges of treason. Then he enticed from a former consul, Marcus Servilius Nonianus (I) and other witnesses precisely the evidence which he had ostensibly wanted to exclude. He also handed over to the consuls Lepida's slaves (who were under army guard); but he forbade their interrogation under torture on any question concerning their own household. Again, he exempted Drusus, the consul-elect, from speaking first in the matter. This was variously interpreted as a non-autocratic step, relieving other speakers from the obligation to agree with Drusus, or as an ominous sign, since only a vote of condemnation would need such a postponement.

The trial was interrupted by Games. While they were on, Aemilia Lepida, accompanied by other distinguished ladies, entered the theatre

时,罗马军队统帅的儿子路奇乌斯·阿普洛尼乌斯·凯西亚努斯便按照父亲的命令率领骑兵和辅助步兵中队,再加上最机动灵活的罗马正规军团士兵,向他们发起了猛烈的进攻,终于打败了努米地亚人,并且将他们赶进了沙漠。

这时,埃米里娅·列庇妲(二世)在罗马受到了控告。列庇妲不但出生于显赫的埃米里乌斯家族,而且还是苏拉和庞培的曾孙女。她的罪名是冒称为一个没有子嗣的富人普布里乌斯·苏尔皮奇乌斯·克维里尼乌斯生了一个儿子。此外还有人控告她和人通奸、放毒以及通过占星术士打探皇帝家族的事情。替她进行辩护的是她的兄弟玛尼乌斯·埃米里乌斯·列庇都斯。尽管她声名狼藉而且又犯了罪,但是由于克维里尼乌斯在和她离婚之后依旧虐待她,因而她得到了人们的同情。

在这次审讯期间,皇帝的态度是不易揣测出来的,因为他的态度是变幻的、不分明的,愤怒和慈祥的表情兼而有之,让人难以捉摸。他最初要求元老院不要受理这一大逆罪的案件,继而又简要地暗示前执政官玛尔库斯·塞尔维里乌斯·诺尼亚努斯(一世)偕同另外一些证人列举出表面上看来他好像是拒绝接纳的证据。他还将(受到了武装监视的)列庇妲的奴隶们交给了执政官;但是不许就他自己的家族的任何问题对这些奴隶进行拷问。他又免除了已被选定为执政官的杜路苏斯在这一事件上首先发言的权利。对此,人们有各种各样的解释,有一些人认为这种做法是一种表示对非专制的让步,因为这样可以使别的发言者不必赞同杜路苏斯的意见。但是也有一些人认为这是一个不祥之兆,因为只有在定罪的时候才需要这样延期。

审讯因运动会而暂时中止。当审讯正在进行的时候,埃米里娅·列庇妲在一些贵族妇女的陪同下进入剧场,她在那里高

and with loud lamentations called upon her ancestors, including Pompey himself whose memorials and statues stood before everyone's eyes. The crowd was sympathetic and tearful, and howled savage curses upon Quirinius as a childless, low-class old man to whom a woman once destined to be Augustus' daughter-in-law (for she had been engaged to Lucius Caesar) was being sacrificed. But then the torture of her slaves disclosed her misconduct. On the proposal of Gaius Rubellius Blandus she was condemned as an outlaw; and, though others had favoured greater leniency, Drusus supported the penalty. However, at the appeal of a senator, Mamercus Aemilius Scaurus, to whom she had given a son, confiscation of her property was waived. It was only now that Tiberius revealed his discovery from Quirinius' slaves that Lepida had tried to poison their master.

So within a short time the Calpurnii had lost Piso, and the Aemilii had lost Lepida. Among these catastrophes to great families the return of Decimus Silanus to the Junii was consoling. His history was briefly this. For all the divine Augustus' good fortune in public affairs, his home life had been unhappy owing to the immorality of his daughter and granddaughter. He expelled them from the city, and executed or banished their lovers. For he used the solemn names of sacrilege and treason for the common offence of misconduct between the sexes. This was inconsistent with traditional tolerance and even with his own legislation. The fates of the other victims I hope to record as part of a general history of the period, if I fulfil my present aim and live to undertake further labours. As for Decimus Junius Silanus, his adultery with Augustus' granddaughter had only been punished by the withdrawal

声哭号,叫着她的祖先们,也包括庞培本人的名字,这座剧场就是为了纪念庞培而修建起来的,一些纪念物和他的半身像就在人们的眼前。群众非常同情她的遭遇,都流下了眼泪,他们号叫着,野蛮地咒骂克维里尼乌斯,这个没有子女的、出身卑微的家伙,竟然使奥古斯都的儿媳妇(因为她被许配给路奇乌斯·恺撒)成为这样的牺牲品。但是后来她的那些受到拷问的奴隶揭发了她的罪行。在盖乌斯·路贝里乌斯·勃兰都斯的建议下,她被判处为一个丧失公权者,别的人虽然倾向于较和缓的处置,但是杜路苏斯却支持这种处罚。然而,后来由于一个元老玛米尔库斯·埃米里乌斯·司考路斯的要求,他和列庇妲生过一个儿子,决定保留她那些本应予以没收的财产。只有在这个时刻,提贝里乌斯才揭露说,他已从克维里尼乌斯本人的奴隶们那里弄清楚,列庇妲确实曾经企图用毒药害死他们的主人。

这样,在不长的一段时间之内,卡尔普尔尼乌斯家族失去了披索,埃米里乌斯家族失去了列庇妲。在这些显赫家族所遭受到的灾难中间,戴奇姆斯·西拉努斯之回到尤尼乌斯家族就是一种安慰。关于他的历史,这里应做一点简单的回顾。圣奥古斯都的政治生活虽然一帆风顺,但是他的家庭生活却由于女儿和外孙女的淫乱而很不幸。他把她们赶出了首都,并且又放逐或处死了她们的情人。由于他将男女之间常犯的这种罪过加上了渎神罪和大逆罪这样严厉的罪名,这就与罗马宽容的传统,甚至与他自己的法律规定不相协调了。至于其他犯罪者的命运,我希望我能在那一时期的通史中作为一部分加以记述,如果我能完成当前这部书并且尚有余年来从事进一步的工作的话。至于戴奇姆斯·尤尼乌斯·西拉努斯,这个与奥古斯都的外孙女通奸的人,所受到的惩罚只是被拒绝了皇帝的友

of the emperor's friendship. But he had realized that this meant exile.

It was not until Tiberius became emperor that Decimus Junius Silanus ventured to appeal to him and the senate. He employed as intermediary his powerful brother Marcus Silanus (I), conspicuous nobleman and speaker. Marcus was thanking the senate for its indulgence when Tiberius intervened. He too, he intimated, was glad that Marcus' brother had returned from his distant travels, as he was entitled to since he had not been banished by the senate or by law; he himself however still felt, unabated, his father's aversion to Decimus —his return had not annulled the wishes of Augustus. Subsequently Decimus lived in Rome, without office.

It was next proposed to mitigate the Papian-Poppaean law. This had been authorized by Augustus in his later years, as a supplement to the Julian legislation, to tighten the sanctions against celibacy, and to increase revenue. It had failed, however, to popularize marriage and the raising of families—childlessness was too attractive. But increasingly many people were liable to penalties, since every household was exposed to informers' technicalities. The danger was now not so much misbehaviour as the law itself.

This prompts me to go into some detail about the origins of law, and the ways in which it developed into our endless and complicated statute-list. Primitive man had no evil desires. Being blameless and innocent, his life was free of compulsions or penalities. He also needed

谊。但是他也已经意识到,这就意味着流放。

直到提贝里乌斯当了皇帝,戴奇姆斯·尤尼乌斯·西拉努斯才敢冒险向皇帝和元老院提出解除流放的请求。他是通过他那有声望的兄弟玛尔库斯·西拉努斯(一世)——一个高贵的人,一个优秀的演说家,做中间人提出他的请求的。当玛尔库斯正在向全体元老表示感谢的时候,提贝里乌斯打断了他,他明白地表示说,他也非常高兴看到玛尔库斯的兄弟能够从远途的旅行中返回。他有权力这样做,因为对他的放逐不是元老院的正式决定,也不是根据某项法律的规定而做出的。但同时他本人也一点都没有减轻他的父亲对这个人所有的厌恶——他的返回并不等于取消奥古斯都的意旨。后来戴奇姆斯便生活在罗马,但未担任官职。

后来又有人建议减轻帕披乌斯·波培乌斯法[1]中的惩罚。这个法律是作为尤利乌斯法案的补充,在奥古斯都晚年时通过的,它的目的就是要严禁独身和增加国库的收入。但是,它并没有奏效,结婚和成家立业并没有成为人们的普遍兴趣。不要孩子对人们太有吸引力了。但是另一方面,越来越多的人有遭受惩处的可能,因为每一个家庭都处在告密者的诡计陷害之中。现在法律本身给人带来的危险,甚至要远远大于过去由于恶习而遭受的灾难了。

这种情况促使我更加深入细致地探讨法律的来源,以及发展成为今天无数的复杂的法律条文的经过。原始的人没有罪恶的欲望,他们天真清白,无需指责,也就不需要有什么强制或是惩罚。人们也并不需要奖赏,因为他们生来就做好事。同样的,因为

---

〔1〕 公元 9 年通过的帕披乌斯·波培乌斯法,是对公元前 18 年制定的鼓励结婚的尤利乌斯法的补充。

no rewards; for he was naturally good. Likewise, where no wrong desires existed, fear imposed no prohibitions. But when men ceased to be equal, egotism replaced fellow-feeling and decency succumbed to violence. The result was despotism—in many countries, permanently. Some communities, however, either immediately or when autocratic government palled, preferred the rule of law. Laws were at first the simple inventions of simple men. The most famous laws are those designed for Crete by Minos, for Sparta by Lycurgus, and then the more extensive and sophisticated code which Solon gave Athens.

We ourselves, when Romulus' autocratic regime ended, were subordinated by Numa to a religious code, to which Tullus Hostilius and Ancus Marcius introduced adjustments. But our outstanding maker of laws—binding even on kings—was Servius Tullius. After Tarquin's expulsion the community took many measures against the ruling class in the interests of freedom and unity. A new Council of Ten, by incorporating the finest elements from all sources, drew up the Twelve Tables. That was the last equitable legislation. For subsequent laws, other than those directed against specific current offences, were forcible creations of class-warfare, designed to grant unconstitutional powers, or banish leading citizens, or fulfil some other deplorable purpose.

Hence arose demagogues like the Gracchi and Lucius Appuleius Saturninus—and the senate's partisans such as Marcus Livius Drusus with their equally comprehensive offers. By these, Italian hopes were raised, only to be dashed by tribunes' vetoes. Even duringthe Social and Civil Wars, contradictory legislation continued. Then the dictator Sulla repealed or altered earlier laws, and passed more himself.

那里根本就不存在错误的欲望,也就用不着用恐吓来禁止他们了。但是公正不复存在了,自尊自大代替了谦逊和克己而屈从于暴力。结果,在许多国家,专制制度就成了永久性的制度了。有一些城市,或者从最初的时候起,或者是在对专制的统治感到厌倦之后,就喜欢法治。最早的法律是头脑简单的人的简单的发明创造,其中最著名的有克里特的米诺斯、斯巴达的李库尔古斯,然后就是比较丰富、比较复杂的雅典的梭伦所制定的法规。

在我们自己这里,罗木路斯的专制统治结束后,努玛把宗教的法典加到我们头上,我们还要屈从于图路斯·赫斯提里乌斯和安库斯·玛尔奇乌斯所制定的法规。然而在我们罗马最著名的制定法律的人却是谢尔维乌斯·图里乌斯,这些法律就是对国王们也有束缚力。在塔尔克维尼乌斯被逐以后,平民们为了保卫自身的自由和确立相互间的团结,采取了很多的措施,来抵抗统治阶级。一个新的十人委员会成立了,这个委员会从各国制度的资源中吸收了最好的因素,制定了十二铜表法,这是最后的一项公平的立法。至于后来的法律,虽然其中也有一些是针对破坏了和平安定的生活的罪行的,但是在更多的情况下,却是由于阶级纠纷而作为暴力产生出来的,其目的在于保障他们非法的权力,或取消市民的中心地位,或是实现其他什么邪恶的目的。

如此就产生了像格拉古兄弟和路奇乌斯·阿普雷乌斯·撒图尔尼努斯那样的政治煽动家——而另一方面,诸如玛尔库斯·里维乌斯·杜路苏斯这样的元老们也在用同样的手段拉拢人心。这样,一直被保民官否决的意大利人的意愿又升起来了。即使在内战期间,大量自相矛盾的法律也仍然在不断出现。直到苏拉建立了自己的独裁统治,用取消或改变早先的法律条文和通过了更

A pause followed; but not for long, since disorder quickly returned owing to the legislation of Marcus Aemilius Lepidus (II), and the tribunes soon regained their power of unlimited popular agitation. Thenceforward measures were concerned with personal instead of national issues. Corruption reached its climax, and legislation abounded.

Pompey, in his third consulship, was chosen to reform public life. But his cures were worse than the abuses; and he broke his own laws. Force was the means of his control, and by force he lost it. During the twenty years of strife that followed, morality and law were nonexistent, criminality went unpunished, decency was often fatal. Finally Caesar Augustus, when consul for the sixth time, felt sure enough of his position to cancel all that he had decreed as Triumvir, in favour of a new order: peace and the Principate.

多的他自己的法律条文的办法,才使这一情况暂时得到了抑制。然而没过多久,这种混乱的状态又因玛尔库斯·埃米里乌斯·列庇都斯(二世)的法案重新搅起了。不久之后,保民官重新取得了在人民群众中间毫无限制地进行鼓动的权力。而这时通过的法案,不是关注国家的利益,而是密切关注着个人的利益。腐败堕落达到极端之时,法律也就多如牛毛了。

第三次担任执政官的庞培被时代选择为社会改革者。然而他所用的治愈社会弊病的办法比社会弊病本身更糟糕。他破坏了他自己制定的法律,武力是他用来控制一切的手段,但同时又因武力而失掉了他的控制权。这以后的充满纷争的 20 年中,道德和法律都不复存在,为非作歹者得不到惩罚,善良公正者却常常遭受到被处死刑的厄运。最后,直到恺撒·奥古斯都第六次当选执政官时,他感到自己的政权已经能够确保稳固,于是才取消了他在三头执政时所发布的命令,并且又制定了一个在承平时期和元首统治时期所需要的法律[1]

---

〔1〕 塔西佗提到的是下列事件:

公元前 451 ~ 前 449 年,十人团制定了十二铜表法。

公元前 133 和公元前 123 ~ 前 122 年,两个格拉古的"民主"改革意图。

公元前 100 年,路奇乌斯·阿普雷乌斯·撒图尔尼努斯进行鼓动活动。

公元前 91 年,玛尔库斯·里维乌斯·杜路苏斯提出了有重大影响并深得人心的建议,被暗杀。

公元前 91 ~ 前 88 年,意大利战争。

公元前 88 ~ 前 82 年,苏拉和马利乌斯间的内战。

公元前 82 年,苏拉的独裁。其独裁统治被玛尔库斯·埃米里乌斯·列庇都斯(公元前 78 年做执政官)和庞培、克拉苏斯(公元前 70 年)摧毁。

公元前 52 年,庞培第三次担任执政官。

公元前 28 年,屋大维第六次担任执政官。

From then onwards restraints were stricter. There were spies, encouraged by inducements from the Papian-Poppaean law, under which failure to earn the advantages of parenthood meant loss of property to the State as universal parent. The spreading encroachments of these informers grievously affected all citizens, whether in Rome, Italy, or elsewhere, and caused widespread ruin and universal panic. To rectify the situation, Tiberius appointed a Commission consisting of five former consuls, five former praetors, and five other senators, chosen by lot. It disentangled numerous legal complexities, and temporarily produced a slight alleviation.

At about the same time the emperor commended to the senate Germanicus' son Nero Caesar, now approaching manhood. Mirth was caused by Tiberius' proposal that Nero Caesar be permitted to stand for the quaestorship five years ahead of the legal age, with exemption from service on the Board of Twenty. The emperor argued that at Augustus' request he himself and his brother had obtained the same concessions. But even at that time, I feel, such applications must have earned secret ridicule. And yet those had been the earliest days of imperial power, when ancient custom had counted for more: besides, Tiberius as grandfather of his candidate, Nero, was a closer connection than Augustus as stepfather of his.

Nero Caesar was also admitted to the Pontifical Order, and on the

但从此以后,各种限制也就更严格了。在人们中间到处都有密探,帕披乌斯·波培乌斯法通过悬赏诱使他们干这样的勾当;按照这一法律,一个人如果不取得做父亲的特权,那么就会失掉他的财产而交给作为一切人的父亲的国家。不过这些告密者贪婪地把自己的侵占活动扩大到所有市民,无论是首都、意大利,还是罗马帝国的其他任何一个角落,人们都受到了他们的进攻。这在各处都引起了毁灭性的事件,全国都笼罩在一片恐怖之中。为了纠正这种情势,提贝里乌斯用抽签的办法选出了五名前任执政官、五名前任行政长官和五名普通的元老组成了一个机构,这个机构专门解决许多法律上的错综复杂的问题,这种举措使人们暂时松了一口气。

大概就在同时,[1]皇帝向元老院推荐日耳曼尼库斯的现在已经成年的儿子尼禄·恺撒,[2]请元老院设法考虑他的问题。提贝里乌斯还提出了一个令人发笑的要求,就是要求元老院允许尼禄比法定年龄早五年候选财务官并解除他在二十人团中的任务。他的理由是,过去由于奥古斯都的要求,他本人和他的兄弟杜路苏斯就都曾经得到了同样的特许。但是我认为,即使是在那个时候,这样的请求也一定会引起人们在暗地里嘲笑的。而且那个时候还是皇帝执政的初期,古代的习俗还受着更高度的重视;此外,提贝里乌斯作为候选人尼禄的祖父,他们之间的关系,是比他与作为他继父的奥古斯都之间的关系更加密切的。

尼禄·恺撒又被授予了祭司长的职位,而在初次荣任之际,

---

〔1〕 指公元 20 年。

〔2〕 尼禄是日耳曼尼库斯的长子,大约生于公元 6 年。

occasion of his official debut there was a free distribution to the public. Their delight to see a son of Germanicus already growing up was increased by his marriage with Drusus' daughter Livia Julia. But that good news was counterbalanced by their dissatisfaction at the betrothal of Claudius' son to the daughter of Sejanus. This was felt to depreciate the nobility of the imperial house, while exalting Sejanus even beyond the excessive hopes which suspicion attributed to him.

At the end of the year two notable Romans died, Lucius Volusius Saturninus (I) and Gaius Sallustius Crispus. Volusius' family, though ancient, had previously never risen above the praetorship, but he contributed a consulship and held censorial functions for the selection of knights as members of the judicature. He was also the first to amass the wealth for which his family became so greatly conspicuous. Crispus was a knight by birth. He took his name from his grandmother's brother, the eminent historian Sallust, who had adopted him. So he had easy access to an official career. But he followed the example of Maecenas and, without senatorial rank, exceeded in power many ex-consuls and winners of Triumphs. Elegant and refined—the antithesis of traditional simplicity—he carried elaborate opulence almost to the point of decadence. Yet underneath was a vigorous mind fit for great affairs, all the keener for its indolent, sleepy mask. So, as a

他便对民众做了一次赠赐。看到日耳曼尼库斯的一个儿子已经长大成人，民众们都十分高兴。而尼禄和杜路苏斯的女儿里维娅·优利娅结婚，更增加了他们的喜悦之情。但是另外又有一件让人心情不悦的事，那就是克劳狄乌斯的儿子与谢雅努斯的女儿订下了婚约，这件事将人们由于前面的好消息而产生的喜悦削弱了一半。这件事给大家的感觉是，这样做无疑是玷污了皇家的尊严，因为如此便自然地提高了被怀疑有野心的谢雅努斯的身份。

就在这年年底，两个著名的罗马人去世了，他们是路奇乌斯·沃路西乌斯·撒图尔尼努斯（一世）和盖乌斯·撒路斯提乌斯·克利司普斯。沃路西乌斯家族虽然是一个古老的家族，但是他们家族中的人，过去获得的官阶从来没有升到过行政长官之上，而他本人却一直做到了执政官，而且，他以一个骑士阶级的出身而成为法官，执行监察官的职责，这种选择也提高了他家族的声望。他还第一个积聚了大量财富，从而使他的家族的声望变得如此显赫。克利司普斯的出身是骑士，他的名字来自于他祖母的兄弟，他就是罗马著名的历史学家盖乌斯·撒路斯提乌斯，盖乌斯把他过继到自己的家里来。如此，他就很容易地取得了一个高级职位。但是他却愿意以迈凯纳斯为榜样，虽然没有元老的头衔，可是势力却超过了许多担任过执政官或接受过凯旋式的人物。他作风的优雅考究和生活的讲求精致与传统的简朴风气截然相反，他那精致的富豪的排场已接近于颓废了。不过这都是表面现象，其实他有一副能够应付重大事件的充满旺盛活力的头脑，而在懒散的、昏昏欲睡的面具下面则是极其敏锐的心灵。因此，作为参与皇帝机密大事的智囊团人物，在迈凯纳斯活着的时候，他仅次于迈凯纳斯；而在迈凯纳斯死后，他就成了第一人了。撒路斯

repository of imperial secrets, he was second only to Maecenas during the latter's lifetime, and thereafter second to none. Sallustius was privy to the murder of Agrippa Postumus. But in his later years his friendship with Tiberius was impressive rather than active. It had been the same with Maecenas. Influence is rarely lasting. Such is its fate. Or perhaps both parties become satiated, when the ruler has nothing more to give, the collaborator nothing more to ask.

The following year witnessed the fourth consulship of Tiberius and the second of Drusus—a noteworthy partnership of father and son. Three years earlier, Germanicus had shared the same position with Tiberius. But they had not been such close relatives, and the association had brought the emperor no pleasure. Now, at the beginning of the year, he withdrew to Campania, ostensibly for his health. Perhaps he was, by degrees, rehearsing for a prolonged, unbroken absence. Or he may have wished by his retirement to leave Drusus as sole consul. Indeed, a small matter which turned into a serious dispute happened to give the prince a chance of popularity. A former practor Cnaeus Domitius Corbulo (I) complained to the senate that a young nobleman, Lucius Cornelius Sulla, had refused to give up his seat to him at

提乌斯是参与了杀死阿格里帕·波司图姆斯这一机密之事的。但是到了晚年,他和皇帝之间的友谊却只是停留在一种印象上,而不是表现在行动中了。这和迈凯纳斯的情况一样。一个人的势力很少能够长久维持下去,它会自然而然地衰亡,这是天数使然。或许是彼此之间都产生了厌倦情绪,有时是皇帝没有更多的东西可以赐予,有时则是宠臣没有更多需要的东西可以请求了。

接下来的一年见证了提贝里乌斯第四次担任执政官和杜路苏斯第二次担任执政官的历史,[1]这是一次值得注意的父亲和儿子之间的著名的合作。[2] 在这之前的三年里,日耳曼尼库斯就和提贝里乌斯一起分担过这样的职位,不过他们之间并没有能够形成这样亲密的关系,而且这次合作带给皇帝的是不愉快的感受。在这一年的年初,提贝里乌斯表面上以身体健康状况不佳为名,退到了康帕尼亚。他这样做,某种程度上,或者正是尝试连续地、长期地离开罗马,或者是因为他希望他的退隐能使杜路苏斯单独完成执政官的职责。而这时的确也发生了一件小事,这件小事后来却演变成一种严重的纠纷,而这却恰巧使这位年轻的执政官取得了很高的声望。原来一个曾经担任过行政长官的名叫科纳乌斯·多米提乌斯·科尔布罗(一世)的人向元老院抱怨说,一个年轻贵族,路奇乌斯·科尔尼利乌斯·苏拉,在观看一场斗剑时拒绝把座位让给他。科尔布罗认为年轻人应该给他让座,理由是他的高

---

〔1〕 公元 21 年,即罗马建城 774 年。

〔2〕 提贝里乌斯前三次担任执政官的合作者是克温提里乌斯·伐鲁斯(公元前 13 年)、格涅乌斯·披索(公元前 7 年)、日耳曼尼库斯(公元 18 年)。在这之后的公元 18 年,又与谢雅努斯共同担任。

a gladiatorial display. Corbulo had on his side age, traditional custom, and the sympathies of the older men. Sulla was supported by his connections, including Mamercus Aemilius Scaurus and Lucius Arruntius. There was a vigorous exchange, and much talk of our ancestors' strict decrees censuring youthful disrespect. Finally Drusus uttered some conciliatory words, which were transmitted to Corbulo by Mamercus Scaurus, Sulla's uncle and stepfather and the most fluent speaker of the day. So Corbulo received satisfaction. However, he then complained about another matter. Many Italian roads, he said, were breached and impassable owing to contractors' dishonesty and slackness among officials. He expressed willingness to initiate prosecutions. But the resulting convictions and compulsory sales destroyed many reputations and fortunes, without corresponding benefit to the public.

A little later, Tiberius wrote to the senate reporting that an incursion by Tacfarinas had again broken the peace in Africa. He requested them to choose a governor who was an experienced commander and physically fit for active service. Sextus Pompeius (II) seized the opportunity of ventilating his dislike of Manius Aemilius Lepidus, whom he described as a lazy degenerate pauper who ought to be excluded from the ballotboth for Africa and for Asia. The senate objected, since it regarded Lepidus as mild rather than lazy, and his irreproachable bearing of an illustrious name—despite inherited poverty—as

龄、传统习惯和对于年长的人应有的同情。跟苏拉有关系的人，包括玛米尔库斯·埃米里乌斯·司考路斯、路奇乌斯·阿尔伦提乌斯，则都为苏拉进行辩护。双方进行了非常激烈的辩论，而且经常谈及我们的祖先为谴责那些不敬老尊上的青年人所制定的严厉的法令。最后杜路苏斯发表了一些调和双方意见的言论，玛美尔库斯·司考路斯将杜路苏斯的演说传达给了科尔布罗，而科尔布罗是苏拉的叔父兼继父、又是那个时代最雄辩的演说家。对其所做的演说科尔布罗感到非常满意。可是接下来，这个科尔布罗又对另一件事进行了指责。他说，由于包工头的虚伪奸诈和官吏的玩忽职守，意大利人的许多道路都断裂毁坏，无法通行了。他表示了立刻对这件事进行追究的意愿。但是最终的判罪和强制的拍卖毁坏了许多人的名誉和财产，而民众却并未得到相应的好处。

不久之后，提贝里乌斯给元老院写了一封信报告说，塔克法里那斯的入侵破坏了阿非利加的和平。他请求元老们挑选一位总督，他既要是一位富有军事经验的指挥官，在体力方面又要能胜任实际的战役行动。塞克斯图斯·彭佩乌斯（二世）于是抓住这个机会发泄自己对玛尼乌斯·埃米里乌斯·列庇都斯的厌恶情绪，他把玛尼乌斯·列庇都斯描述成懒惰的、堕落的乞丐，因此不应当任命这个人到阿非利加和亚细亚去。[1] 元老院对他的意见表示反对，元老院认为，列庇都斯温和而不是懒惰，虽然他继承的财产很少，但是他无可指责地拥有着一个杰出的名字，这是值得称颂

---

〔1〕 亚细亚和阿非利加两地的总督是由资历最高的人来担任的，从前从执政官中选出。

praiseworthy rather than discreditable. So Lepidus was appointed to Asia. With regard to Africa it was decided to let the emperor choose.

During the debate Aulus Caecina Severus proposed that no one appointed to a governorship should be allowed to take his wife. 'My wife and I are good friends', he said, 'and have produced six children. But I have practised what I preach, by keeping her at home in Italy during all my forty years of service in various provinces! The rule which forbade women to be taken to provinces or foreign countries was salutary. A female entourage stimulates extravagance in peacetime and timidity in war. It makes a Roman army resemble an oriental progress. Women are not only frail and easily tired. Relax control, and they become ferocious, ambitious schemers, circulating among the soldiers, ordering company-commanders about. Recently a woman conducted battalion parades and brigade exercises ! Remember that whenever officials are tried for extortion most of the charges are against their wives. The wives attract every rascal in a province. It is they who initiate and transact business. Two escorts are necessary, two centres of government—and the women give the more wilful and despotic orders. They have burst through the old legal restrictions of the Oppian and other laws, and are rulers everywhere—at home, in the courts, and now in the army. '

This speech pleased only a few people. There was a chorus of interruptions, questioning both its relevance to the current discussion and

的而不是耻辱的。于是列庇都斯便被派到亚细亚去了。至于阿非利加,则决定由皇帝来选择一个人去担任总督。

在辩论过程中,奥乌斯·凯奇纳·谢维路斯建议,不能允许任何被分配担任行省任务的高级官吏带妻子上任。"我和我的妻子感情很好,相敬如宾,"他说,"我们俩有六个孩子,但是我依照我所建议的规定,在各个行省参加过的 40 次战役期间,我总是把她留在意大利的家中! 禁止把女人带到行省或外国去的规定是大有裨益的。随从前往的一群妇人在和平时期易于激发奢侈浪费之风,而在战时又易于引起人们的怯懦,并且会使一支罗马的军队看起来像是一支东方的队伍。女人的缺点还不仅仅在于意志薄弱和容易疲倦。如果放松了对她们的控制的话,她们就会变成残忍的、野心勃勃的阴谋家,她们在士兵中间跑来跑去,随便指使那些百人团长。最近就有一个女人主持步兵中队的操练和军团的演习。[1] 请大家想一想,每当高级长官们因勒索罪而受到审判的时候,大多数的指控都是针对着他们的妻子的。在行省那边,长官的妻子总是吸引那些流氓无赖。发动和处理一些事情的也总是她们。因此,需要有两队随从,两个中心,因为妻子们外出时也要带着一批扈从,她们自立一个行政中心,而且女人们发出的是更加任性的和专制的命令。她们冲破了古老的欧庇乌斯法和其他法律的约束,而且在任何地方都成为统治者——在家里、在法庭上、甚至在军队中都颐指气使。"

他的言论只有少数人赞同。但许多人在他发言时打断了他的话,他们对元老院提出这样一个问题来讨论是否适当和凯奇纳

---

〔1〕 这里指披索的妻子普朗奇娜。

Caecina's fitness to be censor in so important a matter. He was answered by Marcus Valerius Messalla Messallinus (I), who possessed some shadow of the eloquence of his father, Marcus Valerius Messalla Corvinus (I). 'Old-fashioned austerity has been satisfactorily mitigated in many ways,' he declared. 'For the city is no longer beleaguered, the provinces no longer hostile. So we make, nowadays, a few concessions to women's requirements—but not the sort to upset their husbands' households, much less the provincials. In all else wives fare like their husbands. And why not, in peace-time? Certainly men must travel light in war. But when they return from their labours they are surely entitled to relax with their wives. Some women, we hear, are schemers or money-grubbers. But officials themselves often show every sort of imperfection: yet governorships are filled. Granted that husbands are often corrupted by bad wives—is bachelorhood the ideal, then?

'The Oppian laws were once accepted because the national situation then required them. Later, they were relaxed and alleviated as expediency suggested. Let us avoid euphemisms for our own slackness. If a woman misbehaves, it is her husband's fault. Besides, the weakness of one or two husbands is no reason to deprive all of them of their wives' partnership in good times and bad. Moreover, that would mean abandoning and exposing the weaker sex to its own temptations and to masculine sensuality. Marriages scarcely survive

作为一个监察官是否具有讨论这样一个重要的问题的资格两方面都提出了质疑。玛尔库斯·瓦列里乌斯·美撒拉·美撒里努斯(一世)立刻就对他的发言做出了回应,在美撒里努斯身上还有他父亲玛尔库斯·瓦列里乌斯·美撒拉·考尔维努斯(一世)的口才的一些影子。他说:"古代的许多严峻的风习都已经以各种方式得到适当的减轻了,因为罗马不再处于战争的环境之中,而周边的各行省也不再是充满敌意了。因此今天我们对于妇女的要求也做出了一些让步——但是并不至于扰乱她们的丈夫的家庭,更不用说各行省了。在其余各方面,妻子也是和丈夫一样共同分享的。在和平时期,为什么不能这样做呢? 当然,在战争中,男人们必须轻装上阵。但是在他们从辛苦征战、劳作中回来的时候,他们确实是最应该从他们的妻子那里得到放松的啊。我们听说,有一些妇女是阴谋家,或是在金钱方面表现得很贪婪。然而有很多高级官吏,他们本人也表现出了各式各样的缺陷和弱点,然而行省长官的职位却永远都是充实着的! 即使我们可以保证,丈夫常常是由于邪恶的妻子而腐化堕落的,那么难道那些独身的人就不犯错误了吗?

"当初我们所以通过了欧庇乌斯法,是因为国家那时的环境要求有这样的法律来约束。后来由于临时情况的需要而把这些法律放松或是减轻了。对于我们自己的松懈,我们是不必找委婉的托词的。如果一个女人行为不端,那么这是由于她丈夫的过错。而且,也没有理由因为一两个丈夫有缺点,就剥夺所有已婚的男子在幸福和灾祸的时候和自己的妻子在一起的权利。而且,这样做就等于把一个生性脆弱的女性抛弃,并使她陷入于别人的诱惑和肉欲之中。就是天天在跟前守着,都几乎很难保证婚

with the keeper on the spot—whatever would happen with some years of virtual divorce to efface them? When reforming abuses elsewhere, remember the immorality of the capital. '

Drusus added a short speech about his own marriage, pointing out that the imperial family often had to visit remote provinces. The divine Augustus, he recalled, had frequently travelled with his wife, to east and west—and he himself had been to Illyricum and if need he would go elsewhere, but not always happily if severed from his beloved wife and all their children. So Caecina's proposal was evaded.

At its next meeting, the senate heard a letter from Tiberius blaming them (by implication) for referring all their difficulties to him, and nominating two men from whom they were to choose the governor of Africa—Marcus Aemilius Lepidus (IV) and Quintus Junius Blaesus. Both then addressed the senate. Lepidus emphatically asked to be excused, pleading ill-health, young children, and a marriageable daughter. He did not mention what was in their thoughts—that Blaesus was beyond competition, being Sejanus' uncle. Blaesus, too, pretended to decline—but less convincingly, and with many flatterers to contradict him.

Next a practice causing widespread secret discontent was made public. Bad characters were increasingly slandering and insulting respectable people and escaping punishment by grasping an effigy of the emperor. Thereby even ex-slaves and slaves had intimidated their

姻的完美,如果多年都不在一起,他们面临的实质上是一种离婚的生活,情况又会如何呢? 在采取措施制止别处的滥用职权的行为时,请好好地想一想在首都的那些不道德的行为吧。"

杜路苏斯又就他自己的婚事,做了一个简短的讲话。他指出,帝王的家庭也不得不经常到很边远的行省去,圣奥古斯都,他回想说,也是经常带着他的妻子利维拉,到西方和东方去旅行的——他自己还曾经到过伊里利库姆,而且如果需要的话,他也准备到任何别的地方去。但是如果要离开他亲爱的妻子,和他们所有的孩子们的话,他也会常常感到不快的。这样一来,凯奇纳的建议也就作罢了。

在元老院的下一次会议上,他们听取了提贝里乌斯发来的一封信中陈述的意见,信里(含蓄地)责备他们把他们的全部困难都推到了他这个皇帝身上。他还指定了两个供元老院选择担任阿非利加的总督的人选,他们是玛尔库斯·埃米里乌斯·列庇都斯(四世)和克温图斯·尤尼乌斯·布莱苏斯。这两个人也都向元老院表示了自己的态度。列庇都斯特别认真地请求免去他这样一个职务,他以自己健康状况不佳、孩子都还年轻以及女儿需要结婚等为理由。但是还有一个他没有讲出来而埋在他心里的一个想法,这就是在竞争中,布莱苏斯的竞争力比他强得多,因为布莱苏斯是谢雅努斯的叔父。布莱苏斯在表面上也予以拒绝,但并不是那么坚定,一些谄媚之徒劝说了一番后,他也就改变了自己的主意。

接下来,又有一件引起了许多人私下里的不满的事情暴露出来了。坏人们越来越肆无忌惮地诽谤和侮辱德高望重的人士,并且靠抓住一个皇帝像来逃避惩罚。因此,甚至被释放的奴隶们和在役的奴隶们也都会以威胁性的语言和姿势使他们的保护人和主人感

patrons and masters with threatening words and gestures. The junior senator Gaius Cestius Gallus (I) raised the matter. Emperors were certainly godlike, he said, but even gods only listened to virtuous petitioners; the Capitol and other Roman temples were not sanctuaries to encourage crime; and it was the height of illegality when Annia Rufilla, convicted for fraud by his agency, should menace and abuse him in the Forum, actually outside the senate, while he could not risk legal proceedings because she clutched an image of the emperor. Similar stories, some more serious, came from all sides. Drusus was begged to inflict exemplary punishment; and summoning Annia, he had her convicted and gaoled in the State prison.

Next, two knights, Considius Aequus and Caelius Cursor, who had made fictitious accusations of treason against the praetor Magius Caecilianus, were punished at the emperor's instigation by a senatorial decree. Both decisions improved Drusus' reputation. Living sociably in Rome, he seemed a moderating influence on his father's solitary designs. Even his youthful extravagances were not unpopular. Better to spend the day enjoying shows and the night banqueting than to lead the emperor's isolated, joyless life of gloomy watchfulness and sinister machinations.

For Tiberius and the accusers were untiring. Ancharius Priscus had impeached the governor of Crete and Cyrene, Caesius Cordus, for extortion—to which was added a charge of treason, now the complement of every prosecution. Again, when a prominent man in Macedonia, Antistius Vetus, was acquitted of adultery, Tiberius rebuked

到十分恐惧。为此年轻的元老盖乌斯·凯司提乌斯·卡尔路斯（一世）发表了自己的看法。皇帝确实是和神一样是神圣不可侵犯的，他说，但是即便是神本身也只听取请求者的正当控诉，卡披托里乌姆神庙和罗马的其他神庙绝不是保护和纵容罪犯的避难所。但是，当被盖乌斯·凯司提乌斯在法庭上判了欺诈罪的安妮娅·卢菲拉在广场上，实际上就是在元老院的门口外面威胁和侮辱他时，他本人却不敢冒险用法律程序制裁她，就因为她手中抓着一个皇帝的像，她便可以这样有恃无恐。类似的事情，甚至是更严重的事情，在各地都时有发生。于是人们都请求杜路苏斯对这类行为施以惩罚，以儆效尤。因此，他不得不下令把安妮娅招来，在证实了她所犯的罪行之后，最后将她囚禁在了国家监狱里。

接着，有两名骑士孔西狄乌斯·埃库斯和凯里乌斯·库尔索尔，他们诬告行政长官玛吉乌斯·凯奇里亚努斯犯了大逆罪。结果在皇帝的请求之下，依照元老院的条令而对他们进行了惩罚。对这两件事的处理提高了杜路苏斯的威信。杜路苏斯在首都罗马的那种善于社交的生活，对于他父亲那些难于捉摸的意图会产生一种中和的影响及效用。人们甚至对他那些年轻放浪的行为也并不计较。在人们看来，杜路苏斯那种随心所欲的，白天看节目，夜晚饮宴的生活，也比皇帝所过的那种笼罩在阴暗多疑和邪恶的诡计之中的孤独的、没有人世欢乐的生活为好。

提贝里乌斯和告密者并没有就此罢手。安卡里乌斯·普利斯库曾经控告克里特和库列涅两地的总督凯西乌斯·科尔杜斯有渎职行为——在这之上又加了一项大逆罪，这是现在每一个指控所必须加上的一条罪状。还有马其顿的一个名叫安提司提乌斯·维图斯的贵族，他被指控强奸的罪名已经宣告不成立了，

the judges and haled the defendant back to be tried for treason as a seditious accomplice of the anti-Roman intentions of Rhescuporis, who had murdered his fellow-monarch Cotys IV. Antistius was outlawed, and banished to an island without access to Macedonia or Thrace.

Meanwhile Thrace, divided between Rhoemetalces II and the children of Cotys IV—with a Roman regent, Titus Trebellenus Rufus, during their minority—was in disorder. The country was unfamiliar with Roman rule; and Rhoemetalces was as forcibly criticized as the regent, for not avenging his people's wrong. Three strong tribes, the Coelaletae, Odrysae, and Dii, opened hostilities. But their leaders did not join forces, and were individually insignificant, so a coalition involving serious war was averted. One contingent plundered its own neighbourhood, another crossed the Balkan mountains to raise the outlying tribes, while the largest and best organized blockaded the king in Philippopolis, a city founded by King Philip II of Macedonia.

When the commander of the nearest Roman army, Publius Vellaeus, heard this news, he sent auxiliary cavalry and infantry against

但是提贝里乌斯对此非常不满,他严厉谴责了这样一种宣判,并且又将被告召了回来,对他的案件以大逆罪进行审理。因为在列司库波里斯企图对罗马人发动战争的时候,他曾经参与了列司库波里斯的阴谋,和这个谋害了共同执政的君主科提斯四世的人一样,心怀叛逆之想。于是安提司提乌斯便被剥夺了公民的政治权利,同时还被流放到一个小岛上,不许进入马其顿和色雷斯。

同时,色雷斯这个王国在莱美塔尔凯斯二世和科提斯四世的孩子们之间进行了分配——在这些孩子尚未成年的时候,由一个叫做提图斯·特列贝列努斯·路福斯的罗马人摄政,在这期间,色雷斯内部一直处于纷乱之中。这个国家不习惯于罗马人的统治,人们对莱美塔尔凯斯的责难像对特列贝列努斯·路福斯的责难一样激烈,因为他没有对他的国人所受的不公正待遇进行报复。三个强大的部族,科埃拉列塔伊人、欧德律撒伊人和迪伊人都公开表示了敌对的立场。但是他们的首领各自拥有武装力量,互不加入、合作,他们本人的身份又都是很卑微的,这就避免了会引起一场严重战争的联合。一部分人不断地抢掠他们邻近的地区;另一部分人则越过了巴尔干山脉把边远地区的部落发动起来;而人数最多、组织得也最好的那一部分人则包围了菲利波波里斯的国王,菲利波波里斯这个城市是马其顿的国王菲利浦二世建立的。[1]

当最近的一支罗马军队的统帅普布里乌斯·维莱乌斯听到这个消息以后,他便派出了辅助骑兵部队和步兵中队去对付那些

---

〔1〕 公元前342年建立在玛利察河上游的这座城市,在历史上一直处于重要的地位,它是以建立者的名字来命名的。

the marauding and recruiting forces, and himself took the main Roman infantry to raise the siege. Each operation was successful. The marauders were annihilated; quarrels broke out in the besieging force, and as the Roman brigade moved up Rhoemetalces made a timely sortie. What followed was not a battle or even a fight, but a massacre of half-armed stragglers, without Roman bloodshed.

In the same year heavy debts drove Gallic communlities into rebellion. Its keenest instigators were Julius Florus among the Treviri and Julius Sacrovir among the Aedui—both noblemen, whose ancestors' services to Rome had earned them citizenship in days when this was scarce and conferred for merit. Secret conferences were attended by desperate characters and penniless, frightened men driven to crime by their evil records. It was agreed that Florus should raise the Belgae and Sacrovir the tribes farther south. There were treasonable gatherings and discussions about endless taxation, crushing rates of interest, and the brutality and arrogance of governors. ' Germanicus' death has demoralized the Roman army! ' they cried. ' Besides, look at the contrast between your strength and Italy' s weakness. Think of the unwarlike population of Rome. How the army needs us provincials! This is an ideal opportunity to regain independence. '

These seeds of rebellion were sown in almost every Gallic community. But the outbreak started among the Andecavi and Turoni. The imperial governor of Lugdunese Gaul, Acilius Aviola, suppressed

到处袭击打劫、掳掠新兵的敌人队伍。他本人则率领着罗马的主力步兵前去解围。罗马人在各方面都取得了胜利。打劫的敌人被消灭了；围攻的军队之间发生了争执；当罗马的军团赶到时，莱美塔尔凯斯立即进行了一次出击，但接下来的，既不成为一场战争，甚至也不是一次战斗，而只是对半武装的四处逃难者的大肆屠杀，而罗马人自己并没有流一滴血。

就在同一年，沉重的债务使得高卢诸行省中的一些城市发生了叛乱。最积极的鼓动者是在特列维里人中间的尤利乌斯·佛洛路斯和在埃杜伊人中间的尤利乌斯·撒克罗维尔。他们两个人都是贵族出身，他们的祖先都曾因对罗马的贡献而获得了罗马的公民权，当时罗马公民权是很少给人而且是在有功时才授予的。绝望的人、贫困的人和那些由于做了坏事而犯罪的害怕惩罚的人们全都参加了秘密会议。在会议上，他们计划让佛洛路斯煽动比尔伽伊人，让撒克罗维尔煽动南方较远的部族。他们多次举行这样的背叛性的集会和讨论，指责那些无休无止的税收、苛刻的利率、长官的残暴与蛮横。"日耳曼尼库斯的被谋杀使罗马的军团意志消沉！"他们说，"但是再看一看你们自己的强有力与意大利的衰弱所形成的鲜明对比吧。想一想那些没有尚武精神的罗马人，他们软弱无力，他们的军队是多么需要我们这些行省人民啊，这正是你们重新取得独立的大好时机！"

这些叛乱行为的种子几乎撒遍了高卢的每一个城市，但是叛乱的爆发最先却是在安迪卡维人和杜罗尼人中间开始的。在路格杜尼斯的帝国统帅阿奇里乌斯·阿维奥拉将他们的叛乱镇压了下去，安迪卡维人是被他所调遣的一个守卫路格杜努姆的城市卫戍步兵中队打败的；杜罗尼人则是被下日耳曼的同僚盖乌斯·维

both, the former with the city-police battalion which garrisoned Lugdunum, and the latter with regular troops sent by his colleague in Lower Germany, Gaius Visellius Varro. To hide their rebellious aims —for which the time was not yet ripe-certain Gallic chiefs supported the disciplinary measures. Sacrovir himself was to be seen encouraging the fighters—on the Roman side. He was bare-headed, ostensibly to attract attention to his valour; but prisoners said it was to show his identity and so avoid being aimed at. Tiberius received this information but disregarded it: his indecision did no good to the war.

Florus, pursuing his plans, tempted a cavalry regiment—raised among the Treviri but serving with us in Roman fashion—to begin hostilities by massacring our business-men. The majority remained loyal, but a few went over. A crowd of debtors and dependants also took up arms. Making for the Arduenna Forest, they were intercepted by brigades sent from opposite directions by the imperial governors of Lower and Upper Germany. The Romans sent ahead a man of rebel nationality, Julius Indus by name, whose loyalty was stimulated by hatred for Florus. This man dispersed the still undisciplined crowd. But Florus escaped in the rout, and his hiding-place proved untraceable. Finally, however, seeing soldiers blocking every exit, he killed himself. So the rebellion among the Treviri ended.

谢里乌斯·瓦罗派出的一队罗马正规军击溃的。为了掩饰他们的背叛意图——因为此时时机尚未成熟，一些高卢的将领也前来辅佐他。撒克罗维尔本人是个很受瞩目的人物，人们看到他亲自在那里激励着部下的士兵勇敢作战——为罗马作战。他头上没有戴头盔，据他自己表面的解释，这是为了使罗马人看到他的勇敢。不过俘虏们却说，他这样做是为了显示出他的身份，以避免成为投枪的目标。提贝里乌斯得悉了这种情况，但他并未予以理会，他的犹豫不决对战争并没有什么好处。

这时，急于实现自己计划的佛洛路斯，企图诱使一支骑兵部队，通过杀害我们罗马商人的办法发动叛乱，这支骑兵是在特列维里征募起来，但却是按照罗马的方式训练并为我们罗马人服役的。他们中大部分的人还是忠实于罗马的，但也有一些人被他争取了过去。另外，还有一群债务人和食客，他们也拿起了武器。他们向一个叫做阿尔杜安纳的森林地区进发，但是维谢里乌斯和盖乌斯·西里乌斯从上、下日耳曼的军队中派出去的队伍在相对的两个方向截住了他们的去路。罗马人先派出去了一个和叛乱者属于同一部族的人，这个人名字叫尤利乌斯·因度斯，他和佛洛路斯的私人仇怨，激起了他对罗马人的忠诚。这个人带领着一队十分精锐的士兵分散到秩序混乱的大群人中间去。佛洛路斯逃脱了追剿，他藏身的地方也十分隐蔽，罗马军队找不到他的踪迹。但是最后，当他看到对方的士兵封锁住了每一个出口，逃出去的希望很渺茫时，他便自杀了。在特列维里人中间发生的这场叛乱就这样平息下去了。

The revolt of the Aedui was more formidable; for they were a richer nation, and less accessible to counter-measures. Sacrovir with an armed force occupied the capital, Augustodunum, and seized the youthful Gallic noblemen who were being educated there. Holding them as pledges to win over their parents and relations, he distributed among them secretly manufactured weapons. His army was forty thousand strong; one-fifth were equipped like Roman soldiers, the rest with hunters' spears, knives, and other such arms. There was also a party of slaves training to be gladiators. Completely encased in iron in the national fashion, these Crupellarii, as they were called, were too clumsy for offensive purposes but impregnable in defence. Reinforcements came in. The neighbouring communities had not yet openly joined, but supplied keen volunters. And the Roman generals were quarrelling; both claimed to control operations. Finally the aged and infirm governor of Lower Germany yielded to his Upper German colleague of more active years, Gaius Silius (I).

At Rome it was said that not the Treviri and Aedui alone but all the sixty-four peoples of Gaul had revolted, that the Germans had joined them, and the Spanish provinces were wavering. As usual, rumour magnified everything. Every respectable Roman citizen deplored his country's difficulties. But many disliked the existing regime and hoped for change so greatly that they even welcomed danger for themselves. They criticized Tiberius for devoting attention to accusers' reports

但是,埃杜伊人发动的叛乱却严重得多,因为他们是更富强的部族,我们罗马的讨伐军更加难以进入。撒克罗维尔带领一支武装的步兵中队占领了这一族的首府奥古斯托杜努姆,[1]他抓住了高卢那些出身望族的年轻子弟,他们正在那里接受着正规的教育。他把他们控制在自己手里,利用他们去争取他们的父母和亲属,同时还把秘密制造的武器分发给他们。他的军队很强大,人数多达四万人,其中有 1/5 是按照罗马正规士兵的标准装备起来的,其余人的装备则是猎人用的长矛、短刀和其他诸如此类的武器。此外,他还将一些原来训练做剑斗士的奴隶们配备成一支队伍。这支队伍中的人都按照本国的习惯身披铁甲,他们被人们称做"克鲁佩拉里人"。他们为了抵御攻击,全身披挂严整,非常不便于进攻,但是这样在防守中就不会受到伤害。这些部队还在不断地增强自己的实力,邻近的各个地区虽然还没有公开地加入进来,但是暗中却输送过来许多热情的志愿者。在罗马的将领中间,却发生了纠纷,他们都声称自己是这次战争的统帅。最后,年老体弱的下日耳曼军统帅瓦罗把这一统率权让给了年轻力壮的上日耳曼军统帅盖乌斯·西里乌斯(一世)。

但是在罗马,人们却传说,不单只是特列维里人和埃杜伊人,而是高卢的 64 个部族全都叛变了,而且还传说,日耳曼也加入了他们的联盟,西班牙也正在动摇。像通常一样,谣言会将一切事情无限夸大。因此每个忧国忧民的罗马公民都感到很痛心,但是许多人不满现状,他们渴望发生大的变乱以致对面临的危险竟然还幸灾乐祸。他们批评提贝里乌斯在这样危险的叛乱局势之下,

---

〔1〕 今天的安敦,那里有奥古斯都建立的一所著名的学校。

during so dangerous a rebellion. 'Was Sacrovir too', they inquired, 'going to appear before the senate for treason? Here at last are men to put a forcible stop to these bloodthirsty imperial letters-and even war is a welcome change from the miseries of peace!' The emperor, however, took all the more pains to appear unperturbed. Profoundly secretive, he allowed neither gesture nor expression to show he was concerned. Or perhaps he knew that the gravity of the trouble had been exaggerated.

Silius sent auxiliaries ahead to ravage villages of the Sequani (a frontier people who were allies and neighbours of the Aedui). Then he himself, with two brigades, moved rapidly against Augustodunum. There was much rivalry among Roman sergeant-majors to reach it first. Indeed, even the ordinary soldiers protested against the usual halts and rests at night. They felt that, once they and the enemy saw each other face to face, victory was as good as won.

On the open ground twelve miles from the town Sacrovir and his forces came into sight. He had stationed his heavily armoured men in front, the fully armed battalions on the wings, and half-armed supporters in the rear. He himself, finely mounted and accompanied by his chiefs, rode round and addressed his men, recalling the ancient triumphs of the Gauls and their successes against the Romans, and contrasting the glorious independence that victory would bring with the even more oppressive servitude that would await defeat.

His words were gloomily received—and cut short. For the Roman army was advancing in line. The Gallic townsmen lacked discipline

居然还把精力集中到告密者的报告上。他们质询说："撒克罗维尔是不是也要站在元老院前来接受大逆罪的审理？但是人们终将会起来用武力制止这些写给皇帝的嗜血如命的告密信的！为了改变和平时期的悲惨景象，人们现在甚至对战争也大加欢迎了！"但是皇帝却忍气吞声，更加装出一副不受干扰的样子。在这些日子里，他深居简出，不动声色，无论是言语姿态还是表情，都丝毫透露不出一点他内心的焦虑。这或许是由于他知道问题并不是像人们所夸大的那样严重。

这时西里乌斯把一支辅助部队派出去作先锋，蹂躏了谢夸尼人的村落[1]。接着，他自己又率领着两个军团，火速地向奥古斯托杜努姆推进。这次进军更像是罗马旗手们看谁先到达目的地的一次比赛，实际上，甚至普通士兵都反对一般中途的休息和夜间的宿营。他们感到，只要他们和叛乱者彼此面对面地发现了对方，就像是已经赢得了胜利一样了。

在离城 12 英里的一片平原上面，撒克罗维尔和他的军队已经清晰可见。只见撒克罗维尔把那些身穿铁甲的士兵配置在前面，将全副武装的步兵中队部署在两翼，而那些武装不齐全的队伍则布置在后卫。他自己则威风凛凛地骑着马，由一队将领陪同着，在他的军队里巡视。他发表演讲，要他们记住高卢人过去的胜利和他们在反对罗马人的战争中所取得的成功，并且对比说，胜利会给他们带来无上光荣的自由，可是，如果他们失败了，那么等待他们的将会是更加难以忍受的压迫和奴役。

他的话很简短，士兵们听了之后反应也十分淡漠，因为罗马军队已经临近并且严阵以待了。高卢市民没有受过军事训练而

---

〔1〕 谢夸尼人住在靠近边界的地区，他们是埃杜伊人的联盟者，并且和埃杜伊人毗邻。

and battle experience; their eyes and ears were no use to them. The Romans' confidence made exhortations unnecessary. However, Silius spoke. It was an affront to the conquerors of Germany, he suggested, to have to march against Gauls—a single battalion had recently suppressed the rebel Turoni, a single cavalry regiment the Treviri, a few troops from this very army the Sequani. 'The wealthy, luxurious Aedui look unwarlike enough', he said. 'You prove that they are what they look! And then when they run, you can spare their lives. '

There was a mighty shout in reply. Our cavalry enveloped the enemy's flanks, while the infantry made a frontal attack. The Gallic flanks were driven in. The iron-clad contingent caused some delay as their casing resisted javelins and swords. However, the Romans used axes and mattocks, and struck at their plating and its wearers like men demolishing a wall. Others knocked down the immobile gladiators with poles or pitchforks, and, lacking the power to rise, they were left for dead. Sacrovir and his closest associates fled first to Augustodunum and then, fearing betrayal, to a house nearby. There he killed himself; and his companions killed each other. The house was set on fire, and the bodies burnt inside it.

At this late stage Tiberius wrote informing the senate simultaneously of the outbreak of the war and its termination. He neither exaggerated nor minimized the facts, commenting that victory was due to the loyal courage of his generals and to his own policy. To explain why he and Drusus had not gone to the war, he stressed the size of the em

且缺乏战争经验,连他们自己的眼睛和耳朵都不灵了。另一方面,罗马人充满信心,根本不需要讲什么激励的话,但是西里乌斯却仍发表了一番讲话。他强调说,日耳曼的征服者还不得不向高卢人兴师动众地进军,这真是一种耻辱——不久之前,仅仅一个步兵中队就平息了杜罗尼人的叛乱;一队骑兵就征服了特列维里人的暴动;这支军队派出的几个骑兵小队就制服了谢夸尼人。"埃杜伊人越富有、越奢侈享乐,就越缺乏尚武精神,"他说,"你们会证明他们正如他们所表现出来的那样不堪一击的!但当他们逃跑时,你们要手下留情,饶了他们的性命。"

士兵们高声做出了强有力的回答。我们的骑兵包围了敌人的两翼,同时步兵则对前卫发起了进攻。高卢人的两翼很快就被攻破了;但是担任前卫的铁甲兵却又延迟了一阵,因为他们身上的铁甲是能够抵挡投枪和剑的。但是这时罗马士兵却抢起了他们的斧头和鹤嘴锄,向着他们的铁甲和头盔猛击,就仿佛是在捣毁墙壁一样。另一些人则用竿子或耙子把这一大群行动不灵活的斗剑士打倒,他们连爬起来的气力也没有了,因此只能躺在那儿等死。撒克罗维尔跟他最忠实的下属起先逃到了奥古斯托杜努姆,后来因为害怕被出卖,又逃到了附近的一座房子里。他在那里自杀了,其他人也相互结束了生命。这座房子被点起了火,他们的尸体也就在这座房子里化为了灰烬。

到了这时,提贝里乌斯才写信给元老院,同时告诉他们战争的爆发和结束。他既没有夸大也没有缩小事实,只是指出,这次胜利的取得,是由于他的将领们的忠诚和勇敢以及他自己所采取的政策。同时为了解释他本人以及杜路苏斯没有亲自去参加这次战役的原因,他着重强调说,帝国的疆域太大了,作为一个治理

pire and the inadvisability of a ruler leaving the centre of government merely because of disturbances in one community or another. Now however (he added) that the motive for his going could not be ascribed to anxiety, he would go—to study the situation, and deal with it.

The senate decreed vows and prayers for his return, and other honours. Only Publius Cornelius Dolabella (I), determined to outshine everybody in ridiculous flattery, proposed that Tiberius should enter the city from Campania with an official ovation. This elicited a letter from Tiberius suggesting that, after conquering the most formidable nations and receiving or declining so many Triumphs in his youth, the emperor was not undistinguished enough to hanker after the empty honour of a suburban parade in his old age.

A little later, Tiberius asked the senate to award a public funeral to Publius Sulpicius Quirinius. He came from Lanuvium, and had no connection with the ancient patrician Sulpician family. But he was a fine soldier, whose zealous services had earned him a consulship and honorary Triumph from the divine Augustus for capturing the fortresses of the Homonadenses on the Cilician borders. Later, appointed adviser to Gaius Caesar during the latter's Armenian commission,

如此广大疆域的统治者,仅仅因为这一个或那一个城市的骚乱就贸然离开作为全国首都的罗马,这也是不明智、不可取的。(他又补充说)不过既然他去那里的动机不会被归因于是焦虑,他还是要去那里调查一下情况,并且会做出及时的处理的。

元老院发布命令,为他的返回罗马向神许愿和祈祷,并且还做出了其他致敬的表示。但是只有普布里乌斯·科尔涅里乌斯·多拉贝拉(一世)为了在荒谬好笑的谄媚方面远远超过其他人,竟然坚决地提出了这样的一个建议:提贝里乌斯应当从康帕尼亚进入罗马来接受一次小凯旋仪式。这使得提贝里乌斯给元老院写了一封信,他在信中表示:他曾经征服过一些最强悍的民族,在年轻时也接受过或拒绝过许多次这样的凯旋式,[1]作为一个皇帝,现在已经到了这样的年纪,更不可能不辨轻重地自己到罗马近郊去,追逐这样的虚荣。

不久之后,提贝里乌斯请求元老院给予普布里乌斯·苏尔皮奇乌斯·克维里尼乌斯以国葬的待遇。他原来是拉奴维乌姆[2]人,和古老的苏尔皮奇乌斯贵族家族并没有什么关系。但他是一名很好的士兵,他在罗马国家所付出的满腔热情的服务,为他赢得了荣誉,终于在圣奥古斯都的治下当上了执政官,并且因为攻占了奇里奇亚边界上的一些赫莫那地人的军事要塞,而取得了凯旋的勋记。后来他虽然再度被任命为当时驻节在亚美尼亚的盖

---

〔1〕 在公元前9年对达尔马提亚人和潘诺尼亚人,公元前7年对日耳曼人,公元12年对伊里利亚人所取得的胜利中,提贝里乌斯曾接受过3次凯旋式。而根据他的颂赞者维列乌斯·帕特尔库路斯的说法,提贝里乌斯曾经接受过7次凯旋式。

〔2〕 在拉提乌姆南部,靠近阿坡亚大道。

Quirinius had treated Tiberius, then living at Rhodes, with respect-
as the emperor now told the senate; and he coupled this praise of
Quirinius' attentiveness with an attack on Marcus Lollius (I), whom
he blamed for Gaius Caesar's perverse quarrelsomeness on that occasion. But others had less agreeable memories of Quirinius, who was a
mean, over-influential old man, and (as I have mentioned) had persecuted Aemilia Lepida (II).

At the end of the year an informer attacked the knight Clutorius
Priscus, who had been subsidized by Tiberius for writing a wellknown
poem about Germanicus' death. Clutorius was now accused of com-
posing another poem while Drusus was ill, for even more lucrative
publication if the prince died. Clutorius had bragged of this in the
house of Publius Petronius, before his host's mother-in-law Vitellia
and many leading women. When the accuser came forward, the other
women were intimidated into admitting this. Vitellia alone said she
had heard nothing. However, the damning evidence was more widely
believed, and the consul-elect Decimus Haterius Agrippa moved for
the death penalty.

Marcus Aemilius Lepidus (IV) opposed this motion. 'If, senators', he argued, 'we only consider the outrageous utterance with which
Clutorius Priscus has degraded himself and his hearers, prison and the

乌斯·恺撒的使节团的一名顾问,但对于当时还居住在罗德岛的提贝里乌斯,他也是正如现在皇帝向元老院所说的那样十分尊敬。他谴责了玛尔库斯·洛里乌斯(一世),指责他当时曾唆使盖乌斯·恺撒采取了固执的、引人争论的态度,与此同时还更加倍赞扬了克维里尼乌斯对他本人的忠诚。不过其他人在想到克维里尼乌斯时态度却并非如此,因为他晚年的行为既卑鄙又飞扬跋扈(并且我曾经说过)他还迫害过埃米里娅·列庇妲(二世)。

在这一年的年底,一个名叫克路托里乌斯·普利斯库斯的罗马骑士被一个告密者控告。这个骑士曾经写过一篇著名的哀悼日耳曼尼库斯之死的诗,他还因此而受到了提贝里乌斯的金钱赏赐。告密信指控克路托里乌斯在杜路苏斯生病的时候,又写了另一首诗,为了赚取到更丰厚的一大笔钱,他准备在杜路苏斯死时发表。克路托里乌斯在普布里乌斯·佩特洛尼乌斯[1]家里,当着主人的岳母维提里娅和许多贵族妇女的面吹嘘他自己的这种做法。当告密者提出控告的时候,其他的贵族妇女惊恐万分,赶忙出来证实此事。只有维提里娅一个人坚持说,她什么也没有听见。不过有利于这一致命控诉的证据反而获得了更广泛的信任,因此已经当选执政官的戴奇姆斯·哈提里乌斯·阿格里帕便建议将其判处死刑。

但是玛尔库斯·埃米里乌斯·列庇都斯(四世)对这个建议表示反对。他说:"元老们,如果我们只考虑到克路托里乌斯·普利斯库斯所讲的那些玷污了他自己和听者的粗暴的言论,那么不论是监

---

noose—or even the tortures reserved for slaves—are not enough for him. Yet, however deplorable and outrageous the offence, the emperor's moderation and your own ancient and modern precedents indicate the mitigation of penalties. Besides, folly is distinguished from crime—and words from deeds. For these reasons, it is legitimate to propose a punishment which will cause us to regret neither overleniency nor harshness. I have often heard our emperor deploring suicides, since they prevent the exercise of his clemency. Clutorius is still alive. His survival will not endanger the State; and his death will convey no lesson. His compositions are senseless, but they are insignificant and ephemeral. A man who betrays his own outrages to impress not men but mere females is no very great danger. I propose, therefore, that we expel him from the city, outlaw him, and confiscate his property, as if he were guilty under the treason law. '

A single ex-consul, Gaius Rubellius Blandus, agreed. But the rest supported Haterius. So Clutorius Priscus was imprisoned and immediately executed.

This drew from Tiberius a characteristically cryptic reproof of the senate. While praising their loyalty in so vigorously avenging even

狱还是绞索,甚至是用来对付奴隶的那种严刑拷打,对他也都是足够宽容的了。尽管他犯下了极大的可悲的罪行,但是皇帝的宽厚和你们自己的祖先以及现代社会的一些先例,也已经表现出了在惩处方面所做出的减缓的努力。而且,如果说愚蠢和邪恶是有所区别的话,那么说坏话和做坏事也是有所不同的。由于这些原因,合理的惩罚提议就应该是,我们既不会过分的宽大,也不会因为过分的严厉而后悔。我常常会听到,我们的皇帝对某一个人的自杀表示深深的遗憾,因为他无法得到皇帝要给予他的宽大处理了。克路托里乌斯还活着,他的存在不会对国家造成任何威胁,而且把他杀死对人民也起不到什么威慑作用。他写的那些东西是荒唐的、毫无意义的,并且很快就会被人忘掉。一个暴露自己的丑行,却只是为了向女人、而不是向男人讨好的人,是不会构成什么大的危险的。因此,我建议把这个人驱逐出罗马,剥夺他的公民权,没收他的财产充公,就好像他是一个犯了大逆罪的罪犯一样给予相应的处罚。"[1]

只有一个曾经担任过执政官的盖乌斯·路贝里乌斯·勃兰都斯同意列庇都斯的意见。但是,其余的人都支持哈提里乌斯的建议。于是克路托里乌斯·普利斯库斯被囚禁起来,而且立刻就被处死了。

这种处理办法引起了提贝里乌斯的回应,他对元老院做了一次颇有特点的含糊其辞的斥责。他称赞元老们是如此忠诚,以致

---

〔1〕 列庇都斯的意思是对克路托里乌斯的罪过是否触犯了大逆法表示怀疑,而且**即使**克路托里乌斯真正触犯了大逆法,法定的惩罚也只是放逐而不至于处死。

minor offences against the emperor, he deprecated so hasty a punishment of a mere verbal lapse. He commended Lepidus—but refrained from criticizing Haterius. The result was a decision that no senatorial decree should be registered at the Treasury for nine days, executions to be delayed for that period. But the senate lacked the freedom to reconsider. And the intervals never softened Tiberius.

The consuls of the following year were Gaius Sulpicius Galba and Decimus Haterius Agrippa. The year was peaceful abroad. But the capital was nervous—for it anticipated stern measures against the current extravagance, which extended unrestrainedly to every sort of outlay. Most of this, however enormous, could be concealed by suppressing prices. But the sums spent on gluttonous eating were widely discussed; and the emperor's old-fashioned austerity inspired fears of rigorous action. On the initiative of Gaius Calpurnius Bibulus, the aediles had argued that the law restricting expenditure was being ignored, that prohibited food prices were increasing daily, and that ordinary measures were helpless against this situation. When the mat-

对于冒犯皇帝这样的非常轻微的言行,也立刻果断地进行了激烈的报复;但是另一方面,对这种仅是口头上的一点过失,却迅速地做出了如此严厉的惩罚,他表示反对。他称赞了列庇都斯,但是也没有批评哈提里乌斯。结果就做出了这样一项决定,即元老院的任何决议都要在整整九天之后才能送交国库注册备案,[1] 所有被判处死刑的犯人在这段期间都应暂缓行刑。[2] 但是元老院并没有重新考虑的权力,而且提贝里乌斯在这期间也从来没有心软过。

接下来的一年,[3] 执政官是盖乌斯·苏尔皮奇乌斯·伽尔巴和戴奇姆斯·哈提里乌斯·阿格里帕。这一年,国外和平安宁,但是在首都罗马,人们却紧张不安。因为奢侈浪费的风气已经毫无节制地蔓延到了每一项花费上面,人们害怕会采取一些严厉的措施来惩治这种不良风气。在这些浪费中间,尽管大多数数目是极为庞大的,但是可以通过压低价格的办法把它们隐瞒下来。但是在大吃大喝方面耗费的大量金钱,是人们广泛议论的话题。皇帝具有的那种旧式苛刻的节约习惯,引起了人们对他向来一丝不苟的作风的恐惧。当营造官盖乌斯·卡尔普尔尼乌斯·比布路斯提出了这个问题的时候,他的同僚们也都支持说,禁止奢侈的法令已经成了一纸空文,食品的黑市价格正在日益上涨,对于这种形势,一般温和的手段已

---

〔1〕 元老院的命令最初是保存在凯列司神庙里,由营造官负责看管,后来才保存在国库中,即协和神庙附近的卡披托里努斯山的撒图尔努斯神庙,命令只有在放进国库后才能生效。

〔2〕 后来延长到30天。

〔3〕 公元22年,即罗马建城775年。

ter was raised in the senate, it was referred without discussion to the emperor. Tiberius often privately doubted whether restraint of these immoderate appetites would be either practicable or beneficial. He knew how undignified it would be to start something which he could not maintain, or could only maintain by humiliating and disgracing eminent men. Finally, he wrote the senate a letter to this effect:

'On all other public questions, senators, it may be desirable for me to be asked, and express, my opinions in your presence. But in regard to this matter, it is well that my eyes are elsewhere. Otherwise, if you indicated the apprehensive faces of men guilty of shameful extravagance, I too might see them, and so find them out. If our energetic aediles had consulted me earlier, I should perhaps have advised them not to tackle such deep—set, flagrant evils—so as not to publish our helplessness against them.

'Yet they have done what I expect from every official, their duty. For me, however, although silence is unfitting, speech is not easy. For I am neither aedile, nor praetor, nor consul. Some grander, more impressive utterance is expected from the emperor. People praise themselves for their good actions but all blame their failings on a single man. And where should I begin my prohibitions and attempted reversions to antique standards? With the vast mansions, or the cosmopolitan hordes of slaves? Or with the ponderous gold and silver

经是无能为力了。当这个问题在元老院提出后,元老院未加讨论便把它直接提交给了皇帝去处理。提贝里乌斯私下里经常怀疑限制这种不加节制的欲望,是否能起到实际的作用,是否是有利的。他清楚如果他开始了这项改革而又不能坚持到底的话,这将是多么有损他的尊严,或者如果他坚持到底的话,他的一些最显赫的臣民就要蒙羞、遭受到侮辱。最后,他就给元老院写了这样一封信,信的主要内容:

"元老们,关于其他任何公众关心的问题,我是非常希望你们能提出问题,并且我也会当众做出回答、表达我的意见的。但是对于这件事情,我认为我还是不参与为好。否则的话,如果你们把那些由于犯下了不光彩的奢侈罪行而惊惶不安的面孔指出来,我或许就可以看到他们,并且因此了解是哪些人犯了这种罪行。如果我们那些充满活力的营造官们早一点儿和我商量这件事的话,我也许会奉劝他们不要去触动这些积重难返的、声名狼藉的恶习,以避免把我们无力克服此种弊端的实际情况昭告于世。

"虽然如此,他们是恪尽了自己的职责的,这也是我所希望每一位高级官吏都能做到的。但是对于我本人来说,尽管沉默不语不太合适,可是要开口讲话也并非易事。因为我既不是营造官,又不是行政长官,也不是执政官。人们对于一个皇帝,所期望的是更伟大,更深刻的言论。人们往往会把成功的荣誉归于他们自身的善行,而把失败的责任都推到一个人身上。我应该从哪里开始着手实行禁令和尝试回复古老的准则呢?从人们修建的大量豪宅,还是从奴隶们满世界的游牧开始呢?[1]或者是从我们大量沉重的黄

---

[1] 当时存在着大量奴隶。

plate, the wonderful pictures and bronze-work, the men's clothes indistinguishable from women's? Or the feminine speciality—the export of our currency to foreign or enemy countries for precious stones?

'I know that at social gatherings these practices are criticized, and their limitation is demanded. But if they were penalized by a law, their present critics themselves would cry that it was a national disaster, a death-blow to distinction, and the conversion of everyone into a potential criminal. Yet the human body, when it has a long and persistently worsening illness, needs a vigorous, radical treatment. And the mind's feverish ailments, too, can only be relieved by remedies as severe as the infection. All our laws—those of our ancestors which are forgotten, those of the divine Augustus which are neglected (and that is worse)—have merely conferred immunity on extravagance. For when you want something that is not prohibited, you fear prohibition. But once you safely ignore a prohibition, fear and shame vanish. Frugality used to prevail because people had self-control—and because we were citizens of one city. Even our domination of Italy did not bring the same temptations. But victories abroad taught us to spend other people's money. Then civil wars showed how to spend our own.

'Besides, the matter to which the aediles' warning relates is inessen-

金和白银开始？或者是从精彩的名画和精美的青铜制品开始？或者是从那些无法与女人的服装相区别的男人的服装开始？或者是从那些特别是让我们的钱源源不断地流入外国或敌国之手的女人的珍贵的珠宝[1]开始吗？

"我知道，在社交集会上，这类事情是会引起人们的批评的，而且人们都要求加以限制。可是，如果用法律手段加以惩处，则现在批评这些东西的人又会叫嚷，说这是国家的一场灾难，是对于显要人物的一种致命的打击，它会使任何一个人都有可能成为罪犯！如果一个人的身体长期患有使身体日渐衰弱的、无法治愈的痼疾，就需要用烈性的猛药来医治。而头脑中的一种热病，就只能用和引起这种热病的情欲同样猛烈的药来医治。我们的祖先所创造的全部法律，我们已经都忘掉了；而圣奥古斯都所制定的全部法律，现在也都被人们忽视了（这种情况更加糟糕）。上述情况只能使人们对于奢侈的恶习更加丧失了免疫力。因为如果你想取得某种尚未被禁止的东西时，你就总是害怕这种东西有一天会被禁止。可是一旦你触犯了禁令而未受到惩罚，你就会胆大妄为，并且毫无羞耻心了。俭朴的作风在过去之所以能够保持，是因为人们都有自制的能力，同时还因为我们只不过是一个城市的市民。甚至在我们成为全部意大利的主人的时候，我们也还没有受到这样的诱惑。但是多次对外战争的胜利，教会了我们花费别人的金钱；而屡次的内战则显示出我们是怎样浪费我们自己的财产。

"除此之外，营造官们提醒大家注意的是多么微小的一件无关

---

〔1〕 当时罗马钱币大量外流，贵金属的不断外流和矿藏的枯竭，导致了硬币成色的降低。

tial—relatively insignificant. Italy's dependence on external re-sources, Rome's subsistence continually at the mercy of sea and storm—those are problems about which there are no speeches. Yet without provincial resources to support master and slave, and supplement our agriculture, our woods and country-houses could not feed us. That, senators, is the emperor's anxiety. Its neglect would mean national ruin. For other troubles, the remedy lies with the individual. If we are decent, we shall behave well—the rich when they are surfeited, the poor because they have to.

'Nevertheless, any officials who can offer enough severity and energy may, with my compliments, relieve me of part of my burdens. But if they want to denounce misbehaviour, take the credit for it, and then leave me the enmities they have created, I intimate to you, senators, that I also do not want to make enemies. When national necessity demands I will face hostility, formidable and often unjust though it may be. But when it is useless and unprofitable—to you as well as myself—I have good reason to decline.'

When the emperor's letter had been read, the aediles were excused from the task.

Since then, however, extravagant eating, which reached fantastic heights during the century between Actium and the disturbances

紧要的事情啊。意大利是依靠着国外的资源来维持的,而且罗马人的持久生存也都是要依赖于海浪和风暴的慈悲。对于这些重大的问题,人们并没有发表任何言论。但是,如果没有行省的资源来支援这里的主人和奴隶,我们自己的田地、我们自己的森林和庄园就很难养活我们!元老们,这就是皇帝所担心的事情。如果我忽视了这些事情,国家就要彻底毁灭了。至于其他的麻烦,就必须靠自己个人来想办法解决了。只要我们行事公正有分寸,我们就能——富人如此是因为他们已经得到了充分的满足,而穷人如此则是因为他们必须这样做。

"尽管如此,如果有哪一位高级官吏能够以足够严厉的手段,以及强有力的措施来纠正这种恶习、卸下我的一部分重担的话,我一定会对他十分感谢,大加赞扬。但是,如果他们想公然抨击腐化堕落的行为并因此而博得人们的信任,可是随后却把招来的怨恨都推到我的身上的话,那么,元老们,我明白地向你们宣布,我也是很不希望给自己树敌的。如果这是国家所必须的要求,则即使这种敌对情绪的确是严重的、而且常常是不公正的,我也将会坦然面对。但是,如果这种敌对情绪毫无意义,不论是对我本人还是对你们大家,都没有任何好处的话,那么我是有充分的理由拒绝遭受这种敌意的。"

皇帝的信宣读之后,营造官们就被解除了这样一项任务。

然而,从那时起,在阿克提乌姆一役之后直到使伽尔巴登上宝座的这整整一个世纪的动乱时期里,[1]人们在吃喝方面挥

---

〔1〕 公元前 31 年至公元 68 年,伽尔巴于公元 68 年登上王位。

which brought Galba to the throne, has gradually become unfashionable. The reasons for the change are worth examining. Old rich families, noble and illustrious, were often ruined by their sumptuous tastes. For, in those days, to court (and be courted by) the public in Rome and the provinces, and by foreign monarchs, was allowed. Fortunes, palaces, and their contents dictated the size of dependent hordes and of reputations. But the reign of terror, when distinction meant death, induced prudence in survivors. At the same time too, the numerous self-made men admitted into the senate from Italian towns (and even from the provinces) brought frugal domestic habits, and, though by good fortune or hard work many of them were rich in later life, they did not change their ideas. No one promoted simplicity more than Vespasian, with his own old-fashioned way of life. For deference to the emperor and the wish to imitate him were more effective than legal penalties and threats.

Or perhaps not only the seasons but everything else, social history included, moves in cycles. Not, however, that earlier times were better than ours in every way—our own epoch too has produced moral and intellectual achievements for our descendants to copy. And

霍奢侈的花费简直是到了惊人的程度,但是在这之后,这种风气便渐渐衰退了。促成这种变化的多种原因倒是值得好好研究的。在先前,富有的家庭,也往往是高贵的、显赫的贵族之家,他们常常由于生活奢侈豪华而导致倾家荡产。因为在那个时代,在罗马以及在外省,向人民大众、向行省居民以及向那些依附罗马的国王们讨好,或是得到他们对自己的奉承,是合法的、为国家和舆论所允许的。一个人所拥有的财产越多、住宅越好、家业越大,依附他的食客也就越多,他的声名也就越盛。但是经过无情的残杀之后,[1]在恐怖统治之下,当声名显赫就意味着死亡的时候,幸存下来的人就非常谨慎了。同时,那些独立创业起家的新人,不断从意大利各城市和移民地(甚至从各个行省)选入元老院来,他们把在本地养成的朴素的生活习惯带到了罗马。而且尽管由于运气好或是由于自己的奋发刻苦,许多人在晚年的时候都变得非常富有,但这并没有改变他们先前的那种勤俭持身的良好作风。促成俭朴风习的最有力的人物是维斯帕西亚努斯,他自己在生活中严格保持着旧式勤俭的作风。从那时开始,对于皇帝的尊敬和模仿他的强烈愿望,就比法律上的惩戒和处罚都更加有效了。

或者也许是,不只是季节的变迁,世界上其他事物,包括社会历史,也都存在着一种循环往复的运动。尽管在我们之前的古代,并非是在各方面都比现代的我们所拥有的好,而我们自己的时代也产生了不少道德上的和文学艺术上的成功典范可供我们的后人模仿。而且,今天我们和古代的这种竞赛也是值得

---

〔1〕 这种残杀发生在提贝里乌斯晚年、卡里古拉、克劳狄乌斯和尼禄4个朝代。

such honourable rivalry with the past is a fine thing.

Tiberius utilized the credit his resistance to the tyranny of informers had gained him by writing to ask the senate to grant Drusus a tribune's authority. This was a designation of supremacy invented by Augustus, who had wanted some title other than 'king' or 'dictator'
which would place him above other officials. In due course Augustus
had chosen associates in this power—Marcus Agrippa, and on his
death Tiberius. That was how he designated his successor, calculating
that this would damp misguided aspirations in others. He was confident of Tiberius' unpretentiousness, and his own pre-eminence.

While Germanicus lived Tiberius had not decided between him
and Drusus. But now he brought Drusus to the top. His letter began
with a prayer that heaven might prosper his plans for the national advantage. Then he wrote in moderate, unexaggerated terms about his
son's character, pointing out that Drusus was a married man with
three children and had reached the age at which he himself had been
called to the same responsibilities by the divine Augustus. Drusus'
promotion, he added, was not premature—after eight years' proba-

尊敬的,是一件非常有益的事情!

对于大批告密者的暴行所进行的抵制,使提贝里乌斯获得了良好的名声,于是他就利用人们的信任给元老院写了一封信,请求他们把保民官的权力授予杜路苏斯。这是奥古斯都发明出来的表示最高大权的称号,因为奥古斯都想要一个比"国王"或"独裁官"更高的名号,从而把自己那种高于其他所有官员的权力和地位表示出来。[1] 奥古斯都曾经选拔玛尔库斯·阿格里帕和他共同掌握这一权力,阿格里帕去世以后,[2] 代替他的是提贝里乌斯。他这样做是为了确定下他的继承人的地位,因为他认为,这种做法可以减弱其他人觊觎王位的渴望。对于提贝里乌斯的谦逊自制和他自己的至高无上,他也是有着充分的信心的。

当日耳曼尼库斯在世的时候,提贝里乌斯对于在他和杜路苏斯两人之间选定谁为继承人这件事犹豫不决。但是现在,提贝里乌斯把杜路苏斯正式推到了继承人的地位上。在这封信中,一开头,他就请求诸神为了国家的利益帮助他实现自己的计划,继而便用几句话以适度的措词,不事夸张地描述了自己儿子的性格。他指出,杜路苏斯已经成婚,并且有了三个孩子,而且他也已经到了先前他本人被圣奥古斯都召回来担任同一职务时那样的年龄。[3] 他还说,他的这种推举并非是一种不成熟的建议,因为杜

---

〔1〕 公元前 23 年 6 月,他终身获得了这一头衔;5 年之后,阿格里帕也取得了这一头衔,一直到公元前 12 年他去世。

〔2〕 这里和事实不符,因为直到公元前 9 年或公元前 6 年,他才取得了为期 5 年的保民官的权力。这权力直到公元 4 年盖乌斯·恺撒死后他被奥古斯都过继为继子的时候才重新恢复。

〔3〕 35 岁。

tion, including the repression of mutinies, completion of wars, a Triumph and two consulships, the prince knew the work he was to share.

The senators, who had foreseen this request, had their complimentary reaction planned. Yet they could think of nothing better than statues of the Caesars, altars to the gods, temples, arches, and other hackneyed gestures. Marcus Junius Silanus (I) was the only exception. For his proposal was that all monuments, public and private, should no longer be dated by names of consuls, but by those of holders of this tribune's authority—to honour the rulers, he degraded the consulship. Quintus Haterius moved that the day's decrees should be engraved in the senate-house in gold lettering. His disgusting sycophancy caused laughter. And since he was so old, it would earn him nothing—except dishonour.

Quintus Junius Blaesus' governorship of Africa was now prolonged. Servius Cornelius Lentulus Maluginensis, the priest of Jupiter, requested the governorship of Asia. It was a common fallacy, he said, that holders of his priesthood could not leave Italy; their legal position was identical with that of the priests of Mars and Quirinus, who were allowed provinces; so why should the priests of Jupiter not have them too? 'There is no law against it,' he said, 'and nothing in the

路苏斯也已经经过了 8 年的考验了。在这期间,他平息过几次叛乱,圆满地完成过几场战斗,接受过一次凯旋式,并且还担任过两次执政官,对他将要承担的工作他已经很熟悉了。

已经预见到这次推举选立的元老们,也早就准备好了一大堆奉承赞美之词。然而他们所能想到的办法,也无非就是为恺撒立像、为诸神修筑祭坛、修造神庙、拱门以及其他陈腐老套的捧场姿态而已。但是唯独玛尔库斯·尤尼乌斯·西拉努斯(一世)是一个例外,他提出了一项新颖的建议,那就是在今后所有的纪念建筑、铭文上——不论是公是私,不再用执政官的名字,而是用拥有保民官大权的那些人物的名字来做纪年,以此来抬高皇帝的权力,从而也就贬低了执政官的地位。克温图斯·哈提里乌斯则建议把这一天的决议用金字铭刻在元老院的房子里,但他令人作呕的奉承引起了人们的嘲笑,在这样大的年纪了还如此极尽谄媚,这除了贻人以讥笑,为自己招致耻辱外,一无所得。

克温图斯·尤尼乌斯·布莱苏斯做阿非利加的总督的期限被延长了,朱庇特神的祭司[1]谢尔维乌斯·科尔涅里乌斯·莱恩图路斯·玛路吉南西斯要求把亚细亚的统治权授予他。他认为,不许担任神父之职的人们离开意大利,这乃是一种常见的错误。他们的法律地位跟玛尔斯神和克维利努斯神的祭司的地位是一样的,而他们获许是可以到各行省去的。如此说来,为什么朱庇特神的祭司就不能也拥有这样的权力呢?他说:"国家的法律并没有明文禁止这一点,在宗教的档案文件中也根本没有这样

---

[1] 十五祭司制起源很古老,他们每人掌管一种特定的祭仪,其中 3 人地位较高,朱庇特神的祭司地位最高。

religious archives. Ordinary priests have often performed the worship of Jupiter when his own priest has been unavailable owing to illness or public business. Moreover, for seventy-five years—after the suicide of Lucius Cornelius Merula—the priesthood was unoccupied. Yet the ceremonies continued without interruption. If the post could remain vacant for so long without detriment to the rites, surely it is easier still for me to be away for one year's governorship ! The Chief Priests used to deny governorships to the priests of Jupiter because of personal rivalries. But today the gods have given us a Chief Priest who is also chief citizen, superior to jealousy, ill-will, or personal considerations. ' Various objections, however, were raised by Cnaeus Cornelius Lentulus (II)—the augur—and others, and it was decided to await the view of the imperial Chief Priest. He, however, postponed his investigation of the matter.

Meanwhile he wrote to the senate modifying the compliments to Drusus in honour of his tribunician power. Tiberius specifically censured the preposterous, un-Roman suggestion of golden lettering. A letter from Drusus also was read. Despite calculated modesty it gave an arrogant impression. Things had come to a pretty pass when a mere youth, awarded so great a distinction, stayed away from Rome's gods and the senate, and did not assume his duties on his native soil.

的记录。当朱庇特神的祭司因病或其他公务而不在场时,一般的祭司就经常代替他向朱庇特神进行礼拜。更何况,在路奇乌斯·科尔涅里乌斯·美路拉自杀[1]之后的75年当中,祭司的职位一直空着,但是祭仪却一直在继续,从来没有中断过。既然在过去的年代里,祭司之职空缺这么长时间也并没有妨碍祭仪的执行,那么我离开这里去担任一年的行省总督也一定更是轻而易举!在先前,主教不许朱庇特神的祭司们担任行省的长官,是由于个人之间的竞争。但是今天,上天把一个全体人民的元首赐予我们当主教,他已经超越于妒忌、恶劣的心情或个人的好恶之上了。"然而,占卜官格涅乌斯·科尔涅里乌斯·楞图路斯(二世)[2]和其他一些人对此提出了各种不同的反对意见,因此最后决定等候皇帝这个主教的意见。但是,提贝里乌斯却迟迟不对此事进行调查。

与此同时,提贝里乌斯还写信给元老院,对为了争取保民官大权而给予杜路苏斯的褒扬做出修改。他特别谴责了哈提里乌斯提出的那种前所未闻的、非罗马式的金字铭刻的建议。元老院还宣读了杜路苏斯的一封来信,尽管在这封信中,杜路苏斯极力想表现得谦逊些,但他却还是给人们一种极其傲慢的印象。人们议论说,世道发生了这样大的变化,甚至一个毛头小伙子都能取得这样大的荣誉,并且既不在罗马神庙,也不在元老院中接受授

---

〔1〕 公元前87年玛利乌斯和秦纳返回罗马时,科尔涅里乌斯自杀,朱庇特的祭司之位就一直空缺着。直到公元前11年,奥古斯都才予以任命。公元前12年,特里乌姆维尔·玛尔库斯·列庇都斯死后,奥古斯都自己成为大主教。

〔2〕 是公元前14年任执政官,公元前1年任亚细亚总督,以豪富著名,但他生性愚钝,语言也迟钝,提贝里乌斯当政时自杀。

'He must be fighting or visiting distant countries.' But he was only touring the Campanian lakes and coasts. So this was the first lesson he learnt from his father—a fine training for the ruler of the world! It was felt that whereas an elderly emperor might shrink from the public gaze, pleading weariness and past labours, Drusus' motive could only be conceit.

Tiberius, while he tightened his control by this conferment on Drusus, allowed the senate a shadow of its ancient power by inviting it to discuss provincial petitions. In Greek cities criminals were increasingly escaping punishment owing to over-lavish rights of sanctuary. Delinquent slaves filled temples. Asylum was granted indiscriminately—to debtors escaping their creditors, even to men suspected of capital offences. Protecting religious observance, these communities were protecting crime itself; and interventions provoked outbreaks which no authority could control. So the cities were requested to submit their charters and their representatives to investigation at Rome.

Some cities then vohuntarily abandoned their unfounded claims. Many however persisted, on the strength of ancient religious myths or their services to Rome. It was a splendid sight, that day, to see the senate investigating privileges conferred by its ancestors, treaties with allies, edicts of kings who had reigned before Rome was a power, even divine cults; and it was flee, as of old, to confirm or amend.

The Ephesians were the first to arrive. They asserted that Apollo and Diana were not, as commonly believed, born at Delos: at Ephesus

勋,甚至就职也不在他故乡的土地上进行。人们也许以为他是由于作战或是由于正在边远的地区巡视而不能来吧。但是,他只是在康帕尼亚的海岸和湖上游玩。这就是他从他父亲那里学到的第一课——这是一种多么好的作为一个全世界的统治者的教育啊!人们认为,一个年事已高的皇帝自然可以不顾公众的需要,以年老体弱和过去的劳苦为由自由隐退。但是在杜路苏斯身上发生这种事,却只有一个原因,那就是傲慢。

提贝里乌斯虽然靠授予杜路苏斯保民官大权的手段,而把独裁大权紧紧地握在自己手里,但又给予元老院一项有名无实的古老权力,那就是要求由元老院来讨论各行省提出的请求。原来在希腊城市里,越来越多的罪犯滥用神庙提供的避难的权力借以逃避惩罚,因此犯罪的奴隶充斥于神庙中,逃避债主的人以及负有大逆罪嫌疑的人也都逃到这里来,免受罪罚。这样,那些享有宗教保护的礼节的地区,同样也就恰恰保护了人间的罪恶,而且对于这种对立所激发的矛盾的爆发,也没有任何一种权威能够控制。于是,这些发生问题的希腊城市被要求派出他们的使节带着文书到罗马来。

接下来,有一些城市自愿放弃了它们那没有什么道理的要求,但是还有许多城市却借口古老的宗教迷信或是它们对罗马有利,而坚持自己的要求。于是就出现了极为壮观的场面,在那一天里,人们看到元老院在仔细审察先人授予他们的各种特权、各个行省的盟约、在罗马崛起成为一大强国之前国王们所发布的各项命令、乃至各种祭神的仪式。和早先一样,元老院有充分的自由对它们给予确认或加以修改。

最先到达的是以弗所人。他们声称,阿波罗和狄安娜并不是像通常人们所认为的那样出生在狄罗斯。在以弗所有一条肯克

there was a river Cenchrius, with an Ortygian grove—it was here that the pregnant Latona, leaning upon an olive-tree which was still standing, had given birth to the twin deities. The grove, they said, had been consecrated by divine order, and there Apollo himself, after killing the Cyclops, had taken refuge from Jupiter's anger. Later Bacchus, after defeating the Amazons, had pardoned those who begged for mercy at the altar, and the temple's sanctity had been further enhanced by permission of Hercules, during his conquest of Lydia. Its privileges had been respected by the Persian governors, Macedonians, and Romans, in turn.

Magnesia on the Maeander—the next delegation—based its claims on the pronouncements of Lucius Cornelius Scipio Asiaticus and Sulla. After their victories over Antiochus III and Mithridates VI respectively, they had rewarded the Magnesians for their loyalty and bravery by granting inviolable right of asylum to the temple of Diana Leucophryene. Then Aphrodisias on behalf of its cult of Venus produced a decree of Julius Caesar, commending its long-standing loyalty to his cause. Stratonicea, too, in support of its shrine of Jupiter and Diana of the Crossroads, quoted a later ordinance of Augustus praising the unshakable devotion to Rome with which they had

里乌斯河和一座欧尔杜吉亚丛林——就在那里,怀孕的拉托娜倚在一棵直到今天还存在着的橄榄树上,生下了这对孪生的天神。他们说,这座丛林也因为神的命令而成了圣地,而阿波罗本人在杀死了库克罗佩斯[1]之后,就是逃到了这里来躲避朱庇特神的愤怒的。后来巴库斯神在打败了亚马逊人之后,在这里赦免了那些躲到祭坛里来请求宽大的亚马逊人。而在赫尔克里士统治吕地亚的时候,经过他的批准,这一神庙获得了更多的神圣特权。这些特权一直依次受到波斯帝国的统治者、马其顿人和罗马人的尊重。

随后而来的是迈安德罗斯河上的玛格涅喜人派出的代表团。他们提出要求的依据是路奇乌斯·科尔涅里乌斯·斯奇比奥·阿西亚提库斯和路奇乌斯·苏拉过去所作的声明。[2]原来在他们分别打败了安提奥库斯三世和米特利达特斯六世之后,为了表彰玛格涅喜人的忠诚和勇敢,而赋予列乌科普利斯的狄安娜的神庙[3]以避难所的神圣不可侵犯的权力。随后,阿普罗狄西亚斯代表维纳斯的信徒们,引证了尤利乌斯·恺撒的一项命令,这项命令是他过去为了表彰他们长期以来对他的事业的忠诚而发布的。而斯特拉托尼凯亚则是为朱庇特和三岔路口的狄安娜[4]的祭仪进行辩护。他举出了圣奥古斯都不久之前发布的一道敕令,敕令中赞扬了在抵抗帕尔提亚人的入侵时,他们对罗马人民所表现出

---

〔1〕 传说中的独眼巨人。

〔2〕 公元前190年和公元前88年,玛格涅喜人分别抵抗了安提奥库斯三世——塞莱乌奇德的独裁者,和庞都斯的米特利达特斯六世后,所签署的声明。

〔3〕 列乌科普利斯就是玛格涅喜人居住的地方。

〔4〕 因为其神庙常常修建在三岔路口的地方,故有此称。

resisted the Parthian invasion.

The representatives of Hierocaesarea had earlier stories of their Persian Diana and her shrine dedicated in the reign of Cyrus I. They recalled that many Roman generals, including Marcus Perperna and Publius Servilius Vatia Isauricus, had recognized the sanctity, not only of the temple, but of the land for two miles round. Then the people of Cyprus made claims for three shrines, the oldest built by Aerias to Venus of Paphos, the next by his son Amathus to Venus of Amathus, and the third by Teucer—fleeing from his father Telamon's anger—to Jupiter of Salamis. Delegations from other cities also were heard.

However, the extensive material and local rivalries proved wearisome. So the senate requested the consuls to investigate the charters for flaws and then report back to itself. Their report approved the cases I have quoted, and added to them an authentic sanctuary of Aesculapius at Pergamum, but intimated that all other stories went back to a past too dim for consideration. Smyrna, for instance, attributed its temple of Venus Stratonicis to instructions from an oracle of Apollo, and Tenos cited another pronouncement from him ordering

的一贯的毫不动摇的忠诚。[1]

希耶洛恺撒利亚的代表谈起了更加古老的事情。原来在他们那里有一位波斯的狄安娜神和一座在居鲁士一世[2]当政时代便奉献给她的神庙。他们回忆了许多罗马将领,包括玛尔库斯·培尔佩那、普布里乌斯·塞尔维利乌斯·瓦提亚·伊扫利库斯,因为这些将领不仅认可这个神庙,而且还承认这一神庙周边两英里的地方都是神圣不可侵犯的。继而,库普利奥提斯人则为3座神庙请命,其中最古老的一座是他们的始祖埃里亚斯建立起来献给帕波司的维纳斯的,第二座是他的儿子阿玛图斯建立起来献给阿玛图斯的维纳斯的,第三座则是为了避开父亲提拉孟的愤怒而逃亡在外的提乌凯尔建立起来献给撒拉米司的朱庇特的。元老院还听取了来自其他城市的代表团的请求。

代表们提出的纷杂的事情,以及他们维护本地区利益的激烈的争吵,使元老们感到十分厌倦。因此最后元老院授权执政官去审查他们要求的豁免权,看看其中有什么可以使其失效的漏洞和缺陷,然后再将结果向元老院汇报。他们的报告证明了我上面所提到的那些城市所提出的要求是合理的;此外,他们还指出,在培尔伽门地方确实还有一座埃司库拉皮乌斯的神庙。但是他们也明白表示,其他所有城市所提出的那些依据都是过于遥远的时代的事情,已经很模糊了,因此难以作为证据。比如说,士麦拿提出的奉献给维纳斯·斯特拉托尼凯的神庙,它是根据阿波罗的一

----

〔1〕 这是公元前40年的事。而事实是,尤利乌斯的命令只涉及阿普罗狄西亚斯的一个地方,奥古斯都的命令也只涉及斯特拉托尼凯亚的一个地方。

〔2〕 波斯国王,公元前559年到公元前529年在位。

the dedication of a statue and shrine to Neptune. The deputation from Sardis, recalling more recent history, ascribed their privilege to the victorious Alexander, and Miletus with equal confidence cited King Darius I. In these cases the cults were of Diana and Apollo respectively. The Cretans made similar claims for a statue of the divine Augustus.

Decrees were then passed in highly honorific terms, but imposing limits. Bronze tablets, too, were to be set up inside the temples as a solemn record—and a warning not to allow religion to become a cloak for inter-city rivalries.

At about this time the Augusta fell dangerously ill; and the emperor had to return urgently to Rome. Either mother and son were still good friends or, if they were not, they concealed it. Indeed shortly beforehand, when dedicating a statue, near the Theatre of Marcellus, to the divine Augustus, she had inscribed Tiberius' name after her own. This was believed to have given him grave, though unexpressed, offence as a slur on his imperial dignity. However, the senate now decreed national prayers and major Games, to be organized by the Pontifical Order, the augurs, and the Board of Fifteen for Religious Ceremonies, assisted by the Board of Seven for Sacrificial Banquets and the Brotherhood of Augustus. Lucius Apronius had proposed that the Fetials should also be among the organizers. But Tiberius opposed this, distinguishing between the functions of the various priesthoods and citing precedents. The Fetials, he said, had never enjoyed such dignity; the priests of Augustus had only been

个神托的提示建立的;提诺斯岛的依据是另一个出自同一来源的预言,预言命令他们把一尊神像和一座神庙奉献给涅普图努斯。撒尔迪斯则举出了时代更近的历史故事,即胜利的亚历山大曾经赐予了他们特权;米利都人以同样的自信引用了国王大流士一世的命令作为依据,在他们列举的这些依据中,他们崇拜的神祇分别是狄安娜和阿波罗。克里特人则又为圣奥古斯都的一座雕像提出了类似的请求。

之后,元老院通过了一系列的决议,这些决议都是用高度尊敬的口吻写出的,然而却仍然做出了一种限制。元老院还命令请求者在神庙内部竖立起一个个铜牌,这样做一则是为了作为一个庄重的纪念,二则是为了提醒大家注意,防止使宗教成为城市内部世俗争吵的掩蔽物。

大约就在同时,优利娅·奥古斯塔病危,皇帝不得不紧急赶回罗马。母子之间的感情看起来还是很好的,如果不是这样的话,那就是他们把彼此间真实的感情深深地隐藏了起来。事实上,就在不久之前,当优利娅在玛尔凯路斯剧场附近的地方为圣奥古斯都建立一座雕像的时候,她曾在铭文上把提贝里乌斯的名字刻在自己名字的后面。人们认为,尽管没有任何表示,提贝里乌斯其实把这种做法当做一种诽谤和侮辱,认为是对自己皇帝尊严的严重冒犯。尽管如此,现在,元老院仍然下令举行全国性的祷告和大赛会。主持大赛会的是祭司、神托官和重大宗教庆典的 15 人团,而以祭宴的 7 人团和奥古斯都祭司团作为辅助。路奇乌斯·阿普洛尼乌斯建议司礼官也应当成为大赛马会的组织成员,但是提贝里乌斯反对这样做,他认为不同祭司团的功能应当有所区别,并且还引证了先前的事例。他说,司礼官是从来没有享受过这样高的尊严的,之所以唯独奥古斯都祭司团的成员被

included because their Brotherhood was attached to the family for which the vows were being fulfilled.

The only proposals in the senate that I have seen fit to mention are particularly praiseworthy or particularly scandalous ones. It seems to me a historian's foremost duty to ensure that merit is recorded, and to confront evil deeds and words with the fear of posterity's denunciations. But this was a tainted, meanly obsequious age. The greatest figures had to protect their positions by subserviency; and, in addition to them, all ex-consuls, most ex-praetors, even many junior senators competed with each other's offensively sycophantic proposals. There is a tradition that whenever Tiberius left the senate-house he exclaimed in Greek, 'Men fit to be slaves!' Even he, freedom's enemy, became impatient of such abject servility.

Then, gradually, self-abasement turned into persecution. Gaius Junius Silanus, accused of extortion by the people of Asia of which he had been governor, was simultaneously assailed by the former consul Mamercus Aemilius Scaurus, the praetor Junius Otho, and the aedile Bruttedius Niger. They charged him with offences against the divinity of Augustus and the imperial majesty of Tiberius. Mamercus quoted as ancient precedents charges made by Scipio Africanus (II), Cato the Censor, and Marcus Aemilius Scaurus against Lucius Aurelius Cotta, Servius Sulpicius Galba (I), and Publius Rutilius

包括进来,是因为这次祷告是为了皇帝家族举行的,而他们正是属于皇帝一家的祭司团。

关于元老院的建议,我认为我只应当提到那些特别值得称赞的和特别可耻的建议。在我看来,一个历史学家的首要职责就是:保证忠实地记录下人们所建立的功业,同时也不能放过那些会遭到后世的责难的邪恶的言论和行动。然而那是一个如此污浊的时代,当时的谄媚奉承之风又是如此的卑鄙无耻,以致最伟大的人物们也不得不靠奴颜婢膝地奉承来保住自己的地位。不仅如此,连所有那些曾经担任过执政官的元老,大部分担任过行政长官的元老,甚至连许多普通元老,彼此都不顾廉耻地争先恐后提出过分谄媚的、令人作呕的建议。人们传说,每当提贝里乌斯离开元老院的时候,他总是习惯于用希腊语说:"真是一群适合于做奴才的人们啊。"甚至他这样一个自由的敌人,对于这种摇尾乞怜、低三下四的奴才相都感到厌烦了。

然后,渐渐地,他们一步一步地从自我作践走向残忍迫害。被控犯了勒索行省居民之罪的亚细亚总督盖乌斯·尤尼乌斯·西拉努斯,同时受到前执政官玛米尔库斯·埃米里乌斯·司考路斯、行政长官尤尼乌斯·奥托和营造官布路提狄乌斯·尼格尔的控诉。他们控诉他冒犯和亵渎了奥古斯都的神圣性和提贝里乌斯的帝王的崇高尊严。但玛米尔库斯竟然引用古人的先例为自己辩护,分别是斯奇比奥·阿非利卡努斯(二世)对路奇乌斯·奥列利乌斯·科塔的控诉,[1]监察官加图对谢尔维乌斯·苏尔皮奇乌斯·伽尔巴(一世)的控诉,[2]玛尔库斯·埃米里乌斯·司考路斯对普布里乌斯·路

---

〔1〕 这是发生在公元前 132 年至前 129 年间的事情。

〔2〕 发生在公元前 149 年。

Rufus respectively—as if there was any comparison with the crimes attacked by Scipio, Cato, or the famous Scaurus, whom this blot on his family, his great-grandson, was now dishonouring with his sordid activities! Junius Otho had formerly kept a school. Later, admitted to the senate by Sejanus' influence, he disgraced even those humble origins by his impudent audacity. Bruttedius Niger was a highly cultured man who, if he had gone straight, would have attained great eminence. But impatience spurred him to outstrip first his equals, then his superiors—and finally his own former ambitions. Impatience has ruined many excellent men who, rejecting the slow, sure way, court destruction by rising too quickly.

The accusers were joined by the two senior members of Silanus' staff in Asia, Gellius Publicola and Marcus Paconius. He was unquestionably guilty of brutality and extortion. But he was involved in circumstances which might have crushed even an innocent man. His enemies in the senate were formidable; and they were supported by the best speakers in the whole province of Asia, selected for this very purpose. Against them he stood alone, an inexperienced speaker, in mortal fear—which incapacitates even practised orators.

Tiberius' words and looks were unrelievedly menacing. So was the

提里乌斯·路福斯的控诉。[1] 但是,他们与这些人的情况并不能相提并论。大家知道,以上所举的事例是斯比奇奥和加图或是玛米尔库斯的曾祖、著名的司考路斯对罪恶进行报复的事,而司考路斯的曾孙玛米尔库斯,却玷污了他的家族,现在因为自己的卑鄙行为而蒙受着耻辱!尤尼乌斯·奥托过去一直办着一所学校,后来靠着谢雅努斯的力量成了元老之后,他的胆大妄为和厚颜无耻甚至使他那本来卑微的出身又加上了一层耻辱。布路提狄乌斯·尼格尔是一个受过很高的教育的人,如果走正路的话,他一定能够取得非常突出的成就。但急于求成的迫切心情促使他先是想超过和他同等身份的人,接着又想超过比他地位高的人,最后竟想超过他自己从前的野心。急躁毁了很多优秀的人,他们不愿意一步一步地、按照正确的途径慢慢进取,结果因为太过迅速地升迁而走向了毁灭。

盖里乌斯·普布利科拉和玛尔库斯·帕科尼乌斯也加入到了控诉者的队伍。他们都是西拉努斯在亚细亚的属下中的高级官员,前者是他的财务官,后者是他的副帅。毫无疑问,被告是犯下了残暴和勒索的罪行。但是他还卷入了许多复杂的事情之中,这些事情甚至是足以使一个无辜者送命的。他在元老院里有许多令人畏惧的强大的敌人,而且还有整个亚细亚行省的最雄辩的演说家支持那些元老院里的对手,这些人都是为对付他而特意选来进行这次控诉的。但是面对着这些人进行答辩的却只是他孑然一人,他既没有演讲的经验,本人又陷入了致命的惊恐之中——就是职业的演说家陷入了这种惊恐情绪的时候,他也会不知所措、无能为力的。

提贝里乌斯的语言和表情,使得这个案件带来的恐惧没有丝

---

[1] 发生在公元前 116 年。

persistence of his interrogations, and the impossibility of negative answers or evasions—even confession was sometimes necessary, so that the emperor should not have asked in vain. Moreover, Silanus' slaves were sold to the Treasury Agent for examination under torture. And not one friend could help him in his peril; for supplementary charges of treason, which were preferred against him, reduced them to compulsory silence. So Silanus, after requesting a few days' adjournment, abandoned his defence. But he ventured to write Tiberius a letter of reproachful entreaty.

The emperor, feeling that a precedent would better justify his proposed action against Silanus, ordered the reading of Augustus' letter and the senate's decree about an earlier governor of the same province, Lucius Valerius Messalla Volesus. Then he asked Lucius Calpurnius Piso (I) for his opinion. Beginning with a prolonged eulogy of the emperor's mercifulness, Piso proposed that Silanus should be outlawed and banished to the island of Gyaros. There was general assent, except for one proposal by Cnaeus Cornelius Lentulus (II)— with which Tiberius concurred-that the property inherited by Silanus from his mother, Atia by name, should be treated separately and allowed to his son.

毫的减轻。此外,他的审问一点也没有中断,步步紧逼地问着这样那样的问题,而这些问题是既不能反驳也不能回避的,甚至有时还需要老老实实地坦白,以便使皇帝不致徒劳无功地审问一场。此外,西拉努斯的奴隶也被正式地卖给了国库官,这样做是为了可以通过严刑拷问对他们进行审讯。在这样危险的时刻,没有一个朋友能够帮他的忙,因为附加上去的正是针对他的大逆罪,使他们不得不保持沉默。因此,西拉努斯在要求给他的几天期限之后,便放弃了为自己进行的辩护,但是他却冒险给提贝里乌斯写了一封带着责备之意的恳求信。

提贝里乌斯认为,历史上的先例能够使自己对西拉努斯的裁决给人以比较好的印象,于是他便下令在元老院宣读圣奥古斯都控诉亚细亚的另一名更早的总督路奇乌斯·沃列苏斯·美撒拉·屋列斯乌斯的一封信,以及元老院就他而发布的一项命令。随后他便征求路奇乌斯·卡尔普尔尼乌斯·披索(一世)的意见。以一大套冗长的对提贝里乌斯的仁慈的赞美之词开头,披索提出自己的主张说,应当剥夺西拉努斯的公民权,并且把他流放到一个叫做吉雅路斯的小岛上去。他的提议得到了一般人的认可,只有格涅乌斯·科尔涅里乌斯·楞图路斯(二世)一人例外,他提议说,既然西拉努斯的财产是从他母亲手里继承过来的,而他的母亲是出生于阿提乌斯家族的,[1]因此在这一方面应当和其他的事情区别对待,并且其财产应当归还给他的儿子。提贝里乌斯同意了他的建议。

---

〔1〕 奥古斯都的母族是阿提乌斯家族,如果盖乌斯·尤尼乌斯·西拉努斯的母亲出生于阿提乌斯家族,那么她大概就与同名的奥古斯都的母亲有密切的关系。他的母亲是玛尔库斯·阿提乌斯·巴尔布斯和恺撒的姊妹优利娅的女儿。

Publius Cornelius Dolabella (I), elaborately sycophantic, included in a denunciation of Silanus the proposal that no one of scandalous life and evil reputation should be eligible for a governorship—the emperor to be judge. For whereas (Dolabella observed) the law punishes offences, it would be much kinder, to offenders and provincials alike, to forestall them. Tiberius, however, disagreed. 'I am aware', he said, 'of the rumours about Silanus. But decisions should not be based on rumours. Many governors have belied people's hopes and fears: important positions stimulate some natures and blunt others. An emperor's knowledge cannot be all-embracing, and intrigues against rivals should not influence him. The law is concerned with what has been done. What will be done is unknown. That is why our ancestors ruled that punishment should follow crime. This was wise, and has always been accepted. Do not reverse it. Emperors have enough burdens—and enough power. Strengthen the executive, and you weaken the law. When one can act by law, the use of official authority is a mistake.'

These constitutional sentiments were welcome, the more so since they were not characteristic of Tiberius. And capable, as he was, of mercy (when not impelled by anger), he proposed that, since Gyaros was a grim, uninhabited island, Silanus—as a concession to his Junian family and former membership of the senate—should be allowed to retire to Cythnos instead. This had been requested, he added, by Silanus' sister Junia Torquata, a priestess of Vesta and a woman of old-

普布里乌斯·科尔涅里乌斯·多拉贝拉(一世)又精心准备了一套献媚之词,他对西拉努斯大加谴责,并且建议说,在生活上有过丑行和名声不好的任何人都不能被选为行省的总督,而皇帝才是仲裁者。(多拉贝拉说)既然法律是用来惩处犯罪的,那么对于犯罪的人,以及对于行省居民来说,要是能够在事先预防他们犯罪的话,那将会更加仁慈!但是,提贝里乌斯不同意他这种说法。他说:"我是知道关于西拉努斯的种种谣传的,但是人们要做出正确的判断不能以谣传为依据。许多做行省总督的人辜负了人们对他的希望或敬畏。显贵的地位激发了人的一些自然本性,同时也使另一些人本性变得迟钝起来。皇帝的知识不可能是无所不包的,针对竞争者的那些阴谋诡计也不会对他产生什么影响。法律制裁的是已经发生的罪行,这是因为将要做的事情是不确定的。这就是我们的祖先为什么会规定,惩罚要针对犯罪行为,这种规定是十分明智的,而且为人们所普遍接受,我们是不应当推翻它的。皇帝们已经有了足够的负担,甚至有了足够的权力。执行者的权力加强了,法律的权威也就削弱了。当一个人依法行事的时候,再使用执政者的权力那就是错误的了。"

这种具有拥护宪法精神的讲话受到了人们的热情欢迎,因为提贝里乌斯的性格很少体现出这种精神。提贝里乌斯(在不为愤怒的情绪所驱遣的时候)还是能尽其所能地做一些富有慈悲心的事情的,因此他建议说,因为吉雅路斯是一个荒凉的、无人居住的小岛,考虑到西拉努斯又是出生于尤尼乌斯家族,并且还曾经是元老院的一名成员,故而可以对他网开一面,做出一些让步,可以准许他退休到库特诺斯岛去。他还说,西拉努斯的姊妹优尼娅·托尔克娃塔是一位维司塔贞女,并且也是一位颇具古风的圣洁的

fashioned saintliness. It was agreed without discussion.

The people of Cyrene were heard next, and Caesius Cordus, accused by Ancharius Priscus, was condemned for extortion. A knight called Lucius Ennius was charged with treason for melting down a silver statue of the emperor for use as plate. Tiberius forbade the prosecution. But Gaius Ateius Capito made a show of independence by openly objecting. He argued that the decision ought not to be taken away from the senate, that so grave a misdeed must not go unpunished, and that the emperor's generosity concerning his personal wrongs should not be extended to condoning offences against the State. But Tiberius understood the sinister implications of this attitude and persisted in his veto. Capito's degradation was especially conspicuous: for he was a learned secular and religious lawyer whose words disgraced his personal talents as well as his official distinction.

A religious problem next arose. In what temple were the knights to lodge the gift vowed by them to Fortune-on-Horseback for the Augusta's recovery from illness? Rome had many temples of Fortune but none with this title. It was discovered, however, that a temple at Antium had the designation—and that all rites, temples, and statues of the gods in Italian towns were under Roman jurisdiction and control. So the gift was deposited at Antium.

Since religious matters were being discussed, Tiberius now produced his deferred answer to the application of Servius Cornelius Lentulus Maluginensis, priest of Jupiter, for the governorship of Asia. Tiberius read a priestly ordinance decreeing that whenever the

女人,她也提出了这样的请求。这项建议未经讨论就通过了。

随后元老院听取了库列涅人的发言。凯西乌斯·科尔杜斯受到安卡里乌斯·普利斯库斯的控诉,他被判犯下了勒索罪。一个名叫路奇乌斯·恩尼乌斯的罗马骑士被控以大逆罪,因为他把皇帝的一座银像熔铸为日用的食器银盘。提贝里乌斯禁止对这件事情进行追究。但是盖乌斯·阿泰乌斯·卡皮托却不附和皇帝的意见,而以独立的姿态公开表示反对。他说,不应该取消元老院做出决定的权力,而且这样一种严重的罪行是一定要受到惩罚的。至于皇帝本人宽宏大度,对自己受到的侮辱可以采取宽大为怀的态度,但是这种宽容不能延及到对国家所犯下的罪行!但是,提贝里乌斯明白卡皮托这种态度中所暗含的险恶的用心,因此便仍然坚持自己的否决意见。在这件事上,卡皮托的堕落特别明显地表现了出来,因为他本人就是一个精通世俗和宗教的法律的法学家,他讲的这种话不仅仅是玷污了他个人的优秀才能,而且也玷污了一位政治家的崇高声望。

接着又出现了一个宗教方面的问题。为了使奥古斯塔早日康复,骑士们奉献给骑着马的幸福女神的礼品要存放在哪个神庙里呢?当时在罗马有许多幸福女神的神庙,但是没有一位幸福女神拥有这样的称号。尽管如此,人们还是发现了,在安提乌姆有一座神庙享有这样的名称。既然在意大利的城市中,所有的祭仪、一切的神庙和神像都是在罗马的管辖和统治之下的,因此他们的礼品也就奉献在安提乌姆神庙托管了。

因为谈到了宗教方面的问题,于是提贝里乌斯现在就顺便对不久之前拖延下来的、关于朱庇特神的祭司,谢尔维乌斯·科尔涅里乌斯·楞图路斯·玛路吉南西斯提出的当亚细亚的总督的要求,

priest of Jupiter was ill he might at the Chief Priest's discretion stay away for a period exceeding two nights, provided that it was not on days of public sacrifice or oftener than twice in one year. This ruling—formulated under Augustus—showed that priests of Jupiter were ineligible for provincial governorships, since these involved a year's absence: the precedent was the ban on the departure of Aulus Posturnius by the Chief Priest Lucius Caecilius Metellus. So Asia was allotted to the ex-consul next after Maluginensis.

At about this time Marcus Aemilius Lepidus (IV) asked the senate's leave to strengthen and beautify, at his own expense, the Hall that was the family monument of the Aemilii, built by Lucius Aemilius Paullus (II). For public munificence was still fashionable. Augustus had allowed enemy spoils, or great resources, to be devoted by Titus Statilius Taurus (I), Lucius Marcius Philippus, and Lucius Cornelius Balbus (II) to the adornment of Rome for the applause of posterity. Now Lepidus, though of moderate means, followed their example by repairing his family memorial. When, however, the Theatre of Pompey was accidentally burnt down, Tiberius undertook to rebuild it himself on the grounds that no Pompeius had the means to do so; but its name was to remain unchanged.

做出了答复。他宣读了祭司的一项命令,命令说,无论何时,朱庇特神的祭司如果生病了,可以在得到祭司长批准的情况之下离开圣职两夜以上,但是不能在国祭期间,而且每年不允许超过两次。在奥古斯都统治时期所做的这一规定表明,朱庇特神的祭司不能到行省去担任总督的职务,因为这样离职一年触犯了对祭司宗教义务的规定。过去也发生过类似的事情,祭司长路奇乌斯·凯奇里乌斯·美提路斯不允许祭司奥路斯·波司图米乌斯离开罗马。[1] 这样,亚细亚便分配给资历次于玛路吉南西斯的一位前任执政官了。

大约就在这个时候,玛尔库斯·埃米里乌斯·列庇都斯(四世)向元老院请假,以便自己出资去加固和装饰那埃米里乌斯家族的纪念建筑物——由路奇乌斯·埃米里乌斯·保路斯(二世)修建的会堂。[2] 私人出钱办公众事情依然是一种风尚。奥古斯都过去曾允许提图斯·斯塔提利乌斯·陶路斯(一世)、路奇乌斯·玛尔库斯·菲利浦和路奇乌斯·科尔尼利乌斯·巴尔布斯(二世)把缴获的战利品或大量资财用来装饰首都罗马,从而受到了后人的称赞。[3] 列庇都斯的财产并不多,但是他现在也以那些人为榜样,重修他们家族著名的纪念性建筑物。同时,对不幸因偶然事故毁于大火的庞培剧场,提贝里乌斯本人亲自出资重修,因为庞培家族中没有任何一个人能有这样的财力来干这件事情,但是庞培的名号却依然保持不变。

---

〔1〕 禁止祭司奥路斯·波司图米乌斯离开罗马是公元前 242 年的事情,但是波司图米乌斯是玛尔斯神的祭司而不是朱庇特神的祭司。

〔2〕 公元前 50 年,列庇都斯的祖父开始修建,列庇都斯的父亲完成并奉献。公元前 14 年毁于大火,后来由奥古斯都和该家族的友人修复。

〔3〕 陶路斯和巴尔布斯分别修建了第一座圆形剧场和一座剧场,菲利浦重建了缪斯的赫尔克里士神神庙。

Tiberius commended Sejanus' energy and watchfulness in preventing the fire from spreading beyond Pompey's Theatre; and the senate voted that his statue be erected there. Again, shortly afterwards, when Tiberius awarded an honorary Triumph to Quintus Junius Blaesus, governor of Africa, the emperor indicated that this was a compliment to the latter's nephew Sejanus. Yet Blaesus' achievements had earned the distinction. For Tacfarinas, despite frequent defeats, had raised reinforcements in the interior and was insolent enough to send representatives to Tiberius demanding land for himself and his army. As the alternative, he offered endless war. No personal or national slur, it is said, ever provoked the emperor more than the sight of this deserter and brigand behaving like a hostile sovereign. Even Spartacus (reflected Tiberius), burning Italy unavenged—at a time when he had destroyed consuls' armies and the nation was convulsed by terrible wars overseas against Quintus Sertorius and Mithridates VI of Pontus—had not been allowed conditions for his surrender. 1 And now, with Roman power at its height, was this bandit Tacfarinas to be bought off by a treaty granting lands?

Tiberius entrusted the matter to the governor Quintus Junius Blaesus. By promising pardon he was to induce the rebels to lay down

　　同时,提贝里乌斯又对谢雅努斯大加称赞,正是由于谢雅努斯的果敢和警觉,才防止了庞培剧场的那场大火的继续蔓延,没有殃及到周围的地区。元老们建议应该在剧场那里给谢雅努斯立像。不久之后,当提贝里乌斯又把凯旋的标记授予阿非利加总督克温图斯·尤尼乌斯·布莱苏斯的时候,皇帝指出,他这样做是为了向谢雅努斯表示祝贺,因为谢雅努斯是布莱苏斯的侄子。尽管这样讲,但是布莱苏斯的功勋也是完全当得起这样的荣誉的。至于塔克法里那斯,尽管他多次被打败,却还在阿非利加的腹地纠合了一批援军,然后竟然放肆到派出使节到提贝里乌斯这里来,为他本人和他的军队要求土地。他说,如果他得不到土地的话,他就会无休无止地发动战争。一个逃亡者和歹徒现在竟然大模大样地装作像一个敌国的首脑那样前来向他提出要求,据说,这种情况所惹起的皇帝的愤怒,比任何他个人或国家受到的侮辱都严重。甚至在斯巴达克斯的战火丝毫没有受到报复地燃遍了整个意大利的时候——这个时候,斯巴达克斯已经歼灭了许多执政官的军队,而共和国正在对克温图斯·谢尔托里乌斯和米特利达特斯六世进行着激烈的殊死战争——甚至在这样的情况下,斯巴达克斯尚且没有获准得到有条件的投降。[1] 而现在,罗马的国力如日中天,这个匪徒塔克法里那斯反而还会被罗马人用缔结和约、割让土地的办法把他打发走吗?

　　提贝里乌斯把这件事交给了总督克温图斯·尤尼乌斯·布莱苏斯。布莱苏斯于是以将会获得宽恕的保证,诱使叛变的人放

---

　　〔1〕 斯巴达克斯领导的奴隶起义是在公元前73年至公元前71年,克温图斯·谢尔托里乌斯在西班牙的反叛是在公元前82年至公元前72年。

arms—except the leader, who was to be captured by any means possible. The amnesty brought many over. Moreover, Tacfarinas was now confronted by methods like his own. Since his army was inferior in fighting power but superior in raiding capacity, he operated with independent groups, avoiding engagements and setting traps. So the Romans, too, attacked with three separate formations. Each had a target of its own. One, under the divisional commander Publius Cornelius Lentulus Scipio (Ⅰ), blocked the route by which the enemy had raided Lepcis, with the Garamantes to fall back upon. On the other flank, a detachment commanded by Blaesus' son protected the communities of Cirta against raids. In the centre was the governor and commander-in-chief himself with selected troops. By planting forts and defences at appropriate spots, he cramped and harassed the enemy. In whatever direction they moved, they found part of the Roman army on front, flanks, and often rear. By these methods many rebels were killed and taken prisoner.

Then Blaesus split up his three formations into smaller bodies, each under a company-commander of distinguished record. It had been customary to withdraw the troops when summer was over, and quarter them in winter camps in Africa proper. Blaesus abolished this

下他们的武器,但对首恶者则绝不宽容,他将用一切可能的办法把他捉拿归案。这种宽大措施使许多人投到了罗马这一边来。这样一来,塔克法里那斯现在就遭遇了和他自己所使用的相似的作战办法。由于塔克法里那斯在大规模的作战能力方面比不上罗马人,但是在小规模的袭击方面占据着优势,他便把自己的兵力分散成若干独立的小队,以避免正面交锋,打完之后就无影无踪,不留下任何痕迹。因此,针对这种情况,罗马人也把队伍分成三个部分,每个部分都有自己的攻击目标,各自分头加以追击。一支由副帅普布里乌斯·科尔涅里乌斯·楞图路斯·斯奇比奥(一世)率领,封锁住敌人进攻列普提斯人之后再退回到伽拉芒提斯人那里去的道路。在另一方面,由布莱苏斯的儿子率领着自己的一支分队,去对付敌人的袭击以保卫奇尔塔的村落。中路则由总督和统帅布莱苏斯亲自率领一支选拔出来的最精锐的军队。他在各个适当的地点都修筑了工事或堡垒,这就在整个地区全面地对敌人构成了强大的压抑和威胁。他们不论跑到什么地方去,都会发现在自己的前面、侧面、甚至还经常在后面,都有罗马的一支军队,就是靠这样的办法,许多叛逆者被歼灭和俘虏了。

接着,布莱苏斯又把他的三支军队分成了更多的小队伍,每支队伍都由战绩卓著的百人团长率领着。按照过去的惯例,每当夏季过后,是要把军队撤回来,让他们到行省阿非利加的冬营中去休整的。[1] 布莱苏斯取消了这个惯例,与此相反,他却修建了

---

〔1〕 阿非利加行省是公元前 146 年迦太基被攻陷以后并入罗马的,公元前 46 年塔普苏斯一役之后,奇尔塔地区和努米地亚的大部分地区另外组成"新阿非利加",直到公元前 25 年,才和"旧行省"合并。

custom. Instead he established a chain of forts—the usual procedure at the beginning, not the end, of a campaigning season. Then, employing mobile columns with desert training, he kept Tacfarinas in a continual state of movement.

Finally, Blaesus captured the rebel leader's brother. Then, however, he withdrew—too soon for the interests of the province, since enough of the enemy were left to revive hostilities. Nevertheless Tiberius treated the war as ended, and even allowed Blaesus the honour of being hailed victor by his army, a traditional distinction granted to successful generals by the spontaneous acclamation of their victorious troops. The distinction was not limited to one commander at a time, and did not confer precedence over others. It had been granted on certain occasions by Augustus. After this award by Tiberius to Blaesus it was never conferred again.

Two eminent men died this year. One was Asinius Saloninus, noteworthy as grandson of Marcus Agrippa and Gains Asinius Pollio (I), half-brother of Drusus, and intended husband of one of Tiberius' granddaughters. The other death that occurred was of Gaius Ateius Capito, whom I have mentioned already. By his distinction as a jurist he had achieved national eminence. Yet his grandfather had only been a company-commander of Sulla, and his father a praetor. Augustus

一连串的工事——而这通常是在作战季节开始时、而非结束时的工作。然后,他又组织了几支素有沙漠作战经验的流动队伍,不停地追击塔克法里那斯,使得塔克法里那斯疲于奔命。

直到最后,布莱苏斯俘虏了判军头目的兄弟之后,才终于撤了回来。但这次撤军仍然是过于仓促,因为行省的安全仍旧不能得到最后的保障,那里保存下来的敌人还有足够的力量重新挑起战争。不过提贝里乌斯却将此当做这次战争的结束,他甚至还给予布莱苏斯以被军团士兵欢呼为统帅的荣誉。这是一种由来以久的给予取得成功的将领们的荣誉,因为在战胜之后,胜利的士兵们是会自发地向他们欢呼的。这种荣誉并非一次仅限于一个指挥官,几个人可以同时拥有这样的头衔,而且拥有这样头衔的人们,他们的地位也并不比他们的同僚们更高。奥古斯都在某些情况下也授予过这样的称号。提贝里乌斯把这个称号授予布莱苏斯以后,就再也没有授予过其他人这样的称号。

这一年,两位著名的人物去世。一个是阿西尼乌斯·撒罗尼努斯,[1]他所以有名是因为他是玛尔库斯·阿格里帕和盖乌斯·阿西尼乌斯·波里欧(一世)的孙子,是杜路苏斯的兄弟,而且他又和提贝里乌斯的一个孙女订了婚。另一个提及的逝者是盖乌斯·阿泰乌斯·卡皮托,关于他,在前面我曾经说起过。由于在法学方面的杰出成就,他在国家中获得了崇高的地位。但是他的祖父只是苏拉手下的一名百人团长,他的父亲也只是一个行政长官。但

---

〔1〕 撒罗尼努斯是阿西尼乌斯·伽路斯和维普撒尼娅(提贝里乌斯的第一个妻子)的儿子,因此是杜路苏斯的兄弟,和日耳曼尼库斯的一个女儿结了婚。

had made him consul before age to give him precedence over another distinguished lawyer, Marcus Antistius Labeo. For these two paragons of the arts of peace were the simultaneous products of a single generation. Labeo's incorruptible independence gave him the finer reputation; Capito's obedience secured him the greater imperial favour. Labeo stopped short at the praetorship. This seemed unfair—and increased his popularity. Capito's consulship, on the other hand, earned him jealousy and dislike. Another death was that of Junia Tertulla, niece of Cato, wife of Gaius Cassius, sister of Brutus—a full sixty-three years after Philippi. Her will caused much discussion, because although she was very rich and included complimentary references to almost every leading Roman she omitted the emperor. However, he showed no autocratic resentment, and did not refuse her a ceremonial funeral, including a eulogy from the official dais. The effigies of twenty highly distinguished families, Manlii, Quinctii, and others equally aristocratic, headed the procession. But Cassius and Brutus were the most gloriously conspicuous—precisely because their statues were not to be seen.

是奥古斯都迅速地在其尚未达到适当的年龄时,就提拔他担任了执政官,从而使得他的声誉超过了另一位著名法学家玛尔库斯·安提司提乌斯·拉贝欧。[1] 这两位和平时代的人文学科的典范人物是在同一个时代里产生的。拉贝欧刚正不阿的独立品格使他在民众当中享有更高的声望,但卡皮托的驯顺和服从则使他更能讨得皇帝的欢心。拉贝欧最高只做到了短暂的行政长官之职,这一点对他似乎是不公平的,但是这却增加了他在人们中的威望。而另一方面,卡皮托虽然做到了执政官,但这也给他招来了嫉妒和怨恨。还有一个人去世了,她就是优尼娅·特尔图拉,她是加图的外甥女、盖乌斯·卡西乌斯的妻子,玛尔库斯·布鲁图斯的妹妹。[2] 她的去世是菲利披之役[3]63 年以后的事情。她的遗嘱引起了许多的议论,因为尽管她非常富有,而说起那些罗马的显要贵族时,她几乎对每个人都大加赞扬,但是偏偏没有提到皇帝。但是皇帝并不曾因这一忽略而显示出丝毫专制者的愤怒,并且也不反对为她举行葬仪,包括在广场的讲坛上宣读对她的颂词。20 个非常显要的家族的胸像走在她的送葬行列的前列,其中有曼里乌斯家族、克温克提乌斯家族以及同样显贵的其他许多贵族家族成员的胸像。卡西乌斯和布鲁图斯二人是最为辉煌著名的,但是他们二人的胸像却没有出现在葬仪中。

---

〔1〕 盖乌斯·阿泰乌斯·卡皮托和玛尔库斯·安提司提乌斯·拉贝欧两个人在法学界都非常著名,他们分别创立了两个学派:撒比尼亚努斯学派和普洛库路斯学派。

〔2〕 加图的姊妹谢尔维里娅起初嫁给了玛尔库斯·尤尼乌斯·布鲁图斯,后来又嫁给戴奇姆斯·尤尼乌斯·西拉努斯。她第一次结婚时生下了暗杀过恺撒的布鲁图斯,第二次结婚后生下了卡西乌斯的妻子特尔图拉。

〔3〕 菲利披之役发生在罗马建城 712 年,即公元前 61 年。

CHAPTER 7

'Partner Of My Labours'

In the consulships of Gaius Asinius Pollio (II) and Gaius Antistius Vetus (I), Tiberius now began his ninth year of national stability and domestic prosperity (the latter, he felt, augmented by Germanicus' death). But then suddenly Fortune turned disruptive. The emperor himself became tyrannical—or gave tyrannical men power. The cause and beginning of the change lay with Lucius Aelius Sejanus, commander of the Guard. I have said something of his influence, and will now describe his origins and personality—and his criminal attempt on the throne.

Sejanus was born at Vulsinii. His father, Lucius Seius Strabo, was a Roman knight. After increasing his income—it was alleged—by a liaison with a rich debauchee named Marcus Gavius Apicius, the boy joined, while still young, the suite of Augustus' grandson Gaius Caesar. Next by various devices he obtained a complete ascendancy over Tiberius. To Sejanus alone the otherwise cryptic emperor spoke

第七章　"我的分忧担劳的好搭档"

　　盖乌斯·阿西尼乌斯·波里奥(二世)和盖乌斯·安提司提乌斯·维图斯(一世)担任执政官的时候,开始了提贝里乌斯在全国安谧和繁荣的情况下进行统治的第九年。[1]（而他认为,日耳曼尼库斯的死亡更加倍促进了国家的繁荣。)但接下来,命运却突然发生了巨大的转变,提贝里乌斯本人变成了暴君——或者把权力交到残暴的人的手中。这种转变的开始和造成这种情况的原因,在于提贝里乌斯的近卫军长官路奇乌斯·埃里乌斯·谢雅努斯。关于他的影响,我在上面已经谈到过了一些情况。现在我就要谈一谈他的出身和品质,以及他那想夺取皇权的罪恶企图。

　　谢雅努斯生于沃尔西尼,[2]他的父亲路奇乌斯·塞乌斯·斯特拉波,是一个罗马骑士。当他的收入增加以后——据称,是靠和一个名字叫做玛尔库斯·伽维乌斯·阿披奇乌斯的有钱的浪荡子弟私通获得的,虽然年纪还小,谢雅努斯却加入了圣奥古斯都的外孙盖乌斯·恺撒的随从。以后,通过各种各样巧妙的手段,他获得了对提贝里乌斯进行控制的完全的优势。只有对谢雅努斯

---

〔1〕　公元 23 年,即罗马建城 776 年。
〔2〕　埃特路里亚的 12 个城市之一,在卡西亚大道旁,现在叫波尔塞那。

freely and unguardedly. This was hardly due to Sejanus' cunning; in that he was outclassed by Tiberius. The cause was rather heaven's anger against Rome—to which the triumph of Sejanus, and his downfall too, were catastrophic. Of audacious character and untiring physique, secretive about himself and ever ready to incriminate others, a blend of arrogance and servility, he concealed behind a carefully modest exterior an unbounded lust for power. Sometimes this impelled him to lavish excesses, but more often to incessant work. And that is as damaging as excess when the throne is its aim.

The command of the Guard had hitherto been of slight importance. Sejanus enhanced it by concentrating the Guard battalions, scattered about Rome, in one camp. Orders could reach them simultaneously, and their visible numbers and strength would increase their selfconfidence and intimidate the population. His pretexts were, that scattered quarters caused unruliness; that united action would be needed in an emergency; and that a camp away from the temptations of the city would improve discipline. When the camp was ready, he gradually insinuated himself into the men's favour. He would talk with them addressing them by name. And he chose their company

一个人，神秘莫测的提贝里乌斯可以自由地谈话，毫无顾忌。这种情况，很难说是由于谢雅努斯的狡诈，因为在这一点上，提贝里乌斯其实是大大超过谢雅努斯的。这样的情况毋宁说是上天降于罗马的愤怒，因为无论是谢雅努斯得势还是垮台，对罗马来说都是一场灾难。这个人有着胆大粗莽的性格和不知疲倦的体格；他善于隐蔽自己的思想，总有办法陷害别人；傲慢和奴性混合在一起；在谦恭谨慎的后面，掩盖着对权力的无穷欲望。这种欲望有时会促使他走向极度的奢侈和浪费，然而在更多的情况下却促使他不断地勤奋工作。而在他想夺取王位的时候，这些品质和奢侈浪费一样都是有害的。

迄今为止，近卫军长官的权力并不大。但是谢雅努斯把分散在整个罗马的那些步兵中队[1]集中在一个营地里，以加强近卫军长官的权力。这样军队能同时接到命令，同时他们明显可知的人数、力量还能够增强他们的自信心，并能够慑服众人。他这样做的借口是，分散的军队不容易控制；而有些情况下需要紧急召集联合行动；而且军营远离城市的引诱，军队的纪律性就会得到加强了。当近卫军的军营准备就绪之后，他便开始逐渐地取得普通士兵的好感，他和他们交谈，叫着他们的名字向他们致敬。同时，他又亲

---

〔1〕 这时共有9个中队，每一个中队由一个将领率领，人数是1000人，并且有补充的骑兵队。从公元41年，他们把克劳狄乌斯拥戴为皇帝，到公元306年他们宣布玛克森提乌斯为皇帝为止，皇帝的立废大权一直在他们手里。六年之后，在穆尔维乌斯桥上几乎被康司坦丁消灭的近卫军被解散，而在城东不远的军营也被摧毁了。

and battalion-commanders himself. Senators' ambitions, too, he tempted with offices and governorships for his dependants.

Tiberius was readily amenable, praising him in conversation—and even in the senate and Assembly—as 'the partner of my labours', and allowing honours to his statues in theatres, public places, and brigade headquarters. Yet Sejanus' ambitions were impeded by the wellstocked imperial house, including a son and heir—in his prime—and grown-up grandchildren. Subtlety required that the crimes should be spaced out: it would be unsafe to strike at all of them simultaneously. So subtle methods prevailed. Sejanus decided to begin with Drusus, against whom he had a recent grudge. For Drusus, violent-tempered and resentful of a rival, had raised his hand against him during a fortuitous quarrel and, when Sejanus resisted, had struck him in the face.

After considering every possibility, Sejanus felt most inclined to rely on Drusus' wife Livilla, the sister of Germanicus. Unattractive in earlier years, she had become a great beauty. Sejanus professed devotion, and seduced her. Then, this first guilty move achieved—since a woman who has parted with her virtue will refuse nothing—he incited her to hope for marriage, partnership in the empire, and the death of her husband. So the grand-niece of Augustus, daughter-in-

自选任他们的百人团长和将领。他还用当他的下属就授予罗马的和行省的官职的办法来引诱元老们的野心。

提贝里乌斯对谢雅努斯百依百顺，他不仅仅在日常的谈话中，甚至在元老院和民众的集会中，都称赞他为"我的分忧担劳的好搭档"，并且使他享有胸像被放置在剧院、广场和军团总部的荣誉。但是谢雅努斯的野心还受着一大群皇室成员的阻挡——包括一位已是成年的儿子和正在成长起来、能够作为继承人的孙子。[1] 此时，聪明的策略就是谋叛的罪行要逐步进行，因为想同时对付所有这些人是非常不安全的，这就需要使用更加狡诈的手段。谢雅努斯决定从杜路苏斯开始下手，因为不久之前他和杜路苏斯之间发生过冲突，谢雅努斯心怀怨恨。杜路苏斯性情暴躁，对忤逆他的人非常恼恨，在偶然发生的一次争吵中，他动手打了谢雅努斯，而在谢雅努斯反抗时，他又给了谢雅努斯一记耳光。

在考虑了各种可能之后，谢雅努斯觉得，要陷害杜路苏斯，最好的办法是依靠杜路苏斯的妻子利维拉，即日耳曼尼库斯的妹妹。虽然她小时候并没有什么吸引力，但长大之后却非常漂亮。谢雅努斯对她大献殷勤，并且诱使她和自己有了奸情。于是，第一桩罪行成功地实施了——一个女人一旦偏离了自己的贞操德行，就无法拒绝任何诱惑了——谢雅努斯又煽动起她想跟自己结婚、分享帝国大权并谋杀自己丈夫的欲望，如此一来，她，奥古斯都

---

〔1〕 皇帝家族中的男子除了提贝里乌斯本人之外，还有尼禄·恺撒、杜路苏斯·恺撒、他的继子日耳曼尼库斯的儿子们，以及杜路苏斯的孪生儿子提贝里乌斯·盖美路斯和日耳曼尼库斯等。

law of Tiberius, mother of Drusus' children, degraded herself and her ancestors and descendants with a small-town adulterer; she sacrificed her honourable, assured position for infamy and hazard. The plot was communicated to Eudemus, Livilla's friend and doctor, who had professional pretexts for frequent interviews. Sejanus encouraged his mistress by sending away his wife Apicata, the mother of his three children. Nevertheless the magnitude of the projected crime caused misgivings, delays, and (on occasion) conflicting plans.

Meanwhile, at the beginning of the year Drusus Caesar, one of Germanicus' children, assumed adult clothing, and the senate's decrees in honour of his brother Nero Caesar were repeated. Tiberius spoke as well, warmly praising his own son Drusus for his fatherly affection to the sons of his 'brother' Germanicus. For, though lofty positions are not easily compatible with friendliness, Drusus was believed to like the young men or at least not to dislike them.

Next there was a revival of the old idea of a tour in the provinces by Tiberius. The emperor justified his proposal (the object of frequent lip-service by him) on the grounds of the numerous soldiers due for release, and the need to fill their places by conscription. There were not enough volunteers, he said, and they lacked the old bravery and discipline, since voluntary enlistment mostly attracted penniless vagrants. Then he briefly enumerated the army formations and the provinces under their protection. I now propose to do the same—in order to give an idea of the Roman armed forces and dependent monarchs at that time, when the empire was so much smaller.

的外孙女、提贝里乌斯的儿媳妇、杜路苏斯的孩子们的母亲,便因为这个小市民出身的奸夫,而玷污了她本人、她的祖先和她的子孙们。她牺牲了当前大受尊敬、又有保障的稳固可靠的地位,而换来了声名狼藉的丑行和危险。利维拉的医生和朋友埃乌德木斯也参与了他们的阴谋,因为他的职业可以为他们经常见面作掩护。为了鼓励自己情妇的信心和勇气,谢雅努斯遗弃了他的妻子阿皮卡塔,他的三个孩子的母亲。然而,所计划的罪行的规模也引起了疑虑、拖延,(有时)甚至是意见上的冲突。

同时,就在这一年年初的时候,日耳曼尼库斯的一个孩子杜路苏斯·恺撒第一次穿上了成人的服装。于是元老院将过去给他的哥哥尼禄·恺撒的贺词又重复了一遍。提贝里乌斯也发表了一篇演说,对他自己的儿子杜路苏斯所表现出的,对他的"兄弟"日耳曼尼库斯的孩子们的真挚深厚的父爱,热情洋溢地大加赞扬。虽然高高在上的地位很难与真诚平等的友爱相容,但是大家认为杜路苏斯对少年人却是喜欢的,至少并不讨厌他们。

接下来,又开始重新讨论起关于提贝里乌斯到各个行省去巡视这样一个老话题来。皇帝证明自己的提议的理由(他常常挂在嘴边的借口)是,有大批服役期满的士兵要退役安置,因而还需要征募大量新兵来代替他们。他说,自愿参加军队的人数不足,而且即使有这样的志愿军,他们也太缺乏过去的军队所有的那种勇敢和纪律性,因为自愿来登记当兵的都是些赤贫的流浪者。然后,他简略地列举了军团的数目和在它们保卫之下的行省。我认为我应当讲一讲的,目的是说明一下当时罗马武装的兵力以及和帝国结盟的有哪些王国,而帝

Italy was guarded by two fleets, one on each sea-board, at Misenum and Ravenna; and other warships—Augustus had captured them in his victorious battle of Actium and sent them, strongly manned, to Forum Julii—defended the near coast of Gaul. But our main strength lay on the Rhine: eight brigades, for protection against Germans or Gauls. Three more occupied the recently pacified Spanish provinces, two each Africa and Egypt (Mauretania had been presented by the Roman State to King Juba II). Then the huge stretch of territory between this end of Syria and the Euphrates was controlled by four brigades, while on the frontiers Roman might also maintained certain monarchies against foreign states, the Iberian and Albanian and others. Another four brigades were on the Danube, two in Pannonia and two in Moesia: Thrace belonged to Rhoemetalces II and the children of Cotys IV. There were two reserve brigades in Dalmatia which had easy access to Italy in an emergency. However, the capital had its own

国当时的疆土比起今天来又是何等狭小。[1]

两支舰队卫护着意大利,一支在米塞努姆海岸,一支在拉温那海岸。而另一些战舰则护卫着邻近的高卢海岸——这些战船都是奥古斯都在阿克提乌姆一役取得胜利时俘获的战利品,而在配备了强有力的水手之后,奥古斯都就把它们派到佛路姆·优里乌姆城[2]去了。但我们的主力却部署在莱茵河上,那里有 8 个军团,是用来对付日耳曼人或高卢人的。三个多军团守卫着不久之前才平定的西班牙诸省。[3] 两个军团守卫着阿非利加,两个军团守卫着埃及(玛乌列塔尼亚作为礼物被罗马国家赠送给了优巴国王二世[4])。从叙利亚边界直到幼发拉底河之间的一片巨大的地区,则由四个军团控制。同时,在边界地区,罗马的威力还保护着伊伯利亚、阿尔巴尼亚和其他王国,使他们不受外国的侵扰。另外四个军团守卫着多瑙河,两个在潘诺尼亚,两个在美西亚:色雷斯属于莱美塔尔凯斯二世和科提斯四世的儿子们管辖。还有两个预备军团配置在达尔马提亚,达尔马提亚处于进入意大利的有利的地理位置,一旦意大利有紧急需要时,他们可以及时给予支援。当然,首都也有它自己的常备军,即三个城市警卫队和 9

〔1〕 这里所指的是从公元 115 年图拉真当政时期帝国扩大到波斯湾和两年之后哈德里亚努斯当政时期后退之间的事情。从奥古斯都以来,主要兼并的是玛乌列塔尼亚(公元 40 年)、不列颠(公元 43 年)、达奇亚(公元101～106 年)、阿拉伯·佩特莱亚(公元 105 年)、亚美尼亚和美索不达米亚(公元 114 年)。

〔2〕 现在的佛列优斯。

〔3〕 它们是公元前 19 年被阿格里帕征服的。

〔4〕 努米地亚的优巴一世的儿子,是继塔普苏斯之后被带到罗马并在罗马受教育的。以博学闻名,普利尼和阿提纳乌等作家都多次引用过他的作品。他娶了安托尼乌斯和克利欧帕特拉的一个女儿为妻。

troops; three battalions of city police, and nine of the Guard, mostly recruited in Etruria, or Umbria, or the old territory of Latin rights and early Roman settlements. Then, at appropriate points outside Italy, the provincials contributed naval crews, and auxiliary cavalry and infantry. Altogether these were about as numerous as the regular army. But I cannot enumerate them since, as circumstances required, they changed stations, or their numbers rose or fell.

This, the year in which Tiberius' rule began to deteriorate, seems an appropriate moment to review the other branches of the government also, and the methods by which they had been administered since his accession. In the first place, public business—and the most important private business—was transacted in the senate. Among its chief men, there was freedom of discussion: their lapses into servility were arrested by the emperor himself. His conferments of office took into consideration birth, military distinction, and civilian eminence, and the choice manifestly fell on the worthiest men. The consuls and praetors maintained their prestige. The lesser offices, too, each exercised their proper authority. Moreover, the treason court excepted, the laws were duly enforced.

Levies of grain, indirect taxation, and the other revenues belonging to the State were managed by associations of Roman knights. But the imperial property was entrusted by the emperor to carefully selected agents—some known to him by reputation only. Once appointed, these were kept on indefinitely, often becoming old in the same jobs. The public suffered, it is true, from oppressive food prices. But that was not the emperor's fault. Indeed, he spared neither money nor labour in combating bad harvests and stormy seas. He ensured also that the provinces were not harassed by new impositions and that

个步兵近卫中队,这些步兵中队的士兵大多数是从埃特路里亚和翁布里亚或是从旧拉提乌姆和早期的罗马居民中征募来的。此外,在意大利以外各个行省的适当地点,还有各行省提供的海军舰队、辅助骑兵部队和步兵中队。这些军队加在一起的数量就相当于一支正规军的规模了。但是我无法一一清楚地列举出他们的数量,因为这些军队由于临时情况的需要,常常要到处移驻,而且他们的人数也是时升时降的。

这是提贝里乌斯的统治开始变坏的一年。因此,我认为这是一个好机会,来回顾一下国家的其他部门以及从他即位以来对他们进行统治的方法。首先,公共事务以及最为重要的私人事务都交给元老院去处理。在元老院的主要人物之间,可以对这些事务展开自由的讨论,而皇帝本人则抓住了他们堕落到奴颜婢膝的弱点。在任命官吏的时候,他考虑到候补者的家世、所建立的军功或是在民事方面的突出业绩,要充分证明接受任命的都是最适当的人选。行政官和执政官保持着他们的威望,甚至地位较低的长官也都能行使他们正当的职权。而且除了涉及大逆罪的案件以外,法律一般还是非常有效的。

公粮的征收、间接税的征收和其他的国家税收由罗马的骑士团体来办理。皇帝把皇家的财产委托给经过仔细挑选出来的代理们去处理,其中有些人甚至皇帝本人都不认识,只是由于这个人声名好才任用的。而这些人一旦被任命,就永远留在这种职位上,经常是在同样的职位上一直到老。民众确实是承受着粮价过高的苦恼,但是这并不是皇帝的过错。为了补偿由于歉收或海上风暴所造成的损失,他确实是既不吝惜金钱又不辞辛苦的。他还确保不再给各行省增加新的赋税,也注意不使旧的赋税

old impositions were not aggravated through official acquisitiveness or brutality; beatings and confiscations did not exist. His estates in Italy were few, his slaves unobtrusive, his household limited to a few ex-slaves. Any disputes that he had with private citizens were settled in the law courts.

Tiberius, in his ungracious fashion—grim and often terrifying as he was—maintained this policy until the death of Drusus reversed it. While Drusus lived, the same methods were employed, because Sejanus in the early stages of his power wanted to gain a reputation for enlightened policy. Moreover, there was an alarming potential avenger in Drusus, who openly showed his hatred and repeatedly complained that the emperor, though he had a son, went elsewhere for his collaborator. Soon, Drusus reflected, the collaborator would be called a colleague—the first steps of an ambitious career are difficult, but once they are achieved helpers and partisans emerge. 'Already Sejanus has secured this new camp—where the Guard are at the disposal of their commander. His statue is to be seen in Pompey's Theatre. The grandsons of us Drususes will be his grandsons too. What can we do now except trust his moderation and pray he will be forbearing?' Drusus often talked like this and many heard him. But even his confidences were betrayed by his wife—to her lover.

So Sejanus decided to act. He chose a poison with gradual effects resembling ordinary ill-health. It was administered to Drusus (as was

负担由于官吏的贪欲或残暴而加重。体罚和没收财产的事情已经不复存在。他在意大利的田产很少,他的奴隶们并不胡作非为,他的家里也只有人数不多的有限的几个被释奴隶。而且当他和普通公民发生纠纷的时候,照例也是要由法庭来解决的。

尽管提贝里乌斯作风冷僻刻板、阴郁,甚至往往是可怕的,但他对这一切还是坚持遵守的。直到杜路苏斯的死亡,他就把这一切做法全都推翻了。当杜路苏斯在世的时候,一切现成的政治措施还没有改变,因为谢雅努斯在他刚刚掌握权力的初期阶段,还想取得开明政治的声誉。而且,他害怕杜路苏斯这样一个潜在的复仇者,因为杜路苏斯经常公开表示出对他的憎恨情绪,他经常抱怨皇帝说,他虽然有一个儿子,却要到别处去找一个人做他的合作者!不久,杜路苏斯又说,这个合作者不久就会被称为同僚了——而一个野心家的生涯在起步阶段是很困难的,可是一旦获得了成功,就不难找到自己的帮手和伙伴了。"谢雅努斯已经得到了一个新的军营,在那里,卫队是由他来调配控制的。在格涅乌斯·庞培的剧场里,也可以看到他的胸像了。我们杜路苏斯一家的孙子也将成为他的外孙了![1]而现在,我们所能做的只能是希望他有些节制,并且祈祷他将来会变得宽容一些而已。"类似的话杜路苏斯经常说起,很多人都曾听到过。甚至他的最机密的事情也被他的妻子泄露给她的情夫了。

因此谢雅努斯决定开始行动,他选用了一种慢性的毒药,药性发作时就好像是一般得病一样。这毒药是宦官吕格都斯给

---

〔1〕 谢雅努斯的女儿嫁给了克劳狄乌斯的儿子。

learnt eight years later) by the eunuch Lygdus. All through his son's illness, Tiberius attended the senate. Either he was unalarmed or he wanted to display his will-power. Even when Drusus had died and his body was awaiting burial, Tiberius continued to attend. The consuls sat on ordinary benches as a sign of mourning. But he reminded them of their dignity and rank. The senators wept. But he silenced them with a consoling oration. 'I know', he said, 'that I may be criticized for appearing before the senate while my affliction is still fresh. Most mourners can hardly bear even their families' condolences—can hardly look upon the light of day. And that need not be censured as weakness. I, however, have sought sterner solace. The arms in which I have taken refuge are those of the State. '

After referring sorrowfully to the Augusta's great age, his grandson's immaturity, and his own declining years, he said that the sons of Germanicus were his only consolation in his grief; and he requested that they should be brought in. The consuls went out, reassured the boys, and conducted them before Tiberius. He took them by the hand, and addressed the senate. 'When these boys lost their father', he said, 'I entrusted them to their uncle Drusus, begging him—though he had children of his own—to treat them as though they were his

杜路苏斯吃下去的（这件事情的真相在 8 年之后才为人们所了解）。他的儿子生病期间，提贝里乌斯还一直参加元老院的集会，这或许是因为他并不感到惊慌害怕，或许是因为他想向人们展示他坚强的意志力。甚至在杜路苏斯已经死去而尸体正在等待下葬的时候，他还依然出席元老院的集会。执政官们坐在普通的长凳上以表示哀悼，[1]但是他却提醒他们不要忘了他们的尊严和官阶。元老们哭了，但是他却让他们安静下来，并安慰他们说："我明白，当我还沉浸在悲痛中的时候来到元老院，也许是要受到人们的非议的。大多数的哀悼者简直是无法承受为自己的亲族举行的吊唁的，甚至几乎不能忍受白天的光亮，我们不能谴责这种做法为懦弱。而我本人却找到了一种更坚强的安慰自己的办法，这就是：把自己的全部心思都投入到国事上面去，以逃避这种痛苦。"

他在悲痛地提到了他的母亲奥古斯塔年事已高，他的诸孙尚未成人，以及他本人也走向了衰老的年龄之后，[2]便说道，日耳曼尼库斯的儿子们是他当前的痛苦中唯一的安慰，并要求将他们抚养长大。执政官们走出去，使孩子们安下心来之后，便把他们带到了提贝里乌斯面前来。他用手拉着他们，向元老们说："元老们，当这些孩子们失去了他们的父亲的时候，我曾经把他们托付给他们的叔父杜路苏斯，并且请求他像对待自己的亲骨肉一样对待他们，尽管他也有自己的孩子。此外，

---

〔1〕 执政官本应当坐在高级长官专用的象牙坐椅上。

〔2〕 根据狄奥·卡西乌斯的说法，这时提贝里乌斯 65 岁，他的母亲 80 岁。

blood, and, for posterity's sake, to fashion them after himself. Now Drusus has gone. So my plea is addressed to you. The gods and our country are its witnesses.

'Senators: on my behalf as well as your own, adopt and guide these youths, whose birth is so glorious—these great-grandchildren of Augustus. Nero and Drusus Caesars: these senators will take the place of your parents. For, in the station to which you are born, the good and bad in you is of national concern. ' This speech was greeted by loud weeping among the senators, followed by heartfelt prayers for the future. Indeed, if Tiberius had stopped there, he would have left his audience sorry for him and proud of their responsibility. But by reverting to empty discredited talk about restoring the Republic and handing the government to the consuls or others, he undermined belief even in what he had said sincerely and truthfully. However, Drusus was voted the same posthumous honours as Germanicus—with the additions expected of flattery's second attempt. The funeral was noteworthy for its long procession of ancestral effigies-Aeneas, originator of the Julian line; all the kings of Alba Longa; Romulus, founder of Rome; then the Sabine nobility with Attus Clausus; finally the rest of the Claudian house.

In describing Drusus' death I have followed the most numerous and reputable authorities. But I should also record a contemporary rumour,

我还请求他为了子孙后代的幸福,把他们教养得和他自己的孩子一样。现在,杜路苏斯已经走了,因此我的请求转而向你们提出,诸位天神和我们的国家作证。

"众位元老,为了我,也为了你们自己,请接受和教育这些孩子吧!他们的出身是如此高贵——他们都是奥古斯都的曾孙。尼禄·恺撒和杜路苏斯·恺撒啊:这些元老今后就是你们的父母了。因为你们生来就处在这样的地位上,你们个人的好坏是与国家的盛衰密切相关的。"听了提贝里乌斯这番话,元老们都放声痛哭起来,随后他们便祈求上天诸神保佑未来一切顺遂。事实上,如果提贝里乌斯及时中止,他一定会使他的听众们对他大起怜悯之情,并且为他们自己所承担的神圣责任而深感自豪的。可是,由于他的话头又回到那些没人会相信的空谈上面去,什么恢复共和呀,他想将统治权交给执政官或其他人啊等等,这样暗中也就破坏了人们对他的信任,甚至对他真心实意说的那些话也不能相信了。尽管如此,杜路苏斯还是被授予了和日耳曼尼库斯一样的哀荣,而且还增加了许多名堂,而这些都是那些善于阿谀奉承的人在第二次要做出的。在葬仪的行列中最值得注意的是走过观众面前的一列长长的祖先的胸像,其中有尤利乌斯一系的始祖埃涅阿斯,有阿尔巴·隆伽的全部国王,有罗马城的建立者罗木路斯,后面则是萨比尼的贵族阿图斯·克劳苏斯,[1]最后是克劳狄乌斯家其他人的像。

在记述杜路苏斯的死亡的时候,我是以那些作品最多、也是最可信的权威作家们的作品为依据的。但是我还要提一下当时

---

〔1〕 根据传说,阿图斯·克劳苏斯是克劳狄乌斯家族的创立者。

strong enough to remain current today. According to this, Sejanus, after seducing Livilla into crime, similarly corrupted the eunuch Lygdus, whose youthful looks had endeared him to his master Drusus and raised him high in the latter's household. Next—the story continues—when the plotters had fixed the place and time for the poisoning, Sejanus had the audacity to change his plan and warn the emperor privately that when dining with his son Tiberius must refuse the first drink offered him, since Drusus intended to poison him. The old emperor, it is alleged, believed this fiction, and at the dinner-party passed the cup he had received to Drusus, who tossed it off as a young man would—in all innocence, but this dyed suspicion deeper since it seemed that Drusus, terrified and ashamed, was inflicting on himself the fate he had designed for his father.

This was widely rumoured. But it is not backed by any reliable authority—and it can be confidently refuted. For no one even of ordinary sense, much less Tiberius with his great experience, would kill his son unheard, by his own hand, leaving no opportunity for second thoughts. Surely Tiberius would rather have tortured the server of the poison and extracted the originator's name. Against his only son— never before convicted of wrong-doing—he would only have proceeded with the characteristic slowness and deliberation which he showed even to strangers. But Sejanus, too much loved by Tiberius and hated by everyone else, passed for the author of every crime; and rumours always proliferate around the downfalls of the great. For such reasons even the most monstrous myths found believers.

流行的一个谣传,这个谣传是如此有力,以至于直到今天还在盛传不已。根据谣传所说,谢雅努斯在引诱利维拉犯下了罪行之后,又同样用不正当的手段贿赂宦官吕格都斯。这个宦官由于年轻貌美而深得他的主人杜路苏斯的喜爱,并且使他取得了在他的侍从中的显著地位。接下来,故事又传说,当阴谋者确定好了一个时间和地点给杜路苏斯下毒药的时候,谢雅努斯竟然胆大到改变了原定的计划,而在私下里警告提贝里乌斯说,在同儿子一道吃饭时,皇帝一定不要喝给他的第一杯酒,因为杜路苏斯想毒死他。据说,年老的皇帝相信了他的谎言,因而在宴会上就座之后,当他接到酒杯的时候,就把它递给了杜路苏斯。当懵然无知的杜路苏斯像青年人那样把酒一饮而尽的时候,提贝里乌斯对他的疑心就变得更深了,因为这看起来好像是,杜路苏斯是由于恐惧和羞愧才使自己遭受了他为他父亲安排的命运。

这种谣言流行得很广泛,但是并没有任何可靠的权威支持这种说法,而且显而易见是不成立的。任何一个稍有头脑的普通人,更不用说像提贝里乌斯这样具有丰富经验的人,也不会不经过事先了解就亲手杀死自己的亲生儿子,并且一点也不给自己留下稍加分析思考的机会的。事实上,提贝里乌斯完全可以拷问提供毒药的人,并且找出他后面的主使者。而且对于过去从来没有因错误的行为而被宣告有罪的独生子,他完全可以从容地、经过深思熟虑后再做出决定,这是他过去一贯的、甚至对陌生人都表现出的一种作风。但是,谢雅努斯由于皇帝特别喜欢他而其他人又十分憎恨他,被看做是一切罪恶的根源,而且在统治者垮掉之后,谣言总是流传得更广。由于这些原因,所以关于他的最骇人听闻的恐怖行为也总会有人深信不疑。

Besides, the real story of the murder was later divulged by Sejanus' wife Apicata, and corroborated under torture by Eudemus and
Lygdus; and no historian, however unfriendly to Tiberius, however
tendentious an investigator of his doings, has accused him of this
crime. My own motive in mentioning and refuting the rumour has
been to illustrate by one conspicuous instance the falsity of hearsay
gossip, and to urge those who read this book not to prefer incredible
tales—however widely current and readily accepted—to the truth unblemished by marvels.

When Tiberius pronounced his son's funeral eulogy from the
platform, the attitudes and tones of mourning exhibited by the senate
and public were insincere and unconvincing. Secretly they were glad
that the house of Germanicus was reviving. However, this awakening
popularity, and Agrippina's ill-concealed maternal ambitions, only
hastened the family's ruin. For when Sejanus saw that Drusus' death
brought no retribution upon the murderers and no national grief, his
criminal audacity grew. The succession of the children of Germanicus
was now certain. So he considered how they could be removed.

To poison all three was impracticable, since their attendants were
loyal—and the virtue of their mother Agrippina unassailable. Her insubordination, however, gave Sejanus a handle against Agrippina. He

再说,这次谋杀的真实经过,后来被谢雅努斯的妻子阿皮卡塔揭发了出来。[1] 而且在拷问之下,埃乌德木斯和吕格都斯也把全部底细都招供出来了。任何一个历史学家,不管对提贝里乌斯多么厌恶,不管对他的所作所为的调查带有多么大的偏见,也绝不会把杀害亲生儿子的罪名加到他的身上的。我自己记载和驳斥这样一种传闻的动机,是要用一个突出事例来说明,口头传说的闲言碎语是不可信的,并且请求那些读到我的这部著作的人们,不要喜欢那些不可信的传闻——无论这些传闻多么广泛地流行和多么容易接受——要认清那些未被传奇歪曲的真实的历史。

当提贝里乌斯在广场的讲坛上对他儿子的葬礼发表悼词的时候,元老和人民就假装做出哀悼的姿态和声调,他们在葬礼上并没有真诚的、令人信任的哀悼。他们在心里暗暗地高兴,因为日耳曼尼库斯的一家又要重新兴旺起来了。但是这一家复苏的声望和阿格里披娜那掩饰不住的母亲的期望,只能加速这个家庭的毁灭。因为谢雅努斯看到杜路苏斯的死亡并没有使谋杀者遭到报复,而全国人民也并没有感到悲痛的时候,他犯罪的胆子也就更大了。日耳曼尼库斯的孩子们将成为皇位的继承人,这一点现在已经是毫无疑问了,因此,谢雅努斯又谋划怎样进一步把他们除掉。

但是要把他们三个人都毒死是不可能的,因为他们的监护人都忠心耿耿,而且他们的母亲阿格里披娜的贞节又是绝对不可侵犯的。但是阿格里披娜的倔强固执这一点,给谢雅努斯留下了把

---

〔1〕 在阿皮卡塔的丈夫和孩子被处死之后,她就在自杀之前把这件事书面报告了提贝里乌斯。

played on the Augusta's longstanding animosity against her, and on Livilla's new complicity. These ladies were to notify Tiberius that Agrippina, proud of her large family and relying on her popularity, had designs on the throne. To this end Sejanus employed skilful slanderers. Notable among them was Julius Postumus, whose adulterous liaison with Mutilia Prisca made him a close friend of the Augusta and particularly apt for Sejanus' purposes; for Prisca had great influence over the old lady, whose jealousy she could use against Agrippina, her granddaughter not by blood like Livilla, but by marriage. Meanwhile Agrippina's closest friends were induced to accentuate her restlessness by malevolent talk.

Tiberius derived comfort from his work. He remained fully occupied with public business—legal cases concerning citizens, and petitions from the provinces. On his initiative, the senate decreed three years' remission of tribute to two cities ruined by earthquakes, Cibyra and Aegium. A governor of Farther Spain, Gaius Vibius Serenus (I), was convicted of violence and deported as a bad character to the island of Amorgos. Carsidius Sacerdos, accused of supplying grain to the enemy Tacfarinas, was acquitted. So was Gaius Sempronius Gracchus (II). He had been taken as a baby by his father to share his banishment on the isle of Cercina. There the son grew up among uneducated expatriates, and later made a living by small trading in Africa and Sicily. Even so, he did not escape the perils of high rank. Indeed, unless his innocence had been vouched for by two governors

柄。他利用奥古斯塔对她的长期的仇恨和利维拉最近与他的共谋,想方设法通过她们让皇帝知道,阿格里披娜以她的大家庭为自豪并且仰仗自己在人民中的声望,计划夺取皇帝的宝座。此外,谢雅努斯还巧妙地利用一些老练的诽谤者。在这些诽谤者之中,特别突出的是尤利乌斯·波司图姆斯,依靠他的情妇木提里亚·普利司卡对奥古斯塔的影响——普利司卡对这个老妇人有很大的影响力,波斯图姆斯同奥古斯塔建立了亲密的关系,普利司卡可以利用奥古斯塔对阿格里披娜的嫉妒来打击她——这个像利维拉一样,虽然不是她的亲孙女但是她的孙媳妇的人。同时,由于他们这些人的恶毒言论,甚至阿格里披娜最亲近的朋友都被挑拨得加重了对她的怨恨。

提贝里乌斯从他的工作中得到了安慰,他完全沉浸在公共事务中,没有半点闲暇——他日夜都在关注着有关市民的案件和来自各行省的请求。在他的建议下,元老院颁布了在三年内豁免遭受地震灾害的两个城市——亚细亚的奇比拉和阿凯亚的埃吉乌姆的税赋的命令。远西班牙的总督盖乌斯·维比乌斯·谢列努斯(一世),也因在施政方面使用暴力而被判罪,并由于他的恶劣作风而被流放到阿莫尔古斯岛去。被控以把粮食供应给罗马公敌塔克法里那斯的卡尔西狄乌斯·撒凯尔多斯被宣告无罪,同样,盖乌斯·谢姆普罗尼乌斯·格拉古斯(二世)也得到了赦免。格拉古还在幼年的时候便随着他父亲被流放到了凯尔奇那岛上。在那里,他就在没有受过任何教育的亡命者中间渐渐长大。后来,通过在阿非利加和西西里做一些小生意,勉强维持自己的生计。甚至即便这样,他也没有能够逃脱掉显贵家族会遇到的危险。老实说,如果不是阿非利加的两位长官路奇乌斯·埃里乌

of Africa, Lucius Aelius Lamia and Lucius Apronius, he would have been destroyed by his famous, tragic name and his father's downfall.

Delegations came this year from two Greek communities, Samos and Cos. They requested the confirmation of sanctuary rights for their temples of Juno and Aesculapius respectively. The Samians relied on a decree of the Amphictyonic Council, the principal arbiter of all matters in the epoch when the Greeks had founded their settlements in Asia and ruled its coast. Cos put forward considerations of equal antiquity, together with a local point. For they had sheltered Roman citizens in the temple of Aesculapius at the time when, on the orders of king Mithridates VI of Pontus, these were being massacred in every island and city in Asia.

Next, after numerous and generally unsuccessful complaints by the praetors, Tiberius addressed the senate on the ill-behaviour of balletdancers and their offences against public order and private morality. The emperor commented that their frivolous popular entertainment, the old Oscan farce, had become so degraded and influential that the senate's authority was needed to repress it. The dancers were then ejected from Italy.

斯·拉米亚和路奇乌斯·阿普洛尼乌斯前来为他的无辜作证的话,他就会由于他那著名的、悲惨的家庭和他父亲的垮台而丧命的。

这一年,又有两个希腊城市撒莫斯和科斯的使团到罗马来。他们分别要求罗马皇帝批准他们的优诺神庙和埃司库拉披乌斯神庙的避难权。撒莫斯人提出这种要求的依据是安披克图昂同盟会[1]的一项命令,这是那个时代的最高裁决。当时,希腊人已经在亚细亚建立了自己的城邦,并且统治了沿海地带。科斯人方面也提出了同样古老的根据,而且,他们还提出了他们自己本地的观点。因为在庞都斯的国王米特利达特斯六世的命令下,在亚细亚的每个岛和每个城市对罗马人进行大屠杀的时候,他们曾经在埃司库拉披乌斯神庙庇护过罗马公民。[2]

接着,在行政长官们做了大量多数是毫无用处的批评之后,提贝里乌斯在元老院发表了演讲。他提出了优伶们的行为不端问题。他说,这些优伶往往冒犯国家的法令,而在私生活中,他们又道德败坏、放荡堕落。皇帝又评论道,作为民众的通俗娱乐的轻佻琐碎的老欧斯卡笑剧,[3]已经如此堕落并具有如此巨大的影响力,以致到了需要元老院利用自己的权力出面制止的程度了,结果那些优伶就被逐出了意大利。

---

　〔1〕　也称近邻同盟会,指住在神庙附近的各族为保卫神庙而结成的同盟,他们每年要召集两次会议。

　〔2〕　此事发生在公元前88年,当时许多神庙都在大屠杀时期被毁掉了。

　〔3〕　康帕尼亚的业余的笑剧,即所谓阿提拉戏,具有固定的角色和乡间的布景。它是在汉尼拔战争之后才被介绍到罗马来的,后来经过文学上的加工后就由职业演员来表演了。在帝国初期,这种戏剧十分流行,戏里常常十分露骨地讽刺皇帝的缺点,诸如提贝里乌斯在卡普利埃的暴饮暴食的行为、尼禄的杀害生母、伽尔巴的贪婪和多米提安的离婚等等。

This year also brought the emperor further bereavement. For one of Drusus' twins died. So did a friend. This was Lucilius Longus, Tiberius' comrade in good and evil fortune, and the only senator who had shared his retirement to Rhodes. So, in spite of his humble origin, Lucilius received a state funeral, and a statue in the Forum of Augustus was allotted him at the national expense by the senate. The senate still handled all manner of business. Even the emperor's agent in Asia, Lucilius Capito, had to defend himself before it when the people of the province prosecuted him. Tiberius insisted that he had only given the agent power over his personal slaves and revenues, and if Capito had assumed the governor's authority and employed military force he was exceeding his instructions: the provincials must be heard. The case was tried, and Capito condemned.

For this act of justice, and the punishment of Gaius Junius Silanus in the previous year, the cities of Asia decreed a temple to Tiberius, his mother, and the senate. Permission was granted. Germanicus' son Nero Caesar expressed the thanks of the cities to the senate and his grandfather—a welcome experience to his listeners, whose still fresh memories of Germanicus created the illusion that it was he whom they

这一年,提贝里乌斯又遇到不幸的丧亡之事,那就是杜路苏斯的一个双生子死了。他的一个朋友也死了,这个朋友名字叫路奇里乌斯·隆古斯,他是曾经和提贝里乌斯共过患难和富贵的朋友,又是同他一起在罗德岛共同度过孤寂岁月的唯一的一位元老。[1] 因此,尽管出身卑微,隆古斯依然受到了国葬的待遇,并且元老院还在奥古斯都广场利用国家的库银给他立了像。而当时元老院还需要处理其他所有方方面面的事情,甚至就连皇帝本人在亚细亚的代理人路奇里乌斯·卡皮托,当行省的人民对他提出控告的时候,也不得不来到元老院为自己进行辩护。提贝里乌斯着重强调说,他授予卡皮托代理的权力只限于他私人的奴隶和个人领地上的收入。如果卡皮托僭夺长官的权力并且动用军事力量的话,那他就违背了他的指示了,因而必须听取行省居民的意见。这个案件经过审理以后,卡皮托被判处有罪。

为了报答这一公正的惩罚,同时也为了报答前一年对盖乌斯·尤尼乌斯·西拉努斯所做的处罚,亚细亚诸城市拟订了一项命令,决定为提贝里乌斯、为他的母亲和元老院修建一座神庙。这项命令得到了批准,因此日耳曼尼库斯的儿子尼禄·恺撒就代表亚细亚各城市对元老院和他的祖父表示感谢,这对听取他的发言的人们来说是一件很高兴的事情,因为日耳曼尼库斯在这些人的头脑中还记忆犹新,因此他们就好像看到了日耳曼尼库斯本人的身影,听到了日耳曼尼库斯本人的声音一样,感到非常欣慰。而

---

〔1〕 这段时间从公元前 6 年开始,一直到公元 2 年路奇乌斯·恺撒去世为止。

were seeing and hearing. And the young man's princely looks and modest bearing were all the more attractive because Sejanus was known to hate him.

At about the same time Tiberius raised the question of replacing the lately deceased priest of Jupiter, Servius Cornelius Maluginensis, and of amending the law governing these appointments. This should be done, he said, either by senatorial decree or by legislation initiated by himself, just as Augustus had modernized other equally hoary usages. Tiberius recalled that the selection had to be made from three simultaneously nominated patricians, born from formal marriages 'by cake and spelt'. This was the tradition, he said, but there were no longer enough candidates since the old wedding ceremony was obsolete or very rare; and he suggested various explanations of this—notably the indifference of both sexes, and their deliberate avoidance of the complicated ritual. Besides, he added, parents objected that their authority no longer applied to holders of this priesthood, or to their wives (who were in such cases transferred to their husbands' control). Consequently, a remedy must be applied either by senatorial decree or by law, just as Augustus, too, had modernized certain heavy relics. After discussion of the religious considerations it was decided not to alter the constitution of the priesthood; but a law was carried providing that the priest's wife, though subject to her husband in regard to her sacred

且这个年轻人有着堂堂皇子的容貌和天生的谦和风度，所有这一切都使他深具魅力。而且尽人皆知，谢雅努斯非常憎恨他，因此他也就更加引人注目了。

大约就在同时，提贝里乌斯提出了选派一个人来代替不久前去世的谢尔维乌斯·科尔涅里乌斯·玛路吉南西斯，担任朱庇特神的祭司职位的问题，同时他还提出了修改有关这种选派的法律问题。他说，或者通过元老院的决定，或者通过法律自身的调整，正好像过去奥古斯都对于一些古老的规定加以修改以适应当时的需要一样。提贝里乌斯回顾了过去的传统后，指出，必须在同时指定的三个贵族中间进行选择，而且这三个人的父母必须是按照"麦饼式"的仪式结婚的。[1] 这种仪式是旧式的，他说，现在再按照这种标准已经找不到足够的候选人了，因为现在已经没有人再以这种古式的婚礼结婚了，即便有也是非常罕见的。对此，他做出了种种不同的解释，而一个主要的原因则是男女双方的冷淡，和人们对这种复杂的仪式本身的故意回避。还有一个原因，那就是父母们反对他们的权威不再诉之于这一祭司职位的担任者或者他的妻子（在这种情况下，妻子是交由担任祭司之职的丈夫保护的）。因而必须通过元老院的命令或者是通过一项特殊的法律规定，就像从前奥古斯都所做的那样，修改一些陈旧腐朽的章程。经过了一番宗教方面问题的讨论之后，最后决定，在祭司的制度方面不再做任何改变，但是要重新制定一项法律，规

---

〔1〕 罗马的正式婚姻主要有三种：男女两人同居已有一年时间的称时效式；视婚姻为一种买卖双方的交易行为者称买卖式；最主要的一种就是此处所说的"麦饼式"，也称"共食式"，举行婚礼时须有至少10名证人在场，新婚夫妇必须在大祭司和朱庇特祭司面前食用供神的麦饼。

functions, should in other respects have the same legal rights as other women. And so the late priest's son was appointed in his father's place. To increase the dignity of priestly offices—and willingness to undertake their ritual—two million sesterces were allocated to the priestess of Vesta, Cornelia, appointed to succeed Scantia. It was also decided that the Augusta, whenever she visited the theatre, should sit in the seats reserved for the Vestal priestesses.

In the next year the consuls were Servius Cornelius Cethegus and Lucius Visellius Varro. Starting with the Pontifical Order, the priestly corporations included Nero Caesar and Drusus Caesar in their prayers for the safety of the emperor. Servility, rather than affection, was the cause. But in a degraded society exaggerated servility is as dangerous as none at all. Tiberius, never warm-hearted to the house of Germanicus, was now particularly irritated that these youths should be coupled with himself, at his advanced age. He sent for the priests and asked them whether they had been influenced by Agrippina's pleas—or threats. They took the blame themselves. However, since many of them were his own relations or distinguished figures, they were only mildly rebuked. But Tiberius warned the senate that in future the young men's susceptible characters should not be tempted to become conceited by premature distinctions. Actually his protest

定,尽管在圣职方面祭司的妻子要服从于她的丈夫,但是在其他方面,她应该和任何其他普通妇女一样享有相同的法律权利。后来,祭司的儿子被指定接替他父亲的职位。而为了提高祭司们的尊严,并且激发他们从事宗教仪节的热情,决定给坎提娅之后担任维司塔贞女的科尔涅里娅拨款二百万谢司特尔提乌斯。而且还规定,每当奥古斯塔来到剧场时,她所坐的座位应该是那些保留给维司塔贞女们的座位。

第二年,[1]是谢尔维乌斯·科尔涅里乌斯·凯提古斯和路奇乌斯·维谢里乌斯·瓦罗担任执政官的一年。祭司们开始依照祭司团命令为皇帝的安宁祈祷发愿,并且把尼禄·恺撒和杜路苏斯·恺撒也加入到他们为皇帝的安全所做的祈祷当中去。他们这样做的原因,与其说是由于对他们两人的敬爱,不如说是一种阿谀奉承的奴性。而在那堕落的社会里,过多的奴性是和根本没有任何奴性一样危险的。提贝里乌斯对于日耳曼尼库斯一家从来都没有什么同情心,而现在他们竟然把一对乳臭未干的孩子和他这个德高望重的人相提并论,因此他特别恼火。他派人把祭司们召了过来,质问他们这样做是不是由于阿格里披娜的请求,或者是威胁,他们说这是他们自己的过失,并自我责备了一番。因为他们中的很多人都是他自己的亲属,或者是国内的显要人物,因此提贝里乌斯只是温和地训斥了他们几句。但是在元老院里,提贝里乌斯却警告说,在今后,任何人不得利用过早的荣誉诱惑这些血气未定的年轻人,以免他们变得骄傲自负

---

[1] 即公元 24 年,罗马建城 777 年。

had been prompted by pressure from Sejanus, who declared that Rome was split as under as though there was civil war: people were calling themselves ' Agrippina ' s party ' —the deepening disunity could only be arrested if some of the ringleaders were removed.

With this motive Sejanus attacked Gaius Silius and Titius Sabinus. They both owed their ruin to Germanicus' friendship. Silius had also been head of a great army for seven years, winner of an honorary Triumph in Germany, conqueror of Sacrovir. So his downfall would be the more spectacular and alarming. Many thought that he had aggravated his offence by imprudence. For he had boasted excessively of his own army's unbroken loyalty when others had lapsed into mutiny. 'If the revolt had spread to my brigades,' he said, 'Tiberius could not have kept the throne. ' The emperor felt that these assertions of an obligation beyond all recompense damaged his own position. For services are welcome as long as it seems possible to repay them, but when they greatly exceed that point they produce not gratitude but hatred.

The emperor also disliked Silius' wife Sosia Galla, because she was a friend of Agrippina. So Sejanus decided that this couple should be the victims. Titius Sabinus could wait a little. The consul Lucius Visellius Varro was set in motion, and with his father's feud against

起来。实际上,他这种强烈的反对态度是由于谢雅努斯在背后极力地怂恿,他声称,国家目前已经处于分裂状态中了,就好像是发生了内战:有人竟然自称是"阿格里披娜派",只有及时除掉那些魁首,才能挽救日益加深的分裂。

在这样的动机之下,谢雅努斯对盖乌斯·西里乌斯和提提乌斯·撒比努斯进行了大肆的攻击。这两个人之所以遭受灭顶之灾,乃是因为他们都是日耳曼尼库斯的朋友。但是西里乌斯遭受攻击还有另一层原因,这就是:他曾经率领过一支庞大的军队长达七年之久、他在日耳曼取得过凯旋的勋记、还战胜过撒克罗维尔。[1] 因此这样一个声名显赫的人物的垮台必然会更加引人注目、更加令人恐惧。许多人认为,他的粗豪鲁莽更加重了他的罪名,因为他曾经过分地吹嘘在别人的军队发生叛乱时,他自己的军队所具有的毫不动摇的忠诚不渝之心。他说:"如果叛乱扩散到我的军团中的话,那么提贝里乌斯的王位就保不住了。"皇帝感到,他所声称的功绩远远不及对自己地位的损害。因为一个人的服务,只有在看起来是能够给予相应的报偿的时候,才是受欢迎的。但是如果这种服务已经远远超过了这个限度的话,那么它们引起的回报就不是感谢,而是憎恨了。

皇帝也不喜欢西里乌斯的妻子索西娅·伽拉,因为她是阿格里披娜的一位好朋友。于是谢雅努斯决定将这一对夫妻作为牺牲品。提提乌斯·撒比努斯的死期因而得以暂时被推迟了。执政官路奇乌斯·维谢里乌斯·瓦罗首先被放出来进行活动,他

---

〔1〕 公元14年,他的身份是上日耳曼的行政长官的副帅;公元15年,取得了凯旋的勋记;公元21年,他击败了撒克罗维尔。

Silius as a pretext sacrificed his own honour to gratify Sejanus' enmity. When accused, Silius requested a brief adjournment until the accuser's consulship should end. But Tiberius opposed this, arguing that officials often proceeded against private citizens, and that there must be no limitation of the rights of the consuls, on whose watchfulness it depended 'that the State takes no harm'. It was typical of Tiberius to use antique terms to veil new sorts of villainy.

So, with many solemn phrases, the senate was summoned as though the charges against Silius had a legal foundation—as though Varro were a real consul, or Rome a Republic! At first, the defendant said nothing. Then, attempting some sort of a defence, he made it clear whose malevolence was ruining him. The prosecution developed its case—longstanding connivance with Sacrovir and cognizance of his rebellion; victory ruined by rapacity; failure to check his wife's criminal acts. In extortion they were undoubtedly both involved. But the case was conducted as a treason trial.

Silius anticipated imminent condemnation by suicide. But his property was dealt with unmercifully. It is true that the provincial taxpayers received nothing back (and none of them requested a refund). But gifts by Augustus were deducted, and the claims of the emperor's personal estate enforced item by item. Never before had Tiberius gone

以西里乌斯同他父亲有仇为借口,不惜牺牲自己的荣誉去迎合谢雅努斯对西里乌斯的敌意。受到控告时,西里乌斯请求稍稍延期到原告执政官任期结束的时候。但是提贝里乌斯不同意他的请求,他说,高级官吏控告普通公民是经常发生的事情,但是执政官的权力却不允许受到任何限制,因为正是要依靠他的警觉"共和国才能不致受到任何损害"。[1] 用过去的词句掩盖他各种各样的新罪行,这是提贝里乌斯的一贯作风。

因此,元老们就被用十分郑重其事的言词召集到了一起,就好像对西里乌斯的控告是有着十分合法的依据似的,而且就好像瓦罗真是一位执政官似的,而罗马国家又真像是一个共和国似的!起初,被告一句话也没有讲,后来他为自己做了一点辩护,为的是要表明他之所以受到控告是因为控告者想置他于死地的恶毒用心。他受控的罪名是:长期纵容撒克罗维尔,认识到了他的反叛野心却置若罔闻;胜利之后贪得无厌;对他妻子的罪行失于检讨。毫无疑问,他们夫妇二人是卷入了勒索罪中了,但是整个案件却是作为大逆罪来审理的。

西里乌斯预料到他最终是逃脱不了悲惨的结局了,于是便自杀了。虽然如此,他的财产也还是被无情地处理掉了。行省的纳税人并没有收回自己付出的任何金钱(他们中间也没有任何人提出过这样的要求);但是奥古斯都赐给他的东西却全被扣除了,皇帝的财库把他的一项项财产都强制予以剥夺。过去提贝里

---

〔1〕 这里提贝里乌斯用了过去的一个提法:执政官应该注意保证共和国不受任何损害。元老院曾利用这种提法先后对付过盖乌斯·格拉古、卡提里那等人。在危机时期,这种决定授予执政官以类似独裁官的权力,类似今天的宣布非常状态。

to such pains regarding other men's property. Gaius Asinius Gallus proposed Sosia's banishment, moving that half of her property should be confiscated and the other half left to her children. Marcus Aemilius Lepidus (IV), however, counter-proposed that a quarter should go to the accusers—as the law required—but that her children should have the rest.

I find that this Marcus Lepidus played a wise and noble part in events. He often palliated the brutalities caused by other people's sycophancy. And he had a sense of proportion—for he enjoyed unbroken influence and favour with Tiberius. This compels me to doubt whether, like other things, the friendships and enmities of rulers depend on destiny and the luck of a man's birth. Instead, may not our own decisions play some part, enabling us to steer a way, safe from intrigues and hazards, between perilous insubordination and degrading servility?

However, Lepidus was contradicted by Marcus Aurelius Cotta Maximus Messallinus, who was of equally noble birth but very different character. At his proposal the senate decreed that officials, however free of guilt or knowledge of guilt themselves, should be punished for their wives' wrongdoing in the provinces as though it were their own.

Then came the case of the aristocratic and independent-minded

乌斯对于别人的财产,从来没有这样斤斤计较过。盖乌斯·阿西尼乌斯·伽路斯建议,将他的妻子索西娅放逐,此外他还建议没收她的一半财产,留下另一半给她的子女。玛尔库斯·埃米里乌斯·列庇都斯(四世)却提出了不同的意见,他建议依照法律规定把1/4的财产赠给原告,剩余的部分都给她的子女。

我发现玛尔库斯·列庇都斯在许多事件当中,都扮演了一个既机智又灵活的著名角色。对于其他人由于讨好而提出的许多残酷不仁的建议,他都能从中进行巧妙的周旋,以减轻他们的残暴。而且,他做事很有分寸、非常适度,因此提贝里乌斯对他一直非常器重和欣赏。这种情况使我怀疑,是否和所有其他的事情一样,国王对一个人的好感和敌意是命中注定的、天生的? 相反,也许命运并不是我们自己能够掌握的,我们能否凭我们自己的力量在危险的执拗和堕落的奴性中间走出一条不受阴谋和危险侵害的道路呢?

另一方面,玛尔库斯·奥列里乌斯·科塔·玛克西姆斯·美撒里努斯[1]有着同样高贵的出身,但是迥然不同的是,他的性格却和列庇都斯形成了鲜明的对比。在他的建议下,元老院公布了这样一项命令,那就是,高级官吏即使他们本人无罪并且不知道别人犯下的罪,但是如果他们的妻子在行省犯了罪,他们也应当受到惩罚,就如同他们自己犯了罪一样。

然后就审理出身高贵而又具有独立思想的路奇乌斯·卡尔

---

〔1〕 他是著名的玛尔库斯·瓦列里乌斯·美撒拉·科尔维努斯的儿子,又是奥维狄乌斯的保护人,在财富和慷慨的作风方面几乎是尽人皆知的。

Lucius Calpurnius Piso (II). This was the man who (as I have mentioned) had insisted to the senate that he would leave the city because of the intrigues of prosecutors, and who, defying the Augusta's might, had dared to hale her friend Urgulania into court from the palace itself. Tiberius had taken this reasonably for the moment. However, though his original bursts of anger might die down, he would turn over resentments in his mind, and did not forget. Quintus Granius charged Piso with treasonable private conversation, adding that he had poison in his house and wore a sword entering the senate-house. The last charge was passed over as too dreadful to be true. But the others—and there was no lack of them—were made into a prosecution, which Piso only avoided by his timely death.

The senate next considered the case of the exiled Cassius Severus. A vicious man of humble origin but an effective speaker, he had earned from the senate, by his unrestrained aggressiveness, a sworn verdict of banishment to Crete. There, by continuing the same practices, he brought upon himself so manyenmities, new on top of old, that he was deprived of his property, outlawed, and ended his days on the rock of Seriphos.

At about this time the praetor Plautius Silvanus, for some unknown reason, threw his wife Apronia out of a window. Haled before the emperor by his father-in-law Lucius Apronius, he answered confusedly that he had been asleep and knew nothing, and his wife must have killed herself. Tiberius instantly proceeded to the house and inspected the bedroom. There signs of violence and resistance were detectable. So Tiberius referred the case to the senate, and it was

普尔尼乌斯·披索(二世)的案件。(就如我在前面所说过的那样)正是这个人曾经坚持向元老院声明说,他要离开罗马这个城市,以抗议告密者的阴谋;也正是这个人,他不畏惧奥古斯塔的势力,竟然敢于将她的朋友乌尔古拉尼娅从皇家的庇护下强行拉到了法庭上。尽管提贝里乌斯当时强压着怒火并没有发作,但是他并没有忘掉这件事,并且把怨恨深深地埋藏在了心底。克温图斯·格拉尼乌斯控告披索说,在他私下的谈话中有诽谤皇帝之言,他还说,披索家中藏有毒药,并且到元老院来的时候身上还佩带着宝剑。最后的一项指控由于太令人厌恶以致难以置信而被撤销了。但是其他的控诉理由——这样的理由又是随处可见,很容易收集到的,却仍旧使他陷入指控之中。只是他那恰逢其时的死亡才使他避免了这场官司。

随后,元老院又考虑被放逐的卡西乌斯·谢维路斯的问题。谢维路斯出身卑微、行为恶劣,但是他具有雄辩的口才。他那毫无顾忌的挑衅行为使得元老院竟然向神宣誓,发布一项命令,把他放逐到克里特去。但他在那里仍然一如既往,因此又给自己招来了许多的新仇旧怨,最后弄得不但被剥夺了财产、公民权,并且又被送到塞里波司岩去终老一生。

大概就在同时,行政长官普劳提乌斯·西尔瓦努斯不知道为了一些什么原因,把他的妻子阿普洛尼娅从窗户里扔了出去。他的岳父路奇乌斯·阿普洛尼乌斯将他扭到了皇帝面前,他含含糊糊、语无伦次地回答说,他自己睡着了,根本不知道发生了什么事情,他的妻子一定是自杀的。提贝里乌斯立刻动身到他家里去,他检查了他的卧室,在那里发现了使用暴力和抗拒的痕迹。因此提贝里乌斯就把这一案件提交给元老院,于是这个案件就进入了审

entered for trial. Then Silvanus was sent a dagger by his grandmother Urgulania. In view of her intimacy with the Augusta, this was regarded as a hint from the emperor. So the accused, after an unsuccessful attempt with the dagger, had his veins opened. Soon afterwards his first wife Numantina was acquitted of driving her husband insane by incantations and philtres.

This year at last freed Rome from the long war with the Numidian Tacfarinas. Previous generals, when they thought they had achieved enough to win honorary Triumphs (already there were three laurelled statues in the city), had let the enemy alone. Yet Tacfarinas continued to ravage Africa; and Mauretanian auxiliaries flocked to him. Their king Ptolemy, the son of Juba II, was too young for responsibility, and they evaded the tyrannical rule of his household's ex-slaves by coming to fight. The king of the Garamantes acted as receiver of Tacfarinas' plunder and joined his raids, not to the extent of heading an army, but by sending light-armed troops—on their long journey, rumour exaggerated their numbers. Moreover, from the province of Africa itself, destitute and disreputable characters flocked to Tacfarinas. This was largely because, after the achievements of Quintus Junius Blacsus, Tiberius had removed one of the garrison's two brigades, the ninth,

理过程中。但是这时西尔瓦努斯的祖母乌尔古拉尼娅却给他送去了一把匕首。由于乌尔古拉尼娅和奥古斯塔的密切关系,因此人们把这看做是皇帝发出的一种暗示。被告用这一武器自杀未遂后,又设法把自己的脉管割断了。在这之后不久,他的第一任妻子,曾经被控告用符咒和春药把自己的丈夫弄疯的努曼提娜得到了赦免。

这一年,罗马人终于从对努米地亚人塔克法里那斯的一场长期战争中解放了出来。早先的统帅们,每当他们认为自己的功勋已经足够取得凯旋的勋记时,也就不再与敌人交手了(这时,城里已经有了三座戴着桂冠的胸像)。然而,塔克法里那斯仍然在劫掠着阿非利加,而且玛乌利塔尼亚人的辅助部队不断地给予着塔克法里那斯增援,他们的国王托勒米,[1]是优巴二世的儿子,他还太年轻不能担当起国家的重任,于是这些玛乌利塔尼亚人就想通过参加战争来逃避国王的被释家奴们对他们的奴役性的专制统治。伽拉芒提斯人的国王为了得到塔克法里那斯掠夺来的物品,也参加了他的袭击,但是还没有达到率领军队在战场上作战的程度,而只是将一些轻武装的军队派遣出去。结果,在他们漫长的行军旅程中,他们的人数也被谣言无限地夸大了。而在行省当地,那些极端贫困的或是声名狼藉的人也都投奔到塔克法里那斯这里来。这种情况之所以产生,主要原因在于,在克温图斯·尤尼乌斯·布莱苏斯取得胜利之后,提贝里乌斯就将驻扎在那里的两个军团之一的第九军团召了回去,就好像阿非利加的敌人已经

---

〔1〕 玛乌利塔尼亚人的最后一位藩王,公元23年至公元40年在位。公元40年,他被召到罗马,他的表兄弟卡里古拉将他处死。

as though Africa were clear of enemies. The governor at the time, Publius Cornelius Dolabella (Ⅰ), had not dared to detain it—fearing the emperor's orders more than the hazards of war.

So Tacfarinas spread rumours that other peoples, too, were dismembering the empire, and so Africa was being gradually evacuated. He declared that such garrison as remained could be cut off—if all who preferred freedom to slavery made a united exertion. His army strengthened, he established an encampment and blockaded the town of Thubuscum. Dolabella, collecting all available troops, managed to raise the siege at the first onset, owing to the terror inspired by Rome—and the Numidians' inability to face an infantry charge. The next stage was to fortify strong points, and execute rebelliously inclined Musulamian chiefs. Then, since several expeditions against Tacfarinas had proved that a single heavy-armed force could never catch so mobile an enemy, Dolabella mobilized Ptolemy and his compatriots as well. Four columns were organized, under Roman generals or colonels; and Mauretanian officers were selected to lead raiding parties. Dolabella himself attended and directed the different units in turn.

It was soon reported that the Numidians had stationed themselves by the half-ruined fort of Auzea (which they themselves had burnt earlier), and pitched their encampment there. This seemed a safe poisition, because of large woods all round. But Dolabella, without revealing a destination, dispatched quick-moving light infantry and cavalry against them. At dawn, with fierce shouts and trumpet-blasts,

完全被消灭了一样。而那一年的阿非利加的总督普布里乌斯·
科尔涅里乌斯·多拉贝拉(一世)对此也不敢加以阻拦,因为对皇
帝的命令的恐惧是更甚于对战争危险的恐惧的。

于是塔克法里那斯就散布谣言说,其他民族也正在瓦解着罗
马帝国,所以罗马军队正在逐渐从阿非利加撤走。他宣称,如此
一来,如果所有渴望自由而不愿被奴役的人们能够联合起来共同
进攻的话,那些留在阿非利加的罗马军队是可以被截断在这里
的。这样,他的军队的力量便增强了,他建起了一座营地,并且包
围了图布斯库姆城。而另一方面,多拉贝拉也将所有可用的兵力
集中了起来,经过奋战,在第一次出击时便击败了围攻的努米地
亚人。这是由于罗马军队对敌人有威慑作用,而努米地亚人也没
有能力抵抗罗马步兵的强有力的攻击。下一步,他又加强了一些
战略据点的防守力量,并且还处决了那些企图谋叛的穆苏拉米人
的首领。接下来,由于对塔克法里那斯的几次远征已经证明,单
纯靠一支重武装部队是绝对不可能制服这样一支流动的敌人的
队伍的,于是多拉贝拉便把国王托勒米和他的国民们召集起来。
他把这些人组成了四个纵队,由罗马副帅或军团将领率领。同
时,他还选拔那些干练的玛乌列塔尼亚人的军官来领导进攻的队
伍,多拉贝拉本人则亲自轮流巡视并指导各个队伍。

不久,有消息说,努米地亚人已经在一座名叫奥吉阿的半毁
的要塞附近驻扎了下来(这座要塞正是他们自己之前放火烧掉
的),而且在那里安下了营地。营地驻所在这里看起来很安全,因
为它的周围都是大森林。多拉贝拉没有说明进军的目的地,便派
遣一些轻武装步兵中队和骑兵中队,让他们全速前进,去进攻努米
地亚人。黎明时分,伴随着阵阵狂叫和喇叭声,他们攻到了还在熟

they fell on the sleepy Numidians, whose horses were still tied up or feeding at a distance. The Roman infantry was in close order, their cavalry troops duly spaced, everything ready for battle. The enemy were taken unawares. They had no weapons, order or plan and were dragged to death or captivity like sheep.

The Roman soldiers resented their hardships, and the enemy's repeated refusals to fight. So they all took their fill of bloody vengeance. The word went round to make for Tacfarinas, a familiar figure after all this warfare: only the leader's death could end the war. His bodyguard fell around him, his son was taken prisoner, and he himself, as the Romans hemmed him in, rushed on to their spearpoints and escaped capture by his death. It had cost the Romans dearly.

But Dolabella's request for an honorary Triumph was rejected by Tiberius out of consideration for Sejanus—to avoid diminishing the glory of the latter's uncle, the former governor Quintus Junius Blaesus. This did not help Blaesus' reputation; but the rebuff increased that of Dolabella, who (with a smaller army) had to his credit important prisoners, the enemy commander's death, and the termination of the war. Accompanying him was a delegation of the Garamantesan unfamiliar spectacle. Disturbed by Tacfarinas' death but regarding themselves as innocent, the tribe had sent the mission to make amends

睡的努米地亚人军中,而此时,努米地亚的马匹还系在马桩上,或是正在遥远的牧场上牧养。罗马这方面的步兵组成了密集的队伍,骑兵也相应的安排好了战阵,战斗所需的一切准备都已经就绪。相反,敌人却毫无知觉,事先一点准备都没有。他们没有武器、毫无秩序、没有应战的计划,就像一群小绵羊一样地被拉去屠杀掉或者是被俘获。

罗马士兵想到自己吃过的苦头,又想到由于敌人的神出鬼没几次都没能进行的战斗,感到非常气恼,因此他们对敌人进行了血腥的报复。通知传达到各营说,要以塔克法里那斯为进攻的目标,因为只有这个反叛首领被杀死以后,战斗才能结束。而在多次战斗之后,他的模样大家都已经很熟悉了。他的卫士都在他的周围倒下了,他的儿子被囚禁起来,而他自己,当罗马士兵将他包围了起来的时候,他就向着他们的长枪直冲过去,以战死疆场摆脱了被俘的命运,但是他也使罗马人付出了沉重的代价。

但是多拉贝拉授予凯旋勋记的要求被提贝里乌斯拒绝了,这是出于对谢雅努斯的考虑,因为这样一来,谢雅努斯的叔父,前任总督克温图斯·尤尼乌斯·布莱苏斯的荣誉相比之下就会逊色得多了,但是这种做法对提高布莱苏斯的声望并没有什么帮助。对授予勋记的请求予以的这种回绝反而更增加了多拉贝拉的声望,因为多拉贝拉(一个率领这样一支弱小的军队的人)俘获了重要的俘虏,杀死了一名头目,结束了这场战争,这不得不使他在人们中获得很高的荣誉。伴随他同来的还有伽拉芒提斯人的一个代表团,这在首都是一种十分罕见的情景。原来塔克法里那斯的死使伽拉芒提斯人感到非常烦恼,但是他们为了免遭相

to Rome. Then, in recognition of the loyal conduct of King Ptolemy of Mauretania during the hostilities, an ancient compliment was revived and a senator dispatched to award him an ivory sceptre and embroidered triumphal robe, and greet him as king, ally, and friend.

In the same summer an incipient slave-war in Italy was only averted by an accident. The instigator was Titus Curtisius, a former Guardsman. By secret meetings at Brundusium and neighbouring towns, followed by openly published declarations, he started inciting the ferocious backwoods slaves to break free. Providentially three patrol ships for the protection of traders in those waters put into harbour. Also in that area was a quaestor, Cutius Lupus, occupying the traditional control-post of the pasture-land. Organizing the crews into a force, he suppressed the rising in its initial stages. A colonel of the Guard called Staius, hastily sent by Tiberius with a strong force, took the ringleader and his most formidable helpers to Rome. There alarm had developed—owing to its vastly increased slave population, in contrast to the continual diminution of free-born inhabitants.

This year also witnessed a terrible instance of tragic heartlessness. Before the senate appeared two men called Vibius Serenus—a son prosecuting his father. The father, dragged back from exile, dirty and shabby and now manacled, had to face the charges of his elegant, brisk young son. Informer and witness in one, he accused his father of plotting against the emperor. Subversive agents, he explained, had been sent to the Gallic rebellion from Spain; funds had been provided by

似的命运，于是派使团前来向罗马人民谢罪。而考虑到玛乌列塔尼亚的国王托勒米在战争期间对罗马的忠诚行为，一位元老被派到他那里去，将一项传统的赠赐，即一支象牙王笏和一件刺绣的凯旋袍送给他，并且按照对待国王、同盟者和朋友的方式向他祝贺。

就在这一年的夏天，一场刚刚在意大利发动起来的奴隶战争，因为一件偶然发生的事件得以避免。煽动叛乱的人是提图斯·库尔提西乌斯，他以前是一名普通近卫军步兵队的士兵。起初他在布伦杜西乌姆和相邻各城市一带地方举行秘密集会，随后他就公开发出了号召，发动那些凶残的、居住在边远的草原地带的奴隶们起来争取自由，但十分幸运的是，在那一带海域上负责保护商旅的三只双层桡船正巧刚刚驶进港口。正在这一地区按照古老的制度管理这一行省的牧地的一位财务官，库提乌斯·路普斯，也起了很大的作用。他把一些水手集合成一支队伍，在这场阴谋开始之初就压制住其上升的趋势。被提贝里乌斯匆忙派来的近卫军长官司泰乌斯率领着一支强大的队伍，把谋叛的首领和比较强硬的同谋者带到了罗马。人们内心感到十分震惊，因为与奴隶人数的剧烈增长相比，生来就为自由人的数量却在显著地减少。

这一年，还见证了一件悲惨无情的惊人例证。在元老院前出现了两个人，其中一个叫做维比乌斯·谢列努斯——一个控告自己父亲的儿子。而父亲，这位刚刚被从放逐的地方召回来，肮脏不堪，又衣衫褴褛，现在身上还戴着镣铐的人，正不得不面对着他那文质彬彬而又聪敏活泼的儿子的指控。谢列努斯兼具告密者和证人的双重身份，他指控他的父亲密谋反对皇帝。他进一步证实道，谋叛的使节曾经从西班牙被派到高卢的反叛者那里

an ex-praetor, Marcus Caecilius Cornutus. Cornutus, finding the anxiety unbearable and regarding prosecution as equivalent to ruin, speedily committed suicide. But the defendant, undaunted, shook his manacles in his son's face and called on the gods of vengeance. 'Give me back my exile,' he prayed them, 'where such fashions were far away! And one day punish my son!'

The elder Serenus insisted that Cornutus was innocent-his panic was caused by a lying charge—if that was not so, let them produce the names of other accomplices besides himself: for surely he had not planned the emperor's murder and revolution with only one associate ! The prosecutor, however, then cited Cnaeus Cornelius Lentulus (II) and Lucius Seius Tubero. This greatly embarrassed the emperor, whose close friends—one extremely old and the other sick-were thus charged with rebellious disturbance of the peace. Both were immnediately exonerated.

Subsequent examinations of the elder Serenus' slaves went against the prosecution. Thereupon the accuser, demented with guilt and terrified by clamorous threats of imprisonment, the Tarpeian rock and a parricide's death, fled from Rome. But he was fetched back from Ravenna and forced to continue the prosecution. For the emperor made no secret of his own longstanding malevolence against the exile. After the condemnation of Marcus Scribonius Libo Drusus, the elder

去。他还说,活动的经费是由前任的行政长官玛尔库斯·凯奇里乌斯·科尔努图斯提供的。科尔努图斯感到这种忧虑的折磨实在是难以承受,而且这种指控就等于要他的命,于是立刻自杀了。但是另一方面,这个被告却一副大无畏的精神,他在自己的儿子面前抖动着身上的镣铐,呼唤着复仇诸神的名字。"请仍然将我放逐回原来的地方吧!"他祈求道,"在那里就会远离这种风气了!而总有一天,我的儿子会受到惩罚的!"

这个老谢列努斯还坚持认为科尔努图斯是无辜的,他的惊恐是由于那撒谎的指控而引起的。他还说,如果不是这样,除了他自己之外,就将其他的那些同谋者的名字也举出来,因为对皇帝的谋杀和叛乱,他自己肯定不能仅仅同一个人勾结起来进行啊!于是,接着原告又举出了格涅乌斯·科尔涅里乌斯·楞图路斯(二世)和路奇乌斯·塞乌斯·图倍罗两个人。这一做法使得提贝里乌斯处于十分为难的境地——这两个人是他的亲密朋友,格涅乌斯·楞图路斯已经年至耄耋,塞乌斯·图倍罗又生病了,然而他们却遭受到这种以武装叛变扰乱国内和平的指控。不过他们立刻就被免除了这样的罪名。

结果,对老谢列努斯的奴隶的拷问推翻了原告的指控。于是,这个原告因为自己的罪行发了疯,而且人们闹嚷嚷发出的恐吓也使他惊恐万分,有人说应当把他送进地牢,有人说应该将他从岩石上扔下去,治他以弑父之罪,于是他吓得逃离了罗马。但是他又被从拉温那捉了回来,被迫继续进行自己的诉讼。提贝里乌斯并不掩饰他对于被放逐者长期以来的怨恨,原来在玛尔库斯·斯科利波尼乌斯·里波·杜路苏斯被判罪之后,老谢列努斯曾给提贝里乌斯写信提出抗议,说只有他的努力白白付出了,而

Serenus had written to Tiberius protesting that his efforts alone had gone unrewarded, and adding comments too insolent for safe address to that haughty, easily offended ear. Now, eight years later, although the stubbornness of the slaves had made their torture disappointing, Tiberius revived the matter, finding additional complaints from the intervening years.

Senators proposed the ancient punishment for the elder Serenus, but the emperor, to mollify ill-feeling, vetoed it. He also rejected Gaius Asinius Gallus' counter-proposal of confinement on Gyaros or Donusa, observing that both islands were waterless and if a man were granted his life he must be allowed the means to live. So Serenus was returned to Amorgos.

Cornutus having committed suicide, it was proposed that the accusers should forfeit their rewards whenever a man prosecuted for treason killed himself before the trial was finished. This proposal was practically carried when Tiberius, quite sharply and with unaccustomed frankness, backed the accusers, protesting that such a measure would invalidate the laws and endanger the nation. 'Better cancel the laws', he said, 'than remove their guardians!' So that breed created for the country's ruin and never sufficiently penalized, the informers, kept their incentives.

没有得到任何奖赏。而且信中还傲慢无礼地说了一些容易带来危险的抱怨的话,这些话在高傲的、容易发怒的皇帝听来,自然是大为恼火。现在,过了8年之后,提贝里乌斯还没有忘记这种旧恨,尽管奴隶们的坚定使得严刑拷打也没有获得所期望的结果,提贝里乌斯还是从这些年来的言行寻找蛛丝马迹,搜集起了其他可以对他发起控诉的证据。

元老们建议,应该按照古老的惯例对老谢列努斯加以惩处,[1]但是提贝里乌斯为了缓和大家对他的恶感而提出了否决意见。盖乌斯·阿西尼乌斯·伽路斯建议,把囚犯拘禁在吉雅罗斯岛或多奴撒岛,提贝里乌斯也表示反对,他提醒说这两个岛上都没有可以饮用的水,如果你要一个人留下性命的话,那就必须满足他能生存下去的一些基本条件。因此,谢列努斯就又被送回了阿莫尔古斯。

由于科尔努图斯自杀了,于是大家便提出了这样一项建议,即每当发生犯有大逆罪的被告在审判结束之前便自杀的情况,就应该没收给予原告的赏金。即将执行这一建议时,提贝里乌斯却非常严厉,并一改往常的习惯,以极其坦率的态度为原告辩解。他反对说,这样一种措施将会使法律失去它的效力,并且还会威胁到国家的安全。他说:"与其取消法律的捍卫者,倒还不如直接取消法律本身。"这样一来,告密者,即那些生来就是要使国家灭亡,而且从来都没有受到过惩罚的人,现在就更有动力了。

---

〔1〕 先是笞打,然后枭首,这种惩罚是以棍子和斧头作为标志的,执政官的权标就是棍束中间的斧头。

These tragedies were interrupted by a comparatively agreeable e-vent. Gaius Cominius, a Roman knight convicted of a poem slande-ring the emperor, was spared by Tiberius as a concession to the pleas of Cominius' brother, a member of the senate. This made it all the more surprising that Tiberius, who was no stranger to better things and understood that mercy was popular, should generally prefer grim-mer courses. And his failures were not because he was unobservant: it is not difficult, when emperors' doings are concerned, to tell whether applause is genuine or insincere. Moreover he himself, usu-ally by no means a fluent speaker-his words seemed to struggle for de-livery- spoke more readily and easily when he urged mercy.

However, when Publius Suillius Rufus, formerly assistant of Germanicus overseas, was convicted of judicial corruption and banned from Italy, Tiberius proposed his relegation to an island, feeling strongly enough to declare on oath that the national interest so re-quired. This was badly received at the time. But later, when Suillius returned, it was favourably regarded. For the next generation was to know him as exceedingly powerful and corrupt, exploiting long and a-bly -but never beneficially—the friendship of Claudius. The same pen-alty was imposed on the junior senator Firmius Catus for falsely accus-ing his sister of treason. It was he, as I have recorded, who trapped Marcus Scribonius Libo Drusus and then produced evidence to de-stroy him. Recalling this service, but alleging other reasons, Tiberius

　　但是在这众多的悲剧中间,却还有一件比较令人高兴的事情。一位罗马骑士盖乌斯·科米尼乌斯被证实犯了写诗诽谤皇帝本人的罪行,皇帝答应了当事人的一位做元老的兄弟向他提出的请求,赦免了他的罪过。这件事使人们大为惊讶,原来提贝里乌斯知道什么是更好的行为,也知道仁慈会使他得到众望,但是他却往往宁肯采取阴鸷的手段。他之所以有这种错误,并不是因为他不善于观察,因为人们对皇帝的行动所给予的喝彩,什么时候出于真心,什么时候是假情假意,这并不难看出。而且,通常提贝里乌斯本人的讲话是很做作的,他讲的每一句话看起来都是经过精心考虑、反复权衡的,但是每当提出一些仁慈的建议的时候,他却讲得比较流利和轻松。

　　尽管如此,当普布里乌斯·苏伊里乌斯·路福斯,一名过去日耳曼尼库斯手下的财务官,因犯了贪赃枉法罪而不许留在意大利的时候,提贝里乌斯却建议把苏伊里乌斯驱逐到一个岛上去。他的这个建议提得如此坚决,以至竟然宣称,他发誓这种要求乃是为了国家的利益而提出的。这种做法在当时引起了人们很大的反感,但是过了不久,在苏伊里乌斯回来以后,提贝里乌斯的做法又得到了人们的支持。因为在下一代的人看来,苏伊里乌斯是克劳狄乌斯的一个大权独揽而又贪污腐败的宠臣,他长时期利用自己和皇帝之间的友谊来巧取豪夺,从来没有做过什么有益的事情。一位资深的元老费尔米乌斯·卡图斯也受到了同样的惩罚,他的罪名是诬告他的姊妹犯了大逆罪。之前我已经说过,就是他,曾经陷害过玛尔库斯·斯科利波尼乌斯·里波·杜路苏斯,后来他又引用一些证据将里波搞垮。提贝里乌斯记得卡图斯过去做过的这件事情,于是就假借一些别的理由为他开脱,终于使

excused Catus from banishment, not objecting, however, to his expulsion from the senate.

I am aware that much of what I have described, and shall describe, may seem unimportant and trivial. But my chronicle is quite a different matter from histories of early Rome. Their subjects were great wars, cities stormed, kings routed and captured. Or, if home affairs were their choice, they could turn freely to conflicts of consuls with tribunes, to land- and corn-laws, feuds of conservatives and commons. Mine, on the other hand, is a circumscribed, inglorious field. Peace was scarcely broken—if at all. Rome was plunged in gloom, the ruler uninterested in expanding the empire.

Yet even apparently insignificant events such as these are worth examination. For they often cause major historical developments. This is so whether a country (or city) is a democracy, an oligarchy, or an autocracy. For it is always one or the other—a mixture of the three is easier to applaud than to achieve, and besides, even when achieved, it cannot last long. When there was democracy, it was necessary to understand the character of the masses and how to control them. When the senate was in power, those who best knew its mind—the mind of the oligarchs—were considered the wisest experts on contemporary events. Similarly, now that Rome has virtually been transformed into an autocracy, the investigation and record of these details concerning

他免遭放逐的惩罚,但是把卡图斯从元老院中开除出去,提贝里乌斯并没有表示反对。

我知道,我已经叙述的和我下面将要叙述的许多事情,也许看起来都是无关紧要的、不值得记述的琐碎之事。但是我所做的编年史工作和人们编写罗马人民的古代历史的工作是不一样的。他们所谈论的题目是:大规模的战争、遭到猛攻的城市、被驱逐或是被俘虏的国王。如果他们选择的是国内事务,他们也会很自如地转入执政官和保民官之间的冲突、土地法、谷物法、贵族和平民的决斗等等。但是我所反映的问题,是从另一个方面着手的,我记述的都是狭窄范围内的不光彩的事情。因为当前是一个长期承平的时代,和平的景象很少遭到破坏,即便有些骚动也是很微不足道的。罗马陷在一种平淡晦暗的气氛之中,皇帝对扩大自己帝国的疆土也并不感兴趣。

但是甚至像我所述的这些看起来毫无意义的事件也是值得深入研究的,因为这些事件表面上看起来没有什么意义,但是它们往往能引起重大历史事件的发生。因为每一个国家(或者城邦),其统治方式不外乎以下三种:或者是民主政体,或者是寡头统治,或者是专制统治。而这三种统治方式适当配合起来的政体是最能得到人们的拥护的,但它却不容易实现,而且即使得以实现,它也不能维持很长的时间。因此,在民主政体下,我们需要去了解群众的性格并研究驾驭他们的办法。但是在元老院掌权的情况下,那些最了解元老院和贵族的性情的人,在当代发生的事件中,就被人们认为是最聪敏、最有智慧的人了。同样的情况,在今天,当罗马世界实质上已经转变成为君主统治的时候,把这些有关君主的琐事加以收集并且按年代编排起来,也仍然是有它的作用

the autocrat may prove useful. Indeed, it is from such studies-from the experience of others—that most men learn to distinguish right and wrong, advantage and disadvantage. Few can tell them apart instinctively.

So these accounts have their uses. But they are distasteful. What interests and stimulates readers is a geographical description, the changing fortune of a battle, the glorious death of a commander. My themes on the other hand concern cruel orders, unremitting accusations, treacherous friendships, innocent men ruined—a conspicuously monotonous glut of downfalls and their monotonous causes. Besides, whereas the ancient historian has few critics—nobody minds if he over-praises the Carthaginian (or Roman) army—the men punished or disgraced under Tiberius have numerous descendants living today. And even when the families are extinct, some will think, if their own habits are similar, that the mention of another's crimes is directed against them. Even glory and merit make enemies—by showing their opposites in too sharp and critical relief.

But I must return to my subject. In the following year the consuls were Cossus Cornelius Lentulus (I) and Marcus Asinius Agrippa. The year began with the prosecution of Aulus Cremutius Cordus on a new and previously unheard-of charge: praise of Brutus in his *History*, and the description of Cassius as 'the last of the Romans'. The prosecutors

的。大多数的人正是通过这种研究——通过对别人的实际经验的分析,得到教训,学会辨别什么是对的、什么是错的,什么是有益的、什么是有害的,很少有人生来就能够辨别对错利害的。

因此,我写的这些东西也是有它们的价值和意义的,但是它们不是那种饶有兴味的东西,不能给人们带来什么愉悦。能够引起读者的兴趣和给读者以强烈刺激的是丰富的地理描述、变幻莫测的战斗场面、光荣牺牲的统帅。但是我所提供给读者的,却是一连串残酷的命运、接连不断的控告、被出卖的友谊、无辜者的惨死,书中到处充斥着这样明显的单调乏味的事件,和造成这种后果的同样单调乏味的原因。而且古代的历史学家很少受到别人的指责,无论对于迦太基的军队,还是对于罗马的军队,给予过分的赞美,人们也不会介意。但是在提贝里乌斯当政时期受过法律惩罚或是贬损的人,他们的许多子孙今天都还活着。甚至即使现在这些家庭都已经灭绝,也仍然会有一些这样的人,如果他们自己也有那样相似的品行,那么提到别人所干的坏事时,他们就会认为是针对他们自己说的。甚至对荣誉和功绩的描述也会招来敌意,因为对它们的热情赞美,也就显示出对它们的对立面的尖锐批评和否定。

但是我还必须回到我的主题上来。接下来的一年,[1]担任执政官的是科苏斯·科尔涅里乌斯·楞图路斯(一世)和玛尔库斯·阿西尼乌斯·阿格里帕。这一年一开始便发生了对奥路斯·科列姆提乌斯·科尔杜斯的一项新颖的和前所未闻的控诉,因为科尔杜斯在他的《历史》一书中,颂扬了布鲁图斯并且描述卡西乌斯

---

[1] 公元25年,即罗马建城778年。

were Satrius Secundus and Pinarius Natta, dependants of Sejanus; that was fatal to the accused man. So was the grimness of Tiberius' face as he listened to the defence. This is how Cremutius, resigned to death, conducted it:

'Senators, my words are blamed. My actions are not blameworthy. Nor were these words of mine aimed against the emperor or his parent, whom the law of treason protects. I am charged with praising Brutus and Cassius. Yet many have written of their deeds—always with respect. Livy, outstanding for objectivity as well as eloquence, praised Pompey so warmly that Augustus called him "the Pompeian". But their friendship did not suffer. And Livy never called Quintus Caecilius Metellus Pius Scipio, Lucius Afranius, and this same pair, bandits and parricides—their fashionable designations today. He described them in language appropriate to distinguished men. '

Gaius Asinius Pollio (I) gave a highly complimentary account of them. Marcus Valerius Messalla Corvinus (I) called Cassius " my commander". Both lived out wealthy and honoured lives. When Cicero

是最后的一名罗马人。控诉人是撒特里乌斯·谢孔杜斯和皮那里乌斯·那塔,这两个人是谢雅努斯的食客,他们的这种身份就决定了被告的命运。还有致命的一点,那就是提贝里乌斯在听取被告的答辩时所表现出的那种阴郁的表情。这就是已把生死置之度外的科列姆提乌斯讲出下面这番话的原因,他说:

"元老们,我的言论受到了谴责,但是我的行为却是不应该受到谴责的。而且我讲的那些话并非针对这些受大逆法保护的人,既不是针对皇帝本人,也不是针对他的父母。我因颂扬了布鲁图斯和卡西乌斯而受到了指控,但是许多人都曾经记述过他们的事迹,而且都是怀着尊敬的心情来记述的。以客观和雄辩而享有盛誉的李维,是那样热情地称赞庞培,以至于奥古斯都称他为'庞培派',但是这并没有破坏他们的友谊。对于克温图斯·凯奇里乌斯·美提尔乌斯·皮乌斯·斯奇比奥,对于路奇乌斯·阿弗拉尼乌斯,[1]对于现在所涉及的这两个人,李维都从来没有像现在流行的称呼那样,称他们为匪徒和弑父者,而是用那些与著名人物相适合的语言来描述他们。"

盖乌斯·阿西尼乌斯·波里欧(一世)[2]的记述给予他们高度的赞扬。玛尔库斯·瓦列里乌斯·美撒拉·科尔维努斯(一世)[3]称卡西乌斯为"我的统帅"。但是波里欧和科尔维努斯在

---

〔1〕 斯奇比奥是庞培的岳父,自杀而死;阿弗拉尼乌斯是他的副帅,公元前46年塔普苏斯惨败之后遭到追击,被俘之后死去。

〔2〕 奥古斯都时代著名的文学家和政治活动家,他所著的历史从公元前60年的三头政治开始。

〔3〕 著名的演说家、军人、文学家和政治家,他是提布路斯、荷拉提乌斯的朋友,晚年又是提贝里乌斯的朋友,提贝里乌斯把他的作品当做拉丁语的典范。

praised Cato to the skies, the dictator Julius Caesar reacted by writing a speech against him—as in a lawsuit. Antony's letters, Brutus' speeches, contain scathing slanders against Augustus. The poems of Marcus Furius Bibaculus and Catullus—still read-are crammed with insults against the Caesars. Yet the divine Julius, the divine Augustus endured them and let them be. This could well be interpreted as wise policy, and not merely forbearance. For things unnoticed are forgotten; resentment confers status upon them.

'I am not speaking of the Greeks. For they left licence unpunished as well as freedom—or, at most, words were countered by words. But among us, too, there has always been complete, uncensored liberty to speak about those whom death has placed beyond hatred or partiality. Cassius and Brutus are not in arms at Philippi now. I am not on the platform inciting the people to civil war. They died seventy years ago! They are known by their statues—even the conqueror did not remove them. And they have their place in the historian's pages. Posterity gives everyone his due honour. If I am condemned, people will remember me as well as Cassius and Brutus. '

生时和死时都享有充分的财富和很高的荣誉！当西塞罗在他的著作中把加图捧上了天的时候,独裁官尤利乌斯·恺撒的反应也只不过是写了一篇书面的演说来进行答辩,就像在公审法庭上发表演说一样。安托尼乌斯的书信里、布鲁图斯的演说中,都包含着对奥古斯都的严重的诋毁;玛尔库斯·福利乌斯·比巴库路斯的和卡图路斯的现在还广为传诵的诗篇里,[1]还充满着对恺撒们的许多侮辱之词。然而,神圣的尤利乌斯和神圣的奥古斯都都容忍了下来,没有惩罚他们。我不知道他们的这种行动是由于他们智慧的策略,还是仅仅由于他们善于克制。因为不放在心上的事情不久就会被忘掉,而怨恨则恰恰会将这些情况加在他们身上。

"我没有提起希腊人的例子。因为在他们那里,书面言论的出格和自由一样都是不会受到惩罚的。对于言语上的冒犯,或者最多也只是以言语来对抗。但是即便在我们中间,对于那些由于自身的死亡而摆脱了别人的怨恨或偏见的人,也能够有完全的自由、不受谴责地发表意见。卡西乌斯和布鲁图斯现在已经不再严阵以待地活跃在菲利披平原上了,我也并不是在讲坛上鼓动人们去发动内战,而布鲁图斯和卡西乌斯 70 年以前就已经去世了！他们的雕像使人们仍然记着他们——甚至就连打败了他们的人都没有将他们一笔抹杀。他们在历史学家的书页中占有着一席之位,后世的人对于每个人都会给予他应有的荣誉。如果我被判有罪的话,人们也将会像纪念布鲁图斯和卡西乌斯一样纪念我的！"

---

〔1〕 比巴库路斯的诗只有很少的残篇,主要保存在苏埃托尼乌斯的著作中;关于卡图路斯,恺撒曾经指出,他写的关于玛木尔拉的诗使自己的名字蒙受了永久的污点,但是当他谢罪时,恺撒就在当天请这位诗人吃饭,并且对卡图路斯的父亲一如既往地采取友好的态度。

Cremutius walked out of the senate, and starved himself to death. The senate ordered his books to be burnt by the aediles. But they survived, first hidden and later republished. This makes one deride the stupidity of people who believe that today's authority can destroy tomorrow's memories. On the contrary, repressions of genius increase its prestige. All that tyrannical conquerors, and imitators of their brutalities, achieve is their own disrepute and their victims' renown.

So continuous was the succession of prosecutions this year that even at the Latin Festival Drusus, as he mounted the platform to be inducted as honorary mayor, was approached with a charge—Calpurnius Salvianus lodged an accusation against Sextus Marius. However, Calpurnius was publicly reprimanded by Tiberius and banished.

Next the community of Cyzicus was accused of neglecting the worship of the divine Augustus and of using violence against Roman citizens. It lost the freedom it had earned during the war against Mithridates VI of Pontus when its bravery (as much as the help of Lucius Licinius Lucullus) beat off the king's besieging force. However Gaius Fontcius Capito (I); former governor of Asia, was acquitted, charges

科列姆提乌斯走出了元老院,绝食而死。元老们命令营造官焚毁他的著作,但还是有一些被保存了下来,这些著作最初还隐藏着,后来就发表了。这一事实使人们更加嘲笑那些自认为自己当前的淫威可以消灭后世人的记忆的人们的愚蠢。相反,对天才的压制反而会提高他的威信。所有那些残暴的征服者以及那些模仿他们的暴行的人,他们所招致的后果只能是使自己声名扫地,而他们的牺牲者却反而获得了崇高的声望。

这一年的时间里,控诉的事件就这样接连不断地发生着,甚至在拉丁节[1]的日子里,当杜路苏斯登上讲坛被宣布正式就任市长之职[2]的时候,都不得不受理一项控诉:卡尔普尔尼乌斯·撒尔维亚努斯对塞克斯图斯·马列乌斯提出了一项控诉。但是,卡尔普尔尼乌斯受到了提贝里乌斯的公开谴责,并且被放逐。

接下来,库吉库斯地方[3]的一个部落被控以藐视圣奥古斯都的尊严,以及对罗马人使用暴力两项罪名,结果他们丧失了他们已经挣得的自由,这是在反对庞都斯的米特利达特斯六世的战争中取得的,当年他们由于勇敢(同样也由于路奇乌斯·里奇尼乌斯·路库鲁斯的帮助),曾击退了国王围攻他们城市的军队。另一方面,亚细亚行省的前任总督盖乌斯·丰提乌斯·卡皮托(一世)

---

〔1〕 在有历史记载的时期里,通常每年4月在阿尔巴山上举行。这个节日是从古代拉提乌姆各部落的一个联合节日演变来的,罗马主要高级官吏都会参加这个节日的庆祝,这时只有一位临时的荣誉市长留在罗马城内执行任务。

〔2〕 日耳曼尼库斯的儿子。关于市长之职,只是实职之外的一种虚衔,主要是给予尚未达到担任元老的年龄的显贵青年人的一种荣誉。

〔3〕 在小普里吉亚,公元前74～前73年,对它的围攻以米特利达特斯的惨败而告终。

laid by the younger Vibius Serenus being demonstrated as fictitious. But this did not hurt Serenus. Widespread detestation actually protected him. For the really aggressive prosecutors became almost impregnable-reprisals only fell upon the insignificant and unknown.

This was the time when Farther Spain sent a delegation to the senate, applying to follow Asia's example and build a shrine to Tiberius and his mother. Disdainful of compliment, Tiberius saw an opportunity to refute rumours of his increasing self-importance. 'I am aware, senators,' he said, 'that my present opposition has been widely regarded as inconsistent with my acquiescence in a similar proposal by the cities of Asia. So I will justify both my silence on that occasion and my intentions from now onwards.

'The divine Augustus did not refuse a temple at Pergamum to himself and the City of Rome. So I, who regard his every action and word as law, followed the precedent thus established-the more readily since the senate was to be worshipped together with myself. One such acceptance may be pardonable. But to have my statue worshipped among the gods in every province would be presumptuous and arrogant. Besides, the honour to Augustus will be meaningless if it is debased by indiscriminate flattery. As for myself, senators, I emphasize to you that I am human, performing human tasks, and content to occupy the first place among men.

'That is what I want later generations to remember. They will do

被宣告无罪,因为年轻的维比乌斯·谢列努斯对他提出的控诉被证明是伪造的。但是这次事件对谢列努斯并没有造成任何损害,广大的人民群众的厌恶对他实际上反而起到保护的作用。因为真正胆大妄为的告密者简直就是不可动摇的,报复只不过是落在那些微不足道的无名小卒身上。

就在这时,远西班牙派了一个使团来到元老院,要求准许他们以亚细亚为榜样,为提贝里乌斯和他的母亲修建一座神庙。一向瞧不起阿谀奉承的提贝里乌斯发现这是一个机会,可以驳斥那种说他越来越追求虚荣的传闻。他说道:"元老们,我知道现在我提出反对意见,会被普遍地当成是反复无常。因为就在不久之前,我默许了亚细亚各城市所作的相同的请求。因此现在我要说明,为什么在那一次我会表示沉默,以及从此以后我对这类事情所持的态度。

"既然圣奥古斯都过去没有禁止人们在培尔伽门为他本人以及为罗马城修建一座神庙,因此,把他的每一个行动和言论都看成是法律的我,才遵照他的先例也这样修建起了一座神庙。但是我更高兴的是,对我本人的崇拜将与对元老院的尊敬联系在一起。接受一次这样的要求也许是可以谅解的,但是若让我的像在所有的行省里都当成神像来崇奉,那就是虚荣和妄自尊大了。如果我们给予奥古斯都的荣誉被许多庸俗无聊的谄媚贬低,那么这种荣誉就会变得没有什么意义了。至于我本人,元老们,我要向你们强调的是,我是一个凡人,履行的职责是一个人所尽的职责,而且在人们中我所处的地位是最主要的,我已经感到很满足了。

"这就是我希望我们的后人能够记住的东西。如果他们认为

more than justice to my memory if they judge me worthy of my ancestors, careful of your interests, steadfast in danger and fearless of animosities incurred in the public service. Those are my temples in your
hearts, those my finest and most lasting images. Marble monuments,
if the verdict of posterity is unfriendly, are mere neglected sepul-
chres. So my requests to provincials and Roman citizens, and heav-
en, are these. To heaven—grant me, until I die, a peaceful mind
and an understanding of what is due to gods and men. To mortals—
when I am dead, remember my actions and my name kindly and favourably. '

Later, too, even in private conversation, he persisted in rejecting such veneration. Some attributed this to modesty, but most people thought it was uneasiness. It was also ascribed to degeneracy, on
the grounds that the best men aimed highest—that was how Romulus,
like Hercules and Liber (Bacchus) among the Greeks, had been admitted to the gods. ' Augustus had done better than Tiberius ', it was
said, ' by hoping. Rulers receive instantly everything else they want.
One thing only needs to be untiringly worked for—a fair name for the
future. Contempt for fame means contempt for goodness. '

我能够配得上我的祖先，关心你们的利益，在危险中表现得很坚定，为了公众的幸福不怕别人对自己的敌意，就是对我做出的最公正不过的评价了。这些就是在你们心里为我修造的神庙，这些就是我的最美好和最持久的像。如果后人的看法是冷漠的，那些石造的纪念物也只会被视为坟墓！因此，我对各行省、对罗马的公民们，以及对上天诸神所提出的请求都是这样：我恳求上天诸神，直到我临死的时候，都给予我一个宁静的心灵，并且让我懂得天上和人间的律条。人总有一死，当我死了的时候，希望你们能够怀着亲切和赞美的心情来怀念我的事业、记住我的名字。"

后来，甚至于在私人的谈话当中，他也都坚持拒绝将这种神圣的荣誉加到自己的身上。一些人将他这种态度归因于他的谦逊，但是大多数人却认为这是由于心神不安，还有少数人则认为这是一种堕落。他们的理由是，最优秀的人物，他们的目标也是最崇高的。这就是我们罗马人中的克维利努斯，[1]之所以像希腊人中的赫尔克里士与里倍尔（巴库斯）[2]一样，被列进了诸神的行列的原因。"由于有这种愿望，奥古斯都比提贝里乌斯做得好，"人们认为，"只要愿意，皇帝们是能够立刻就得到想要的所有的东西的。但是有一件东西却只有经过长期的不倦的努力才能取得，这就是后人对他的公正评价。因为人们对于名誉的蔑视，也正是意味着对他的德行的蔑视。"

---

〔1〕 他原来是萨比尼人部落的地方神，这个部落并入罗马之后，他和朱庇特、玛尔斯并列为罗马的国家神。

〔2〕 即巴库斯，罗马的酒神。

Sejanus' judgement now became affected by too great success; and feminine ambition hustled him, since Livilla was demanding her promised marriage. He wrote a memorandum to the emperor. (It was customary at that time to address him in writing even when he was at Rome.) This is what Sejanus said:

'The kindness of your father Augustus, and your own numerous marks of favour, have accustomed me to bringing my hopes and desires to the imperial ear as readily as to the gods. I have never asked for brilliant office. I would rather watch and work, like any soldier, for the emperor's safety. Yet I have gained the greatest privilege—to be thought worthy of a marriage—link with your house. That inspired me to hope: besides, I have heard that Augustus, when marrying his daughter, had not regarded even knights as beneath his consideration. So please bear in mind, if you should seek a husband for Livilla, your friend who would gain nothing but prestige from the relationship. For I am content with the duties I have to perform; satisfied-for my children's sake-if my family is safeguarded against the unfounded malevolence of Agrippina. For myself, to live my appointed span under so great an emperor is all the life I desire. '

In reply Tiberius praised Sejanus' loyalty, touched lightly on his own favours to him, and asked for time, ostensibly for unbiased reflection. Finally, he answered. 'Other men's decisions', he wrote, 'may be based on their own interests, but rulers are situated differently, since in important matters they need to consider public opinion. So I

这时,谢雅努斯由于取得了极大的成功而头脑发昏,自以为是;而且,一个野心勃勃的女人还在催促着他,因为利维拉一直在要求谢雅努斯履行他允诺的婚约。因此,他就给皇帝写了一份报告(因为按照那时的习惯,凡是向皇帝陈事,即使他本人在罗马,也要用书面的形式)。谢雅努斯是这样说的:

"由于您的父亲奥古斯都的仁爱,以及您本人对我的许多支持和照顾,我已经形成了这样一种习惯,那就是将我的任何希望、任何誓愿,都像告诉诸神那样地乐于告诉皇帝听。我从来不曾要求过花哨的官职,我宁愿像皇帝的任何一名普通卫兵一样,为了皇帝的安全而日夜警戒、勤苦工作。然而我却得到了意想不到的最大的权力,这就是,我竟然被认为有资格同您的亲族联姻。除此之外,这种情况也激励我产生了新的希望,那就是,我曾听说,当奥古斯都在安排他女儿的婚事的时候,甚至并没有鄙视罗马骑士,从而也将他们作为考虑的对象。因此,如果您要为利维拉选择一位丈夫的话,恳求您不要忘记您的一个朋友,这个朋友只是希望从这一联姻中取得荣誉,别的一无所求。但是我并不想推卸我必须承担的责任,我要为我的孩子们着想,只要我的一家能够有足够的力量防止阿格里披娜对我们的仇视,我就感到十分满足了。至于我本人,则终生在您这样一位伟大的皇帝手下效劳,才是我一生的心愿。"

在回信中,提贝里乌斯赞扬了谢雅努斯的忠诚,还略微谈了谈他本人对他的喜爱,并且说,他需要有一点时间来充分地、不带偏见地考虑这个问题。最后,他做出了答复,他写道:"其他人在做出决定时,是以他们自己的利益为出发点的,但是作为皇帝来说,情况就完全不同了,因为在处理最重大的事件时,皇帝就必须要

do not resort to the easy answer, that Livilla can decide for herself whether she should fill Drusus' place by remarrying, or stay in the same home. Nor shall I reply that she has a mother and grandmother who are her more intimate advisers than myself. I shall be more frank. In the first place Agrippina's ill-feelings will be greatly intensified if Livilla marries; this would virtually split the imperial house in two. Even now, the women's rivalry is irrepressible, and my grandsons are torn between them. What if the proposed marriage accentuated the feud?

'You are mistaken, Sejanus, if you think that Livilla, once married to Gaius Caesar and then to Drusus, would be content to grow old as the wife of a knight—or that you could retain your present status. Even if I allowed it, do you think it would be tolerated by those who have seen her brother and father, and our ancestors, holding the great offices of state? You do not want to rise above your present rank. But the officials and distinguished men who force their way in upon you and consult you on all matters maintain openly that you have long ago eclipsed all other knights and risen above any friend of my father's. Moreover, envying you, they criticize me. '

'Augustus, you say, considered marrying his daughter to a knight. But he foresaw that the man set apart by such an alliance

考虑到公众的意见。因此我不能用一个最现成的答案来为自己作借口，这就是，在杜路苏斯死后，改嫁他人、还是留在自己原来的家里，利维拉可以自己做出决定。而且我还可以推托说，她有她自己的母亲和祖母，对于利维拉来说，她们是比我更适合、更亲密的顾问。我还可以更加坦白地说：首先，如果利维拉重新结婚的话，将会更加增强阿格里披娜的恶感，因为这种婚姻实质上会把皇帝的家族分裂为二。甚至在现在这种情况下，女人们的嫉妒都是无法抑制的，而且我的孙子们也会夹在她们中间互相争斗。如果你提出的这种婚姻加剧了这一争端的话，那又怎么办呢？

"谢雅努斯，如果你以为利维拉在嫁给盖乌斯·恺撒，继而又嫁给杜路苏斯之后，还会满足于做一个罗马骑士的妻子而终老一生，或者你以为你可以保持你当前的地位，那你就错了。即使我个人准许了你的请求，你以为见过她的兄弟、她的父亲的那些人，以及我们那些担任过国家的最高职位的祖先会容忍这种情况吗？你自己不想再升任比你目前更高的职位，但是那些用尽各种手段出现在你面前仰仗你，并且同你商讨每一件事情的高级官吏和显要人物，他们会公开坚持自己的这样一种看法的，那就是：很久以来，你就已经凌驾于其他所有骑士的地位之上了，并且也远远高于我父亲的朋友之上了[1]。进而，出于对你的嫉妒，他们也会对我进行指责的。

"你说奥古斯都曾考虑过把他的女儿嫁给一个罗马骑士，但是

---

〔1〕 这里指骑士出身的元老，如迈凯纳斯、撒路斯提乌斯·克利司普斯和其他诸如此类的人物。

would be enormously elevated; and is it surprising, therefore, that those he had in mind were men like Gaius Proculeius, noted for their retiring abstention from public affairs? Besides, if we are noting Augustus' delay in making up his mind the decisive consideration is that the sons-in-law whom he actually chose were Marcus Agrippa and then, in due course, myself. I have spoken openly, as your friend. However, what you and Livilla decide, I shall not oppose. Of certain projects of my own, and additional ties by which I plan to link you with me, I shall not speak now. This only shall I say: for your merits and your devotion to me, no elevation would be too high. When the time comes to speak before the senate and public, I shall not be silent. '

Sejanus was alarmed, not just for his marriage but on graver grounds. He replied urging Tiberius to eschew suspicion and ignore rumour and malignant envy. Then, unwilling either to shut out his stream of visitors—which would mean loss of influence—or by receiving them to give his critics a handle, he turned his attention to persuading Tiberius to settle in some attractive place far from Rome. He foresaw many advantages in this. He himself would control access to the emperor—as well as most of his correspondence, since it

奥古斯都预见到,由于这样的联姻,这个男子会脱离他原来的身份,而在与他同等的人们中间极大地提高起来。因此,令人吃惊的是,他所考虑的是像盖乌斯·普罗库列乌斯[1]那样,以毫不过问国事的离群索居的退隐生活而著名的人!而且,如果我们注意到了奥古斯都在考虑这个问题时的迟疑不决的态度,我们更应该看到这样一个事实,那就是:他明确地选择了玛尔库斯·阿格里帕做他的女婿,后来,在适当的时候,又将她嫁给了我本人。作为你的朋友,我是开诚布公地对你讲出这番话的。尽管如此,对于你和利维拉的决定,我是不会表示反对的。关于我本人的一些想法,以及在今后加强你和我之间的联系的另外一些计划,我现在还不打算说。我要说的只有一点,那就是,论你的优点以及你对我的忠诚,给予你任何高位都是不过分的。在时机成熟时,不论是在元老院、还是在人民群众的面前,我是不会保持沉默的。"

谢雅努斯感到非常惊讶,不仅仅是由于婚姻的事情,而且还由于更深刻的原因。于是他又复信,劝提贝里乌斯不要理会那些毫无根据的怀疑、谣言以及那些恶意的嫉妒。与此同时,他既不愿意把大批前来拜会他的人拒之门外——因为这样会削弱他自己的影响;另一方面,又不愿意接待这些人,因为这样做会给批评他的人留下把柄,于是他便转而劝说提贝里乌斯,到远离罗马的某个赏心悦目的地方去居住一段时间。他预见到这样做会有许多好处,通过这种做法,他可以控制人们对皇帝的接近,还可以监视皇帝的

---

[1] 奥古斯都的亲密朋友,在阿克提乌姆一役之后曾代表他到安托尼乌斯和克利欧帕特拉那里去。

would be transmitted by Guardsmen. Besides, the ageing monarch, slackening in retirement, would soon be readier to delegate governmental functions. Meanwhile Sejanus himself would become less unpopular when his large receptions ceased—by eliminating inessentials, he would strengthen his real power. So he increasingly denounced to Tiberius the drudgeries of Rome, its crowds and innumerable visitors, and spoke warmly of peace and solitude, far from vexation and friction: where first things could come first.

Tiberius wavered. At this moment, a trial happened to take place which made him anxious to avoid the senate's meetings. For the evidence included offensive (and often accurate) remarks about himself, repeated to his face. For while the able and well-known Votienus Montanus was being tried for abusing the emperor, a soldier called Aemilius who was one of the witnesses, eager to prove the case, perseveringly spared no detail. Despite loud protests, Tiberius had to hear the insults to which, in private, he was subject. Greatly upset, he cried that he must clear his reputation immediately, or at least before the case ended. He was only calmed with difficulty by his friends' entreaties

大部分来往信件,因为这些信件都是由近卫军士兵传递的。[1] 除此之外,这位已届衰年的皇帝,因为隐居的生活而日益懒散,这样,不久之后,他便会更愿意把统治大权交给别人去支配了。而与此同时,谢雅努斯本人,由于停止了与各色人等的大量交接,会减轻人们对他的恶感。而且取消那些无关紧要的虚荣,反而会加强他的实权。这样,他就逐渐开始向提贝里乌斯抱怨在罗马的各种麻烦:熙熙攘攘的人群、没完没了的来访者;另一方面,又热情赞扬那种可以远离烦恼和摩擦的、和平而又清静的生活,并且说,在那种地方,最重要的事情能够得到最先的处理。

提贝里乌斯动摇了。而就在这个时候,又恰巧发生了一次使他急于想回避的元老院会议组织的审判,因为在这次审判的证据中,包含着一些直接针对他的(还很尖刻的)批评,而这些批评又是切中要害的,这就是对于很有才能而又很有声望的沃提耶努斯·蒙塔努斯[2]的审判。原来当沃提耶努斯被控以侮辱皇帝之罪的时候,证人之一,一个热切地希望证实这一案情的名叫埃米里乌斯的士兵,便不屈不挠地将事情的全部经过事无巨细、毫无遗漏地叙述了出来。尽管有人在会场上高声抗议,提贝里乌斯还是真切地听到了人们在私下里对他进行侮辱的那些话。这些话使他极为烦躁,以致他高声叫道,至少是在审判结束之前,他必须立即予以澄清,恢复他的声誉。在他的朋友们的极力恳求、再加上所有在场的人们的谄媚之下,提贝里乌斯好不容易才平静了

---

〔1〕 这是近卫军的一支特殊的骑兵队伍,这支骑兵队伍是由谢雅努斯直接控制的。

〔2〕 纳尔波的一位演说家。

and a chorus of flattery. Votienus paid the penalty of treason. Imputa-
tions of his excessive severity to defendants only made Tiberius severer
still. He exiled a lady named Aquilia for adultery-though one of the
consuls—designate, Cnaeus Cornelius Lentulus Gaetulicus, had only
requested condemnation under the Julian law-and struck a senator
called Apidius Merula off the roll for not swearing obedience to the
acts of the divine Augustus.

Deputations from Sparta and Messene were now heard concerning the ownership of the temple of Diana Linmatis. The Spartan assertion, backed by historical records and poems, was that whereas
their ancestors had consecrated it on their own territory, it had been
forcibly taken from them by Philip II of Macedon during their war a-
gainst him; and afterwards they had received it back by rulings of
Julius Caesar and Antony. The Messenians, on the other hand, cited the ancient partition of the Peloponnese among the descendants of
Hercules, by which the Denthaliate area—in which the shrine stands-
had been allotted to their king. This, they added, was confirmed by
ancient bronze and stone records; if appeal was to be made to poets
and historians, the more numerous and reliable authorities were on
their side; and Philip's judgement had not been arbitrary but objec-
tive—King Antigonus III Doson and the Roman commander Lucius

下来。沃提耶努斯受到了大逆罪的惩处。人们指责提贝里乌斯对待被告过分严酷,但是这却使他更加顽固地坚持这种严酷的做法。一个名叫阿克维里娅的女子由于与人通奸,被提贝里乌斯判处了放逐的处分,而科涅乌斯·科尔涅里乌斯·楞图路斯·盖图里库斯,一个当选而尚未就职的执政官,提出的只根据尤利乌斯法来处理她的建议并没有得到采纳。一个名叫阿庇狄乌斯·美路拉的元老,由于没有发誓效忠于圣奥古斯都的法令,结果就被提贝里乌斯剥夺了元老的称号。

元老院现在听取来自斯巴达和美塞涅的代表的发言,他们所争论的是狄安娜·利姆纳提斯的一座神庙[1]应归谁所有的问题。斯巴达人以历史的记载和诗人的诗篇为证,断言是他们的祖先在他们自己的土地上奉献了这座神庙。但是,在他们反对马其顿的菲利浦二世的战争中,这座神庙被马其顿的军队从他们手里夺走了。后来,由于尤利乌斯·恺撒和安东尼的决定,他们又将这座神庙收了回来。但是另一方面,美塞涅人则提出了往古时代在赫尔克里士的子孙们之间对伯罗奔尼撒地区的分配问题。他们说,由于这次分配,顿塔里亚特,这座神庙所在的地区,被分配给了他们的国王。现在还有古老的青铜铭刻和石刻可以证明。如果要求他们证诸于诗歌和历史的证据的话,那在他们这一方面有着更大量、更可靠的有力证据。菲利浦的决定并不是专断的,而是客观的。国王

---

〔1〕 尼顿河上游边界地区的一座神庙,美塞涅和拉科尼亚两地的人都崇奉它。按照传统的说法,引起第一次美塞涅战争的争吵就是在这里发生的。

Mummius had decided similarly, and the same verdict had been reached by the city of Miletus, officially appointed as arbitrator, and again by Atidius Geminus governor of Achaia. The Messenians won their case.

Segesta appealed for the reconstruction of its temple of Venus on Mount Eryx. When the well-known story of this antique ruin was repeated, Tiberius was pleased and on grounds of kinship gladly undertook the task. Next, a petition from Massilia was considered. Volcacius Moschus, an exile at that city, had become naturalized and left his property to it as his own country. His bequest was confirmed in view of the precedent of an earlier exile, Publius Rutilius Rufus, who had become a citizen of Smyrna.

This year witnessed the deaths of two noblemen, Cnaeus Cornelius Lentulus(II) and Lucius Domitius Ahenobarbus (I). Leutulus, in addition to his consulship and honorary Triumph won against the Getae, was honoured for poverty patiently endured, followed by great wealth respectably acquired and modestly employed. Domitius derived prestige from his father's sea-power during the civil war: subsequently he had joined first Antony and then the future Augustus. His grandfather had fallen on the aristocratic side at Pharsalus. He himself had

安提戈努斯三世多松〔1〕和罗马统帅路奇乌斯·穆米乌斯也做出了相似的决定,当时被官方指定为仲裁者的城市米利都也做出了同样的决定,还有阿凯亚的长官阿提狄乌斯·盖米努斯也都做出了类似的决定。因此,最终是美塞涅人赢了这场诉讼。

塞盖斯塔尼人也要求重修埃律克斯山上的维纳斯神庙,当他们重复叙述这个为人熟知的古老神庙遭到毁坏的故事时,提贝里乌斯听了很高兴。而且因为和塞盖斯塔尼人有亲属关系,提贝里乌斯很乐意承担此事。接下来,元老院又在考虑玛西里亚〔2〕送来的一份请愿书。被放逐于那个城市的乌尔卡奇乌斯·莫斯库斯已经逐渐顺化于玛西里亚,他把自己的财产赠给了那个城市,并且已经把它视为自己的祖国。根据普布里乌斯·路提里乌斯·路福斯的一个先例,这一请求得到了批准,原来路提里乌斯曾在依法被放逐之后,取得了士麦拿的公民权。

这一年,两个著名的贵族格涅乌斯·科尔涅里乌斯·楞图路斯(二世)和路奇乌斯·多米提乌斯·埃诺巴尔布斯(一世)〔3〕去世。楞图路斯除了曾担任过执政官和战胜过盖塔伊人而取得凯旋的勋记之外,还因为以下原因获得了很高的荣誉:他曾经很有忍耐力地过着贫苦的生活,后来他正当取得了巨大的财富,但是却依旧谦逊有节制。多米提乌斯取得了声望则是由于他在内战时期称雄海上的父亲,但是后来,他先是追随了第一个安东尼,继而又投奔了以后的奥古斯都。他的祖父在帕尔撒鲁斯战役〔4〕中是

---

〔1〕 马其顿国王安提戈努斯三世,公元前229～前220年当政。
〔2〕 今天法国的马赛。
〔3〕 皇帝尼禄的祖父。
〔4〕 公元前48年,恺撒打败庞培的一次决定性的战役。

been chosen as husband for Augustus' niece, Octavia's daughter, Antonia (I). Later he had won an honorary Triumph by conducting an army across the Elbe and penetrating deeper into Germany than anyone before him.

Another death was that of Lucius Antonius, of famous but ill-starred family. Only a boy when his father lullus Antonius was executed for adultery with Augustus' daughter Julia (III), that emperor (his great-uncle) had dismissed him to Massilia, where study could be a cloak for exile. However, he was given an honourable funeral, and by the senate's decree his remains were placed in the tomb of the Octavii.

In the same year a savage crime was committed in Nearer Spain. As Lucius Calpurnius Piso (III), imperial governor of the province, was travelling-unguarded, since conditions were peaceful—he was suddenly attacked by a peasant from Termes, and killed with one blow. His assailant escaped to wooded country on a swift horse, which he there turned loose, evading pursuit in steep pathless country. But not for long. The horse was found and taken round the neighbouring villages, until its master was identified. Arrested, and tortured to reveal his associates, he shouted in his native tongue that investigation was

站在贵族的阵营作战而阵亡的。他本人被选为奥古斯都的外甥女，即屋大维娅的女儿安托尼娅（一世）[1]的丈夫。后来，因为他率领一支军队渡过了易北河，比在他之前的所有人还要更深入地开进了日耳曼，因此，被授予了凯旋的勋记。

路奇乌斯·安托尼乌斯也去世了。安托尼乌斯出生于一个著名的、然而又是很不幸的家庭中，当他还是一个小男孩儿的时候，他的父亲优路斯·安托尼乌斯[2]便由于和奥古斯都的女儿优利娅（三世）通奸而被处死，他也因此被皇帝流放到玛西里亚去了。在那里，他借口研究学问来掩饰自己被放逐的事实。尽管如此，他的葬仪还是享有哀荣的。根据元老院的命令，他的遗体被安葬在屋大维家族的墓地里。

同一年里，在近西班牙发生了一件野蛮的罪行。皇帝的行省长官路奇乌斯·卡尔普尔尼乌斯·披索（三世），因为当地的环境和平安宁，便毫无戒备地各处游览。特尔美斯部落的一个农民出其不意地袭击了他，而且一击就把他杀死了。凶手骑着一匹快马逃进了一片森林地区，在那里，他把马放开，为了逃避人们的追捕，他走进了陡峭险峻、没有道路的荒野。但是没过多久，他的马被人发现了。于是，这匹马被牵到附近的各个村落去，最后确认出了它的主人。凶手被逮捕后，经受了种种拷问，逼他供出同谋者，他却用本地话高声喊道，审讯是没有用的，他的同伴可以

---

〔1〕 安托尼娅两姊妹是三头之一的安托尼乌斯和奥古斯都的姊妹屋大维娅二人所生的女儿。嫁给路奇乌斯·多米提乌斯·埃诺巴尔布斯的是大安托尼娅，而嫁给提贝里乌斯的兄弟杜路苏斯的是小安托尼娅。

〔2〕 他是安托尼乌斯和福尔维娅的儿子，但是他是由继母屋大维娅在罗马抚养长大的。公元前2年被处死。

useless-his partners could safely stand by and watch; no amount of pain would make him confess. Next day while he was being dragged back for further torture, he tore himself away from his guards and dashed his head against a rock, dying immediately. Nevertheless, Piso's death is attributed to conspirators from Termes. For public funds had been stolen, and he was recovering them with a strictness which seemed intolerable to natives.

Next year the consuls were Cnaeus Cornelius Lentulus Gaetulicus and Gaius Calvisius Sabinus. The year began with the award of an honorary Triumph to Gaius Poppaeus Sabinus for suppressing Thracian mountain tribesmen. The causes of the rebellion were their uncivilized and intractable temperaments, and their refusal of the conscription system which drafted their best men into our forces. Their loyalty even to their own kings was capricious—such contingents as they sent the kings were under their own chieftains and only employed against neighbours. It was now rumoured that the tribes were to be broken up, mixed with other peoples, and transported to far countries.

However, before opening hostilities the Thracians sent envoys to stress their friendship and obedience, which would remain intact, they said, if no new burdens were imposed. But if, they added, they were enslaved like conquered men, they had the weapons, warriors, and determination to be free or to die. They pointed to their fortresses on

安全地站在旁边观望,多少折磨、多么大的痛苦,都不会使他屈服招供的。第二天,当他再被拖去进行进一步拷问的时候,他突然从看守人的手中挣脱了出来,他迎头向一块大石头上用力撞去,当场便撞死了。然而,人们仍然将披索的死归因于特尔美斯人的阴谋。因为公家的钱被盗了,于是披索就用极为严厉的手段要他们赔偿,看来,当地人是不能容忍了。

下一年,[1]担任执政官的是格涅乌斯·科尔涅里乌斯·楞图路斯·盖图里库斯和盖乌斯·卡尔维西乌斯·撒比努斯。这一年的年初,元老院决定把凯旋的勋记授予盖乌斯·波培乌斯·撒比努斯,因为他制服了色雷斯山地的部落居民。这些居民暴动的原因是因为他们野蛮的、桀骜不驯的反叛性格。除此之外,还因为他们不愿意接受罗马军队的军事征募,不愿把他们最优秀的壮丁都选派入罗马的军队之中。他们甚至连对自己国王的忠诚也往往都是反复无常的,因为他们派到国王那里去的部队,要由他们自己的头目率领,并且只对同他们相邻的部族作战。但这时突然又有一个谣传,说他们的部落将要被拆散,和其他部族混合在一起,然后,再被迁居到遥远的国度去。

不过在使用武力之前,色雷斯人还是派出了一个使团来到罗马。他们强调了他们过去与罗马人的友谊和服从,并且还说,如果不再给他们增加新的税赋负担,他们还仍将保持对罗马人的友谊和忠诚。但是,如果他们像被征服的人们那样,被当做奴隶看待,那么,他们手中有锋利的武器、有坚强的战士、也有要么争取到自由要么就慷慨赴死的决心。他们又指着他们在山顶上的要塞

---

[1] 公元 26 年,罗马建城 779 年。

hilltops, where their parents and wives were lodged; and they threatened a difficult, arduous, bloody war.

Sabinus gave conciliatory replies until his forces were collected. But when a brigade under Pomponius Labeo reached him from Moesia and King Rhoemetalces II added loyal native auxiliaries, he led them and his own troops against the enemy. These had collected in wooded ravines. A few ventured to show themselves on open hillsides, but Sabinus attacked and easily routed them—inflicting little loss, however, since cover was near. Next Sabinus made his headquarters into a fortified camp. Then, taking a considerable force, he seized a narrow mountain-ridge which stretched, even and unbroken, to the nearest enemy fortress. This was defended by numerous armed Thracians, including irregulars. Against the fiercest of them, as they capered and chanted in front of their lines according to national custom, he detached picked archers. At long range these archers scored many hits without loss. But at closer quarters an unexpected sortie routed them. They were rescued by a battalion of Sugambri stationed by Sabinus nearby owing to its effectiveness in emergencies; it was as savage as the enemy in its chanting and clashing of arms.

Then the camp was moved closer to the enemy. The Thracian

对罗马人说,那里安顿着他们的父母、妻子。他们威胁道:如果要开战,那将是一场艰苦卓绝的、血流满地的残酷战争。

撒比努斯一直等到把他自己的兵力集合起来时,才对他们做出了温和的答复。但是当彭波尼乌斯·拉贝欧率领的一个军团从美西亚赶到他这里来,而同时,国王莱美塔尔凯斯二世也率领一队忠于罗马的地方辅助队伍赶了过来的时候,他便让这些军队和他自己的军队一起向敌人发起进攻。敌人都集中在林木茂密的峡谷里,几个比较大胆的人则公然在开阔的山坡上面露面。撒比努斯发起了进攻很容易就将这些人赶跑了。他们受到的损失很小,因为在他们附近都有掩护场所。接下来,撒比努斯就在那里建立了一座筑有防御工事的营地。随后他便率领着一支强大的军队,占领了一条狭窄的山脊,这条山脊比较平坦,中间又没有中断,它一直延伸到最近的一座敌人的工事那里,而在这座工事里,有大量全副武装的色雷斯军队和一些非正规军担任防守任务。与此同时,当敌人正在他们的堡垒前面,按照他们本国的风俗,一面放声歌唱,一面雀跃狂舞的时候,撒比努斯又选派了一队精锐的弓手,去对付最勇敢的那一部分敌人。只要弓手们在远距离的地方作战,他们就能够毫无伤亡地给予敌人有力的打击。但是当他们向前逼进的时候,他们却遭到了一次出其不意的袭击,结果队伍被搅乱了。幸而苏甘布列人的一个步兵中队及时接应了他们,这个步兵中队被撒比努斯配置在附近不远的地方,为的就是让他们在危急的时刻能够迅速地予以接应,而且他们的歌声和武器的撞击声也和敌人的一样凶蛮。

于是,营地又向更加接近敌人的地方移过去。我在上面提到

auxiliaries who, as I mentioned, had joined our side were left in the previous camp, and allowed to ravage, burn, and loot, provided that their plundering was restricted to the daylight and that they spent the night safe and watchful in the camp. At first this proviso was observed. But later, loaded with booty, they became self-indulgent and abandoned sentry duty in favour of dissipation, or lay drunkenly sleeping. The enemy learnt of their slackness and organized two detachments, one to attack the Thracian plunderers while the other assaulted the Roman camp. They did not expect to capture it but hoped that amid the shouting and clash of weapons every soldier would be too intent on his own peril to hear the other battle. To intensify the alarm the attack was to be by night. However, the attempt on the Roman fortifications was easily driven off. But the Thracian auxiliaries, lying along the earthworks, or in most cases drifting about outside, were terrified by the sudden raid, and slaughtered—with particular savagery, since they were condemned as traitorous deserters fighting to enslave themselves and their country.

On the next day Sabinus paraded his force on the plain. He hoped that the natives might be tempted by the night's success to risk battle. But they would not leave the fortress and its surrounding hills. So he proceeded to hem them in by strong-points, which—conveniently enough-he had already begun to construct. Linking these by a ditch and breastwork four miles in circumference, he gradually narrowed and tightened the loop, to cut off the defenders' water and fodder. He also began work on a mound from which boulders, spears, and torches could reach the now adjacent enemy. But their worst hardship

的已经加入到了我们这方面来的色雷斯人,被配置在以前的营地上。而且,只要他们将劫掠限制在白天,而夜里能够安全而警觉地守卫在营地里,就允许他们任意烧杀掠夺。起初,他们还遵守这种规定,可是后来,由于劫掠了大量物品而大发横财,他们便自我放纵,将警卫之责抛在了脑后而四散去享乐,或是在酩酊大醉之后便倒在地上呼呼大睡。敌人了解到他们放松了戒备的松懈状态,便组织了两支队伍,一支进攻色雷斯的打劫者,同时另一支则进攻罗马的营地。他们并没有打算占领这一营地,而只是希望通过他们的呼啸声和武器的碰撞声使每个罗马人都全神贯注在自己的安全上,从而顾不上再去注意别的地方的战斗。为了增加这种惊恐情绪,他们便趁夜间发起了进攻。然而,这种进攻罗马军团工事的企图是很容易被击退的。但是色雷斯的辅助部队,他们或者倚着工事睡着了,或者在大部分时候散在外面游荡,却被这次突然的袭击吓坏了,结果他们就遭到了极其野蛮的屠杀,因为他们被认为是举兵奴役自己的同胞的卖国贼和背叛自己祖国的逃亡者。

第二天,撒比努斯就让他的军队在平原上面列开队形,他想诱使由于夜间的成功而得意洋洋的敌人冒险出来作战,但是敌人并没有离开自己的工事和周围的山岭。于是他就开始用强大的据点把他们包围起来,凑巧的是,这些据点他早已经开始修建了。随后他便修造了一道壕沟和土墙,将这些据点连接在了一起,周边全长有4英里。最后,他就逐步紧缩包围圈,以此来切断敌人的水源和粮草的供应。同时,他还开始着手修筑一道土堤,从这上面可以把石块、投枪和火把之类引火物大量投到现在已经和他们相毗连的敌人那里去。但是他们面临的最大困苦还是口渴,

was thirst, since there was now only one spring for a great crowd of warriors and non-combatants. Meanwhile, their horses and cattle, shut in with them in accordance with native custom, were dying of starvation. Beside them lay corpses, victims of wounds and thirst. The whole place stank with putrefaction and infection.

The troubles of the Thracians were intensified by the supreme misfortune of dissension. One party favoured surrender, another death at each other's hands, while a further section, insisting that a price should be paid for their deaths, demanded a sortie. Opposing views were not limited to the ranks, but came from a chieftain the aged Dinis, whose long experience of Roman power and mercy led him to urge that the only solution to their plight was surrender. He took the initiative by giving himself up to the victors with his wife and children. The old and young and the women, and those who preferred life to glory, followed him.

The younger men, however, were split between Tarsa and Turesis. Both were determined to die rather than lose their freedom. Tarsa cried out for a quick end, an end of fears as well as hopes, and set the example by plunging his sword into his breast. Others followed his lead. But Turesis and his supporters waited for darkness. The Roman commander, aware of their plan, reinforced his outposts. Night fell stormily. On the enemy's side savage cries alternated with complete stillness. The besiegers were perplexed. But Sabinus went round warning them not to let mysterious noises or pretended inactivity make them vulnerable to surprise—every man must stand firmly at his post

因为现在只剩下一眼泉水来供应这样大批的战斗人员和非战斗人员的饮水了。与此同时,按照蛮族的习惯和他们自己关在一起的马牛等牲畜,由于缺乏秣草也快要饿死了。在他们身边倒着一具具的尸体,他们是受伤而死或是渴死的,伴随着腐败物和瘟疫,到处都散发着臭味。

色雷斯人的麻烦,还由于内部不和这一最大的不幸而更加突出了。一派主张投降,而另一派则建议相互杀死,更有甚者还有人认为他们应该死得有价值,因此建议进行一次出击。主张投降的意见,不只是来自一般的高级将领,还来自一个年长的首领,这个人名字叫做狄尼斯,由于长期的切身经验,他对罗马的威力和仁慈有着深刻的体会,因此他便建议说,解决目前困境的唯一办法就是投降。他自己首先带着他的妻子、儿女向胜利者投降。妇女老幼,以及那些为了活命而放弃荣誉的人都追随着他向对方投降了。

另一方面,比较年轻的人却分成了塔尔撒和图列西斯两派。这两派人都抱定了丧失自由毋宁死的决心。塔尔撒大声疾呼,要求从速结束自己的性命,这样也就可以结束那些恐惧和希望,他把剑插入自己的胸膛,为他人树立了榜样,他的支持者们也追随他的榜样自杀了。图列西斯和他的追随者则在等待着黑夜。罗马统帅意识到了他们的计划,于是便加强了前哨据点的力量。夜幕降临时下起了一阵暴雨,在敌人方面,凶残的叫声和死一样的沉寂交替着,包围他们的人们对这种情况感到颇为困惑。但是撒比努斯到处巡视着他的工事,他警告自己的士兵们,不要为这种神秘的呼叫声或是伪装的沉寂所迷惑,从而给敌人留下突袭的机会。每个人都必须坚守在自己的岗位上,而且不要向着实

and not throw weapons at non-existent targets.

Then the Thracians, in groups, charged down the slope. Some hurled boulders, fire-hardened stakes, and boughs hacked from trees at the palisade. Another party filled the ditch with branches, hurdles, and corpses. A small detachment brought ready-made gangways and ladders up to the turrets, which they grasped and overturned in hand-to-hand fighting. The Romans pushed them back with spears and shields, and hurled siege-javelins and showers of stones. Our men felt confident that the battle was won—and knew the disgrace (more conspicuous on our side) that defeat would bring upon them. As for the enemy, this was their supreme crisis. Moreover, many of them were spurred on by the wailing of their mothers and wives nearby.

Night gave the Thracians fresh heart. But it terrified the Romans. Striking out aimlessly, struck unpredictably, they could not tell friend and enemy apart. Shouts echoing back from the mountain clefts seemed to come from the rear; and they abandoned some of their defences, believing them overrun. However, only very few Thracians broke through. The remainder, their best men dead or wounded, were pushed back at dawn to their hill-fortress. There they were finally forced to surrender. The surrounding population submitted voluntarily. The remaining rebels were saved from successful assault or blockade by the severe, untimely winter of the Balkan mountains.

In Rome, convulsions shook the imperial house. The chain of events leading to Agrippina's end was initiated by the trial of her second

际上并不存在的目标投掷武器。

就在这个时候,成群结队的色雷斯人冲下了山坡。一部分人朝着工事的栅栏猛掷石块、用火烧尖的木棍,和从树上削下来的橡木棒。另一部分人则用树枝、篱笆和尸体等东西将壕沟填平。还有一小队人带着事先准备好的渡桥和梯子向着塔楼进攻。他们抓住塔楼,把它们掀翻,和守卫者展开了面对面的肉搏。守卫的罗马军队则用枪和盾牌把他们击退,并且把围攻的投枪和大量的巨石雨点般向敌人猛烈地投掷过去。双方都有足够的动力鼓起自己的勇气来:在我们这一方面,我们的士兵坚信胜利是属于我们的,而且很清楚失败会带给他们怎样的耻辱。至于敌人方面,这是他们面临的最大的一次危机。而且,他们中的许多人的妻子和母亲正在近旁哀哭着,这激励着他们进行殊死的搏斗。

黑夜使色雷斯人精神振奋,但却使罗马人感到恐慌。他们毫无目标地乱击一气,无法预料到会造成怎样的伤害,也无法区别哪些是朋友、哪些是敌人。从峡谷间反射回来的呼叫声,听起来好像是从后面传出来的。这使得罗马人放弃了自己的一些阵地,因为他们认为周围到处是敌人。不过实际上,只有很少的色雷斯人杀出了重围。其余的人——在他们中间最勇敢的那些人,不是战死、就是负了伤,在天明时又被逼回到山上的要塞里去了。最后,他们不得不在那里缴械投降了。附近地区的居民自愿地投降了,其余地区的叛变者则由于巴尔干山脉过早到来的严冬,从而避免了在进攻或包围之下被征服的命运。

但是,在罗马,骚乱动摇了皇帝的家族。引起阿格里披娜的毁灭的一连串事件,是以对她的表姊妹克劳狄娅·普尔克拉的控

cousin Claudia Pulchra. The prosecutor was Cnaeus Domitius Afer- an undistinguished recent praetor, ready to commit any crime for advancement. The charges were immorality (adultery with Furnius), attempted poisoning of the emperor, and magic spells against him. Agrippina, always violent, was upset by her relative's predicament, and hastened to Tiberius. She found him sacrificing to his adoptive father, and used this as the text of her reproaches. 'The man who offers victims to the deified Augustus', she said, 'ought not to persecute his descendants. It is not in mute statues that Augustus' divine spirit has lodged-I, born of his sacred blood, am its incarnation! I see my danger; and I wear mourning. Claudia Pulchra is an idle pretext. Her downfall, poor fool, is because she chooses Agrippina as friend! She forgot Sosia Galla—who suffered for just that. '

These words goaded the secretive Tiberius to one of his infrequent pronouncements. Grasping her, he quoted a Greek line: it was not *an injury that she did not reign.* Pulchra and Furnius were condemned. Afer became a leading advocate. His talents had been seen; and Tiberius had commented that he was a born speaker. Subsequently, in prosecution and defence alike, Afer's speeches greatly deteriorated in old age. It lessened his powers, but not his inability to-remain silent.

Agrippina, resentful as ever, became physically ill. When Tiberius visited her, at first she wept long and silently. Then she broke into embittered appeals. 'I am lonely', she said. 'Help me and give me a

诉为开端的。控诉者是格涅乌斯·多米提乌斯·阿菲尔,一个没有什么地位、新近才担任行政长官职务的人,但是为了能够飞黄腾达,他是准备进行任何罪恶的行动的。他控告她不守贞节(和福尔尼乌斯通奸),还企图用毒药谋害皇帝的性命,并以魔法魇镇皇帝。一向性情暴烈的阿格里披娜对自己亲属所处的危险处境,感到十分焦急,于是她便匆匆忙忙地赶到提贝里乌斯那里去。恰巧,她发现他正在祭奠他的继父,于是她便利用这一点作为她责难提贝里乌斯的借口。她说:"一个向圣奥古斯都献祭的人,不应该同时却迫害他的后人。奥古斯都的圣灵并不是寄存于不能讲话的石像中,出生于他的神圣血统中的我本人就是他真正的化身!我明白我自己的危险处境,所以我才穿上了丧服。克劳狄娅·普尔克拉只是一个毫无意义的借口,她之所以倒霉,是因为可怜的她愚蠢地选择了阿格里披娜做她的亲密朋友!她忘记了正是由于这样的原因而丧命的索西娅·伽拉。"

这些话刺激一向神秘莫测的提贝里乌斯发表了一次少见的谈话。他拉住阿格里披娜,引用了一句希腊语道:"一个妇女如果没有得到王位,她就不会受到伤害。"普尔克拉和福尔尼乌斯被定了罪。阿菲尔成了著名的辩护人,他的天才也显露了出来,而且提贝里乌斯也称他是一位天生的演说家。后来,不管是作为检举人还是辩护人,他的口才都因他的高龄而大大地退化了。这使他的权力也受到了削弱,然而却仍旧不能消除他那不能保持缄默的习惯。

仍然像从前一样心怀怨恨的阿格里披娜,身体变得虚弱多病。当提贝里乌斯前来探视她时,她先是长时间默默地流泪,随后就带着更痛苦的语气恳求说:"我很孤独,请帮帮我,再给我找

husband! I am still young enough, and marriage is the only respectable consolation. Rome contains men who would welcome Germanicus' wife and children. ' Tiberius recognized the political implications of this—but did not want to show either anger or fear. So her persistence remained unanswered. This incident, ignored by the historians, I found in the memoirs of Agrippina's daughter (mother of the emperor Nero), in which she recorded for posterity her life and her family's fortunes.

Distressed and impetuous, Agrippina was further upset by Sejanus. His agents now warned her—ostensibly as friends-against schemes to poison her: she must avoid dining with her father-in-law Tiberius. Agrippina was bad at pretending. Next to the emperor at table, she remained silent and expressionless, her food untouched, until he happened to notice (or perhaps he was told). When fruit was placed before him, the emperor—requiring a more conclusive test-praised it and himself offered it to her. This accentuated her suspicions and she passed it to her slaves uneaten. Tiberius said nothing publicly. But he turned to his mother and asked if it was surprising that he envisaged somewhat stern measures against a woman who alleged he was poisoning her. It was accordingly rumoured that the emperor planned Agrippina's death, but-not daring to murder her openly—was trying to find a secret method.

To distract gossip, Tiberius attended the senate regularly. He spent

一个丈夫！我还不算太老,结婚是对我这样的女人唯一的安慰。我相信,罗马帝国一定会有愿意接受日耳曼尼库斯的遗孀和他的孩子的男人的。"提贝里乌斯当然清楚她这番话所具有的政治含义,但是他既不愿流露出愤怒也不愿流露出恐惧的感情。因此,尽管阿格里披娜一再坚持,提贝里乌斯也没有做出答复。这个被历史学家们忽略的事件,我是从阿格里披娜的女儿(即尼禄皇帝的母亲)的回忆录中发现的。在这篇回忆录中,她为后世子孙记录了她一生的生活以及她的家族荣辱升沉的命运。

本来内心已经非常痛苦并且性格又急躁的阿格里披娜,由于谢雅努斯的捣鬼,就更加烦躁不宁了。谢雅努斯派人表面上装成知心朋友的样子,去警告阿格里披娜,说有人计划毒死她,为了躲避这种阴谋,她最好是不要和自己的公公提贝里乌斯一起进餐。阿格里披娜从来不会装腔作势,因此听了这种话后,当在餐桌前坐在提贝里乌斯身旁的时候,她就总是面无表情一句话也不讲,她的食物也一动不动。最后,提贝里乌斯偶然(或许是有人告诉了他)注意到了这种情况。于是,他就故意地试探她,一次,当一盘水果摆到他面前的时候,他就称赞这些果物的鲜美,并且亲自把这果物递给了阿格里披娜。这更加重了阿格里披娜的怀疑,她没有尝一尝,就给了自己的奴隶。对此,提贝里乌斯没有任何公开的表示,但是他却转而到他的母亲那里去了,并且问道,如果他决定用点儿严厉的手段去对付一个指控他放毒的女人,是否会令人感到吃惊?因此便又有谣传说,皇帝正准备除掉阿格里披娜,不过他却不敢公开谋害她,只是在暗地里寻找机会。

为了转移外界的闲言碎语,提贝里乌斯照例出席元老院的会

several days hearing deputations from Asia arguing about which community should erect his temple. Eleven cities, of varying importance,
competed with uniform keenness for this privilege. Their pleas all
dwelt on ancient origins and services to Rome in the wars against Perseus, Aristonicus and other foreign princes. Four, Hypaepa, Tralles,
Laodicea on the Lycus, and Magnesia on the Maeander, were passed
over as too unimportant. Even Ilium, boasting Troy as Rome's mother-
city, was insignificant apart from its glorious antiquity. The assertion
of Halicarnassus that it had stood firm, undisturbed by earthquakes,
for twelve hundred years, and that the foundations of its temple would
rest on natural rock, attracted attention briefly. The delegates from
Pergamum cited their temple of Augustus; but this was thought distinction enough. Ephesus and Miletus were adjudged fully occupied
with their state-cults of Diana and Apollo respectively.

So the choice rested between Sardis and Smyrna. The Sardians

议。他花了好几天的时间来听取来自亚细亚各城市的使节们的辩论,他们争论的是应在他们的哪个城市为提贝里乌斯修建神庙的问题。11 个有着不同实力的城市,都在以同样的渴望争取着这一权力。这些城市的代表都详细叙述了自己城邦古老的起源,以及在对佩尔谢乌斯[1]、阿里斯托尼库斯[2]和其他外族行省的战争当中他们为罗马所作出的贡献等等。以下四个城市,即哈帕埃帕、[3]特拉列斯[4]以及里库斯的拉欧狄凯亚[5]和迈安德的玛格涅西亚[6],因为它们都是一些太不重要的小城市而不予讨论。甚至伊利昂,虽然它吹嘘特洛伊城是罗马的母城,但是它除了光荣的过去以外,别的无足称道。哈利卡尔纳索斯人则声称,他们的城市很坚固,1200 年来没有遭到过地震的破坏,因此神庙的基址可以建立在天然的岩石上面,但是这并没有引起人们多大的注意。培尔伽门人以他们已经有了奥古斯都的一座神庙为理由,但是人们认为这一荣誉对他们来说已经足够了。以弗所和米利都两座城市则被认为,他们各自已经完全将崇祀集中在狄安娜和阿波罗两个神的身上了。

于是在这件事上的考虑便落到撒尔迪斯和士麦拿这两座城

---

〔1〕 罗马对佩尔谢乌斯的战争,即所谓马其顿战争,结束于公元前 168 年的披德纳一役,佩尔谢乌斯战败。

〔2〕 培尔伽门的埃乌美尼斯二世的私生子阿里斯托尼库斯的起义,是在公元前 168 年,被玛尔库斯·培尔佩那和玛尔库斯·阿克维里乌斯镇压下去的。

〔3〕 在吕地亚,今天土耳其的厄代米什附近。

〔4〕 在卡里亚,今天的阿伊登。

〔5〕 在普利吉亚,今天的拉塔基亚。

〔6〕 迈安德罗斯河上的玛格涅西亚,其地在吕地亚,今天的玛格尼撒。

claimed kinship with the Etruscans, quoting a decree of the latter. They explained that the original nation, owing to its size, had been divided between the sons of King Atys—Tyrrhenus, who had been dispatched to create new homes, and Lydus, who had stayed in his fatherland—the two countries, in Italy and Asia, taking the names of their rulers; while the Lydians had extended their power by planting settlements in that part of Greece later called the Peloponnese after Pelops. The Sardians went on to quote Roman commanders' letters and treaties made with Rome during the Macedonian war; and they stressed their rich rivers, temperate climate, and fertile surrounding territory.

The deputation from Smyrna traced back their origins-whether Jupiter's son Tantalus, or Theseus (also of divine birth), or an Amazon was their founder—and then passed to their most confident arguments: their services to Rome, including the dispatch of naval forces for wars abroad and even in Italy; and their initiative in founding a Temple of Rome, in the consulship of Marcus Porcius Cato the Censor, at a time when our power although already considerable had not reached its height, since Carthage still existed and Asia still had powerful kings. They also cited Sulla's acknowledgement that, when

市上了。撒尔迪斯人宣读了埃特路里亚的一项法令,证明撒尔迪斯和埃特路里亚有亲属关系。他们说,起初,他们的民族由于幅员辽阔,才由国王阿图斯的两个儿子第勒努斯和吕都斯把全国分开。第勒努斯出去开辟了一个新的家园,吕都斯则留在了他祖先的国土上。因此,意大利和亚细亚两个国家也就从他们各自的领袖那里取得了自己的名字。吕地亚人在希腊那块后来因伯罗普斯而称为伯罗奔尼撒半岛的地方开辟了一些移民地,因而大大扩展了自己的势力。撒尔迪斯人又继续引用了罗马统帅的书信,引用了在马其顿战争时期同罗马缔结的条约。他们还着重提到了他们水量充沛的河流、温和宜人的气候以及城市周边地区土地的肥沃。

另一方面,士麦拿的代表回溯了他们自己城市的历史:它的建立者也许是朱庇特的儿子坦塔路斯,也许是提谢乌斯(他也是神的后裔),也许是一位亚马逊人。随后他们就提出了最有信心的论据:他们曾为罗马人民提供过忠诚的服务。他们不仅派遣舰队帮助罗马人民进行国外的战争,[1]甚至是在意大利进行的内战中,他们也出过力。[2] 士麦拿人第一个为罗马城建立了一座神庙。在玛尔库斯·波尔奇乌斯·加图[3]担任执政官的时候,罗马的国运虽然说是蒸蒸日上,但是还没有达到如日中天的程度,因为那时迦太基还存在着,而且亚细亚也还有很有势力的国王。

---

〔1〕 对叙利亚的安提奥库斯三世的战争。

〔2〕 公元前90～前87年间的同盟战争,即意大利本土诸同盟市为争取罗马公民权而进行的战争。

〔3〕 玛尔库斯·波尔奇乌斯·加图,即担任监察官的大加图。他和路奇乌斯·瓦列里乌斯·佛拉库斯是公元前195年度的执政官。

his army was suffering critically from inadequate clothing in a bitter winter, a public announcement of this fact at Smyrna caused the whole audience to strip off its clothes and send them to our soldiers.

The senate voted in favour of Smyrna. It was proposed by Gaius Vibius Marsus that the governor of Asia, Marcus Aemilius Lepidus (IV), should be allotted a supernumerary official in charge of the new temple. As the governor modestly declined to make the choice himself, lots were cast and a former praetor, Valerius Naso, was appointed.

Now, after long consideration and frequent postponements, Tiberius at last left for Campania. His ostensible purpose was the dedication of temples to Jupiter and Augustus at Capua and Nola respectively. But he had decided to live away from Rome. Like most historians, I attribute his withdrawal to Sejanus' intrigues. Yet, since he maintained this seclusion for six years after Sejanus' execution, I often wonder whether it was not really caused by a desire to hide the cruelty and immorality which his actions made all too conspicuous. It was also said that in old age he became sensitive about his appearance. Tall and abnormally thin, bent and bald, he had a face covered with sores and often plaster. His retirement at Rhodes had accustomed him to unsociability and secretive pleasures.

他们还用苏拉表示感谢的话来作证据,苏拉说,当他的军队在严寒的冬天承受着缺少衣服的痛苦,因而处于极为危急的关头时,士麦拿人召开了一次集会,公开宣布了这个事实,这引起了全体听众的同情,他们立刻就把自己身上的衣服脱下来,送给了我们的军团士兵。

元老院投票表决,支持士麦拿。盖乌斯·维比乌斯·玛尔苏斯建议,要派一位特任的副帅到亚细亚行省总督玛尔库斯·埃米里乌斯·列庇都斯(四世)那里去,负责这一神庙。由于列庇都斯谦逊地表示不能由他自己来选择,因此就用抽签的办法,选出了前任行政长官瓦列里乌斯·纳索,并把他派出去了。

这时,在经过了长时间的考虑,并且又几经推迟之后,提贝里乌斯终于离开罗马到康帕尼亚去了。表面上,他此行的目的是为了在卡普亚把一座神庙献给朱庇特,在诺拉把一座神庙献给奥古斯都。[1] 但实际上却是,他已经决心到远离罗马的地方去生活。关于他这次从罗马退隐的动机,我的看法也和大多数历史学家的说法一样,认为是出于谢雅努斯的阴谋。但是联想到在谢雅努斯被处死之后,他也曾同样离群索居达六年之久这样的事实,我就会常常怀疑,他是否是出于这样的一种希望,那就是希望借此来掩盖他那由于自己的行动而过于昭著的残酷和淫乱。另外据说,在他老年的时候,他对自己的外貌也变得特别敏感。他长得很高,又出奇的瘦,背有些弯曲,脑袋上一根头发也没有,脸上又长着脓疮,还经常涂着膏药。他在罗德岛的隐居生活,使他习惯于不和人们交往,而只是自己偷偷地享乐。

---

〔1〕 这里奉献的是奥古斯都去世时住的房屋。

According to another theory he was driven away by his mother's bullying: to share control with her seemed intolerable, to dislodge her impracticable—since that control had been given him by her. For Augustus had considered awarding the empire to his universally loved grand—nephew Germanicus. But his wife had induced him to adopt Tiberius instead (though Tiberius was made to adopt Germanicus). The Augusta harped accusingly on this obligation—and exacted repayment.

Tiberius left with only a few companions: one senator and exconsul, Marcus Cocceius Nerva the jurist, one distinguished knight, Curtius Atticus—and Sejanus. The rest were literarymen, mostly Greeks whose conversation diverted him. The astrologers asserted that the conjunction of heavenly bodies under which he had left Rome precluded his return. This proved fatal to many who deduced, and proclaimed, that his end was near. For they did not foresee the unbelievable fact that his voluntary self-exile would last eleven years. Time was to show how narrow is the dividing-line between authentic prediction and imposture: truth is surrounded by mystery. For the first assertion proved authentic—though he came to adjacent points of the countryside or coast, and often approached the city's very walls. But the prophets' foreknowledge was limited, for he lived to a great age.

A dangerous accident to Tiberius at this time stimulated idle gossip, and gave him reason for increased confidence in Sejanus' friendship and loyalty. While they were dining at a villa called The Cave, in a

根据另外一种说法称,他是被他母亲的专横逼走的,与母亲分享统治权,他不能容忍;将自己的母亲除掉,又是不可能的事情,因为他的统治权正是母亲给予他的。原来奥古斯都过去曾经考虑过将帝位授予他姊妹的外孙日耳曼尼库斯,因为他是一个受到普遍爱戴的人物。但是他的妻子却诱使他把提贝里乌斯收为继子(日耳曼尼库斯则过继为提贝里乌斯的继子)。奥古斯塔常常带着责备的口吻唠唠叨叨地反复提起这件事,并希望取得报偿。

提贝里乌斯只带着少数几个陪同离开了罗马:一位曾担任执政官的元老、法学家玛尔库斯·科凯乌斯·涅尔瓦,一位地位较高的罗马骑士库尔提乌斯·阿提库斯,还有谢雅努斯,其他的就是一些文人,其中主要是希腊人,他们是陪着提贝里乌斯聊天给他解闷娱乐的人物。占星术士说,从他离开罗马时行星相互间的位置的联系来看,他是不可能再回来了。这对于许多推断并且宣称提贝里乌斯不久就会死去的人来说,是一种致命的打击,因为他们没有预见到这样一件不可相信的事实,那就是,他自愿的自我放逐竟然持续了 11 年之久。时间不久就会证明,真实的预测和诈骗之间的界限是多么小,而真相总是掩盖在神秘的面纱之下。第一种断言,即说他永远不会再回到罗马来,这话基本是正确的,尽管他经常是就要进入罗马了:他时而在城市郊区,时而在附近的河岸,而且还常常就在城墙脚下。但是预言家的先知也是有限的,因为他活到很大的年纪。

正在这时,提贝里乌斯遇到了一件十分危险的偶然事件,这件事引起了人们各种各样的闲言碎语,并且使皇帝有理由更加相信谢雅努斯的友谊和忠诚。当他们正在一座名叫"洞窟"的庄园住宅

natural cavern between the sea at Amyclae and the hills of Fundi, there was a fall of rock at the cave-mouth. Several servants were crushed, and amid the general panic the diners fled. But Sejanus, braced on hands and knees, face to face, warded the falling boulders off Tiberius. That is how the soldiers who rescued them found him. The incident increased Sejanus' power. Tiberius believed him disinterested and listened trustingly to his advice, however disastrous.

Towards Germanicus' family Sejanus adopted the role of judge. Agents suborned as accusers were to direct their main onslaught against Nero Caesar, heir to the throne, who though youthfully unpretentious often forgot the care which the circumstances demanded. His ex-slaves and dependants, impatient for power, urged him to show vigour and confidence. Rome and the armies wanted it, they said, and no counter-stroke would be risked by Sejanus, whose targets were juvenile ineffectiveness and senile passivity.

Nero Caesar listened. His intentions were harmless. But he sometimes made thoughtless, disrespectful remarks. Spies noted, reported, and exaggerated these, and he was given no opportunity to explain. People began to show disquiet in various ways. They avoided him, or turned away after greeting him, or, very often, broke off conversations abruptly. Sejanus' partisans stood and watched, sneering. Tiberius treated Nero Caesar grimly, or smiled insincerely-the young

里吃饭的时候——这座庄园修建在阿米克莱湾和富安狄山之间的天然洞窟里面,洞口的一块岩石突然落了下来。几个仆人被落下的岩石压死了,大家惊恐万状,正在就餐的人四散逃去。但这时只有谢雅努斯一个人,张开手臂和膝盖,面对面地护拥着提贝里乌斯,遮盖着他不受落下来的石块的伤害。直到前来救援他们的士兵们来到这里时,发现他还在这样保护着提贝里乌斯。这次事件大大增强了谢雅努斯的权力,提贝里乌斯相信他是一个毫不利己的人,对他总是言听计从,哪怕他提出的是会带来灾难的意见。

对于日耳曼尼库斯一家人,谢雅努斯扮演了法官的角色。被他收买担任控告者的那些人,他们直接的、主要的攻讦对象就是皇位的直接继承人尼禄·恺撒。这个年轻人尽管谦逊有礼、并不张扬,但他却往往忘记了他所处的险恶环境所要求的加倍的小心。他的那些被释奴隶和食客,急于谋取权力,不断地怂恿他要他振作起来并且要有信心。他们说,罗马人民和罗马军队都需要他这样做,而且谢雅努斯是不敢冒险加以反击的,因为他只是践踏老年人的驯顺和青年人的无能!

尼禄·恺撒在听到这些话后,并没有受到什么有害的影响。但是他有时却说出一些未加思考的、不够尊敬的话来。安置在他身边的奸细们听到这些话,就赶忙前去打小报告,并且还添油加醋地给予夸大,而尼禄却连给自己申辩的机会都没有。因此人们又开始表现出各种各样的忧虑。他们极力回避他,或者向他例行地打过招呼之后就匆忙离开,而更经常的是,他们会突然地就中止和他的谈话。而谢雅努斯的同党们却站在那里观望,并且还对他冷嘲热讽。提贝里乌斯对尼禄·恺撒的态度是阴冷的,或者

man seemed equally guilty whether he spoke or remained silent. Even night-time was not safe. For whether he slept, or lay awake, or sighed, his wife Livia Julia told her mother Livilla, and she told Sejanus. Sejanus even made an accomplice of the young man's brother Drusus Caesar—tempting him with supreme power if only he could eliminate his already undermined elder brother. Drusus Caesar's degraded character was animated by power-lust, and the usual hatred between brothers—also jealousy, because his mother Agrippina preferred Nero Caesar. But Sejanus'cultivation of Drusus Caesar did not exclude plans to begin his destruction too, since the youth, as he knew, was hot-headed and could be trapped.

The end of the year witnessed the deaths of Marcus Asinius Agrippa, who had lived worthily of his distinguished (though not ancient) house, and Quintus Haterius, of senatorial family. His oratory impressed his contemporaries, though surviving examples are less esteemed today. Indeed, his success was due to vigour rather than pains. Other men's careful, laborious work attains posthumous repute. Conversely, Haterius'resonant fluency died with him.

In the following year the consuls were Marcus Licinius Crassus Frugi and Lucius Calpurnius Piso (IV). A sudden disaster which now

只是皮笑肉不笑。这个年轻人是动辄得咎,不论是开口说话,还是保持沉默,看起来都是罪过。甚至就是夜间也不安全,因为不管他是睡着还是醒了躺在那儿,还是叹息,他的妻子利维拉·优利娅都会事无巨细地报告给她的母亲利维拉,而利维拉再告诉谢雅努斯。谢雅努斯甚至还与这个年轻人的兄弟杜路苏斯·恺撒同谋。他诱惑杜路苏斯说,只要他能除掉他那处境已经岌岌可危的兄弟,这皇帝之位就是他的了。强烈的权力欲激活了杜路苏斯恶劣的品性,而常有的兄弟之间的不和也是他陷害哥哥的一个原因,还有对尼禄的嫉妒,因为他的母亲阿格里披娜对尼禄非常偏爱。谢雅努斯尽管看起来是对杜路苏斯·恺撒极力栽培,但是他心里却已经在盘算着将来除掉他的计划了,因为他知道,杜路苏斯这个年轻人头脑简单冲动,是很容易被设计陷害的。

这年年底,又死了两位著名人物:一个是玛尔库斯·阿西尼乌斯·阿格里帕,阿格里帕出生于一个光荣(虽然并不古老)的家族;一个是克温图斯·哈提里乌斯,哈提里乌斯出生于元老家族,他的演讲口才虽然名闻当代,但是后人对他的评价却并不太高。事实上,他在演说方面所取得的成功,与其说是由于刻苦努力,毋宁说是由于他在演说中表现得感情充沛、铿锵有力。其他的人在演说方面付出的长期的、刻苦的钻研,使他们在死后反而获得了声誉,相反,哈提里乌斯当时所取得的反响,却随着他的死亡而消失了。

接下来的一年里,[1]担任执政官的是玛尔库斯·李奇尼乌斯·克拉苏斯·福路吉和路奇乌斯·卡尔普尔尼乌斯·披索(四世)。这

---

〔1〕 公元 27 年,罗马建城 780 年。

occurred was as destructive as a major war. It began and ended in a moment. An ex-slave called Atilius started building an amphitheatre at Fidenae for a gladiatorial show. But he neither rested its foundations on solid ground nor fastened the wooden superstructure securely. He had undertaken the project not because of great wealth or municipal ambition but for sordid profits. Lovers of such displays, starved of amusements under Tiberius, flocked in—men and women of all ages. Their numbers, swollen by the town's proximity, intensified the tragedy. The packed structure collapsed, subsiding both inwards and outwards and precipitating or overwhelming a huge crowd of spectators and bystanders.

Those killed at the outset of the catastrophe at least escaped torture, as far as their violent deaths permitted. More pitiable were those, mangled but not yet dead, who knew their wives and children lay there too. In daytime they could see them, and at night they heard their screams and moans. The news attracted crowds, lamenting kinsmen, brothers, and fathers. Even those whose friends and relations had gone away on other business were alarmed, for while the casualties remained unidentified uncertainty gave free range for anxieties. When the ruins began to be cleared, people rushed to embrace and kiss the corpses—and even quarrelled over them, when features were unrecognizable but similarities of physique or age had caused wrong identifications.

时，一件突发的灾害带来的灾难竟然具有像是大规模的战争那样的毁灭性。这场灾难的开始和结束都是一刹那的事情。一个名叫阿提里乌斯的被释奴隶在费迪纳修建了一座用来进行剑斗表演的半圆形剧场。但是他既没有将这座剧场建立在坚固的地基上面，也没有将建筑的木架结构紧密、安全地接合在一起。他从事这个工程并不是因为他太有钱，也不是因为具有市政的热情，而是由于他利欲熏心地妄图贪求不正当的利益。爱好这种表演的人们，不分男女老幼，都拥到了这里来。由于提贝里乌斯统治时期禁止娱乐，而人们又渴望娱乐，因此来的人特别多，已经达到了这个城市人口容量的极限，这就更加加重了这场惨剧的严重性。里面挤满了人的庞大建筑物突然倒塌下来向里或是向外轰然倒塌，结果把大量观众和站在四周旁观的人猛地摔了下来，压倒在了下面。

那些在惨剧刚一发生就被灾祸压死的人至少是没有受到痛苦的折磨，人们遇到这类的灾祸也只能是认命。更可怜的是那些被砸伤了身体但还没有死的人，他们知道他们的妻子和儿女也躺在那里。白天，他们还能够看到他们的妻子儿女，但是在夜里，他们就只能听着妻子儿女的尖叫声和呻吟声了。许多人闻讯赶来，他们为自己的亲戚、兄弟和父母而痛哭。甚至那些有朋友或亲属因其他原因而离开了家的人也感到非常惊恐，因为人们还不知道罹祸的都是哪些人，而这种未能确定受害者的情况使得更多的人感到焦虑。当人们开始清理倒塌现场的废墟时，周围的人们便冲过去，紧紧拥抱着他们亲人的尸体并亲吻着他们。他们甚至时时为了面前的尸体而发生争吵，因为尸体的面貌模糊不清、难以辨认，但是体形和年龄的相仿却使人们错认了亲人。

Fifty thousand people were mutilated or crushed to death in the disaster. The senate decreed that in future no one with a capital of less than four hundred thousand sesterces should exhibit a gladiatorial show, and no amphitheatre should be constructed except on ground of proved solidity. Atilius was banished. Immediately after the catastrophe, leading Romans threw open their homes, providing medical attention and supplies all round. In those days Rome, for all its miseries, recalled the practice of our ancestors, who after great battles had lavished gifts and attentions on the wounded.

This calamity had not been forgotten when Rome suffered an exceptionally destructive fire, which gutted the Caelian Hill. This was a fatal year, people said. Fastening on a scapegoat for chance happenings (as the public does), they detected an evil omen in the emperor's decision to leave Rome. Tiberius disarmed criticism by distributing money in proportion to losses incurred. This earned him votes of thanks in the senate by eminent members, and, as the news got round, a feeling of gratitude among the general public, because the donations were made without respecting persons or favouring relatives' petitions: sometimes the beneficiaries were unknown victims applying in response to the emperor's invitation. It was proposed that the Caelian should in future be called the Augustan Hill, since while flames roared on all sides the one thing unharmed was a statue of Tiberius in the house of a senator named Junius. The same thing, it was remarked, had once happened to Claudia Quinta, whose image, twice spared by conflagrations, our ancestors had dedicated in the temple of the Mother of the Gods: the Claudian house was holy and honoured by heaven, and the place where the gods had so con-

在这次惨祸中,有5万多人负伤残废或者是被砸死。于是,元老院做出了一项决定,规定在今后,拥有财产的数量少于40万谢司特尔提乌斯的人不得举办剑斗比赛,而且除非其地基的坚固程度已经经过了严格的试验确证,不得在上面建筑半圆形剧场。阿提里乌斯受到了放逐的处分。在惨祸发生之后,罗马的显赫家族立即全部打开了大门,他们倾其所有地为周围各处的人提供医疗用品和所需的物资。在那些日子里,罗马的景象尽管十分凄惨,但是却令人联想到了我们祖先的做法,他们过去在大规模战争之后,对于负伤者总是慷慨地赠送礼物并给予热情关注的。

在人们对这次灾祸还仍然记忆犹新的时候,罗马城又遭到了一场非同寻常的造成了极大破坏的大火,整个凯利乌斯山都被烧光了。人们议论说,这一年是个灾难年,人们总喜欢为偶然发生的事件找一个替罪羊(就像群众经常会做的那样),于是他们将皇帝离开罗马的决定视为是罪恶的征兆。为了消除人们对他的指责,提贝里乌斯按照人们所遭受到的不同损失发放了抚恤金。这种行为为他赢得了普遍的赞誉,显贵们在元老院里对他表示感谢;当这个消息传开以后,普通的人民群众也充满了感激之情。因为这次的赠赐是无需任何显贵或亲属的请托的,甚至有些受害者只是受到皇帝的感召而前来请求,他们与皇帝素不相识,但依然得到了皇帝的慷慨赠赐。还有人建议今后应将凯利乌斯山改称为奥古斯都山,因为当火焰在四面八方飞舞的时候,只有一件东西没有受到损伤,那就是在元老尤尼乌斯家中的一座提贝里乌斯的胸像。据人们说,同样的事情过去也曾经发生在克劳狄娅·克温妲身上。她的胸像,曾经两次逃脱了火灾的厄运,我们的祖先就把它奉献在诸神之母的神庙中。克劳狄乌斯家族是神圣的、是

spicuously favoured the emperor should be accorded increased veneration.

It may be appropriate to record here that the hill was originally called Oak Hill because of its dense growth of oak trees, and was later named 'Caelian' after Caeles Vibenna, an Etruscan chief who, for helping Rome, had been granted the hill as a residence by Tarquinius Priscus- or another king; here writers disagree. But there is no doubt about the extensive Etruscan settlement, which also comprised the flat ground near the Forum; it was after these immigrants that the Tuscan Street was given its name.

Accidents, then, were alleviated by leading men's public spirit and the emperor's generosity. But there was no alleviation of the accusers, who became more formidable and vicious every day. Quinctilius Varus, a wealthy relation of Tiberius, was accused by Cnaeus Domitius Afer who had secured his mother Claudia Pulchra's condemnation. After long poverty Afer had made money and misused it, and it surprised no one that he now had further infamous designs. But it was remarkable that his partner in the prosecution was Publius Cornelius Dolabella (I), an aristocrat and Varus' relative—setting out to ruin his own class and blood. However, the senate sought their only tem-

上天特别惠佑的,因而对于诸神如此特别惠顾皇帝的地方,相应的也就应当特别加以崇敬。

在这里也许应该记述一下这样一个事件,那就是,这座山在先前由于生长着密集的橡树而被称为"橡树山",后来,因埃特路里亚的一个名叫凯列斯·维本纳的首领而得名为凯利乌斯山。维本纳由于帮助过罗马而从塔尔克维尼乌斯·普利斯库斯或者是从另一位国王那里取得了这个地方作为定居地,也有的作家不同意这种说法。但是关于埃特路里亚人其余的广阔的居住地却是无可怀疑的:维本纳的人数众多的军队也曾定居在罗马广场附近平坦的平原地带,而且图司库斯街的名称就是根据这些移民而命名的。

但是,当事故所造成的损失,由于贵族们表示的大公无私的精神和皇帝的慷慨而得以减轻的时候,那变得越来越猖獗、越有危害的告密者的活动,却丝毫也没有减弱。克温克提里乌斯·伐鲁斯,[1]提贝里乌斯的一个富有的亲戚,也受到了那个招致自己的母亲克劳狄娅·普尔克拉被判了罪的格涅乌斯·多米提乌斯·阿菲尔的控告。在多年的贫困之后,阿菲尔因告密获得了不少的赏金,但随即又挥霍浪费了。因此,现在,看到阿菲尔又在准备新的罪恶计划,人们也就不感到惊讶了。不过令人吃惊的却是,普布里乌斯·科尔涅里乌斯·多拉贝拉(一世)却和他成了一同控告的伙伴。他是一名贵族,又是伐鲁斯的亲戚,这样一来,他就开始诋毁自己的高贵身份和血统了。元老院以须等待皇帝回来做出裁决为借口,对他们的控告采取了抵制。他们也只能以这样的办法来

---

〔1〕 奥古斯都的一位统帅的儿子,曾一度同日耳曼尼库斯的女儿订婚。

porary escape from tragedy by opposing action pending the emperor's return.

Tiberius was dedicating the temples in Campania. He issued an edict forbidding the disturbance of his privacy, and troops were posted in the towns to prevent crowds. He detested these towns, and indeed the whole mainland. So he took refuge on the island of Capreae, separated from the tip of the Surrentum promontory by three miles of sea. Presumably what attracted him was the isolation of Capreae. Harbourless, it has few roadsteads even for small vessels; sentries can control all landings. In winter the climate is mild, since hills on the mainland keep off gales. In summer the island is delightful, since it faces west and has open sea all round. The bay it overlooks was exceptionally lovely, until Vesuvius' eruption transformed the landscape. This was an area of Greek colonization, and tradition records that Capreae had been occupied by the Teleboi.

On this island then, in twelve spacious, separately named villas, Tiberius took up residence. His former absorption in State affairs ended. Instead he spent the time in secret orgies, or idle malevolent thoughts. But his abnormally credulous suspicions were unabated. Sejanus, who had encouraged them even at Rome, whipped them up,

暂时逃避一下迫在眉睫的恐怖。

提贝里乌斯在康帕尼亚奉献了一些神庙。他曾发布敕令,不许人们打搅他的私生活,并且把军队配置在各自的自治市,以阻挡大群前来拜会的人们。他十分讨厌那些自治市,实际上是陆地上的一切,因此他才躲避到卡普利埃岛[1]上来,这个小岛以3英里宽的一道海峡同苏尔伦图姆海角[2]相隔。可以推知,卡普利埃岛这个地方对提贝里乌斯的吸引力,主要是因为它的偏僻。四周没有一个海港,甚至连停泊小船的一些临时碰泊处也很少,但哨兵在上面对于整个陆地的情况却可以一览无余。冬天,气候温和,因为陆地上的山脉把冷风都挡住了。夏天,岛上则风光宜人,因为柔和的西风拂面吹来,四周又全是辽阔的大海。它所面临的海湾极其美丽可爱,但是后来维苏威火山的爆发改变了这一优美的景色。[3]康帕尼亚曾经是希腊人的一块殖民地,据传统记载,卡普利埃被提列波伊斯人占据着。

提贝里乌斯住在这里时,卡普利埃岛上有12座雄伟广大的别墅,每个别墅都有它自己的名字。提贝里乌斯过去专心于国事的生活结束了,取而代之的是天天沉溺于秘密的荒淫享乐的私生活和满脑子无聊的恶毒思想。但是,提贝里乌斯那种疑心极大而又轻信人言的特点,却丝毫没有减轻。谢雅努斯在罗马的时候就不断刺激、煽动他的这种疑心,现在则进一步扰乱他的头脑。现

---

[1] 公元前29年奥古斯都用伊司奇亚从那不勒斯换来了这个岛,从此它就成了皇帝的私产。

[2] 今天的索伦托。

[3] 指公元79年的那次大喷火,在这次火山爆发中,庞培城和赫尔库拉涅乌姆城全部毁灭。

and now openly disclosed his designs against Agrippina and Nero Caesar. Soldiers attached to them reported with a historian's precision their correspondence, visitors, and doings private and public. Agents incited them to flee to the German armies, or-in the Forum at its peak hour-to grasp the divine Augustus' statue, and appeal to senate and public. They dismissed such projects: but were accused of them.

The next year, in which the consuls were Gaius Appius Junius Silanus and Publius Silius Nerva, began deplorably. A distinguished knight called Titius Sabinus was dragged to gaol because he had been Germanicus' friend. Sabinus had maintained every attention to Germanicus' widow and children, visiting their home, escorting them in public-of their crowds of followers he was the only survivor. Decent men respected this, but spiteful people hated him. His downfall was planned by four ex-praetors ambitious for the consulship, Lucanius Latiaris, Marcus Porcius Cato, Petilius Rufus and Marcus Opsius. For the only access to this lay through Sejanus; and only crimes secured Sejanus' goodwill.

The four arranged that, with the others present as witnesses, one of them, Lucanius Latiaris (who knew Sabinus slightly), should trap him with a view to prosecution. So Latiaris after some casual remarks com-

在,谢雅努斯公然表示出了他反对阿格里披娜和尼禄·恺撒的阴谋。紧跟着他们的士兵们,用编年史家那样准确的记录记下了他们的来往信件、拜访者、他们公开的和秘密的行动,将这些情况报告给谢雅努斯。谢雅努斯的那些密探甚至诱劝他们到日耳曼的军队中去避难,或者是在罗马广场,乘人最多的时候,抱住圣奥古斯都的胸像,向元老院和人民请求帮助。他们拒绝了这样的建议,但他们仍然以这样的罪名被控告。

下一年,[1]在这个盖乌斯·阿披乌斯·尤尼乌斯·西拉努斯和普布里乌斯·西里乌斯·涅尔瓦担任执政官的一年里,一开始就发生了一件可耻的事情。一位名叫提提乌斯·撒比努斯的著名的罗马骑士,被拖进了牢狱,就因为他是日耳曼尼库斯的朋友。撒比努斯对日耳曼尼库斯的未亡人和孩子们一直非常关心,他照旧到他们家里去,在公开的场合护卫着他们。在他们过去的一大群追随者中,撒比努斯是唯一一个依然故我地对待他们的人。他的这种做法,使正直的人给予他尊敬,而那些卑鄙小人则对他心生忌恨。他是被四个曾担任过行政长官而又热切追求执政官职位的人选中为陷害对象的:这四个人是鲁卡尼乌斯·拉提亚里斯、玛尔库斯·波尔奇乌斯·加图、佩提里乌斯·路福斯和玛尔库斯·奥普西乌斯。因为只有通过谢雅努斯,他们才能获得执政官的职位,而只有通过罪恶手段,他们才能博得谢雅努斯的好感。

他们四个人计划,由鲁卡尼乌斯·拉提亚里斯(同撒比努斯比较熟悉)设圈套,制造一个可以提出指控的证据,其他三人则出面作证。因此,拉提亚里斯就去接近撒比努斯。在同撒比努斯谈

---

〔1〕 公元28年,罗马建城781年。

plimented Sabinus on his unshaken adherence, in its misfortunes, to the family he had supported in its prosperty-and he commented respecfully about Germanicus, sympathetically about Agrippina. Sabinus burst into tearful complaints; for misery is demoralizing. Latiaris then openly attacked Sejanus as cruel, domineering, and ambitious-and did not even spare Tiberius. These exchanges of forbidden confidences seemed to cement a close friendship. So now Sabinus sought out Latiaris' company, frequenting his house and unburdening his sorrows to this outwardly reliable companion.

The four partners next considered how to make these conversations available to a larger audience. The meeting-place had to appear private. Even if they stood behind the doors, they risked being seen or heard or detected by some suspicious whim. So in between roof and ceiling they crammed three Roman senators. In this hiding-place-as undignified as the trick was despicable—they applied their ears to chinks and holes. Meanwhile Latiaris had found Sabinus out of doors and, pretending to have fresh news to report, escorted him home to Sabinus' bedroom. There Latiaris dwelt on the unfailing subject of past and present distresses, introducing some fresh terrors too. Sabinus embroidered at greater length on the same theme: once grievances find expression, there is no silencing them. Acting rapidly, the accusers

话时,他先是随便谈了几句,然后就称赞撒比努斯,说在这个家族繁荣的时候,他支持他们,而在这个家族遭遇不幸的时候,他依然毫不动摇地站在他们这一边。与此同时,拉提亚里斯还十分尊敬地谈到了日耳曼尼库斯,又带着同情的语气谈到了阿格里披娜。撒比努斯于是就一面哭一面抱怨,因为有过悲惨经历的人情绪是很低落的。看到这种情况,拉提亚里斯就开始公然攻击起谢雅努斯来,他责骂他残酷、狂妄、野心勃勃,甚至把提贝里乌斯也没有放在眼里。对内心深处不敢表露的信任的这样一种交流,看起来像是更加牢固地加强了他们之间亲密的友谊。于是,自此以后,撒比努斯就主动去和拉提亚里斯交朋友,他常常到他家里去,把自己心里的痛苦倾诉给这个外表看来好像是非常值得信赖的朋友。

这四个同伙又考虑下一步该用什么办法使更多的人听到这些谈话了。约会的地点必须是一个隐秘的私人住的地方。而且,如果他们站在门后面的话,他们也会有被人看见、被人听到,或是引起别人怀疑的危险。于是这三个元老就钻到天花板和屋顶中间的空隙里面去,就如同他们卑鄙的阴谋一样,把耳朵贴在裂口和有空隙的地方偷听。同时,拉提亚里斯也在街上找到了走出家门的撒比努斯。拉提亚里斯以刚刚得到了新消息要告诉撒比努斯为借口,匆匆忙忙地拉着他回了家,直接就进了撒比努斯的卧室。在这里,拉提亚里斯把过去成功蒙骗了撒比努斯的老话重述了一遍,又详细叙述了现在所遭到的痛苦,还把新近发生的恐怖事件也活灵活现地描述了一番。撒比努斯于是就同一个话题打开了话匣子,更详尽、更具体地说了起来。一个人内心的痛苦一旦找到了发泄的渠道,他的宣泄就难

wrote to Tiberius and disclosed the history of the trap and their own deplorable role. At Rome there was unprecedented agitation and terror. People behaved secretively even to their intimates, avoiding encounters and conversation, shunning the ears both of friends and strangers. Even voiceless, inanimate objects—ceilings and walls-were scanned suspiciously.

In a letter read in the senate on January 1st Tiberius, after the customary New Year formalities, rounded upon Sabinus, alleging that he had tampered with certain of the emperor's ex-slaves and plotted against his life. The letter unequivocally demanded retribution. This was hastily decreed. The condemned man was dragged away, crying (as loudly as the cloak muffling his mouth and the noose round his neck allowed) that this was a fine New Year ceremony—this year's sacrifice was to Sejanus! But wherever his eye rested or his words carried, there was a stampede: all roads and public places were evacuated and deserted. Some, however, reappeared and showed themselves again-alarmed because they had displayed alarm. For it seemed that no day would be free of convictions when, at a season in which custom forbade even an ominous word, sacrifices and prayers were attended by manacles and nooses. Tiberius had incurred this indignation deliberately, people said—it was a purposeful, premeditated action to show that the newly elected officials who opened the religious year could also open the death-cells.

以抑制了。告密者于是立刻迅速行动起来,他们给提贝里乌斯写了一封信,信中陈述了他们安排这一阴谋的详细经过以及他们在其中所担任的可耻角色。这一事件在罗马引起了前所未有的骚乱和恐惧,人们对自己最亲近的人都谨言慎行,严格保密。亲友或者陌生人之间也都尽量回避,不在一起交谈,因为他们同样害怕别人的耳朵的窃听。即使是没有声音、没有生命的东西,诸如天花板和墙壁,也都被投以怀疑的目光。

1月1日元旦,在元老院宣读的一封信里,提贝里乌斯在例行的新年祝福之后,便转到了撒比努斯身上。皇帝指控他贿赂过自己的几名被释奴隶,并且还阴谋伤害他的生命。这封信以不容商量的口吻要求给予撒比努斯严厉的处罚。于是,元老院立刻发布命令进行处罚。这个被判罪的人被拉出去处死(尽管罩布蒙住了他的嘴巴和鼻子,而绞索又套在他的脖子上),他用尽力量呼喊说,这是一个多么好的新年的庆祝仪式,这种新年的牺牲就是奉献给谢雅努斯来讨他的欢心的!然而不管他向着哪个方向看,不管他的话讲给什么人听,面前出现的只是一个人群轰然而散的场面,人们都逃离了街道和广场,所到之处空无一人。然而却也有人重新走了出来,他们因为刚刚表现出的惊恐情绪而更加感到惴惴不安。世界上没有哪一天是可以免除死罪的,因为在一个按风俗习惯,甚至是连一句不吉利的话也不许讲的日子里,在祭祀和祈祷之际,都可以给人戴上镣铐和绞索!人们认为,提贝里乌斯完全是有意招致这样不光彩的事情的,因为这是一次有目的的、事先经过周密计划的行动,目的是向人们昭示,新当选的高级官吏在新年伊始这样一种宗教性的庆典中,也会毫无顾忌地打开死亡之牢的。

The emperor wrote again, thanking the senate for punishing a public danger, and adding that he had grave anxieties and reasons to suspect disaffected persons of plotting. He mentioned no names. But Nero Caesar and Agrippina were undoubtedly meant. If I did not propose to record each event under its own year, I should have liked to anticipate and recount immediately the fates of the four criminal plotters against Sabinus—partly in the reign of Gaius, and partly also under Tiberius. For Tiberius, unwilling though he was for others to destroy his villainous agents, frequently wearied of them and, when new recruits became available, eliminated their distasteful predecessors. However, this punishment of guilty men, and other similar cases, I shall describe at the proper time.

Gaius Asinius Gallus, of whose children Agrippina was aunt, now proposed that the emperor should indicate his fears to the senate, and permit their removal. Now of all his self-ascribed virtues Tiberius cherished none more dearly than dissimulation. So he greatly disliked disclosing what he had suppressed. However Sejanus calmed him, not from affection for Gallus, but to let the emperor's hesitations take their course. For, as Sejanus knew, Tiberius reached decisions slowly, but once the outburst occurred there was a rapid transition from grim

　　随后,皇帝又写来了一封信,对元老院处决了一个危害国家的人表示感谢。他还说他自己充满了忧虑,而且也有理由怀疑那些不忠诚的人会策划杀害他的阴谋。虽然他并没有提起任何人的名字,但是毫无疑问,他的这些话指的是阿格里披娜和尼禄·恺撒。我并没有打算把这一年里的每一件事情都记载下来,但是我愿意预先谈一谈并且立刻记载下那四个陷害撒比努斯的罪恶的阴谋者的结局,这些内容一部分是在盖乌斯·恺撒即位以后的事,而一部分是提贝里乌斯生前的事情。提贝里乌斯虽然不愿意为了别人将替他行凶作恶的代理人毁掉,但是他本人对这些人却也常常会感到厌倦,因此当在这方面又有了新手可以利用的时候,他就将那些先前使他感到讨厌的人除掉了。但是,对于这些罪行累累的人所受到的惩罚以及其他诸如此类的事件,以后在适当的时候我还要提到的。

　　这时盖乌斯·阿西尼乌斯·伽路斯—阿格里披娜是他的孩子们的姨母,[1]对皇帝建议说,皇帝应该把他所害怕的事情告诉元老院,并且允许元老院去消除他的隐患。在颇为自诩的全部本领当中,提贝里乌斯自己最欣赏的莫过于他那作伪的本领,因此他特别讨厌别人把他自己深深压在心底的想法给抖搂出来。谢雅努斯使他的心情平静下来,但是并不是因为他喜爱伽路斯,而是为了让皇帝在反复考虑之后再做出自己的决定。因为谢雅努斯知道,提贝里乌斯要做出一个决定是需要很长一段时间的慢慢斟酌的,但是一旦他做出了决定,那么他那阴郁的言语就会立

---

　　〔1〕　伽路斯的妻子维普撒尼娅和阿格里披娜是同母姊妹。维普撒尼娅是提贝里乌斯的第一个妻子,她在同提贝里乌斯离婚之后就嫁给了伽路斯。

words to terrible action.

This was about the time when Julia (IV) died. Convicted of a-dultery, she had been condemned by her grandfather Augustus to banishment on the island of Trimerum off the Apulian coast. There she had endured exile for twenty years. The Augusta had helped her: after secretly ruining her step-daughter's family when they prospered, she openly showed pity for them in their ruin.

In this year, across the Rhine, the Frisian tribe broke the peace. The cause was Roman rapacity rather than Frisian insubordi-nation. Bearing their povety in mind, Nero Drusus had assessed their taxation leniently: ox-hides were requested, for military purposes. No one had stipulated their dimensions or quality until Olennius, a senior staffofficer who was in charge of them, interpreted the requirements as buffalo-hides. This demand, severe enough for any community, was particularly oppressive in Germany where, though the forests abound in huge beasts, domestic animals are small. So first the Frisians lost their cattle, next their lands, and finally their wives and children went into slavery. Distressful complaints produced no relief. So they resorted to war. Soldiers collecting the tax were gibbeted. Olennius anticipated the Frisians' angry intentions by taking refuge in a fort called Flevum,

刻转变成令人恐惧的行动的。

　　大约就在这个时候,优利娅(四世)[1]去世了。由于被指控犯了通奸罪,她曾经被她的外祖父奥古斯都判罪,流放到离开阿普里亚海岸的特利美路斯岛上去。她在那里忍受了20年的流放生活的痛苦,这期间,奥古斯塔却给予了她一些生活上的帮助:奥古斯塔在她的继女一家家境兴旺时暗中陷害他们,在将他们毁掉后却又故意公开表示对他们的怜悯。

　　就在这一年,莱茵河对岸的一个部族弗里喜人又挑起了战争。战争的原因是他们受不了罗马人的掠夺之苦,而不是由于他们的不驯服。由于他们国内的资源太贫乏,杜路苏斯对他们的税赋政策是非常宽大的,只不过是为了军队的需要,要求他们缴纳一些牛皮。过去任何人都不曾对牛皮的质量或尺寸做出过要求和规定,后来有一个名叫欧伦尼乌斯的高级百人团长负责管理他们,他指定要缴纳一种欧罗克野牛的皮。这种要求对于任何一个部落来说都是苛刻的,对于日耳曼压力就更大了,因为在那里的森林中虽然有许多巨大的野兽,但驯养的牲畜却都是很小的。因此,弗里喜人开始时是失去了他们的牲畜,随后又失去了他们的土地,最后连他们的妻子和儿女也遭到了奴役。他们痛苦的抱怨并没有使他们的处境得到丝毫改善,于是他们便诉诸武力。前来征收税物的士兵们被吊在绞刑台上绞死了,而欧伦尼乌斯早就预感到了弗里喜人的愤怒会使他们做出什么样的打算,因而事先逃到了一个叫做佛列乌姆的要塞去,在那里有相当大的

──────────

　　〔1〕　她是玛尔库斯·维普撒尼乌斯·阿格里帕和老优利娅的女儿,因此是阿格里披娜的姊妹。

where a considerable concentration of Roman and auxiliary troops guarded the North Sea coast.

When Lucius Apronius, imperial governor of Lower Germany, heard the news, he summoned detachments from Roman brigades in Upper Germany, together with picked auxiliary horse and foot, and brought the combined force down the Rhine against the Frisians. Finding the siege of Flevum raised, and the rebels gone to defend their own property, he constructed causeways and bridges across the adjacent coastal marshes for the transportation of his heavy columns. A ford was discovered; and German cavalry belonging to the tribe of the Canninefates, together with such of their auxiliary infantry as was serving with us, were ordered to take the enemy in the rear. The Frisians however, in battle-formation, repulsed our cavalry—and also regular cavalry dispatched in support. Then Apronius sent in three of the infantry battalions from Germany, followed by two more, and finally (after an interval) the main auxiliary cavalry. If they had attacked simultaneously, this would have been sufficient strength. But, arriving piecemeal, they failed to rally the disorganized horsemen. Indeed, the reinforcements themselves became involved in the panic-stricken retreat.

Then Apronius put the remaining auxiliaries under Cethegus Labeo, commander of the fifth division. Labeo, seriously endangered by his men's plight, sent messengers urgently requesting extensive regular reinforcements. But his men rushed forward ahead of the rest, drove back the enemy after a vigorous fight, and rescued the wounded and exhausted cavalry and infantry. The Roman general did not

一支罗马的军事力量，还有一支行省的辅助部队，这些士兵们在守卫着北海的海岸。

下日耳曼的长官路奇乌斯·阿普洛尼乌斯听到了这个消息，便把上日耳曼军团的几个小队，还有精锐的辅助步兵部队和骑兵部队都召了来，并且带领这支联合部队沿着莱茵河下行，去对付弗里喜人。看到包围佛列乌姆的军队已经撤走了，叛变的弗里喜人离开这里前去保卫他们自己的财产去了，路奇乌斯·阿普洛尼乌斯于是穿过附近的河口地区，修建了堤路，构筑了桥梁，为大军的通行做好充分的准备。这时人们发现了一个渡口，于是他就下令属于坎宁尼法提斯人的日耳曼骑兵部队，连同在我们的军队中服役的日耳曼辅助步兵去攻打敌人的后方。这时，已经列好了战阵的弗里喜人击退了辅助骑兵部队，而且又击退了前去增援的正规军团骑兵部队。路奇乌斯·阿普洛尼乌斯于是就派出了三个日耳曼步兵中队，随后又派出了两个，最后，（在间隔了不久之后）又把辅助骑兵部队的主力也派了上去。如果让这些军队同时向敌人发起进攻的话，那它们的力量的确是非常强大。但是，这样分期分批地派出，不但不能重整秩序已经混乱的军队，而且连这些援军也反而被卷到仓皇退却的士兵洪流里去了。

于是阿普洛尼乌斯便把第五军团的副帅凯提古斯·拉贝欧统率之下的最后一批辅助军队也派了出去。看到自己这方面的军队情况十分危急，拉贝欧便派出使节去紧急要求增援大批正规军队。拉贝欧的士兵们勇往直前地冲在其他军队的前面，在一次激烈的战斗中他们打退了敌人，并且**挽救**了那些伤亡惨重、筋疲力尽的步兵中队和骑兵中队。尽管许多著名的军团

attempt retaliation, or bury his dead, although many regular and auxiliary colonels and senior company-commanders were killed. Later deserters reported that nine hundred Romans who had prolonged the battle till next day had been slaughtered in the Baduhenna wood, while
another body four hundred strong had occupied the villa of an ex-sol-
dier of ours named Cruptorix, but fearing treachery had killed each
other. Germany glorified the Frisians for these doings. However,
rather than appoint a commander for the war, Tiberius suppressed the
losses.

The senate, too, had more pressing concerns than a frontier setback. Metropolitan terrors were what preoccupied them. From these
they sought relief in flattery. Though assembled to consider some unrelated business, they voted the erection of altars to Mercy and
Friendship the latter to be flanked by statues of Tiberius and Sejanus.
The senate also repeatedly begged them to vouchsafe a view of themselves. But neither came into Rome, or near it. They thought it sufficient to leave their island and show themselves on the Campanian
coast opposite. There flocked senators and knights and large crowds of
ordinary people-anxiously regarding Sejanus.

Access to him was harder now. It was only procurable by intrigue
and complicity. His arrogance obviously battened on the sight of this
blatant subservience. At Rome people circulate, and the city's size
conceals the purposes of their errands. But there in Campania, huddled

将领、指挥官和百人团长都阵亡了，可是罗马统帅并没有打算报复，也没有掩埋那些阵亡者。不久之后，逃出来的人们传说道，一直坚持战斗到第二天的 900 名罗马士兵，在巴杜痕那树林里被屠杀了。同时，另一支四百多人的队伍占领了一个名字叫克鲁普托里克斯的士兵的别墅，这个士兵曾在我们的军队中服过役，但是后来这些士兵却由于害怕被出卖而自相残杀了。弗里喜人由于这些行动的成功，因而在日耳曼取得了荣誉。而我们这方面，提贝里乌斯不但没有委派任何人去指挥这场战争，而且还将我方遭受重大损失的消息给严密封锁了起来。

元老院这时也正在为另一些比帝国在边境受挫更加迫切的事情焦虑着，弥漫全国的惊恐情绪侵蚀着每一个人，因此，他们也正在极尽阿谀谄媚之能事以求摆脱这种恐怖情绪。尽管元老们集会讨论的是一些互不相关的事情，但他们却提议为仁慈和友谊修建祭坛，而且在友谊祭坛的每一面都有恺撒和谢雅努斯的像，他们还反复地请求他们两人答应和他们见面的许诺。但是，他们两个人谁也没有来到罗马或是罗马的附近，因为在他们看来，离开他们居住的小岛，并且出现在康帕尼亚离岛最近的海岸上，让他们看一下就足够了。一群元老和骑士，以及大批的人民群众蜂拥而至，他们来到康帕尼亚，急不可待地想见一见谢雅努斯。

现在要想接近谢雅努斯更加困难了。只有通过阴谋和与他进行同谋共犯的罪恶勾当的人才能见到他。看到人们竞相表示出来的这种令人作呕的奴才相，他的傲慢之态也很明显地大大增长起来。在罗马，大家对此已经习以为常，而且在规模如此巨大的罗马城市，那些熙熙攘攘的信使来回穿梭的真正意图也被

indiscriminately on land and shore, men endured, day and night, the patronage and self-importance of his door-keepers. Finally they were denied even that, and returned to Rome. Anxiety gnawed those whom he had not deigned to address or see. Others were elated. But they were misguided, for their ill-omened friendship was soon to end disastrously.

Tiberius had personally entrusted his grandchild Agrippina (II) , daughter of Germanicus, to Cnaeus Domitius Ahenobarbus. Now the emperor ordered the marriage to be celebrated in the capital. His choice, Domitius, was a man of ancient family and a blood-relation of the Caesars; for his grandmother was Octavia, and Augustus his great-uncle.

In the following year, when Gaius Fufius Geminus and Lucius Rubellius Geminus were consuls, the aged Augusta died. By her own Claudian family, and her adoption into the Livii and Julii, she was of the highest nobility. Her first husband, and the father of her children, had been Tiberius Claudius Nero, who, after emigrating in the Perusian

掩盖了起来。但是在康帕尼亚,他们却乱糟糟地拥挤在陆地上或是海岸上,不分昼夜地奉承着谢雅努斯的门卫,忍受着他们神气十足的恩人面孔和傲慢之态。最后,他们甚至连这样的权力也被取消了,于是他们就回到了罗马。那些没能够屈尊去奉承他说话、恭维他脸色的人便害怕得战栗起来;而其他一些得以奉承的人则得意洋洋,但是他们受到的是误导,他们没有料到所得到的是一种不祥的友谊,而这种友谊不久就带来了灾难性的后果。

提贝里乌斯本人还把他的孙女阿格里披娜(二世),即日耳曼尼库斯的女儿嫁给了格涅乌斯·多米提乌斯·阿海诺巴尔布斯。现在,皇帝发出命令,婚礼要在首都罗马举行。他所选择的这个多米提乌斯不仅出生于一个古老的家族,而且和恺撒们有血统关系,因为他的外祖母是屋大维娅,而奥古斯都则是他的外舅祖父。

下一年,[1]盖乌斯·富斐乌斯·盖米努斯和路奇乌斯·路贝里乌斯·盖米努斯担任执政官,这一年,年迈的奥古斯塔去世。[2]因为奥古斯塔出生于克劳狄乌斯家族,并且又被过继到了里维乌斯和尤利乌斯家族中,所以她拥有着最高贵的身世。[3] 她的第一个丈夫是提贝里乌斯·克劳狄乌斯·尼禄,[4]并且她和他生过孩

---

〔1〕 公元 29 年,罗马建城 782 年。

〔2〕 死时 86 岁。

〔3〕 奥古斯塔的父亲是克劳狄乌斯家族中的一员,曾经被过继为在公元前 91 年进行改革的保民官,玛尔库斯·里维乌斯·杜路苏斯的继子,因此有了玛尔库斯·里维乌斯·杜路苏斯·克劳狄亚努斯的名字。奥古斯塔本人名字叫利维拉·杜路西拉,后来由于奥古斯都的遗嘱,被过继为尤利乌斯家族的一员并被加上了奥古斯塔的称号。

〔4〕 皇帝提贝里乌斯的父亲。

war, returned to Rome when peace was concluded between Sextus Pompeius (Ⅰ) and the Triumvirate. The future Augustus, fascinated by her beauty, removed her from him—with or without her encouragement—and hastily conducted her to his own home even before the baby she was expecting (the future Nero Drusus) was born. That was her last child. But her connection with Augustus through the marriage of her grandson Germanicus to his granddaughter Agrippina gave them great-grandchildren in common. Her private life was of traditional strictness. But her graciousness exceeded old-fashioned standards. She was a compliant wife, but an overbearing mother. Neither her husband's diplomacy nor her son's insincerity could outmanoeuvre her.

The implementation of her will was long delayed. At her modest funeral, the obituary speech was pronounced by her great-grandson Gaius, soon to be emperor. Tiberius did not interrupt his own selfindulgences for his mother's last rites, but wrote excusing himself and pleading important business. Moreover, when the senate decreed extensive honours to her memory, he curtailed them in the name of moderation, conceding only a few. Tiberius added that she was not

子。提贝里乌斯·克劳狄乌斯·尼禄在佩路西亚战争[1]时迁居到外地,直到塞克斯图斯·彭佩乌斯(一世)和三头之间缔结了和约,[2]他才返回了罗马。后来,奥古斯都因为迷恋于她的美丽,就把她从她的丈夫手里夺了过来。或者出于她的怂恿,也或者不是这个原因,甚至在她怀孕还没有分娩的时候(这个孩子就是尼禄·杜路苏斯),奥古斯都就迫不及待地把她接到自己家里来了。他是她最后的一个孩子,她和奥古斯都结婚后就没有再生育。不过后来,她的孙子日耳曼尼库斯和奥古斯都的外孙女阿格里披娜结了婚,这样一来就使她和奥古斯都有了共同的重孙,从而他们俩也就有了血统上的联系。她在私生活方面秉持着传统的严格习惯,但是她的宽厚仁慈却超过了旧式妇女的标准。她虽然是一个百依百顺的妻子,但却是一位蛮横专断的母亲。不管是丈夫的计谋,还是儿子的不诚实,都无法胜过她的机智聪明。

她的遗嘱长时期都没有得到遵照执行。在为她举行的简朴的葬仪中,致悼词的是她的重孙盖乌斯·恺撒,他在不久之后就做了皇帝。提贝里乌斯并没有因自己母亲最后的葬礼而暂时中止沉迷于荒淫的生活,他只是写了一封信,以有重要事务为借口为自己不能参加母亲的葬礼辩护。此外,当元老院决定给予奥古斯塔更多的哀荣的时候,提贝里乌斯还以要有节制为理由给予了大量的削减,他只是认可了他们很少的几项决定。另外,提贝里乌斯还补充规定,不要把她列为神明,因为奥古斯塔本人并

---

[1] 是屋大维和路奇乌斯·安托尼乌斯之间的战争,公元前40年,这一战争因佩路西亚城断粮投降而结束。

[2] 他们于公元前39年缔结了和约。

to be deified-she herself had not wished it.

The same letter contained strictures on ' female friendships '. This was an implied criticism of the consul Gaius Fufius Geminus, whom the Augusta's patronage had elevated. Fufius could attract women. Moreover, his sharp tongue had often ridiculed Tiberius with sarcastic jokes such as autocrats long remember.

Now began a time of sheer crushing tyranny. While the Augusta lived there was still a moderating influence, for Tiberius had retained a deep-rooted deference for his mother. Sejanus, too, had not ventured to outbid her parental authority. Now, however, the reins were thrown off, and they pressed ahead. A letter was sent to Rome denouncing Agrippina and Nero Caesar. It was read so soon after the Augusta's death that people believed it had arrived earlier and been suppressed by her.

Its wording was deliberately harsh. However, the youth was accused not of actual or intended rebellion but of homosexual indecency. Against his daughter-in-law Tiberius dared not invent similar charges, but attacked her insubordinate language and disobedient spirit. The senate listened in terrified silence. But opportunists can always turn national disasters to advantage, and finally a few men to whom integrity offered no incentives demanded that the question should be put. Marcus Aurelius Cotta Maximus Messallinus was ready enough with a savage proposal. Other leading men, especially officials, felt anxiety. For Tiberius, despite his savage strictures, left

不希望这样做。

在同一封信里,他还对"女人的友谊"进行了苛刻的评论。他这是间接地指责执政官盖乌斯·富斐乌斯·盖米尼乌斯,因为富斐乌斯就是仰仗着奥古斯塔的庇护才得到提拔的。富斐乌斯除了很有办法吸引女人之外,还有一副尖酸刻薄的伶牙俐齿,他常常用讽刺性的玩笑嘲弄提贝里乌斯,这些玩笑话久久地留在那些权要人物的记忆里。

现在,一个严酷而残暴的专制统治时期就这样开始了。当奥古斯塔在世的时候,她还能起到一些节制的作用,因为提贝里乌斯对他的母亲保持着一种根深蒂固的敬畏,谢雅努斯也不敢冒险去挑战她做母亲的威严。但是现在,这种约束得到了摆脱,他们可以为所欲为了。一封指责阿格里披娜和尼禄·恺撒的信被送到了罗马,在奥古斯塔死后不久,这封信就被公开宣读了,因此人们普遍认为,这封信是早就送到了罗马的,只不过之前被奥古斯塔压了下来。

他的话故意讲得十分严厉。不过皇帝对这个年轻人的指控并不是他有什么叛乱的行为,也不是有发动政变的阴谋,而是说他搞同性恋道德堕落。对于他的儿媳妇,提贝里乌斯不敢捏造相同的罪名,但是却斥责她出言不逊、脾气固执不驯顺。元老们非常惊恐地听着对这封信的宣读,一个个默不作声。但是,总会有一些野心家要以国家的灾难作为自己的晋身之阶的,最后几个毫无诚实可言的人竟然要求把这个问题提出来。玛尔库斯·奥列里乌斯·科塔·玛克西姆斯·美撒里努斯就做出了充分的准备来提出这种残暴的建议。但是其他显要人物,特别是那些高级官吏,却感到非常忧虑。因为提贝里乌斯尽管进行了野蛮

his intentions obscure.

One member of the senate, Junius Rusticus, had been chosen by Tiberius to keep its minutes and was believed to understand his secret thoughts. Rusticus had never shown courage before. But fate now impelled him. Or perhaps, in his anxiety about future uncertainties, misplaced cunning blinded him to immediate peril. For Rusticus, joining the hesitant senators, advised the consuls not to put the question. Vital issues depend on a touch, he said—the aged emperor might one day regret the elimination of Germanicus' family. Meanwhile, crowds with statues of Agrippina and Nero Caesar pressed round the senate-house. Cheering Tiberius, they cried that the letter was a fabrication-the emperor could not favour plots to destroy his family!

So on that day there were no tragic developments. Forged attacks on Sejanus circulated, their alleged authors ex-consuls-anonymity lent impudence to many imaginations. This infuriated Sejanus and gave him fresh material for his charges. The senate, he said, had scorned the emperor's distress, and the populace had been disloyal. Rebellious speeches and senatorial decrees were being heard and read. Next they would be seizing arms and hailing as leaders and commanders those whose statues they had followed like standards.

Tiberius again denounced his grandson and daughter-in-law. Then he reprimanded the Roman populace by edict. To the senate he expressed regrets that a single member's duplicity should have resulted in a public affront to the imperial majesty. However, he reserved the

的责骂，但他的真正意图是什么仍然是含糊不清楚的。

在元老院里有一个名叫尤尼乌斯·路斯提库斯的元老，他曾经被提贝里乌斯选拔出来担任修纂议事录的工作，因此大家相信他是明白皇帝一些内心的想法的。路斯提库斯先前从来没有表现出过自己的勇气，但是现在，命运使然，他竟毅然挺身而出。这或许是由于对未来难以捉摸的情况过于害怕，因而他那狡诈的小聪明才用错了地方，使他看不到迫在眉睫的危险。他竟然掺和到那些犹豫不决的元老们中间，劝执政官们不要提出这样的问题。他说，生死攸关的事情是发生在一念之间的。年老的皇帝也许有朝一日会后悔消灭日耳曼尼库斯一家的行动的。同时，人民群众也带着阿格里披娜和尼禄·恺撒的胸像把元老院议事厅围了起来。他们向提贝里乌斯呼吁，哭喊着说，这封信是伪造的，皇帝是绝不会赞同这种消灭自己的家族的阴谋的！

因此，在那一天里没有任何惨剧发生。外面还流传着伪造的对谢雅努斯的攻击，据说这种攻击的制造者是曾经担任过执政官的人们。因为攻击者都是匿名的，所以他们可以毫无顾忌地展开各种各样的想象。这种情况大大激怒了谢雅努斯，并且为他的控诉提供了新的材料。他说，元老院蔑视皇帝的痛苦，民众也已经不忠诚了。人们听到和读到了背叛性的言论和元老院背叛性的决定，下一步，他们就会拿起武器，紧紧追随那些他们把其胸像奉为旗帜的人，而这种人也就会被他们拥戴为统帅和皇帝了。

提贝里乌斯再一次斥责了他的孙子和儿媳妇，然后又发布敕令谴责罗马人民。对于元老院，他表示了这样的遗憾：只是一位元老的不忠诚，就导致了全国人民都蔑视皇帝的尊严的恶果。尽管如此，他还是要求把全部问题都留给他本人来处理。元

entire matter for his own decision. Without further discussion the senate proceeded, not to death sentences (these had been forbidden them), but to protestations that only the emperor's command was restraining their eagerness for vengeance.

[*There is now a gap of two years in our manuscript of Tacitus. First Agrippina, Nero Caesar, and Drusus Caesar are exiled; and Nero Caesar dies. Then Tiberius, believing Sejanus himself (now consul) guilty of conspiracy, has him arrested in the senate and executed. Sejanus' divorced wife Apicata now reveals to Tiberius that his own son Drusus had been poisoned by Sejanus and Livilla; and Livilla too is killed or kills herself.*]

老院没有就这个问题做更进一步的讨论,也没有做出死刑的判决(因为这样的手段对他们来说是受到禁止的),但这表明他们是热切希望对这件事进行报复的,只是由于皇帝的命令,才抑制了他们的这种愿望。

〔在我们所掌握的塔西佗的原稿中,这里中间两年所发生的事件的一些材料都佚失了。首先是阿格里帕、尼禄·恺撒和杜路苏斯·恺撒被流放;尼禄·恺撒去世。接下来是提贝里乌斯与谢雅努斯担任执政官,这期间,提贝里乌斯证实了正是谢雅努斯本人才是阴谋反叛的共谋者,于是提贝里乌斯在元老院将谢雅努斯逮捕并处死。与谢雅努斯离婚的妻子阿皮卡塔向提贝里乌斯揭露了他自己的儿子杜路苏斯被谢雅努斯和利维拉毒死的真相;利维拉也被处死,或者是自杀。〕

CHAPTER 8

The Reign Of Terror

Forty-Four speeches were delivered about the punishment of Livilla. A few were prompted by anxiety, most by routine servility. But a
partisan of Sejanus defended himself. ' That Sejanus should be disgraced,' he said, ' and my friendship with him become shameful,
did not cross my mind. Destinies are reversed! The man who called
Sejanus his colleague and son-in-law pardons himself. Everyone else
proceeds from humiliating sycophancy to outrageous abuse. Which is
the more lamentable, to accuse a friend or to be accused because of
him? I do not know! I shall not test whether anybody is cruel or merciful. A free man, undisturbed in conscience, I shall forestall my destruction. Remember me, please, happily, not sorrowfully. Add my
name to those who have honourably withdrawn themselves from the
harrowing national scene. '

He spent part of the day with his friends. If they wished to stay and
talk, he let them. When they left, he bade them farewell. Then, while

第八章　恐怖统治

关于对利维拉的处理[1]这一问题,大家发表了 44 篇演说,其中少数几篇是由于内心的忧虑使然,大多数则是出于惯于阿谀奉承的奴性。但是,谢雅努斯的一个同伙为自己辩护说:"我明白,谢雅努斯是可耻的,我与他的友情也是令人感到耻辱的。时运翻转,那个称谢雅努斯为同僚和女婿的人,[2]自己却将责任推卸得一干二净。其余的那些过去曾经恬不知耻地对他大加谄媚的人,现在却摇身一变,反过来对他进行无情的谩骂和诽谤。我不知道,指控一个朋友或者是为了与他的友谊而受人指控,这二者哪一种情况更可悲? 我不愿意试验任何人看他是残酷还是仁慈,作为一个意识没有被扰乱的自由人,我预感到了自己的毁灭。请你们在想起我的时候要高兴,不要难过。请把我的名字加到那些以自己光荣的死亡而使国家摆脱痛苦的人们中间去吧。"

白天,他一部分时间和朋友们待在一起。如果他们愿意,他就让他们留下来,和他们交谈。当他们离开的时候,他就和他们

---

〔1〕　公元 31 年,罗马建城 784 年。

〔2〕　公元 31 年,谢雅努斯和提贝里乌斯共同担任执政官。提贝里乌斯曾打算让谢雅努斯和杜路苏斯的女儿优利娅·利维拉订婚而成为自己的孙女婿,而不是这里所说的女婿。

many still remained, gazing on his unperturbed features and not knowing the end was near, he drew a sword concealed in his clothing and fell upon it. Tiberius did not assail the dead man with the slanders and insults with which he had so savagely attacked Sejanus' uncle, Quintus Junius Blaesus.

Next came the cases of Publius Vitellius and Publius Pomponius Secundus. The former was charged with offering the keys of the Treasury (of which he was controller) and Military Treasury for seditious projects. Pomponius was accused by the former praetor Considius of friendship with Aelius Gallus who had sheltered in his garden, as the safest hiding-place, after Sejanus' execution. The only support of Vitellius and Pomponius in this predicament was the fearlessness of their brothers, who went bail for them. But after numerous adjournments Publius Vitellius found his hopes and fears unendurable. Requesting a pen-knife (he wanted to write, he said) he put an end to his distress by a slight incision of his veins. Pomponius, however—a distinguished, high-principled intellectual—patiently endured misfortune, and outlived Tiberius.

The general rage against Sejanus was now subsiding, appeased by the executions already carried out. Yet retribution was now decreed against his remaining children. They were taken to prison. The boy

道以永别。当还留在那里的人们望着他那刚毅不屈的表情,还没有意识到死亡就要来临的时候,他却抽出了他藏在衣服里面的一把刀自杀了。提贝里乌斯并没有对死者进行侮辱和诽谤性的攻击,但是对谢雅努斯的叔叔克温图斯·尤尼乌斯·布莱苏斯他却做出了十分猛烈的攻击。[1]

随后,又讨论普布里乌斯·维提里乌斯和普布里乌斯·彭波尼乌斯·谢孔都斯的问题。普布里乌斯·维提里乌斯被人控告说,他曾经把国库的钥匙(他负责看管)以及军用库的钥匙交出来帮助叛逆者。彭波尼乌斯则受到前任行政长官孔西狄乌斯的控诉,他说彭波尼乌斯·谢孔都斯和埃里乌斯·伽路斯[2]有着深厚的交情,在谢雅努斯被处决之后,伽路斯曾躲藏在谢孔都斯的花园里,把它当做他最安全的避难所。在这种危险的时刻,对维提里乌斯和彭波尼乌斯他们两个人的唯一的支持,就是他们大无畏的兄弟,他们出面为他们做出了坚定的保证。后来,他们的案件一拖再拖,普布里乌斯·维提里乌斯感到再也承受不了希望与恐惧的折磨了,他请人给他一把修笔的小刀子(他说他想写些东西),他用这把小刀轻轻割断了自己的动脉,从而结束了自己痛苦的生命。但是,杰出的、才华出众的彭波尼乌斯却以坚忍的耐力忍受着自己的不幸命运,结果活的时间比提贝里乌斯还要长。

人民群众对谢雅努斯的愤怒现在正在平息下去,已经做出的一批处决也使大部分人的情绪都得到了缓和,但对谢雅努斯还活着的子女还是做出了处罚的决定,他们被带进了监狱。那个男孩

---

[1] 谢雅努斯的叔父,也被处死了。

[2] 此人很可能是谢雅努斯的长子。

understood what lay ahead of him. But the girl uncomprehendingly repeated: 'What have I done? Where are you taking me? I will not do it again!' She could be punished with a beating, she said, like other children. Contemporary writers report that, because capital punishment of a virgin was unprecedented, she was violated by the executioner, with the noose beside her. Then both were strangled, and their young bodies thrown on to the Gemonian Steps.

At this juncture Asia and Achaia were alarmed by a short-lived but vigorous rumour that Drusus Caesar, Germanicus' son, had been seen in the Cyclades archipelago, and then on the mainland. It was really a youth of similar age whom certain of the emperor's former slaves had seditiously pretended to recognize. Joining him, they collected an ignorant following, attracted by the great name and their Greek taste for novelties and marvels. The story was invented-and instantly believed-that he had escaped from prison and was making for his father's armies, to invade Egypt or Syria. Surrounded by young supporters and enthusiastic crowds, he was delighted with his progress and over-optimistic. The matter was now reported to Gaius Poppaeus Sabinus, imperial governor of Macedonia and also Achaia. Determined to nip the story in the bud-whether it was true or false-he moved rapidly. Hastening past the gulfs of Torone and Thermae, the island of Euboea in the Aegean, and Piraeus in Attica, then landing on the isthmus of Corinth and crossing it, he moved into the Ionian Sea, and proceeded to the Roman colony of Actium near Nicopolis. There

知道摆在他面前的将会是怎样的命运，但是那个女孩子一点也不能理解，她反复问："我到底做错了什么事？你们要把我带到什么地方去？放了我吧，我再也不会做错事了！"而且她还哀求道，她可以像其他孩子那样忍受责打的惩罚的。据当时作家的记载，因为把一个处女判处极刑是前所未闻的事情，因此在绞索旁边，刽子手就将她奸污了。这两个孩子都被绞死了，他们年轻的尸体就被抛弃在盖莫尼埃台阶上。

这时，就在亚细亚和阿凯亚相连接的地方，一个为时不久然而很有影响力的谣传使人们感到非常惊恐。谣言说，有人看见日耳曼尼库斯的儿子杜路苏斯·恺撒出现在基克拉季斯岛，不久之后又出现在了大陆上。实际上，这个人只是一个和杜路苏斯年龄相仿佛的年轻人，但是皇帝以前的一些奴隶别有用心地假称认出他就是杜路苏斯。他们和他一起，依靠杜路苏斯很高的名气，并利用希腊人对新奇事物特别感兴趣的特点，将一群不明真相的人召集在了一起。这个故事一经捏造出来，便立刻得到了人们的信任，他们说：杜路苏斯是从监狱中逃出来的，他直奔到他父亲的军队那里去，打算向埃及或叙利亚发动进攻。被年轻的追随者和热情的人群簇拥着，面对自己所取得的进展和过于乐观的前景，这个青年人兴高采烈。这时，这个消息传到了马其顿、也是阿凯亚的行政长官盖乌斯·波培乌斯·撒比努斯那里。于是，不管这个传闻是真是假，他决定，在它刚刚开始的萌芽时期，就立刻将这个传闻消除掉。他迅速动身起程，匆忙地穿过了托罗尼湾和提尔玛伊湾，穿过了爱琴海上的优卑亚岛，阿提卡岸上的披莱乌斯，然后又登上并穿过了科林斯的海岸和地峡而进入了爱奥尼亚海，之后，他又到了罗马的移民地尼科波利斯附近的

he learnt that skillful questioning about his identity had induced the impostor to describe himself as the son of Marcus Junius Silanus (I) ; and that after losing many of his adherents he had taken ship, ostensibly for Italy. Poppaeus reported this to Tiberius. But I have no further information about the incident, either in its early or its final phases.

At the end of the year, ill-feeling that had long been developing between the consuls found open expression. Lucius Fulcinius Trio, a quarrelsome lawyer, had implied criticism of Publius Memmius Regulus for slackness in suppressing Sejanus' partisans. Regulus, an unassuming man until provoked, not only refuted his colleague but proposed his investigation for complicity in the plot. Many senators begged them to drop this feud with its calamitous prospects. But they persisted in exchanging hostile threats until they went out of office.

When next year's consuls, Cnaeus Domitius Ahenobarbus and Lucius Arruntius Camillus Scribonianus, had assumed their functions, Tiberius crossed the channel between Capreae and Surrentum and coasted along Campania, undecided whether to enter Rome-or determined not to, and therefore pretending that he would. He made frequent landings near the city, and visited Caesar's Gardens on the Tiber. But then he regained his secluded sea-cliffs. For his criminal

埃克提乌姆。在那里,他获悉,当这个骗子被人巧妙地询问他的身份的时候,他被诱导说出了他是玛尔库斯·尤尼乌斯·西拉努斯(一世)的儿子。他还发现当这个人的许多追随者都溜掉了的时候,他便乘上了一条船,这只船表面上看起来是向意大利驶去的。波培乌斯于是将这些情况写信汇报给了提贝里乌斯。但是关于这一事件的起源和结果,我没有找到任何更进一步描述的材料。

这年年底,长期以来一直存在于两位执政官之间的不和终于找到了爆发口。一向喜欢争吵的法学家路奇乌斯·富尔奇尼乌斯·特里奥曾转弯抹角地责难普布里乌斯·美米乌斯·列古路斯,说他在镇压谢雅努斯的同党的问题上过于松懈。列古路斯,如果不受到挑衅的时候,是一个很谦逊的人,他不仅仅驳斥了他的同僚的攻击,而且还建议元老院对参加这一阴谋行动的共犯做出调查。许多元老都劝他们不要再争吵,向前看言归于好,以免惹起致命的灾祸,但是直到离任,他们两个人也依旧是相互敌视、威胁。

当下一年[1]的执政官,格涅乌斯·多米提乌斯·阿海诺巴尔布斯和路奇乌斯·阿伦提乌斯·卡米路斯·司克里波尼亚努斯就任的时候,提贝里乌斯已经渡过了卡普利埃岛和苏尔伦图姆之间的海峡,并且到达了康帕尼亚的沿岸地带。难以确定他是要进入罗马,还是由于他已经决定不到罗马来,而做出要到罗马来的样子。他经常在罗马附近的地方登陆,登临台伯河岸上皇帝的庭园,但是,随后他又返回了海上的孤岛。他对于自己罪恶的

---

[1] 公元 32 年,罗马建城 785 年。

lusts shamed him. Their uncontrollable activity was worthy of an oriental tyrant. Free-born children were his victims. He was fascinated by beauty, youthful innocence, and aristocratic birth. New names for types of perversion were invented. Slaves were charged to locate and procure his requirements. They rewarded compliance, overbore reluctance with menaces, and—if resisted by parents or relations—kidnapped their victims, and violated them on their own account. It was like the sack of a captured city.

As the year began at Rome, one might have thought Livilla's longpunished crimes newly discovered, so savage were the measures against even her statues and her memory. Sejanus' property was to be withdrawn from the Treasury and transferred to the emperor's personal estate—not that it made any difference. These motions were being pressed in identical or similar language by men with the grand names of Scipio, Silanus, Cassius, when suddenly Togonius Gallus inserted his undistinguished person among them. He proposed that the emperor should be urged to nominate senators from whom twenty should be chosen by lot to protect his life, armed, whenever he entered the senate-house. His speech caused laughter. Evidently he had taken literally Tiberius' request for a consul as bodyguard when he travelled from Capreae to Rome.

Tiberius, who liked to blend seriousness and humour, thanked the senators for their kindness. 'But who among you', he asked, 'are to be included in my bodyguard, and who excluded? Are they always to be the same, or will there be rotation? Will they be junior or senior

情欲感到非常羞愧,那些无法抑制的行为使得他就像一个东方的暴君那样。自由人家的孩子们成了他的淫欲的牺牲品,他不仅仅是迷恋年轻美丽的清纯,还迷恋高贵的出身,现在,人们还为这种性变态创造出了一些新名词。奴隶们按他的要求负责去给他搜索对象,如果对方顺利合作的话就给予赏赐,如果不情愿就以威胁相压服,并且如果遭到其父母或者是亲族的抗拒的话,那么就对这些孩子进行劫夺、强暴,完全不负任何责任,就好像对被攻占的城市进行洗劫一样。

但是年初的时候,在罗马,对利维拉早已受到惩处的罪行,好像是刚刚才被发现似的,甚至对她的胸像以及对有关她的纪念物,人们也都采取了十分粗暴的措施对待。谢雅努斯的财产将从国库中提出来,归到皇帝私人的财库——这二者之间并没有什么区别。这些建议得到了有着斯奇比奥、西拉努斯和卡西乌斯这样的显赫名字的人们的热烈赞同,他们以一致或是相似的发言敦促着此建议的执行。这时在他们中间,突然插入了托哥尼乌斯·伽路斯这样一个无名的小人物。他建议说,应该敦请皇帝任命一批元老,在他们中间,再用抽签的办法选出 20 人来,他们可以带着武器,在皇帝进入元老院时保护皇帝的安全。他的建议引起了人们的哄堂大笑。很显然,他正是相信了提贝里乌斯在信里提出的要求,提贝里乌斯说,当他从卡普利埃岛回到罗马的时候,请求一位执政官来做他的保镖。

虽然如此,喜欢把严肃和幽默混合在一起的提贝里乌斯仍然对元老们的好意表示了感谢。他问道:"但是,你们当中应当选哪些人、又不选哪些人来做我的贴身护卫呢? 选出来的那些人是一成不变呢,还是要轮流交替人选呢? 是选择年轻的、还是选择年

officials or private persons? And what a sight they will be, putting on their swords at the senate-house door! If my life needs arms to protect it, it does not seem to me worth having. ' As regards Togonius the emperor's reply was lenient, no request being made other than the cancellation of the proposal.

Junius Gallio, on the other hand, who had moved that ex-Guardsmen should be entitled to sit in the fourteen rows at the theatre reserved for the knights, was sternly reprimanded. What, wrote Tiberius-as if addressing him to his face—had Gallio to do with the soldiers? They were entitled to receive their orders and rewards from the emperor only. How clever of Gallio to discover something which the divine Augustus had neglected! Or was he an agent of Sejanus fomenting rebellion in simple hearts—seeming to offer privileges, his real aim the subversion of discipline? So the reward for Gallio's careful sycophancy was ejection from the senate immediately, from Italy later. He chose the famous and agreeable island of Lesbos for his exile. But it was protested that life would be too pleasant for him there. So he was dragged back to Rome and lodged in private custody by officials.

Tiberius' letter about Gallio also, to the senate's great satisfaction, assailed the former praetor Sextius Paconianus, an evil, violent rooterout of secrets. The revelation that Sextius had been Sejanus' chosen participant in his plot against Gaius released pent-up hatreds, and he only escaped the death-sentence by turning informer. When he

老的人？是选择官吏还是选择普通人？而且,元老们带着刀剑站在元老院议事厅的门口,那会是个什么样的场景？如果我的生命必须用武力加以保护的话,那么我看起来也就没有什么价值了。"对于托哥尼乌斯的建议,皇帝的回答是十分温和的,他取消了这个建议,也没有再提其他建议。

但是,另一方面,尤尼乌斯·伽里奥的建议却受到了严厉的斥责,他的建议是:在剧院里,退役的近卫军士兵应当有坐到为骑士准备的 14 排里面去的权利。[1] 提贝里乌斯在信里用仿佛是当着他的面讲话的口吻问他,伽里奥到底和这些士兵有什么关系？士兵们只有接受皇帝的命令以及赏赐的权利,而没有任何其他权利！多么聪明的伽里奥,竟然发现了圣奥古斯都所没有注意到的事情！否则的话,他就是谢雅努斯的一个代理人,头脑简单地妄图煽动叛乱,其目的就是颠覆军队的纪律吧？伽里奥精心逢迎所得到的奖励,就是马上被赶出了元老院,后来又被赶出了意大利。伽里奥选择了著名的和宜人的列斯波司岛做他的流放之所,但是在那里的生活对他来说,是太惬意了,因此他又被拖回罗马,在一些高级官吏的私邸中被软禁起来。

在提贝里乌斯斥责伽里奥的同一封信里,使元老们感到非常满意的是,他猛烈攻击了前任行政长官塞克斯提乌斯·帕科尼亚努斯,这是一个邪恶的、专门揭发别人隐私的人物。他是谢雅努斯在陷害盖乌斯·恺撒的阴谋中特别选出来的得力助手,当这一点被揭发出来以后,人们长久以来对他的怨恨立刻爆发了出来,

---

〔1〕 根据公元前 67 年制定的罗斯奇乌斯法,剧院里观众席的前 14 排是为骑士们准备的。

denounced Lucanius Latiaris, there was the agreeable spectacle of defendant as unpopular as his accuser. Latiaris, as I recorded, was chiefly responsible for the downfall of Titius Sabinus. He was also the first to pay for it.

While this was under way, Decimus Haterius Agrippa attacked the consuls of the previous year. Why, he asked, after assailing each other with accusations, were they now quiet ? Evidently, he observed, mutual fears and bad conscience bound them to silence-but the senate, after what it had heard, could not keep silence. Publius Memmius Regulus replied that he was biding his time for retaliation, and would pursue the matter before the emperor. Lucius Fulcinius Trio suggested that this friction between colleagues, and remarks provoked by their quarrel, had best be forgotten. When Haterius persisted, an ex-consul Quintus Sanquinius Maximus urged the senate not to multiply the emperor's worries by hunting up further troubles-when solutions were needed, the emperor was capable of providing them. This saved Regulus, and postponed Trio's fate. Haterius, a somnolent creature (and, when awake, depraved), was all the more loathsome because, as he over-ate and debauched—too inactive for any imperial atrocity to threaten himself- he plotted the downfall of his betters.

Next, at the first opportunity, Marcus Aurelius Cotta Maximus Messallinus was accused of uttering reflections on Gaius' manliness; of describing a priest's banquet, which he himself had attended on the

而且,如果不是他转而还要告发其他人的话,他早就被叛处死刑了。当他把鲁卡尼乌斯·拉提亚里斯的名字揭发出来的时候,看到被告是和原告一样可憎的人物,人们都十分高兴。正如我所说过的那样,拉提亚里斯是整垮提提乌斯·撒比努斯的主凶,而现在他又是第一个遭到了报应。

正在这个时候,戴奇姆斯·哈提里乌斯·阿格里帕对前一年的执政官发动了攻击。他问道,他们为什么在过去控诉时相互攻击,而现在却沉默了? 很显然,他评论道,他们相互间都害怕受到对方的揭发,他们所做的亏心事,使他们不得不保持沉默。但是,元老院在听取了发言之后,却不能保持沉默。普布里乌斯·美米乌斯·列古路斯回答说,他正在等候着适当的时机进行报复,并且要到皇帝面前去对此事进行控诉。路奇乌斯·富尔奇尼乌斯·特里奥则说,同僚之间的这种小摩擦,以及相互之间争吵时讲的那些话,最好还是不要记在心上。当哈提里乌斯坚持不懈地追问下去的时候,曾经担任过执政官的克温图斯·桑克维尼乌斯·玛克西姆斯便请求元老们不要再惹起更多的事端来给皇帝增加多重烦恼。在必要的时候,皇帝自己是有能力来处理好这些事情的。这话拯救了列古路斯,同时也延缓了特里奥灭亡的命运。但是哈提里乌斯,这个终日昏昏欲睡(但在醒着时又十分腐化堕落的家伙)却引起了人们更大的憎恶,因为这个人狂饮暴食、放荡淫逸,竟然懒散到连皇帝的任何残暴行径的威胁都吓不倒他的程度。但是他却还在想着搞垮比他更有声望的人。

随后,在刚刚有机会的时候,玛尔库斯·奥列里乌斯·科塔·玛克西姆斯·美撒里努斯便受到了控诉,因为就是他发表了盖乌斯的性别有问题的看法。同时,在同祭司们一起参加奥

Augusta's birthday, as a funeral feast; and, when complaining of the influence of Marcus Aemilius Lepidus (IV) and Lucius Arruntius, his opponents in a money-dispute, he was said to have added: 'The senate will back them. My sweet little Tiberius will back me!' The charges were brought home and pressed by outstanding figures; but Cotta appealed to the emperor. Soon afterwards Tiberius wrote to the senate. In self-defence he traced back to its beginning his friendship with Cotta, whose many services he recalled, urging that words maliciously distorted, or loosely uttered at table, should not be regarded as damning evidence.

The opening of Tiberius' letter attracted attention. 'If I know what to write to you at this time, senators,' he said, 'or how to write it, or what not to write, may heaven plunge me into a worse ruin than I feel overtaking me every day!' His crimes and wickedness had rebounded to torment himself. How truly the wisest of men used to assert that the souls of despots, if revealed, would show wounds and mutilations-weals left on the spirit, like lash-marks on a body, by cruelty, lust, and malevolence. Neither Tiberius' autocracy nor isolation could save him from confessing the internal torments which were his retribution.

The senate was then instructed to investigate one of its members,

古斯塔的生日宴会时，他还称那次宴会为葬礼前夜的宴会。还有一次，当他在抱怨与他在金钱上有争执的对手玛尔库斯·埃米里乌斯·列庇都斯（四世）和路奇乌斯·阿尔伦提乌斯的影响时，他还说道："元老院会支持他们，但是我可爱的小提贝里乌斯却是会支持我的。"对他的全部控诉都切中要害，而且都有非常杰出的人出来作证。但是科塔向皇帝求助，而且不久之后，提贝里乌斯就给元老院写了一封信。在这封信里，作为一种自我辩护，提贝里乌斯在回想了科塔所做出的许多功绩的同时，回顾了他本人和科塔之间的友谊是如何开始的，并且要求元老院，不要把他那些遭到恶意歪曲的话，或者是在饭桌旁不经意说出的言语，当做罪证来对待。

提贝里乌斯这封信的开头部分非常引人注目。他在信的开头部分是这样写的："元老们，如果在这个时候，我知道我要给你们写什么，怎样写它，或者是不写什么，那么就让上天将我投入到比我自己每天感到的毁灭更惨的毁灭中吧！"他的罪恶和他的丑行已经使他遭到了报应，并将他自己也陷入到痛苦之中了。第一位哲人[1]经常讲的话是多么富有真理性啊！他说，如果将暴君们的灵魂暴露在光天化日之下的话，人们将会看到那上面满是裂口和伤痕；残暴、欲望和恶意，也会像鞭子在身体上留下的伤痕那样，在人的精神上留下累累的鞭痕的。提贝里乌斯所拥有的专制的权力，和他所处的隔绝状态，都无法阻止他坦白自己内心的痛苦，他无法逃避自己应得的惩罚。

元老们继而奉命处理一位名叫盖乌斯·凯奇里亚努斯的元

---

〔1〕 指苏格拉底。

Gaius Caesilianus, who had provided the chief evidence against Cotta. He was condemned to the same penalty as Aruseius and Sangurius, who had accused Lucius Arruntius. This was the climax of Cotta's honours. Beggared (though a nobleman) by extravagance, disgraced by evil-doing, he received the compliment of a vengeance which equated him with the immaculate Lucius Arruntius.

The next defendants were Quintus Servaeus, a former praetor who had been on Germanicus' staff, and a knight called Minucius Thermus. They attracted particular sympathy because both had been friends with Sejanus, and neither had abused the fact. But Tiberius denounced them as leading criminals. He then requested a senator, Gaius Cestius Gallus (I), who had written privately to the emperor, to communicate the contents of his letter to his colleagues. The senator duly prosecuted Servaeus and Thermus before them. It was, indeed, a horrible feature of the period that leading senators became informers even on trivial matters-some openly, many secretly. Friends and relatives were as suspect as strangers, old stories as damaging as new. In the Forum, at a dinner-party, a remark on any subject might mean prosecution. Every one competed for priority in marking down the victim. Sometimes this was self-defence, but mostly it was a sort of contagion, like an epidemic. In this case the two condemned men turned informer, and two others, Julius Africanus of the Santones tribe in Gaul, and Seius Quadratus, were dragged into the net.

老的问题,因为反对科塔的主要证据都是由他提出来的。他被判处和路奇乌斯·阿尔伦提乌斯的控诉者阿路谢乌斯和桑克维里乌斯相同的惩罚。这对于科塔来说,是一种莫大的荣誉。(虽然出身高贵)但由于奢侈荒淫而一贫如洗,由于作恶多端而声名扫地的科塔,现在却因为一次报复而取得了荣誉,而这次报复竟使他得以和清白无辜的阿尔伦提乌斯相提并论。

接下来受到审讯的是克温图斯·谢尔瓦埃乌斯,他曾担任过行政长官,并在日耳曼尼库斯的军队中服过役;还有一个名叫米努奇乌斯·提尔穆斯的骑士。他们两个人都引起了人们的特别同情,因为他们虽然都是谢雅努斯的朋友,但都不曾滥用过这种友谊。但是提贝里乌斯却指责他们为罪魁祸首,盖乌斯·凯司提乌斯·伽路斯(一世)曾私下里给皇帝写过一封信,提贝里乌斯要求他把这封信的内容传达给元老院的同僚。于是凯司提乌斯就在元老面前对谢尔瓦埃乌斯和提尔穆斯两个人提出了控诉。而实际上,这一时期令人感到恐惧的是,那些著名的元老们都成了告密者,甚至是对一些微不足道的小事情也提出控告。有一些人是公开地,而多数人则是在暗地里用最卑鄙的方式进行控告。亲戚朋友也和陌生人一样令人怀疑,过去的陈年旧事也和现在新发生的事情一样具有危害性。在广场上、在晚餐的宴会上,对任何事情的谈论都有被控诉的危险,因为每个人都争先恐后地去搞垮别人。这有时是出于自卫,但是在大多数的情况下,是一种像传染病一样流行的社会风气。在这个事件中,两个被认为有罪的人,米努奇乌斯和谢尔瓦埃乌斯又转而成了控告者,他们又把另外两个人拉到了里面,一个是出生于高卢的桑托尼斯人部落的尤利乌斯·阿非利卡努斯,另一个是塞乌斯·克瓦德拉图斯。

I realize that many writers omit numerous trials and condemna-
tions, bored by repetition or afraid that catalogues they themselves
have found over-long and dismal may equally depress their readers.
But numerous unrecorded incidents, which have come to my attention, ought to be known. For instance at this juncture, when everyone
else was untruthfully disclaiming friendship with Sejanus, a knight
called Marcus Terentius bravely accepted the imputation. 'In my position', he observed to the senate, 'it might do me more good to deny the accusation than to admit it. And yet, whatever the results, I
will confess that I was Sejanus' friend: I sought his friendship, and
was glad to secure it. I had seen him as joint-commander of the Guard
with his father. Then I saw him conducting the civil as well as the
military administration. His kinsmen, his relations by marriage,
gained office. Sejanus' ill-will meant danger and pleas for mercy. I
give no examples. At my own peril only, I speak for all who took no
part in his final plans. For we honoured, not Sejanus of Vulsinii, but
the member of the Claudian and Julian houses into which his marriage
alliances had admitted him—your future son-in-law, Tiberius, your
partner as consul, your representative in State affairs. '

'It is not for us to comment on the man whom you elevate above
others, and on your reasons. The gods have given you supreme control—to us is left the glory of obeying ! Besides, we only see what is
before our eyes: the man to whom you have given wealth, power, the

　　我发现,很多历史学家略去了过去大量审判和惩处的史实,这或者是因为材料太多,会造成重复的麻烦,或者是害怕他们自己认为冗长而令人感到沉闷的那个名单,会同样使他们的读者感到压抑。但是我却把那些别人没有记述,但引起了我注意的大量的东西都记下来了。例如,正当这种紧要关头,当其他的人都在虚伪地否认同谢雅努斯的友谊的时候,一个名叫玛尔库斯·提伦提乌斯的罗马骑士却勇敢地站出来承担了这样的罪名。他在对元老院的发言中说:"在我这种处境中,否认这一指控比承认这一指控对我来说更加有利。然而不管后果如何,我也愿意承认,我是谢雅努斯的朋友! 是我自己努力争取他的友谊,而且我也十分高兴我获得了这种友谊。我曾经看到他和他的父亲一起联合做近卫军的统帅。后来,我又目睹了他主持民政的和军事的事务,与他有血缘关系的亲人和有姻亲关系的亲属都获得了显要的官职。但是,另一方面,谢雅努斯的厌恶却意味着危险,遭到他厌恶的人就要向他乞求宽恕,我就不举具体的例证了。但我要为那些没有参加过谢雅努斯最后的谋叛计划的人作出证明,一切风险均由我自己承担。因为我们所尊敬的并不是沃尔西尼人谢雅努斯,而是谢雅努斯通过联姻而得以参加进来的克劳狄乌斯家族和尤利乌斯家族的成员,也就是说,我们所尊重的是您未来的女婿,提贝里乌斯,是和您一同担任执政官的合作者,是您国内事务的代理人!

　　"我们没有资格对那位您提拔得比其他任何人都要高的人做出评论,也没有资格来追问您这样做的理由。诸神给了您主宰一切事物的最高统治权,而给予我们的,只有服从的光荣! 此外,我们只能看到我们眼前的东西,也就是说,您给予了财富、权力的

greatest potentialities for good and evil—and nobody will deny that Sejanus had these. Research into the emperor's hidden thoughts and secret designs is forbidden, hazardous, and not necessarily informative. Think, senators, not of Sejanus' last day, but of the previous sixteen years. We revered even Satrius Secundus and Pomponius. We thought it grand even if Sejanus' ex-slaves and door-keepers knew us. You will ask if this defence is to be valid for all, without discrimination. Certainly not. But draw a fair dividing-line ! Punish plots against the State and the emperor's life. But, as regards friendship and its obligations, if we sever them at the same time as you do, Tiberius, that should excuse us as it excuses you. ' This courageous utterance, publicly reflecting everyone's private thoughts, proved so effective that it earned Terentius' accusers, with their criminal records, banishment and execution.

Tiberius next wrote denouncing an intimate friend of his brother Nero Drusus—the former praetor Sextus Vistilius, whom he had transferred to his own entourage. Vistilius was charged, rightly or wrongly, with criticizing Gaius' morals. For this the emperor excluded him from his company. Vistilius made a senile attempt to cut his veins, then bound them up and wrote Tiberius an appeal. But the reply was unrelenting, and he opened them again.

人,是有着最大的潜力去做好事或是坏事的人,而没有人能够否认,谢雅努斯兼有这一切!要想探索皇帝深藏于内心的想法和他暗中拟订的计划,这是遭到禁止的,也是危险的,而且这种探索也不一定会有什么结果。元老们,请不要只考虑谢雅努斯最后的一些日子,请想一想他在这之前的16年吧!我们甚至是非常崇敬撒特里乌斯·塞坎都斯和彭波尼乌斯的,甚至如果谢雅努斯的被释奴隶和他的门卫知道了我们,我们都会认为是一件了不起的事情!您也许会问我,这次辩护是不是没有任何差别地对所有人都有效?当然不是这样!但是,让我们划出一条公正的界限吧!对背叛国家和皇帝的阴谋罪行要给予严厉的惩罚,但是关于友谊和它的责任,如果我们像您一样在同一个时期做出相同的选择的话,提贝里乌斯,那么我们也就应该和您本人得到了原谅一样,也应该得到谅解的。"他这些勇敢地公开反映了每个人内心的真实想法的讲话,给人们带来了如此强烈的影响,以至于为那些控告提伦提乌斯的人们赢得了他们应得的下场,他们都因为自己的罪恶记录,而被放逐或被处死了。

提贝里乌斯于是就写了一封信,责难曾经是他的兄弟尼禄·杜路苏斯的一位密友、后来被他罗致到了自己身边的、曾经担任过行政长官的塞克斯图斯·维司提里乌斯。维司提里乌斯之所以遭到正确或者是错误的责难,是因为他对盖乌斯的道德所作的批评。正由于这个原因,皇帝将他从自己身边的陪同中排除了出去。维司提里乌斯用刀子割断了自己的动脉,然后又把它包扎了起来,并且给提贝里乌斯写了一封信请求他的原谅,但是他得到的回答却是冷酷无情的,于是他又把包扎的地方松开了。

Then five senators, including a father and son Gaius Annius Pollio and Lucius Annius Vinicianus, were bracketed in one comprehensive charge of treason. All were of leading families, some of the highest official rank. Other senators felt extremely nervous. For few of
them were unrelated by marriage or friendship to such distinguished
men. However, two of them, Gaius Appius Junius Silanus and Gaius
Calvisius Sabinus, were rescued by the evidence of a commander of a
city police battalion, Julius Celsus, who was one of the informers. Tiberius adjourned the other three cases for investigation by himself in
consultation with the senate. However, his letter contained ominous
allusions to one of the defendants, Mamercus Aemilius Scaurus.

Even women were in danger. They could not be charged with aiming at supreme power. So they were accused of weeping: one old lady, Vitia, was executed for lamenting the death of her son, Gaius
Fufius Geminus. The senate decided this case. The emperor, however, sentenced to death two of his oldest friends, Vescularius Flaccus
and Julius Marinus, his inseparable companions at Rhodes and Capreae respectively. One had been the emperor's go-between in the plot
against Marcus Scribonius Libo Drusus, the other Sejanus' associate
in ruining Curtius Atticus. So there was particular satisfaction that
their practices had recoiled on themselves.

At about this time, Lucius Calpurnius Piso (I), member of the

接着，又有五个元老被控以叛国的罪名，包括一个父亲盖乌斯·安尼乌斯·波里欧和他的儿子卢奇乌斯·安尼乌斯·维尼奇安努斯，也被牵连到了里面。他们全都是出身名门世家，其中的一些人还担任过最高级的官吏。其他的元老们也感到极度的紧张不安，因为和这样著名的人物没有姻亲或是朋友关系的人是微乎其微的。不过这时，他们当中的两个人，盖乌斯·阿庇乌斯·尤尼乌斯·西拉努斯和盖乌斯·卡尔维西乌斯·撒比努斯却摆脱了危险，解救他们的人，是一个城防步兵中队将领、作为控告者之一的尤利乌斯·凯尔苏斯。而提贝里乌斯却将其他三个人的案件的审查暂时中止下来，因为他个人要同元老院共同做出决定。不过在他的信中，对其中一个被告玛米尔库斯·埃米里乌斯·司考路斯所做出的暗示，却是包含着不祥的征兆。

甚至妇女也会陷入危险之中，她们不可能被控以想夺取最高权力的罪名，因而她们就因为哭泣而受到控告。一个年老的妇人维提娅，就是因为在自己的儿子盖乌斯·富斐乌斯·盖米努斯被处死的时候哭了，而被处以死刑，这是元老院判决的一个案件。但是，皇帝也对他的两个最老的朋友判处了死刑，这两个人是维斯库拉里乌斯·佛拉库斯和尤利乌斯·玛利努斯，在罗德岛和卡普利埃岛，他们都曾分别伴随在他左右，是他不可分离的伙伴。维斯库拉里乌斯曾经在陷害玛尔库斯·斯科利波尼乌斯·里波·杜路苏斯的阴谋中为皇帝出过力，玛利努斯则曾和谢雅努斯一起联合摧毁了库尔提乌斯·阿提库斯。因此，当大家知道曾经谋害过别人的人也害了自己，得到了被处死的下场时，都特别得高兴。

大约就在这个时候，祭司路奇乌斯·卡尔普尔尼乌斯·披索

Pontifical Order, died a natural death—a rare end for one so distinguished. He had never initiated any sycophantic proposal; and in face of irresistible pressure he had showed wise moderation. Son of a man whose censorship I have recorded, he won an honorary Triumph in Thrace, and lived to eighty.

But his particular distinction was the outstanding discretion which he showed as City Prefect. This office was unpopular, and obedience to it grudging, since it had only recently become permanent. Long ago, when kings or later officials left Rome, continuity of government had been ensured by a temporary official to administer the law and meet emergencies. Thus Denter Romulius is said to have been appointed by Romulus, Numa Marcius by Tullus Hostilius, and Spurius Lucretius by Tarquinius Superbus. Subsequently consuls made similar appointments, and a relic still survives in the nomination of a man to act as consul during the Latin Festival. Then in the civil wars the future Augustus entrusted Rome and Italy to a knight, Gaius Maccenas, of the Cilnian family. Later, when Augustus became sole ruler, the size of the

（一世）自然死亡，那时，像他这样有名望的人，是很少能够得到善终的。他从来没有主动地提出过任何阿谀奉承的建议，并且在不可抗拒的压力面前，他也仍然能够保持自己的审慎。在前面我已经说过，他的父亲曾经担任过监察官，在色雷斯曾经获得过一次凯旋的荣誉，并且一直活到80岁高龄。

但是他的特别突出之处，是他在市长任上〔1〕行使职权时所显示出的卓越的处理事务的能力。他担任的这一职务并不是一个受人喜欢的职务，当时人们还没有形成服从的习惯，只是到了最近，它才成为了一个常设的职务。很久以前，当国王或者是后来的高级长官不得不离开罗马时，为了使政府工作的连续性能够得到保证，因此便设置一个临时性的官吏，主持法庭事务和应付临时发生的情况。据说，因此罗木路斯就曾任命过丹特尔·罗木里乌斯，后来图路斯·荷司提里乌斯任命过努玛·玛尔奇乌斯，塔尔克维也纳尼乌斯·苏培尔布斯也曾任命过司普里乌斯·卢克列提乌斯。后来，执政官也可以给予类似的任命。旧制度的残余还保存在这样一件事上面，那就是在拉丁节期间，都要任命一个人在城内担任执政官的任务。以后，在内战时期，未来的奥古斯都又委托骑士阶级出身的奇尔尼乌斯·迈凯纳斯总领罗马和意大利的全部事务。后来，当奥古斯都成了一个独裁的统治者的

〔1〕 最初设置市长这一职务的目的是应付国王或后来的执政官不在时发生的临时事件。公元前367年设置城市行政长官时，这一职务即不再需要。但当高级长官与元老们每年去阿尔巴山参加拉丁节时，仍然要指派一名长官临时维持城内秩序。在奥古斯都时期，这一职务又重新恢复，提贝里乌斯退居卡普利埃之后，便成为常设的职务，由曾经担任过执政官的人担任。市长负责维持罗马市的秩序，并率领三个（后来是四个）城防步兵中队，市长由皇帝亲自任命，但在皇帝死的时候，便不得不空下来了。

population and tardiness of legal remedies induced him to appoint a former consul to discipline the slaves and those other inhabitants who need threats of force to keep them in order. The first to receive these powers was Marcus Valerius Messalla Corvinus (I) ; but he resigned them after a few days, alleging ignorance of their application. Then Titus Statilius Taurus (I), old though he was, had made an excellent Prefect. Finally Lucius Calpurnius Piso (I) occupied the post no less creditably for twenty years. The senate honoured him with a public funeral.

A tribune, Quinctilianus, now consulted the senate about a book of Sibylline oracles. Lucius Caninius Gallus, a member of the Board of Fifteen for Religious Ceremonies, desired the senate to vote its inclusion among the Sibyl's prophecies. The senate agreed without discussion. But Tiberius wrote mildly criticizing the tribune for juvenile ignorance of traditional custom, and reprimanding Caninius. For Caninius' familiarity with religious lore and ritual (the emperor said) should have warned him not to raise the matter in a poorly attended senate, and on unreliable authority; he had not awaited his Board's decision or the usual perusal and consideration by its executive committee. Tiberius also recalled that, because of the many forgeries circulating with the prestige of the Sibyl's name, Augustus had required their notification to the city praetor before a certain date, private retention becoming illegal. (A similar decision had been taken in an earlier generation—after the burning of the Capitol during the Social War—when the poems of the Sibyl, or Sibyls, were collected from

时候,由于人口众多而又法纪松弛,他便选派一名过去曾担任过执政官的官吏,去约束奴隶和那些需要用武力来震慑的自由民阶级,以维护社会秩序。第一个被授予这种权力的是玛尔库斯·瓦列里乌斯·美撒拉·科尔维努斯(一世),但是这些权力他仅仅拥有了几天后,就不得不失去了,因为他没能恰当地行使这些权力。后来,提图斯·司塔提里乌斯·陶路斯(一世)虽然年纪已经很大了,但是他担任这一职务却干得非常出色。最后,路奇乌斯·卡尔普尔尼乌斯·披索(一世)非常称职地担任这一职务长达20年之久,在他死的时候,元老院给予他国葬的待遇。

现在,平民保民官克温提里亚努斯就一部西比拉预言书的问题向元老院提出建议。十五人团的成员路奇乌斯·卡尼尼乌斯·伽路斯,也向元老院提出要求,希望元老院发布命令,把这部预言书也收到这位女预言者西比拉的其他预言诗里面去。元老院没有经过讨论便同意了这个建议。但这时提贝里乌斯却写来了一封信,信中对保民官进行了温和的批评,批评了他由于年轻而对传统习俗的忽视。同时,对伽路斯也提出了谴责,(皇帝说)他对宗教学说和仪节非常熟悉,应该能够非常谨慎,不要根据那不可靠的权威并且不通过十五人团而自行做出决定,不应该没有等待主持人做出决定或者按惯例对预言诗加以诵读,并且也没有让主持仪节的人加以考虑,就把这个问题提交给了出席人数很少的元老院。同时提贝里乌斯还提醒说,由于有许多伪造的预言假借西比拉这个名字的声望在外面流传,所以奥古斯都过去便要求在一个规定的日期之前,把这些预言诗都交到城市行政长官那里去,私藏是非法的。(甚至在更早的时候,即在同盟战争时期卡拔托里乌姆神庙遭到火灾以后,也曾做出过一个类似的

Samos, Ilium, Erythrae, and even Africa, Sicily, and Greek settlements in Italy, and the priests were charged to do everything humanly possible to identify authentic examples.) So the collection of oracles recommended by Caninius was duly referred to the Board of Fifteen.

In the same year the high price of corn nearly caused riots. In the theatre, for several days, sweeping demands were shouted with a presumption rarely displayed to emperors. Upset, Tiberius reproved the officials and senate for not using their authority to restrain popular demonstrations. He enumerated the provinces from which he was importing corn—more extensively than Augustus. So the senate passed a resolution of old-fashioned strictness censuring the public. The consuls too issued an equally severe edict. Tiberius was silent. However, this was taken not for modesty as he hoped, but for arrogance.

At the end of the year three knights, Geminius, Celsus and Pompeius, succumbed to charges of conspiracy. Geminius had gained Sejanus' friendship through his extravagance and effeminacy, but no serious offence was involved. Another defendant, the city police colonel Julius Celsus, loosened the chain with which he was bound and looping it round his own throat strained against it until he broke his neck. Rubrius Fabatus was arrested for attempting flight to the mercy of the Parthians in despair of Rome. Intercepted at the Sicilian Strait and conducted back by a staff-officer, he could not plausibly explain his ambitious travelling plans. However, he was left alive, not pardoned but forgotten.

决定。当时从撒莫斯、伊利乌姆、埃律特莱,甚至在阿非利加、西西里和意大利的希腊移民地,也都搜集到了一种或多种西比拉预言诗。祭司们被指派用一切力所能及的办法去对这些预言的真伪进行辨别。)因此,这次卡尼尼乌斯所提出的西比拉预言书的收集,也必须要交给十五人团去审查。

在同一年里,粮价过高几乎引起了暴动。接连好几天,人们在剧场里高声呼喊提出了许多要求,表现出以前很少有的对皇帝的放肆态度。提贝里乌斯严厉谴责高级长官和元老院没有利用国家的权力来制服群众的示威。此外他还列举了向意大利输送粮食的行省,而且,现在输入粮食的规模比奥古斯都时期要大得多。因此,为了对民众进行监控,元老院发布了一项具有古代风尚的严苛的决定,执政官也发布了同样严厉的命令。提贝里乌斯本人却一直保持沉默。不过这种表示并没有像他自己所希望的那样,被认为是一种民主的宽容,而被认为是一种傲慢。

年底,三个罗马骑士盖米努斯、凯尔苏斯和彭佩乌斯死于密谋叛逆罪的指控。盖米努斯曾由于生活挥霍浪费和女子气的娇媚而赢得了谢雅努斯的赏识,但是他并没有什么严重的犯罪行为。另一名被告,一个城防军将领尤利乌斯·凯尔苏斯,松开了绑在身上的锁链,然后把它套在自己的脖子上,紧紧地锁住了咽喉,直到把自己勒死。卢布里乌斯·法巴图斯则是因为不满意罗马的现状而想投奔到慈悲的帕尔提亚人那里去,因而被逮捕。他是在西西里海峡的附近被搜捕到的,并且被一名百人团长押解回罗马的。他无法合理地解释,为什么要跑到那儿去。但是他还是保全了一条性命,不过这并非是由于宽大,而是由于他被忘记了。

Tiberius had long been meditating the choice of husbands for his marriageable granddaughters, Julia Livilla and Drusilla. Next year, when the consuls were Servius Sulpicius Galba (II) and Marcus Vinicius, he selected Lucius Cassius Longinus and Marcus Vinicius. Vinicius came from the town of Gales. His father and grandfather had become consuls, the rest of the family were knights. He was mild in character, with an elaborate oratorical style. Cassius came of an ancient and respected, though plebeian, family. Although sternly brought up by his father, he was more conspicuous for pliancy than vigour. To these men, then, Tiberius gave Germanicus' daughters; and he wrote to the senate perfunctorily complimenting the bridegrooms.

Next, after vague excuses for his absence, he turned to graver matters. Emphasizing the enmities he had incurred in the national interest, he requested that whenever he entered the senate a small escort should attend him—including the Guard commander, Quintus Naevius Cordus Sutorius Macro, colonels, and staff-officers. The senate passed a comprehensive resolution without specifying the num-

提贝里乌斯很长时间以来就在反复思考权衡,为他那些已到结婚年龄的孙女们——优利娅·利维拉和杜路西拉〔1〕选择佳婿。第二年,在谢尔维乌斯·苏尔皮奇乌斯·伽尔巴(二世)和玛尔库斯·维尼奇乌斯担任执政官的那一年里,〔2〕他选定了路奇乌斯·卡西乌斯·朗吉努斯和玛尔库斯·维尼奇乌斯为她们的丈夫。维尼奇乌斯出生在卡列司的一个乡村,他的父亲和祖父都做过执政官,他家族中其他的人则属于骑士阶级。他的性情温和,而且语言谈吐非常讲究。卡西乌斯虽然出身为平民,但来自一个古老而受人尊敬的罗马家族。在早年,他的父亲虽然曾给予他非常严格的教育,但是后来他却是以善于体会别人的意思而不是以严厉而著名。于是,提贝里乌斯就把日耳曼尼库斯的两个女儿分别许配了这两个人,并且就这件事写信给元老院,敷衍地把这两个新郎称赞了一番。

然后,他在含糊其词地为他不留在罗马提出了一些借口之后,就转而谈起了一些比较严重的问题。他着重强调了他为国家的利益而招致的一些敌意,并且要求每当他进入元老院的时候,应当由近卫军长官克温图斯·奈维乌斯·考尔都斯·苏托里乌斯·玛克罗〔3〕以及一些军团将领与百人团长组成的护卫队陪伴着他。元老院于是没有详细说明这个护卫队的人数和组成人员,就发布了一项内容广泛的命令。尽管如此,提贝里乌斯还

----

〔1〕 日耳曼尼库斯的两个女儿,她们的第三个姊妹阿格里披娜已经嫁给了格涅乌斯·多米提乌斯。卡西乌斯八年后被卡里古拉杀害,维尼奇乌斯则是在公元46年被美撒里娜毒死。

〔2〕 公元33年,罗马建城786年。

〔3〕 克温图斯·奈维乌斯·考尔都斯·苏托里乌斯·玛克罗曾经执行了逮捕谢雅努斯的任务,因此就代替他担任了近卫军长官,但是这个人比谢雅努斯还要恶劣。

bers or composition of this bodyguard. Even so, Tiberius never again entered Rome, much less an official meeting. He often circled round his city by devious routes—only to recoil.

Accusers were now intensely active. Their present targets were men who enriched themselves by usury, infringing the law by which the dictator Julius Caesar had controlled loans and land-ownership in Italy. Since patriotism comes second to private profits, this law had long been ignored. Money-lending is an ancient problem in Rome, and a frequent cause of disharmony and disorder. Even in an earlier, less corrupt society steps had been taken against it. At first, interest had been determined arbitrarily by the rich, but then the Twelve Tables had fixed the maximum at 10%. Next, a tribune's law had halved the rate. Finally loans on compound interest were forbidden completely. Fraudulence, attacked by repeated legislation, was ingeniously revived after each successive counter-measure.

Now, however, the praetor Sempronius Gracchus (II), responsible for the investigation, was compelled by the num – bers of potential defendants to refer the matter to the senate. That body-being implicated to a man-nervously entreated the emperor's indulgence. It was granted. Eighteen months were allowed in which all private finances had to be brought into line with the law. The result was a shortage of money. For all debts were called in simultaneously; besides, the many convictions and sales of confiscated property had concentrated currency in the Treasury and its imperially controlled branches. To meet this situation the senate had instructed that creditors should invest

是没有再进入罗马,更不用说参加国家的正式会议了。然而他却经常围绕着罗马城,在偏僻的小路上漫步,然后就返回卡普利埃岛而始终不进入罗马。

这个时候,控诉者的活动更加积极了。他们现在的目标是那些由于放高利贷而增加了自己的财富的人,因为这些人违反了独裁官尤利乌斯·恺撒为控制借贷以及在意大利本土保有的地产而制定的一项法律。由于公共利益被置于私人利益之下,因此这项法律很久以来就一直为人们所忽视。在罗马,高利贷的问题由来已久,它是造成叛乱与不和的惯常的原因。甚至在较早的,还不是那样腐化堕落的社会里,就已经采取各种办法进行反对了。开始,是有钱的人随意规定贷款的利息;继而十二铜表法做出规定,年息最高不得超过10%;后来,一条保民官的法律又将利率降低了一半;最后这样一种利滚利的高利贷行当就被完全禁止了。虽然,在过去也有许多法令力图制止各种诈骗行为,但它们总是屡禁不止,每次遭到压制以后,又巧妙地重兴起来。

但是在目前,由于被牵连进来的人数过多,负责审理这一案件的行政长官谢姆普罗尼乌斯·格拉古(二世),便被迫将它提交到了元老院。而在这一案件面前,元老院的主要人物也都暗中被牵连了进去,因此他们紧张地请求皇帝的宽恕。皇帝准许了他们的请求,规定在今后的18个月内所有私人的资金必须根据法律的规定进行调整。这种措施引起的后果就是现金的缺乏,因为所有的债务同时被收回,而大量的判罪和被没收的财产被出售之后,国库或是皇帝的财库又集中了大量所变卖的现金。为了应对这样的情况,元老院指示,每一个债权人都必须把他用来生息的2/3的资金拿出来在意大利投资,而债务人则要立即

two-thirds of their capital in Italy, and debtors immediately pay the same proportion of their debts.

However, creditors demanded payment in full, and debtors were morally bound to respond. The first results were importunate appeals to money-lenders. Next, the praetor's court resounded with activity. The decree requiring land purchases and sales, envisaged as relief, had the opposite effect since when the capitalists received payment they hoarded it, to buy land at their convenience. These extensive transactions reduced prices. But large-scale debtors found it difficult to sell; so many of them were ejected from their properties, and lost not only their estates but their rank and reputation.

Then Tiberius came to the rescue. He distributed a hundred million sesterces among specially established banks, for interest-free three year state loans, against security of double the value in landed property. Credit was thus restored; and gradually private lenders, too, reappeared. However, land transactions failed to adhere to the provisions of the senatorial decree. As usual, the beginning was strict, the sequel slack.

Earlier fears now revived. Considius Proculus was accused of treason. While unperturbedly celebrating his birthday, he was dragged to the senate-house, and instantly condemned and executed. His sister Sancia was outlawed. Her accuser was Quintus Pomponius, a neurotic who claimed that he undertook these and similar cases in order to gain the emperor's favour and rescue his brother Publius Pomponius Secundus from danger. Another woman, Pompeia Macrina, was exiled. Tiberius had already ruined her husband and father-in-law, Argolicus and Laco, leading Greeks. Now her father, a

按照同样的比例支付他所负的债务。

债权人既然要求偿清全部债款,债务人从道义上来说就应该被给予相应的赔偿。开始的时候,债务人不断地请求允许延期偿还。接下来,行政长官的法庭就忙碌地运作起来了。要求买卖土地的法令下达后,又产生了另外相反的后果,因为放高利贷的富豪们把自己放贷的流动资金收回来以后,就趁机去购买土地了。市场上物资的过剩引起了物价的下跌,因而负债极重的人是很难把自己的货物卖出去以偿还债务的,而如此一来,这些人便不仅丧失了财产,也丧失了他们原有的地位和名誉。

提贝里乌斯终于出来拯救困境了。他把 1 亿谢司特尔提乌斯分配给各个特设的银行,借款人可以得到免息三年的国家贷款,但他必须能提出价值相当贷款一倍的土地作为抵押保证。信用贷款就这样重新恢复起来了,而私自贷款的人也渐渐地又重新出现了。然而,土地交易也不按照元老院的规定执行了。像往常一样,这次仍然以虎头蛇尾的结果不了了之。

先前的恐惧现在又重新恢复起来了。孔西狄乌斯·普洛库路斯被控以叛逆罪,正在他泰然自若地庆祝自己的生日的时候,却被拖到了元老院,并且马上就在那里定了罪并立即处决了。他的姊妹桑奇娅被剥夺了公民权,控告她的人是克温图斯·彭波尼乌斯,一个神经病人,他声称他做这些事以及诸如此类的其他勾当,目的就是为了博得皇帝的喜欢,以解救他的兄弟普布里乌斯·彭波尼乌斯·谢孔都斯面临的危险。还有一个叫做彭佩娅·玛克里娜的女人受到了流放,她的丈夫阿尔哥里库斯和公公拉科,都是知名的希腊人,他们都已经被提贝里乌斯除掉了。

distinguished knight, and her brother a former praetor, saw condemnation ahead and killed themselves. Their offence was that the latter's Mytilenean great-grandfather Theophanes had been a close friend of Pompey and had been deified posthumously by sycophantic Greeks. Then Sextus Marius, the richest man in Spain, was thrown from the Tarpeian Rock. The charge was incest with his daughter. But the real cause of his ruin was his wealth. This became clear from Tiberius' personal appropriation of his gold—and copper-mines—though the State was ostensibly their confiscator.

Frenzied with bloodshed, the emperor now ordered the execution of all those arrested for complicity with Sejanus. It was a massacre. Without discrimination of sex or age, eminence or obscurity, there they lay, strewn about-or in heaps. Relatives and friends were forbidden to stand by or lament them, or even gaze for long. Guards surrounded them, spying on their sorrow, and escorted the rotting bodies until, dragged into the Tiber, they floated away or grounded—with none to cremate or touch them. Terror had paralysed human sympathy. The rising surge of brutality drove compassion away.

This was about the time when Gaius, who had accompanied his grandfather to Capreae, received in marriage Junia Claudilla, a daughter of Marcus Junius Silanus (I). A deceitful discretion concealed Gaius' horrible character. His mother's condemnation, his brother's destruction, elicited no word from him. He faithfully reflected Tiberius' daily

现在,她的父亲———一个罗马高级骑士,和她的兄弟———以前的行政长官,看到就要面临着被判罪的危险,就都自杀了。他们的罪名是:后者的曾祖父是米提利涅人提欧帕涅斯,他是庞培的一个亲密朋友,而且在他死后,阿谀奉承的希腊人又把他追捧为神明。之后,塞克斯图斯·马利乌斯,这个西班牙最富有的人,被从塔尔培亚岩上扔了下去。他受到指控的罪名是同他自己的女儿通奸,但是使他丧命的真正原因是他的财富。从提贝里乌斯的私人收入看出,很明显,元老院没收他的金矿和铜矿进了提贝里乌斯的私囊。

杀人成狂的提贝里乌斯,现在下令将所有因和谢雅努斯同谋的罪名而被逮捕的人都处死。这是一次大规模的屠杀,不分男女老少,不分富贵贫贱。他们的尸体躺在地下,或是散在各处,或是堆在一起。亲戚或朋友都不许靠近他们,不许为他们哭泣,甚至不允许长久地凝望。周围到处都有放哨的卫兵在那里监视着人们,侦察着他们的伤心的情绪,守护着这些腐烂的尸体,一直到他们被拖进了台伯河。之后,这些尸体就被水流冲走或是被冲上了岸,但是没有人敢火化这些尸体或是碰他们。恐怖使人类的同情心都瘫痪了,残暴升起的地方,同情就被驱走了。

大约就在这个时候,陪伴着自己的祖父到卡普利埃岛去的盖乌斯同玛尔库斯·尤尼乌斯·西拉努斯(一世)的女儿优尼娅·克劳狄娅结了婚。一种虚假的谦虚掩饰着盖乌斯那极为凶残的性格。他的母亲的判刑、他的兄弟的毁灭,都没有从他口里引出过一句话。他只是每天无比忠实地反映着提贝里乌斯的情绪,甚至是每一句话。这促使了后来一个著名的警句的诞生,这是一位

moods-almost his words. This later prompted the famous epigram by Gaius Sallustius Passienus Crispus that there had never been a better slave or a worse master.

Tiberius' prophecy about the consul Servius Sulpicius Galba (II) deserves mention. After sending for Galba and sounding him in various fashions Tiberius said to him in Greek: ' You too, Galba, shall one day have a taste of empire. ' This prophecy of Galba's late, brief principate was based on Tiberius' knowledge of Chaldaean astrology, taught him at Rhodes by Thrasyllus. He had tested Thrasyllus' knowledge in this way. When seeking occult guidance Tiberius would retire to the top of his house, with a single tough, illiterate former slave as confidant. Those astrologers whose skill Tiberius had decided to test were escorted to him by this man over pathless, precipitous ground; for the house overhung a cliff. Then, on their way down, if they were suspected of unreliability or fraudulence, the ex-slave hurled them into the sea below, so that no betrayer of the secret proceedings should survive.

Thrasyllus, after reaching Tiberius by this steep route, had impressed him, when interrogated, by his intelligent forecasts of future events-including Tiberius' accession. Tiberius then inquired if Thrasyllus had cast his own horoscope. How did it appear for the current year and day? Thrasyllus, after measuring the positions and distances of the stars, hesitated, then showed alarm. The more he looked, the greater became his astonishment and fright. Then he cried

演说家盖乌斯·撒路斯提乌斯·帕西耶努斯·科里斯普斯说出的,这句名言说道:"世界上从来没有见过更好的奴隶,更坏的主人。"

在这里应该谈一谈提贝里乌斯关于对当时担任执政官的谢尔维乌斯·苏尔皮奇乌斯·伽尔巴(二世)的预言。他派人把伽尔巴召来,在听他谈了各种各样的时事后,提贝里乌斯用希腊语对他说:"伽尔巴啊,将来有一天你也会尝到当皇帝的滋味的。"提贝里乌斯所以能做出伽尔巴很晚才做了很短一段时间的皇帝这样的预言,是因为在罗德岛的时候,特拉西路斯曾教他学会了一些迦勒底的占星术的知识。他曾用这种办法来试验过特拉西路斯教他的本领。每当他占星寻求那种神秘的指引的时候,提贝里乌斯就到他的别墅中最高的地方去,只带着一个身体强壮的、不识字的被释奴隶作为亲信侍候着他。那些为提贝里乌斯决定试验其本领的占星术士们,就由这个奴隶领着,到一座无路可通而又十分险峻的高山上去,因为他的房屋就修建在俯临大海的悬崖上。接着,在回来的路上,如果怀疑这个占星术士的本领不可靠或者是有欺诈,这个被释奴隶就把他扔到下面的大海里去,这样这一秘密的泄露者就不会存在了。

特拉西路斯当时也是沿着这条陡峭的山路被带到提贝里乌斯这里来的,当提贝里乌斯询问他一些未来的事件,也包括他自己的帝位问题时,他做出的高妙预言给了提贝里乌斯很深的印象。继而提贝里乌斯就问他,他是否给自己看过星象,而他今年和今天的星象是怎样的。特拉西路斯在测量了一下星位和星距之后,先是犹豫了一会儿,然后他就现出了惊恐的表情,他越是往下仔细地推算,就越是感到惊讶和恐惧。随后他就哭了,说道,

that a critical and perhaps fatal emergency was upon him. Tiberius clasped him, commending his divination of peril and promising he would escape it. Thrasyllus was admitted among his closest friends; his pronouncements were regarded as oracular.

When I hear this and similar stories I feel uncertain whether human affairs are directed by Fate's unalterable necessity—or by chance. On this question the wisest ancient thinkers and their disciples differ. Many insist that heaven is unconcerned with our births and deaths-is unconcerned, in fact, with human beings-so that the good often suffer, and the wicked prosper. Others disagree, maintaining that although things happen according to fate, this depends not on astral movements but on the principles and logic of natural causality.

This school leaves us free to choose our lives. But once the choice is made, they warn that the future sequence of events is immutable. Yet in regard to those events they claim that the popular ideas of good and evil are mistaken: many who seem afflicted are happy, if they endure their hardships courageously; others (however wealthy) are wretched, if they employ their prosperity unwisely. Most men, however, find it natural to believe that lives are predestined from birth, that the science of prophecy is verified by remarkable testimonials, ancient and modern; and that unfulfilled predictions are due merely to ignorant

一个危险的、也许是致命的危机正逼临到他身上来。提贝里乌斯立刻过去紧紧拥抱了他,称赞他对这一危险的预测,并答应放了他。特拉西路斯在今后也就成了提贝里乌斯最亲近的朋友之一,[1]他的预言也被提贝里乌斯看做是神所启示的预言。

当我听到这件事情以及诸如此类的故事时,我无法确定,人间的事物到底是决定于不能选择和改变的命运呢,还是决定于偶然的事件呢? 在这个问题上最有智慧的古代思想家和他们的门徒之间,意见是不同的。许多人坚信上天和我们的生死没有关系,事实上,也就是和人类没有关系,因此,好人才总是受苦,而坏人却往往得意。另一些人则不同意这种观点,认为,尽管事情的发生是由命运决定的,然而命运并不依赖于星辰的运行,而是依赖于自然的因果关系和原则必然过程。

这一派给予我们自主地选择我们的生活的自由。不过一旦我们做出了一种选择,他们提醒道,那么相应的未来的事情就不能再改变了。对于事情的看法,他们还说,大家普遍所认为的是好事和坏事的意见其实是错误的。许多从表面上看来正遭受着折磨的人却是快乐的,如果他们能够勇敢地忍受他们目前的艰难生活的话。另一些人(尽管很富有)反而很不快乐,因为他们不能明智地使用自己的财富。不过大多数人是很自然地会相信命运的,他们认为,一个人的生活遭遇是在他刚刚出生时便被确定了的。在古代以及在现代,都有许多著名的试验证明了预言的科学性。那些没有应验的预言,仅仅是由于并不相信预言

---

[1] 他被赐名提贝里乌斯·克劳狄乌斯·特拉西路斯,并且一直陪伴提贝里乌斯,他比皇帝早死一年。

impostors who discredit it. Not here-for I must not extend this digression-but in its place I will record the forecast of Nero's reign made by Thrasyllus' son.

In the same year it became known that Gaius Asinius Gallus was dead. He died of starvation—whether self-inflicted or forcible was undiscovered. Tiberius, asked if he would permit the burial of Asinius, unblushingly authorized it, adding his regrets at the circumstances which removed the defendant before investigation by himself. In three years, apparently, no time had been found to try this elderly ex-consul and father of consuls.

The next to perish was Drusus Caesar. For eight days he had staved off death on pitiable nourishment—by gnawing the stuffing of his mattress. It has been suggested that the emperor had ordered Macro, if Sejanus attempted rebellion, to free the youth from the Palatine-where he was incarcerated—and display him to the people as a leader. Later, however, because of rumours that Tiberius had relented towards Drusus Caesar and his mother Agrippina, the emperor's lenient second thoughts were again superseded by severity.

Even when Drusus Caesar was dead, Tiberius attacked him. The charges included immorality, plots to murder his relatives, designs against the government. He also ordered reports of the prince's daily doings and sayings to be posthumously recited. This seemed the supreme cruelty. That agents had stood by Drusus all these years noting every look and groan, even private mutterings; and that his grandfather could have heard, read, and published the whole story,

的骗子乱讲一通而致。但是现在我不能把话题扯得太远。关于这个特拉西路斯的儿子对尼禄要做皇帝的事情所做的预言,我还要在适当的地方加以叙述。

在同一年里,广为人知的一件事情就是盖乌斯·阿西尼乌斯·伽路斯的死亡。他是饿死的,不过是由于想不开自杀,还是被别人强迫造成的,这就难以确定了。当人们询问提贝里乌斯,他是否允许埋葬阿西尼乌斯的时候,他竟然恬不知耻地应允了,并且还对于被告在还没弄清自己的罪名之前便发生了这种情况表示遗憾。在三年之中,很显然,是没有时间来审问这位老年的前任执政官和许多位执政官的父亲的。

下一个突然死亡的是杜路苏斯·恺撒。在他饿死前整整8天的时间里,他仅仅是靠着咀嚼他褥子里的填充物可怜地维持着生命。据说,皇帝曾经命令玛克罗,如果谢雅努斯企图反叛的话,就把这个青年人从被监禁的皇宫中释放出来,并且使他成为人民的首领。后来,外面又有谣传,说提贝里乌斯对杜路苏斯·恺撒和他的母亲阿格里披娜变得温和了,因而他的一点慈悲心又被残忍暴虐所取代了。

甚至在杜路苏斯·恺撒死后,提贝里乌斯也仍然没有停止对他的攻击。攻击的内容包括:他不道德的恋爱,攻击他阴谋杀害他的亲人,以及阴谋反对政府。甚至还在他死后下令公开宣读这位王子每日言行的记录。这是一种极端残酷的行为!这么多年以来,那些密探们时刻在杜路苏斯身边,监视着他的一举一动,把他的每一个表情、每一声叹息,甚至喃喃自语的话都记录下来。而他的祖父则警惕地听取着、批阅着有关他的一切的报告,并且将它们全部公之于世,这种情况简直是令人难以相信!然而我们却明明白

was scarcely credible. Yet there were the reports of a staff-officer of the Guard and an ex-slave, named Attius and Didymus respectively, and in them the names of the slaves who had struck and intimidated Drusus Caesar whenever he tried to leave his room. The officer had e-ven noted his own brutal language—as something creditable.

He also recorded the dying man's words. First, feigning mad-ness, Drusus Caesar had screamed apparently delirious maledictions upon Tiberius. Then, despairing of his life, he had uttered an elabo-rate and formal curse: that for deluging his family in blood, for mas-sacring his daughter-in-law, nephew, and grandchildren, Tiberius might pay the penalty due to his house—to his ancestors and descend-ants. The senators interrupted, as though horrified. What really horri-fied them—and amazed them—was that one formerly so astute, so se-cretive a concealer of his crimes as Tiberius should unflinchingly snatch away the prison walls and show his grandson battered by an of-ficer, beaten by slaves, vainly begging the bare necessities of life.

This tragedy was still fresh when news came of Agrippina's end. After Sejanus' death hope, I suppose, was what had kept her alive. But even then her cruel treatment was not mitigated. So she killed herself-unless food was denied so that her death should look like sui-cide. From Tiberius came an outburst of filthy slanders, accusing her of adultery with Gaius Asinius Gallus, and asserting that she had wea-ried of living when Asinius died. (Actually, Agrippina knew no femi-nine weaknesses. Intolerant of rivalry, thirsting for power, she had a man's preoccupations.) It'should be recorded, Tiberius continued,

白地看到过百人团长阿提乌斯和被释奴隶狄杜穆斯的报告。这份报告中记录了一些奴隶的名字,他们在杜路苏斯想离开他的房间时,就打他或是对他进行威胁。这个百人团长甚至还把他自己野蛮的言词也加了上去,似乎这就是他了不起的功劳。

他还记录下了这个行将死亡的人的一些话。起初,杜路苏斯·恺撒佯装发狂,疯疯癫癫、大喊大叫地咒骂提贝里乌斯。后来,当知道自己已经没有了活命的希望的时候,他就对提贝里乌斯做了经过精心思考的、正式的诅咒:由于提贝里乌斯使他的一家浸泡在血泊里,由于他对自己的儿媳妇、侄子、孙子的屠杀,他必将会使他家的祖先和后代遭到惩罚。元老们好像很害怕的样子,打断了对这种报告的宣读。但实际上真正使他们感到恐怖和惊讶的是,像提贝里乌斯这样机警、这样善于严密隐藏自己的罪行的人,竟然这样果断坚定地撕开了他的监狱的围墙,显示出自己的孙子去受一个百人团长的折磨,受奴隶们的殴打,徒劳地去乞求生存最起码的一些需要的惨状。

在人们对这一悲惨事件还记忆犹新的时候,又传来了阿格里披娜逝世的消息。谢雅努斯的死使她还抱着一线希望,我认为,这是她所以顽强活了下来的原因。但是,后来当她看到甚至那时她所受到的残酷对待也还没有减轻的时候,她就自杀了——除非是人们不给她食物,这样看起来就好像是自杀而死了。提贝里乌斯用污言秽语对阿格里披娜进行了恶毒的诽谤,他指责她不贞,说她和盖乌斯·阿西尼乌斯·伽路斯通奸,并声称正是看到阿西尼乌斯死了,她才厌世轻生(但实际上,阿格里披娜并没有女性常有的这种弱点,她不能忍受别人对她的敌意,渴望权力,她所具有的是男人的争强好胜之心和专注的神志)。提贝里乌斯继续说,

that she died on the very day of Sejanus' execution two years earlier. He claimed credit for not having Agrippina strangled or hurled on to the Gemonian Steps. For this, he was voted thanks, and it was resolved that henceforward on every eighteenth of October, the day of both deaths, a sacrifice should be made to Jupiter.

Shortly afterwards Marcus Cocceius Nerva, the emperor's companion, an expert in secular and religious law, decided to die-his position unthreatened, his health sound. When Tiberius heard this he sat beside Nerva, inquired his reasons, and implored him to desist, declaring that his own feelings and reputation would suffer grievously if his most intimate friend chose to die without cause. Nerva declined to speak, and persisted in refusing nourishment. Those who knew his mind asserted that his close sight of Rome's calamities had impelled him, in indignation and terror, to seek an honourable death.

Curiously enough Agrippina's destruction brought down Plancina, widow of Cnaeus Calpumius Piso. Openly delighting at Germanicus' death, she had been rescued, after Piso's downfall, by the Augusta's intercessions and Agrippina's hostility. Now that her patroness and her enemy were both gone, justice prevailed. Charged with her notorious offences, Plancina met by her own hand her well-deserved, overdue end.

As the country mourned its calamities, it was a contributory grievance that Livia Julia, daughter of Drusus and widow of Nero Caesar, married into the family of Gaius Rubellius Blandus, whose grandfather

还应该给予记录的是,她死的那天正是谢雅努斯两年前被处死的那天。他还自我炫耀地宣称他没有把阿格里披娜绞死或者是把她的尸体拖到盖莫尼埃台阶上。因此,提贝里乌斯获得了正式的致谢,并且决定,从此以后,每年的 10 月 18 日,也就是这两人死亡的日子,都要向朱庇特神奉献一个祭品。

不久之后,玛尔库斯·科凯乌斯·涅尔瓦,皇帝的伙伴,一位精通世俗和宗教法律的人,在地位并没有受到什么威胁和健康状况正常的情况下决心寻死。提贝里乌斯听到了这样的事情之后,就坐到涅尔瓦的身旁,询问他其中的原因,接着就恳求他断绝此念,他说,如果他最亲近的朋友没有什么理由就要寻死,那么他的感情和名誉都将会受到严重的伤害。涅尔瓦拒绝回答,而且继续坚持拒绝进食,一直到死。那些了解他的思想的人说,他对罗马所发生的各种灾难的密切观察促成了他的自杀,因为他陷入了深深的愤慨和恐惧之中,因此就决定体面地死去。

奇怪的是,阿格里披娜的去世还导致了普朗奇娜的死亡。普朗奇娜是格涅乌斯·卡尔普尔尼乌斯·披索的寡妇,在日耳曼尼库斯死的时候公然表现出欣喜若狂的感情,因此得救。披索死后,她又由于奥古斯塔的干预和阿格里披娜对她的敌视而得救。现在,既然她的同伙和敌人都离去了,正义也就行使它的权力了。她因臭名昭著的罪行而受到控告,于是普朗奇娜就用自己的手结束了她罪恶的生命,得到了她罪有应得,而且为时还太晚的报应。

正当这个国家为它遭到的种种灾难而悲伤的时候,又发生了一件憾事,这就是杜路苏斯的女儿利维拉·优利娅,也就是尼禄·恺撒的寡妇,现在嫁到盖乌斯·路贝里乌斯·勃兰都斯的家里

was widely remembered as a mere knight from Tibur. The last days of
the year witnessed the death and state funeral of Lucius Aelius Lamia,
who, finally released from his fictitious imperial governorship of Syri-
a, had become City Prefect. Nobly born, vigorous in old age, he had
gained in prestige by not being allowed to take up his governorship.
Then, on the death of Lucius Pomponius Flaccus who had succeeded
Lamia in Syria, a letter was read from Tiberius complaining that every
distinguished man capable of commanding an army declined the post,
and that he was reduced to entreaties in order to persuade former consuls to accept a province. He forgot that Lucius Arruntius was, for the
tenth successive year, being prevented from proceeding to his Spanish
governorship.

The death of Marcus Aemilius Lepidus (IV) also occurred in
this year. I have already commended on his good sense and wisdom-
and his aristocratic origin needs little description. The Aemilii have
always produced good Romans. Even the family's bad characters
have shared its distinction.

Next year the consuls were Paullus Fabius Persicus and Lucius
Vitellius (I). It was now, at the conclusion of an age-long cycle,
that the phoenix appeared in Egypt, a remarkable event which occasioned much discussion by Egyptian and Greek authorities. I will indicate the facts on which there is agreement, and certain others which
are doubtful but not wholly fantastic. The phoenix is sacred to the sun.

去。勃兰都斯的祖父,人们都还记得,只是提布尔地方的一名罗马骑士。在这一年的最后几天里,路奇乌斯·埃里乌斯·拉米亚去世了,并且进行了国葬。他在最后终于被解除了本来是虚有其名的叙利亚长官的职务,但随即又被任命为市长官。他出身于贵族家庭,年事已高但仍然精力旺盛,并且由于他没有担任行省长官之职而获得了更良好的声望。接着,在接替拉米亚担任叙利亚长官的路奇乌斯·彭波尼乌斯·佛拉库斯去世的当时,元老院宣读了提贝里乌斯写来的一封信,信中抱怨说,每一个能够统率军队的著名人物都拒绝担任这样一个职务。因此他不得不纡尊百般恳求,以说服一位曾担任过执政官的人来担负起行省长官的任务。但是他忘记了,路奇乌斯·阿尔伦提乌斯之所以连续 10 年被留在罗马,就是为了防止他到西班牙去。

还是在这一年里,玛尼乌斯·埃米里乌斯·列庇都斯(四世)也去世了。在前面,我已经谈到了这个人的聪明和智慧,而且对他的高贵出身也无需再做很多的说明。埃米里乌斯家族已经产生出了许多优秀的罗马人,甚至这一家族中那些品行不好的人都分享着这一家族的荣誉。

接下来的一年里,[1] 担任执政官的是保路斯·法比乌斯·皮尔西库斯和路奇乌斯·维提里乌斯(一世)。现在,在经过了多年的周期之后,一只长生鸟在埃及出现了,这一奇异的事件引起了埃及和希腊的学者们的极大兴趣。我要指出的事实就是,他们的观点有些是可以接受的,而有些还有很多可疑之处,不过这些可疑的论点也不完全是荒诞不经的。这种长生鸟是献给太阳神的圣鸟。那些

---

[1] 公元 34 年,罗马建城 787 年。

Those who have depicted it agree that its head and the markings of its plumage distinguish it from other birds. Regarding the length of its life accounts vary. The commonest view favours 500 years. But some estimate that it appears every 1461 years, and that the three last seen flew to Heliopolis in the reigns of Sesosis, Amasis, and Ptolemy III (of the Macedonian dynasty) respectively, escorted by numerous ordinary birds astonished by its unfamiliar aspect. Its earliest appearances are unverifiable; but since between Ptolemy and Tiberius there were less than 250 years some have denied the authenticity of the Tiberian phoenix, which did not, they say, come from Arabia or perform the traditionally attested actions. For when its years are complete and death is close, it is said to make a nest in its own country and shed over it a procreative substance—from which rises a young phoenix. Its first function after growth is the burial of its father. This is habitually done as follows. After proving, by a long flight with a load of myrrh, that it is capable of the burden and the journey, it takes up its father's body, carries it to the Altar of the Sun, and burns it. The details are disputed and embellished by myths. But that the bird sometimes appears in Egypt is unquestioned.

At Rome the massacre was continuous. Pomponius Labeo, whose imperial governorship of Moesia I have mentioned, opened his veins and bled to death, followed by his wife Paxaea. Such deaths were readily resorted to. They were due to fears of execution, and because people sentenced to death forfeited their property and were forbidden burial, whereas suicides were rewarded for this acceleration by burial

描述过这种鸟的形状的人们都说,它的头部和羽毛的五色斑斓的色彩是它区别于其他鸟的特征所在。至于它生命的年限,记载各不相同。最普遍的观点认为是 500 年,然而也有一些人估计这种鸟每隔 1461 年才出现一次。人们较晚见到过的三次,分别是在谢索西斯的统治时期、阿玛西斯的统治时期、托勒米三世的统治时期(马其顿王朝),飞到了赫里波利斯城的,而且是有大量对它的新奇外貌感到惊叹的普通鸟的陪伴。它最早出现时的情况虽然已经不能确证,但是因为从托勒米到提贝里乌斯,这之间不到 250 年,所以一些人便不相信,这是那个真正的长生鸟,他们说,它不是来自阿拉伯,它的行动同古代所验证的行动也不相符。因为据传说,当它天年已尽而死亡来临的时候,它要在它的本国做一个巢,把一种具有生殖力的物质洒在上面,这样一只小长生鸟就会从那里生出来了。小长生鸟长大之后,它所做的第一件事情就是把它的父亲埋葬起来。它做这件事习惯上是按照以下的程序进行的:它先带着一定量的没药长时间地飞行,以证明它已经有能力负重远行了;下一步它就背起父亲的尸体,把它带到太阳神的祭坛那里,然后就把它烧掉。关于详细的情况,人们还存在着争议,并且传说也都将它们进行了夸大。但是这种鸟时常在埃及出现,这一点却是毫无疑问的。

在罗马,残杀仍在继续不断。彭波尼乌斯·拉贝欧——我在前面已经说过了关于他治理美西亚的事情——割断了自己的动脉,流血而死,继而他的妻子帕克赛娅也追随他而死。由于人们害怕被判罪,而且因为当一个人被判处死刑的时候,财产会被没收并且尸体也得不到埋葬,所以自杀也就很容易成为人们的选择。而另一方面,自杀的人还能够得到埋葬尸体的待遇,并且他

and recognition of their wills. Tiberius, however, wrote to the senate recalling that Romans of earlier days, when excluding someone from their friendship, had terminated relations by forbidding him their houses. That, he said, was what he had done in this case: but Labeo, charged with misgovernment of his province and other offences, had tried to conceal his crime by maliciously implying persecution and unnecessarily alarming his wife, who—though guilty—had been in no danger.

Next came the second indictment of Mamercus Aemilius Scaurus. This aristocratic and eloquent, but dissolute, personage was ruined not by Sejanus' friendship but by the no less lethal enmity of Macro. Stealthily imitating his predecessor, Macro had denounced the subject-matter of a tragedy written by Scaurus, citing verses alleged to reflect on Tiberius. But the ostensible charges, brought by Servilius and Cornelius, were adultery with Livilla and magic. Scaurus, worthily of the Aemilii of old, anticipated his condemnation, encouraged and joined by Sextia his wife.

And yet, when occasion arose, retribution overcame accusers too. The ill-famed destroyers of Scaurus were outlawed and banished to the islands for accepting bribes to drop a charge against Varius Ligur. Likewise an ex-aedile named Abudius Ruso was actually condemned and banned from Rome, while menacing Cnaeus Cornelius Lentulus Gaetulicus (under whom he had commanded a brigade) for having betrothed his own daughter to a son of Sejanus. At this time Gaetulicus

的遗嘱也将会得到许可。不过提贝里乌斯在写给元老院的一封信里，回忆古罗马时代说，那时，当人们和某一个人绝交时，便会禁止这个人到他们家里来，从而与他彻底断绝一切关系。他说，他本人对拉贝欧也是这样做的，因为拉贝欧被控以在他的行省中滥用职权以及其他罪行后，却企图通过恶意地暗示他受到了迫害，并毫无必要地引起他妻子的恐惧等手段，来掩盖他自己的罪行。他的妻子虽然也是有罪的，不过并没有生命的危险。

接下来的就是对玛米尔库斯·埃米里乌斯·司考路斯的第二次的控诉。这个有着贵族出身，又有着极高的口才，但是在私生活方面却很放荡的人，他的毁灭并不是由于他和谢雅努斯的友谊，而是同样由于遭到了玛克罗致命的敌视。玛克罗暗暗地模仿着他的前辈谢雅努斯，他指控司考路斯所写的一个悲剧的主题，说里面引用的一些诗句是暗讽提贝里乌斯的。但在表面上，却是由塞尔维里乌斯和科尔涅里乌斯对他提出控告，指控的罪名是同利维拉通奸和使用魔法。司考路斯无愧于古老的埃米里乌斯家族，他预料到自己会被判罪，因而在他的妻子塞克司提娅的鼓励和陪同之下自杀了。

虽然如此，在机会来临的时候，报应也会降临到控告者头上。臭名昭著，阴谋陷害司考路斯的人被剥夺了公民权，并且被放逐到岛上去，因为他们收纳了贿赂而中止了对瓦里乌斯·里古斯的控诉。同样的，先前担任过营造官的阿布狄乌斯·路索也被判了罪，并且被逐出罗马，因为他对科涅乌斯·科尔涅里乌斯·楞图路斯·盖图里库斯（路索本人曾在盖图里库斯手下担任过军团将领）进行威胁，说盖图里库斯曾把自己的一个女儿许配给谢雅努斯的一个儿子，因此要控告他。这

commanded the army of Upper Germany. It loved him dearly for his generous kindness and leniency. He was also popular with the neighbouring army of Lucius Apronius, his father-in-law. It was persistently asserted that Gaetulicus had ventured to write to Tiberius. 'My connection with Sejanus,' he was believed to have said, 'was not my idea, but yours. I could be deceived as easily as you. The same mistake could not be considered harmless in some, a capital offence in others. My own loyalty is undiminished and permanent—unless I am plotted against. But I should regard my supersession as a death-warning. Let us strike a bargain—that you rule everywhere else, and I keep my province.'

The story is remarkable. Yet it is corroborated by Gaetulicus' retention—alone among Sejanus' connections—of life and favour. Tiberius knew that he himself, old and unpopular, reigned by prestige more than by actual power.

In the next year, when the consuls were Gaius Cestius Gallus (I) and Marcus Servilius Nonianus (II), certain Parthian noblemen visited Rome, unknown to their king Artabanus III. That monarch, while he had Germanicus to fear, had been faithful to Rome and just towards his own people. But then successful warfare against neighbouring nations encouraged him—and he despised Tiberius as old and

时,盖图里库斯正在上日耳曼统率着一支军队,因为他慷慨仁慈、宽厚善良,所以士兵们都非常爱戴他。由于他的岳父路奇乌斯·阿普洛尼乌斯的关系,他在相邻部队中也享有很高的声望。一些人坚持认为,盖图里库斯曾经冒险给提贝里乌斯写过信,并且还坚信他曾在信中这样说:"我和谢雅努斯结亲,并不是出自我的本意,而是由于您的劝告。我是和您一样容易被欺骗的。同样的错误,不能在一种情况下被看做是无害的,而在另一种情况下就是致命的罪行。我本人的忠诚丝毫没有减弱,而且,除非我被阴谋陷害,我的忠诚也是会保持到永远的。如果有人来接替我的话,我会把它看做是我死亡的一个警告。让我们订立一个合约,皇帝您统治所有其他的地方,而我本人则保留行省的统治权。"

这个说法是耸人听闻的。但是从盖图里库斯的职位得以保留这一事实来看,它又得到了确证,因为在同谢雅努斯有联系——包括与他有亲属关系和得到他的欣赏的人们中间,只有盖图里库斯安然无恙。提贝里乌斯知道,年事已高又不得人心的他,需要靠的是威信而不是实际拥有的权力来统治这个帝国。

第二年,是盖乌斯·凯司提乌斯·盖路斯(一世)和玛尔库斯·塞尔维里乌斯·诺尼亚努斯(二世)担任执政官的一年,[1] 在这一年中有一些帕尔提亚的贵族们访问了罗马,他们是瞒着他们的国王阿尔塔巴努斯三世而来的。这一位君主,尽管对于日耳曼尼库斯心存恐惧,但是,正如他对于本国人民的态度一样,他对于罗马还是很忠诚的。但是,接着他与邻近的几个国家进行了几次战争,并且大获全胜,这使得他的欲望膨胀了起来,而且根本就不把年迈而

---

〔1〕 公元 35 年,罗马建城 788 年。

unwarlike. So Artabanus became insolent to us, and brutal to his subjects. He wanted Armenia, and on the death of its monarch Artaxias
III installed his eldest son Arsaces on its throne, sending delegates
with an insulting demand for the treasure the exiled King Vonones I
had left in Syria and Cilicia. Artabanus added menacing boasts about
the old frontiers of the Persian and Macedonian empires, promising to
seize the lands that Cyrus and Alexander had ruled.

The secret Parthian mission to Rome was chiefly inspired by the
wealthy nobleman Sinnaces, supported by Abdus, a eunuch (for a-
mong orientals that condition, far from being despised, is actually a
source of power). Other leading men, too, had been consulted. They
could find no one of the Parthian royal house to elevate to the throne -
Artabanus had killed many of them, and the rest were minors. So
they requested Prince Phraates (son of Phraates IV, a former Parthian
king) from Rome. All that was needed, they said, was a name and
an authorization: the name of a Parthian royalty—to show himself on
the Euphrates—and the authorization of Tiberius. This was what Tiberius wanted. True to his policy of manipulating foreign affairs by astute diplomacy without warfare, he subsidized and equipped Phraates.

Meanwhile Artabanus discovered the conspiracy. Panic and passion for revenge seized him in turn. Though natives regard hesitation
as servile, and expect instant action from a king, Artabanus acted prudently. Abdus, invited with ostensible friendliness to dinner, was dis-

且不再适宜于战争的提贝里乌斯放在眼里。于是阿尔塔巴努斯对我们采取了傲慢的态度,而对其臣民也采取了残暴的政策。他对亚美尼亚存有野心,因此在亚美尼亚国王阿尔塔克西亚斯三世去世之后,就将自己的长子阿尔撒凯斯扶上了王位,同时派出使节提出了侮辱性的要求,要求取得遭到驱逐的国王沃诺尼斯一世所遗留在叙利亚和奇里奇亚的财宝。阿尔塔巴努斯还进行威胁,夸大其词地谈起了旧日波斯帝国和马其顿帝国的边界,发誓要夺取居鲁士和亚历山大曾经统治过的地区。

帕尔提亚的密使之所以能够到罗马来,主要是受了富有的贵族辛纳凯斯的鼓动,并且是得到了宦官阿布都斯的支持的。(原来在东方的部落中间,宦官不但不会受到轻视,而且还是拥有实权的。)他们还征求过其他一些政要人物的意见。他们在帕尔提亚的王室家族当中无法找到一个可以登上王位的人,因为他们当中的许多人被阿尔塔巴努斯杀死了,而剩下的其他的人都还没有成年,于是他们便要求王子普拉提斯从罗马回来(普拉提斯是帕尔提亚前国王普拉提斯五世的儿子)。他们说,他们所需要的只是一个名字和一种授权:帕尔提亚王室的名字,和王室人员出现在幼发拉底河的河岸上,以及提贝里乌斯的授权。这也正是提贝里乌斯所想的事情。实际上提贝里乌斯一心想通过外交权术,而不是依赖战争来操纵外交事务,于是他给予普拉提斯资金和装备上的支持。

与此同时,阿尔塔巴努斯发现了这一阴谋。惊恐和渴望复仇的念头在他的内心相互交织着。虽然对于这些外族人来说,犹豫观望在他们看来就是奴隶的特征,大家都以为国王会迅速采取行动,但是,阿尔塔巴努斯却采取了随机应变的策略。阿布都斯以

abled by a slow poison. Disingenuous tactics, including presents, distracted Sinnaces; and he was kept busy. Then, in Syria, Phraates, abandoning the Roman way of life—to which he had been accustomed for many years—in favour of his Parthian countrymen's customs, could not tolerate these, fell ill, and died.

But Tiberius persevered. Another royal prince, Tiridates III, was selected to dispute Parthia with Artabanus. Simultaneously Mithridates, a brother of Pharasmanes the king of Iberia in the Caucasus, was reconciled with his brother and sent to recover Armenia from Artabanus' son Arsaces. The eastern situation as a whole was entrusted to Lucius Vitellius (I). Though his reputation at Rome was admittedly bad, and much scandalous behaviour was attributed to him, his provincial government showed old-fashioned integrity. But after his recall, fear of Gaius and friendship with Claudius were to make Vitellius so deplorably servile that, to subsequent generations, he is a byword for degraded sycophancy. His first doings are effaced by his last - his youthful distinction by his scandalous later years.

The violent and treacherous princeling Mithridates took the initiative in persuading his brother Pharasmanes to help him recover the

增进友谊为借口,被邀请来参加宴会,其结果就是由于中毒而慢慢变成了一个残废。而对于辛纳凯斯则使用了包括送礼等在内的各种欺诈性的措施,使其整日奔波而分散了他的注意力。接着就是普拉提斯,他在叙利亚已经放弃了多年来所习惯了的罗马的生活方式,以便能够适应帕尔提亚国人的习俗,结果是无法适应,最终病倒而去世。

但是,提贝里乌斯仍然坚持自己的原计划,选中了另一个帕尔提亚王室成员提里达特斯三世到帕尔提亚去与阿尔塔巴努斯展开竞争。与此同时,伊伯利亚人米特利达特斯,即在卡乌卡苏斯的伊伯利亚国王帕拉斯玛尼斯的兄弟,在与其国王兄弟取得了和解之后,受命被派往亚美尼亚,将亚美尼亚从阿尔塔巴努斯的儿子阿尔撒凯斯手里解放出来。东方的全部事务都授予了路奇乌斯·维提里乌斯(一世)[1]负责管理。虽然在罗马他的名声很臭,而且有许多恶行都可以找到他的头上去,但是他在治理行省的过程之中却表现出了古老的正直诚实的风尚。但是在他被召回了罗马之后,出于对卡里古拉的恐惧和与克劳狄乌斯亲密的友谊关系,使维提里乌斯堕落到了如此讨厌的奴性十足的程度,以至于他之后的人们都将他视做是一个阿谀奉承的典范。他早年时突出的高尚都被他自己晚年的恶行掩盖了,从而使人们所记住的都是他晚年的所作所为,而不是早期的情况。

米特利达特斯作为王室的成员却采用了暴力和欺骗的手段,以诱使自己的兄弟帕拉斯玛尼斯帮助他重新夺回亚美尼亚国王

---

〔1〕 这是克劳狄乌斯一个臭名昭著的宠臣,他是前一任的执政官,又是未来皇帝的父亲。

Armenian throne. Agents were found to induce the Armenians (at a heavy price) to murder Arsaces. Simultaneously a strong Iberian force broke into Armenia and seized the capital, Artaxata. Artabanus, learning the news, appointed another son Orodes to exact retribution, gave him Parthian troops, and sent representatives to hire auxiliaries.

Pharasmanes responded by enlisting the Albani and calling on the Sarmatians, whose chiefs, as is the national custom, accepted gifts from, and enlisted on, both sides. But the Iberians controlled the strong-points and speedily rushed their Sarmatians over the Caucasian pass into Armenia. They easily blocked those of the Sarmatians who had joined the other side. For the Iberians closed every pass except one, and that one-between the outermost Albanian mountains and the sea—is impassable in summer since the seaboard is flooded by Etesian gales: in winter south winds drive back the water, and the sea's recession drains the shallows.

Orodes, short of allies, was now challenged to fight by the heavily reinforced Pharasmanes. He refused. However, the enemy harassed Orodes, riding close to the camp, plundering his sources of forage, and often virtually blockading him with a ring of outposts. Orodes' Parthians, unaccustomed to such insolence, pressed round him and

的地位。他们(花大价钱)买通了亚美尼亚人以刺杀阿尔撒凯斯。与此同时,一支强大的伊伯利亚军队却攻入了亚美尼亚,并占领了亚美尼亚的首都阿尔塔克撒塔城。阿尔塔巴努斯听到了这一消息之后,就任命他的另一个儿子欧洛狄斯组织军队准备报复,将帕尔提亚的军队交给了他,而且派人出去雇佣辅助部队。

帕拉斯玛尼斯的对策就是与阿尔巴尼亚结为同盟,另外还将撒尔玛提亚人召集起来,而撒尔玛提亚人的"持杖者"[1]则是按照本民族的传统习惯,接受了双方各自的礼物,从而加入了双方的阵营。但是伊伯利亚军队占据了战略要点,而且驱使他们所控制的撒尔玛提亚人迅速推进,越过了卡乌卡西亚路而进入了亚美尼亚。他们轻易地就将那些已经加入到了另一方的撒尔玛提亚人给截住了。因为伊伯利亚军队已经将所有的其他通道都给封锁了,只留下了一条,这条通道位于阿尔巴尼亚山脉的最外端和大海之间。每到夏天,这条通道根本就不可能通行,因为埃提西亚风[2]所带来的洪水将海岸都给淹没了。而冬天则盛行南风,海水又会退回去,而随着海水的退出,浅海地面又会露出来。

欧洛狄斯缺少联盟者,现在面对着拥有强有力支持的帕拉斯玛尼斯的挑战,他退却了。但是敌军却不断地骚扰欧洛狄斯,骑兵们推进到他的军营附近,抢掠他的秣草场,而且经常用一队队的前哨部队对他形成包围之势。欧洛狄斯手下的帕尔提亚人部队根本就不能容忍如此的侮辱,因而他们围着国王坚决要求出

---

〔1〕 原来是指波斯皇宫之中的大宦官,后来则是指某些西徐亚的小国王。

〔2〕 埃提西亚风是每年夏天在地中海上空所刮的一种季节风。

demanded battle. Their whole strength lay in their cavalry. But Pharasmanes had useful infantry as well as cavalry, since the highland
life of the Iberians and Albanians has given them exceptional tough-
ness and endurance. They claim Thessalian origin, dating from the
time when Jason, after leaving with Medea and their children, returned to the empty palace of Aeetes and the kingless Colchians. They
have many stories about him, and maintain an oracle of Phrixus; and
as he is said to have been carried on a ram (whether it was the animal
or a ship's figurehead), the sacrifice of rams is forbidden.

When both sides had drawn up their battle-line, Orodes addressed his men, glorifying the Parthian empire and its royal family's
grandeur, in contrast with the humble Iberians and their mercenaries.
Pharasmanes, however, reminded his troops that they had never submitted to Parthia—the loftier their aspirations, he said, the greater
would be the honour of victory, and the disgrace and peril of defeat.
Contrasting his own formidable warriors with the enemy in their
goldembroidered robes, he cried: ' Men on one side-on the other,
loot ! '

Nevertheless, among the Sarmatians, their Iberian commander's
was not the only voice. This must not be a bowman's engagement,
men shouted; better to rush matters by a charge, and then fight hand-
tohand! So the battle was confused. The Parthian cavalry, expert at
withdrawals as well as pursuits, opened ranks to allow themselves
room to shoot. But the Sarmatian horsemen on the other side, instead
of shooting back—their bows being inferior in range-charged, with

战。他们整个的力量就在于骑兵身上了。但是帕拉斯玛尼斯不仅拥有一支强大的骑兵部队，而且也拥有一支有效的步兵，因为伊伯利亚人和阿尔巴尼亚人多年的山地生活环境使他们具有一种特别坚强和特别能忍耐的精神。他们自称是帖撒利亚人的后裔，他们的祖先可以追溯到亚逊，那时候亚逊和美狄娅以及他们的孩子们离开之后，又返回到了阿埃提斯空荡荡的宫殿之中和没有国王的科尔齐斯人之中去。对于亚逊，他们有许多传说，这其中包含了一个普利克苏斯的神托：由于传说中普利克苏斯是由一只公羊托着（当然到底是一只动物还是一艘刻着公羊头的船头雕饰，还不清楚），所以用公羊作祭品的事情是绝对不允许的。

在双方拉开战线准备开战时，欧洛狄斯对他手下的士兵们发表了讲话，他详细地谈起了帕尔提亚帝国及其皇家家族的伟大，并将这与卑微的伊伯利亚人和他们的雇佣军队进行了比较。而帕拉斯玛尼斯则提醒他的军队，他们从来就没有向帕尔提亚人屈服过。他说，他们的勇气越足，就越能够取得更为巨大的胜利的光荣，而假如战败的话就会面临着屈辱和危险了。将自己手下的这支令人生威的部队与敌方的那支穿着金绣外袍的部队进行了比较之后，他喊道："这边的是英雄好汉，那边的只是一些战利品！"

但是，在撒尔玛提亚人的队伍之中，发言的却不仅仅是他们的伊伯利亚将领，他们高喊道，这场战争不能成为弓箭手之间的较量，最好是采取先发制人的措施，然后再开展一次白刃战。于是，战争的局势就变得错综复杂起来了。帕尔提亚人的骑兵部队，擅长于撤退，而且也能巧妙地追击，他们拉开了自己的骑兵部队的队形，从而留出了一块可以投掷长枪的地区。但是，另一方的撒尔玛提亚人的骑兵队伍由于他们的弓箭射程不远，所以就不用

pikes and swords. At one moment it was like an orthodox cavalry battle, with successive advances and retreats. Next the riders, interlocked, shoved and hewed at one another. At this juncture, the Albanian and Iberian infantry struck. Gripping hold of the Parthian riders, they tried to unsaddle them. The Parthians were caught between two fires-infantry grappling with them at close quarters, and Sarmatian horsemen attacking them from higher ground.

Pharasmanes and Orodes were conspicuous, supporting the staunchest fighters and rescuing those in trouble. Then they recognized each other and charged. Pharasmanes' onslaught was the more violent, and he pierced the Parthian's helmet and wounded him. But he failed to deliver a second blow, since his horse carried him past; and the wounded man's bravest officers protected him. Still, false reports of Orodes' death were believed; the Parthians were panic-stricken, and conceded victory.

Artabanus then mobilized his kingdom's entire resources for retaliation. But the Iberians had the better of the fighting, since they knew the Armenian terrain. Nevertheless, the Parthians were only induced to retire because Lucius Vitellius concentrated his divisions in a feint against Mesopotamia. Artabanus could not face war against Rome, and he evacuated Armenia. Vitellius then secured his downfall by enticing his subjects to abandon him. For indeed Artabanus was as disastrously unsuccessful in war as he was savage in peace. So Sinnaces, already (as I have mentioned) the enemy of Artabanus, per-

射击的方法,而是拿着枪和剑勇猛地向前冲。战争一会儿就像传统的骑兵战一样,骑兵们不断地交替进攻与后撤。紧接着,骑兵们互相混战了起来,他们或是击退敌人,或是被敌人所击退。就在这时,阿尔巴尼亚人和伊伯利亚人的步兵们也加入了战斗,他们用手抓住帕尔提亚人的骑兵,极力地将他们从马鞍上拖下来。现在的帕尔提亚人遭受了双重的危险,步兵靠近他们向他们展开了攻击,而撒尔玛提亚人的骑兵部队则是从上面向他们进攻。

帕拉斯玛尼斯和欧洛狄斯分别带领军队各自支援自己的正在作战的士兵或救援那些处于危险之中的战士。他们在队伍当中非常突出,于是彼此认出了对方,并向对方发起了攻击。帕拉斯玛尼斯的厮杀更加凶猛,他刺穿了对方的头盔而使之负了伤,但是他却没有机会发起第二次进攻,因为他的战马将他带离了战场。而受了伤的欧洛狄斯受到了他手下的最勇猛的卫士的保护。接着,传来了一个错误的消息,说欧洛狄斯已经战死,而且大伙都相信了。这一消息使帕尔提亚人情绪上感到非常惊恐沮丧,于是就承认自己战败了。

接着,阿尔塔巴努斯就动员了整个王国的兵力前来报复。但是伊伯利亚人已经了解了亚美尼亚的地形情况,于是他们在战争之中取得了优势。然而,直到路奇乌斯·维提里乌斯集中了他手下的所有军团,并假装摆出了一副要进攻美索不达米亚的样子,阿尔塔巴努斯才被迫撤军。由于阿尔塔巴努斯不敢直接与罗马开战,所以从亚美尼亚撤军了。接着,维提里乌斯就诱使他的臣民背叛了他,从而促使他下了台。因为说实话,阿尔塔巴努斯尽管在平时极其残忍凶暴,而在战场上却是极其可怜而无能。于是,(正如我已经提及的那样)早已经是阿尔

suaded his own father Abdagaeses to revolt, together with other accomplices encouraged to rebel by continuous Parthian reverses. They
were gradually joined by men who had supported Artabanus from fear
rather than goodwill and plucked up courage now that leaders had appeared. Soon all that Artabanus had left were his foreign guards, expatriates unconcerned with right and wrong-paid instruments of crime.
With these he hastily fled to the remote borders of Scythia, hoping to
obtain help from marriage connections among the Hyrcanians and Car-
manians of that region. Meanwhile the Parthians—always impatient of
present rulers, fond of absent ones—might penitently change their
minds.

However, Artabanus had fled, and his countrymen were now inclined for a new king. So Vitellius advised Tiridates III to seize his
opportunity, and led the bulk of his regular and auxiliary troops to
the Euphrates. There sacrifices were performed. Vitellius offered to
Mars the Roman boar, ram, and bull; Tiridates propitiated the river
with a finely harnessed horse. Though no rain had fallen, the inhabitants reported a spontaneous and remarkable rise in its waters. Moreover, its white foam seemed to form circles, like diadems, which
were said to prophesy a successful crossing. Others offered a shrewder

塔巴努斯的敌对者的幸纳凯斯,便诱使自己的父亲阿布达伽伊塞斯也起来造反,与他们一起的同谋者是一些不断地遭受厄运从而受到了鼓励起来改变命运的帕尔提亚人。既然出现了领导反叛阿尔塔巴努斯的人,那些过去投靠阿尔塔巴努斯是由于恐惧而不是出于心甘情愿的人也就勇气高涨了起来,他们纷纷加入到了叛乱者的队伍之中。不久,阿尔塔巴努斯不得不在一些外国卫士的保护之下离开了,这些人只是依靠替他人从事犯罪活动而挣钱谋生的,在他们的观念之中是不存在对与错之分的。带着这些人,他匆匆忙忙地逃到了遥远的西徐亚〔1〕边疆地区去了,希望利用那一地区之中的叙尔卡尼亚人和卡尔玛尼亚人与自己的婚姻关系而获得支持。那些习惯于反抗现存统治者而喜欢被驱逐走的统治者的帕尔提亚人,此时或许又在后悔从而改变自己的主意。

然而,阿尔塔巴努斯已经逃跑了,他的国人们现在正急于寻找一位新国王。于是维提里乌斯劝告提里达特斯三世要抓住这一机会,而将其正规军团与辅助部队带到幼发拉底河沿岸地区。接着就举行了献祭仪式,维提里乌斯向玛尔斯神祭献了公猪、公羊、公牛等祭品;而提里达特斯也用一匹精良的战马向幼发拉底河献了祭。虽然没有下雨,但是附近的居民却来报告说,幼发拉底河水突然自动地高涨了起来,而且涨得令人惊奇。而且河水的白色泡沫形成了看似圆圈的东西,就像一顶王冠,据说这是可以顺利渡河的象征。其他一些人则是做出了更加巧妙的解释,说

---

〔1〕 西徐亚是指古时候里海以东的地区,当时在这一地区居住的是叙尔卡尼亚人,紧接在他们北面的是达阿伊人,而卡尔玛尼亚人当时居住在波斯湾沿岸地区。

interpretation-the enterprise would prosper at first, but briefly; omens of earth or sky were more reliable, but rivers being fluid no sooner displayed a portent than they obliterated it.

A bridge of boats was constructed, and the army crossed. The first to join them was Omospades, with a large force of cavalry. Formerly an exile, he had seen distinguished service under Tiberius in the Dalmatian war and received Roman citizenship, and later, restored to his king's friendship and high favour, had become governor of Mesopotamia, the plain enclosed by the famous Tigris and Euphrates. Soon afterwards Tiridates was joined by Sinnaces and Abdagaeses. The latter, the pillar of their cause, brought the court treasure and regalia. Vitellius concluded that his display of Roman might was sufficient. Exhorting Tiridates to remember all the great qualities of his royal grandfather Phraates IV and his imperial foster-father, he urged his supporters to remain loyal to their king, respectful to Rome, and true to their own honour and good faith. Then Vitellius marched his army back to Syria.

I have merged the events of two summers, to allow some respite from Roman miseries. Three years had passed since Sejanus' execution. But influences which soften other hearts-time, entreaties,

这次出征一开始会很成功,但是稍纵即逝,因为天地所提供的征兆会更加可信,而流动的河水不久就会将吉兆冲刷掉,从而展示出凶兆来。

河面上用小舟构筑的桥梁建起来了,部队也通过了。第一个加入到他们部队来的是欧尔诺司帕狄斯,他带来了一支规模巨大的骑兵部队。以前他曾经是一个被驱逐者,进而在达尔马提亚战役[1]之中在提贝里乌斯手下服役,并立了赫赫战功,从而获得了罗马公民权。以后,他又依靠与国王的友谊以及深受国王的器重,成为包括底格里斯河与幼发拉底河在内的美索不达米亚平原的统治者。不久之后,提里达特斯的军队之中又融入了辛纳凯斯和阿布达伽伊塞斯所率领的军队,而后者作为他们事业的支柱,带来了宫廷所有的财富和王室所有的标志。维提里乌斯认为,只要显示了罗马的威风就足够了,于是就向提里达特斯提出了忠告,要他牢记自己的王室祖父普拉提斯四世和作为皇帝的养父,要记住这两个人的伟大的品质;他要求提里达特斯的支持者们要对国王保持忠心,要对罗马保持尊敬之心,而且要真正与他们所具有的荣誉和诚意相符合。随后,维提里乌斯就率领着自己的部队返回了叙利亚。

我是将两个夏季所发生的事情放在一起进行叙述的,目的是为了让人们暂时不管罗马所发生的那一些悲惨事件。尽管谢雅努斯被处决[2]已经过去三年了,但是,时间、请求、厌烦这些足以使

---

satiety—did not dissuade Tiberius from punishing disputable, outdated offences as though they were fresh and terrible. Lucius Fulcinius Trio, alarmed, escaped imminent prosecution by killing himself. He left a will savagely criticizing Naevius Sutorius Macro and Tiberius' leading ex-slaves, and attacking the emperor himself as a dotard who, by reason of his long absence, was virtually an exile. Fulcinius' heirs wanted this suppressed. But Tiberius had it read to show his toleration of free speech—and indifference to his own reputation. Or perhaps, warned by his long unawareness of Sejanus' crimes, he now favoured publicity for every kind of assertion, so that abuse failing other methods—should reveal the truth which servility hides.

Further senators now fell. One, Granius Marcianus, accused by Gaius Sempronius Gracchus (II) of treason, committed suicide. A former praetor called Tarius Gratianus was sentenced to death for the same offence. Two others, Titus Trebellenus Rufus and Sextius Paconianus, met similar ends, one killing himself, the other strangled in gaol for verses he had composed there criticizing the emperor. When Tiberius heard of these events he was not, as hitherto, across the sea, receiving messengers from afar, but near the city where he could answer the consuls' letters on the same day—or after a single night—and could almost gaze at the homes deluged in blood, and the execu-

人心软的东西并没有使提贝里乌斯心软,从而停止对那些尚有争议的过错进行残酷的处罚,那些很久之前对他的微小的冒犯就像是刚刚犯下的,并且是罪大恶极令人可怕的罪行似的。对此,路奇乌斯·富尔奇尼乌斯·特里奥非常惊恐,为了逃避那不可避免的迫害,他自杀了。他留下了一份遗嘱,里面猛烈地抨击了纳尔维乌斯·苏陀利乌斯·玛克罗以及皇帝的主要被释奴隶;而且抨击皇帝,将他说成是一个年老昏庸的人,并且由于长年不在罗马,从而实际上已经成为了一个流亡犯。富尔奇尼乌斯的继承人想将这份遗嘱保存起来,但是提贝里乌斯却命令他当众宣读,以表明容许他人自由发表言论,并且对于自己的恶名不屑一顾。或许是他想通过自己多年来对于谢雅努斯罪行的一无所知而警告自己,现在他宁愿将每一种攻击性的言论公之于众;这样,假如不是通过其他的方法的话,也可以通过谩骂性的言词而认识到被奴性的奉承所掩盖的真理。

现在,更多元老们相继垮台了。其中之一就是格拉尼乌斯·玛尔奇亚努斯,他被盖乌斯·塞姆普罗尼乌斯·格拉古斯(二世)指控为叛国罪,从而自杀了。名叫塔里乌斯·格拉提亚努斯的前任行政长官也因为同样的罪名而被判处了死刑。另外两名元老,提图斯·特列贝列努斯·路福斯和塞克斯提乌斯·帕科尼亚努斯也遭受了同样的结局,一个是自杀而终,另一个则是因为写了反对皇帝的诗篇而被关进了监狱进而被绞死。当提贝里乌斯听到这些消息的时候,他并不是像从前一样从遥远的地方,跨过海洋而得到这些消息的,他就在罗马城附近,在那儿他可以当天就能够收到元老院的报告,并做出批示,最迟也不过就隔一夜的时间。尤其是他几乎就能够亲眼看到他们所流淌的鲜血,或者是能够看到剑

tioners at work.

The last days of the year witnessed the death of Gaius Poppaeus Sabinus. Humbly born, he had owed his consulship and honorary Triumph to the friendship of emperors. He had been retained as imperial governor of important provinces for twenty-four years-not for any outstanding talent, but because he was competent and no more.

The following year the consuls were Quintus Plautius and Sextus Papinius Allenius. Tragedies had now become so frequent that the executions of Lucius Aruseius and others caused little shock. Yet it was alarming when the knight Vibulenus Agrippa, after the completion of a hearing against him, drew poison from his clothing, swallowed it in the senate-house itself, collapsed, and was rapidly taken by attendants to prison. There the noose was tightened round his neck-though he was already dead. Not even ex-king Tigranes IV of Armenia was saved by his royal rank from prosecution and the fate common to Roman citizens. The former consul Gaius Sulpicius Galba and the two sons of Quintus Junius Blaesus died by suicide. Galba had received an ominous letter from Tiberius excluding him from the ballot for governorships. As for the Blaesi, priesthoods destined for them while their family prospered, and deferred when the crash came, had now been treated by Tiberius as vacant and given to others. They saw that this meant death, and acted accordingly. Aemilia Lepida (III),

子手们在处决他们。

这一年的年底,盖乌斯·波培乌斯·撒比努斯过世。他尽管出身卑微,却获得了执政官的地位,而且由于与皇帝之间的友谊而获得了凯旋的荣耀。他担当皇帝所任命的行政长官而统治各大行省达 24 年之久。他之所以能够做到这一点,并不是因为他有什么突出的才能,而仅仅是因为他能够胜任这一官职。

下一年,是克温图斯·普劳提乌斯和塞克斯图斯·帕皮尼乌斯·阿列尼乌斯担任执政官的一年。[1] 在这一年里,惨剧的发生是如此频繁,以至于路奇乌斯·阿路谢乌斯和其他人的被处死这样的恐怖事件,也几乎没有引起任何震动。但是也还是有过令人惊恐的场面:当罗马骑士维布列努斯·阿格里帕听完了控诉者对他的控告之后,就从衣服里面取出毒药吞了下去,从而倒在了元老院里,而旁边的侍从仍然迅速地将他拖到地牢去了。虽然他现在已经气绝身亡,刽子手却仍然把绞索紧紧地套在了他的脖子上。甚至曾经担任过亚美尼亚国王的提格拉尼斯四世,他的国王头衔也都不能使他逃脱一个普通罗马公民所受到的被控告的悲惨命运。担任过执政官的盖乌斯·苏尔皮奇乌斯·伽尔巴和克温图斯·尤尼乌斯·布莱苏斯的两个儿子自杀了。伽尔巴曾经收到过提贝里乌斯写给他的一封不祥的信,他一个行省也没有分配给伽尔巴。而在布莱苏斯家族的兴盛时期指定给两个布莱苏斯的祭司职位,在这一家族垮台之后便被延迟了下来,而现在提贝里乌斯把这些位置作为空缺给了其他的人。人们将此理解为处以死刑的暗示,因此就加以执行了。埃米里娅·列庇妲(三世)——

---

〔1〕 公元 36 年,罗马建城 789 年。

whose marriage with Drusus Caesar I have recorded, had showered slanders on her husband and lived, execrable but unpunished, while her father Marcus Aemilius Lepidus (IV) survived. Now accusers prosecuted her for adultery with a slave. Since her guilt was beyond question, she did not defend herself but committed suicide.

At this period the Cietae, a tribe subject to the Cappadocian prince Archclaus the younger, resisted compulsion to supply property-returns and taxes in Roman fashion by withdrawing to the heights of the Taurus mountains where, aided by the nature of the country, they held out against the prince's unwarlike troops. But the divisional commander Marcus Trebellius, sent by Lucius Vitcllius (imperial governor of Syria) with 4,000 regulars and picked auxiliary forces, constructed earthworks round two hills held by the natives (the smaller called Cadra, the larger Davara). After killing some who attempted to break out, Trebellius forced the rest to surrender.

Meanwhile with Parthian approval Tiridates III occupied Mesopotamian towns, including Macedonian foundations (Nicephorium, Anthemusias, and others with Greek names) and some places of Parthian origin (Halus and Artemita). This caused satisfaction among those who loathed the cruelty of the Scythia-bred Artabanus III and hoped Tiridates had been civilized by Roman culture. The supreme sycophancy came from Seleucia on the Tigris, a powerful walled city which, remembering its founder Seleucus, had not decayed into barbarism. Its senate numbers three hundred men, selected for their wealth or intelligence. The public, too, have prerogatives of their own.

她与杜路苏斯·恺撒的婚姻前面我已经记述过了,在对她的丈夫进行了一连串的诽谤后,虽然非常令人厌恶,但她并没有受到惩罚,当时她的父亲玛尔库斯·埃米里乌斯·列庇都斯(四世)还活着。现在,控告者控诉她和一个奴隶通奸。因为她的罪行是毫无疑问的,因此她没有为自己辩护就自杀了。

就在这个时候,奇耶塔伊人,一个臣服于卡帕多奇亚年轻国王阿尔凯拉乌斯的部落,由于不愿意被迫按照罗马的惯例缴纳财产税和贡物,而迁居到了陶路斯山脉的高原地带。他们借着那一地区的自然形势,抗拒着国王统治下那些没有什么斗志的部队。但是,(叙利亚长官)路奇乌斯·维提里乌斯派遣了他的副帅玛尔库斯·特列贝里乌斯率领 4000 名正规军团士兵和一支精锐的辅助步兵队伍赶了过来。特列贝里乌斯围绕着奇耶塔伊人占领的两座小山(较小的一座山叫卡德拉山,较大的一座叫达瓦拉山)修筑了大量的工事,在杀死了一些妄图突围出去的人后,其余的人便在特列贝里乌斯的威逼之下被迫投降了。

正在这个时候,在帕尔提亚人的许可之下,提里达特斯三世占领了美索不达米亚各城市,包括马其顿人建立的城市(尼凯波里乌姆、安提木西亚斯和其他带有希腊名称的城市),和帕尔提亚的发源地(哈路斯和阿尔提米塔)。人们不满于受过西徐亚式训练的阿尔塔巴努斯三世的残酷,而且对受到罗马文化教育的提里达特斯充满了希望,因此他们对此十分高兴。提格里斯的塞琉西亚,这个有城墙围绕的强大城市,虽然谄媚之风盛行,但仍然记着建城者塞琉古的遗教,没有堕落成为野蛮之邦。它的元老院由300 人组成,他们都是以其财产丰富或智慧超群而被选拔出来的。人民也有他们自己的特权。

When senate and public agree, Seleucia despises Parthia. When they disagree, each calls in help against the other, and one side's external helper overwhelms both sides alike. That had recently happened during the reign of Artabanus III. He had sacrificed the public to their leaders; this was in his interests, since democracy approximates to freedom, whereas arbitrary absolutism feels closer to oligarchy.

So the Seleucian people welcomed Tiridates with royal honours, ancient and modern. They abused Artabanus as low-born, being royal on his mother's side only. Tiridates established democratic government at Seleucia. Then however, as he was considering which day to select for his formal accession to the throne, he received letters from two of the most powerful governors, Phraates and Hiero, requesting a brief postponement. It was decided to move to the capital Ctesiphon and there to await these important personages. One deferment followed another, but finally the hereditary commander-in-chief (or Surenas) with traditional ritual, before a large and enthusiastic crowd, crowned Tiridates with the royal diadem.

If he had immediately proceeded to the other peoples in the interior, all waverers' doubts would have vanished and the Parthian empire would have been his. Instead he besieged the fortress in which Artabanus had lodged his treasury and harem. This allowed time for agreements to be broken; and Phraates and Hiero, with others who had not participated in the coronation, went over to Artabanus—some because they feared him, others through jealousy of Abdagaeses (now Court Minister) and Tiridates. Artabanus was discovered in Hyrcania,

　　只要元老院和人民这两个阶级齐心协力,塞琉西亚人就完全可以藐视帕尔提亚人了。但是如果他们发生不和,那么每一方面都会寻求帮助来反对另一方,而结果,被一方召请来援助的外来者却征服了双方全体的人民。这样的事情不久之前就发生在了阿尔塔巴努斯三世统治的时期。他为了贵族阶层的目的,而牺牲了民众的利益。他这样做是从他自己的利益出发的,因为民主就意味着自由,而少数派的统治与一个国王的专断是非常接近的。

　　因此,塞琉西亚人用过去给予古代国王的荣誉以及当前比较喜欢用的新式荣誉来欢迎提里达特斯的到来。同时他们又辱骂阿尔塔巴努斯出身的卑微,因为在他的家族中只有他的母亲是一个王室成员而已。提里达特斯按照塞琉西亚的统治方式建立了民主统治。但是,接下来,当他正在考虑选择哪一天正式登上王位时,他收到了从两个最强大的藩王普拉提斯和希耶洛那里送来的信,来信要求暂时推迟一下登位的日期。人们建议把首府迁往克提西丰,并且在那里等候这些重要人物。但是他们一天一天地拖延下去,最后,一个首领(或者是苏列纳)就按照传统的方式,在一大群热情的群众面前,把皇冠加到了提里达特斯的头上。

　　假如他即刻向国内的其他部落发动进攻的话,所有那些观望怀疑的人将会马上消除疑虑,进而整个帕尔提亚帝国将会掌握在他的手中。相反,他包围了阿尔塔巴努斯借以安置其金钱和后宫的要塞,这一举动就造成了借以撕毁协议的时间,而普拉提斯和希耶洛,连同其他的没有参加加冕仪式的人一同投靠到了阿尔塔巴努斯一边去了,一些人是出于对他的恐惧,另外一些人则是因为嫉妒(现在已经成为了宫廷大臣的)阿布达伽伊塞斯以及新国王提里达特斯。阿尔塔巴努斯是在叙尔卡尼亚发现的,当时他满身

a grimy figure, eating what his bow procured him. At first, in alarm, he suspected a trap. Convinced, finally, that the aim of their visit was his restoration, he recovered confidence and inquired the cause of this sudden change. Hiero criticized Tiridates as a mere boy, and complained that the power was not in the hands of the royal family: Tiridates had the empty title, but foreign luxury had made him effeminate -and Abdagacscs. ' family was supreme.

Artabanus' experience of rulership told him that, however spurious their affection, their hatreds were genuine. Waiting only to collect Scythian allies, he took the field-too quickly to allow enemy intrigues, or second thoughts by friends. To enlist popular sympathy, he retained his filthy appearance. Using every means—appeals and menaces alike—to attract waverers and encourage supporters, he approached Seleucia with a large force.

Unnerved by news of his approach, and by his arrival very soon afterwards, Tiridates hesitated. Should he engage Artabanus, or aim at a war of attrition? Those favouring battle and a speedy decision argued that the enemy troops, dispersed and weary after their long march, were not even psychologically united in loyalty to Artabanus - they backed him now, but recently they had betrayed and opposed him. Abdagaescs, however, counselled retreat to Mesopotamia, where, protected by the Tigris, they could first raise the Armenians and other outlying peoples such as the Elymaei, and then, with allied and Roman support, put matters to the test. This advice prevailed. For Abdagaeses was all-powerful—and Tiridates had no taste for

污泥,靠一张弓所猎获的东西而生存。一开始,阿尔塔巴努斯非常惊恐害怕,怀疑这是一个陷阱,最后在得到对方的保证,是为了迎接他重新登上王位之后,他恢复了自信,并询问造成这一突然变化的原因。希耶洛猛烈批评提里达特斯,说他只是一个孩子,并抱怨统治权并没有掌握在王室家族手中:提里达特斯只是一个空头衔的国王,多年居住在外国所养成的奢华的生活习惯已经使他懦弱无能,而阿布达伽伊塞斯家族已经是高高在上。

多年的统治经验告诉阿尔塔巴努斯,尽管他们对他的拥护是假装的,但是他们的憎恨之情却是真的。一旦等到他将西徐亚的联盟部队集中起来,马上就以一种令敌人迅雷不及掩耳之势或者令朋友们来不及改变想法的速度展开了攻击。为了争取大众们的同情支持,他保留了他那肮脏的外表。他将各种可以利用的手段都用上了,包括恳求和欺骗,以吸引迟疑观望者,鼓励支持者,同时他带领一支强大的军队逼近了塞琉西亚。

提里达特斯在听到阿尔塔巴努斯正在迫近边疆和不久之后他就有可能率部到达的消息之后,吓得失魂落魄,犹豫不决。是应该马上就与阿尔塔巴努斯交战呢,还是要与之展开一场消耗战?那些主张作战并迅速做出决定的人认为,经过了长途行军之后,敌人的军队已经分散并疲劳至极,甚至根本就不可能团结一心,对阿尔塔巴努斯保持忠心。现在他们虽然支持他,可不久以前他们曾经背叛并反对他。但是,阿布达伽伊塞斯却主张撤退到美索不达米亚地区,在那儿有底格里斯河可以作为屏障,而且可以首先将亚美尼亚人以及其他一些边远的民族,例如埃律迈安人发动起来,接着在联盟军队和罗马军队的支持之下,就可以与敌军一见高低了。这个意见占据了上风,因为阿布达伽伊塞斯掌握了决定一切

danger. But the retirement virtually became a flight. First the Arabi-ans, then the rest, left for their homes—and for Artabanus' camp. Fi-nally Tiridates relieved them from the dishonour of desertion by retur-ning, with a few followers, to Syria.

In the same year there was a serious fire at Rome. The Aventine and adjacent parts of the Circus Maximus were devastated. Tiberius acquired prestige from the calamity by defraying the value of the hou-ses and apartment-blocks destroyed. This generosity cost him one hundred million sesterces. It was all the more popular because his own building activities were slight. His only two public works were the Temple of Augustus and a new stage for Pompey's Theatre-and e-ven these he was too contemptuous of his reputation to dedicate, or too old. To estimate individual losses in the fire, he appointed a com-mission comprising the husbands of his four granddaughters, Cnaeus Domitius Ahenobarbus, Lucius Cassius Longinus, Marcus Vinicius, and Gaius Rubellius Blandus, with one additional member, Publius Petronius, nominated by the consuls. The emperor was voted every compliment that senators' ingenuity could devise. But his reactions, favourable or negative, were never known. For his end was near.

Shortly afterwards, the last consuls of his reign, Cnaeus Acerro-nius Proculus and Gaius Petronius Pontius Nigrinus, entered office.

的权力,而提里达特斯也不想冒风险。但是这次撤退最终变成了一次逃跑。首先是阿拉伯人,接着其他的人都跟着跑回家去了,而有的则是直接逃到阿尔塔巴努斯的军营之中去了。最后提里达特斯在一些追随者的陪同下逃回到了叙利亚,这样就免除了所有的人都逃跑了的耻辱。

在同一年,罗马城发生了一场严重的火灾。阿文提努姆以及与它相连接的大竞技场的部分都烧毁了。提贝里乌斯因为按照被烧毁的房屋和住宅区的价值给予人们赔偿,从而为自己获得了名誉。这一次的慷慨行动花费了他 1 亿谢司特尔提乌斯,因为他自己在住宅方面一直是花费很少的,所以这一举动更得到了人民群众的欢迎。他所建筑的仅有的两座公共建筑是奥古斯都神庙和庞培剧院的新舞台,而且即使是在那些地方他都没有去进行献祭活动,或许是因为他对名声非常蔑视,也或许是因为他已太老了而无法搞这一活动。为了准确地估计在这次火灾之中每家所造成的损失,他特地任命了自己的四个孙女的丈夫,即格涅乌斯·多米提乌斯·埃诺巴尔布斯、路奇乌斯·卡西乌斯·隆吉努斯、玛尔库斯·维尼奇乌斯以及盖乌斯·路贝利乌斯·勃兰都斯组成了一个委员会,管理此事。另外,执政官们又任命了一个叫普布里乌斯·佩特罗尼乌斯的人参与此事。元老们穷其所能,精心设计了各种各样的荣誉献给了皇帝,但是他对此是接受了还是予以拒绝了,我们不得而知,因为他临终的日子就要来到了。

不久之后,在他统治时期的最后的两名执政官格涅乌斯·阿凯罗尼乌斯·普罗库鲁斯和盖乌斯·佩特罗尼乌斯·庞提乌斯·尼格里努斯宣誓就职。[1]

---

〔1〕 公元 37 年,罗马建城 790 年。

Macro had become excessively powerful. Never neglectful of Gaius' favour, now Macro cultivated him more strenuously every day. After the death of Junia Claudilla—whose wedding with Gaius I recorded elsewhere—Macro induced his own wife Ennia to pretend she loved the prince and entice him into a promise of marriage. Gaius had no objection if it helped him towards the throne. Temperamental though he was, intimacy with his grandfather had taught him dissimulation.

The emperor knew this—and hesitated about the succession. First, there were his grandsons. Drusus' son Tiberius Gemellus was nearer to him in blood, and dearer. But he was still a boy. Gaius was in the prime of early manhood. He was also popular, being Germanicus' son. So his grandfather hated him. Claudius too was considered. He was middle-aged and well-meaning, but his weakminindedness was an objection. Tiberius feared that to nominate a successor outside the imperial house might bring contempt and humiliation upon Augustus' memory and the name of the Caesars. He cared more for posthumous appreciation than for immediate popularity.

Soon, irresolute and physically exhausted, Tiberius left the decision to fate. It was beyond him. Yet, by certain comments, he showed understanding of the future. When he reproached Macro for abandoning the setting for the rising sun, his meaning was clear. And when Gaius, in casual discussion, slighted the memory of Sulla, Tiberius fore-

　　玛克罗已经拥有了巨大的权力。他从来就没有敢于忽视过盖乌斯对他的好感，现在却日复一日地强烈地想得到这些东西。关于朱尼娅·克劳狄娅嫁给盖乌斯的事情我在前面曾经做过讲述，而自从她死后，玛克罗就唆使自己的妻子恩尼娅，假装已经爱上了这一王子，并用一个与他结婚的诺言来拴住他。而对于盖乌斯王子来说，只要是有助于他取得王位，什么事情他都不会反对的。他虽然是一个脾气暴躁的人，但是面对着自己的祖父，他还是尽量地伪装而不露出马脚。

　　皇帝对此非常了解，在对于选定继承人的问题上他犹豫不决。首先，他所考虑的是他自己的孙子。在他们中间，杜路苏斯的儿子提贝里乌斯·盖美路斯论血缘关系来说，和他更近一些，而且他也非常地疼爱他。但是，他还只是一个未成年的孩子。盖乌斯正处于青春期，而且是精力旺盛。同时作为日耳曼尼库斯的儿子，还深得人们的喜爱。而这正是他的祖父讨厌他的地方。克劳狄乌斯也被作为考虑对象。他正处于中年，而且颇具修养，但是他的脑子不够灵活，这是他的一个缺点。提贝里乌斯还生怕假如任命一位皇室之外的人作为继承人的话，那么对于奥古斯都的追忆和恺撒们的名字都只会变成人们嘲笑和蔑视的对象。他所关心的是后世的人们对他的称赞，而不是当前人们对他的欢迎。

　　不久之后，犹豫不决以及体力上的虚弱，使得提贝里乌斯放弃做出决定，而听任命运的安排。他实在无能为力了。然而，在一些漫不经心的评论之中，他也表露出了对于未来变化的一些看法。当他责备玛克罗，因为对方抛弃了快要落下的太阳而只关心正要升起的太阳，他所暗含的意思再清楚不过了。在一次偶然

told that Gaius would have all Sulla's faults and none of his virtues. Then, weeping bitterly and clasping his grandson Tiberius Gemellus, he said to the frowning Gaius: 'You will kill him! And someone else will kill you!' However, despite failing health, Tiberius did not ration his sensualities. He was making a show of vigour to conceal his illness; and he kept up his habitual jokes against the medical profession, declaring that no man over thirty ought to need advice about what was good or bad for him.

At Rome, meanwhile, were sown the seeds of bloodshed in later reigns. Acutia, the former wife of Publius Vitellius, was charged with treason by Decimus Laelius Balbus. But after her conviction, the proposal to reward her accuser was vetoed by a tribune, Junius Otho-whose downfall the feud thus created ultimately brought about. Then Albucilla, earlier married to Satrius Secundus, who had divulged Sejanus' conspiracy, was denounced for disloyalty to the emperor. She was notorious for her many lovers, and Cnaeus Domitius Ahenobarbus, Gaius Vibius Marsus, and Lucius Arruntius were cited for complicity and adultery with her. Of Ahenobarbus' lineage I have spoken. Marsus too could claim ancient family, as well as literary

的探讨中,当盖乌斯嘲笑苏拉的记忆力时,提贝里乌斯就预言似的说,盖乌斯将会具备苏拉的所有的缺点,而没有他身上的一点优点。接着,他大哭着紧紧抱住自己的孙子提贝里乌斯·盖美路斯,对盖乌斯说:"你会杀死他!而另外会有人将你杀死!"[1]尽管自己的健康状况日渐恶化,提贝里乌斯对于自己的放荡行为却一点儿也没有节制。他向世人展现自己的活力以掩盖自己的疾病。对于医疗技术,他还是保持着其惯有的态度,对此极尽嘲讽之能事,并宣称任何人只要是已过了30岁,就没有必要让别人告知哪些东西对自己的身体有利,哪些有害。

与此同时,在罗马正在酝酿着后来的皇帝方能见到的血腥事件。戴西姆斯·莱利乌斯·巴尔布斯指控普布利乌斯·维提里乌斯的前妻阿库提娅犯有大逆罪,但是在她被处决之后,对于控告者进行奖赏的提议却被保民官尤尼乌斯·奥托给否决了,他们两人之间的仇恨直到奥托丧命之后才最后消除。接着就是阿尔布奇拉,她早年曾经嫁给过告发谢雅努斯阴谋叛乱的撒特里乌斯·谢孔都斯,[2]现在她被戴西姆斯·莱利乌斯·巴尔布斯指控对皇帝不敬。她因为有许多情夫而臭名昭著,这其中,格涅乌斯·多米提乌斯·埃诺巴尔布斯、盖乌斯·维比乌斯·玛尔苏斯、路奇乌斯·阿尔伦提乌斯,都作为她的同谋犯和奸夫而受到了起诉。对于埃诺巴尔布斯的高贵出身我在前面已做过讲述。玛尔苏斯也有值得称道的地方,就是他那古老的家族以及本人在文学

---

〔1〕 他所说的这两句预言都实现了,前一句被盖乌斯在一年之内就实现了,后一句则是在公元41年被卡西乌斯·凯列亚实现了。

〔2〕 撒特里乌斯·谢孔都斯告发谢雅努斯阴谋刺杀提贝里乌斯和盖乌斯,并抢夺皇位的罪行。

distinction. Memoranda submitted to the senate indicated that the interrogation of witnesses and torture of the slaves had been supervised by Macro. But there was reason to suspect that Macro, known to hate Arruntius, had forged much of the evidence.

Perhaps the invalid emperor did not know this. For no instructions came from him. So Ahenobarbus and Marsus were able to stay alive—the former preparing his defence, the latter ostensibly starving himself to death. Arruntius' friends urged him, too, to procrastinate. But his answer was that different things suited different people. 'I have lived long enough', he said. 'My only regret is that insults and perils have made my old age unhappy. Sejanus long hated me; and Macro does now. There is always some powerful figure against me. It is not my fault; it is because I dislike criminality. '

'Certainly I might survive the few days until Tiberius dies. But in that case, how can I avoid the young emperor ahead? If Tiberius, in spite of all his experience, has been transformed and deranged by absolute power, will Gaius do better? Almost a boy, wholly ignorant, with a criminal upbringing, guided by Macro—the man chosen to suppress Sejanus, though Macro is the worse man of the two and responsible for more terrible crimes and national suffering. I foresee even grimmer slavery ahead. So from evils past, and evils to come, I am escaping. '

With these prophetic words he opened his veins. What followed showed the wisdom of his death. Albucilla, after unsuccessfully wounding herself, was consigned to prison by the senate. One of her

上的杰出才能。但是送交元老院的备忘录之中却说,玛克罗曾经主持对目击证人的审问以及对奴隶的拷打工作。既然众所周知玛克罗非常憎恨阿尔伦提乌斯,那么就有理由怀疑所谓的证据都是捏造出来的。

也许是皇帝生病了,并不知此事,因为他未对此事做出批示。因此埃诺巴尔布斯和玛尔苏斯仍然活着,前者在忙于准备自己的辩护,后者则是摆出了一副要绝食至死的架势。阿尔伦提乌斯的朋友们也劝告他要进行拖延。但是他的回答却是说不同的事情适合于不同的人。他说:"我活的时间已经足够长了,我唯一感到遗憾的事情就是侮辱和威胁使我的晚年生活很不幸福。谢雅努斯长久以来就憎恨我,而现在又是玛克罗。总有一些当权的人物来反对我,这并不是我的过错,而只是我疾恶如仇的缘故。

"确实是,在提贝里乌斯死亡之前的这段不长的日子里,我还可以活着。但是,即便如此,我又怎么能够逃得过即将登位的年轻的皇帝呢?假如提贝里乌斯尽管拥有了各种各样丰富的经验都会被绝对的权力而扭曲或改变了性格的话,难道盖乌斯会不这样吗?他几乎还只是一个孩子,根本就不懂事,是在一个违法犯罪的环境之中长大的,尤其是在玛克罗的监护之下长大的,此人是选出来以镇压谢雅努斯的,而实际上两者相比他更坏,应该对许许多多的令人发指的犯罪行为以及国家的灾难负责。我甚至可以预言,更加苛刻的奴役就在眼前,因此我是要从过去以及未来的邪恶之中逃脱出来。"

说完这些带有预言性质的话之后,他就切断了自己的血管。从后来所发生的事件来看,他的死亡是一个明智之举。阿尔布奇拉在自杀没有成功之后,就被元老院下令关进了监狱。她的

lovers, a former praetor named Carsidius Sacerdos, was deported to an island, another, Pontius Fregellanus, deprived of senatorial rank. But so was her prosecutor Decimus Laelius Balbus-to the general satisfaction, since he was noted for his malignant eloquence, readily utilized against innocent men. At this time, too, Sextus Papinius-son of a man who had been consul-hurled himself headlong to a sudden and undignified death. The blame fell on his mother. Long divorced, she had indulged his extravagances to a point at which death was his only escape. Charged in the senate, she prostrated herself before the senators and made a long and piteous appeal, pleading especially the anguish which anybody, particularly a weak woman, must feel at a bereavement such as hers. However, she was banned from Rome for ten years, until her younger son had passed the dangerous years of youth.

Tiberius' health and strength were now failing. But his stern will and vigorous speech and expression remained. So did his powers of dissimulation. To conceal his obvious decline, he assumed an affable manner. After numerous moves he settled in a villa on Cape Misenum which had belonged to Lucius Licinius Lucullus. There his end was discovered to be approaching. For an eminent doctor called Charicles, though not employed to treat the emperor's illnesses, had made himself available for consultation. Ostensibly taking his leave to attend to private affairs, he grasped the emperor's hand-and under cover of this respectful gesture felt his pulse. Tiberius noticed, ordered the

一个情夫名字叫卡尔西狄乌斯·撒凯尔多斯,是一个前任行政长官,被流放到一个岛上去了;另一个情夫名叫彭提乌斯·佛列盖拉努斯,则是被剥夺了元老的头衔。而令大伙感到普遍满意的是对她提出指控的戴西姆斯·莱利乌斯·巴尔布斯也遭到了同样的惩罚,因为此人是以恶毒的讲话而闻名的,并随时都在攻击陷害无辜的人。也是在这些日子里,一个曾经担任过执政官的人的儿子名字叫塞克斯图斯·帕披尼乌斯突然就从窗户里跳了出去,非常不体面地死去了。此事的责任应该归咎于他的母亲,她很早就离婚了,并且非常纵容自己的儿子,以至于自己干出了只有一死才能逃脱的丑事。当在元老院受到起诉之时,她便跪在元老们的面前,进行了长时间的、令人同情的辩解,说任何人遇到这样的事情都会感到悲伤的,尤其是像她这样一个无力的女人,在丧失了自己的亲人之后会感到更加悲伤。尽管如此,她还是被判 10 年之内不准返回罗马,一直到她的小儿子度过了危险的年轻阶段为止。

现在,提贝里乌斯的体质和气力逐渐地垮了。但是,他那坚强的意志、生动的演讲以及表达能力尚存在着。为了将自己那明显已不行了的身体状况掩盖起来,他假装出了一种平易近人的作风。经过多次改换居住地之后,他最后住在了一幢别墅之内,这幢别墅位于米塞努姆海角上,过去属于路奇乌斯·里西尼乌斯·路库鲁斯。在那儿人们发现他的死期就要来临了。因为有一位著名的医生名字叫卡里克列斯,虽然不是雇来专门为皇帝治疗疾病的,却经常被召来为皇帝提供咨询。表面上,他以参加私人的事务为借口来向皇帝请假,并抓住了皇帝的手,而此举看似是为了表示尊重,实际上是为了把皇帝的脉搏。提贝里乌斯觉察到了

dinner to be prolonged, and stayed up later than usual. This was allegedly in honour of his departing friend. But he may well have been annoyed, and so taken special pains to conceal his annoyance.

However, Charicles assured Macro that Tiberius was sinking and would not last more than two days. There were conferences, and dispatches to imperial governors and generals, hurriedly making all arrangements. On March 16th the emperor ceased to breathe, and was believed to be dead. Gaius, surrounded by a congratulatory crowd, issued forth to begin his reign. But then it was suddenly reported that Tiberius had recovered his speech and sight, and was asking for food to strengthen him after his fainting-fit. There was a general panic-stricken dispersal. Every face was composed to show grief- or una-wareness. Only Gaius stood in stupefied silence, his soaring hopes dashed, expecting the worst. Marco, unperturbed, ordered the old man to be smothered with a heap of bed-clothes and left alone.

So Tiberius died, in his seventy-eighth year. The son of Tiberius Claudius Nero, he was a Claudian on both sides (his mother was successively adopted into the Livian and the Julian families). From birth he experienced contrasts of fortune. After following his proscribed father into exile, he entered Augustus' family as his stepson only to suffer from many competitors, while they lived: first Marcellus and Agrippa, then Gaius Caesar and Lucius Caesar. His own brother Nero Drusus was more of a popular favourite. But Tiberius' position

此举的目的,于是就下令延长宴会的时间,并且在宴席上待到比平时更晚的时间。并宣布这是在为自己临行的朋友饯行。但是,或许是因为他确实被激怒了,因而特别用力地掩饰着自己的怒气。

然而,卡里克列斯肯定地对玛克罗说,提贝里乌斯的身体正在衰竭,不会支撑过两天了。于是紧急召开了会议,匆匆忙忙地做了各种安排,并通过信使通知了各地总督和军队统帅。在3月16日那一天,皇帝停止了呼吸,大家都认为他已经死了。于是,盖乌斯在祝贺的人群的簇拥之下准备登基事宜。但是,这时突然传来报告说提贝里乌斯已经醒过来了,能够说话、看东西了,并要求进食,以便在晕厥之后可以加强一下自己的体力。大家都惊慌失措地分散开了,每个人的脸上都写满了悲伤或对此事毫不知情的样子。只有盖乌斯站在那儿,呆若木鸡一言不发,他那爬上高峰的希望摔碎了,并在等着最坏的结局。而玛克罗却镇定自若,下令用一大摞被子将这位老人压住使他窒息而死,而且没有人敢管这事。

就这样,提贝里乌斯在自己78岁那一年死去了。他是提贝里乌斯·克劳狄乌斯·尼禄的儿子,他的父母双亲都是克劳狄乌斯家族的人(他的母亲则是相继过继到了里维乌斯家族和尤利乌斯家族)。从出生那一刻起,他就经历了跌宕起伏的命运历程。一开始,他伴随着自己的父亲遭受了驱逐,之后就进入了奥古斯都家族做了继子,当那些竞争对手还活着的时候,他遭受了他们许许多多的折磨:一开始是玛尔凯路斯和阿格里帕,接着就是盖乌斯·恺撒和路奇乌斯·恺撒。他自己的亲兄弟杜路苏斯都比他更加受到了国人的爱戴。但是,即使他与奥古斯都的女儿

became most delicate of all after his marriage to Augustus' daughter Julia (III). For he had to choose between enduring her unfaithfulness or escaping it. He went to Rhodes. When he returned, he was undisputed heir in the emperor's home for twelve years. Then he ruled the Roman world for nearly twenty-three.

His character, too, had its different stages. While he was a private citizen or holding commands under Augustus, his life was blameless; and so was his reputation. While Germanicus and Drusus still lived, he concealed his real self, cunningly affecting virtuous qualities. However, until his mother died there was good in Tiberius as well as evil. Again, as long as he favoured (or feared) Sejanus, the cruelty of Tiberius was detested, but his perversions unrevealed. Then fear vanished, and with it shame. Thereafter he expressed only his own personality—by unrestrained crime and infamy.

优利娅(三世)结婚之后,他的地位还是最为不稳固的,因为这时他必须对于妻子的不贞要么能够容忍,要么进行逃避。他去了罗德岛。而当他回来并在皇室之中待了 12 年之后,成为无人能够竞争的帝位继承人。接着,他统治了整个罗马世界将近 23 年。

而他的性格的变化也可以分成不同的阶段。当他还是一个普通公民的时候,或者是在奥古斯都统治之下的一个军事统帅的时候,他的生活可以说是无可指责的;而他的名声同样也是崇高的。当日尔曼尼库斯和杜路苏斯还活着的时候,他将真实的自我掩盖了起来,表现了其伪善的品德。而且即使到母亲去世的时候,提贝里乌斯身上既有好的一面,也有邪恶的一面。进而,当提贝里乌斯喜欢(或者说是恐惧)谢雅努斯的时候,人们所讨厌的也只是他的残忍,而他的淫欲却是被隐藏了起来。下一步,恐惧感也就消失了,羞耻感也就不存在了。之后,他也就完全按照自己的本性而为所欲为,而不惧怕于任何的犯罪和丑行了。[1]

---

〔1〕 本书的内容从这儿一直到第二部分的开始,也就是一直到第九章的开始,中间的内容全部佚失了,佚失的部分包括了从公元 37 年到公元 47 年的内容,主要的事件有:(1)公元 37 年,盖乌斯继位;(2)公元 38 年,民会在名义上恢复;(3)公元 39 年,持续发生了处死和财产充公的事件;(4)公元 40 年,盖乌斯皇帝在里昂的一些事迹;(5)公元 41 年,盖乌斯皇帝被暗杀,克劳狄乌斯宣布继承皇位;(6)公元 42 年,玛乌列塔尼亚被分裂成了由代理官所治理的两个行省;(7)公元 43 年,奥劳斯·普劳提乌斯·西尔瓦努斯率领军队进攻不列颠;(8)公元 44 年,克劳狄乌斯凯旋;(9)公元 45 年,米特利达特斯在博斯普鲁斯叛乱;(10)公元 47 年,克劳狄乌斯和维提里乌斯担任监察官。

PART Two Claudius And Nero

CHAPTER 9
The Fall Of Messalina

[*The manuscript breaks off at the death of Tiberius, and Tacitus'*
description of the four years' reign of the unbalanced Gaius (Caligu-
la) is lost. So is his account of the first six years of Caius' successor
and uncle Claudius. Claudius has married his own cousin Messalina
(his third wife). Their children are Octavia and Britannicus, who are
about six and five respectively when Tacitus' surviving narrative is re-
sumed. Poppaea Sabina is a wealthy and fashionable beauty of whom
Messalina is jealous.]

Messalina believed that Decimus Valerius Asiaticus, twice consul, had been Poppaea Sabina's lover. Messalina also coveted the
park which had been begun by Lucius Licinius Lucullus, and which
Asiaticus was beautifying with exceptional lavishness. So she directed
Publius Suillius Rufus to prosecute both of them. He was to be associated in this with Britannicus' tutor, Sosibius. The task of the ostensibly well-meaning tutor was to warn Claudius to beware of another's power-of resources too formidable for an emperor's comfort.
'Asiaticus', declared Sosibius, 'was the principal instigator of the
murder of Gaius ! At an Assembly meeting he fearlessly admitted the
crime, and claimed glory for it. So he is famous at Rome. Moreover, rumours throughout the provinces tell of a projected visit to the

第二部分　克劳狄乌斯和尼禄

第九章　美撒里娜之死

〔手稿中提贝里乌斯之死的记述中断了,而且对盖乌斯(卡里古拉)四年统治的不平衡的记述也遗失了。因此接下来的是对盖乌斯的继任者和他的叔叔克劳狄乌斯第一个六年统治时期的记录。克劳狄乌斯和他的堂妹美撒里娜结婚(她是他的第三个妻子),他们的孩子是奥克塔维娅和布列塔尼库斯。当塔西佗的记述重新恢复时,他们分别是六岁和五岁。波培娅·萨比娜是一个富有而又时尚的漂亮女人,美撒里娜非常嫉妒她。〕

美撒里娜相信,曾两次担任执政官的狄奇姆斯·瓦列里乌斯·亚细亚提库斯先前是波培娅·萨比娜的情夫。美撒里娜也同样地垂涎路奇乌斯·里奇尼乌斯·路库鲁斯修建的、并为亚细亚提库斯装饰得极为豪华瑰丽的那座花园,因此,她便指使普布里乌斯·苏伊里乌斯·路福斯去控诉这一对情人。路福斯还同不列塔尼库斯的教师索西比乌斯勾结在一起。表面上仿佛是好心的索西比乌斯警告克劳狄乌斯,要他注意防备那对皇帝们来说是非常可怕的另一种权力的源泉,他说:"亚细亚提库斯是谋杀盖乌斯·恺撒的主谋! 在一次群众集会上,他毫不畏惧地承认了此事,甚至还声称为此感到光荣。就这样,他在罗马出了名,而且各个行省都在传说他准备去巡视日耳曼的军队。因为他生于高

armies of Germany. For his birth at Vienna in Gaul, and his powerful connections in that country, make it easy for him to rouse his own people's tribes.'

Without further inquiry Claudius sent the commander of the Guard, Rufrius Crispinus, with enough troops to suppress a rebellion. Proceeding at full speed, Crispinus found Asiaticus at Baiae and took him to Rome in chains. Refused access to the senate, Asiaticus was examined in a bedroom, with Messalina present. Publius Suillius Rufus accused him of corrupting the army and using bribes and sexual entanglements to commit the soldiers to unbounded atrocities. Adultery with Poppaea Sabina was a supplementary charge. Another was effeminacy. At this accusation the prisoner found his voice. 'Ask your sons, Suillius,' he said. 'They will confirm my masculinity.'

Then Asiaticus began his defence. It greatly moved Claudius-and even extracted tears from Messalina. She left the room to dry them, warning Lucius Vitellius (I) not to let the defendant elude her. Then she rapidly organized Poppaea Sabina's destruction. Agents were suborned to threaten Poppaea with imprisonment, and thus terrorize her into suicide. Claudius knew nothing of this. When Poppaea's husband Publius Cornelius Lentulus Scipio (I) was dining with him a few days later, the emperor asked him why he had come without his wife. The answer was that she was dead.

卢的维也纳,他的权力与那一地区有着密切的联系,在那里,他可以很容易地在本地各民族之间挑起事端。"

克劳狄乌斯并没有进一步进行调查,就赶忙派近卫军长官路福里乌斯·克利司披努斯率领着一支力量非常强大的部队,前去镇压叛乱。克利司披努斯立即出发,部队全速前进,他在拜阿伊找到了亚细亚提库斯之后,就给他上了镣铐,把他押解回了首都罗马。亚细亚提库斯被拒绝进入到元老院去,就在一间寝室中接受了审判,审判时有美撒里娜在旁。普布里乌斯·苏伊里乌斯·路福斯对他进行控诉,控诉的罪名是:使军队作风败坏,使用贿赂和性纠缠等手段指使士兵们毫无节制地作恶;和波培娅·撒比娜通奸;另外,他还是个像姑。[1] 最后这一条控诉使得被告提出了抗议,他说:"去问一问你的儿子们,苏伊里乌斯,他们会证实我是一个男子汉的!"

接着,亚细亚提库斯开始为自己进行辩护,他的发言深深地感动了克劳狄乌斯,甚至连美撒里娜听后都被感动得落泪了。美撒里娜离开房间擦掉了眼泪,她提醒路奇乌斯·维提里乌斯(一世)小心,不要让囚犯从她的手里溜掉了。接下来,她自己则迅速着手安排毁掉波培娅·撒比娜,她唆使她的奸细用地牢相威胁,撒比娜非常惊恐地被迫自杀了。克劳狄乌斯则完全不知道这件事情,几天之后,当波培娅的丈夫普布里乌斯·考尔尼利乌斯·楞图路斯·斯奇比奥(一世)同他一起吃晚饭时,皇帝还问斯奇比奥为什么没有和自己的妻子一同前来,斯奇比奥回答说她已经死了,直到这时他才知道她已经不在人世了。

---

〔1〕 指具有柔弱女人气质的男人。

Lucius Vitellius, asked by Claudius whether he thought Asiaticus should be acquitted, first tearfully recalled their long friendship and partnership in devotion to the emperor's mother, Antonia (II). Then, reviewing Asiaticus' public services—including recent military activity against the British—and every other mitigating consideration, Vitellius urged that he should be allowed to choose his own death. Claudius' decision was to the same merciful effect. Asiaticus' friends recommended to him the unforcible method of self-starvation, but he proposed to dispense with that favour. After gymnastic exercises as usual, he bathed and dined cheerfully. Then, remarking that it would have been more honourable to die by the wiles of Tiberius or the violence of Gaius than by a woman's intrigues and Vitellius' obscene tongue, he opened his veins. First, however, he inspected his pyre and ordered it to be moved so that the flames should not damage the foliage of the trees. For he remained calm to the end.

The senate was then summoned, and Publius Suillius Rufus proceeded to add to the list of accused personages two distinguished knights of the name of Petra. The real reason for their deaths was the supposition that they had lent their house as a meeting-place for the ballet-dancer Mnester (I) and Poppaea Sabina. But the ostensible charge against one of the two men was a dream in which he had seen Claudius wearing a wheaten wreath with inverted ears. This Petra had interpreted as portending a corn shortage. The wreath was otherwise described as of whitening vine leaves, predicting the emperor's death

但是,当克劳狄乌斯向路奇乌斯·维提里乌斯征求意见是否要除掉亚细亚提库斯的时候,维提里乌斯却先是含着眼泪回忆了他们两人之间长期的友谊,以及他们对皇帝的母亲安托尼娅(二世)所表示的同样的忠诚。继而,他又细数了亚细亚提库斯为国家所做过的事情,他最近对不列颠人作战的功勋和所有其他有可能引起皇帝怜悯之心的事情。维提里乌斯要求皇帝允许亚细亚提库斯自己选择死亡的方式。克劳狄乌斯的决定也同样具有仁慈的效果。当亚细亚提库斯的一些朋友建议他用绝食的办法慢慢自杀时,亚细亚提库斯却不想接受这种恩惠。像平常一样,他先做了一些体格上的运动锻炼,然后就去洗了洗澡,高高兴兴地吃了晚饭。之后,他说,死于提贝里乌斯的阴谋或是死于盖乌斯·恺撒的暴虐之下,比死于妇人的欺诈和维提里乌斯的挑拨性的下流语言之下更体面些,接着他就切开了自己的血管。然而,在他切开血管之前,他先到他的柴木堆那里去检查了一下,下令把它们挪到别的地方,以防止烈火毁坏那些茂密的树叶。他在临死之前,一直非常的从容沉着!

接着元老院召开了一次会议。普布里乌斯·苏伊里乌斯·路福斯进而又把名为佩特拉的两名著名的罗马骑士加到了被控诉者的名单上去。处死他们的真正原因,据说是因为他们曾经将他们自己所住的房屋出租出去,作为优伶莫涅斯特和波培娅·撒比娜的幽会之所。但其中的一个人受到控诉,表面上的原因是因为他的一个梦,在梦中他看见克劳狄乌斯戴着小麦编的王冠,麦穗向下。这个佩特拉把他的梦解释作是粮食歉收的预兆。有一些人说,他梦里看到的是带着发白的叶子的葡萄蔓编织的花环,这预示着皇帝在秋末将要死亡。无论是什么情况,可以肯定的一点就

in the autumn. In any case, it was certainly some dream which destroyed him and his brother.

One and a half million sesterces, and an honorary praetorship, were voted to Rufrius Crispinus. Lucius Vitellius proposed the award of a further million to Sosibius for helping Britannicus with his instruction and Claudius with his advice. Publius Cornelius Lentulus Scipio (I), asked for his opinion, answered: 'Since I share the general view about Poppaea Sabina's misdeeds, take it that I say what everyone says' —a graceful compromise between husbandly love and senatorial compulsion.

Now Suillius continued his prosecutions with unremitting ferocity. Moreover, his unscrupulousness had many imitators. For the emperor's absorption of all judicial and magisterial functions had opened up extensive opportunities for illicit gain. The most readily purchasable commodity on the market was an advocate's treachery. One distinguished knight named Samius fell on his sword at Suillius' house after paying him four hundred thousand sesterces and then finding Suillius was in collusion with the other side.

After this the senators, led by the consul-designate Gaius Silius (II) (whose power and downfall I shall describe in the appropriate place) , rose and demanded enforcement of the ancient Cincian law forbidding the acceptance of money or gifts for legal services. Those affected by the measure protested. Silius, however, violently assailed Suillius—whom he hated. Silius recalled the ancient orators who had wanted no rewards for their eloquence except present and future fame. 'What would otherwise be the first and finest of talents', he said, 'is defiled by mercenary hire—an eye on profits means double-dealing. If no one paid a fee for lawsuits, there would be less of them! As it is,

是,这个梦会毁掉他本人和他的兄弟的性命。

元老院决定把 150 万谢司特尔提乌斯和行政长官的标记赠予路福里乌斯·克利司披努斯。路奇乌斯·维提里乌斯则建议再把 100 万给予索西比乌斯,奖励他用教诲帮助过不列塔尼库斯,用劝告帮助过克劳狄乌斯的行为。被征询过意见的普布里乌斯·考尔尼乌斯·楞图路斯·斯奇比奥(一世)回答说:"关于波培娅·撒比娜的罪行,我的想法和大家的想法相同,可以认为我要说的话也正是大家所说的话!"丈夫之爱和元老之责之间得到了极美妙的折中。

现在,苏伊里乌斯继续以毫不懈怠的残酷无情干着他控告的勾当,而且他的这种肆无忌惮的做法还吸引了许多人的效仿,因为皇帝将法律上和行政上的全部权力集于一身,这就给非法获得各种利益大开了方便之门,制造了各种各样的机会。市场上最容易买卖的商品就是辩护者的背叛行为,一个著名的骑士撒米乌斯付给了苏伊里乌斯 40 万谢司特尔提乌斯,随后却发现他竟然同对方勾结在一起,于是他就在辩护人苏伊里乌斯的家里用剑自杀了。

这个事件以后,元老院根据业已任命的执政官盖乌斯·西里乌斯(二世)的建议,(关于西里乌斯的权力和垮台,我将要在适当的时候再来叙述。)提起并要求执行古老的秦奇乌斯法。这项法律规定,在为某一案件进行辩护时,禁止接受金钱或者是礼物。当受到此种措施影响的元老们起来反对的时候,西里乌斯便对他憎恨的苏伊里乌斯进行了一次猛烈的抨击,并且援引了古代那些把现在和将来的名誉当做自己口才的惟一报酬的演说家的范例,他说:"最重要和最优秀的才能都受到了唯利是图行为的腐化,因为一只眼睛总盯着利益就会获得双倍的利益。如果没有人付给诉

feuds, charges, malevolence, and slander are encouraged. For just as physical illness brings revenue to doctors, so a diseased legal system enriches advocates. Remember that the great orators reached the top of their profession without degrading themselves or their eloquence. ' And he cited Gaius Asinius Pollio (I) and Marcus Valerius Messalla Corvinus (I), and among later figures Lucius Arruntius and Marcus Claudius Marcellus Aeserninus.

This speech by the consul-designate was applauded, and a motion was prepared inculpating offenders under the extortion law. Suillius and Cossutianus Capito, and others like them, saw that this meant not just trial—they were obviously guilty—but punishment. So they flocked round Claudius urging forgiveness of the past. Allowed to plead their case, they argued that advocates, like anyone else, cannot just hope for eternal fame: they have to work to meet people's practical needs, and ensure that nobody succumbs to a powerful litigant through lack of an advocate.

' But eloquence', they added, ' is not acquired for nothing. To attend to other people's affairs means neglecting one's own. Other senators often earn their living by military service, or agriculture. No calling attracts candidates unless they can reckon its emoluments beforehand. It was easy for men like Gaius Asinius Pollio (I) and Marcus Valerius Messalla Corvinus (I), gorged with the spoils of Augustus' war with

讼者小费的话,诉讼的人就会大大减少了。但实际的情况却是,仇视、指控、恶意和诽谤,都得到了极大的鼓励。因为,就好像身体上的疾病能给医生带来收入一样,病态的法律体制也能使辩护人发家致富。让我们记住那些在他们的专业上已经达到了最高的造诣,但是他们自己和他们的辩才却没有任何污点的最伟大的演说家们吧!"于是,他就列举了盖乌斯·阿西乌斯·波里欧(一世)和玛尔库斯·瓦列里乌斯·美撒拉·科尔维努斯(一世),在现代的著名人物中,他则列举了路奇乌斯·阿尔伦提乌斯和玛尔库斯·克劳狄乌斯·玛尔凯路斯·埃塞尔尼努斯。

已经任命但未到任的执政官的这番话得到了人们的喝彩,于是他便起草一项决议,准备对那些违犯了反勒索法的罪犯实行制裁。苏伊里乌斯、科苏提亚努斯·卡皮托和其他诸如此类的人物,看到这一决定对他们来说不只是意味着审讯——他们的罪行是显而易见的,而且是意味着惩处时,他们便围在克劳狄乌斯身边,请求他赦免他们过去的罪行。皇帝准许了他们的请求,他们便为他们自己的案件进行辩护说,像其他任何人一样,辩护人也不能只希望取得不朽的声名,因为他们必须努力满足人们的实际需要,并且保证任何人都不会由于缺少辩护人的辩护而屈从于强有力的诉讼人。

他们还说:"但是,口才并不是不花一文钱就能得来的东西,因为一个人为别人的事情奔走,也就是意味着忽略了他私人的事务。许多元老是依靠服军役来维持他们的生活,或者经营他们的农庄,只有那些能预计给人带来相当的报酬的行业,才能吸引人们去从事。对于像盖乌斯·阿西尼乌斯·波里欧(一世)和玛尔库斯·瓦列里乌斯·美撒拉·科尔维努斯(一世)这样,在奥古斯都与安东尼

Antony, or for men such as Marcus Claudius Marcellus Aeserninus and Lucius Arruntius, the heirs of wealthy families, to appear high-minded. Besides, one can equally point to former orators like Publius Clodius and Gaius Scribonius Curio who received huge fees for speeches. We, however, are senators of moderate means who, in a peaceful state, only seek peace-time incomes. Besides, think of the humble people who win distinction by pleading. Remove a profession's incentives, and the profession perishes.' Less idealistic though these arguments were, Claudius saw some point in them. He decided to establish a maximum fee often thousand sesterces: those who accepted more were to be guilty of extortion.

At this period Mithridates, whose accession to the Armenian throne and imprisonment by Gaius I have mentioned, returned to his kingdom with Claudius' encouragement, backed by the resources of his brother Pharasmanes, king of Iberia. The latter had reported that, since Parthia was again plunged in civil war, all lesser matters there were neglected in the fight for supremacy. For the king of Parthia Gotarzes II, among many other atrocities, had had one of his own brothers, Artabanus by name, murdered, together with his wife and son. So the other Parthians, alarmed, called in a further brother, Vardanes. Vardanes, always ready for adventures, covered 350 miles in two days, routed the unsuspecting and panic-stricken Gotarzes, and speedily occupied the adjacent provinces. Only Seleucia on the

的战争中大发横财的人，或者像玛尔库斯·克劳狄乌斯·玛尔凯路斯·埃塞尔尼努斯和路提乌斯·阿尔伦提乌斯之流豪富家族的后人们，做出慷慨的姿态是很容易的事情。但除此之外也同样还需要指出，以前的演说家，像普布里乌斯·克洛狄乌斯或盖乌斯·斯科里波尼乌斯·库利欧，在发表演说时的收费也是很高的。而我们，这些在没有战争的时期除了和平的报酬之外没有得到任何东西的人，都是些家境平平的元老。请再考虑一下那些由于辩护的活动而成名的出身卑微的人吧！如果刺激他们研习这门学问的动机消失了，这门学问也就会灭亡了。"尽管这些观点少了一些高尚的理想主义色彩，但是克劳狄乌斯也认识到其中一些观点还是不无道理的。于是，他便规定辩护人所收的费用最多不能超过10000谢司特尔提乌斯，如果谁收取的费用超过了这个数目，那就是犯了勒索罪。

就在这个时期，米特利达特斯——前面我已经提到了他获得亚美尼亚的王位和盖乌斯将他逮捕的事情，在克劳狄乌斯的鼓励下，靠着他的兄弟伊伯利亚国王帕拉斯玛尼斯的力量支持，返回了他的王国。帕拉斯玛尼斯宣称，由于帕尔提亚人又陷入了内战，大家忙于争夺王位的战斗，所有的小事情都无人过问。因为帕尔提亚国王哥塔尔吉斯二世，在他做过的许多残暴的事情之中，其中一件是杀死他的兄弟阿尔塔巴努斯及其妻儿，所以其他的帕尔提亚人感到非常惊恐，于是，他们召来了他的另一个兄弟瓦尔达尼斯。瓦尔达尼斯，这个总是喜欢冒险行动的人，在两天里便走了350英里的路程，赶跑了没有想到瓦尔达尼斯会来进攻因此惊慌失措的哥塔尔吉斯，并且迅速地攻占了毗邻的一些省份，只有提格里斯的塞琉西亚拒绝对他臣服。与其说是

Tigris refused homage. Less for immediate advantage than from irritation (it had deserted his father Artabanus III too), Vardanes involved himself in a siege of this powerful and well-provisioned city, with its protections of river and walls. Meanwhile Gotarzes, mobilizing reinforcements among the Dahae and Hyrcanians, renewed the struggle. Vardanes was forced to raise the siege, and withdrew to Bactria.

This major disunion in the east, and its uncertain outcome, gave Mithridates his chance of seizing Armenia. While Roman troops actively reduced mountain fortresses, Iberian forces overran the plains. The Armenians unsuccessfully risked an engagement under Demonax, and then laid down arms. Some delay was caused by Cotys, the king of Lesser Armenia, to whom certain Armenian leaders had turned. However, a letter from Claudius restrained him, and Mithridates established himself. But his severity was inadvisable for a new monarch.

The rival Parthian leaders were preparing for battle when Gotarzes II discovered a conspiracy among their followers-and revealed it to Vardanes. Thereupon the two brothers abruptly concluded a truce. Their first meeting was hesitant. But then they clasped hands and swore, over the altars of the gods, to punish the treachery of their enemies and achieve a compromise with each other. Vardanes was thought the more suitable to be king. Gotarzes, to avoid rivalry, with-

出于对自己切身利益的考虑,毋宁说是(对这一座也背弃了他的
父亲阿尔塔巴努斯三世的城市)感到愤怒,瓦尔达尼斯亲自率部
围攻这座城市。这是一座实力雄厚、粮草充足,又有着一条河流
和围墙作屏障的设防坚固的城市,因此久攻不下。就在这时,哥
塔尔吉斯得到了达阿伊人和叙尔卡尼亚人的兵力援助,又重新投
入了战斗。瓦尔达尼斯被迫加强了围攻的力量,撤退到巴克妥利
亚的平原上扎下营地。

　　东方大部分的政权都处于分裂状态,而结果尚难以确定,这
种局面给了米特利达特斯以极好的占领亚美尼亚的机会。因为
这时罗马军队正在积极活跃地摧毁山上的要塞,而伊伯利亚的军
队此时在忙于蹂躏平原地区。当地居民亚美尼亚人在狄莫纳克
斯率领下,冒险迎战,失败后就放下了武器。一些亚美尼亚贵族
所依附的小亚美尼亚[1]国王科提斯造成了一些延迟,但是,不久
之后,克劳狄乌斯写来的一封信就将他压制了下去,于是米特利
达特斯就登上了王位。但他表现得过于严厉,这对于一个新即位
的君主来说并不是明智之举。

　　对手一方的帕尔提亚的将领们正在准备作战,这时,哥塔尔
吉斯二世发现了他们的追随者中间的一件叛国阴谋,并向瓦尔
达尼斯透露了这一消息,因此他们兄弟之间就突然缔结了一项
条约。他们在第一次会见时还有点犹豫,但是后来便相互握住
对方的手,并在神坛前面发誓,对他们的敌人的叛逆行动进行惩
罚,并且彼此间都做出了让步。瓦尔达尼斯被认为更适合做国
王,而为了避免发生任何敌对行动,哥塔尔吉斯则撤退到遥远的

---

〔1〕　在亚美尼亚本土西部。

drew into remote Hyrcania. Vardanes returned to Seleucia, which surrendered. Its revolt had lasted seven years. This prolonged defiance by one city had humiliated the Parthians.

Vardanes then toured the principal provinces. He was also enthusiastic to visit Armenia, but was checked by a threat of war from the imperial governor of Syria, Gaius Vibius Marsus. Meanwhile Gotarzes had regretted giving up the throne. Invited back by the nobles-who find subordination particularly intolerable in peacetime-he collected an army. Vardanes marched against him and won a hard-fought battle at a crossing of the river Barferush. Then, by a series of further successes, he reduced one tribe after another up to the river Tedzhen, the frontier between the Dahae and Arii.

Finally, however, his conquests ended because the Parthians, though victorious, disliked distant service. So, after erecting monuments glorifying his power and the subjection of peoples never before under Parthian monarchs, Vardanes returned home. But his triumphs had made him more overbearing and autocratic. So, while unsuspectingly out hunting, he was assassinated. He was still very young; yet in renown he would have had few equals, however long-lived, if only he had sought to inspire as much affection in his people as terror in his enemies.

The murder of Vardanes created anarchy among the Parthians, who were divided concerning his successor. Many wanted Gotarzes II, others a descendant of King Phraates IV called Meherdates who was

叙尔卡尼亚内地去。瓦尔达尼斯返回塞琉西亚，这个城市终于投降了，而这时它的叛乱已经延续了七个年头。一个城市对他们的蔑视竟然延续了这么长的时间，这极大地污辱了帕尔提亚人。

瓦尔达尼斯于是巡视了主要的各省，他也热切希望参观亚美尼亚，但是由于害怕这会引起和叙利亚的副帅盖乌斯·维比乌斯·玛尔苏斯发生冲突而不得不把这种野心收敛起来。就在这时，哥塔尔吉斯又后悔放弃了王位，在那些特别不能忍受在和平环境中处于藩属地位的贵族的教唆下，他又征募起一支军队。而瓦尔达尼斯也命令军队开拔前去和哥塔尔吉斯作战，在巴尔费路士河渡口的一场激烈战斗中，他取得了胜利，之后，他又取得了一系列的成功。他征服了一个又一个部族，直到信德河的地方，而信德河则是达阿伊人和雅利安人之间的边界。

然而，最终他对其他部族的征服就到那里为止了，因为虽然取得了胜利，但帕尔提亚人不喜欢远征作战。因此他建立了许多颂扬他的威势的纪念物，在这种纪念物上记载着那些向他臣服的民族，这是之前任何一个帕尔提亚君主都不曾做到过的。之后，瓦尔达尼斯便十分光荣地班师回朝了。但是他为所取得的胜利洋洋自得，对自己的臣民更加横傲，更加专断了。因此，在一次外出打猎时，一个预谋的背叛行动出其不意地将他杀害了。这个国王当时虽然还十分年轻，但是已经是非常有名了，如果他能像给敌人造成的恐惧那样强烈地得到自己人民的深深爱戴的话，那么那些长寿的国王也很少有人能够与他相匹敌的。

瓦尔达尼斯被杀以后，在帕尔提亚人中间产生了混乱，因为大家对于继承者的人选问题，意见产生了分歧。许多人倾向于哥塔尔吉斯二世，但还有一些倾向于国王普拉提斯四世的后人美赫

in our hands as a hostage. Gotarzes prevailed, and occupied the palace. But his cruelty and dissipation impelled the Parthians to dispatch a secret appeal to the Roman emperor, urging that Meherdates should be released to assume the crown of his forefathers.

This year being the eight hundredth since Rome's foundation, Secular Games were celebrated, sixty-four years after those of Augustus. The calculations undertaken by the two emperors I omit, since they have been sufficiently described in my account of Domitian's reign. For he too celebrated Secular Games, with which I was closely concerned as a member of the Board of Fifteen for Religious Ceremonies and praetor for the year. I mention this not from vanity but because these celebrations have since ancient times been administered by the Board, special responsibility for the ceremonies falling to those of its members who are officials.

The Games held by Cladius included performances in the Circus, where in the emperor's presence youthful horsemen of noble birth performed the Troy Pageant. Among them were the emperor's son Britannicus and Lucius Domitius Ahenobarbus, soon to be adopted heir to the throne with the name of Nero. The greater applause re-

尔达特斯,这个人正在我们这里做人质。但是哥塔尔吉斯捷足先
登取得了胜利,占领了宫廷。但是他的残酷和放纵使得帕尔提亚
人不得不秘密地把一份请愿书送到罗马皇帝那里去,请求把美赫
尔达特斯释放出来,让他取得他的先人留下的王位。

这一年,是罗马建城 800 年的时候,[1] 罗马举行了一次百年
祭,[2] 这一次是在奥古斯都前一次举办百年祭的 64 年之后。两位
皇帝所用的计算方法我就不再详谈了,因为在对多米提安统治时期
的论述中,我已经充分地记述过这些计算方法了。因为他也举行过
百年祭,而作为十五人祭司团的成员和这一年的行政长官,我对这
件事是特别关注的。我提起这件事并不是出于虚荣心,而是因为从
古代的时候,这项任务就是由十五人祭司团负责的,而特别是那些
同宗教仪式有关的职务,则由高级长官负责执行。

在克劳狄乌斯所举办的运动会中包括了在大竞技场所举行的
表演赛。在这儿,皇帝亲自出席,而豪门出身的少年子弟则组成了
一个马队,表演特洛伊战争。在他们中间,就有皇帝的儿子不列塔
尼库斯和路奇乌斯·多米提乌斯·阿诺巴尔布斯,[3] 多米提乌斯
不久就过继为皇帝的继承人,并且被定名为尼禄。多米提乌斯所受
到的人民群众的热烈欢迎则被看做是具有预言的性质。还有一个

---

〔1〕 公元 47 年,执政官是克劳狄乌斯和维提里乌斯。

〔2〕 百年祭大约是公元前 249 年制定的,每百年举行一次。第二次是在
公元前 146 年,比规定晚了三年,但在公元前 46 年却没有举行。奥古斯都利
用西比拉预言书中所说的 110 年的世纪和十五祭司团的传统,设法在公元前
17 年举行了百年祭。克劳狄乌斯又恢复了百年的世纪。多米提安采用了奥
古斯都的办法,但是他提前六年举行了祭礼。

〔3〕 即未来的皇帝尼禄,他是格涅乌斯·多米提乌斯·埃诺巴尔布斯
和日耳曼库斯的女儿阿格里披娜所生的儿子。

ceived by the latter was regarded as prophetic. A further story, that in his infancy serpents had watched over him, was a fable adapted from foreign miracle-tales. Nero himself—who was not over-modest-used to say that just one snake had been seen in his bedroom.

His popularity was an inheritance from Germanicus, of whom he was the only surviving male descendant. Moreover, pity was increasingly felt for his mother Agrippina (II), owing to her persecution by Messalina. The latter, always Agrippina's enemy and now particularly virulent, was only distracted from launching prosecutions and prosecutors by a new and almost maniacal love affair. She was infatuated with the best-looking young man in Rome, Gaius Silius (II). Forced by Messalina to divorce his aristocratic wife Junia Silana—so that her own adulterer should be disengaged—Silius realized the scandal and the peril. But refusal meant certain death. Besides, there was some hope of avoiding detection. And the affair was lucrative. So, banishing thoughts of the future, he took comfort and enjoyment from the present. Messalina, spurning secrecy, repeatedly visited his house with numerous attendants, clung to him when he went out, showered wealth and distinction upon him. Finally, as though the empire had changed hands, there were to be seen in her lover's home imperial slaves and ex-slaves and furniture.

Claudius, unaware of his matrimonial complications, was busy with the functions of censor. A former consul and playwright Publius Pomponius Secundus, and high-ranking ladies, had been insulted in the theatre: the emperor issued edicts sternly rebuking audiences for their unruliness. He also passed a law against harsh treatment of debtors,

更离奇的传说,说在他幼年的时候曾经有一些蛇前来看护他。这是模仿外国的奇迹故事而改编的一种神话,因为尼禄本人——他并不是一个过分谦逊的人——就常常说在他卧室里发现的正是一条蛇。

他的声望是来自于人们对日耳曼尼库斯的追忆,因为他是唯一尚存的日耳曼尼库斯的男性后裔。而且,由于他的母亲阿格里披娜(二世)受到美撒里娜的迫害,他也就越发的得到了人们的同情。一直以来都是阿格里披娜的敌人、而且现在又对她充满恶意的美撒里娜,目前却顾不上对阿格里皮娜提出控诉和教唆控诉者了,因为她最近几乎疯狂般地爱上了一个人,她爱上了罗马的一个最漂亮的青年盖乌斯·西里乌斯(二世)。在美撒里娜的逼迫下,西里乌斯不得不和他出身显要的妻子优尼娅·西拉娜离婚。这样一来,美撒里娜的情夫现在就已经是无拘无束的自由之身了。西里乌斯也知道这样的丑闻是多么不堪和自己将会面临的危险,但是由于拒绝就意味着必死无疑,而且由于还存有一线不会暴露出来的希望,并且他得到的报酬也是非常丰厚的,因此他便不再考虑未来的后果,只图眼前的享受,及时行乐。但是,美撒里娜却不屑于隐瞒,她经常带领着她的大群门客到他家里去。当他外出的时候,她也总是紧挨在他身边,并且赠给他数不清的财富和荣誉。最后,好像皇帝的大权已经转到了他的手中似的,在美撒里娜的奸夫的家中,人们可以看到宫廷的奴隶、被释奴隶和各种设施。

这时,克劳狄乌斯还不知道自己的婚姻发生了问题,他正忙于自己监察官的工作。曾经担任过执政官的剧作家普布里乌斯·彭波尼乌斯·塞坎都斯和一些有地位的女士们,在剧场中遭到了侮辱,因此,皇帝就发布了严峻的敕令,斥责那些观众的放肆行为。他还通过了一项法律来制裁债权人的勒索行为,禁止在父亲

forbidding loans to minors for repayment after their fathers' deaths. Claudius next ordered the construction of an aqueduct to convey streams from the Simbruine hills into Rome. Then, influenced by the discovery that even the Greek alphabet was a gradual creation, he introduced and popularized new Latin characters.

The first people to represent thoughts graphically were the Egyptians with their animal-pictures. These earliest records of humanity are still to be seen, engraved on stone. They also claim to have discovered the alphabet and taught it to the Phoenicians, who, controlling the seas, introduced it to Greece and were credited with inventing what they had really borrowed. The story is that Cadmus, arriving with a Phoenician fleet, taught the still uncivilized Greeks how to write. According to other accounts, Cecrops of Athens, or Linus of Thebes, or Palamedes of Argos in the Trojan war, invented sixteen letters, the rest being introduced later, notably by Simonides. In Italy, the Etruscans learnt writing from Demaratus the Corinthian, the Aborigines from Evander the Arcadian. The Latin characters resemble those of the earliest Greeks. Their letters, like ours, were originally few, and subsequently increased—thus affording Claudius a precedent. However, after employment in his reign the three letters that he invented became obsolete. But they can still be seen on bronze inscriptions in public squares and temples.

Claudius then proposed to the senate the establishment of a Board of Soothsayers. 'This oldest Italian art', he said, 'ought not to die out through neglect. The advice of soothsayers, consulted in time of disaster, has often caused the revival and more correct subsequent ob-

去世后将债务转给他未成年的儿子偿还。克劳狄乌斯接下来又下令挖掘一条水沟,把西姆布路伊尼山上的泉水引到罗马城里。接着,他发现就连希腊字母也是一步一步逐渐创造出来的,受此启发,于是他就创造并普及了一些新的拉丁字母。

最早用图画符号表示思想的民族,是用动物图画来表示思想的埃及人。直到今天,我们还可以看到这些刻在石头上的、人类历史最早的记录。他们还声称,是他们发明了字母,并将其传播到菲尼基人那里。而曾经称雄海上的菲尼基人,将其带到了希腊,并被认为是字母的发明者,而这种声誉实际上是从埃及人那里借来的。据传说,是随着一支菲尼基船队到来的卡德木斯,教会了当时还没有开化的希腊各民族怎样去使用文字书写。还有一种说法则是,雅典的凯克罗普斯,或者是底比斯的里努斯,或者是特洛伊战争时代阿尔哥斯的帕拉米狄斯,发明了 16 个字母,其余的字母则是后来发明的,特别是著名的西莫尼德斯陆续增加的。在意大利,埃特路里亚人从科林斯人戴玛拉托斯那里学到了文字,阿波里吉尼斯人从阿尔卡地亚人伊凡德尔那里学到了文字。拉丁字母和最早的希腊字母是很相像的。就像我们自己的字母一样,他们的字母起初数目也不多,后来才逐渐增多了。这就给克劳狄乌斯提供了一个先例,他又加上了三个字母。这三个字母虽然在他的统治时期很流行,可是后来就作废了,不过在广场和神庙的青铜牌上我们现在还仍然可以看到它们。

后来,克劳狄乌斯又向元老院提议建立一个卜人团的问题,他说:"这种最古老的意大利的技艺不应该由于遭到忽视而失传。在国家遭到灾难的时候,他们这些卜人常常被招来,他们经常能很好地恢复宗教的礼节,并且能比较准确地预见到未来的事情。

servance of religious ceremonies. Moreover leading Etruscans, on their own initiative—or the Roman senate's—have kept up the art and handed it down from father to son. Now, however, public indifference to praiseworthy accomplishments has caused its neglect; and the advance of foreign superstitions has contributed to this. At present all is well. But gratitude for divine favour must be shown by ensuring that rites observed in bad times are not forgotten in prosperity. ' So the senate decreed that the priests should consider which institutions of the soothsayers required upkeep or support.

In the same year the tribe of the Cherusci asked Rome for a king. Civil wars having annihilated their nobility, the only surviving royal prince was Italicus, son of Flavus (Arminius' brother) and of a daughter of Actumerus, chief of the Chatti. Italicus was kept at Rome—a handsome man, trained to fight and ride in both German and Roman style. Claudius subsidized him, provided an escort, and encouraged him to enter upon his heritage, adding that Italicus was the first man born at Rome as a citizen—not a hostage—to proceed to a foreign throne.

At first the Germans welcomed him. Free of partisanships, he favoured all equally, and gained prestige and respect—sometimes by the generally popular qualities of affability and moderation; more often by the drunkenness and lustfulness which natives admire. His reputation reached neighbouring states, and beyond. But men who had

而且,埃特路里亚的贵族们已经自愿地或者是由于罗马元老院的邀请,保存了这一技艺,并且将其在家族中祖祖辈辈地传播了下来。但是现在,由于人们都不关心这种值得称颂的技艺,结果这方面的工作就做得越来越疏忽了,而外来迷信的盛行更加重了这一状况的恶化。现在,一切情况都很好。但是对于上天的垂爱,我们必须通过这样的方式来表示我们的感谢,那就是我们要保证,在国家危急的时候所遵守的那些宗教仪节,在繁荣兴旺的时候也同样不会被忘记。"因此元老院便通过了一项命令,责成祭司们予以考虑斟酌:在卜人的训练中,哪些部分是需要保存的,哪些部分又是需要给予加强的。

同年,凯路斯奇人的部族到罗马来要求给他们派一个国王,因为国内的斗争已经把他们的贵族消灭了,而唯一还在的皇族成员就只剩下这一个意大利库斯了,他的父亲是(阿尔米尼乌斯的兄弟)弗拉乌斯,他的母亲则是卡提伊人的国王阿克图美路斯的女儿。意大利库斯被留在罗马,他人长得很漂亮,又受过良好的日耳曼式的和罗马式的军事训练和骑术训练。克劳狄乌斯送给他一笔钱作资助,并拨给他一队护卫人员,还鼓励他鼓起勇气开始继承起他们家族的光荣传统。克劳狄乌斯还说,他是作为一个出生在罗马的罗马公民,而不是一个人质,前去国外接受王位的第一人。

起初,日耳曼人对他的到来确实是十分欢迎。他没有党派之见,并且对所有的人都一视同仁,表现出关切的态度,因此他获得了很高的声望和尊重。他有时表现得和蔼亲切、彬彬有礼,很受人欢迎,但是他更经常的是表现出那种使当地部族感到羡慕的酗酒和淫乱。他的声誉已经开始传到相邻的各邦,并且传到了更远

found disunion profitable envied his power. 'Rome is encroaching,' they said to the adjacent communities which they sought out. 'Germany's ancient freedom is being destroyed. Is there really no home-born person eligible for the kingship? Do we have to give first place to the son of Flavus, a mere Roman military policeman? It is no good talking of Arminius. Even if his own son had returned to reign after growing up in enemy country, there would be reason to fear the contagion of foreign upbringing, slave-labour, dress, and everything else. Besides, if Italicus takes after his father, no one ever fought against his own country and its god more violently than Flavus did !'

Such arguments attracted numerous supporters. Italicus' following, however, was just as large. He reminded them that he had not intruded against their will, but had been invited because his birth made him pre-eminent. A test of his courage, he added, would find him worthy of his uncle and grandfather-and he was not ashamed of his father, who had steadfastly maintained obligations to Rome which he had entered with German approval: the word 'freedom' was hypocritically put foward by low characters whose politics were a menace and whose only hope was national disunion.

These assertions were enthusiastically applauded. There followed a battle-important by native standards—which Italicus won. But success made him arrogant, and he was ejected. Subsequently, with the

的地方。但是在这个时候，那些想制造分裂从而牟求私利的人开始嫉妒他的权力，他们到相邻的部落里去，在那里发表他们的抗议宣言说："罗马正在吞食侵占各处，日耳曼的古老的自由正在被毁坏。在与他们一样诞生在同一块土地上的人们当中，难道就没有一个人能当国王吗？难道我们非得把那个弗拉乌斯的儿子、一个十足的罗马军事探子捧在众人头上不可吗？对于这种情况难道阿尔米尼乌斯人就无话可说了吗？祈求阿尔米尼乌斯的名字是没有用的。即使他自己有一个儿子在敌国长大成人之后，又回来统治这个王国，人们也有理由担心这是一个受到外国的教育、奴役、衣着以及其他一切都被玷污的青年！而且，如果说意大利库斯像他的父亲的话，那么没有任何一个人能够像他的父亲弗拉乌斯那样，对他自己的祖国和上帝进行过那样残暴的战争！"

诸如此类的号召吸引了许多的支持者。然而，意大利库斯支持者的力量也毫不逊色。他提醒他们说，他并没有强迫他们的意志，而是由于他自己有着比对手们更加高贵的出身才被召来的。至于他的勇气，他们可以试验一下，他继续说，他们将会看到，他是配得上他的叔叔阿尔米尼乌斯和他的祖父阿克图美路斯的！他也并没有为他的父亲感到羞愧，因为他的父亲是在得到了日耳曼人的赞同的情况下，坚定地履行了对罗马所承担的义务。"自由"这一词汇正在被一些卑贱的人利用来作为不诚实的借口，这些人一向危害国家，他们唯一的希望就是制造国家的分裂。

这些宣言得到了群众热烈的欢呼。接下来就进行了一场战争，就像一场部族间的战争那样规模巨大的战争，意大利库斯取得了胜利。但是胜利使得他变得骄傲自大起来，结果被赶了出去。

backing of the Langobardi, he was restored. But in good and bad fortune alike he proved disastrous to the Cherusci.

At this period the Chauci, free from internal dissension, took advantage of the death of the imperial governor of Lower Germany,
Quintus Sanquinius Maximus, to raid that province before his successor Cnaeus Domitius Corbulo (II) arrived. Their commander was
Gannascus of the tribe of the Canninefates, an auxiliary deserter and
now a pirate with small ships plundering, in particular, the Gallic
coast, which he knew to be both wealthy and unwarlike. On arrival in
the province Corbulo's careful methods soon won him the fame that
dates from this campaign. Bringing up warships by the main channel
of the Rhine, and other craft (according to their build) by creeks and
canals, he sank the enemy's boats and ejected Gannascus.

His Roman soldiers were enthusiastic looters but slack and reluctant workers. So, when the immediate situation was remedied, Corbulo revived traditional standards of discipline. Falling out on the
march, and fighting without orders, were prohibited. Picket and sentry duty—all tasks day and night—were performed under arms. One
soldier is said to have been executed for digging at the earthwork without side-arms, another for wearing his dagger only. These stories are
exaggerated, and perhaps invented. But Corbulo's strictness inspired
them; and a man credited with such severity over details must have
been vigilant and, for serious offences, inexorable.

The terror he caused had opposite effects on our men and the Ger-

但是后来,依靠着朗哥巴狄的军队,他又重新取得了王位。但是,不论他是在顺境中还是在逆境中,他都是凯路斯奇人的祸害。

这个时期,卡乌奇人已经结束了内部的纷争,趁着下日耳曼军统帅克温图斯·桑克维尼乌斯·玛克西姆斯刚刚死去,而继任者格涅乌斯·多米提乌斯·科尔布罗(二世)还没有到来的有利时机,卡乌奇人在干纳斯库斯的率领下,先发制人地对下日耳曼发动了进攻。干纳斯库斯是一个坎宁尼法提斯人,曾在罗马的辅助部队里服过役,后来当了逃兵,而现在则带领着一小队轻便船只在海上以打劫为生。他的活动范围主要是在高卢沿岸一带,因为他对于这里的财富和非战情绪是非常熟悉的。科尔布罗从一进入行省,就采取了极为谨慎的措施,不久就取得了这次战争开始以来便享有的盛誉。他把他的战船全部集中在莱茵河干流上,其他船只则(按照它们的吃水量大小)分别停泊在河口和支流上面。他击沉了敌人的船只,将干纳斯库斯驱赶了出去。

他的罗马士兵们热切地盼望劫掠财物而十分松懈,并且对劳苦和军务感到厌烦。因此,当他把事情就地安排妥当之后,科尔布罗就重申了那些古老法律的条款,要军团士兵们记住:在进军时离开队伍,不遵守命令而自行发动战斗,这些都是法律所严格禁止的。不论放哨还是值班,不论白天还是夜晚,执行所有的任务时都要佩带着武器。据说,一个士兵是因为在掘土修建工事时没有佩剑受到死刑的处分,另一个士兵则是因为在干这一工作时只带着一把匕首。这种说法未免是夸大其词了,也可能是杜撰的,但正是科尔布罗的严厉激起了这样的想象力。对于小事都这样严厉的一个人,对于重大的罪行就更是毫不宽容了。

他激起的这种恐怖情绪对我们罗马士兵以及对日耳曼人却发生

mans. It made the Romans better soldiers, and weakened the morale of the natives. The Frisians, hostile or disloyal since the revolt they had launched by defeating Lucius Apronius, gave hostages and settled on lands delimited by Corbulo. He also allocated to them a senate, officials, and laws—and constructed a fort to ensure obedience.

Then Corbulo sent agents to induce the Greater Chauci (the eastern branch) to surrender, and to trap and kill Gannascus. The trap was successful. Being directed against a deserter who had broken faith, it was not dishonourable. Yet it upset the Chauci, and provoked them to rebellion. Some Romans welcomed this policy, others deplored it. 'Why provoke the enemy?' they said. 'If he fails, Rome will be the loser. If he wins, such a distinguished soldier will offend the inactive emperor—and so endanger peace. '

And indeed Claudius forbade further aggression against the Germans, and even ordered the withdrawal of our garrisons to the west bank of the Rhine. These instructions took Corbulo by surprise. He received them when he was already building a camp in enemy country. Many consequences crowded into his mind-peril from the emperor, scorn from the natives, ridicule from provincials. However, his only comment was: 'Earlier Roman commanders were fortunate!' Then he sounded the retreat. But to keep the troops occupied he made them dig a twenty-three-mile Meuse-Rhine canal, to bypass the hazards of the North Sea.

Though he had forbidden the war, Claudius awarded Corbulo an

了恰恰相反的效果。这样的办法使得罗马人的军队更加强大，但对外族人来说，却削弱了他们的士气。弗里喜人曾因战胜了路奇乌斯·阿普洛尼乌斯而发生了叛乱，自从那时以后，弗里喜人便采取敌对或不满的态度。而此时，他们交出了人质，并且移居到科尔布罗限定的地区去。科尔布罗也给他们成立了一个元老院，设置了一名高级官吏，并且还给他们制定了法律，又在那里设置了一个设防的据点，以保证他们服从。

然后，科尔布罗又派遣使节到大卡乌奇人（东方的一支卡乌奇人）那里去劝说他们投降，并且要他们诱捕并杀死干纳斯库斯。这种计策获得了成功，对付这样一个不忠诚的逃兵，这算不上是可耻的举动。但是干纳斯库斯的被杀惹恼了卡乌奇人，激起了他们的反叛之心。一些罗马人支持这种策略，而另一些人则表示痛惜。他们说："为什么要树敌呢？如果他失败了，那么国家就要遭受到损失。而如果他胜利了，这样一位杰出的士兵又将会冒犯敏感的皇帝，因此就会危及和平。"

的确如此，克劳狄乌斯十分坚定地禁止对日耳曼发动更进一步的侵略，甚至还下令我们的卫戍部队撤退到莱茵河的西岸。这些命令使科尔布罗感到十分吃惊，当他已经开始在敌人的土地上修建营地的时候，他收到了这些命令。尽管他想到了这些命令会带来的许许多多的后果——来自皇帝那里的危险，各部族方面的蔑视，行省居民的讥笑，但是，他却只讲了这样一句话："以前的罗马将领是多么幸运啊！"随后他就下令撤退了。但是为了使士兵们有事可做，他让他们在莱茵河和摩撒河之间挖掘一条 23 英里长的运河，这样便可以避开来自北海上的危险。

克劳狄乌斯虽然不许科尔布罗作战，却仍然赐给他一个凯

honorary Triumph. Soon afterwards the same honour was awarded in Upper Germany to Curtius Rufus. He had sunk a mine in the territory of the Mattiaci to find silver. Its products were scanty and shortlived, though the troops suffered and toiled, digging channels and doing underground work which would have been laborious enough in the open. This forced labour covered several provinces. Worn out by it, the men secretly appealed to the emperor, in the name of all the armies, begging him to grant honorary Triumphs to commanders *before* giving them their armies.

Some said Curtius Rufus was a gladiator's son. I do not want to lie about his origin but would be embarrassed to tell the truth. When he grew up he had been employed by the assistant to the governor of Africa. At Hadrumetum, while he was strolling alone at midday in a deserted colonnade, a female figure of superhuman stature appeared to him and said: 'Rufus, you will come to this province as governor.' Encouraged by the omen he left for Rome, where his energetic personality, aided by subsidies from friends, won him the quaestorship. Then, defeating noble competitors, he became praetor. Tiberius backed him, palliating his inglorious birth with the remark 'Curtius Rufus' achievements are paternity enough.' Surly though cringing to his superiors, bullying to his inferiors, ill at ease with his equals, Curtius lived to an advanced age, gained the consulship, an honorary Triumph, and finally the governorship of Africa-where, his destiny fulfilled, he died.

旋的标记。不久之后，在上日耳曼，库尔提乌斯·路福斯也取得了同样的荣誉，因为他为了寻找银矿，在玛提乌姆地区开发了一处矿山。尽管军团士兵在挖水道和修建十分艰巨的地下矿坑设备时——这种工作在露天进行也已经够艰巨的了，吃了很大的苦头，但是矿山的产量却很少，而且维持的时间也不长。这种强劳动力的苦役覆盖了好几个行省，从事这种劳动的人们为这种过度紧张的工作而累得疲惫不堪，于是他们就以全军的名义秘密上书皇帝，请求他在把他们的军队交给统帅们之前，先赐给他们凯旋的荣誉。

有些人说库尔提乌斯·路福斯是一个剑斗士的儿子。关于他的出身，我不想说假话，但说出真实情况又是一件比较尴尬的事情。在长大成人的时候，他被阿非利加总督手下的一名财务官所雇佣做事情。在阿杜路美图姆，一天中午，当他正独自在一个荒废的柱廊下漫步时，一个高大得超乎常人的妇女出现在他的面前对他说："路福斯，你将来会来到这个行省担任长官的。"为这一征兆所鼓舞，于是他就离开这个城市来到了罗马。在罗马，由于他自己果敢的性格，再加上他的朋友们的慷慨解囊相助，他取得了财务官的职位。随后，他又击败了贵族出身的竞争对手而取得了行政长官的职位。提贝里乌斯对他给予了支持，为了给他并不光彩的出身作开脱，他曾经说过这样的话："库尔提乌斯·路福斯所取得的成功是足以光宗耀祖的。"尽管对上恭恭敬敬、逢迎巴结，对下蛮横无理，而在同僚当中又颇为难对付，但是库尔提乌斯却能在他年纪轻轻的时候就爬上了执政官的高位，取得了凯旋的标记，最后终于担任了阿非利加的总督职位。在阿非利加，他命中注定的官运应验了，而他也就死在了那里。

Meanwhile at Rome a knight called Cnaeus Nonius was found wearing a sword at the emperor's morning reception. No motive became evident, then or later. Under torture, he did not deny his guilt. But he revealed no accomplices; whether he had any to hide is unknown.

In the same year Publius Cornelius Dolabella (II) proposed that an annual gladiatorial display should be defrayed by the quaestors. Offices had traditionally been the reward of merit, and every respectable citizen, however young, could stand for them. There had been no lower age-limit for consulships or dictatorships. The quaestorship had been founded in the regal period, as is shown by Lucius Junius Brutus' restatement of the Assembly's original law. Selection remained with the consuls until this and other offices passed to popular vote. The first quaestors to be appointed by the new method—sixty-three years after the expulsion of the Tarquins—were Valerius Potitus and Aemilius Mamercus (to supervise the war-chest). Then, as business increased, two more quaestors were added for duties at Rome. Soon, with taxes coming in from Italy and the provinces, the number was again doubled. Next, twenty more were appointed by Sulla—to enlarge the senate, which he had invested with criminal jurisdiction. Later these judicial functions were recovered by the order of knights. Yet, even after that, quaestorships still depended not on payment but on merit and popularity. But Dolabella's proposal virtually put them up for auction.

同时,在罗马,人们发现一个名叫格涅乌斯·诺尼乌斯的骑士在皇帝早朝时身上佩带着宝剑。但是他这样做的动机是什么,无论是当时还是以后都没有弄清楚。在严刑拷问之下,他不得不供认了自己的罪行,但是并没有招供任何共谋犯,他是否有一些什么东西想隐瞒也不得而知。

在同一年里,普布里乌斯·考尔尼里乌斯·多拉贝拉(二世)建议道,每年一度的剑斗表演比赛的费用都应当由已经当选的财务官支付。传统上,官职是一个人的功业的报偿,每一个值得尊敬的正直的公民,即使他还非常年轻,也都能合法地竞选长官职位。关于担任执政官或独裁官的最低年龄,并不曾有过什么限制。财务官这一职位,早在国王统治时期就已经设置了,路奇乌斯·尤尼乌斯·布鲁图斯对库里亚大权法的恢复就显示出了这一点。选任的权力掌握在执政官手里,直到这一官职和其他官职都转由人民来选举产生的时候。在塔尔克维尼乌斯被逐后63年,由新办法选出的第一任财务官是瓦列里乌斯·波提图斯和埃米里乌斯·玛美尔库斯(他们的职责是掌理战时军队的财政)。后来由于他们的事务越来越多了,在罗马又增设了两位财务官。不久,由于意大利以及各行省向罗马缴纳的税收也日益增加,因此财务官的数目又增加了一倍。在这之后,根据苏拉的一项法律,又任命了20多名财务官,用来扩大元老院的规模,因为他已经把刑事法庭的审判权交给元老院了。后来,这一审判权又为骑士们所重新获得。此后,财务官一职也仍然不是靠金钱得到的,而是有赖于竞选者的功业和他在人民中的威望。但是实际上,多拉贝拉的这个建议却无疑是将这个官职作为商品拍卖了。

In the following year the consuls were Aulus Vitellius and Lucius Vipstanus Poplicola. During debates that were now held about enlarging the senate, the chief men of 'long-haired' (northern and central) Gaul—belonging to tribes with long-standing treaties with Rome, of which they themselves were citizens—claimed the right to hold office in the capital. The question aroused much discussion, and the opposing arguments were put to the emperor.

'Italy is not so decayed', said some, 'that she cannot provide her own capital with a senate. In former times even peoples akin to us were content with a Roman senate of native Romans only; and the government of those days is a glorious memory. To this day, people cite the ancient Roman character for their models of courage and renown.

'Is it not enough that Venetian and Insubrian Gauls have forced their way into the senate? Do we have to import foreigners in hordes, like gangs of prisoners, and leave no careers for our own surviving aristocracy, or for impoverished senators from Latium? Every post will be absorbed by the rich men whose grandfathers and greatgrandfathers commanded hostile tribes, assailed our armies in battle, besieged the divine Julius Caesar at Alesia. Those are recent memories. But are we to forget our men who, beside Rome's Capitoline citadel, were killed by the ancestors of these very Gauls? Let them, by all means, have the title of Roman citizens. But the senate's insignia, the glory of office, they must not cheapen.'

在接下来的一年里，[1]奥路斯·维提里乌斯和路奇乌斯·维普斯塔努斯·波普里考拉担任执政官。这期间，讨论了补充元老院名额的问题。所谓长发高卢（北方的和中部的）的首要公民，由于长时间以来就与罗马签订了和约，而他们本身又是罗马公民，所以他们要求取得在首都担任官职的权利。这个问题引起了人们热烈的讨论，而不同观点的激烈辩论也提交到了皇帝面前。

有的人说："意大利还没有衰败到连为首都罗马提供一个元老院的能力都没有的程度。在过去，对于那些和我们有血统关系的民族来说，一个由罗马本民族的人组成的罗马的元老院也就足够了，而且在那段日子里，共和国也创造了辉煌的历史。直到今天，人们还引用古老的罗马品格为世人提供勇气和荣誉的范例！

"维尼提人和印苏布里高卢人[2]已经冲进了元老院，难道这还不够吗？难道我们还要把大群的外国人引进来，就好像一群囚徒一样吗？我们难道就不给我们罗马贵族的后裔和来自拉提乌姆的贫穷的元老留下任何位置吗？所有的重要职位都要被那些有钱人占有了，然而这些人的祖父、曾祖父却曾经统率着同罗马为敌的部落，在战争中攻击我们的军队，并曾在阿列西亚包围过圣尤利乌斯·恺撒。而且这都是不久之前才发生的事情啊！难道我们就忘记了那些在罗马的卡皮托里乌姆神庙边被杀害的同胞了吗？而杀害我们的同胞的正是这些高卢人的祖先啊！就让他们享有罗马公民的头衔吧，但是元老的标记和长官的荣誉，绝对不能被他们玷污！"

---

〔1〕 公元 48 年，罗马建城 801 年。
〔2〕 公元前 49 年，尤利乌斯·恺撒曾授予他们以公民权。

These and similar arguments did not impress Claudius. He contradicted them on the spot, and then summoned the senate and made this speech:

'The experience of my own ancestors, notably of my family's Sabine founder Clausus who was simultaneously made a Roman citizen and a patrician, encourage me to adopt the same national policy, by bringing excellence to Rome from whatever source. For I do not forget that the Julii came from Alba Longa, the Coruncanii from Camerium, the Porcii from Tusculum; and, leaving antiquity aside, that men from Etruria, Lucania, and all Italy have been admitted into the senate; and that finally Italy herself has been extended to the Alps, uniting not merely individuals but whole territories and peoples under the name of Rome.'

'Moreover, after the enfranchisement of Italy across the Po, our next step was to make citizens of the finest provincials too: we added them to our ex-soldiers in settlements throughout the world, and by their means reinvigorated the exhausted empire. This helped to stabilize peace within the frontiers and successful relations with foreign powers. Is it regretted that the Cornelii Balbi immigrated from Spain, and other equally distinguished men from southern Gaul? Their descendants are with us; and they love Rome as much as we do. What proved fatal to Sparta and Athens, for all their military strength, was their segregation of conquered subjects as aliens. Our founder Romulus, on the other hand, had the wisdom—more than once—to transform

　　这一番话以及其他一些类似的言论，都没有给克劳狄斯带来多大的影响。他当场就提出了自己的反对意见。之后，他又召集了一次元老院会议，发表了下面的讲话：

　　"我自己的先人就有着同样的经历，我们萨比尼家族的创建者高贵的克劳苏斯，他在成为一个罗马公民的同时，又取得了贵族的称号。我的祖先的这种经历激励着我采取同样的政策，那就是把一切真正优秀的东西都吸收进我们的罗马来，而不论它来自什么地方。因为我不会忘记：尤利乌斯家族是从阿尔巴·隆格到我们这里来的，科伦卡尼乌斯是从卡美里乌姆来的，波尔齐乌斯家族是从图司库路姆来的；且不说远古时代的事情，就是现在，那些来自埃特路里亚、路卡尼亚以及整个意大利的人们不也已经被接纳为元老院的元老们了吗？而且最后，意大利本身也已经扩展到了阿尔卑斯山，因此不仅仅是个人，就是整个地区和民族也都完全联合并入到罗马的名下了。"

　　"而且，当波河对岸各地区的意大利居民取得了公民权以后，我们接下来的任务就是把最强壮的行省居民，我们的退役军人已遍布于天下各地，再把这些人加到他们中间去，这样就给我们凋敝的帝国重新注入了强大的力量。这样做可以帮助我们在国内建立巩固的和平，与外面的强国建立良好的外交关系。科尔尼利·巴尔布斯一家是从西班牙迁来的，和他们同样显赫的一些家族则是从南方的高卢来的，难道这也是遗憾的事情吗？这些人的子孙现在都和我们在一起，他们对他们的祖国罗马的爱也和我们一样深挚。斯巴达和雅典都拥有着强大的军事力量，可是终于免不了灭亡的命运，正是因为他们始终把被征服者当做外人看待而采取种族隔离政策的缘故。但是另一方面，我们自己的始

whole enemy peoples into Roman citizens within the course of a single day. Even some of our kings were foreign. Similarly, the admission to former office of the sons of slaves is not the novelty it is alleged to be. In early times it happened frequently. '

' "The Senonian Gauls fought against us," it is objected. But did not Italians, Vulsci and Aequi, as well? "The Gauls captured Rome" you say. But we also lost battles to our neighbours—we gave hostages to the Etruscans, we went beneath the Samnites' yoke. Actually, a review of all these wars shows that the Gallic war took the shortest time of all-since then, peace and loyalty have reigned unbroken. Now that they have assimilated our customs and culture and married into our families, let them bring in their gold and wealth rather than keep it to themselves. Senators, however ancient any institution seems, once upon a time it was new! First, plebeians joined patricians in office. Next, the Latins were added. Then came men from other Italian peoples. The innovation now proposed will, in its turn, one day be old: what we seek to justify by precedents today will itself become a precedent. '

The senate approved the emperor's speech. The first Gauls who thereby obtained the right to become Roman senators were the Aedui. They owed this privilege to their ancient treaty with Rome and their position as the only Gallic community entitled ' Brothers of

祖罗木路斯却是比从前的一切人都明智,他竟然在一天的时间里就将整个敌对的民族转变成了罗马公民!甚至我们的一些国王也都是外国人,同样,允许奴隶的儿子担任官职,这也并不像人们所想象的那样是什么新鲜事情。早在古代,这样的事情就经常发生。"

"有人可以反驳说,'高卢的谢诺尼人同我们打过仗',但是难道意大利人、沃尔斯奇人和埃魁人就没有和我们打过仗吗?也许还会有人反驳说,'高卢人曾经占领过罗马',可是我们也曾在与邻国的作战中失利,把我们的人质送到托司卡尼人那里去,并且从撒姆尼特人的轭下穿过去。实际上,如果回顾一下我们过去的历次战争,就会发现,对高卢人的战争所用的时间最短,而且从那时起,那里就一直保持着和平和忠诚。现在他们已经吸收了我们的风俗习惯、文化的营养,深受其化育,并且通过婚姻关系而融入于我们的家族中了,让他们把他们自己的黄金和财富带进来,而不要排斥在我们的国境之外留在他们自己那里吧!元老们,古代的任何制度,都曾经有一个时期看起来是全新的!起初,是平民加入贵族的行列担任高级长官;后来,又有了拉丁人担任长官,而拉丁人之后又有了来自意大利其他民族的高级长官。我们的提议在今天是个创举,但将来有一天它也会成为过去的一个构成部分,而今天我们引证前例努力加以辩护的事情,在将来也会成为被引证的前例。"

元老们对皇帝的发言表示赞同,结果埃杜伊人就成为首先在首都担任罗马元老的高卢人。他们之所以能取得这样的权利,是因为他们很早就已经和罗马签订了盟约关系,而且在高卢人的城市里,只有他们拥有着"罗马人民的兄弟"这样的地位。就在这

the Roman People'. At this period Claudius also elevated senators of particularly long standing and illustrious birth to patrician rank, which few surviving families possessed. They comprised what Romulus had called 'the Greater' and Lucius Junius Brutus 'the Lesser' Houses. Even the families which the dictator Caesar and Augustus promoted in their place, under the Cassian and Saenian laws respectively, had died out. The action of Claudius was welcomed as beneficial, and the imperial censor enjoyed performing it.

But Claudius was worried about how to expel notorious bad characters from the senate. Rejecting old-fashioned severity in favour of a lenient modern method, he advised individuals concerned to consider their own cases and apply for permission to renounce senatorial rank— which would readily be granted. He would then publish expulsions by the censors *and* resignations in a single list—so that the humiliation of those expelled should be mitigated by association with those who had modestly volunteered to withdraw. For this one of the consuls, Lucius Vipstanus Poplicola, proposed that Claudius should be called Father of the Senate—since others too were called Father of the Country, whereas new services to the country deserved new titles. But the emperor vetoed the proposal as too flattering. Then he concluded the ritual of the census, which showed a citizen body of 5,984,072 persons.

And now ended Claudius' ignorance of his own domestic affairs. Now he had, ineluctably, to discover and punish his wife's excesses (as a preliminary to coveting an incestuous substitute). Messalina's adultery was going so smoothly that she was drifting, through boredom, into unfamiliar vices. But now fate seemed to have unhinged Gaius Silius; or perhaps he felt that impending perils could only be

期间,克劳狄乌斯又把那些长期任职和门第非常显赫的元老们提拔为贵族,因为原来拥有这种荣誉的家族这时已经所剩无几了,这些家族就是罗木路斯所说的"大家族"和路奇乌斯·优尼乌斯·布鲁图斯所说的"小家族"。甚至在独裁官恺撒和皇帝奥古斯都在位时,分别根据卡西乌斯法和赛尼乌斯法选出来的那些家族,现在也都零落殆尽了。克劳狄乌斯这一措施大有裨益,因此深受欢迎,于是皇家监察官便欣然地承担起了这样一项任务。

不过怎样把那些臭名昭著的坏人从元老院中排除出去,却是克劳狄乌斯非常焦虑的事情。他放弃了过去时兴的那种严厉的办法,而采用了一些温和的现代手段。他劝告每个有关的人自己考虑他们自己的问题,然后申请准予放弃元老的职务——这种申请自然很快地就得到了批准。继而,他就在同一个名单上同时发表了被监察官开除的和被批准退职的元老的名字。如此把由监察官开除的人和谦虚的自动退职的人混合在一起公布,被开除的人们的耻辱也就相应的减轻了。为此,执政官路奇乌斯·维普斯塔努斯·波普里科拉建议,克劳狄乌斯应取得"元老院之父"的称号。因为其他人已经被称做"祖国之父",而为国家作出新的贡献的人应该享有新的尊称。但是皇帝本人却否决了这一建议,认为他太过阿谀奉承了。之后,他还主持了一次的人口调查的结束仪式,调查结果表明罗马公民现有5984072人。

现在,克劳狄乌斯对于他自己国内的事情不再是一无所知了。于是,他就不可避免地发现并且惩罚了他妻子的越轨行为(然而这只不过是代之以后来的一次乱伦的结合的开端)。美撒里娜的奸情进行得太顺利了,以至于让她感到厌烦,因此又不断地翻新一些罪恶的新花样。但是现在似乎命运注定要使盖乌斯·西

met by perilous action. He urged that concealment should be dropped. 'We do not have to wait until the emperor dies of old age!' he told her. 'Besides, only innocent people can afford long-term plans. Flagrant guilt requires audacity. And we have accomplices who share our danger. I am without wife or child. I am ready to marry, and to adopt Britannicus. Your power will remain undiminished. Peace of mind will only be yours if we can forestall Claudius. He is slow to discover deception—but quick to anger.'

Messalina was unenthusiastic. It was not that she loved her husband. But she feared that Silius, once supreme, might despise his mistress, and see the crime prompted by an emergency in its true colours. However, the idea of being called his wife appealed to her owing to its sheer outrageousness—a sensualist's ultimate satisfaction. So, waiting only until Claudius had left to sacrifice at Ostia, she celebrated a formal marriage with Silius.

It will seem fantastic, I know, that in a city where nothing escapes notice or comment, any human beings could have felt themselves so secure. Much more so that, on an appointed day and before invited signatories, a consul designate and the emperor's wife should have been joined together in formal marriage-'for the purpose of rearing children'; that she should have listened to the diviners' words, assumed the wedding-veil, sacrificed to the gods; that the pair should have taken their places at a banquet, embraced, and finally

里乌斯丧失理智，或许是由于他感觉到只有冒险一搏才能应付得了将要临头的危险，盖乌斯不断地催促美撒里娜索性把事情公开。他告诉她说："我们不能干等着皇帝年老而死！只有清白无辜的人才能耗得起时间去做长时间的谋划；而恶名昭彰的罪行是需要大胆地豁出去干的。我们有很多同谋者，他们和我们共同承担着风险。我没有妻子儿女，我准备结婚，并且把不列塔尼库斯过继过来。你的权力将会保持不变，不会有什么削弱。而且，如果我们能先动手除掉克劳狄乌斯的话，你的心灵只会得到宁静而不会遭受痛苦。要知道，虽然克劳狄乌斯不会那样快发现对他的欺骗，但他却是很容易发怒的。"

美撒里娜的反应很冷淡，这倒不是因为她还爱着自己的丈夫，而是因为她担心西里乌斯一旦得到了最高的权力，就会把自己的情妇抛弃。同时，她也在冷静地分析，为紧急情况所驱使就贸然采取行动，犯下这样的罪行，到底值不值得。然而成为他的妻子的渴望促使她做出最丑恶的行径，她不知廉耻地追求着肉欲上的最大的欢乐。因此，她只是默默地等待着时机，直到克劳狄乌斯离开罗马到奥斯蒂亚去主持牺牲奉献式，她就和西里乌斯举行一个正式的、隆重的婚礼。

我知道，在一座任何事情都瞒不过人们的耳目、逃不过人们的议论的城市里，任何人如果认为自己是十分安全的，那简直就是异想天开。更不用说，在一个指定的日子里，当着在婚书上盖章的证人的面，一位当选的执政官和皇帝的妻子公然举行正式的婚礼结合在一起了——"为了生养孩子的目的"；她还听从占卜师的话，戴上了结婚的面罩，向诸神奉献了牺牲；两个人还举行了庆祝宴会，在宴会上接吻拥抱，最后就作为一对夫妇在夜里同床共

spent the night as man and wife. But I am not inventing marvels. What I have told, and shall tell, is the truth. Older men heard and recorded it.

The imperial household shuddered—especially those in power, with everything to fear from a new emperor. There were secret conferences. Then indignation was unconcealed. 'While a ballet-dancing actor violated the emperor's bedroom', they said, 'it was humiliating enough. Yet it did not threaten Claudius' life. Here, on the other hand, is a young, handsome, intelligent nobleman, consul-to-be-but with a loftier destiny in mind. For where such a marriage will lead is clear enough.' When they thought of Claudius' sluggish uxoriousness, and the many assassinations ordered by Messalina, they were terrified. Yet the emperor's very pliability gave them hope. If they could convince him of the enormity of the outrage, Messalina might be condemned and eliminated without trial. But everything, they felt, turned on this—would Claudius give her a hearing? Could they actually shut his ears against her confession?

Callistus, who has already been mentioned in connection with Gaius' murder, Narcissus, who had contrived the death of Gaius Appius Junius Silanus, and Pallas, who was now basking in the warmest favour, conferred together. They discussed whether, pretending ignorance of everything else, they could secretly frighten Messalina out of her affair with Silius. But this scheme was abandoned by Pallas and Callistus as too dangerous for themselves. Pallas' mo-

枕共度良宵！然而,这绝不是我自己杜撰的耸人听闻的神奇故事,我所说的和我将要说的,都是事实,这些事都是年长的人亲耳听到和亲笔记录下来的。

皇室家族的人战栗了,特别是那些掌握着权力的人,因为这些人对一个新皇帝的一切都感到恐慌。开始,他们只是在私下的谈话中表示不满,后来就公开表现出了自己的愤怒情绪了。他们说:"当一个优伶玷污了皇帝的卧室的时候,虽然也已经是够丢脸的了,不过还不至于威胁到克劳狄乌斯本人的生命安全。但是现在,情况不同了,这是一位年轻潇洒、聪明机智的贵族,一位当选的执政官,他心里正在准备着实现自己更大的目的。因此,这次结婚会引起什么样的后果,已经是足够清晰明朗的了!"当他们想到克劳狄乌斯对美撒里娜的那种愚钝糊涂的疼爱,他在美撒里娜的命令之下所进行的多次屠杀的时候,他们就不禁深感害怕。然而,皇帝的温驯的性格本身又给了他们以希望。如果他们能使他认识到这种侮辱性的行为的严重性,那么美撒里娜就可以在得到审判之前就被判罪、除掉。但是他们也认识到,所有这一切都要看克劳狄乌斯肯不肯听取她给自己辩护,以及他们是否能阻止得了他,不让他去听取她的忏悔之词。

卡利司图斯(这个人我已经提到过,与盖乌斯的被杀有关系)、纳尔奇苏斯(这个人设法杀死了盖乌斯·阿庇乌斯·尤尼乌斯·西拉努斯)和帕拉斯(这个人是当时最受宠信的炙手可热的人物)三人聚在一起商量办法。他们讨论,如果他们假装对所知道的一切其他情况都可以置之脑后,是否可以在私下里恐吓美撒里娜,让她离开她的情夫西里乌斯。但是这个计划遭到了帕拉斯和卡利司图斯的反对,因为这样做对他们自己本身来说太危险。帕

tive was cowardice. Callistus had learnt from his experience dating from the previous reign that power was better safeguarded by diplomatic than by vigorous methods. Narcissus, however, persevered in taking action-with this new feature: she was to be denounced without forewarning of charge or accuser. Narcissus watched for an opening. Then, as Claudius prolonged his stay at Ostia, he induced the emperor's two favourite mistresses to act as informers. They were persuaded by gifts, promises, and assurances of the increased influence that Messalina's downfall would bring them.

One of the women, Calpurnia (I), secured a private interview with Claudius. Throwing herself at his feet, she cried that Messalina had married Silius—in the same breath asking the other girl, Cleopatra (who was standing by ready), for corroboration: which she provided. Then Calpurnia urged that Narcissus should be summoned. 'I must excuse my earlier silences', said Narcissus, 'about Vettius Valens, Plautius Lateranus, and the like—and now, too, I do not propose to complain of her adulteries, much less impel you to demand back from Silius your mansion, slaves, and other imperial perquisites. *But are you aware you are divorced?* Nation, senate, and army have witnessed her wedding to Silius. Act promptly, or her new husband controls Rome!'

Claudius summoned his closest friends. First he interrogated Gaius Turranius, controller of the corn supply, then Lusius Geta, commander of the Guard. They confirmed the story. The rest of the emperor's

拉斯是由于胆怯,卡利司图斯则是因为从对前朝统治经验的总结中深切体会到,用灵活机动的策略提出自己的看法,较之采取生硬的措施更能稳妥地保持住自己的权力。纳尔奇苏斯则坚持要采取行动,只是对自己的计划作了一些新的改进:在事先根本不告诉她要控告她和谁控告她的情况下对她提出指控。纳尔奇苏斯在窥伺着一个有利的时机。后来,因为克劳狄乌斯在奥斯蒂亚那里待着延迟了回罗马的日期,于是他就诱使皇帝最宠爱的两个情妇充当告密者。他送给她们厚礼,对她们许诺,并且向她们保证说美撒里娜的垮台一定会带给她们自己势力的增强的。

这两个女人的其中之一,名字叫做卡尔普尔尼娅(一世)的女人获得了与克劳狄乌斯私下约见的机会。她扑通一声跪倒在地,便哭着告诉皇帝说,美撒里娜已经嫁给了西里乌斯。并且同时,她又问另一个女人克利欧帕特拉(这个女人就站在身旁,已经做好了充分的准备以回答问题),是否也听到了这样的事情,来证实她的说法。在克利欧帕特拉作出了肯定的回答之后,卡尔普尔尼娅便请求皇帝召见纳尔奇苏斯。纳尔奇苏斯说:"我必须请求您宽恕我过去的沉默,因为我没有向您提起过关于维提乌斯·瓦伦斯、普劳提乌斯·拉提拉努斯以及诸如此类的人物的事情。甚至现在,我也仍不打算责备这个女人的淫荡,更不想催促您把皇宫、奴隶和其他的皇家物什从西里乌斯手中要回来。但是,您知道您已经离婚了吗?全国人民、元老院和军队都看到了她和西里乌斯的婚礼。就请您赶快行动吧,否则她的新丈夫就掌要握罗马了!"

于是,克劳狄乌斯召见了他的一些最亲密的朋友们。首先向粮务官盖乌斯·图尔拉尼乌斯,接着又向近卫军长官路奇乌斯·盖塔询问此事,他们都证实了这件事情。皇帝的其他随从则高声

entourage loudly insisted that he must visit the camp and secure the Guard—safety must come before vengeance. Claudius, it is said, was panic-stricken. 'Am I still emperor?' he kept on asking. 'Is Silius still a private citizen?'

Meanwhile, Messalina was indulging in unprecedented extravagances. It was full autumn; and she was performing in her grounds a mimic grape-harvest. Presses were working, vats overflowing, surrounded by women capering in skins like sacrificing or frenzied Maenads. She herself, hair streaming, brandished a Bacchic wand. Beside her stood Silius in ivy—wreath and buskins, rolling his head, while the disreputable chorus yelled round him. Vettius Valens, the story goes, gaily climbed a great tree. Asked what he saw, his answer was: 'A fearful storm over Ostia !' There may have been a storm. Or it could have been a casual phrase. But later it seemed prophetic.

Rumours and messengers now came pouring in. They revealed that Claudius knew all, and was on his way, determined for revenge. So the couple separated, Messalina to the Gardens of Lucullus, Silius—to disguise his alarm—to business in the Forum. The others too melted away in every direction. But they were pounced on and arrested separately by staff-officers of the Guard, in the streets or in hidingplaces. Messalina was too shaken by the catastrophe to make any plans. But she instantly decided on the course that had often saved her-to meet her husband and let him see her.

叫喊着，坚持要求皇帝到军营去，先得到近卫军的保护——在复仇之前必须要先保障皇帝的安全。据说，证实了这一事实后，克劳狄乌斯当时就惊呆了。他一直在不停地在问："我还是一个皇帝吗？西里乌斯还是一个普通的公民吗？"

但是，与此同时，美撒里娜却是沉浸于前所未有的放荡奢侈之中。现在正是仲秋时节，她正在她私邸的园地里举行一个模仿葡萄收获的表演。榨葡萄汁机正在工作着，大桶里装满了葡萄汁，满得溢了出来，戴着常春藤编织的花环、披着皮子的妇女则围在旁边，像奉献牺牲时或疯狂的酒神女祭司美娜达那样跳跃着。美撒里娜自己则在那里披散着瀑布似的头发，挥动着酒神杖。西里乌斯站在她的身旁，戴着常春藤冠、穿着优伶穿的厚底靴，摇晃着他的头，而同时合唱队则围在他的周围放荡地胡乱叫着。传说维提乌斯·瓦伦斯兴高采烈地爬到了一株高大的树上去。当别人问他，他看到了什么的时候，他的回答是："奥斯蒂亚上空的一场可怕的暴风雨！"也许是那里真正下了一场暴风雨，也许是偶然间随便讲出来的一句话，但后来这句话却成了一句谶语。

这时谣传和报信的人从四面八方铺天盖地地来了。他们透露消息说，克劳狄乌斯已经知道了一切，并且正在往这里赶来，要坚决地进行报复。于是他们俩就分手了，美撒里娜到路库鲁斯的花园去，西里乌斯则为了掩饰他内心的惊恐，到广场上办事去了，其余的人也都四散而去溜之大吉。但是他们却纷纷被百人团长们发觉并逮捕了起来，有的是在街道上，有的是在躲避的地点。美撒里娜因大难临头而手足无措，但她立刻决定采用那种她过去经常使用的方法，那就是去见她的丈夫，并且让他看到自己，这种方法过去总能使她脱困得救。

She also sent word that Britannicus and Octavia should go and seek their father's embraces. She herself begged the senior priestess of Vesta, Vibidia, to obtain the ear of the emperor as Chief Priest and urge pardon. Meanwhile, with only three companions-so rapidly was she deserted—she walked from end to end of the city. Then she started along the Ostia road—in a cart used for removing garden refuse. People did not pity her, for they were horrified by her appalling crimes.

On Claudius' side there was just as much agitation. Lusius Geta, the Guard commander, followed his own caprices, regardless of right and wrong. No one trusted him. So Narcissus, supported by others as afraid as he was, asserted that there was only one hope of saving the emperor's life: the transference of the Guard, for that one day, to the command of a freed slave-himself; for he offered himself as commander. Then, afraid that Claudius, during the return journey to Rome, might have his mind changed by his companions Lucius Vitellius and Gaius Caecina Largus, Narcissus asked for a place in the same carriage, and sat with them.

Claudius, it was widely said afterwards, contradicted himself incessantly, veering from invective against Messalina's misconduct to reminiscences of their marriage and their children's infancy. Lucius Vitellius would only moan 'How wicked, how sinful!' When Narcissus pressed that he should reveal his mind honestly and unambiguously, Vitellius, undeterred, still responded with cryptic exclamations which could be taken in two ways. Caecina Largus did the same.

她还派人给不列塔尼库斯和屋大维娅带口信,让他们立刻去寻找并且投到他们的父亲的怀抱里去。接着,她又亲自去恳求年长的维司塔贞女维比狄娅,请维比狄娅作为最高祭司为她向皇帝说情,请求他的宽恕。而这时陪同她的同伴一共只有三个人——她如此迅速地就遭到了人们的遗弃!她徒步从城市的这一端走到另一端,然后乘上一辆用来清理花园垃圾的马车,沿着欧斯提亚大道出发了。没有一个人同情她,因为人们都感到,她所犯的这种骇人听闻的罪行实在是太可怕了!

在克劳狄乌斯这一方面,也同样惊恐不安。他的近卫军长官路奇乌斯·盖塔,是一个反复无常、见风使舵,根本不考虑什么是对、什么是错的人,因此没有人会信任他。于是纳尔奇苏斯就在同他一样感到惊恐的那些人的支持下,正式向皇帝进言说,只有一个办法才能挽救皇帝的生命,这就是,在那一天,把近卫军的统率权交给他的一名被释奴隶,也就是他自己。他主动提出由他自己担任近卫军长官。接下来,由于担心克劳狄乌斯在返回罗马的途中,会由于陪伴他的路奇乌斯·维提里乌斯和盖乌斯·凯奇纳·拉尔古斯的劝说而改变主意,纳尔奇苏斯就要求和皇帝同乘一辆马车,跟他们坐在一起。

后来,人们普遍传说,当时克劳狄乌斯本人也是十分矛盾的。他一会儿大骂美撒里娜的淫乱行为,一会儿却又怀念起他们过去的婚姻生活,怜惜起他们孩子们的年幼。路奇乌斯·维提里乌斯一路上只是在不断地叫道:"多么无耻邪恶啊,多么深重的罪行啊!"纳尔奇苏斯让他忠诚地把他心里的真话说出来,而维提里乌斯不为所动,仍然是那种模棱两可、含糊其辞的话。凯奇纳·拉尔古斯也一样。

Now Messalina came into view. She cried and cried that Claudius must listen to the mother of Octavia and Britannicus. Narcissus shouted her down with the story of Silius and the wedding, simultaneously distracting the emperor's gaze with a document listing her immoralities. Soon afterwards, at a point near the city, the two children were brought forward. Narcissus ordered their removal. But he could not remove Vibidia, who demanded most indignantly that a wife should not be executed unheard. Narcissus replied that the emperor would hear Messalina—she would have a chance to clear herself—and that meanwhile Vibidia had better go and attend to her own religious duties.

Claudius remained strangely silent. Lucius Vitellius looked as if he did not know what was happening. The former slave, Narcissus, took charge. He ordered the adulterer's home to be opened and the emperor to be taken there. First, in the forecourt, Narcissus pointed out a statue of Silius' condemned father, placed there in defiance of senatorial decree. Then he pointed to the heirlooms of Neros and Drususes that had come to the house among the wages of sin. This angered the emperor; he became threatening. Narcissus conducted him to the camp and delivered a preliminary statement. Then Claudius addressed the assembled Guard—but only briefly, because, just though his indignation was, he could hardly express it for shame.

The Guardsmen shouted repeatedly for the offenders to be named and punished. Silius was brought on to the platform. Without at-

现在,美撒里娜出现在了他们面前。她一直在向克劳狄乌斯哭喊着,要求他听一听屋大维娅和不列塔尼库斯的母亲的话。纳尔奇苏斯便提高嗓门儿大声讲述西里乌斯和这次婚礼的事情,以盖过美撒里娜的呼喊声。同时为了引开皇帝的视线,他把列举了她的各种放荡罪行的文件交给他看。不久之后,在就要进入罗马的一个地方,早就被带到了前面的两个孩子在等着见他们的父亲。纳尔奇苏斯下令把他们领走。但是他却不能使维比狄娅走开,她极为愤怒地要求道,一个妻子不能在不经审问的情况下就被处死。纳尔奇苏斯回答她说,皇帝正准备审问美撒里娜,她会有为自己辩解的机会的,同时他又奉劝贞女维比狄娅最好还是回去照管好自己的宗教事务。

克劳狄乌斯始终奇怪地保持着沉默,路奇乌斯·维提里乌斯看起来则好像对所发生的事情一点儿都不知道的样子,一切事情都任凭被释奴隶纳尔奇苏斯去处理。他下令把奸夫的住宅打开,并且把皇帝请到那里去。在那里,他首先把一座西里乌斯父亲的半身像指给皇帝看,它正放在入口的地方,这里原是元老院明令禁止放置的。随后他又指出那些尼禄家族和杜路苏斯家族的传家宝,它们都是在两人进行罪孽的活动时作为报酬而送到西里乌斯家里来的。这使皇帝勃然大怒,他说了许多威胁的话。纳尔奇苏斯于是便把他领到了军营,在他讲了几句开场白之后,克劳狄乌斯便向集结的近卫军发表了讲话,但他只说了几句,因为尽管他的气愤是理所应当的,但是羞愧之心却使他几乎说不出话来。

近卫军士兵反复地呼叫着,要求他把罪犯的名字讲出来,并对他们加以惩罚。西里乌斯被带到了台上,他既不想为自己进行

tempting defence or postponement, he asked for a quick death. Certain distinguished knights showed equal courage. They too desired a speedy end. The execution of accomplices was ordered: Titius Proculus - appointed Messalina's 'guardian' by Silius-Vettius Valens, who confessed, and two further members of the order of knights, Pompeius Urbicus and Saufeius Trogus. The same penalty was visited on the commander of the watch, Decrius Calpurnianus, the superintendent of a gladiator's school, Sulpicius Rufus, and a junior senator, Juncus Vergilianus.

Only Mnester (I) caused hesitation. Tearing his clothes, he entreated Claudius to look at his whip-marks and remember the words with which the emperor had placed him under Messalina's orders. Others, he urged, had sinned for money or ambition, he from compulsion—and if Silius had become emperor he, Mnester, would have been the first to die. Claudius had an indulgent nature and this moved him. But the ex-slaves prevailed upon the emperor not, after executing so many distinguished men, to spare a ballet-dancer——when crimes were so grave it was irrelevant whether they were voluntary or enforced.

Rejection, too, awaited the defence of an unpretentious but goodlooking young knight, Sextus Traulus Montanus, whom within a single night Messalina, as capricious in her dislikes as in her desires, had sent for and sent away. Plautius Lateranus escaped the death sentence owing to an uncle's distinguished record. So did Suillius Caesoninus, because of his own vices—at that repulsive gathering his had been merely a female part.

辩护,也不想拖延,只是要求速死。一些比较显要的罗马骑士也表现出了同样的勇气,他们也要求立刻将自己处死。于是皇帝下令将同谋者处死,他们是:提提乌斯·普洛库路斯,这个人曾被西里乌斯指定为美撒里娜的"监护人";维提乌斯·瓦伦斯,他对所有的罪行供认不讳;还有同谋的两个骑士彭佩乌斯·乌尔比库斯和撒乌费乌斯·特洛古斯。城市守卫队长官戴克里乌斯·卡尔普尔尼亚努斯、剑奴训练所高级监督苏尔皮奇乌斯·路福斯,还有一个年轻的元老雍库斯·维尔吉里亚努斯也受到了同样的惩罚。

只有对莫涅斯特(一世)的处理引起了皇帝的犹豫。因为他撕开了自己的衣服,请求克劳狄乌斯看他身上的鞭痕,并且让克劳狄乌斯回想一下他命令他一切要听美撒里娜的使唤的那些话。他说,别人犯罪是为了金钱或是为了满足自己的野心,但他却是被逼无奈,而且,如果西里乌斯篡取了皇帝之位,那么毫无疑问,他,莫涅斯特,将会是第一个丧命的人。克劳狄乌斯天性就是宽容的,这些话打动了他,但是他身边的被释奴隶劝说皇帝道,在处死了这样多显要人物之后,不能赦免这样一个优伶,因为当罪行如此严重的时候,是出于自愿的还是被迫参与,就都无关紧要了。

塞克斯图斯·特劳路斯·蒙塔努斯的辩护也被驳回。这是一个谦逊而且又非常漂亮的年轻骑士,他曾在一天夜里突然被美撒里娜召去,又在同一夜里被她打发走,因为美撒里娜是一个喜怒无常的人。但是普劳提乌斯·拉提拉努斯却由于他的叔父的杰出功绩免于一死;苏伊里乌斯·凯索尼努斯也被赦免,而他被赦免的原因却是因为他本身的无耻行为,因为在这一群无耻之徒中,他只是扮演着一个女人的角色。

Meanwhile at the Gardens of Lucullus Messalina was fighting for her life. She composed an appeal. Its terms were hopeful and even at times indignant, so shameless was her insolence to the very end. Indeed, if Narcissus had not speedily caused her death, the fatal blow would have rebounded on her accuser. For Claudius, home again, soothed and a little fuddled after an early dinner, ordered 'the poor woman' (that is said to have been his phrase) to appear on the next day to defend herself. This was noted. His anger was clearly cooling, his love returning. Further delay risked that the approaching night would revive memories of conjugal pleasures.

So Narcissus hurried away. Ostensibly on the emperor's instructions, he ordered a Guard colonel, who was standing by, and some staff officers to kill Messalina. A former slave, name Euodus, was sent to prevent her escape and see that the order was carried out. Hastening to the Gardens ahead of the officers, he found her prostrate on the ground, with her mother Domitia Lepida sitting beside her. While her daughter was in power they had quarrelled. But in her extremity, Lepida was overcome by pity. She urged Messalina to await the executioner. 'Your life is finished,' she said. 'All that remains is to make a decent end.' But in that lust-ridden heart decency did not exist. Messalina was still uselessly weeping and moaning when the men violently broke down the door. The officer stood there, silently. The ex-slave, with a slave's foulness of tongue, insulted her. Then, for the first time, it dawned on Messalina what her position really was. Terrified, she took a dagger and put it to her throat and then

　　这时,在路库鲁斯花园中,美撒里娜正在为保全自己的性命进行着最后的挣扎。她写了一份请愿书,言词间还充满着希望,有时甚至还表现出激愤情绪,这个女人是如此无耻,在生命的最后时刻竟然还是这样霸道。说实话,如果纳尔奇苏斯不赶快将她处死,致命的打击将会很快落到她的控诉者的身上。原来克劳狄乌斯回到宫里,提早吃了晚饭之后,他的心情已经平息了下来,他又带着一点醉意,便接着下令要人去通知那个"可怜的女人"(据说这是他当时的原话),让她在第二天亲自到他这里来为自己辩护。人们注意到,他的怒气显然已经开始消失,他对她的爱情又回来了。因此,如果继续拖延下去,即将到来的黑夜就会使皇帝重新回忆起他们的闺房乐事。

　　于是纳尔奇苏斯就赶快跑了出去,他伪称是皇帝的命令,命令正站在一旁的一名近卫军将领和几名百人团长立刻去杀死美撒里娜。一名被释奴隶埃沃都斯被派去防止她的逃跑,并去探看一下他们是否执行了命令。他比所有其他人都要早地急忙跑到花园时,发现美撒里娜正伏在地上,她的母亲多米提娅·列庇妲则坐在她的身旁。列庇妲在她的女儿得势时,两人经常争吵,但是在她遇到危难时,列庇妲对她的怜悯心又战胜了过去的一切不合。她劝美撒里娜静等刽子手的到来,她说:"你的生命是结束了,你现在所能做的只能是尽量死得体面些。"但是在那个淫荡堕落的女人的心里,已经没有什么荣誉和体面存在了。当人们粗暴地破门而入的时候,美撒里娜却还在毫无用处地哭泣和呻吟。近卫军的将领站在她的面前,默不作声,而被释奴隶则以奴隶骂大街那样的语气狠狠地辱骂着她。于是,美撒里娜才第一次明白了自己实际上处于什么样的地位。她惊恐万状,抓起一把匕首刺

her breast-but could not do it. And so the officer ran her through. The body was left with her mother. Claudius was still at table when news came that Messalina had died; whether by her own hand or another's was unspecified. Claudius did not inquire. He called for more wine, and went on with his party as usual.

On the days that followed, the emperor gave no sign of hatred, satisfaction, anger, distress, or any other human feeling-even when he saw the accusers exulting, and his children mourning. His forgetfulness was helped by the senate, which decreed that Messalina's name and statues should be removed from all public and private sites. It also awarded Narcissus an honorary quaestorship. But this was the least reason for conceit to a man who exceeded even Pallas or Callistus in power.

The vengeance on Messalina was just. But its consequences were grim.

向自己的咽喉,又刺向自己的胸脯,但是都没有刺中,最后,那个近卫军将领一刀把她刺死了,把她的尸体留给了她的母亲。当美撒里娜已死的消息传来时,克劳狄乌斯还在吃饭,她是自杀的还是由别人把她杀死的,没有做出说明。克劳狄乌斯也没有追问,他又要了一些酒,像往常一样继续进行他的宴会。

在这之后的一些日子里,人们在皇帝身上看不出憎恨,也看不出满意,看不出愤怒,也看不出悲哀以及人的所有其他感情的迹象。甚至当他看到控诉者欢欣鼓舞,而他的孩子却在那里悲泣的时候,也是一样面无表情。元老院设法帮助他忘掉这件事,发布命令让人们把美撒里娜的名字和胸像从一切公众的和私人的地点除掉。元老院还把财务官的标记授予了纳尔奇苏斯。但是对于权力已经超过了帕拉斯和卡利司图斯的人物来说,这样的荣誉一点也没有什么可骄傲的。

对美撒里娜的报复是公正的,但它所产生的后果却是冷酷无情的。

CHAPTER 10

The Mother Of Nero

Messalina's death convulsed the imperial household. Claudius was impatient of celibacy and easily controlled by his wives, and the ex-slaves quarrelled about who should choose his next one. Rivalry among the women was equally fierce. Each cited her own high birth, beauty, and wealth as qualifications for this exalted marriage. 'The chief competitors were Lollia Paulina, daughter of the former consul Marcus Lollius (II), and Germanicus' daughter Agrippina (II). Their backers were Callistus and Pallas respectively. Narcissus supported Aelia Paetina, who was of the family of the Aelii Tuberones. The emperor continually changed his mind according to whatever advice he had heard last.

Finally, he summoned the disputants to a meeting and requested them to give reasoned opinions. At the meeting, Narcissus reminded Claudius that he had been married to Aelia Paetina before; that the union had been productive (a daughter, Claudia Antonia, had been born to them); that remarriage would necessitate no domestic innovations; and that, far from entertaining a stepmother's dislike for Britannicus and Octavia, Paectina would cherish them next to her own children. Callistus objected that Claudius had divorced Pactina long

第十章　尼禄的母亲

美撒里娜的死震动了皇室。克劳狄乌斯对独身生活失去了耐心,他是很容易被他的妻子控制的,因此,在为他选择另一个妻子的问题上,他的被释奴隶们发生了争执。女人们的竞争也同样激烈,人人都在极力夸耀自己出身的高贵、容貌的美丽和家境的富有,以证明自己配得上这一高贵的婚姻。主要的竞争者是洛里娅·宝琳娜,她是担任过执政官的玛尔库斯·洛里乌斯(二世)的女儿,还有日耳曼尼库斯的女儿阿格里披娜(二世)。她们的支持者分别是卡利司图斯和帕拉斯。纳尔奇斯乌斯则支持埃里娅·帕提伊娜,她是埃里伊·图倍罗家族的成员。皇帝对每个人的建议都觉得有理,不断地因后来者的举荐改变着自己的主意。

最后,他把争论的各方都召集到一起举行了一次会议,要求他们各自发表自己的意见并说出充分的理由。在会上,纳尔奇苏斯提醒克劳狄乌斯以下几点:他以前就和埃里娅·帕提伊娜结过婚;而他们的这种结合也已经有了结果(他们俩共同生了一个女儿克劳狄娅·安托尼娅);这次重新结合将不会给他的家庭生活带来什么变化;而且她对不列塔尼库斯和屋大维娅也绝对不会有继母的那种厌恶之情,帕提伊娜会仅次于对待自己的孩子一样的爱护这两个孩子的。卡利司图斯反对说,克劳狄乌斯和埃

ago and that this disqualified her—remarriage would make her arrogant, and Lollia was far more eligible since, being childless, she
would be a mother to her stepchildren without jealousy. Pallas, proposing Agrippina, emphasized that the son whom she would bring with
her was Germanicus' grandson, eminently deserving of imperial rank;
let the emperor ally himself with a noble race and unite two branches
of the Claudian house, rather than allow this lady of proved capacity
for child-bearing, still young, to transfer the glorious name of the
Caesars to another family.

These arguments prevailed. Agrippina's seductiveness was a
help. Visiting her uncle frequently—ostensibly as a close relation—
she tempted him into giving her the preference and into treating her,
in anticipation, as his wife. Once sure of her marriage, she enlarged
the scope of her plans and devoted herself to scheming for her son Lucius Domitius Ahenobarbus, whose father was Cnaeus Domitius Ahenobarbus. It was her ambition that this boy, the future Nero, should
be wedded to the emperor's daughter Octavia. Here criminal methods
were necessary, since Claudius had already betrothed Octavia to Lucius Junius Silanus Torquatus (I)—and had won popularity for his distinguished record by awarding him an honorary Triumph, and giving a
lavish gladiatorial display in his name. But with an emperor whose
likes and dislikes were all suggested and dictated to him, anything
seemed possible.

Lucius Vitellius had an eye for future despots. Using his post as
censor to cloak his servile fabrications, he sought Agrippina's favour

里娅·帕提伊娜很久以前就离婚了,她已经没有这种资格了,因为重婚将会使她变得骄傲自大。而洛里娅就合格得多了,因为她自己没有孩子,因此她会成为她的继子的母亲,而毫无嫉妒心。帕拉斯提议阿格里披娜,他着重强调道,她所带来的儿子是日耳曼尼库斯的外孙,他是最有资格继承皇位的;让皇帝与这一名门望族联姻,将克劳狄乌斯家族的两个分支结合到一起,这比眼睁睁看着这位确实还能生儿育女的、年轻的妇人将恺撒的光荣名字再传给另一个家族要好得多。

帕拉斯的论辩占据了优势,阿格里披娜本人的魅力也大有帮助。她以亲近的关系为借口,经常去拜见她的叔叔,并诱惑他使他对自己特别偏爱,她这样有成效地迷住了她的叔父,以至于皇帝早就期待着把她当做自己的妻子了。当她确信她的婚事有了把握的时候,就立刻开始扩大自己的计划,她全部精力都投入到为她自己的儿子路奇乌斯·多米提乌斯·埃诺巴尔布斯的谋划中——他的父亲是格涅乌斯·多米提乌斯·埃诺巴尔布斯。她野心勃勃地想,这个孩子,也就是以后的尼禄,应该和皇帝的女儿屋大维娅结婚。因此她就不惜使用一些罪恶的手段,因为克劳狄乌斯已经把屋大维娅许给了路奇乌斯·尤尼乌斯·西拉努斯·托尔库瓦图斯(一世),而且还曾把凯旋的勋记授予了他,并且还曾经以他的名义举行过一次隆重的剑斗表演比赛,这些光荣的记录使他获得了很高的声望。但是,在这样一个好恶总容易受人影响,特别容易为别人摆布的皇帝面前,没有什么事情是不可能的。

路奇乌斯·维提里乌斯密切关注着未来的专制君主。他利用自己监察官的名义为自己卑鄙无耻的勾当打掩护,拼命地向

by involving himself in her projects and prosecuting Lucius Junius Silanus Torquatus. Silanus'attractive but shameless sister, Junia Calvina, had until lately been married to Vitellius' son: using this as a handle, Vitellius put an unsavoury construction on the unguarded (but not incestuous) affection between Silanus and his sister. Claudius, particularly ready to suspect the future husband of the daughter he loved, gave attention to the charge. Silanus, unaware of the plot, happened to be praetor for the year. Suddenly, though the roll of senators and the ceremonies terminating the census were long complete, an edict of Vitellius struck him off the senate. Simultaneously, Claudius cancelled Octavia's engagement with Silanus, and he was forced to resign his office and was superseded for the one remaining day, in favour of Titus Clodius Eprius Marcellus.

Next year the consuls were Gaius Pompeius Longinus Gallus and Quintus Veranius (II). Rumour now strongly predicted Claudius' marriage to Agrippina; so did their illicit intercourse. But they did not yet dare to celebrate the wedding. For marriage with a niece was unprecedented—indeed it was incestuous, and disregard of this might, it was feared, cause national disaster. Hesitation was only overcome when Lucius Vitellius undertook to arrange matters by methods of his own. He asked Claudius if he would yield to a decree of the Assembly and the senate's recommendation. The emperor replied that he was a citizen himself and would bow to unanimity. Then Vitellius, requesting him to wait in the palace, entered the senate and stating

阿格里披娜讨好。他设法使自己参与到阿格里披娜的计划中去，并向路奇乌斯·尤尼乌斯·西拉努斯·托尔库瓦图斯提起控诉。西拉努斯的美貌但是不知羞耻的妹妹优尼娅·卡尔维纳不久之前刚刚嫁给了维提里乌斯的儿子。拿这件事作为把柄，维提里乌斯就无耻地捏造诬陷之词说，西拉努斯和他的妹妹之间有不正当的感情（但不是乱伦）。克劳狄乌斯对自己深爱的女儿未来的丈夫特别容易产生怀疑，因此密切关注着这次控告。对这一阴谋一无所知的西拉努斯，恰好是这一年的行政长官。尽管元老院的名单已经定好，为长时间进行的人口调查的完成而举行的庆典也已经结束了，但是维提里乌斯的一纸命令却突然地将西拉努斯开除出了元老院。同时，克劳狄乌斯取消了奥克塔维娅与西拉努斯的婚约，西拉努斯被迫辞去了自己的高级官职，把剩下的任期交给了提图斯·克劳狄乌斯·埃普里乌斯·玛尔凯路斯。

下一年，[1]是盖乌斯·彭佩乌斯·朗吉努斯·噶尔路斯和克温图斯·维拉尼乌斯（二世）担任执政官的一年。外面的传闻都煞有介事地说克劳狄乌斯要和阿格里披娜结婚了，而他们两人私通的事实也确实证明了这一点。但是他们却没有胆量正式举行婚礼，因为叔父同侄女结婚的事情是史无前例的，事实上这是一种乱伦的关系。如果不考虑这一点的话，恐怕就会引起全国性的灾难。直到路奇乌斯·维提里乌斯自己想办法来安排这件事时，才不再徘徊观望了。维提里乌斯问克劳狄乌斯是不是愿意服从人民大会的命令，是不是愿意服从元老院的决定。克劳狄乌斯回答说，他自己也是一个罗马公民，他当然愿意服从人民的决定。于是，维提里乌斯要求他

---

〔1〕 公元49年，罗马建城802年。

that it was a matter of the highest national importance, asked permission to speak first.

'In his exceedingly arduous duties,' Vitellius said, 'which cover the whole world, the emperor needs support, to enable him to provide for the public good without domestic worries. Could there be a more respectable comfort to our Censor—a stranger to dissipation or self-indulgence, law-abiding since earliest youth-than a wife, a partner in good and bad fortune alike, to whom he can confide his inmost thoughts, and his little children?'

These winning preliminaries were warmly applauded by the senate. Then Vitellius proceeded. 'We agree unanimously, then, that the emperor should marry. The chosen lady must be aristocratic, capable of child-bearing, and virtuous. Agrippina's exceptionally illustrious birth is indisputable. She has demonstrated her fertility. Her morals are equally outstanding. For the emperor—who knows no man's wives but his own—her widowhood is welcome and providential. You have heard from your parents, indeed you have yourselves known, of the abduction of men's wives at an emperor's whim. The respectable arrangement which I propose is strikingly different. We can create a precedent: the nation presents the emperor with a wife! Marriage to a niece, it may be objected, is unfamiliar to us. Yet in other countries it is regular and lawful. Here also, unions between cousins, long unknown, have become frequent in course of time. Customs change as circumstances change-this innovation too will take root.'

在宫中等着,他自己则到元老院去,宣布说有一件头等重要的国家大事,要求元老院允许他第一个发言。

维提里乌斯说道:"皇帝治理天下,在遇到极其艰巨的工作时,也需要有人来帮助,这样才可以使他不用为家务事操心,而专心致力于国家事务。对于我们的监察官,也就是这位从小就对放荡或享乐的生活非常陌生,而严守法律的皇帝来说,还有比娶一个能和他荣辱与共,能够向她倾诉内心最深处的想法,并可以对之托付他幼小的孩子的妻子更好的安慰吗?"

这样娓娓动听的开场白,赢得了元老院热烈的趋奉。维提里乌斯又继续说道:"既然我们大家都一致赞同,那么皇帝就应该结婚。而入选的女子应该出身贵族,能够养育儿女,而且品德高尚。阿格里披娜突出的高贵出身自然是毫无争议的,事实也已经证明了她很好的生育能力,她美好的品德也是同样优秀杰出。对于除去自己的妻子以外没有接触过任何女人的皇帝来说,阿格里披娜的寡妇生活正是上天给他准备的良缘。你们从你们的父亲那里听到过,而且实际上你们自己也亲眼看到过,过去的皇帝是怎样凭着自己一时的高兴来诱娶别人的妻子的。这种粗暴的做法与我现在这种值得尊敬的建议相比简直是天壤之别。我们能够创造一个前例,这就是:我们罗马人民献给皇帝一个妻子!也许会有人反对,因为叔父和侄女通婚,在我们这里还是从来没有过的事情,可是在别的国家里,这样的做法是正常的,是法律所许可的。表兄妹结婚的事情虽然在过去很久都没有听说过,但现在已经是司空见惯了。时代环境变了,人们的风俗习惯也会随之发生变化,今天没有前例的革新正是将来引以为据的惯例。"

At this, some senators ran out of the house enthusiastically clamouring that if Claudius hesitated they would use constraint. A throng of passers-by cried that the Roman public were similarly minded. Claudius delayed no longer. After receiving the crowd's congratulations in the Forum, he entered the senate to request a decree legalizing future marriages with a brother's daughter. However, only one other seeker after this sort of union is identifiable—a knight named Alledius Severus, whose motive was believed to be the hope of Agrippina's favour.

From this moment the country was transformed. Complete obedience was accorded to a woman—and not a woman like Messalina who toyed with national affairs to satisfy her appetites. This was a rigorous, almost masculine despotism. In public. Agrippina was austere and often arrogant. Her private life was chaste—unless power was to be gained. Her passion to acquire money was unbounded. She wanted it as a stepping-stone to supremacy.

On the wedding-day Lucius Junius Silanus Torquatus committed suicide. For that day finally terminated his hopes of life—or perhaps he chose it to increase ill-feeling. His sister Junia Calvina was banished from Italy. Claudius ordained ritual prescribed by King Tullus Hostilius, including expiatory ceremonies by priests at the Grove of Diana. The emperor's resuscitation, at this juncture, of punishments and expiations for Silanus' incest provoked universal ridicule. Agrippina, however, was anxious not to be credited with bad actions only. So she now secured the recall of Lucius Annaeus Seneca from exile and his appointment to a praetorship. She judged that owing to his

　　这时,一些元老跑出元老院去闹哄哄地热烈表示,如果克劳狄乌斯还在犹豫不决的话,他们便要使用强迫的手段了。一大群各色各样的过路人也都集合到一处,声称罗马公众有着同样的心愿。于是克劳狄乌斯不再延迟,他到广场上来接受人们的祝贺,然后便走进了元老院,要求公布一项命令,使人们在今后和兄弟的女儿的结合行为成为合法。不过,也只有另一个人是热心模仿这种婚姻方式的,这就是罗马骑士阿列狄乌斯·谢维洛斯,人们认为他这样做的动机只不过是想讨好阿格里披娜而已。

　　从这个时候开始,国家的情况就改变了。全部国家大事都听从于一个女人的安排,不过这个女人与美撒里娜不同,美撒里娜为了满足自己的嗜欲而将罗马帝国玩弄于股掌之中。这是一种严酷的、几乎是男子统治的暴政。在公开场合,阿格里披娜不仅是严厉的,而且常常是非常傲慢的。她的私生活是贞节的,除非是为得到权力。她获取金钱的热情简直没有极限,因为她认为这是取得专制权力的坚强基石。

　　皇帝举行婚礼那天,路奇乌斯·尤尼乌斯·西拉努斯·托尔库瓦图斯自杀了。因为这一天断绝了他活命的希望,也许他选择这一天来结束自己的性命,是为了让自己的死亡更增加他们的反感。他的姊妹优尼娅·卡尔维娜被逐出了意大利。此外,克劳狄乌斯还下令按照国王图路苏斯·赫斯提里乌斯的规定颁布的仪式举行献牲式,并且由祭司们在狄安娜圣林中举行赎罪的仪式。皇帝偏偏在这样一个时刻,惩罚和去除西拉努斯近亲通奸的罪恶,这种做法引起了人们普遍的嘲笑。但是,阿格里披娜却在担心人们会以为她只会干坏事,因此她就把路奇乌斯·安奈乌斯·塞内加从流放地召回来并且赐给他行政长官的职位。她认为塞内加

literary eminence this would be popular. She also had designs on him as a distinguished tutor for her young son Lucius Domitius Ahenobarbus (the future Nero). Seneca's advice could serve their plans for supremacy; and he was believed to be devoted to her—in gratitude for her favours—but hostile to Claudius whose unfairness he resented.

It was now decided to act without further delay. A consul-designate, Lucius Mammius Pollio, was induced by lavish promises to propose a petition to Claudius, begging him to betroth Octavia to Domitius—an arrangement compatible with their ages and likely to lead to higher things. The arguments used closely resembled those recently employed by Lucius Vitellius. The engagement took place. In addition to their previous relationship, Domitius was now Claudius' future son-in-law. By his mother's efforts—and the intrigues of Messalina's accusers, who feared vengeance from her son-he was becoming the rival of Britannicus.

I have mentioned that a Parthian delegation had been sent to Rome to ask for Meherdates—a hostage in our hands—as their king. It now appeared before the senate. The delegates described their mission in these terms:

'We know of the treaty between our two countries. Nor do we come as rebels against the Parthian royal house. We are calling upon the son of Vonones I, the grandson of Phraates IV, to destroy the tyranny of Gotarzes II, which nobles and populace alike find unendur

突出的学识会使她的这一行动博得人们的好评,同时她也打算让他给她即将长大成人的儿子路奇乌斯·多米提乌斯·埃诺巴尔布斯(未来的尼禄)作导师。另外,塞内加的意见还会对帮助他们策划夺取皇位发挥重要的作用,因为人们相信塞内加是忠于阿格里披娜的,他感激她的恩情,但他对于克劳狄乌斯给予他的那些不公正的待遇是心怀怨恨的。

现在,格里披娜决定不再耽搁而立即采取行动。当选的执政官路奇乌斯·玛米乌斯·波里欧在极为丰富的许诺的引诱下,向克劳狄乌斯提出申请,请求他把屋大维娅许配给多米提乌斯,因为这种安排对他们两人的年纪来说是合适的,而且这还很可能会带来更加重大的意义。波里欧这一建议的理由,和不久之前路奇乌斯·维提里乌斯所提出的理由是如此相像。不久就举行了订婚仪式。这样一来,在和皇帝本来就有亲属关系的基础上,多米提乌斯现在又成了克劳狄乌斯未来的女婿。一方面由于他母亲的努力,另一方面,也是因为美撒里娜的那些控告者们,害怕美撒里娜的儿子将来会对他们报复而进行密谋,多米提乌斯于是便和不列塔尼库斯并驾齐驱,成为他强有力的竞争对手了。

我已经说过,这时有一些帕尔提亚的使节被派到罗马来,要求我们把在我们手里的人质美赫尔达特斯放回去做他们的国王。他们现在来到了元老院,使节们用以下的言词陈述他们此行的任务:

"我们知道我们两国之间缔结的条约,我们到这里来也不是因为背叛了帕尔提亚王族,我们是前来召请沃诺尼斯一世的儿子、普拉提斯四世的孙子去摧毁哥塔尔吉斯二世的暴政的,因为无论是贵族还是平民都已经不能再忍受了。他已经残害了他的

able. He has exterminated his brothers and other near relations—not to speak of more distant kinsmen. Now he is turning even upon pregnant women and small children. A slovenly administrator and unsuccessful commander, he plunges into brutality to disguise his inertia. '

'You and we have an old, officially inaugurated friendship. We, your allies, rival you in power but take second place out of respect. Now we need your help. That is why Parthian kings' sons are given you as hostages: so that, if our rulers at home become distasteful, we can apply to emperor and senate and receive a monarch trained in your culture. '

In response to these and similar assertions Claudius spoke about Roman supremacy and Parthian homage. He compared himself to the divine Augustus, recalling that Augustus too had been asked for a Parthian king. (About Tiberius, who had likewise sent one, he said nothing.) Meherdates was present: Claudius advised him to think of himself not as an autocrat among slaves, but as a guide of free men, and to be merciful and just—virtues all the more welcome to natives because of their unfamiliarity. Then, turning to the deputation, he commanded Rome's foster-son as having hitherto shown exemplary character. But, he added, kings have to be endured however they are, since continual changes are undesinable; and Rome, having taken her fill of glory, wanted other countries also to be peaceful. He then instructed Gaius Cassius Longinus, imperial governor of Syria, to conduct the prince to the bank of the Euphrates.

兄弟和其他一些近亲，更不用说那些远亲，现在他甚至连那些怀孕的女人和年幼的孩子也不放过。一个懒散、无所作为的统治者，一个失败的指挥官，但是他却想用残酷来掩饰自己的懒惰和怯懦。"

"我们和你们之间有着由来已久的由两国正式缔结的友谊。我们，作为你们的联盟，在实力上也堪与你们匹敌，但是出于对你们的尊敬，我们屈居你们之下。现在我们需要你们的帮助了，这就是帕尔提亚的国王们把他们的儿子交给你们做人质的原因：如果我们国内的统治者给我们的国人带来的是灾难的话，我们可以到罗马皇帝和元老院这里来请求，接回一位在你们的文化教养之下成长起来的国王。"

为了答复这些以及诸如此类的说法，克劳狄乌斯就罗马的至高无上的地位和帕尔提亚所表示的服从和敬意做了讲话。他把他自己和圣奥古斯都相提并论，回顾道，以前帕尔提亚人也曾向奥古斯都要求过一位国王（提贝里乌斯也曾把国王派到那里去，他却没有提起）。美赫尔达特斯当时也在场，于是克劳狄乌斯便劝告他说，不要把自己当做奴隶们的残酷的统治者，而要成为自由的人民的领路人，并且要仁慈、公正——这些美德是那些民族更欢迎的，因为他们对此很缺乏。随后，他又向使节们称赞这个罗马培养出来的儿子，说他到当时为止在各方面都表现出可以为人效仿的优秀品格。但是他又说，无论国王们的品性如何，人们都应该忍受，因为不断地改换国王并没有什么好处。已经充分享有了极大光荣的罗马，希望其他国家也同样安定和平。然后，他就派遣叙利亚的长官盖乌斯·卡西乌斯·朗吉努斯护送这个青年人到幼发拉底河的河岸。

At this period Cassius was pre-eminent as a jurist-military quali-ties are unrecognized in peace-time, in which good and bad soldiers are indistinguishable. Yet Cassius, as far as he could without a war, revived ancient discipline, organized manoeuvres, and took as much trouble and forethought as if an enemy were upon him. He felt he owed this to his ancestors, the Cassian family, of which the fame ex-tended to that area. Summoning the men who had instigated the mis-sion, Cassius encamped at Zeugma, the site of the most convenient river-crossing. The Parthian dignitaries joined him; so did Acbarus (Abgar V), the Arab king of Edessa. Cassius warned Meherdates to press on, since delay cools oriental enthusiasm and produces treacher-y. But the advice was disregarded by the ingenuous young man, who thought kingship meant self-indulgence, and allowed himself to be de-tained for many days at Edessa by its deceitful ruler. Carenes, gover-nor of Mesopotamia, invited him in, stressing that everything would be easy if he came quickly. Yet instead of taking the short route to Mesopotamia, Meherdates made a detour to Armenia, which in that season, at the outset of winter, is forbidding.

Finally, exhausted by snow-bound mountainous territory, he and his men joined up with Carenes' force near the plains. Crossing the Tigris, they went on through Adiabene; its king, Izates, had ostensi-bly allied himself with Meherdates but was privately a loyal supporter of

在这个时候,作为法学家卡西乌斯是最著名的:在天下太平时期,军事才能是不为人所注意的,一个好的士兵和坏的士兵没有什么区别。但是,尽管没有什么战争,卡西乌斯也仍然尽其所能地恢复旧时的纪律。他严格操练他的军团,就像敌人在眼前似的深谋远虑,未雨绸缪。他认为只有这样,才无愧于他的祖先,无愧于声名甚至远达那些地区的卡西乌斯家族。[1] 于是他将那些建议到罗马来请派一个国王的人们召请来,并且在一个最方便的渡口丘格玛那里设下了他的营地。在帕尔提亚的权贵们和依德撒的阿拉伯国王阿克巴路斯(伽阿布尔五世)都来到他这里之后,卡西乌斯便提醒美赫尔达特斯,要他立刻行动,因为尽管现在东方部族的热情很高,但是如果耽搁下来,他们的热情便会冷却,甚至会引起背叛。但是这样的忠告却被这个单纯的年轻人置之脑后,因为这个未经世故的年轻人认为,作为一个国王就可以自由地沉迷于放荡的生活,并且可以在这样一个由欺诈的统治者统治的依德撒城停留许多日子。甚至当美索不达米亚的长官卡列尼斯前来邀请,并着重指出,如果他们能尽快地赶到,则一切事情就都会很顺利的时候,美赫尔达特斯都没有走近路去美索不达米亚,而是绕道去了亚美尼亚,而在那个季节,由于严冬已经降临,那里是无法通行的。

最后,他们这些因为在大雪覆盖的高山地区行走,而累得筋疲力尽的人们,在平原附近和卡列尼斯的军队会合到了一起。他们渡过了底格里斯河之后,便继续穿过阿狄亚贝尼人的地区。阿

---

〔1〕 这是因为,他的祖先盖乌斯·卡西乌斯曾经是弥库斯·里奇尼乌斯·克拉苏斯手下的一名属官。盖乌斯就是后来刺杀恺撒的人,他在克拉苏斯死后,在公元前53年在卡尔莱战役之后曾经成功地击退帕尔提亚人对叙利亚的进攻。

Gotarzes. During the journey, Meherdates and Carenes captured the ancient Assyrian capital Ninos, and the famous fortress where the Persian Darius Ⅲ had been finally defeated by Alexander. Meanwhile Gotarzes offered vows to the mountain deities on Mount Sunbulah. The chief cult is that of Hercules. At regular intervals he warns his priests by dreams to prepare, beside his temple, horses equipped for hunting. With quivers full of arrows fastened on them, these are let loose in the forest and only return at night, panting violently, their quivers empty. In a second dream the god reveals the course he has followed in the woods; and all along it wild beasts are found struck down.

Since, however, Gotarzes' army was not yet strong enough, he took up a position protected by the river Adhaim (?) , and, in spite of envoys taunting him to fight, contrived delays—moving from place to place, and sending agents to bribe the enemy forces to change sides. The monarchs of Adiabene and then Edessa deserted to him with their armies. Disloyalty was their national habit; besides, experience has shown that natives are readier to invite kings from Rome than to keep them.

Deprived of these powerful allies, and suspecting treason in his other associates too, Meherdates decided that his only hope was to stake everything on an engagement. Gotarzes felt confident after these defections, and accepted battle. The struggle was bloody, and long undecided. But finally Carenes, after routing his opponents, advanced too

狄亚贝尼人的国王伊札提斯表面上和美赫尔达特斯结成联盟,但是在暗中,他却是哥塔尔吉斯忠诚的支持者。在旅途中,美赫尔达特斯和卡列尼斯占领了亚述的古都尼诺斯,还占领了一座著名的要塞,在那里,波斯国王大流士三世最终被亚历山大打败。这时哥塔尔吉斯正在桑布洛斯山向当地诸神许愿,主要的祭仪是赫尔克里士的祭仪,赫尔克里士每当要光顾这里的时候,便会托梦给他的祭司们,预先告知他们,并让他们在他的神庙旁边给他准备一些装备好的马,以备狩猎之用。这些马驮着满装着箭的箭筒,被放到林中空地上。到了夜里,它们气喘吁吁地回来了,而这时箭筒也全都空了。在第二个梦中,赫尔克里士神向祭司们指出他在森林中所经过的道路,而在他经过的道路上,到处都是被打倒在地的野兽。

因为哥塔尔吉斯这时的兵力还不够强大,所以他便利用阿得哈伊姆河[1]来做一道天然的屏障,而尽管对方派人辱骂他向他进行挑战,他却故意设法拖延,不断地把军队从一个地方转移到另一个地方,并且派遣间谍去贿赂敌人的军队,唆使他们改变立场。阿狄亚贝尼人和伊德撒的军队先后溜走了,见异思迁是这些不忠诚的民族的一贯作风,而事实和经验表明,这些部族一向都喜欢向罗马帝国要求国王,而不想让已有的国王稳定地保持其统治。

美赫尔达特斯失掉了这些有力的同盟者,又怀疑其他同盟者会背叛自己,他觉得唯一的希望就是通过战争来决定自己的命运。哥塔尔吉斯看到敌人削弱了,信心便增强了起来,他勇敢地接受了挑战。战斗进行得很激烈,双方伤亡都很惨重,血流成河,

〔1〕 庇格里斯河东部支流,具体地点不详。

far; and fresh troops cut off his return. Meherdates, desperate, listened to the promises of a vassal of his father, Parraces, who then treacherously surrendered him in chains to the victorious Gotarzes. Gotarzes, sneering at Meherdates as no relative of his, no Parthian royalty but an alien Roman, allowed him to live—with his ears cut off. This was a demonstration of his clemency and our humiliation.

Gotarzes II soon fell ill and died. He was succeeded by the king of Media Atropatene, Vonones II, whose short and undistinguished reign contained no noteworthy victories or reverses. His successor was his son Vologeses I.

The king of the Crimean Bosphorus, Mithridates, had been deposed and was homeless. He now learnt that most of the kingdom's Roman garrison under Aulus Didius Gallus had been withdrawn. Only a few battalions, under a Roman knight, Gaius Julius Aquila, were left with the exile's young and inexperienced brother, King Cotys I. Mithridates despised both. He raised the tribes, enticed deserters, and finally collected an army and seized control of the neighbouring tribe, the Dandaridae, expelling its king. At this news Cotys and Aquila feared invasion was imminent. But they were conscious of their weakness. Zorsines, chief of the Siraci, had resumed hostilities against them; and now they too sought outside assistance, sending envoys to

长时间无法决定胜负。最后,卡列尼斯击溃了抗击他的敌军,但是由于他的部队又向前推进得太远了,被增援的敌军切断了退路。美赫尔达特斯彻底绝望了,只好相信了他的父亲的一个臣属、帕尔拉凯斯的许诺,结果却被这个帕尔拉凯斯出卖,他被戴上了镣铐,送到胜利的哥塔尔吉斯那里去了。哥塔尔吉斯嘲笑美赫尔达特斯,说他既不是自己的亲属,也不是帕尔提亚王族的成员,只不过是一个异邦人、罗马人。但是哥塔尔吉斯却没有杀死他,只是割下了他的两只耳朵。这是他的宽宏大量的表现,但却是我们的耻辱。

不久,哥塔尔吉斯二世病死了。他的继任者是米地亚的阿特洛帕提尼国王沃诺尼斯二世。他短暂、平庸的统治没有什么成就,也没有遇到过什么挫折。他的继任者是他的儿子沃洛吉西斯一世。

这时,克里米亚·博斯普鲁斯国王米特利达特斯由于失去了王位而到处漂泊、无家可归。他现在得知罗马的统帅奥路斯·狄第乌斯·伽路斯已经率领着他的主力军团撤走了,只剩下了罗马骑士盖乌斯·尤利乌斯·阿克维拉统率下的几个步兵中队,陪伴着他这位年轻而又未经世故的兄弟国王科提斯一世留在他的新王国里。米特利达特斯根本不把这两个人放在眼里,他鼓动各个部落,把逃亡者吸收进来,最后集合起了一支队伍,赶跑了丹达里达伊人的国王,控制了他的这个邻近的部族。当这个消息传了出去,科提斯和阿克维拉非常担心米特利达特斯很快就会进攻博斯普鲁斯,但是他们知道他们自己的兵力很弱,而西拉奇人的国王佐尔西尼斯对他们又重新采取了敌对的军事行动,因此他们也走出去,向外面去寻求援助,他们派使节到强大的欧尔喜人的

Eunones, chief of the Aorsi. Cotys and Aquila could point to the power of Rome, ranged against the rebel Mithridates; and an alliance was easily negotiated.

It was arranged the Eunones should fight cavalry battles, while all sieges were undertaken by the Romans. The combined forces advanced, Eunones' tribesmen in the van and rear, auxiliary battalions and Bosphorans (armed in Roman fashion) forming the main body. They drove back the enemy and took Soza, a town of the Dandaridae which Mithridates had evacuated. Owing to the dubious loyalty of its inhabitants they decided to garrison it. Then they made for Zorsines' tribe, crossed the river Panda, and besieged Uspe. This hill-town possessed a wall and moat. But the wall, being made not of stone but of wickerwork hurdles with earth between, was poor protection against attack; and it suffered from our firebrands and spears launched from lofty siege-towers. Indeed, only the interruption of hostilities by nightfall prevented the conclusion of the battle within a single day.

Next day, the townsmen of Uspe sent envoys asking for the free population to be spared but offering to hand over ten thousand slaves. The victorious Romans rejected this proposal on the grounds that it was barbarous to slaughter men who had surrendered, but hard to provide guards for such large numbers—better that they should be slain in normal warfare. So the soldiers, who had scaled the defences on ladders, were given orders to kill; and the inhabitants were exterminated.

This terrified the surrounding population. Armaments, fortifications, natural heights and obstacles, rivers, and cities had all failed to check invasion; nothing seemed safe. Zorsines long hesitated whether

首领优诺尼斯那里去。因为科提斯和阿克维拉可以依靠罗马的力量来对付背叛的米特利达特斯,因此这一联盟很容易地缔结起来了。

他们做出了这样的安排:优诺尼斯负责骑兵的战斗,而所有的围攻任务则由罗马人来承担。于是他们把兵力联合起来向前进军,欧尔喜部族的人担任先锋和后卫,罗马步兵中队和(罗马式装备的)博斯普鲁斯军队则组成中坚力量。他们击退了敌人,并且占领了米特利达特斯的一个市镇索札,这时,丹达里达伊人已经从这里撤走了。因为不知道这里的居民是否对他们忠诚,因此他们决定把一支卫戍部队留在该镇驻防。随后,他们便向佐尔西尼斯人的地区进发。他们渡过了庞达河,包围了乌斯佩。这座山城由城墙和壕沟护卫着,但是这座城的城墙不是石造的,而是用树枝编成的篱笆夹着泥土造成的,因此它的防守很不牢固,经不起攻击。从我们高高的攻城塔中发射出去的火把和投枪,使城里的卫戍部队遭受了极大的痛苦。老实说,如果不是黑夜阻止了这次战斗的话,只在一天内这次进攻就可以结束了。

第二天,乌斯佩人派代表出城要求赦免自由居民,并愿意交出一万名奴隶。胜利的罗马人拒绝了这个条件,因为屠杀投降的人是一种野蛮残暴的行为,但是要在这样多的人四周设置上警戒人员也是非常困难的,最好还是让他们死在战争的进程之中吧!因此从云梯攻上去的士兵就接到命令,对敌人格杀勿论,于是城中的居民惨遭屠杀。

对乌斯佩居民的屠杀使周围其他地区的居民深感恐慌,既然军队的武器和工事、自然的高山和屏障、河流和城市都不能阻挡敌人的进攻,就没有什么办法能取得安全的保障了。佐尔西

to support Mithridates in his extremity or save his own ancestral kingdom. Finally he put his own people's interests first, gave hostages, and prostrated himself before the emperor's statue. This was an important success for the Roman army. Unscathed and triumphant, it is reliably reported to have reached a point only three days from the river Don. But its return was less satisfactory. For on the voyage back, some ships went aground on the Crimean coast, where natives surrounded them and killed a battalion commander and numerous auxiliaries.

Resistance being hopeless, Mithridates considered to whose mercy he should appeal. He distrusted his brother Cotys I, who had betrayed him and then fought against him. And no Roman of sufficient importance for his promises to carry weight was available. So Mithridates turned to Eunones, who had no personal feud with him and had become stronger since his alliance with Rome. Adapting his dress and appearance as best he could to his critical situation, Mithridates entered Eunones' palace and fell at his feet, crying : ' Mithridates, whom the Romans have sought on land and sea for many years, voluntarily presents himself! Treat as you will the descendant of mighty Achaemenes. That descent is all my enemies have left me. '

尼斯长时期犹豫不决,不知道他是应当去帮助陷于绝境的米特利达特斯,还是应当去拯救他从自己祖先手里接受的王国。但是最后,他还是以本国人民的利益为重交出了人质,并且匍匐在罗马皇帝的胸像前面。这是罗马军队取得的不同寻常的成功,因为他们是在没有受到任何伤亡的情况下取得了胜利,而且据可靠的消息说,他们只用了三天的时间便从塔纳伊斯河出发到达了那个地方。不过他们在回师的时候却不是那么顺利,因为在从海路返回的途中,一些船只被吹到了克里米亚海岸一带。在那里,当地的一些部族将他们包围起来,杀死了他们的一个中队队长和许多辅助部队的士兵。

这时,抵抗也已经毫无取胜的希望了,米特利达特斯便考虑他应当向谁请求宽恕的问题。他并不信任他的兄弟科提斯一世,因为科提斯曾经背叛过他,后来又公然同他作战。在当地的罗马人中间,也没有一个人有足够的威信可以给予他能够实现的许诺。于是米特利达特斯就转而到优诺尼斯那里去,因为优诺尼斯和他之间并没有什么个人的恩怨,而且优诺尼斯还因为不久之前同罗马缔结的联盟而大大加强了自己的力量。他竭尽所能地使他的衣着和表情与他当前的危急处境相适应,然后,便走进了优诺尼斯的宫廷。米特利达特斯跪倒在国王的面前,向他说道:"罗马人多年来在海上和陆上一直在寻求的米特利达特斯,他自愿地把自己呈现在这里了!任凭你怎样处置这位伟大的阿凯美尼斯[1]的后裔吧,这一头衔是我所有的敌人都没有从我手中夺走的。"

---

〔1〕 波斯王家的始祖、冈比西斯的祖父、居鲁士的父亲。博斯普鲁斯国王米特利达特斯的祖先,米特利达特斯一世自称是他的后人。

Eunones was moved by his distinction, reversed fortunes, and dignified plca. Raising the suppliant, he congratulated Mithridates for trusting him and his tribe with such an appeal. Eunones then sent envoys to Claudius with a letter. 'Friendships between Roman emperors and the kings of great nations', he wrote, 'originate from their comparable grandeur. You and I are also partners in victory. The happiest ending of a war is a pardon; Zorsines, for example, though conquered, was not despoiled. Mithridates deserves harder treatment, and for him I ask no power or royal position. But spare him a triumphal procession or capital punishment.'

Claudius was generally conciliatory to foreign notables. But he could not decide whether to accept Mithridates as a prisoner, with the promise of his life, or to recapture him by force. Resentment of his aggression, and the desire for revenge, inclined the emperor to the latter course. But on the other side it was argued that the war involved would be in a land without roads or harbours, against savage chieftains of nomad tribes in barren country. Delays would be wearisome, haste perilous-victory inglorious, but defeat humiliating. Better, ran this argument, to seize the opportunity offered, and let Mithridates live, as a destitute exile to whom every further day of life would be an additional punishment.

Claudius was impressed by these points, and wrote informing the ex-king's captor that though Mithridates merited a death sentence,

优诺尼斯被他高贵的出身、不幸的遭遇以及他富有尊严的请求感动了。优诺尼斯把他扶了起来，并且向米特利达特斯表示祝贺，祝贺他对他本人和他的部族如此信任、向他做出这样的请求。接着，优诺尼斯便派遣了一个使团带着一封信，到克劳狄乌斯那里去。他在信中说道："罗马皇帝与大国国王之间的友谊产生于他们之间大体相当的高贵地位，我本人和您也是共同取得胜利的伙伴。战争最令人满意的结果是能够达成谅解。比如说，佐尔西尼斯虽然被打败，却没有遭到剥夺。米特利达特斯应当受到更加严厉的惩罚，我既不是为他要求权力，也不是为他要求王位，我只是向您请求不要把他放到凯旋的行列里，不要让他受到处死的惩罚。"

一般情况下，克劳狄乌斯对外国权贵是宽大为怀的，但是这次对米特利达特斯他却犹豫不决，他在想，到底是在保留他性命的条件下接受他为俘虏呢，还是用武力再把他抓来？他对米特利达特斯的冒犯感到憎恶和愤慨，并且很想进行复仇，因此他倾向于选择后者。但是另一方面他又考虑到，如果要把他抓来，那么就要在一个没有道路、没有港口的地方，在那荒瘠不毛的土地上，同那些游牧部落的野蛮嗜杀的国王们作战。拖延下去会引起人们的厌烦情绪，轻举妄动又会陷入危险，胜利不会给罗马带来什么光荣，但是失败却会给罗马人带来耻辱。最好还是不放过机会，留米特利达特斯一条活命，让他过贫困的、颠沛流亡的生活吧，对于过着这种生活的人来说，每过一天也就是多受一天的惩罚。

克劳狄乌斯基于以上考虑拿定了主意，于是他便写信通知逮捕这个前国王的人说，尽管米特利达特斯按罪确实应当处死，

and the emperor had the means to enforce it, it was traditional Roman policy to show mercy to suppliants no less than resolution against enemies: 'it was against whole nations and kingdoms, not individuals, that Triumphs were earned'. Then Mithridates was handed over and conducted to Rome by the imperial finance agent in Pontus, Junio Chilo.

However, he is reported to have addressed the emperor with more spirit than his situation warranted. One observation became publicly known: 'I have not been brought back to you; I have come back. If you disbelieve this, let me go—and then try to catch me !' When he was displayed to the public beside the platform in the Forum among his guards, his expression remained undaunted. The insignia of consul and praetor respectively were conferred upon Junius Chilo and Gaius Julius Aquila.

Agrippina hated Lollia Paulina as a rival for the emperor's hand; and Agrippina was a relentless enemy. In this same year she found an accuser to prosecute Lollia. The charges were association with Chaldaean astrologers and magicians, and the consultation of Apollo's statue at Clarus concerning Claudius' marriage. The emperor did not give the defendant a hearing. He himself spoke at length about her noble connections-omitting her marriage with Gaius, but pointing out that her mother was the sister of Lucius Volusius Saturninus (I), her great-uncle Marcus Aurelius Cotta Maximus Messallinus, and she herself the former wife of Publius Memmius Regulus. But he added that her projects were a national danger and that her potentialities for mischief must be eliminated. She must therefore, he said, have her

而且皇帝他自己也有办法施加这种惩罚,但是罗马的传统遗训却要求,对求情的人要宽大仁慈,就像对敌人要进行坚决斗争一样:"只有征服整个民族和王国,而不是征服一个一个人,才是取得了胜利。"于是米特利达特斯便被移交给罗马,押送他的是皇帝在庞都的财务代理官尤尼乌斯·奇罗。

据说,他在皇帝面前所讲的话,表现出与他目前所处的地位所不允许的那种倔强精神。有一句话广为流传,他说道:"我不是被押回到你这里来的,我是自己回来的。如果你不相信这话,你就把我放走,再试试看能否抓我回来!"当他在一群卫兵的监视下,被带到广场上的讲坛旁示众的时候,他脸上表现出大无畏的不屈神色。执政官的标记授予了尤尼乌斯·奇罗,行政官的标记授予了盖乌斯·尤尼乌斯·阿克维拉。

洛里娅·帕乌里娜曾经同阿格里披娜争夺皇帝的宠爱,对此,阿格里披娜怀恨在心。而且,阿格里披娜对自己的敌人绝对是残酷无情的。就在这些执政官执政的同一年里,她收买了一个人对洛里娅提出控诉。洛里娅的罪名是同迦勒底的星象家和魔法师有来往,并且到克拉路斯的阿波罗神的神像那里,去询问有关克劳狄乌斯大婚的事情。皇帝没有听取被告的申诉,他自己在元老院里先发表了长篇的演说,谈论她一家的高贵身世。他故意避而不谈她同盖乌斯·卡里古拉结婚的事情,但却指出,她的母亲是路奇乌斯·沃路西乌斯·撒图尔尼努斯(一世)的姊妹,她的叔祖是玛尔库斯·奥列里努斯·科塔·玛克西姆斯·美撒里努斯,她本人曾经是普布里乌斯·美米乌斯·列古路斯的妻子。他还说她的计划对国家是极其危险的,必须剥夺她那恃以作恶的财产。因此,他说,必须没收她的财产并且把她逐出意大利。结果就只给

property confiscated and leave Italy. She was left with five million sesterces out of her vast property. Another noblewoman, Calpurnia (II), was struck down because the emperor had praised her looks. Since, however, he had spoken casually and without designs on her, Agrippina's anger stopped short of extreme measures. In Lollia Paulina's case, however, a colonel of the Guard was sent to enforce her suicide.

Also condemned at this time was Gaius Cadius Rufus, a governor of Bithynia, who was charged by its people for extortion. Another province, Narbonese Gaul, received a privilege for its deferential attitude to the senate: senators originating from it were allowed to visit their homes without the emperor's permission, as was already permitted to members from Sicily. Ituraea and Judaea, on the deaths of their monarchs, Sohaemus and Agrippa (I) respectively, were incorporated in the province of Syria.

It was decided to reintroduce and perpetuate the 'Augury for the Welfare of Rome', suspended for the last seventy-five years. Claudius also extended the city boundary. Here he followed an ancient custom whereby those who have expanded the empire are entitled to enlarge the city boundary also. Yet no Roman commander except Sulla and the divine Augustus had ever exercised this right, however great their conquests.

There are various traditions concerning the pretensions or renown of the kings in this respect. The original foundation, and Romulus' boundary, are noteworthy. The furrow indicating the city's limits started from the Cattle Market, because oxen are employed for ploughing (the bronze statue of a bull is displayed there), and ran outside

她留下了 500 万谢司特尔提乌斯作为放逐后的生活费用,其余的巨额财产则全部被没收。还有一个出身显贵的女人卡尔普尔尼娅(二世)也遭到了打击,就因为皇帝在谈话中曾经称赞过她的美貌。不过因为皇帝的话是随便说出口的,并不是对她怀有什么企图,阿格里披娜便没有对她采取极端的措施。但是对于洛里娅·帕乌里娜,阿格里披娜毫不留情,她派了一名近卫军将领去逼迫她自杀了。

同时,还有一个名字叫盖乌斯·卡狄乌斯·路福斯的比提尼亚的行政长官被判罪,因为比提尼亚人控告他对他们有勒索行为。另一个行省纳尔波高卢,由于对罗马元老院恭敬尊重的态度而取得了这样一项特权:这一行省出身的元老事先无须取得皇帝的允许,就可以回家去探视,这和西西里行省出身的元老们已经获得的权利一样。伊图莱亚和犹太分别在它们的国王索海木斯和阿格里帕(一世)死的时候,被并入了叙利亚行省。

过去 75 年来一直被废置的"罗马福祉的占卜式"决定重新恢复起来,并且在今后也将永远继续下去。克劳狄乌斯还扩大了城市的疆界,因为按照古老的风俗,如果有谁将帝国的疆域扩大了,那么他也有权力相应的扩大城市的疆界。不过甚至在征服了若干强国之后,除了路奇乌斯·苏拉和圣奥古斯都二人以外,也没有任何罗马统帅行使过这项权力。

关于各个国王在这方面的虚荣或光荣,有种种不同的说法,但是城市的最初建立和罗木路斯的城界,是值得好好研究的。从青铜牛像的牛场开始的犁沟表明了城市的疆界,因为驾犁耕地的牛(青铜牛像就设置在那里)正是作为疆界的起点,这道犁沟一直向外延伸到赫尔克里士的大祭坛处。从那一地点开始,沿着帕

the great altar of Hercules. Then there were stones at regular intervals marked along the base of the Palatine Hill to the altar of Consus, the old Council House, the shrine of the Lares, and the Forum. The Forum and Capitol are believed to have been included in the city not by Romulus but by Titus Tatius. Subsequently the city boundaries grew as Roman territory expanded. The limits established by Claudius are easily traceable and are indicated in public records.

In the following year Gaius Antistius Vetus (II) and Marcus Suillius Nerullinus became consuls. The adoption of Lucius Domitius Ahenobarbus was now hurried forward. Pallas, pledged to Agrippina as organizer of her marriage and subsequently her lover, took the initiative. He pressed Claudius to consider the national interests and furnish the boy Britannicus with a protector: 'Just as the divine Augustus, though supported by grandsons, advanced his stepsons, and Tiberius, with children of his own, adopted Germanicus; so Claudius too ought to provide himself with a young future partner in his labours. ' The emperor was convinced. Echoing the ex-slave's arguments in the senate, he promoted Lucius Domitius Ahenobarbus above his own son, who was three years younger.

Thanks were voted to the emperor. More remarkable was the compliment that the young man received: legal adoption into the Claudian family with the name of Nero. Authorities noted that this was the first known adoption into the patrician branch of the Claudii, which

拉提努斯山的山麓,直到康苏斯的祭坛,从那里经过库里亚老会堂、拉列斯神庙而到罗马广场,每隔一定距离便设立一些界石。人们认为广场和卡披托里乌姆神庙不是被罗木路斯,而是被提图斯·塔提乌斯并入城界之内的。后来,城界便由于罗马地区的扩大而日益扩大了。现在由克劳狄乌斯所规定的城界是很容易确定的,而且在正式的官方记录中,也有着明确的记载。

下一年,[1]是盖乌斯·安提司提乌斯·维图斯(二世)和玛尔库斯·苏伊里乌斯·涅路里努斯担任执政官的一年,路奇乌斯·多米提乌斯·埃诺巴尔布斯过继为克劳狄乌斯的继子的问题被迫切地提了出来。过去曾为阿格里披娜的婚事出过力,后来又成为她的情人的帕拉斯是始作俑者,现在他不断促使克劳狄乌斯要为国家的利益着想,并且给年少的不列塔尼库斯配备一位可靠的保护者。他说:"正如圣奥古斯都的家庭那样,尽管他有孙子可以依靠,但他还是优先考虑他的继子。提贝里乌斯也有他自己的孩子,然而他还是过继了日耳曼尼库斯为继子。因此,克劳狄乌斯也应当给自己指定一位年轻的共治者,和他共同分担治理国家大事的辛苦。"皇帝被说服了,答应了他的请求,并且在元老院里把他的被释奴隶所提出来的理由重述了一遍,将路奇乌斯·多米提乌斯·埃诺巴尔布斯安置在他的儿子之上,他的儿子比多米提乌斯小三岁。

于是,元老院向皇帝表达了感激之情。更加值得一提的是,他们极力恭维皇帝过继了这一位年轻人,而且通过了一项法律,把他正式地过继到了克劳狄乌斯家族来,给他起名叫尼禄。据权威人士认为,在这之前,克劳狄乌斯家族的贵族的一支从阿

---

〔1〕 公元50年,罗马建城803年。

had come down without a break from Attus Clausus. And now Agrippina, too, was honoured with the title of Augusta. After these developments no one was hard-hearted enough not to feel distressed at Britannicus' fate. Gradually deprived even of his slaves' services, Britannicus saw through his stepmother's hypocrisy and treated her untimely attentions cynically. He is said to have been intelligent. This may be true. But it is a reputation which was never tested, and perhaps he only owes it to sympathy with his perils.

Agrippina now advertised her power to the provincials. She had a settlement of ex-soldiers established at the capital of the Ubii and named after her. This was her birthplace. Incidentally, it had been her grandfather Agrippa to whom the tribe had submitted after crossing the Rhine.

At this time, too, a marauding raid by the Chatti alarmed Upper Germany. The imperial governor Publius Pomponius Secundus sent German levies from the tribes of the Vangiones and Nemetes, and auxiliary cavalry, with orders to cut off the raiders or, if they dispersed, to surround them unawares. The troops carried out his orders keenly. They divided into two columns. The left-hand column surprised a newly returned enemy band, somnolent after an orgy over the spoils. Particularly satisfactory was the recovery, after forty years of enslavement, of a few survivors from the disaster of Publius Quinctilius

图斯克劳苏斯以来世代相传,绵延不绝,从来就没有发生过过继的事情。而现在,阿格里披娜也被称之为奥古斯塔的尊号。在这些事情过去之后,没有一个人的心肠会硬到不为不列塔尼库斯的遭遇感到难过的地步。逐渐地,他身边的奴隶也被减少了很多,而不列塔尼库斯也已经看穿了他的继母的虚伪,对她那矫揉造作的关照只是感到很可笑。据说他一直是一个很聪明的孩子,这种说法也许是真的。但是,这一名声从来也没有得到检验,也许是大伙出于对他的危险处境的怜悯,才说出这样的话的。

现在,阿格里披娜也在开始向各行省显示自己的权威。她在乌比伊人的首都建了一座老兵移民地,而且以她自己的名字命名这一移民地。这一地方也是她的出生地。巧合的是,那位渡过莱茵河,将对岸的部落征服收归罗马的人就是他的外祖父阿格里帕。

正在这时,卡提伊人发动的掠夺性的进攻也引起了上日耳曼地区人的惊慌。行政长官普布里乌斯·彭波尼乌斯·塞坤都斯派遣了从万吉欧尼斯和涅米提斯两个部落所征集的日耳曼兵,以及辅助骑兵,命令他们截击这些掠夺者,假如他们要溃逃的话,就出其不意地包围他们。士兵们非常机智地执行了他的作战命令。整个军队分作了两队。一队向左方行进,他们突然袭击了一队刚刚掠夺归来的敌兵,而此时的敌军在一顿大吃大喝之后正在昏昏欲睡。特别令人感到满意的是,在普布里乌斯·克温科

Varus. The contingent which had taken the shorter, right-hand, route inflicted a worse defeat on the enemy, which had risked an open engagement. Laden with plunder after this achievement, the column returned to the Taunus mountains.

Pomponius was waiting there with his Roman brigades. He hoped that eagerness to retaliate might induce the Chatti to risk battle. But they were afraid of being trapped between the Romans and their perpetual enemies the Cherusci. So they sent a delegation to Rome with hostages. Pomponius was awarded an honorary Triumph- a small part of his reputation with posterity, which values his poetry more.

At the same period Vannius was ejected from the kingdom of the Suebi which Drusus had given him. In the early years of his reign his people had loved and honoured Vannius. Then continuous power had made him tyrannical; and internal disputes, combined with the enmity of his neighbours, brought him down. His downfall was due to Vibilius, king of the Hermunduri, and to his own sister's sons, Vangio and Sido. Claudius received repeated appeals from Vannius, but refused to intervene between the native combatants. However, he promised Vannius a safe refuge if he were ejected. The emperor also instructed the imperial governor of Pannonia, Sextus Palpellius Hister, to post a division with picked local auxiliaries on the Danube bank, in order to protect the losers-and intimidate the winners, in case success

提里乌斯·伐鲁斯惨败[1]之后,一些幸存者在遭受了 40 年的奴役之后又被解救了出来。从右路出击的一支军队,抄近路行军,敌人竟然冒险公开与罗马军队展开正规战,结果他们遭受了更为惨烈的损失。获胜之后,他们带着战利品光荣地返回了陶努斯山。

彭波尼乌斯正带着自己手下的罗马军团在那儿等着。他原以为强烈的复仇愿望会使卡提伊人冒险前来公开挑战。但是,他们害怕受到罗马人和他们的夙敌凯路斯奇人的双面夹击,于是,派遣了一个使团带了人质到罗马去讲和。于是,彭波尼乌斯被授予了凯旋荣誉奖章,这一荣誉在他的一生之中只不过是占很小的一部分,与此相比,他的诗人的名声更大一些。

与此同时,被杜路苏斯任命来统治苏埃比王国的万尼乌斯被驱逐出了他的王国。在万尼乌斯统治之初,他还是受到了他的人民的爱戴和拥护的。然而,随着继续掌权,他变得残暴起来。这就导致了国内的冲突和邻国的仇视。他的垮台是由赫尔孟都利国王维比里乌斯和自己姐妹的儿子万吉欧和西多促成的。万尼乌斯多次向克劳狄乌斯求救,但是克劳狄乌斯拒绝介入外族之间的战争。然而,他向万尼乌斯做出保证,一旦他战败了,可以为他提供一个安全的避难所。皇帝还向潘诺尼亚的行政长官塞克斯提乌斯·帕尔佩里乌斯·希斯特尔写了一封信,命令他将一个罗马军团和一支当地的精锐辅助部队驻扎在多瑙河的河岸上,目的是既要保护战败者,也要震慑胜利的一方,从而防止战胜方变

---

〔1〕 伐鲁斯,公元前 13 年的执政官,公元 9 年,作了莱茵地区的长官,当他率领三个军团的士兵从威悉河附近的夏营回师之时,在无路可逃的地区遭受到了阿尔米尼乌斯人的伏击,结果兵败自杀。

emboldened them to break the peace with Rome also.

For numberless hordes, Lugii and other tribes, were closing in, drawn by the reputation of the opulent kingdom which Vannius had enriched for thirty years by plunder and taxation. Since his own infantry and Sarmatian cavalry from the tribe of the Jazyges were no match for the enemy's numbers, he decided to gain time by conducting defensive warfare from his strongholds. His cavalry, however, had no patience for sieges, and wandered over the surrounding plains. There the hostile Lugii and Hermunduri converged on them, and a battle became unavoidable. Vannius came down from his fortresses, but was defeated—though applauded, in his misfortune, for fighting personally at close quarters and receiving frontal wounds.

Vannlius took refuge with the Roman fleet waiting on the Danube. His dependants soon followed and were settled, with grants of land, in Pannonia. His nephews shared his kingdom. To us they were steadfastly loyal. With their subjects, they were popular while winning power, unpopular (more markedly) after they had won it. Their characters had changed—or absolutism was producing its results.

In Britain the situation inherited by the imperial governor Publius Ostorius Scapula was chaotic. Convinced that a new commander, with an unfamiliar army and with winter begun, would not fight them, hostile tribes had broken violently into the Roman province. But Ostorius knew that initial results are what produce alarm or con

得过分放纵起来,破坏与罗马之间的和平关系。

这时,有无数的游牧部落的士兵,包括路吉人和其他一些部落的人,正在迅速逼近国境,因为过去的 30 年,万尼乌斯通过抢掠和横征暴敛而积累了大量的财富,因而他的王国以富有而闻名,这极大地吸引了他们。因为他自己手下的步兵和从雅泽吉人部落那儿征集来的撒尔玛提亚骑兵部队在人数上是没法与敌军相抗衡的,最后,他决心要在自己的要塞之中抗击敌人,以寻求战机。然而,他手下的骑兵部队因为被围困而失去了耐心,不断地到周围的平原上漫游。在那儿,敌对的路吉人和赫尔孟都利人向他们发动了进攻,就这样,不可避免地爆发了战斗。万尼乌斯带领人从要塞之中冲了下来,但是被击败了。然而,尽管他运气不佳,却由于近距离地与敌人展开厮杀,而且身体的前半部分也受了伤,所以还是得到了人民的赞扬。

万尼乌斯逃到了在多瑙河上相候的罗马舰队中来避难。他的臣属们不久也跟着来了,并且也都安排在了潘诺尼亚,每人给了一块土地。他的外甥们将他的王国瓜分了,而他们对我们罗马帝国倒是非常忠诚的。他们的臣民们,在他们争夺统治权的过程之中,对于他们是拥戴的,但是在他们夺取了统治权之后,就对他们特别地憎恨了。或许是因为他们的性格发生了变化,也或许是因为他们进行了残暴的统治所导致的结果。

在不列颠,行政长官普布里乌斯·欧司托里乌斯·斯坎普拉发现所继承的局势十分混乱。那些敌对的部落认为刚刚来了一位新的军事统帅,他对于自己的军队还不熟悉,尤其是冬天已来临了,因此是不会与他们开战的,所以就猛烈地攻入了罗马所控制的行省。但是,欧司托里乌斯很清楚,初战所取得的结果对于加

fidence. So he marched his light auxiliary battalions rapidly ahead, and stamped out resistance. The enemy were dispersed and hard pressed. To prevent a rally, or a bitter treacherous peace which would give neither general nor army any rest, Ostorius prepared to disarm all suspects and reduce the whole territory as far as the Trent' and Severn.

The first to revolt against this were the Iceni. We had not defeated this powerful tribe in battle, since they had voluntarily become our allies. Led by them, the neighbouring tribes now chose a battlefield at a place protected by a rustic earthwork, with an approach too narrow to give access to cavalry. The Roman commander, though his troops were auxiliaries without regular support, proposed to carry these defences. At the signal, Ostorius' infantry, placed at appropriate points and reinforced by dismounted cavalrymen, broke through the embankment. The enemy, imprisoned by their own barrier, were overwhelmed—though with rebellion on their consciences, and no way out, they performed prodigies of valour. During the battle the governor's son, Marcus Ostorius Scapula, won the Citizen's Oak-Wreath for the saving of a Roman's life.

This defeat of the Iceni quieted others who were wavering between war and peace. The Roman army then struck against the Decangi, ravaging their territory and collecting extensive booty. The enemy did not venture upon an open engagement and, when they tried to

剧军队的恐惧感还是增强军队的自信心,具有关键的作用。于是,他率领着轻武装的辅助中队快速推进,对于抵抗的敌军予以击破。敌军被驱散了,而且面临着很大的压力。为了防止敌军的重新集结,也为了防止签订一项既不能使统帅也不能使士兵们得到安宁的、令人不满意而又含有阴谋的和约,欧司托里乌斯准备将所有可疑的人都解除武装,而且将敌人所控制的地区一直压缩到特伦特河和塞佛恩河一带地区。

对此最先起来造反的是伊凯尼人,对于这一强大的部落,我们罗马军队还没有在战争中将其击败过。那是因为他们已经主动地与我们结为了盟友。现在,在他们的带领之下,周围各个部落选择了一个作战地点准备与我们决战。他们所选择的地点布满了土石树枝之类的东西作为防卫,而入口非常狭窄,骑兵们根本就无法进入。虽然手下都是一些辅助部队,没有正规军队的支持,罗马统帅却决心要攻破这一工事。欧司托里乌斯将他手下的步兵们配置在了各个合适的进攻地点,并命令骑兵们下马,帮助他们进攻。接着一声信号,军队迅速地突破了敌人的工事,而敌人则是被自己所修建的工事所困,很快就被击败了。尽管敌人由于叛乱而感到十分愧疚,但在感到没有出路的情况之下,还是进行了英勇的战斗。战争期间,统帅的儿子玛尔库斯·欧司托里乌斯·斯坎普拉由于救了一名罗马人的性命而赢得了罗马公民的橡冠。

伊凯尼人被战败之后,那些动摇于战争与和平之间的部落也都安静了下来。于是,罗马军队就对第凯安吉人发动了进攻,蹂躏了他们的国土,抢掠了许多战利品。敌人不敢冒险公开与罗马军队开战了,而假如试图伏击罗马军队的话,他们的阴谋就会

ambush the column, suffered for their trickery. Ostorius had nearly reached the sea facing Ireland when a rising by the Brigantes recalled him. For, until his conquests were secured, he was determined to postpone further expansion. The Brigantes subsided; their few peace-breakers were killed, and the rest were pardoned.

But neither sternness nor leniency prevented the Silures from fighting. To suppress them, a brigade garrison had to be established. In order to facilitate the displacement of troops westward to man it, a strong settlement of ex-soldiers was established on conquered land at Camulodunum. Its mission was to protect the country against revolt and familiarize the provincials with law-abiding government. Next Ostorius invaded Silurian territory.

The natural ferocity of the inhabitants was intensified by their belief in the prowess of Caratacus, whose many undefeated battles—and even many victories—had made him pre-eminent among British chieftains. His deficiency in strength was compensated by superior cunning and topographical knowledge. Transferring the war to the country of the Ordovices, he was joined by everyone who found the prospect of a Roman peace alarming. Then Caratacus staked his fate on a battle. He selected a site where numerous factors—notably approaches and escape-routes—helped him and impeded us. On one side there were steep hills. Wherever the gradient was gentler, stones were piled into a kind of rampart. And at his front there was a river without easy crossings. The defences were strongly manned.

The British chieftains went round their men, encouraging and

受到严重的惩罚。欧司托里乌斯率军几乎赶到了与爱尔兰隔海相望的地带,这时不列刚提斯人所发动的叛乱又迫使他率军赶了回来。对他来说,除非能够确保被征服地区的安定,否则他是不会发动新的进攻的。不列刚提斯人被征服了,他们当中一些破坏和平的少数分子被处死了,其余的都得到了宽恕。

然而,不论是严厉的手段还是宽大的政策,都不能阻止西里鲁斯人的叛乱。为了镇压他们,不得不建立一座军团的营地。为了便利于替换向西挺进的军队管理这些地方,于是在被征服的土地上的卡木洛杜努姆这一地方,设置了一个由老兵们防守的强大的移民地,老兵们的任务就是应对叛乱,保护这一地区,并使行省的居民们能够熟悉法律遵从政府的管理。接着,欧司托里乌斯就侵入了西里鲁斯人的地区。

这些人生来骁勇善战,再加上他们非常相信卡拉塔库斯的勇猛,这就更增强了他们的勇敢。卡拉塔库斯多次取得的胜利甚至是大胜,使自己成为不列颠领袖人物之中最为突出的一个。他在兵力上的不足通过他那超人的智谋和对当地地形的熟悉得到了弥补。他把战场转移到了欧尔多维凯斯人居住的地区,他联合了每一个对于罗马的和平前景感到惊恐的人。于是,卡拉塔库斯就决定将自己的命运押在一场战争上。他选择了一处地点,这一地点的许多因素,包括入口和逃生的路线都对他们作战有利,而对我们很不利。一边是高耸的群山,而凡是山坡的坡度较缓的地方,就堆上各种各样的防护物,以堵着道路。在敌军的前面是一条小河,小河上没有任何方便跨越的渡口。整个的防御体系非常坚固。

不列颠的这些部落领袖们到处巡视自己的部队,鼓舞并激励

heartening them to be unafraid and optimistic, and offering other stimulants to battle. Caratacus, as he hastened to one point and another, stressed that this was the day, this the battle, which would either win back their freedom or enslave them for ever. He invoked their ancestors, who by routing Julius Caesar had valorously preserved their present descendants from Roman officials and taxes—and their wives and children from defilement. These exhortations were applauded. Then every man swore by his tribal oath that no enemy weapons would make them yield-and no wounds either.

This eagerness dismayed the Roman commanders disconcerted as he already was by the river-barrier, the fortifications supplementing it, the overhanging cliffs, and the ferocious crowds of defenders at every point. But our soldiers shouted for battle, clamouring that courage could overcome everything; and their colonels spoke to the same effect, to encourage them further.

After a reconnaissance to detect vulnerable and invulnerable points, Ostorius led his enthusiastic soldiers forward. They crossed the river without difficulty, and reached the rampart. But then, in an exchange of missiles, they came off worse in wounds and casualties. However, under a roof of locked shields, the Romans demolished the crude and clumsy stone embankment, and in the subsequent fight at close quarters the natives were driven to the hill-tops. Our troops pursued them closely. While light-armed auxiliaries attacked with javelins, the heavy regular infantry advanced in close formation. The British, unprotected by breastplates or helmets, were thrown into disorder. If they stood up to the auxiliaries they were cut down by the swords and spears of

他们要藐视困难,不要悲观,以及其他诸如此类的战争动员。急匆匆到处奔跑的卡拉塔库斯则强调指出,今天这个日子以及这场战争具有重要的意义,要么会使他们夺回自由,要么就会遭受永久的奴役。他提及了他们的列祖列宗们,是他们击退了优利乌斯·恺撒的入侵,他们英勇顽强的战斗使现在的后人们免遭罗马残暴的政治统治和苛捐杂税的折磨,也使自己的妻子儿女们免遭蹂躏。这些激励的话语获得了热烈的欢呼。然后,每一个人都按照本部落的誓言发了誓,表示任何武力都不能使他们屈服,不论多么严重的伤势都不会退缩。

敌人的这种作战热情使罗马的军事将领们感到非常苦恼,而早已经使他们感到头痛的情况还有:河岸上有大量工事防守的河流作为屏障、陡峭的山崖、处处都布置着英勇顽强的守军。但是,我们的士兵们高喊着要出战,他们嚷着勇敢可以克服任何的困难。而他们的将领们的讲话也产生了同样的效果,进一步鼓舞了他们的斗志。

经过仔细观察研究,确定了哪些地方可以攻破,那些地方无法攻破之后,欧司托里乌斯就率领着那些斗志昂扬的士兵们出发了。他们毫不费劲地就渡过了河,到达了敌人的工事前面。但是,在那儿所进行的相互投枪的战斗中,罗马军队的伤亡更加惨重。然而,他们用盾牌紧密地摆成了一个保护平台,以此推进,他们摧毁了敌人用石头堆积而成的粗糙的防御工事,随之就展开了肉搏战,这些外族人被迫撤到了山顶上。我们的军队在后面紧紧地追击。当轻武装的辅助部队用标枪向敌军展开进攻的时候,重武装的正规部队则是排成了密集的队形继续前进,不列颠的士兵没有胸甲和头盔的掩护,因而陷入了一片混乱

the regulars, and if they faced the latter they succumbed to the auxiliaries' broadswords and pikes. It was a great victory. Caratacus' wife and daughter were captured; his brother surrendered. He himself sought sanctuary with Cartimandua, queen of the Brigantes. But the defeated have no refuge. He was arrested, and handed over to the conquerors.

The war in Britain was in its ninth year. The reputation of Caratacus had spread beyond the islands and through the neighbouring provinces to Italy itself. These people were curious to see the man who had defied our power for so many years. Even at Rome his name meant something. Besides, the emperor's attempts to glorify himself conferred additional glory on Caratacus in defeat. For the people were summoned as though for a fine spectacle, while the Guard stood in arms on the parade ground before their camp. Then there was a march past, with Caratacus' petty vassals, and the decorations and neck-chains and spoils of his foreign wars. Next were displayed his brothers, wife, and daughter. Last came the king himself. The others, frightened, degraded themselves by entreaties. But there were no downcast looks or appeals for mercy from Caratacus. On reaching the dais he spoke in these terms.

'Had my lineage and rank been accompanied by only moderate success, I should have come to this city as friend rather than prisoner, and you would not have disdained to ally yourself peacefully with one so nobly born, the ruler of so many nations. As it is, humiliation is my lot, glory yours. I had horses, men, arms, wealth. Are you surprised I am sorry to lose them? If you want to rule the world, does it follow

之中,假如他们抗击辅助部队,就会被正规部队的刀剑和长矛打倒在地,而假如他们攻击后者的话,他们就被辅助部队的弯刀和长枪击毙。这是一次巨大的胜利,卡拉塔库斯的妻子和女儿被俘,他的兄弟也投降了。他本人则是逃到了不列刚提斯人女王卡尔提曼杜娅那儿寻求避难。但是,战败的人是不可能找到避难所的,他被捕了,并且押送到了征服者的手里。

这已经是不列颠开战以来的第九个年头了。为此,卡拉塔库斯声名远播,名声早已经超出了不列颠群岛,穿越了各个行省,到达了意大利本土。人们都怀着好奇的心情,想看一看这一位敢于公然与我们强大的军队作战多年的人。即使是在罗马,他的名字也是响当当的。除此之外,皇帝为了提高自己的声誉,另外也使被战败的卡拉塔库斯获得了声誉。当卫兵们在平地的军营前边武装列队的时候,民众们也召集了起来,像要看一个壮观的场面。然后就走来了一大队士兵,里面押着卡拉塔库斯的少数臣仆,以及一些他对外作战之时所获得的饰物、项链和战利品。后面过来的是他的兄弟们、妻子和女儿,最后过来的是国王本人。其他一些人由于惊恐,在非常低贱地不断求饶。但是,卡拉塔库斯既没有显得垂头丧气,也没有可怜巴巴地求饶。来到讲坛之上,他发表了以下的演讲:

"假如我的身世和我的地位能够同我胜利之时的谦逊结合在一起,那么我就会以朋友的身份而不是以犯人的身份来到这座城市,那么你们也就不会愿意同一位有如此高贵的出身、如此多民族的统治者缔结和平的联盟了。现实情况是我的命运的屈辱,而对于你们来说则是光荣。我拥有马匹、人员、武器、财富。假如丢失了我会感到难过的,这在你们看来难道是很奇怪的现象吗?

that everyone else welcomes enslavement? If I had surrendered without a blow before being brought before you, neither my downfall nor your triumph would have become famous. If you execute me, they will be forgotten. Spare me, and I shall be an everlasting token of your mercy!'

Claudius responded by pardoning him and his wife and brothers. Released from their chains, they offered to Agrippina, conspicuously seated on another dais nearby, the same homage and gratitude as they had given the emperor. That a woman should sit before Roman standards was an unprecedented novelty. She was asserting her partnership in the empire her ancestors had won.

Then the senate met. It devoted numerous complimentary speeches to the capture of Caratacus. This was hailed as equal in glory to any previous Roman general's exhibition of a captured king. They cited the display of Syphax by Publius Cornelius Scipio Africanus and of Perseus by Lucius Aemilius Paullus(I). Ostorius received an honorary Triumph. But now his success, hitherto unblemished, began to waver. Possibly the elimination of Caratacus had caused a slackening of energy, in the belief that the war was over. Or perhaps the enemy's sympathy with their great king had whetted their appetite for revenge.

In Silurian country, Roman troops left to build forts under a divisional chief of staff were surrounded, and only saved from annihilation because neighbouring fortresses learnt of their siege and speedily sent help. As it was, casualties included the chief of staff, eight com

假如你们想统治全世界的话，难道随之就会让人人都欢迎遭受奴役吗？假如我不做任何的抵抗就向你们缴了械，然后被带到了你们的跟前，那么就不会使我的失败和你们的胜利如此闻名遐迩了。假如你们处决了我，这一切也就被遗忘了。但是假如宽恕了我的话，我将永远牢记你们的仁慈的。

克劳狄乌斯对此做出了回应，赦免了他、他的妻子和弟兄们。他们被去掉了脚镣之后，就走过去向阿格里披娜致敬。此时阿格里披娜非常显眼地坐在了皇帝身边的另一个讲坛座上，他们对她致以了与皇帝同样的称颂和感谢。一个女人竟然坐在了罗马军旗前面，这可是以前从来就没有过的新鲜事。她想以此来表明，在他的祖先所创立的帝国之中，她自己也有一份管理权。

接着，元老院召开了会议，就卡拉塔库斯被捕一事发表了许多赞扬性的演说。他们认为，这次的军事胜利所获得的光荣完全可以同以前罗马统帅所进行的任何一次抓获国王的光荣相媲美，在以前的光荣战绩之中他们列举了普布利乌斯·考尔奈里乌斯·斯奇比奥·阿非利加努斯擒获西法克斯、路奇乌斯·埃米里乌斯·保路斯（一世）擒获佩尔谢乌斯。欧司托里乌斯被授予凯旋荣誉勋章。但是，以前一直很顺利的欧司托里乌斯，现在的事业却遭受了重大的打击。或许是因为消灭了卡拉塔库斯之后，大家都认为战争已经结束了，因而对敌人的警惕也就放松了。也或许是因为敌人对于他们的国王被捕深表同情，从而激发了他们强烈的复仇欲望。

在西路里斯地区，留下的罗马军队的一支步兵中队在一位营帅的带领下正在修筑要塞，他们被敌人包围了。附近各个要塞的罗马士兵听说了他们被围困的消息之后，火速派兵增援，他们才勉强免于全军覆没的厄运。即使如此，但是损失非常惨重，包括

pany-commanders, and the pick of the men. Shortly afterwards a Roman foraging party was put to flight. So were cavalry toops sent to its
rescue. Ostorius threw in his light auxiliary battalions, but even so
did not check the rout until the regular brigades joined in. Their
strength made the struggle equal and eventually gave us the advantage. However, night was coming on, so the enemy escaped almost
undamaged.

Battle followed battle. They were mostly guerrilla fights, in
woods and bogs. Some were accidental-the results of chance encounters. Others were planned with calculated bravery. The motives were
hatred or plunder. Sometimes these engagements were ordered by the
generals; sometimes they knew nothing of them.

The Silures were exceptionally stubborn. They were enraged by a
much-repeated saying of the Roman commander that they must be utterly exterminated, just as the Sugambri had once been annihilated or
transplanted to the Gallic provinces. Two auxiliary battalions, which
their greedy commanders had taken plundering with insufficient precautions, fell into a trap laid by the Silures. Then they began, by
gifts of spoils and prisoners, to tempt other tribes to join their rebellion.

At this point, exhausted by his anxious responsibilities, Ostorius
died. The enemy exulted that so considerable a general, if not defeated in battle, had at least been eliminated by warfare. On hearing of
the governor's death the emperor, not wanting to leave the province
masterless, appointed Aulus Didius Gallus to take over. Didius made

这位营帅、八位百人团长和一些精锐士兵都阵亡了。之后不久，一支征集马料的部队也全军覆没了。而派出去增援的一支骑兵部队也遭受了同样的命运。欧司托里乌斯将他手下的轻武装辅助中队全部投入了战争，但是，即使如此也没有平息这次叛乱，直到正规军团加入了战斗，情况才有所好转。敌军的力量和我们旗鼓相当，最终还是我们取得了优势。然而，当夜幕降临的时候，敌军几乎毫发未损地逃脱了。

战争不断地发生着。其中大多数都是发生在森林和沼泽地带的游击性质的战斗。其中有一些是偶然发生的战争，两军不期而遇就开了火。有些是事前就计划好的，士兵们英勇地投入了战斗。开战的目的不是为了报仇，就是为了抢夺战利品。有些时候，这些战争是在统帅们的命令下展开的，有些时候则是在统帅们不知情的情况之下展开的。

这些西路里斯人非常顽强。他们感到非常气愤，因为罗马统帅们一直在不断地说，既然过去苏甘布利人曾经被消灭，或者是被迁移到了高卢诸行省，那么西路里斯人的名字就应该消失。有两个辅助步兵中队由于他们的军官贪得无厌，让士兵们忙于抢掠，而没有保持足够的戒备，结果就陷入了由西路里斯人所设计的埋伏。于是，西路里斯人通过用赠送战利品和俘虏的办法，引诱其他一些部落也加入了他们的反叛队伍之中。

这时，欧司托里乌斯则由于操劳过度而精疲力竭过世了。敌人为如此重要的一位统帅的去世而欢欣鼓舞，尽管不是在战斗之中将他击毙的，最起码也是在整个战役的过程之中使他消失的。皇帝听说了欧司托里乌斯的死讯，感到不能使这一行省处于无人掌管的状态，于是任命奥路斯·狄第乌斯·伽路斯去接

for Britain rapidly. But he found a further deterioration. For in the interval a Roman brigade commanded by Manlius Valens had suffered a reverse. Reports were magnified—the enemy magnified them, to frighten the new general; and the new general magnified them to increase his glory if he won, and improve his excuse if resistance proved unbreakable. Again the damage was due to the Silures: until deterred by Didius' arrival, they plundered far and wide.

However, since Caratacus' capture the best strategist was Venutius who as I mentioned earlier, was a Brigantian. While married to the tribal queen, Cartimandua, he had remained loyal and under Roman protection. But divorce had immediately been followed by hostilities against her and then against us. At first, the Brigantes had merely fought among themselves. Cartimandua had astutely trapped Venutius' brother and other relatives. But her enemies, infuriated and goaded by fears of humiliating feminine rule, invaded her kingdom with a powerful force of picked warriors. We had foreseen this, and sent auxiliary battalions to support her. The engagement that followed had no positive results at first but ended more favourably. A battle fought by a regular brigade under Caesius Nasica likewise had a satisfactory ending. Didius, of impressive seniority and incapacitated by age, was content to act through subordinates and on the defensive.

(These campaigns were conducted by two imperial governors over a

替他的职务。狄第乌斯火速赶往不列颠。但是,他发现那儿的情况进一步恶化了。因为由曼里乌斯·瓦伦斯率领的一个罗马军团又被敌人击败了。整个情况都被夸大了,敌人夸大的目的是为了震慑住新来的统帅;而新统帅夸大的目的则是,假如他能够取胜的话就可以提高自己的荣耀,而假如不能击败叛军的话也能为自己找更多的借口。西路里斯人再一次给我们制造了很大的损失,而当狄第乌斯赶到并将他们击退的时候,他们已经在广大范围之内进行了掠夺。

然而,自从卡拉塔库斯被俘以后,最为优秀的战略家就要数维努提乌斯,此人我在前面已经提及过,他是一位不列刚提斯人。当他娶了部落女王卡尔提曼杜娅之后,就保持着对罗马的忠诚,并一直由罗马军队为他提供保护。但是,在他们离婚之后,他就对她采取了敌视的态度,接着也就开始反对起我们来了。一开始,不列刚提斯人只是在他们自己内部开战。女王卡尔提曼杜娅非常巧妙地捕获了维努提乌斯的兄弟和其他一些亲戚,但是,她的敌人们对此事感到非常气愤,同时感到要屈辱地受一位女人的统治非常痛苦,于是他们组织了一支强大的精锐部队对女王的王国进行了攻击。我们早已经预见到了这种情况,所以就组织了一些辅助步兵中队去支援她。接着就发生了激战,一开始我们并没有取得理想的战果,但最后却获得了胜利。由凯西乌斯·纳西卡所统帅的一个正规军团与敌军经过一场激战,同样也取得了满意的战果。而狄第乌斯由于地位特别显贵,又年事已高行动不便,只能看着下属们进行战斗,也只能防守而不能进攻。

(这一系列的战役是分别由两位行政长官指挥的,而且是跨

period of years. But I have described them in one place since piece-meal description would cast a strain on the memory. Now I return to the chronological succession of events.)

Next came the year when Claudius held his fifth consulship (his colleague was Servius Cornelius Salvidienus Orfitus) ; Nero now prematurely assumed adult costume, to qualify himself for an official career. The emperor willingly yielded to the senate's sycophantic proposal that Nero should hold the consulship at nineteen and meanwhile, as consul-designate, already possess its status outside the city, and be styled Prince of Youth. Furthermore gifts were made to the troops and public in Nero's name, and at Games held in the Circus he was allowed to attract popular attention by wearing triumphal robes, whereas Britannicus was dressed as a minor. So the crowd, seeing one in the trappings of command and the other in boy's clothes, could deduce their contrasted destinies.

Now, too, all colonels, staff-officers, and company-commanders of the Guard who showed sympathy with Britannicus' predicament were eliminated on various fictitious grounds; sometimes promotion was the pretext. Even former slaves loyal to him were removed. The excuse for this was a meeting between the two boys at which Nero had

越了好几年。但是我在这儿集中起来讲述,因为假如分开来描述的话,就不能使读者获得深刻的印象。现在,我再回过头来按照事件所发生的年代顺序来讲。)

让我们回到克劳狄乌斯第五次担任执政官的那一年[1](当时和他一块担任执政官的同僚是谢尔维乌斯·科尔涅里乌斯·塞尔维迭努斯·奥尔费图斯)。而此时尼禄则是提前接受了成人的外袍,[2]使自己获得了参与政治生活的资格。元老院提出了谄媚性的请求,要求尼禄在19岁的时候就担任执政官,[3]而在正式担任政官之前就以罗马城之外行省的代表的身份作为当选执政官,而且要被冠以"青年之王"的光荣称号。皇帝非常高兴地批准了。此外,又以尼禄的名义向军队和公众赠送了礼物,而且在大竞技场召开赛会期间,允许尼禄通过穿着凯旋的外袍的方式吸引公众的注意力,而不列塔尼库斯还要穿着未成年人的服装。因此,看到一个戴着最高统帅的标记,而另一个穿着少年人的衣着,公众们就能够推断出两个人完全不同的命运。

还有,现在所有对不列塔尼库斯表示了同情的将领、百人团长以及禁卫军指挥都被以各种捏造的理由而消除了,有一些则是以提升为借口被调走了。甚至有一些对他忠诚的被释奴隶也被驱逐走了。理由是这两个孩子在见面的时候,尼禄向对方打招呼时称呼不列塔尼库斯的名字,而不列塔尼库斯则是称

---

〔1〕 罗马建城804年,即公元51年。

〔2〕 在上一年的12月15日,尼禄13岁,而要想穿上成人的外袍则是至少要14岁方可。

〔3〕 按照奥古斯都所制定的规矩,要想担任执政官,年龄至少也要33岁。

greeted Britannicus by that name, but Britannicus addressed him as 'Domitius'. Agrippina complained vigorously to her husband. This was a first sign of unfriendliness, she said, a contemptuous neglect of the adoption, a contradiction—in the emperor's own home—of a national measure, voted by the senate and enacted by the people. Disaster for Rome would ensue, she added, unless malevolent and corrupting teachers were removed. Disturbed by these implied accusations, the emperor banished or executed all Britannicus' best tutors and put him under the control of his stepmother's nominees.

Nevertheless, Agrippina did not yet venture to make her supreme attempt until she could remove the commanders of the Guard, Lusius Geta and Rufrius Crispinus, whom she regarded as loyal to the memory of Messalina and to the cause of Messalina's children. So Agrippina asserted to Claudius that the Guard was split by their rivalry and that unified control would mean stricter discipline. Thereupon the command was transferred to Sextus Afranius Burrus, who was a distinguished soldier but fully aware whose initiative was behind his appointment. Agrippina also enhanced her own status. She entered the Capitol in a ceremonial carriage. This distinction, traditionally reserved for priests and sacred emblems, increased the reverence felt

呼他为"多米提乌斯"〔1〕 对此,阿格里披娜对她的丈夫提出了强烈的不满。她说,这是不友好的第一个信号,是对过继这一事件的轻蔑和忽视,在皇帝自己的家里所发生的这一事件,与元老院的决定和人民的命令却形成了鲜明的对比。她进一步说道,罗马肯定是要遭难的,除非把这些向他灌输敌视情绪的人的有害影响全部消除掉。皇帝被这些含蓄的控告弄得很不安宁,于是就将不列塔尼库斯所有最好的教师要么驱逐走,要么处死,让他的儿子由其继母所选定的人来监护。

　　然而,阿格里披娜还不敢冒险拿出她最为狠毒的一招,因为她还没有将两位近卫军将领路西乌斯·盖塔和路福里乌斯·克利司披努斯挤走,对于他们两个人,她认为他们还会牢记着对美撒里娜的忠诚,因而也会忠诚于美撒里娜的儿子的。于是,阿格里披娜对克劳狄乌斯说道,近卫军由于两个人的对立而分裂了,只有统一管理才能够严格纪律。于是近卫军长官的职位就落到了塞克斯提乌斯·阿弗拉尼乌斯·布路斯手上来了,这是一位杰出的军人,但是他完全明白这一次的任命是由谁提议的。阿格里披娜还想办法来提高自己的地位。她乘辇〔2〕出入卡披托里乌姆神庙,而在传统上来说这种待遇只有祭司和圣物才能够享受到。而这也增强了一个女人的自尊感,她到今天为止仍然是历史

---

〔1〕 阿格里披娜之所以感到恼火,是因为尼禄在过继给了皇帝之后就不应该再称之为"路奇乌斯·多米提乌斯·埃诺巴而布斯",而应该称之为"提贝里乌斯·克劳狄乌斯·尼禄·恺撒"。

〔2〕 这是一种双轮彩盖车,元老院过去曾经准许美撒里娜乘坐这种车,而提贝里乌斯为了表彰利维娅也让她乘坐过这种车。

for a woman who to this day remains unique as the daughter of a great commander and the sister, wife, and mother of emperors.

However, her chief supporter, Lucius Vitellius, greatly influential but extremely old, was now prosecuted by a junior senator, Junius Lupus—so precarious is a great man's position. The charges were treason and designs on the throne. The emperor would have listened but for the pleas, or rather menaces, of Agrippina, who instead induced him to outlaw the accuser. Vitellius had not asked for more than that.

This year witnessed many prodigies. Ill-omened birds settled on the Capitol. Houses were flattened by repeated earthquakes, and as terror spread the weak were trampled to death by the panic-stricken crowd. Further portents were seen in a shortage of corn, resulting in famine. The consequent alarm found open expression when Claudius, administering justice, was surrounded by a frenzied mob; driven to the far corner of the Forum, he was hard pressed until a detachment of troops forced a way for him through the hostile crowd. It was established that there was no more than fifteen days' supply of food in the city. Only heaven's special favour and a mild winter prevented catastrophe. And yet surely Italy once exported food for the army to distant provinces ! The trouble, now, is not infertile soil. The fact is that

上唯一的一位既是统帅的女儿,[1]也是皇帝的妹妹、皇帝的妻子以及皇帝的母亲的人。[2]

然而,阿格里披娜的主要支持者,地位极为显赫却又年事过高的路奇乌斯·维提利乌斯却遭到了一位年轻的元老尤尼乌斯·路普斯的指控。看来大人物的地位也是不稳固的呀!对他的指控的罪名就是大逆罪和谋夺皇位的罪行。皇帝原来是想听取路普斯的意见而对其定罪的,但是由于阿格里披娜的求情甚至是威胁,皇帝宣布控告者不受罗马法律的约束,从而使维提利乌斯没有被定罪。而这正是维提利乌斯所希望得到的。

这一年出现了许多怪异的事件。不吉利的鸟栖息在了卡披托里乌姆神庙上面,接连发生的地震使许多房屋都倒塌了,恐怖的气氛在四处散播着,这导致了惊慌失措的人们四散逃命,使许多年老体弱之人被践踏致死。更为严重的是粮食短缺,导致了饥荒的发生。随之出现了令人惊恐的现象,群众的不满情绪开始公开地发泄出来,于是克劳狄乌斯这一位统治者被一群狂呼乱叫的人给包围了起来。人们一直将他逼到罗马广场最远的一个角落里,并言辞激烈地责问他,到后来一队士兵拼命为他挤开了一条道路,让他从愤怒的人群之中走了出来。据估计,罗马城的粮食供应只能够维持 15 天了。只是由于老天爷特别地开恩,这是一个温暖的冬季,罗马城才没有出现大灾难。以前意大利还要向驻扎在边远行省的军队供应粮食,而现在的问题不是在于土地不够肥沃,而在于我们将

---

〔1〕 她的父亲日耳曼尼库斯曾经从提贝里乌斯那儿得到过这一称号。

〔2〕 阿格里披娜是卡里古拉的妹妹、克劳狄乌斯的妻子、尼禄的母亲。

we prefer to cultivate Africa and Egypt--thereby staking Rome's survival on the hazards of navigation.

In this year war broke out between the Armenians and Iberians, and seriously disturbed relations between Rome and Parthia. The king of Parthia was now Vologeses I, a Greek concubine's son, who had obtained the throne with the agreement of his brothers. Pharasmanes had long ruled over Iberia. His brother Mithridates held Armenia with our support. Pharasmanes had a son Radamistus, a tall handsome youth of great physical strength, skilled in his countrymen's accomplishments and well thought of among the adjacent peoples. Frequently and violently—too much so for his ambitions to remain a secret—he complained that his father's longevity kept him off the humble Iberian throne.

Pharasmanes, in his advancing years, felt nervous about his son's popularity and eagerness for power. So he diverted the young man's hopes to Armenia—recalling that he himself, after routing the Parthians, had put his brother Mithridates there. But force, he said, must wait-better set a trap and catch Mithridates unawares. So Radamistus counterfeited a breach with his father and, alleging that he could not face his stepmother's hostility, proceeded to his uncle Mithridates. There he was treated with great friendliness and honoured as a son—while he seduced the Armenian noblemen into rebellion against his unsuspecting host.

The next step was a pretended reconciliation with his father. Radamistus returned to Pharasmanes, reporting that all that plotting could do had been done, and force must do the rest. Pharasmanes invented

耕种的重点放在了阿非利加和埃及,这样就使得罗马的生死存亡依赖于海上航运了。

在这一年,在亚美尼亚人和伊伯利亚人之间爆发了战争,这使得罗马和帕尔提亚之间的关系变得非常紧张起来。现在,帕尔提亚的国王是沃洛吉西斯一世,一位希腊侍妾所生的儿子,在弟兄们的同意之下,他获得了王位。而帕拉司玛尼斯长久以来一直统治着伊伯利亚。他的兄弟米特利达特斯统治着亚美尼亚,并得到我们的支持。帕拉司玛尼斯有一个儿子叫拉达米司图斯,他是一位高大、年轻、力大无比的年轻人,精通本国的才艺,而且深得相邻各民族人民的赞扬。他毫不掩饰自己的野心,不断地、抱怨他的父亲老而不死,使他长时间不能够得到这个弱小国家的王位。

帕拉司玛尼斯随着年事日高,对于儿子受到国人的拥护并且拥有强烈的权力欲感到非常焦虑。于是他想法将儿子的野心转移到亚美尼亚,他回忆说,以前他在驱逐了帕尔提亚人之后,使自己的兄弟米特利达特斯做了亚美尼亚的国王。他说,目前还不能使用武力,最好是能设计一个圈套,乘米特利达特斯不备之时将其抓获。于是,拉达米司图斯假装和他父亲决裂,他宣称自己不能忍受继母的仇视,就到了自己的叔父米特利达特斯这儿来了。在此,叔父对他特别好,就像对待自己的儿子一样尊重他。而他却唆使亚美尼亚的贵族们起来反抗对他一点儿也没起疑心的叔父。

下一步就是拉达米司图斯假装与父亲和解,于是回到了帕拉司玛尼斯的身边,他向父亲汇报说,他所能够做的一切阴谋诡计都已经做好了,接下来就应该采取军事行动了。帕拉司玛尼

a pretext for war. He alleged that, during hostilities against the neighbouring king of Albania, his brother Mithridates had opposed his appeal for Roman help, and must pay for this with his life. Then, at the head of a large force given him by his father, Radamistus suddenly burst into Armenia.

He drove the terrified Mithridates out of the open country into the fortress of Gomeae. Strongly situated and well garrisoned, it was under the Roman commander of an auxiliary battalion, Caclius Pollio, and a company-commander Casperius. Natives are totally ignorant of that branch of military art which we understand so thoroughly, siegeequipment and tactics, and Radamistus' attacks on the fortifications proved costly failures. So he began a blockade. But force created no impression, so he tried tempting Caelius Pollio's acquisitiveness. Casperius protested against this criminal bribery, aimed at the overthrow of an allied king and the Armenian realm given him by Rome. But his superior officer pleaded the enemy's strength; and Radamistus pleaded his father's orders. Casperius arranged a truce and left, intending to deter Pharasmanes from war, or, failing that, to report the Armenian situation to the imperial governor of Syria.

Relieved of supervision now that the company-commander had gone, Caelius Pollio urged Mithridates to make terms. He stressed the bonds of brotherhood, Pharasmanes' seniority, and their other family ties (Mithridates was married to a daughter of Pharasmanes, and Rada

斯就开始寻找战争的借口,他宣称在与邻近的阿尔巴尼亚国王开战的过程之中,他的兄弟米特利达特斯曾经反对他向罗马求援,因此他必须为此付出生命的代价。于是,拉达米司图斯从父亲的手里接过了一支大军,他就带领着这支队伍突然攻入了亚美尼亚。

他带领军队将惊慌失措的米特利达特斯从这个国家的开阔地带驱逐出去,使他被迫退守到一个名叫戈尔尼埃的要塞。这个要塞非常坚固,地形险要,而且驻守着一支装备精良的卫戍部队,这支部队是由一名罗马附属中队长凯里乌斯·波里欧和百人团长卡司佩里乌斯指挥。这些外族人根本就不懂,而我们非常熟悉的一门作战技术就是围攻时所使用的各种设备和技巧,因此,拉达米司图斯对要塞的围攻付出了惨重的代价。在此之下,他将要塞封锁了起来。既然武力不能产生任何效果,他就瞅准了凯里乌斯·波里欧贪财的弱点,想收买他。但是,卡司佩里乌斯对这一罪恶的贿赂行为坚决予以反对,这一行为旨在颠覆一个与罗马结盟的国王的统治,而且亚美尼亚的国土又是罗马赠予他的。但是他的上司坚持以敌人势力太过强大为借口,拉达米司图斯则坚持说这是父亲的命令,他必须要执行。卡司佩里乌斯只得要求先行停战,然后就离开了。他此举的目的就是为了阻止帕拉司玛尼斯发动战争,或者是,假如做不到这一点,他就到叙利亚长官那儿汇报亚美尼亚的局势。

由于卡司佩里乌斯已经走了,无人监视了,凯里乌斯·波里欧就督促米特利达特斯鉴订一项条约。他强调指出自己与帕拉司玛尼斯的兄弟关系(帕拉司玛尼斯的尊贵,以及其他一些亲属关系,包括米特利达特斯娶了帕拉司玛尼斯的女儿,而拉达米

mistus to a daughter of Mithridates), and argued that the Iberians, though at present in the ascendancy, were inclined for peace. 'You know Armenian treachery,' he said. 'Your only protection is an ill-provisioned fort. Do not attempt the hazards of warfare ! Accept a bloodless agreement.' Mithridates hesitated, suspecting the intentions of Caelius, who had seduced one of his royal concubines and was considered purchasable for any outrage.

Meanwhile Casperius reached Pharasmanes, and demanded that the Iberians should raise the siege. Their king's public answers were ambiguous but on the whole acquiescent. Privately, however, Pharasmanes warned Radamistus by messenger to prosecute the siege with all urgency. The wage of treachery was therefore raised, and Pollio by secret bribery induced his men to demand peace and threaten to lay down arms. Mithridates was forced to agree to a day and place for a meeting; and he left the fort.

When they met, Radamistus threw himself into Mithridates' arms with pretended devotion, greeting him as father-in-law and parent, and swearing that neither by the sword nor by poison would he attack him. Then Radamistus conducted him into a wood nearby; everything was ready for a sacrifice there, he said, so that the gods might witness and ratify their agreement. By tradition, kings meeting to become allies join hands and have their thumbs tied and fastened tightly by a knot. The blood, flowing into the extremities, is released by a slight cut and licked by the two participants. The exchange of blood is held to confer a mystic sanction on the alliance. On this occasion, the man fastening the cords pretended to slip, and grasping Mithri

司图斯则是娶了米特利达特斯的女儿）。他还强调指出，伊伯利亚人尽管目前占着优势地位，却愿意与你们缔结和平条约。他说：“你应该知道亚美尼亚人的背叛行为，而你唯一借以保护自己的只不过是一个缺乏粮食供应的要塞。不要冒险开战，应该接受一项没有流血牺牲的合约。”米特利达特斯犹豫不决，因为他怀疑凯里乌斯的目的何在，此人曾经勾引过自己的一名侍妾，而且被认为是一个为了金钱而无恶不作的人。

　　与此同时，卡司佩里乌斯赶到了帕拉司玛尼斯那儿，要求伊伯利亚人解除包围。表面上，国王的回答尽管是模棱两可，但总体上还是默认了他的要求。然而，在暗地里，帕拉司玛尼斯却派人通知拉达米司图斯，要求他用一切可能的办法加紧围攻。这样一来阴谋背叛的代价就相应的提高了，波里欧暗中行贿唆使他手下的人提出缔结和平条约，而且以放下手中的武器相威胁。米特利达特斯被迫答应与对方在某一天的某一地点会面，而且也离开了要塞。

　　见面的时候，拉达米司图斯假装非常热情的样子，紧紧拥抱了米特利达特斯，以岳父和叔父的礼节向对方表示了致意，并且发誓说，他既不会用刀剑也不会用毒药来谋害他。然后，拉达米司图斯将米特利达特斯带到了附近的一个森林之中。他说，奉献牺牲的所有用品都已经准备好了，这样诸神就会见证并批准他们之间的合约。按照传统的办法，国王们相会结盟的时候，应该拉着手并将拇指用绳子系在一起，然后用一个结将他们紧紧勒紧，当血液都流向拇指尖的时候，便轻轻地将拇指的那个地方割破使血流出来，两个誓盟的人再用舌头舔。用舔血的办法来确认联盟条约是一种十分神秘的办法。但此时，给他们系结的人假装摔倒，

dates round the knees pulled him down. Then others ran up and shackled him. He was dragged away by his fetters-natives consider this particularly degrading-amid insults and blows from the populace who had suffered from his stern rule. Others, however, felt pity for this overwhelming change of fortune.

Mithridates' wife followed with their small children, filling the air with her cries. They, too, were imprisoned, in separate covered carriages, to await Pharasmanes' orders. In his criminal heart brotherly and fatherly feelings were outweighed by acquisitiveness. However, Pharasmanes spared himself the sight of the murders. Radamistus apparently remembered his oath. He employed neither sword nor poison against his sister and uncle. Instead, he heaped heavy clothing on their prostrate bodies and smothered them. Mithridates' sons too were killed, for weeping at their parents' deaths.

When Gaius Ummidius Durmius Quadratus, imperial governor of Syria, learnt that Mithridates had fallen by treachery and that his murderers held Armenia, he summoned his council. Reporting what had happened, he asked for advice whether punitive action should be taken. A few members were concerned for our national honour. Most, however, advocated prudence. Their argument was that foreigners' crimes were to be welcomed and that discord should actually be inculcated: indeed emperors had often made a gift of this same Armenia, ostensibly from generosity, really to unsettle the natives. Let Radamistus, they suggested, keep his ill-gotten gains, secured at the price of loathing and infamy—that was better for Rome than if he had won them gloriously. This view was accepted. However, for fear of seeming to condone the crime—or receiving contrary

抱住米特利达特斯的膝盖,将他摔倒了。然后其他的人就迅速地跑过来给他戴上了脚镣。就这样他戴着脚镣被带走了。外族的人都认为这是一个非常卑鄙的行为。那些遭受过他的残酷统治的民众们对他进行了侮辱和殴打。而其他的一些人对他的命运发生的翻天覆地的改变则表示同情。

而带着几个年幼的孩子的米特利达特斯的妻子则是大声哭泣,大家都能够听见她的哭声。他们也都被抓了起来,分别被装入有盖的车内,等待着帕拉司玛尼斯的命令。很明显,拉达米司图斯还没有忘掉自己的誓言,既不会用刀剑也不会用毒药来谋害姐姐和叔父。而是采用了把他们拖倒在地,用大量的衣服压到他们身上,使他们窒息而死的方法。米特利达特斯的儿子们也都被杀死了,理由是在处死他们的父母的时候他们流了眼泪。

当叙利亚长官盖乌斯·翁米狄乌斯·杜尔米乌斯·克瓦德拉图斯听说米特利达特斯已经被阴谋推下了台,而且在亚美尼亚被谋杀的消息后,就召集了一次会议。在会上他将所发生的上述事情作了报告之后,询问大家是否应该采取惩治性措施。有一些人对于我们国家的荣誉表示关切,然而,大多数人都建议要慎重行事。他们认为,对于外国人的犯罪行为我们应该欢迎,实际上就应该在他们之间撒播仇恨的种子。历代的罗马皇帝都曾将这同一个亚美尼亚作为礼物赠送出去,表面上是慷慨大方,实际上是为了使这些外族人之间产生不和。他们建议道,就让拉达米司图斯保持他那非法所获得的一切吧,其代价必然是遭受憎恨和谩骂。而这对于罗马来说,要比他们光荣地获得这一切要有利得多。这个意见被采纳了。但是由于害怕这样看起来是默许这一犯罪行为,又担心克劳狄乌斯的命令与他们的意见相反,于是派遣

orders from Claudius-a delegation was sent to bid Pharasmanes evacuate Armenia and recall his son.

The governor of Cappadocia was a knight called Julius Paelignus. Though as contemptible for his stupidity as for his absurd appearance, he was extremely intimate with Claudius, who before his accession had amused his idle leisure with the company of such buffoons. Paelignus now collected local auxiliaries with a view to recovering Armenia. However, his ravages caused the provincials worse suffering than the enemy. Then his troops deserted him. Left defenceless against native attacks he fled to Radamistus—who gave him costly presents. Captivated, Paelignus urged Radamistus to assume the insignia of kingship; and the ceremony took place, with Paelignus standing by as authorizer and henchman.

When this disgraceful news became known, Quadratus felt it must be shown that all Romans were not like Paelignus; and he sent a division to handle the disturbed position as circumstances suggested. Crossing the Taurus mountains rapidly, its commander, Helvidius Priscus (I), dealt with the situation, more by diplomacy than by force. But then he was recalled to Syria, in case he provoked a Parthian war.

For Vologeses believed that he had an opportunity to invade Armenia-once ruled by his ancestors, now criminally seized by a foreigner. He collected an army and prepared to establish his brother Tiridates on the throne (this would mean that every branch of his family had

了一个使团到帕拉司玛尼斯那儿去,要求他从亚美尼亚撤军,并召回自己的儿子。

卡帕多奇亚的长官是尤利乌斯·帕伊里格努斯,虽然此人愚蠢而古怪的外表同样令人厌恶,但他却跟克劳狄乌斯保持了极为亲密的关系,因为克劳狄乌斯在担任皇帝之前就是与这些小丑一起打发那些无聊的闲暇时光的。现在,帕伊里格努斯征集了当地的辅助部队宣布要收复亚美尼亚。然而,他的劫掠行为使之遭难的是行省的居民,而不是敌人。于是他手下的军队就抛弃了他。这样就使他面对外族的进攻时毫无还手之力,他逃到了拉达米司图斯那儿去了,而后者对他非常慷慨大度。深受感动的帕伊里格努斯就力劝拉达米司图斯采用国王的标记,而且在举行这一仪式的时候,帕伊里格努斯就站在那儿作为委任人和心腹的身份出席。

当这一丑闻传开之后,克瓦德拉图斯感到必须要通过行动来表明并不是所有的罗马人都像帕伊里格努斯一样可耻,于是他派遣了一个军团的兵力,让他们根据情况的需要来处理这一混乱的局面。军团统帅赫尔维狄乌斯·普利斯库斯(一世)带领士兵们迅速地穿过了陶路斯山,对于那儿的情况他更多的是采用了外交手段而不是武力的办法进行处理。但是,接着他就被召回了叙利亚,以防他引起一场帕尔提亚战争。

因为此时的沃洛吉西斯相信现在他有一个进攻的机会,这一地方以前是自己的祖先所统治的领土,而现在却被一个外国人运用邪恶的手段夺走。他集合了一支军队,准备将自己的兄弟提里达特斯扶上王位去(这样一来自己家族的每一支便都有自己的王

its kingdom). The Parthians crossed the frontier. The Iberians were driven back without a fight, and Artaxata and Tigranocerta submitted. Then, however, followed a terrible winter; and the inefficient supply system of the Parthians caused an epidemic. Vologeses was compelled to evacuate the country and Armenia was once more without a government. In came Radamistus, more savage than ever-treating the people as traitors who would, in time, revolt again.

However, though slavery was nothing new, the patience of the Armenians was not unlimited. They surrounded the palace in arms. Swift horses were all that saved Radamistus. They carried him and his wife away. But she was pregnant. At first she endured the journey as best she could, for terror of her enemies and love of her husband. But the continuous galloping soon shook and jarred her so terribly that she begged to be rescued from the humiliations of captivity by an honourable death. Radamistus admired her courage: sick with fear of leaving her to someone else, he embraced, comforted and encouraged her. But he was a man of violence; and finally, in the vehemence of his love, he drew his sabre, stabbed her, dragged her to the bank of the river Aras, and hurled her in—so that even her corpse should not be taken. Then he rode full speed to his own land of Iberia.

But Zenobia (that was his wife's name) was found by shepherds in a backwater. She lived; she was still breathing. Concluding from her noble appearance that she was someone distinguished, they bandaged her wound and applied rustic remedies. When they learnt her name

国了)。[1] 帕尔提亚人快速地推进到了前线,而伊伯利亚人没有经过一次像样的作战就撤退了,阿尔塔克撒塔和提格拉诺凯尔塔这两个城市也投降了。接着就是一个严冬,粮食供应的不足使帕尔提亚人中出现了流行病。这使得沃洛吉西斯被迫从这一地区撤退了,亚美尼亚再一次陷入无人统治的境地。于是,拉达米司图斯又回来了,而他对于这个曾经背叛了他,以后有机会还有可能再次背叛他的民族进行了更加残暴的统治,

　　然而,亚美尼亚人虽然依旧是奴性十足,但其忍耐性也不是无限的,他们拿起武器包围了王宫。多亏了马跑得快,拉达米司图斯才得救。马载着他和他的妻子逃跑了。一开始,她因为惧怕他的敌人以及深深地爱着自己的丈夫,她还是尽自己最大的可能忍受着疼痛坚持着,但是,随着马匹持续地飞奔,很快,剧烈的摇晃就震得她实在受不了,于是她恳求丈夫把她杀死,让她光荣地死去,以免被捕后受辱。拉达米司图斯非常欣赏她的勇敢,却又害怕将她留下会被别人占有,就不断地拥抱她、安抚她、鼓励她。但是,他毕竟是一个非常残暴的人,最终,在强烈的爱情支配之下,他抽出了佩刀砍到她身上,然后就将她拖到了阿拉克西斯河的河岸,将她扔进了河里,这样即使她的尸体也不会被敌人取走了。而他则骑马全速跑回了自己的祖国伊伯利亚。

　　但是,吉诺比娅(这是拉达米司图斯妻子的名字)被一些牧人在一片死水之中发现了。她还活着,而且还在呼吸。他们从她那高贵的外表看得出她是一位地位显赫的人,就将她的伤口包扎起来,并用乡村的土办法对她进行治疗。当他们得知了她的名字

---

〔1〕　沃洛吉西斯的另一个兄弟帕科路斯治理着米地亚阿特罗帕提尼。

and story they took her to the city of Artaxata. From there she was officially conducted to Tiridates, who received her kindly and gave her royal honours.

In the following year the consuls were Faustus Cornelius Sulla Felix and Lucius Salvius Otho Titianus. Lucius Arruntius Furius Scribonianus was now exiled for inquiring from astrologers about the emperor's death. The charge was also extended to his mother, Vibia, recalcitrant (it was alleged) against her earlier sentence of expulsion. The fact that Scribonianus' father, Lucius Arruntius Camillus Scribonianus, had rebelled in Dalmatia was cited by the emperor to illustrate his mercy in again sparing this disaffected family. But the exile did not survive long. Did Scribonianus die naturally or by poison? People spread their own beliefs. The senate passed a severe, but futile, decree banning astrologers from Italy.

The emperor, in a speech, praised senators who voluntarily abandoned their rank through poverty. Those however who, by not retiring, showed shamelessness as well as indigence were expelled. Next Claudius proposed to the senate that women marrying slaves should be penalized. It was decided that the penalty for such a lapse should be enslavement, if the man's master did not know, and the status of an ex-slave if he did. The emperor revealed that this proposal was due to Pallas; to whom accordingly rewards of an honorary

和她的遭遇之后,就将她送到了阿尔塔克撒塔城去了。从那儿她被很隆重地护送到了提里达特斯那里去,而后者很友好地接待了她,并且以王后之礼款待她。

第二年,是由法乌司图斯·科尔涅里乌斯·苏拉·费里克斯和路奇乌斯·撒尔维乌斯·奥托·提提亚努斯担当执政官。[1]在这一年,路奇乌斯·阿伦提乌斯·福利乌斯·司克里波尼亚努斯遭到了驱逐,因为他竟敢向占星术师探寻皇帝的死期问题。这个案件中,他的母亲维比狄娅也被牵连进去,(据说)她的罪名是她对放逐他的那个判决感到不服。事实上是因为司克里波尼亚努斯的父亲路奇乌斯·阿伦提乌斯·卡米路斯·司克里波尼亚努斯曾经在达尔马提亚发动过武装叛乱,而这件事曾经被皇帝拿来说明自己的宽宏大量,因为他再一次宽恕了这个与他为敌的家族。但是这一次放逐并没有使他们的性命维持很长的时间。到底司克里波尼亚努斯是自然死亡的还是被毒死的,人们各有各的看法。元老院颁布了一项严厉的法令,要将占星术师从意大利驱逐出去,但是这一命令实际上没有任何效果。

在一次演讲中,皇帝盛赞了那些由于贫穷而自动放弃职位的元老们,而那些不自动退休,表现得既贫穷又无耻的人,则被逐出了元老院。接着,克劳狄乌斯向元老院提议,要严厉惩罚那些与奴隶们结婚的女人。决议于是规定,假如奴隶的主人不知道这件事,就将与奴隶结婚的女人降为奴隶;而假如主人知道,就将其地位降为被释奴隶。皇帝说这项议案最初是由帕拉斯提出来的,于是相应的授予了他行政长官的标记和

---

〔1〕 罗马建城 805 年之际,即公元 52 年。

praetorship and fifteen million sesterces were proposed by the consul-designate Marcius Barea Soranus. Publius Cornelius Lentulus Scipio (II) added the suggestion that Pallas should be given the nation's thanks because, though descended from Arcadian kings, he preferred the national interests to his antique lineage, and let himself be regarded as one of the emperor's servants. Claudius reported that Pallas was content with that distinction only, and preferred not to exceed his former modest means. So the senate's decree was engraved in letters of bronze; it loaded praises for old—world frugality on a man who had once been a slave and was now worth three hundred million sesterces.

Pallas' brother, the knight Antonius Felix, who was the governor of Judaea, showed less moderation. Backed by vast influence, he believed himself free to commit any crime. However, the Jews had shown unrest and had rioted when Gaius ordered the erection of his own statue in the Temple. Gaius died before the order had been carried out, but there remained fears that a later emperor would repeat it. Moreover, Felix stimulated outbreaks by injudicious disciplinary measures. His bad example was imitated by Ventidius Cumanus, who controlled part of the province. For Judaea was divided: the Samaritans came under Felix and the Galileans under Ventidius.

These tribes had a long-standing feud, which their contempt for their present rulers now allowed to rage unrestrained. They ravaged each other's territory with invading robber gangs, setting traps for one another and sometimes openly clashing, and then depositing their

1500万谢司特尔提乌斯,而这一奖励的提议者则是当选执政官玛尔奇乌斯·巴列亚·索拉努斯。普布里乌斯·科尔涅里乌斯·楞图卢斯·斯奇比奥(二世)则进一步提议道,帕拉斯应该接受全国人民的感谢,因为他虽然是阿尔卡地亚国王的一名后裔,但是他却将国家的利益置于自己古老显贵的家族之上,而他本人也将自己看做是皇帝的一名奴仆。克劳狄乌斯则说,帕拉斯只对所授予他的荣誉感兴趣,而不想使自己的生活水平超过以前的简朴生活。于是,元老院颁布了一项命令,并将命令刻在了铜板上,对这位以前是奴隶,而现在拥有了3000万谢司特尔提乌斯的人的简朴古风给予了充分的赞扬。

帕拉斯的兄弟是罗马骑士安托尼乌斯·费里克斯,此人是犹太的长官,他所表现出的节制就要差远了。有这样大的势力做靠山,他认为自己就可以胡作非为而不受制裁了。然而,过去当盖乌斯命令在神庙之中树立自己的雕像之时,犹太人却是为表现自己的不满而发动过暴乱。这一项命令在还没有执行之前,盖乌斯就死了,但是他们还是害怕以后的某一个皇帝会做出同样的指示。更何况,费里克斯竟然用一些错误的惩罚措施进一步刺激了暴乱的爆发。而他的行径又为控制该行省另一部分的一位长官文提狄乌斯·库玛努斯树立了极坏的榜样,使他极力模仿。因为对犹太这一行省的管理进行了分工,撒玛利亚由费里克斯管理,而迦利里则是由文提狄乌斯管理。

这些部落的居民们很久以来就相互不和。而当他们各自蔑视自己现在的管理者之时,这种敌视情绪就愈发难以遏制了。他们都派了一些专事抢劫的暴徒到对方的领土上进行掠夺,有时候相互伏击,有时则是公开进行对抗,然后就将这些偷来或抢

thefts and plunder with the Roman officials. At first the two men were pleased. Then, as the situation became graver, they intervened with troops-which suffered reverses. War would have flamed up throughout the province if the imperial governor of Syria had not intervened.

Jews who had ventured to kill Roman soldiers were executed without hesitation. The cases of Cumanus and Felix were more embarrassing. For Claudius, learning the causes of the revolt, had empowered Quadratus to deal with these officials himself. He displayed Felix as one of the judges, his position on the bench being intended to silence his accusers. Cumanus was condemned for the irregularities of both. Then the Judaean province was peaceful again.

Shortly afterwards the wild Cilician tribes of the Cietae, which had often caused disturbances, fortified a mountainous position under their chief Troxoboris, and descended from it upon the cities and the coast. There they boldly attacked cultivators, townsmen, and often traders and ship-owners. They besieged Anemurium, and defeated a cavalry force under Curtius Severus sent to its relief from Syria; for the rough ground impeded cavalry operations and favoured the Cilicians who were on foot. Finally Antiochus Epiphanes IV of Commagene, the dependent monarch who controlled the coast, by offering inducements to the rank and file and tricking their leader, split the native forces, and after executing the chief and a few of his associates pardoned and pacified the rest.

A tunnel through the mountain between the Fucine Lake and the river Liris had now been completed. To enable a large crowd to see this impressive achievement a naval battle was staged on the lake

劫来的东西献给他们的罗马长官。一开始,这两位长官对此非常高兴。然而,随着形势的日益严峻,他们开始派遣军队对他们之间的冲突进行干涉,却各吃了败仗。假如不是叙利亚的皇家统治者介入此事的话,战火将会燃及整个犹太行省。

那些胆敢杀死罗马士兵的人将会被毫不犹豫地处死。但是如何处理库玛努斯和费里克斯这一件事情却让人颇感为难。因为克劳狄乌斯在得知了叛乱的起因之后,就授权克瓦德拉图斯亲自来处理这两位官员。他让费里克斯作为一名审判员出席了这次审判会,而他作为审判员的职位使那些控告他的人被迫保持沉默,不再控诉。库玛努斯则承担了两个人的罪责,从而被判有罪。这样犹太这一行省就又恢复了和平。

之后不久,经常发生骚乱的奇里奇亚地区野蛮的奇耶塔伊人诸部落在他们的领袖特洛克索波尔的带领之下,在山上设置了一个营地,他们从山上冲下来,一直进攻到城市和海滨,他们野蛮地攻击农民和市民,也经常攻击商人和船主。他们包围了阿涅木里乌姆城,并且击败了一支由库尔提乌斯·谢维卢斯所率领的从叙利亚赶来救援的骑兵部队。因为崎岖的路面不适于骑兵作战,而有利于那些步行作战的奇耶塔伊人。最终,孔玛盖尼的安提奥库斯·埃批帕尼斯四世,也就是控制沿海地区的藩王,通过用授予官职来诱惑普通士兵以及欺骗他们的将领的办法破坏了这些外族军队的团结,并在处死了首领以及一些主要的助手之后,宽恕并安抚了其余所有的人。

现在,穿越富奇努斯湖和利里斯河之间的山脉的一条隧道已经建成了。为了使大量的群众能够看到这一巨大的成就,克劳狄乌斯就模仿奥古斯都曾经在与台伯河相连接的人工湖上所举行

itself, like the exhibition given by Augustus on his artificial lake adjoining the Tiber, though his ships and combatants had been fewer. Claudius equipped warships manned with nineteen thousand combatants, surrounding them with a circle of rafts to prevent their escape. Enough space in the middle, however, was left for energetic rowing, skilful steering, charging, and all the incidents of a sea-battle. On the rafts were stationed double companies of the Guard and other units, behind ramparts from which they could shoot catapults and stonethrowers. The rest of the lake was covered with the decked ships of the marines.

The coast, the slopes, and the hill-tops were thronged like a theatre by innumerable spectators, who had come from the neighbouring towns and even from Rome itself—to see the show or pay respects to the emperor. Claudius presided in a splendid military cloak, with Agrippina in a mantle of cloth of gold. Though the fighters were criminals they fought like brave men. After much blood-letting, they were spared extermination.

After the display, the waterway was opened. But careless construction became evident. The tunnel had not been sunk to the bottom of the lake or even halfway down. So time had to be allowed for the deepening of the channel. A second crowd was assembled, this time to witness an infantry battle fought by gladiators on pontoons. But, to the horror of banqueters near the lake's outlet, the force of the outrushing water swept away everything in the vicinity-and the crash and roar caused shock and terror even farther afield. Agrippina took advantage of the emperor's alarm to accuse Narcissus, the controller of the project, of illicit profits. He retorted by assailing her

的海战演习那样,在富奇努斯湖上也举行了一次海战演习。当然奥古斯都所举行的那一次在参加演习的船舶和人数上都相对少一些。这次克劳狄乌斯在战舰上配备了 19000 名演习人员,在这些战舰的周围环绕着许多船筏,以防止演习人员逃跑。在湖泊的中央则是留出了一块非常大的水面,以表演激烈的划船、掌舵技巧、进攻以及在海战过程中所有可能发生的情节。船筏上驻守着两个禁卫军和其他兵种的连队,他们站在防御墙后面,可以从那儿投掷长枪和发射弩石。湖面的其他地方则是挤满了驻扎着海军士兵的铺着甲板的船只。

湖岸、山坡和山顶都挤满了人,这儿就像一个有无数观众的剧院一样,他们是从附近各个城市赶来的,有的甚至是从罗马城赶来的,他们是为了看演习,也是为了向皇帝表示敬意而来的。克劳狄乌斯亲自主持了这一演习,他身穿一件豪华的军服,阿格里披娜也来了,她穿着一件绣金外袍。虽然参加演习格斗的都是一些罪犯,但是他们却像一些勇敢的士兵一样进行了演习。他们在进行了一场血腥的表演之后,就被免除了死刑。

演习结束之后,就将水道打开,开始放水。但是,这时在修建过程中所出现的疏忽就表现出来了。隧道没有开到湖底,甚至是没有到湖水一半深的地方。因此,不得不再花费时间以挖深隧道。人群第二次被召集起来了,这一次是为了让他们看一群剑奴在浮桥上表演步兵的战斗。但是,令那些在湖水泄口处举行宴会的人感到惊恐的是,泄出的湖水的巨大威力将这附近所有的东西都冲光了,崩裂声以及湖水的咆哮声令离这儿很远的人也感到惊惶不已。阿格里披娜趁皇帝恐慌不安的时候,就借机攻击这一工程的督造官纳尔奇苏斯,说他非法营私舞弊。他则是反唇相讥,

dictatorial, feminine excess of ambition.

Next year, when the consuls were Decimus Junius Silanus Torquatus and Quintus Haterius Antoninus, Nero, aged sixteen, married the emperor's daughter Octavia. Eager to make a brilliant name as learned and eloquent, Nero successfully backed Ilium's application to be exempted from all public burdens, fluently recalling the descent of Rome from Troy and of the Julii from Aeneas, and other more or less mythical traditions. Nero's advocacy also secured for the settlement of Bononia, which had been burnt down, a grant often million sesterces. Next the Rhodians-continually liberated or subjected in accordance with their services in foreign wars, or lapses into disorder at home-recovered their freedom. And Phrygian Apamea, overwhelmed by an earthquake, was granted remission of taxes for five years.

But Agrippina's intrigues were still driving Claudius to the most brutal behaviour. Titus Statilius Taurus (II), famous for his wealth, had gardens which she coveted. So she broke him. The prosecutor she used as her instrument was Tarquitius Priscus. When Taurus was governor of Africa, Tarquitius had been his deputy; now that they were back he accused Taurus of a few acts of extortion but more especially of magic. Unable any longer to endure undeserved humiliation by a lying accuser, the defendant, without awaiting the senate's verdict, took his own life. The senate, however, so detested the

攻击她作为一个女人太过专横,野心太大。

下一年,[1]戴奇姆斯·尤尼乌斯·西拉努斯·托尔克瓦图斯和克温图斯·哈提里乌斯·安托尼努斯担任执政官。那一年,16岁的尼禄与皇帝的女儿屋大维娅结了婚。因为急于想博得多才多艺和能言善辩的名声,尼禄为伊利乌姆人作了辩护,并成功地支持他们取得了免除一切赋役的特权。他娓娓动听地谈到罗马人民的祖先是特洛伊人,说尤利乌斯家族的祖先是埃涅阿斯人,并提到了其他各种或多或少带点神话色彩的传说。尼禄的辩护使得遭到大火的波诺尼亚得到了 1000 万谢司特尔提斯的补助金。接着,罗得岛人重新取得了他们的自由——他们常常由于帮助罗马对外作战而取得自由,或者由于国内的叛乱而被剥夺了自由。受到地震灾害的福里吉阿帕美亚,被免除了其后五年中的赋税。

但是另一方面,阿格里披娜的阴谋却促使克劳狄乌斯不断地干着最残暴野蛮的事情。以家拥万贯之财而著名的提图斯·司塔提里乌斯·陶路斯(二世)的庭院引起了阿格里披娜的垂涎,因此她就想毁掉他。她利用塔尔克维提乌斯·普利斯库斯当控告人,对陶路斯进行控告和陷害。当陶路斯作亚细亚总督的时候,普利斯库斯是他的副帅。现在,在他们回来之后,普利斯库斯便控诉陶路斯有一些勒索的行为,但更为严重的还是他沉湎于对魔法的迷信。陶路斯再也无法忍受一个满口谎言的控诉者对他所进行的不应有的侮辱,没有等到元老院的判决公布他就自杀了。虽然如此,因为元老们非常讨厌这个控告者,因此,尽管阿格里披娜是

---

[1] 公元 53 年,罗马建城 806 年。

informer that they expelled him—although Agrippina was his supporter.

On several occasions this year the emperor was heard saying that the decisions of knights who were his agents should be as valid as his own judgements. And in case these should be regarded as chance utterances, the senate decreed on the subject in more detailed and comprehensive terms than hitherto. The divine Augustus had conferred jurisdiction on those who governed Egypt, their judgements to rank with those of senatorial officials. Later, in other provinces and in Rome as well, knights were ceded many judicial cases hitherto heard by governors and praetors respectively. Now Claudius handed over to the knights all the powers which had so often caused rioting and fighting, as, for instance, when the laws of Gaius Sempronius Gracchus (I) gave them a monopoly of places on the Bench and the law of Quintus Servilius Caepio restored them to the senate. This was the principal issue in the fighting between Marius and Sulla. In earlier days, however, the struggle had been between classes, and the results extorted applied to a whole class. Julius Caesar's protégés, Gaius Oppius and Lucius Cornelius Balbus (I) , were the first individuals important enough to decide issues of peace and war. Later names of powerful members of the order, such as Gaius Matius and Publius Vedius Pollio, are not worth mentioning since Claudius now gave even exslaves, placed in control of his personal estates, equal authority with himself and the law.

Next he proposed to exempt Cos from taxation. In a lengthy discourse about its ancient history, he said that its first inhabitants had been Argives-or perhaps Coeus, the father of the goddess Latona; then Aesculapius had brought the art of healing, which had achieved

他的支持者,元老院也仍然决定将他驱逐出元老院。

这一年,人们在许多场合都听皇帝说过,作为他的代理官的骑士们所做的决定,将和他本人所做的决定具有同等的效力。为了不使这些话被当做是偶然发表的议论,元老院就这个问题做了比先前任何时候更加详细、更加广泛的规定。过去圣奥古斯都曾下令把审判权交给统治埃及的骑士,他们所做的决定就和罗马的高级长官所做的决定一样。后来,在其他各行省以及在罗马,过去一直由总督和行政官审理的大量案件也都转到骑士的手里去了。现在,克劳狄乌斯又把那些经常引起动乱或战争争夺的审判权全部交给了骑士。比如说,当盖乌斯·塞普洛尼乌斯·格拉克乌斯(一世)的法律把法庭的独裁权交给了骑士等级的时候,当克温图斯·塞尔维里乌斯法·凯皮欧的法律又把这些法庭交回给元老院的时候,甚至是在马利乌斯和苏拉的时代,这也是一条主要的原则。在早先的时代,争斗乃是在各个等级之间进行的,胜利的结果却是对各个等级都普遍适用的。在尤利乌斯·恺撒的权力的支持下,盖乌斯·欧庇乌斯和路奇乌斯·科尔涅里乌斯·巴尔布斯(一世)是能够在他们的行省中有权决定和战的足够重要的人物。在他们之后的人,那些拥有极大势力的罗马骑士,诸如盖乌斯·玛提乌斯、普布里乌斯·维狄乌斯·波里欧等人就不用说了,因为克劳狄乌斯现在甚至给那些被释奴隶以很高的权力,任命他们来管理自己的财产,他们甚至都拥有着同他本人以及同法律同等的权力了。

接着,他又建议豁免科斯岛居民的赋税。对于他们古代的历史,他详尽地进行了叙述。他说,科斯岛的最古老的居民是阿尔哥斯人,也可能是拉托娜女神的父亲科厄斯。后来,埃司库拉皮乌斯带来了医疗的技术,而他的后人又进一步发扬光大,使医疗

remarkable distinction among his descendants. The emperor indicated their names and the periods at which each had lived. Then he added that a member of the same family was his own doctor, Gaius Stertinius Xenophon: in response to whose petition the people of Cos would in future be exempted from all taxation, holding their island as a sacred place, and serving the god alone. Claudius might, of course, have recalled their frequent assistance to Rome, and the victories they had shared with us. But he preferred not to disguise behind external arguments the favour which, with his usual indulgence, he had conceded to an individual.

The Byzantines, on the other hand, when their protests against oppressive burdens were given a hearing, reviewed all their services to Rome. Beginning with their treaty with Rome at the time of our war against the king of Macedonia known, owing to his dubious origin, as pseudo-Philip, they then recounted their services against Antiochus III, Perseus, and Aristonicus, their assistance to Marcus Antonius Creticus in the Pirate War, to Sulla, Lucius Licinius Lucullus, and Pompey, and finally, in more recent times, to the Caesars. The reason for these services had been their situation at a convenient crossingpoint for generals and their armies and supplies. For the Greeks had founded Byzantium at the narrowest part of the strait between Europe and Asia. When they asked Pythian Apollo where to found a city, the oracle replied 'opposite the land of the blind'. This riddle referred to Chalcedon, whose inhabitants had arrived in the region

的技术取得了极高的声誉。皇帝在这里举出了他们的名字,以及他们每个人在一些时期的主要活动。接着,他还说,出生于这一家族的盖乌斯·斯特尔提尼乌斯·色诺芬就是经常为他治病的御医。而应色诺芬的请求,在今后应该免去科斯岛人的一切赋税,并且允许他们把他们的岛当成是只奉祀他们的神的神圣的地方。当然,克劳狄乌斯还列举了大量事实说明该岛居民曾经为罗马做了许多事情,曾经帮助罗马取得过多次的胜利。但是克劳狄乌斯却不愿意用外部的理由来掩饰他自己出于惯常的好意而给予某个人的恩惠。

另一方面,对本身所负担的过重的赋税表示抗议的拜占庭人,受到了元老院的接见,元老院还听取了他们的陈述,也回顾了他们为罗马所作出的贡献。他们一开头就叙述了在我们对马其顿国王——他的可疑的身世使他以伪菲利浦的名字而著名,作战时他们同我们所缔结的条约,继而他们又回顾了他们派遣军队协助我们对安提奥库斯三世佩尔谢乌斯和阿里斯托尼库斯作战的事情,回顾了他们曾经对玛尔库斯·安托尼乌斯·科列提库斯与海盗的战斗中提供的帮助,对苏拉、路奇乌斯·里奇尼乌斯·路库鲁斯和庞培的协助,以及最近对恺撒们所提供的服务。他们之所以能够提供这样的服务,是因为他们占据着有利的地势,可以便利统帅和他们的军队从陆地上或海上的通行,并且对于军用物资的运输也同样提供了便利条件,因为希腊人过去把拜占庭建立在了欧罗巴和亚细亚之间的那个海峡的最狭窄的地段。当希腊人向佩提亚的阿波罗请示,他们应当在什么地方建立一座城市的时候,神使的回答指示他们"到盲人国土的对面去"。这个谜指的是卡尔凯东,那里的居民比他们更早地来到了这一地区,并且

earlier and had seen the superb site first but chosen an inferior one. Byzantium had originally been rich and prosperous. It has a fertile soil and a productive sea, since great numbers of fish, coming from the Black Sea and scared by shelving rocks under the surface on the winding Asiatic coast, swim away from it into the harbours on the European side. But subsequently financial burdens became oppressive; and now they begged for exemption or alleviation. The emperor supported them, arguing that their exhaustion from recent wars in Thrace and the Crimean Bosphorus entitled them to relief. A remission of tribute was granted for five years.

In the following year the consuls were Marcus Asinius Marcellus and Manius Acilius Aviola. A series of prodigies indicated changes for the worse. Standards and soldiers' tents were set on fire from the sky. A swarm of bees settled on the pediment of the Capitoline temple. Half-bestial children were born, and a pig with a hawk's claws. A portent, too, was discerned in the losses suffered by every official post: a quaestor, aedile, tribune, praetor, and consul had all died within a few months. Agrippina was particularly frightened-because Claudius had remarked in his cups that it was his destiny first to endure his wives' misdeeds, and then to punish them. She decided to act quickly.

First, however, out of feminine jealousy, she destroyed Domitia Lepida, who regarded herself as Agrippina's equal in nobility—she was daughter of Antonia (I), and grand-niece of Augustus; cousin once removed of Agrippina; and sister of Agrippina's former husband

更早地发现了这一上好的建城地址,但他们最后选定的却是较差的一个地方。拜占庭地区一开始就是一个繁荣富庶的城市,那里有肥沃的土地和水产丰富的海洋,因为一群群大量从黑海游出来的鱼害怕海面下倾斜的石坡,便离开了曲曲折折的亚细亚海岸,而游到对岸欧罗巴的各个港湾里来。但是后来,赋税的负担变得越来越沉重了,于是现在他们才到元老院请求豁免或者是减轻他们的赋税。皇帝本人对他们的请求表示支持。皇帝向元老院指出,不久以前,与色雷斯和克利米安·博斯普鲁斯的战争已使他们筋疲力尽,故而理应减轻他们的赋税负担。这样就豁免了他们在今后五年里的赋税。

下一年,[1]是玛尔库斯·阿西尼乌斯·玛尔凯路斯和玛尼乌斯·阿奇里乌斯·阿维奥拉担任执政官的一年。在这一年里,一系列的征兆表明,局面会更加坏下去:军队的队旗和士兵的营帐突然被一把天火烧毁了;一群蜜蜂聚在卡披托里乌姆神庙正面的三角墙上;一些半人半兽的孩子出生;还有一只长着鹰爪的猪出生。人们还认为这样一件事也是一种预兆,即每一种官职都有人死掉:在几个月的时间里,就死了一位财务官、一位营造官、一位保民官,还有一位行政长官和一位执政官。阿格里披娜更是感到特别害怕,因为克劳狄乌斯在他喝醉酒的时候说道,他命中注定要在开头的时候忍受他妻子的丑行,但后来就要对她们进行惩罚的。阿格里披娜于是下决心立即动手。

首先,她出于女人之间的嫉妒,害死了多米提亚·列庇妲。因为列庇妲认为自己的出身和阿格里披娜一样高贵:她是小安托尼娅(一世)的女儿;奥古斯都是她的外舅祖父;阿格里披娜是她的堂表姊妹,她又是阿格里披娜的前夫格涅乌斯·多米提乌斯·埃诺巴

---

[1] 公元 54 年,罗马建城 807 年。

Cnaeus Domitius Ahenobarbus. In beauty, age, and wealth there was little between the two women. Moreover both were immoral, disreputable, and violent, so they were as keen rivals in vicious habits as in the gifts bestowed on them by fortune. But their sharpest issue was whether aunt or mother should stand first with Nero. Lepida sought to seduce his youthful character by kind words and indulgence. Agrippina on the other hand, employed severity and menaces-she could give her son the empire, but not endure him as emperor.

However, the charge against Lepida was attempting the life of the empress by magic, and disturbing the peace of Italy by failing to keep her Calabrian slave-gangs in order. On these charges she was sentenced to death—in spite of vigorous opposition by Narcissus. His suspicions of Agrippina continually grew deeper. 'Whether Britannicus or Nero comes to the throne', he was said to have told his friends, 'my destruction is inevitable. But Claudius has been so good to me that I would give my life to help him. The criminal intentions for which Messalina was condemned with Gaius Silius have re-e-merged in Agrippina. With Britannicus as his successor the emperor has nothing to fear. But the intrigues of his stepmother in Nero's interests are fatal to the imperial house—more ruinous than if I had said nothing about her predecessor's unfaithfulness. And once more there is unfaithfulness. Agrippina's lover is Pallas. *That* is the final proof that there is nothing she will not sacrifice to imperial ambition-neither decency, nor honour, nor chastity.'

Talking like this, Narcissus would embrace Britannicus and pray

尔布斯的姊妹。在容貌、年龄和财富上,这两个女人之间都没有什么太大的差别。而且,两个人也是同样不守贞节、同样声名狼藉、同样凶狠残暴,因此双方便激烈地较量看谁的恶行更多,就如同她们互不相让地较量看谁受到命运的眷顾更多一样。但是她们最激烈的竞争却集中在这样一个焦点上,这就是:姑母和母亲最先得到尼禄的欢心。原来列庇妲正在努力用美妙的言词和沉迷于个人享受来诱惑这个年轻人的品德,另一方面,阿格里披娜却是严峻的、令人畏惧的,她虽然能够给她的儿子一个帝国,却不能容忍他做这样一个皇帝。

但是,对列庇妲所提出的控诉理由却是:她曾使用魔法谋害皇帝的伴侣的性命,此外由于她疏于管束自己的卡拉布里亚的奴隶队伍,致使意大利的和平被搅乱了。尽管纳尔奇苏斯坚决表示反对,但还是根据这些理由对她做出了死刑的判决。纳尔奇苏斯对阿格里披娜的猜疑越来越重,据说他曾经对他的朋友们说:"我的死亡是注定不可避免的,但是克劳狄乌斯对我太好了,因此我甘愿牺牲自己的生命去帮助他。已经受到了惩罚的美撒里娜和盖乌斯·西里乌斯所犯的罪行,目前又在阿格里披娜身上重演了。如果继位者是不列塔尼库斯的话,那么皇帝本人是不会有什么危险的,但是他的继母的阴谋目的在于为了尼禄的利益倾覆整个皇室,这个事件的后果所带来的危险,与如果我对她丈夫的前妻的不忠诚保持缄默相比,造成的毁灭性的危险会更大。现在,阿格里披娜再次对皇帝有不忠诚的行为,她的情人是帕拉斯。这一点就清楚地证明了,为了取得皇位,她是不惜牺牲她自己的一切的,不管是她的尊严、她的荣誉还是她的贞洁,都是可以抛弃的。"

每当他说起这样的话的时候,他就把不列塔尼库斯搂到怀里,

he would soon be a man. With hands outstretched-now to the boy, now to heaven—he besought that Britannicus might grow up and cast out his father's enemies, and even avenge his mother's murderers. Then Narcissus' anxieties caused his health to fail. He retired to Sinuessa, to recover his strength in its mild climate and health-giving waters.

Agrippina had long decided on murder. Now she saw her opportunity. Her agents were ready. But she needed advice about poisons. A sudden, drastic effect would give her away. A gradual, wasting recipe might make Claudius, confronted with death, love his son again. What was needed was something subtle that would upset the emperor's faculties but produce a deferred fatal effect. An expert in such matters was selected—a woman called Locusta, recently sentenced for poisoning but with a long career of imperial service ahead of her. By her talents, a preparation was supplied. It was administered by the eunuch Halotus who habitually served the emperor and tasted his food.

Later, the whole story became known. Contemporary writers stated that the poison was sprinkled on a particularly succulent mushroom. But because Claudius was torpid—or drunk—its effect was not at first apparent; and an evacuation of his bowels seemed to have saved him. Agrippina was horrified. But when the ultimate stakes are so alarmingly large, immediate disrepute is brushed aside. She had already secured the complicity of the emperor's doctor Xenophon; and now she called him in. The story is that, while pretending to help Claudius to vomit, he put a feather dipped in a quick poison down his throat.

祈祷他快快长大成人。他伸出双手,时而是伸向上天,时而是伸向不列塔尼库斯,恳求他快快长大起来,除掉他父亲的敌人,甚至向谋杀他母亲的凶手进行报复!因此,过多的忧虑损害了纳尔奇苏斯的健康。于是他退下来到西努埃撒去疗养,在那个不但气候温和宜人,而且还有可以疗病的泉水的地方恢复体力。

阿格里披娜长久以来就已经决定进行谋杀。现在她看到她的机会来了,就立刻开始动手。为她做事的人都早已准备好了,但她需要一个好的建议,就是采用哪种毒药。阿格里披娜担心,如果用烈性的、可以立即见效的毒药,会使她自己露出马脚;如果使用一种慢性的、消耗性的毒药,那么克劳狄乌斯在死前又可能会重新爱他自己的儿子。因此她需要的是这样一种巧妙的毒药,这种毒药可以削弱皇帝的功能,但是又不会很快将皇帝致死。于是她挑选了一个在这方面颇为精到的人物,一个名叫洛库丝塔的女人,这个女人不久之前虽曾因为放毒案而被判罪,但是却又被留了下来,在今后的长时期里为皇室服务。依靠她的聪明才智,这个女人做了巧妙的准备,这件事情由宦官哈洛图斯具体实行,他的职务就是侍奉皇帝的饮食起居,并事先为皇帝尝菜。

后来,阴谋的全部经过大家都知道了。当时的作家们都记载说毒药是撒到特别新鲜的蘑菇上的。但是由于克劳狄乌斯或是因为天生迟钝,或是因为喝醉了酒,药性在起初并不明显,而且他的一次排便好像已经拯救了他的生命。阿格里披娜非常惊恐,但是既然这事的后果会极其严重,她眼前也就将所有的脸面都抛弃在一边了。她已经取得了皇帝的医生色诺芬的暗中协助,这时她把他叫了进来。据人们说,当他假意地帮助克劳狄乌斯呕吐的时候,把一枝浸上了烈性毒药的羽毛伸到了克劳狄乌斯的喉咙里

Xenophon knew that major crimes, though hazardous to undertake, are profitable to achieve.

The senate was summoned. Consuls and priests offered prayers for the emperor's safety. But meanwhile his already lifeless body was being wrapped in blankets and poultices. Moreover, the appropriate steps were being taken to secure Nero's accession. First Agrippina, with heart-broken demeanour, held Britannicus to her as though to draw comfort from him. He was the very image of his father, she declared. By various devices she prevented him from leaving his room and likewise detained his sisters, Claudia Antonia and Octavia. Blocking every approach with troops, Agrippina issued frequent encouraging announcements about the emperor's health, to maintain the Guard's morale and await the propitious moment forecast by the astrologers.

At last, at midday on October the thirteenth, the palace gates were suddenly thrown open. Attended by Sextus Afranius Burrus, commander of the Guard, out came Nero to the battalion which, in accordance with regulations, was on duty. At a word from its commander, he was cheered and put in a litter. Some of the men are said to have looked round hesitantly and asked where Britannicus was. However, as no counter-suggestion was made, they accepted the choice offered them. Nero was then conducted into the Guards' camp. There, after saying a few words appropriate to the occasion—and promising gifts on the generous standard set by his father—he was hailed as emperor. The army's decision was followed by senatorial decrees. The provinces, too, showed no hesitation.

Claudius was voted divine honours, and his funeral was modelled

去。因为色诺芬清楚地知道，从事重大的犯罪虽然要冒险，然而结果却是大为有利可图的。

元老院召集了会议，执政官和祭司为了皇帝的安全向神许愿。但是与此同时，克劳狄乌斯已经停止了生命的尸体正在被裹进毯子和保温的绷带里面。而且，同时又采取必要的措施以便保证尼禄顺利即位。在开头的时候，装作伤心欲绝的样子的阿格里披娜把不列塔尼库斯拉到自己的胸前，好像要从他身上求得安慰似的。她说，他正是他父亲的影子。她用各种各样的办法，阻止不列塔尼库斯离开自己的屋子，并同样地使她的姊妹克劳狄娅·安托尼娅和屋大维娅也不要离开自己的屋子。阿格里披娜用军队把所有的通路都封锁起来，并不时鼓舞人心地说，皇帝的病情正在好转，以维持军队的士气，并且等待占星术士所预言的那个吉利的时刻。

最后，在10月13日的正午，宫廷的大门突然打开了。尼禄在近卫军长官塞克斯图斯·阿福拉尼乌斯·布路斯的陪伴下，走出皇宫来到近卫军那里，近卫军按照规定是永远处于戒备状态的。在那里，通过近卫军长官的语言发动，他受到了近卫军的欢呼，并且随即被放到一个肩舆上面。据说有一些人当时看起来还有些犹豫，他们回过头来问不列塔尼库斯在什么地方。但是，后来既然没有人出头对此表示反对，他们便接受了提供给他们的这一选择。尼禄于是被抬到了近卫军的军营中去，在那里，他按照当时的情况讲了一些话，并且答应他会像他父亲一样慷慨地向士兵进行颁赐的。在这之后，他便正式被拥立为皇帝了。军队的决定随后就得到了元老院的批准，各行省也毫不迟疑地立刻表示同意了。

克劳狄乌斯被授予神圣的荣誉，他的隆重的葬礼也以圣奥古斯

on that of the divine Augustus-Agrippina imitating the grandeur of her great-grandmother Livia, the first Augusta. But Claudius' will was not read, in case his preference of stepson to son should create a public impression of unfairness and injustice.

都的葬礼为标准举行;阿格里披娜则尽力效仿她的曾祖母利维拉的尊荣。但是克劳狄乌斯的遗嘱并没有宣读,这是为了防止他那偏爱继子的做法会给民众的心中造成一种不合理、不公正的印象。

【英汉对照全译本】

THE ANNALS OF IMPERIAL ROME

罗马帝国编年史

[古罗马]塔西佗 著

贺 严 高书文 译

（三）

中国社会科学出版社

CHAPTER 11

The Fall Of Agrippina

The first casualty of the new reign was the governor of Asia, Marcus Junius Silanus (II). His death was treacherously contrived by Agrippina, without Nero's knowledge. It was not provoked by any ferocity of temper. Silanus was lazy, and previous rulers had despised him—Gaius used to call him 'the Golden Sheep'. But Agrippina was afraid he would avenge her murder of his brother, Lucius Junius Silanus Torquatus (I). Popular gossip, too, widely suggested that Nero, still almost a boy and emperor only by a crime, was less eligible for the throne than a mature, blameless aristocrat who was, like himself, descended from the Caesars. For Silanus was a great-great-grandson of the divine Augustus—and this still counted. So he was murdered. The act was done by a knight, Publius Celer, and a former slave, Helius, the emperor's agents in Asia. Without the precautions necessary to maintain secrecy, they administered poison to the governor at dinner.

Equally hurried was the death of Claudius' ex-slave Narcissus. I

第十一章　阿格里披娜之死

　　新皇帝上台之后的第一个牺牲者就是亚细亚总督玛克乌斯·尤尼乌斯·西拉努斯(二世)。此人是在尼禄不知情的情况之下，被阿格里披娜设计陷害致死的。其死亡并不是由脾气暴烈而引起的。西拉努斯是一个懒散的人，以前的皇帝根本就没有将他放在眼里。盖乌斯·恺撒过去经常称他为"金绵羊"〔1〕但是由于阿格里披娜害死了他的兄弟路奇乌斯·尤尼乌斯·西拉努斯·托尔库瓦图斯(一世)，从而害怕他会报复。因为人们普遍认为，尚未成年而且是通过罪恶的手段谋取到帝位的尼禄，要论适合于帝位，尚不及一个年已成熟的、品行毫无指摘之处的贵族，一个跟尼禄一样出生于恺撒家庭的人。对于西拉努斯来说，他也是奥古斯都的曾孙一辈，这一点很重要。因此他就被谋杀了。这次谋杀行动是由一名叫普布里乌斯·凯列尔的骑士和一名叫赫里乌斯的被释放奴隶干的，他们是皇帝派往亚细亚的财务官。他们是在晚餐时用毒药将总督害死的，做这件事他们甚至感到没有保守秘密的必要。

　　同样的，克劳狄乌斯的被释放奴隶纳尔奇苏斯也很快就被迫

---

　　〔1〕　盖乌斯·恺撒用这一比喻是在嘲笑玛克乌斯·尤尼乌斯·西拉努斯是一位富有而又懒散的人。

have described his feud with Agrippina. Imprisoned and harshly treated, the threat of imminent execution drove him to suicide. The emperor, however, was sorry: Narcissus' greed and extravagance harmo-
nized admirably with his own still latent vices.

Other murders were meant to follow. But the emperor's tutors,
Sextus Afranius Burrus and Lucius Annaeus Seneca, prevented them.
These two men, with a unanimity rare among partners in power,
were, by different methods, equally influential. Burrus' strength lay
in soldierly efficiency and seriousness of character, Seneca's in amia-
ble high principles and his tuition of Nero in public speaking. They
collaborated in controlling the emperor's perilous adolescence; their
policy was to direct his deviations from virtue into licensed channels of
indulgence. Agrippina's violence, inflamed by all the passions of ill-
gotten tyranny, encountered their united opposition.

She, however, was supported by Pallas, who had ruined Claudius by instigating his incestuous marriage and disastrous adoption. But
Nero was not disposed to obey slaves. Pallas' surly arrogance, anoma-
lous in a man of servile origin, disgusted him. Nevertheless, publicly, Agrippina received honour after honour. When the escort-com-
mander made the customary request for a password, Nero gave: 'The
best of mothers.' The senate voted her two official attendants and the
Priesthood of Claudius.

For Claudius was declared a god. A public funeral was to come first.
On the day of the funeral the emperor pronounced his predecessor's praises. While he recounted the consulships and Triumphs of the dead

结束了自己的生命。他与阿格里披娜的矛盾我在前边已做过讲述。他被关进了监狱并受到了严刑折磨,在死刑的威逼之下他被迫自杀了。对此,皇帝感到很难过,因为纳尔奇苏斯的贪婪和奢侈生活与尼禄尚未显露出来的恶习相一致。

谋杀还在继续着,但是皇帝的两位老师,塞克斯图斯·阿弗拉尼乌斯·布路斯和路奇乌斯·安奈乌斯·塞内加站出来阻止了这一举动。这两个人在共同执掌政权的时候,很少取得一致意见,但这一次却通过不同的途径对皇帝施加了同样的影响。布路斯的影响力在于其军事方面的才能和一丝不苟的性格,而塞内加则在于和蔼可亲的态度以及他作为尼禄的演说技能。他们共同协作对皇帝年轻时的邪恶品性进行了控制,他们所制定的策略就是对皇帝的放纵享乐进行引导,从而使其达到社会可以允许的范围之内。阿格里披娜那被非法获得政权的激情所激发的残暴遭到了他们的共同抵制。

但是她却获得了帕拉斯的支持,此人曾经怂恿克劳狄乌斯犯了近亲乱伦性的结婚以及灾难性地过继了尼禄。但是尼禄是不愿意听从奴隶们的建议的。帕拉斯那种傲慢的、与原本是一个奴隶的身份极不相符的神态使尼禄感到非常讨厌。而在公开的场合,一种接着一种的荣誉授予了阿格里披娜。当一位近卫军将领根据规章要求向尼禄请示口令的时候,尼禄回答道:"最好的母亲。"元老院通过了决议,赠予了她两名官方的侍从,并让她担当了负责祭奠克劳狄乌斯的女祭司。

由于宣布克劳狄乌斯为神,所以首先为他举行了国葬。在举行葬礼的那一天,皇帝极力赞扬了他的前任。当他追述死者的祖先们所担任的执政官职位以及所取得的胜利之时,他以及在场的

man's ancestors, he and his audience were serious. References to Claudius' literary accomplishments too, and to the absence of disasters in the field during his reign, were favourably received. But when Nero began to talk of his stepfather's foresight and wisdom, nobody could help laughing.

Yet the speech, composed by Seneca, was highly polished-a good example of his pleasant talent, which admirably suited contemporary taste. Older men, who spent their leisure in making comparisons with the past, noted that Nero was the first ruler to need borrowed eloquence. The dictator Julius Caesar had rivalled the greatest orators. Augustus spoke with imperial fluency and spontaneity. Tiberius was a master at weighing out his words-he could express his thoughts forcibly, or he could be deliberately obscure. Even Gaius' mental disorders had not weakened his vigorous speech; Claudius' oratory, too, was graceful enough, provided it was prepared. But from early boyhood Nero's mind, though lively, directed itself to other things-carving, painting, singing, and riding. Sometimes, too, he wrote verses, and thereby showed he possessed the rudiments of culture.

Sorrow duly counterfeited, Nero attended the senate and acknowledged its support and the army's backing. Then he spoke of his advisers, and of the examples of good rulers before his eyes. 'Besides, I bring with me no feud, no resentment or vindictiveness,' he asserted. 'No civil war, no family quarrels, clouded my early years.' Then, outlining his future policy, he renounced everything that had occasioned recent unpopularity. 'I will not judge every kind of case myself', he said, 'and give too free rein to the influence of a few individuals by

所有听众都表情肃穆。当提及克劳狄乌斯的文学成就以及在他统治时期农田里没有遭受过重大的灾难之时,也得到了相当的肯定。但是当尼禄开始谈论他继父的先见之明和聪明智慧的时候,人人都忍不住要发笑了。

然而,由塞内加所起草的这篇演讲,其内容是相当洗练的,这是他那惹人喜爱的才华的一个良好的典范,十分符合当时人们的口味。老人们喜欢在闲暇时拿过去的事例与现在的事例进行比较,他们指出,尼禄是第一个用别人的稿子进行演说的皇帝。独裁者尤利乌斯·恺撒可以和最伟大的演说家相媲美;而奥古斯都则是用一位君主所应有的机智和流利的口才进行演说;提贝里乌斯则十分善于斟酌演说时的词句,既能非常有力地表达出自己的思想,也能有意地将自己不想表达的思想含糊其辞而过;即使是盖乌斯那混乱无序的头脑,也没有削弱他那生动活泼的演讲。而假如克劳狄乌斯事先做了准备的话,也能够做出足够精彩的演讲。然而尼禄从幼年时期开始,他那活泼的头脑就被其他一些事物,例如雕刻、绘画、唱歌和骑马等吸引去了。有些时候他也写一些诗歌,而这些诗歌则表明他是有一定的文化功底的。

尼禄在装模作样地做了哀悼之后,就开始谈起元老院,他非常感谢元老院对他的支持和军队对他的声援。接着,他谈起了他身边的顾问们,还有浮现在眼前的为他树立了良好榜样的前任诸位皇帝。他宣布:"除此之外,我没有遭受任何侮辱、没有任何个人怨恨、没有任何复仇的愿望,这是因为我的早年生活过程中,没有经历任何内战以及家庭纠纷的惨剧。"随后,他概括性地说明了他今后的施政方针,却有意避开了最近以来所发生的引起了民众强烈不满的所有事情。他接着说:"我永远也不会把处理一

hearing prosecutors and defendants behind my closed doors. From my house, bribery and favouritism will be excluded. I will keep personal and State affairs separate. The senate is to preserve its ancient functions. By applying to the consuls, people from Italy and the senatorial provinces may have access to its tribunals. I myself will look after the armies under my control. '

Moreover, these promises were implemented. The senate decided many matters. They forbade advocates to receive fees or gifts. They excused quaestors—designate from the obligation to hold gladiatorial displays. Agrippina objected to this as a reversal of Claudius' legislation. Yet it was carried—although the meeting was convened in the Palatine, and a door built at the back so that she could stand behind a curtain unseen, and listen. Again, when an Armenian delegation was pleading before Nero, she was just going to mount the emperor's dais and sit beside him. Everyone was stupefied. But Seneca instructed Nero to advance and meet his mother. This show of filial dutifulness averted the scandal.

At the end of the year there were disturbing rumours that the Parthians had broken out and were plundering Armenia-Radamistus, who had so often seized control of that country and been ejected, had again given up the struggle. So in Rome, where gossip thrives, people asked how an emperor who was only just seventeen could endure or

切案件的权力抓在我一个人的手里,我也不会将原告和被告关在我家紧闭的门后,而任凭几个人在那儿为所欲为地使用自己手中的权力。任何接受贿赂和徇私枉法的事情都要被横扫出我的家门。我会将个人的事情和国家的事情区别对待的。元老院将会继续保持它过去的权力。来自于意大利以及元老院所属行省的人民只要是向执政官提出申请,都有机会加入到审判员席上来。至于我所控制的军队,我会仔细照看管理的。"

更何况,所做的这一系列诺言是会得到贯彻落实的。元老院有权力对许多事情做出决定。元老们有权力禁止为他人做辩护的人收取酬金和礼品;有权力免除当选财务官必须举行剑斗比赛的义务。阿格里披娜对后一条规定表示了反对,因为这违背了克劳狄乌斯所制定的法律,但还是被元老院通过了。尽管当时的会议是在帕拉提乌姆皇宫中举行的,在会场的后面还开了一扇门,这样,阿格里披娜就可以在不被人看见的情况之下,站在门帘后边倾听会议内容。还有,当亚美尼亚的外交使节在尼禄面前为本国做着辩护的时候,她则是正准备登上皇帝的座坛坐在皇帝的身边。在场的人都惊呆了。但是塞内加却指示尼禄走上前去迎接自己的母亲,这一举动可以表示自己真诚的孝心,以应对外界对他的诽谤。

这一年的年底,传来了一些令人恐慌不安的谣言,说帕尔提亚人又挑起了战争,并正在洗劫亚美尼亚,拉达米司图斯这位过去多次掌握这个国家的统治权接着就被赶走的国君,现在已经是又一次放弃了抵抗。于是,在罗马这一座喜欢闲聊的城市之内,人们提出了这样的疑问:一个年龄刚刚17岁的皇帝能否忍受或者是打退这样令人震惊的威胁;一位在女人的掌控之下的年轻

repel the shock. A youth under feminine control was not reassuring. Wars, with their battles and sieges, could not be managed by tutors.

However, there was also a contrary view, which regarded it as better than if the responsibilities of command had fallen to the lazy old Claudius, who would have been ordered about by his slaves. Burrus and Seneca, it was recalled, were known to be highly experienced men, and Nero was nearly grown up; Pompey had conducted a civil war at seventeen, and the future Augustus at nineteen. 'At the top', said supporters of this opinion, 'command and planning count more than weapon-wielding and physique. We shall see whether his advisers are good or bad if he appoints the best man as commander, ignoring that man's jealous critics and pressure, from wealthy or influential rivals.'

While this was the talk, Nero commanded the eastern divisions to be raised to full strength by drafts from the adjacent provinces, and to proceed towards Armenia. Two dependent kings, namely Agrippa II and Antiochus Epiphanes IV (of Commagene), were instructed to prepare an army to invade Parthia, and orders were given that the Euphrates should be bridged. Lesser Armenia and Sophene were given to Aristobulus and Sohaemus, with royal status. Opportunely, there was a revolt against Vologeses led by a son of Vardanes I; and the

人看来是没有什么指望的;充满了激战与围攻的战争是不能够靠那些教师们来指挥处理的。

然而,也有一部分人持相反的观点,他们认为,假如现在全国还是由迟钝而又年迈的克劳狄乌斯来指挥的话,情况会更糟糕,因为对于这一切,他将会由其奴隶们任意摆布的。至于布路斯和塞内加,大家都知道,他们都是具有丰富经验的人,而且尼禄也眼看就要长大成人了。庞培在 17 岁的时候就已经能够灵活处理内战了,[1] 而以后的奥古斯都处理同样的问题之时,也只有 19 岁。[2] 那些支持者们发表了这样的观点:"要做好指挥和谋划的事情,更多的不是依靠武器和体力。只要他不顾来自于那些本性嫉妒的人的批评和压力,不顾那些富人们和具有相当影响力的对手们的反对而任命一位最杰出的人担当统帅,这样就可以看出他身边的顾问们到底是优秀还是拙劣了。"

当人们争执不下的时候,尼禄命令从相邻各行省征集人员以增强东部各军团的军事力量,让他们全部开赴亚美尼亚前线。同时,两位藩王,名字叫阿格里帕二世和(孔玛盖尼国王)安提奥库斯·埃披帕尼斯四世,也接到了命令要准备一支军队攻击帕尔提亚;尼禄还命令他们要在幼发拉底河上建一些桥。小亚美尼亚地区和索佩尼地区则分别给予了阿里斯托布路斯和索海木斯进行管理,而且他们两个人都取得了国王的地位。恰巧在这时,沃洛吉西斯的一个名叫瓦尔达尼斯一世的儿子领兵起来反叛自己的

---

〔1〕 实际上这是发生在公元前 84 年的事情,而庞培出生于公元前 106 年,当时庞培已经是 22 岁了,塔西佗将庞培的年龄少算了五岁。

〔2〕 这是公元前 44 年的事情。

Parthians evacuated Armenia. Their intention was to fight later. But the senators performed exaggerated celebrations, proposing days of thanksgiving on which the emperor should wear the triumphal robe, enter the city in ovation, and have his statue in the temple of Mars the Avenger-of the same size as the god's. Besides habitual sycophancy there was satisfaction because the man appointed to secure Armenia was Cnaeus Domitius Corbulo (II) —a sign that promotions were to be by merit.

The disposition of the eastern armies was as follows. Two brigades with part of the auxiliaries were to remain in the province of Syria under its imperial governor, Gaius Ummidius Durmius Quadratus. Corbulo was to have a combined regular and auxiliary force of the same size, with the addition of the auxiliary infantry and cavalry wintering in Cappadocia. The allied kings were instructed to serve wherever hostilities required; their inclination was to follow Corbulo. He, to follow up his prestige—a vital matter in new undertakings-rapidly proceeded to Cilicia. Quadratus came there to meet him at Aegeae, so that Corbulo should not enter Syria to take over his army,

父亲。于是帕尔提亚人就从亚美尼亚撤兵了。他们的目的就是以后有机会再开战。但是元老们却夸大其词地召开庆祝会,并提议要举行全国性的感恩祭日,在这一天,皇帝要穿上象征凯旋的外袍,用小凯旋式的仪式入城;并且要在复仇之神玛尔斯的神庙之中为尼禄设立一个雕像,其尺寸大小与玛尔斯神像一样。除了因为是例行性的谄媚话语之外,尼禄也确实是做出了一项令人满意的决定,那就是他任命格涅乌斯·多米提乌斯·科尔布罗(二世)〔1〕去拯救亚美尼亚,而这是一种信号,表明个人是可以凭着其业绩而获得提升的。

东方部队的分配情况如下:两个军团的士兵和一部分辅助部队的士兵被留在了叙利亚行省,由行省长官盖乌斯·翁米狄乌斯·杜尔米乌斯·克瓦德拉图斯率领;科尔布罗要带领一支同样规模的正规军团士兵和辅助部队,此外还包括一部分在卡帕多奇亚过冬的辅助步兵部队和辅助骑兵部队;而联盟的诸王们则被命令随时待命,任何地方爆发了战争需要他们的时候就要提供援助,他们的倾向是追随科尔布罗的。科尔布罗为了建立个人威望,因为个人威望对于刚刚承担一项新的任务来说是至关重要的,他火速推进赶到了奇里奇亚。而克瓦德拉图斯则赶往那里并在埃吉阿伊城与科尔布罗会了面,他这样做的目的是为了防止科尔布罗进入叙利亚从而将他自己的军队给接管了,这样的话,科尔布罗就会

---

〔1〕 格涅乌斯·多米提乌斯·科尔布罗,古罗马帝国时期著名的军事家和政治家,公元 39 年补缺而担任了执政官;公元 47 年担任了下日耳曼副帅;公元 50 年之后不久开始担任亚细亚总督。在本书之中的本卷和后面两卷叙述了他在东方率领军队开展的战役。公元 67 年他被尼禄召到了希腊,最后为了逃避被处死的命运而自杀。

thus becoming the focus of attention. Corbulo's appearance was impressive, and so was his oratory-superficial advantages matching his experience and ability.

Both commanders sent messengers advising Vologeses to choose peace not war, and to demonstrate, by giving hostages, the respect his predecessors had been accustomed to show for Rome. Vologeses duly handed over leading Parthian royalties. He wanted to select his own time for hostilities. Perhaps, too, he wanted, under the guise of hostages, to eliminate suspected rivals. The hostages were received by Insteius Capito, a junior Roman staff officer, who chanced to have been sent by Quadratus to see Vologeses concerning some previous matter. Corbulo, hearing this, ordered a battalion commander, Arrius Varus, to go and take over the hostages. This caused an altercation between the two envoys.

To cut short this exhibition before foreigners, the officers left the decision to the hostages themselves and their escorts. They chose Corbulo on account of his freshly won reputation (indeed, he was popular even among enemies). So the two generals quarrelled. Quadratus declared himself robbed of the fruits of his own negotiations. Corbulo asserted that the Parthian decision to give hostages had been subsequent to his own appointment to conduct the war-which had converted the king's optimism into alarm. To terminate the dispute Nero had it announced that the imperial fasces should be wreathed with laurel 'owing to the successes of Quadratus and Corbulo'. (I have here described events extending into the next year.)

成为众人瞩目的焦点。科尔布罗的外表给人留下了深刻的印象，他的口才也同样如此；而他的经验和才能与他外部所表现出来的过人之处也令人称赞。

两位统帅都派遣了使节去劝告沃洛吉西斯，让他要选择和平而不要选择战争，要通过交给罗马人质的办法以表达自己要像自己的先祖们一样尊敬罗马。于是沃洛吉西斯及时地将帕尔提亚王室中的一些头面人物交了出来。他或许是在选择自己认为合适的开战时机，或者是想通过交出人质作为伪装以消除对手的猜疑。印斯泰乌斯·卡佩托是一位较低级的罗马百人团长，他碰巧被克瓦德拉图斯派遣去拜访沃洛吉西斯，以商谈一些以前的事情，于是印斯泰乌斯就接受了这些人质。科尔布罗听说了这个消息之后，就命令一名叫阿里乌斯·伐鲁斯的中队长赶去接管人质。于是这两名使节之间发生了争执。

为了减少在外国人面前争吵露丑，这两名军官就决定让人质们和与他们相伴的人们自己进行选择。他们选择了科尔布罗，是因为科尔布罗不久之前所取得的巨大的声誉（实际上，即使是在敌人之中他也是受到尊重和喜爱的）。于是，这两名统帅之间便发生了矛盾。克瓦德拉图斯坚持认为自己的谈判果实被他人抢掠去了；而科尔布罗则宣称，帕尔提亚人之所以决定要交出人质是因为自己被任命为统帅，负责指挥处理这场战争，而正是这使国王原有的乐观情绪变成了恐惧，随之才交出了人质。为了结束他们之间的争论，尼禄做出决定，宣布："由于克瓦德拉图斯和科尔布罗所取得的辉煌成就"，要在皇帝的棍束[1]上加上月桂的花环。（在此，我所叙述的这些事情都是已经进入到了第二年的事情。）

---

〔1〕 公元前19年奥古斯都接受了终身执政官的职位，这时候元老院按规定给了他12名执棍束的侍从，以后的皇帝都有这一规定。

In the same year the emperor requested the senate to authorize statues of his late father Cnaeus Domitius Ahenobarbus and his guardian Asconius Labeo. He declined an offer to erect statues of himself in solid gold or silver. The senate had decreed that future years should begin in December, the month of his birth. But he retained the old religious custom of starting the year on January 1st. He refused to allow the prosecution of a Roman knight, Julius Densus, for favouring Britannicus-or of a junior senator, Carrinas Celer, who was accused by a slave. Consul in the next year, Nero exempted his colleague Lucius Antistius Vetus from swearing allegiance, like the other officials, to the emperor's acts. The senate praised this vigorously; they hoped that if his youthful heart were elated by popularity for minor good deeds he might turn to greater ones. Then he showed leniency by readmitting to the senate Plautius Lateranus, who had been expelled for adultery with Messalina. Nero pledged himself to clemency in numerous speeches; Seneca put them into his mouth, to display his own talent or demonstrate his high-minded guidance.

Agrippina was gradually losing control over Nero. He fell in love with a former slave Acte. His confidants were two fashionable young

同一年,皇帝向元老院提出要求,通过决议以授权为他已故的父亲格涅乌斯·多米提乌斯·埃诺巴尔布斯和他的监护人阿司科尼乌斯·拉贝欧树立雕像。对于有人提议为他设立一座纯金或纯银雕像的问题,他谢绝了。元老院做出了一项决议,命令新的一年要从每年的 12 月份开始,因为尼禄就诞生在这一月。但是,他还是按照古老的宗教传统,把 1 月 1 日作为一年的开始。因为罗马骑士尤尼乌斯·邓苏斯对于不列塔尼库斯的偏爱,有人便对他进行迫害,对此,尼禄制止了这一追究;他还制止了一名奴隶对于资历较浅的元老卡尔里那斯·凯列尔所进行的指控而引起的追究。担任执政官的第二年[1],尼禄坚决不允许他的同事,执政官路奇乌斯·安提司提乌斯·维图斯也像其他的行政官员一样,向他的法律条令宣誓效忠。对此,元老院给予了热烈的赞扬,他们这样做的目的就在于使皇帝这颗年轻的心假如因为小事得到好评从而感到高兴的话,就有可能以后会做更大的好事了。然后,他通过让普劳提乌斯·拉提拉努斯重新回到元老院从而表现了他的宽大,拉提拉努斯过去是因为与美撒里娜通奸从而被驱逐出元老院的。尼禄还在许许多多的演说之中表示自己要做一个宽大仁慈的皇帝;塞内加为尼禄起草了这些演说稿,而通过尼禄之口向公众充分地证明了塞内加本人所具有的杰出才能,也展示了他的教导有方。

慢慢地,阿格里披娜就失去了对尼禄的控制。尼禄爱上了一名叫阿克提的前奴隶。他有两名年轻漂亮的心腹:一名叫玛尔库

---

〔1〕 罗马建城 808 年,即公元 55 年。

men, Marcus Salvius Otho, whose father had been consul, and Claudius Senecio, son of a former imperial slave. Nero's secret, surreptitious, sensual meetings with Acte established her ascendancy. When Nero's mother finally discovered, her opposition was fruitless. Even his older friends were not displeased to see his appetites satisfied by a common girl with no grudges. Destiny, or the greater attraction of forbidden pleasures, had alienated him from his aristocratic and virtuous wife Octavia, and it was feared that prohibition of his affair with Acte might result in seductions of noblewomen instead.

Agrippina, however, displayed feminine rage at having an ex-slave as her rival and a servant girl as her daughter-in-law, and so on. She refused to wait until her son regretted the association, or tired of it. But her violent scoldings only intensified his affection for Acte. In the end, deeply in love, he became openly disobedient to his mother and turned to Seneca—one of whose intimates, Annaeus Serenus, had screened the first stages of the liaison by lending his own name as the ostensible donor of the presents which Nero secretly gave Acte. Agrippina now changed her tactics, and indulgently offered the privacy of her own bedroom for the relaxations natural to Nero's age and

斯·塞尔维乌斯·奥托，[1]他的父亲以前曾经做过执政官；一个是克劳狄乌斯·塞内奇奥，他的父亲以前做过皇帝的奴隶。尼禄与阿克提的秘密的、偷偷摸摸的、放荡不羁的交往极大地提高了阿克提的身份。而当尼禄的母亲发现了这件事情之后，她的反对已不起作用了。即使是他的老朋友们对于他们之间的交往也不反对，因为他们认为这样一个普通的女孩子就可以满足他的欲望，而这也不会引起其他人的嫉妒。也不知是命运的缘故还是由于非法的通奸具有更大的吸引力，总而言之他开始讨厌起自己那具有高贵身份并且是贞节的妻子屋大维娅来了。这样大伙都担心，要是禁止他与阿克提的交往，这件事的结果就很有可能是导致他诱奸其他贵族女人作为代替品。

然而，阿格里披娜出于女人的本能，对于一个被释放的奴隶竟然成为自己的对手、而且把一个侍女当作自己的儿媳妇，还有其他一些不称心的事情感到十分生气。她不想等她的儿子赶到后悔或者是感到厌倦的时候再来管此事。但是她那激烈的责备只是越发的加重了尼禄对于阿克提的热爱之情。最后，出于对阿克提的深爱，他开始公开地不再听从母亲的话了，他转而把自己交到塞内加的手上。塞内加的一个亲密的朋友，名字叫安奈乌斯·谢列努斯，为了给皇帝的第一次偷情进行掩护，把自己假装成正在和此被释放女奴隶谈恋爱，并不惜利用自己的名义将尼禄暗中送给阿克提的大量的礼物当着他人给了她。现在阿格里披娜转变了策略，对他极力放纵，甚至为他提供了自己的私人寝室以供皇帝那刚刚成年以及帝王的地位所应该

---

〔1〕 这位奥托就是公元 69 年做了皇帝的那位奥托。

position. She admitted that her strictness had been untimely, and placed her resources—which were not much smaller than his own—at his disposal. This change from excessive severity to extravagant complaisance did not deceive Nero—and it alarmed his friends, who urged him to beware of the tricks of this always terrible and now insincere woman.

One day Nero was looking at the robes worn by the resplendent wives and mothers of former emperors. Picking out a jewelled garment, he sent it as a present to his mother—a generous, spontaneous gift of a greatly coveted object. But Agrippina, instead of regarding this as an addition to her wardrobe, declared that her son was doling out to her a mere fraction of what he owed her-all else but this one thing was kept from her. Some put a sinister construction on her words.

Nero, exasperated with the partisans of this female conceit, deposed Pallas from the position from which, since his appointment by Claudius, he had virtually controlled the empire. As the ex-slave left the palace with a great crowd of followers, the emperor penetratingly commented 'Pallas is going to swear himself out of his state functions'. In fact, Pallas had substituted for that customary oath of high officials a stipulation that there should be no investigations of his past conduct, and that his account with the State should be regarded as balanced.

具有的寻欢作乐。她承认她自己以前的严厉是太不合时宜了,而且她还将自己所具有的财物拿出来供皇帝支配使用,而她自己的私蓄是并不比皇帝本人少的。阿格里披娜对于尼禄的管教从过分的严厉一下子转变为过度的放纵,这并没有欺骗了尼禄,而且也引起了他的朋友们的警惕,他们提醒他要当心这样一个一贯残酷无情而现在又表现出虚情假意的女人的骗局。

有一天,尼禄正在观看先皇们的妻子和先皇们的母亲所遗留下来的豪华的外袍时,他选中了一件上面带有珠宝的衣服作为礼品派人送给了自己的母亲。这是一件慷慨的,并且是发自内心而送出的礼物,是一件极其珍贵的礼品。但是,阿格里披娜却没有将这件礼品看做是增添了她衣柜里的衣服,说他的儿子此举只是将他所欠她的东西的一部分还给她,而除了这份礼品之外其他东西都被尼禄给夺走了。于是,有些人就非常恶毒地将这些话重新编造之后说给了尼禄听。

由于尼禄对于傲慢的阿格里披娜的同党感到非常生气,于是就撤销了帕拉斯的职务,而他自从被克劳狄乌斯任命而担任了这一职务以来,实际上已经控制了整个的罗马帝国。当这一位被释奴隶被一大批随从簇拥着离开皇宫之时,皇帝尖刻地评说道:"帕拉斯是要去宣誓交卸职务的。"[1]实际上,帕拉斯在离任之时没有按照传统的高级官员离任之时进行宣誓的做法,而是提出了要求:不能对他过去的行为进行追查,他和国家之间的账目算是两

---

〔1〕 当时,高级长官的卸任都要正式宣誓:"未做任何违法的事情。"而且宣誓要有一大批朋友相伴;而这儿的长官是一名被释奴隶,友人则是一群食客,代替誓言的则是自己在离任之时所提出的一个条件,所以尼禄对此进行了讽刺。

Agrippina was alarmed; her talk became angry and menacing. She let the emperor hear her say that Britannicus was grown up and was the true and worthy heir of his father's supreme position-now held, she added, by an adopted intruder, who used it to maltreat his mother. Unshrinkingly she disclosed every blot on that ill-fated family, without sparing her own marriage and her poisoning of her husband. 'But heaven and myself are to be thanked', she added, 'that my stepson is alive! I will take him to the Guards' camp. Let them listen to Germanicus' daughter pitted against the men who claim to rule the whole human race—the cripple Burrus with his maimed hand, and Seneca, that deportee with the professorial voice!' Gesticulating, shouting abuse, she invoked the deified Claudius, the spirits of the Silani below-and all her own unavailing crimes.

This worried Nero. As the day of Britannicus' fourteenth birthday approached, he pondered on his mother's violent behaviour—also on Britannicus' character, lately revealedby a small indication which had gained him wide popularity. During the amusements of the Saturnalia the young men had thrown dice for who should be king, and Nero had won. To the others he gave various orders causing no

清了。

阿格里披娜对此非常惊恐,她的话语里面开始带有愤怒和威胁的成分了,她要让皇帝听到她所说的话。她说,布列塔尼库斯已经长大成人了,而实际上他才有资格继承他父亲的最高统治地位。她进一步告诉尼禄,他作为一个继子而插进来,之所以能够掌握最高权力,完全是靠自己母亲的犯罪行为。她绝不会畏惧将这一不幸家庭的所有污点都公之于众的,即使自己的婚姻以及毒死自己丈夫的罪行也毫不保留。她还说:"但是应该感谢上天以及我的明智之举,我的继子还活着。我要带着他到禁卫军的军营中去,让他们听一听日耳曼尼库斯的女儿是如何与那些自称要统治全部人类的人展开斗争的,他们就是布路斯和塞内加,残疾的布路斯用他那残废了的手、而塞内加则是用他那教书匠一般的舌头,妄图实现他们的野心的。"她打着手势,不断地谩骂着,并召请圣克劳狄乌斯以及西拉努斯一家那地下的灵魂,把自己所犯的那些什么也没有获得的罪行也全都当场说了出来。

这使尼禄感到非常焦虑。伴随着布列塔尼库斯 14 岁生日[1]那一天的临近,尼禄一会儿想起了自己母亲的暴烈举动,一会儿又考虑到了布列塔尼库斯的个性特点,尽管他的性格只是在一些小事上有所表现,却让他赢得了广泛的同情。在撒图尔那里亚节[2]的娱乐活动之中,年轻人都在一起玩掷骰子游戏,以决出谁能

---

〔1〕 按照古罗马的传统习惯,14 岁是罗马少年接受成年人的外袍的年龄,也就是进入了官方所承认的成人的年龄。

〔2〕 古罗马时所设置的撒图尔那里亚节是从每年的 12 月 17 日开始,持续 15 天。

embarrassment. But he commanded Britannicus to get up and come into the middle and sing a song. Nero hoped for laughter at the boy's expense, since Britannicus was not accustomed even to sober parties, much less to drunken ones. But Britannicus composedly sang a poem implying his displacement from his father's home and throne. This aroused sympathy—and in the frank atmosphere of a nocturnal party, it was unconcealed. Nero noticed the feeling against himself, and hated Britannicus all the more.

Though upset by Agrippina's threats, he could not find a charge against his stepbrother or order his execution openly. Instead, he decided to act secretly-and ordered poison to be prepared. Arrangements were entrusted to a colonel of the Guard, Julius Pouio, who was in charge of the notorious convicted poisoner Locnsta. It had earlier been ensured that Britannicus' attendants should be unscrupulous and disloyal. His tutors first administered the poison. But it was evacuated, being either too weak or too diluted for prompt effectiveness. Impatient at the slowness of the murder, Nero browbeat the colonel and ordered Locusta to be tortured. They thought of nothing but public opinion, he complained; they safeguarded themselves and regarded his security as a secondary consideration. Then they swore that they would produce effects as rapid as any sword-stroke; and in a room adjoining Nero's bedroom, from well-tried poisons, they concocted a mixture.

够做国王,结果尼禄就赢了。对于其他一些年轻人,他作出了各种各样的指示,这些命令都不令人难堪。但是他却命令布列塔尼库斯站起来,走到游戏场地的中央,唱一首歌。尼禄想将布列塔尼库斯作为嘲笑的对象,因为这个孩子在清醒的人之间都感到不习惯,更不用说是在醉汉们之间了。但是这一次布列塔尼库斯却唱了一首由诗歌所谱成的歌曲,内容中暗示自己从父亲的家中以及王位上被赶了出来。这引起了大家的同情,尤其是在彻夜的晚会之后大家处于坦率的氛围之中,这种同情就更加无遮无拦了。

尼禄知道布列塔尼库斯的这种情绪是针对于他的,因而对他的憎恨之情就更加剧烈了。尼禄虽然对于阿格里披娜的威逼非常反感,但是却难以找出罪名来控告自己的异父母的兄弟,更不敢公然将他处死。但是,他却决定暗中下手,他命人准备毒药将他毒死。奉命干此事的人是一名叫尤利乌斯·波里欧的近卫军将领。而他负责看管那一位臭名昭著且被判有罪的制造毒药的人洛库丝塔。很早被安排在布列塔尼库斯身边的侍从就是一些肆无忌惮的狂徒和一些毫无信义可言的人。第一个给他投毒的人就是他的老师,但是,或许是因为毒药太稀了,或许是因为毒性不够,从而没有马上发挥作用,而被排泄出来了。尼禄对于谋杀行动迟迟不能得手感到非常不耐烦,就威逼这位将领,并命人对洛库丝塔进行严刑拷打。尼禄抱怨这些人眼里只有公众对他们的看法,他们在想办法确保自己的安全,而把皇帝的安全放在了次要的地位。在这种情况之下,他们做出了保证,他们将立即采取行动,并使之产生像剑刺一样的立竿见影的效果。于是在与尼禄的卧室相连接的一间房子里,经过多次试验,他们配置出了一种混合型的毒药,效果非常好。

It was the custom for young imperial princes to eat with other noblemen's children of the same age at a special, less luxurious table,
before the eyes of their relations: that is where Britannicus dined. A
selected servant habitually tasted his food and drink. But the murderers thought of a way of leaving this custom intact without giving themselves away by a double death. Britannicus was handed a harmless
drink. The taster had tasted it; but Britannicus found it too hot, and
refused it. Then cold water containing the poison was added. Speechless, his whole body convulsed, he instantly ceased to breathe.

His companions were horrified. Some, uncomprehending, fled.
Others, understanding better, remained rooted in their places, staring
at Nero. He still lay back unconcernedly—and he remarked that this
often happened to epileptics; that Britannicus had been one since infancy; soon his sight and consciousness would return. Agrippina tried
to control her features. But their evident consternation and terror
showed that, like Britannicus' sister Octavia, she knew nothing.
Agrippina realized that her last support was gone. And here was Nero
murdering a relation. But Octavia, young though she was, had learnt
to hide sorrow, affection, every feeling. After a short silence the banquet continued.

Britannicus was cremated the night he died. Indeed, preparations

按照传统习惯,年幼的皇子们要跟其他一些与他们同龄的贵族子弟们当着亲属们的面吃饭,饭是在一张特制的、比较简朴的桌子面前吃的,而布列塔尼库斯也在此进食[1]。通常情况之下,会有一个挑选出来的侍从为布列塔尼库斯尝试饭菜和汤,于是,杀手们想出了一个办法,既可以避免改变这一传统规定,也可以避免使主仆二人同被毒死,从而不使自己的阴谋败露。他们首先递给了布列塔尼库斯一道无毒的汤,而且负责品尝的人也已经品尝过了。但是布列塔尼库斯发现这道汤太热了,就拒绝喝。然后就有人在里面加了一些掺了毒药的冷水。毒药在布列塔尼库斯的全身发作起来,接着就不能说话了,很快他就停止了呼吸。

与他一起吃饭的同伴们吓呆了。一些头脑简单的人吓得四散而逃。而另一些具有良好理解力的人则是坐在了原地没有动,拿眼睛盯着尼禄;他却是一副若无其事的样子倚靠在床上,并对此评论说,这种情况对于一个癫痫病人来说是常有的现象,而布列塔尼库斯从幼儿时期就患有这种疾病,过不了多久就会睁开眼睛、恢复神智的。阿格里披娜尽力地控制自己的面部表情,但是这些表情明显地带有痛苦和恐怖的神态,这就表明,她跟布列塔尼库斯的姐姐屋大维娅一样,对此事毫不知情。这时,阿格里披娜意识到她自己最后的支柱也失去了。而在此杀害自己亲属的人就是尼禄。但是对于屋大维娅来说,尽管还很年轻,却学会了将自己的悲伤、爱以及各种感情掩藏起来。晚宴在经过了短暂的沉默之后,接着又继续进行下去。

布列塔尼库斯在死亡的当天晚上就被火葬了。实际上,他那

---

[1] 按照当时宫廷的规矩,比他们年长的人则是倚在床上的。

for his inexpensive funeral had already been made. As his remains were placed in the Field of Mars, there erupted a violent storm. It was widely believed that the gods were showing their fury at the boy's murder—though even his fellow—men generally condoned it, arguing that brothers were traditional enemies and that the empire was indivisible. A number of contemporary writers assert that for a considerable time previously Nero had corrupted his victim. If so, his death might have seemed to come none too soon, and be the lesser outrage of the two.

Such was this hurried murder of the last of the Claudians, physically defiled, then poisoned right among the religious emblems on the table, before his enemy's eyes—without time even to give his sister a farewell kiss. Nero justified the hasty funeral by an edict recalling the traditional custom of withdrawing untimely deaths from the public gaze and not dwelling on them with eulogies and processions. Now that he had lost his brother's help, he added, all his hopes were centred on his country; senate and people must give all the greater support to their emperor, the only remaining member of his family, exalted by destiny. Then he distributed lavish gifts to his closest friends. Some were shocked when, at such a juncture, men of ethical pretensions accepted his distribution of town and country mansions like loot. Others thought they had no choice since the

简朴的丧礼所使用的用品事先早就准备好了。当他的骨灰被安置在玛尔斯原野[1]之时,发生了一场暴风雨。大家普遍认为,这是神灵对于这个孩子的被谋杀而表示出的愤怒。但是尼禄手下的人都在为他辩解,认为通常情况之下兄弟们都是仇敌,而皇权是不能够分享的。当时的许多作家则认为,在这个孩子死之前的相当长的一段时间之内,尼禄一直在折磨这一牺牲品。假如是这样的话,那么他的死亡就不能看做是太早,也不能看做是太过残酷的事情。

奥古斯都家族的最后一名男孩就这样急匆匆地死了,他在身体上经常遭受玷污,接着就在神圣的餐桌旁、在敌人的眼皮底下被毒死了,死之前甚至来不及向自己的姐姐拥抱、吻别。尼禄发表了一道敕令,解释为什么要匆忙地举行丧礼,他说回顾罗马的传统,是不能够让公众们看到这些夭折、早亡的孩子们的丧礼的,而且不能用对死者的赞辞和丧礼的绵长来拖延孩子的下葬时间。他进一步说,现在他已然丧失了兄弟的帮助,那么自己全部的希望就寄托在国家上面了,元老院和民众们必须要给他们的皇帝以更大的支持,因为命中注定要统治这个国家的家族的人之中,现在只有他一个人在世了。随后,他把丰厚的礼品赏赐给自己那些最亲密的朋友。有些人对此事感到非常的震惊,认为在这样的一个时刻,那些自命为道德高尚的人士竟然像分赃一样地接受皇帝所分给他们的在城中或乡下的房产。其他一些人则认为,他们是被迫接受的,因为皇帝在杀死了自己的弟弟之后,良心上感到非常的内疚,希望能够通过用慷慨赠赐的办法,使那些对于他

---

[1] 也就是说,他被安葬进了奥古斯都的陵墓之中。

emperor, with his guilty conscience, hoped for impunity if he could bind everyone of importance to himself by generous presents.

However, no generosity could mollify his mother. She became Octavia's supporter. Constantly meeting her own friends in secret, Agrippina outdid even her natural greed in grasping funds from all quarters to back her designs. She was gracious to officers, and attentive to such able and high-ranking noblemen as survived. She seemed to be looking round for a Party, and a leader for it. Learning this, Nero withdrew the military bodyguard which she had been given as empress and retained as the emperor's mother, and also the German guardsmen by which, as an additional compliment, it had recently been strengthened. Furthermore, he terminated her great receptions, by giving her a separate residence in the mansion formely occupied by Antonia (II). When he visited her there, he would bring an escort of staff-officers, hurriedly embrace her, and leave.

Veneration of another person's power, if it is ill-supported, is the most precarious and transient thing in the world. Agrippina's house was immediately deserted. Her only visitors and comforters were a few women, there because they loved her—or hated her. One of them was Junia Silana, whose separation from her husband Gaius Silius (II) by Messalina I have described. Noble, beautiful, and immoral, she had long been an intimate friend of Agrippina. Recently, however, an unspoken enmity had arisen between them, because Agrippina had

来说极端重要的人物都能够对他感恩戴德，从而取得他们肯定的宽恕。

然而，任何慷慨的赏赐都不能平息他的母亲的怒火。突然之间，她成为屋大维娅的支持者。阿格里披娜经常在私下里接见自己的朋友们，她甚至超出了平时的贪婪本性，更加疯狂地从四面八方敛取金钱，以为自己所策划的阴谋准备款项。她变得对官员们宽宏大量，对那些幸免于难的德高望重的贵族们则表示了尊重。这一些都在表明她正在到处拉拢人以成立一个党派，并想自己做此组织的领袖。对此，尼禄下令撤销她身边的一支军事卫队，这一卫队是她在做皇后时所配备，而做了皇太后之后仍然保留了下来的。尼禄又下令撤销了她身边的另一支卫队，这是一支日耳曼人卫队，是尼禄为了表示尊敬而给她配备的，而最近这支卫队的力量又得到了加强。而且，尼禄通过给予她一套单独的房子让她居住的办法，使她无法再召开大型的宴会。这套房子以前是属于安托尼娅（二世）的。当他到那儿去看望她的时候，总要带去一大批的百人团长，并且只是匆匆忙忙地与她拥抱一下就离开了。

以他人的力量而获得的尊荣，假如这一支持又很不可靠，那么这种尊荣就是世上最不稳固、最易消逝的东西。马上，阿格里披娜的住所就门可罗雀了。只有一些女人还去拜访她、安慰她，但是她们去的目的到底是因为爱她还是因为恨她则不得而知了。她们当中有一个名叫优尼娅·西拉娜的，前边我曾经讲过，她被美撒里娜从她的丈夫盖乌斯·西里乌斯（二世）身旁赶走了。作为一个高贵、美丽、放荡的女人，很久以来她就是阿格里披娜的亲密朋友。然而，最近一段时间，她们两人在心底里产生了敌对的情

deterred a young nobleman, Titus Sextius Africanus, from marrying Silana by describing her as immoral and past her prime. Agrippina did not want him for herself, but wanted to keep him from obtaining the childless Silana's wealth.

Silana now saw her chance of revenge. She put up two of her dependants, Iturius and Calvisius, to prosecute Agrippina. They avoided the old, frequently heard charges of her mourning Britannicus' death or proclaiming Octavia's wrongs. Instead they accused her of inciting Rubellius Plautus to revolution. This man, through his mother, possessed the same relationship to the divine Augustus as Nero did. Agrippina, the allegation was, proposed to marry Plautus and control the empire again. Nero's aunt Domitia-who was Agrippina's deadly rival-had a freed slave Atimetus who heard this story from the two prosecutors and urged the ballet-dancer Paris (another of Domitia's former slaves) to go speedily and divulge the plot to the emperor, in sensational terms.

It was late at night when Paris entered. Nero had long been drinking. This was the time Paris usually came, to enliven the emperor's dissipations. Tonight, however, Paris wore a gloomy expression; and he told his story in detail. The emperor, listening in

绪,原因就是阿格里披娜曾经阻止一个名叫塞克斯提乌斯·阿非利卡努斯的年轻贵族与西拉娜结婚,她把西拉娜描绘成为一位道德堕落、人老珠黄的女人。阿格里披娜之所以这样做,并不是为了将这一位年轻人留作自己享用,而是不想让这一位年轻人获得没有子嗣的西拉娜的巨额财富。

西拉娜现在终于找到报仇的机会了。她唆使自己手下的两名食客伊图里乌斯和卡尔维西乌斯站出来控告阿格里披娜。他们控告阿格里披娜的罪名并不是像长久以来就不断传说的那样,即说她哀悼布列塔尼库斯的死或者是公开宣布屋大维娅所遭受的不公正的待遇。实际上,他们控告她的罪名是她鼓动过路贝里乌斯·普劳图斯发动叛乱,普劳图斯从其母亲一方的血缘关系来看,与圣奥古斯都的关系与尼禄与圣奥古斯都的关系是相同的。[1] 控告者说阿格里披娜想嫁给普劳图斯进而再度控制这个帝国。尼禄的姑姑是多米提娅,她一直是阿格里披娜的死对头,她有一个被释奴隶叫阿提美图斯,他从这两个控告者的嘴里听说了这件事情之后,就唆使芭蕾舞演员帕利斯(多米提娅的另一个被释奴隶)赶忙赶到皇帝那儿去,用一些耸人听闻的话语将这一阴谋泄露给了皇帝。

当帕利斯赶到的时候已经是深夜,而尼禄已经狂饮很长时间了。帕利斯通常都是在这一时间赶来的,目的是为了给皇帝的放荡生活增加乐趣。然而今天晚上,帕里斯的表情却装出一副非常悲伤的样子,他把这一阴谋非常详细地告诉了尼禄。皇帝听后非常害

---

〔1〕 因为他是路贝里乌斯·勃兰都斯和杜路苏斯的女儿优利娅的儿子,因此他是提贝里乌斯的曾孙辈,是提贝里乌斯的继父奥古斯都的玄孙辈,而尼禄作为母系的直接后裔同奥古斯都处于同样的亲属关系。

terror, resolved to kill his mother, to kill Plautus, and also to depose Burrus from the command of the Guard, as being a supporter and nominee of Agrippina. One historian, Fabius Rusticus, claims that Nero had actually written a letter of appointment to a proposed successor of Burrus, Gaius Caecina Tuscus, and that it was only through Seneca's influence that Burrus retained his post. But this authority favours Seneca, whose friendship had made his career; and two others writers, Pliny the Elder and Cluvius Rufus, report no doubts of Burrus' loyalty. (My plan is to indicate such individual sources only when they differ. When they are unanimous, I shall follow them without citation.)

Nero was so alarmed and eager to murder his mother that he only agreed to be patient when Burrus promised that, if she was found guilty, she should die. But Burrus pointed out that everyone must be given an opportunity for defence—especially a parent; and that at present there were no prosecutors but only the report of one man, from a household unfriendly to her. Nero should reflect, he added, that it was late and they had spent a convivial night, and that the whole story had an air of recklessness and ignorance.

This calmed the emperor's fears. Next morning, Burrus visited Agrippina to acquaint her with the accusation and tell her she must refute it or pay the penalty. Burrus did this in Seneca's presence; certain ex-slaves were also there as witnesses. Burrus named the charges

怕,下定决心要杀死自己的母亲、杀死普劳图斯,另外还决心要解除布路斯的近卫军长官的职务,因为他是阿格里披娜的支持者,同时近卫军长官的职务也是阿格里披娜任命的。根据一位名字叫法比乌斯·路斯提库斯的历史学家的说法,尼禄确实曾经发布过一道诏令,任命盖乌斯·凯奇纳·图斯库斯作为继承者从而代替布路斯,是由于塞内加的干涉,布路斯才得以保住自己的职位。无论如何,布路斯都过分盛赞塞内加,他是因为与塞内加的友谊而得以步步高升的;而另外两位作家,老普利尼和克路维乌斯·路福斯则对于布路斯的忠诚毫不怀疑。(而我的写作计划是只要这些作家们的说法出现了不同,我就会将他们每个人的说法都列举出来;当他们的说法都一样时,我就会遵从他们的说法,不再引用原话。)

尼禄是如此惊恐,他急于想杀死自己的母亲,直到布路斯向他作出了保证,只要是发现阿格里披娜确实有罪,马上就会处死她,这时才同意再忍耐一会儿。但是,布路斯指出,每一个人都应该得到机会为自己作出辩解,尤其是作为一个皇帝的母亲;而且,在目前的情况下,没有其他人对此提出指控,只有一个来自阿格里披娜仇人家中的人所进行的控告。他进一步说,尼禄应该考虑到,夜已经很深了,而且他们度过了一个狂欢之夜,在此时整个的事件都带有一种轻率和无知的氛围。

这些话使尼禄那惊恐的心情平静了下来。第二天早晨,布路斯就到阿格里披娜那儿去了,就对她指控的事情向她进行了询问,然后告诉她必须举出例子加以反驳或者是承认自己的罪行而接受处罚。布路斯是当着塞内加的面说这些话的,还有一些被释奴隶也在场,可以作为证人。布路斯将对她的指控和指控者的

and the accusers, and adopted a menacing air. But Agrippina displayed her old spirit. ' Junia Silana has never had a child ' , she said, ' so I am not surprised she does not understand a mother's feelings ! For mothers change their sons less easily than loose women change their lovers. If Silana's dependants Iturius and Calvisius, after exhausting their means, can only repay the hag's favours by becoming accusers, is that a reason for darkening my name with my son's murder, or loading the emperor's conscience with mine?

' As for Domitia, I should welcome her hostility if she were competing with me in kindness to my Nero—instead of concocting melodramas with her lover Atimetus and the dancer Paris. While I was planning Nero's adoption and promotion to consular status and designation to the consulship, and all the other preparations for his accession, she was beautifying her fish-ponds at her beloved Baiae.

' I defy anyone to convict me of tampering with city police or provincial loyalty, or of inciting slaves and ex-slaves to crimes. If Britannicus had become emperor could I ever have survived? If Rubellius Plautus or another gained the throne and became my judge, there would be no lack of accusers! For then I should be charged, not with occasional indiscretions-outbursts of uncontrollable love-but with crimes which no one can pardon except a son! '

Agrippina's listeners were touched, and tried to calm her excitement. But she demanded to see her son. To him, she offered no defence,

名字作了陈述后，就开始采用一种威胁性的态度向她问话。但是，阿格里披娜将她过去所具有的那种精神展现了出来，她说："优尼娅·西拉娜从来就没有生过孩子，因此我对她不了解一个母亲的感情这件事情一点儿也不感到吃惊。对于一个母亲来说，更换自己的孩子这件事情的难度并不比女人失去了自己的情人小。假如优尼娅·西拉娜的两位食客伊图里乌斯和卡尔维西乌斯在耗尽了自己所有的家产之后，想通过变成一个控告者的方式来报答这一老丑妇的关爱的话，难道说这就成为一个理由来控告我要谋杀我的儿子从而损坏我的名声，或者说使皇帝谋杀自己的母亲从而加重其良心的负担的一个理由？

"至于说多米提娅，假如她想与我展开竞赛看谁更疼爱我的尼禄，而不是勾结她的情夫阿提美图斯和芭蕾舞演员帕利斯一起来上演这一幕喜剧的话，我倒是欢迎她这种敌对行为的。当我正在设法使尼禄得以过继，得以提升为总督，以及得以就任执政官的时候，以及做着各种各样的谋划以为他获取皇位的时候，她则是正在她所喜欢的拜阿伊那里美化自己的鱼池呢。

"至于有人控告我，说我贿赂罗马城的守卫、损害行省的忠诚、引诱奴隶和被释奴隶进行违法犯罪活动，对此我公然予以蔑视。假如布列塔尼库斯成为皇帝，我就能够幸免于难？假如路贝里乌斯·普劳图斯或其他任何的人获得了帝位而对我进行审问的话，肯定不会缺少控诉者的！而到那时，我所受到的指控就不是由于难以自控的爱而偶然说出的不得体的话，而是除了一个儿子之外没有人肯原谅的罪名了。"

阿格里披娜的话使在场的人听了都很感动，他们都极力平息她的激动情绪。但是她提出了要求去见自己的儿子。面对着皇帝，她

no reminder of her services. For the former might have implied misgivings, the latter reproach. Instead she secured rewards for her supporters—and revenge on her accusers. Junia Silana, on the other hand, was exiled, her dependants Iturius and Calvisius expelled, Atimetus executed. Paris played too important a part in the emperor's debaucheries to be punished. Rubellius Plautus was left unnoticed- for the present. Publius Antcius, appointed imperial governor of Syria, was put off by various devices and finally kept in Rome. Faenius Rufus was given control of the food supply, Arruntius Stella given the Games projected by the emperor, and Tiberius Claudius Balbillus made imperial governor of Egypt.

Pallas and Burrus were charged with conspiring to give the empire to Faustus Cornelius Sulla Felix, because of his great name and marriage link with Claudius, whose daughter Claudia Antonia was his wife. The accusation originated with a certain Pactus, notorious for acquiring confiscated properties from the Treasury. His story was clearly untrue. But Pallas's innocence did not cause much satisfaction because of the disgust provoked by his arrogance. For when certain ex-slaves in his household were denounced as his accomplices, Pallas replied that all orders in his home were given by nods or waves of the hand-when more detailed instructions were required he wrote them, to avoid personal contact. Burrus, though himself among the accused, was one of the judges, and pronounced acquittal. The informer was banished, and his records unearthing forgotten debts to the Treasury were burnt.

既没有为自己进行辩护,也没有提及自己的功劳。因为前者会表明自己的担惊害怕,而后者会含有责备的意味。相反,她为支持她的人谋取了奖励,而对于那些控告她的人则是进行了报复。另一方面,优尼娅·西拉娜遭到了驱逐,她的两名食客伊图里乌斯和卡尔维西乌斯则被开除,阿提美图斯则被处死,而芭蕾舞演员帕利斯因在皇帝的放荡生活之中扮演了过分重要的角色,而免于处罚。路贝里乌斯·普劳图斯没有予以追究,但这也只是暂时的事情。普布里乌斯·安泰乌斯被任命为叙利亚的长官,但是他提出了各种借口进行拖延,最终也就留在了罗马。法伊尼乌斯·路福斯授权管理粮食供应问题,阿尔伦提乌斯·司提拉受皇帝之命主持筹备之中的赛会,提贝里乌斯·克劳狄乌斯·巴尔比路斯被任命为埃及长官。

有人控告帕拉斯和布路斯阴谋拥立法乌司图斯·科尔涅里乌斯·苏拉·费里克斯做皇帝,因为他具有高贵的出身以及与克劳狄乌斯具有联姻关系,克劳狄乌斯的女儿克劳狄娅·安托尼娅就是他的妻子。提出这一控告的是一个名叫帕克图斯的人,此人因经常从国库之中购买被没收的财产而臭名昭著。很明显,他所捏造的这一罪名是不真实的。但是,帕拉斯的无罪并没有引起大众太多的高兴,因为他的傲慢引起了人们的反感。当他的一些被释奴隶被指控与他一起阴谋叛乱的时候,他则回答道,在他的家里,所有的命令都是通过点头或者是摇手的方式传达的,当需要进一步作出详细的指示的时候,他会写出来让他们看,这样就能避免与他们有过于亲密的接触。而布路斯虽然也是被告之一,但是却参加了审判。提出指控的人被判处放逐的处罚,但是,他的账目却烧毁了,里面记录了那些已经揭露出来的、人们已经忘记了的应该上缴国库的债务。

At the end of the year the battalion of the Guard customarily present at the Games was withdrawn. The intention was to give a greater impression of freedom, to improve discipline by removing the Guardsmen from the temptations of public displays, and to test whether the public would behave respectably without their restraint. The temples of Jupiter and Minerva were struck by lightning.

The emperor consulted diviners and on their recommendation conducted a purification of the city.

The consuls for the following year were Quintus Voluaius Saturnius and Publius Cornelius Lentulus Scipio (Ⅱ). The year was a time of peace abroad, but disgusting excesses by Nero in Rome. Disguised as a slave, he ranged the streets, brothels, and taverns with his friends, who pilfered goods from shops and assaulted wayfarers. Their identity was unsuspected: indeed, as marks on his face testified, Nero himself was struck. When it became known that the waylayer was the emperor, attacks on distinguished men and women multiplied. For, since disorderliness was tolerated, pseudo-Neros mobilized gangs and behaved similarly, with impunity. Rome by night came to resemble a conquered city.

A senator called Julius Montanus, who had not yet held office, assaulted by the emperor in the dark, hit back vigorously. But then Montanus recognized his assailant and apologized. However his

这一年的年底,通常会在赛会期间出现的大队的近卫军撤销了。此举的目的是为了给人留下更加自由的印象,是为了不使近卫军士兵们受到剧场中观众的不文明行为的诱惑而败坏了纪律,同时也是为了考验一下公众们在没有近卫军对他们的行为进行监视的情况下举止是否彬彬有礼。

朱庇特神庙和米涅尔瓦神庙遭受了雷击。皇帝让占卜人进行了占卜,在他们的建议之下,皇帝为罗马城举行了驱邪仪式。

下一年,是由克温图斯·沃路西乌斯·撒图尔尼乌斯和普布里乌斯·考尔奈里乌斯·楞图路斯·斯奇比奥(二世)担任执政官。[1] 在这一年的时间里,国外没有战争,处于和平时期。但是,尼禄在罗马城却是放荡不羁。在一群朋友的陪伴之下,他将自己打扮成为一名奴隶,游荡于街头、妓院、酒楼。他们经常偷窃商店里的货物、攻击路上的行人。大伙都不知他们的身份,尼禄本人就曾遭受过攻击,而被打得鼻青脸肿就是明证。当知道了在街上打劫的人就是皇帝本人以后,大众对于显贵的男女的攻击就越来越多了。既然为所欲为的事情容许存在,于是一些人就假借尼禄的名义鼓动一些狐朋狗党做出跟尼禄他们同样的举动,也没有人处罚他们。夜晚的罗马变得就像敌人占据之下的一座城市。

一名还没有担任过官职的元老尤利乌斯·蒙塔努斯,在黑暗中受到了皇帝的攻击,于是进行了激烈的还击。但是当蒙塔努斯认出了向他攻击的人是谁的时候,赶忙赔礼道歉;然而,他的

---

〔1〕 罗马建城 809 年,即公元 56 年。

apology was interpreted as a slur, and he was forced to commit suicide. Yet the incident diminished Nero's boldness. In future he surrounded himself with soldiers and masses of gladiators, and these, while holding aloof from minor semi-private brawls, intervened forcibly whenever the victims showed vigorous resistance.

In the theatre, there were brawls between gangs favouring rival ballet-dancers. Nero converted these disorders into serious warfare. For he waived penalties and offered prizes-watching in person, secretly and on many occasions even openly. Finally, however, public animosities and fears of worse disturbances left no alternative but to expel these dancers from Italy and station troops in the theatre again.

About this time the senate discussed the offences offormer slaves. It was demanded that patrons should be empowered to re-enslave undeserving ex-slaves. The proposal had widespread support. But the consuls did not dare to put the motion without consulting the emperor, to whom they wrote stating the senate's view. Since his advisers, though few, were divided, Nero hesitated to give a ruling. One side denounced the disrespectfulness of liberated slaves. 'It goes to such lengths', they said, 'that former slaves confront their patron with the choice of yielding them their rights by legal argument, as equals, or by force. Freed slaves even lift their hands to strike their former master-and sarcastically urge their own punishment. For all that an injured patron may do is to send his freed slave away beyond the hun-

道歉被看成是一种辱骂,于是他被迫自杀了。但这一事故也使尼禄减少了自己的鲁莽行为。以后再出去时,身边就有一些士兵和一大批剑奴相伴,假如与他人发生了半私人性质的、小规模的争吵,他们就会站在一边旁观,而如果遭受攻击的人进行了猛烈的抵抗,他们就会以武力进行干预。

在剧院里,在捧角的人和芭蕾舞演员们之间经常发生争吵。尼禄使得这些争吵简直就达到了正规战争的程度,因为他对此不是给予惩罚,而是给予奖励。他经常亲自去观看他们之间所发生的争吵,有时候是秘密的,也有许多时候甚至是公开地观看。最后由于民众的憎恨情绪以及怕由此引起更大的骚乱,当局别无选择,只好把这些演员们驱逐出意大利,并且又重新在剧院内驻扎了军队。

大约在同时,元老院讨论了被释奴隶冒犯自己的主人的问题。有人提议,假如被释奴隶不能配得上这一称号,他先前的主人就有权利重新使他变为奴隶。这一提议得到了广泛的支持。执政官们将元老院的意见写信向皇帝作了汇报,但是在没有皇帝的批准之前,他们又不敢进行表决。尼禄身边的顾问们虽然很少,但却各自持有不同的意见,这使得尼禄很犹豫,难以做出决定。一方的观点认为,被释奴隶简直是目无尊长,无法无天。他们说:"事情已经发展到了非常严重的程度,以至于被释奴隶们迫使他们的旧主人们做出抉择:要么通过法律控诉的方法,要么通过武力的手段使主人们做出让步,从而授予他们平等的权利。取得了自由的奴隶们有时候甚至还动手打他们以前的主人,而且挖苦地说这是他们理应得到的惩罚。对于被释奴隶的这一切所作所为,受到了伤害的旧主人们唯一的办法就是将他们遣送到100英里

dredth milestone-to the Campanian beaches! In all other respects the two men are legally equal and identical. Patrons ought to be given a weapon which cannot be disregarded. It would be no hardship for the liberated to have to keep their freedom by the same respectful behaviour which won it for them. Indeed, blatant offenders ought to be enslaved again, so as to frighten the ungrateful into obedience. '

The opposite argument went thus: ' The guilty few ought to suffer, but not to the detriment of freed slaves' rights in general. For ex-slaves are everywhere. They provide the majority of the voters, public servants, attendants of officials and priests, watchmen, firemen. Most knights, many senators, are descended from former slaves. Segregate the freed-and you will only show how few free-born there are! When our ancestors fixed degrees of rank, they were right to make everyone free. Besides, two sorts of liberation were instituted to leave room for second thoughts or favour. Some were liberated "by the wand", those who were not remained half-slaves. Slave-owners ought to consider individual merits, but be slow to grant what is irrevocable. '

之外的地方去,送到康帕尼亚的海岸地带去![1] 在其他所有的方面,旧主人和被释奴隶都具有平等的甚至是完全相同的法律权利。应该授予旧主人们武器使他们保护自己不受轻视。被释奴隶们用使自己取得自由的恭恭敬敬的行为,保持自己的自由地位,这将不是一件很困难的事情。确实是,那些肆无忌惮的罪犯们理应再次沦为奴隶,这样才能够震慑住那些忘恩负义的小人,从而使他们变得驯服起来。"

另一些人表达了与此相反的观点:"对于少数的罪犯,理应予以惩罚。但不要使全部取得自由的奴隶的权利受到损害。因为社会上处处充满了被释奴隶。投票人、公职人员、官僚和祭司们的助手、巡夜人以及消防员,这些人绝大多数是被释奴隶。而且大多数的骑士、许多元老们也都是被释奴隶的后裔。假如将被释奴隶划出去,你就会发现真正的自由人是多么少啊!我们的祖先在确定各个阶级的地位之时,他们非常明智地规定每个人都有机会获得自由。除此之外,又规定了两种解放奴隶的方式,[2]以便于为主人们改变想法或施恩留有余地。一些奴隶是通过'杖式解放'的方式获得自由的,而另一些没有经过此一仪式的,可以说仍旧处于半奴隶的身份。奴隶主们应该对每一个奴隶的优缺点进行认真的考虑,要慎重授予那一旦给予就不可收回的自由。"

---

〔1〕 因为这里是意大利最舒适的地方,也是犯了罪的人最喜欢去的地方,所以这种说法含着讽刺的意味。

〔2〕 当时解放奴隶的方法分为正式、彻底的方法和非正式、非彻底的方法。前者又可以分作:(1)"杖式解放",主人将杖放在奴隶的头上以示给予他们自由;(2)检察官将奴隶们的名字列入公民的名单之中;(3)通过正式立下遗嘱的方式。后者包括:(1)作口头的声明,但必须要有证人在场;(2)签署一项文书;(3)奴隶和其主人共餐。

This opinion prevailed. Nero wrote asking the senate to give separate consideration to every charge by a patron, but not to diminish the rights of ex-slaves in general. Soon afterwards his aunt Domitia was deprived of the patronage of her former slave Paris, ostensibly on legal grounds. He was pronounced free-born, on the orders of the emperor-whose reputation suffered thereby.

Nevertheless there were still signs of a free country. A dispute arose between a praetor, Vibullius, and a tribune, Antistius Sosianus, because the latter had ordered the release of some of the disorderly followers of ballet-dancers. The praetor had imprisoned these hangers-on, and the senate backed him, censuring the tribune for irregularity. They also forbade tribunes to encroach on the authority of praetors and consuls, or to summon Italian litigants to Rome in cases where local settlement was practicable. The consul-designate Lucius Calpurnius Piso (V) added proposals that tribunes should not exercise their powers in their own homes, and that fines imposed by them should not be entered in the Treasury records for four months, during which time objections could be lodged for adjudication by the consuls. The powers of aediles, too, were curtailed, limits being fixed to the sums which 'curule' aediles and aediles of the people could distrain or fine. Moreover a quaestor in charge of the Treasury, Helvidius Priscus (II), was quarrelling with a tribune, Obultronius Sabinus, who charged him with over-rigorous compulsory sales of poor men's property. Thereupon the emperor transferred the Treasury and public accounts from quaestors to commissioners who were experienced former praetors. The control of the Treasury has undergone numerous changes. Augustus entrusted it to commissioners selected by the senate. Later, when

后一种观点取得了胜利。尼禄向元老院写了回信,要求对那些旧主人们对于被释奴隶所提出的每一种指控要区别对待,不要整个地取消他们的权利。不久之后,他的姑姑多米提娅便被剥夺了对于被释奴隶帕利斯的主人的身份,从表面上来看,这一行动是有法律依据的。皇帝发了一道诏令,宣布他是生而自由的人,此举对于皇帝的声誉造成了严重的损害。

虽然如此,还是有一些自由国家的氛围的。行政长官维布里乌斯和保民官安提司提乌斯·索西亚努斯之间发生了一次争吵,因为后者下令将一些闹事的芭蕾舞演员们的追随者释放了。是行政长官下令将这些食客们关进监狱里去的,元老院支持这一举动,同时谴责了保民官的多事。他们还做出了规定,禁止保民官干涉行政长官和执政官们所具有的权限;同时规定,假如在当地可以自行解决的问题就不要将意大利的诉讼当事人传唤到罗马城来。新当选的执政官路奇乌斯·凯尔普尔尼乌斯·披索(五世)又提出了一项建议,要求保民官不能在自己的家中行使自己的权力,他们所罚的款项,只有在登记注册4个月之后才可以进入国库,在此期间人们可以提出反对的意见,而由执政官做出最后的裁决。营造官的权力也受到了限制,对于高级营造官或平民营造官所能规定的保证金和罚款金进行了具体的限制。还有,由于保民官奥布尔特罗尼乌斯·撒比努斯控告管理国库的财务官赫尔维狄乌斯·普利斯库斯(二世),说他过分无情地强迫拍卖穷人的财产,由此两人发生了争吵。于是,皇帝将管理国库和公共财物的权力从财务官手中转移到了以前曾经担任过行政长官的国库官的手中。国库的管理权已经经历了多次的变化。奥古斯都委任由元老院选举所

improper canvassing was suspected, they were chosen by lot from the praetors. But the lot could fall on incompetent men, so this arrangement too was short-lived. Claudius returned the post to quaestors. However, thinking they might prove inactive through fear of giving offence, he promised them exceptional promotion. But the young men lacked the maturity for so important a first post.

A governor of Sardinia, Vipsanius Laenas, was found guilty of fraudulence (also in this year). However, a governor of Achaia, Cestius Proculus, charged by the Cretans with extortion, was exonerated. The fleet-commander at Ravenna, Publius Palpellius Clodius Quirinalis, who had inflicted his savagery and debauchery on Italy as if it were the humblest of subject territories, poisoned himself to forestall condemnation. Cininius Rebilus, outstanding in legal learning and wealth, escaped the miseries of invalid old age by opening his veins. No one had thought he had the courage for this, because of his notorious effeminacy. Lucius Volusius Saturninus (II) also died, leaving a distinguished reputation and a great fortune, honestly won. He had lived to ninety-three and avoided the malevolence of every emperor.

Next year, when the consuls were Nero (for the second time) and Lucius Calpurnius Piso (V), little worth recording occurred, except in the eyes of historians who like filling their pages with praise of the foundations and beams of Nero's huge amphitheatre in the Field of Mars. But that is material for official gazettes, whereas it has traditionally been judged fitting to Rome's grandeur that its histories should

产生的官员担任国库官。后来由于害怕发生营私舞弊的行为,就改为从行政长官之中通过抽签的方式决定人选。但是,中签者很有可能是那些不能够胜任的人,因此,这一方法施行了很短的时间。克劳狄乌斯又将这一权力交回给了财务官,但是,考虑到这些官员们有可能因为怕得罪人而消极怠工,他向他们许诺,他们可以获得破格升迁的机会。但是,一开始担任这一如此重要职位的人都是一些缺乏经验的年轻人。

撒丁尼亚长官维普撒尼乌斯·莱纳斯被发现犯有贪污受贿的行为(也就是在这一年)。然而,被克里特人控告犯有勒索罪的阿凯亚长官凯司提乌斯·普洛库鲁斯被宣告无罪。驻扎在拉温那的舰队司令是普布里乌斯·帕尔博尔里乌斯·克洛狄乌斯·克维里那里斯,此人曾经野蛮而残暴地蹂躏过意大利,就好像意大利是一个最为卑贱的人所居住的地区,他在遭到控告而没有作出判决之前就服毒自尽了。奇尼尼乌斯·列比路斯是一个在法律学识和财富方面都很突出的人物,为了逃避多病的老年岁月的不幸而切断血管自杀了。因为他那臭名昭著的浑身所散发出来的女人气,没有人会相信他有勇气做出这一事情。路奇乌斯·沃路西乌斯·塞图尔尼努斯(二世)也过世了,身后留下了光荣的名声、通过诚实劳动所获得的巨额财富,他一直活到 93 岁,巧妙地避开了每一个皇帝所造成的恶毒的伤害。

第二年是尼禄(这是第二次了)和路奇乌斯·凯尔普尔尼乌斯·披索(五世)担任执政官的一年,[1] 在这一年里,没有发生什么值得记录的大事。但是在历史学家的眼里,也许会喜欢将尼禄在玛尔斯原野所修建的巨大的半圆形剧场的基座和粗大的横梁的赞

---

〔1〕 罗马建城 810 年、即公元 57 年。

contain only important events. Drafts of ex-soldiers were sent to two I-talian settlements, Capua and Nuceria. The city population were given a bonus of four hundred sesterces a head. Forty million sesterces were paid into the Treasury to maintain public credit. The 4 per cent tax on the purchase of slaves was waived (though its removal was a fiction, since the tax was only shifted to the dealers, who increased their prices accordingly).

The emperor also published instructions that no provincial official, in his province, should give shows of gladiators or wild beasts, or any other display. For hitherto this ostensible generosity had been as oppressive to provincials as extortion, the governors' intention being to win partisans to screen their irregularities. The senate also passed a ptmitive and precautionary measure. If a man was murdered by his slaves, those liberated by his will—if they were in the house-were to be executed with the rest.

At this time a former consul Lurius Varus, formerly convicted of extortion, was restored to his rank. The distinguished lady Pomponia Graecina, wife of Aulus Plautius—whose official ovation for British victories I have mentioned—was charged with foreign superstition and referred to her husband for trial. Following ancient tradition he decided her fate and reputation before her kinsmen, and acquitted her. But her long life was continuously unhappy. For after the murder, by Messalina's intrigues, of her relative Livia Julia—daughter of Drusus—she wore mourning and grieved unceasingly for forty years. This escaped punishment under Claudius, and thereafter gave her prestige.

美之词写在自己所编的史册上。但是,这类事件只能作为官方的记录素材,而按照传统上罗马人的尊严,历史家们所值得记录的应该只是一些重大的历史事件。一批老兵被送到了卡普亚和努凯里亚这两个意大利移民地去了;所有的城市人每人都获得了400谢司特尔提乌斯的赏赐;4000万谢司特尔提乌斯被缴入国库,以维持公共信誉;购买奴隶时所征收的4%的税也被取消了(但是这种取消也只是一种骗局,因为这部分的税全部转到了卖者的身上去了,而卖者也就相应的提高了出卖价格)。

皇帝还发布了诏令,规定任何的行省官员,在本省之内都不得举办剑斗、同野兽的搏斗以及其他任何的表演。因为,以前的这一表面上的慷慨做法与对于行省居民们的压迫剥削和勒索同样严重。而行省官员们这样做的目的只不过是为了讨好民众,以掩盖他们的违法乱纪的行为而已。元老院还通过了一项惩罚性和预防性的措施。假如一个人被他自己的奴隶谋杀了,那些根据主人的遗嘱已经获得了解放的奴隶,假如他们还留在主人家中的话,就要同其他所有的奴隶一道被处死。

在这一时候,以前因为勒索罪而被撤了职的前执政官路里乌斯·法鲁斯又官复原职。在前面我所提及的那位在不列颠之战中获得了胜利,从而举行了小凯旋仪式的奥路斯·普劳提乌斯的妻子彭波尼娅·格莱奇娜,是一位出身高贵的夫人,她被指控为从事外国的宗教迷信,从而交由自己的丈夫进行审讯。奥路斯·普劳提乌斯在她的亲属们面前对她进行了审问,以决定她的命运和名誉,并最终宣布她无罪。但是,她那漫长的一生却不断地处于悲伤之中。因为,自从她的亲戚杜路苏斯的女儿利维娅·优利娅被美撒里娜设计谋害之后,40年来,她一直穿着

The same year witnessed several prosecutions. Publius Celer was accused by the province of Asia. He, as I have mentioned, had been the murderer of his governor Marcus Junius Silanus (II)—a great e-nough crime to overshadow his other misdeeds. Nero could not acquit him. Instead he protracted the case until Celer died of old age. Coss-utianus Capito was indicted by the Cilicians. This vicious and disrep-utable individual believed he could behave as outrageously in his province as in Rome. Defeated, however, by determined prosecutors, he abandoned his defence and was condemned under the extortion law. The Lycians claimed damages from Titus Clodius Eprius Marcel-lus. But his intrigues were so effective that some of his accusers were exiled for endangering an innocent man.

Nero's colleague in his third consulship was Marcus Valerius Messalla Corvinus (II), whose great-grandfather, the orator of the same name, a few old men remembered as consular colleague of Ne-ro's great-great-grandfather the divine Augustus. The reputation of Messalla's distinguished family was now buttressed by an annual grant of half a million sesterces to enable him to support his poverty honestly. The emperor also conferred annuities on two other senators, Aurelius Cotta and Quintus Haterius Antoninus, though both had squandered their inherited fortunes by extravagance.

At the beginning of the year the war between Rome and Parthia

丧服,悲伤不已。而这一举动不但没有受到克劳狄乌斯的处罚,而且后来还成了她的荣耀。

这一年,见证了许多人遭受迫害。亚细亚行省的居民们对普布里乌斯·凯列尔进行了指控。对于此人,我在前面已经作过交代,他谋杀了自己的长官,亚细亚总督玛尔库斯·尤尼乌斯·西拉努斯(二世),这一罪行如此之大,以至于将他所犯的其他罪行都遮盖住了。连尼禄都无法为他开脱。于是,皇帝对此案件一直拖延,直到凯列尔老死为止。而奇里奇亚的人则控告了科苏提亚努斯·卡皮托,这个邪恶而又令人讨厌的家伙竟然认为在自己的行省之中,可以像在罗马一样胡作非为。但是,在坚决顽强的控告者们的努力之下,他败诉了,只好放弃了辩护,并依照反勒索法而被宣判有罪。吕奇亚人要求提图斯·克劳狄乌斯·埃普里乌斯·玛尔凯路斯对他们所造成的伤害进行赔偿。但是他所施展的阴谋手段如此有效,以至于使一些控告他的人被判因为陷害无辜的人而被流放。

尼禄第三次担任执政官时[1]的同僚是玛尔库斯·瓦列里乌斯·美撒拉·科尔维努斯(二世),他的曾祖父是一位与他同样出名的演说家,一些老人还依稀记得,他作为执政官是与尼禄的高祖圣奥古斯都作同僚。现在,美撒拉每年从国家领取 50 万谢司特尔提乌斯作为补助,以支持他那诚实但很贫穷的生活,这使他的显贵家族的声誉可以得到提升了。对于其他两名元老奥列里乌斯·科塔和库伊恩图斯·哈提里乌斯·安托尼努斯,尼禄还每年给他们提供补助,尽管这两个人是由于奢侈腐化而将所继承的家产挥霍殆尽。

---

〔1〕 罗马建城 811 年,即公元 58 年。

for the possession of Armenia, in abeyance after a half-hearted start, was energetically resumed. For Vologeses I of Parthia would allow his brother Tiridates neither to lose the Armenian throne, which he had given him; nor to hold it as the gift of a foreign power; whereas Cnaeus Domitius Corbulo (II) felt that the grandeur of Rome required the recovery of the territories once conquered by Lucius Licinius Lucullus and Pompey. Furthermore, the Armenians were divided in allegiance and asked both sides in. But their geographical position and way of life inclined them to the Parthians; and with Parthians they had intermarried. So those were the masters they preferred. Of freedom they knew nothing.

Corbulo found his own men's slackness a worse trouble than enemy treachery. His troops had come from Syria. Demoralized by years of peace, they took badly to service conditions. The army actually contained old soldiers who had never been on guard or watch, who found ramparts and ditches strange novelties, and who owned neither helmet nor breastplate—flashy money-makers who had soldiered in towns. Corbulo discharged men who were too old or too weak, and filled their places with Galatian and Cappadocian recruits, augmented by a brigade from Germany with auxiliary infantry and cavalry. The whole army was kept under canvas through a winter so severe that ice had to be removed and the ground excavated before tents could be pitched. Frostbite caused many losses of limbs. Sentries were frozen to death. A soldier was seen carrying a bundle of firewood with hands so frozen that they fell off, fastened to their load.

这一年的开始,罗马和帕尔提亚为了争夺亚美尼亚而展开了战争,开始的时候战争半死不活,接着就是拖拖拉拉,但是现在战争变得非常激烈了。因为帕尔提亚的沃洛吉西斯一世既不想让他的兄弟提里达特斯失去他所赠予的亚美尼亚王位,也不想把这一王位看做是外国所赠予的礼物;而格涅乌斯·多米提乌斯·科尔布罗(二世)却认为,罗马的尊严要求恢复占领以前路奇乌斯·里奇尼乌斯·路库鲁斯和庞培所曾经征服过的领土。而且,亚美尼亚人将自己的忠诚分作了两半,要求双方的军队都进入本国。但是,从地理位置和生活方式来看,他们更倾向于帕尔提亚人。而且他们与帕尔提亚人互相通婚。因此,他们更愿意选择帕尔提亚人作为他们的主人。他们对于所谓的自由根本就一无所知。

科尔布罗发现,对于他手下的人来说,更大、更紧迫的困难在于克服那种松散无纪律的状态,而不是击败敌人的阴谋。他手下的军队来自叙利亚,由于多年的和平环境使这些军人变得萎靡不振,他们对于服役的环境感到非常讨厌。实际上,这支部队包括了一些从来就没有放过哨或担任过值班任务的老兵。在他们看来,壁垒和壕沟就是一些奇怪而又新鲜的东西,而且他们既没有头盔也没有胸甲,他们是一些只在城市中服过役,并且只知穿戴和敛钱的士兵。科尔布罗将那些年纪太老、身体太过虚弱的士兵从部队中清洗掉了,然后将他们的位置用一些从加拉提亚和卡帕多奇亚人之中征集来的部队予以补充,然后又从日耳曼调来了一个军团,加上这一军团的辅助步兵和骑兵。全军在营地之中度过了整个冬季,而这一年的冬天是如此的寒冷,必须要掘开冻土才能安营扎寨。一些士兵在冻伤之后,四肢就失去了,而有一些放哨的士兵则是冻死了。人们看见一个士兵背着一捆木柴,手紧紧地与木柴冻在了一起,以至于木柴与手一起从胳膊上掉了下来。

Corbulo himself, thinly dressed and bare-headed, moved among his men at work and on the march, encouraging the sick and praising efficiency—an example to all. But the harsh climate and service produced many shirkers and deserters. Corbulo's remedy was severity. In other armies, first and second offences were excused: Corbulo executed deserters immediately. Results showed that this was salutary and preferable to indulgence. For he had fewer deserters than lenient commanders.

Corbulo kept his troops in camp until spring was under way. Auxiliary infantry were suitably distributed, with orders not to provoke battle. These outposts were put under a senior staff-officer, Paccius Orfitus. He reported that the natives were unguarded and conditions were suitable for an engagement; but he was instructed to stay behind his defences and await reinforcements. When, however, a few small units reached him from neighbouring forts and ignorandy clamoured to fight, Paccius flouted his orders and attacked. He was routed. The troops who should have supported him took fright at his defeat and withdrew headlong to their respective entrenchments. Corbulo was angry. Reprimanding Paccius, he ordered him and his staff and men to encamp outside the fortifications, and in that degrading position they were kept until a unanimous petition secured their release.

Tiridates, now supported by his brother Vologeses' forces as well as his own dependants, dropped concealment and openly ravaged Armenia. As he moved rapidly, plundering communities he believed to be pro-Roman and evading detachments sent against him, his repu-

科尔布罗本人也是穿得很薄,头上几乎没戴东西,与士兵们一起干活或者一起行军时,就不断地鼓励那些伤病的人,并表扬那些勇敢的人在全军之中起了模范带头作用。但是,由于恶劣的气候条件和繁重的军务,产生了许多拒不从命的士兵或者是逃兵。科尔布罗采取了严厉的手段加以补救。在其他部队之中,初犯或是再犯的士兵还可以得到宽恕,而科尔布罗对于逃兵则是立即处决。结果表明这一做法是有效的,比纵容更为可取。因为他手下的逃兵比那些宽大为怀的统帅手下的逃兵要少。

科尔布罗让他手下的军队一直待在军营里,一直到春天来临。辅助步兵被分到了各自适宜的地点,并命令他们不要挑起战争。而这些卫戍据点则由一名叫帕克奇乌斯·奥尔菲图斯的主力百人团长负责把守。他报告说,这些外族人缺少戒备,因而条件非常适合发动进攻。但是,他却得到命令,要他待在防御工事的后面等着增援部队的来临。然而,当从附近各防守据点来了几小队士兵之后,帕克奇乌斯就不顾没有作战经验而要求出战,于是他不顾科尔布罗的命令而发动了攻击,结果被敌人击溃了。本来应该赶来支援他的部队被他的失利吓坏了,于是撤回到各自的防守据点中去。科尔布罗对此大为恼火,对帕克奇乌斯进行了严厉的批评,之后就命令帕克奇乌斯和他手下的军官、士兵在工事的外边扎营,他们一直处于那种丢人的处境之中,直到大家一致为他们求情才得到了赦免。

现在的提里达特斯得到了自己的臣属和自己的兄弟沃洛吉西斯的武力支持,就不再偷偷摸摸地,而是公开地对亚美尼亚进行蹂躏。由于他的部队推进非常迅速,对于那些他认为忠于罗马的地区进行了劫掠,而一旦派部队对其作战的时候,他就快速地

tation (rather than any warlike feats) terrorized the country. Corbulo tried persistently to force an engagement, but failed. Instead he was forced to imitate the enemy and enlarge the theatre of war, dispersing his formations so that their commanders could deliver co-ordinated attacks at different points. So the king of Commagene, Antiochus Epiphanes IV, was ordered to invade the regions nearest his border. Pharasmanes, king of Iberia, also demonstrated his friendship to us by reviving his longstanding feud with the Armenians; he had executed his son Radamistus as a traitor. The tribe of the Heniochi, too, inaugurated their record of keen loyalty to Rome by overrunning certain remote areas.

Tiridates' plans were upset. Envoys from him demanded, in his and Parthia's name, why after he had recently given hostages and reaffirmed friendship he was being expelled from his longstanding occupancy of Armenia. Vologeses, they added, had not acted yet because they preferred to rely on their rights rather than force; but if the Romans persisted in fighting, then the Parthian royal house would again be as valorous and successful as numerous Roman disasters had proved it. But Corbulo knew that Vologeses was occupied with a rebellion in Hyrcania. So he urged Tiridates to petition the emperor. 'You might win a secure throne bloodlessly', he suggested, 'if you abandon distant far-off ambitions and take the better chance that is now offered you.'

These exchanges, however, did not bring peace any nearer. So it was decided to fix the place and time for a meeting. Tiridates said he

转移了,他用流言蜚语(而不是武力)使得整个国家变得惶惶不可终日。科尔布罗不断寻求机会以同敌人进行决战,但都失败了。于是,他被迫模仿敌人的做法,扩大了作战区域。他将自己的部队进行了分散,目的在于使各个部队的指挥官可以发布命令同时对于不同的地点发动进攻。他还向孔玛盖尼国王安提奥库斯·埃披帕尼斯四世下达了命令,让他进攻与他的国界最为接近的地区。伊伯利亚国王帕拉司玛尼斯也正在想处理一下与亚美尼亚人的夙怨,这也是在向我们表明与罗马的友谊。他已经将自己的儿子拉达米司徒斯作为一名叛国者处决了。黑尼奥奇人部落也第一次开始向亚美尼亚某一遥远的地区发动了进攻,以此来表明对于罗马的真诚的忠心。

提里达特斯的作战计划就被打乱了,于是他就以他本人和帕尔提亚的名义派遣了使节来进行询问:为什么在最近他已经交出了人质和重新确定了与罗马的友谊之后,却被赶出了他长久占据的亚美尼亚。他们接着说,沃洛吉西斯之所以还没有采取行动,其原因就是他们更愿意依赖他们理应具备的权利,而不是依靠武力。但是,假如罗马人坚持开战的话,那么帕尔提亚王室将会再一次表现出自己的勇猛顽强,并取得最终成功;而罗马人的无数次灾难就证明了这一点。但是科尔布罗知道,沃洛吉西斯正忙于镇压叙尔卡尼亚人的起义,于是他就力劝提里达特斯向罗马皇帝进行请求。他还建议道:"假如你能够抛弃那遥远而又毫无希望的野心,好好抓住当前为你提供的机会,你或许不用流血就能获取稳固的王位。"

然而,这些意见的交换,并没有使和平进一步落实下来。于是确定了双方首领会面的地点和时间。提里达特斯说他将会带

would bring a thousand cavalry as escort-Corbulo could bring as many men as he liked, of whatever kind, provided that they came peaceably, without breastplates or helmets. Anyone, and best of all a wary veteran commander, could see a cunning native trick in the proposal to restrict his own numbers but allow Corbulo more. For any number of unarmed men, exposed to trained bowmen on horseback, would be useless. Pretending not to understand, Corbulo replied that these national issues were best discussed in front of their whole armies. The site he chose was between gently sloping hills suitable for infantry movements and level ground on which cavalry could deploy.

On the appointed day Corbulo arrived first. On his flanks were auxiliaries from the provinces and dependent kingdoms, in the centre the sixth brigade strengthened by an admixture of three thousand men from the third—these summoned from another camp by night but put under the same Eagle to look like a single brigade. It was evening when Tiridates appeared; but he stayed in the distance-visible yet not audible. So there was no meeting. Corbulo ordered his men to return to their respective camps. Tiridates moved away hastily. Either the dispersal of the Roman army made him suspect treachery, or he wanted to intercept provisions reaching us by the Black Sea by way of Trapezus. In this, however, he failed since the supply-line across the mountains was in Roman hands.

To avoid a long unprofitable campaign and put the Armenians on the defensive, Corbulo prepared to destroy their forts. Leaving smaller ones to two subordinates, the divisional commander Cornelius

1000名骑兵伴随,而科尔布罗自己愿意带多少兵、何种类型的兵都可以,只要是为了和平的目的而来,不披着胸甲、戴着头盔就可以了。任何人,尤其是一位最杰出的、久经沙场而且有远见的统帅,当然能够看得出,这些狡猾的外族人严格限制自己一方的士兵数目,而允许科尔布罗带更多的士兵,这里面所含的阴谋诡计。因为对于没有武装的人来说,假如暴露在一批骑在马背上的历经训练的弓箭手面前,人数再多也将是毫无用处的。对此,科尔布罗假装不懂敌人的阴谋诡计,回答道,讨论国家大事最好是当着双方的全部军队进行。他选择了一面是适于骑兵运动作战的坡势较缓的小山,另一面是适于骑兵展开活动的平原中间地带作为会面地点。

到了约定的那一天,科尔布罗首先到达。在他的两翼是来自于各行省和各藩国的辅助部队;中间则是第六军团和从第三军团所抽调的3000名士兵,这3000人是晚上从另一个营地之中派遣来的,不过却打一面军旗,这样看起来就是一个军团了。而当提里达特斯出现的时候,已经是傍晚了;但是,他却停在了可以看见但听不见的远处。于是,就无法见面了。科尔布罗命令自己的军队返回了各自的军营。提里达特斯也匆匆忙忙地撤走了。也许是四散的罗马军队使他怀疑里面有什么阴谋,或许是想切断罗马军在黑海之滨通过特拉佩佐斯城的粮食供应线。但是,对于这一点他没有能够做到,因为通过山脉的粮食供应线控制在罗马士兵的手里。

为了避免一场旷日持久的战争,也为了将亚美尼亚人逼入防守的境地,科尔布罗准备毁掉他们的要塞。在留下了一两个较小的要塞交由自己的下属——军团将领科尔涅里乌斯·佛拉库斯

Flaccus and Insteius Capito, now chief-of-staff, he himself tackled the strongest in the region, Volandum by name. After reconnoitring its fortifications he planned the assault. He urged his men to strike for glory and also for plunder, and expel this shifty enemy who wanted neither war nor peace but admitted their treachery and cowardice by fleeing. Corbulo divided his force into four detachments. One he massed in tortoise-formation and set to destroying the rampart. Another had orders to move ladders to the walls. A further large party was to shoot torches and javelins from engines. Finally, two kinds of slingers were allotted positions to discharge lead bullets at long range.

The intention was to press the enemy at every point so that no unit in difficulties could be relieved from elsewhere. The attack was so energetic that, before the day was one-third gone, the Armenian defenders were swept from the walls, their barricades at the gates flattened, fortifications scaled and taken, every adult male killed-without the loss of one Roman soldier, and with very few wounded. The noncombatant population were sold as slaves. Everything else went as spoils to the victors. The other two commanders were equally successful. The storming of three forts in one day caused the remaining garrisons to surrender in panic—or in some cases willingly.

This encouraged Corbulo to attack the Armenian capital Artaxata. But the direct route would have involved crossing the river Aras by a bridge right under the city walls and exposed to missiles. So his force

和印斯泰乌斯·卡皮托,由他们率部负责攻击之外,科尔布罗亲自率领主要的军团对付该地区最为坚固的、被称为沃兰杜姆的要塞。视察完了防御工事之后,科尔布罗就制定了进攻计划。他鼓励自己的部下,要为了荣誉和抢夺战利品而战,要将这些反复无常的敌人赶出这些地区。敌人既不想开战,也不想缔结和约,而只能通过逃跑向世人证明自己的卑鄙和怯懦。科尔布罗将自己的军队分作了四个部分,第一部分摆成了密集的龟形战阵,负责进攻破坏敌人的阵地;第二部分则是负责向城墙上架云梯;第三部分人数更多,负责用军事器械投射火把和标枪;最后一部分则是负责两种投射器,它们被安置在不同的阵地上,从远处向敌人发射铅弹。

这样安排的目的就是为了从各个方向向敌人施加压力,从而使处于困境之中的一部分敌人不能从另外的地方获得增援。进攻是如此猛烈,以至于还不到一天的1/3时间,负责守卫城墙的帕尔提亚士兵就全被消灭了,城墙门口的防卫栅栏被摧毁了,防御工事也被从云梯上攻上来的士兵占领了;在没有一名罗马士兵阵亡,而只有少数几人受伤的情况之下,他们杀死了对方所有的成年男子。那些没有参战的人也都被卖为奴隶。其他的东西也都成了战胜者的战利品。另两位将领也同样获得了胜利。而三座要塞在猛攻之下一天之内就被攻陷的事实使得其他各个要塞的守兵在惊恐之下也都投降了,有的则是出于自愿而投降的。

这一战果鼓励了科尔布罗,使他下定了决心要进攻亚美尼亚的首都阿尔塔克撒塔,但是,假如部队抄近路的话就要通过阿拉斯河上的桥,而桥正好位于阿尔塔克撒塔城墙底下,那样就容易

instead crossed by a wider ford some way off. Tiridates was torn between pride and fright. Acquiescence in a siege would make him look
helpless. But intervention would mean entangling himself and his cavalry on difficult ground. Finally he decided to display battle order
and, as opportunity offered, to fight or lure the enemy into an ambush, by pretending to retreat. By the latter means he suddenly enveloped the Roman army.

But Corbulo was not taken by surprise. His forces were as ready
for fighting as for marching; on the right flank stood the third brigade,
on the left the sixth, with picked troops of the tenth in the centre.
The baggage was brought within the lines. A thousand cavalry protected the rear, with orders to resist hand-to-hand attack but not to follow
if the enemy withdrew. On the wings were the remaining cavalry and
foot-archers. The left wing was extended along the foot of the hills so
that enemy penetration could be outflanked as well as met frontally.
Tiridates approached the Roman front line. He kept out of range, but
by alternately threatening attack and simulating alarm tried to detach
our formations so that he could fall on them separately. However, the
Roman ranks remained cautiously closed. Only the commander of a
cavalry section advanced too impetuously; he fell transfixed. But this
example merely strengthened the general obedience. As darkness approached, Tiridates withdrew.

Corbulo pitched camp where he was. Supposing Tiridates to have
retired to Artaxata, he thought of marching his forces there by night

遭受敌人投枪的袭击。于是他带领部队在较为遥远的地方,从一个较为宽阔的渡口过了河。此时的提里达特斯在豪气和胆怯之间徘徊煎熬:假如他默许了科尔布罗的此次围攻,就会使他显得软弱无能;但是假如干预此次进攻的话,又会使他和他的骑兵陷入困难的境地。最终,他下定了决心将自己的部队摆成战争方阵,假如有机会的话,就向敌人开战,或者是通过假装撤退寻找机会以伏击敌人。而通过后一种办法,他突然地将罗马军队包围了起来。

但是,科尔布罗对此毫不惊慌。他的军队对于作战和行军已经做好了准备:部队的右侧是第三军团;左侧是第六军团;第十军团的精锐部分则配备在中央;所携带的辎重被放在了队阵的里面;安排1000名骑兵用来保护部队的尾翼,给他们的命令是在遭受到进攻的情况之下要进行抵抗,但是在敌人撤退时不要尾随追击;其余的骑兵和徒步的弓箭手安排在了两翼,左翼的士兵沿着一些小山的山脚伸展开去,假如敌人的部队突入的话,他们就既可以侧翼包围,也可以正面还击。提里达特斯率领部队靠近了罗马部队的前沿阵地,他将部队带到了罗马军方的射击范围以外,他们时而威胁要进攻,时而装出一副惊恐的样子,想以此将罗马的军队分散开,然后就能够分别加以攻击。但是,罗马军队非常警惕,仍然保持着紧密的队形。只有一位骑兵队长过于莽撞地攻了出去,很快就倒在了敌人的乱箭之下。但是,这件事情为其他所有的士兵树立了一个榜样,从而更加强了他们的服从意识。夜幕降临的时候,提里达特斯就撤退了。

科尔布罗就地安扎了军营。他想:假如提里达特斯早已经撤到了阿尔塔克撒塔,那么他就必须要抛弃重的辎重而带领士兵急行

without heavy baggage and investing the town. But intelligence reports indicated that the king was on a long journey, either to Media Atropatene or to Albania. So Corbulo awaited daytime. Meanwhile he sent light-armed auxiliaries ahead to surround the walls and begin the siege from a distance. But the inhabitants of Artaxata voluntarily opened the gates and surrendered themselves and their property to the Romans, thus saving their lives.

The city was set on fire and razed to the ground. Its extensive walls could only have been held by a considerable garrison, and the Roman army was not numerous enough to provide garrisons as well as fighting. If, however, the town had been left unscathed and unguarded, its capture would have brought neither glory nor benefit. Besides, a divine portent seemed to occur. While the sun shone brightly all round the walls, the arca of the city itself was suddenly enveloped in a dark cloud with unearthly lightning-flashes. It was believed that the angry gods were consigning Artaxata to destruction.

For these achievements Nero was officially hailed as victor. The senate decreed thanksgivings. They voted the emperor statues, arches, and a succession of consulships. The days of the victory and its announcement were to rank as festivals. Following further extravagant decrees of the same sort, Gaius Cassius Longinus—who had supported the other honours—observed that if the gods were to be thanked worthily for their favours the whole year was too short for their thanksgivings: so a distinction should be made between religious festivals and working days on which people might perform religious duties without neglecting mundane ones.

军,连夜赶往阿尔塔克撒塔,并将它包围起来。但是,侦察兵的报告表明,国王正在进行长途行军,要么是到米地亚,要么是到阿尔巴尼亚。于是,科尔布罗就等着破晓时分的来临。与此同时,他将一些轻武装的辅助部队作为先锋,将这座城市包围了起来,而且从一定的距离开始对其展开了进攻。但是,阿尔塔克撒塔城的居民们却是自愿地打开了城门,并且将自己以及他们的财产交给了罗马人,以此而保全了性命。

这座城市被火焚烧,并被夷为了平地。因为它那绵延的城墙需要驻扎一支庞大的军队来保卫,而罗马的军队人数除了作战之外,不足以再留出一支强大的卫戍部队。然而,假如这座城市保留完好而又没有卫戍部队防守,那么对这座城市的占领就既不会带来荣誉也不会带来利益。除此之外,上天似乎也昭示了不祥之兆。当围绕着整个城墙的地方还是阳光明媚的时候,突然城市的内部地区被一团黑云包围了,而且还夹杂着可怕的闪电。人们都认为,神仙的发怒表明阿尔塔克撒塔城注定要被摧毁了。

由于这一系列的胜利,尼禄被官僚们欢呼为获胜者。元老院发布命令,要举行感恩祭。他们通过了决议,要为皇帝树立雕像、建造拱门,并选他连任执政官。获胜的日子以及宣告胜利的日子都被列入了节日的行列,以示纪念。在这些提议之后,紧接着又提出了许多过分的提议。例如,盖乌斯·卡西乌斯·朗吉努斯,他在支持了其他所有的授予荣誉的提议之后,接着又指出,假如我们必须向诸神给予我们的恩惠进行足够的谢恩的话,那么一整年用来表示对他们的感恩还是时间太短了,因此,我们应当将宗教节日和工作日区别开来,在平时的工作日之中,人们也可以在没有忽略了俗务的情况之下举行宗教仪式。

Now came the condemnation of Publius Suillius Rufus. He had earned much hatred in his stormy career. Nevertheless his fall brought discredit upon Seneca. Under Claudius the venal Suillius had been formidable. Changed times had not brought him as low as his enemies wished. Indeed, he envisaged himself as aggressor rather than suppliant. It was to suppress him—so it was said—that the senate had revived an old decree under the Cincian law, penalizing advocates who accepted fees. Suillius protested abusively, reviling Seneca with characteristic ferocity and senile outspokenness.

'Seneca hates Claudius' friends, said Suillius. 'For under Claudius he was most deservedly exiled! He only understands academic activities and immature youths. So he envies men who speak out vigorously and unaffectedly for their fellow-citizens. I was on Germanicus' staffwhile Seneca was committing adultery in his house! Is the acceptance of rewards a dependant offers voluntarily, for an honourable job, a worse offence than seducing imperial princesses? What branch of learning, what philosophical school, won Seneca three hundred million sesterces during four years of imperial friendship? In Rome, he entices into his snares the childless and their legacies. His huge rates of interest suck Italy and the provinces dry. I, on the other hand, have worked for my humble means. I will endure prosecution, trial, and everything else rather than have my lifelong efforts wiped out by this successful upstart!'

There were people to tell Seneca of these words, or exaggerated

现在,普布里乌斯·苏伊里乌斯·路福斯被判有罪。在其变化多端的一生之中,招致了他人的大量憎恨。然而,他的垮台无论如何对于塞内加来说都造成了一定的损害。在克劳狄乌斯统治时期,贪污腐败的苏伊里乌斯就是一个令人头疼的人物。时代的变换并没有使他像他的敌手们所想象的那样垮了台。实际上,此人宁愿将自己作为一个侵略者,也不愿将自己弄成一个可怜的祈求者。据说为了将他整倒,元老院引用了一条古老的法规,这条法规是出自于辛希安法,规定辩护人收取费用的话将会受到惩罚。对此,苏伊里乌斯坚决反对,他破口大骂,凶狠地,并且是倚老卖老地咒骂塞内加。

苏伊里乌斯说:"塞内加憎恨克劳狄乌斯的所有朋友,因为在克劳狄乌斯统治时期,他遭受了完全是罪有应得的驱逐! 他只是对学术活动和幼稚的年轻人有所了解。因此,他对于那些为国民进行生动而朴实的辩护的人非常嫉妒。塞内加曾经是日尔曼尼库斯手下的一名官员,却在人家的家中犯了通奸的罪行。辩护人作为一种可尊敬的职务,难道说接受诉讼者所自愿给予的报酬所犯的罪行会比诱奸皇帝的女儿更严重吗? 以哪一门学识、哪一个哲学流派作为依据,使塞内加在与皇帝保持四年的友谊之内,就可以获取30000万谢司特尔提乌斯的家产? 在罗马,他将那些没有子嗣的人的全部遗产都搜进了自己的罗网,他的巨大的高利贷利息已经将整个意大利和各个行省的血都吸干了。另一方面,我那有限的财产是靠我辛辛苦苦地工作挣来的,我宁愿忍受控诉、审讯以及其他的折磨,也不愿意用我一生辛苦所挣来的东西在他这一位新贵面前屈膝。"

有人将这些话都告诉了塞内加,甚至还添油加醋、夸大

versions of them. Accusers were found. They charged Suillius with fleecing the provincials as governor of Asia, and embezzling public funds. The prosecution was granted a year for investigation. Meanwhile it was thought quicker to begin with charges relating to Rome— for which witnesses were available. They accused Suillius of forcing a former consul, Quintus Pomponius Secundus, into civil war by his savage indictments, driving Livia Julia, daughter of Drusus, and Poppaea Sabina to their deaths, striking down Decimus Valerius Asiaticus and two other ex-consuls, Quintus Lutetius Lusits Saturninus and Cornelius Lupus, and convicting masses of knights—in a word, all the brutalities of Claudius.

Suillius' defence was that he had invariably acted not on his own initiative but on the emperor's orders. But Nero cut him short, declaring that his father Claudius had never insisted on any prosecutions—his papers proved it. Suillius then alleged instructions from Messalina. But this defence too broke down. For why (it was asked) had just Suillius, and no one else, been selected to speak for that barbarous harlot? —the instrument of atrocities, the man who was paid for crimes and then blamed them on others, must be punished.

Half his estate was confiscated. His son, Marcus Suillius Nerullinus, and granddaughter were allowed the other half, as well as what they had inherited from their mother and grandmother. Suillius himself was exiled to the Balearic islands. Neither ordeal nor aftermath broke

其词。于是塞内加找到了一些控告者。他们控告苏伊里乌斯在担任亚细亚总督的时候，进行欺诈活动和侵吞公款的活动。针对这次控告，进行了一年时间的调查。因此大家认为假如从他在罗马所犯的罪行进行调查的话，速度会更快一些的，因为在此很容易就可以找到证人。这些人控告苏伊里乌斯通过恶毒的告发的手段逼迫前执政官克温图斯·彭波尼乌斯·塞库恩杜斯发动了内战；逼死了杜路苏斯的女儿利维娅·优利娅和波培娅·萨比娜；曾经陷害过戴奇姆斯·瓦列里乌斯·亚细亚提库斯和另外两名执政官克温图斯·路特提乌斯·路西乌斯·撒图尔尼乌斯、科尔涅里乌斯·路普斯；另外，他还宣判过大批的骑士有罪。总而言之，把克劳狄乌斯的所有暴行都算到了苏伊里乌斯的头上。

苏伊里乌斯对此进行了辩驳，他说以上的各种行为都不是出自自己的意愿，而是奉皇帝的命令干的。但是，尼禄打断了他的话，说自己的父亲从来就没有强迫对任何人进行控诉，这一点从他遗留下来的文书就可以得到证明。于是苏伊里乌斯就说这些都是奉了美撒里娜的命令而干的。但是这一辩解也很快就被戳穿了。因为，(有人就问他)为什么恰好是你苏伊里乌斯，而不是别人被选做了这位杀人淫妇的代言人？作为实施这些残暴行为的工具，作为靠犯罪而谋取收入、却又将自己的罪行推卸到他人身上的人，必须要接受处罚。

于是他的财产的一半被没收了。他的儿子玛尔库斯·苏伊里乌斯·奈路里努斯和他的孙女允许保留另一半，而从他们的母亲和祖母那儿继承来的遗产也留下了。苏伊里乌斯本人则是被驱逐到了巴利阿里群岛上去了。不论是对他的审判还是对他的

his spirit. His retirement was known to be sustained by comfortable self-indulgence. When accusers, relying on Suillius' unpopularity, prosecuted his son for extortion, the emperor felt vengeance was satisfied and vetoed the proceedings.

At about this time the tribune Octavius Sagitta, madly in love with a married woman called Pontia, paid her vast sums to become his mistress and then to leave her husband. He promised to marry her, and secured a similar promise from her. But once she was free she procrastinated, pleading her father's opposition and evading her promise—a richer husband now being in prospect. Octavius remonstrated, threatened, and appealed—his reputation and money were both gone (he said), and his life, all that he had left, he put in her hands. But she remained unmoved.

He pleaded for one night—as a consolation and to help him control himself in future. The night was fixed. Pontia had a maid in attendance who knew of the affair. Octavius arrived with a former slave. Under his clothes was a dagger. Love and anger took their course. They quarrelled, pleaded, insulted each other, made it up. For part of the night they made love. Then, ostensibly carried away by passion, he stabbed the unsuspecting woman with his dagger. A maid ran in and fell wounded by him. Then he fled.

When day came the murder was discovered. They were proved to have been together; the murderer was unmistakable. The ex-slave, however, claimed that the action was his, undertaken to avenge his

惩罚,都没有击溃他的精神。据说他在退隐时期仍然保持着那种舒适而又放纵的生活。当控告者因为苏伊里乌斯的垮台而控告他的儿子犯有勒索罪的时候,皇帝认为报复已经足够了,就制止了进一步的控告行为。

大约在同时,保民官奥克塔维乌斯·撒吉塔疯狂地爱上了一个已婚妇女彭提娅。他给了她大量的金钱使她变成了自己的情妇,然后又让她离开了自己的丈夫。他发誓要娶她,而她也作出了同样的保证。但是她在获得了自由之后,却将婚事拖了下来,还找理由说是自己的父亲反对此事,最终就不承认自己的誓言了,因为她又找了一位更富裕的男人做她的对象。而奥克塔维乌斯则是不断地规劝、威胁,甚至是请求,他说他的声誉、金钱都已经没有了,而他的生命以及他所剩余的其他东西都交由她来处理。但是,她仍然对此无动于衷。

于是,他请求再给他一晚上的机会,作为对他的安慰,以及帮助他未来可以控制住自己。约会的晚上也确定了。彭提娅让一位知道他们之间事情的侍女在身边侍候。奥克塔维乌斯在一位被释奴隶的陪伴之下赶来了,他在外衣底下藏了一把匕首。在见面的这一段时间,他们之间充满了爱和恨。他们争吵、请求,彼此责难,又相互道歉。这一晚上的一部分时间,他们进行做爱。接着,他看来已经是被激情冲昏了头脑,就用匕首刺死了这位毫不起疑的女人。侍女跑了进来,但也被刺伤了,然后他就逃跑了。

当天亮的时候,这一谋杀案就被发现了。由于有人证明他们曾经在一起,所以杀人的罪行就确定无疑了。而他的被释奴隶却宣布这一谋杀举动是他干的,他之所以采取这一举动,是为他的

patron's wrongs. Many were convinced by his devotion. But the maid recovered from her wound and revealed the truth. Octavius was charged before the consuls by his victim's father. He ceased to be tribune and was condemned by senatorial decree and under the law of murder.

An equally conspicuous case of immorality in the same year brought grave national disaster. There was at Rome a woman called Poppaea. Friendship with Sejanus had ruined her father, Titus Ollius, before he held office, and she had assumed the name of her brilliant maternal grandfather, Gaius Poppaeus Sabinus, of illustrious memory for his consulship and honorary Triumph. Poppaea had every asset except goodness. From her mother, the loveliest woman of her day, she inherited distinction and beauty. Her wealth, too, was equal to her birth. She was clever and pleasant to talk to. She seemed respectable. But her life was depraved. Her public appearances were few; she would half-veil her face at them, to stimulate curiosity (or because it suited her). To her, married or bachelor bedfellows were alike. She was indifferent to her reputation-yet insensible to men's love, and herself unloving. Advantage dictated the bestowal of her favours.

While married to a knight called Rufrius Crispinus-to whom she had borne a son-she was seduced by Marcus Salvius Otho, an extravagant youth who was regarded as peculiarly close to Nero. Their liaison was quickly converted into marriage. Otho praised her charms and graces to the emperor. This was either a lover's indiscretion or a

主人所遭受的不公正对待而报仇。他的忠诚使许多人都相信了他的话。但是受了伤的那位侍女在苏醒之后将事实的真相揭露了出来。奥克塔维乌斯被死者的父亲告到了执政官那儿,他被撤销了保民官的职务,然后依据元老院的命令和有关谋杀的法律条款而被判了罪。

在同一年,发生了一件同样不道德的引人注目的事件。在罗马城有一位妇女名字叫波培娅。她的父亲提图斯·欧里乌斯在没有担任官职之前,就因为与谢雅努斯的友谊而被毁掉了。波培娅采用的是自己的辉煌的外祖父盖乌斯·波培乌斯·撒比努斯的名字。撒比努斯因为担任过执政官和取得过光荣的凯旋标记而在历史上声名卓著。波培娅除了不具备良好的道德品质之外,具备了女人的其他一切优点。她的母亲是她那个时代最迷人的女人,而她则是继承了母亲的名誉和美貌,还有那与高贵的门第相匹配的巨额财富。她聪明机智又谈吐迷人。她表面上看起来尊贵高雅,但实际上生活堕落不堪。她很少在公共场合中露面,出现在公众面前时也会用纱巾半遮着脸,目的是为了引起他人的好奇心(也或许是因为这种方式就适合于她)。对于她来说,已婚的床友和未婚的床友是完全一样的。她对于自己的名声根本就不关心,对于男人是否爱她,她是否爱对方也毫不在乎,利益是她所有爱情的指南针。

她在嫁给了一名叫路福里乌斯·克利司披努斯的骑士并且为他生了一个儿子之后,她就被玛尔库斯·塞尔维乌斯·奥托勾引去了,奥托是一个放荡的年轻人,他被视作是皇帝身边的亲信。而且,他们很快就由姘居关系而转变成了夫妻关系。奥托经常对皇帝盛赞自己妻子的迷人和优雅。其原因或许是因为一个陷于

deliberate stimulus prompted by the idea that joint possession of Poppaea would be a bond reinforcing Otho's own power. As he left the emperor's table he was often heard saying he was going to his wife, who had brought him what all men want and only the fortunate enjoy - nobility and beauty.

Under such provocations, delay was brief. Poppaea obtained access to Nero, and established her ascendancy. First she used flirtatious wiles, prtending to be unable to resist her passion for Nero's looks. Then, as the emperor fell in love with her, she became haughty, and if he kept her for more than two nights she insisted that she was married and could not give up her marriage. 'I am devoted to Otho. My relations with him are unique. His character and way of living are both fine. *There* is a man for whom nothing is too good. Whereas you, Nero, are kept down because the mistress you live with is a servant, Actc. What a sordid, dreary, menial association!'

Otho lost his intimacy with the emperor. Soon he was excluded from Nero's receptions and company. Finally, to eliminate his rivalry from the Roman scene, he was made governor of Lusitania. There, until the civil war, he lived moderately and respectably-enjoying himself in his spare time, officially blameless.

At this juncture Nero stopped trying to justify his criminal misdeeds. He particularly distrusted Faustus Cornelius Sulla Felix, whose

爱情中的人的不经意,也或许是为了有意刺激皇帝的情欲,使他们两人共同占有波培娅,从而使奥托本人的权力可以得到加强。每当他离开皇帝的饭桌时,总听见他在说,他要回去看自己的妻子,因为他的妻子为他带来了所有的男人都想得到的,而只有幸运的人才能够享受得到的东西,那就是高贵和美丽。

在这样的刺激之下,其效果很快就出现了。波培娅获得了接近尼禄的机会,并建立了自己的势力。一开始,她采用了一种甜言蜜语的欺骗手段,假装说自己面对着皇帝那美貌的外表,根本就不能控制自己的情欲,而当皇帝深深地迷上了她之后,她又故作矜持起来,如果皇帝留她过夜超过两个晚上,她就要坚持回去,说自己已经结婚了,并且不想放弃自己的婚姻。她说:"我忠于奥托,我和他之间的关系是无与伦比的。他的个性和生活方式都是很优秀的,他是一个不断追求完美的人。而你,尼禄,却在自贬,因为你在与一个女奴阿克提通奸。你们的交往是多么的肮脏、庸俗、卑贱呀!"

很快,奥托就失去了他与皇帝的亲密关系。不久,他就不能再见到皇帝并陪伴在皇帝的身边了。最后,尼禄为了将自己的情敌驱逐出罗马,就任命奥托做了路西塔尼亚的长官。在那儿,他一直待到内战[1]爆发,在此期间,他过着既正直而又受人尊重的生活,他的业余生活很惬意,公务上也无可指摘。

在这之后,尼禄就不再尽力地掩饰自己那罪恶的放荡行为了。他特别不信任法乌司图斯·科尔涅里乌斯·苏拉·费里克

---

[1] 指公元58~68年古罗马帝国所发生的内战。

stupidity he wrongly interpreted as well-concealed cunning. This suspicion was intensified by the fabrication of an old former imperial slave Graptus, familiar with the palace since Tiberius' reign. At this time the Milvian Bridge was notorious for its night resorts. Nero used to go there; he could enjoy himself more riotously outside the city. On his way home by the Flaminian road one night, a few young revellers, typical of the times, caused groundless alarm among his attendants. 'There had been a plot to attack Nero!' lied Graptus. 'Only a providential detour to the Gardens of Sallust had saved himand the plotter was Sulla!' No slave or dependant of Sulla was identified, and his wholly timid and despicable character was incapable of such an attempt. However, he was treated as if proved guilty, exiled, and confined to Massilia.

This year Puteoli sent two opposing delegations to the senate, one from the town council and one from the other citizens. The council complained of public disorderliness, and the populace of embezzlement by officials and leading men. There had been riots, with stone-throwing and threatened arson. Gaius Cassius Longinus was appointed to prevent armed warfare and find a solution. But the town could not stand his severity, and at his own request the task was transferred to two brothers, Publius Sulpicius Scribonius Proculus and Sulpicius Scribonius Rufus. They were allocated a battalion of the

斯,他错误地理解了苏拉的愚蠢笨拙,将这视作是深深掩藏的一种奸诈。这一怀疑被皇帝的一位年老的被释奴隶格拉普图斯所编造的谎言进一步加重了,此人自从提贝里乌斯担任皇帝开始,就一直在皇宫之内,所以对于宫廷之内的事情非常了解。当时,穆尔维乌斯桥地区由于夜游者经常光顾而变得臭名昭著。尼禄也经常到那儿去;因为到了城外,他就可以肆无忌惮地玩乐了。有一天晚上,在他经过佛拉米尼大道回家时,遇见了一批年轻人酗酒闹事,这在当时本来是很平常的事情,但皇帝身边的侍从们却虚惊一场。格拉普图斯对此却编造谎言道:"本来此地有一场针对尼禄的阴谋刺杀活动,正是由于神意的保佑使他转到了撒路斯提乌斯花园,因而救了他的性命。而阴谋策划者就是苏拉!"在这些闹事者之中没有找出任何苏拉手下的奴隶或者是食客,而苏拉那胆怯而又卑下的性格也不可能做出这一举动。但是,他所遭受的对待就好像是已经证明真的犯了罪似的,他遭到了驱逐,被拘押到了玛西里亚地区。

在这一年,菩提欧里派了两个彼此互相对立的代表团来到了元老院,其中一个是由市议会派来的,另一个则是由其他市民派来的。市议会代表团抱怨民众目无法纪、扰乱社会;而民众代表团则控告官吏们和社会上的头面人物。这场冲突很激烈,已经发展到了双方互相扔石块和以纵火相威胁的严重地步。盖乌斯·卡西乌斯·朗吉努斯受命来阻止这一武装冲突并找到解决问题的办法。但是,市议会代表团忍受不了他的严酷手段,于是在他的请求之下,任务转交由普布里乌斯·苏尔皮西乌斯·司克里波尼乌斯·普罗库鲁斯和苏尔皮西乌斯·司克里波尼乌斯·路福斯这兄弟两人来处理。调拨给了他们一支近卫军

Guard, fear of which-supplemented by a few executions-restored harmony.

The senate also passed a decree authorizing the city of Syracuse to exceed the numbers allowed at gladiatorial displays. This would be too insignificant to mention had not the opposition of Publius Clodius Thrasea Paetus given his critics a chance to attack his attitude. 'If', they said, 'Thrasea believes Rome needs a free senate, why does he pursue such trivial matters? Why does he not argue one way or the other about questions of war and peace, taxation, legislation, and other matters of national importance? When a senator is called upon to speak, he may speak about anything and demand a motion about it. Is the prevention of extravagance at Syracusan shows the only reform we need? Is everything else in the empire as good as if Thrasea and not Nero were its ruler? If significant matters are passed over and ignored, surely trivialities ought to be left alone. ' Thrasea, asked by his friends to justify himself, replied that it was not through ignorance of the general situation that he offered criticism on such a subject, but because he respectfully credited the senate with understanding that men who attended to these details would not fail to show attention to important matters also.

In this year there were persistent public complaints against the companies farming indirect taxes from the government. Nero contemplated a noble gift to the human race:he would abolish every indirecttax.

中队,军队通过处死了几个人发挥了威慑作用,使他们感到了恐惧,于是双方就答应实现和解。

元老院还通过了一项命令,允许西拉库赛城参加剑斗比赛的人数超过规定的数目。这原本是一件毫无意义的事情,并不值得记录,但是,我之所以记录于此是由于普布里乌斯·克劳狄乌斯·特拉塞亚·帕伊图斯不同意此一命令,从而给了其批评者们对其观点进行攻击的机会。他们说:"假如特拉塞亚相信罗马需要一个自由的元老院的话,那么他为什么要关心如此琐碎的事情呢? 他为什么不讨论一下有关战争与和平问题、税收问题、法律问题以及其他有关国计民生的大事情的种种处理办法? 任何元老在讲话之时,都会针对某一件事情而发表自己的观点,并要求对自己所谈及的问题进行讨论。反对过分扩大西拉库赛城参加剑斗比赛的人数,难道这是我们所需要的唯一的改革吗? 难道说帝国之中的所有事务都要合于特拉塞亚的理想,就好像帝国的统治者不是尼禄而是他特拉塞亚一样? 假如重要的事情都要忽略、无人去管的话,那么看来就只能管这些无关紧要的、琐碎的事情了。"当朋友们要求特拉塞亚对此进行辩解的时候,他回答道,在他对于此问题做出要求修改的意见之时,并没有忽视当时的形势,但是,他非常敬重地相信元老院会明白,只有在人们对于那些具体细微的事情予以关照的情况之下,才会真正地关心重大的事情。

在同一年,公众们不断抱怨,反对由政府所包出去的、由包税机构所征收的间接税,[1]对此,尼禄考虑要取消所有的间接税,以此作

---

[1] 整个罗马的税收分作两部分,一部分是由政府官吏所征收的直接税,另一部分是由罗马骑士们所征收的间接税,包括关税和港口税等税收都算作是间接税。

But the senators whom he consulted, after loudly praising his noble generosity, restrained his impulse. They indicated that the empire could not survive without its revenues, and that abolition of the indirect customs dues would be followed by demands to abolish direct taxation also. Many companies for collecting indirect taxes, they recalled, had been established by consuls and tribunes in the freest times of the Republic; since then such taxation had formed part of the efforts to balance income and expenditure. But Nero's advisers agreed that tax-collectors' acquisitiveness must be restrained, to prevent novel grievances from discrediting taxes long endured uncomplainingly.

So the emperor's orders were these. Regulations governing each tax, hitherto confidential, were to be published. Claims for arrears were to lapse after one year. Praetors at Rome, governors in the provirces, must give special priority to cases against tax-collectors. Soldiers were to remain tax-free except on what they sold. There were other excellent provisions too. But they were soon evaded-though the abolition of certain illegal exactions invented by tax-collectors, such as the two and a half percent and two per cent duties, is still valid. Overseas transportation of grain was facilitated, and it was decided to exempt merchant ships from assessment and property-tax.

At this juncture two ex-governors of Africa, Quintus Sulpicius Camerinus and Marcus Pompeius Silvanus, were tried by the emperor and acquitted. Camerinus was charged not with embezzlement but with brutal acts towards a few individuals; Silvanus was beset by a

为送给人类的一项高贵的礼物。但是,当他向元老院征求意见之时,元老们在高度地赞扬了他高贵的慷慨大方之后,就否决了这一心血来潮的想法。他们说,假如没有税收的话,帝国是不可能存在下去的,而假如取消了间接性质的进口关税,紧接着就会有人要求取消直接税。他们回忆说,当罗马共和国尚处于全盛的时期,就建立了许多由执政官和保民官负责征收间接税;自那以后,此类税收就成为调节平衡收入与支出的一种有效的手段。但是,尼禄的顾问们也同意,对于那些包税人贪得无厌的举动也必须要加以限制,以防止使人们多年来一直毫无怨言地忍受下来的一种税收制度,由于新式的严酷措施而遭到民众的强烈不满。

于是,皇帝下了以下的敕令。规定过去一直是保密的,关于每种税收的征收条例,现在都要公开;对于尚未付清的税款,一年之后再提出要求就算是无效了;罗马的行政长官、各个行省的总督,在审理案件之时,要优先审理对于包税人的指控案件;士兵们仍旧不用交税,但是对于他们出售东西的所得则是除外;此外,还做出了其他一些极好的规定,可是这些规定很快就没有人遵守了。取消包税人自己所制定的某些非法的规定,例如取消"1/40税"、"1/50税",这些法令却是有效地得到了执行。海外的粮食运输方便多了,同时规定,商船不再列入商人的资产项目之内,免除商船的财产税。

同时,两个前阿非利加行省的总督,克温图斯·苏尔皮奇乌斯·卡美里努斯和玛尔库斯·彭培乌斯·西尔瓦努斯,受到了皇帝的审判,并被无罪释放。有一些人对卡美里努斯提出控告,其罪名并不是贪污受贿,而是针对他的残酷统治;但是控告西尔瓦努斯的人却是很多,他们要求再给他们留出时间以便于收

crowd of accusers who requested time to collect witnesses. But he insisted on an immediate hearing, and being rich, old, and childless,
was successful. Moreover, he outlived the legacy-hunters whose scheming had secured his acquittal!

Up to now, Germany had been peaceful because, prodigal a-
wards having cheapened the honorary Triumph, our generals looked
for greater glory from maintaining peace. To keep the troops busy, the
imperial governor of Lower Germany, Pompeius Paulinus, finished the
dam for controlling the Rhine, begun sixty-three years previously by
Nero Drusus. His colleague in Upper Germany, Lucius Antistius Vetus, planned to build a Saône-Moselle canal. Goods arriving from the
Mediterranean up the Rhône and Saône would thus pass via the Mo-
selle into the Rhine, and so to the North Sea. Such a waterway, joining the western Mediterranean to the northern seaboard, would eliminate the difficulties of land transport. But the imperial governor of
Gallia Belgica, Aelius Gracilis, jealously prevented his neighbour in
Lower Germany from bringing his army into the province he governed.
'This would be currying favour in Gaul, and would worry the emper-
or,' he objected-using an argument which often blocks good projects.

The prolonged inaction of the Roman armies led to a rumour
that their commanders had been forbidden to open hostilities. So the
Frisians, led by Verritus and Malorix—their kings (in so far as Germans have any)—advanced to the Rhine bank. Moving their fighting
men over swamps and woods, and shipping the young and old across

集他的罪证。但是被告则坚持要求马上就召开听证会，最终由于他的富有、他的高龄以及没有子嗣等原因使他获得了这场诉讼的胜利。而且，他比那些觊觎他财富的人活得还要长久，那些人害他的计划反而成了确保他无罪获释的有力证据。

直到现在，日耳曼地区一直保持着和平安宁的状况，这是因为罗马的军事统帅们对于获得光荣的凯旋标记的奖励这件事情，已经觉着无足轻重了，他们想通过维持和平以获取更大的荣耀。为了不使军队无所事事，下日耳曼地区的行政长官彭培乌斯·保里努斯，就让士兵们修建63年前由尼禄·杜路苏斯开始修建的莱茵河大坝，以控制莱茵河的洪水。他的上日耳曼地区的同僚路奇乌斯·安提司提乌斯·维图斯，则是计划在阿拉尔河与摩泽尔河之间修建一条运河。这样，货物运输就可以从地中海出发，上行经过罗纳河和阿拉尔河，这样就可以经过摩泽尔河进入莱茵河，并最终到达北海。修建这样一条水道，就可以将西地中海地区与北部海岸之间联结起来，从而消除陆路运输所带来的困难。但是，盖里亚·比尔吉卡行省的行政长官埃利乌斯·格拉奇里斯嫉妒此事，禁止邻近的下日耳曼地区的长官带领军队进入自己所管辖的行省。他反对说："这种做法是在讨好高卢人，而这会引起皇帝的猜疑的。"使用了阻挡好事所常用的一种借口。

罗马军队长期以来的闲散无事，导致了谣言四起，说他们的统帅已经被剥夺了率军对敌作战的权力。于是，弗里喜人在他们的首领（这种首领就是类似于日耳曼人所说的国王）维尔里图斯和玛洛里克斯的带领之下移居到了莱茵河的沿岸地区，那些有作战能力的人是穿过森林、跨过沼泽地而到达目的地的，而那些年

the lakes, they settled in lands reserved for Roman troops. There they erected houses, sowed fields, and tilled the land as if they had inherited it. However, a new imperial governor of Lower Germany, Lucius Duvius Avitus, threatened them with the power of Rome unless they returned to their old lands or had new ones granted by the emperor.

Verritus and Malorix decided to appeal. They went to Rome. While waiting for Nero, who was engaged, they visited Pompey's Theatreone of the sights usually shown barbarians—to see the huge crowd. There, to pass the time (for they had not the education to enjoy the show), they inquired about the seating arrangements and distinctions between orders—where senators had their places and where knights sat. They saw, seated among the senators, men in foreign clothes. On inquiry they learnt that these were delegates who received this compliment because their nations were conspicuous for courage, and friendship for Rome. Crying that no race on earth was braver and more loyal than the Germans, they moved down and sat among the senators. The spectators liked this fine, impulsive, old-fashioned pride

幼和年老的人则是从湖泊上坐船过来的,最后,他们定居在了为
罗马军队所保留的一些地方去了。在那儿,他们建造房屋、播撒
种子、翻耕土地,就好像这些地方是他们从祖上那儿继承下来的
一样。然而,下日耳曼地区的新任行政长官路奇乌斯·杜比乌
斯·阿维图斯却使用罗马的武力对他们进行威胁,命令他们要么
退回到原来的土地上去,要么在获得了皇帝的授权之后方才可以
居住在这一新地区。

　　维尔里图斯和玛洛里克斯决定到罗马去请愿,于是他们赶往
了罗马。尼禄非常繁忙,于是他们在等待皇帝召见前的这一段时
间里,就去参观了庞培大剧院,那是一个蛮族人[1]经常去参观的
地方,在那儿他们见到了大量的拥挤的观众。在那儿为了消磨
时光(由于他们没有接受过欣赏戏剧表演的教育),他们开始探
讨有关剧院之内坐席的安排,以及两个显要阶级次序的安排,即
元老们的座位在哪里,而骑士们又会坐在哪里,他们发现,坐在
元老们中间的有一些穿着外国服装的人。经过询问他们才知
道,这些人是一些民族的代表,他们之所以能够得到这样的尊
敬,是由于这些民族以勇敢而闻名天下,并且与罗马保持了友好
的关系。听了这些话之后,他们就叫了起来,嚷着说,世界上没
有任何一个民族在作战勇敢和对罗马的忠诚方面能够超过日耳
曼人,于是他们就移动了座位,坐到了元老们的席位上去了。在
座的人对他们表示了欢迎,对于这种炫耀式的、非常冒失的举动
做出了善意的解释,认为这种古朴的举动完全出自于一个争强好

---

　　〔1〕　蛮族人或者是野蛮人,是古希腊、古罗马时期对于非本民族人的
一种蔑称,类似于中国古时候汉人将少数民族称为"胡人"、"戎人"一样。

of race; and Nero made them both Roman citizens. All the same, he ordered the Frisians to evacuate the land. And when they ignored this instruction, auxiliary cavalry arrived unexpectedly and enforced his commands, capturing or killing obstinate resisters.

Then the Ampsivarii occupied the territory. They were a larger tribe, and inspired sympathy in neighbouring peoples since they had been expelled from their lands by the Chauci, and were homeless petitioners for a safe place of exile. Their spokesman was the proRoman Boiocalus, a well-known figure among these tribes. ' When the Cherusci rebelled', he reminded us, ' Arminius imprisoned me. I served under Tiberius and Germanicus. Now, as the climax to fifty years of loyalty, I am bringing my people into your empire. How little of this land would ever be used for the eventual grazing of Roman soldiers' flocks and herds! Reserve pasturage for cattle-if you must though men are starving: but not, surely, to the extent of thinking desert wastes more useful to you than friendly nations! This used to be the territory of the Chamavi tribe, and then the Tubantes, and then the Usipi. Just as heaven belongs to the gods, the earth belongs to man: and tenantless land can be occupied. ' He raised his eyes to the sun; he invoked all the heavenly bodies. ' Do you like looking at empty land?' he pretended to ask them. ' Then flood it-rather than expel us! And drown those who take other men's soil !'

胜的民族自尊心。对于他们两人,尼禄都授予了罗马公民权,但是,他命令弗里喜人撤出他们所占据的地区。而当他们不听从皇帝的命令的时候,为了实施皇帝的决定,就突然有一支辅助骑兵队伍赶到,并向他们发动了进攻,那些顽强抵抗的人不是被捕就是被杀。

　　然后,安普西瓦里人占领了这一地区。他们是一个更加强大的部落,而且由于已经被卡乌奇人赶出了自己的家园,他们成为一个无家可归、渴望获得一个安全避难所的民族,所以得到了邻近诸部落的同情。替他们说话的是一个名叫波约卡路斯的人,此人对罗马非常忠诚,而且在这些部落之中是一个非常闻名的角色。他提醒我们道:"当凯路斯奇人发动叛乱的时候,阿尔米尼乌斯将我关进了监狱。后来我又在提贝里乌斯和日耳曼尼库斯的领导之下服过役,现在,作为对你们50年忠诚的最高表示,我正在率领着我们整个的民族归顺你们罗马帝国。这一块地方你们留出来仅仅用作放牧罗马军队的畜群的,如此其价值就显得多么小啊!假如你们一定要这么做的话,一定要将这个地区用来放牧牲畜而不管那些仍然在挨饿的人的话,那么可不要真正到了认为荒废的土地比友好的民族更为重要的地步。以前这个地方是卡玛维人的领土,然后又被图邦提斯人占领,接着又被乌西批人占有。正如天空归属于诸神一样,大地是属于人类的。没有人居住的土地是人人都可以占有的。"他抬头仰望着太阳,向所有的天体作着祈求,仿佛是在向他们进行质问似的:"难道你们喜欢荒无人烟的土地吗?假如那样的话,就不要把我们赶走,而用洪水将土地淹没吧,将那些强占土地的人都淹死吧。"

Lucius Duvius Avitus was impressed. But he replied that men must obey their betters, that the gods they invoked had empowered the Romans to decide what to give and take away and to tolerate no judges but themselves. That was his official answer to the Ampsivarii. To Boiocalus himself, however, he promised land on the strength of his loyal record. The German rejected this as the wage of treachery. 'We may have nowhere to live', he commented, 'but we can find somewhere to die !' And they parted on bad terms.

The Ampsivarii urged the Bructeri, the Tencteri, and even more distant tribes, to fight at their side. Avitus wrote requesting the imperial governor of Upper Germany, Titus Curtilius Mancia, to cross the Rhine and menace their rear. Then Avitus invaded their potential allies the Tencteri, successfully threatening annihilation if they joined in. The Bructeri were likewise intimidated, and the other tribes proved equally unwilling to involve themselves in other people's dangers. The Ampsivarii fell back on the Usipi and Tubantes, who compelled them, however, to move on to the Chatti and then to the Cherusci. In their protracted wanderings, the exiles were treated as guests, then as beggars, then as enemies. Finally, their fighting men were exterminated, their young and old distributed as booty.

路奇乌斯·杜比乌斯·阿维图斯对这些话感到很不高兴,但是,他却回答道,人必须要服从比他们高贵的人的命令,他们所祈求的诸神已经做出了规定,授予罗马人权力,对于给予什么、剥夺什么,应该由罗马人说了算,除了罗马人之外,诸神是不会容忍任何人做出决定的。这就是他对于安普西瓦里人的请求所做出的回答,而对于波约卡路斯本人,他保证看在他多年对罗马忠诚的分上,给予他一块土地。这个日耳曼人拒绝了,因为在他看来,这是背叛的报酬。他进一步说:"我们可以没有谋生的土地,但我们却可以找到死亡的地方。"就这样,他们在恶语相对之中分手了。

安普西瓦里人极力劝说布路克提里人和腾可提里人,甚至是更远的一些部落,请他们与自己并肩作战。阿维图斯给上日耳曼地区的行政长官提图斯·库尔提里乌斯·曼奇亚写了一封信,请他率军渡过莱茵河,以便威胁敌军的后方。然后,他率部侵入了安普西瓦里人潜在的联盟部落腾可提里人所在的地区,威胁说,假如他们与安普西瓦里人结盟的话,就会把他们整个的民族杀光,并最终取得了成效。在同样的威胁之下,布路克提里人也屈服了。而其他的各个部落也同样不愿意为了他人的事情而使自己卷入危险之中。安普西瓦里人只好退到乌西批人和图邦提斯人所居住的地区,然而,他们又被从这些地方驱赶了出来;之后,又相继搬迁到卡提伊人和凯路斯奇人所住的地方去。在他们漫长的流浪过程之中,所到之处,起初被视为客人,接着就被当作乞丐,再接着就被看做是敌人了。最终,他们之中能够作战的人都在异国他乡战死了,而孩子和老人都被当作了战利品而被分配了。

The same summer, the Hermunduri and Chatti fought a great battle. Each wanted to seize the rich salt-producing river which flowed between them. Besides their passion for settling everything by force, they held a religious conviction that this region was close to heaven so that men's prayers received ready access. And by divine favour, they believed, salt in this river and these woods was produced, not as in other countries by the evaporation of water left by the sea, but by pouring it on heaps of burning wood and thus uniting the two opposed elements, fire and water. In the battle, the Chatti were defeated—with catastrophic effects. For both sides, in the event of victory, had vowed their enemies to Mars and Mercury. This vow implied the sacrifice of the entire beaten side with their horses and all their possessions. So the threats of this anti-Roman people recoiled on themselves.

But a friendly tribe also, the Ubii, were overwhelmed by a sudden disaster. Flames bursting out of the ground devoured farmhouses, crops, and villages far and wide, right up to the walls of the recently founded settlement named after Agrippina. Neither rain nor river norăny other water could quench the fire. Finally a few desperate and distraught peasants hurled rocks into the flames, and, as they subsided, advanced and fought them with clubs and other implements, as one would fight wild animals. Finally, they tore off their clothes and heaped them on. The oldest and dirtiest garments were most effective as extinguishers.

同一年的夏天,赫尔孟都利人和卡提伊人之间爆发了一场激烈的战争。双方都想抢夺一条富含食盐的流过两个部落之间的河流。除了热切地希望通过武力来解决所有的问题之外,他们还有一个宗教信念,认为这一地区离天神更近一些,这样他们所做的祷告就容易被天神听到。他们认为,通过神的恩赐,使得这条河和这一森林地区的产盐方式与其他地区不同,其他地区生产盐是用将海水引到海岸上,再进行蒸发的办法,但是这一地区则是通过将河水浇在一堆燃烧的木柴上,因此就将水和火这两种对立的元素结合在了一起,而生产出了食盐[1]。在战争中,卡提伊人被打败了,因而面临着灾难性的后果。因为他们双方都发过誓,只要是自己获得了胜利,就要将他们的敌人献给玛尔斯神和麦库利神,而这一誓言的含义就是要将被战败一方的所有人员以及他们所有的马匹、所有的财产统统地消灭掉。这样这一反对罗马人的民族的威胁就回报到自己身上了。

但是,与罗马保持友好关系的一个叫乌比伊的部落突然遭受了一场灭顶之灾。从地底下冒出来的火烧毁了农家的住宅、粮食、村落,火势又快又猛,很快就烧到了不久之前刚刚建立的以阿格里披娜的名字而命名的一座城墙的墙根。天上的雨、河里的水以及其他任何形式的水都不能扑灭这场大火。最后,一些孤注一掷的、情绪非常激动的农民猛烈地往大火里面投掷石块,而且,当火势稳定下来之后,他们走上前去,用木棍或其他的工具抽打,就像在跟野兽搏斗一样。最后,他们脱下衣服,捂在火上。那些又脏又破的衣服就成了最有效的灭火工具。

---

〔1〕 实际上,这不过是一种靠加热蒸发而生产盐的过程。

The fig-tree called 'Ruminalis', in the Place of Assembly, which 830 years earlier had sheltered the babies Romulus and Remus, suffered in this year. Its shoots died and its trunk withered. This was regarded as a portent. However, it revived, with fresh shoots.

When the new year came, and Gaius Vipstanus Apronianus and Gaius Fontcius Capito (II) became consuls, Nero ceased delaying his long-meditated crime. The longer his reign lasted, the bolder he became. Besides, he loved Poppaea more every day. While Agrippina lived, Poppaea saw no hope of his divorcing Octavia and marrying her. So she nagged and mocked him incessantly. He was under his guardian's thumb, she said—master neither of the empire nor of himself. 'Otherwise', she said, 'why these postponements of our marriage? I suppose my looks and victorious ancestors are not good enough. Or do you distrust my capacity to bear children? Or the sincerity of my love?

'No! I think you are afraid that, if we were married, I might tell you frankly how the senate is downtrodden and the public enraged by your mother's arrogance and greed. If Agrippina can only tolerate daughters-in-law who hate her son, let me be Otho's wife again! I will go anywhere in the world where I only need hear of the emperor's humiliations rather than see them-and see you in danger, like myself!'

在民会会场上有一株名叫"卢米那里斯"的无花果树,它就是830年之前曾经荫庇过罗木路斯和列穆斯的那一株树,[1]在这一年遭受了灾难。它的树根已经死了,树干枯萎了。这被看成了是某一种征兆。然而,它又抽出了新枝,复活了。

新年来临的时候,盖乌斯·维普斯塔努斯·阿普洛尼亚努斯和盖乌斯·丰提乌斯·卡皮托(二世)开始担任执政官。[2]尼禄决定不再将自己蓄谋已久的罪恶行动拖延下去了。统治时间越长,他的胆量也就变得越大。而且,他对波培娅的迷恋也在日复一日地增长着。波培娅发现,只要是阿格里披娜还活着,就没有希望使尼禄与屋大维娅离婚,进而使尼禄娶自己。于是她不断地对皇帝进行责备甚至是嘲笑,她说他完全受自己的监护人的支配,既不是帝国的主人,也不能替自己做主。她说:"假如不是这样的话,那么为什么我们的婚事还这样一直拖着呢?我想是因为我的容貌没有足够的漂亮,我的祖先没有足够的凯旋的荣耀。难道你怀疑我不能为你生孩子?还是怀疑我对你的真挚的爱情?

"不,我想你害怕的是一旦我们结了婚,我将会把元老院如何遭受压制以及公众对于你母亲的横暴和贪婪是如何愤怒都坦白地告诉你。假如阿格里披娜只能容忍一个仇视她儿子的人做她的儿媳妇的话,那么就让我重新做奥托的妻子好了!只要我只是听到而不至于亲眼见到皇帝所遭受的羞辱,不会亲眼见到你处于危险之中,就犹如我处于危险之中一样,那么我愿意到任何地方

----

〔1〕 传说之中,罗马人的始祖罗木路斯和列穆斯就是在这棵无花果树下吮吸母狼的奶水的,还传说这棵树是自发的从帕拉提努斯山脚下的卢佩卡尔洞穴迁移到元老院对面的民会会场上来的。

〔2〕 罗马建城812年,即公元59年。

This appeal was reinforced by tears and all a lover's tricks. Nero was won. Nor was there any opposition. Everyone longed for the mother's domination to end. But no one believed that her son's hatred would go as far as murder.

According to one author, Cluvius Rufus, Agrippina's passion to retain power carried her so far that at midday, the time when food and drink were beginning to raise Nero's temperature, she several times appeared before her inebriated son all decked out and ready for incest. Their companions observed sensual kisses and evilly suggestive caresses. Seneca, supposing that the answer to a woman's enticements was a woman, called in the ex-slave Acte. She feared for Nero's reputation—and for her own safety. Now she was instructed to warn Nero that Agrippina was boasting of her intimacy with her son, that her boasts had received wide publicity, and that the army would never tolerate a sacrilegious emperor.

Another writer, Fabius Rusticus, agrees in attributing successful intervention to Acte's wiles, but states that the desires were not Agrippina's but Nero's. But the other authorities support the contrary version. So does the tradition. That may be because Agrippina really did intend this monstrosity. Or perhaps it is because no sexual novelty seemed incredible in such a woman. In her earliest years she had employed an illicit relationship with Marcus Aemilius Lepidus (V) as a means to power. Through the same ambition she had sunk to be Pallas' mistress. Then, married to her uncle, her training in abomination was complete. So Nero avoided

去。"这一哭诉通过眼泪和各种媚术而增强了效果,尼禄被征服了,他没有进行任何的反对意见。所有的人也都渴望阿格里披娜结束其在全国范围内的支配地位。但是也没有人相信她的儿子会恨她到要杀死她的地步。

根据一位作家克路维乌斯·路福斯的说法,阿格里披娜在保住自己的权力的强烈欲望的驱使之下,竟然干出了这样的丑事:每当正午吃饭时分,尼禄喝酒已经喝得激情澎湃的时候,她有好几次将自己打扮得花枝招展出现在自己已经微醉的儿子面前,准备干那近亲相奸的勾当。他们身边伴随的人已经观察到了那些色情的接吻和那些预示着犯罪的爱抚。塞内加想到了要抵制一个女人的诱惑只有利用另一个女人,于是将被释奴隶阿克提召了进来。她非常害怕尼禄此举会毁了尼禄本人的名声,也非常害怕自己的危险处境。现在,她按照指示提醒尼禄,阿格里披娜到处炫耀自己与儿子的乱伦行为,她的夸耀使公众们都知道了这件事情,而军队是永远也不会容忍一个亵渎神灵的皇帝的统治的。

另一位作家法比乌斯·路斯提库斯同意多亏了阿克提的聪明机智才破坏了他们的丑行这一说法,但是他认为,想通奸的不是阿格里披娜,而是尼禄。但是,另外一些作家则是支持与之相反的观点,而传统的说法也是与克路维乌斯·路福斯的说法相同。或许是因为阿格里披娜本人确实是想进行这样的罪恶勾当,也或许是因为大家认为在这样一个女人身上不发生淫乱的新奇故事是根本就不可能的事情。最早的时候,她为了获取权力,就与玛尔库斯·埃米里乌斯·列庇都斯(五世)发生了通奸的行为。接着,为了同样的目的,她又委身于帕拉斯,做了他的情人。然后,又与自己的叔父结了婚,她的举动简直就是可恶之极。因此,尼禄就

being alone with her. When she left for her gardens or country mansions at Tusculum and Antium, he praised her intention of taking a holiday.

Finally, however, he concluded that wherever Agrippina was she was intolerable. He decided to kill her. His only doubt was whether to employ poison, or the dagger, or violence of some other kind. Poison was the first choice. But a death at the emperor's table would not look fortuitous after Britannicus had died there. Yet her criminal conscience kept her so alert for plots that it seemed impracticable to corrupt her household. Moreover, she had strengthened her physical resistance by a preventive course of antidotes. No one could think of a way of stabbing her without detection. And there was another danger: that the selected assassin might shrink from carrying out his dreadful orders.

However, a scheme was put forward by Anicetus, an ex-slave who conunanded the fleet at Misenum. In Nero's boyhood Anicetus had been his tutor; he and Agrippina hated each other. A ship could be made, he now said, with a section which would come loose at sea and hurl Agrippina into the water without warning. Nothing is so productive of surprises as the sea, remarked Anicetus; if a shipwreck did away with her, who could be so unreasonable as to blame a human agency instead of wind and water? Besides, when she was dead the emperor could allot her a temple and altars and the other public tokens of filial duty.

避免和自己的母亲单独在一起了。当她到她在图司库路姆和安提乌姆的花园和别墅去的时候，她休养的意图就受到了他的赞美。

然而，尼禄最终得出了结论，不论阿格里披娜在什么地方，始终是一个令人无法忍受的祸害。他决心要杀死她。他唯一还在迟疑的是，究竟要用毒药还是用刀子还是要用其他的办法下手。首先，他选择了下毒的办法。但是，要让她死在皇帝的餐桌旁，公众们就绝对不会认为这是偶然的事情了，因为布列塔尼库斯已经是这样死了。而要想收买阿格里披娜身边的仆人看来也是行不通的，因为她早已经习惯于犯罪，这使得她的意识之中对于陷害她的阴谋保持着高度的警惕性。更何况，为了预防自己被毒死，她已经服用了解毒药，进而增强了自己身体的抗毒药性。如果刺杀，则没有人可以想出可以使她觉察不到的办法。而且这样做还存在着一个危险，那就是他所挑选出来的杀手很有可能拒绝执行他这一可怕的命令。

正在这时，一名叫阿尼凯图斯的被释奴隶，此人担任过米塞努姆的海军舰队指挥官，他向尼禄提出了一个谋杀计划。在尼禄的少年时代，他曾经担任过尼禄的教师，而且他与阿格里披娜彼此互相仇恨。他对尼禄说，可以制造这样的一艘船，当轮船航行在大海之中的时候，它的一部分会自行松动脱落，从而使阿格里披娜在毫不知情的情况之下掉入大海。阿尼凯图斯强调说，任何地方都不及大海那样容易发生令人惊恐的事故。假如她在船难事故之中丧命的话，谁还会强词夺理地指责这是人为的谋杀而不将这看做是风浪所造成的意外呢？而且，当她死后，皇帝要为她修建神庙、祭坛以及其他的可以表示孝心的公共建筑。

This ingenious plan found favour. The time of year, too, was suitable, since Nero habitually attended the festival of Minerva at Baiae. Now he enticed his mother there. ' Parents' tempers must be borne! ' he kept announcing. 'One must humour their feelings. ' This was to create the general impression that they were friends again, and to produce the same effect on Agrippina. For women are naturally indined to believe welcome news.

As she arrived from Antium, Nero met her at the shore. After welcoming her with outstretched hands and embraces, he conducted her to Bauli, a mansion on the bay between Cape Misenum and the waters of Baiae. Some ships were standing there. One, more sumptuous than the rest, was evidently another compliment to his mother, who had formerly been accustomed to travel in warships manned by the imperial navy. Then she was invited out to dinner. The crime was to take place on the ship under cover of darkness. But an informer, it was said, gave the plot away; Agrippina could not decide whether to believe the story, and preferred a sedan-chair as her conveyance to Baiae.

There her alarm was relieved by Nero's attentions. He received her kindly, and gave her the place of honour next himself. The party went on for a long time. They talked about various things; Nero was boyish and intimate—or confidentially serious. When she left, he saw her off, gazing into her eyes and clinging to her. This may have been a final piece of shamming-or perhaps even Nero's brutal heart was affected

　　这一精心的计划完全可行,而且时机也非常合适,因为尼禄通常要到拜阿伊去庆祝米涅尔瓦节。[1] 现在,他极力引诱她的母亲到那里去。他不断地声明:"在父母发火的时候,一定要忍耐,一定要体谅父母的感情。"他说这些话的目的就是要给对方留下深刻的印象,他们已经和好了。而这对于阿格里披娜也确实产生了这样的效果。因为女人们通常情况下都易于相信顺心事的。

　　当她从安提乌姆赶来的时候,尼禄在海岸边迎接她。尼禄伸出手来扶住了她,并且拥抱了她,之后就陪她到包利去。包利是位于米塞努姆海角和拜阿伊湖之间的一个海湾之上的一座别墅。那儿排列了许多的船,其中有一艘比其他的船都要漂亮,很明显这是皇帝对母亲的尊敬之情的另一种表达方式,因为以前她习惯乘坐的是一艘由一批皇家水手掌控的战舰。接着,她就被要求出船舱进行晚宴。但是,据说早就有人将这一阴谋泄露给她了。阿格里披娜还没有做出决定,到底该不该相信这一说法。她选择了肩舆作为交通工具赶到了拜阿伊。

　　在那儿,尼禄的招待减轻了她的恐惧之心。他热情地接待了她,并让她享受了坐在皇帝身旁的殊荣。宴会进行了很长时间,他们对各种问题进行了交谈,尼禄则有时候像个孩子一样会非常亲昵,有时又很严肃地谈一些问题。当阿格里披娜要离开的时候,他为她送别,并亲吻她的眼睛,紧紧地将她拥抱。尼禄此举或

---

　　〔1〕　这是每年的3月19日为米涅尔瓦神所举行的节日,节日举行5天,由于工作性质的原因而受这位女神保护的人,可特别的进行庆祝,这个节日也是学校的放假日。

by his last sight of his mother, going to her death.

But heaven seemed determined to reveal the crime. For it was a quiet, star-lit night and the sea was calm. The ship began to go on its way. Agrippina was attended by two of her friends. One of them, Crepereius Gallus, stood near the tiller. The other, Acerronia, leant over the feet of her resting mistress, happily talking about Nero's remorseful behaviour and his mother's re-established influence. Then came the signal. Under the pressure of heavy lead weights, the roof fell in. Crepereius was crushed, and died instantly. Agrippina and Acerronia were saved by the raised sides of their couch, which happened to be strong enough to resist the pressure. Moreover, the ship held together.

In the general confusion, those in the conspiracy were hampered by the many who were not. But then some of the oarsmen had the idea of throwing their weight on one side, to capsize the ship. However, they took too long to concert this improvised plan, and meanwhile others brought weight to bear in the opposite direction. This provided the opportunity to make a gentler descent into the water. Acerronia ill-advisedly started crying out, 'I am Agrippina! Help, help the emperor's mother!' She was struck dead by blows from poles and oars and whatever ship's gear happened to be available. Agrippina herself kept quiet and avoided recognition. Though she was hurt-she had a wound in the shoulder—she swam until she came to some sailing-boats. They brought her to the Lucrine lake, from which she was taken home.

There she realized that the invitation and special compliment had been treacherous, and the collapse of her ship planned. The collapse

许是因为想将这出戏演到底,也或许是即使是尼禄这样残忍成性的人也因为最后看一眼行将丧命的母亲而心有感触。

但是,似乎上天也想将这一罪行揭露似的,因为这是一个安宁、繁星满天的夜晚,海面上也极为平静。轮船开始起航了。阿格里披娜有两个好友相伴,一个是克列培莱乌斯·伽路斯,就站在舵柄的旁边。另一个是阿凯罗尼娅,偎依在横卧着的皇太后的脚下,而阿格里披娜则正在兴奋地谈论着尼禄的幡然悔悟,以及他的母亲重新建立的对他的影响。这时候传来了信号,在沉重的铅块的压力下,船顶塌落了下来。克列培莱乌斯被砸中了,接着就死去了,而阿格里披娜和阿凯罗尼娅被床两侧的挡板给救了,因为恰巧床板非常结实,足以抵抗这一压力。而且,轮船也没有破裂。

这时船上一片混乱,参与这次阴谋的人也被许多不知内情的人给挡住了,而无法下手。但是,这时一些水手想出了一个办法,他们站在船的一面将他们的重量加在一块将船压翻。但是,对于这一临时的决定他们花费了太多的时间,甚至还没有来得及统一意见,这时已经有一些人将他们的重量加到了相反的方向上去了,这使得这些谋害者慢慢地滑落进水去了。而这时阿凯罗尼娅开始鲁莽地大喊道:"我是阿格里披娜,救命! 快来救皇帝的母亲!"她就被竿子、船桨以及船上任何能够摸到的东西给打死了。而阿格里披娜未发一言,也就没有被辨认出来,虽然她被打了一下,伤了肩膀,但她一直在游着,直到被一些渔船救起。他们将她载到了路克里努斯湖,从那儿她被带回了家。

在那儿她充分地认识到,尼禄对她的邀请以及对她的异乎寻常的敬重,原来都是一次骗局,轮船的塌陷也是早已经设计好的,

had started at the top, like a stage-contrivance. The shore was close by, there had been no wind, no rock to collide with. Acerronia's death and her own wound also invited reflection. Agrippina decided that the only escape from the plot was to profess ignorance of it. She sent an ex-slave Agerinus to tell her son that by divine mercy and his lucky star she had survived a serious accident. The messenger was to add, however, that despite anxiety about his mother's dangerous experience Nero must not yet trouble to visit her-at present rest was what she needed. Meanwhile, pretending unconcern, she cared for her wound and physical condition generally. She also ordered Acerronia's will to be found and her property sealed. Here alone no pretence was needed.

To Nero, awaiting news that the crime was done, came word that she had escaped with a slight wound-after hazards which left no doubt of their instigator's identity. Half-dead with fear, he insisted she might arrive at any moment. 'She may arm her slaves! She may whip up the army, or gain access to the senate or Assembly, and incriminate me for wrecking and wounding her and killing her friends! What can I do to save myself?' Could Burrus and Seneca help? Whether they were in the plot is uncertain. But they were imme diately awakened and summoned.

For a long time neither spoke. They did not want to dissuade and be rejected. They may have felt matters had gone so far that Nero had to strike before Agrippina, or die. Finally Seneca ventured so far as to turn to Burrus and ask if the troops should be ordered to kill her. He replied that the Guard were devoted to the whole imperial house and

轮船就像一个设计好了的舞台一样突然从上面塌了下来。而且就在离海岸很近的地方，当时海上既没有起风，轮船也没有触礁。阿格里披娜又回忆了一下阿凯罗尼娅的死亡以及自己受伤的经过，她认识到唯一能够从这一阴谋之中逃命的办法就是装作对此事不知内情。她派一名被释奴隶阿盖尔穆斯给她的儿子捎信，告诉他，由于上天的怜悯和自己福星的护佑，她已经躲过了一场严重的灾难。在信里面她还加了一条，告诉尼禄，尽管他会对于母亲的危险经历感到焦虑万分，但是，还是不用麻烦他来看望她，因为当前她最需要的是休息。她假装若无其事的样子，开始照料自己的伤口和自己的身体状况。她还派人去搜寻阿凯罗尼娅的遗嘱，并把她的财产封存了起来。这一举动倒没有必要假装。

尼禄正在等着阴谋的执行情况，这时传来了消息说他的母亲已经逃命了，只是受了一点儿轻伤。受到了伤害之后，却使她弄明白了谋害者的真实身份。尼禄对此吓得半死，他不断地在想阿格里披娜有可能会随时来找他。"她有可能将自己手下的奴隶武装起来，她有可能煽动军队造反，或许她回到元老院或民会那里去控告我在船上所布置的谋杀以及使她受伤和杀死她的朋友的事情。我应该采取什么行动以自保呢？"布路斯和塞内加可以帮忙吗？而他们是否参与了这次阴谋也还不清楚。但是，尼禄还是马上派人将他们叫醒并传唤了来。

他们两个很长一段时间沉默不语。他们不想劝阻皇帝，因为那样也是无用的。他们认为事情已经发展到如此严重的地步了，最后，塞内加鼓足勇气，把脸转向了布路斯，询问他是否可以命令部队处死她。布路斯对此回答道，近卫军对整个皇室都非常效

to Germanicus' memory; they would commit no violence against his offspring. Anicetus, he said, must make good his promise. Anicetus unhesitatingly claimed the direction of the crime. Hearing him, Nero cried that this was the first day of his reign—and the magnificent gift came from a former slave! 'Go quickly!' he said. 'And take men who obey orders scrupulously!'

Agrippina's messenger arrived. When Nero was told, he took the initiative, and staged a fictitious incrimination. While Agerinus delivered his message, Nero dropped a sword at the man's feet and had him arrested as if caught red-handed. Then he could pretend that his mother had plotted against the emperor's life, been detected, and-in shame-committed suicide.

Meanwhile Agrippina's perilous adventure had become known. It was believed to be accidental. As soon as people heard of it they ran to the beach, and climbed on to the embankment, or fishing-boats nearby. Others waded out as far as they could, or waved their arms. The whole shore echoed with wails and prayers and the din of all manner of inquiries and ignorant answers. Huge crowds gathered with lights. When she was known to be safe, they prepared to make a show of rejoicing.

But a menacing armed column arrived and dispersed them. Anicetus surrounded her house and broke in. Arresting every slave in his path, he came to her bedroom door. Here stood a few servants-the rest had been frightened away by the invasion. In her dimly lit room a single maid waited with her. Agrippina's alarm had increased

忠,并且十分怀念日耳曼尼库斯,因此,他们不会愿意对他的后人下毒手的。他说,阿尼凯图斯应该认真履行他的诺言。于是,阿尼凯图斯毫不犹豫地宣布他会执行这一犯罪行为的。听到了他的话,尼禄就叫喊了起来,说今天他才真正地获得了统治大权,而这份丰厚的礼物是来自于一个被释奴隶。他说:"马上就去办!要带一批绝对服从命令的人去处理此事!"

这时,阿格里披娜的信使赶到了,尼禄知道之后,就采取了先发制人的方法,编织了一个会构成大逆罪的圈套。当阿盖尔穆斯向他转达阿格里披娜的信息时,尼禄将一把剑扔在了此人的脚底下,然后命人将他逮捕,就好像是抓住了一名现行谋杀犯一样。然后他就可以散布谣言,说他的母亲派人来要谋害皇帝的性命,被发觉之后,由于羞愧难当自尽了。

与此同时,阿格里披娜遇险的消息也传开了。大家都认为,这只是一次偶然的事故。当民众听说了这一消息之后,他们就跑向了海滩,爬上了海边的堤岸,或者是登上了附近的渔船。还有一些人则是尽可能地涉足走向海水,直到不能再往里走为止;还有一些人则是张开了双臂。整个海岸边充满了号泣和祈祷以及各种各样询问的和含混不清的回答的回响声。大批的人群手里拿着火把拥挤到了这里。当他们知道她很安全的时候,就准备举行一次庆祝演出。

但是,一支森严可畏的武装部队赶到了这里,把他们驱散了。阿尼凯图斯将她的住所团团包围起来,然后就闯了进去。把所遇见的每一名奴隶都抓起来之后,他来到了她的卧室门口。在那儿站了一些奴仆,而其余的人在军队闯进来之时都已经吓跑了。在她那点着昏暗的灯光的卧室里面,只有一名女仆陪伴

as nobody, not even Agerinus, came from her son. If things had been well there would not be this terribly ominous isolation, then this sudden uproar. Her maid vanished. ' Are you leaving me, too? ' called Agrippina. Then she saw Anicetus. Behind him were a naval captain and lieutenant named Herculcius and Obaritus respectively. ' If you have come to visit me ' , she said, ' you can report that I am better. But if you are assassins, I know my son is not responsible. He did not order his mother' s death. ' The murderers closed round her bed. First the captain hit her on the head with a truncheon. Then as the lieutenant was drawing his sword to finish her off, she cried out: ' Strike here! ' pointing to her womb. Blow after blow fell, and she died.

So far accounts agree. Some add that Nero inspected his mother' s corpse and praised her figure; but that is contested. She was cremated that night, on a dining couch, with meagre ceremony. While Nero reigned, her grave was not covered with earth or enclosed, though later her household gave her a modest tomb beside the road to Misenum, on the heights where Julius Caesar' s mansion overlooks the bay beneath. During the cremation one of her former slaves, Mnester (II) , stabbed himself to death. Either he loved his patroness, or he feared assassination.

This was the end which Agrippina had anticipated for years. The prospect had not daunted her. When she asked astrologers about Nero,

在她的身边。由于没有任何人,甚至连阿盖尔穆斯在内,也没有从她的儿子那儿传过话来,所以她的恐惧之心逐渐地剧烈起来。假如事情还顺利的话,就不会出现如此可怕的不吉利的孤寂。接着就传来了一片喧闹声,她身边的女仆也逃跑了。于是,阿格里披娜喊道:"你也要离开我吗?"这时她看见了阿尼凯图斯,而在他身后的是一名叫赫丘列乌斯的海军船长和一名叫奥巴里图斯的海军百人团长。她说道:"假如你们是来看望我的,就向皇帝汇报说我比以前好多了。但是,假如你们是来谋杀我的话,那么我知道我的儿子不可能对此负责,他不可能命令杀死自己的母亲的。"杀手们将她的床包围了起来,一开始,船长用木棍击中了她的头部,然后,当百人团长抽出剑要结束她的性命的时候,她指着自己的腹部喊道:"刺这儿呀!"一剑接着一剑地刺下去之后,她就死了。

对于以上事件的历史记载都是相同的。有一些记载中则是说,当尼禄见到他母亲的尸体的时候,曾经称赞她的体形很美。但有人对此予以了否认。当天晚上,她的尸体就被放在了一个用餐的卧榻上,用非常简单的仪式就地火化了。在尼禄统治期间,她的坟墓上既没有填土,也没有圈起来。直到后来,她的一位仆人才在米塞努姆的大道旁边给她修建了一座最为简陋的墓地。而离墓地不远的高地上就是那俯视下面海湾的尤利乌斯·恺撒的别墅,在阿格里披娜的尸体被火化的时候,她的一位被释奴隶,名字叫莫涅斯特尔(二世),拔刀自杀了。或许是出于对前主人的爱戴,也或许是惧怕遭受陷害的缘故。

对于自己这样的结局,阿格里披娜多年之前就已经料到了。当年她请占星术士占卜一下尼禄的未来,占星术士们回答

they had answered that he would become emperor but kill his mother. Her reply was, ' Let him kill me—provided he becomes emperor!' But Nero only understood the horror of his crime when it was done. For the rest of the night, witless and speechless, he alternately lay paralysed and leapt to his feet in terror—waiting for the dawn which he thought would be his last. Hope began to return to him when at Burrus' suggestion the colonels and captains of the Guard came and cringed to him, with congratulatory handclasps for his escape from the unexpected menace of his mother's evil activities. Nero's friends crowded to the temples. Campanian towns nearby followed their lead and displayed joy by sacrifices and deputations.

Nero's insincerity took a different form. He adopted a gloomy demeanour, as though sorry to be safe and mourning for his parent's death. But the features of the countryside are less adaptable than those of men; and Nero's gaze could not escape the dreadful view of that sea and shore. Besides, the coast echoed (it was said) with trumpet blasts from the neighbouring hills—and wails from his mother's grave. So Nero departed to Neapolis.

He wrote the senate a letter. Its gist was that Agerinus, a confidential ex-slave of Agrippina, had been caught with a sword, about to murder him, and that she, conscious of her guilt as instigator of the crime, had paid the penalty. He added older charges. ' She had wanted to be coruler—to receive oaths of allegiance from the Guard, and to subject senate and public to the same humiliation. Disappointed of this, she had hated all of them—army, senate and people. She had opposed

道,他将来会成为皇帝的,但是会杀死自己的母亲。她的回答则是:"那就让他杀了我吧,只要他能成为皇帝就行。"但是,当这一罪行完成了之后,尼禄所感到的只有恐惧。那天晚上的剩余时间里,他或者是呆呆地一句话也不说,或者是吓得疯了似的从床上跳起来,等候着黎明的到来,他认为黎明就是他的末日来临了。但是,当将领们以及近卫军百人团长们在布路斯的提议之下相继走上前来,与他握手,祝贺他从自己母亲的罪恶的、想出其不意地谋害皇帝的险境之中逃了出来的时候,他又恢复了希望。尼禄的朋友们又簇拥着到了神庙之中,在他们的带领之下,康帕尼亚附近的各个城镇也用奉献牺牲和派遣代表团的方式表达自己的喜悦。

尼禄的伪装则是采用了一种不同的方式。他装出一副非常悲伤的样子,似乎对于自己还安然在世感到极为遗憾,而对于母亲的去世则是痛心疾首。但是,河山的面貌不可能像人的面貌那样容易改变,而且尼禄的视线总是离不开大海和海岸那可怕的景色。除此之外,(据说)海岸边还经常能听见从附近的群山中传来的喇叭声和从她母亲的坟墓中传来的哭泣声。于是,尼禄决定离开这儿到那不勒斯去。

他给元老院写了一封信,大意是说,阿格里披娜所信赖的一名被释奴隶阿盖尔穆斯手里拿着一把剑,准备刺杀他的时候被抓住了,事后,阿格里披娜意识到自己主使这次谋杀罪行的严重,就自杀了。他把旧账全部翻出来对她进行控诉:"她想成为共同的统治者,要整个近卫军向她宣誓效忠,同时也想逼迫元老院和民众蒙受同样的耻辱。当这一企图没有得逞之后,她就对所有的人产生了憎恨之情,包括对军队、对元老院、对民众。她一直反对

gratuities to soldiers and civilians alike. She had contrived the deaths of distinguished men. ' Only with the utmost difficulty, added Nero, had he prevented her from breaking into the senate-house and delivering verdicts to foreign envoys. He also indirectly attacked Claudius' regime, blaming his mother for all its scandals. Her death, he said, was providential. And he even called the shipwreck a happy accident. For even the greatest fool could not believe it accidental—or imagine that one shipwrecked woman had sent a single armed man to break through the imperial guards and fleets. Here condemnation fell not on Nero, whose monstrous conduct beggared criticism, but on Seneca who had composed his self-incriminating speech.

Nevertheless leading citizens competed with complimentary proposals—thanksgivings at every shrine; annual games at Minerva's Festival (during which the discovery of the plot had been staged); the erection in the senate-house of gold statues of Minerva and (beside her) the emperor; the inclusion of Agrippina's birthday among illomened dates. It had been the custom of Publius Clodius Thrasea Pactus to pass over flatteries in silence or with curt agreement. But this time he walked out of the senate—thereby endangering himself without bringing general freedom any nearer.

Many prodigies occurred. A woman gave birth to a snake. Another woman was killed in her husband's arms by a thunderbolt. The sun suddenly went dark. All fourteen city-districts were struck by lightning.

对士兵进行奖赏,对平民也是如此。她还曾经致许多社会显贵人物于死地。"尼禄还说,他尽了最大的努力才使她不能闯进元老院以接见外国使节。对于克劳狄乌斯的统治时期他也间接给予了指责,说他的母亲应该对当时的所有丑事负责。他说,他母亲的死是国家的一件幸事,甚至轮船事故也是国家之福。然而,即使是世界上最傻的人也不会相信这是一次偶然的事故,也难以想象一个遭受了船难事故的女人,会派遣一个人手拿凶器只身闯过禁卫军和海军的重重防线而刺杀皇帝。此时,舆论的谴责声就不再集中在尼禄的头上了,因为他的凶残已经使人无从谴责,而是落在了塞内加的头上,因为是他给尼禄起草的这份招认自己有罪的辩护稿。

然而,社会上的头面人物却在竞相提出溜须拍马的提议:在每个神庙之中都要开展感恩祭;在米涅尔瓦节(即发现刺杀皇帝阴谋的那一天),每年都要举行赛会;在元老院的会议室里面给米涅尔瓦女神竖一座金像,(在她的旁边)再给皇帝竖一座。阿格里披娜的生日那一天也被列入了凶煞日的行列[1]普布里乌斯·克劳狄乌斯·特拉塞亚·帕伊图斯过去习惯于使各种提案获得通过,对于各种阿谀奉承的提议要么沉默不语,要么只是敷敷衍衍地表示自己的同意。但是,这一次他走出了元老院,而这一做法只是使自己陷于危险的境地,并不能增加任何一点自由的氛围。

这时候,出现了许多古怪的预兆:一位妇女生了一条蛇;另一位女人在她丈夫的怀抱里却被雷劈死;太阳突然隐去了,天空一片黑暗;罗马城的14个街区都遭受了雷击。但是,这些征兆本身

[1] 11月6日。

But these portents meant nothing. So little were they due to the gods that Nero continued his reign and his crimes for years to come.

However, to intensify his mother's unpopularity and indicate his increased leniency now she had gone, he brought back two eminent women, Junia Calvina and Calpurnia (II), and two former praetors, Valerius Capito and Licinius Gabolus, whom she had exiled. He even permitted Lollia Paulina's ashes to be brought home, and a tomb erected. He also allowed back Junia Silana's two dependants, Iturius and Calvisius, whom he had recently banished. Silana herself had died at Tarcntum, having returned from her distant exile when Agrippina, whose malevolence had struck her down, became less vindictive—or less powerful.

Nero lingered in the cities of Campania. His return to Rome was a worrying problem. Would the senate be obedient? Would the public cheer him? Every bad character (and no court had ever had so many) reassured him that Agrippina was detested, and that her death had increased his popularity. They urged him to enter boldly and see for himself how he was revered. Preceding him—as they had asked to— they found even greater enthusiasm than they had promised. The people marshalled in their tribes were out to meet him, the senators were in their gala clothes, wives and children drawn up in lines by sex and age. Along his route there were tiers of seats as though for a Triumph. Proud conqueror of a servile nation, Nero proceeded to the

毫无意义,它们也几乎没有代表诸神的意旨,因为在这之后尼禄又统治了好多年,还在继续着他的罪恶行径。

然而,为了加深人们对她母亲的憎恨之情,以及表示在她死后自己那逐步宽容的胸怀,他将被阿格里披娜驱逐出罗马的两位显要的妇女优尼娅·卡尔维娜和卡尔普尔尼娅(二世)以及两名前行政长官瓦列里乌斯·卡皮托和李奇尼乌斯·伽波路斯都召回了罗马。他甚至允许将洛里娅·宝琳娜的骨灰运回家,并为她修了一座坟墓。最近刚刚遭到驱逐的优尼娅·西拉娜手下的两名食客伊图里乌斯和卡尔维西乌斯也被允许回到了罗马。西拉娜本人则是已经在塔伦特过世了,她在阿格里披娜尚在世的时候已经从遥远的流放地回来了。阿格里披娜那恶毒的复仇心理使她狠狠地击垮了西拉娜,而以后这一心理不那么坚决了或者是不那么强烈了,所以才让她回来。

尼禄还在康帕尼亚的各个城市之中徘徊,返回罗马仍然是一件让他焦虑不安的事情。元老院会服从他的命令吗?民众们会不会欢迎他?每个坏人(世界上任何宫廷之中都从未出现过如此众多的恶棍)都在鼓励他,说阿格里披娜遭到了人民的憎恨,她的死亡提高了皇帝的声誉。他们敦促他勇敢地回到罗马,看一下自己受到了多么大的敬仰。正如他们在先前所布置的那样,在皇帝的面前他们看到了比他们向皇帝所保证的还要热烈得多的欢迎场面。各个部落的民众都走出家门集合起来夹道迎接他;元老们都穿上了节日的盛装;妇女和儿童按照性别和年龄列起队伍欢迎他。沿着他所走过的路线,搭起了一排排的座位,好像是在欢迎一场胜利的凯旋。尼禄感到了自己就是一个奴性十足的民族的征服者,于是豪情万丈地赶到了朱庇特神

Capitol and paid his vows.

Then he plunged into the wildest improprieties, which vestiges of respect for his mother had hitherto not indeed repressed, but at least impeded.

庙,在那儿还了愿。

接着,尼禄又开始了他那无法无天的罪恶举动。而到目前为止,他对于母亲的那一点点尊敬之情,虽然实际上根本就约束不了他,但起码也推迟了他的各种犯罪活动。

CHAPTER 12

Nero And His Helpers

Nero had long desired to drive in four-horse chariot races. Another equally deplorable ambition was to sing to the lyre, like a professional. 'Chariot-racing', he said, 'was an accomplishment of ancient kings and leaders-honoured by poets, associated with divine worship. Singing, too, is sacred to Apollo: that glorious and provident god is represented in a musician's dress in Greek cities, and also in Roman temples.'

There was no stopping him. But Seneca and Burrus tried to prevent him from gaining both his wishes by conceding one of them. In the Vatican valley, therefore, an enclosure was constructed, where he could drive his horses, remote from the public eye. But soon the public were admitted—and even invited; and they approved vociferously. For such is a crowd: avid for entertainment, and delighted if the emperor shares their tastes. However, this scandalous publicity did not satiate Nero, as his advisers had expected. Indeed, it led him on. But if he shared his degradation, he thought it would be less; so he brought on to the stage members of the ancient nobility whose poverty made

第十二章　尼禄及其帮凶

　　尼禄很久以来就渴望能够参加四匹马的马车比赛。另一个同样令人可笑的愿望就是像一位专业歌手一样在竖琴的伴奏之下进行演唱。他说："马车比赛是古代国王们和统帅们的一项才艺,是由于诗人们的称颂而扬名的,是一项祭祀诸神的活动。而唱歌同样是为了献给阿波罗神的,因为这位伟大而又有先见之明的神灵不论是在希腊的城市中,还是在罗马的神庙中,出现的时候都穿着歌手的服装。"

　　没有人可以劝阻住他。但是塞内加和布路斯想通过在其中一方面让步的方法而不让他在两个方面都得逞。于是,他们在梵蒂冈谷地圈了一块土地进行建设,可以使尼禄在远离人民视线的情况之下驾驭他的马车。但是不久之后,公众就获准,甚至是被邀请来参观他的驾车表演了,而他们对尼禄大加赞扬。民众们就是这样的,渴望各种娱乐活动,而假如皇帝和他们有同样的嗜好,他们一定会很高兴的。然而尼禄的这种丑恶可耻的公开露面并没有像他的顾问们所想的那样使他得到满足。事实上,这让他进一步发展下去。他认为,假如别人和他同样地堕落的话,就会使他自己的堕落显得不那么突出了。于是他便让那些出生于古老

— 925 —

them corruptible. They are dead, and I feel I owe it to their ancestors not to name them. For though they behaved dishonourably, so did the man who paid them to offend (instead of not to do so). Well-known knights, too, he induced by huge presents to offer their services in the arena. But gifts from the man who can command carry with them an obligation.

However, Nero was not yet ready to disgrace himself on a public stage. Instead he instituted 'Youth Games'. There were many volunteers. Birth, age, official career did not prevent people from acting-in Greek or Latin style—or from accompanying their performances with effeminate gestures and songs. Eminent women, too, rehearsed indecent parts. In the wood which Augustus had planted round his Naval Lake, places of assignation and taverns were built, and every stimulus to vice was displayed for sale. Moreover, there were distributions of money. Respectable people were compelled to spend it; disreputable people did so gladly. Promiscuity and degradation throve. Roman morals had long become impure, but never was there so favourable an environment for debauchery as among this filthy crowd. Even in good surroundings people find it hard to behave well. Here every form of immorality competed for attention, and no chastity, modesty, or vestige of decency could survive.

的显要家族却由于贫穷而堕落的人登上了舞台进行演出。[1] 他们已经过世了,但我看在他们祖先的面上就不把他们的名字写出来了。因为,虽然他们的行为非常不光彩,而那些给他们钱让他们干缺德事(而不是不让他们干缺德事)的人同样也很无耻。他还用丰厚赏赐来引诱那些著名的骑士到斗兽场上进行表演。但是,从一个占据统治地位的人手里接受赏赐而进行的活动,是带有强制性的。

然而,尼禄还没有打算到公共舞台上进行表演以使自己丢人。不过,他创立了"青年竞赛会",[2] 有许多人自愿参加了这一赛会。不论任何出身、任何年龄、任何从政经历的即制都不能阻止人们在希腊风格或拉丁风格的戏剧之中扮演角色,也不能阻止他们用女人般的身段和唱腔进行表演。显要的贵妇人们也扮演下流的角色。在奥古斯都于他的海军湖四周所种植的树林里,建了许多约会的地点和小酒馆,而各式各样的用于刺激淫欲的东西在展示出售。更何况,还有金钱赏赐。那些德高望重的人是被迫才这样做的,而那些臭名昭著的人则是乐此不倦。荒淫与无耻的行为在社会上快速地繁衍着。罗马的道德早就肮脏不堪了,然而也从来没有出现过像今天这样的助长恶棍们荒淫放荡的环境。即使是在良好环境之中成长起来的人也很难做到洁身自好了。这是一个大伙竞相作恶的时代,任何的贞操、谦逊甚至哪怕是一点点体面都难以保存。

---

〔1〕 在古罗马,优伶的社会地位是很低的,即使可以出名也会让人瞧不起,因此真正的罗马人是不允许干这一行的。

〔2〕 尼禄创立这一赛会是为了纪念自己第一次剃胡须。

The climax was the emperor's stage debut. Meticulously tuning his lyre, he struck practice notes to the trainers beside him. A battalion attended with its officers. So did Burrus, grieving—but applauding. Now, too, was formed the corps of Roman knights known as the Augustiani. These powerful young men, impudent by nature or ambition, maintained a din of applause day and night, showering divine epithets on Nero's beauty and voice. They were grand and respected as if they had done great things.

But the emperor did not obtain publicity by his theatrical talents only. He also aspired to poetic taste. He gathered round himself at dinner men who possessed some versifying ability but were not yet known. As they sat on, they strung together verses they had brought with them, or extemporized—and filled out Nero's own suggestions, such as they were. This method is apparent from Nero's poems themselves, which lack vigour, inspiration, and homnogeneity. To philosophers, too, he devoted some of his time after dinner, enjoying their quarrelsome assertions of contradictory views. There were enough of such people willing to display their glum features and expressions for the amusement of the court.

At about this time there was a serious fight between the inhabitants

这一切的高潮出现在皇帝初次登台演出之时。他细心地调试了一下他的竖琴,向他身旁的师傅们唱了几个定音的调子。一个近卫军中队在其长官们的带领之下也参与了。尽管曲调伤心叹气,但人们在鼓掌叫好。在这期间,又成立了一个称作为奥古斯提亚尼的罗马骑士团体。[1] 这些年轻力壮的小伙子们或许是出于天性,或许是出于个人的野心,他们整日整夜厚颜无耻地为尼禄的表演喝彩,把奉献给神灵的那些形容词用来歌颂他的外貌和嗓音。他们高贵而又受人尊重,就像他们在从事伟大的事业似的。

但是皇帝不仅仅是以戏剧方面的天才而闻名,他还有创作诗歌的兴趣。在晚宴上,他在自己身边聚集了一批会写押韵的诗歌但还没有出名的人物。他们一入席,就开始将一些自己随身携带的诗句凑合到一起或是即兴朗诵,把尼禄按照自己的想法填充的一些东西凑在一起,他们所谓的诗歌就是这样。这种做诗方法从尼禄本人所创作的诗歌之中也可以清楚地看得出:没有活力,没有灵感,没有统一的风格。晚饭之后,他还会拿出一部分时间跟哲学家们待在一起,以他们各持己见进行争论作为一种享受。也不缺少这样的人,他们将自己装扮得性格忧郁、表情严肃以供皇帝消遣之用。

大约也就是在这一时候,在罗马的两个移民地努凯里亚和庞

---

〔1〕 这个团体除了骑士之外,还包括了 4000 名精壮的平民。其头目有固定的薪水,规定有成套的喝彩方法,打扮上也有特别的规定:头发要搽油、左手上不能带戒指等。

of two Roman settlements, Nuceria and Pompeii. It arose out of a tri-fling incident at a gladiatorial show given by Livineius Regulus (II), whose expulsion from the senate I have mentioned elsewhere. During an exchange of taunts-characteristic of these disorderly country towns-abuse led to stone-throwing, and then swords were drawn. The people of Pompeii, where the show was held, came off best. Many wounded and mutilated Nucerians were taken to the capital. Many bereavements, too, were suffered by parents and children. The emperor instructed the senate to investigate the affair. The senate passed it to the consuls. When they reported back, the senate debarred Pompeii from holding any similar gathering for ten years. Illegal associations in the town were dissolved; and the sponsor of the show and his fellow-instigators of the disorders were exiled.

Cyrene secured the expulsion of a governor, Pedius Blaesus, from the senate for violating their treasury of Aesculapius and accepting bribes and solicitations to falsify the recruiting rolls. Cyrene also prosecuted another ex-praetor, Acilius Strabo, who had been sent by Claudius to adjudicate on the ancestral royal estates which had been left, with the whole kingdom, to Rome by King Ptolemy Apion. Neighbouring landowners who had occupied these estates cited their longstanding usurpation as fair title. The adjudicator decided against them. So they reviled him. The senate answered that it did not know

培之间发生了严重的武装冲突。这次冲突发生在李维涅乌斯·
列古路斯(二世)主办的一次剑斗比赛上,是因为一个小小的事故
而引起的。而关于列古路斯被逐出元老院的事件我已经在别处
做过说明了。[1] 这次冲突的起因首先是他们用外地城市之中那
些无法无天的公民的典型方式进行了互相嘲弄,继而从谩骂发展
为相互抛石块,然后就是拔剑相斗。由于比赛是在庞培举行的,
那儿的人就占据了上风。许多受伤和致残的努凯里亚人被抬到
了首都罗马。许多父母和孩子为丧失了亲人而痛苦。皇帝下令
元老院对此事展开调查。元老院又转交给执政官进行处理。案
件回报给元老院之后,元老院做出了判决,今后 10 年之内禁止庞
培再举行此类的集会,城内所有的非法团体都要解散,而这次赛
会的举办者和其手下对这次混乱进行煽风点火的人则被驱逐
出境。

库列涅人控告他们的长官培狄乌斯·布莱苏斯侵犯了他们
的埃司库拉披乌斯的宝藏,并且在招募军队的过程之中收受贿
赂,徇私枉法。库列涅人还控告另一位前行政长官阿奇里乌斯·
斯特拉波,此人曾被克劳狄乌斯派遣来处理由托勒密·阿披昂国
王连同整个王国一同赠送给罗马[2]的古老的皇家地产,邻近的已
经占有这些地产的地主们将他们长久以来被默许的占据视做是
一种合法的举动。处理者做出了对他们不利的判决。于是他们
对他心怀忌恨。元老院对此的答复是他们还不知道克劳狄乌斯

---

〔1〕 本书中塔西佗对此事件说明的部分已经遗失了。

〔2〕 托勒密·阿披昂国王是库列奈卡王国的最后一位国王,他是埃及
的托勒密七世的私生子,死于公元前 96 年,他曾在公元前 96 年按照其父的
计划将库列奈卡王国遗赠给罗马。

Claudius' instructions-reference must be made to the emperor. Nero upheld the adjudicator, but wrote that nevertheless he would help the provincial landowners by legalizing their occupation.

The deaths now occurred of two famous men, Cnaeus Domitius Afer and Marcus Servilius Nonianus (II). Both were great orators with distinguished records, Domitius as advocate, Servilius—after a long legal career—as Roman historian; also as man of taste, wherein he displayed a marked contrast with his otherwise equally brilliant rival.

In the following year, when Nero (for the fourth time) and Cossus Cornelius Lentulus (II) were consuls, a five-yearly stage-competition was founded at Rome on the Greek model. Like most innovations, its reception was mixed. Some recalled with approval the criticism of Pompey, among his elders, for constructing a permanent theatre, whereas previously performances had been held with improvised stage and auditorium, or (to go back to the remoter past) spectators had stood-since seats, it was feared, would keep them idle for days on end. ' As for the shows, ' said objectors, ' let them continue in the old Roman way, whenever it falls to the praetors to celebrate them, and provided no citizen is obliged to compete. Traditional morals, already gradually deteriorating, have been utterly ruined by this imported laxity! It makes everything potentially corrupting and corruptible

做出了怎样的指示,因此必须向皇帝作请示。尼禄支持克劳狄乌斯的处理决定,但是写了一封信表示无论如何他会帮助行省的地主们使他们所占领的地产合法化。

现在出现了两个显要人物去世的事件,他们是格涅乌斯·多米提乌斯和玛尔库斯·塞尔维里乌斯·诺尼亚努斯(二世)。两个人都作为雄辩的演说家而永载史册。多米提乌斯的闻名是由于其辩护活动;而塞尔维里乌斯则是在经历了长时间的法律职业生涯之后,还作过罗马历史学家,这一切使他闻名于世,而他有着丰富的生活经历,这一点又使得他与和他同样杰出的人形成了鲜明的对比。

第二年,是尼禄(第四次)和科苏斯·科尔涅里乌斯·楞图路斯(二世)开始担任执政官的一年,[1]在这一年罗马举行了一种希腊式的、五年一度的舞台表演比赛。[2] 和对于一切新鲜事物一样,人们对于它的态度各不相同。有些人回想起了在庞培想建立一座永久性的剧院之时所受到的自己长辈们的批评,因为在他之前的表演都是在临时性的舞台上举行的,而观众席也是临时的;(再往前追溯的话)或者观众们都是站着的,因为人们担心座位会诱使人们连续数日而无所事事。反对者们说:"只要表演是由行政长官来主持,只要没有任何公民被强迫去竞争,那么最好还是按照罗马古老的方式进行演出。传统的道德水准已经逐渐地堕落下去了,现在又被舶来的放荡作风完全地毁坏了。这使得每一种可以使人堕落的或者是本身会堕落的东西都会在首都罗马出现。而且国

---

〔1〕 罗马建城 813 年,即公元 60 年。

〔2〕 这是尼禄按照希腊人的方式所创办的一种包括音乐、角力和赛马的比赛,每五年举办一次,因为这种比赛是尼禄第一次介绍到罗马来的,所以命名为"尼禄尼亚"。

flow into the capital-foreign influences demoralize our young men into shirkers, gymnasts, and perverts.

'Responsibility rests with emperor and senate. They have given immorality a free hand. Now they are compelling the Roman upper class to degrade themselves as orators or singers on the stage. It only remains to strip and fight in boxing-gloves instead of joining the army. Does expert attention to effeminate music and songs contribute to justice, or does it make the knights who serve as judges give better verdicts? And this vileness continues even at night! Good behaviour has no time left for it. In these promiscuous crowds, debauchees are emboldened to practise by night the lusts they have imagined by day. '

This licence was just what most people approved-though they put it more respectably. 'But our ancestors, too,' they suggested, 'did not shrink from such public entertainment as contemporary resources permitted. Ballet-dancers were imported from Etruria, horse-racing from Thurii. Ever since the annexation of Greece and Asia, performances have become more ambitious. Two hundred years have passed since the Triumph of Lucius Mummius—who first gave that sort of show here-and during that time no upper-class Roman has ever demeaned himself by *professional* acting. As for a permanent theatre, it was more economical than the construction and demolition of a new one every year, at vast expense.

外这些影响会使我们的年轻人变成懒汉、体育爱好者和淫乱的人。

"皇帝和元老院要对这种情况负责。他们已经对于非道德的行为放任自流了,现在他们又强迫罗马的上流人士作为演说家或歌唱家登台来玷污自己。对他们来说,唯一要做的事就是脱光衣服、带上拳击手套表演拳击,而不是去参加军队。[1] 难道那些对于女人气十足的音乐和歌曲很在行的人就会对于公正有所裨益吗?难道让骑士们担任法官就会做出更为公正的宣判?即使是在黑夜这种卑鄙肮脏的举动也在持续着,没有任何培养良好举止的余地。在这些乱七八糟的人群之中,那些流氓无赖们在黑夜里是敢大胆做出他们白天向往的事情的。"

这种放纵的行为恰恰是绝大多数人所喜欢的,他们甚至将其装扮得非常高雅体面。他们说:"即使我们的祖先,在当时财力许可的条件之下也不反对举行这类公共娱乐活动。芭蕾舞演员是从埃特路里亚来的,赛马是从图里伊学来的。自从格雷斯和亚细亚并入罗马以来,[2]演出越来越经常了。第一个把这一剧目介绍到罗马的人,路奇乌斯·穆米乌斯,取得成功以来已经过去200年了,[3]在这期间没有一个高贵的罗马人会以演戏作为终生的职业。而且建一座永久性的剧院,其花费比每年都要花大量金钱建一座新的临时性的剧院而后又拆掉要节约得多。

----

〔1〕 在希腊人看来,自由人是完全可以参加拳击比赛的,但罗马人却把这看做是和剑斗同样卑下的事情。在他们看来,具有一定的价值而又不玷污自己的唯一的体力训练就是军事训练。

〔2〕 它们分别是公元前146年和公元前133年并入罗马的。

〔3〕 这是公元前415年的事。

'If—as now suggested—the State pays for shows, it will save the purses of officials and give the public less opportunity to ask them for Greek contests. Prizes for oratory and poetry will encourage talent. And why should it be degrading even for a judge to listen with legitimate enjoyment to fine words? These nights—not many, out of a period of five years are for gaiety, not immorality. Besides, in such a blaze of lights, surreptitious immorality is impossible.'

Certainly, the display took place without any open scandal. Nor was there any partisan rioting, since the ballet-dancers, though allowed back on the stage, were banned from these sacred contests. The first prize for oratory was not awarded, but the emperor was declared winner. Greek clothes, which had been greatly worn during the competition, subsequently went out of fashion.

A brilliant comet now appeared. The general belief is that a comet means a change of emperor. So people speculated on Nero's successor as though Nero were already dethroned. Everybody talked of Rubellius Plautus, a Julian on his mother's side. His personal tastes were old-fashioned, his bearing austere, and his life respectable and secluded. Retirement, due to fear, had enhanced his reputation. The talk about the comet was intensified by equally superstitious reactions to a flash of lightning, which struck and broke the table at which Nero was

"假如跟我们现在所建议的那样,演出的费用由国家来支付,既可以节约官员们的费用开支,也可以使公众们减少机会要求长官们举行希腊式竞赛。[1] 演说家和诗人所取得的奖励会鼓励他们才能的发挥。假如一位法官将倾听高雅的戏剧作为合法的娱乐活动,那么为什么会感到下贱呢? 在这五年之中晚上给人们提供欢乐,不是经常的事情,也不是什么不道德的事。而且在这灯火通明的环境之下,根本就不可能做出什么偷偷摸摸不道德的事情。"

确实是,在赛会举行期间没有发生什么公开的丑闻,也没有发生任何为捧角而相互争吵的事件,因为那些芭蕾舞演员们虽然被允许回到舞台上,却被禁止参加一些神圣的比赛。没有颁发演说比赛的第一名的奖赏,但是皇帝却被宣布为获胜者。在比赛期间所盛行的希腊式服装,随之就不再流行了。

这时,天空出现了一颗明亮的彗星。按照传统的看法,彗星的出现将预示着皇帝要有所变换。于是,人们就推测谁将是尼禄的继承人,就好像尼禄已被废黜了似的。大家提到路贝里乌斯·普劳图斯,此人的母亲出生于尤利乌斯家族。他个人的观点是属于传统保守型的,他举止严肃,个人生活正派而又不声张。他由于畏惧而过着退隐的生活,这提高了他的声誉。人们对于彗星的讨论由于对一次雷电的同样迷信的反应而更加激烈了。尼禄在西姆布路伊尼湖畔的苏布拉奇乌姆别墅就餐时,出现了一次雷

---

〔1〕 罗马共和国时期,官员们为了讨好民众争取选票而出钱举行比赛,这是造成他们贪污受贿的原因之一。在罗马帝国时期,这种官吏自己出钱的情况实际上已不存在了。

dining in his mansion at Sublaqueum near the Simbruine Lakes. Since this was near Tibur, the birthplace of Plautus' father, the belief arose that the Divine Will had marked Plautus out. He was frequently courted by those whose devouring and often misguided ambitions attach them prematurely to new and hazardous causes. Nero was worried. He wrote asking Plautus, in the interests of the city's peace, to withdraw from malevolent gossip to enjoy his youthful years in the safety and calm of his family estates in Asia. So there Plautus went, with his wife, Antistia Pollitta, and his closest friends.

Nero, in these days, endangered and discredited himself by an extravagent eccentricity: he bathed in the source of the Marcian Aqueduct. His immersion therein was held to have polluted the sanctity of its holy waters. The divine anger was apparent when he became seriously ill.

When Cnaeus Domitius Corbulo (II) had demolished Artaxata, he decided to utilize the panic thus created in order to capture Tigranocerta. For if he destroyed it, he would increase the enemy's terror; if he spared it, he would be praised as merciful. So he started out. Without relaxing precautions, he avoided hostilities so that the Armenians might hope to be pardoned. He knew they were unstable-slow to face danger, but quick to change sides when opportunity offered. The natives, according to their dispositions, offered submission, or evacuated their villages and withdrew into the wilds. Some hid themselves and their families in caves.

Corbulo varied his treatment. To suppliants he was lenient; fugitives he chased. Those in hiding he ruthlessly burnt out after stuffing

电,雷电击中了他的餐桌并将其击碎了。由于这发生在提布尔附近,而提布尔正好是普劳图斯父亲的出生地,大伙相信神的旨意就是指定让普劳图斯担任皇位继承人。普劳图斯受到了那些热切的但又怀有不切实际的野心的人的支持,这些人往往会非常幼稚地产生一些新奇的但又很危险的想法。尼禄对此非常担忧。于是他给普劳图斯写了一封信,请他为了罗马城的和平而离开这些造谣生事的人,要求他到安全而又宁静的亚细亚去,那儿有他的家产,他可以在那儿享受自己的青春年华。于是普劳图斯带着自己的妻子和一些最亲密的朋友到亚细亚去了。

在那些时候,尼禄由于自己的过分放纵,使自己面临险境,并使自己声名狼藉。他到玛尔奇的克温图斯源头去游泳。有人把尼禄到那儿沐浴视做是对圣水的神圣性的玷污。后来他得了重病,有人就认为是神发怒的明证。

当格涅乌斯·多米提乌斯·科尔布罗(二世)将阿尔塔克撒塔夷为平地之后,就决定利用给敌人所造成的恐慌以夺取提格拉诺凯尔塔城。因为只要摧毁了这座城市,就能增加敌人的恐惧心理;而若赦免了它,就可以为自己赢得仁慈的美名。于是就率部出发了。他没有放松警惕,尽量避免采取敌对行动,这样就可以使亚美尼亚人怀有获得赦免的希望。他知道这些人是易变的,虽然面对危险反应迟钝,但是一旦有机会就会迅速改变立场。这些民族的人依据自己不同的性情要么向他屈服投降,要么逃离了自己的村庄而跑散到荒野之中去。而有一些人则是将自己和家人隐藏于山洞之中。

科尔布罗对此采取了不同的策略。对求饶者,他予以赦免;对逃跑者,予以追击。而对于那些躲藏起来的人,它采取了无情

the mouths and exits of their caves with bushes and faggots. The Mardi, experienced brigands, harassed him as he skirted their borders. Mountains protect their country from attack, but Corbulo launched the Iberians to devastate it, and thus punished the tribe's rash hostility without sacrificing Roman lives. Nevertheless, though he and his army suffered no losses in battle, over-exertion was wearing them out - also inadequate rations, for meat was all that kept them alive. Moreover, water was short, it was a blazing summer, and marches were long. The only compensation was the endurance of the general, who bore as much as the rank and file, and more.

Finally, however, they reached cultivated territory, where they harvested the crops. Here the Armenians had taken refuge in two forts. One was successfully assaulted, the other taken by siege. When they passed on to the district of Tauraunitis, Corbulo escaped from an unexpected threat to his life. A native of some importance was discovered near his tent with a weapon. Under torture he disclosed a conspiracy to murder Corbulo, incriminating others as well as himself. These plotters of treachery behind friendly appearances were tried and executed.

Soon afterwards a deputation from Tigranocerta announced that its gates were open and its population awaited Corbulo's orders. They

的政策,用灌木和树枝将他们藏身的山洞的入口和出口都堵了起来,然后就点起了火。玛尔地人[1]具有丰富的打劫经验,当科尔布罗的军队经过他们的边界之时,遭到了他们的骚扰。他们的国家有许多山脉可以作为保护自己防止敌人进攻的屏障,于是科尔布罗就派了伊伯利亚人对他们进行了蹂躏,这样,就在没有牺牲罗马人的生命的前提下,对这个部落的胆大妄为的行为进行了惩罚。尽管他及其军队在战斗中没有遭到损失,但是过度的劳苦已经使他们精疲力竭了,而且由于缺粮,他们就只能靠吃肉来维持生命,[2]更何况还缺水。这又是一个炎热的夏季,行军距离非常遥远。他们唯一感到安慰的是他们统帅的吃苦耐劳,他和士兵们同甘共苦,甚至比士兵们吃苦还多。

尽管如此,最终他们还是到达了农耕地区,就在那儿他们收割了庄稼。那里的亚美尼亚人通过两座要塞进行抵抗。一座被顺利地攻占了,另一座由于敌人的投降也攻克了。当他们继续前进,到达陶洛尼特人控制的地区时,科尔布罗躲过了一次没有预想到的危险。一个地位较为重要的外族人,手里拿着武器,出现在了他的帐篷附近。经过严刑拷打,他供认了包括其他一些人和自己在内的一次谋杀科尔布罗的阴谋。于是,那些躲在朋友身后的变节的阴谋家们受到了审讯并被判了刑。

不久之后,从提格拉诺凯尔塔城来了一位使节,说城门已经打开了,那儿的人们在等待着科尔布罗的命令。为了表示欢迎,

---

〔1〕 分布在波斯和亚美尼亚境内的库尔狄什人,其分布范围极其广泛。

〔2〕 罗马军队的食物主要是谷物,口粮每人每月是未碾过的 36 公斤谷物,士兵们一般拒绝吃过多的肉类食物。

gave him a golden crown as a sign of welcome. He accepted it politely and spared the citizens' property, hoping thereby to win their loyalty. However, another fortress, Legerda, manned by a formidable garrison, was not overcome without a fight. The defenders even risked battle in the open. Then, driven inside their walls, they only capitulated when the Romans erected a siege-mound and forced an entrance.

These victories came the more easily because Parthia was engaged in a war with the Hyrcanians. These sent a mission to the emperor requesting an alliance and citing as a pledge of friendship their diversion of Vologeses. On their return journey Corbulo feared the Hyrcanian delegates would be intercepted by enemy forces if they crossed the Euphrates. So he gave them an escort to the Caspian sea, across which they returned home without entering Parthian territory.

However, Tiridates now entered Armenia on the far side, from Media Atropatene. But Corbulo, sending auxiliaries ahead under Lucius Verulanus Severus and himself following rapidly with Roman troops, forced him to withdraw and abandon all hope of fighting. Burning and ravaging districts known to be unfriendly, Corbulo was occupying Armenia when Tigranes V-Nero's nominee for its throne-made his appearance. Through a member of the Cappadocian royal family (he was the great-grandson of Archclaus), Tigranes' long residence at Rome as a hostage had made him as docile as a slave. In any case, the Parthian royal house still had its supporters. So his welcome was not unanimous. However, the majority loathed Parthian

他们赠给了他一顶黄金打造的王冠。他很有礼貌地接受了,并宣布要赦免市民们的财产而不予没收,他希望通过这种办法来赢得他们对罗马的忠诚。然而,另一座名叫列吉尔达的要塞却是由一队勇敢的士兵守卫着,他们是通过激烈的战斗才将其攻克的。要塞的守卫者甚至敢冒险到城外的开阔地带作战,接着他被赶回了城内,而直到罗马军队堆起攻城用的土山,并发起了猛攻之后,他们才被征服了。

这些胜利之所以来得较为容易,是因为帕尔提亚人正忙于同叙尔卡尼亚人进行战争。他们派遣一名使节拜见了罗马皇帝,要求结为同盟,并把将对沃洛西吉斯的牵制作为友谊的保证。科尔布罗非常担心叙尔卡尼亚人的外交使节在回国的途中渡过幼发拉底河之时,会遭受到敌军的截击,因此他调遣了一队士兵把他们一直护送到里海,从那里他们就可以不用经过帕尔提亚人的地区而直接返回自己的家园了。

然而,现在提里达特斯通过米地亚·阿特洛帕特尼从亚美尼亚遥远的另一侧进入了。而科尔布罗派路奇乌斯·维路拉努斯·塞维路斯率领着辅助部队作为先头部队出发了,随后自己率领着罗马军队也迅速赶来,他们迫使国王后撤,并使其抛弃了一切作战的希望。对于那些不友好的地区进行了烧毁和蹂躏之后,科尔布罗占领了亚美尼亚,直到尼禄任命的国王提格拉尼斯五世到达了这儿为止。尽管提格拉尼斯是卡帕多奇亚王室的成员(他是国王阿尔凯拉乌斯的重孙子),但是由于长期待在罗马作为人质已使他变得像奴隶一样的驯顺。但是,无论如何帕尔提亚王室还是有着大量的支持者,因而他没有受到普遍的欢迎。不过那些对于帕尔提亚人的骄横非常反感的人之中,绝大多数还是欢迎罗马

arrogance and preferred a king appointed by Rome.

Tigranes was given a guard of a thousand Roman regulars, three auxiliary battalions of infantry, and two cavalry regiments. The new ruler was further protected by the allocation of Armenia' s frontier zones to the adjoining kings, Pharasmanes of Iberia, Polemo II of Pontus, Aristobulus of Lesser Amenia, and Antiochus IV Epiphanes of Commagene. Corbulo retired to Syria, the imperial governorship of which was open to him, its incumbent, Gaius Ummidius Durmius Quadratus having died.

In the Asian province one of its famous cities, Laodicea, was destroyed by an earthquake in this year, and rebuilt from its own resources without any subventicn from Rome.

In the same year, in Italy, the ancient town of Puteoli was given the status of a Roman settlement and named after Nero. The settlements at Tarentun and Antium, too, were augmented by ex-soldiers. But this did not arrest their depopulation. For most of the settlers emigrated to the provinces in which they had served-leaving no children, since they were unaccustomed to marrying and bringing up families. Once these settlements had consisted of whole brigades of soldiers drawn up in their ranks behind their officers—a new community based on consent and comradeship. But now colonists came from various units and were imknown to each other. Without leaders, without loyalty, they were a mere concentration of aliens rather than a Roman settlement.

所任命的国王的。

提格拉尼斯获准拥有一支卫戍部队,这支部队是由 1000 名罗马正规军、三个辅助步兵中队和两个骑兵中队所组成。为了进一步警惕这位新国王,科尔布罗将亚美尼亚与其他王国接壤的地区,分别交由一些王国的国王管理,这些国王包括:伊伯利亚国王帕拉司玛尼斯、本都国王波列莫二世、小亚美尼亚国王阿里斯托布路斯以及孔玛盖尼国王安提奥库斯四世埃披帕尼斯。科尔布罗撤回到了叙利亚,由于叙利亚的长官盖乌斯·翁米狄乌斯·杜尔米乌斯·克瓦德拉图斯已经死了,这一行政职务就由他来代理了。

在这一年,亚细亚行省有一座著名的城市叫拉欧狄凯亚毁于地震,而它的重建全靠自己的力量而没有依靠罗马的协助。

同一年,在意大利有一座叫普提欧利的古老的城市,获得了罗马移民地的地位,并依照尼禄的名字取了名[1] 还有塔伦特和安提乌姆这两个移民地也用退役的士兵来补充人口,但是这也没有阻止人口的减少。因为这些移居者之中的绝大多数已经移民到了他们服役过的行省中去了,而且由于他们不习惯于结婚养家,在这些移民地中没有留下任何子女。在过去,这些移民地是由整个的军团,包括长官和士兵一起所组成的,这是在协商一致和同志般的友谊的基础之上所组成的新的共同体。而现在的移民来自不同的单位,他们彼此根本就不认识。他们没有领袖,没有忠诚,只是一些外来人集中在一块而已,根本就不像罗马人的移民地。

---

〔1〕 但实际上这一地区早在公元前 194 年就已经成为罗马的移民地。

At this year's election of praetors at Rome there were three more candidates than posts, and feelings were accordingly violent. Praetors were normally elected by the senate. Now, however, the emperor restored harmony by appointing the three supernumeraries to brigade commands. He increased the senate's prerogatives by ordering that its appellants from civil courts must deposit the same sum as those appealing to himself (previously appeals to the senate had been unrestricted and subject to no sanction). At the end of the year a knight called Vibius Secundus was convicted for extortion on a charge brought by the Mauretanians, and expelled from Italy. The influence of his brother Quintus Vibius Crispus saved him from a worse sentence.

The following year, when the consuls were Lucius Cacsennius Paetus and Publius Petronius Turpilianus, witnessed a serious disaster in Britain. The imperial governor Aulus Didius Gallus had, as I have said, merely held his own. His successor Quintus Veranius (II) had only conducted minor raids against the Silures when death terminated his operations. His life had been famous for its austerity. But his testamentary last words were glaringly self-seeking, for they grossly flattered Nero and added that Veranius, if he had lived two years longer, would have presented him with the whole province.

The new imperial governor of Britain was Gaius Suetonius Paulinus. Corbulo's rival in military science, as in popular talk-which makes everybody compete—he was ambitious to achieve victories as glorious

此时在罗马行政长官的选举中,有三个人是不能当选的,[1]因而选举的气氛十分激烈。行政长官通常是由元老院选举产生的。而现在皇帝通过任命三个多余的候选人为军团统帅的方法平息了这一争端。他提高了元老院的威信,规定从民事法庭向元老院上诉的人,必须缴纳保证金,这与向皇帝上诉之时所缴纳的保证金数量相同。(以前对向元老院上诉一直未作任何规定,而且也没有任何法律条款可以依据。)在这一年年底,玛乌列塔尼亚人以勒索罪而起诉一名叫维比乌斯·谢孔都斯的骑士,他被宣判有罪而被驱逐出了意大利。他没有受到更为严厉的惩罚,是由于他的兄弟克温图斯·维比乌斯·克利司普斯的影响。

第二年,当路奇乌斯·凯森尼乌斯·帕伊图斯和普布里乌斯·佩特罗尼乌斯·图尔披里亚努斯担任执政官的时候,[2]不列颠遭受了巨大的灾难。正如我在前边所说的,行政长官奥路斯·狄第乌斯·盖路斯只能守住已经征服了的领土,而他的继任者克温图斯·维拉尼乌斯(二世)也只能对西路里斯人展开小规模的进攻,而他的死亡就使这一军事行动停止了。他一生以严正而闻名,但是从他所留遗嘱的最后一些话来看,他是一个相当喜爱追求私利的人,在这些话里他非常肉麻地奉承尼禄,而且维拉尼乌斯还表示,假如他还能够再活两年的话,他本来是会把整个行省都平定的。

不列颠新的行政长官是盖乌斯·苏埃托尼乌斯·保里努斯。他在军事才能以及最能够激发每个人的好胜心的公众舆论之中,都是科尔布罗的劲敌。他野心勃勃,想取得胜利以获取与征服亚

---

[1] 行政长官的名额是 12 名,候选人是 15 人。
[2] 罗马建城 814 年,即公元 61 年。

as the reconquest of Armenia. So Suetonius planned to attack the island of Mona, which although thickly populated had also given sanctuary to many refugees.

Flat-bottomed boats were built to contend with the shifting shallows, and these took the infantry across. Then came the cavalry; some utilized fords, but in deeper water the men swam beside their horses. The enemy lined the shore in a dense armed mass. Among them were black-robed women with dishevelled hair like Furies, brandishing torches. Close by stood Druids, raising their hands to heaven and screaming dreadful curses.

This weird spectacle awed the Roman soldiers into a sort of paralysis. They stood still—and presented themselves as a target. But then they urged each other (and were urged by the general) not to fear a horde of fanatical women. Onward pressed their standards and they bore down their opponents, enveloping them in the flames of their own torches. Suetonius garrisoned the conquered island. The groves devoted to Mona's barbarous superstitions he demolished. For it was their religion to drench their altars in the blood of prisoners and consult their gods by means of human entrails.

While Suetonius was thus occupied, he learnt of a sudden rebellion in the province. Prasutagus, king of the Iceni, after a life of long and renowned prosperity, had made the emperor co-heir with his own two daughters. Prasutagus hoped by this submissiveness to preserve his kingdom and household from attack. But it turned out otherwise.

美尼亚同样的殊荣。因此,苏埃托尼乌斯计划进攻莫纳岛,该岛虽然人口稠密,却给许多难民提供了避难所。

为了对付水浅多变,他建造了一些平底船,用它们把陆军载过海去。跟在后边的是骑兵,其中一些是涉水而过,到了深水的地方就靠在马边上游泳而过。敌人全副武装密集地排在海岸边列阵应战,其中有一些穿着黑色长袍、披散着头发而像复仇女神[1]的妇女,她们手里挥动着火把。在她们身边则是站着一些德鲁伊德[2],双手伸向天空,嘴里发出了许多可怕的诅咒。

这种凄厉恐怖的场面吓坏了罗马士兵,使他们惊呆了,他们站在那儿一动不动,成为敌人进攻的靶子。但是,他们接着就开始互相激励起来,(而统帅也极力鼓励他们,)表示不能在一群疯狂的妇女面前胆怯。在队旗的指引之下,他们击败了敌人,将敌人包围在自己的火把的火光之中。苏埃托尼乌斯在这座被征服的岛屿上设置了防守部队,并将莫纳人用来进行其野蛮的迷信活动的小树林给摧毁了。原来,按照他们的宗教信仰,要用所俘获的人的鲜血浇灌他们的祭坛,并用人的心脏来向神占卜。

当苏埃托尼乌斯正忙于这些事务的时候,得到报告,说行省[3]突然发生了叛乱。长期以骄奢淫逸而闻名的伊凯尼人的国王普拉苏塔古斯把皇帝和自己的两个女儿指定为共同的继承人。普拉苏塔古斯想通过这种恭敬的方式以保护自己的王国和家庭

---

〔1〕 希腊神话中有复仇三女神,她们分别是提西福涅、阿勒克托和墨盖拉。传说中她们的形象十分可怕,头上散乱的头发是一条条的毒蛇,一手拿着火把,一手拿着匕首。

〔2〕 德鲁伊德,古时不列颠的巫师。

〔3〕 这儿所谓的行省是指不列颠之中已被征服的部分。

Kingdom and household alike were plundered like prizes of war, the one by Roman officers, the other by Roman slaves. As a beginning, his widow Boudicca was flogged and their daughters raped. The Icenian chiefs were deprived of their hereditary estates as if the Romans had been given the whole country. The king's own relatives were treated like slaves.

And the humiliated Iceni feared still worse, now that they had been reduced to provincial status. So they rebelled. With them rose the Trinobantes and others. Servitude had not broken them, and they had secretly plotted together to become free again. They particularly hated the Roman ex-soldiers who had recently established a settlement at Camulodunum. The settlers drove the Trinobantes from their homes and land, and called them prisoners and slaves. The troops encouraged the settlers' outrages, since their own way of behaving was the same and they looked forward to similar licence for themselves. Moreover, the temple erected to the divine Claudius was a blatant stronghold of alien rule, and its observances were a pretext to make the natives appointed as its priests drain the whole country dry.

It seemed easy to destroy the settlement; for it had no walls. That was a matter which Roman commanders, thinking of amenities rather than needs, had neglected. At this juncture, for no visible reason, the statue of Victory at Camulodunum fell down-with its back turned as though it were fleeing the enemy. Delirious women chanted of destruction at hand. They cried that in the local senate-house outlandish yells had been heard; the theatre had echoed with shrieks; at the mouth of the Thames a phantom settlement had been seen in ruins. A blood-red colour in the sea, too, and shapes like human corpses left

免遭侵害。但结果适得其反,王国和家庭都像战利品一样遭到了抢劫,罗马军官们侵占了他的国家,而奴隶们掠夺了他的家庭。一开始,他的妻子布狄卡被鞭打,而他们的女儿则遭到了强奸。伊凯尼人的所有显要人物的世袭财产都被没收了,似乎整个国家的财产都是罗马人所给予的。而国王本人的所有的亲戚都受到了奴隶般的对待。

既然已经被降为了一个行省,遭受屈辱的伊凯尼人担心自己今后的生活会变得糟糕,于是他们开始造反了。和他们一块起事的有特利诺班提人和其他部落的人,奴役并没有摧毁他们,他们曾经秘密联合起义,以重新获得自由。他们特别痛恨那些罗马的退役士兵,这些人最近在卡木洛杜努姆建立了一个移民地。这些移民者将特利诺班提人赶出了自己的家园和故土,并把他们称为"俘虏"和"奴隶"。军队纵容移民者的残暴行为,因为他们之间的行为方式是相同的,而且他们希望将来自己也可以拥有同样的权利。而且,为神圣的克劳狄乌斯所修建的神庙也被看成了外族统治的显要的堡垒,且被任命在这座神庙中担任祭司的人会在宗教的借口之下榨干整个国家的血液。

看来要摧毁这块移民地是很容易的事情,因为它没有围墙保护。这是那些讲究舒适而轻视实用的罗马统帅们所忽略的一个问题。就在这时,也不知出于什么原因,在卡木洛杜努姆的一座胜利女神雕像倒了,她的背部向上,好像是在逃离敌人似的。神志不清的妇女们高喊着毁灭就在眼前,她们喊叫说在当地人的元老院之中听到了外国人的叫声,剧院里面回荡着尖叫声,在泰晤士河的河口曾经看见过一个已成为废墟的移民地的幻象。还有,在海洋中出现了血红的颜色,海水退潮时把一些外形像人的尸首

by the ebb tide, were interpreted hopefully by the Britons-and with terror by the settlers.

Suetonius, however, was far away. So they appealed for help to the imperial agent Catus Decianus. He sent them barely two hundred men, incompletely armed. There was also a small garrison on the spot. Reliance was placed on the temple's protection. Misled by secret prorebels, who hampered their plans, they dispensed with rampart or trench. They omitted also to evacuate old people and women and thus leave only fighting men behind. Their precautions were appropriate to a time of unbroken peace.

Then a native horde surrounded them. When all else had been ravaged or burnt, the garrison concentrated itself in the temple. After two days' siege, it fell by storm. The ninth Roman division, commanded by Quintus Petilius Cerialis Caesius Rufus, attempted to relieve the town, but was stopped by the victorious Britons and routed. Its entire infantry force was massacred, while the commander escaped to his camp with his cavalry and sheltered behind its defences. The imperial agent Catus Decianus, horrified by the catastrophe and by his unpopularity, withdrew to Gaul. It was his rapacity which had driven the province to war.

But Suetonius, undismayed, marched through disaffected territory to Londinium. This town did not rank as a Roman settlement, but was an important centre for business-men and merchandise. At first, he hesitated whether to stand and fight there. Eventually, his numerical

的东西留在了岸边。所有这一切在不列颠人看来都是充满了希望的事情,而在移民者们看来则是令人恐惧的。

然而,苏埃托尼乌斯还在遥远的地方。于是,他们到皇帝的代理官卡图斯·德奇亚努斯那儿去请求援助。他只能给他们不到200名还没有完全装备起来的士兵。还有一小支部队随时待命。他们把希望完全寄托在神庙的庇护上。那些秘密地支持叛乱的人,为了阻止他们的防卫计划,误导他们抛弃了防守的壕沟或壁垒。他们也忽略了,应该将老人和妇女转移走而只把具有作战能力的男人留在这儿。他们的预防措施就跟天下太平的日子里差不多。

接着一支外族军队将他们重重包围了,当所有的一切都被掠夺走或者被焚烧掉之后,这一小支军队还集中在神庙之内,但是经过两天的猛烈攻击之后,神庙也陷落了。第九军团在克温图斯·佩提里乌斯·凯里亚里斯·卡西乌斯·路福斯的带领下,试图救援这一城镇,但被获胜的不列颠人阻击并击败了,凯里亚里斯手下的步兵全被歼灭了,而他本人和骑兵则逃回了军营,躲在了防御工事的后面。皇帝的代理官卡图斯·德奇亚努斯被这惨败的场面和反对他的呼声吓坏了,撤到了高卢。正是他的贪婪才把整个行省拖入了战争之中。

但是,苏埃托尼乌斯没有灰心,他带领军队穿过了敌人占领的地区向伦狄尼乌姆城[1]推进。这个城镇虽然没有列入移民地的行列,但却是一个重要的商人和商业集中的中心。一开始,他很犹豫是否应该在这儿驻扎并将其作为作战中心。最终,考虑到人数

---

[1] 就是今天的伦敦城。

inferiority-and the price only too clearly paid by the divisional commander's rashness-decided him to sacrifice the single city of Londinium to save the province as a whole. Unmoved by lamentations and appeals, Suetonius gave the signal for departure. The inhabitants were allowed to accompany him. But those who stayed because they were women, or old, or attached to the place, were slaughtered by the enemy. Verulamium suffered the same fate.

The natives enjoyed plundering and thought of nothing else. Bypassing forts and garrisons, they made for where loot was richest and protection weakest. Roman and provincial deaths at the places mentioned are estimated at seventy thousand. For the British did not take or sell prisoners, or practise other war-time exchanges. They could not wait to cut throats, hang, burn, and crucify-as though avenging, in advance, the retribution that was on its way.

Suetonius collected the fourteenth brigade and detachments of the twentieth, together with the nearest available auxiliaries-amounting to nearly ten thousand armed men—and decided to attack without further delay. He chose a position in a defile with a wood behind him. There could be no enemy, he knew, except at his front, where there was open country without cover for ambushes. Suetonius drew up his regular troops in close order, with the light-armed auxiliaries at their flanks, and the cavalry massed on the wings. On the British side, cavalry and infantry bands seethed over a wide area in unprecedented numbers. Their confidence was such that they brought their wives with them to see the victory, installing them in carts stationed at the edge of the battlefield.

Boudicca drove round all the tribes in a chariot with her daughters in front of her. 'We British are used to woman commanders in war,'

上的劣势以及记忆犹新的军团长官凯里亚里斯的冒失进攻所带来的惨痛教训,他决定牺牲伦狄尼乌姆城这一城市,而去援救整个行省。苏埃托尼乌斯没有被当地人们的哭诉和留下来的请求所动,他发出了指示,命令部队开拔,而居民允许跟随他出发。但是那些妇女、老人以及依恋故土的人都留了下来,他们都遭到了敌人的洗掠。而维路拉米乌姆市也遭受了同样的命运。

叛乱的这些居民只知道抢掠,对其他的事情毫不感兴趣。他们绕过要塞和守卫的据点,而去攻击那些可以掠取最丰富的战利品且又防守最为薄弱的地方。上述地区所死亡的罗马及外省人的总人数已有7000人,因为这些不列颠人既不收容战俘也不将战俘卖掉,而且也不在战时进行其他交换。他们迫不及待地将敌人切断喉咙、绞死、烧死和磔杀,就好像是报仇的时机即将到来,而他们在提前进行似的。

苏埃托尼乌斯将第十四军团、二十军团的一部分以及最近的地区所能够征集的附属部队集合在了一起,士兵总数接近10000人。他毫不迟疑,马上决定展开进攻。他将一条隘路附近的地区选做阵地,后面则是森林。他知道除了前方之外不可能有敌人,而前方非常敞亮,没有地方可以做隐蔽之用。苏埃托尼乌斯将他手下的正规军组成了密集的队形,两边是轻武装的辅助部队,而骑兵则集合在两翼。在对面的不列颠人一方,骑兵和步兵在一片广阔的土地上活动着,人数不计其数。他们的自信是如此之高,以至于竟然将妻子也带来观看他们的胜利,并将她们安置在了那些停在战场边沿的马车里。

布狄卡驾驶着马车到所有的部落之中进行游说,并将自己的女儿们放在她的前面。她哭道:"在战争中,我们不列颠人习

she cried. 'I am descended from mighty men! But now I am not fighting for my kingdom and wealth. I am fighting as an ordinary person for my lost freedom, my bruised body, and my outraged daughters. Nowadays Roman rapicity does not even spare our bodies. Old people are killed, virgins raped. But the gods will grant us the vengeance we deserve! The Roman division which dared to fight is annihilated. The others cower in their camps, or watch for a chance to escape. They will never face even the din and roar of all our thousands, much less the shock of our onslaught. Consider how many of you are fighting—and why. Then you will win this battle, or perish. That is what I, a woman, plan to do! —let the men live in slavery if they will. '

Suetonius trusted his men's bravery. Yet he too, at this critical moment, offered encouragements and appeals. 'Disregard the clamours and empty threats of the natives!' he said. 'In their ranks, there are more women than fighting men. Unwarlike, unarmed, when they see the arms and courage of the conquerors who have routed them so often, they will break immediately. Even when a force contains many divisions, few among them win the battles—what special glory for your small numbers to win the renown of a whole army! Just keep in close order. Throw your javelins, and then carry on: use shield-bosses to fell them, swords to kill them. Do not think of plunder. When you have won, you will have everything. '

The general's words were enthusiastically received: the old battle-experienced soldiers longed to hurl their javelins. So Suetonius confidently gave the signal for battle. At first the regular troops stood their

惯于由女人做统帅,我从跟随一个伟大的男人降落到如此悲惨的地步!而我现在不是为了我的王国和财富而战,而是作为一个普通人为了我所失去的自由、我所遭受鞭打的躯体以及我所遭受奸污的女儿而战。现在罗马人的贪婪竟然发展到了连我们的躯体都不放过的地步。老年人被杀了,少女们遭到了强奸。不过神灵会同意我们进行应有的报复的。敢于出战的那一个罗马军团已经被歼灭了,其余的要么躲进了他们的营地,要么寻找机会准备逃跑。他们甚至不敢面对我们千千万万人的吵声和怒吼,更不用说在我们猛烈攻击之下,他们肯定会胆战心惊了。只要考虑到你们已有多少人以及为什么参战,就知道这场战争是非胜即死。这是我一个女人计划要做的事情,而男人们假如愿意,就让他们去做奴隶吧!"

苏埃托尼乌斯对其手下士兵的勇敢怀有信心。然而在这紧急关头,他还是进行了鼓励和作了要求。他说:"我们决不能将这些蛮族们的喧闹和虚张声势放在眼里。他们没有斗志,没有装备,当他们看到屡次将他们击败的征服者所拥有的装备和勇气的时候,他们马上就会被打垮的。即使一支部队包括许多军团,那也只有少数人才能取得胜利,假如你们能以少数人去获取一整支大军才能获取的胜利,那该是多高的殊荣!只需要保持住紧密的战斗序列,投出手中的投枪,然后用盾牌的牌心将他们击倒,用剑将他们杀死。不要考虑掠夺,只要能够获胜就可以得到一切了。"

统帅的话得到了士兵们的热情支持。那些久经沙场的老兵们长久以来就渴望掷出手中的投枪。于是苏埃托尼乌斯满怀信心地发出了作战的命令。一开始正规军们站立不动,固守隘路,

ground. Keeping to the defile as a natural defence, they launched their javelins accurately at the approaching enemy. Then, in wedge formation, they burst forward. So did the auxiliary infantry. The cavalry, too, with lances extended, demolished all serious resistance. The remaining Britons fled with difficulty since their ring of wagons blocked the outlets. The Romans did not spare even the women. Baggage animals too, transfixed with weapons, added to the heaps of dead.

It was a glorious victory, comparable with bygone triumphs. According to one report almost eighty thousand Britons fell. Our own casualties were about four hundred dead and a slightly larger number of wounded. Boudicca poisoned herself. Poenius Postumus, chief-of-staff of the second division which had not joined Suetonius, learning of the success of the other two formations, stabbed himself to death because he had cheated his formation of its share in the victory and broken regulations by disobeying his commander's orders.

The whole army was now united. Suetonius kept it under canvas to finish the war. The emperor raised its numbers by transferring from Germany two thousand regular troops, which brought the ninth division to full strength, also eight auxiliary infantry battalions and a thousand cavalry. These were stationed together in new winter quarters, and hostile or wavering tribes were ravaged with fire and sword. But the enemy's worst affliction was famine. For they had neglected to sow their fields and brought everyone available into the army, intending to seize our supplies. Still, the savage British tribesmen were disinclined for peace, especially as the newly arrived imperial agent Gaius Julius Alpinus Classicianus, successor to Catus Decianus, was on bad terms with Suetonius, and allowed his personal animosities

将其作为一道天然的防卫屏障,而当敌人们逐渐靠近之时,他们就准确地投出手中的投枪。接着他们就以楔形队列向敌人猛冲过去,辅助性步兵也冲了过去。而骑兵也将长枪刺了出去,将各种坚决的抵抗势力都摧毁了。幸存的不列颠人要想逃跑也是件很困难的事情,因为他们自己四面的马车将路给堵住了。罗马人甚至连妇女都没有放过。驮畜也都用武器刺死了,并将其与死人的尸体堆在了一起。

这是一次巨大的胜利,可以跟以前的任何一次胜利相媲美。根据一份报告说,不列颠人死亡接近80000人,而我们这一方的阵亡者大约只有400人,受伤者稍微多一些。布狄卡服毒自尽。第二军团的营帅波伊尼乌斯·波司图姆斯没有率部加入到苏埃托尼乌斯的这次战斗,当听说了另外两个军团所取得的胜利的消息之后,他就拔剑自杀了,因为他欺骗了他手下的军团,使之不能够享受这次胜利的光荣,而且他不服从统帅的命令,这也违反了军规。

现在全部军队都被集中在一起,苏埃托尼乌斯让他们安营扎寨以处理战争的善后事宜。罗马皇帝增强了这支部队的人数,从日耳曼调来了2000名正规军士兵,这使第九军团的名额得以补全;还有8个辅助性步兵中队和1000名骑兵。这些士兵都被安置在冬营里,而那些敌对或观望的部落都被烧杀。但是,敌人所受的最大的灾难就是饥荒,因为他们早已经忽略了种植农田而使每一个可以参军的人都加入了战斗,以图抢掠我们的给养。更何况,野蛮的不列颠诸部落都不愿意谋求和平,尤其是新任的皇帝的代理官是盖乌斯·尤利乌斯·埃尔披努斯·克拉西奇亚努斯,即卡图斯·德奇亚努斯的继任者,此人与苏埃托尼乌斯不

to damage the national interests. For he passed round advice to wait for a new governor who would be kind to those who surrendered, without an enemy's bitterness or a conqueror's arrogance. Classicianus also reported to Rome that there was no prospect of ending the war unless a successor was appointed to Suetonius, whose failures he attributed to perversity-and his successes to luck.

So a former imperial slave, Polyclitus, was sent to investigate the British situation. Nero was very hopeful that Polyclitus' influence would both reconcile the governor and agent and pacify native rebelliousness. With his enormous escort, Polyclitus was a trial to Italy and Gaul. Then he crossed the Channel and succeeded in intimidating even the Roman army. But the enemy laughed at him. For them, freedom still lived, and the power of ex-slaves was still unfamiliar. The British marvelled that a general and an army who had completed such a mighty war should obey a slave.

But all this was toned down in Polyclitus' reports to the emperor. Retained as governor, Suetonius lost a few ships and their crews on the shore, and was then superseded for not terminating the war. His successor, the recent consul Publius Petronius Turpilianus, neither provoking the enemy nor provoked, called this ignoble inactivity peace with honour.

The same year witnessed two noteworthy crimes at Rome. One of the audacious perpetrators was a senator, the other a slave. Domitius Balbus was a former praetor whose age, wealth, and childlessness

和,结果就因个人的仇恨而损害了国家的利益。他到处宣传,说应该派一位新的行政长官,此人会对降敌采取友善的政策,既没有敌人的狠毒也没有征服者的狂傲。克拉西奇亚努斯还向罗马报告说,除非重新任命一个人来代替苏埃托尼乌斯,否则要结束这场战争是毫无希望的事情。他将苏埃托尼乌斯的失败归因于刚愎自用,而所取得的成功也仅仅是出于侥幸而已。

于是,皇帝以前的一位奴隶波里克利图斯受命来调查不列颠的情况。尼禄非常希望通过波里克利图斯的影响,不仅能够调解好行政长官和皇帝代理官之间的关系,而且能够平息当地居民的叛乱情绪。波里克利图斯手下带了一大批人,这对于意大利和高卢来说,是一场灾难。他渡过了海峡,成功地震慑住了他人,甚至连罗马军队也给吓住了。但是,敌人却极力嘲笑他。对他们来说,自由的精神还存在着,他们对一个被释放奴隶所拥有的权威仍然不能接受。令不列颠人感到惊奇的是,完成了如此重大的一场战役的一位统帅和一支军队竟然听命于一个奴隶。

但是所有这些嘲笑声和批评声都通过波里克利图斯做的报告而传达给了皇帝。苏埃托尼乌斯继续留任行政长官,后来由于在海岸上损失了一些船只和一些水手,就以战争还没有结束为借口派人替代了他的官职。他的继任者是刚刚担任过执政官的普布里乌斯·佩特洛尼乌斯·图尔披里亚努斯,他既不向敌人挑战,也没有受到敌人的挑战,而他却以这种可耻的无所事事的和平为荣。

同一年,在罗马发生了两件引人注目的犯罪行为。这两个胆大妄为的罪犯中,一个是一名元老,另一个是一个奴隶。多米提乌斯·巴尔布斯曾经担任过行政长官,他的年龄、他的财富和没

exposed him to fraudulence. His relative Valerius Fabianus (a man destined for an official career) forged Domitius' will. Two knights, Vinicius Rufinus and Terentius Lentinus, who were Valerius' accomplices, brought in Marcus Antonius Primus, a man ready for anything, and Marcus Asinius Marcellus, who had the distinction of being the great-grandson of Gaius Asinius Pollio (I) and was respected-apart from his belief that poverty was the supreme misfortune. So with these associates, and others of less account, Valerius sealed the document. When this was proved in the senate, the forgers were all convicted under the Cornelian law against falsification, except Marcellus, who escaped punishment owing to the emperor's intervention in memory of his ancestors. Disgrace he did not escape.

On the same day a young ex-quaestor, Pompeius Aelianus, was condemned for complicity in the same crime and banned from Italy and his home country, Spain. Valerius Ponticus was excluded from Italy for conducting prosecutions before the praetor to avoid trial by the City Prefect-a procedure which, while preserving legality for the time being, aimed at ultimate acquittal by collusion. A clause was added to the relevant senatorial decree making anyone who bought or sold such connivance liable to the same penalty as if convicted by false accusation in a criminal case.

有儿女的情况都使他成为他人陷害的对象。他的一位亲戚名叫瓦列里乌斯·法比雅努斯(这是一位注定要走上仕途的人物),他伪造了巴尔布斯的遗嘱。两个骑士维尼奇乌斯·路菲努斯和提伦提乌斯·楞提努斯,是瓦列里乌斯的同党。他们两个又将另外两个人拉进了他们的阴谋之中,这两人分别是:玛尔库斯·安托尼乌斯·普利姆斯,这是一个胆大妄为的人;玛尔库斯·阿西尼乌斯·玛尔凯路斯,此人是盖乌斯·阿西尼乌斯·波里欧(一世)的重孙子,因而地位颇为显要且受人尊重,但他也有一个缺点,就是相信贫穷是最大的不幸。于是,瓦列里乌斯在这些人,还有其他一些不怎么知名的人的作证之下,将这封伪造的文书密封了起来。当这封遗嘱在元老院被证明是伪造的之后,所有的伪造者都依据科尔涅里乌斯法[1]中反伪造条例而被定了罪。只有玛尔凯路斯除外,由于皇帝念在他祖先的面上对此事进行干预,他才免于受处罚,但他却不能洗掉自己的耻辱。

在同一时期,一位曾经担任过财务官的年轻人,名字叫彭培乌斯·埃里亚努斯,在上述案件之中作为同犯而被宣判有罪,他被驱逐出了意大利和自己的故乡西班牙。而瓦列里乌斯·彭提库斯也被驱逐出了意大利,原因在于,他为了使被告避免受到市长官的审问而将案件转移到了行政长官的手中,此举在于通过合法程序而将案件暂时拖延,最终可以通过共谋而宣判无罪。在元老院相关的命令之中又加了一条,规定任何行贿或受贿以图共谋的人都要接受与刑事法庭对诽谤罪所做出的同样的处罚。

---

〔1〕 公元前81年苏拉所制定的法律,其目的在于制止与反对遗嘱之中的各种形式的诈骗行为。

Soon afterwards the City Prefect, Lucius Pedanius Secundus, was murdered by one of his slaves. Either Pedanius had refused to free the murderer after agreeing to a price, or the slave, infatuated with some man or other, found competition from his master intolerable. After the murder, ancient custom required that every slave residing under the same roof must be executed. But a crowd gathered, eager to save so many innocent lives; and rioting began. The senate-house was besieged. Inside, there was feeling against excessive severity, but the majority opposed any change. Among the latter was Gaius Cassius Longinus, who when his turn came spoke as follows:

' I have often been here, senators, when decrees deviating from our ancestral laws and customs were mooted. I have not opposed them. Not that I had any doubts about the superiority—in every matter whatsoever-of ancient arrangements, and the undesirability of every change. But I did not wish, by exaggerated regard for antique usage, to show too high an opinion of my own profession, the law. Nor did I want, by continual opposition, to weaken any influence I may possess. I wanted to keep it intact in case the country needed my advice.

' It needs it today! A man who has held the consulship had been deliberately murdered by a slave in his own home. None of his fellowslaves prevented or betrayed the murderer, though the senatorial decree threatening the whole household with execution still stands. Exempt them from the penalty if you like. But then, if the City Prefect was not important enough to be immune, who will be? Who will

之后不久，市长官路奇乌斯·佩达尼乌斯·谢孔都斯被自己的一名奴隶给谋杀了。或许是因为双方在谈妥了某一价格之后，佩达尼乌斯仍然拒绝给这个奴隶以自由的身份的缘故；也或许是因为这个奴隶爱上了某一个娈童，而不能容忍其主人跟他竞争的缘故。案发之后，按照古老的传统，市长官家中的奴隶要被全部处死。但是大批的民众聚集起来了，想挽救如此多的无辜者的生命，甚至开始了骚乱。元老院也被包围起来了。在元老院内部，尽管有一部分人反对这一过分严厉的处罚，但是绝大多数元老反对做出任何的更改。后者之中有一个叫盖乌斯·卡西乌斯·朗吉努斯的人，当轮到他时，他做了如下的发言：

"诸位元老，我经常来参加元老院会议，听到所要求的一些命令完全违背了我们祖先的法律和习俗，对此我也没有提什么反对意见。这并不是因为我对下列问题存有疑虑：一是古代对于每一件事情上所做的安排的正确性，一是任何改变都是不受欢迎的。但是，我不希望通过过分尊重古时的习惯来表示我好像是在抬高我本人的职业，即高估法律。同时我也不希望，我所具有的任何的影响会被他人的持续不断的反对而遭到削弱。我希望我的影响能够完整地保存下来，一直到国家需要我提出建议的时候。

"今天就是需要我提出建议的时候了。一位曾经担任过执政官的人在自己的家里竟然被一位奴隶蓄意谋杀了。尽管元老院在出现这一情况之时威胁要处死全体奴隶的命令仍然持续有效，但是，他手下的奴隶们没有任何一位出来阻止或揭露这一谋杀犯。假如你们愿意的话，就赦免他们而不予惩罚吧。但是，假如市长官高贵的地位都不足以使自己免于受害的话，那么谁又能保证自己呢？假如佩达尼乌斯拥有了400名奴隶都嫌过少的话，那么诸位谁会

have enough slaves to protect him if Pedanius' four hundred were too few? Who can rely on his household's help if even fear for their own lives does not make them shield us?

'Or was the assassin avenging a wrong? For that is one shameless fabrication. Tell us next that the slave had been negotiating about his patrimony, or he had lost some ancestral property! We had better call it justifiable homicide straightaway.

'When wiser men have in past times considered and settled the whole matter, will you dare to refute them? Pretend, if you like, that we are deciding a policy for the first time. Do you believe that a slave can have planned to kill his master without letting fall a single rash or menacing word? Or even if we assume he kept his secret—and obtained a weapon unnoticed—could he have passed the watch, opened the bedroom door, carried in a light, and committed the murder, without anyone knowing? There are many advance notifications of crimes. If slaves give them away, we can live securely, though one among many, because of their insecurity; or, if we must die, we can at least be sure the guilty will be punished.

'Our ancestors distrusted their slaves. Yet slaves were then born on the same estates, in the same homes, as their masters, who had treated them kindly from birth. But nowadays our huge households are international. They include every alien religion—or none at all. The only way to keep down this scum is by intimidation. Innocent people will die, you say. Yes, and when in a defeated army every tenth man is flogged to death, the brave have to draw lots with the others.

拥有足够的奴隶来保护自己呢？假如即使担心自己的生命安全都不能促使奴隶们来保护我们,那么谁还会依赖自己所养的奴隶的帮助呢？

"要是这一暗杀行为只是为了报复自己所受到的不公正待遇呢？这也只是一种恬不知耻的胡编乱造的谎言。接着你们就会说这位奴隶一直对于其祖传的财产在进行协商,或者是他已经将祖先的一部分财产给丢失了。我们就最好说这次谋杀是一次公正合理的行为。

"对于古时那些比我们更有智慧的人都已考虑过并都已解决了的问题,难道你们还敢驳斥？假如你们愿意的话,就假定我们是第一次在制定一项政策。你们相信竟然会有在不走漏一点儿口风,不说一句威胁的话的情况之下,一个奴隶就会谋划杀掉他的主人？或者即使我们假定他能够保守秘密,而且在他人不知道的情况之下弄到了武器,那么他能够在他人毫无知觉的情况之下躲过门卫,打开寝室的门,手里拿着灯而实施这一犯罪行为吗？犯罪行为事先都是有许多迹象的。假如奴隶们能够把这些迹象揭露出来,我们就可以安全地生活着。尽管一个主人生活在许多奴隶之间,他们还要为自己的安全而感到不安。退一步来说,即使我们注定都会死去,我们起码也要使犯罪行为得到应有的惩罚。

"我们的祖先一直不信任他们的奴隶,即使奴隶们跟自己的主人出生在同一个田庄里、同一个家里,而且自从一出生,主人对他们就一直很友善。但是,现在我们拥有众多的奴隶,他们来自不同的国家。他们有着不同的宗教信仰,或者没有任何宗教信仰。只有用恐吓的办法才能制服这一些渣滓。你们会说,无辜的人也会因此而死去。是的,是这样的。要知道战败的军队之中每

Exemplary punishment always contains an element of injustice. But individual wrongs are outweighed by the advantage of the community. '

No one dared speak up against Cassius. But there were protesting cries of pity for the numbers affected, and the women, and the young, and the undoubted innocence of the majority. Yet those favouring execution prevailed. However, great crowds ready with stones and torches prevented the order from being carried out. Nero rebuked the population by edict, and lined with troops the whole route along which those condemned were taken for execution. Then it was proposed by Cingonius Varro that the ex-slaves, too, who had been under the same roof should be deported from Italy. But the emperor vetoed this—the ancient custom had not been tempered by mercy, but should not be aggravated by brutality.

Bithynia, this year, secured the condemnation of its governor, Tarquitius Priscus, for extortion. The senate, remembering that he had once accused his own governor, Titus Statilius Taurus (II), was delighted. In Gaul, a census was carried out by Quintus Volusius Saturninus, Titus Sextius Africanus, and Lucius Trebellius Maximus. The aristocratic Volusius and Sextius were rivals, and both despised Trebellius, who took advantage of their bickering to get the better of them.

Publius Memmius Regulus now died. His influence, dignity and good name had attained the greatest glory which the all-overshadowing imperial grandeur permits. Indeed, when Nero was ill, and sycophantic courtiers declared that his death would mean the end of the

十个人要有一个人被鞭打致死,而勇敢的士兵也不得不与其他人一起抽签。警惕性的惩罚都会包括不公正的因素。但是个人遭受过分严重不公正的待遇会有利于整个国家的。"

没有一个人敢出来大声反对卡西乌斯。但是也有一些抗议的声音,表示对如此多的卷入者的怜悯,对于这些妇女、年轻人以及绝大多数毫无疑问是无辜的人的怜悯。但是,那些支持处死的人的意见还是占了上风。然而,大群的民众手里拿着石头和火把准备要阻止这次判决的执行。尼禄发布了敕令对民众进行了斥责,并派军队守住了押送犯人到刑场去的全部道路。接着,提格尼乌斯·瓦罗提出了建议,共同在死者家中服过役的被释放的奴隶也要被驱逐出意大利。但是皇帝把这一项提议否决了,因为虽然古老的习俗不能因为仁慈而放松了要求,但也不能通过残忍而使之加重。

这一年,比提尼亚人对他们的长官塔尔科维提乌斯·普里斯库斯提出了指控,控告他的勒索罪行。元老院想起了此人曾经控告过自己的长官提图斯·司塔提里乌斯·陶路斯(二世),因而很高兴。在高卢,克温图斯·沃路西乌斯·撒图尔尼努斯、提图斯·塞克斯提乌斯·阿非里卡努斯和卢奇乌斯·特列贝里乌斯·玛克西姆斯进行了一次人口调查。贵族出身的沃路西乌斯和阿非里卡努斯彼此之间是对手,但是两人又都瞧不起特列贝里乌斯,而后者又利用了两人的彼此排挤而超越了两人。

这一年,普布里乌斯·美米乌斯·列古路斯死去了。他的影响、节操和他良好的声誉使得他取得了最大的荣誉,这种荣誉甚至超过了至高无上的皇帝的尊严。确实是,在尼禄生病的时候,他身边相伴的那些奸佞小人说,皇帝的死将意味着整个帝国的灭

empire, the emperor answered that the State had a support; and when they asked what he meant, he replied: 'Memmius Regulus.' Yet Regulus survived unharmed. For he was inactive, his family was only recently ennobled, and his resources were too insignificant to attract envy.

Another event of this year was the dedication of a gymnasium by Nero. Oil was distributed to senators and knights on a truly Greek scale of extravagance. In the following year, when the consuls were Publius Marius Celsus and Lucius Afmius Gallus, the practor Antistius Sosianus, whose disorderly behaviour as tribune I have mentioned, wrote verses satirizing the emperor, and read them aloud at a large dinner-party given by Marcus Ostorius Scapula. Antistius was charged with treason by Cossutianus Capito, who on the entreaty of his father-in-law Gaius Ofonius Tigellinus had recently been made a senator. This was the first revival of the treason law. The intention-people believed-was not so much to ruin Antistius as to enable the emperor to gain credit by using his tribune's authority to veto the senate's adverse verdict.

亡,皇帝对此的回答是国家还会有一个人来支撑。当这些人问皇帝是指谁时,尼禄就说:"是美米乌斯·列古路斯。"然而,列古路斯幸免于难,毫发未损地活了下来,因为他淡泊名利,他的家庭是最近才显贵起来的,而且他的财产也远没有到引起他人嫉妒的地步。

　　这一年里所发生的另一件事情是尼禄奉献了一座大竞技场,[1]并按照真正的希腊慷慨之风将油[2]免费赠送给了元老和骑士。第二年,是普布里乌斯·马利乌斯·凯尔苏斯和路奇乌斯·阿非尼乌斯·盖尔路斯担任执政官的一年,行政长官安提司提乌斯·索斯亚努斯——关于这个人在担任保民官之时的不良行为,我在前面已做过交代——写了一些诗篇对皇帝进行诽谤,而且在由玛尔库斯·欧司托里乌斯·司卡普拉所举办的很多人参加的大规模晚宴之中,高声朗诵这些诗篇。为此,科苏提亚努斯·卡皮托指控安提司提乌斯犯有叛国罪。卡皮托是依仗着自己的岳父盖乌斯·奥佛尼乌斯·提盖里努斯[3]的支持最近才成为了一名元老。这是第一次恢复实施叛国罪的条款。人们认为,这样做的目的并不仅仅是为了毁掉安提司提乌斯,更重要的是能够提高皇帝的声誉,因为他能够利用保民官的权力否决元老院所做出的判处安提司提乌斯死刑的决定。

---

〔1〕　是尼禄为尼禄尼亚节比赛建造的,位于玛尔斯广场尼禄尼亚温泉附近。

〔2〕　这种油是在体育比赛时用的,是擦在身上的,在雅典,这种油是由节日主办者免费赠送的。

〔3〕　提盖里努斯是尼禄时期最受宠爱的一位佞臣,是尼禄的近卫军的统帅,对尼禄的政治生活产生了巨大的影响,在奥托统治时自杀。

The host testified that he had heard nothing. Yet contrary witnesses were believed, and one of the consuls-designate, Quintus Junius Marullus, moved Antistius' deposition from the praetorship, to be followed by execution in the ancient manner. There was general agreement. But Thrasea, after highly complimenting Nero and vigorously blaming Antistius, argued that under so excellent an emperor the senate was liable to no compulsion, and need not inflict the maximum punishment deserved. The executioner and the noose were obsolete, said Thrasea; the laws had extablished penalties which exempted judges from brutality and avoided undesirable anachronisms; so let Antistius have his property confiscated and be sent to an island, where every prolongation of his guilty life would intensify his personal misery but splendidly illustrate official mercy.

Thrasea's independence made others less servile. So his proposal, when the consul put the vote, was carried. Among the few dissentients the worst sycophant was Aulus Vitellius. Like other cowards he insulted anyone decent, but kept quiet when answered back. However, the consuls did not venture to confirm the senate's decree, but wrote informing Nero of the general view. Anger and discretion fought within him. Finally he sent the following reply: ' Antistius, unprovoked, has grossly abused the emperor. The senate was asked to punish him. It ought to have fixed a punishment fitting the enormity of the crime. But I will not amend your leniency. Indeed, I should not

主人作证说,他什么也没有听到。但是,大家所相信的是相反的证词,于是当选的执政官克温图斯·尤尼乌斯·玛儒路斯提出建议,剥夺安提司提乌斯的行政长官的职务,并按照古老的方式予以处决。这一提议得到了元老们的普遍赞同。但是,特拉塞亚在高度颂扬了尼禄和猛烈地抨击了安提司提乌斯之后却认为,在一位如此英明皇帝的统治之下,元老院应该在没有压力的情况之下作出判决,这时所做出的处罚不必非得是所应得的极刑。特拉塞亚说,刽子手和绞索早已经过时了,按照以前的法律所做出的处罚既可以使审判官们免受残暴之名,又可以避免不受欢迎的与时代不相符的措施。因此,没收安提司提乌斯的财产,并将他驱逐到一座岛屿上去,这样,在那儿他那有罪的生命越延长,就越会加深他的痛苦,也会越能作为范例而显示国家的仁慈。

特拉塞亚的独立性使其他一些人多多少少地减少了一些自己的奴性。因此,在元老院对此进行表决时,他的提议就通过了。在少数不同意的人之中,最臭名昭著的谄媚者就是奥路斯·维提里乌斯,[1]就如其他所有的胆小怯懦之辈一样,他对那些品德高尚的人进行辱骂攻击,而一旦受到反击,就会沉默不言了。然而,执政官们也不敢正式批准元老院的命令,而是向尼禄写了一封信,通报了大多数人的观点。尼禄的心里交织着愤怒和谨慎的情绪,最终他派人送来了一封回信,内容如下:"安提司提乌斯无缘无故地就对皇帝展开了恶劣的辱骂攻击,元老院受命对此事做出判罚。元老院理应做出一项与他所犯的严重的罪行相适应的惩处,但是,我不会对你们所做出的宽大处理进行修正的,实际上,我本

---

〔1〕 此人就是以后的皇帝维提里乌斯。

have allowed anything else. Decide as you please. You could have acquitted him if you wished. '

These and similar comments were read out. Nero was clearly offended. Yet the consuls did not change the motion. Thrasea did not alter his proposal, and the others, too, adhered to their decision. Some wanted to avoid showing the emperor in an unfavourable light. The majority saw safety in numbers. Thrasea was showing his usual resolution-and conformity with his reputation.

Aulus Didius Gallus Fabricius Veiento fell to a similar charge, namely the inclusion in a so-called will of numerous insults against senators and priests. His accuser, Gaius Terentius Tullius Geminus, added that Veiento had accepted bribery, in return for his influence with the emperor regarding official promotions. This led Nero to deal with the case himself. He found Veiento guilty, expelled him from Italy, and ordered his writings to be burnt. These were eagerly sought for and read-while it was dangerous to have them. When, later, the ban became obsolete, they were forgotten.

The situation of the country was deteriorating every day; and a counteracting influence now vanished, with the death of Burrus. Whether natural causes or poison killed him is uncertain. The

来就不应该对此事说三道四。请按照你们自己的意愿作决定吧，假如你们愿意的话，甚至也可以将他赦免。"

这些以及相类似的话在元老院公开宣读了。很明显，尼禄似乎受到了冒犯，很不高兴。然而，元老院并没有改变所做出的决定；特拉塞亚也没有更改自己的提议，其他的人仍然是各持己见。有一些人想尽力避免使皇帝处于招人忌恨的地步，而大多数人则是由于自己一方的人多而感到很安全。特拉塞亚则展现了自己一贯所具有的坚定不屈的性格，而这与他的声誉是相符合的。

奥路斯·狄第乌斯·盖尔路斯·法布里奇乌斯·维伊安托也受到了同样的指控，他在一部所谓《遗言》[1]的书里面，对元老和祭司们进行了大肆的侮辱。控告者盖乌斯·特莱恩提乌斯·图里乌斯·盖米努斯还进一步说，维伊安托一贯收取他人贿赂，而作为报答，就是利用自己对皇帝的影响力而使行贿者得以升官。这就使得尼禄决定亲自出马来处理这一案件。他宣布维伊安托有罪，将其驱逐出了意大利，而且发布命令将他的书籍予以烧毁。尽管拥有和阅读这些书籍要冒很大的风险，这样的处理却反而促使人们热切地寻找和阅读这些书籍。后来，当禁令解除之后，人们也就遗忘了。

整个国家的道德情况正日渐堕落。现在，伴随着布路斯的去世，一个可以力挽狂澜的力量也消失了。他到底是自然死亡的，还是被人毒死的，这件事很难确定。有些人认为他是自然病死

---

〔1〕 也就是说，这是一篇假想性的遗嘱，在里面他写了一些攻击和侮辱大人物的话语。在罗马帝国时期，很多人在遗嘱之中对大人物进行攻击，因而在死后出版遗嘱才是最安全的。

gradually increasing tumour in his throat, which blocked the passage and stopped his breathing, suggested natural causes. But the general view was that Nero, ostensibly proposing a medical treatment, had instructed that Burrus'throat should be painted with a poisonous drug. The patient, it was said, had detected the crime, and when the emperor visited him had turned his face away and only answered Nero's inquiries with the words: '*I* am doing all right. '

The death of Burrus caused great public distress. His merits were dwelt on-also the inferiority of his successors, one harmless but ineffective and the other a notorious criminal. For the emperor now appointed two commanders of the Guard-Faenius Rufus because he was popular (having managed the corn supply without personal profit), and Gaius Ofonius Tigellinus because Nero found his unending immoralities and evil reputation fascinating. Each commander behaved as expected. Tigellinus was the more influential with the emperor, in whose private debaucheries he participated. Rufus was liked by Guardsmen and civilians: which went against him with Nero.

Burrus' death undermined the influence of Seneca. Decent standards carried less weight when one of their two advocates was gone. Now Nero listened to more disreputable advisers. These attacked Seneca, first for his wealth, which was enormous and excessive for any subject, they said, and was still increasing; secondly, for the grandeur of his mansions and beauty of his gardens, which outdid even the emperor's; and thirdly, for his alleged bids for popularity. They also charged Seneca with allowing no one to be called eloquent but himself. 'He is always writing poetry,' they suggested, ' now that Nero has become fond of it. He openly disparages the emperor's

的,是由于喉咙里的肿块越来越大,最终堵住了他的气管,使他窒息而死。但是大家普遍认为,在治疗布路斯的喉咙的时候,尼禄指使人以此为借口,将一层毒药涂在了他的面皮上。据说,病人早已察觉了这一阴谋,当皇帝来探视他的病情之时,他将脸转了过去,对于尼禄的问候只说了一句:"我很好。"

布路斯的死亡引起了公众们极大的悲伤。他的光辉形象在人们心中永存,同时大家也知道他的继承者们的卑贱:一个老实却又无能;另一个是一个罪大恶极的罪犯。因为现在尼禄任命了两位近卫军长官:一位是法伊尼乌斯·路福斯,此人的升迁是因为他颇得民众的好感(他在掌管罗马粮食供应之中没有牟取个人私利);另一位是盖乌斯·奥佛尼乌斯·提盖里努斯,此人的升迁是因为他放荡无耻因而获得了尼禄的好感。他们两人都分别按照人们所了解的方式行事。其中提盖里努斯对皇帝的影响更大。他参与了尼禄秘密的放荡行为。路福斯受到了近卫军和人民的欢迎,这使得他与尼禄的关系很紧张。

布路斯的死破坏了塞内加的影响力。两位高尚风气的提倡者之一的去世使得高尚风气失去了力量。现在的尼禄就更愿意倾听那些声名狼藉的顾问们的建议。他们对塞内加进行了攻击,首先攻击他的地方就是他的财富,说他的财富非常庞大,超过了应有的限度,而且还在继续增长。其次,他们攻击他的别墅的宏伟和花园的美丽方面甚至已经超过了皇帝。他们攻击塞内加的第三点,是说他正在极力争取人民的好感。他们还指责塞内加,说他说过除了自己之外没有人可以称作是演说家。他们说:"由于尼禄喜欢诗,所以他也就一直在写诗。他公开对皇帝的娱乐活动进行挑剔,看不起皇帝的驾车本领,而且对皇帝的歌唱极尽嘲

amusements, underestimates him as a charioteer, and makes fun of his singing. How long must merit at Rome be conferred by Seneca's certificate alone? Surely Nero is a boy no longer! He is a grown man and ought to discharge his tutor. His ancestors will teach him all he needs. ' Seneca knew of these attacks. People who still had some decency told him of them. Nero increasingly avoided his company.

Seneca, however, requested an audience, and when it was granted, this is what he said. ' It is nearly fourteen years, Caesar, since I became associated with your rising fortunes, eight since you became emperor. During that time you have showered on me such distinctions and riches that, if only I could retire to enjoy them unpretentiously, my prosperity would be complete.

' May I quote illustrious precedents drawn from your rank, not mine? Your great-great-grandfather Augustus allowed Marcus Agrippa to withdraw to Mytilcne, and allowed Gaius Maecenas the equivalent of retirement at Rome itself. The one his partner in wars,

笑之能事。似乎只有塞内加所发明的东西才是好东西,这种情况要持续到什么时候呢? 实际上,尼禄已经不再是一位不懂事的孩子了,他已经是一位成人,应该将自己的老师打发走了。他的祖先会教给他所需要的一切知识的。"塞内加知道了这些针对他的攻击,那些还有正义感的人将这些攻击告诉了他;尼禄也逐渐地与他疏远了。

于是,他要求尼禄给他一次见面的机会。当批准之后,他就对尼禄说了如下的一段话:"恺撒啊! 自从我与你那具有美好前程的幼年相伴以来,时间已经过去将近 14 年了,而自从你成为皇帝也已经八年了。在这一段时间之内,你将如此多的荣誉和财富赐给了我,以至于只要我能够退休以谨慎地享受这些东西,也就可以拥有完美的幸福了。

"我可以从你的身份的方面,而不是从我的身份方面来引用一些先辈的例子来说明问题吗? 你祖父的祖父奥古斯都[1]允许玛尔库斯·阿格里帕退居到米提利涅去,[2]而允许盖乌斯·迈凯纳斯在罗马本城退了休,其中之一是他在战争之中的搭档,而另一

---

〔1〕 尼禄是小阿格里披娜的儿子,而小阿格里披娜是老阿格里披娜的女儿,老阿格里披娜是奥古斯都的女儿优利娅的女儿,因而,尼禄与奥古斯都的祖孙关系主要是在母系方面。而由于尼禄的外祖父日耳曼尼库斯被提贝里乌斯过继为继子,而提贝里乌斯又曾被奥古斯都过继为继子,所以在父系方面有了祖孙关系。

〔2〕 奥古斯都为了能够建立一个王朝,把自己的女儿嫁给了其妹妹的儿子玛尔凯路斯,想在自己去世之后将帝位传给他。在公元前 23 年奥古斯都生病之时,由于觉得玛尔凯路斯年纪太轻而难以担当重任,便把自己带有图章的戒指给了阿格里帕。这样就使阿格里帕产生了野心,并与玛尔凯路斯的关系紧张起来了。奥古斯都病好了之后,为了调解两者的关系,找了一个借口将阿格里帕调到东方去了,阿格里帕负气到米提利涅去了。

the other the bearer of many anxious burdens at Rome, they were greatly rewarded, for great services. I have had no claim on your generosity, except my learning. Though acquired outside the glare of public life, it has brought me the wonderful recompense and distinction of having assisted in your early education.

'But you have also bestowed on me measureless favours, ınd boundless wealth. Accordingly, I often ask myself: "Is it I, son of a provincial knight, who am accounted a national leader? Is mine the unknown name which has come to glitter among ancient and glorious pedigrees? Where is my old self, that was content with so little? Laying out these fine gardens? Grandly inspecting these estates? Wallowing in my vast revenues?" I can only find one excuse. It was not for me to obstruct your munificence.

'But we have both filled the measure-you, of what an emperor can give his friend, and I, of what a friend may receive from his emperor. Anything more will breed envy. Your greatness is far above all such mortal things. But I am not; so I crave your help. If, in the field or on a journey, I were tired, I should want a stick. In life's journey, I need just such a support.

'For I am old and cannot do the lightest work. I am no longer equal to the burden of my wealth. Order your agents to take over my property and incorporate it in yours. I do not suggest plunging myself into poverty, but giving up the things that are too brilliant and dazzle me. The time now spent on gardens and mansions shall be devoted to the mind. You have abundant strength. For years the supreme power

个在罗马为他分担了许多的忧愁,他们因为自己所取得的丰功伟绩而获得了巨大的报酬。除了我所拥有的学识之外,我没有任何东西值得你给予如此慷慨的赠赐。虽然这些学识是在我孤独之中苦读得来的,但是它在你早年的教育中为你提供了帮助,并因此为我带来了丰厚的报酬和巨大的荣誉。

"但是你又给予了我莫大的信任,给了我无数的财富。因而,我经常自问:一个像我一样出生于外省的骑士家庭的人不是已经成为了一名国内显要的权贵了吗? 我原本默默无闻的名字不是已经与那些古老而又光荣的家族同样地显赫了吗? 原来那个极易满足的我到哪儿去了? 为什么要修建如此豪华的花园? 隆重地巡视这些地产是为什么? 仰仗着我那巨大的财产要过一种奢华的生活吗? 我只能找到一种借口,那就是我不能拒绝你的慷慨赠予。

"但是我们两个都已经相互尽了本分了,你作为一个皇帝,把自己所能够给予的一切都已经给予了朋友;而我作为一个朋友,也已经得到了皇帝所给予的一切。再进一步就会引起他人的嫉妒了。你的伟大早已经远远地超越了所有的凡人所具有的嫉妒之类的东西。但是,我却没有如此的伟大,因此需要你的帮助。就像在田间劳作、旅途奔波一样,我累了,我需要援助之手,在生活的旅途上,我也需要如此的援助。

"因为我已经年老了,连最轻微的工作也不能做了。我也不能够再承担我的财产的重负了。给你的代理官下令,接管我的财产而收归于你的名下吧。我不是想使自己重新陷入贫穷之中,而是要放弃那些太过于奢侈而使我眩晕的东西。现在用于照料花园和别墅的时间将会用于精神活动。你拥有无穷的力量,而且已经

has been familiar to you. We older friends may ask for our rest. This, too, will add to your glory—that you have raised to the heights men content with lower positions. '

The substance of Nero's reply was this. 'My first debt to you is that I can reply impromptu to your premeditated speech. For you taught me to improvise as well as to make prepared orations. True, my greatgreat-grandfather Augustus permitted Agrippa and Maecenas to rest after their labours. But he did so when he was old enough to assure them, by his prestige, of everything—of whatever kind—that he had given them. Besides, he certainly deprived neither of the rewards which they had earned from him in the wars and crises of Augustus' youthful years. If my life had been warlike, you too would have fought for me. But you gave what our situation demanded: wisdom, advice, philosophy, to support me as boy and youth. Your gifts to me will endure as long as life itself! My gifts to you, gardens and mansions and revenues, are liable to circumstances.

'They may seem extensive. But many people far less deserving than you have had more. I omit, from shame, to mention ex-slaves who flaunt greater wealth. I am even ashamed that you, my dearest friend, are not the richest of all men You are still vigorous and fit for State affairs and their rewards. My reign is only beginning. Or do you think you have reached your limit? If so you must rank yourself below

拥有了控制国家最高权力的多年的经验。我们这些老朋友们可以请求休息了，而这也会增加你的光荣，那些你提拔到高级职位上来的人同样也会满足于较低的地位。"

尼禄回答的大意是这样的："我对你的第一个义务就是我能够立即回答你的一番经过了精心构思的演说。因为你教育过我不仅仅要做好精心准备的演说，也要能够做到即席演讲。确实是，我的祖父的祖父奥古斯都在阿格里帕和迈凯纳斯他们为国辛劳一生之后允许他们退休。但是他如此做的时候，他的年龄加上他的威信已经使他足以确保他能够给予他们一切东西，而且也不论是什么性质的东西。除此之外，他确实没有剥夺自己所授予他们的任何奖品；这些东西是奥古斯都年轻的时候，他们通过自己在战争以及在危机的关头所作出的贡献而争取到、并由奥古斯都奖励给他们的。假如我的生命之中曾经经历过战争的话，你也肯定会为我奋勇而战。但是，你确实也给予了当时我们的形势所需要的东西，你用你的智慧、忠告和哲理抚育了我的童年和青年。你所给予我的礼物将会与我终生相伴，而我所给予你的礼物，如花园、别墅和金钱之类的东西会随着环境的变化而过时的。

"这些东西也许看起来是很珍贵的，但是许多品格远不如你的人却获得了比你更多的东西。我耻于再提及那些以比你的财富多而夸耀的被释放的奴隶了。我更加引以为耻的是，你作为我最亲密的朋友，竟然不是所有的人之中最为富有的人。你的生命仍然充满了活力，可以担任国家要职，并取得与此相适应的报酬。而且我本人的统治也刚刚才开始。难道你认为自己已经达到了生命的极限吗？假如是如此的话，你就应该认为自己的地位比不

Lucius Vitellius, thrice consul, and my generosity below that of Claudius, and my gifts as inferior to the lifelong savings of Lucius Volusius Saturninus (II).

'If youth's slippery paths lead me astray, be at hand to call me back! You equipped my manhood; devote even greater care to guiding it! If you return my gifts and desert your emperor, it is not your unpretentiousness, your retirement, that will be on everyone's lips, but *my* meanness, your dread of *my* brutality. However much your self-denial were praised, no philosopher could becomingly gain credit from an action damaging to his friend's reputation. '

Then he clasped and kissed Seneca. Nature and experience had fitted Nero to conceal hatred behind treacherous embraces. Seneca expressed his gratitude (all conversations with autocrats end like that). But he abandoned the customs of his former ascendancy. Terminating his large receptions, he dismissed his entourage, and rarely visited Rome. Ill-health or philosophical studies kept him at home, he said.

After Seneca's elimination it was easy to bring down the commander of the Guard Faenius Rufus, who was accused of friendship with Agrippina. Faenius' colleague Tigellinus became more powerful every day. But he felt that his criminal aptitudes—the only qualities he possessed—would influence the emperor more if he could make them partners in crime. Studying Nero's fears, Tigellinus found he chiefly dreaded Rubellius Plautus and Faustus Cornelius Sulla Felix. One

上曾经三次担任过执政官的路奇乌斯·维提里乌斯,而我的慷慨程度还比不上克劳狄乌斯,我所给予你的礼物也比不上路奇乌斯·沃路西乌斯·塞图尼努斯(二世)长年来所节省下来的财富。

"假如因为年轻而使我有脱离正轨的迹象,就请随时给我指正。既然是你指导我长大成人的,就请进一步地关心和指导我的成长。假如你将我所赠赐的礼物都归还给我,而且抛弃了我——你的皇帝,那么人们挂在嘴边进行议论和非难的将不是你的谦逊、你的退隐,而是我的贪婪以及你对我的残暴的恐惧之情。不管人们对你的自我克制精神进行了怎样的颂扬,一位智者是不会从损害自己朋友名声的举止之中获取良好信誉的。"

然后他就拥抱并吻别了塞内加。天性以及多年的历练已经使尼禄完全可以将自己的憎恨掩饰在虚伪的亲切之下。塞内加向对方表达了谢意(与一位独裁者所进行的对话就以这种方式全部结束了)。但是,他抛弃了以前所习惯的那种讲排场的生活方式,不再举办大型宴会,解散了身边的大量随从人员,并很少到罗马来进行拜访。他说,由于糟糕的健康状况和全身心地投入到哲学研究之中,使他只能待在家里。

自从打发走了塞内加之后,要想整垮近卫军长官法伊尼乌斯·路福斯就是一件很容易的事情了,因为有人控告他与阿格里披娜保持了友谊关系。而法伊尼乌斯的同事提盖里努斯的势力却是逐日在增强。因为,他认为自己唯一所具有的天赋才能就是作恶有术,而如果他能将这些才能用来与皇帝一同做罪恶的勾当,他就可以加强自己对皇帝的影响。提盖里努斯在认真研究了尼禄所恐惧的对象之后,发现皇帝所害怕的主要人物是路贝里乌斯·普劳图斯和法乌司图斯·科尔涅里乌斯·苏拉·费里克斯。

had been recently removed to Asia, the other to southern Gaul. Tigellinus enlarged on their aristocratic origins, and their present proximity to the armies of the east and of Germany respectively.

'I have no divided allegiance like Burrus,' he said. 'My only thought is your safety! At Rome this may in some degree be ensured by vigilance on the spot. But how can one suppress sedition far away? The dictator Sulla's name has excited the Gauls. For the peoples of Asia Drusus' grandson is just as unsettling. Sulla's poverty increases his daring. He pretends to be lazy—yet he is only biding his time for a *coup*. Plautus is rich, and does not pretend to like retirement. He parades an admiration of the ancient Romans, but he has the arrogance of the Stoics, who breed sedition and intrigue. '

Action was not long delayed. Five days later, Sulla was murdered at dinner. Assassins had reached Massilia before the alarm. His head was transported to Nero, who joked that it was disfigured by premature greyness.

The plans for Plautus' death were less secret. More people were interested in his safety. Besides, the length and duration of the land and sea journeys encouraged rumours. The story was invented that Plautus had escaped to Corbulo who, having mighty armies behind him, would be in the gravest peril if there was to be a massacre of blameless

最近,他将其中之一调到了亚细亚,另一个调到了南高卢地区。提盖里努斯有意地夸大了他们的贵族身份和他们各自分别与东方的以及日耳曼的军队的接近。

他说:"我不像布路斯一样怀有异心,我全心全意关注的就是你的安全。在罗马可以通过我的亲自值勤守卫,使你的安全在某种程度上有所保证。但是如何才能镇压远处的叛乱呢?独裁者苏拉的名字曾经鼓舞了高卢人[1]对于亚细亚各族人民来说,杜路苏斯的外孙的名字同样也使他们激动不已[2]苏拉的贫困加强了他的胆量。他假装出一副懒散的样子,而其唯一的目的就在于寻找机会以谋政变。普劳图斯家境富裕,根本就没有隐退的打算。他不仅极力模仿某些古罗马人,而且还拥有了斯多噶派的高傲,这一派就是专门教人搞叛乱和耍阴谋的。"

尼禄毫不拖延,马上就采取了行动。五天之后,苏拉在就餐时就被暗杀了。杀手在对方对危险毫无知觉的情况之下就已经赶到玛西里亚了。他的首级被运回来交给了尼禄,尼禄对此开玩笑地说,他那过早出现的灰白头发使他的面部都变形了。

谋杀普劳图斯的计划很难秘密进行。更多的人在关心他的安全。除此之外,陆地和海洋路程的遥远以及由此产生的执行任务的时间拖延使得谣言四起。有人编造故事,说普劳图斯已经逃到科尔布罗那儿去了,而科尔布罗手下拥有强大的军队。假如一个未犯有任何过错的显要人物在他那儿被谋杀,那科尔布罗将是一个最危险的人物了。还有人传说,整个亚细亚在普劳图

---

〔1〕 上面所提及的苏拉就是独裁者苏拉的后人。

〔2〕 普劳图斯就是杜路苏斯的外孙,他是杜路苏斯的女儿优利娅的儿子。

notables. Asia, it was said, had risen in Plautus' support; the few, unenthusiastic, soldiers sent to murder him had failed to carry out their orders and had joined the rebellion. Idle credulity, as usual, amplified these fictitious rumours.

Meanwhile an ex-slave of Plautus, helped by favourable winds, outstripped the staff-officer of the Guard who had been sent against him, and brought a message from Plautus' father-in-law Lucius Antistius Vetus. 'Escape a passive end while there is a way out!' advised Antistius. 'Sympathy for your great name will make decent men back you and brave men help you. Meantime, disdain no possible support. Sixty soldiers have been sent. If you can repulse them, much can happen—even a war can develop-before Nero receives the news and sends another force. In short, either you save yourself by this action, or at least a bold end is as good as a timid one. '

But Plautus remained unimpressed. Either he felt helpless-an unarmed exile—or the suspense wearied him. Or perhaps he believed that his wife and children, whom he loved, would be more leniently treated if the emperor were not upset by an alarm. One account states that his father-in-law sent further messages saying that Plautus was in no danger. Or his philosophical friends, the Greek Coeranus and the Etruscan Gaius Musonius Rufus, may have recommended an imperturbable expectation of death rather than a hazardous anxious life.

The killers found him at midday, stripped for exercise. Supervised by the eunuch Pelago whom Nero had put in charge of the gang-

斯的支持之下已经造反了;而那被派去谋杀他的几个士兵本来就不热心,在不能完成自己的任务的情况之下也加入到叛军之中去了。像通常的情况一样,这些编造的谣言被那些无聊的轻信者夸大其词地传播着。

与此同时,普劳图斯的一名释放了的奴隶借着顺风的帮助,超过了一名受命来谋杀普劳图斯的近卫军的百人团长,并且从普劳图斯的岳父路奇乌斯·安提司提乌斯·维图斯那儿带来了一封信。安提司提乌斯在信中说:"当有办法逃生的时候,决不能被动地等死!出于对你那伟大的名声的同情,有身份的人会站出来支持你,而勇敢的人会帮助你。同时,千万不要拒绝别人所给予的任何可能的帮助,已经有60名士兵被派来谋杀你,假如你能够击退他们的话,那么在消息传到尼禄那儿而他派出另一支军队之前,还会发生更多的事情,甚至有可能招致战争。总而言之,你或者是用这一办法来营救自己,或者是采取勇敢的举动,而这一办法也不会比一个懦夫的举动更差。"

但是普劳图斯对此无动于衷。或许是他对于自己作为一个没有武装的被驱逐者已感到毫无生还的希望;或许是焦虑严重地折磨着他,使他厌倦了;也或许是他认为只要是皇帝的日常生活不被惊恐所打乱,他就会宽大对待自己所深爱的妻子和孩子。还有一种说法,说他的岳父派人又送来了一封信,说普拉图斯不再有生命之忧了。或者他的哲学朋友,希腊人科伊拉努斯和图司奇人盖乌斯·穆索尼乌斯·路福斯可能对他做过劝告,要他勇敢地迎接死亡,而不要在惊恐焦虑之中生活。

当凶手发现他的时候,他脱了衣服在锻炼身体。从旁监视的是宦官佩拉戈,他是尼禄派来监视这些人的,他就像君主的一位

like a slave set over a monarch's underlings-the officer slew him as he was. The victim's head was brought to Nero. I will quote the actual words he uttered when he saw it. 'Nero,' he said, 'how could such a long-nosed man have frightened you?'

Indeed, the fears which had caused the emperor to postpone his wedding with Poppaea were now dispelled. He planned to marry her quickly, after eliminating Octavia his wife. Octavia's conduct was unassuming; but he hated her, because she was popular and an emperor's daughter. First Nero wrote to the senate emphasizing his perpetual solicitude for the national interests, and—without admitting their murder-denouncing Sulla and Plautus as agitators. On these grounds the senate voted a thanksgiving, and the two men's expulsion from the senate. This was a mockery which caused greater disgust even than the crimes. Hearing of their decree, Nero concluded that all his misdeeds were accounted meritorious. So he divorced Octavia for barrenness, and married Poppaea.

Dominating Nero as his wife, as she had long dominated him as his mistress, Poppaea incited one of Octavia's household to accuse Octavia of adultery with a slave—an Alexandrian flute-player called Eucaerus was designated for the role. Octavia's maids were tortured, and though some were induced by the pain to make false confessions, the majority unflinchingly maintained her innocence. One retorted that the mouth of Tigellinus, who was bullying her, was less clean than any part of Octavia. Nevertheless, she was put away. First, there was an ordinary divorce: she received the ominous gifts of Burrus,

奴才在监视着自己的臣属一样,在这种情况之下,百人团长将普劳图斯杀死了。死者的首级被带回来交给了尼禄,我所引用的话是尼禄在看见首级之时的原话,他说:"尼禄啊,这样一个长着长鼻子的人怎么会吓着你了呢?"

实际上,现在皇帝已经清除了使他与波培娅结婚被迫延期的各种顾虑了。在遣送走了妻子屋大维娅之后,他计划马上与她结婚。尽管屋大维娅举止性情很柔顺,但是尼禄非常憎恨她,因为她深得人民的爱戴,而且是皇帝的女儿。首先,尼禄给元老院写了一封信,强调自己永远在关注国家的利益,并且指责苏拉和普劳图斯为叛乱犯,而没有提及自己已将他们谋杀的事情。为了这个缘故,元老院表决通过了一项决议,在全国举行了一次感恩节祭日,宣布将这两人开除出元老院。这种嘲弄所引起的侮辱甚至比犯罪还要严重。听到元老们所发出的命令之后,尼禄得出了这样一个结论,那就是自己所有的违法乱纪行为都会被描述成崇高的。于是他以屋大维娅不能生育为借口而与她离了婚,并娶了波培娅。

现在波培娅以妻子的身份控制了尼禄,正如长久以来就以情妇的身份控制着他一样。在这种情况之下,波培娅唆使屋大维娅的一名仆人控告屋大维娅同一名奴隶通奸,一个名叫优凯路斯的亚历山大笛师受命扮演了这一奸夫的角色。于是,屋大维娅的侍女们受到了严刑拷问,虽然有一些侍女熬不过疼痛的折磨而被迫做了虚假的招供,但是,绝大多数都坚定地说屋大维娅是清白无辜的。其中有一个面对威逼她的提盖里努斯大骂,说他的嘴不及屋大维娅身体的任何一部分干净。然而,屋大维娅还是被撵走了。开始,这只是作为一件普通的离婚案来对待,她获得了两样并不吉

house and Rubellius Plautus' estates. Soon, however, she was banished to Campania, under military surveillance.

Now indiscretion is safer for the Roman public than for their superiors, since they are insignificant; and they protested openly and loudly. This seemed to recall Nero to decency, and he proposed to make Octavia his wife again. Happy crowds climbed the Capitol, thankful to heaven at last. They overturned Poppaea's statues and carried Octavia's on their shoulders, showering flowers on them and setting them in the Forum and temples.

Even the emperor was acclaimed and worshipped again. Indeed a noisy crowd invaded the palace. But detachments of troops clubbed them and forced them back at the point of the sword. Then the changes the rioters had inspired were reversed, and Poppaea reinstated. Always a savage hater, she was now mad with fear of mass violence and Nero's capitulation to it. She fell at his feet crying: ' Now that things have reached this pass, it is not marriage I am fighting for, but what, to me, means less than my marriage—my life. It is in danger from Octavia's dependants and slaves! They pretend to be the people of Rome! They commit, in peace-time, outrages that could hardly happen even in war! The emperor is their target-they only lack a leader. And once disorders begin one will easily be found, when she leaves Campania and proceeds to the capital! Even her distant nod causes riots.

' What have *I* done wrong? Whom have I injured? Or is all this because I am going to give an authentic heir to the house of the

利的财产:布路斯的房子和路贝里乌斯·普劳图斯的地产。然而之后不久,她就在军队的监视之下而被驱逐到了康帕尼亚。

现在,对于罗马公众来说,采取轻率的行为要比那些显要人物采取同样的行为安全得多,于是他们对此举动采取了公开的反对活动,并将这一反对大声地喊了出来。据说因此尼禄感到了自己行为的不得体,又打算将屋大维娅召回来重新做自己的妻子。欢呼雀跃的人群爬上了卡披托里乌姆神庙,最后,他们向上天表示了感谢。他们推翻了波培娅的雕像,并把屋大维娅的雕像抬在肩上,把花撒在了这些雕像的上面,并把他们安置到了广场和神庙之中。

他们甚至对皇帝也进行欢呼并表示了致敬。确实是有一大群吵嚷的人众挤到皇宫之中来了。但是,这时出现了一队队的士兵,他们用棍棒抽打群众,并用刀尖逼迫他们往后退。于是,这一事件所促成的变化又倒转过来了,波培娅又恢复了荣誉。此人一向是一个残忍的报复者,现在,对群众强烈抗议的恐惧和尼禄对此抗议的妥协使她疯狂了。她跪倒在尼禄的脚下哭喊道:"既然事情已经发展到了这个地步,我就不再争取与你结婚了,尽管对我来说这场婚姻比我的生命还重要。屋大维娅的食客和奴隶们已经使我的生命处于危险之中! 他们把自己假扮成罗马人民! 他们在和平时期所做出的暴行即使是战争时期也难以发生! 他们将皇帝列为攻击目标,他们只是缺少一个领袖罢了。而一旦爆发了骚乱,这时只要她离开了康帕尼亚来到首都,就很容易选出一位领袖了! 即使是她从远处点一点头,就能够引起一场暴乱。

"我做错了什么事情? 又曾经伤害到谁了? 或者说所发生的这一切难道都是因为我将要为恺撒家族生一位嫡亲后人? 难道

Caesars? Would Rome prefer an Egyptian flute-player's child to be introduced into the palace? If you think it best, take back your directress voluntarily—do not be coerced into doing so. Or else, safeguard yourself! Punish suitably. No severity was needed to end the first troubles. But now, once they lose hope of Nero keeping Octavia, they will find her another husband.'

Poppaea's arguments, playing on Nero's alarm and anger in turn, duly terrified and infuriated him. But the suspicions concerning Octavia's slave came to nothing; the examination of her servants proved fruitless. So it was decided to extract a confession of adultery from someone against whom a charge of revolution could also be concocted. A suitable person seemed to be the aforementioned Anicetus, fleet-comniander at Misenum and instrument of Nero's matricide. After the crime he had been fairly well regarded. Later, however, he was in serious disfavour; for the sight of a former accomplice in terrible crimes is a reproach.

Nero summoned him, and reminded him of his previous job-Anicetus alone had protected his emperor against his mother's plotting. Now, said Nero, he could earn equal gratitude by climinating a detested wife. No violence or weapons were needed. Anicetus only had to confess adultery with Octavia. Great rewards were promised-though at present they were unspecified—and an agreed place of retirement. Refusal would mean death. Anicetus' warped character found no difficulty in a further crime. Indeed, the confession which he made to Nero's friends, assembled as a council of state, even exceeded his instructions. Then he was removed to comfortable exile

说罗马宁愿选择一位埃及笛师的孩子进入皇宫做皇子？假如你认为这样做最好的话，就将你的女主人招回来吧，只要是出于自愿而不是被迫这样做的。或者是为自己的安全考虑，而采取适当的惩罚措施。叛乱刚刚开始，不用太过严厉的手段就可以镇压下去的。但是现在，一旦群众失望地看到尼禄没有留住屋大维娅，他们会为她另外再寻找一位丈夫的。"

波培娅原来用以激起尼禄的恐惧和恼怒的话语立刻将他吓住并激起他的激怒了。但是对屋大维娅奴隶的怀疑不会带来任何结果；而对其侍从的审问也证明是白费力气。于是，尼禄决定找一个人使他承认自己和屋大维娅通奸，此外还可以将编造的叛乱者的罪名加在他的头上。看来最合适不过的人选就是我以前所提及的阿尼凯图斯，他是米塞努姆的舰队长官，他就是帮助尼禄弑杀母亲的凶犯。谋杀之后，他被尼禄重重地赏了一笔。然而后来，尼禄就非常讨厌他了，因为一看到自己先前的同谋犯，可怕的犯罪感就会浮现在他的心头。

尼禄将他招来，提起了阿尼凯图斯以前的举动，表扬他说只有他在皇帝反对母亲的阴谋陷害之中保护过皇帝的安全。尼禄说，现在他有了一个同样使自己感恩不尽的机会，那就是替皇帝铲除一个邪恶的妻子。既不能使用暴力也不能使用武器。而阿尼凯图斯只要坦白自己与屋大维娅通奸就行了。虽然没有具体说明是什么报酬，但尼禄已许诺给他丰厚的报酬，另外还给他一个舒适的场所作为退休之用。假如拒绝的话，就意味着死亡。阿尼凯图斯生性邪恶，犯罪对他来说是小菜一碟。于是，在尼禄所召集的并由他本人的密党所组成的国务会议上，阿尼凯图斯做了供认，甚至于编造了超过指示要他说的东西。于是，他被驱逐流放

in Sardinia, where he died a natural death.

Nero reported in an edict that Octavia had tried to win over the fleet by seducing its commander, and then, nervous about her unfaithfulness, had procured an abortion (the emperor forgot his recent charge of sterility). She was then confined on the island of Pandateria.

No exiled woman ever earned greater sympathy from those who saw her. Some still remembered the banishment of the elder Agrippina by Tiberius and, more recently, of Julia Livilla by Claudius. Yet they had been mature women with happy memories which could alleviate their present sufferings. But Octavia had virtually died on her wedding day. Her new home had brought her nothing but misery. Poison had removed her father, and very soon her brother. Maid had been preferred to mistress. Then she, Nero's wife, had been ruined by her successor. Last came the bitterest of all fates, this accusation.

So this girl, in her twentieth year, was picketed by company-commanders of the Guard and their men. She was hardly a living person any more—so certain was she of imminent destruction. Yet still she lacked the peace of death. The order to die arrived a few days later. She protested that she was a wife no longer—Nero's sister only. She invoked the Germanici, the relations she shared with Nero. Finally she even invoked Agrippina, in whose days her marriage had been unhappy, certainly, but at least not fatal. But Octavia was bound, and all her veins were opened. However, her terror retarded the flow of blood. So she was put into an exceedingly

到了撒丁尼亚,在那里过着舒适的生活,得以寿终正寝。

尼禄发布敕令,宣布屋大维娅为了能够取得海军舰队,就勾引舰队长官,而后来由于对自己的不忠而惴惴不安,从而做了流产。(皇帝竟然忘记了自己不久之前还说她不能生育。)于是她被囚禁到庞达提里亚岛去了。

那些见过她的人说,没有任何一个被流放的女人曾经像她那样令人同情。有些人还仍然记得提贝里乌斯流放老阿格里披娜的事情,以及再近一点的克劳狄乌斯放逐优利娅·里维拉的事情。但是她们两人都已经是成熟的女性,曾经有过幸福的回忆,而这会减轻她们当时的痛苦。但是对于屋大维娅来说,实际上,她结婚的日子就是她死亡的日子。她的新家给她带来的除了灾难之外一无所有。毒药已经夺走了自己父亲的生命,而自己的兄弟不久也死于同一个方式。女仆人竟然代替了女主人,于是,她作为尼禄的妻子被其继任者完全毁掉了。最后则是面临着最为悲惨的命运,她被起诉了。

于是,这位女孩在自己20岁的时候,被近卫军的百人团长和其手下的士兵包围起来了。她已经难以再过一种正常人的生活了,她很明白自己的生命不可避免地将要毁灭了。然而即使死她也没有获得安宁。处死她的命令几天之后就到达了。她对于被称做尼禄的妻子表示了抗议,宣布自己已不再是尼禄的妻子,而只是他的一个妹妹。她向作为自己与尼禄的亲戚的日耳曼尼库斯家族的人祈求保佑;最后她又向阿格里披娜祈求保佑,因为她在世的时候,她的婚姻生活当然也算不上幸福,但起码还不是致命的。但是,屋大维娅被捆绑了起来,全身的血管都被切断了。然而她的恐惧却使血液不能顺利地流淌出来。于是她被抬

hot vapour-bath and suffocated. An even crueller atrocity followed. Her head was cut off and taken to Rome for Poppaea to see.

How long must I go on recording the thank-offerings in temples on such occasions? Every reader about that epoch, in my own work or others, can assume that the gods were thanked every time the emperor ordered a banishment or murder; and, conversely, that happenings once regarded joyfully were now treated as national disasters. Nevertheless, when any senatorial decree reaches new depths of sycophancy or abasement, I will not leave it unrecorded.

In the same year Nero was believed to have poisoned two of his most prominent ex-slaves-Doryphorus for opposing the emperor's marriage with Poppaea, and Pallas for reserving his own immense riches for himself by living so long.

Seneca was secretly denounced by Romanus as an associate of Gaius Calpurnius Piso. But Seneca more effectively turned the same charge against his accuser. However, the incident alarmed Piso-and by so doing initiated a far-reaching, disastrous conspiracy against Nero.

到一个极热的蒸汽浴室之中窒息而亡。接着就发生了一个更加残忍的行径。她的头颅被砍下来送到了罗马,供波培娅过目。

为了这类事件,在神庙之中向诸神奉献牺牲祭品以表示感谢,对此我还要继续记录多长时间呢?关于那段历史,不论是在我的作品之中,还是在他人的作品之中,每一位读者都可以看得出,每一次只要是皇帝下令要驱逐或处死某一个人,诸神就要受到谢恩;而相反,以前认为是高兴的事情,现在就应被视作是国家的灾难。无论如何,不论元老院的命令会谄媚和卑鄙到何种新的程度,我是永远也不会放过而不作记录的。

在同一年,我们相信尼禄又毒死了他的两个最重要的被释奴隶,多律弗路斯和帕拉斯。多律弗路斯是因为反对皇帝与波培娅的婚姻,而帕拉斯则是因为占有了巨额的财富,而本人的寿命又是如此之长的缘故。

塞内加被洛玛努斯秘密地控告了,他被指责与盖乌斯·卡尔普尔尼乌斯·披索相勾结。但是,塞内加又用同样的罪名反过来对付控告他的人,而且卓有成效。然而这件事情却把披索吓坏了,于是就发动了一场反对尼禄的涉及广泛又是灾难性的阴谋叛乱。

CHAPTER 13
Eastern Settlement

The Parthian king Vologeses I had now heard of Corbulo's activities and Rome's award of the Armenian throne to the foreigner
Tigranes V. Vologeses wanted to avenge the slur cast on the Parthian
royal house by the expulsion of his brother Tiridates from Armenia.
Yet Roman power, and his respect for the longstanding treaty with us,
put him in two minds. Hesitant by nature, Vologeses was also embarrassed by the rebellion of the formidabl Hyrcanian people and the numerous resultant campaigns. As he wavered, however, news of a further humiliation provoked him to action. Tigranes had left Armenia
and subjected its neighbour Adiabene to devastation too protracted and
comprehensive to be regarded as a mere raid.

This was too much for the Parthian grandees. 'Are we so utterly
despised,' they said, 'that we are invaded not even by a Roman
commander but by an impudent hostage who has long been considered
a slave?' The king of Adiabene, Monobazus, further inflamed their
resentment. 'Where,' he asked, 'from what quarter, can I find
protection? Armenia is gone! The borderlands are following! If Parthia

第十三章　东方移民地

　　现在,帕尔提亚国王沃洛吉西斯一世知道了科尔布罗的战绩和罗马将亚美尼亚王位作为奖励授予了外国人提格拉尼斯五世的事情之后,沃洛吉西斯就想为阿尔撒奇达伊王族报仇,以雪由于自己的弟弟提里达特斯被驱逐出亚美尼亚而蒙受的耻辱。但是罗马实力的强大,以及他对于他与罗马所缔结的长期条约的尊重,使他左右为难。沃洛吉西斯生性优柔寡断,而且可怕的叙尔卡尼亚部族的人民起义以及对他们所展开的多次镇压也使他受到了很大的牵制。然而正当他犹豫不决的时候,一件使他进一步遭受侮辱的消息促使他采取了行动。提格拉尼斯已经离开了亚美尼亚侵入了他的邻邦阿狄亚贝尼,对那儿的人民进行了抢劫蹂躏,其时间之长和规模之大,绝对不能看做是一般的抢劫。

　　这种举动使帕尔提亚的贵族们实在忍受不了了,他们说:"我们遭受了彻底的贬损,不仅仅是罗马统帅敢于入侵我们,而且一位多年来一直就被看做是奴隶的厚颜无耻的人渣也敢来欺凌我们,难道不是吗?"阿狄亚贝尼人的国王莫诺巴佐斯则是煽风点火,进一步激发了他们的不满。他问道:"我可以到哪里寻求,从什么方向上得到保护呢? 亚美尼亚已经丢失了,相邻的地区接着

will not help, we must give in to Rome, and make the best of it-avoid conquest by surrendering. ' The silence, and restrained reproaches, of the dethroned exile Tiridates were even more effective. 'Passivity does not preserve great empires,' he said. 'That needs fighting, with warriors and weapons. When stakes are highest, might is right. A private individual can satisfy his prestige by holding his own—but a monarch can only do it by claiming other people's property. '

Vologeses was moved by these pleas. Calling a council, he placed Tiridates next to himself. 'When this man,' said Vologescs, 'whose father was mine too, renounced the supreme position to me as the elder, I awarded him the third-ranking kingdom, Armenia; for Pacorus had already been given Media Atropatenc. By abandoning the tradition of brotherly feuds and family strife, I thought I had settled the affairs of our family satisfactorily. But the Romans, though they have never broken the peace to their advantage, are breaking it once again. It will mean their destruction!

'I admit I should have preferred to rely on right and inheritance, not on sanguinary warfare, to keep what my ancestors won. But if I have delayed mistakenly, my prowess henceforward will make a-mends. Your might and renown, gentlemen, are undiminished. You have gained a name, also, for moderation. No man is exalted enough to scorn moderation; and the gods too honour it. ' So saying, he placed the diadem on Tiridates' head. Then, entrusting his royal cavalry

就要被侵占。假如帕尔提亚不能给我们提供保护的话，我们就要向罗马投降，我们必须要设法这样，即通过屈服以免遭受抢掠。"

已被剥夺了王位并遭受驱逐的提里达特斯沉默寡言，提出的抗议也很有节制，但是却更有效，他说："消极忍让不是伟大的帝国所应该做的事情，它需要勇士们拿起武器进行战斗。当面临最危险的境地的时候，实力才是唯一有权力说话的东西。个人可以通过保存自己的财产而获取声誉，而一个君主只有获取其他民族的财产才能赢得光荣。"

沃洛吉西斯被这些话打动了，于是召开了一次会议，他让提里达特斯坐在了自己的身边。沃洛吉西斯说："这个人与我是同一个父亲所生，当年因为我年长的原因，他把最高的王位让给了我，而我则是把第三等的王国亚美尼亚作为奖励授予了他，因为米地亚·阿特洛帕提尼已经送给了帕科路斯。[1] 我认为我已经圆满地处理了我们家庭的事情，而没有出现通常那种兄弟相互仇恨、家庭冲突的现象。尽管破坏和平从来也没有给罗马人带来任何好处，但是他们却又一次破坏了，而这将意味着他们的毁灭！

"我承认，我宁愿采取公正合理的办法与继承的方法来保存我的先辈们所赢得的产业，而不想诉诸血腥的战争。但是，假如我错误地延误了战机的话，那么我的勇气可以进行补偿。诸位绅士们，你们的实力和名誉没有受到任何损害。同时你们还获得了一种谦逊的美誉。任何高贵的人都不敢蔑视这种谦逊的品德。诸神也以它为荣。"说完之后，他把王冠戴在了提里达特斯的头

---

〔1〕 他的另一个兄弟，被分配到了阿尔撒奇达伊王的一个属邑米地亚·阿特洛帕提尼（在亚美尼亚和米地亚本土之间）。

escort or auxiliaries from Adiabene to a nobleman called Monaeses, Vologeses ordered Tiridates to expel Tigranes from Armenia. Vologeses himself, waiving his dispute with the Hyrcanians, mobilized his home forces for major operations against the Roman provinces.

When Corbulo received reliable information of these measures, he sent two divisions to support Tigrancs. But Corbulo secretly instructed their commanders, Lucius Verulanus Severus and Marcus Vettius Bolanus, to act warily and not to hustle. For he wanted to have a war on hand rather than to fight one. Moreover, since Syria would be the chief sufferer from invasion by Vologeses, he had written recommending Nero to appoint a separate commander to defend Armenia. Meanwhile Corbulo posted his remaining divisions on the Euphrates, improvised an armed force of provincials, and blocked every possible entrance-point with troops. Water being so scarce in the area, he built forts to protect certain springs, and destroyed others by filling them with sand.

During these preparations for the defence of Syria, Monaeses advanced rapidly, hoping to reach Tigranes before his approach was announced; but he did not catch Corbulo unawares or unprepared. Tigranes had occupied Tigranoccrta. This city was powerfully garrisoned and fortified. Parts of its walls were protected by a considerable river, the Nicephorius, while a large fosse surrounded the remaining circumference. Inside were Roman troops, and stores already collected. A few of their collectors, advancing rashly, had been surprised and cut off by the enemy. However, this irritated rather than intimidated

上。然后,沃洛吉西斯将自己身边的一支皇家骑兵护卫队和一支来自于阿狄亚贝尼的辅助部队交给了一个名叫莫纳伊西斯的贵族,并命令提里达特斯将提格拉尼斯从亚美尼亚赶出去。沃洛吉西斯则是将他与叙尔卡尼亚的争吵搁置在一边,亲自动员了国内的兵力,准备全力以赴地进攻罗马各行省。

当科尔布罗接到了这些事件的准确情报之后,就派出了两个军团去援助提格拉尼斯。但是科尔布罗在暗地里却对两个军团统帅路奇乌斯·维路拉努斯·谢维路斯和玛尔库斯·维提乌斯·波拉努斯进行了吩咐,要他们行动谨慎,不可鲁莽。因为他宁愿迎接一场战争,也不愿去挑起一场战争。更何况,由于沃洛吉西斯将主要的进攻地点选在了叙利亚地区,他便给尼禄写了一封信,要求另外再选派一位统帅来保卫亚美尼亚。与此同时,科尔布罗将自己手下的其余军团布置在了幼发拉底河沿岸,将一支来自于各个行省的部队武装起来,并用军队将敌人可能用于进攻的每一个地方都封锁了起来。由于这一地区极度缺水,他就将某些泉水建起要塞加以保护,而另外的泉水则通过用填沙子堵塞的方法加以破坏。

正当罗马军为保护叙利亚而做着这些准备措施的时候,莫纳伊西斯也在迅速地向前推进,他希望在被发现之前能够接近提格拉尼斯。但是他发现科尔布罗已经做好了戒备,并已准备好了迎敌。提格拉尼斯早已占据了提格拉诺凯尔塔城,这座城市拥有强大的卫戍士兵和牢固的工事。而且一部分城墙还被一条相当宽阔的尼凯波里乌斯河环绕保护着,而在没有河水的地方则有一条巨大的壕沟环绕着。里面的守军是罗马部队,而且战略物资早已经储备好了。在搜集物资的时候,他的一些人走得太过于匆忙也太遥远了,被一些突然出现的罗马军切断了归路。然而这种情况

their fellow-soldiers.

The Parthians lacked the hand-to-hand courage to prosecute a siege. Their sporadic discharge of arrows deluded no one but themselves; it did not frighten the Roman garrison. And when the Adiabenians brought up ladders and siege-engines they were easily thrown back, and then roughly handled by a sortie. But Corbulo decided to take no great advantage of the successes. Instead he wrote to Vologeses protesting against his invasion of the province and blockade of an allied, friendly king and Roman troops. Either Vologeses must raise the siege, said Corbulo, or he himself would likewise occupy enemy territory. The staff-officer Casperius who took the letter found the Parthian king at Nisibis, thirty-seven miles from Tigranocerta, and spiritedly delivered his message in person.

It was Vologeses' longstanding and firm policy to avoid war with Rome. Besides, his affairs were not going well. The siege had failed. Tigranes was well-garrisoned and supplied. The assaulting party had been routed. Moreover, Roman divisions had been dispatched to Armenia, while others were on the Syrian frontier ready for an offensive. His own cavalry, however, was suffering from lack of fodder, since an invasion of locusts had destroyed all leafage and grass. Afraid—but hiding it—Vologeses gave a conciliatory reply: he would send envoys to the Roman emperor, to discuss the Parthian claim to Armenia and the conclusion of a stable peace. Then the king ordered Monaeses to abandon the attempt on Tigranocerta, and also withdrew himself.

This was generally regarded as a triumph, achieved by Corbulo's threats and Vologeses' fears. Some, however, alleged a secret agree-

却激怒了他们的战友,而不是把他们给吓倒了。

进行围攻的帕尔提亚人缺少同敌人短兵相接的勇气。他们只是自欺欺人地偶尔乱射一些箭,根本就没有吓倒守城的罗马军队。当阿狄亚贝尼人架起梯子和攻城器械时,他们很容易就被击退,然后被城中出击的部队迅速击溃。但是科尔布罗却决定不再乘胜追击,相反,他给沃洛吉西斯写了一封信,抗议他对罗马行省的侵犯和他对于罗马盟军和友好国王以及罗马军队的包围。科尔布罗说,沃洛吉西斯必须停止围攻,否则他自己将率军攻到敌人的领土上去。百人团长卡司佩里乌斯带着信在离提格拉诺凯尔塔37英里的尼西比斯城中见到了帕尔提亚国王,并且精神抖擞地亲自向对方转达了科尔布罗的意见。

长久以来沃洛吉西斯所制定的一项坚定的原则就是要避免同罗马开战。除此之外,他自己的一些事务也并没有处理好。围城遭到了失败。提格拉尼斯受到了严密的保护,并且有充足的粮食供应。攻击部队已经被击败了。而且一些罗马军团已经被布置在了亚美尼亚,其他一些军团则集结在了叙利亚边境,随时准备进攻。并且,由于发生了蝗虫灾害,所有的树叶和草都被吃光了,他的骑兵缺少草料。尽管沃洛吉西斯非常后怕,但他将这种恐惧埋藏在心底,用一种温和的语调做了回答,说他将会派使节去见罗马皇帝,以讨论帕尔提亚对于亚美尼亚所提出的权利问题,并签订两国之间巩固持久和平的协议。接着国王就命令莫纳伊西斯放弃了对于提格拉诺凯尔塔城的进攻,自己也率军后撤了。

多数人认为这是一次由于科尔布罗的威胁和沃洛吉西斯的恐惧而取得的胜利。然而,有一些人却认为,他们秘密签订了一项协定,规定双方结束军事行动,而沃洛吉西斯和提格拉尼

ment whereby each side should suspend hostilities and both Vologeses and Tigranes should leave Armenia. 'Otherwise', they argued, 'why had the Roman army evacuated Tigranocerta? Was it better to have wintered on the Cappadocian frontier, in hastily erected huts, rather than in the capital of the kingdom they had just saved? No, surely the war was postponed so that Vologeses should encounter a different opponent. Corbulo clearly had no intention of hazarding any more the honours that his long service had won him. '

For Corbulo, as already stated, had requested a separate appointment for the defence of Armenia. Lucius Caesennius Paetus was reported to be on his way. When he arrived, the forces were divided. Paetus received the first brigade which had recently been summoned from Moesia, and the fourth and twelfth, and all the auxiliaries from Pontus, Galatia, and Cappadocia. Corbulo retained the third, sixth and tenth brigades, and the original Syrian army. The remaining troops were to be shared or allotted as circumstances required. However, Corbulo was impatient of rivals. Paetus, for his part, might well in other circumstances have been satisfied to take second place—but he had formed a low estimate of what his colleague had achieved. There had been no killing or plundering, said Paetus—the storming of cities had been purely nominal: *he* intended to impose, not merely a phantom king, but the tribute and law and government of Rome.

At this juncture Vologeses' envoys, whose mission to the emperor I mentioned, returned unsuccessful. So Parthia started undisguised

斯双方都要撤离亚美尼亚。他们论辩说:"否则为什么罗马军队要撤离提格拉诺凯尔塔城?宁愿在卡帕多奇亚的边界地带,在仓促修建的茅屋里过冬,[1]却不愿在他们刚刚解放的王国的首都里过冬,这难道是更好的选择吗?不,事实绝非如此,而是他们将战争推迟了,这样沃洛吉西斯就可以对付另一个对手了,很明显科尔布罗不愿意拿他多年辛苦所挣来的荣誉进行冒险。"

正如在前面说过的那样,科尔布罗曾经要求另外派一位统帅来保卫亚美尼亚。而且听说凯森尼乌斯·帕伊图斯正在赶往目的地的路上。到达之后,他们就将兵力进行了分配。帕伊图斯管辖刚刚从美西亚征召而来的第一军团以及第四军团和第十二军团,再加上来自于本都、加拉提亚和卡帕多奇亚的辅助部队;而科尔布罗则管辖第三、第六和第十军团,以及原有的叙利亚部队。其余部队要分还是要合,这要根据具体的情况而作决定。然而,科尔布罗是容不下他的对手的。就帕伊图斯来说,或许在其他情况之下,坐上第二把交椅就已经很满足了,但是他对于他的搭档所取得的成就十分瞧不起。帕伊图斯说,既没有杀死敌人,也没有夺得战利品,攻打城池更属空穴来风。他则是打算不仅仅安置一名有名无实的国王,而且想把罗马的税赋、法律以及统治全部加到这一地区。

正在这时,沃洛吉西斯所派出的使节一无所获地返回去了,关于他们到皇帝那儿所负的使命我在前面已经讲过了。于是帕

---

〔1〕 同沃洛吉西斯的协议是在年底达成的,因此冬天是公元 61 年到公元 62 年的冬天,而后边的说明则是公元 62 年春天或夏天的事情。

warfare. Pactus was willing, and entered Armenia with two divisions, the fourth under Lucius Funisulanus Vettonianus, and the twelfth under Calavius Sabinus. But the omens were sinister. For while crossing the Euphrates bridge the horse carrying the consular insignia took fright for no apparent reason, and bolted to the rear. Then a victim due for sacrifice when the construction of the winter camp was complete escaped outside the rampart before the work was done. Moreover, some soldiers' javelins caught fire—a particularly significant portent since the Parthian enemy fights with missiles.

But Paetus disregarded the omens. Without adequately fortifying his winter camp or arranging to store corn, he hurried his army across the Taurus range, proposing to recover Tigranocerta and devastate the areas which Corbulo had left unravaged. A few forts were captured and some credit gained, also loot; though Pactus claimed immoderate credit, and wasted the loot. But during his long marches over territory he could not hold, the corn he had seized became spoilt. Winter was approaching. So Paetus withdrew his army and composed a dispatch to Nero. It was grandly phrased—as if the war was over-but empty of substance.

Corbulo had guarded the Euphrates bank vigilantly. Now he reinforced its protection. A bridge was also constructed. To prevent inter

尔提亚发动了公开的战争,帕伊图斯也很乐意开战,于是率领两个军团开进了亚美尼亚,这两个军团分别是:由路奇乌斯·富尼苏拉乌斯·维托尼亚努斯指挥的第四军团和由卡拉维乌斯·撒比努斯指挥的第十二军团。但是出现了一些不吉利的征兆。原来罗马军队正在过幼发拉底河大桥的时候,带有执政官标记的那匹马突然莫名其妙地受了惊吓,跑到后边去了。然后就是在正在修建的冬营之中,有一匹用作祭祀的牲畜在工事修完之前跑到堡垒外边去了。还有,一些士兵的长枪着了火,这一征兆特别引人注目,因为作为敌人一方的帕尔提亚人是使用投枪打仗的。

但是帕伊图斯对这些征兆不屑一顾。在冬营还没有进行充分的防守以及没有安排好足够的粮食之时,帕伊图斯就匆忙挥师越过了陶洛斯山脉,扬言要收复提格拉诺凯尔塔城,并蹂躏科尔布罗尚未蹂躏过的地区。他确实攻占了一些据点,取得了一些荣誉,俘获了一些战利品。然而帕伊图斯却贪图过多的荣誉,并造成了战利品的浪费。但是,当他的军队长途奔袭在无法坚守的广大地区之时,他所掠夺的粮食就全部毁掉了,而且冬天正逐步来临。于是帕伊图斯就撤军了,并给尼禄写了一封急报信。里面的措辞是非常动听的,好像战争已胜利结束,但内容却是非常空洞的。

科尔布罗早已十分警觉地防守在幼发拉底河岸,[1]而现在他又大大增强了防守力量,同时还在建造了一座大桥。敌人的骑兵

〔1〕 他的阵地在丘格玛,那是该河最著名的渡河地点,而他所建立的桥头堡,进可以攻入美索不达米亚地区,退可以据守,又可以阻止敌人对叙利亚的攻击。正因为这一桥头堡的建立,以尼西比斯为根据地的沃洛吉西斯才改变了进攻方向,向北攻入了亚美尼亚,并打算在冬天真正到来之前的短时间内同帕伊图斯决一胜负。

ference by the enemy cavalry-already manoeuvring impressively near-by-he moved across the river large ships joined by poles and fortified with turrets. On these were stationed engines and catapults which repulsed the Parthians: their discharge of stones and spears outranged the enemy's arrows. The bridge was then completed, and the hills opposite occupied, first by auxiliaries and then by a brigade camp. The speed and power displayed were so imposing that the Parthians abandoned their preparations for invading Syria and concentrated all their hopes on Armenia.

Paetus was unaware of the threat. The fifth brigade was in distant Pontus, The others were weakened by excessive grants of leave. Then came news that Vologeses was approaching with a large and formidable force. Paetus summoned up the twelfth brigade. But this action, designed to give an impression of strength, only revealed his weakness. Yet with such a force, if only he had followed a consistent policy-his own or that of his advisers—he could have held the camp, or frustrated the Parthians by delaying action. As it was, emboldened to face the emergency by his staff, he adopted a different, inferior plan-to show his independent judgement. Asserting that the means given him to resist the enemy were not ditches and ramparts but men and weapons, he abandoned the winter camp and led out his army as though for a battle.

After losing a small reconnaissance detachment under a company-

早已经威风凛凛地出现在了附近,而为了使建桥工作不受这支骑兵的骚扰,他沿着河流用木板将一些大船连接到了一起,并在船上面建了一些塔楼。而在塔楼上所架设的弩机和投石机将帕尔提亚人击退了,因为他们所投掷的石头和长矛的威力是敌人发射的箭所无法比拟的。桥就这样建成了,然后就攻占了河对岸的一些小山,最初是由联盟的辅助部队,然后就是一个军团,占据了这些小山。他们推进时显示出了惊人的速度和力量,因此帕尔提亚人将他们进攻叙利亚的准备工作也抛弃了,而把他们的全部希望都寄托在了进攻亚美尼亚方面。

帕伊图斯尚不知道即将到来的危险。他的第五军团还在遥远的本都。而其余的军队[1]也由于过度的分散而大大削弱了战斗力。不久就传来了新消息,说沃洛吉西斯正率领着一支规模巨大、十分可怕的部队向他这边发起进攻。帕伊图斯将第十二军团召集了起来。这一举动的目的在于显示自己力量的强大,但是恰好将自己的弱点暴露了出来。然而,即使面对如此的情况,只要他能够始终不渝地贯彻他自己的或者是手下的参谋们所制定的政策,也还是能够保住阵地的,甚至如果采取拖延的战略的话,还可以击败帕尔提亚人。但实际情况却是,他手下的将士们刚刚使他获得了面对险情的勇气,他就为了显示自己具有独立的判断能力,而采取了一种不同的但对自己更加不利的措施。他宣布,他用来对付敌人的手段不是壕沟和堡垒,而是士兵和武器,于是他抛弃了冬营,仿佛要率领军队出发去作战。

后来,一名百人团长所率领的一支小规模的侦察部队失踪

---

〔1〕 指他手下的第四和第十二军团,他们同第五军团是分开驻守的。

commander, he returned in alarm. But Vologeses' omission to press the pursuit restored his baseless confience. So Paetus posted three thousand picked infantry on the nearest spur of the Taurus to bar Vologeses' approach, stationed the best of his cavalry from Pannonia on the neighbouring plain, and shut his wife and son into the fort of Arsamosata, which was garrisoned by one battalion. If concentrated, Paetus' troops might well have held the enemy's sporadic attacks; but he scattered them.

Only very reluctantly, it is said, did he agree to admit his danger to Corbulo. But Corbulo did not hurry. The graver the peril, he felt, the more glorious the rescue. Nevertheless, he told a thousand regular troops from each of his three brigades, eight hundred cavalry, and eight hundred auxiliary infantry, to stand by for marching orders.

Vologeses knew that Paetus had blocked his route with infantry on one flank and cavalry on the other. But the Parthian adhered to his plan. Frightening off the cavalry by a threat of force, he overwhelmed the Roman infantry. Only one company-commander, Tarquitius Crescens, put up a fight for the tower he was defending. After numerous sorties, and the destruction of every oriental who approached, he fell beneath showers of firebrand. Surviving infantrymen fled far into the wilderness. The wounded regained the camp with terrified, exaggerated stories of the king's prowess and the ferocity of his numerous peoples. These tales were readily believed by listeners who felt the same terrors. The general himself collapsed under his difficulties. Paetus neglected military duty, but wroteagain to Corbulo, urging speed to save the Eagles, standards, and

了,这样他才在惊慌之中返回了营地。但是由于沃洛吉西斯并没有紧紧追赶,帕伊图斯就又恢复了他那盲目的自信。于是帕伊图斯将3000名精锐步兵布置在最近的陶洛斯山坡上,以阻止沃洛吉西斯的进攻。将手下最精锐的来自于潘诺尼亚的骑兵布置在邻近的平原上。而将自己的妻子和儿子安排在阿尔撒莫撒塔要塞之中,由一个步兵中队守卫着。假如帕伊图斯能够将他的部队集中在一起,是很有可能战胜敌人的神出鬼没的进攻的,但是,他却将他们分散开了。

据说,在他人的劝说之下,帕伊图斯才极不情愿地向科尔布罗承认自己已处于危险的境地。但是科尔布罗没有马上采取行动。他认为,帕伊图斯越处于危险境地,他的援救才越光荣。然而,他还是命令他手下的三个军团每个军团各出1000名士兵,再加上800名骑兵,以及800名辅助步兵随时整装待命。

沃洛吉西斯得知了帕伊图斯在一侧已经用步兵封锁了自己进攻的路线,而在另一侧则用骑兵封锁,但是这位帕尔提亚人仍然坚持自己的进攻计划。他用武力相威胁,将对方的骑兵部队吓跑了,接着就打垮了罗马的步兵部队。只有一位名叫塔尔克维提乌斯·克列司肯斯的百人团长在为保卫他所据守的塔楼而坚持战斗。经过了数次出击,并多次打败了四面八方进攻的敌人之后,最终他倒在了火把的攻击之下。一些幸免于难的步兵逃到遥远的荒野地区去了。那些受伤的士兵惊恐地逃回军营之中后,夸大地讲述着国王的勇敢以及他的臣民们的凶猛。他们的讲述很容易就被那些同样是惊恐不已的听者们所相信。身处如此的困境,统帅本人也崩溃了。帕伊图斯忘记了自己所有的军事责任,只知道向科尔布罗写信,要求火速来援救军队和他的这支

remaining prestige of his unhappy army-whith would hold out loyally,
he said, until it perished.

Corbulo was not alarmed. Leaving part of his army in Syria to
hold the Euphrates defences, he proceeded to Armenia by the shortest
provisioned route, by way of Commagene and Cappadocia. His usual
military equipment was supplemented by numerous camels carrying
corn; for measures to resist famine, as well as the enemy, were necessary. The first of the defeated force whom he encountered was a
senior company-commander Paccius Orfitus, then numerous soldiers.
They offered various exccuses for their flight. But Corbulo ordered
them to return to their units and see if Pactus would forgive them.
Personally, he added, he was unindulgent, except to battle-winners.

Addressing his own troops, he encouraged them with reminders
of past glories, and hopes of more. 'Our worthwhile objectives', he
said, 'are not Armenian towns and villages but a Roman camp containing two Roman brigades. Any of you private soldiers can win from
the emperor's own hand the glorious wreath for saving a citizen's
life. But how infinitely honourable if this army could win it corpora-
tively for saving a force as large as itself!' His address inspired unanimous enthusiasm. Besides, some soldiers had personal incentives-
brothers and other relatives in danger. They marched at top speed,
night and day.

Vologeses intensified the siege, bringing pressure alternately on
the camp defences and the fort containing the non-combatants. He approached closer than Parthians usually do, hoping by this boldness to
lure the enemy into an engagement. But the Romans could hardly be

不幸的军队所剩下的名誉,他说这支军队将一直保持其忠诚,一直到灭亡。

科尔布罗没有惊慌。在把一部分军队留在叙利亚以保护幼发拉底河防线之后,他沿着一条最近的并有粮食供应的路线,经过孔玛盖尼地区和卡帕多奇亚地区向亚美尼亚地区进发。他的军队除了通常的军事装备之外,还有一大批驮着粮食的骆驼。这样就既可以预防饥饿,而当遇到敌人的时候,骆驼也很有用处。他所遇见的败军之中,第一个是主力百人团团长帕克奇乌斯·奥尔菲图斯,然后是大群的士兵。他们为自己的逃跑找出了各种理由,但是科尔布罗却命令他们返回各自的部队,看一看帕伊图斯是否能够原谅他们。他进一步说,除了战胜者之外,对其他的人他是绝不会宽恕的。

对于自己的军队,科尔布罗发表了讲话,鼓励他们要想起过去的光荣,并争取获得更多的光荣。他说:"我们争取的目标并不是亚美尼亚的城镇和乡村,而是为了我们自己拥有两个罗马军团的军营,你们当中的任何一名士兵只要能够救了一名公民的性命,罗马皇帝就会亲手为他带上光荣的花冠。可是假如这支军队能够集体地救出同样数量的另一支部队,那将是多么无限光荣的事情。"他的讲话极大地鼓舞了士兵们的斗志。除此之外,有一些士兵还有个人的动机:他们的兄弟们及其亲属正处于危险之中。他们不分昼夜地以最快的速度行军。

沃洛吉西斯展开了更加猛烈的进攻,有时候向营地的守卫部队施压,有时候又选非战斗人员藏身的要塞作为进攻的对象。他所采取的作战方法与帕尔提亚人平时的做法不同,更加逼近敌人,希望用这种大胆的举动诱使敌人出战。但是罗马人很难

enticed out of their tents, other than to man the defences. In some cases the motive was obedience to their general. Others were cowards. They claimed to be waiting for Corbulo. But the prospect of an enemy onslaught made them think of past catastrophes like the Caudine Forks or Numantia—'and there the conquerors had been the Samnites, one Italian tribe, whereas the Parthians are a power rivalling imperial Rome itself. Even the brave, admired ancient Romans had taken thought for their lives when fortune deserted them.'

Paetus succumbed to the general hopelessness, and wrote to Vologeses. But his first letter was less a petition than a protest against this forcible support of Armenia, which, he claimed, had always been subject to Rome or to a king chosen by the emperor. Peace, he urged, was mutually beneficial. The king must look beyond the immediate circumstances. He had brought the whole strength of his kingdom against two brigades, but Rome had the rest of the world to support her warfare.

Vologeses replied evasively that he must await his brothers Pacorus and Tiridates, that this was the time and place fixed for deciding Armenia's future, and that heaven had added the task-befitting his house-of deciding the fate of the Roman army. Paetus then sent messengers requesting an interview with the king. Instead, Vologeses sent his cavalry-commander Vasaces. To him, Paetus emphasized the

被引出营地,而只是在防守他们的阵地。有时候一些人采取这一做法是出于对统帅的命令的服从,而另一些人则是怯懦使然。他们声称是在等着科尔布罗援兵的到来。但是敌人有可能发起的猛攻却使他们禁不住想起了罗马过去所经历的战败,如考地尼·佛科斯之辱[1]和努曼西亚之败[2]。他们想:撒姆尼特只不过是意大利的一个部落,却一直作为征服者,而帕尔提亚人实力强大,足以与整个罗马帝国相抗衡。即使那些勇敢、令人敬佩的古罗马人,当命运抛弃他们的时候,也会考虑自己的生命问题。

帕伊图斯被全军的失望情绪弄得非常灰心,于是给沃洛吉西斯写了一封信。但是,他所写的第一封信与其说是在请求,不如说是在抗议这次为了支持亚美尼亚而采取的军事行动。他说,亚美尼亚一直臣服于罗马,或由罗马皇帝选任一位国王进行统治。他进一步说,和平对于双方都有好处,国王不能只顾眼前。他调集了整个王国的兵力来对付两个军团,但是全世界其余的国家都在支持罗马进行战争。

沃洛吉西斯则用含糊其辞的方式做了回答:他说他必须等待他的兄弟帕科路斯和提里达特斯的到来,而此时此地应该解决亚美尼亚未来的命运了;另外上天还给他们家族增加了一项新的任务,那就是要决定罗马军队的命运。然后,帕伊图斯派出了信使,要求同国王会晤。而沃洛吉西斯则是派出了自己的骑兵将领瓦撒凯斯作为代表。帕伊图斯向他强调了罗马对亚美尼亚的占领,

---

〔1〕 公元前321年,罗马军队在考地尼·佛科斯地区被撒尼特人战败,并屈辱地从他们轭门之下穿过。

〔2〕 公元前137年,罗马执政官盖乌斯·荷司提里乌斯·曼奇努斯在西班牙的努曼西亚地区被凯尔提贝里人战败。

history of Rome's occupations and disposals of Armenia by Lucius Licinius Lucullus, Pompey, and the emperors. The Parthian objected that these had been purely nominal; the real power had belonged to his compatriots. After long discussion, Monobazus, the king of Adiabene, was brought in next day to witness an agreement. The siege was to be raised, all Roman troops evacuated from Armenia, forts and provisions ceded to the Parthians; after all of which, Vologeses was to be authorized to send envoys to Nero.

Paetus next bridged the river Arsania alongside the camp. Ostensibly this was for his own retreat, though in reality the Parthians had ordered its construction to commemorate their victory. For it was they who utilized it. Our army took a different route. Rumour added that the Roman troops suffered indignities befitting their humiliation, including the yoke. The behaviour of the Armenians was in keeping with such reports. They entered the defences before the Roman column left, and lined the roads, identifying and intercepting slaves and cattle our men had earlier plundered. Even clothing was torn off, and weapons seized from the terrified soldiers. To avoid any pretext for a battle, the Romans acquiesced.

To commemorate our defeat, Vologeses piled up the arms and corpses of the fallen. But he refrained from viewing the Roman army's withdrawal. His pride satisfied, he desired a name for moderation. He forded the river on an elephant, while horses swam across with his staff. For the rumour had spread that the bridge had been treacherously

以及路奇乌斯·里奇尼乌斯·路库路斯、庞培和罗马皇帝们对亚美尼亚事务的处理。而这位帕尔提亚人则说,以上所说的罗马的权力只是名义上的,而真正的实权却掌握在他的同胞帕尔提亚人手里。经过长时间的谈判之后,第二天,阿狄亚贝尼人的国王莫诺巴佐斯来作为证人监督双方签订条约。条约规定:解除对罗马军队的包围,所有的罗马军队都要从亚美尼亚撤出,而要塞和粮食则移交给帕尔提亚人。在完成了所有这一切之后,沃洛吉西斯获准派使节去面见尼禄。

接着帕伊图斯在沿着营地的阿尔撒尼亚斯河上建了一座桥。表面上看,这座桥是为了自己撤退之用的,实际上是帕尔提亚人命令他修建的,以纪念他们的胜利。因为他们使用了这座桥,而我们的军队则沿着相反的方向撤退。还有谣言说,罗马军队遭受了很大的屈辱,甚至是从轭门之下穿过的。[1] 这些谣言与亚美尼亚人的行为确实相符,他们在罗马军队尚未撤离之前就已开进了我军所防守的阵地,而且还站在道路的两边,把以前我们的士兵从他们那儿掠夺来的奴隶和牲畜辨认出来并且领走。惊慌失措的士兵们甚至被剥光了衣服,抢走了武器。为了避免再挑起战端,罗马士兵们都默默忍受了。

沃洛吉西斯将武器和阵亡者的尸体堆积在一起,作为我们罗马人战败的标记。但是,他没有亲眼去看罗马军队的撤退,在自尊心得到了满足之后,他想获得一个谦逊的美名。他骑在一头大象上趟过了河,而他手下的人则是骑着战马追随着他。因为流传

---

〔1〕 战争中,获胜一方举牛轭命令战俘们从下面通过,以示他们的服从。

built to collapse beneath a weight. But those who ventured on it found it solid and reliable.

The besieged, it became known, had been so well provided with corn that they burned their granaries. The Parthians, however-according to Corbulo—were about to raise the siege owing to the exhaustion of their supplies and forage: and he was only three days' march away. He added that Pactus swore, before the standards (and witnesses sent by the kings) , that no Roman should cnter Armenia until Nero had written back saying whether he accepted the peace. Even assuming that these stories were invented to heighten Pactus' disgrace, the other reports are certainly true; in one day Paetus marched forty miles, abandoning his wounded as he went—a panic—striken flight as disgraceful as running away in battle.

Corbulo and his troops met them at the Euphrates. There was no display of decorations or arms to point a censorious contrast. Corbulo's men, in sad sympathy for their fellow soldiers, wept so bitterly that they could hardly manage to utter a greeting. The incentives produced by success—rivalry in valour and ambition for glory—just were not there. Instead, in the lower ranks especially, the prevailing emotion was pity.

The generals had a brief conversation. 'My work is wasted!' said Corbulo. 'The war could have been ended, and the Parthians routed. ' 'Nothing is lost for either of us,' replied Paetus. 'Let us turn our Eagles round and jointly invade Armenia, which is powerless now

着一个谣言,说大桥修建得不结实,重东西一旦压上去就会倒塌。但是那些冒险走上去的人却发现大桥是结实牢靠的。

逐渐地人们才知道,被围困的军队有如此充足的粮食供应,以至于他们还烧掉了他们的一些谷仓。然而,依据科尔布罗的记载,帕尔提亚人却由于粮食和秣草的耗竭准备要撤走他们的包围军队了。而他所率领的军队离那儿也只有三天的路程了。他进一步说,帕伊图斯还在队旗(还有国王们所派来的证人)面前发誓,在接到尼禄就是否接受这一和平条约的回信之前,任何一个罗马人都不许进入亚美尼亚。即使这些说法都是编造出来以加重帕伊图斯的耻辱的,那么其他的一些说法则肯定是真实的:在一天之内帕伊图斯就行军走了 40 英里,[1]而且一路上到处抛弃伤员;逃兵们惊慌奔逃就如同正在开战中败逃的士兵们一样丢人。

在幼发拉底河岸,科尔布罗和他的军队遇见了这些败军。他没有炫耀自己麾下的军事标记和武器,以免与对方相较而使他们难看。科尔布罗手下的军人们,对于战友们所遭受的悲惨境遇深表同情,他们太难过了,哭得几乎都不能行军礼了。勇气的比试、获取荣誉的野心,这些激励成功的感情,都已荡然无存了。相反,主要是怜悯的感情,尤其是那些级别较低的士兵。

两个统帅进行了简短的交谈。科尔布罗说:"我所做的一切都白费了。战争本应该结束了,而帕尔提亚人应该能被解决掉的。"帕伊图斯回答道:"我们两个都完好无损。让我们掉转军旗,联合起来一起向亚美尼亚发动进攻。由于沃洛吉西斯的撤退,那

---

〔1〕 在当时,正常的行军是每天 20 英里,在特殊情况之下也只有 24 英里,因而帕伊图斯的行军速度就是正常行军速度的两倍,或接近两倍。

Vologeses has gone. ' But Corbulo answered that the emperor had given him no such orders. ' I only left my province through anxiety for your army. Parthian plans are unpredictable! I must return to Syria. Even as it is, my infantry is exhausted by protracted marching-and we shall need luck to intercept their powerful cavalry, which moves so much faster on the level ground. '

Paetus wintered in Cappadocia. Vologeses sent envoys to Corbulo requesting the suppression of his forts across the Euphrates and its re-establishment as the frontier. Corbulo then insisted that all Parthian garrisons should evacuate Armenia; and finally the king gave way. Corbulo's fortifications across the Euphrates were then demolished, and the Armenians were left without interference.

At Rome, however, trophies and arches for victory over Parthia were erected in the centre of the Capitoline hill. Voted by the senate while the war was still undecided, they were not abandoned now. Unmistakable facts were ignored in favour of appearances.

As a further distraction from the grave foreign situation, certain corn that had been intended for the inhabitants of Rome but had deteriorated in storage was dumped by Nero in the Tiber. This was to inspire confidence that supplies were abundant. However, nearly two hundred corn ships—actually in harbour—had been destroyed by a violent storm, and a hundred more were accidentally burnt when already up the Tiber. Yet the emperor did not increase the price. But he proceeded to appoint three ex-consuls, Lucius Calpurnius Piso (V), Aulus Ducenius Geminus, and Pompeius Paulinus, to control the

儿毫无战斗力。"但是科尔布罗回答道,皇帝还没有向他下达这样
的命令,"我只是为你的部队处于危险之中而感到焦虑才离开我
驻守的行省的。帕尔提亚人的计划难以预料,我必须返回叙利亚
去。即使这样,我们也应祈求好运,希望我手下的这支因长途行
军而已极度疲倦的步兵能够截住敌人精锐的骑兵,因为这支骑兵
在平地上行进的速度比他的步兵快多了。"

帕伊图斯在卡帕多奇亚扎下了冬营。沃洛吉西斯派遣使节
去见了科尔布罗,要求他撤掉跨过幼发拉底河的哨所,重新将该
河作为边界线。于是,科尔布罗坚持要求所有的帕尔提亚人的卫
戍部队应该从亚美尼亚撤走。最终国王作了让步,而科尔布罗也
拆除了跨过幼发拉底河的哨所,而亚美尼亚人则可以自行处理自
己的事务了。

然而在罗马,在卡庇托里努斯山的中央,为了纪念对帕尔提
亚人所取得的胜利的记功碑和凯旋门已经开始修建了。当战争
还没有决出胜负的时候,元老院就已表决通过了修建这些东西的
决议,现在这些决议仍然没有取消。为了保全面子,尽人皆知的
事实只好置之不理。

为了进一步将民众的注意力从日益严重的国外局势之中吸
引开,尼禄将为罗马城的民众而准备的,但由于储藏时间过长而
发霉坏了的一些粮食倒进了台伯河里。这一举动是为了证明罗
马的粮食供应是非常充足的。虽然有将近二百艘已经进入港口
的运粮船被一阵猛烈的暴风摧毁了,还有一百多艘沿着台伯河而
上的船在中途不慎着火烧毁了,但是皇帝不准提高粮食价格。而且
他还任命了三位前执政官路奇乌斯·卡尔普尔尼乌斯·披索(五
世)、奥路斯·杜肯尼乌斯·盖米努斯和彭佩乌斯·保里努斯管理国

national revenues. Nero utilized this occasion to criticize previous emperors for their ruinous expenditure in advance of income, and to emphasize his own annual gifts of sixty million sesterces to the nation.

At this period there was a widespread harmful practice whereby, when an election or ballot for governorships was impending, childless persons fictitiously adopted sons, and then, when they had won practorships or provinces as fathers of families, immediately emancipated the adopted persons. The senate received angry appeals from real parents. These contrasted the unnatural, fraudulent brevity of these adoptions with the natural claims of themselves, who had suffered the anxieties of bringing up children. The childless were amply consoled, they argued, by the ready ease with which, carefree and unburdened, they acquired influence and office; whereas their own legal privileges, after protracted waiting, became a farce when some irresponsible so-called father—whose lack of children did not come from bereavement-effortlessly achieved the longstanding ambitions of authentic parents. So the senate decreed that, when offices or even inheritances were at stake, fictitious adoptions should carry no weight.

Next came the trial of a Cretan, Claudius Timarchus. Most of the charges against him were those habitually brought against mighty

库的收入。利用这一机会，尼禄对以前的诸位皇帝进行了批评，批评他们的灾难性消费已经超过了收入，而突出强调了自己将每年拿出6000万谢司特尔提乌斯作为礼物赠送给国家。

在这一时期，普遍流行着一个坏习惯：当面临着选举或选派高级行政官员的时候，没有孩子的那些人都会采用欺骗的办法假装过继儿子，[1]然后，当他们以家长的身份赢得了行政长官或行省长官的职位之后，就会立即将过继的人抛弃。元老院就会收到来自于孩子真正家长的愤怒控诉。他们将这些过继行为的弄虚作假和短暂的欺骗性质与自己辛辛苦苦抚养孩子的煎熬加以对此从而对孩子拥有的天赋权利进行了比较。他们认为，这些无孩子的人已经得到了足够的补偿，因为他们根本就不用操心而且不用负担什么责任，就可以轻易地获得势力和官职；而他们自己的经过了长久等待之后才拥有的合法权利却成了一种笑柄。因为一些所谓的父亲根本就不用承担父亲的责任，他们没有孩子却不是失去了孩子的缘故，这样的人竟然很轻易地获得了真正的父亲长久以来的愿望。于是元老院发布了一项命令，规定在竞选官职，甚至是在继承遗产时，欺骗性的过继将会无效。[2]

接着就发生了审判克里特人克劳狄乌斯·提玛尔库斯的事件。对他的指控绝大部分就是那些通常的对于显贵的行省居民

[1] 因为在公元9年罗马制定了帕披乌斯·波塔乌斯法，该法规定，在竞选或者被选派担任行政官之时，有孩子的人与无孩子的人相比享有优先权，所以很多政客会采用欺骗的办法过继儿子。

[2] 帕披乌斯·波塔乌斯法规定，除非死者和独身者的关系在特定亲等之内，否则将禁止其取得任何遗产。即使结了婚但没有孩子的人，继承遗产时，也只能获得一半遗产。

provincials whose enormous wealth inflates them into oppressors. But he had also made a remark (more than once) which constituted an insult to the senate: 'Whether a governor of Crete receives the thanks of our Provincial Assembly depends on me!' Thrasea utilized the occasion to the national advantage. Proposing the defendant's banishment from Crete, he reminded the senate how experience showed that, among right-thinking men, good laws and beneficial precedents are prompted by other men's misdeeds. Punishments, he pointed out, come after crimes, and rectifications after abuses. He quoted the Cincian bill originating from the excesses of advocates, the Julian laws from corruption among candidates, and the Calpurnian enactments from the rapacity of officials.

'So let us face this unprecedented provincial arrogance', he urged, 'with a measure befitting Roman honour and dignity. Without diminishing our protection of provincials, we must recover the conviction that a Roman's reputation depends on Romans only. Once we used to send praetors and consuls, and even private citizens, to inspect provinces and report on everyone's loyalty. Then nations trembled for the verdict of one man! But now we court and flatter foreigners. Some individual makes a sign, and they thank our governor-or, more likely, prosecute him!

'But even granting that we must continue to let provincials display

的指控,由于他们具有无数的财富,所以他们非常骄横,从而压迫他人。但是提玛尔库斯曾经作过一番讲话,(而且不只一次地说过,)这些话对元老院造成了侮辱。他说:"克里特的长官能否得到我们行省公民大会的感谢,这完全取决于我。"特拉塞亚想把这一事件转变成对国家有利的事件。在提议将被告驱逐出克里特之后,他提醒元老院要注意以往的经验,因为经验证明,在思想正直的人之中,良好的法律和有益的先例是由于别人的过失而促使其产生出来的。他指出,犯罪之后才需要惩罚,出现了弊端才需要矫正。他举例说,秦奇乌斯法的产生就是因为辩护人的放肆行为,尤利乌斯法的产生则是因为竞选者的贪污腐败,卡尔普尔尼乌斯法[1]的产生则是由于官吏们的贪得无厌。"

他说:"因此,面对着行省居民的这种前所未有的骄横行为,我们应该制定一条与我们罗马的荣誉和尊严相适应的措施。在不损害对行省居民保护的前提下,我们必须要纠正一种错误看法,认为罗马人的荣誉只有靠罗马人自己来维持。过去我们常常派遣行政长官或执政官,甚至是普通公民到各个行省去进行监督,并就每一个公民是否忠诚做出报告。然后,许多民族都在战战兢兢地等待着一个人所做出的判决。但是,现在我们却要向外国人讨好、献媚。他们当中某一个人示意一下,他们才会对我们的长官表示感谢,或者更有可能的是对长官进行告发。

"但是,即使如此,我们也必须继续让行省居民通过这种方式展

---

〔1〕 卡尔普尔尼乌斯法是在公元前149年所通过的一项法律,提出这一法案的是保民官路奇乌斯·卡尔普尔尼乌斯·披索。根据这一法律的规定,各行省的居民都有权利向罗马要求赔偿长官们所勒索的金钱,并为此设立了一个常设法庭。

their power in this way, we should nevertheless frown on governors winning empty eulogies, extracted by entreaties. We should judge this as severely as ill-intentioned or brutal government. To oblige is often as harmful as to offend. Indeed, some virtues provoke hatred. Unbending strictness and incorruptibility do. That is why our officials usually start well and end badly; like election candidates, they begin looking round for support. Stop this, and provincial administration will be fairer and steadier. Prohibit votes of thanks, and popularity-hunting will collapse—just as acquisitiveness is repressed by fear of the extortion laws. '

These opinions received warm approval. But no senatorial decree could be carried, since the consuls ruled that no question on the subject was before the House. Later, however, on the emperor's initiative, a decree was passed forbidding votes of thanks to governors at Provincial Assemblies, or the participation by provincials in missions conveying such votes.

This, too, was the year in which the Gymnasium was struck by lightning and burnt down. A statue of Nero inside was melted into a shapeless bronze mass. An earthquake also largely demolished the populous Campanian town of Pompcii. Laelia, priestess of Vesta, died, and her place was taken by Cornelia, of the family of the Cossi.

现他们的权利,无论如何我们也应该杜绝长官们通过请求的方式而得到空洞的赞美之辞。我们应该将这视做与无赖行为或残酷统治一样严重的行为。通常情况下,施恩和伤害会对他人造成同样的恶果。实际上,某些美德会招致他人的憎恨。不屈不挠的严厉和永不腐化堕落就属于这种美德。这就是为什么我们的官员们新上任之时还清正廉洁,而到卸任之时就会腐化堕落的原因;因为那时他们就像候选人竞选那样,开始四处为自己寻求支持。制止这些做法,行省就能治理得更好、更稳定。禁止人们提出表示感谢性的提议,讨好他人的行为也就可以消除了,这就像只要人们对于勒索行为的法律处罚深感恐惧就会制止自己的贪婪行为一样。"

这些建议受到了热烈的支持,但是,因为执政官们裁定不能将这一问题提交给元老院进行讨论,所以元老院还不能发布命令。然而,后来在皇帝的提议之下通过了一项决议,规定禁止任何人在行省的公民大会之中提议向长官们表示感谢,禁止任何行省派遣代表到罗马来表达这种谢意。[1]

也是在这一年,罗马竞技场遭到了雷击,被烧毁了。里面的一座尼禄雕像被烧成了一堆不成样子的废铜。还发生了一次地震,严重地摧毁了康帕尼亚的一座人口众多的城市庞姆普西。维司塔贞女莱利娅死了,而她的职位由来自科苏斯家族的科尔涅里娅接替。

---

〔1〕 当时各个行省经常派代表到元老院来,向返回罗马的总督或行政长官表示谢意,感谢在他们的统治之下,给那儿的人民带去了"幸福"。这是一种为卸任的长官捞取名誉的做法。

Next year the consuls were Gaius Memmius Regulus and Lucius Verginius Rufus. Poppaca now bore Nero a daughter. His joy exceeded human measure, and mother and child were both named Augusta. The infant was born at Nero's own birthplace, the Roman settlement of Antium. The senate had already asked heaven's blessing on Poppaea's pregnancy and made official vows. Now these vows were discharged, with additions including a thanksgiving. A temple of Fertility was decreed, and a competition modelled on the Actian Victory Festival. Golden statues of the Two Fortunes of Antium were to be placed on the throne of Capitoline Jupiter, and Antium was to have Circus Games in honour of the Claudian and Domitian houses, like the Games in honour of the Julian house at Bovillae.

But it was all ephemeral; for within less than four months the baby was dead. Then followed new forms of sycophancy. She was declared a goddess and voted a place on the gods' ceremonial couch, together with a shrine and a priest. The emperor's delight had been immoderate; so was his mourning.

Shortly after the birth, the whole senate had flocked out to Antium. But Thrasea had been forbidden to attend. It was noticed how calmly he received this affront—though it foreshadowed his own impending death. Nero, it is said, subsequently boasted to Seneca that he was reconciled with Thrasea; and Seneca congratulated Nero. The

第二年,盖乌斯·美米乌斯·列古路斯和路奇乌斯·维尔吉尼乌斯·路福斯担任了执政官。现在波培娅为尼禄生了一个女儿。尼禄的兴奋超过了人类的极限,他将"奥古斯塔"这一名字赐给了母亲和孩子。这个女孩的出生地跟尼禄本人的出生地是相同的,是罗马的安提乌姆移民地。元老院曾经祈求诸神保佑怀孕时的波培娅,并且以官方的名义许了愿。现在这些许愿都已加了码,另外又增加了一次感恩仪式。元老院又发布命令,修建了一座丰产神庙,还按照阿克提乌姆节的样式举行了一次竞赛。[1] 安提乌姆两位命运女神的金像被安置到了卡披托里乌姆神庙朱庇特神的宝座上。而为了纪念克劳狄乌斯家族和多米提乌斯家族,还要在安提乌姆举行赛马会,这就和在波维莱为了纪念尤利乌斯家族而举行的赛会一样。

但所有这一切都是转瞬即逝,因为不到四个月,这孩子就死了。接着就出现了新的谄媚花样。波培娅死去的孩子被宣布为女神,而且在诸神之间给她留下了一个神座,为她修了一座神庙,配置了一名专门的祭司。皇帝不能控制自己的欢乐,同样也不能控制自己的悲伤。

尼禄的女儿出生不久,元老院全体人员都涌向了安提乌姆。但是他却禁止特拉塞亚前去庆祝。尽管这对特拉塞亚来说就意味着死亡的来临,但是他对这种公然的侮辱却表现出了惊人的镇静。据说,随之尼禄就向塞内加夸口说,自己已经与特拉塞亚重归于好,而塞内加向尼禄表示了祝贺。这一事件虽然提高了这两名显赫人物

---

[1] 是古罗马时期由奥古斯都设立的一种体育和音乐比赛,是为了纪念公元前31年9月2日他在阿克提乌姆战役之中所取得的胜利而设立的,每五年举行一次,竞赛地点是在尼科波利斯。之后成为古罗马的一种盛会。

incident increased both these eminent men's prestige, but also their peril.

At this time, the beginning of spring, there arrived the Parthian delegation bringing Vologeses' message and a letter confirming it. 'I say nothing now about my frequently repeated claim to Armenia,' ran the communication, 'since the gods, who direct the fates even of the greatest nations, have handed the country to the Parthians, not without Roman ignominy. When, recently, I besieged Tigranes, I could have destroyed Lucius Caesennius Pactus and his army. But I let them go free. I have sufficiently demonstrated my power; and I have also given proof of my clemency. Tiridates, too, would not decline to come to Rome and receive his diadem, if this were not prevented by taboos connected with his priesthood. He would attend the emperor's standards and statues, and inaugurate his reign before the Roman army.'

It was hard to reconcile this message with Paetus' report that the position was inconclusive. A Roman staff-officer escorting the delegates was interrogated concerning the situation. He replied that all Romans had left Armenia. The ironical character of the orientals' request for what they had already seized was clear. Nero consulted his council: was it to be a hazardous war, or a humiliating peace? The unhesitating decision was war. To prevent a further disaster from the incompetence of some new general—for they were disgusted with Pactus-the sole command was given to Corbulo, with his long

的声誉,但也使他们处于更加危险的境地。

这时候,也就是初春时节,帕尔提亚的外交使团赶到了,他们带来了沃洛吉西斯的口信以及一封正式的信函。信函的内容是这样写的:"现在,对于我经常提起、不断重复的占有亚美尼亚的要求,我不想再说什么了。因为即使支配最强大的国家命运的诸神,也早已经将亚美尼亚交给帕尔提亚人来管理了,而没有顾及罗马人的面子。最近,当我包围了提格拉尼斯的时候,我本来完全有能力消灭路奇乌斯·凯森尼乌斯·帕伊图斯及其军队,但是我却让他们逃命了。我已经充分地展现了我的实力,也完全证明了我的仁慈。假如提里达特斯不是因为与他所担任的祭司这一职务有关联的一些顾忌的话,[1]他是不会拒绝亲自来罗马接受自己的王冠的。他会当着罗马皇帝的军旗和雕像,在罗马军队面前宣誓自己的就任的。"

这封信与帕伊图斯的报告难以吻合,因为报告称战争局面仍旧是难决胜负。于是他就战争局势问题询问了一位陪同外交使节一起来的百人团长。他回答说,所有的罗马人都已经撤离了亚美尼亚。东方人要求取得他们早已经取得的东西,这一做法的讽刺效果是非常明显的。是进行一场冒险的战争,还是要接受这一可耻的和平?尼禄与他的顾问们进行了商讨,毫不犹豫所做出的决定就是要开战。由于大家对帕伊图斯早就厌倦了,而又怕派遣一位新的统帅会造成更加深重的灾难,所以基于科尔布罗拥有多

---

〔1〕 因为提里达特斯是一位玛哥斯僧人,按照他们的信仰,是不能渡海的,"因为精通魔法的人照例是不允许向海里吐痰或是用人身不可免的其他任何排泄物玷污海水的"(普利尼:《自然史》,第30卷,第2章,第16节),所以他无法来面见罗马皇帝。

experience of active service.

So the delegates were dismissed, their purpose unaccomplished. But they were given presents to encourage the hope that, if Tiridates made the same appeal in person, it would be favourably received. Corbulo's army was reinforced by a brigade from Pannonia under the command of Marius Colsus. Gaius Cestius Gallus (II) was made imperial governor of Svria. Instructions were sent to vassal kings and princes, and neighbouring governors of all ranks, to obey Corbulo's orders. His powers were virtually increased to those the state had granted to Pompey for the Pirate War. Paetus, back in Rome, expected the worst. But Nero contented himself with a sarcastic rebuke. He was pardoning the general immediately, he intimated, because prolonged suspense would damage so timid a person's health.

Corbulo sent Paetus' fourth and twelfth brigades to Syria, considering that the loss of their best men and demoralization of the remainder had made them unfit to fight. His invasion force for Armenia included his own two fresh brigades, the sixth and third, toughened by long and successful service. To these Corbulo added the recently arrived fifteenth brigade from Pannonia, and the fifth which had been stationed in Pontus and so had escaped the disaster, picked detachments from Illyricum and Egypt, and auxiliary infantry and cavalry, including contingents from the dependent kings. These forces were concentrated in Melitene at the point where he planned

年的实战经验,决定将唯一的统帅权授予他。

于是外交使节们就被遣送回国了,他们的目的并没有实现。但是他们获得了一些礼物,以激发他们产生这样的希望:假如提里达特斯亲自来做出同样的要求的话,其目的是可以实现的。科尔布罗的军队得到了加强,新补充了由马利乌斯·凯尔苏斯所率领的潘诺尼亚第十五军团,叙利亚的行政长官则是由盖乌斯·凯司提乌斯·噶尔鲁斯(二世)担任。命令传达到了藩王、诸侯,以及相邻各省的各级行政长官,[1]要他们都听从科尔布罗的命令。实际上他的权力已扩大到了与庞培对海盗进行作战[2]时所授予的权力的程度。帕伊图斯返回了罗马,已想好了自己最糟糕的结局。但是,尼禄只是用开玩笑的方式责备了他。他立刻就宽恕了这位统帅。他说,因为长时间的拖延会损伤一位如此胆小的人的健康。

科尔布罗将帕伊图斯手下的第四和第十二军团调到了叙利亚,因为他认为这两个军团已经损失了最勇敢的士兵,而剩余的士兵都缺乏纪律性,根本就不再适于作战。他用来进攻亚美尼亚的军队里新增了两个军团,第六军团和第三军团,他们都经受过长久的严格训练,并有过成功的作战经验。除此之外,科尔布罗又增添了最近从潘诺尼亚赶来的第十五军团和一直驻守在本都故而没有遭受重大损失的第五军团。还有从伊里利库姆和埃及调来的独立部队和一部分附属的步兵、骑兵,另外包括了来自于藩王的部队。这些军队都集中于米利提尼,因为他打

---

〔1〕 这里所说的各级行政长官,包括了奇里亚、吕奇亚、潘披里亚和加拉提亚各行省的行政长官,他们都衔副帅之职。

〔2〕 公元前67年庞培率军队与海盗进行了战争。

to cross the Euphrates. Then-after the customary purification ritual - Corbulo addressed the army. His own achievements under the emperor's auspices received grandiloquent allusions. Reverses he blamed on Paetus' inexperience. His words had that authoritative ring which, in a military man, takes the place of eloquence.

Soon his advance began along the road originally opened up by Lucius Licinius Lucullus. Obstructions formed in the course of time had to be cleared. When envoys arrived from Tiridates and Vologese to discuss peace, he did not rebuff them but sent them back with Roman staff-officers bearing conciliatory messages. 'Matters have not reached the point', he said, 'when war to the finish is unavoidable. Rome's many successes, Parthia's successes, too, are warnings against arrogance. To accept his kingdom as a gift, undevastated, is to Tiridates' advantage. Vologeses, too, will serve Parthian interests better by alliance with Rome than by a policy of mutual injury. I know the internal dissensions of your kingdom, with its formidable, lawless nations—a contrast to my emperor, whose territories are uniformly peaceful. This is his only war. '

Advice was reinforced by intimidation. The Armenian chiefs who had first revolted against Rome were driven from their homes, and their fortresses demolished. In highlands and lowlands, among strong

算从那儿渡过幼发拉底河。在行过了通常的被除礼之后,科尔布罗便向军队作了讲话。他将自己在皇帝恩德的庇护之下所取得的功勋夸大其词地说了一番,反过来又极力指责了帕伊图斯的无能。他的讲话含有一种威严,这种威严在一个军事家身上完全取代了口才的作用。

不久,他的军队就开始沿着由路奇乌斯·里奇努斯·路库鲁斯所开拓的道路[1]行进了。一路上由时间所造成的各种障碍必须要认真清除。当提里达特斯和沃洛吉西斯所派来的商谈和解问题的使节到达的时候,他没有拒绝他们,而是派遣了几位带着他的和解指示的罗马百人团长随他们一同回去了。他对使节们说:"事情远没有发展到必须用战争作为最后解决问题的手段的地步。罗马拥有许多的成功,而帕尔提亚也有许多的成功,这就警告我们要坚决反对狂妄自大。对于提里达特斯来说,接受一个不曾遭受过蹂躏的自己的王国作为赠礼,是一件非常有利的事情。对于沃洛吉西斯来说,与罗马结成同盟要远比奉行互相伤害的政策更加符合帕尔提亚人的利益。我知道你们王国的内部存在着严重的倾轧,各民族非常强悍,又不遵守法纪。与此相反,对我们的皇帝来说,他所治理的国土内到处充满了和平。这场战争是他所进行的唯一的一场战争。"

为了增强劝说的效果,又使用了恐吓的办法。那些最早起来反对罗马的亚美尼亚贵族都被赶出了家园,而他们的要塞也都被摧毁了。不论是在高地还是平原,不论是在坚强的人还是懦

---

〔1〕 这是他在公元前 69 年所开拓的一条进军提格拉诺凯尔塔的道路。

and weak, there was panic. But the enemy felt no bitterness or hostility towards Corbulo. They trusted his advice. So Vologeses avoided showing intransigence on the main issue, and requested a truce in certain provinces; while Tiridates requested that a day and place should be fixed for a conference. An early date was arranged. As the place, the orientals selected the scene of Paetus' recent blockade with his army; this was to commemorate their victory. Corbulo did not object. Their contrasted fortunes seemed to accentuate his own glory. How little Paetus' discredit distressed him, he clearly showed by ordering the latter's son, a colonel, to take a detachment and bury the remains of the disastrous battle.

On the appointed day a distinguished knight, Tiberius Julius Alexander, who was attached to the campaign in an advisory capacity, and Corbulo's son-in-law, Annius Vinicianus, who, though below senatorial age, was acting as commander of the fifth brigade, entered Tiridates' camp. Their visit was both a compliment and a pledge against treachery. Then Tiridates and Corbulo, each with an escort of twenty cavalry, went to meet each other. When he saw the Roman, Tiridates was the first to dismount. Corbulo quickly did the same. On

弱的人的心中都充满了恐惧不安。但是敌人对于科尔布罗既不感到痛恨也不仇视。他们就相信了他所提出的建议。因此沃洛吉西斯在主要问题上尽力避免表现出一种固执己见的做法,而在某些行省之中要求停战。提里达特斯则是要求将会谈的日期和地点确定下来。会谈的日期定得很早,至于地点问题,东方人选择了最近包围帕伊图斯的地方,这是为了庆祝他们的胜利。科尔布罗没有反对。因为他们从不同的命运对比看来是可以提高自己的荣耀的。不论帕伊图斯的耻辱有多么的严重,都没有使科尔布罗悲观;他命令帕伊图斯的儿子和一名军团将领,率领一队士兵将战败中死去但尚没有掩埋的尸首进行埋葬这件事就清楚地表明了他这一情绪。

到了约定的那一天,被任命为这次出征的顾问官的是一位名叫提贝里乌斯·尤利乌斯·亚历山大的显要骑士,[1]另一位是虽然还没有达到担任元老的年龄,却已担任了第五军团统帅的科尔布罗的女婿安尼乌斯·维尼奇亚努斯,[2]两人一起进入了提里达特斯的军营。他们的造访,既是一种问候,也是一种不要阴谋的保证。然后,提里达特斯和科尔布罗各在 20 名骑兵的保护之下来会面了。当提里达特斯看到罗马人的时候,首先就从马上跳了下来,而科尔布罗也迅速地跳了下来,两个人站着握起了手。一开

---

〔1〕 提贝里乌斯·尤利乌斯·亚历山大是庇洛·犹太乌斯的侄子,但他是一名异教徒;公元 46 年作了犹太的代理官,公元 67 年又作了埃及的长官,公元 69 年 7 月 1 日带头承认维斯帕西亚努斯的皇帝地位;在围攻耶路撒冷的战斗中作过提图斯的副帅。

〔2〕 他后来还奉命随提里达特斯到罗马去;这一年他才 25 岁,还不够担任元老的年龄,但按规定军团统帅必须是一名元老,通常是由一名曾经担任过行政长官的人来担任。

foot, they clasped hands. Corbulo began by complimenting the young ruler on his rejection of adventure and adoption of a safe, beneficial policy. The king, after long preliminaries concerning the nobility of his family, spoke in moderate terms. He would go to Rome, he said, and bring the emperor an unfamiliar distinction—the homage, following no Parthian reverse, of a Parthian royal prince. It was then arranged that Tiridates should lay the royal diadem before the emperor's statue, to resume it only from Nero's hand. The interview ended with an embrace.

A few days later both armies paraded in splendid array. On the Parthian side was troop after troop of cavalry, with their national ensigns. On the other side stood our brigades, with their glittering Eagles and standards; and all the images of gods made one think of a temple. On the do is in the middle was a Roman official chair, bearing Nero's effigy. To this Tiridates advanced. When the customary sacrifices had been made, he took the diadem from his head and laid it at the feet of the statue. This caused a profound and universal impression, the more so since the picture of Roman armies slaughtered and besieged had not faded from people's eyes. Now, it seemed, the situation was reversed. Tiridates was going to make a world-wide exhibition of himself; he was little short of a prisoner.

Corbulo improved his already glorious reputation by courtesy and entertainment. For every novelty he saw, the king requested explanations-for instance a company-commander announcing the new watch; the bugle-note terminating the banquet; the torch which lit the altar before the commander-in-chief's tent. Corbulo's grandiose replies fired Tiridates with admiration for ancient Roman customs. Next day,

始科尔布罗就对于年轻的统治者抛弃冒险的作法而采取了安全而又有利的政策表示了赞扬,而国王一开始则用了很长一段时间来讲述自己家族的显赫,接着用一种很有节制的语言进行了讲话。他说,他很愿意到罗马去,以给罗马皇帝带去与众不同的礼物,那就是遵照帕尔提亚人的意愿,奉献上帕尔提亚王室的效忠。然后就做了安排,规定提里达特斯将他的王权标记放到尼禄的雕像前,象征着只有从尼禄的手中才能够重新获取它。最后,在互相拥抱之中结束了这次会谈。

几天之后,两支军队都举行了盛大的列队游行。在帕尔提亚人方面,参加游行的是一队队带着本国标帜的骑兵,而在另一面,则是站立着我们的军团士兵,他们手里拿着各种光辉灿烂的军旗和队旗,而挥舞的各种神像则使人误以为是一座神庙。在中间的高台上则是放了一把罗马长官的坐椅,上面安放了尼禄的像。整个队伍的最前面是提里达特斯,他在作了传统的献祭仪式之后,将王冠从自己的头上摘了下来,然后放在了尼禄的雕像前面。这一举动给全场留下了深刻而又普遍的印象,尤其是当人们眼前还浮现着罗马军队遭屠杀和被包围的情景之时,这一印象就更深刻了。现在,似乎形势已经转变了,提里达特斯将要把自己向全世界展示:他目前跟一名囚犯差不多。

科尔布罗通过自己的彬彬有礼和对客人的一次招待在自己本来就已取得的巨大声誉上面又增添了不少光辉。国王对于所看到的每一件新鲜而有趣的事物,例如,百人团长宣布夜班值勤换岗,用号角宣布宴席停止,用火把点燃统帅军营前边祭坛上的火,这些都要求科尔布罗给予解释。而科尔布罗那渲染夸张的回答则是点燃了提里达特斯对于古罗马传统习俗的敬仰羡慕。

however, he requested time to visit his brothers and mother before the long journey. Meanwhile, he gave his daughter as a hostage, and presented his petition for Nero.

Tiridates then went to find Vologeses and his other brother Pacorus, who were at Ecbatana and in Media Atropatene respectively. Concerned for Tiridates' interests, the Parthian king had sent envoys to Corbulo asking that his brother should not be exposed to any external signs of subjection—that he should keep his sword, be entitled to embrace governors, not be kept waiting at their door, and at Rome receive a consul's honours. Vologeses was accustomed to foreign ostentatiousness. Clearly he did not understand how we Romans value real power but disdain its vanities.

Other events of this year were the award of Latin rights to the tribes of the Maritime Alps, and the allocation to Roman knights of places in the circus in front of the ordinary people's seats. Hitherto the order of knights had possessed no separate seats in the circus because the Roscian law allotting them 'the first fourteen rows' applied only to the theatre.

第二天,他要求在远行之前,留出时间去拜访自己的兄弟并看望自己的母亲。与此同时,他将自己的女儿作为了人质,而且呈献给尼禄一封请求信。

接着,提里达特斯就去拜访了沃洛吉西斯和他的另一个兄弟帕科路斯,他们分别居住在埃克巴塔纳和米地亚。帕尔提亚国王非常关心自己弟弟的利益,他已经派专使去见科尔布罗,请求不要将任何藩臣的外部标记加到自己弟弟身上,即他要保留自己的佩剑,他应该有权拥抱行政长官而不能侍立在长官的门外等候、在罗马要取得与执政官同样的荣誉。沃洛吉西斯已经习惯于国外那种虚炫的排场。很显然,他不知道罗马人看重的是实权,而不屑于那种虚荣的排场。

在这一年里还发生了另外一些事情:沿海阿尔卑斯各族人民被授予了拉丁权,[1]在竞技场内罗马骑士的座位被安排在了普通平民座位的前面。在这以前,在竞技场内骑士们是没有与百姓分离的座位的,因为罗司奇乌斯法规定他们的座位只限于剧场之内的"前14排"。

---

〔1〕 这是同盟战争以来在意大利就已不复存在的一种部分公民权,但这种权利却受到了行省人民的重视,因为这是取得全部公民权的一个步骤。

CHAPTER 14

The Burning Of Rome

THE same year witnessed gladiatorial displays on a no less magnificent scale than before, but exceeding all precedent in the number of distinguished women and senators disgracing themselves in the arena. When the new year began, with Gaius Laecanius Bassus and Marcus Licinius Crassus Frugi (II) as consuls, Nero showed daily-increasing impatience to appear regularly on the public stage. Hitherto, he had sung at home, or at the Youth Games held in his Gardens. But he began to disdain such occasions as insufficiently attended and too restricted for a voice like his. Not venturing, however, to make his debut at Rome, he selected Neapolis, as being a Greek city. Starting there, he planned to cross to Greece, win the glorious and long-revered wreaths of its Games, and thus increase his fame and popularity at home.

The Neapolitan theatre was filled. Besides the local population, it contained visitors from all around attracted by the notable occasion.

第十四章　罗马大火

在同一年里,还举行了规模不比以前小的剑斗比赛。但是,从数量上来说,真正超过以前的是,有许多显要的妇人和元老在比赛之中使自己受到了侮辱[1]。在新年开始的时候,伴随着盖乌斯·莱卡尼乌斯·巴苏斯和玛尔库斯·里奇尼乌斯·格拉苏斯·福路吉(二世)开始担任执政官,尼禄一天比一天更加忍耐不住了,他想在公开的舞台上正式露面。直到这时为止,他只是在自己的宫殿里唱歌,或者是在青年竞赛节期间在自家的花园里唱歌。但是他开始对这种场合的演出感到厌倦了,因为观众人数太少了,而且也过分限制了像他一样的好嗓音。然而这时他的勇气还不足以使自己在罗马正式表演,他选择了那不勒斯这座希腊城市。他打算,从那儿开始,穿越整个希腊,在歌唱竞赛之中赢得光荣的和长久以来受到人们尊重的桂冠,这样就可以提高自己的声誉,受到国人们的拥护。

那不勒斯的剧场爆满了。除了当地的观众之外,也包括了被这一盛大场面吸引而从周围各地赶来的参观者。还有为了赶来

---

[1]　每一次,尼禄都是要求 400 名元老和 600 名罗马骑士参加剑斗比赛和对野兽搏斗。他还邀请维司塔贞女参观角力比赛,他认为在古希腊奥林匹亚赛上,凯列司的女祭司就可以参观表演。

Present, too, were those who attend the emperor out of respect or to perform various services—and even units of troops. The theatre now provided what seemed to most people an evil omen, but to Nero a sign of divine providence and favour. For when it was empty (the crowd having left), it collapsed. But there were no casualties; and Nero composed a poem thanking the gods for the happy outcome of the incident.

Then, on his way to cross the Adriatic, he stopped for a while at Beneventum. There large crowds were attending a gladiatorial display given by a certain Vatinius. This outstanding monstrosity of the court had originated from a shoe shop. Deformed in body and scurrilous in wit, he had first been taken up as a butt for abuse. But then he gained power enough to eclipse any scoundrel in influence, wealth, and capacity for damage. He rose by attacking decent people.

But even at his pleasures, attending this man's show, Nero took no vacation from crime. For enforced death now came to Decimus Junius Silanus Torquatus. This was because, in addition to the nobility of his Junian house, he could claim the divine Augustus as a great-great-grandfather. The accusers were instructed to charge Torquatus with generosity so extravagant that revolution had become his only hope. Censure was also to be directed against the titles which he gave some of his former slaves—Secretary-General, Petitions Secretary, and Financial Secretary. These, it was alleged, were titles of an imperial houschold; Torquatus must be preparing for one. His confidential exslaves were arrested and removed. Seeing conviction ahead, he opened

向皇帝致敬和从事各种事务而追随皇帝到这里来的人,还有一队队的士兵。但是剧场里发生了一件事情,在大多数人看来这是一个不祥之兆,而在尼禄看来,却是上天所赐的一个祥兆。原来,空荡荡的剧场(人群已经退场了)突然倒塌了,但是没有任何人受到伤害;于是尼禄为这次事故没有发生悲惨的结局而写了一首诗以感谢诸神。

然后,在渡过亚得里亚海的时候,他在贝内文托逗留了一段时间。在那里有大量民众正在参观一场剑斗比赛,举办者是一个名叫瓦提尼乌斯的人。瓦提尼乌斯是宫廷之中最为丑陋的人之一,他来自于一个鞋匠之家。身躯已变形,而趣味低级下流。起初他只是一个被人嘲弄的对象,但是后来他取得了巨大的势力,足以在权势、财富以及害人的本领方面使任何的流氓恶棍为之黯然失色。他的发迹是通过对好人的攻击陷害而取得的。

尼禄参观了此人的表演,但是即使是在欢乐之时,他也没有停止其犯罪行为。现在到了要迫害戴奇姆斯·尤尼乌斯·西拉努斯·托尔克瓦图斯,并将其致死的时候了。这样做的原因除了他那出生于尤尼乌斯家族的高贵身份之外,还因为他竟然宣称圣奥古斯都是他的高祖。指控者受到了指示,说托尔克瓦图斯在他人身上花钱如此大手大脚,以至于叛乱成为他唯一的愿望。此外还提出了其他指控,这些指控说他从他以前的奴隶之中任命了一些人担任秘书长、法律秘书、财务秘书等官职,据说这些官职只有皇室的人才能担当,托尔克瓦图斯必定是在为当皇帝作准备。他的一些被释放的心腹奴隶都被逮捕并遭到了杀害。眼见死亡已是近在眼前的事了,他就切断了自己的脉管。于是,

his veins. Nero made the usual pronouncement indicating that, however guilty and rightly distrustful of his defence Torquatus had been, he would nevertheless—if he had awaited his judge's mercy-have lived.

Before long Nero, for some reason unknown, postponed his visit to Greece, and returned to Rome. But he still planned to visit the eastern provinces, particularly Egypt; and his secret thoughts dwelt on them. After announcing by edict that his absence would be brief and all branches of government would carry on with undiminished efficiency, he proceeded to the Capitol for consultation about his journey. After worshipping the Capitoline gods, he entered the shrine of Vesta. But there all his limbs suddenly began to tremble. The goddess frightened him. Or perhaps he was always frightened, remembering his crimes. At all events, he abandoned this journey too.

His patriotism came before everything, Nero asserted; he had seen the people's sad faces and heard their private lamentations about the extensive travels he planned—even his brief absences they found unendurable, being accustomed (he added) to derive comfort in life's misfortunes from the sight of their emperor. Just as in private relationships nearest are dearest, he said, so to him the inhabitants of Rome came first: he must obey their appeal to stay! The people liked such protestations. They loved their amusements. But their principal interest was the corn supply: and they feared it would run short if Nero went away. Senators and leading men were uncertain whether he was more abominable present or absent. Subsequently, as happens when men undergo terrifying experiences, the alternative that had befallen them seemed the graver.

尼禄又按照惯例发表了声明,宣布不管被告托尔克瓦图斯犯了多么严重的罪行,也不管他的辩护有多么不值得信任,假如他能够等待他的法官对他做出宽恕的话,无论如何他还是可以活下去的。

不久之后,也不知出于什么原因,尼禄放弃了希腊之行,而回到了罗马。但是他仍然在打算着到东方诸行省去,尤其是埃及;这一秘密想法一直在他脑海之中萦绕着。他发布了敕令,宣布自己离开罗马只是很短一段时间,而在此期间国家的行政机构将会一如既往地运转着。接着,他来到了卡披托里乌姆神庙,对这次出行进行请示。在向卡披托里乌姆诸神作了祷告之后,他走进了维司塔神室,但是在那里他的四肢突然开始发起抖来。或许是因为女神使他感到惊怕,也或许是因为他突然想起了自己所犯的罪行而感到了惊恐。总而言之,他也就放弃了这次出行。

尼禄宣布,他的爱国主义情怀胜过了一切;对于自己所设定的远行计划,他看到了民众悲伤的面孔,听到了他们所发出的低声的怨言,因为哪怕是皇帝最短时间的离开都是他们所无法忍受的。(他进一步说,)民众们早已习惯于在身处不幸之时一看到他们的皇帝就深感安慰了。他说,正如在私人关系方面最接近的人也就是最亲爱的人一样,对他来说,罗马人是最为重要的,他必须要服从他们的意愿而留下来。民众们就喜欢这样的表白。他们喜欢使自己快乐的各种娱乐活动。但是他们首先关心的还是粮食供应问题,他们害怕一旦尼禄外出,就会出现粮食供应短缺的问题。元老们和那些显要人物则不知道到底是他待在罗马还是外出更为可怕。随之,正如人们所经历的可怕体验一样,那些既成事实的选择就是最为恶劣的选择。

Nero himself now tried to make it appear that Rome was his favourite abode. He gave feasts in public places as if the whole city were his own home. But the most prodigal and notorious banquet was given by Tigellinus. To avoid repetitious accounts of extravagance, I shall describe it, as a model of its kind. The entertainment took place on a raft constructed on Marcs Agrippa's lake. It was towed about by other vessels, with gold and ivory fittings. Their rowers were degenerates, assorted according to age and vice. Tigellinus had also collected birds and animals from remote countries, and even the products of the ocean. On the quays were brothels stocked with high-ranking ladies. Opposite them could be seen naked prostitutes, indecently posturing and gesturing.

At nightfall the woods and houses nearby echoed with singing and blazed with lights. Nero was already corrupted by every lust, natural and unnatural. But he now refuted any surmises that no further degradation was possible for him. For a few days later he went through a formal wedding ceremony with one of the perverted gang called Pythagoras. The emperor, in the presence of witnesses, put on the bridal veil. Dowry, marriage bed, wedding torches, all were there. Indeed everything was public which even in a natural union is veiled by night.

Disaster followed. Whether it was accidental or caused by a criminal act on the part of the emperor is uncertain—both versions have supporters. Now started the most terrible and destructive fire which Rome had ever experienced. It began in the Circus, where it adjoins the Palatine and Caelian hills. Breaking out in shops selling inflam-

现在,尼禄本人正在作出一种样子,似乎罗马就是他最喜欢的住所。他在公共场所举办宴会,好像全城都是他自己的宫殿似的。但是最为奢侈、最为臭名昭著的那次宴会则是由提盖里努斯举办的。为了避免一再地叙述这些宴会的奢侈的麻烦,我就将它作为一个具有代表性的例子加以描述。这次宴会是在一只木筏上举办的,而木筏则建在了玛尔克斯的阿格里帕湖上。这只木筏被另外一些用黄金和象牙装饰的船只在湖上拖着运行。这些船上的划手都是一些男妓,完全是按照他们的年龄和纵淫的本领加以安置的。提盖里努斯还从遥远的国度里搜集了各种鸟兽,甚至包括了大洋里的水产。在码头各处都设有妓馆,里面都是一些高贵的妇女。在她们的对面就可以看到裸体的妓女们,她们正在摆着各种淫荡的姿态和做着各种猥亵的动作。

在夜幕降临的时候,湖边的森林和附近的房子里边就有歌声开始飘荡,闪烁着灯光。尼禄早就被这些自然的和非自然的淫行腐化了。但是,现在他却拒绝了任何可能使他达到登峰造极的罪恶生活的勾当。原来,几天之后他跟他身边的一名恶棍举行了一场正式的婚礼,这名恶棍名叫毕达哥拉斯。在证婚人的伴随之下,皇帝戴上了新娘的面纱。嫁妆、结婚用的床、婚礼用的火把都有。实际上,甚至是在一次自然的婚姻结合之中需要用夜幕来掩盖的东西,在这里也全部都公开了。

紧接着就发生了一场灾难。究竟是偶然发生的,还是由于皇帝的罪行所引起的,还很难说。两种说法都各有其支持者。现在来看,这是罗马城所经历过的一次最为恐怖、最具破坏性的火灾。最先开始燃烧的大竞技场,是在比邻着帕拉提努斯山和凯利乌斯山的地方。火是从堆积着易燃商品的商店里烧起来的,借着风势

mable goods, and fanned by the wind, the conflagration instantly grew and swept the whole length of the Circus. There were no walled mansions or temples, or any other obstructions, which could arrest it. First, the fire swept violently over the level spaces. Then it climbed the hills—but returned to ravage the lower ground again. It outstripped every counter-measure. The ancient city's narrow winding streets and irregular blocks encouraged its progress.

Terrified, shrieking women, helpless old and young, people intent on their own safety, people unselfishly supporting invalids or waiting for them, fugitives and lingerers alike-all heightened the confusion. When people looked back, menacing flames sprang up before them or outflanked them. When they escaped to a neighbouring quarter, the fire followed—even districts believed remote proved to be involved. Finally, with no idea where or what to flee, they crowded on to the country roads, or lay in the fields. Some who had lost everything—even their food for the day—could have escaped, but preferred to die. So did others, who had failed to rescue their loved ones. Nobody dared fight the flames. Attempts to do so were prevented by menacing gangs. Torches, too, were openly thrown in, by men crying that they acted under orders. Perhaps they had received orders. Or they may just have wanted to plunder unhampered.

Nero was at Antium. He only returned to the city when the fire was approaching the mansion he had built to link the Gardens of Maecenas to the Palatine. The flames could not be prevented from overwhelming the whole of the Palatine, including his palace. Nevertheless, for the relief of the homeless, fugitive masses he threw open the Field of Mars, including Agrippa's public buildings, and even his

火猛烈地燃烧起来,大火持续不断地烧着,很快就将整个大竞技场烧毁了。因为那里没有任何可以抵挡火灾的用围墙围起来的大房子和神庙,也没有任何其他类似的建筑。一开始,大火猛烈地将平坦的地区都吞噬了,接着就烧到了山上,再接着又烧回到了低地。任何抵抗措施都不能赶上它的蔓延速度。而古老的罗马那狭窄而又曲折的街道以及不规则的建筑又加快了火势的蔓延。

到处都是惊恐哭叫的妇女,到处都是无助的老人、孩子;有的只管自己的安全在逃命,也有的在无私地帮着那些病弱的人或等着他们赶上,不论是走得快的还是走得慢的同样都加重了这一混乱。当人们回头看的时候,猛烈的火焰就会从其前面或四周扑过来。当他们逃到一个邻近地区之时,大火也会接踵而至,即使那些他们认为是远离危险的地区,原来也已经被火焰所包围了。最终,他们确实也不知哪里可以逃生或如何逃生了,于是就拥挤到乡下的大道上,或趴在田野里。有些人已经把所有的东西都丢光了,甚至包括每天的口粮,在这种情况之下,即使可以逃生的人也宁愿死去。其他一些人也是如此的心情,因为他们不能把自己的亲人从火灾之中救出来。没有人敢去救火。许多试图救火的人都被那些发出威胁的人所制止了。还有一些人竟然在公开地将火把乱投,他们喊叫着说,他们是奉命这样做的。也许他们确实已接到了命令,也许这样做是为了可以趁火打劫。

这时尼禄正在安提乌姆。直到大火扑向了他建筑用来把帕拉提努斯山和迈凯纳斯花园联结起来的那幢房屋的时候他才回到了罗马。很快要烧光帕拉提努斯山以及他自己的宫殿的大火看来是不可能扑灭了。为了收容那些无家可归的大量的逃亡者,尼禄将玛尔斯广场、阿格里帕的那些公共建筑物,甚至是自己的

own Gardens. Nero also constructed emergency accommodation for the destitute multitude. Food was brought from Ostia and neighbouring towns, and the price of corn was cut to less than 1/4 sesterce a pound. Yet hese measures, for all their popular character, earned no gratitude. For a rumour had spread that, while the city was burning, Nero had gone on his private stage and, comparing modern calamities with ancient, had sung of the destruction of Troy.

By the sixth day enormous demolitions had confronted the raging flames with bare ground and open sky, and the fire was finally stamped out at the foot of the Esquiline Hill. But before panic had subsided, or hope revived, flames broke out again in the more open regions of the city. Here there were fewer casualties; but the destruction of temples and pleasure arcades was even worse. This new conflagration caused additional ill-feeling because it started on Tigellinus' estate in the Acmilian district. For people believed that Nero was ambitious to found a new city to be called after himself.

Of Rome's fourteen districts only four remained intact. Three were levelled to the ground. The other seven were reduced to a few scorched and mangled ruins. To count the mansions, blocks, and temples destroyed would be difficult. They included shrines of remote antiquity, such as Servius Tullius' temple of the Moon, the Great Altar and holy place dedicated by Evander to Hercules, the temple vowed by Romulus to Jupiter the Stayer, Numa's sacred residence, and Vesta's shrine containing Rome's household gods. Among the losses, too, were the precious spoils of countless victories, Greek

花园都开放了。尼禄还建立了许多紧急收容所来收容那些无家可归的难民。食品从奥斯蒂亚和邻近的各城市运来了,粮食的价格则是降到了每磅不到 1/4 谢司特尔提乌斯。然而这些措施,尽管对人民群众有利,却没有收到相应的效果。因为有一个谣言到处在散播,说当大火在焚烧的时候,尼禄却早已经登上了自己的私人舞台,而且他竟然唱起了特洛伊被毁的故事,将当前的灾难与古时候的灾祸进行了比较。

第六天,凶猛的大火在造成了大量的毁坏之后,随之碰到了一片空地和空旷的天际,蔓延到了埃司克维里埃山山脚下的火终于停了下来。但是,在人们的惊恐完全平静下来,或重新获得希望之前,在城内人口较为稀疏的地方,又发生了一些火灾。在这些地方造成的人员伤亡相对较少。但是神庙和用于休息的柱廊所造成的毁坏却更严重。这一次新的火灾引起了更大的非议,因为它是从埃米里乌斯区提盖里努斯的房子那儿开始燃烧的。民众开始相信尼禄野心勃勃,想建立一座以他的名字命名的新城市。[1]

在罗马的十四个区之中,只有四个区保持得完好无损。三个区已经被夷为平地。其他七个区则只剩下了烧焦的、破烂的断垣残壁。要想计算一下被火灾损坏的私人住宅、房区、神庙,将是一件十分困难的事情。其中包括一些远古时代的神庙,例如谢尔维乌斯·图里乌斯所建筑的月神庙,伊凡德尔为赫尔克里士神所建的大祭坛和神庙,罗木鲁斯为了还愿而为朱庇特·斯塔托尔修建的神庙,努玛圣地,包括罗马人民的家神的维司塔圣所。在所有的损失物之中,还包括因战争获胜而掠得的珍贵战利品、

---

〔1〕 他想建立的新首都的名字是尼禄诺波里斯。

artistic masterpieces, and authentic records of old Roman genius. All the splendour of the rebuilt city did not prevent the older generation from remembering these irreplaceable objects. It was noted that the fire had started on July 19th, the day on which the Senonian Gauls had captured and burnt the city. Others elaborately calculated that the two fires were separated by the same number of years, months, and days.

But Nero profited by his country's ruin to build a new palace. Its wonders were not so much customary and commonplace luxuries like gold and jewels, but lawns and lakes and faked rusticity-woods here, open spaces and views there. With their cunning, impudent artificialities, Nero's architects and engineers, Severus and Celer, did not balk at effects which Nature herself had ruled out as impossible.

They also fooled away an emperor's riches. For they promised to dig a navigable canal from Lake Avernus to the Tiber estuary, over the stony shore and mountain barriers. The only water to feed the canal was in the Pontine marshes. Elsewhere, all was precipitous or waterless. Moreover, even if a passage could have been forced, the labour would have been unendurable and unjustified. But Nero was eager to perform the incredible; so he attempted to excavate the hills adjoining Lake Avernus. Traces of his frustrated hopes are visible today.

希腊的艺术杰作,以及古老的罗马天才们所作的不朽的文献记录。重建的罗马城所具有的所有的金碧辉煌都不能阻挡老一辈人对于那些不可恢复的东西的怀念。有人指出,火灾发生在 7 月 19 日,而这一天正好是谢洛尼人攻占并焚烧罗马城的日子。另有一些人经过精心计算得出,这两次大火是被同样的年代、月份、日子所隔开的。[1]

但是尼禄却趁国家处于灾难之机而为自己修了一座新的宫殿。这座宫殿的惊人之处,不在于具有早已为人民所熟知的例如黄金和珠宝等奢侈品,而在于那些草地、湖泊以及处处由林地、空地所组成的人造的乡间景色。尼禄的建筑师和工程师是谢维路斯和凯列尔,以他们所具有的精心和厚颜无耻的勇气,不顾大自然的规律,尽其可能地试验他们的技艺。

他们还耗费掉了一位皇帝的财富。因为他们设计从阿维尔努斯湖到台伯河河口的地方,跨过那石质的海岸和那些绵延的大山,开凿一条可以通航的运河。唯一可以向运河提供水源的是彭普提努斯沼地。其余都是悬崖和干涸的地方。而且即使能够在这儿开凿一条通道,所需要付出的劳动的艰辛也是令人所无法忍受的,而且也没有理由来说明白为什么要这样做。但是尼禄却要极力完成这一令人难以置信的工程;于是他努力要把与阿维尔努斯湖相连的那些小山凿通。他这一徒劳无益的工程在今天还可以看到。

---

[1] 公元前 390 年,阿里亚河之战后,高卢人火烧了罗马城,到这次大火的公元 64 年,在这两次大火之间正好是 454 年,按每年 12 个月,每月 31 天,则可以计算成 418 年加上 418 月再加 418 日。

In parts of Rome unfilled by Nero's palace, construction was not-as after the burning by the Gauls—without plan or demarcation. Street-fronts were of regulated alignment, streets were broad, and houses built round courtyards. Their height was restricted, and their frontages protected by colonnades. Nero undertook to erect these at his own expense, and also to clear debris from building-sites before transferring them to their owners. He announced bonuses, in proportion to rank and resources, for the completion of houses and blocks before a given date. Rubbish was to be dumped in the Ostian marshes by corn-ships returning down the Tiber.

A fixed proportion of every building had to be massive, untimbered stone from Gabii or Alba (these stones being fireproof). Furthermore, guards were to ensure a more abundant and extensive public watersupply, hitherto diminished by irregular private enterprise. Householders were obliged to keep fire-fighting apparatus in an accessible place; and semi-detached houses were forbidden—they must have their own walls. These measures were welcomed for their practicality, and they beautified the new city. Some, however, believed that the old town's configuration had been healthier, since its narrow streets and high houses had provided protection against the burning sun, whereas now the shadowless open spaces radiated a fiercer heat.

So much for human precautions. Next came attempts to appease heaven. After consultation of the Sibylline books, prayers were addressed to Vulcan, Ceres, and Proserpina. Juno, too, was propitiated. Women who had been married were responsible for the rites-first

在罗马城,在尼禄准备建宫殿的那些地方,重建工作不像高卢大火之后那样毫无计划、毫无秩序地进行。所设计的街道井然有序;马路宽阔,房屋周围都有庭院;建筑物的高度都有严格限制,而且在它们的正面都有柱廊作为保护物。尼禄是用自己的钱来做这些重建工作的,而且他归还给原主之前将那些建筑地上的瓦砾堆进行了清理。他还为那些在规定的日子之前能够完成房屋或房区重建工作的人,依照地位的高低和财富的多少悬赏了奖金。垃圾按照指令要倒入欧斯提亚沼地,沿着台伯河驶离罗马的运粮船必须要运走垃圾。

每一幢建筑物的组成部分必须是结实的,要使用从伽比努斯山或阿尔巴努斯山运来的石料建构(因为这些石头可以防火)。更何况,为了能够确保更丰富的、更大范围之内的公共用水的供应,还专门设置了许多卫兵,杜绝私人非法截水所造成的供水不足。规定家长们必须将消防器材摆放在容易触及的地方,而不允许建造相互连接的房屋,每家的房屋都必须要有自己的围墙。这些措施因为其实用性而广受欢迎,而且也美化了新罗马城。然而,仍有一些人认为旧城的格局更有利于健康,因为狭窄的街道和高大的建筑可以抵挡阳光的曝晒,然而现在所建的开阔地带却缺少阴凉地,从而就更加酷热了。

人类所能够做到的防范措施也就是如此了。下一步所应做的就是要平息天神的恼怒。在向西比拉预言书作了请示之后,祷告者们向武尔卡努斯[1]、凯列司[2]和普罗西尔皮娜[3]进行了祈祷。优诺也得到了抚慰:那些已婚的妇女们一开始所选中的地点是卡披托神庙,

---

[1]　火与锻冶之神,是朱庇特神和优诺女神的儿子,维纳斯女神的丈夫。

[2]　农业和谷物之神。

[3]　朱庇特神和凯列司女神所生的女儿,是地狱之神普鲁托的妻子。

on the Capitol, then at the nearest sea-board, where water was taken to sprinkle her temple and statue. Women with husbands living also celebrated ritual banquets and vigils.

But neither human resources, nor imperial munificence, nor appeasement of the gods, climinated sinister suspicions that the fire had been instigated. To suppress this rumour, Nero fabricated scapegoats-and punished with every refinement the notoriously depraved Christians (as they were popularly called). Their originator, Christ, had been executed in Tiberius' reign by the governor of Judaea, Pontius Pilatus. But in spite of this temporary setback the deadly superstition had broken out afresh, not only in Judaea (where the mischief had started) but even in Rome. All degraded and shameful practices collect and flourish in the capital.

First, Nero had self-acknowledged Christians arrested. Then, on their information, large numbers of others were condemned—not so much for incendiarism as for their anti-social tendencies. Their deaths were made farcical. Dressed in wild animals' skins, they were torn to pieces by dogs, or crucified, or made into torches to be ignited after dark as substitutes for daylight. Nero provided his Gardens for thespectacle, and exhibited displays in the Circus, at which he mingled with the crowd—or stood in a chariot, dressed as a charioteer. Despite their guilt as Christians, and the ruthless punishment it deserved, the victims were pitied. For it was felt that they were being sacrificed to one man's brutality rather than to the national interest.

Meanwhile Italy was ransacked for funds, and the provinces were

然后又在离海岸最近的可以汲水的地方,用汲上来的水喷洒女神的神庙和雕像。有夫之妇们也要参加宗教宴会和守夜仪式。

但是不论是人为的各项措施,皇帝的慷慨大度,还是为了平息天神的恼怒所作的各件事情,都不能消除人们之中所存在的一种可怕的怀疑,怀疑这场火灾是有人故意放的。为了平息谣言,尼禄就把那些因为臭名昭著而受到人们憎恶的基督徒(被人们称之为此)当作了替罪羊,并且用极其残酷的手段进行了惩罚。他们的创始人是基督,在提贝里乌斯统治时期就被一名叫彭提乌斯·彼拉图斯的总督给处死了。尽管这一致命性的迷信活动被一时压制住了,但是不仅在犹太人(即这一灾害的发源地),而且在罗马又再度流行起来。所有世上下流和可耻的活动都会在首都集中并猖獗起来。

开始的时候,尼禄将所有自称为基督徒的人都抓了起来。然后依据他们的招供,又有其他大量的一些人被定了罪。这与其说是他们纵火,倒不如说是由于他们对社会的敌视倾向。他们的死亡真是滑稽可笑:或者是被披上了野兽的外皮,然后让狗给撕成了碎片;或者是被钉死在十字架上;或者是被制成了火把在天黑的时候被点亮以作照明之用。尼禄将自己的花园提供给众人以作游览之景点,并在大竞技场举办比赛;在竞赛过程中,他将自己打扮成了一个马夫,要么混在人群之中,要么站在马车上。尽管基督徒们所犯罪行严重,而且对他们所进行的残酷处罚也是罪有应得,但他们的死亡也确实是令人十分的同情。因为民众觉得他们是在某一个人的残忍之下而牺牲的,而不是为了国家的利益。

与此同时,意大利到处受到了搜刮以勒索金钱,而各个行省

ruined-unprivileged and privileged communities alike. Even the gods were included in the looting. Temples at Rome were robbed, and emptied of the gold dedicated for the triumphs and vows, the ambitions and fears, of generations of Romans. Plunder from Asia and Greece included not only offerings but actual statues of the gods. Two agents were sent to these provinces. One, Acratus, was an ex-slave, capable of any depravity. The other, Secundus Carrinas, professed Greek culture, but no virtue from it percolated to his heart.

Seneca, rumour went, sought to avoid the odium of this sacrilege by asking leave to retire to a distant country retreat, and then—permission being refused—feigning a muscular complaint and keeping to his bedroom. According to some accounts one of his former slaves, Cleonicus by name, acting on Nero's orders intended to poison Seneca but he escaped-either because the man confessed or because Seneca's own fears caused him to live very simply on plain fruit, quenching his thirst with running water.

At this juncture there was an attempted break-out by gladiators atPraeneste. Their army guards overpowered them. But the Roman public, as always terrified (or fascinated) by revolution, were already talking of ancient calamities such as the rising of Spartacus. Soon afterwards a naval disaster occurred. This was not on active set vice; never had there been such profound peace. But Nero had ordered the fleet to return to Campania by a fixed date regardless of weather. So, despite heavy seas the steersmen started from Formiae. But when they

和同级别的联盟单位都因遭到了毁坏而开始衰败了。即使是诸神也在劫难逃。罗马城里的神庙都遭到了抢劫,里面所存的世世代代的罗马人在欢庆胜利和还愿时、在为了能够实现个人的野心或驱除个人的恐慌之时,所捐献的黄金都被劫掠一空。在亚细亚和阿凯亚,被劫掠的不仅仅有供物,甚至还有诸神的雕像。有两个代表被派往了这些行省。一个名叫阿克拉图斯,是一个被释放的奴隶,此人几乎无恶不作;另一个人名叫谢孔都斯·卡尔里那斯,自称精通于希腊文化,但实际上他的心灵一点也没有受这种文化的影响。

谣言在继续着,说塞内加为了使自己能够避免染上这一亵渎神灵的罪行所引起的憎恨的情绪,要求退休离开罗马到一个遥远的乡下去过一种隐退的生活;在要求遭到了拒绝之后,他就开始假装肌肉疼痛而待在寝室里不出来了。依据一些人的记载,他的一个以前的奴隶,名字叫克里欧尼库斯,奉了尼禄之命要将塞内加毒死,但是塞内加躲开了这一次谋杀;这或许是因为此人坦白了的缘故,或许是因为塞内加本人的警觉而使自己在饥饿的时候只食用野生的果子,口渴的时候只喝流动的水。[1]

在同一时期,在普列涅斯特城有一群剑奴企图发动暴动,当地的武装驻军将他们的起义镇压下去了。但是那些常常受到这些叛乱的惊吓(或者是诱惑)的罗马民众们早已在谈论过去的灾祸,例如斯巴达克斯起义等。不久,海军又发生了一次灾难。这次灾难不是在战争的过程之中发生的,因为以前从来就没有像现在这样完全处于和平状态。但是尼禄却不顾天气的状况而强行命令海军舰队在规定的期限之内返回到康帕尼亚。于是,舵手们不管海上的狂风海浪,就从弗尔米埃出发了。但是,当他们试图绕过米

---

〔1〕 指泉水和河水。

tried to round Cape Misenum a south-westerly gale drove them ashore near Cumae and destroyed numerous warships and smaller craft.

As the year ended omens of impending misfortune were widely rumoured-unprecedentedly frequent lightning; a comet (atoned for by Nero, as usual, by aristocratic blood); two-headed offspring of men and beasts, thrown into the streets or discovered among the offerings to those deities to whom pregnant victims are sacrificed. Near Placentia a calf was born beside the road with its head fastened to one of its legs. Soothsayers deduced that a new head was being prepared for the world—but that it would be neither powerful nor secret since it had been deformed in the womb and given birth by the roadside.

塞努姆海岬的时候,一阵西南风把他们吹到了库麦附近的海岸上去,使他们损失了许许多多的战舰和小船。

当这年年底到来的时候,到处都在谣传着预示灾难即将到来的恶兆:空前频繁的雷电现象;一颗彗星(对于这一恶兆,尼禄跟以前一样,都是用贵族的鲜血加以抵偿的);人和野兽结合所生的双头怪胎或者是被人丢在了大街上,或者是在怀孕的屠宰献祭用的牺牲的腹内被发现。在普拉肯提亚附近的路边生了一头小牛,小牛的头和一条腿紧紧地长在了一起。预言家们就断言道,还会有一头小牛将会诞生于这个世界上,但是由于它在子宫之内已经长成了畸形,而且出生在路边,所以它将既不会强壮,也不会是秘密的。

CHAPTER 15
The Plot

THE consuls for the following year were Aulus Licinius Nerva Silanus Firmus Pasidienus and Marcus Julius Vestinus Atticus. As soon as they had assumed office, a conspiracy was hatched and instantly gained strength. Senators and knights, officers, even women, competed to join. They hated Nero; and they liked Gaius Calpurnius Piso. His membership of the aristocratic Calpurnian house linked him, on his father's side, with many illustrious families. Among the masses, too, he enjoyed a great reputation for his good qualities, real or apparent. For he employed his eloquence to defend his fellow-citizens in court; he was a generous friend—and gracious and affable even to strangers; and he also possessed the accidental advantages of impressive stature and a handsome face. But his character lacked seriousness or self-control. He was superficial, ostentatious, and sometimes dissolute. But many people are fascinated by depravity and disinclined for austere morals on the throne. Such men found Piso's qualities attractive.

However, his ambitions were not what originated the conspiracy.

第十五章 阴 谋

在紧接着的一年里,[1]奥路斯·里西努斯·涅尔瓦西拉努斯·费尔姆斯·帕西狄埃努斯和玛尔库斯·尤利乌斯·维司提努斯·阿提库斯担任了执政官。他们一上任,就发生了一次阴谋叛乱,而且马上就发展成为了一支巨大的力量。元老们、骑士们、官僚们甚至是妇女们都竞相参与了这次活动。原因是由于他们憎恨尼禄,也由于他们喜爱盖乌斯·卡尔普尔尼乌斯·披索。披索出生于贵族世家,在父系的血统之中与卡尔普尔尼乌斯家族紧密相连,他身上集中了好多显贵家族的血统。他在民众之中享有极高的威望,因为他具有崇高的道德品质,且不论这种崇高性是真正的还是表现出来的。因为他曾经利用其杰出的口才在法庭上为其国人进行过辩护,还因为他对于朋友宽宏大量,哪怕是对于陌生人也非常地和蔼可亲;他还具有其他人所不具备的优点:身材上给人留下深刻的印象,容貌上英俊潇洒。但是他的性格之中缺少严肃凝重,缺乏自控。他非常肤浅,喜爱炫耀,有时候又很放荡。但是有许多人容易被邪恶的东西所迷惑,而且不喜欢君王的性格过分严峻。这样的人会发现披索的性格颇具吸引力。

然而,这一次阴谋并不是他野心勃勃所策动的。到底谁是阴谋

---

[1] 罗马建城818年,即公元65年。

Who did, who initiated this enterprise which so many joined, I could not easily say. Subrius Flavus, a colonel of the Guard, and Sulpicius Asper, company-commander, were in the forefront—as their courageous deaths showed. Violent hatred was what brought in Lucan and Plautius Lateranus. Lucan's animosity was personal. For Nero had the impudence to compete with Lucan as a poet, and had impeded his reputation by vetoing his publicity. Lateranus joined from no personal grievance; his motive was patriotism. Two other senators, Flavius Scaevinus and Afranius Quintianus, belied their reputations by becoming leaders in so important a project. For Scaevinus' brain was ruined by dissipation, and he led a languid sleepy life. Quintianus was a notorious degenerate who had been insulted by Nero in an offensive poem, and desired revenge.

These men talked to each other, and to their friends, about the emperor's crimes and his reign's imminent close. They were joined by seven Roman knights: Claudius Senecio, Cervarius Proculus, Volcacius Araricus, Julius Augurinus, Munatius Gratus, Antonius Natalis and Marcius Festus. Senecio was Nero's close associate, and so his position was especially perilous since they were still ostensibly friends. Natalis shared all Piso's secrets. The rest looked to revolution for personal advancement. Nor were Flavus and Asper the only officers involved. Other accomplices were the Guard colonels Gaius Gavius Silvanus and Statius Proxumus, and company-commanders,

的发起人,是谁策划了这一次有这么多人参加的阴谋,我确实很难说清楚。苏布里乌斯·弗拉乌斯,作为近卫军的一名将领,苏尔皮奇乌斯·阿司佩尔作为一名百人团的团长,则始终站在了战斗的最前线,他们英勇不屈的死亡就充分证明了这一点;安奈乌斯·路卡努斯和普劳提乌斯·拉提拉努斯则是怀着强烈的仇恨参加了这次阴谋。路卡努斯是出于私人的动机,因为尼禄恬不知耻,曾经自视为一名诗人与路卡努斯展开竞争,而且通过禁止公开发表他的诗作的方式以压制他的诗名。拉提拉努斯的参与则毫无个人的恩怨,其动机纯粹就是热爱祖国。而另外两个元老,佛拉维乌斯·司凯维努斯和阿弗拉尼乌斯·克温提亚努斯为了掩盖自己的臭名从而在如此重要而又冒险的举动之中成为带头人。因为司凯维努斯生活放荡使其脑子反应迟钝,整天就是过着一种昏昏欲睡的生活。克温提亚努斯是一个臭名昭著的恶棍,他曾经被尼禄在一首带有攻击性的诗篇中侮辱过,从而渴望进行报复。

这些人在彼此之间,以及向他们的朋友们宣传着皇帝的罪行和他的统治已危在旦夕的流言。有几个罗马骑士也加入到了他们的行动之中来,他们是:克劳狄乌斯·塞内奇奥、凯尔瓦里乌斯·普洛库路斯、沃尔卡奇乌斯·阿拉里库斯、尤利乌斯·奥古里努斯、穆纳提乌斯·格拉图斯、安托尼乌斯·纳塔里斯以及玛尔奇乌斯·费司图斯。这其中塞内奇奥是尼禄的一位密友,既然两者还保持着表面上的友谊关系,因此他的处境就特别危险。纳塔里斯参与了披索所有的秘密计划,而其他那些骑士参与阴谋暴乱的目的就是为了寻求个人的出路。卷入其中的官员不仅仅有弗拉乌斯和阿司佩尔,其他参与这次阴谋的还有近卫军将领盖乌斯·伽维乌斯·

Maximus Scaurus and Venetus Paulus, were also in the plot. But the mainstay was felt to be Faenius Rufus, commander of the Guard. His respectability and good reputation had made less impression on Nero than the cruelty and depravity of his colleague Tigellinus-who persecuted Faenius with slanders, reiterating the alarming allegation that he had been Agrippina's lover and was intent on avenging her.

So when the conspirators were satisfied by Faenius' own repeated assurances that he was with them, serious discussion began about the date and place of Nero's murder. Subrius Flavus, it was said, had felt tempted to attack Nero when the emperor was singing on the stage or rushing from place to place during the night, unguarded, while his palace burned. Flavus had been attracted in the latter instance by Nero's opportune solitude, and in the former, conversely, by the large crowds which would witness the noble deed. But what held him back was that hindrance to all mighty enterprises, the desire for survival.

The plotters hesitated, still hoping and fearing. A woman called Epicharis, who had extracted their secret-it is not known how, for she had never before interested herself in anything good-kept urging them on and assailing them. Finally, happening to be in Campania and becoming impatient with the slowness of the conspirators, she attempted to unsettle and implicate the naval officers at Misenum. She began with a rear-admiral named Volusius Proculus, who had helped Nero with his mother's murder and felt his promotion had fallen short of so tremendous a crime. Whether their friendship was

西尔瓦努斯和司塔提乌斯·普洛克苏木斯以及百人团长玛克西姆斯·司考路斯和维尼图斯·保路斯。但是人们认为主要的力量还是要依靠近卫军长官法伊尼乌斯·路福斯。他那令人尊敬的举止和良好的声誉在尼禄眼里看来是远远比不上法伊尼乌斯的同事,那残暴而又贪婪的提盖里努斯的。后者用诽谤的方式迫害法伊尼乌斯,他散播着令人惊恐的谣言,说法伊尼乌斯一直是阿格里披娜的情夫,因此要为她报仇。

因此,当阴谋叛乱者们非常高兴地得知法伊尼乌斯本人已多次声明要坚定地支持他们的时候,就开始严肃认真地探讨谋杀尼禄的时间和地点。据说苏布里乌斯·弗拉乌斯就曾经试图在尼禄登台演唱的时候,或者是在他的身边没有侍卫而皇宫里正起大火,而他一个人在夜间到处乱跑之时,向他发动攻击。对于后一种情况,吸引弗拉乌斯的地方就在于恰好尼禄一个人独处时便于下手;而前一种情况则正好相反,使他神往的是有大批的民众可以目睹他的壮举和英勇的牺牲。但是使他没有敢于采取诸如此类的举动的是他对于活下去的渴望。

阴谋者们还在犹豫,仍然在希望和恐惧之中徘徊着。一个名叫埃皮卡里丝的女人得知了这一阴谋,也不知道她是从哪儿听说的,因为她以前对于任何积极向善的东西从来不感兴趣,而此次则鼓励他们,并责备他们还不采取行动。最后,她对于阴谋叛乱者们还迟迟不动手感到忍无可忍了,而恰好她正在康帕尼亚,就开始极力劝说米塞努姆的海军军官,试图把他们也拉进这次举动之中。她是从一个名叫沃洛西乌斯·普洛库路斯的海军将领身上着手的。此人曾帮助过尼禄谋杀自己的母亲,在他看来,他所得到的职位上的升迁绝对抵不上自己在如此重大的罪行之中所做

longstanding or recent is unknown. At all events Proculus told the woman of his services to Nero and their inadequate reward, and expressed not only discontent but the determination to have his own back if the chance occurred. This raised hopes that Proculus might be induced to act, and bring others in. The fleet could be extremely useful and provide valuable opportunities, since Nero enjoyed going to sea off Puteoli and Misenum.

So Epicharis went further. Enlarging on the emperor's abolition of the senate's rights and whole criminal record, she revealed the plan to avenge Rome's destruction at Nero's hands—only let Proculus make ready to do his part by winning over the best men, and he should be worthily rewarded. But she did not disclose the names of the conspirators. So, when Proculus proceeded—as he did-to report what he had heard to Nero, his information was useless. Epicharis was summoned and confronted with Proculus, but in the absence of witnesses easily refuted him. However, she herself was kept in custody. For Nero suspected that the story, though unproven, might not be untrue.

The conspirators were now tormented by fears of betrayal. They wanted to perform the assassination quickly—at Piso's villa at Baiae. For Nero appreciated its charms and often came for a bathe or banquet, without guards or imperial pomp. But Piso refused, arguing that to stain the sanctity of hospitality with the blood of an emperor, however evil, would cause a bad impression. The city would be a

的贡献。也不知道他们的友情已保持了很长一段时间了,还是最近刚刚开始。反正普洛库路斯向这位女人透露了自己是如何帮助尼禄以及所得到的可怜的回报,他不仅大发牢骚,而且决定只要有机会就会向尼禄讨回公道。这就表明很有希望将普洛库路斯拉进这次举动之中,而且有希望将其他一些人也拉进来。因为尼禄喜欢在普提欧里和米塞努姆附近的海面上游玩,所以海军舰队的参与对这次行动会极为有利,可以提供方便的下手机会。

于是埃皮卡里丝采取了进一步的行动。她指出皇帝已经将自己的权力扩大到了极致而剥夺了元老院的所有权力,并列举了皇帝的所有罪行。她将大家要采取行动以推翻尼禄在罗马的毁灭性统治的计划透露给了普洛库路斯。而普洛库路斯的任务则是只要赢得机会带领他手下的那些最优秀的人参与这次行动就可以邀功请赏了。但是她没有将这次参加叛乱的名字透露给他。因此当普洛库路斯着手并且也确实将自己的所闻向尼禄作了汇报之后,他所提供的信息价值不大。埃皮卡里丝被传唤并与普洛库路斯对质,但是由于缺少证人,所以她很容易地就将他的控告驳倒。然而,她本人还是被拘押了起来,因为尼禄怀疑,这件事情虽然没有证据来证明它的真实性,但也不一定就是假的。

现在密谋者们非常害怕被出卖了,他们想赶快采取刺杀行动,地点就选在了披索在拜阿伊的一所别墅之中。因为尼禄很欣赏这座别墅的风光,经常过来洗澡和参加宴饮,既没有卫兵也没有皇帝的仪仗。但是披索拒绝了,理由是尽管这是一个罪恶深重的皇帝,假如用他的血将这圣洁的宴饮之地给玷污了,那也将留下不快的印象。他说,罗马城是较理想的下手的地方,或者是在

better place, he said—that detested palace Nero had plundered his people to build; or, since their deed would be in the public interest, a public centre.

That was what Piso said aloud. But secretly he was afraid of a rival claimant to the throne—Lucius Junius Silanus Torquatus (II). The illustrious birth of Torquatus, and his upbringing by Gaius Cassius Longinus, fitted him for the highest destiny. Moreover non-conspirators, who might pity Nero as the victim of a crime, would back Torquatus readily. Some thought that Piso had also wished to prevent the lively consul, Marcus Julius Vestinus Atticus, from leading a Republican movement or insisting that the next emperor should be chosen by himself. For Vestinus was not one of the conspirators—though Nero used the charge to gratify his longstanding hatred of an innocent man.

They finally decided to execute their design at the Circus Games, on the day dedicated to Ceres. For though Nero rarely left the seclusion of his palace and gardens, he often attended Circus performances, and was more accessible in their festive atmosphere. The attack was planned as follows. Plautius Lateranus, ostensibly petitioning for financial assistance, was to prostrate himself before the unsuspecting emperor and then-being both resolute and muscular-bring him down and hold him. As Nero lay pinned down, the military men among the plotters, and any others sufficiently daring, would rush up and kill him. The leading role was claimed by Flavius Scaevinus, who had taken a dagger from a temple of Safety or (according to other reports) from the Shrine of Fortune at Ferentum, and wore it as the dedicated instrument of a great enterprise.

Meanwhile Piso was to wait at the temple of Ceres, from which

尼禄掠夺其国民而修建的令人厌恶的宫殿之内,或者是既然他们所采取的行动是为了公共利益,就将行动的地址选在公共中心地区。

以上是披索所公开申明的,但是在私下里他是防着路奇乌斯·尤尼乌斯·西拉努斯·托尔库阿图斯来争夺皇位,因为西拉努斯出身高贵,而且受过盖乌斯·卡西乌斯·朗吉努斯的教育,这使他可以出任任何显赫的职位。更何况,那些没有参与此次阴谋的人很有可能出于对尼禄在这次谋杀中的去世而深表同情,会转而拥戴他作皇帝。一些人认为披索也曾经希望能够阻止现任执政官玛尔库斯·尤利乌斯·维司提努斯·阿提库斯领导一场共和运动,或者是坚持下一个皇帝由他自己来挑选。因为维司提努斯并不是阴谋叛乱分子,尽管尼禄后来曾经向这个无辜的人发泄了他长久以来的憎恨情绪。

最后他们决定将行动的日期定在了敬献给凯列司神的赛马大会的那一天。因为尽管尼禄过着一种封闭的生活而很少离开自己的宫殿和花园,但是他经常参加赛马比赛,而在这种节日的气氛之中,要接近他也更容易一些。所谋划的进攻措施如下:普劳提乌斯·拉提拉努斯假装请求财政上的援助,跪倒在还没有起疑的皇帝面前,然后将皇帝掀翻在地,并将其抓住,因为普劳提乌斯·拉提拉努斯勇猛顽强,而且强壮有力。一旦尼禄被压在地上不能动,参与这次阴谋的具有军事作战能力的人以及其他具有足够胆量的人就要冲上来将其杀死。弗拉维乌斯·司凯维努斯则宣称要担任这些刺客中的带头人,他从费伦提努姆城之中的安全神庙取了一把匕首,而另一些人则说他是从幸福神庙取的。他将匕首带在身上,作为要完成一项伟大事业时所使用的神奇的武器。

与此同时,披索将会在凯列司神庙等候着,从那儿法伊尼乌

Faenius Rufus and the rest were to fetch him to the Guards' camp. The elder Pliny adds that, to win popular favour for Piso, Claudius' daughter Claudia Antonia was to accompany him. True or false, I have felt that this statement ought at least to be recorded. Yet it seems absurd either that Claudia Antonia should have staked her name and life on so hopeless a project, or that Piso, famous for his devotion to his wife, could have pledged himself to another marriage-unless indeed the lust for power outblazes all other feelings combined.

The secret was astonishingly well kept, considering the differences of the conspirators in social and financial position, rank, age, and sex. But betrayal came in the end—from the house of Flavius Scaevinus. The day before the attempt, he had a long conversation with Antonius Natalis. Then Scaevinus returned home and signed his will. Taking the aforesaid dagger from its sheath, and complaining that it was blunt with age, he gave it to his freed slave Milichus to be sharpened and polished on a stone. Then came a dinner-party, more luxurious than usual, at which Scaevinus freed his favourite slaves and gave others presents of money. He maintained a desultory conversation with superficial gaiety. But he was evidently anxious and seriously preoccupied. Finally, he instructed the same Milichus to prepare bandages and styptics for wounds.

Perhaps Milichus was in the secret, and had hitherto proved trustworthy. Alternatively (and this is the usual version) he knew nothing, but his suspicions were now aroused. At all events his slave's brain considered the rewards of treachery and conceived ideas of vast wealth and power. Then morality, his patron's life, gratitude for his freedom,

斯·路福斯和其余的人将会带他到近卫军的军营。年长的普利尼说,为了能够赢得公众的支持,克劳狄乌斯的女儿克劳狄娅·安托尼娅要陪伴着他。不论真假,我认为这一说法至少应该被记录下来。然而下列两种情况看来都是荒唐的:一是克劳狄娅·安托尼娅竟然会将自己的名誉和生命押在一桩如此不可靠的赌注上;一是以忠诚于妻子而闻名的披索竟然会同另外一个女人结婚,除非是他的权力欲望确实是压倒了其他所有欲望的总和。

尽管这些阴谋叛乱者有着不同的社会地位、经济地位、等级、年龄和性别,保密却取得了令人吃惊的成效。但是最后还是在弗拉维乌斯·司凯维努斯家中败露了。在举事的前一天,他曾经和安托尼乌斯·纳塔里斯进行了一次长谈。然后司凯维努斯就回到了家中,签署了自己的遗嘱。当他把前面所提及的那把匕首从鞘中拔出之时,就抱怨说它已经多年未用,已经钝了,于是他把它交给了他的一名被释放的名字叫米利库斯的奴隶,命令他去磨刀石上将它磨快、磨亮。然后又举办了一次比平时要奢华的晚宴,在宴会上司凯维努斯给了他最喜欢的一些奴隶以自由,而把金钱赏赐给了其他一些在场的奴隶。他强作欢笑,同宴会上的人漫无边际地闲谈着。但是很明显他是焦虑不安的,而且在严肃地思考着什么。最后,他又吩咐米利库斯去准备包扎伤口用的绷带和止血用品。

或许是米利库斯已经知道了秘密,而到目前为止他还是值得信任的。或许是他对此事一无所知,但现在他开始怀疑了起来,而这是一般人通常所持的观点。总而言之,他那奴性未除的大脑里面所考虑的是出卖主人之后所得到的报酬,以及眼前所浮现的大量的财富和无限的权力。然后,什么道德良心、什么主人

counted for nothing. His wife's womanly, sordid advice implanted a further motive, fear. Many slaves and former slaves, she recalled, had been there and seen the same happenings-one man's silence would be useless, and the rewards would go to the informer who spoke first.

So at daybreak Milichus left for the Servilian Gardens. At first he was kept out. Finally, however, after insisting on the dreadful gravity of his news, he was taken by the doorkeepers to Nero's freed slave Epaphroditus—who conducted him to Nero. Milichus then revealed the resolute determination of the senators, the danger to Nero's life, and everything else he had heard or guessed. Exhibiting the dagger destined for Nero's murder, Milichus urged that the accused man be fetched. Scaevinus was arrested by soldiers. But he denied his guilt.

'The weapon concerned in the charge', he said, 'is a venerated heirloom kept in my bedroom. This ex-slave Milichus has stolen it. As to my will, I have often signed new clauses without particularly noting the date. I have given slaves their freedom and money-gifts before. This time the scale was larger because, with reduced means and pressing creditors, I feared my will would be rejected. My table has always been generous, my life comfortable—too comfortable for austere critics. Bandages for wounds I did not order. But the man's allegations of patent untruths are so unconvincing that he has added

的生命安全、什么自己从主人那儿所获得的自由,统统都抛在了脑后。他妻子的妇人之见则是令人恐慌的,她提出了一个卑鄙的建议以进一步说明应该采取如此行动的原因。她回忆说,许多奴隶和许多被释放了的奴隶在此都看到过同样事情的发生:一个人的沉默不会带来任何好处,而只有第一个告密的人才会得到奖赏。

于是,天一亮米利库斯就赶忙动身赶往塞尔维廉花园。一开始他被拒之于门外,然而他一再坚持说他有极其可怕的重大消息要汇报,这样最终才被门卫们带到了尼禄的被释放了的奴隶埃帕普洛狄图斯面前,埃帕普洛狄图斯又领他去拜见了尼禄。于是米利库斯就将元老们所做出的不顾一切的决定,将要对尼禄的生命安全所造成的危害,以及他所听到和猜测到的另外一些情况统统透露了出来。米利库斯将用来刺杀尼禄的匕首拿了出来,坚持认为应该将被告带来。司凯维努斯被士兵们抓了起来,但是他否认曾经犯过这样的罪行。

他说:"在控告中所提及的那把匕首,是我珍藏在我的寝室之中的一个十分珍贵的传家宝。米利库斯这个我所释放了的奴隶却将他偷走了。至于说我的遗嘱问题,我往往将一些新的条款加上去,所以不需要注明什么特别的日期。以前我曾经给一些奴隶以自由和赏赐给他们一些金钱作为礼物。这一次我所做的规模大了一点,是因为伴随着我所拥有的财产的减少和债权人紧迫的逼债,我怕我的遗嘱被废弃了。我的饭食一直很奢华,因为我追求一种享乐的生活,这种生活在那些提倡简朴的批评家们看来是太过于奢了。我没有让人准备包扎伤口用的绷带。但是此人显然不值得信任的控告太不能令人信服了,因此才捏造上了这

this charge merely because it rests wholly on his own evidence. '

Scaevinus spiritedly reinforced this defence by assailing the exs-lave as an infamous rascal. His self-possessed tones and features would have annihilated the accusation if Milichus' wife had not remin-ded her husband that Scaevinus had spoken privately and at length with Antonius Natalis, and that both of them were associates of Gaius Calpurnius Piso. So Natalis was summoned, and he and Scaevinus were interrogated separately about their conversation and its subject. The discrepancy between their replies aroused suspicion, and they were put in chains.

At the threat and sight of torture they broke down-Natalis first. With his more intimate knowledge of the whole conspiracy (and greater cunning as an accuser) , he began by denouncing Piso-then Seneca. Either Natalis had really acted as intermediary between Sen-eca and Piso or he hoped to conciliate Nero, who loathed Seneca and sought every means to destroy him. Scaevinus was equally unheroic-or he may have thought that since all was known silence held no ad-vantages. At all events, when told of Natalis' confession, he named the remaining conspirators. Of these, Lucan, Afranius Quintia-nus, and Claudius Senecio long refused to incriminate themselves. But finally, tempted by a bribe of impunity, they confessed. What they said explained their hesitation, for Lucan denounced his own

一罪状,因为这样的事情完全是他信口开河的一面之词。"

司凯维努斯通过把这个被释放了的奴隶说成是一个臭名昭著的恶棍而进一步激烈地为自己辩护。他那充满了自信的声调和表情眼看就要将告密者的话给击溃了,但这时米利库斯却想起了他妻子提醒的话:司凯维努斯曾经与安托尼乌斯·纳塔里斯私下里进行过长时间的密谈,而且他们俩都与盖乌斯·卡尔普尔尼乌斯·披索交往密切。于是纳塔里斯被传唤了,并将他和司凯维努斯分开来询问他们所交谈的内容和主题。由于他们的答案不能够合到一块去,所以引起了怀疑,于是他们就被关进了监狱。

在严刑拷打的威胁和亲眼看到拷打的情况之下,他们就崩溃了,纳塔里斯是第一个投降的人。由于他更加熟悉阴谋的全部内情,而且他也是一个更加老练的控告者,于是他开始指证,先是供出了披索,接着又是塞内加。或许是因为他确实曾经担当过塞内加和披索之间的调解人,或许是因为他知道尼禄早就憎恨塞内加,一直在寻找各种办法将其除掉,因而这样就有希望讨好尼禄了。或许是因为司凯维努斯同样是一个软骨头,或许是因为他认为既然一切都已被人所知了,再保持沉默也是毫无益处,无论怎样,他是在纳塔里斯招供之后,就将其余的密谋者的名字全部都供了出来。在这些人之中,路卡努斯、阿弗拉尼乌斯·克温提亚努斯、克劳狄乌斯·塞内奇奥很长时间一直拒不承认自己参与过此一罪行。但是最后,他们经受不住以不予惩罚作为回报的诱惑而招供了。他们对于自己迟迟不肯招供各自的原因做出了解释,路卡努斯的理由是他要指控自己的母亲阿奇里娅,而他的两

mother Acilia, and his two partners implicated their closest friends, Glitius Gallus and Annius Pollio.

Nero now remembered the information of Volusius Proculus and consequent arrest of Epicharis. Thinking no female body could stand the pain, he ordered her to be tortured. But lashes did not weaken her denials, nor did branding—nor the fury of the torturers at being defied by a woman. So the first day's examination was frustrated. Next day her racked limbs could not support her, so she was taken for further torments in a chair. But on the way she tore off her breast-band, fastened it in a noose to the chair's canopy, and placed her neck inside it. Then, straining with all her weight, she throttled the little life that was still in her. So, shielding in direst agony men unconnected with her and almost strangers, this former slavewoman set an example which particularly shone when free men, Roman knights and senators, were betraying, before anybody had laid a hand on them, their nearest and dearest. For Lucan and Senecio and Quintianus gave away their fellow-conspirators wholesale.

Nero became increasingly frightened. His guard had been redoubled. Indeed, the whole of Rome was virtually put in custody-troops manned the walls, and blockaded the city by sea and river. Roman public squares and homes, and even neighbouring towns and country districts, were invaded by infantry and cavalry. Among them were Germans; being foreigners, the emperor trusted them particularly.

Line after line of chained men were dragged to their destination at

个同伙则分别要指控他们自己最亲密的朋友格里提乌斯·伽路斯和安尼乌斯·波里欧。

尼禄这时候想起了由于沃洛西乌斯·普洛库路斯的告密而随之将埃皮卡里丝逮捕的事情。他认为一个女人的柔弱之躯是经受不了痛苦的，就下令对她进行严刑拷问。然而不论是鞭打，还是火烙，抑或是拷问者因被一位女人公然蔑视而暴跳如雷，都不能使她承认自己的罪行。因此第一天的拷问一无所获。第二天，她那受伤了的肢体已经无法使自己站立起来了，于是就将她放在一把椅子上进一步进行拷问。但是，在这一过程中，她将自己胸前的带子解了下来，把它系成了一个环子而挂在了椅子上方的顶盖上，并将自己的脖子伸了进去，然后就将自己全身的重量都挂在了绳子上，结束了那已经奄奄一息的生命。因此，这一位被释放的前奴隶在严刑折磨之下掩护了同她没有丝毫关系的而且几乎是素不相识的男人们，这样她就树立了一个特别光辉的榜样。这一榜样使得那些所谓的自由的男子们、罗马的骑士们、元老们显得黯然失色，因为他们在没有经受任何拷打逼问的情况之下，就将自己最亲近的、最亲密的人统统出卖了。而对于路卡努斯、塞内奇奥、克温提亚努斯来说，却是将自己的同谋者全部都出卖了。

尼禄的恐惧逐日剧增，他加倍增强了自己的近卫部队。实际上，整个罗马城都处于戒严状态：城墙之上配备了成队的士兵，而通向罗马城的海路和河路都被封锁了；步兵和骑兵们在罗马城的公共广场、住宅，甚至是在邻近的城镇和乡村地区到处搜索着。在这些士兵之中，有一部分是日耳曼人，由于他们是外国人，所以皇帝特别信任他们。

一队接着一队的带着手铐脚镣的人被带到了尼禄花园的门

the gates of Nero's Gardens. When they were brought in to be interrogated, guilt was deduced from affability to a conspirator, or a chance conversation or meeting, or entrance to a party or a show together. Fierce interrogation by Nero and Tigellinus was supplemented by savage attacks from Faenius Rufus. No informer had denounced him yet; so, to establish his independence of his fellow-conspirators, he bullied them. When Subrius Flavius, who was standing by, inquired by a sign—in the middle of an actual trial-if he should draw his sword and assassinate Nero, Faenius Rufus shook his head and checked Subrius' impulse as his hand was already moving to the hilt.

After the betrayal of the plot, while Milichus was talking and Scaevinus hesitating, Piso was urged to go to the Guards' camp and test the attitude of the troops, or mount the platform in the Forum and try the civilians. 'If your fellow-conspirators rally round you', it was argued, 'outsiders will follow. Once a move is made the publicity will be immense—a vitally important point in revolutions. Nero has taken no precautions against this. Unforeseen developments intimidate even courageous men, so how could forcible countermeasures be feared from this actor-with Tigellinus and Tigellinus' mistresses as his escort! Many things that look hard to timid people can be done by trying.

'It is useless to expect loyal silence when so many accomplices are involved, body and soul. Tortures and rewards find a way anywhere. You too will be visited and put in chains—and ultimately to a degrading death. How much finer to die for the good of your country, calling

口接受审问。当他们被带进来接受审问的时候,只要是他们曾经向阴谋者流露过亲切的表情,或者是曾经谈过话,或者是在一块举行过集会,甚至是在一起聚会、在一起看演出,都被认为是有罪。尼禄和提盖里努斯在进行着无情的审问,除此之外,法伊尼乌斯·路福斯也在进行着野蛮的拷问。现在还没有告密者出来控告他;为了表明自己与这些同谋者们无关,他对他们进行了恐吓谩骂。在真正的拷问过程之中,当站在他身旁的苏布里乌斯·弗拉乌斯用一个暗号向他询问是否应该抽出宝剑来将尼禄杀死的时候,法伊尼乌斯·路福斯连忙摇头,并抑制住了苏布里乌斯的这一冲动,而这时他已经将自己的手伸向了剑柄。

阴谋被出卖了之后,当米利库斯在进行控诉的时候,斯凯维努斯也在那里迟疑,这时有人就劝披索到军营之中去,探视一下军队的情绪倾向,而另有一些人则劝他登上广场的讲坛去探视一下大众的情绪倾向。他们说:"假如你的同谋者重新集合到你的身边,局外人士也会跟着做的。而一旦采取了这一举动,就将会不可避免地公开出去,这对于这次政变将起着至关重要的作用。而尼禄绝不会提防这一招的。即使勇敢的人遇到了猝不及防的事件之时也会手足无措的,何况只有一个提盖里努斯和他的情夫作为助手,又如何能够用武力来对抗我们!有许多事情对于那些胆怯的人看来也许是困难的,但是假如敢于尝试的话,或许会成功的。

"有如此多的人参与了这次举动,期望人人都全心全意地忠诚而保持沉默那是根本就不可能的事情。严刑拷打和奖赏总能找到突破口的。你也会被抓住而被戴上手铐脚镣的,而且会被极不光彩地处死。假如为了你自己国家的利益或为了号召人民

for men to defend its freedom! The army may fail you, the people a-
bandon you. But you yourself—if you must die early—die in a way of
which your ancestors and posterity could approve!'

But Piso was unimpressed. After a brief public appearance, he
shut himself in his house and summoned up courage for his end, waiting for the Guardsmen. Nero, suspicious of old soldiers as likely supporters of Piso, had selected new or recent recruits as his assassins.
But Piso died by opening the veins in his arms. He loaded his will
with repulsive flattery of Nero. This was done because Piso loved his
own wife Satria Galla, though she was low-born and her beauty her
only asset. He had stolen her from her former husband, a friend of
his called Domitius Silus, whose complaisance-like her misconduct-
had increased Piso's notoriety.

The next to be killed by Nero was the consul-designate Plautius
Lateranus. His removal was so hasty that he was not allowed to embrace his children or given the customary short respite to choose his
own death. Hurried off to the place reserved for slaves' executions,
Lateranus was dispatched by a Guard colonel, Statius Proxumus. He
died in resolute silence-without denouncing the officer's equal guilt.

Seneca's death followed. It delighted the emperor. Nero had no
proof of Seneca's complicity but was glad to use arms against him
when poison had failed. The only evidence was a statement of Antonius Natalis that he had been sent to visit the ailing Seneca and com-

去保卫自由而死,这样的死是多么高尚啊!你所领导的军队有可能失败,所领导的人民有可能将你抛弃,假如你必须要过早死去,那么就以一种你的祖辈和后人们看来是很值得的方式去赴死!"

但是披索毫无所动。他在公开的场合出现了一会儿之后,就将自己关在自己的家中,等待着近卫军的到来,鼓足勇气迎接死亡的来临。由于怀疑那些老兵们有可能是披索的支持者,尼禄就选了一些新的、最近才补充进来的士兵作为这次行动的执行者。但是披索却已通过切断自己手臂上的脉管的方式而死去了。他所留下的遗嘱之中充满了对尼禄的令人作呕的谄媚之词。披索之所以这样做,是因为他爱自己的妻子撒特里娅·伽拉,尽管她出身低微,除了自己的美貌之外一无所有。她是他从她的前夫,他的一位名叫多米提乌斯·西路斯那里勾引来的。西路斯的讨好和她的淫荡行为更加重了披索的寡廉鲜耻。

尼禄接着处死的人是刚刚当选的执政官普劳提乌斯·拉提拉努斯。他的被处决是如此的匆忙,以至于连拥抱自己的孩子和按照通常的习惯来选择自己死亡的方式的时间都没有。拉提拉努斯被匆匆地带到了处决奴隶的地方之后,就被一名近卫军将领司塔提乌斯·普洛克苏木斯处死了。他选用了坚定的沉默不言的方式结束了自己的生命,甚至于不愿揭露这一位将领同样也是这一阴谋叛乱的参与者。

下一个被处死的是塞内加,这件事令皇帝高兴万分。虽然尼禄没有证据说明塞内加参与了这一阴谋,但是在毒药没有将对方毒死的情况之下,他却很高兴用武器将他处死。唯一的证据是安托尼乌斯·纳塔里斯在陈述之中提到了他;说自己曾经被人派遣

plain because Seneca had refused to receive Piso. Natalis had conveyed the message that friends ought to have friendly meetings; and Seneca had answered that frequent meetings and conversations would benefit neither: but that his own welfare depended on Piso's.

A colonel of the Guard, Gavius Silvanus, was ordered to convey this report to Seneca and ask whether he admitted that those were the words of Natalis and himself. Fortuitously or intentionally, Seneca had returned that day from Campania and halted at a villa four miles from Rome. Towards evening the officer arrived. Surrounding the villa with pickets, he delivered the emperor's message to Seneca as he dined with his wife Pompeia Paulina and two friends. Seneca replied as follows: ' Natalis was sent to me to protest, on Piso's behalf, because I would not let him visit me. I answered excusing myself on grounds of health and love of quiet. I could have had no reason to value any private person's welfare above my own. Nor am I a flatterer. Nero knows this exceptionally well. He has had more frankness than servility from Seneca!'

The officer reported this to Nero in the presence of Poppaea and Tigellinus, intimate counsellors of the emperor's brutalities. Nero asked if Seneca was preparing for suicide. Gavius Silvanus replied that he had noticed no signs of fear or sadness in his words or features. So Silvanus was ordered to go back and notify the death-sentence. According to Fabius Rusticus, he did not return by the way he had come but made a detour to visit the commander of the Guard, Faenius Rufus; he showed Faenius the emperor's orders, asking if he should obey them; and Faenius, with that ineluctable weakness which they all revealed, told him to obey. For Silvanus was himself one of the con-

去看望生病了的塞内加,并向他大发牢骚,但是塞内加拒不接待披索。纳塔里斯曾经表达过朋友应该经常亲密地接触的话语。而塞内加的回答是朋友之间经常见面交谈对于双方来说都没有什么好处,除非自己的生命依赖于披索的安全。

一名近卫军将领盖乌斯·伽维乌斯·西尔瓦努斯奉命将这些报告转达给塞内加,问他是否承认有关纳塔里斯和自己所说过的这些话的真实性。也不知是偶然的还是有意的,那一天塞内加正好从康帕尼亚返回,并且在一个离罗马四英里的别墅之中做逗留。黄昏时分,这位将领抵达了这里。派哨兵将这座别墅包围起来之后,他就将皇帝的话向他做了转达。而此时的塞内加正在与妻子彭佩娅·宝琳娜和两个朋友吃晚饭。对此塞内加做了如下回答:"纳塔里斯是被派往这里代表披索来表达抗议的,因为我不让披索来拜访我。我答复的借口是基于我健康的考虑和因为我喜欢安静。我没有任何理由将我自己的安全寄托在其他任何人的帮助之上。而且我也不是一个谄媚者。对于这一点,尼禄比他人知道得更清楚。他从塞内加身上所看到的更多的是坦诚而不是奴颜婢膝。"

这位将领将这一切汇报给了尼禄,当时在场的有波培娅和提盖里努斯,他们是皇帝实施暴行的亲密顾问。尼禄问塞内加是否准备自杀,伽维乌斯·西尔瓦努斯回答道,在塞内加的言谈与表情之中看不出有任何恐惧和悲伤的表情。于是西尔瓦努斯被命令赶回去宣布皇帝对他判处的死刑。依据法比乌斯·路斯提库斯的话来说,他没有按照原来来时的道路返回去,而是绕道到了近卫军长官法伊尼乌斯·路福斯那儿去拜访,他向法伊尼乌斯出示了皇帝的命令,询问他是否应该遵从这一命令。因为命中注定他们都是胆怯的人,所以法伊尼乌斯就告诉他要听从这一命令。因为西

spirators—and now he was adding to the crimes which he had conspired to avenge. But he shirked communicating or witnessing the atrocity. Instead he sent in one of his staff-officers to tell Seneca he must die.

Unperturbed, Seneca asked for his will. But the officer refused. Then Seneca turned to his friends. 'Being forbidden', he said, 'to show gratitude for your services, I leave you my one remaining possession, and my best: the pattern of my life. If you remember it, your devoted friendship will be rewarded by a name for virtuous accomplishments.' As he talked—and sometimes in sterner and more imperative terms—he checked their tears and sought to revive their courage. Where had their philosophy gone, he asked, and that resolution against impending misfortunes which they had devised over so many years? 'Surely nobody was unaware that Nero was cruel!' he added. 'After murdering his mother and brother, it only remained for him to kill his teacher and tutor.'

These words were evidently intended for public hearing. Then Seneca embraced his wife and, with a tenderness very different from his philosophical imperturbability, entreated her to moderate and set a term to her grief, and take just consolation, in her bereavement, from contemplating his well-spent life. Nevertheless, she insisted on dying with him, and demanded the executioner's stroke. Seneca did not oppose her brave decision. Indeed, loving her wholeheartedly, he was reluctant to leave her behind to be persecuted. 'Solace in life was what I commended to you,' he said. 'But you prefer death and glory. I will not grudge your setting so fine an example. We can die

尔瓦努斯是阴谋叛乱者之一,而现在他又要在他一直要阴谋报复的罪行的基础之上增加新的罪行。但是他没有忍心亲口宣布这一死刑并目睹塞内加的死亡,相反,他派遣了其手下的一名百人团长去宣布塞内加的死刑。

塞内加毫无惧色,让人把他的遗嘱拿来。但是这位将领拒绝了这一要求。于是塞内加就转向了他的朋友,说道:"由于无法向你们的服务表示感谢,我就只能把我所拥有的一件,也是最为美好的一件东西留给你们,那就是我的生活方式。假如你们能够将这一方式记住的话,你们那真诚的友谊将会因为道德上的完善而得以赢得声誉。"在演说中,有时他用跟平时一样的语气,有时他用较为严厉的,甚至是强制性的语气说话,他叫他们要收起眼泪,鼓起勇气来。他问他们的哲学理论都到哪儿去了?他们多年来所学到的对付面临的灾难之时应该具有的理智态度到哪里去了?他进一步说:"确实是,无人不知尼禄的残暴,自从杀死了自己的母亲和弟弟之后,对他来说唯一想做的事情就是要杀死自己的老师和监护人。"

很明显,这些话是想让公众们听的。然后,塞内加就拥抱了自己的妻子,并用一种与平时的冷静的语气极度不同的温柔的口气祈求她,要节哀,不要过度悲伤,而只要想到了他那过得富有意义的崇高的一生,这样即使失去了丈夫,也会得到公正的安慰的。然而她无论如何总是坚持要与他一起去死,并要求刽子手将两人一块杀死。塞内加没有再反对她这一勇敢的举动。实际上,由于全身心地爱着她,他也不愿意让她一个人单独留下而遭受迫害。他说:"生活之中我已经为你指明了安慰的办法,但是你宁愿选择死亡和光荣。你想树立一个光辉的榜样,我就不反对了。我们可

with equal fortitude. But yours will be the nobler end. '

Then, each with one incision of the blade, he and his wife cut their arms. But Seneca's aged body, lean from austere living, released the blood too slowly. So he also severed the veins in his ankles and behind his knees. Exhausted by severe pain, he was afraid of weakening his wife's endurance by betraying his agony-or of losing his own selfpossession at the sight of her sufferings. So he asked her to go into another bedroom. But even in his last moments his eloquence remained. Summoning secretaries, he dictated a dissertation. (It has been published in his own words, so I shall refrain from paraphrasing it.)

Nero did not dislike Paulina personally. In order, therefore, to avoid increasing his ill-repute for cruelty, he ordered her suicide to be averted. So, on instructions from the soldiers, slaves and ex-slaves bandaged her arms and stopped the bleeding. She may have been unconscious. But discreditable versions are always popular, and some took a different view—that as long as she feared there was no appeasing Nero, she coveted the distinction of dying with her husband, but when better prospects appeared life's attractions got the better of her. She lived on for a few years, honourably loyal to her husband's memory, with pallid features and limbs which showed how much vital blood she had lost.

Meanwhile Seneca's death was slow and lingering. Poison, such as was formerly used to execute State criminals at Athens, had long been prepared; and Seneca now entreated his experienced doctor

以以同样勇敢的方式去死亡。但是你的死亡将会更加高贵。"

然后,他和他的妻子每人就各用一把小刀割断了自己手臂上的血管。但是塞内加年事已高,而且平素生活俭朴,身躯很虚弱,因此血液往外流淌得很慢。于是他猛烈地将脚踝和膝盖后面的血管都切断了。剧烈的疼痛折磨得他奄奄一息,由于担心他所表现出来的痛苦会使妻子的忍耐力受到削弱,或者担心当自己看到妻子的痛苦之时会使自己受不了,因此,他就请妻子到另一间寝室之中去了。但是,即使是在他的最后时刻,他的口才也依然如故。叫来了秘书之后,他口述了长篇的谈话。他的原话已经公开发表,我就不再赘述了。

对于宝琳娜个人来说,尼禄并没有不喜欢她。为了避免扩大他那残暴的坏名声,因而他下令阻止她的自杀。于是在这位军官的命令之下,奴隶和被释放了的奴隶们包扎住了她的手臂,止住了她的血。或许她早已经不省人事了。但是,在通常情况之下,大家更愿意相信坏的说法,于是一些人提出了不同的见解,认为她在以为尼禄不会饶过她的时候,就选择了与丈夫同归于尽的光荣壮举,但是当情况出现了良好的转机的时候,活下去的愿望又战胜了她原来的想法。她又活了几年,深深怀念着自己的丈夫,对他保持了令人崇敬的忠诚,那苍白无力的面孔和四肢就证明了她的生命力已经衰竭到什么程度了。

与此同时,塞内加的死却是迟缓而久久不能咽气。毒药,例如以前在雅典用来执行城邦法庭所宣判的死罪时所使用的那一种,早就准备好了[1]。于是,塞内加就将一位富有经验的、名字叫安奈乌

---

[1] 这种毒药,就是精选的毒芹。

Annaeus Statius, who was also an old friend, to supply it. But when it came, Seneca drank it without effect. For his limbs were already cold and numbed against the poison's action. Finally he was placed in a bath of warm water. He sprinkled a little of it on the attendant slaves, commenting that this was his libation to Jupiter. Then he was carried into a vapour-bath, where he suffocated. His cremation was without ceremony, in accordance with his own instructions about his death-written at the height of his wealth and power.

It was rumoured that Subrius Flavus and certain company-commanders of the Guard had secretly plotted, with Seneca's knowledge, that when Nero had been killed by Piso's agency Piso too should be murdered, and the throne given to Seneca: it would look as though men uninvolved in the plot had chosen Seneca for his moral qualities. Flavus was widely quoted as saying that, in point of disgrace, it made little difference to remove a lyre-player and replace him by a performer in tragedies. For Nero's singing to the lyre was paralleled by Piso's singing of tragic parts.

But the respite of the army conspirators was at an end. Finding Faenius Rufus' dual role as plotter and inquisitor intolerable, those who had turned informers longed to betray him. So while he pressed and threatened Scaevinus the latter retorted sneeringly that no one was better informed than Faenius himself—he should demonstrate his gratitude voluntarily to his excellent emperor. Words failed Faenius in reply. So did silence; a stammering utterance betrayed his terror. The remaining conspirators, especially the knight Cervarius Proculus, pressed for his conviction. The emperor ordered a soldier named

斯·塔提乌斯的医生请来给自己服食毒药,此人是他的一位老朋友。但是当毒药拿来,塞内加服下之后,一点儿效果也没起。因为他的四肢早已经冰凉了,这就抑制了药性的发挥。最后,他被抬进了一盆热水里面。他把一些水撒在身边服侍的奴隶身上,并说这是向解放者朱庇特神行灌奠之礼。接着他被抬着去洗蒸汽浴,在那儿他窒息而死。依照他在处于财富和权力顶峰时所写下的如何处理他的死亡的指示,在对他的火葬过程之中没有举行任何仪式。

有谣言说,苏布里乌斯·弗拉乌斯和近卫军之中的某一些百人团长在塞内加知悉的情况之下,曾经密谋过,一旦披索一派的人杀死了尼禄,接着就要杀死披索,然后将帝位交给塞内加。这样做就显得好像是塞内加由于他那崇高的道德品性而被一些未卷入这次阴谋叛乱的人推举而坐上宝座的。还广泛传说,弗拉乌斯曾经这样说过,就无耻这一点而论,赶走一个竖琴歌手而用一名悲剧演员来代替他,这两者根本就没有什么区别。因为尼禄弹着竖琴歌唱和披索在悲剧之中的演唱是完全可以相互媲美的。

但是,即使是军队里的那些阴谋叛乱者也面临着灭顶之灾。那些已经背叛了的人发现法伊尼乌斯·路福斯那种既是阴谋叛乱者又做审问者的双重身份时,就渴望出卖他。因此,当法伊尼乌斯在那儿又申斥又恐吓的时候,司凯维努斯却对他嘲笑地反驳道,任何人对于阴谋都没有法伊尼乌斯那样了解得一清二楚,他应该主动地向他的仁慈的皇帝表示感谢。法伊尼乌斯答不上话来,又不能保持沉默。而他那结结巴巴的话又将他的罪行暴露无遗。其他一些还活着的阴谋者,尤其是骑士凯尔瓦里乌斯·普洛库路斯,开始控诉他的罪行。皇帝就命令一名叫卡西乌斯的

Cassius, who was in attendance because of his great physical strength, to seize Faenius and bind him.

The evidence of the same fellow-conspirators next destroyed the Guard colonel Subrius Flavus. His first line of defence was difference of character: a soldier like him would never have shared such an enterprise with these effeminate civilians. But, when pressed, Flavus admitted his guilt, and gloried in it. Asked by Nero why he had forgotten his military oath, he replied: 'Because I detested you! I was as loyal as any of your soldiers as long as you deserved affection. I began detesting you when you murdered your mother and wife and became charioteer, actor, and incendiary!' I have given his actual words because they did not obtain the publicity of Seneca's; yet the soldier's blunt, forceful utterance was equally worth recording. Nothing in this conspiracy fell more shockingly on Nero's ears. For although ready enough to commit crimes, he was unaccustomed to be told about them.

A fellow-colonel, Veianius Niger, was detailed to execute Flavus. But when he ordered a grave to be dug in a field nearby, Flavus objected it was too shallow and narrow. 'More bad discipline,' he remarked to the soldiers in attendance. Then, bidden to offer his neck firmly, he replied: 'You strike equally firmly!' But the executioner, trembling violently, only just severed the head with two blows. However he boasted of his ferocity to Nero, saying he had killed Flavus with 'a stroke and a half!'

Another officer of the Guard, the company-commander Sulpicius

士兵将法伊尼乌斯抓住并捆绑了起来,这位士兵之所以选来做皇帝的侍卫,就因为他体格特别的高大有力。

通过这些同样的阴谋者的作证,接着又搞垮了近卫军将领苏布里乌斯·弗拉乌斯。一开始他用来为自己辩护的是性格上的不同:一个像他这样的军人是不可能参与到这些女人气十足的家伙们的冒险活动之中的。但是,当面临进一步审讯的时候,弗拉乌斯就承认了自己的罪行,并以此为自豪。当尼禄问他为什么将自己所发下的一名军人的誓言给忘记了的时候,他回答道:"因为我恨你。只要你值得拥护,我就会像你的任何一位军人一样对你忠诚。当你杀死了自己的母亲、妻子的时候,当你变成了一个车夫、一名演员、一个纵火犯的时候,我就开始恨你。"我之所以要将弗拉乌斯的原话公布于此,是因为这些话不同于塞内加的话,并没有公之于众。但是一位军人的真诚而又有力的话语同样是值得记录在册的。在这次阴谋叛乱之中,没有什么别的话比这更令尼禄感到刺耳了,因为尽管尼禄敢于做出任何罪恶的行为,但是他却不习惯于被人谈论他所干的勾当。

一个名叫维亚尼乌斯·尼格尔的军队将领奉命去处死弗拉乌斯。但是当尼格尔下令在附近的土地上挖一个墓穴时,弗拉乌斯提出了抗议,嫌它太浅太窄,他向身边的士兵们评论说:"在这儿训练也是更糟糕的了。"然后,当命令将脖子伸直不动的时候,他答复道:"你们的动作也应该同样干脆。"但是浑身抖得厉害的行刑人用了两刀才好不容易将他的头给砍了下来。然而,他却向尼禄夸耀自己的残暴,说自己只用了"一刀半"就将弗拉乌斯给杀死了。

接着,另一名近卫军将领苏尔皮奇乌斯·阿司佩尔,一名百人

Asper, was the next to show exemplary courage. For when Nero asked why he had plotted to kill him, Asper replied that it was the only way to rescue Nero from evil ways. He was convicted and executed. His equals likewise died without disgracing themselves. But Faenius Rufus was less brave-and could not keep lamentations even out of his will.

Nero was also expecting the incrimination of the consul Marcus Julius Vestinus Atticus, whom he regarded as revolutionary and disaffected. But none of the conspirators had confided in Vestinus. Some had longstanding feuds with him; others thought him impetuous and independent. Nero hated him as a result of their intimate association. For Vestinus knew and despised the emperor's worthlessness, while Nero feared this outspoken friend, who made him the butt of crude jokes; when they are based on truth, they rankle. Besides, Vestinus had added a further motive by marrying Statilia Messalina, although he knew her to be one of Nero's mistresses. Yet no accuser came forward, and there was no charge.

So Nero could not assume the judge's role. Accordingly, he behaved like an autocrat instead, and sent a battalion of the Guard. Its commander, Gerellanus, was ordered to forestall the consul's designs, seize his 'citadel', and overpower his picked young followers. For the house where Vestinus lived overlooked the Forum, and he kept handsome slaves, all young. Vestinus had finished his consular duties for the day and was giving a dinner-party-unsuspecting, or pretending

团的团长又树立了一个威武不能屈的范例。因为当尼禄问他为
什么要谋杀他的时候,阿司佩尔回答到,这是能够将尼禄从深重
的罪恶之中解救出来的唯一的办法。他被宣判有罪并被处决了。
他的同级官僚们的死跟他一样都没有玷污自己的人格。但是法
伊尼乌斯·路福斯却没有表现出同样的勇敢,即使在遗嘱里面他
都没有抑制住他的悲伤的情绪。

　　尼禄还想将罪名加在执政官玛尔库斯·尤利乌斯·维司提
努斯·阿提库斯的身上,他认为他是一名造反者而且也不喜欢
他。但是没有一个阴谋者相信维司提努斯。有些人是因为长久
以来就与他不和,而另外一些人则认为他刚愎自用,而且难以相
处。尼禄之所以恨他,是因为他们之间有过亲切的交往。对于维
司提努斯来说,他非常了解和鄙视尼禄的卑鄙,而尼禄则非常害
怕这位直言坦率并经常用粗鲁的玩笑来嘲弄他的朋友。假如这
些玩笑都有事实为依据的话,那么就会激起人的怨恨的。除此之
外,维司提努斯之所以遭到忌恨,还有一个更深的原因,那就是虽
然他知道司塔提里娅·美撒里娜是尼禄的情妇之一,却把她娶了
过来。然而由于没有原告出来指控他,就没法定他的罪。

　　因此,尼禄不能扮演审判官的角色。于是他转而采用专制独
裁的手段,派出一中队卫兵去抓他。这些卫兵的将领叫盖列拉努
斯,他受命去对这位当选执政官采取先发制人的措施,占领其"城
堡",并镇压他手下的一支从年轻人之中挑选出来的追随部队。
原来维司提努斯所居住的房子可以俯视广场,而且他还保留了一
支全部由年轻的英俊奴隶所组成的部队。那一天他处理完了执
政官的公务之后,正在举办晚宴,当士兵们进来告诉他说,他们的
将领要找他有事时,他没有丝毫疑虑,也许是假装的,反正他马

to be-when the soldiers entered and said the commander wanted him. He instantly rose and rapidly initiated all his arrangements. Shutting himself in his bedroom, he called his doctor and had his veins cut. Before the effects were felt, he was carried to a vapour-bath, and plunged into hot water. No word of self-pity escaped him. Meanwhile his dinner-companions were surrounded by Guardsmen and not released until late at night. It amused Nero to picture their expectation of death after dinner. But finally he ruled that they had been punished enough for their consular party.

Then he ordered Lucan to die. When he felt loss of blood numbing his feet and hands, and life gradually leaving his extremities (though his heart was still warm, and his brain clear), Lucan remembered verses he had written about a wounded soldier who had died a similar death. His last words were a recitation of this passage. Claudius Senecio, Afranius Quintianus, and Flavius Scaevinus were the next to die. Their deaths belied their effeminate lives. Then, without memorable words or actions, the remaining conspirators perished.

Executions now abounded in the city, and thank-offerings on the Capitol. Men who had lost their sons, or brothers, or other kinsmen, or friends, thanked the gods and decorated their houses with laurel, and fell before Nero, kissing his hand incessantly. Interpreting this as joy, he pardoned Antonius Natalis and Cervarius Proculus for their prompt information. Milichus was richly compensated, and adopted the Greek word for 'Saviour' as his name. One colonel of the Guard,

上就站了起来,[1]快速地安排好了一切。他把自己关在寝室里,把医生叫了进来将他的血管切断。在没有死亡之前,他被抬到了蒸汽浴室,被投到热水里去,一句自叹自怜的话也没有讲。与此同时,同他一块参加晚宴的客人们,被卫兵们包围了起来,直到深夜才被放回。一想到他们在晚宴之后在不安之中等待丧命的场景,尼禄就高兴得要命。但是,最终他还是宣布这些人为出席了执政官的宴会已经得到了足够的惩罚。

接着他下令处死路卡努斯。当路卡努斯感到了血在流失,手脚开始变凉,生命正逐渐地消失时(尽管心脏还热着,脑子还算清醒),他想起了自己曾经写过的一首诗,里面描写了一个以同样方式死去的士兵的情形。于是他在背诵这些诗句的过程之中死去了。接着,克劳狄乌斯·塞内奇奥、阿弗拉尼乌斯·克温提亚努斯和佛拉维乌斯·司凯维努斯都被处死了。他们的死亡完全不同于他们平时的怯懦表现。那么,至于其他阴谋者的死亡,就没有任何值得回忆的言论和举动了。

现在,城里面到处都有将人处死的景象,而在卡披托里乌姆神庙里则是堆满了献祭之时用的牺牲。那些失去了不论是儿子还是兄弟、还是其他亲人、还是朋友的人们,都在感谢天神,并用月桂花环装饰着他们的房屋,他们跪在了尼禄面前不断地亲吻他的手。尼禄把这些认为是欢乐的表现,因为安托尼乌斯·纳塔里斯和凯尔瓦里乌斯·普洛库路斯及时地将阴谋通报给了他,于是就饶恕了他们。米利库斯因为通风报信而得到了大量的补偿,因而富了起来,并且采用了希腊语"救星"一词作为自己的名字。

---

[1] 罗马人在吃饭时是采用半卧式的,一排卧床围在饭桌的周边。

Gavius Silvanus, was acquitted but killed himself, and another, Statius Proxumus, frustrated the imperial pardon by a melodramatic suicide. Four more, Pompeius, Cornelius Martialis, Flavius Nepos, and Statius Domitius, were deprived of their rank. They did not hate the emperor: but it was believed that they did.

Three unimplicated men, Decimus Novius Priscus, Glitius Gallus and Annius Pollio, were disgraced and exiled-the first of them because he was Seneca's friend. Priscus and Gallus were accompanied by their wives, Artoria Flaccilla and Egnatia Maximilla respectively. Egnatia's departure was to her credit, because her wealth was not confiscated-and its later confiscation did her credit too. Rufrius Crispinus was banished. The ostensible reason was conspiracy, but it was really because Nero hated him as Poppaea's ex-husband. Two more, Verginius Flavus and Gaius Musonius Rufus, went because of their distinction as professors of rhetoric and philosophy. The massive list continues with five more: Cluvidienus Quietus, Julius Agrippa, Blitius Catulinus, Petronius Priscus, and Julius Altinus. They were permitted to live in the Aegean islands. Caesennius Maximus and Caedicia, the wife of Scaevinus, only learnt of their trial when they received their sentence: exclusion from Italy. Lucan's mother, Acilia, was ignored-unacquitted, but unpunished.

When this was all done, Nero addressed the Guard and presented

一个近卫军将领,伽维乌斯·西尔瓦努斯虽然被免了罪,却自杀了;而另一位将领,斯塔提乌斯·普洛克苏木斯尽管被皇帝赦免了,却已感到心灰意冷,因而用一种离奇的手段自杀了。还有四位:彭佩乌斯、科尔涅里乌斯·玛尔提亚里斯、佛拉维乌斯·涅波斯和斯塔提乌斯·多米提乌斯都被免了职。尽管他们没有憎恨皇帝,却有人说他们如此。

而三个与阴谋无关的人:德西姆斯·诺维乌斯·普里斯库斯、格里提乌斯·伽路斯和安尼乌斯·波里欧也受到了屈辱并被放逐了。其中第一个人因为是塞内加的朋友。伴随着普里斯库斯、伽路斯的是他们各自的妻子,她们分别是:阿尔托里娅·佛拉奇拉,埃格纳提娅·玛克西米拉。埃格纳提娅遭驱逐是因为她的声誉,她拥有巨大的财产,一开始还没有没收,但是后来就被没收了,这一切都更加提高了她的声誉。路福里乌斯·克利司披努斯也遭到了驱逐,所谓的参加阴谋只是一个借口,真正的原因则是因为他是波培娅的前夫,因而尼禄憎恨他。还有两个人,即:维尔吉尼乌斯·弗拉乌斯和盖乌斯·穆索尼乌斯·路福斯,他们之所以遭到驱逐则是因为他们分别是杰出的修辞学和哲学的教师,从而具有巨大的声誉。长长的被惩罚者的名单上还有五个人,他们分别是:克路维狄耶乌斯·克维耶图斯、尤利乌斯·阿格里帕、布利提乌斯·卡图里努斯、佩特洛尼乌斯·普利斯库斯和尤利乌斯·阿尔提努斯,他们被驱逐而获准在爱琴海诸岛屿上居住。而司凯维努斯的妻子凯森尼乌斯·玛克西姆斯和凯迪奇娅直到收到了被驱逐出意大利的判决之后才知道她们已经受到了审判。路卡努斯的母亲阿奇里娅则是被忽视了:既没有被赦免,但也没有遭受惩罚。

当这一切都处理完了之后,尼禄对近卫军的士兵进行了犒

each man with two thousand sesterces and free corn (they had hitherto paid the market price). Then, as though to announce a military victory, he summoned the senate and awarded honorary Triumphs to the former consul Publius Petronius Turpilianus, the praetor-designate Marcus Cocceius Nerva, and the commander of the Guard Tigellinus. The two last were also awarded statues in the Palace, as well as triumphal effigies in the Forum. An honorary consulship was bestowed on Nymphidius Sabinus. This is his first appearance, so I must dwell on him for a moment—for he was to be deeply involved in Rome's imminent calamities. His mother was an attractive ex-slave who had hawked her charms among the slaves and freed slaves of emperors. His father, he claimed, was Gaius. For Nymphidius happened to be tall and grim-faced. And it was certainly possible that his mother had taken part in the amusements of Gaius, whose tastes ran to prostitutes.

After his speech in the senate, Nero published an edict appending the statements of the informers and confessions of the convicted. For widespread popular attacks charged him with murdering even innocent men from jealousy or fear. However, the initiation, development, and suppression of the conspiracy are fully documented in reliable contemporary writings; and exiles who returned to Rome after Nero's death told the same story.

In the senate, there was abundant congratulation-especially from those with most to lament. Its manifestations included attacks on Lucius Annaeus Junius Gallio. Terrified by his brother Seneca's death and appealing for his life, Gallio was denounced as a public enemy and

赏,每人奖励了 2000 谢司特尔提乌斯,以及可以免费获得口粮,而在以前他们是按照市场的价格进行购买的。然后,似乎是为了表明获得了一次军事胜利,他召开了元老院会议,在会上将凯旋的荣誉授予了前执政官普布里乌斯·佩特洛尼乌斯·图尔披里亚努斯,当选的行政长官玛尔库斯·科凯乌斯·涅尔瓦以及近卫军长官提盖里努斯。后两者还获得了殊荣,被奖励在皇宫里给他们立雕像以及在广场里给他们树立穿着凯旋服装的像。荣誉执政官的标记被授予了尼姆披狄乌斯·撒比努斯。此人在本书中第一次出现,因此我必须对他做一叙述,因为他还是一个深深地卷入了罗马即将到来的悲剧之中的人物。他的母亲是一个被释放了的奴隶,长相迷人,过去就曾经在皇帝手下的奴隶和被释放了的奴隶之间干卖淫的勾当。尼姆披狄乌斯宣称自己的父亲就是盖乌斯,因为他恰巧也生得身材高大,而且面色阴沉。也许他的母亲曾经跟盖乌斯一道取乐过,因为盖乌斯喜欢寻花问柳。

尼禄在元老院发表了讲话之后,还发布了一道敕令,他在敕令中公布了告发者的供述和被定罪者的认罪状。因为人们在广泛地流传着对他的攻击和指责,说他出于嫉妒和恐惧才大开杀戒,甚至连无辜的人也被杀死。然而,这次叛乱从其发生、发展一直到镇压不但在当时可靠的记录材料之中完全可以得到证实,即使那些在尼禄死后返回罗马的遭受过驱逐的人那里同样也可以证明这次阴谋的存在。

在元老院,到处充满了祝贺之词,尤其是出自那些最为悲伤者之口的贺词最为突出。这些献媚的表现形式包括对路奇乌斯·安奈乌斯·尤尼乌斯·伽里奥的攻击。伽里奥本来就被自己的兄弟塞内加之死吓得胆战心惊,正在设法保全自己的生命,这

parricide. But the prosecutor, Salienus Clemens, had to bow to the senate's unanimous refusal to let him utilize-as it seemed-national misfortunes for private animosities by reviving brutal measures concerning matters settled or dismissed by the clemency of the emperor.

Then thank-offerings were decreed to the gods for miraculously uncovering the conspiracy: and particularly to the Sun-who has an ancient temple in the Circus Maximus (where the crime was planned). The Circus Games of Ceres were to be enlarged by additional horse-races. The month of April was to take Nero's name. A Temple of Welfare was to be constructed, also a memorial in the temple from which Scaevinus had taken the dagger. Nero himself dedicated that weapon on the Capitol, to Jupiter 'Vindex' the Avenger. At the time this went unnoticed. But after the revolt of Gaius Julius Vindex it was interpreted as a sign portending future retribution.

I find in the senate's minutes that the consul-designate Gaius Anicizs Cerealis proposed that a temple should be erected, as a matter of urgency, to the Divine Nero. The proposer meant to indicate that the emperor had transcended humanity and earned its worship. But Nero himself vetoed this in case the malevolent twisted it into an omen of his death. For divine honours are paid to emperors only when they are no longer among men.

时又被控告为国家的公敌和弑亲者。但是对其进行迫害的人撒利耶努斯·克利门斯最后不得不放弃了这一举动,因为元老们一致不同意他这样做。他们指出,这样做似乎是在通过对于皇帝业已宽大处理或取消了的事情上重新采取残酷手段的方式,来利用国难以报私仇。

然后,向诸神举行了感恩和献祭仪式,感谢他们的神力揭露了这场阴谋。特别是向太阳神感恩、献祭。在大竞技场,(也就是计划发动阴谋叛乱的地方),有一座古老的太阳神神庙。纪念凯列司女神的赛马大会另外又增加了比赛的场次。而 4 月这个月份将以尼禄的名字命名。一座纪念幸福女神的神庙又被建立了起来,这儿也是司凯维努斯取得他的匕首的地方。尼禄亲自将这把兵刃献给了卡披托里乌姆神庙,在上面刻上了"献给复仇者朱庇特神"的字样。这件事情在当时并没有引起人们的注意,但是在发生了盖乌斯·尤利乌斯·温代克斯("复仇者")的叛乱之后,就被看成是未来报应的一种征兆了。

我在元老院的议事纪录之中发现,当选执政官盖乌斯·阿尼奇乌斯·凯里亚里斯曾经作过提议,作为一项紧急的事务,应该给圣尼禄建一座神庙。这项提议表明,皇帝已经超凡入圣,赢得了人民的崇拜。但是尼禄本人否决了这一提案,以防那些怀有恶意的人将它曲解为预示皇帝死亡的征兆。因为神圣这一光荣称号只能授予那些已经不在人世的皇帝。

CHAPTER 16

Innocent Victims

But fortune was about to make a fool of Nero. For he credulously believed a lunatic Carthaginian named Caesellius Bassus. This man put faith in a dream, left for Rome, and bribed his way into the emperor's presence. Addressing Nero, he alleged the discovery on his estate of an immensely deep cave containing masses of gold, not in coin but in ancient, unworked bullion. There were ponderous ingots lying about and standing like columns, he said—all hidden centuries ago. His explanation of this windfall from antiquity was this: after her flight from Troy and foundation of Carthage, Phoenician Dido had hidden the treasure in case too much wealth might corrupt her young nation, or the already hostile Numidian kings, coveting the gold, might go to war.

Nero failed to check the man's credibility or to send investigators to confirm its truthfulness. Instead, his imagination exaggerated the report, and he dispatched men to fetch the spoils he believed were lying ready to hand. Warships were allocated, with picked rowers to accelerate their journey. This was the outstanding current subject of conversation. The public were optimistic, sensible people the reverse.

第十六章　无辜的牺牲者

　　但命运还是捉弄了尼禄。他竟然轻易相信了一个精神错乱的迦太基人所作的各种承诺,这个人的名字叫凯谢里乌斯·巴苏斯。他把他在夜里所作的一个梦竟然当作了完全可以实现的事情,于是离开了家来到罗马,他通过贿赂的方式,得到了皇帝的召见。他向尼禄解释说,他在自家的土地里发现了一个非常深的洞,里面存在着大量的黄金,这些黄金都不是金币的形式,而是古时候未经加工的金块。他进一步说,那儿的地面上原来就有沉重的金块,这些黄金堆成了一个个圆柱的样子,所有的黄金都是几个世纪之前埋藏起来的。他对这笔古代留下来的横财是这样解释的:腓尼基人狄多在逃离特洛伊并建立了迦太基之后,就把这些宝藏埋了起来,因为她非常害怕过多的财产会使她那年轻的国家过上奢侈的生活,或者是因为害怕敌对的努米地亚国王觊觎她的黄金而有可能向她发动战争。

　　尼禄没有认真地考虑这个人的报告,也没有派人去调查他所报告的事情本身是否属实。相反,他有意地夸大了这一报告,于是就派人去取这笔他认为是唾手可得的埋藏品。他派了一些战舰,并挑选了一些精壮的划手以加快航行的速度。在当时,这成了一个热门话题。民众们都持乐观的态度,审慎的人则是持相反的态

It happened to be the year of the second five-yearly Neronian Games, and speakers, in their panegyrics of the emperor, made this a leading theme: 'Earth', they said, 'is now producing not only her accustomed crops, not only gold mixed with other substances—she is teeming with a new kind of fertility ! Wealth unsought is sent by the gods!'-and every other invention which eloquent sycophants could devise. They were confident of their imperial listener's credulity.

These vain hopes increased Nero's extravagance. Existing resources were squandered as though the material for many more years of wastefulness were now accessible. Indeed, he already drew on this imaginary treasure for free distributions; his expectation of wealth actually contributed to the national impoverishment. Meanwhile Bassus dug up his ground—and a wide area round about—declaring that this or that was the location of the promised cave. The soldiers accompanied him, together with a horde of rustics engaged to undertake the work. Finally, however, he recovered from his delusion-expressing amazement that, after all his other hallucinations had come true, this one alone had deceived him. He sought escape from his shame and fright in suicide. (According to other sources, he was arrested but soon released, his property however being confiscated in compensation for the imaginary Royal Treasure.)

The five-yearly Games were now close. The senate tried to avert scandal by offering the emperor, in advance, the first prize for song, and also conferred on him a crown 'for eloquence' to gloss over the degradation attaching to the stage. But Nero declared that there was no need for favouritism or the senate's authority; he would compete on equal terms and rely on the conscience of the judges to award him the prize he deserved. First he recited a poem on the stage. Then, when

度。而且这时候恰逢第二届五年一次的尼禄尼亚赛会,而那些演说家们则是把这件事情当作了他们歌颂皇帝的主题,他们说道:"现在大地不仅是在生产常见的谷物,也不仅是在生产同其他金属合到一起的黄金,她又拥有了一种新产品!上天在没有收到祈求的时候就送来了财富!"此外,他们还施展了雄辩的口才,表现了其所有能够做到的阿谀谄媚。他们相信,这个头脑简单的皇帝很轻易就会听信他人的话的。

这些毫无根据的希望加剧了尼禄的奢侈浪费。长时期以来积累起来的财富被浪费得一干二净,因为他相信他会取得另外一笔可供他挥霍多年的财富。实际上,他早已经仗着这笔想象之中的财富来大量赏赐了;他对财富的期盼实际上已经造成了国家的贫困。与此同时,巴苏斯在他自己家的一片宽阔的土地上以及周围的土地上挖着,说这里或那里就是他所说的那个洞穴的地点。跟他在一起的有士兵还有一大群农民,他们是被征召来干这一工作的。然而,他最后还是放弃了自己的梦想,十分吃惊地表示,他的其他所有的梦都变成了现实,唯独这一次欺骗了他。为了避免受辱,他在惊吓之下自杀了。(另一种说法则是,他被关了起来,但不久就被释放了,但是他的财产却被充公了,以补偿他所说的那位女王的财富。)

五年制赛会马上就要举行了。元老院为了掩盖丑闻而提前将胜利的歌曲作为奖赏授予了皇帝,同时还将一项"雄辩演说家"的荣冠奖给了他,以掩饰他登台而必然要发生的耻辱。但是尼禄却宣布,他既不需要他人的偏袒,也不需要元老院的威信来支持他。他将会以平等的身份参与比赛,他要通过裁判员的良心而取得他理应获得的奖赏。开始他在舞台上背诵了一首诗,而

the crowd shouted that he should 'display all his accomplishments' (those were their actual words), he made a second *entrée* as a musician.

Nero scrupulously observed harpists' etiquette. When tired, he remained standing. To wipe away perspiration, he used nothing but the robe he was wearing. He allowed no moisture from his mouth or nose to be visible. At the conclusion, he awaited the verdict of the judges in assumed trepidation, on bended knee, and with a gesture of deference to the public. And the public at least, used to applauding the poses even of professional actors, cheered in measured, rhythmical cadences. They sounded delighted. Indeed, since the national disgrace meant nothing to them, perhaps they were.

But people from remote country towns of austere, old-fashioned Italy, or visitors from distant provinces on official or private business, had no experience of outrageous behaviour; they found the spectacle intolerable. Their unpractised hands tired easily and proved unequal to the degrading task, thereby disorganizing the expert applauders and earning many cuffs from the Guardsmen who, to prevent any momentary disharmony or silence, were stationed along the benches. Numerous knights, it is recorded, were crushed to death forcing their way up through the narrow exits against the crowd. Others, as they sat day and night, collapsed and died. For absence was even more dangerous than attendance, since there were many spies unconcealedly (and more still secretly) noting who was there—and noting whether their expressions were pleased or dissatisfied. Humble offenders received instant punishment. Against important people the grudge was momentarily postponed, but paid later. Vespasian, the story went, nodded somnolently; he was reprimanded by an ex-slave called Phoebus, and only rescued by enlightened intercession. Nor was this the last time he was in peril. But his imperial destiny saved him.

当在场的群众向他高呼"把所有的才艺都表演出来"的时候(这就是当时他们的原话),他便像一位艺人一样再次走上舞台。

尼禄完全按照职业艺人的规则进行表演。即使累了,他也坚持站着。他只用自己穿的长袍擦拭汗水,极力使自己口中的唾沫和鼻涕不被观众看见。最后,他跪了下来,装成惊恐的样子等着裁判员的裁定,并向公众们做出各种致敬的动作。于是公众们用所习惯的欢呼一般职业演员的方式,至少是以整齐而又有节奏的欢呼声祝贺起来。这些人看起来似乎非常高兴,实际上,他们或许真的很高兴,因为他们根本就不关心国家的耻辱。

但是,那些从偏远的、还保持着古老风尚的意大利外地城市来的观众,以及那些来自于遥远的行省以处理公事或私事的人,从来就没有经历过这种狂放的行为,他们感到这种场面是难以容忍的。他们那未经训练的手很快就疲倦了,他们的动作跟那些卑劣的举止不相协调,打乱了那些职业喝彩者的节奏,因此就会遭受到那些安排在长凳上以防止任何时候有可能出现的失去节奏的喝彩以及出现沉默场面的卫兵们的惩罚。据记载,有许多骑士在密集的人群之中挤过狭窄的过道时被挤死。另外一些人,由于整日整夜地坐着,在板凳倒塌之后就死去了。与参加赛会者相比,那些缺席者就更危险了,因为有许多公开的侦探(还有更多的密探),在关注着在场者的名字以及人们的表情是欢乐还是忧郁。下等的冒犯者立刻就会遭到惩罚。至于显要人士则会遭受嫉恨,虽一时不会显露出来,但随后会遭到报复。据传说,维斯帕西亚努斯在看演出时犯了瞌睡,就遭到了一位名叫佩布斯的被释放的奴隶的斥责,只是在许多重要人物的斡旋之下才免于被治罪。对他来说,这也不是最后一次处于险境之中,只是他注定要成就大业的

Soon after the Games Poppaea died. She was pregnant, and her husband, in a chance fit of anger, kicked her. Some writers record that she was poisoned; but this sounds malevolent rather than truthful, and I do not believe it—for Nero wanted children and loved his wife. She was buried in the Mausoleum of Augustus. Her body was not cremated in the Roman fashion, but was stuffed with spices and embalmed in the manner of foreign potentates. At the State funeral, Nero mounted the platform to praise her looks, her parenthood of an infant now deified, and her other lucky assets which could be interpreted as virtues.

Publicly Poppaea's death was mourned. But those who remembered her immorality and cruelty welcomed it. However, Nero's action caused disgust, which was accentuated when he forbade Gaius Cassius Longinus to attend the funeral. This was the first sign of impending trouble: and it came quickly. Lucius Junius Silanus Torquatus (II) became involved. His only offence was to be a respectable young member of the highest nobility; those of Cassius were his remarkable ancestral wealth and outstanding character. Nero wrote to the senate requesting that both should be expelled from public life. He charged Cassius with revering, among the statues of his ancestors, a representation of Gaius Cassius, labelled "Leader of the Cause"— thus planting the seeds of civil war and treason to the house of the Caesars.

But (the emperor added) a hated name was not enough material for revolution, so Cassius had taken on the unbalanced young nobleman Lucius Silanus as the rebellion's figurehead. Then Nero attacked Silanus (as he had earlier attacked his uncle, Decimus Junius Silanus Torquatus) for already allocating imperial responsibilities by designating his ex-slaves Financial Secretary, Petitions Secretary, and

命运拯救了他。

赛会过后,波培娅就死了。她怀有身孕,而她的丈夫由于一次偶然的发火,将她踢倒了。据一些作者的记载她是被毒死的。这似乎是出于恶意而不是出于事实,因而我不相信这一说法。因为尼禄是很想要孩子的,而且也很爱他的妻子。她被安葬在了尤利乌斯家族的陵墓之中。她的尸体并没有按照罗马的传统方式火化,而是按照外国宫廷的惯例塞上香料涂上油膏。在举行国葬的那一天,尼禄登上广场的讲坛,盛赞她的美貌,盛赞她是一位已被列入诸神之中的女婴的母亲,以及其他可以被称之为美德的幸运的资产。

公众们对于波培娅的死表示了哀悼。但是那些知道她的放荡和残忍的人,却是欢迎至极。然而,尼禄的一件行为却招致了众人的憎恨,那就是他禁止盖乌斯·卡西乌斯·朗吉努斯参加这一葬礼。这是灾难的第一个征兆,这一灾难很快就到了。卢奇乌斯·尤尼乌斯·西拉乌斯·托尔克瓦图斯(二世)也卷入其中。西拉乌斯唯一的冒犯之处就在于他受人尊敬、年轻而且出身高贵;而卡西乌斯则在于有一笔巨大的世袭家产和鲜明的个性。尼禄给元老院写了一封信,要求不许他们俩人参加政治活动。他控告卡西乌斯的罪名是:在他所供奉的祖先的雕像之中,有盖乌斯·卡西乌斯的胸像,像上刻着"党派领袖"的字样;而这会播撒内战的种子,背叛恺撒家族。

但是,(皇帝还进一步说)仅仅怀念一个被憎恨的名字还不足以证明他的背叛,他竟然还将一位性格莽撞的年轻贵族卢奇乌斯·西拉乌斯也拉入做他的伙伴,他完全应该承担背叛的罪名。然后,尼禄又攻击西拉努斯(像以前攻击西拉努斯的叔父戴奇姆斯·尤尼乌斯·西拉努斯·托尔克瓦图斯一样),说他已经在通过释

Secretary-General. The charge was fatuous. It was also untrue. For Silanus, besides feeling the effects of the prevalent terror, had been frightened by his uncle's death into extreme caution. Next, so-called informers fabricated against Cassius' wife, Junia Lepida, accusations of black magic and incest with her brother's son—Lucius Silanus. Two senators, Volcacius Tertullinus and Cornelius Marcellus, and a knight, Gaius Calpurnius Fabatus, were charged with complicity. But they avoided imminent condemnation by appealing to Nero. For he was preoccupied with important crimes, and they were eventually saved by their insignificance.

For Cassius and Silanus, the senate decreed banishment. Concerning Junia Lepida the emperor was to decide. Cassius was deported to Sardinia, where old age was left to do its work. Silanus was first removed to Ostia, with Naxos as his supposed destination; but he was instead confined in the Apulian country town of Barium. There, as he philosophically endured his thoroughly undeserved misfortune, a company-commander of the Guard was sent to kill him. Seized and told to open his veins, he answered that he was ready to die but would not excuse his assassin the glorious duty. The officer, however, noting that though unarmed he was very strong and far from intimidated, ordered his men to overpower him. Silanus did not fail to resist, hitting back as much as his bare hands allowed. Finally the commander's sword struck him down, and he fell, wounded in front, as in battle.

Lucius Antistius Vetus, and his mother-in-law Sextia and daughter Antistia Pollitta, died just as courageously. All three appeared detest-

放奴隶来掌管财务大臣、通信大臣、文书总管的方式在分配帝国的职务。这一指控太荒唐了，与事实毫不相符。对于西拉努斯来说，除了已经感觉到了当前的恐怖状况之外，他还一直受他叔父之死的惊吓，因而对任何事情都非常小心谨慎。接着，那些所谓的告密者又被带到了元老院，对西拉努斯的妻子尤尼娅·列庇妲进行了控告，指控她使用了巫术，并且与其内侄卢奇乌斯·西拉乌斯发生了奸情。元老院的两名元老乌尔卡其乌斯·图利努斯和科尔涅利乌斯·马尔凯路斯和一名叫盖乌斯·卡尔普尔尼乌斯·法巴图斯的骑士被检举共同谋反。但是由于他们求救于尼禄而免于定罪。尼禄说他们所犯罪行不太严重，最终他们就获救了。

对于卡西乌斯和西拉努斯，元老院判处了流放。对于尤尼娅·列庇妲的案件由皇帝亲自来裁断。卡西乌斯被流放到了撒丁尼亚岛上，任凭他老死在那里。西拉努斯则被放逐到了奥斯蒂亚，似乎将纳克索斯作为最终的流放地；但是他最终被囚禁在阿普里亚一个名叫巴里乌姆的小城里。在那里他利用他的哲学信念坚持忍受着这不白之冤，而一位百人团团长则被派到那儿去刺杀他。当他被擒并被命令割断自己脉管的时候，他回答道，对于死他早已做好了准备，但是绝不容许凶手来执行这一光荣的任务。这位团长注意到尽管对方手无寸铁，但是体格健壮，而且面对死亡毫无畏惧之色，于是他命令其手下的士兵们制服西拉努斯。西拉努斯没有放弃抵抗，使尽了全力以赤手空拳进行还击。最终百人团长用剑将他击倒，他像在战场上前线作战那样因身受重伤而倒下了。

路奇乌斯·安提司提乌斯·维图斯及其岳母塞克司提娅和他的女儿安提司提娅·波利塔，也同样勇敢地死去了。这三个人

able to the emperor as living reproaches for his murder of Vetus' so-nin-law, Rubellius Plautus. A chance for Nero to display his brutality was afforded by a former slave of Vetus named Fortunatus. This person, after stealing his patron's money, turned accuser, mobilizing an individual named Claudius Demianus who had been imprisoned for criminal actions by Vetus during his governorship of Asia but subsequently released by Nero as a reward for this accusation. When Vetus heard this, and knew he had to face the ex-slave on equal terms, he withdrew to his estate at Formiae, under secret military surveillance.

With him was his daughter. Besides the imminent peril, she was embittered by sorrow. This had lasted unceasingly ever since she had seen her husband Rubellius Plautus assassinated. She had clasped his bleeding neck, and kept his bloodstained clothes-an unkempt widow grieving incessantly, eating barely enough to stay alive. Now, at her father's plea, she went to Neapolis. Refused access to Nero, she lay in wait for him at the door. When he came, she entreated him to hear an innocent man, and not surrender his former fellow-consul to a man who had been a slave. She cried like a woman. She also screamed in unwomanly fury. But appeals and reproaches alike left the emperor cold.

So she sent her father word to abandon hope and accept the inevitable. Simultaneously there came forewarning of a trial in the senate, and a harsh verdict. Some advised Vetus to name the emperor as his principal heir, thus securing the residue for his grandchildren. But he

都是皇帝所讨厌的,因为他们的存在就意味着对他杀死维图斯的女婿路贝里乌斯·普劳图斯的指责。以前是维图斯的一个奴隶,名字叫佛尔图那图斯的人给尼禄提供了一个展示其凶残的机会。此人在偷窃了主人的钱财之后,现在却摇身一变成为了控告者,并且动员一个名叫克劳狄乌斯·德米亚努斯的人来做他的帮凶。他在维图斯担任亚细亚总督时曾经由于犯下了罪行而被维图斯关押了起来,但随后却被尼禄释放了,作为他提出控告的补偿。当维图斯得知这一消息之后,他知道他要同他以前的奴隶在平等的地位上进行诉讼,他便回到了他在佛尔米埃的别墅,并受到了军队的暗中监视。

跟他在一起的是他的女儿。除了面临的危险之外,她还陷入深深的伤痛之中。自从她眼见其丈夫路贝里乌斯·普劳图斯被谋杀的那一天开始,这种伤痛就没有停止过。当时她抱着他流血的脖子,并一直保存着他那沾满鲜血的袍子。她毫不打扮的过着寡妇的生活,没有一点儿慰藉,而进食也几乎不能维持生命。现在,在她父亲的恳求之下,她到了那不勒斯,在拜见尼禄的请求被拒绝之后,她就在门口躺在地下等他。当他出来的时候,她就向他呼吁,希望他能够倾听一位无辜者的申诉,而不要使一个曾经和他一起担任过执政官的同僚被一个以前曾经是奴隶的人所毁掉。她像一位妇女一样哭泣,又用男子一样的口吻进行威胁。但是皇帝对她的请求和斥责全都无动于衷。

于是她让人给她父亲传话,说事情已经没有希望了,只能准备一死了。与此同时,又传来了消息,说元老院正在安排一次审讯,将会做出严厉的判决。有些人建议维图斯将皇帝作为主要的财产继承人,这样做就可以保证他的子孙能得到剩余的一些家产。但是

scorned to spoil what had mostly been a life of freedom by servility at its close. So he distributed his ready cash among his slaves, and bade them remove everything portable for themselves, keeping only three couches for the end.

Then, in one room, with a single weapon, all three of them— Vetus, his mother-in-law, and his daughter—opened their veins. Wearing a single garment each for decency's sake, they were hastily carried into the bath. The young woman gazed long at her father and grandmother, and they at her. All three prayed to cease their feeble breathing speedily and be the first to die—but not be long outlived. Fate observed the right order. First the two eldest perished, then the young Antistia. After burial, they were denounced, and condemned to punishment in the ancient fashion. Nero intervened, allowing them to die unsupervised. But this farce was subsequent to their deaths.

A knight called Publius Gallus was outlawed for being on good terms with Vetus as well as a close friend of Faenius Rufus. The ex-slave who had preferred the charge against Vetus was rewarded by a seat in the theatre among the attendants of the tribunes. The names of the months following 'Neroneus'—otherwise April—were changed. May became 'Claudius', June 'Germanicus'. According to the o-riginator of the proposal, Servius Cornelius Orfitus by name, the latter change was necessary because the execution of two Junii Torquati had made the name 'June' ill-omened.

他一生自由,在临终之时却要被他的奴隶污陷,并要奴颜婢膝地结束生命,对此他极为蔑视。于是,他把他可以动用的所有的钱都分给了他的奴隶,而且让他们把一切可以搬动的东西都拿去使用,只留下了三张床供临终之时使用。

然后,在一间房子里,维图斯、他的岳母以及他的女儿三个人全部用唯一的一件兵器切断了自己的脉管;他们被匆匆地抬进了浴室,而为了体面的原因,每个人都被裹进了一件外袍里。这位年轻的妇女一直在望着他的父亲和外祖母,而他俩也在望着她。三个人都在祈祷着尽快结束他们那越来越微弱的生命,使自己早死,而不要使这段时间太长以至于比另外两者晚结束生命。命运安排了适当的次序:两位老者先过世了,然后才是年轻的波利塔。埋葬之后,他们受到了起诉,并宣判以古老的方式予以惩罚。尼禄进行了干预,允许他们在不受监视的情况之下死去。不过这一幕喜剧是在他们死后才上演的。

一位名叫普布里乌斯·伽路斯的骑士被剥夺了公民权,原因就是他同维图斯以及法伊尼乌斯·路福斯保持了亲密的朋友关系。控告维图斯的那位被释放了的奴隶受到了奖赏,他在剧场之内在将领侍从们的座位之中被赐予了一个座位。4月也被称之为"尼禄尼乌斯月",这之后的各月都重新改了名字。5月为"克劳狄乌斯月",6月为"日尔曼尼库斯月"[1] 这一建议的提议者名字叫塞尔维乌斯·科尔尼利乌斯·奥尔菲图斯,根据他的解释,之所以将6月("June")的名字改掉,是因为两个尤尼乌斯·托尔克瓦图斯已经

---

[1] 这些名字都是属于尼禄本人的,因为他的全名就是克劳狄乌斯·恺撒·日耳曼尼库斯。

Heaven, too, marked this crime-stained year with tempest and pestilence. Campania was ravaged by a hurricane which destroyed houses, orchards, and crops over a wide area and almost extended its fury to the city. At Rome, a plague devastated the entire population. No miasma was discernible in the air. Yet the houses were full of corpses, and the streets of funerals. Neither sex nor age conferred immunity. Slave or free, all succumbed just as suddenly. Their mourning wives and children were often cremated on the very pyres by which they had sat and lamented. Senators and knights were not spared. But their deaths seemed less tragic; for by dying like other men they merely seemed to be forestalling the emperor's bloodthirstiness.

In this year the Roman army in the Illyrian provinces, weakened by discharges due to age and unfitness, was replenished by recruiting in Narbonese Gaul, Africa, and Asia.

A disastrous fire at Lugdunum was alleviated by an imperial gift of four million sesterces to repair the town's damage-the same sum as its people had contributed to Rome's similar misfortunes.

When, in the following year, Gaius Suetonius Paulinus and Gaius Luccius Telesinus became consuls, Antistius Sosianus, who, as I have mentioned, was in exile for writing offensive poems about Nero, noted the rewards paid to informers and the emperor's readiness for bloodshed. A restless opportunist by nature, he utilized the similarity of their fortunes to make friends with a fellow-exile at the same place, called Pammenes. The latter's fame as an astrologer had won him many

使"尤尼乌斯"[1]这一名字不吉利了。

这一年,上天也被这些可耻的犯罪行为激怒了,降以暴风雨和疾病。康帕尼亚遭到了旋风的袭击,将大范围内的房屋、牧场以及农田毁坏了,并且几乎将它的威力扩展到城里。在罗马,一场瘟疫夺去了各个阶层的大批人的生命。空中看不出任何瘴气的迹象,而房子里到处都堆满了尸体,街上处处在忙着埋葬。任何年龄、任何性别的人都难以幸免于难。奴隶和自由人同样突然就倒毙了。死者悲伤的妻子和儿女们往往在哀悼的时候由于传染上瘟疫倒下,也和他们一起在同一堆柴火上火化了。元老和骑士们也不能幸免,但是他们的死亡看起来并没有那么悲惨;因为他们即使和他人一样地死去,似乎却能够躲过皇帝血腥的手掌。

这一年,在驻扎在伊里利库姆行省的罗马军队中,许多因为年老或有病而丧失作战能力的人都退役了,为了补充,就在纳尔波尼斯高卢、阿非利加、亚细亚进行了征兵。

为了安慰路格杜努姆的火灾,皇室拨给了 400 万谢司特尔提乌斯,以补偿该城的损失。这笔钱恰好等于以前该城的人民为援助受灾的罗马而提供的那笔钱。

第二年,[2]在盖乌斯·苏埃托尼乌斯·波利努斯和盖乌斯·路克奇乌斯·提列西努斯担任执政官的一年里,我前面所提及的由于写作侮辱尼禄的诗而遭到驱逐的安提司提乌斯·索西亚努斯得知了告密者所能取得的荣誉和皇帝喜欢血腥屠杀的情况。这个生性

---

[1] 因为在拉丁语之中 6 月为"Junius"(尤尼乌斯)。
[2] 罗马建城 819 年,即公元 66 年。

friends. Sosianus noted that messengers were continually arriving to consult him—and deduced that there must be a purpose behind their visits.

He also learnt that Pammenes received an annual subsidy from Publius Anteius. Nero hated Anteius (Sosianus knew) as a friend of Agrippina, and might well covet his wealth—a frequent cause of fatalities. Sosianus therefore intercepted a letter from Anteius. He also stole from Pammenes' secret files documents giving Anteius' horoscope and destiny. He likewise found there papers relating to the birth and life of Marcus Ostorius Scapula. Then he wrote to the emperor, intimating that, if he were granted a brief respite from his banishment, he would bring information vital to Nero's safety. For Anteius and Ostorius, he said, were studying their own and the emperor's destinies—and thus imperilling the empire.

Fast ships were immediately sent, and Sosianus was soon there. When his denunciation became known, Anteius and Ostorius were regarded less as defendants than as persons already condemned. Indeed, no one would witness Anteius' will until Tigellinus sanctioned this-after warning the testator to complete the formalities speedily. Anteius took poison, but impatient with its slowness obtained a quicker death by cutting his veins.

Ostorius was at the time at a remote estate on the Ligurian border. There a staff-officer of the Guard was dispatched to kill him rapidly. The reason for this haste was Nero's fear of a personal attack. Always cowardly, he was more terrified than ever since the recently discovered conspiracy. Besides, Ostorius was of huge physique and an expert with weapons-his distinguished military record included the oak-

不安分而又喜欢投机的人就利用了相同的命运这一点,同一个也是被驱逐到当地的,名叫帕姆梅尼斯的人结为了朋友。后者因为是占星术士,所以结交了许多朋友。索西亚努斯注意到有许多使者不断来向他请教,就认定在他们拜访的背后肯定隐藏着秘密。

他还得知,帕姆梅尼斯每年都要接收到来自普布里乌斯·安泰乌斯的一笔钱。(索西亚努斯知道)尼禄憎恨安泰乌斯,因为他曾经是阿格里披娜的好朋友,或许是因为觊觎他的财富,而这是许多人丧命的原因。于是,索西亚努斯截获了安泰乌斯的一封信,还从帕姆梅尼斯的文件夹里偷取了记载有安泰乌斯星命和流年的文件。同时,他还在这些文件之中发现了有关玛尔库斯·欧司托里乌斯·司卡普拉的生辰和流年的一些记载。于是他就向皇帝写信,请求说,假如给他一些简短的期限让他从流放地赶回来,他就会带回对尼禄的安全至关重要的一些消息。他说,安泰乌斯和欧司托里乌斯正在占卜他们自己和皇帝的命运,因此会危及整个帝国。

快船马上就被调派去,索西亚努斯很快就赶到了罗马。当他的指控被他人知道后,人们都认为安泰乌斯和欧司托里乌斯就不仅仅是受到了控告,而是已经被判了刑。结果是,直到提盖里努斯预先通知立遗嘱人赶忙办完最后的手续,并批准了这一行动的时候,才有人愿意给安泰乌斯的遗嘱签字作证。安泰乌斯服了毒药,但是他嫌毒性太慢,又切断了自己的脉管以求速死。

此时,欧司托里乌斯正在遥远的利古里亚边界地区的一幢别墅里。有一名百人团长被派去速速将他处死。之所以这么匆忙就因为尼禄害怕遭受个人攻击。他一直比较怯懦,而自从最近发

wreath for saving a citizen's life in Britain. The officer arrived; and closing every exit from the house, he told Ostorius of the emperor's orders. The courage he had often demonstrated against the enemy Ostorius turned upon himself. Because his veins, when opened, let the blood out too slowly, he ordered a slave to hold up his hand firmly with a dagger in it—nothing more. Then Ostorius pulled the slave's hand on to his own throat.

Even if I were describing foreign wars and patriotic deaths, this monotonous series of events would have become tedious both for me and for my readers. For I should expect them to feel as surfeited as myself by the tragic sequence of citizen deaths—even if they had been honourable deaths. But this slavish passivity, this torrent of wasted bloodshed far from active service, wearies, depresses, and paralyses the mind. The only indulgence I would ask the reader for the inglorious victims is that he should forbear to censure them. For the fault was not theirs. The cause was rather heaven's anger with Rome-and not an isolated burst of anger such as could be passed over with a single mention, as when armies are defeated or cities captured. And let us at least make this concession to the reputation of famous men: just as in the manner of their burial they are distinguished from the common herd, so when their deaths are mentioned let each receive his separate, permanent record.

Within a few days there fell, one after another, Annaeus Mela, Gaius Anicius Cerealis, Rufrius Crispinus, and Petronius. Mela and Crispinus were Roman knights who enjoyed the status of senators.

现了阴谋之后,他更加惊恐万状了。而且,欧司托里乌斯身躯高大,善于使用各种兵器,他在军事上有相当高的威望,并在不列颠获得过公民荣冠。[1] 百人团长赶到之后,就封锁了别墅的所有出口,并向欧司托里乌斯宣读了皇帝的命令。欧司托里乌斯表现出了他过去常常在敌人面前所表现出来的勇敢。他切断脉管之后发现鲜血流得太慢,就命令一个奴隶紧紧地握住一把匕首,其他什么事情都不用做,然后欧司托里乌斯抓住奴隶的手刺向了自己的喉咙。

即使我所描述的是对外战争和为共和国献身的事迹,对于这些事件的千篇一律的叙述,我以及我的读者们也都会感到厌倦的。因为我能够想象得出他们和我一样已经过多地听到了罗马人接二连三地悲惨死去的故事,尽管那些人也许是勇敢地死去的。但是,这种奴才式的忍耐以及容忍白白流血而不采取反抗的行动,会使人的思想感到厌倦、压抑以及麻木。我唯一请求读者原谅的是,请他们允许我谅解那些死得如此卑怯的人。因为这不是他们的过错,而是上天恼怒于罗马的结果:这跟军队被战败或城市被攻占之时的情况不同,对于上天怒火的发作,是不能一次就解释清楚的。最起码让我们把这一特权给予那些显贵家族的后代吧,正如他们的殡仪和普通民众的不同一样,因此当提及他们的死亡之时,就让他们每一个人都取得并保持住自己的纪录吧。

仅仅在几天之内,相继死去的有安奈乌斯·梅拉、盖乌斯·阿尼奇乌斯·凯里亚里斯、路福里乌斯·克里司披努斯和佩特洛尼乌斯。其中梅拉和克里司披努斯还是罗马骑士,他们

---

〔1〕 拯救了罗马公民性命的人就可以获得公民荣冠。

The latter, formerly commander of the Guard-and an honorary consul-but recently exiled to Sardinia on a charge of conspiracy, received the order to die, and committed suicide. Mela, brother of Seneca and of Lucius Annaeus Junius Gallio, had refrained from seeking office owing to his perverse ambition to achieve a consul's influence while remaining a knight. He had also seen a shorter road to wealth in becoming an agent handling the emperor's business. The fact that he was Lucan's father greatly enhanced his reputation. But after his son's death Mela called in Lucan's debts so harshly that one of the latter's intimate friends, Fabius Romanus, denounced him, fabricating a charge that father and son had shared complicity in the plot. The evidence was a forged letter from Lucan, which Nero examined: then he sent it to Mela, whose wealth he coveted.

Mela died in the fashionable way, opening his veins. First, however, he recorded large bequests to Tigellinus and the latter's son-in-law Cossutianus Capito-hoping to save the residue. He added a postscript protesting against his unfair fate, and contrasting his undeserved death with the survival of Crispinus and Cerealis, the emperor's enemies. But the postscript was regarded as a fabrication, Crispinus figuring because capital punishment had already been inflicted on him, and Cerealis to ensure its infliction. Soon afterwards Cerealis duly committed suicide—less pitied than the rest, because he was remem-

都享有元老级别的待遇。[1] 后者以前曾经担任过禁卫军的统帅，以及名誉执政官，但是近来却由于被指控犯有阴谋罪而被驱逐到了撒丁尼亚，他在收到被判死刑的命令之后就自杀了。梅拉是塞内加和路奇乌斯·安奈乌斯·尤尼乌斯·伽里奥的亲兄弟，以前曾经拒绝寻求官职，因为他有一个荒唐的野心，那就是尽管是一个骑士的身份却想取得一个执政官的影响。他还看到了一个聚集财富的捷径，就是担任为皇帝处理私事的代理官。而他作为路卡努斯父亲的这一事实又大大地提高了他的声望。在他的儿子死后，梅拉以严厉的手段追缴路卡努斯的债务，致使后者的一位亲密朋友，名叫法比乌斯·洛玛努斯的人捏造了一项罪名来控告他，法比乌斯编织了一项罪名说父亲和儿子都参加过阴谋，并且编造了路卡努斯的一封信作为证明。尼禄早就觊觎梅拉的财富，于是在检查了这封信之后，就派人给他送去。

于是梅拉切断了自己的脉管，用一种流行的方法死去了。但是，在这之前他曾经写下遗言，要把一大笔钱赠给提盖里努斯和他的女婿科苏提亚努斯·卡皮托，想以此来保住剩余的财产。在遗言中，他加了一个附录对他所受到的不公正遭遇表示了抗议，与他无辜的死亡相比，皇帝的敌对者路福里乌斯·克里司披努斯和阿尼奇乌斯·凯里亚里斯却还活着。但是这一附录被认为是伪造的，因为就克里司披努斯来说，他早已经被处死了；而对于凯里亚里斯来说，肯定也会遭受这一处罚的。果然不久之后凯里亚

---

〔1〕 安奈乌斯·梅拉、路福里乌斯·克里司披努斯都是骑士，虽然不是元老，却能够与元老院的成员们并列，因为他们具备了元老院的财产资格要求。

bered to have betrayed a conspiracy to Gaius.

Petronius deserves a brief obituary. He spent his days sleeping, his nights working and enjoying himself. Others achieve fame by energy, Petronius by laziness. Yet he was not, like others who waste their resources, regarded as dissipated or extravagant, but as a refined voluptuary. People liked the apparent freshness of his unconventional and unselfconscious sayings and doings. Nevertheless, as governor of Bithynia and later as consul, he had displayed a capacity for business.

Then, reverting to a vicious or ostensibly vicious way of life, he had been admitted into the small circle of Nero's intimates, as Arbiter of Taste: to the blase emperor nothing was smart and elegant unless Petronius had given it his approval. So Tigellinus, loathing him as a rival and a more expert hedonist, denounced him on the grounds of his friendship with Flavius Scaevinus. This appealed to the emperor's outstanding passion—his cruelty. A slave was bribed to incriminate Petronius. No defence was heard. Indeed, most of his household were under arrest.

The emperor happened to be in Campania. Petronius too had reached Cumae; and there he was arrested. Delay, with its hopes and fears, he refused to endure. He severed his own veins. Then, having them bound up again when the fancy took him, he talked with his friends-but not seriously, or so as to gain a name for fortitude. And he listened to them reciting, not discourses about the immortality of the soul or philosophy, but light lyrics and frivolous poems. Some slaves received presents—others beatings. He appeared at dinner, and dozed, so that his death, even if compulsory, might look natural.

里斯就正式自杀了。他的死所得到的同情要比其他死者少,因为人们并没有忘记他曾经向盖乌斯揭发过一次阴谋。

对于佩特洛尼乌斯,我们有必要作一个简短的回顾。他白天睡觉,晚上却处理公务和享受生活。其他人是通过勤奋而获得名声的,佩特洛尼乌斯却由于懒惰而闻名。其他一些纨绔子弟被看作是放荡而又奢侈浪费,而他与他们不同,他被认为是一位精于享乐之道的人。他不拘小节,言行放荡不羁,但其质朴的表现却引起了人们的好感。虽然如此,在他担任比提尼亚总督以及后来担任执政官期间,却展示了其处理公务的高超的能力。

后来,由于染上了做坏事的生活习惯,或者是模仿做坏事的生活习惯,他就钻进了尼禄亲信之中的小圈子,成了尼禄的风雅顾问。对这位已经玩腻了的皇帝来说,只有在佩特洛尼乌斯所称赞的东西里才能发现一点漂亮和优雅的东西。提盖里努斯非常嫉妒他,因为他是一个明显的对手,而且在享乐方面更具专业性。于是提盖里努斯指控他同弗拉乌斯·司凯维努斯结交了朋友。这就激起了皇帝的主导情绪:他的残忍凶暴。佩特洛尼乌斯的一个奴隶被收买指控了他,他没有获得任何辩护的机会,而且同时他的家人大部分也被捕了。

皇帝偶然来到了康帕尼亚。佩特洛尼乌斯也到了库麦,在那里他被逮捕了。佩特洛尼乌斯不愿意再在希望和恐惧之中拖延时日了,他切断了自己的脉管。然后他突发奇想,又将它们包扎了起来,开始与他的朋友们轻松地交谈起来,看来或许是为了获取坚定地面对死亡的美誉。他听他们的朗诵,内容不是有关灵魂不朽的对话,也不是有关哲学的对话,而是轻松的抒情歌曲和轻薄的诗章。一些奴隶收到了礼物,其他一些则遭到了责打。他参加了晚宴,并打了一个盹,因此他的死尽管是由于强迫的,但看起来却像是寿终正寝。

Even his will deviated from the routine death-bed flatteries of Nero, Tigellinus, and other leaders. Petronius wrote out a list of Nero's sensualities—giving names of each male and female bed-fellow and details of every lubricious novelty—and sent it under seal to Nero. Then Petronius broke his signet-ring, to prevent its subsequent employment to incriminate others. Nero could not imagine how his nocturnal ingenuities were known. He suspected Silia, a woman of note (she was a senator's wife) who knew all his obscenities from personal experience—and was a close friend of Petronius. For breaking silence about what she had seen and known, she was exiled. Here the grievance was Nero's own. It was to Tigellinus' malevolence, however, that he sacrificed a former praetor, Minucius Thermus (Ⅱ). A freed slave made criminal charges against this man; the ex-slave's penalty was torture, the patron's an undeserved death.

After the massacre of so many distinguished men, Nero finally coveted the destruction of Virtue herself by killing Thrasea and Marcius Barea Soranus. He had long hated them both. Against Thrasea there were additional motives. He had, as I mentioned, walked out of the senate during the debate about Agrippina. He had also been inconspicuous at the Youth Games. This gave all the more offence because during Games (the festival instituted by Antenor the Trojan) at his birthplace, Patavium, he had participated by singing in tragic costume. Besides, on the day when the praetor Antistius Sosianus was virtually condemned to death for writing offensive verses about Nero, he had proposed and carried a more lenient sentence. Again,

　　甚至是他的遗嘱也同一般自杀者对尼禄、提盖里努斯和其他统治者们所进行的谄媚方式不相同。佩特洛尼乌斯在遗嘱中详细列举了尼禄的淫荡行为和他所采取的每种淫行的新花样,而在其中首先是把各个陪床的娈童和女人的名字标出来,并在盖章之后将这一文件交给了尼禄。然后佩特洛尼乌斯将自己的图章戒指毁坏了,以防止这东西后来可能给别人带来麻烦。尼禄想不明白为什么自己在夜间的那些丑事会公之于众。他怀疑西里娅,这个女人颇有名望(她是一个元老的妻子),此人与尼禄发生过肉体关系而且知道他所有的纵欲方式,她还是佩特洛尼乌斯的好友。由于不能对所见所闻的事情保守秘密,她便遭到了驱逐。这是出于尼禄自己的不满。然而,出于他的忌恨,尼禄就将其前行政长官米努奇乌斯·提尔穆斯(二世)处死了。提尔穆斯的一个被释放了的奴隶对提盖里努斯进行了一些罪行指控,这位被释放的奴隶遭到了严刑拷打,而其主人则被无辜处死。

　　在屠杀了如此多的显要人物之后,尼禄最后想将道德本身完全毁灭,因为他竟然要杀死特拉塞亚·帕伊图斯和玛尔奇乌斯·巴里埃·索拉努斯。长久以来,他一直憎恨他们。而他对特拉塞亚的憎恨还有其他原因。正如我所提及的那样,在讨论阿格里披娜问题的过程中,特拉塞亚曾经走出过元老院。他对于参加青年节也一直不热心。下一个事件使尼禄感到受到了更大的冒犯,因为在特拉塞亚的故乡帕塔维乌姆所举行的竞赛节日之中(由特洛伊人安提诺尔过去所发起),特拉塞亚竟然穿着悲剧的服装演唱。除此之外,当行政长官安提司提乌斯由于写诗讽刺尼禄而被

after Poppaea's death, he had deliberately stayed away when divine honours were voted to her, and was not present at her funeral.

Cossutianus Capito kept these memories fresh. For that criminal bore Thrasea a grudge for helping a Cilician deputation to convict him for extortion. So now Capito added further charges: 'At the New Year, Thrasea evaded the regular oath. Though a member of the Board of Fifteen for Religious Ceremonies, he absented himself from the national vows. He has never sacrificed for the emperor's welfare or his divine voice. Once an indefatigable and invariable participant in the senate's discussions—taking sides on even the most trivial proposal - now, for three years, he has not entered the senate. Only yesterday, when there was universal competition to strike down Lucius Junius Silanus Torquatus (II) and Lucius Antistius Vetus, he preferred to take time off helping his dependants.

'This is party-warfare against the government. It is secession. If many more have the same impudence, it is war. As this faction-loving country once talked of Caesar versus Cato, so now, Nero, it talks of you versus Thrasea. And he has his followers—or his courtiers rather. They do not yet imitate his treasonable voting. But they copy his grim and gloomy manner and expression: they rebuke your amusements. He is the one man to whom your safety is immaterial, your talents unadmired. He dislikes the emperor to be happy. But even your unhappiness, your bereavements, do not appease him. Disbelief in Poppaea's divinity shows the same spirit as refusing allegiance to the acts of the divine Augustus and divine Julius. Thrasea rejects religion, abrogates law.

'In every province and army the official Gazette is read with special

判处死刑之时,他却建议并通过了一项较轻微的处罚。还有,当波培娅死后,元老院投票决定要授予她死后的荣誉之时,他却有意离开了,在她的葬礼上他也没有露面。

克苏提亚努斯·卡皮托经常不断地向尼禄提及这些事情。他生性就带着犯罪的因素,他十分忌恨特拉塞亚,因为特拉塞亚曾经利用自己的影响帮助奇里奇亚人指控他的勒索行为,而且被定了罪。于是卡皮托提出了更加严重的指控:"在新年初,特拉塞亚没有参加例行的宣誓;他虽然是15人祭祀团的一名成员,却缺席全国发愿的祭奠;他从来就没有为皇帝的幸福和神圣的嗓音做出过任何牺牲;过去他对于元老院之中所做出的哪怕是琐碎的决定,都积极参与争论,总是明确表示自己的赞同或反对的意见,但现在他已经三年没有来元老院了;就是在昨天,当元老们一致争取击败路奇乌斯·尤尼乌斯·西拉努斯托尔库瓦图斯(二世)和路奇乌斯·安提斯提乌斯·维图斯的时候,他却选择抽出时间以帮助其食客。

"现在已发展到党派林立、与政府公然为敌、搞分裂的局面了。假如许多人都这样胆大妄为的话,就意味着战争了。正如这个经常发生内乱的国家过去所谈论的是恺撒对加图,那么现在,尼禄呀,人们所谈论的便是你本人对特拉塞亚了。而且他有他的追随者,或者说是他的臣仆。虽然这些人还没有模仿他的与他人相左的作风,但是他们很欣赏他的严厉、忧郁的风采以及容貌,目的就在于谴责你的放荡。他是一个不关心你的安全、不尊重你的天才能力的人。他不希望皇帝获得幸福;即使是你遇到了不幸,遭受了痛苦,他都感到不解恨。不相信波培娅是神,这就体现出了跟拒绝向圣奥古斯都和圣尤利乌斯的法令宣誓效忠一样的精神。他拒绝宗教信仰,废除了法律。

"在每一个行省和全体军队之中,人们都特别仔细地阅读官

care-to see what Thrasea has refused to do. If his principles are better, let us adopt them. Otherwise, let us deprive these revolutionaries
of their chief and champion. This is the school which produced men
like Quintus Aelius Tubero and Marcus Favonius-unpopular names e-
ven in the old Republic. They acclaim Liberty to destroy the imperial
regime. Having destroyed it, they will strike at Liberty too. Your removal of a Cassius was pointless if you propose to allow emulators of
the Brutuses to multiply and prosper. Finally-write no instructions a-
bout Thrasea yourself. Leave the senate to decide between us. ' Nero
whipped up Cossutianus' hot temper still further, and associated with
him the bitingly eloquent Titus Clodius Eprius Marcellus.

The prosecution of Marcius Barea Soranus had been claimed by
Ostorius Sabinus, a knight, on the grounds of alleged incidents during
the defendant's governorship of Asia. The energy and fairness of Bar-
ca Soranus in that post had increased the emperor's malevolence. He
had industriously cleared the harbour of Ephesus, and had refrained
from punishing Pergamum for forcibly preventing an ex-slave of Nero
called Acratus from removing its statues and pictures. However the
charges against him were friendship with Rubellius Plautus and cour-
ting the provincials with revolutionary intentions. His conviction was
timed just before Tiridates' arrival to receive the Armenian crown.
This was to divert attention from domestic outrages to foreign affairs -
or, perhaps, to display imperial grandeur to the visitor by a truly royal massacre of distinguished men.

All Rome turned out to welcome the emperor and inspect the king.
Thrasea's presence, however, was forbidden. Undismayed, he wrote

报,想了解一下特拉塞亚拒绝做一些什么事情。假如他的建议是
更可取的,那么就让我们采纳吧。否则的话,我们就应该将这些
企图叛乱的人的首脑和煽动者予以铲除。这一派产生了诸如克温
图斯·艾利乌斯·图倍罗和玛尔库斯·法沃尼乌斯之流,这样的人
即使是在古老的共和国之中也是不受欢迎的。为了毁坏帝国的统
治,他们提出了自由的口号;而真的获得了之后,他们也会扼杀自由
本身。假如你容许这些同布鲁图斯之流相媲美的人不断地增多和
强大起来,那么消除一个卡斯乌斯也无关大局。总之,对于特拉塞
亚,你无须亲手写什么指示,留给元老院我们这些人来做决定吧。"
尼禄则是进一步煽动科苏提亚努斯的激动情绪,还要让言语尖刻的
提图斯·克劳狄乌斯·埃普里乌斯·玛尔开路斯来协助他。

对于玛尔奇乌斯·巴列亚·索拉努斯的迫害,则是发生在他
担任亚细亚总督之时,有一个名叫欧司托里乌斯·撒比努斯的骑
士对他提出了指控。巴列亚·索拉努斯在担任总督期间的能力
和公正性早就加深了皇帝对他的忌恨。他精心清理了以弗所的
港口;对于培尔伽门城的人们使用武力阻止尼禄的一名叫阿克拉
图斯的被释放了的奴隶抢走该城的雕像和绘画之事,巴列亚·索
拉努斯没有进行惩罚。然而对他的控告却是针对他同路贝里乌
斯·普劳图斯的友谊以及他在行省中讨好居民以发动政变的罪
名。宣判日期正好选择在了提里达特斯前来接受亚美尼亚王冠
之前。这样做无非就是为了将人们注意的焦点从国内的罪行转
到对外事务上,或者也许是为了通过皇帝对显要人物的杀戮以向
参观者显示皇帝的威严。

整个罗马城都出来迎接皇帝并去看国王。然而却禁止特拉
塞亚参加这次欢迎活动。他没有垂头丧气,他给尼禄写了一封信,

to Nero inquiring what the charges against him were and insisting that he would clear himself if he were told them and given an opportunity to dispose of them. Nero took the letter eagerly, hoping Thrasea had been frightened into some humiliating statement that would enhance the imperial prestige. But this was not so. Indeed, it was Nero who took fright, at the innocent Thrasea's spirited independence; so he convened the senate.

Thrasea consulted his friends whether he should attempt or disdain to defend himself. The advice he received was contradictory. Some said he should attend the senate. 'We know you will stand firm,' they said. 'Everything you say will enhance your renown! A secret end is for the feeble-spirited and timid. Let the people see a man who can face death. Let the senate hear inspired, superhuman utterances. Even Nero might be miraculously moved. But if his brutality persists, at least posterity will distinguish a noble end from the silent, spiritless deaths we have been seeing. '

Other friends, while equally complimentary to himself, urged him to wait at home, forecasting jeers and insults if he attended the senate. 'Avert your ears from taunts and slanders,' they advised. 'Cossutianus and Eprius are not the only criminals. Others are savage enough not to stop at physical violence—and fear makes even decent men follow their lead. You have been the senate's glory. Spare them this degrading crime; leave their verdict on Thrasea uncertain. To make Nero ashamed of his misdeeds is a vain hope. Much more real is the danger of his cruelty to your wife and daughter and other dear ones.

询问指控他的罪名是什么。并且坚持，只要给他一个机会让他与他们面对面进行对话，他会将他们驳倒从而洗清自己的罪名。尼禄急切地将他的来信读完了，他原以为特拉塞亚会因受到惊吓而写一些玷污自己声望的东西，从而提高皇帝的声誉。但事实绝非如此。反倒是尼禄对于无辜的特拉塞亚所表现出来的独立的精神人格所震惊。于是他召开了元老院会议。

特拉塞亚向自己的朋友们请教：他是应该努力还是不屑于为自己进行辩护。他得到了截然相反的建议。有些人认为他应该出席元老院会议，他们说："我们知道你很坚强，你的讲话会提高你的光荣。悄无声息地死去是懦弱和胆怯的所为。让国人们看一位敢于面对死亡的男人吧。让元老院听一次受到神的启示而且由一位超人所作的演讲吧。甚至尼禄也许会被神奇般地感动的。但是假如他坚持自己的残暴行为，至少后世的人会了解我们所见到的一次高贵的死亡和一次沉默而又缺少骨气的死亡之间的区别的。"

其他一些朋友，尽管对他持同样的赞誉之词，却力劝他在家里等着，因为他到元老院去是会遭受嘲弄和侮辱的。他们说："你最好不要去听那些谩骂和侮辱的言辞，想对你施加罪恶的不只是科苏提亚努斯和埃普里乌斯两个人。其他一些野蛮成性的人也许会禁不住向你动起粗来；即使那些体面的人也会出于安全的考虑而追随他们。你曾经是元老院的光荣和自豪。你最好不要使元老们犯下这样可耻的罪行，看他们对特拉塞亚做出怎样的判决吧。要想让尼禄为自己的错误而感到羞耻那只是痴人说梦。而更加现实的危险是他会残暴地对待你的妻子、女儿以及其他亲

No-die untarnished, unpolluted, as gloriously as those in whose foot-steps and precepts you have lived!

One of those present, the fervent young Lucius Junius Arulenus Rusticus, sought glory by proposing, as tribune, to veto the senate's decree. Thrasea rejected his enthusiastic plan as futile-fatal to its au-thor, and not even any help to the accused. 'My time is finished,' he said. 'I must not abandon my longstanding, unremitting way of life. But you are starting your official career. Your future is uncom-promised, so you must consider carefully beforehand what political cause you intend to adopt in such times.' The advisability of his own presence or absence he reserved for personal decision.

Next morning, two battalions of the Guard, under arms, occu-pied the temple of Venus Genetrix. The approach to the senate-house was guarded by guards in civilian clothes displaying their swords. Troops too were arrayed round the principal forums and the law-courts. Under their menacing glares, the senators entered the build-ing. The emperor's address was read by his quaestor. Without men-tioning any name he rebuked members for neglecting their official du-ties and setting the knights a slovenly example. What wonder, he said, if senators from distant provinces stayed away, when many ex-consuls and priests showed greater devotion to the embellishment of their gardens?

The accusers seized the weapon which this gave them. Cossutia-nus began the attack. Eprius Marcellus, following with even greater violence, claimed that the issue was one of prime national importance. The emperor's indulgence, he said, was hampered by the insubordina-tion of those beneath him, and the senate had hitherto been overle-nient. 'For you have allowed yourselves', he said, 'to be ridiculed

人。你应当死得清白、死得无瑕,应当像你平时为人处世之时最佩服的人一样光荣地死去!"

出席这次会议的人之中,有一位年少气盛的人名字叫路奇乌斯·尤尼乌斯·阿路列努斯·路斯提库斯;这个渴望获得荣誉的人,作为一名保民官,提议否决元老院的决议。特拉塞亚拒绝了这一热情的建议,因为这是毫无意义的:它会给提议者本人带来致命性伤害,而即使对于被告也不会有任何帮助。他说:"我的生命已经结束了。我不能放弃我多年来一直遵守的、从未间断过的生活方式。但是你的政治生涯才刚刚开始。你的未来不能遭到任何损害,在这样的一个年代里,你必须要认真考虑一下当前你所采取的政治立场以及由此而带来的后果。"至于他是否应该出席元老院会议,待自己考虑之后再作决定。

第二天早上,两个近卫军中队,在全副武装之下占领了维纳斯·盖尼特利克斯的神庙。元老院的门口被一对对在托迦袍里面藏着佩剑的人把守着。士兵们也被安置在了各个广场和会堂的附近。就是在这种威吓的气氛之下,元老们进入了会堂。皇帝的财务官代他宣读了致辞。在致辞中,没有提及任何人的名字,却批评元老们玩忽职守,从而给骑士们树立了一个懒惰的榜样。他说,假如许多前执政官和祭司们整日沉溺于装点自己的花园,那么那些遥远的行省之中的元老们不愿到元老院来有什么可感到惊奇的呢?

控告者们抓住了皇帝所给予他们的进攻的武器。科苏提亚努斯首先进行了攻击。紧接着,埃普里乌斯·玛尔凯路斯进行了更为激烈的攻击,声称所讨论的这一问题是国家最为重要的问题。他说,皇帝的宽容早已经被其手下那些倔强不顺从的人给糟蹋了。到目前为止,元老院对这些人太过放任了。他进一步说:"你们竟然让怀有叛逆之心的特拉塞亚愚弄而不予以惩处;与特拉塞亚

with impunity-by the rebellious Thrasea, his equally infatuated son-in-law Helvidius Priscus (II), Gaius Paconius Agrippinus (heir to his father's hatred of emperors), and that scribbler of detestable verses Curtius Montanus. I insist that a former consul should attend the senate; a priest take the national vows; a citizen swear the oath of allegiance. Or has Thrasea renounced our ancestral customs and rites in favour of open treachery and hostility?

'In a word: let this model senator, this protector of the emperor's critics, appear and specify the reforms and changes that he wants. His detailed carpings would be more endurable than the universal censure of his silence. Does world-peace give him no satisfaction, or victories won without a Roman casualty? Do not gratify the perverted ambitions of a man who deplores national success, thinks of courts, theatres, and temples as deserts—and threatens to exile himself. Here is a man to whom senatorial decrees, public office, Rome itself, mean not a thing. Let him sever all connection with the place he has long since ceased to love, and has now ceased even to honour with his attendance!'

While Eprius Marcellus spoke in this vein, grim and blustering as ever, fanatical of eye, voice, and features, the senators did not feel any genuine sadness: repeated perils had made the whole business all too familiar. And yet as they saw the Guardsmen's hands on their weapons, they felt a new, sharper terror. They thought of Thrasea's venerable figure. Some also pitied Helvidius, to suffer for his guiltless

同流合污的还有:与他一样晕头晕脑的女婿赫尔维狄乌斯·普利斯库斯(二世),盖乌斯·帕科尼乌斯·阿格里披努斯(从他父亲那里继承了对皇帝们的憎恨),以及写下了许多可恶的诗篇的库尔提乌斯·蒙塔努斯。我坚持认为,作为一个前执政官应该出席元老院会议;作为一个祭司应该出席全国的发愿的祭典;作为一个公民应该参加效忠宣誓。难道是特拉塞亚已经抛弃了我们祖先的制度和仪典,而公然背叛和敌视祖国与人民?

"总而言之,让这个自诩为模范的元老,这个皇帝批评者的保护人来参加会议吧,陈述一下他所想进行的改革和变化,他那不厌其烦的挑剔比他那不吭一声却否定一切的做法倒更容易让人能够忍受。是不是天下太平惹他不高兴了,或者是罗马人不损失一兵一卒而取得的胜利惹他不高兴了? 对于一个对国家的胜利感到悲伤的人,对一个把广场、剧院和神庙看做是荒地的人,对一个用亡命天涯来威胁他人的人,这样的人的邪恶的野心我们决不能让其得到满足。这儿却有一个人,对于什么元老院的决议、什么公众长官、什么罗马,都看得一钱不值。让他从这个很久以来不再热爱、而现在甚至于连看一眼也不愿意的地方消失吧!"

当埃普里乌斯·玛尔凯路斯用这种腔调讲话的时候,他就像往常一样阴森而又令人恐怖,眼睛、声音、面容都透露着狂热,而这却没有让元老们产生丝毫的悲痛之感,因为一再重复出现的危险使他们对于所有这一切都太熟悉了。但是当他们看到近卫军士兵们的手抓向了武器的时候,他们却感到了一种新的、更加强烈的可怕。他们想起了特拉塞亚那令人尊敬的形象。对于赫尔维狄乌斯,有些元老们也持同情的态度,因为他即将为一次纯洁的婚姻关系而遭难。当阿格里披努斯的父亲落难的时候,他本人

marriage relationship. And what was there against Agrippinus except his father's downfall? -for he too, though as innocent as his son, had succumbed to imperial cruelty under Tiberius. The worthy young Montanus, too, was no libellous poet. The cause of his banishment was his manifest talent.

Next Ostorius Sabinus, the accuser of Barea Soranus, entered and began to speak. He denounced the defendant's friendship with Rubellius Plautus, and claimed that Barea's governorship of Asia had been planned not to serve the public interest but to win popularity for himself- by encouraging the cities to rebellion. That was stale. But there was also a new charge involving Barea's daughter, Servilia, in his ordeal. She was said to have given large sums to magicians. This was true; but the cause was filial affection. Young and imprudent, she had consulted the magicians out of love for her father-but only a-bout the prospects of her family's survival, and of Nero's compassion, and of a happy outcome to the senate's investigation. So she too was summoned before the senate. There, at opposite ends of the consul's dais, stood the elderly father and his teenage daughter, un-consolable for the loss of her exiled husband Annius Pollio-and unable even to look at her father, whose perils she had clearly intensified.

The accuser demanded whether she had sold her *trousseau* and taken the necklace from her neck in order to raise money for magical rites. At first she collapsed on the ground, weeping incessantly and not answering. But then she grasped the altar and its steps, and cried: 'Never have I called upon forbidden gods or spells! My unhappy pray-ers have had a single aim: that you, Caesar, and you, senators, should spare my dear father. I gave my jewels and clothes-the things

又遭受到了什么迫害呢？父亲跟儿子一样，虽然都是无辜的，却都惨遭提贝里乌斯的杀害。正派的年轻人蒙塔努斯，也从没有写过中伤性的诗，而他之所以遭到了驱逐，则是由于他所表现出的才华。

接着欧司托里乌斯·撒比努斯，也就是控告巴里埃·索拉努斯的那个人，进入元老院并开始发言。他指责被告与路贝里乌斯·普劳图斯的友谊，并控告被告在亚细亚的统治时期心中所盘算的不是国家的利益，而是通过鼓励城市叛乱的方式以使自己获取他人的好感。这是老生常谈了，但是为了折磨索拉努斯，于是对他的女儿谢尔维利亚却提出了新的控告。指控她把大批金钱送给了魔法师们。这是事实，但却完全是出于女儿的一片孝心。因为少不更事，而且又深爱着自己的父亲，所以她向魔法师请教，但是所询问的问题只是有关她一家人的安全问题；还有尼禄是否对此要宽大处理的问题；以及元老院的调查会不会做出悲惨的判决。于是她也被传唤到了元老院。在执政官座坛的相对两端，分别坐着年老的父亲和年幼的女儿。她已经感到了孤独，因为她的丈夫安尼乌斯·波里欧已遭到了驱逐。现在她甚至不敢抬头看一眼自己的父亲，她显然已经加重了父亲的危险。

控诉人问她是否曾经将自己的嫁妆出售，是否从脖子上摘下自己的项链换取金钱以举行魔法仪式。起初她倒在地上，在不断地抽泣，并不作答。但接着她就手抓着座台和台阶，哭喊道："我从来就没有向被禁止的神和魔法求助过！我那可怜的祈祷只有一个目标，那就是你恺撒，还有你们诸位元老们，能够宽恕我那亲爱的父亲。假如魔法师们需要的话，我就会把像我这样地位的妇女所拥有的珠宝和外袍捐献给他们，就像需要的话我会献出我的

that a woman in my position owns—as I would have given my blood and my life if the magicians had wanted them! I did not know the men before. They must answer for their own reputations and methods; that is not for me to do. I never mentioned the emperor except as a god. And everything was done without my poor father's knowledge. If it was a crime, I alone am to blame!'

Soranus broke in with the plea that she had not gone with him to the province, was too young to have known Rubellius Plautus, and was ummplicated in the charges against her husband. 'Her only crime is too much family affection,' he urged. 'Take her case separately—for me any fate will be acceptable.' Then he moved towards his daughter to embrace her, and she towards him. But attendants intervened and kept them apart.

Evidence was then heard. The brutality of the prosecution aroused compassion-which was only equalled by the indignation felt against one of the witnesses, Publius Egnatius Celer. He was a dependant of Soranus bribed to ruin his friend. Though professing the Stoic creed, he was crafty and deceitful at heart, using a practised demeanour of rectitude as a cover for viciousness and greed. But money was capable of stripping off the mask. Egnatius became a standard warning that men of notorious depravity or obvious deceit yield nothing in nastiness to hypocritical pseudo-philosophers and treacherous friends. However, the same day provided a model of integrity—Cassius Asclepiodotus, the richest man in Bithynia. Having honoured Soranus when he prospered, he would not desert him in his fall. So he was deprived of his whole fortune and ordered into exile-thus affording a demonstration of heaven's impartiality between good and evil.

鲜血和生命一样。以前我并不认识这些人。他们必须对他们自己的声誉和魔法负责;而不应该由我来负责。我一直把皇帝看作是一个神灵。但是所有的这一切事情都是我在我那可怜的父亲不知情的情况之下做出来的。假如这是罪过的话,就由我一个人来承担吧!"

在她还在诉讼的时候,索拉努斯插话了,他说她从来就没有跟自己到过行省;她的年龄太小,不可能认识路贝里乌斯·普劳图斯;而且她也没有卷入对她的丈夫的控诉之中。他申辩道:"她唯一的罪行就是太孝顺了,应该对她进行个案处理;至于我,任何命运我都会接受。"然后他就向他的女儿那边冲过去想拥抱他,而她也向他那边跑过去。但是侍卫们介入将他们隔开了。

接着证人出席了。假如迫害的残暴性能够引起深深的同情,只有普布里乌斯·埃格纳提乌斯·凯莱尔作证时所引起的激愤才能与之相匹敌。他原来是索拉努斯的一名食客,现在被收买来对朋友进行迫害。虽然装扮成一名斯多噶派的信徒,其实内心深处是一个阴险狡诈的人,在公正而又廉洁的举止和表情下面掩藏的是淫乱和贪欲。但是金钱可以戳穿他的假面目。埃格纳提乌斯就是一个例子,足以向世人证明,应当警惕的与其说是那些臭名昭著的堕落者或是显然为罪行所玷污的坏人,毋宁说是那些想用高尚的学识来掩盖自己的虚伪和出卖朋友的丑恶的人。但是,在同一天却又出现了一位崇高人格的典范:卡西乌斯·阿司克列皮奥多图斯,他是比提尼亚最有钱的人。当索拉努斯处于兴旺发达的时候,他就一直崇拜索拉努斯;而在索拉努斯落难的时候,他也不愿背弃他。因此,他被剥夺了全部家产,并且被驱逐了,而这一点就足以说明上天对好人和坏人是不作区别对待的。

Thrasea, Soranus, and Servilia were allowed to choose their own deaths. Helvidius and Paconius were banned from Italy. Montanus was spared for his father's sake, with the stipulation that his official career should be discontinued. The accusers Eprius and Cossutianus received five million sesterces each, Ostorius twelve hundred thousand and an honorary quaestorship.

The consul's quaestor, sent to Thrasea, found him in the evening in his garden. In his company were numerous distinguished men and women. His attention, however, was concentrated on a Cynic professor, Demetrius. To judge from Thrasea's earnest expression, and audible snatches of their conversation, they were discussing the nature of the soul and the dichotomy of spirit and body. A close friend, Domitius Caecilianus, came and informed him of the senate's decision. Thrasea urged the weeping and protesting company to leave rapidly and avoid the perils of association with a doomed man. His wife Arria, like Arria her mother, sought to share his fate. But he told her to stay alive and not deprive their daughter of her only protection.

Thrasea walked to the colonnade. There the quaestor found him, happy rather than sorrowful, because he had heard that his son-in-law Helvidius Priscus was merely banned from Italy. Then, taking the copy of the senate's decree, he led Helvidius and Demetrius into his bedroom, and offered the veins of both his arms. When the blood began to flow, he sprinkled it on the ground, and called the quaetor nearer. 'This is a libation', he said, 'to Jupiter the Liberator. Look, young man ! For you have been born (may heaven avert the omen!) into an age when examples of fortitude may be a useful support. '

特拉塞亚、索拉努斯、谢尔维里娅获准自己选择死亡方式。赫尔维狄乌斯和帕科尼乌斯被驱逐出意大利；蒙塔努斯则由于父亲的缘故而获得了宽恕，但条件是不能再继续他的行政生涯。控告者埃普里乌斯和科苏提亚努斯每人获得了 500 万谢司特尔提乌斯的奖金；欧司托里乌斯则获得了 120 万谢司特尔提乌斯和荣誉财务官的奖赏。

执政官的财务官被派往特拉塞亚那儿，黄昏时分财务官在他的花园里见到了他。与他在一起相伴的是许许多多显赫的男女。然而他的注意力却集中到了犬儒学派的一位大师戴米特里乌斯身上。从特拉塞亚严肃认真的表情以及从他们的谈话的偶然可以听到的片言只语中，可以判断得出，他们正在探讨灵魂的本质和精神与躯体相分离的问题。多米提乌斯·凯奇里亚努斯是他的一位密友，他将元老院所做出的判决向特拉塞亚作了通报。特拉塞亚就力劝那些正在哭泣和叹息的同伴们赶快离开，以免除被一位业已定罪者牵连的危险，他的妻子阿里娅也想学自己的母亲阿里娅一样陪自己的丈夫同死。但是他却劝她继续活下去，以免使他们的女儿失去了唯一的保护人。

特拉塞亚向柱廊走去。在那里财务官发现与其说他是悲伤，倒不如说他是幸福，因为他已经听说了他的女婿赫尔维狄乌斯·普里斯库斯仅仅是被驱逐出意大利。然后他带着元老院所做出

Then, as his lingering death was very painful, he turned to Demetrius ...

[*The manuscript breaks off here. The lost part of the work described the visit of King Tiridates, the beginning of the Jewish revolt, Nero's visit to Greece, the suppression of the revolt of Gaius Julius Vindex in Gaul, and the final desertion of Nero by the senate in favour of Galba, imperial governor of Nearer Spain. Nero fled to a villa of his freed slave Phaon, four miles outside Rome. There he died, his hand guided by another former slave Epaphroditus.*]

的决定,把赫尔维狄乌斯和戴米特里乌斯带进了自己的卧室。他让他们把自己双臂的脉管切开。当鲜血开始外流的时候,他把它洒到地上,并且把财务官叫到跟前,他对他说:"这是向解放神朱庇特行灌奠之礼。快看,年轻人(但愿上天不要垂示这样的征兆),对你来说,已经生活在这样一个时代,坚定的榜样或许是一种有益的支持。"

在他充满痛苦地慢慢死去的时候,他将眼光转向了戴米特里乌斯……

〔手稿在此中断。**遗失的部分所描写的主要内容是:国王提里达特斯的拜访;犹太人反叛的开始;尼禄巡视希腊;盖乌斯·尤利乌斯·文戴克斯在高卢的反叛被镇压;元老院同意西班牙总督伽尔巴的建议废弃尼禄;尼禄逃到离罗马四英里远的一个名叫法恩的被释奴隶的近郊别墅中;在那儿尼禄死去,他的另一个被释奴隶伊帕菲罗蒂图斯执着他的手指引着他。**〕

译者后记

塔西佗的《罗马帝国编年史》是一部影响巨大的古希腊历史学名著,迄今为止已经出版了多种英译本,其中"企鹅丛书"(Penguin Books)中迈克尔·格兰特(Michael Grant)的英译本、"洛布古典丛书"(The Loeb Classical Library)中约翰·杰克逊(John Jackson)的拉英对照本、"万人丛书"(Everyman's Library)中阿瑟·墨菲(Arthur Murphy)的英译本都产生了比较大的影响。

格兰特英译本的译文富有文采,英译者为了方便读者的阅读和理解,在原文比较难于理解的地方,有时加入一些阐释性的语言,使文意更加鲜明、语言更加流畅。因此,格兰特译本在基本保持塔西佗原著主要风貌的基础上,更加通俗易懂,一部板滞的历史学著作也因此增添了几分生动。

商务印书馆曾出版过王以铸、崔妙因两位先生翻译的《罗马帝国编年史》,这部中译本是根据 1951 年英国"洛布古典丛书"中约翰·杰克逊的英译本译出的。"洛布丛书"英译本稍乏文采,但忠实于原著,别具一格。王以铸、崔妙因两先生的汉译本注释颇详,学术价值很高,此次中英文对照本的汉译注释对两位先生的译注成果也有所吸收。

这次《罗马帝国编年史》的译著因为是以英汉对照本的形式

出版,所以译文尽量采用直译的方式,力求忠实于英译本的原貌。同时,也参考了多种汉译本,特别是注释部分,查阅了大量相关资料,力求史实准确。对于此书的翻译,译者尽了很大的努力,审慎从事,但是由于译者功力所限,肯定还有许多不准确、甚至是谬误之处,就正于方家,也请广大读者批评指正。

另外,本书的译稿承蒙中国社会科学出版社的丁玉灵先生反复审阅,提出了许多宝贵的意见,在此一并表示感谢!

贺　严　高书文

2006 年 7 月